»The N.W.O.B.H.M. Encyclopedia«

Malc Macmillan

© I.P. Verlag Jeske/Mader GbR
Haydnstr. 2
12203 Berlin
Germany

pages@ip-verlag.de

All rights reserved.

No part of this publication may be reproduced, stored in a retrieval system, or transmitted in any form or by any means, electronic, mechanical, photocopying, recording or otherwise, without the prior permission of the publisher.

Cover artwork by Marco Thiel at NW-GRAFIX

"Beatus Aurora est, provisor caloris et lucis."

ISBN 978-3-931624-16-3
Sixth Edition February 2025
Printed at TZ; www.tz-verlag.de

Table Of Contents

Part I
Prologue 7
Preface 12
Introduction 15
NWOBHM – The British Perspective 18
NWOBHM – The State Of The Market 24

Part II
A
ACE LANE 28
AFTER DARK 29
AFTER HOURS 30
ALEC JOHNSON BAND 31
ALKATRAZZ 31
AMAZON 32
ANGEL STREET 33
ANGEL WITCH 34
ANTHEM 41
APOCALYPSE 42
ARAGORN 43
ARC 43
A.R.C. ROCK BAND 44
ARGUS 45
ATLANTIS RISING 45
ATOMKRAFT 46
AIIZ 48
AURORA 50
AVALANCHE 50
AVALON 51
AVENGER 51
AVENUE 53
AXIS 54

B
BABY TUCKOO 55
BACKLASH 57
BADGE 57
BADGER 58
BASELINE 59
BASHFUL ALLEY 60
BATTLEAXE 61
BATTLEZONE 63
BEG TO DIFFER 65
BERLIN RITZ 65
BIG DAISY 66
BILL THE MURDERER 67
BITCHES SIN 68
BLACK AXE 70
BLACKMAYNE..................................... 71
BLACKOUT 72
BLACK ROSE 72
BLACKWYCH 75
BLADE RUNNER 76
BLAZER BLAZER 78

BLEAK HOUSE 79
BLITZ, THE 80
BLITZKRIEG 80
BLOOD MONEY 85
BLOODSHOT EYES 86
BLUE BLUD 87
BOLLWEEVIL 88
BOMBAY 89
BOULEVARD 90
BRIAR 91
BRONZ 93
BROOKLYN 96
BRUNEL 96
BUFFALO 97
BUZZARD.. 99

C
CAGEY BEE 100
CAMARGUE 100
CANIS MAJOR 101
CATCH 22 (I) 102
CATCH 22 (II) 102
CEFFYL PREN 103
CENTURION 103
CHAINSAW (I) 104
CHAINSAW (II) 105
CHALLENGER 105
CHARGER 106
CHARIOT..107
CHARLIE 'UNGRY 109
CHASAR 110
CHASE 111
CHASER 112
CHATEAUX 112
CHEEKY 114
CHEMICAL ALICE 114
CHEVY 115
CHINA DOLL 117
CHINATOWN 117
CHINAWITE 120
CHROME MOLLY 120
CLIENTELLE 123
CLOVEN HOOF 124
COBRA (I) 127
COBRA (II) 127
COVENANT, THE 128
CRACKED MIRROR 129
CRAZY BLAZE 130
CRUCIFIXION 130
CRY 131
CRYER 132
CRYS..134
CYNIC 135

D
DAMASCUS 136
DARK HEART 137

DARK STAR	138
DAWN TRADER	140
DAWNWATCHER	141
DEADLY ATLANTIC RUN	143
DEALER	144
DEDRINGER	145
DEEP SWITCH	147
DEF LEPPARD	148
DEMOLITION	154
DEMON	155
DEMON PACT	161
DENIGH	162
DESOLATION ANGELS	164
DESPERATE OATES	165
DESTROYER	166
DEUCE (I)	166
DEUCE (II)	168
DIAMOND HEAD	169
DIANNO	180
DIAWLED	182
DICK SMITH BAND	183
DIE LAUGHING	183
DISTRAINERS	184
DORCAS	185
DRAGONFLY	185
DRAGONSLAYER	186
DRAGSTER	188
DRIVESHAFT	189
DUCHESS	190
DUMPY'S RUSTY NUTS	192

E

EARTHBOUND	194
EAZIE RYDER	195
EAZY STREET	195
EF BAND	196
ELIXIR	197
EMERSON	201
ENERGY	201
ERIC BELL BAND	203
E.S.P.	204
ETHEL THE FROG	204
EVERYONE ELSE	205
EXCALIBUR	206
EXOCET	207
EXPLORER	208
EXPORT	209
EXPOZER	210
EZY MEAT	211

F

FACTORY	214
FAIR WARNING	214
FALSE IDOLS	215
FAST KUTZ	216
FILTHY RICH	217
FIREBIRD	218

FIREBRAND	219
FIRECLOWN	219
FIST	220
5 A.M.	222
FLASH HARRY	223
FLASHPOINT	223
FLIGHT 77	224
FORCE	224
FORGER	225
FOUNDED	226
FOUR WHEEL DRIVE	227
FRAMED	228
FRENZY	229
FRIENDS	230
FUGITIVE	231
FULL MOON	232
FURY	232

G

GARBO	233
GASKIN	234
GEDDES AXE	236
GEMAGE	238
GENERAL WOLF	238
GENGHIS KHAN	239
GIRL	239
GIRLSCHOOL	243
GLASGOW	252
GOGMAGOG	253
GOLDSMITH	255
GOLGOTHA	256
GRAND PRIX	258
GRIM REAPER	261
GROUND ATTACK	264
GUNSLINGERS	265
GYPP	267

H

HAMMER	267
HAMMERHEAD	268
HANDSOME BEASTS	269
HARD, THE	271
HARLEQUYN	272
HARRIER	273
HAZE	274
HAZZARD	276
HEADBANGERS	277
HEAVY PETTIN	277
HELL	280
HELLANBACH	282
HELLRAZER	283
HELL'S BELLES	284
HERETIC	286
HERITAGE	287
H.G.B.	288
HIGH RISK	288
HIGH TREASON	289

HOGGS	290
HOLLAND	291
HOLLOW GROUND	292
HOLOCAUST	294
HOLOGRAM	299
HORIZON	300
HORSEPOWER	300

I

IDLE FLOWERS	301
IDOL RICH	302
INCUBUS	303
INFLUENCE	304
INTERNATIONAL HEROES	304
IONA	305
IPANEMA KATZ	306
IRON MAIDEN	307
ISENGARD	319

J

JAGUAR	319
JAMESON RAID	323
JANINE	325
JEDDAH	325
JESS COX	326
JJ'S POWERHOUSE	327
JODEY	329
JODY ST.	330
JOE LETHAL	332
JOKER	332
JOKERS WILD	333
JONAH	334
JUNO'S CLAW	334

K

KARRIER	335
KICK	336
KNIGHTRIDER	337
KNOCK UP	337
KOOGA	338
KOREA	340
KRAKEN	340
KRUZA	341

L

LADY JANE	341
LAST FLIGHT	342
LAUTREC	343
LAW, THE	344
LÉARGO	345
LEFT HAND DRIVE	346
LEGEND (I)	346
LEGEND (II)	347
LE GRIFFE	349
LIAISON	350
LIGHTNING RAIDERS	352
LIMELIGHT	353

LIONHEART	356
LONELY HEARTS	358
LONE WOLF (I)	359
LONE WOLF (II)	359
LORELEI	360
LOST FAMOUS	361
LOST PROPERTY	361
LOTUS CRUISE	361
LYADRIVE	362
LYNX	365

M

MAD DOG	365
MADE IN ENGLAND	367
MAINEEAXE	368
MAISON ROUGE	369
MALLET	370
MAMA'S BOYS	370
MAMMATH	375
MAMMOTH	376
MARIONETTE	377
MARQUIS DE SADE	378
MARSEILLE	379
MARZ	381
MASAI	382
MASS	383
MASTERSTROKE	384
MAYDAY	384
MAYHEM	385
McCOY	386
MEANSTREAK	387
MEGATON	388
MENDES PREY	389
METAL MIRROR	392
METAL VIRGINS	392
MIDAS	393
MILLENNIUM	394
MITHRANDIR	395
MOBY DICK	396
MONEY	396
MORE	397
MOSELLE	400
MOTHER'S RUIN	401
MOURNBLADE	402
MOVIE STARS	404
MYTHRA	405

N

NATIONAL GOLD	408
NATO	409
NEON SPIRIT	409
NEVER AMBER	410
NEXT BAND	410
NICKY MOORE BAND	411
NIGHT GAMES	412
NIGHTIME FLYER	413
NIGHTWING	414

NO FAITH	416
NO QUARTER	416
NORTH STAR	418
NO SWEAT	419
NUTHIN FANCY	420

O

OMEGA	420
OMEN SEARCHER	422
100% PROOF	422
ONSLAUGHT	423
ORAL	423
ORE	424
ORIGINAL SIN	425
ORION	426
OVERDRIVE	427
OVERKILL	428
OXYM	429

P

PAGAN ALTAR	430
PALI GAP	432
PANZA DIVISION	433
PARADYNE	434
PARALEX	434
PARIAH	436
PAUL DALE BAND	438
PENETRATIONS	438
PERSIAN RISK	439
PET HATE	442
PHASSLAYNE	443
PHEETUS	444
PHOENIX RISING	444
PHYNE THANQUZ	445
PRAYING MANTIS	446
PREDATOR	452
PREDATÜR	453
PRESENCE	453
PREYER	454
PROWLER (I)	455
PROWLER (II)	456
PURPLE HAZE	457
PYRAMID	458

Q

QUARTZ	458

R

RADAR	462
RADIUM	462
RAGE	463
RAMPENT	465
RANKELSON	465
RAVEN	467
RAW DEAL (I)	473
RAW DEAL (II)	474
RED	475

RED ALERT	476
RED RAGE	477
REINCARNATE	477
RENEGADE (I)	478
RENEGADE (II)	479
REQUIEM	480
RHABSTALLION	480
RICOCHET	482
ROADSTER	483
ROCK GODDESS	484
ROGUE MALE	488
ROKKA	491
ROLLIN' THUNDER	491
ROUGH JUSTICE (I)	492
ROUGH JUSTICE (II)	493
ROX	494
RUNESTAFF	496

S

SABRE	497
SACRED ALIEN	498
SAIGON	499
SALEM	500
SAMSON	501
SAM THUNDER	510
SAMURAI	511
SAPPHIRE	512
SARACEN	513
SATAN	514
SATANIC RITES (I)	519
SATANIC RITES (II)	520
SAVAGE	520
SAXON	525
SCARAB (I)	533
SCARAB (II)	534
SCORCHED EARTH	534
SCORPIO	535
SEDUCER	536
SEVENTH SON	537
SEVERED HEAD	540
SHADER	541
SHADOWFAX	542
SHADOWLANDS	543
SHE	544
SHEER KHAN	545
SHERWOOD	546
SHIVA	546
SHOCK TREATMENT	548
SHOGUN	549
SHY	550
SHYWOLF	553
SIAN	554
SIDEWINDER	555
SIEGE	555
SILVERWING	556
SINGAPORE	558
SINNER	559

SKITZOFRENIK	560
SLEDGEHAMMER	561
SLENDER THREAD	563
SLOWTRAIN	563
SMART	564
SMOKIN' ROADIE	565
SNAKEBITE	566
SNATCH-BACK	567
SNOWBLIND	567
SOLDIER	568
SO WHAT	570
SPARTA	571
SPARTAN WARRIOR	572
SPEED	573
SPEED LIMIT	573
SPIDER	574
SPITFIRE	576
SPITZBROOK	578
SPLIT BEAVER	578
SPLITCROW	579
SQUASHED PYRANNAH	580
STAGEFRIGHT	581
STAMPEDE (I)	581
STAMPEDE (II)	583
STARFIGHTERS	583
STATETROOPER	586
STATIC	588
STEEL	589
STOLEN THUNDER	590
STORMCHILD	591
STORMQUEEN	592
STORMTROOPER	593
STORYTELLER	593
STRATEGY	594
STRATUS	595
STREETFIGHTER	596
STREET LEGAL	597
STRUTZ	598
STRYDER	599
SURFACE	599
SUSPECT	600
SWEET SAVAGE	601
SYAR	605
S.Y.Z.	606

T

T34	607
TANK	607
TARGET UK	612
TEMPEST	614
TERRAPLANE	615
THIN END OF THE WEDGE	617
THUNDERSTICK	618
TITAN (I)	620
TITAN (II)	621
TNT	622
TOAD THE WET SPROCKET	623

TOBRUK	624
TOK-IO ROSE	626
TOKYO BLADE	627
TOKYO ROSE	634
TOO MUCH	635
TORA TORA	635
TORTURE	637
TOSH	638
TOUCHED	639
TRACER	640
TRACK 4	641
TRADER	642
TRAITORS GATE	642
TRANS AM	643
TRAXX	644
TREDEGAR	644
TRESPASS	647
TRIARCHY	650
TRIDENT	651
TROBWLL	652
TROJAN (I)	653
TROJAN (II)	654
TRUFFLE	656
TRUX	657
TRYDAN	658
TURBO	658
TUTCH	660
TUXEDO	660
20/20 VISION	661
TWISTED ACE	661
TYGA MYRA	662
TYGERS OF PAN TANG	663
TYRANT	671
TYSONDOG	672
TYTAN	674

U

URCHIN	676
US	678

V

V8	678
VAGABOND	679
VALHALLA (I)	679
VALHALLA (II)	680
VARDIS	680
VENOM	684
VERMILION	694
VHF	695
VIRGINIA WOLF	695
VIRGIN STAR	696
VIRTUE	697
VOLTZ	699
VOYAGER UK	701

W

WARFARE	702

WAR MACHINE	706	WOLF (I)	735
WARRIOR (I)	707	WOLF (II)	736
WARRIOR (II)	708	WRATHCHILD	737
WARRIOR (III)	709		
WARRIOR (IV)	710	**X**	
WEAPON	711	XERO	740
WENDY HOUSE	712		
WHITEFIRE	713	**Y**	
WHITE HEAT	714	YOUNG BLOOD	742
WHITE LIGHTNING	715		
WHITE SPIRIT	717	**Z**	
WIDOW	720	ZENITH	744
WIKKYD VIKKER	721	ZORRO	744
WILDFIRE (I)	722		
WILDFIRE (II)	723	**Part III**	
WILD HORSES	725	Compilations	746
WILDSMITH ST.	726	Local-band Compilations	784
WINTER'S REIGN	727	Epilogue	796
WITCHES BREW	728	Acknowledgements	798
WITCHFINDER GENERAL	728	N.W.O.B.H.M. Survey	800
WITCHFYNDE	730		

Prologue

My time with IRON MAIDEN was fantastic, one moment we were playing small clubs around the UK, then suddenly we went straight into the charts with a Number One album! After that it was Hammersmith Odeon, a tour of Europe with KISS, 'Top Of The Pops' etc. Half the time I didn't know if I was coming or going, but it was the greatest experience a young guy could ever have had, and it got even better when British Metal began to achieve global domination, because the NWOBHM was without a doubt the most vibrant and happening music scene that this country has ever known.

Paul Dianno, June 2001

The New Wave Of British Heavy Metal – it's like classic rock meets punk rock! Some of the skill and arrangements of ZEPPELIN, SABBATH, PURPLE, PRIEST and RUSH mixed in with the energy of the PISTOLS, CLASH, RAMONES and THE JAM. Their *'do-it-yourself'* attitude gave us a kick, along with the fact that some fresh, newish acts (AC/DC, UFO, LONE STAR) were now playing the smaller venues, and suddenly there were loads of like-minded young bands playing gigs and releasing their own records. I remember when DEF LEPPARD made the front page of 'Sounds', Geoff Barton wrote a massive piece on them and IRON MAIDEN, and every week there seemed to be something else to do with the NWOBHM. I liked the movement, especially since we could be a part of it, and when LEPPARD got signed it gave us such a kick. We thought, *'right, we can do this!'*

Brian Tatler, June 2001

What the hell's a DEF LEPPARD?! What a stupid name! I thought to myself sitting outside bassist Rocky's parents house reading a centre spread two-page feature on this unknown band in Sounds after a band rehearsal in the summer of 1979. This was my introduction to the existence of another young rock act in the UK. Our band was called the TYGERS OF PAN TANG – we'd been together for ten months, had done 50 or so local pub gigs and were armed with one 3-track demo. We even had a manager – Tom Noble. 'Manager' was probably a bit of a grand title at that time as Tom was a full time school teacher/part time local DJ and music writer. What he did have was, like all of us, boundless enthusiasm, a love of music and the perverse bloody-mindedness and belief that the band was destined for greater things: quite what, no one knew. Until now that is.

'They sound like you,' said Tom after reading the said same article, 'we'll send 'Sounds' your demo.' After scouring the paper for an address off our tape went and the next week we were in 'Sounds' with (I think) four other acts: IRON MAIDEN, SAMSON, DEF LEPPARD and, maybe, SAXON. Writer Geoff Barton was busy enthusing about this New Wave explosion of young metal acts in the UK and coined the now legendary mantra: New Wave Of British Heavy Metal.

Until that point none of us knew anything about any other rock acts playing metal around the UK and I'm quite sure that none of our future NWOBHM colleagues knew or cared about the existence of each other either. In retrospect, metal was probably pretty unfashionable in the UK at the time (what's new?!). We were all aged between 18 and 20 and had grown up with DEEP PURPLE, BLACK SABBATH, LED ZEPPELIN etc and then had got into the prog scene with bands like YES, GENESIS and ELP, the off the wall acts of BOWIE, ROXY MUSIC and ALICE COOPER and on to the West Coast sound of THE EAGLES, SPRINGSTEEN and LITTLE FEET. The UK had just come out of the punk era and was into a Ska thing in '79 with acts like MADNESS, THE SPECIALS and THE SELECTER all over the radio. So being in a metal band was not that cool! Why did we do it and how did this explosion of new metal acts springing up at the same time across the UK happen?

Well, the truth probably was not that there

NEAT RECORDS

Venom, Raven, Tygers Of Pan Tang,

Blitzkrieg, Jaguar, Shy, Savage,

Al Atkins, Gaskin, Holocaust,

Sweet Savage, Witchfynde, Tyson Dog, Artillery, Marshall Law,

Cronos, Fist, Satan, Warfare.

22 years of bringing you the best in NWOBHM.

Buy online or order a free catalogue from:

Neat Records, 71 High Street East, Wallsend,

Tyne & Wear NE28 7RJ, England

Tel: 0044 191 262 4999   Fax: 0044 191 240 2580

E-mail: miffy101@hotmail.com   neatrecords.com

was a plethora of heavy metal acts emerging in the UK in '79, rather there was just a handful: LEPPARD in Sheffield; MAIDEN, ANGEL WITCH and SAMSON in London; SAXON in Barnsley and us in Newcastle. The rest came along, albeit at a great pace, after the first Geoff Barton NWOBHM piece in Sounds. Even now, a powerful media type could probably call for metal demos from young acts in the UK, pull together an act in each town, call it a movement, give it a name, push it through the media and cross their fingers that it takes off. That could me being old(er) and cynical – but it's more or less true. Having said that, today they wouldn't find the diversity and originality of acts. What they'd get now is ten LIMP BIZKITS. Not that there's anything wrong with LIMP BIZKIT – but ten of them? '79 saw and celebrated such a diversity in the NWOBHM scene for several reasons:

In '79 metal bands didn't expect to get 'signed'. It just didn't happen then – they had no main act to copy so that they could attract a label. They just played what they liked in naive bliss without the artistic restraint of trying to sound like the 'in' acts. IRON MAIDEN didn't sound like DEF LEPPARD who in turn sounded nothing like the TYGERS. Probably another factor was the influence of the melting pot of music that had gone before. You didn't just listen to 50 metal acts all sounding the same. Your record collection might consist of older rock acts like PURPLE/SABBATH, some USA West Coast bands like CHEAP TRICK and THE TUBES with a sprinkle of the more diverse acts like ZAPPA, LITTLE FEET and early ROXY and ALICE COOPER. You probably also had a thick collection of punk albums and 7" singles. Throwing all this music together with the do-it-yourself-anyone-can-be-in-a-band punk attitude it's not surprising that young rock acts in the UK sounded so different and were busy going off to their local recording studios to record their demos etc for 50 quid: results can be seen in LEPPARD's debut EP on Bludgeon Riffola, MAIDEN's »Soundhouse Tapes« and the TYGER's »Don't Touch Me There« 7" on Neat Records.

Importantly, and another factor why metal bands didn't sound like each other, there was no rock on the radio, TV or in the press in the '70's! It was a time of pre-MTV, Internet or specialist print mags. There was no 'Kerrang' (later to become the NWOBHM specialist weekly bible). There were three music broadsheets ('Sounds', 'NME' and 'Melody Maker'). That was it. Until Geoff Barton's intervention in Sounds you had no metal music in any of these publications. The NWOBHM scene happened because kids who liked metal went and took a leaf out of the punk movement – they made their own sounds and formed their own labels from which they could release their own singles: DEF LEPPARD and MAIDEN's labels are examples. HOLOCAUST also had Phoenix Records – Phoenix was actually the name of the record shop where the then HOLOCAUST vocalist Gary Lettice worked. It was the embracing of NWOBHM by the major labels, always on the lookout to exploit the next big scene, which really kicked off the metal explosion. With MAIDEN and ANGEL WITCH going to EMI, LEPPARD went to Phonogram and the TYGERS went to MCA. Others followed, but the majors lost interest by '82. Bar MAIDEN/LEPPARD/SAXON, a lot of these acts were dropped.

It must be said, of course, that other newly formed independents signed and developed a lot of the talent before (and long after) the heyday of the NWOBHM. Neat Records was (even though I now own the label myself!) the most successful and prolific: originally launching the careers of the Tygers and bringing the likes of VENOM, RAVEN, BLITZKRIEG, WHITE SPIRIT, FIST and JAGUAR, to name a few, to the world. The label is based in Newcastle upon Tyne in the North East of England and signed so many New Wave acts that 'Sounds'/'Kerrang' actually originally called this phenomenon the (NE)NWOBHM (as in North East). The label had all the ingredients to succeed. Firstly, they had their own in-house studio called Impulse and, secondly, the area had an abundance of young metal acts. One act, VENOM, not only became the label's flagship act but, prior to the evil ones even striking their first note, Cronos (or Conrad as he was known then) was the junior studio assistant! TYSONDOG lived a few streets away. The TYGERS, RAVEN, VENOM, FIST, WHITE SPIRIT et al. all lived within 15 minutes drive of Neat Records.

The bands were literally queuing up at the door! RAVEN were brought to Neat by the TYGERS' manager; VENOM had a 'foot in the door', as I said, with Conrad being employed at Impulse. Others like AVENGER, for example, were brought by VENOM's manager whose brother was the vocalist. It wasn't all sweetness and light, of course, with the bands competing for dominance over each other: rivalries were, to say the least, razor sharp! As the vocalist with the TYGERS I know that certain acts did,

9

and probably still do to this day, resent the TYGERS 'succeeding' by being signed to MCA. David Wood, the then label owner, had a large three foot mount made for Neat offices of me on stage – which basically became used for darts practise by other Neat acts when they visited! I remember playing our big homecoming gig at Newcastle's Mayfair Ballroom on the 'Wild Cat Tour' to 2,000 fans – only to see members of FIST throwing glasses at us from the middle of the crowd! I can laugh at these things now (not that we really gave them a second thought at the time either!), but it does somewhat tarnish the myth that all the bands of the NWOBHM were some kind of big happy family.

Other labels that flew the flag at the time were mainly Heavy Metal Records in Wolverhampton and Ebony Records in Hull. Heavy Metal were responsible for such classic acts as the HANDSOME BEASTS (what an album cover for their first album »Bestiality« – marvellous!), WITCHFINDER GENERAL, SPLIT BEAVER (charming!) and SHIVA to name a few. Ebony, of course, released a clutch of classics including SAVAGE's debut »Loose 'N' Lethal«. They also gave us albums by the brilliant GRIM REAPER and CHATEAUX. Again, these labels had an abundance of local acts and owned in-house studios. Sadly, Ebony went bust years ago although Neat has re-released SAVAGE's (and SHY's) debut and is ready to get the CHATEAUX catalogue back out there on CD for the first time through Edgy Records.

I've already highlighted other 'also ran' labels like Phoenix in Edinburgh (HOLOCAUST), but there were others such as Rondelet (GASKIN, WITCHFYNDE), Reddington's Rare Records (QUARTZ) and Guardian (who were responsible for rare but highly collectable 7" and compilation albums including SATAN's debut single »Kiss Of Death«). To this day Heavy Metal Records are still in existence under the name Revolver Records but it's only really Neat Records who have kept the true spirit and sound of those days, releasing some 40+ albums in recent years by acts like HOLOCAUST, TYGERS OF PAN TANG, BLITZKRIEG, JAGUAR, SAVAGE and GASKIN. Not only have they released the back catalogues of these acts but they have also recorded and put out new albums by all these bands over the last few years including HOLOCAUST (who are, as I write this, touring America).

In places like Germany and Japan (God bless you Pony Canyon!) the NWOBHM never really went away. The spirit has also been kept alive by a group of fans who have gone on from the scene to become label bosses, magazine editors, concert and festival promoters and managers. With the seeming demise of the sometimes-bland metal scene of recent years (hardcore/black/death etc.) and the revival of interest around the world for hard rock once again, I know there is a new interest in this great period for rock music. With Spitfire Records in the USA and Sanctuary with its Metal-Is label in the UK continuing to champion true metal there may be some chance that a second wave of metal acts may just be around the corner. It won't be called the NWOBHM and it can't come from the pen of Geoff Barton at 'Sounds', but someone or some event will spark off a revival and bring a new audience to a new scene with fresh new acts. Quick someone and think of a name!

Of course, that's the possible future. For now, what you have here in this book is a faithful documentation of the histories and discographies of every NWOBHM act (and many others) who picked up an instrument, not to change the world or get a record deal, but to be the best metal act in Scunthorpe, Wigan, Basildon or Whitley Bay! The rising of American 'poodle rock' in the mid-80's effectively killed off the NWOBHM: depending on your point of view this colloquial, naivety amongst these British acts could very well have been the movement's Achilles heel – or, in my opinion, it could be its most endearing legacy.

Jess Cox, April 2001

Rare Records

The N.W.O.B.H.M. Specialist

Rarities, Overstocks & Memorabilia
Vinyl & CD

Currently in stock (July 2001):

AIIZ »The Witch of Berkley« LP	40,- Euro
BLITZKRIEG »10 Years« LP	30,- Euro
DEMON »Liar« 7" Single	30,- Euro
EZY MEAT »Not for Wimps« LP	70,- Euro
EZY MEAT »Not for Wimps« CD with 5 bonus tracks	15,- Euro
EZY MEAT »Rock your Brains« LP	70,- Euro
IRON MAIDEN »Maiden Mania« 5 x 12" Box Greece	250,- Euro
IRON MAIDEN »Live Castle Donington« 3 LP's	70,- Euro
JAMESON RAID »7 Days of Splendour« 7" Single	60,- Euro
LEGEND »Same« LP	130,- Euro
LEGEND »Limited Edition« 12" EP	50,- Euro
MAD DOG »Same« LP	30,- Euro
MENDES PREY »Wonderland« 7" Single	60,- Euro
SEVENTH SON »Sound and Fury« 7" Single	70,- Euro
SEVENTH SON »Northern Boots« 7" Single	40,- Euro
SEVENTH SON »Factory Girls« 7" Single	30,- Euro
SEVENTH SON »What more do you want?« 12" EP	30,- Euro
SHERWOOD »Riding the Rainbow« 12" EP	60,- Euro
SWEET SAVAGE »Killing Time« 7" Single	160,- Euro
VENOM »Doomed to Hell« LP	120,- Euro
VENOM »French Assault« LP	70,- Euro
VENOM »Scandinavian Assault« LP	70,- Euro
V.A. »Torn in Two« LP (incl. unreleased SEVENTH SON)	50,- Euro

New titles in weeks!
Free 14-page list from:
I.P. Verlag Jeske/Mader GbR
Haydnstr. 2
12203 Berlin
Germany
e-mail: pages@ip-verlag.de

tel. 0049/30/86 20 09 81
fax 0049/30/86 20 09 82

Preface

The offer to write a book about the New Wave Of British Heavy Metal era came out of the blue, although I had been ruminating about the possibility of some such project for several years. It started out as a request for a third volume (covering the really obscure outfits of the time) to complement the German-language books which had already been published by 'IRON PAGES', namely 1995's 'NWOBHM - The Glory Days' and its successor, 1997's rather more comprehensive 'NWOBHM Vol.2'. Along the way, however, this third instalment evolved into a markedly more ambitious venture, as it became apparent that devotees all over the world wanted an English-language text on the subject. As a result, the notion of a straight translation of 'NWOBHM Vol.2' was briefly entertained, after which the additional obscurities could be added to create something resembling the encyclopaedia you see before you. This idea duly metamorphosed into a complete revision of the original German texts, given that a certain (ahem) big-headed individual reached the conclusion that he might actually make a better job of it if he started more or less from scratch. This isn't to say that the earlier volumes were poorly-researched or badly-written (quite the contrary), and these books were truly invaluable when it came to plonking myself in front of a computer and attempting to create a worthy addition to the series. Just as 'NWOBHM Vol.2' owed a fundamental debt to 'NWOBHM - The Glory Days', this mighty tome should be regarded as yet another continuation, even if the words have changed along the way.

When it comes down to hard facts, there's unquestionably a distinct lack of detailed knowledge among enthusiasts, compared to most other genres, although this is by no means a criticism. Rather, it's simply a reflection of the fact that no especially thorough research has been undertaken for all but the best-known outfits of the era, with memories of the minor acts growing ever more hazy as time has passed. Generalised reference books which mention *bona fide* NWOBHM bands at all (and these are few and far between) usually tend to be vague about histories and personnel changes, concentrating instead on easily-established facts and discographies. Again, this is completely forgivable, as none of those responsible have (as far as I'm aware) set themselves up as an authority on the subject, and have merely included a few early 80's outfits as a matter of routine. Furthermore, the sad truth remains that the NWOBHM phenomenon has, in recent years, been pushed to the back of the British public's memory, while aficionados in other parts of the world have greeted the music with boundless enthusiasm. While such individuals have kept the original spirit alive, it hasn't been easy for them to get hold of interesting or reliable information, and it would, perhaps, be slightly unreasonable to expect someone on the other side of the globe to pen a comprehensive critique on the activities of a bunch of long-forgotten amateur musicians on a small island, just as it would be a virtually impossible task to assemble a meaningful reference tome on the history of Tamla-Motown music from a council house in Birmingham, for instance. As a result, people have had to wait a long time for well-informed books on this particular subject.

Having said all this, there are some hugely knowledgeable fans outwith the UK, and the 'IRON PAGES' crew have performed heroics throughout the past decade, tracking down many of the musicians involved and digging up valuable details relating to quite a few of the more popular NWOBHM groups, allowing their individual stories to be pieced together with an awe-inspiring degree of accuracy and completeness at long last. However, the ground-breaking 'NWOBHM - The Glory Days' and 'NWOBHM Vol.2' made no claims of being totally all-encompassing in terms of content, and neither does this one, as there are always more bands to be discussed, more details to be unearthed, more anecdotes to be recounted and more stories to be told. Here's where I come in. Having been into the scene since its inception, and being based in Britain throughout, the past twenty years have allowed me to be exposed to a vast amount of NWOBHM music, on both vinyl and tape, encountering like-minded contacts in the collecting field as time passed. Added to the fact that I've crossed paths/swords with numerous dealers, musicians, traders, shop-owners, fanzine editors and general scenesters over the years, it's not totally unreasonable to suggest that I have a decent perspective on what took place during that unique period of supernova-style activity. Whether or not my unashamedly verbose writing style lends itself to creating an informative-but-readable reference source remains open to debate, though. If you feel yourself lapsing into a coma or losing the will to live, stop reading.

You will presumably have noticed that this is quite a large book. Indeed, the overall objective

Black Widow
Via Del Campo 6 R - 16124 GENOVA
Tel. 010.2461708 - 010.2544500
blackwidow@tin.it / www.blackwidow.it

IL SEGNO DEL COMANDO
Der Golem

AGONY BAG
Feelmazumba

HIGH TIDE
Open Season

MALOMBRA
Dissolution Age

PRESENCE
Gold

NORTHWINDS
Masters of Magic

BLACK WIDOW
Return to the Sabbat

THE BLACK
Golgotha

BLACK WIDOW TRIBUTE

DEATH SS TRIBUTE

NECROMANDUS
Orexis of Death

BLUE CHEER TRIBUTE

News:
the fifth album of the Gods of Heavy-Doom
PENTAGRAM - Sub-Basement

has been to document almost all of those NWOBHM acts who made it to the vinyl stage during the period in question. Fair enough, you say, people will always be interested in the major-players of any movement, but is there really a need for such obsessive research regarding the official releases and biographical minutiae of apparently insignificant bands? Unquestionably, the reasons being twofold. Firstly, it's just fundamentally exhilarating (and hopefully semi-interesting) to read about hopelessly obscure groups, or to discover a novel snippet of information about one of your favourites, as it has the potential to increase your appreciation of the music no end. Given that a relatively large proportion of information seems to reside in the crania of a handful of individuals (erudition is a sin, so they say), it's surely a worthwhile exercise putting everything down on paper for the masses to appreciate. Secondly, this genre has (as with certain others) been extremely prone to rumour-mongering and wild speculation over the years, and it's irritating to see someone setting themselves up as an *'armchair expert'* on the grounds that they possess two TYGERS OF PAN TANG albums. In most cases, this activity is fairly harmless (you'll encounter some real garbage on the internet, even on supposedly *'official'* band pages), although it does, on occasion, make us vulnerable to those who would seek to profit.

Record dealers thrive on the sheer scarcity of this stuff, and many have been getting away with murder for years, touting around non-rare and non-listenable obscurities from the period as wallet-emptying rarities which outclass every other release of the time. Let's face it, these types are hardly paragons of objectivity, and, even in the unlikely eventuality that they've actually played the record, they're probably not in a position to give you a remotely meaningful description of its contents. Once again, here's where I come in. This volume covers almost every release from the era that you're likely to encounter on your travels, with well over five hundred groups (two hundred more than the mighty 'NWOBHM Vol.2') being discussed in detail. I've set out to include as much relevant information as humanly possible, covering history, development and vinyl output, plus the fundamentally-important description of each band's general sound, quoting reference points within (and sometimes outwith) the NWOBHM field. You may disagree with certain comparisons (I'm always amazed how the same piece of music can be interpreted in so many different ways), and I make no apologies whatsoever for the unashamedly opinionated nature of a few entries, but I hope it makes a refreshing change from the uncritical, infuriatingly-vague phrases (*'mid-paced rock with female vocals'*) that you'll often find elsewhere. Since I have no vested interest in selling NWOBHM records or promoting bands of any description, there's no reason for dishonesty or hyperbole, so if a release is described as particularly good or bad, you have no fundamental grounds to distrust this assertion.

The music reference book field has become fairly lucrative for some (those who sell many thousands of copies), with there being an incredible level of competition amongst authors in one or two areas. I don't view this as being a potential problem in our case, however, as the NWOBHM market is extremely limited and specialised in relation to all-encompassing genres such as rock, jazz or blues. Given that I've spent such a ludicrous amount of time on this particular project, there shouldn't, in all modesty and honesty, be much scope for competition (although there will always be room for enhancement), as I simply don't accept that it would be feasible for any one person or group of individuals to assemble a more comprehensive or informative reference source *from scratch*. I could be completely wrong. On the other hand, it may be tempting to *'borrow'* the odd entry for inclusion in more general texts. Be *very* careful if you're tempted to do so. The data presented here have been assimilated from numerous sources, both written (for reasons outlined below, other reference books cannot generally be trusted with any certainty and have therefore not been used in this capacity) and verbal, and have been checked for corroboration at every possible opportunity. I can tell you precisely where each snippet of information originates from, and I seriously doubt that anyone else could do the same. If anything resembling any part of this volume appears elsewhere (either in print or on the net) without my express written permission, I'll want to know why. I'm perfectly happy for people to use certain material, assuming they have the decency to ask, as long as the publishers and myself are credited.

Comparing a variety of reference books during the course of compiling this volume, it was disturbing to note what appears to be the almost universally-employed device of *'deliberate mistake inclusion'* as a means of thwarting intellectual property theft. I wholeheartedly object to this for several reasons. Firstly, it simply doesn't work. It just means that untruths are perpetuated and created unnecessarily (perversely, defeating the purpose of a reference source in the first place), when authors should be more concerned about making their publications as watertight as possible. Secondly, it's a *'get out of jail'* card. Rather than holding their hands up and admitting the possibility that their books might contain inaccuracies (heaven forfend), writers can contest that you've merely spotted a *'deliberate'* mistake that they knew about all along. Lastly, it's just downright childish, but it appears to go with the territory and the churlish *'I'm better than you and I've got a bigger record collection as well'* mentality. Perversely, though, those who make the loudest noise about copyright (you know who you are) are clearly the ones who are happiest to *'borrow'* things themselves. It merely takes one person to miscredit a song title or list a record that was never pressed, and it suddenly appears in half a dozen other sources. I hope this book is different. It will, due to the very nature of the subject, surely have inaccuracies from time to time, and it's entirely possible that some colloquialisms and/or misguided attempts at humour will lose something in translation, but there are no deliberate measures to mislead or confound. Neither does this represent anyone's record collection (least of all mine), so don't start getting jealous or feeling inferior. One of the nicest things about NWOBHM is the observation that major-league rarities are distributed fairly evenly among collectors. Nobody on earth possesses every record in this book, and they probably never will.

Well, that's about the size of it, so just settle down with this paperweight and enjoy a few gentle revelations. I sincerely hope that the demystification of one or two legendary outfits doesn't ultimately lessen anyone's appreciation of their music, but I suspect that the reverse situation is rather more likely. It's taken a while (well, around twice as long as I originally anticipated) to get the finished article together in its present form, but I've enjoyed every last minute of it, so (unlike some self-pitying characters in a similar position) I'm not going to whinge about how much *'work'* was involved or the *'sacrifices'* I had to make in the process. Lastly, if you have any corrections or anything at all to add (no matter how inconsequential it may seem), please don't just sit there feeling smug, kindly get in touch with those nice chaps at 'IRON PAGES' and we can improve all the relevant entries when/if additional volumes or revised editions are published. I've learned a lot from this book, I'm sure you will too.

Malc Macmillan, November 2000

Introduction

This volume, the third instalment in the 'IRON PAGES' series of NWOBHM reference texts, is, in most respects, highly similar in structure to its predecessors, and will hopefully appeal to the same cross-section of people who purchased the original German-language publications. If you possess either/both of the earlier books, you might want to skip the preamble and head straight for the individual entries. If not, you might (especially if you're something of a newcomer to the music) wish to plough through all the introductory waffle instead. Following the general overview, the first part includes 'NWOBHM – The British Perspective', which seeks to elaborate upon the background, development, importance and legacy of the New Wave Of British Heavy Metal phenomenon as a whole. After that, 'NWOBHM – The State Of The Market' explores the manner in which the collecting scene has evolved over the years, with reference to the activities of dealers, labels and collectors themselves. Although these topics have broadly been covered in previous volumes, you might find that the additional inclusion of these sections, delivered from a uniquely British perspective, actually complements the Eurocentric nature of the earlier discourses (not that they were fundamentally flawed in any way), giving a more balanced and international view of the phenomena involved. Towards the end of the book, you'll find a comprehensive review of those compilation releases with notable NWOBHM content, followed by an introduction to the little-known area of local-band samplers, many of which contain material of considerable interest. Rounding things off is a discussion of what might come next, in which readers are invited to express their opinion as to whether this volume has achieved its aims, and what might ultimately succeed it.

Quite clearly, the main body of this work is contained in an alphabetically-arranged section which covers the individual band entries. Approximately two-thirds of the groups mentioned were present in 'NWOBHM Vol.2', whereas the remainder are being featured for the first time, although each individual entry has been completely rewritten from first principles. This wholesale revision of the preceding volume has largely been undertaken in view of significant additional facts having become established, although changes have also been necessary in view of the minor inaccuracies, inconsistencies or unfortunate misunderstandings which have since come to light. Moreover, it seems more logical to have the entire volume written in a consistent style by one person, rather than attempting to amalgamate contributions from various sources. With regard to the entirely novel entries, the vast majority comprise extremely obscure acts with little-known private releases, several of which were previously outlined in the 'completion list', but were unconfirmed or unobtainable at that time. Of the remainder, some were presumably overlooked or accidentally omitted, although others were earlier to be found on the infamous 'black list'. In the interests of fairness, the latter was re-evaluated, whereupon certain acts gained a last-minute reprieve. In all cases, though, the inclusion/exclusion of a particular group is based upon their overall relevance to NWOBHM collectors; it's not uncommon, for instance, for a four track EP to feature one semi-decent composition (BLACKMAIL and ANNIVERSARY, to name but two examples), even though the record as a whole doesn't qualify as NWOBHM.

As ever, the choice of which artists to cover is extremely subjective; one person's NWOBHM is another person's pub rock or punk crossover, and so on. I concede that several of the groups featured herein may be contentious (in the sense that they have a foot in more than one genre, or were merely operating on the periphery of the metal scene), to say the very least, but we're never going to attain universal consensus as to what constitutes a genuine NWOBHM concern. I think we're sufficiently independent of thought to be able to determine what appeals to our specific sensibilities, and can collectively reject any proposition which blatantly fails to meet the relevant criteria. Having said that, there are always anomalies, such as URCHIN (too early), BLAZER BLAZER (hardly even rock, let alone metal) and the EF BAND (two-thirds Swedish), which, for various reasons, become established as NWOBHM when they are actually nothing of the sort. Also, some would seriously question the inclusion of VERMILION, MAYHEM and their ilk in the previous volumes, but we're back in the realms of 'crossover' appeal, aren't we? There has, nevertheless, been rather less of a tendency to feature punk-influenced groups than before, with an accompanying gentle shift towards including more progressively-inclined acts (but hopefully stopping short of out-and-out prog rock). Admittedly, a small quantity of rather more lightweight outfits are also featured, but, with a bit of luck, these shouldn't include anyone who belongs solely in the AOR or pub rock categories.

In the main, those covered in this tome are basically heavy rock/metal acts from the British Isles (not UK outfits based in Europe, nor *vice versa*) who released vinyl (either on recognised labels or privately) in the period 1979 – 86 (which has, over the ensuing years, become largely synonymous with the term 'new wave of British heavy metal'), although there are literally a couple of exceptional entries from outwith this general catchment area. Although many of the bands featured may not have been affiliated with the NWOBHM movement at the time (remember, the main period of activity is generally regarded as being 1979 – 81, although it tailed off over a number of years), their musical style and/or relation to earlier outfits still allows them to be afforded the generalised label of 'NWOBHM'. If you're a hardliner, nobody's forcing you to read about the later acts, but you'll be missing out on some very talented groups. A comparatively broad spectrum of styles are encompassed, from the archetypal sound associated with the likes of JAGUAR or the TYGERS OF PAN TANG (which, to be honest, applies to an extremely limited selection of bands), to certain more progressively-inclined (but still heavy) acts and traditional heavy rock/metal combos, but also including some of those who would more commonly be defined as melodic rock, biker rock, boogie/blues, lightweight punk/metal and glam-influenced. It's a wide-ranging remit, admittedly, but this has always been the case, it's not as though we're becoming increasingly less selective (or more desperate to find something else to seek out) as time goes by. As many dealers have found to their cost, we're not as gullible as they might think, and we're perfectly capable of making up our own minds as to what constitutes NWOBHM, thank you very much.

The entries for individual bands are in much the same style as before (these incorporate full references and credits for any quotes taken from other sources), including the earliest known recording line-up (this may refer to the personnel responsible for a pre-vinyl demo or session) wherever possible, a detailed band history (or as much as is currently known) in terms of the geographical location (generally given in terms of a region or county, as a great number of bands featured musicians from more than one town or city), musical style, non-vinyl recordings (in particular, important radio appearances and live broadcasts are discussed within each entry, rather than in a separate section as before), personnel changes, vinyl releases (including notes on whether or not picture sleeves are known to have been issued, and approximate quantities pressed, wherever possible), notable live activities and tours, shifts in direction, previous/later activities of individual members etc., followed by as complete a discography as is possible with regard to singles, EP's, LP's, CD's (including details of important variations in vinyl colour, sleeve designs and foreign issues, if these differ significantly in any way) and compilation appearances. Mind you, for a few of the scene's major names (the likes of IRON MAIDEN, DEF LEPPARD, SAXON and VENOM), there's little or no point in even attempting to chronicle the multifarious foreign pressings, bootleg albums, merchandise and compilation appearances. If you're particularly concerned about such things, there are specialist publications available elsewhere which will doubtless disclose the relevant information.

In contrast to the preceding volumes, however, use of the ambiguous word *'unreleased'* has been kept to an absolute minimum, as this term has, in the past, been used to mean both (a) a cut from a single which didn't feature on an official LP, and (b) a track from a compilation which is otherwise entirely unavailable. In any case, *'unreleased'* more accurately refers to a track which failed to appear officially in any form and is languishing in the vaults of some record company. The more regular convention, which has been adopted in the present work, is to utilise the phrases *'non-LP'* (referring to a B-side which isn't taken from a regular album, for example) and *'exclusive'* to mean a compilation track which didn't otherwise appear on any of the band's own releases. This system isn't perfect, though, and there are still a couple of entries where confusion may arise (for example, if a certain composition is originally non-LP, but subsequently appears on a CD reissue, although explanatory details will be provided under such circumstances). Also, if a compilation or single cut, for example, differs significantly from its album counterpart (being either an edited/extended version, for instance, or if it is an entirely different take), this will also be stated explicitly in the discography. Feel free to correct me if I've overlooked the fact that two apparently-similar solos were actually played on different guitars (yes, some characters take great pleasure in pointing out this kind of inconsequential detail), but I'm not a musician or a particularly tragic case.

Furthermore, the normal convention for classifying records is dependent on the number of tracks featured, not the size of the vinyl (the previous method was to ascribe the term *'single'* to everything on 7" and *'maxi'* to all 12" releases except LP's, which tends not to be employed outside mainland Europe), which has necessitated some major changes in the current text. Hence, a record featuring two tracks is now referred to as a *'single'* (either 7", 10" or 12"), whereas any record with three or four is an *'EP'* (*'extended play'*). A five or six track 12", on the other hand, usually tends to be classed as a mini-LP. Once the playing time of any 12" approaches forty minutes, however, it almost invariably becomes classified as a proper LP, regardless of the number of tracks thereon. With respect to discographies, the inclusion of video-format material has been deemed neither necessary nor appropriate (although mention of such footage may be made within the individual entries themselves), such was the semi-professional/unofficial nature of the medium in the vast majority of cases. Since there is no fundamental justification for defining either bootleg audio tapes or recordable CD's as collectable releases (given that these items can be duplicated indefinitely), there's no compelling reason to mention anything other than officially-sanctioned, long-form videos (due to the expense of the format at the time, only the most popular bands got involved) which were sold on general release. And don't get me started on laser discs.

I'm aware of several limitations and criticisms which may be levelled at this volume. First, a significant number of the acts featured are so horrendously obscure that very few details have thus far emerged concerning their history. As a result, a few entries cover little more than a musical critique of their known vinyl releases. Hopefully, in due course, some scraps of information may be forthcoming about one or two of these small-time hopefuls, meaning that we can do them justice in any later editions. Also, I hope that the necessary evil of *obscurum per obscurius* (describing the musical style of one esoteric band in terms of an equally unrenowned ensemble) isn't too frustrating, and I've endeavoured to quote more generalised reference points wherever feasible, in an attempt to make the text accessible to as great a readership as possible. Secondly, it may be regarded as rather elitist to be affording so much attention and column space to bands which very few people may ever get the chance to hear, and who probably exerted little influence on the scene at the time. Even so, I believe it's still worth documenting these outfits and allowing them to occupy their own, tiny space in an important area of musical history. On a purely altruistic level, just think of all those once-hopeful musicians who may, in due course, find their names included in a reference source such as this and be able to point out their long-forgotten achievements to friends and families. Aaah.

Finally, you will appreciate that this particular volume reveals the identities of numerous minor personalities from the NWOBHM era, many of which have not been common knowledge until now. Certain individuals may, therefore, be enormously tempted to wade through a mountain of telephone directories, searching for some of the more unusual surnames featured. To be brutally honest, I wouldn't encourage you to do so. Apart from the fact that you'll almost certainly run up an astronomical phone bill if you attempt to locate any of these characters, you might be left sorely disappointed in the long run. Even if you conspire to beat the odds and make contact with someone who was once in a small-time metal band in the early 80's, please remember that precious few of these people now have any connection whatsoever with the music business and might be slightly taken aback that a complete stranger wants to interrogate them about an ensemble they played with for six months while in their formative years. Please be extraordinarily polite and respectful if you decide to go ahead and play amateur detective; some folks don't have good memories, others simply don't want to relive the past, some may even be hostile (I could tell you a few horror stories...) that their youthful indiscretions are being put under the microscope twenty years on. Be aware that, in all probability, they *don't* have a crate of singles in their garage, and, even if they once did, someone has almost certainly beaten you to it. Whatever you do, *don't* phone from the other side of the world when it's three o'clock in the morning in the UK.

Well, that's the boring preamble out of the way, maybe now you can enjoy your book. If you like it, hate it, think it hits the wrong note (it's supposed to be light-hearted, but it's not intentionally derisory) or could be improved in terms of layout, contents or whatever, please get in touch *via* the 'IRON PAGES' address. I'm sure many of you could make a serious contribution to future editions, so don't be ashamed to offer any information or ideas you might have. Finally, on a personal note, there's a couple of things which cause me a minor level of concern. First, comparatively few women seem to be lending an ear to NWOBHM, for reasons I don't fully understand. Surely it's not only for sad, ugly blokes who don't get out much? Nah, there's no reason why the fairer sex can't come out of the closet and admit they get a kick out of hairy geezers singing nonsensical lyrics, wearing bad clothes and playing loud guitars, so think about introducing one or two of your lady acquaintances to the wonderful world of NWOBHM. Secondly, some of us take NWOBHM (and metal in general) *far* too seriously. Honestly, folks, it's time to put things in perspective, as the SPINAL TAP lads would say. If you can come to terms with the absolute absurdity of metal, it doesn't make you any less of a fan, quite the reverse. Neither does admitting to liking the odd bit of something completely different. I don't know about you, but I worry about those individuals who listen to nothing but rock music (some of whom restrict themselves to just one or two sub-genres) all the time, and who interact only with similarly-minded characters. There's a world of music out there, and there's good and bad in all corners. Lend an ear to something else occasionally, and you'll be a better person for it. Trust me.

NWOBHM – The British Perspective

Well, what's this peculiar NWOBHM thing all about, then? Twenty years on and debate still rages; was it a movement or a musical style? Has its true significance been misconstrued or inflated out of all proportion in the intervening years? Moreover, does anyone really still care about the exploits of various amateur musicians in the dim and distant past? If so, why? Well, we all have our individual opinions on these matters, and it's often a fundamental mistake to over-analyse certain aspects of cultural phenomena, but for what it's worth, I'll give you my own view of how and why it all happened, how the scene evolved, and whether or not it left any significant musical legacy. Some of this has undoubtedly been said before (I'm certainly not claiming these particular thoughts to be unique), some of it possibly hasn't; I don't profess to have read everything that's been written on the subject in the past couple of decades. Feel free to disagree wholeheartedly with this text (it appears, broadly speaking, to echo the feelings of most of the original fans and band members I've spoken to over the years), but remember, we were actually there...

For those who would write generalised reference books about the history of music, the combined genres of rock and metal are, on the whole, marginalised to an extraordinary extent, and the NWOBHM in particular seems to have been the unfortunate victim of *'selective memory syndrome'* on the part of most journalists and historians. Anyone misguided enough to swallow the dubious version of events frequently trotted out will be led to believe that the late 70's (or, in some cases, the entire decade) were utterly dominated by punk culture and the accompanying sounds of musical rebellion, after which there was a conveniently-seamless transition to the electronic and new romantic phase in the early 80's. Piffle. It may be deeply unfashionable to admit this, but the whole punk phenomenon (which burned itself out very quickly indeed, although numerous apologists regularly claim that it was hijacked by the middle classes) really *has* been blown out of all proportion in the decades since its demise, and was *never* as big as disco, no matter what anyone may say. New romanticism, on the other hand, might have been all the rage in a handful of elitist clubs in some of England's major conurbations (London, Sheffield and Birmingham, for example, which were a law unto themselves), but it wasn't a nationwide phenomenon and its pretension simply didn't appeal to the working classes at all. Well, if that's the case, then what sort of music was a remarkably large percentage of the youthful British populace listening to at the turn of the decade? Ooh, you'll never guess.

Throughout the 70's, home-grown rock/metal stalwarts such as BLACK SABBATH, UFO, JUDAS PRIEST, THIN LIZZY, LED ZEPPELIN, BUDGIE, BAD COMPANY, NAZARETH, DEEP PURPLE and STATUS QUO had, primarily through their album releases, elevated heavy music to an almost unprecedented level of popularity, although this was largely ignored by the media in favour of the more fashionable or lucrative markets of the day such as disco, glam, mod, new wave or electronic music, which tended to dominate the singles charts but were, in terms of individual acts, fairly transient. The inevitable result of this media favouritism was a widely-held belief that rock and metal were a spent force, an outmoded and irrelevant musical style which was now in serious and permanent decline. Nevertheless, from the mid-70's onwards, various bands (mostly based in England's larger cities) had been inspired to form in an attempt to emulate their heroes, additionally taking influences from weighty imports such as AC/DC, KISS, AEROSMITH, MONTROSE, the RUNAWAYS, RUSH and BLUE ÖYSTER CULT. Towards the end of the decade, however, the likes of WHITESNAKE, MOTÖRHEAD and RAINBOW had finally started to dent the mainstream charts, achieving success with several singles as well as albums, and rock duly became a high-profile market which could no longer be ignored. Around the same time, the number of small-time outfits who decided to play heavy music (many of whom did, admittedly, take on board some of punk's energy, speed and attitude) began to grow exponentially, so that the metal sound now encompassed the whole of the UK, from the major population centres to the smallest towns. Furthermore, after the BBC's legendary 'Friday Rock Show' was launched at the tail end of 1978, the nation was able to appreciate a solid chunk of rock music (giving exposure to vinyl released by less well-known outfits and also promoting home-grown talent in the shape of specially-recorded sessions) on their radios once a week.

Eventually, towards the middle of 1979, the media finally cottoned on to the fact that something a bit new and exciting seemed to be happening, and certain journalists focused on the activities of a few of the more high-profile, youthful outfits such as IRON MAIDEN, SAXON, DEF LEPPARD, GIRLSCHOOL and SAMSON, enlightening the readers as to the extent of this grass-roots activity. As we know, Geoff Barton of 'Sounds' wrote an article about the phenomenon, in which the phrase *'New Wave Of British Heavy Metal'* was invoked for the first time. At this point, it was simply a throwaway line, nothing more. However, the public latched onto these words with astonishing vigour, acknowledging the fact that there really was a whole new generation of bands who were doing their own thing. As time went on, therefore, the unpronounceable acronym *'NWOBHM'* became a byword for rock/metal which stood alone and wasn't rooted in the past. Although some had originally been influenced by weighty acts from earlier in the decade, the overwhelming shift was towards faster, shorter, less bass-heavy numbers, owing a debt to albums such as JUDAS PRIEST's »Killing Machine« and MOTÖRHEAD's eponymous debut. In this respect, we have a kind of duality; in its formative days, NWOBHM became regarded as both a movement *and* a musical style, even though those spawned as a result evolved into a multitude of different variants. Over the next couple of years, so many bands formed that it was practically impossible to keep abreast of developments. Gigs were organised at an incredible rate, and entrepreneurs such as Neal Kay (the chap who would put together the seminal and influential »Metal For Muthas« compilation for EMI, which raised the profile of several young bands to a major extent) duly identified a pre-

Vinyl Tap Mail Order Music

1 Minerva Works, Crossley Lane, Kirkheaton, Huddersfield, W Yorks, England HD5 0QP

Tel.: 0044 1484 421446   Fax: 0044 1484 531019

E-Mail: sales@vinyltap.demon.co.uk   Website: http://www.vinyltap.co.uk/

Specialising in rare and collectable CDs, Vinyl and memorabilia

Over 75,000 items currently in stock

Let us know what artists/groups you collect, CDs and Vinyl or both

Write, Phone or Fax for FREE Lists

http://www.vinyltap.co.uk/

Lists now available by e-mail – just ask   Website updated weekly

viously-unexploited niche for rock discos with his legendary 'Heavy Metal Soundhouse' (where many of the NWOBHM upstarts were introduced to the masses, although it's worth stating that the old stagers were still favoured by some). It's difficult to convey precisely how popular rock/metal became (certainly among teenagers and young adults) during this period, and it should be stated that most people weren't quite as partisan then as they are now (back then, you could happily buy a single by IRON MAIDEN at the same time as a single by THE JAM), but it's fair to say that, in many parts of the country, the headbangers were outnumbering the devotees of other genres in no uncertain terms.

With the UK now playing host to literally thousands of rock and metal outfits who were performing straightforward, energetic, exuberant and unpretentious music just for the sheer hell of it, it was inevitable that a significant percentage would ultimately conclude that there was no overwhelming reason why they couldn't release their own product to sell to local fans at the rapidly-expanding series of gigs which allowed minor NWOBHM hopefuls to participate. With enterprising companies such as SRT, Ellie Jay and Lyntone now offering very limited pressings of 7" singles at a reasonable cost (they had previously restricted themselves to large runs and albums, which were considerably more expensive), it became a financial viability for many emergent acts to issue their own product (usually a modest two-tracker) over the next year or two, and only now are fans beginning to appreciate the sheer scale of this activity; it wasn't a few dozen groups who were releasing self-financed records, it was *hundreds*. Britain had become a turbulent place by the tail end of the 70's, rife with unemployment, strikes, political upheavals and widespread social unrest, all of which would continue until the summer of 1981 (culminating in the infamous series of riots in Brixton, Toxteth *etc.*) or thereabouts. It may be a coincidence that the main period of the NWOBHM explosion spanned approximately the same timescale (and, given that the aforementioned disturbances were predominantly a reaction to some sickening racist attacks, we're probably skating on remarkably thin ice here), but it may indeed reflect the fact that certain young people saw energetic music as a means of venting their anger and frustration, rather than resorting to violence.

Within a fairly short space of time, it became apparent to the larger record companies that, with this proliferation of new musical talent, there had to be scope for making a bit of money.

While most of the major players such as EMI, MCA, RCA, Polydor, Vertigo, Atlantic *etc.* were each prepared to promote one or two of the new crop of heavy bands (some of whom were staggeringly unsuccessful, it must be said), none were ready to take a chance on the NWOBHM movement as a whole. However, this situation was soon remedied with the advent of more specialist labels such as Neat, Ebony and Heavy Metal (plus, to a markedly lesser extent, Guardian, Future Earth and Avatar), each of whom would provide exposure (and, vitally, the opportunity for some lucky hopefuls to record a full album, which was beyond the means of the vast majority of self-financing outfits) for a considerable number of newer groups. Furthermore, since ready cash was being raked in from the music itself, NWOBHM-devoted publications duly became a lucrative possibility. With several underground rock fanzines having appeared by 1981, the big boys decided to get in on the act, and the famous 'Kerrang' magazine was launched (originally as a one-off publicising the NWOBHM scene and the rock *'revival'* in general) as a spin-off from the more wide-ranging 'Sounds'. The public reaction was unprecedented (and entirely unforeseen), the result being that the metallers' bible soon became a regular sight on the shelves of newsagents nationwide.

By late 1982, however, things had cooled off quite tangibly (the situation wasn't exactly helped by a number of long-standing or more peripheral outfits shamelessly attempting to jump on the bandwagon in a desperate attempt to get themselves noticed by the major record companies), and most regarded the NWOBHM phenomenon as having burned itself out completely, as punk had done several years earlier. In fact, the world had simply returned to a more manageable state, as there was no way the previous supernova of intense activity could have sustained itself for a particularly long period of time. However, from 1983 onwards, the music press based in the UK itself (with one or two exceptions, notably the fledgling 'Metal Forces', which would later play a pivotal role in allowing the tape-trading scene to flourish) would form the collective opinion that the NWOBHM-influenced metal scene (*i.e.* virtually every outfit then operating in the British/European underground) was now in serious decline, and basically deserted its patronage of home-grown acts (although some, particularly IRON MAIDEN and DEF LEPPARD, were to remain incredibly popular) in favour of imports such as Y&T, TWISTED SISTER, ANVIL, RIOT, MÖTLEY CRÜE *etc.*, relegating practically any hapless ensemble with the remo-

21

test NWOBHM connection to the most cursory (often derogatory) of mentions.

In fact, while the whole NWOBHM experience might have been rapidly fading from the British public's memory (rock music has never since attained anything like a similar level of adulation in this country), its bequest was far from forgotten elsewhere, with the European market (having embraced the movement with open arms at its inception) continuing to accommodate both the major names and also newer additions to the fold. Indeed, such was the overwhelming enthusiasm of countries such as Holland and France, that even minor UK outfits with no official releases could often find gigs there. Of course, the metal scene in mainland Europe has always been remarkably strong, with many home-grown examples of talent in virtually every territory, but let's just say that they were slightly less xenophobic about welcoming visitors from overseas than were some places. Furthermore, European magazines such as 'Metal Hammer' and 'Aardschok' (which boasted enviably-high circulations at their peak) were instrumental in keeping the music alive in the ensuing years. The NWOBHM boom also extended to the likes of North America (where significant sections of the population were rapidly tiring of being force-fed a steady diet of insipid, mainstream rock) and Japan (plus, eventually, South America, Australia etc.), inspiring heavy acts to form (with the same 'let's do our own thing regardless of commercial viability' ethos) and inciting aficionados to seek out the original vinyl releases from the UK.

As we're all aware, outfits such as METALLICA and MEGADETH (to name two particularly facile and familiar examples) took the basics of NWOBHM to new extremes, building on the foundations of bands such as DIAMOND HEAD, SAVAGE, ANGEL WITCH etc. and coming up with faster, heavier arrangements which went down a storm in their native land (and, eventually, virtually everywhere else). It would be stretching the truth to breaking point to affirm (as some have done) that the NWOBHM was entirely responsible for the development of the thrash scene, but it was certainly a notable influence for some of its more prominent exponents, even if most were rather less voluble than Ulrich and his cohorts. Meanwhile, back in the UK, the weekly rock press were now tending to favour considerably more commercial outfits, prompting many an original NWOBHM unit to change direction towards melodic, keyboard-filled commerciality. While a handful of concerns successfully managed this musical about-turn, many others just resigned themselves to the fact that their chance had apparently gone, and went back to their day jobs. A few newer acts, such as ELIXIR, CHARIOT and the DESOLATION ANGELS (often confusingly referred to as 'second wave NWOBHM'), hoping for a return to 'true metal' (whatever that may have been), attempted to recapture the original spirit, albeit with limited success, since the dominant musical style was soon to shift from melodic rock towards more extreme sleaze or thrash. At this point, therefore, it seemed as though the now-redundant NWOBHM might eventually become a distant memory with no bearing on the subsequent rock/metal scene as it gradually evolved into new variants.

By the second half of the 80's, however, many heavy outfits (who wanted to distance themselves from the melodic rock/sleaze influx as much as possible), particularly in good old mainland Europe (where persevering stalwarts such as DEMON, SATAN, RAVEN and TOKYO BLADE continued to tour successfully, despite having been long forgotten in their homeland), were clearly doing their utmost to keep the NWOBHM dream alive. The likes of KREATOR and SODOM duly acknowledged the pioneering influence of the original bands (particularly TANK and the TYGERS OF PAN TANG), even going so far as to immortalise covers of selected NWOBHM classics, as had METALLICA since their earliest days. Towards the end of the decade, Lars Ulrich took full responsibility for raising public awareness of the NWOBHM in major fashion, electing himself the music's champion and saviour. After countless interviews spent extolling the virtues of his prized record collection, he went as far as to compile (with the assistance of Geoff Barton, who seldom gets equal credit) a commemorative anthology of NWOBHM material, a time-consuming 'labour of love' which was seemingly undertaken without motives of profit-making or self-promotion. Love him or hate him, there's no question that his considerable efforts were not in vain. In spite of the fact that the set was pressed in fairly limited quantities (some cynics have cruelly suggested that the record company involved were merely humouring him), it has since become apparent that this compilation found its way into the hands of many an inquisitive fan, a considerable proportion of whom were spurred on to seek out further material from the bands featured.

On the back of this compilation release, and with 'Kerrang' having now experienced a complete change of heart with regard to the NWOBHM, leading to a commemorative supplement celebrating the movement's '10th Anniversary' (which, surprisingly, actually went a bit further than merely reminding people of the main contenders from the era), a large number of people began to collect some of the more highly-regarded records from scratch. This isn't to say that certain individuals hadn't been collecting up to this point, but most had tended to be fairly selective in terms of the bands they favoured. Suddenly, however, it appeared that some peculiar people wanted *everything*, even all those laughably-bad releases by long-forgotten no-hopers. It didn't take certain dealers long to cotton on to the fact that a new market had materialised, and records which had been cluttering up the second-hand shops were now frequently presented for sale as coveted items. In the early 90's, the prices being charged for some *'rarities'* verged on the absurd (see 'NWOBHM – The State Of The Market'), although things have now calmed down a bit, fortunately. Nevertheless, the fact that some self-financed singles were pressed in truly minuscule quantities has created a pronounced *'two-tier'* hierarchy, with standard issues (such as those on familiar labels such as Neat, Heavy Metal or Ebony) tending to peak at around twenty pounds, whereas selected obscurities which are known to exist in terms of only a handful of examples can still, on occasion, fetch a couple of hundred pounds or more.

Aside from a few obsessive collectors, though, does anyone *really* still care about the NWOBHM in the 90's? Certainly, with further high-profile advocates of the movement having come out of the closet, notably DEATH's Chuck Schuldiner, Bill Steer (of CARCASS, FIREBIRD *etc.*) and PANTERA mainman Phil Anselmo, their patronage of the genre might conceivably result in some younger fans of more extreme music checking out several of the acts who originally influenced their heroes. Furthermore, the legacy of NWOBHM extends quite significantly further within the present metal climate, with certain bands having been cited as chiefly responsible for the emergence (or re-emergence) of particular genres, such as the New Wave Of Scandinavian Death Metal (which even has its own, equally silly acronym, NWOSDM), where groups such as DARK TRANQUILLITY, DISSECTION or IN FLAMES have adopted the technical twin-guitar riffing of IRON MAIDEN or ELIXIR, for instance. Elsewhere, the extraordinary resurgence of Black Metal has resulted in numerous outfits acknowledging the trailblazing evilness of VENOM (strange, therefore, that most appear to have more in common with BATHORY), whereas a considerable proportion of modern-day doom fanatics continue to cite WITCHFINDER GENERAL as inspirational figures (incredibly, they seem to be mentioned more often than BLACK SABBATH), which is surprising, since they were by no means an outstandingly popular or influential act at the time. Moreover, the similarity between certain NWOBHM bands and some of the melodic punk ensembles from across the Atlantic (the OFFSPRING, HÜSKER DÜ, GOO GOO DOLLS and their tuneful ilk) is undeniable, although I reckon we'll wait a long time before any of them admits a penchant for NWOBHM music while retaining a straight face. Maybe it's just a coincidence.

Also in the 90's, the unanticipated success of the famous series of bootleg compilation CD's (using immensely obscure and rare singles from the era), which first surfaced in Japan back in 1992, took us all by surprise, and clearly demonstrated that there really were many aficionados who just desperately wanted to hear as much of the original music as possible, irrespective of format. Furthermore, several of the godfathers of the NWOBHM scene (notably IRON MAIDEN, SAXON, DEMON and RAVEN) have either persevered, with varying degrees of success (whereas some, such as the all-conquering DEF LEPPARD, have successfully distanced themselves from their original roots) or reformed, capitalising on the latest wave of interest in their music, with labels such as the resurrected Neat Metal going so far as to issue brand-new material by the likes of SAVAGE, HOLOCAUST, BLITZKRIEG and SWEET SAVAGE, and also helping to promote the occasional gig by these revitalised luminaries. Furthermore, European festivals such as Wacken have afforded warm receptions to reunited bands (GASKIN, GRIM REAPER, the TYGERS OF PAN TANG, JAGUAR *etc.*), so you can't suggest that any of these acts have overstayed their welcome or have no place in the modern metal world. Moreover, with labels such as British Steel, Zoom Club and Vinyl Tap identifying the potential of the market in terms of CD releases, and with such highly-regarded music publications as 'IRON PAGES', 'Snakepit' and 'Singing Swords' all lending their weight to the promotion of NWOBHM, in both its original and revived forms, there seems to be little danger of our beloved music fading into obscurity or disrepute.

In conclusion, it looks as though NWOBHM music is here to stay, even though the rock/metal scene has changed beyond all recognition in the intervening years. Despite the fact that the labels, journalists and publications who originally championed the movement have now mostly moved on, and either look back on the phenomenon with fond memories or utter derision, it appears that new devotees of all ages are still cropping up constantly. Thanks largely to the massive expansion of the internet (which, in addition to keeping the fans informed about the present-day activities of high-profile outfits and relevant record labels, has allowed die-hard metalheads from all over the world to make contact with one another, demonstrating just how surprisingly widespread the general interest in NWOBHM actually is), it has become possible for anyone who shows a bit of curiosity in the subject to find out about the bands and hear their music. Given that it has become deeply unfashionable for younger rock fans to admit to owning any music which is more than six months old, let alone something from a previous decade, maybe it's about time we had another NWOBHM revival and a bit of belated appreciation for some truly outstanding bands.

NWOBHM – The State Of The Market

There's no doubt whatsoever that NWOBHM has now become firmly established as an eminently collectable genre, although, sadly, the market is completely misunderstood by many. I can't really comment on what goes on outside the UK, but here's the story in Britain itself. When the serious collecting scene began to take shape in the late 80's/early 90's, it was widely believed that virtually everything vaguely heavy from the era was now worth silly money. Certain individuals, working on the faulty premise that all you had to do was stockpile any vinyl with the remotest NWOBHM association, mark up the price by a factor of ten and wait for the money to roll in from gullible, insatiable fans, have had their fingers burned in major fashion. The main stumbling block for British dealers (*i.e.* the ones who are most likely to unearth the stuff in the first place) is that, generally speaking, there aren't many serious collectors in the UK itself, and even fewer are prepared to spend more than about ten pounds on anything, no matter how rare. Given that many record dealers have no overseas contacts, they are therefore left with a dilemma: either try to sell the items for the maximum amount at fairs in small British towns (a process which can take years), or pass them on to more specialist dealers at a fraction of the price. You'll see those who have chosen the former option at every provincial fair the length and breadth of the UK, safe in the unshakeable knowledge that, one day, someone really will come along and gleefully hand over thirty quid for that tatty LIMELIGHT album.

For those more knowledgeable dealers with numerous customers and contacts overseas, things might look a bit brighter, but it's still not all plain sailing. It was originally believed that non-British collectors (particularly those in the USA and Japan, who many still clearly regard as having *'more money than sense'*) were so plentiful and utterly non-discriminating that Britain's entire supply of NWOBHM vinyl would soon be exhausted, having been sold to rich individuals who just wanted to accumulate something rare and exotic, whether it was records, stamps or antiques. Not only was this assumption wholly inaccurate, it's also grossly unfair; I've never encountered any evidence whatsoever to suggest that some of those who collect NWOBHM aren't totally into the music, and there are certainly no individuals who acquire vinyl purely for the sake of it and who don't even listen to the records once they have them in their possession. The dealers have discovered, through painful experience, that NWOBHM aficionados are indeed discriminating creatures. Furthermore, they now recognise that, if you're going to charge big money for this stuff, then you'd better have precisely the right items for sale and not mislead the punters.

Just who exactly decides the value of NWOBHM records, you may ask, and using which criteria? Good question. Going back to the mid-80's, it wasn't uncommon to encounter such artefacts in second-hand shops, at much the same price as any other piece of vinyl. More often than not, the pieces you'd see were fairly run-of-the-mill items such as singles by SAXON, ANGEL WITCH, DIAMOND HEAD, TYGERS OF PAN TANG and PRAYING MANTIS (*i.e.* the ones which had sold in notable quantities in the first instance), alongside the usual motley selection from the Neat and Heavy Metal labels. Occasionally (and I *mean* occasionally), you might just have been lucky enough to come across something a tad more esoteric (a 7" on Guardian, perhaps, or even one of those self-financed issues). Since these weren't generally regarded as being more interesting (in fact, they were often seen as less collectable) than the bog-standard NWOBHM artefacts, the asking price didn't tend to vary from the usual nominal value, so it really was possible to find ultra-rare singles at affordable prices. Contrary to tantalising stories spun by some rather cruel characters, though, Britain's vinyl shops were never, at any point in time, filled with dirt-cheap rarities! Ultimately, however, some astute person no doubt noticed that there was a growing trade in NWOBHM vinyl (records were even making their way to mainland Europe and beyond in the long term), and presumably began wondering if there might be a niche for the more unusual pieces.

Almost overnight, the prices being charged for relatively obscure NWOBHM singles (and the odd album) went through the roof. This has, on occasion, happened in certain other genres (notably, 70's progressive rock), although it's more common for the value of records in self-contained musical areas to rise and fall at a more controlled rate, as competition among collectors varies. Whenever any hyper-inflation of this type occurs, therefore, you have to ask whether a modicum of *'reverse psychology'* might have come into play *i.e.* dealers, rather than collectors, have decided what's worth shelling out for, creating an artificial demand with arbitrarily high prices. Whatever the mechanism, it seems to have worked. Collectors appeared from nowhere (having said that, only a tiny proportion were actually prepared to pay these exorbitant prices) and were hooked by loquacious tales of monumentally rare and astoundingly listenable records by utterly unknown bands, so large sums of money were often handed over in exchange for just one or two of these legendary pieces of vinyl. At this time, the dealers happily exploited the almost illicit secrecy of it all, revelling in their ability to unearth immensely obscure artefacts and foist them upon voracious aficionados of the genre. Mind you, they didn't have it all their own way for long. Predictably, the high prices suddenly being charged for collectable NWOBHM items caused several eyebrows to be raised at the offices of 'Record Collector' magazine, the mainstay of vinyl devotees worldwide, who approached some of the bigger players in the dealing world to write an exposé on this phenomenon, asking them to reveal a few details of the mysterious bands involved, what their music was actually like, how limited the pressings were, and so forth. Time and again, the dealers refused.

Now, I don't want to paint all dealers as the unscrupulous villains that they are often made out to be, but, by refusing to attempt to justify the outlandish prices they were now charging, they didn't do themselves any favours at all. As time went on, NWOBHM enthusiasts carried out their own investigations and drew their own conclusions about all the records which were suddenly being offered for sale at ludicrous prices. Some of them turned out to be musically atrocious (which hadn't deterred those who sought to make a profit), some simply weren't genuine NWOBHM at all (they were either undated late 80's releases, foreign acts or groups who had no affiliation with the movement whatsoever), and several weren't nearly as scarce as had been intimated (in extreme cases, boxes of unsold copies had been obtained from the band in question, but the dealers still made out that they only had a solitary example in their possession). As a result, things rapidly cooled off, with collectors becoming considerably more wary about parting with their hard-earned cash. Nevertheless, a few items (generally speaking, those which are musically worthy and genuinely rare) have held up quite respectably in terms of monetary value, maintaining their approximate figure of around five years ago, when the market appears to have hit its peak, whereas the asking price for others has dwindled dramatically. Having approached various other individuals, 'Record Collector' finally got their NWOBHM article in the late 90's, courtesy of Matthias Mader himself, after which the values of some obscure releases duly found their way into the price guides, resulting in markedly more standardised pricing among dealers. While the theoretical values at the top end of the market have continued to fluctuate wildly over the years, however, the global demand for common items has been remarkably stable, with these prices (tending to peak at around fifteen to twenty pounds) remaining reassuringly constant throughout.

As pointed out in the previous section, only now are we beginning to come to terms with the sheer quantity of amateur-hour acts who contrived to make their mark on the vinyl world during the NWOBHM era. New discoveries continue to be unearthed, albeit at an ever-decreasing rate, and so the completists will just have to accept that they will never possess everything, as we genuinely don't know what's still out there. It's become apparent that certain pressings were extraordinarily limited (a couple of hundred copies, in a few cases), with some bands only selling their records through tiny shops or at the occasional local gig. To be brutally honest, however, there's a remarkably straightforward explanation as to why certain acts didn't sell many records; they weren't very good. If somebody offers you a hopelessly obscure single by an outfit that only shifted a few copies, you have to ask yourself why it sold so poorly in the first place. There may be a few hidden treasures out there, but these are few and far between, and seldom challenge the major players for musical superiority. Mind you, perfection isn't what everyone wants; some of us simply wish to hear the ramshackle, poorly-produced material which, in terms of energy and enthusiasm, allows the wannabes to come to the fore and to compensate for their musical shortcomings.

It's inevitable that, wherever there's money to be made, a few shady characters will come out of the woodwork to do their evil work. In fact, NWOBHM has, thus far, been very fortunate to have been affected by relatively little in the way of underhand activities. Although the odd LP has been illegally mastered onto CD by labels such as Reborn Classics and Mausoleum Classix, this was perhaps (as with the much-praised series of Japanese bootleg compilations) more a case of satisfying the niche market demand in the face of legitimate label indifference than anything more sinister. Furthermore, aside from a tiny number of live bootlegs which appeared on vinyl in the early 80's, very little in the way of unreleased material has found its way into the public's hands without the artists' consent, and, with the exception of a couple of 'reissues' of dubious legality, there's no evidence to suggest that any of the original vinyl items have yet been counterfeited on any scale. It may still happen, admittedly, but I reckon that we've all become a lot more cautious in recent years, and would be reluctant to part with hard cash for suspiciously new-looking rarities (twenty years on, there aren't many mint records with pristine sleeves around) or highly questionable 'white labels'. It's almost certain, however, that some people have been tempted to fabricate sleeves for singles which weren't originally issued as such, either for their own amusement or with the deliberate intention to defraud. This is a tricky area, as some releases of the time had genuine, promo-only sleeves which, often being hand-made, tended to be pretty flimsy and haphazardly-constructed. If in doubt, don't pay more for one of these than you would for a standard issue, particularly if the sleeve has the appearance of a photocopy and doesn't carry any information which isn't given on the record itself.

Following the example of various enterprising companies and individuals who were illegally manufacturing CD's with seemingly notable success, companies such as British Steel, High Vaultage, Zoom Club and Vinyl Tap decided to

get in on the act, licensing various archive material for release on disc format. These have been worthwhile enough ventures, although they further reinforce the general opinion that, if a longplayer wasn't a particularly popular choice originally, it's highly unlikely to break the bank the second time around. In fact, collectors appear to have been more impressed with compilations and releases featuring obscure or otherwise-unavailable material. With labels such as Neat Metal and (to a considerably lesser extent) Heavy Metal/Revolver having returned from the dead to re-release old albums and also promote resurrected NWOBHM outfits alongside newer bands, aficionados of the genre are being treated to the option of acquiring prime-era NWOBHM on officially-sanctioned CD's for the first time. Various other material has emerged on disc from smaller labels, including worthy albums by the likes of ANGEL WITCH, TRESPASS, PAGAN ALTAR, PARIAH, BUFFALO, LYADRIVE, AFTER DARK and SEVENTH SON, which can only be a good thing, although the limited distribution networks of many of the emergent companies concerned means that the fans may encounter considerable difficulty getting hold of (or even finding out about) such releases. Again, with the growth of the internet, things undoubtedly have the potential to improve quite substantially, and I firmly believe that if someone were able to establish themselves as a reliable and comprehensive resource for new NWOBHM releases, then they would do very well in the global market.

To conclude, I'd offer a couple of humble pieces of advice to those whose lives are touched by NWOBHM.

(a) To dealers: be realistic. Acknowledge the painful fact that the NWOBHM market isn't as capacious as many once thought, and that there are several different levels of collecting; for every thousand people who might purchase a TYGERS OF PAN TANG, DIAMOND HEAD or VENOM record (at a reasonable price, mind), there might only be a tiny handful who would consider buying a METAL MIRROR single, for example. Of these, only one or two might be prepared to stump up a three-figure asking price for such an item. Let's face it, you're unlikely to meet these devotees at a provincial record fair. Don't be greedy. If the only way to make a profit is to sell to another dealer, then you'd be well advised do so, or you're likely to have unsaleable records in your possession for years to come. Also, if you're tempted to inflate the price of a completely obscure and unknown record to extreme values, be aware that you might suffer a customer backlash in the long run if it turns out to be a turkey.

(b) To labels: don't get carried away. You might be offered the rights to reissue everything under the sun, but half of it just won't sell. You should know by now that NWOBHM collectors can't be fobbed off with unnecessary reissues or ropy compilations of easily-obtained material just by slapping a prominent 'NWOBHM' sticker on the cover. Do a bit of market research, find out what people really want in their collections, you might be surprised. If you can identify a genuine demand for certain album reissues, you'd be amazed how much difference a few bonus tracks can make. If, on the other hand, you can successfully secure the rights to unissued material, there's no point making your finished product look like a shabby bootleg. Get someone fairly knowledgeable (or, at the very least, keen) to write some informative sleeve notes, include a biography or discography, photos, anything rather than just the bare details.

(c) To collectors: don't let market forces dictate what you have in your record collection. If you really can't live without the rare stuff then you might want to give serious consideration as to what you're actually getting for your money. Having splashed out on this book (or either of the previous 'IRON PAGES' NWOBHM volumes), you've hopefully got the information you need at your fingertips. Unless you're extremely well-off (no, me neither), you'll find it immensely difficult to justify blowing a hundred pounds (or more) on what might be a hyped-up single, so digest the group's entry and form a mental opinion of what it probably sounds like in advance. Make sure it's got a picture cover if it's supposed to have one, but beware of *'promotional'* sleeves which might have been knocked up at a later stage. Shop around. Even for mid-priced items, there can be a considerable disparity in prices among different dealers. If you appreciate the efforts of the companies who are putting NWOBHM out on CD, let them know about it. If you're not happy with their choice of material, or if you have any suggestions, get in touch with those involved, they're not mind-readers. If we can finally establish a modicum of two-way communication, the future could be pretty bright for NWOBHM addicts.

ACE LANE

Mick Clarke (v)
Paul Brook (g)
Gary Sleet (g)
Stef Prokopczuk (b)
Roy Whyke (d)

The rather perplexing name of ACE LANE represented a young bunch of hopefuls who first came into existence at some point in 1982, following Stef Prokopczuk's defection from GASKIN to collaborate with vocalist Mick Clarke (who had, as it turns out, also been involved with GASKIN in the preceding few months, but things hadn't quite worked out as planned) in an attempt to create a sophisticated rock outfit. After searching throughout Yorkshire and the East Midlands for a suitable set of musical accomplices, the duo's new venture soon established itself as a stand-alone unit whose own compositions bore little resemblance to the high-concept works of their previous employers. Within a remarkably short space of time, ACE LANE had managed to wangle a deal with the Expulsion concern (the latest home of WITCHFYNDE), whereupon the lads were invited to enter the studio towards the end of the year and encouraged to capture an album's worth of material on tape. Their selection of originals met with Expulsion's approval, and so the debut ACE LANE long-player was duly released (under the GRIM REAPER-baiting title of »See You In Heaven«) early in 1983. From the opening moments of "Emotion", however, it's pretty clear that ACE LANE were very much 'the band who aspired to be DIAMOND HEAD', coming across (in places, if not throughout) as a highly-similar NWOBHM proposition who were perfectly happy to operate in this distinctive, post-ZEPPELIN/FREE/PURPLE enclave of melodic-but-powerful metal.

The »See You In Heaven« set is actually an enjoyable enough album as a whole, although most of the individual compositions (some of which are considerably more lightweight, and bring the likes of MEANSTREAK to mind) simply don't have the personality, structure or technical prowess of the semi-analogous material penned by the aforementioned Stourbridge gods. In a funny way, much of it seems closer to the music featured on the latter's »Canterbury« (a long-player which hadn't actually been recorded at that time), although ACE LANE's NWOBHM-era reference points would generally tend to favour slightly later groups such as TARGET UK and SURFACE. All things considered, though, it's fair to say that there weren't too many British outfits doing this sort of thing back in 1983, so let's give some credit where it's due and acknowledge those strong-willed groups who didn't merely follow the trends. While »See You In Heaven« eventually emerged on a grand total of three European labels (after it was picked up by both Roadrunner and Mausoleum), presumably in a concerted attempt to maximise exposure for the outfit, it wasn't a great commercial success in any part of the world, and there was never any serious talk of a follow-up.

Two of the album's more capable tracks ("Never The Same" and "Emotion") were, incidentally, also issued on Mausoleum's poorly-received »Metal Prisoners« sampler (alongside the likes of ACID, SEDUCER, FACTORY and CHINAWITE), leading to speculation that this pairing might additionally have appeared as a single in their own right, although I've never actually heard of a copy being offered for sale. It looks as though ACE LANE had finally disintegrated (in the wake of continued public disinterest) by the end of 1984 at the very latest, although vocalist Mick Clarke persevered with various minor club acts, and even went on to front an eponymous project at one stage. Drummer Roy Whyke also kept himself fairly busy in the music business, picking up the odd bit of session work here and there, including a stint backing little-known indie personality MARK JACKSON, who contributed a track to the obscure »Bites And Stabs« compilation a short time later. More recently, the obliging sticksman has been assisting former TURBO vocalist Des Horsfall in some of his dodgy solo ventures, but I wouldn't bother seeking out any of those releases unless you're partial to a bit of country rock!

LP's
»See You In Heaven« Expulsion 1983/Roadrunner 1983
[UK/Dutch issue]
»See You In Heaven« Mausoleum 1983
[Alternate European issue in different cover]

CD's
»See You In Heaven« Mausoleum Classix 1994
[Unofficial release]

Compilation Appearances
"Never The Same" on »Metal Prisoners« LP Mausoleum 1983
"Emotion" on »Metal Prisoners« LP Mausoleum 1983

AFTER DARK

Steve Annetts (v)
Mick Hare (g)
J.C. (g)
Ian King (b)
Andy Harris (k)
John Metcalfe (d)

On the face of it, Berkshire's talented AFTER DARK (not to be confused with a lightweight pop act who recorded a private album on SRT in the early 80's) appeared to have everything going for them: a capable and experienced set of musicians, an extensive and varied repertoire of original material, plus the ambition and determination to achieve their major-label destiny in the long term. As with so many others, however, the unfortunate outfit fell victim to the harsh reality of the horrendously unfair rock scene of the early 80's, where the Darwinian *'survival of the fittest'* hypothesis was taken to fairly ludicrous extremes. For the six musicians involved with the AFTER DARK venture at the outset, their relationship with the rock scene had all started back in the mid-to-late 70's with various long-forgotten local bands (vocalist Steve Annetts, for example, had spent many happy years fronting a bluesy club act called HEARTBREAKER, whose not-remotely-predictable speciality was performing an abundance of FREE covers), before they eventually gravitated together at some point in 1980, their collective intention being to establish a contemporary outfit who could hold their own with the more high-profile exponents of the NWOBHM archetype.

With little or no fanfare, the six-piece proposition went on to become something of a regional favourite over the coming months, and they were soon tempted to issue some self-financed vinyl product to sell to their rapidly-swelling fan base. Their first release took the form of a three track EP, featuring "Evil Woman", "Johnny" and "Lucy", and clearly showed the lads to have retained something of a 70's influence in their sound as opposed to jumping on the NWOBHM bandwagon wholesale. In particular, the excellent "Evil Woman" (later featured on the »NWOBHM Vol.4« bootleg) went a long way towards proving that, if WHITE SPIRIT were the bastard offspring of Gillan-era DEEP PURPLE, then AFTER DARK were surely more aligned with the aforementioned outfit in their more raunchy, Coverdale-fronted period. Apart from WHITE SPIRIT, however, there would be additional NWOBHM comparisons with the likes of BABY TUCKOO (in particular), XERO, LAUTREC and the HANDSOME BEASTS, although AFTER DARK were a talented bunch whose musical prowess and charismatic vocalist had the potential to carry them a long way in the rock world. The remaining tracks on the EP (the paired "Johnny" and "Lucy", two titles which had earlier appeared together on the OVERLORD 7", but it seems to be nothing more than a spooky coincidence) weren't quite up to the standard of "Evil Woman", although both were considerably more accomplished than the haphazard tunes being churned out by many of their contemporaries. Nowadays, the first AFTER DARK release (issued in a monochrome picture sleeve showing something vaguely resembling a dragon's head) is a highly-valued rarity, although a fair few copies have surfaced over the years.

On the back of this first release, the lads began to pick up useful support slots with touring acts such as DIAMOND HEAD, GILLAN, SAMSON and TRUST, after which the ambitious bunch began giving serious thought to the possibility of releasing an album of their own. Clearly, however, with no label sponsorship having come their way, it seemed that the only option would be to record the whole affair in advance and then either tout the tapes around the minor companies or save their collective pennies for another self-financed piece of vinyl. Backed by their management team, the outfit proceeded to immerse themselves in a writing/recording frenzy for several months during 1983, and soon had well over an album's worth of material at their disposal. At first, AFTER DARK formulated tentative plans to issue an LP (»Masked By Midnight«) on their own Lazer Records label, and duly set about creating something of a buzz by pressing a limited quantity of promotional picture discs, featuring two of the tracks from the forthcoming long-player. On the evidence of this release, however, it would appear that AFTER DARK had branched out into rather more powerful territory, with "Deathbringer", in particular, being a forceful effort with elements of DRAGONSLAYER, BLADE RUNNER or Hampshire's LONE WOLF. Mind you, "Call Of The Wild", a blatant attempt at an epic power ballad, was somewhat less inspiring, but at least it was a departure from the rudimentary, 70's-inspired musings which had shaped their early material. This promo-only 7" was, as you would expect, pressed in modest quantities, and isn't exactly a commonly-sighted beast these days, although its current value is considerably lower than that of the debut EP.

By the spring of 1984, the group had completed their studio sessions and had also undertaken a notable amount of productive gigging further afield (including more appearances with DIAMOND HEAD, this time on the latter's recent UK tour), so things were hunky-dory in that sense. With regard to getting their LP into the shops, however, they had apparently reached something of an impasse, and it soon became painfully clear that any notion of releasing »Masked By Midnight« was now little more than a pipe-dream after all. With the outfit's management having lost faith and cold-heartedly deserted them in their hour of need, the lads saw the proverbial rug pulled from beneath their feet, and they were left with little option but to place the whole project on hold until their circumstances (financial or otherwise) improved. Sadly, however, things never really got all that much better for the luckless AFTER DARK, although the central characters still continued to write and record together (it's believed that they almost ended up with enough usable material for a second album) while attempting to maintain something resembling a stable line-up. In the end, however, personnel instability and creeping disillusionment finally drove the musicians apart, and the last incarnation of AFTER DARK eventually ground to a halt in around 1985. In the wake of their demise, guitarist Mick Hare moved on to the ill-fated IRON HEART, who called it a day after just one release, the semi-decent »Running Away« 12" from 1988. Vocalist Steve Annetts, on the other hand, proceeded to sing in a couple of minor melodic rock acts before throwing his weight behind a little-remembered project called DANGEROUS AGE in the early 90's. This bunch even got as far as releasing a full album (a seldom-seen, mediocre affair called »Troubled Times«), which appeared on a German label, Long Island.

Interestingly, however, the vocalist's affiliation with the company eventually led to negotiations for the AFTER DARK master tapes, and a small-scale bidding war broke out among some of the more prominent, NWOBHM-friendly concerns of the day. In the end, Germany's Art Of Music put the best offer on the table, and the »Masked By Midnight« album finally saw a belated CD release, a decade after the group had bitten the dust. It was a lovingly-prepared issue, with decent artwork, lyrics etc., and the whole package came across as a fitting tribute to the band rather than a hastily-assembled cash-in. Steve Annetts was keen to give his reaction to the renewed interest in his former outfit: 'The whole NWOBHM revival came as a great surprise to me. As far as AFTER DARK were concerned, there's no denying that we all still hoped to get a second chance eventually, given that we were such a strong outfit with so much good material of our own. It's just such a pity that real rock music counts for nothing in England.' (Ref: Iron Pages No.35, 1996). The album was sympathetically-received by many reviewers, although its comparatively limited distribution outside Germany meant that only a small percentage of fans were initially made aware of its existence. Once copies had finally made it into wider circulation, however, there were suggestions that a revamped version of AFTER DARK might return from the wilderness and play a few comeback shows to promote the release. Almost inevitably, though, the initial enthusiasm soon wore off, and there has been little or no musical activity from any of the original members since then.

7" EP's
»Evil Woman« SRT 1981

7" Singles
»Deathbringer« Lazer Records 1983
[Most issued as promotional picture discs, a few as black vinyl test pressings]

CD's
»Masked By Midnight« Art Of Music 1995
[Features unreleased studio material from early 80's]

Compilation Appearances
"Evil Woman" on »NWOBHM Vol.4« Bootleg CD 1992

AFTER HOURS

Bayley
Carter

If nothing else, this humble volume should prove, once and for all, that the influence of women on the NWOBHM movement extends significantly beyond the usual reference points of GIRLSCHOOL and ROCK GODDESS. For our first example, we present AFTER HOURS, an obscure, female-fronted proposition (not to be confused with the Hampshire ensemble who offered the world an album or two of AOR in the late 80's) who released their »All Over Town« two-tracker at the very height of the NWOBHM explosion in 1980. One of the heavier records to feature a lady vocalist during the early part of the decade, the A-side showcases a fairly raunchy performance (from what sounds like a very young chantress indeed) along the general lines of ROCK GODDESS or AVENUE, while "Suspicious", on the reverse, is a slower, more bluesy number (featuring a double-female vocal in places), undeniably similar in its construction to AMAZON's "Hypnotising You". The single (issued in a cheaply-printed, cut-out picture cover) hasn't turned up in significant quantities thus far, rendering it a semi-collectable rarity amongst NWOBHM aficionados. No additional details of the band's personnel or activities on the scene are available at present (I'm assuming that the JSG label refers to the Bradford studio of the same name, which tends to suggest that AFTER HOURS were based somewhere in the Yorkshire area), and no other material is known to have been immortalised on vinyl, so it looks as though their existence was probably pretty brief. Further information would, as ever, be appreciated...

7" Singles
»All Over Town« JSG Records 1980

ALEC JOHNSON BAND

Alec Johnson (g)
Steve Bartley (d)

I've always had a bit of a fundamental problem with eponymous projects, particularly when the individual in question isn't exactly a household name to start off with. I mean, what sort of impression does it give Joe Public if you're either too big-headed or unimaginative to think up an original handle for your outfit? Anyway, the ALEC JOHNSON BAND established themselves in the North West of England during the late 70's, having evolved from an earlier rock concern called DESTINY, who, at one point, apparently featured personnel from the best-known of the various bands called ENGLAND. Their one and only single (issued without a picture sleeve) was released in mid-1979 (the group going out on a short tour of minor venues to promote the release shortly afterwards), and coupled the easy-going "Busman's Holiday" with "My Lady". Produced by the ever-obliging Gordon Rowley of local lads STRIFE, the music is only marginally NWOBHM, being rather more in tune with various other North West rockers of the day such as EXPORT, NUTZ and the aforementioned STRIFE. It's quite enjoyable, though, with the bluesy, good-time sound and fairly decent vocal effort also bringing the likes of NUTHIN FANCY and TRACK 4 to mind. Clearly, old Gordon Rowley was quite impressed by their collective talents, as he later recruited Johnson and drummer Steve Bartley to the fold as he was putting together his NIGHTWING project. Presumably, the ALEC JOHNSON BAND had already ceased to exist by this point, and the other musicians involved in this musical venture (assuming there were any, that is) remain unknown for the time being.

7" Singles
»Busman's Holiday« RFP Records 1979

ALKATRAZZ

Craig Stevens (v)
Bob Jenner (g)
Gary Bevan (b)
Nick Parsons (d)

It's somewhat ironic that one of Kent's least innovative (but still undeniably talented) rock outfits could have become the region's major success story, but it looks as though ALKATRAZZ (not to be confused either with Graham Bonnet's ALCATRAZZ or with the MAN offshoot ALKATRAZ) just happened to be in the right place at precisely the right time when the giant RCA corporation came sniffing around in their search for new talent towards the end of 1980. Having formed at more or less the height of the NWOBHM explosion (from the ashes of an unsuccessful minor bunch called INTERFACE), the emergent group gained some early credibility through a handful of relatively successful support slots with the likes of MAGNUM and the TYGERS OF PAN TANG, and it's fair to say that the tuneful bunch did, on occasion, share a rather similar musical outlook to that of future labelmates GRAND PRIX. With the coveted RCA deal in the bag, the musicians were encouraged to pen an album's worth of original material at their convenience, after which the ambitious quartet duly entered the recording studio to lay the foundations for their imminent assault on an unsuspecting rock scene.

While ALKATRAZZ might not have set out to promote themselves as *bona fide* new metal contenders in the first instance, their debut long-player (the »Young Blood« effort from 1981) turned out to be a capable enough offering which revealed the ensemble to be only slightly removed from the rough'n'ready NWOBHM archetype. In particular, such listenable compositions as the excellent "Rockin' High" (also utilised as the basis of a tie-in single, as was the weaker "You And The Night"), "Deadline" and "Crazy Dancer" all bring to mind contemporaries such as MOTHER'S RUIN, LAUTREC and early DEF LEPPARD, while the outstanding "Run Wild" (which, bizarrely enough, appeared as the flipside on *both* of their first two singles) is a markedly more powerful inclusion, and is undeniably similar to certain material found on the first SPARTAN WARRIOR album. Elsewhere, however, things seem a bit too sanitised and polished to have satisfied the whims of the denim-clad hordes of the day, and the initial batch of ALKATRAZZ vinyl appears to have been largely overlooked at the time, in spite of the best efforts of RCA to promote them. Still, the lads managed to hitch a ride on a lengthy tour organised by labelmates SAMSON, but they didn't exactly blow the headliners away. Having said all that, however, »Young Blood« is a pretty competent release which still has the potential to appeal to a fair proportion of modern-day fans of the NWOBHM genre.

The outfit were retained by RCA, despite mediocre sales of their debut, and album number two, issued a year later, saw an almost inevitable move away from their original roots towards considerably more commercial material, although the puzzlingly-titled »Radio 5« once again represented a competent enough set of recordings. In spite of the keyboards (contributed by guest musician Jo Julian, who also produced the whole affair, and who went on to provide the same service on PAUL SAMSON's »Joint Forces« album) and the grand, harmonised choruses, however, the lads were just about saved from the tag of *'SURVIVOR wannabes'* by a couple of more rocking numbers, notably "Long Time No Love" and "Short Change". Overall, though, if we're talking in terms of facile DEF LEPPARD comparisons, it's definitely one for fans of »Pyromania« rather than »On Through The Night«. As something of a cost-cutting exercise, just one single was trotted out to promote the new album, featuring the radio-friendly "Think It Over" as the lead track, but this release ultimately failed to dent the charts. By this stage, it looked as though ALKATRAZZ were already well on their way to becoming an out-and-out AOR proposition, destined to churn out numerous formulaic albums of inoffensive rock and receive endless *'heavy rotation'* on American radio stations. Oddly enough, it didn't happen.

The last known piece of ALKATRAZZ recording activity appears to have been a summer visit to the BBC's studios, the lads having been invited to lay down their first session for the 'Friday Rock Show'. Broadcast on the 6th of August 1982, the session allowed the band to showcase four tracks from their latest album, namely "Miles Away", "Blinded", "Long Time No Love" and "Communication". By this juncture, however, they had already lost original bassist Gary Bevan, his immediate replacement being an unfamiliar chap called Philip Tame. Furthermore, they were now also utilising the services of keyboard player Kirk Pinkney, another new addition to the fold. In the long term, it looks as though this personnel instability might have contributed to the eventual disintegration of the outfit, and it's not currently known whether or not they were ever offered the opportunity to record a third album for RCA. Whatever the story, no further releases ever materialised, and they appear to have called it quits for good by 1983, after which the one-time members all kept a remarkably low profile for many years. There were, however, reliable reports that various ex-ALKATRAZZ personnel became involved with a little-remembered, early 90's venture called FLYING ANVIL (conceived by erstwhile NICKY MOORE BAND stalwart Leigh Highwood), although nobody seems to recall which of them might have played a part, so that will have to remain a mystery for now.

LP's
»Young Blood« RCA 1981
»Radio 5« RCA 1982

7" Singles
»Rockin' High« RCA 1981
»You And The Night« RCA 1981
»Think It Over« RCA 1982
[Also issued as limited edition picture disc]

Compilation Appearances
"Blame It On The Night" on »Hot Shower« LP RCA 1982
"Short Change" on »Hot Shower« LP RCA 1982

AMAZON

Lori Chacko (v)
Gerry Moffett (g)
Andy Bown (b)
Richard Cottle (k)
Peter Van Hooke (d)

London's AMAZON gained a fairly healthy following amongst the capital's rock fraternity in the early 80's, undoubtedly helped along by the presence of the statuesque Lori Chacko, the owner of a powerful set of lungs and some inadvisably minuscule stage outfits. Not that this was the outfit's main selling point or anything, perish the thought. Plucked from relative obscurity after a year or two on the club circuit by the emergent (but short-lived) Megamusic label, who evidently had pretty big plans for the group, a promotional-only 7" (a double A-sided effort featuring "Hypnotising You" and "Fallen Angel") was circulated to various influential parties in 1981, but the introductory two-tracker largely failed to elicit the required response. Clearly, the British public wasn't regarded as crying out for a melodic rock proposition with PAT BENATAR-style vocals (precisely the same fate befell such similarly-inclined acts as AFTER HOURS, SIAN, LOST PROPERTY and AVENUE, for instance), and the various members went their separate ways soon afterwards, dejected by their lack of success in the short term.

Having had time to reconsider the situation, however, the plucky vocalist ultimately decided to have another bite at the cherry, and reassembled a working version of AMAZON in 1983 (using mainly session musicians to serve as a backing band this time), with Chacko's immediate intention being to record a long-player (tentatively titled »Branded«) at Riverside Studios in London. The singer certainly had some talented helpers joining in the fun, notably Richard Cottle (one of JOHN SLOMAN's long-time associates) and journeyman bassist Andy Bown, both of whom had previously been employed by PETER FRAMPTON, plus the much-travelled Peter Van Hooke of STACKRIDGE, MIKE AND THE MECHANICS *et al.*, but things evidently just didn't work out when it came to the recording sessions. Certainly, no further vinyl product seems to have materialised under the original AMAZON name (the *'reformation'* was, by virtue of its rather unofficial nature, a relatively evanescent affair), suggesting that world domination was never a particularly realistic possibility for Chacko at that stage. If, however, you should encounter a copy of their single, especially with its flimsy sleeve depicting the vocalist herself, you can rest assured that you're unlikely to see a rarer record from the period. As with LAUTREC's debut, only pressed as white-label copies, the number of AMAZON promos known to exist today can be counted on the fingers of one hand.

Ms. Chacko had presumably had her fill of the UK by around 1984, and subsequently made the pilgrimage across the Atlantic to the land of the free in order to pursue a combined career in both the musical and thespian arts. Over the ensuing months, she touted her wares around the majors and was, surprisingly enough, eventually offered the chance to deliver a full album's worth of ostensibly *'solo'* material. The resultant long-player, simply entitled »Chacko«, was apparently released by the mighty Polydor concern in around 1985 or thereabouts (I think there was even a tie-in single or two), but doesn't really seem to have shifted enough units to justify all the effort and expenditure, and the ambitious lass was last heard of trying her luck in a variety of minor Stateside film appearances in her inexorable quest for fame and fortune.

7" Singles
»**Hypnotising You**« Megamusic Records 1981

ANGEL STREET

Dave Colwell (g)
Dave Page

Disappointingly scant information has been forthcoming about the enigmatic ANGEL STREET (although they were almost certainly based in the East End of London), whose sole contribution to the music industry seems to have been the undated »Midnight Man« single, apparently released in the pre-explosion days of the late 70's. Issued on the small-time Motor label without the unnecessary extravagance of a picture sleeve, but pressed (rather unusually for an independent rock release of the time) on coloured (blue) vinyl, this is a prime example of good-time rock'n'roll in the grand old British tradition. The A-side is the more rocking of the two numbers, evoking early TERRAPLANE or TRUX, whereas the reverse ("Running Away") is a bit more restrained, in a kind of *'BAD COMPANY meets the EAGLES'* manner. Possibly not quite heavy enough for those weaned on the likes of SATAN and VENOM, but a reasonable enough effort for fans of RAGE (UK version), all the same. Given the fact that nobody seems to recall ANGEL STREET being particularly high-profile faces on the capital's rock scene at the time, however, I reckon that the fly-by-night outfit must have splintered within a remarkably short timescale, having made little or no impression upon the movers and shakers. Maybe they would have enjoyed a bit more longevity if they'd started out a year or so later...

ANGEL STREET axeman Dave Colwell (a veteran of minor act HOTLINE, who employed various future NWOBHM stalwarts) became involved with the short-lived 720 (who somehow managed to wangle a support slot with the mighty BLACK SABBATH after MORE dropped out) in around 1982 before going on to assist (briefly) in the studio activities of TERRAPLANE. The in-demand guitarist also found time to help out in the NEW TORPEDOS and MICK RALPHS BAND before joining SAMSON/PAUL SAMSON'S EMPIRE in the mid-80's and subsequently (as well as penning the odd effort such as "Reach Out" for IRON MAIDEN) playing a part in Adrian Smith's short-lived ASAP project. Indeed, it's entirely possible that he was even briefly involved with the fortunes of either URCHIN or the BROADWAY BRATS in the dim and distant past, given that Adrian Smith was keen to find work for many of his former colleagues at one time or another. More recently, Colwell has been recruited as a touring member of the rejuvenated BAD COMPANY, and still keeps himself busy in terms of session work. The ANGEL STREET single, meanwhile, isn't regarded as a major-league rarity, but further information would, nevertheless, still be appreciated. Good name, though!

7" Singles
»Midnight Man« Motor Records 1979
[Issued as limited edition on blue vinyl]

ANGEL WITCH

Kevin Heybourne (v,g)
Rob Downing (g)
Kevin 'Skids' Riddles (b)
Dave Hogg (d)

While the music of DIAMOND HEAD will forever be associated with inspiring Lars Ulrich to form METALLICA, it would appear that his former colleague, Dave Mustaine, was originally far more attuned to the heavier sounds of ANGEL WITCH, the legendary bunch of East End heroes who first got the music bug back in 1977. Originally adopting the unholy name of LUCIFER, the quartet (the brainchild of youthful guitarist Kev Heybourne) decided to set about taking the doomy framework of BLACK SABBATH, adding a pinch of JUDAS PRIEST-style dynamism and updating the whole concoction to create something which would be both listenable and powerful, yet still satisfyingly heavy to scare away all those nasty punk upstarts. For the first couple of years on the capital's rock scene (during which time the lads settled on the more individualistic identity of ANGEL WITCH), their live sets were still rapidly evolving from the cover-dominated early affairs (with the ever-popular SABBATH standard "Paranoid" and UFO's "Lights Out", for example), but a repertoire of impressive originals (formative efforts such as "Into The Dark" and "Help Yourself" were soon being superseded by newer, even heavier numbers such as "Extermination Day" and "Baphomet") was steadily accruing, as was a truly fervent fan base who accompanied the protagonists to many a memorable outing. Certain promoters soon identified ANGEL WITCH and their *'rent-a-crowd'* following as a potentially-lucrative support act, so the outfit were soon being invited to hook up with a wide variety of more established touring concerns.

After paying their dues by slogging away on the largely-unrewarding pub/club circuit (playing the usual variety of dives throughout the capital) for the best part of two years, the lads were delighted to be able to showcase their music to a far wider audience at these well-attended shows, and their *'management'* (*i.e.* Heybourne's father) was soon touting ANGEL WITCH around as the next big thing, especially once the seeds of the forthcoming NWOBHM explosion had well and truly germinated. By late 1978, the foursome began making their first trips to the recording studio, and were soon laying down embryonic versions of compositions such as "Sorceress" and "White Witch", which would be attracting the interest of various record companies before long. By the second half of 1979, by which time the band had amassed a huge tally of gigs in and around the capital, a demo tape featuring a selection of newly-recorded material drew the attention of EMI (*via* local DJ/entrepreneur Neal Kay), who were in the process of assembling a one-off compilation to celebrate this fleeting interest in new British metal. This culminated in their "Baphomet" composition being lifted for inclusion on the »Metal For Muthas« album in the early part of 1980, allowing the public to hear the full might of ANGEL WITCH on vinyl for the first time. It was a substantial effort, with bludgeoning riffs, an interesting structure and more than a nod towards BLACK SABBATH (both musically and lyrically), in spite of the group's repeated attempts to distance themselves from such facile and oft-made comparisons. Nevertheless, there wasn't exactly an abundance of British outfits attempting such a heavyweight interpretation of the genre, so it's fair to say that the likes of ANGEL WITCH and DEMON were certainly paving the way for similarly-minded acts such as WITCHFINDER GENERAL, SATAN and the DESOLATION ANGELS in years to come.

By the time the compilation hit the shops, ANGEL WITCH had already dispensed with their second guitarist, Rob Downing, and elected to continue as a trio (Kev Heybourne being assisted by the rather more experienced Kevin Riddles and Dave Hogg) from that point onwards. Fortunately, the slimmed-down version still had the ability to carry off their material with a great deal of conviction, and their overall sound altered little as a result. To promote their appearance on »Metal For Muthas«, ANGEL WITCH were swiftly invited to lay down a session for the 'Fri-

day Rock Show', where they unveiled "Sweet Danger", "Angel Witch", "Angel Of Death" and "Extermination Day" (broadcast on the 14th of March 1980), an excellent selection of material which was soon drawing considerable praise from the listeners, with "Extermination Day" subsequently being plucked for inclusion on the BBC's »Metal Explosion« album of session highlights later in the year. With the public having now taken to ANGEL WITCH in major fashion, EMI decided to get in on the action, allowing the trio to lay down their debut single shortly thereafter. The record would be based around the upbeat "Sweet Danger", with "Flight Nineteen" as the flipside and the lengthy (and superbly-titled) "Hades Paradise" as a bonus on the 12" version, the whole thing being packaged in an imposing sleeve with the baphomet image that ANGEL WITCH used on most of their T-shirts, patches, and so forth. »Sweet Danger« proved to be an immensely popular purchase among metal fans, with many thousands of units being shifted within a matter of weeks. In fact, it was such a huge success that it even made it into the mainstream charts (and pitifully few of the acts featured in this book can lay claim to such a

feat), but this notable achievement was, ludicrously enough, to have an adverse effect on the future career of the luckless ANGEL WITCH.

Here's the deal. Each week, the mainstream singles charts listed the 75 top-selling, major-label records which had been made available to the public, a few of which would remain in the charts for some time and many of which would disappear from sight almost immediately. The nightmare scenario, therefore, would be for a hapless act to hit number 75 and stay there for just one week. Guess who became the first ever bunch to do it? Yep, good old ANGEL WITCH. If they had only reached number 76, nobody would have been any the wiser, but they went into the history books (the 'Guinness Book Of Hit Singles' and even the 'Guinness Book Of Records'), where they were cruelly identified as the 'least successful chart act of all time', which a considerable number of halfwits seem to have interpreted as 'least successful act of all time'. It was all a bit of a laugh back then, although this claim to infamy has been the source of widespread media obloquy in later years (particularly among certain journalists who seem to have had something of a personal vendetta against the group), and is something which ANGEL WITCH have found quite difficult to live down. It was an example of cruel irony, considering the fact that these charts represented the most popular musical acts of the day, not the also-rans, and it's also particularly galling that nobody ever mentions the fact that the »Keep On Believing« 7", released by GRAND PRIX three years later, achieved *exactly* the same thing. Undeterred by their *'failure'* to achieve a 'Top 10' placing, ANGEL WITCH went from strength to strength in the live environment, and were soon enjoying support slots with the likes of APRIL WINE, KROKUS and BLACK SABBATH, although it came as something of a disappointment when EMI decided to concentrate on pushing IRON MAIDEN, leaving acts such as ANGEL WITCH, SAMSON and ETHEL THE FROG without a deal.

By the summer of 1980, however, ANGEL WITCH were in serious negotiations with several labels, and an announcement concerning their future career seemed to be imminent. First of all, though, the band were to enjoy a high-profile appearance at the Reading Festival, where they set the stage for headliners DEF LEPPARD and WHITESNAKE by delivering an immensely well-received set featuring such compositions as "Angel Of Death", "Sorceress", the anthemic "Angel Witch" and the seldom-performed "Guillotine". With ANGEL WITCH having proved to be one of the more successful acts on the day, the interest of the various labels was additionally piqued, and a contract with Bronze was signed shortly thereafter. Sensing a hot proposition, the label ushered ANGEL WITCH into the studio almost immediately, whereupon the lads finally began work on that long-awaited debut album. After several weeks of hard graft, the trio emerged with a long-player to take the world by storm, and Bronze prepared a taster in the shape of the »Angel Witch« 7" (b/w "Gorgon") to whet the public's appetite. Understandably, with the single being based around a particular live favourite, sales were brisk once again, and the powerful flipside turned out to be just as popular with the fans. Strangely, there were two separate pressings of the 7" (with different labels and mastered off different plates, although there's no particularly obvious difference in the sound), one of which claimed that the tracks were 'taken from the forthcoming album »Surprise, Surprise«'. Well, that notion seems to have fallen by the wayside at some stage, and the long-player subsequently emerged as an eponymous effort. Fortunately, the single failed to make the mainstream listings this time, and so ANGEL WITCH were returned to their rightful place as an immensely popular metal band as opposed to a horrendously unsuccessful chart proposition.

The first ANGEL WITCH album appeared towards the end of 1980, and featured a healthy quota of live favourites, some of which had been unveiled on their singles and sessions, but some of which were being heard in studio form for the very first time. It was all immensely listenable (and surprisingly varied), with powerful compositions such as "Atlantis" "Angel Of Death" and "Gorgon" contrasting effectively with the rather more subtle and restrained sections contained within "Sorceress", "White Witch" and the outstanding "Free Man" (later reworked by DEATH SS member STEVE SYLVESTER on a solo LP). »Angel Witch« really was a ground-breaking album ("Confused", mooted as a possible single at one stage, was subsequently covered by both ONSLAUGHT and TROUBLE), and sales were soon mounting up, much to the delight of Bronze, who sensed that they really were onto a winner with ANGEL WITCH. After a handful of gigs to promote the release, however, founder member Dave Hogg departed for pastures new, whereupon immensely experienced sticksman Dave Dufort was cheekily poached from the EF BAND, making his first appearance at the beginning of 1981. The lads couldn't have wished for a more capable drummer, since the much-travelled Dufort had been plying his trade in the music business since the late 60's, having worked with such diverse acts as PAPER BLITZ TISSUE, EAST OF EDEN, ALEX HARVEY and KEVIN AYERS along the way. He slotted into the ranks with consummate ease, although some of the fans were soon asking themselves who this 'old boy' at the back was, something which must have amused the youthful Heybourne and Riddles.

After a few gigs supporting MAX WEBSTER with the new line-up, ANGEL WITCH began making tentative plans for their second album, and the prolific outfit soon had enough usable material at their disposal. Live, they were already trying out new numbers such as "Evil Games" and "They Wouldn't Dare" (both slightly more accessible than the majority of their early compositions), and one of their performances from around this time was recorded and issued as a limited edition fan club cassette entitled »Give It Some Tickle« (don't ask). For some strange reason, however, the name of ANGEL WITCH was soon making fewer and fewer appearances in the gig guides, suggesting that something wasn't quite right in the camp. The band had originally been very keen to undertake a European tour to satisfy their fervent overseas fan base, but it looks as though Bronze failed to stump up the cash for such a jaunt. Even the previously-numerous British dates tailed off pretty quickly, though, and this once-prolific touring act were now relegated to little more than a studio project. Still, they managed to come up with an EP to keep the fans happy, the three-tracker featuring new efforts "Loser", "Suffer" and "Dr. Phibes", although the latest ANGEL WITCH numbers seemed to be drifting into perilously melodic waters ("Suffer" sounds like THE SWEET, for pity's sake) at times. "Loser" was an enjoyable enough song, admittedly, but the new, lightweight ANGEL WITCH failed to win the hearts of their fanatical followers, and it was soon crisis time for the outfit and their label.

In fact, it looks as though Bronze swiftly backed out of their agreement to sponsor a second long-player, fearing that a pretty significant loss of popularity was on the horizon. The dejected ANGEL WITCH struggled to maintain any great level of enthusiasm thereafter, and soon existed in name only, with one of their last undertakings together coming in the shape of a studio appearance on (wait for it) East German television (!), a bizarre scenario which saw the pride-swallowing ANGEL WITCH performing (well, miming) a handful of numbers in front of a bemused audience of schoolchildren and respectable middle-aged couples. Unintentionally hilarious. The lads must surely have wondered what the hell was going on by that stage, and the end came within a couple of months. The musicians might have reached the end of their tether as far as ANGEL WITCH was concerned, but all three were keen to play a further part in the music business, with Dufort and Riddles swiftly getting their all-new TYTAN (see separate entry) project of the ground, achieving a similar level of success initially but running into problems when it came to issuing their own debut album. Heybourne, meanwhile, inveigled his way into the ranks of London's legendary DEEP MACHINE as an extremely convenient replacement for departed founder member Bob Hooker. The guitarist remained with the outfit for only a short period, however (playing a handful of gigs and bringing a couple of his own compositions into the set list), before getting itchy feet and succumbing to the irresistible temptation to reform his beloved ANGEL WITCH at the beginning of 1982.

With a truly staggering level of audacity, Heybourne took two DEEP MACHINE cohorts with him (vocalist Roger Marsden and drummer Ricky Bruce) when he left, although the bewildered DEEP MACHINE soon re-established themselves after more or less merging with fellow strugglers BURN. In fact, Heybourne had tried to get bassist Andy Wrighton too, but the latter elected to stay with DEEP MACHINE instead (what a loyal chap), whereupon the all-new ANGEL WITCH roped in former REMUS DOWN BOULEVARD stalwart Gerry Cunningham to fill the bass vacancy. The luckless Roger Marsden was unexpectedly ousted after a mere one or two gigs, however (he later attempted to find fame and fortune with BORDELLO, KAMIKAZE and NEVADA FOXX before finally hooking up with the EF BAND for their »One Night Stand« LP), whereupon Heybourne assumed vocal duties once again and the outfit happily continued as a three-piece. Soon, they were getting back into the swing of things on the live front (getting out on the road with S.O.S. and SAMSON), and were rewarded for their efforts with a slot on the bill of the Mildenhall Festival in the summer of 1982, playing alongside the likes of MAGNUM and SAMSON (again). It proved to be a highly successful outing, and the canny bunch had arranged for their performance to be professionally recorded, the intention being to release a live album (Polydor had expressed an interest in issuing it) a short time later. In the event, the possibility of releasing the set in its original form was scuppered by a few serious technical hitches (poor sound and glitches in a couple of tracks), so the plan fell through. Undeterred, the lads laid down three studio compositions ("They Wouldn't Dare", "Nowhere To Run" and "Evil Games") for release as a comeback EP. Again, however, the initial idea came to nothing and the revived ANGEL WITCH fell apart (amidst a fair bit of internal friction) once more by the end of 1982.

There was little chance that Heybourne would remain out of the limelight for long, however, and he soon established a new outfit, this time taking the name BLIND FURY. He was joined by a completely new set of accomplices, namely erstwhile MARQUIS DE SADE bassist Pete Gordelier, former SARACEN (»Roksnax« version) vocalist Lou Taylor and unknown drummer Steve Coleman, and the four-piece burst forth upon the live scene in the early months of 1983, their sets consisting predominantly of freshly-penned material and just one or two ANGEL WITCH originals. The outfit didn't exactly exhaust themselves with constant gigging, though, but they still made it into the studio to lay down new versions of "Evil Games" and "Nowhere To Run", with Taylor's distinctive vocals (although capable enough) seeming a bit too over-the-top for this type of material. Nevertheless, the band still intended to release some vinyl, and took tentative steps towards getting an EP entitled »Fire And Fury« into the shops at some point before the year was out. Almost inevitably, it failed to happen, and further disappointment was to come their way when Lou Taylor was lured away by an offer to join Geordie heavyweights SATAN (who subsequently used the soon-to-become-redundant BLIND FURY moniker to reinvent themselves), whereupon Heybourne took over vocal duties yet again and resurrected the ANGEL WITCH identity for the umpteenth time. Steve Coleman was soon to throw in the proverbial towel, however, and old mucker Dave Hogg was somehow roped in to help out at short notice.

After around a year's worth of inconspicuous activity on the rock scene, the revitalised ANGEL WITCH (who managed to retain a stable line-up for some time before yielding to temptation and bringing in new vocalist Dave Tattum) finally got themselves a brand-new deal with the Killerwatt label, and soon disappeared off into the studio to lay down their long-awaited second album. It all happened with fairly minimal publicity, though, and even the die-hard fans (I should know, I was one of them) were quite surprised to discover a new long-player suddenly appearing in the racks. The feebly-titled »Screamin'n'Bleedin'« (they must have been having a sale at the apostrophe shop) showcased a selection of almost entirely unfamiliar ANGEL WITCH compositions (although perennial live favourite "Evil Games" finally achieved its vinyl destiny), and saw a move into rather more accessible territory, with the majority of tracks coming across as similar to some of the less interesting numbers on the TYTAN (ironically enough) and PERSIAN RISK albums. It wasn't a bad effort, and Dave Tattum was a more-than-capable frontman, with numbers such as "Reawakening", "Whose To Blame" and the title track all representing listenable enough songs. Elsewhere, there were some pleasingly heavy riffs and occasional glimpses of their original doomy style (in fact, "Waltz The Night" and "Child Of The Night" are even vaguely reminiscent of CANDLEMASS), although (for reasons which aren't entirely easy to pin down) the album just didn't acquit itself particularly well as a whole.

In terms of sales, the ANGEL WITCH comeback release turned out to be extremely disappointing (even taking into account a licensing deal with the American JCI label which allowed some of their newer material to be made available in the States), and some decidedly mixed reviews didn't help matters. The consensus of opinion was that there was little energy or enthusiasm, and it was all generally a bit too ponderous and uninspiring to win the hearts of many metal fans. Even Kevin Heybourne's own opinion of the second album was disarmingly frank: 'Well, I spent like five years with my head up my arsehole so I didn't know what was happening at the time, which was wrong. At the time I was quite pleased with the album, but listening to it now I think it's a bit too commercial and a bit laid back.' (Ref: Metal Forces No.22, 1987). Surprisingly, Killerwatt even plucked one of the more accessible numbers from the long-player ("Goodbye") to form the basis of a scarcely-sighted two-tracker, although the tiny quantity sold can barely have justified the effort. Still, the outfit were retained by their label, and they eventually started thinking about another LP. Dave Hogg, however, was to play no further part in the activities of ANGEL WITCH, and was shown the door (due to 'his lack of enthusiasm') shortly after the second album was recorded. After a handful of promotional showcases to underline the fact that ANGEL WITCH were still a going concern (with new sticksman Spencer Hollman, whose main claim to infamy was a brief stint with DEXY'S MIDNIGHT RUNNERS, being introduced to the public at these events), the lads entered the studio at the beginning of 1986 to prepare the necessary groundwork for that 'difficult third album'.

Fortunately, the upbeat »Frontal Assault« (recorded at AVM Studios in Stoke with DEMON's Les Hunt producing once more, and local UNITED NATIONS keyboard player Chris Stonier helping out on a couple of tracks) was a considerably better-received effort, and represented a clear attempt to recapture the heavy, powerful spirit of their youth. ANGEL WITCH continued the tradition of delivering a strong title track, and the likes of "Undergods" (originally played live as early as 1982), "Straight From Hell" and "Rendezvous With The Blade" (hardly surprising, since it was a reworked "Guillotine") all came across as extremely worthwhile inclusions. Reviews were slightly kinder this time, but the media response failed to spark much renewed interest in ANGEL WITCH in the UK, leaving them to promote the album with some dismally-attended (reports of half a dozen paying customers at one event) shows at home. Still, there was always still the ever-dependable European following to fall back upon, and ANGEL WITCH were soon putting in a triumphal appearance at the Dynamo Festival, where the rapturous reaction from the assembled masses confirmed that they had plenty of hardcore fans left after all. Disappointingly, however, neither of the Killerwatt albums proceeded to sell in particularly noteworthy quantities (the monumentally awful sleeve artwork didn't help) as a result of their live exertions, but the group carried on regardless, undertaking a reasonably productive European tour with SATAN towards the end of 1986. By this time, though, the rights to the early ANGEL WITCH material had passed from Bronze to Castle, which resulted in a shoddily-packaged reissue of the first album (with the »Loser« tracks as a bonus) emerging on the Raw Power subsidiary. The lads weren't remotely impressed, and saw this cash-in as doing a genuine disservice to their current attempts to re-establish themselves, but there wasn't all that much they could do about it.

With the lads having parted company with Killerwatt, who were now actively promoting SURFACE as their major act, ANGEL WITCH gigged throughout 1987 (losing Dave Tattum to NIGHTWING along the way) with the likes of ELIXIR, CHROME MOLLY and SATAN, occasionally unveiling compositions such as "Time To Die" and "Psychopathic", which, to the surprise of many casual onlookers, appeared to be taking the outfit into more thrashy territory. They even demoed some of this forceful material officially at around this point, although few labels expressed the remotest interest in the three-piece's future activities. The flirtation with heavier genres proved to be brief, though, as Heybourne later confirmed: *'There was a time when I thought the stuff we did on the first album was a bit laid back and we needed to do something faster. So we were trying out some new stuff but it was turning out a bit too thrashy. I was screaming a helluva lot and I just don't have that kind of voice.'* (Ref: Kerrang No.248, July 1989). Admittedly, they may have originally inspired the likes of MEGADETH, but were hardly the sort of act who should now be trying to emulate them! After keeping a remarkably low profile for the whole of 1988, however, ANGEL WITCH suddenly jetted off to the States early the following year, whereupon they hooked up with LAAZ ROCKIT for a well-attended tour. By this time, they had expanded to a quartet once again (via the recruitment of former T. BONE guitarist Grant Dennison), and were playing a selection of old favourites, with no post-1980 numbers featuring in their sets at all. The jaunt turned out to be such an unanticipated success (with one of the gigs later surfacing as the cunningly-titled »Angel Witch Live« album, released through an arrangement between Metal Blade and Music For Nations) that band mainman Heybourne soon elected to remain in the States and re-establish yet another new version of ANGEL WITCH under the auspices of an influential American management company.

In 1990, Heybourne formed an alliance with erstwhile LAAZ ROCKIT bassist John Torres, and swiftly brought in former EXODUS drummer Tom Hunting to complete the favoured power trio line-up. Within a remarkably short space of time, a demo (featuring "Twist Of The Knife", "Psychopathic" and "Slowly Sever") was hurriedly recorded, and, with the tape creating a bit of a media buzz from the outset, it looked as though the all-new ANGEL WITCH had every chance of being picked up sooner or later. With the subsequent arrival of HEATHEN's Doug Piercy as second guitarist, ANGEL WITCH (once the epitome of quintessentially-British metal) seemed to be metamorphosing into some sort of *'Bay Area supergroup'* (not an entirely unwise move in view of the immense transatlantic popularity of such outfits), although the luckless Heybourne was soon identified as an *'undesirable'* of some kind or another, and was rapidly deported back to Britain. ANGEL WITCH pretty much fell apart in the early 90's as a result, although Heybourne and Torres continued to swap ideas and collaborate on new material *via* some sort of long-distance arrangement, although none of the more recent compositions were made available to the public (or even recorded

properly, in all probability). Still, there was a significant market for older ANGEL WITCH material, and the CD's soon started appearing, including a further reissue of the first album by Castle and a considerably more ambitious set from High Vaultage, whose »'82 Revisited« CD assembled the long-lost live show from Mildenhall (with all the bugs now ironed out) plus the three demo tracks from around the same time.

There was more to come, however, as the Heybourne/Torres partnership soon began making some of their work available to fans on tape (initially) and then CD-R, with newer, late 90's efforts (where Heybourne and Torres were helped by Tom Hunting and mystery guitarist Myk Taylor) such as "Scrape The Well" and "Inertia" attracting considerable interest from the metal world. A collection of demo recordings has also recently appeared as an official CD entitled »Resurrection«, released by Crook'd Records in the States and subsequently picked up by Zoom Club in the UK. The latter concern has additionally compiled a CD of unreleased studio/live material from the early days (»Sinister History«), with some entertaining, Heybourne-penned sleeve notes, although a few of the details seem somewhat inaccurate. Selections such as the seldom-performed "The Night Is Calling" are credited as coming from a show at the Marquee in October 1981 (try October 1982, lads, since Kev was in DEEP MACHINE that time the previous year), and even the tracks lifted from the »Give It Some Tickle« tape are incorrectly dated (it was January 1981, not February), which is a shame. Sorry to be such a horrendously smug and anal-retentive git, folks, but these clearly aren't simple misprints, so I'd tactfully suggest that a bit of double-checking is always a prudent idea in such circumstances. Believe me, I'm painfully aware how easy it is to overlook things…

With any luck, though, there will be even more ANGEL WITCH archive releases to come (a recently-recorded live set has been made available latterly), but let's hope that the relevant labels can get hold of some genuinely exclusive material and take steps to ensure that they avoid the slippery descent into the continual repackaging of original albums and the incessant production of all those shabby, hastily-assembled, retrospective collections which (particularly in the case of groups such as GIRLSCHOOL and VENOM) are designed merely to fleece the fans and make money for avaricious companies. Mind you, there's also a pretty good chance that some freshly-penned material will be recorded at some stage, given that Kev Heybourne has now assembled a revamped touring version of ANGEL WITCH once more, with Richie Wicks (b), Scott Higham (d) and Keith Herzberg (g) lending a hand at their recent comeback gigs (a couple of high-profile shows with SAMSON and one or two low-key London appearances as headliners), which seem to have been received remarkably favourably by those lucky souls in attendance. Here's hoping that they go from strength to strength (a rapturously-received performance at Wacken 2000 didn't do them any harm at all) and win a modicum of deserved recognition from the notoriously-hostile rock press.

LP's
»**Angel Witch**« Bronze 1980
»**Screamin'n'Bleedin'**« Killerwatt Records 1986
»**Frontal Assault**« Killerwatt Records 1986
»**Doctor Phibes**« Raw Power 1986
[Reissue of »Angel Witch« LP in different cover with »Loser« EP tracks as bonus]
»**Frontal Assault**« JCI Records 1988
[US album featuring mix of tracks from »Frontal Assault« and »Screamin'n'Bleedin'«, with different cover to either]
»**Angel Witch Live**« Metal Blade Records 1990
[Live release]

12" EP's
»**Sweet Danger**« EMI 1980
[Both "Flight 19" and "Hades Paradise" non-LP, "Sweet Danger" different to album version]

7" EP's
»**Loser**« Bronze 1981
[All three tracks originally non-LP, but subsequently appeared on »Doctor Phibes« reissue]

7" Singles
»**Sweet Danger**« EMI 1980
[A-side different to album version, B-side "Flight 19" non-LP]
»**Angel Witch**« Bronze 1980
[A-side different to album version, issued with either cream paper labels or green moulded labels]
»**Angel Witch**« Victor 1980
[Japanese issue with different sleeve]
»**Goodbye**« Killerwatt Records 1985

CD's
»**Doctor Phibes**« Raw Power 1986
[Reissue of »Angel Witch« LP in different cover with »Loser« EP tracks as bonus]
»**Screamin' Assault**« Killerwatt Records 1987
[Combination of »Screamin'n'Bleedin'« and »Frontal Assault«, with five tracks omitted, completely unique sleeve]

»**Frontal Assault**« JCI Records 1988
[US release, includes material taken from »Frontal Assault« and »Screamin'n'Bleedin'«, with different cover to either]
»**Angel Witch**« Teichiku 1989
[Japanese issue]
»**Angel Witch Live**« Metal Blade Records 1990
[Live release]
»**Angel Witch**« Castle Communications 1991
[UK issue in original cover]
»**Angel Witch**« Victor 199?
[Japanese issue]
»**'82 Revisited**« High Vaultage 1996
[Compilation of unreleased live and studio material]
»**Paranoid**« Midas Touch 1996
[Bootleg release of »Give It Some Tickle« official live tape from 1981]
»**Angel Witch**« Castle Communications 1998
[With six bonus tracks from singles and compilations]
»**Sinister History**« Zoom Club Records 1999
[Compilation of unreleased live and studio material]
»**Resurrection**« Crook'd Records 2000
[Original US issue, compilation of unreleased studio recordings from late 80's and 90's]
»**Resurrection**« Zoom Club Records 2000
[UK issue in different cover]
»**Angel Witch 2000: Live at the LA2**« Zoom Club Records 2000
[Live release, double disc]

Compilation Appearances
"**Baphomet**" on »Metal For Muthas« LP EMI 1980/CD Airraid Records 2000 + »The Bible Of Hard Rock« CD Toshiba 1990
[Exclusive studio recording, different version appears on »Sinister History« CD, live version appears on »Angel Witch Live« album]
"**Extermination Day**" on »Metal Explosion« LP BBC Records 1980 + »NWOBHM '79 Revisited« Do-LP/Do-CD Phonogram 1990
[Exclusive session recording, different version appears on »Sinister History« CD, live version appears on »Angel Witch Live« album]
"**Angel Witch**" on »A Quiet Night In« LP Bronze 1981 + »Hammer« LP Ariola 1981 + »Giants Of Rock-The Metal Decade Vol.1« Do-CD Teldec 1990 + »Metal Mania« Do-CD Duet 1995 + »The Metal Box« 3-CD Box Kaz Records 1995 + »The Bronze Story« Do-CD Essential 2000
"**Loser**" on »A Quiet Night In« LP Bronze 1981 + »N.W.O.B.H.M. Metal Rarities Vol.1« CD British Steel 1996
"**Screamin'n'Bleedin'**" on »Metallergy« LP Bandit Records 1985
"**Dr. Phibes**" on »Metal Inferno« LP Castle Communications 1985 + »N.W.O.B.H.M. Metal

Rarities Vol.1« CD British Steel 1996
"Hades Paradise" on »NWOBHM Vol.1« Bootleg CD 1992
"Flight 19" on »NWOBHM Vol.6« Bootleg CD 1992
"Free Man" on »Rock Legends Volume 1« CD Castle Communications 1992 + »Giants Of Rock« Cassette Castle Communications 1993 + »Rock Classics« CD Castle Communications 1995
"Sweet Danger" on »The Metal Box« 3-CD Box Castle Communications 1993 + »Metal Mania« Do-CD Duet 1995 + »The Metal Box« 3-CD Box Kaz Records 1995
"Devil's Tower" on »Rock Legends Volume 2« CD Castle Communications 1992 + »Wild Thing« CD Kaz Records 1995 + »The Metal Box« 3-CD Box Kaz Records 1995
"Straight From Hell" on »Give 'Em Hell« CD Nectar Masters 1995
"Suffer" on »N.W.O.B.H.M. Metal Rarities Vol.1« CD British Steel 1996
"White Witch" (live) on »NWOBHM Live« CD Emporio 1997
"Angel Of Death" (live) on »NWOBHM Live« CD Emporio 1997
"Angel Witch" (live) on »NWOBHM Live« CD Emporio 1997
"They Wouldn't Dare" on »The Best Of British Metal« CD Delta Music 1999
"Sorceress" (live) on »The Best Of British Metal« CD Delta Music 1999

ANTHEM

John Pattison (v)
Phil Kershaw (g)
Paul John Wilson (b)
Mick Sanderson (d)

The little-known British version (as opposed to the considerably more familiar and successful Japanese group) of ANTHEM were an extraordinarily obscure four-piece concern from Lancashire who paused only long enough to issue the three track (bewilderingly, labelled as a *'double A-side'*) »England« EP (the quartet's roots can apparently be traced back to an equally unrenowned outfit who themselves operated under the identity of ENGLAND) in 1981 before disappearing back into the utter anonymity from whence they came. As brought to the attention of modern-day aficionados on the »NWOBHM Vol.8« bootleg, the main focus of attention is an epic, anthemic composition whose verses are actually uncannily similar to PETER GABRIEL's "Games Without Frontiers", although the track itself is quite a heavy and metallic affair in the general style of ARC or OMEGA. Still, the lyrics on this particular number are fairly heartfelt and poetic, the following excerpt being a prime example of the ANTHEM mindset:
*'Grave mother of majestic works
From her Isle-Altar gazing down
Who God-like grasps the triple forks
And King-like wears the orb and crown.'*
After this overblown opening gambit, therefore, it comes as a considerable surprise to discover that the pair of compositions tucked away on the flipside bear absolutely no relation to the title track, and these reveal a completely different

aspect to ANTHEM's music. In fact, "Some Like It Hot" is a no-frills, good-time rocker reminiscent of SINNER, while "Do You Mind If We Butt In?" is a faster, boogie-tinged number in the rudimentary manner of NO FAITH or VARDIS. An eclectic bunch, obviously...

ANTHEM's one-off EP is an incredibly scarce slice of vinyl nowadays, reflecting an extremely limited pressing and equally restricted sales (with the band having been a studio project, there wasn't even an opportunity to shift copies at local gigs), and the handful of examples unearthed in recent times have been known to fetch stratospheric prices amongst excitable collectors. Just to make matters worse for obsessive completists, however, the makeshift picture sleeve (featuring the group's logo, where the central 'T' has been transformed into a glinting sword in true metal fashion) exists in two different colour variations, with the double-sided brown version (which, in all probability, only accompanied a tiny quantity of promotional copies) being observed even less frequently than the single-sided black one. Also, as with the METAL MIRROR single, for example, the sleeve helpfully informs us that the record was actually a *'limited edition'*, which is reassuringly sensible, as manufacturing an infinite number of copies would probably have been unnecessarily time-consuming.

7" EP's
»England« Private 1981
[Issued in both black and brown sleeves, black more common]

Compilation Appearances
"England" on »NWOBHM Vol.8« Bootleg CD 1996

APOCALYPSE

Nick Brent (v,g)
Steve Grainger (g)
Dave Robertson (b)
Robertson (d)

London's APOCALYPSE (not to be confused either with the Swiss thrashers or with a later British outfit who also chose to adopt the identity) were one of the heavier bands to have emerged from the early 80's metal scene in the UK. Having toured around the capital and Home Counties for a year or two before issuing a well-received three track demo in 1981, the group had steadily developed a style of metal resembling a somewhat more forceful version of PRAYING MANTIS or TRESPASS. The emergent quartet's early compositions (including such offerings as "Nightstalker", "Midnight Train" and the epic "The Child") all demonstrated an inventiveness and confidence that no doubt served them well in the live environment, and the group ultimately built upon this initial exposure by releasing their »Stormchild« single (b/w "Chosen Few") on the microscopic Gate label the following year. Although the music of APOCALYPSE was, by this time, beginning to draw comparisons with yet more powerful outfits such as ARC and SOLDIER, the lads again managed to stamp their own commanding identity on the material, and their two-tracker represented a laudable vinyl debut. The record itself was issued in a rather makeshift-looking, one-sided picture cover featuring the lyrics to both songs, which provides us with an insight into the band's despondency, as the following excerpt from "Chosen Few" admirably illustrates:

'Across the plain the soldiers came

Wearily they shuffled through the dust
Guns hung loosely from their shoulders
Bloodstains turned to rust
Underground, underground they hide.
Searching through the wreckage of a
city they used to call their home
Realising slowly that their families
and livelihoods have gone
Underground the warlords watch them cry.'

I reckon it's just as well this bunch never collaborated with the equally miserable TRACER, or sales of razor blades would surely have gone through the roof! Mentioned, but not exactly praised, in the 'Singles' section of 'Kerrang', the reviewer's query *'do they have to take it all so seriously?'* was quite pertinent, but there's nothing wrong with a bit of doom and gloom every now and then. Needless to say, however, the two-tracker is a scarce and highly-valued piece on the current NWOBHM collecting scene, and relatively few collectors actually own a copy. Incidentally, it's worth pointing out that APOCALYPSE was a surprisingly common name in the early 80's, and various other minor bands of that identity apparently issued vinyl product at around the same time, although none of these are at all related to the outfit in question, and most aren't even in the rock/metal bracket at all. Notwithstanding the limited success of their debut release, the musicians evidently concluded that a few changes needed to be made, and the name of APOCALYPSE was soon being laid to rest. At the beginning of 1983 or thereabouts, having now dumped their original drummer (the unlucky brother of bassist Dave Robertson) and drafted in new sticksman Graham Roberts (an erstwhile member of Paul Dianno's BIRD OF PREY as well as the heavy London version of GBH), APOCALYPSE evolved into OMEGA (see separate entry), an undeniably similar (albeit markedly more diverse and technical) proposition. After contributing one of their early tracks to an Ebony compilation several months later, OMEGA also inked a deal with the Gate concern in 1984 (as publicised in 'Kerrang' at the time), although this arrangement seems to have run into trouble at some point thereafter, and their LP finally appeared on the larger Rock Machine label (an early subsidiary of Metal Masters) a year later.

7" Singles
»Stormchild« Gate Records 1982

Compilation Appearances
"Stormchild" on »NWOBHM Vol.8« Bootleg CD 1996

ARAGORN

Chris Dunne (v)
John Hull (g)
Dale Lee (b)
Mike Ellis (d)

Cheshire's ARAGORN (not to be confused with various outfits who called themselves ARAGON) were one of Neat's earliest signings in the NWOBHM era, although they were unfortunate enough to be struck by personnel problems soon afterwards, meaning that they were obliged to enlist the services of a guest bassist in order to get their first single released in the early months of 1981. Featuring "Black Ice" and "Noonday", the record is in a pretty basic, mid-tempo NWOBHM style, with similarities to both SACRED ALIEN and TRAXX, although rather less technical and imaginative than either outfit. "Noonday" was also featured on Neat's »Lead Weight« sampler a few months later, before the lads decided to establish more of a stable line-up (original guest bassist Dale Lee, incidentally, later ended up in BLOOD MONEY). To this end, new recruits Chris White (b) and Andy Halliwell (g) were duly recruited to the fold in order to form a much chunkier quintet. With the newly-expanded ARAGORN (their identity being taken from Tolkien's writings) having already written some novel material by mid-1981, the outfit were asked about their progress and ambitions in an early issue of 'Kerrang', where bassist Chris White was keen to offer an opinion of the over-saturated metal scene: 'We know full well the situation regarding new bands in England today. Nobody is signing new heavy bands. They have hundreds of good bands on their books, the record companies, and we won't kid ourselves. It's the aftermath of the Geoff Barton New Wave of whatever, a couple of years ago. We are realistic.' (Ref: Kerrang No.2, August 1981).

The youngsters were, by this stage, attempting to progress beyond the limitations of their humble vinyl debut by aiming for a proper deal, and so it wasn't long before the revised line-up circulated a brand-new demo (featuring recently-penned selections such as "Night Is Burning", "Hungry For Love" and "Tickets On The Wall") to see if anyone might take the bait. Although the members of ARAGORN seemed to regard this batch of material as undisputed evidence of their collective ability, it wasn't exactly a ground-breaking show of talent by any means, and the shorter, snappier arrangements ultimately failed to find favour either with Neat or with anyone else, leaving the dejected ensemble to return to the drawing board. Sadly, they failed to last the distance, and soon began to fragment (Andy Halliwell and Mike Ellis both fled the sinking ship, the latter being succeeded by one-time SAM THUNDER drummer Chris Dadson, who soon moved over to CHATEAUX), the curtain having fallen by 1983. The erstwhile guitarists went on to find alternative employment, however, with Andy Halliwell teaming up with Pete Wadeson in an early incarnation of TROJAN (the pair would also briefly work together in SWEET SIN towards the end of the decade), while John Hull proceeded to establish the TOUCHED project in nearby Manchester. Original drummer Mike Ellis, on the other hand, elected to remain a bit further North, eventually taking his place in the ranks of Cumbria's RAW DEAL, one of numerous groups to adopt the identity, but probably one of the least successful.

7" Singles
»Black Ice« Neat 1981

Compilation Appearances
"Noonday" on »Lead Weight« LP Neat 1981/CD Teichiku 1992

ARC

John Whitbread (v)
Mike Whitbread (g)
Dennis Paszkowec (g)
Steve Slater (b)
Geoff Whitbread (d)

Worcestershire's ARC (not to be confused either with the A.R.C. ROCK BAND from Lincolnshire or an earlier ARC who recorded for Decca in the 70's) are a prime example of an outfit who improved immeasurably between their first and second singles, although it transpires that rather fewer examples of their sophomore effort seem to be in circulation, which is a bit odd. Having formed in around 1978 and touted their musical wares around the Midlands for a couple of years, the lads eventually started thinking about releasing some self-financed vinyl of their own. Along the way, they had replaced original guitarist Dennis Paszkowec with new recruit Phil Lynch, while Steve Potter stepped in to succeed the departed Steve Slater, who had moved over to rival heavyweights REQUIEM, dextrously switching from bass to lead guitar in the process. The quintet's debut vinyl offering (a double A-sided release from 1980), featuring the pairing of "For My Next Kick" and "Tribute (To Mike Hailwood)" (which is a tiny bit spooky, considering the aforementioned motorcycling ace didn't actually die until 1981), is a somewhat ramshackle performance in terms of musicianship, although the vocals (in the general style of BLOOD MONEY or even the aforementioned REQUIEM themselves) help things along to some extent, even if they sound a bit strained at times.

Still, it was a reasonable way for these hopefuls to kick off their career, and the record seems to have done the trick as far as publicity was concerned. Indeed, the band even appea-

red in session on BRMB (Midlands local radio station) in May of the same year, showcasing the original music of ARC (another family affair, by the looks of things) to a wider audience. By the time the group's outstanding »War Of The Ring« effort was unleashed upon an unsuspecting public the following year, however, ARC's vocalist had become far more accomplished and confident in his delivery, and the A-side ('dedicated to the inspirational works of J.R.R. Tolkien', a literary source of stimulus which was also to shape quite a few of BLIND GUARDIAN's lyrics in due course) comes across as an excellent mixture of TYRANT, IRON MAIDEN and VAGABOND. With the track being built upon the foundations of an incredibly heavy riff (we're talking real ST. VITUS stuff here) and monastic choral backing (cf. the intro to TYTAN's "Blind Men And Fools"), it's fair to say that ARC were more than capable of showing today's doom hopefuls precisely how this sort of thing should be done. In fact, I'd even stick my neck out and say this particular number was heavier than anything WITCHFINDER GENERAL ever committed to vinyl, but I suspect that relatively few of you will believe me. To be honest, though, the record's flipside (the nonsensically-titled "Ice Cream Theme") fails to achieve quite the same standard of excellence, and constitutes a rather more melancholic and less intense affair, but it's still an enjoyable enough effort all the same.

Sadly, the weighty ensemble don't seem to have progressed any further in terms of getting additional vinyl product into the shops thereafter (although they were still playing live in their locality as late as 1983), and ARC probably failed to make much of an impression outwith the Midlands, which is a great pity. It looks as though the participants probably took their leave of the rock scene in later years, having decided that they weren't going to become superstars by playing such a heavy form of music. It's fair to say that doom metal wasn't a popular genre (particularly in the UK) in the early 80's, so ARC's ultimate failure to make a global impact is perfectly understandable, although I suspect that such acts might have slightly better luck nowadays. So come on lads, how about chucking in the soul-destroying day jobs and reforming? I'm sure CATHEDRAL's Lee Dorrian would sign you up for an album or two on his Rise Above label in no time and you could put all these second-rate KYUSS clones to shame. Only the second ARC two-tracker (now an incredibly scarce and coveted piece) was ever issued with a picture sleeve, incidentally, and featured an intricate fantasy image with the outfit's logo superimposed on some ancient, mystical writings. I guess it's not something you'd easily fail to notice...

7" Singles
»For My Next Kick« Orcrist Records 1980
»War Of The Ring« Slipped Disc 1981

A.R.C. ROCK BAND

Klaus Brunnenkant (v,g)
A. Howe-Haysom (v,b)
C. Ashcroft (d)

Well, there's nothing like laying your cards firmly on the table and announcing yourself as a 'rock band', is there? The A.R.C. ROCK BAND (or just plain old A.R.C., as they're identified on the record itself), from Lincolnshire, issued a rare single in 1979 (predictably enough, on the Rock label, but not the same one that put out the

SLENDER THREAD 7") which predates both releases by the Worcestershire ensemble ARC, although, predominantly due to the scarcity of the former, the two outfits have been regularly misconstrued as being one and the same by many collectors over the years. A hand-written sleeve amendment (on some copies, at least) suggests that the band later adopted the name SPLIT, so maybe there was even confusion amongst fans at the time (or maybe the lads just realised their original moniker was bollocks). In fact, a truly minimal number of copies of the A.R.C. ROCK BAND single (housed in a fairly unremarkable, fold-open sleeve) seem to have come out of the woodwork over the past decade, and this item would probably be a pretty high-ranking collectable were it not for the fact that so few modern-day NWOBHM fans are aware of its existence.

The threesome's music was, on the basis of this unassuming opening gambit, fairly primitive, with the raw, gravelly vocals on "Home Made Wine" conjuring up a musical mixture of MOTÖRHEAD, TANK and SABRE, with numerous *'gotta get me a taste of that home made wine'* references included during the course of the song. The slower number on the reverse ("The Chase") has a more polished vocal performance, however, with decent guitar breaks ensuring that the tune isn't quite as mawkish as the ill-advised ballads attempted by some of their NWOBHM rivals. It would appear that this short-lived concern had precisely zero appeal to the major labels, and failed to achieve all that much media recognition (either as the A.R.C. ROCK BAND or SPLIT) during the course of their existence, but they no doubt developed a loyal following in their locality, and probably didn't lose too much sleep when the dream finally ended. These musicians obviously liked their drink, though, further evidenced by the beer-swigging photos on the front and back sleeves. Cheers!

7" Singles
»Home Made Wine« Rock Records 1979

ARGUS

Line-up unknown

Humberside's little-remembered ARGUS (not a unique identity by any means, although most of their namesakes were of overseas origin) ultimately failed to achieve their dreams of stardom during their relatively short time on Britain's restructuring post-NWOBHM rock scene, although the musicians must have come to the conclusion that they were doing something right when mail-order sales of a humble five track demo tape began racking up in no uncertain terms. With a few handy quid in the ARGUS coffers as a result, the ensemble merrily went off to a nearby studio facility and laid down a vinyl two-tracker of their own, coupling "Holocaust" with "The Widow", a release which made its way into the shops before the end of 1984. Mind you, it was something of an oddity, and the group's semi-progressive musical style (with a vaguely theatrical feel from time to time) was generally quite difficult to pin down, although there were elements of oddball acts such as MARQUIS DE SADE, CHEMICAL ALICE, GOLGOTHA and early MOURNBLADE thrown into the melting pot.

With regard to the pair of compositions committed to vinyl by the mysterious members of ARGUS, "Holocaust" is the better number by far, benefitting from an interesting structure and a few novel ideas thrown in along the way, although it certainly wasn't typical British metal in any sense. The more restrained flipside, however, represented an immensely annoying listening experience as a consequence of the constant beeping noise (it's actually supposed to signify a life-support machine) throughout, which really gets on your nerves within a matter of seconds. It's all a bit over-the-top, if you ask me, especially with various other sound effects chucked in for good measure, and it's not a track which stands up too well after all this time. The single (some examples of which came with a rudimentary picture sleeve featuring the band's unremarkable logo) appears to have sold in reasonable quantities by mail order over the ensuing months (it's a scarce artefact today, though), but ultimately didn't serve to propel ARGUS into the superstar bracket, leaving them to call it a day within a year or two.

7" Singles
»Holocaust« ABS Records 1984

ATLANTIS RISING

D. Radford
G. Matcham
N. Milton

Behind the extremely promising name of

ATLANTIS RISING (not to be confused with a little-known FIFTH ANGEL offshoot from the early 90's) lies a rather lightweight, progressively-inclined concern who appear to have been from the London area (neither should they be confused with minor hopefuls ATLANTIS, who were from the same neck of the woods but who almost certainly didn't get to the vinyl stage), although their activities on the music scene must have been decidedly low-profile at the time. Their only known vinyl release, a two-tracker comprising "Tightrope" and the pretentiously-titled "Reverie: A Vision", brings forth comparisons with the likes of CHEMICAL ALICE, LIAISON, CHASE and occasionally FRIENDS, although there's also a distinct throwback to the 70's, with a few additional influences coming from YES, PINK FLOYD and (particularly) SUPERTRAMP. On the basis of this particular release, it looks as though ATLANTIS RISING weren't exactly a prog outfit in the sense of MARILLION, for example, given that they weren't predisposed to widdly keyboard sections and convoluted arrangements, but they were certainly rather more sophisticated than most of the NWOBHM hopefuls doing the rounds at the time. Issued (at some point in 1983) without a picture sleeve, a minimal number of copies of »Tightrope« have surfaced thus far, and those responsible are likely to remain something of a mystery for the foreseeable future.

7" Singles
»Tightrope« CMI Records 1983

ATOMKRAFT

Tony Dolan (v,b)
Rob Mathew (g)
Ged Wolf (d)

Amazing as it may seem, the original version of Geordie heroes ATOMKRAFT (their name being taken from a German term relating to nuclear weaponry) was actually conceived as long ago as 1979, although it was very much a part-time outfit (with ever-changing personnel) at the outset. Having taken a range of punk and metal influences on board, the ensemble (led by frontman Tony Dolan) struggled to develop a particularly strong sense of identity in the early stages (with the band's own honest admission that they could barely play in tune), eventually becoming something of a semi-thrash proposition in

around 1982. Inevitably, accusations would soon be made that they were merely jumping on the VENOM bandwagon (especially since the two outfits rapidly struck up a friendly rapport), but it was a fairly natural and non-contrived progression from ATOMKRAFT's semi-punk beginnings. The original guitarist, Steve White, left to form WAR MACHINE (see separate entry) in around 1983, however, and it wasn't until late the following year (in the wake of a failed attempt by Dolan to start afresh in Canada) that a stable three-piece line-up of Tony Dolan (v,b), the extremely youthful Rob Mathew (g) and former TYSONDOG stalwart Ged Wolf (d) was established. By 1985, the outfit had become something of a serious concern (having largely abandoned their early compositions), and the trio had circulated a demo or two (notably »Total Metal« and »Pour The Metal In«) by the time Neat Records finally stepped in with a coveted deal, the lads being offered (fairly atypically) the opportunity to start off their career with a full LP.

In the summer of 1985, the trio were lucky enough to secure a support slot with SLAYER at the Marquee in London, although the partisan crowd gave them a less-than-easy ride. As a consequence of the hostile audience reaction and various equipment snarl-ups, the petulant youths trashed their kit after just three numbers and casually walked off stage to the bemusement of the assembled masses. Nevertheless, they were subsequently offered the chance to tour Europe in support of VENOM (whether or not they were ever actually VENOM's roadies is open to debate, although it seems to be a widely-held belief), and their debut album was released to coincide with this particular series of shows. »Future Warriors« was a capable slice of vinyl, very much in the VENOM and WARFARE scheme of things in places (predictably, it soon found favour with the many fans of those two outfits), although it was their more distinctive material (such as "Starchild" and "This Planet's Burning", both with some pretty decent guitar work) that served to identify the outfit as something rather more substantial than mere speed metal wannabes or sub-VENOM imitators. Furthermore, it was plain for all to see that each of the individual members had indeed learned to play their instruments by this juncture, and ATOMKRAFT swiftly became established as one of Neat's more popular acts of the mid-80's.

Moving into 1986, the band were invited to record an EP for Neat, and one of the tracks ("Your Mentor") scheduled to appear was even featured on one of the label's promotional cassettes at the time, suggesting that the recording sessions took place as intended. For some reason, however, the release (which was also due to feature "Funeral Pyre" and "Demolition") was cancelled, presumably as a consequence of the personnel instability which began at around this time. Mainman Tony Dolan wasn't entirely happy with the group's situation, and decided to go off and do his own thing for a while, later revealing his motivation: *'It happened because I wanted to go down to London but the others wanted to stay in Newcastle. We also had arguments about the direction because I didn't really want the band to follow along the lines of VENOM, which is what some people wanted us to do, so we split but both wanted to keep the name. It was all pretty petty really! I recorded some new stuff with some people I was working with but it just didn't work out.'* (Ref: Metal Forces No.21, 1986). To take its place, two new members were recruited, namely bassist DC Rage (who, in all probability, was none other than one-time AVENGER drummer Darren Kurland) and erstwhile SATAN/AVENGER vocalist Ian Davison Swift. The group's plans were rapidly reconsidered, and they duly re-emerged with the »Queen Of Death« mini-LP, a five-tracker which marked a drift in style towards even more thrashy territory (although "Funeral Pyre" was a more restrained effort), so it seemed as though the revamped ATOMKRAFT were now making a concerted effort to sell themselves as one of Britain's heavier acts of the period.

Clearly, however, new recruit DC Rage was unsettled in the ranks of ATOMKRAFT, and had already left by the end of the year, making way for none other than Tony Dolan himself, who returned in the capacity of bassist only, leaving Swift to continue to front the band. Over the following year, the lads began picking up support slots with some of the heavier touring acts, notably NUCLEAR ASSAULT and AGENT STEEL, and also won an appearance at the prestigious Dynamo Open Air Festival, which consolidated their position as favourites in mainland Europe. The quartet subsequently announced that they had written a variety of new numbers such as "Aftermath" and "Annihilate The Bride", and revealed plans to issue a full album (to be titled »Atomized«) before the end of 1987. In the event, however, time constraints meant that this project eventually metamorphosed into another mini-LP (»Conductors Of Noize«), something that the lads could complete at short notice and promote on their already-arranged tour. It was made clear, however, that they intended to return to the recording of their »Atomized« opus after their various touring commitments had been honoured, the release date for the delayed LP now being estimated as the spring of 1988. Meanwhile, the »Conductors Of Noize« set was hitting the shops, and it was essentially an all-out thrash assault from start to finish, the lads showing (particularly on "The Cage") that they were more than ready to take on the likes of OVER KILL (American version) and ANTHRAX in the moshability stakes. Without doubt, ATOMKRAFT were certainly among the pioneers of the thrash movement in the UK, so it's something of an injustice that they didn't receive the appropriate press attention at the time.

Sadly, the group's second full album was to be postponed indefinitely, as their activities gradually wound down over the following two years. Having said that, 1988 began well enough, the outfit enjoying support slots with the likes of EXUMER and NASTY SAVAGE, both in Europe and the UK itself. It also saw the return of bassist DC Rage, which led to the versatile Tony Dolan moving to rhythm guitar (his original weapon of choice) and the group experimenting as a five-piece for a while. New material was consistently being written at this stage, including such novel efforts as "Dance Of The Immortals" (which the group intended to issue as a single in its own right at some point in the future), "No Escape", "Sell It Fast", "Phobia", "Atomized", "Apocalyptic Tendencies", "Devil's Rain" and "Tsunami (Storm)", although these compositions were never to be issued in official form. ATOMKRAFT limped into 1989 without a deal or firm plans for the future, having lost their way somewhat in the preceding few months, and it was only a matter of time before they were put out of their misery. Indeed, it looks as though ATOMKRAFT had ceased to exist long before Tony Dolan went on to join forces with the revamped VENOM in the latter half of the year.

LP's

»**Future Warriors**« Neat 1985/Roadrunner 1985
[UK/Dutch issue]
»**Atomkraft**« Tonpress 1987
[Polish release with selection of tracks from both mini-LP's]

Mini-LP's

»**Queen Of Death**« Neat 1986/Roadrunner 1986
[UK/Dutch issue]
»**Conductors Of Noize**« Neat 1987

Exclusive Compilation Appearances

"**Your Mentor**" on »Powertrax« Cassette Neat

1986 + »Heavy Metal Collection 2« CD X-Tra Collection 1993

Compilation Appearances
"Demolition" on »A Rather Nasty Dream« LP RKT Records 1989
"Future Warriors" on »Metal Masters« 4-CD Box Castle Communications 1993

A II Z

Dave Owens (v)
Gary Owens (g)
Cam Campbell (b)
Karl Reti (d)

Manchester's A II Z were one of the lucky few outfits who came to prominence at precisely the right time, and were picked up by one of the major companies (in their case, Polydor) remarkably shortly after their initial formation in 1979. It seemed like an improbable chain of events, although Gary Owens was to confirm the story which led to their rapid rise to major-label status: 'It was mainly myself who organised that. We got a band together and we were really useless, even though we reckoned we were good at the time, like you would do. We did a few gigs around the pubs in Manchester suburbs. But those weren't the right places for us to be playing-we didn't enjoy it, and so we began organising gigs in local school halls. The first one we played drew four hundred, the next time there were eight hundred there and then we got nearly a thousand so we were obviously going down well.' (Ref: Kerrang No.7, January 1982). After somehow selling themselves to this influential label, the four-piece were encouraged to start off their vinyl career with a full album, which Polydor decided to record live (suggesting that they weren't prepared to gamble in terms of studio time for an untested bunch who might not be able to deliver the goods when it came to the crunch), a sneaky procedure which was again utilised when later signings STAMPEDE were introduced to the masses.

In due course, a well-attended local A II Z gig was captured for posterity, and edited highlights were subsequently used to compile »The Witch Of Berkeley«, the group's debut long-player. It was a low-budget, rough'n'ready effort which failed to show the band at their strongest, although the quartet's upbeat brand of SAVAGE/EXCALIBUR-style metal still shone through on numbers such as "Lay Down",

"U.X.B." and the title track itself. Mind you, the likes of "Glastonbury Massacre" and "The Romp" (which no doubt went down a storm live) just didn't have the desired effect on vinyl, and these should certainly have been rejected in favour of something rather more substantial. In spite of its shortcomings, however, the album brought the name of A II Z to the public's attention (serving its main purpose) and proceeded to sell in pretty respectable quantities, whereupon the outfit steadily grew in stature and began earning themselves a series of prestigious support slots. In due course, they hit the road with the likes of GIRLSCHOOL (one of these performances was even recorded by the BBC for future use on the 'In Concert' series of radio broadcasts) and BLACK SABBATH, a memorable experience which (despite the observation that the latter outfit didn't exactly go out of their way to communicate with the youngsters) can't have done them any harm at all.

It didn't all go entirely according to plan, mind you, and there was soon a rather nasty 'exposé' in the 'N.M.E.' at the beginning of 1981, which practically attempted to identify the musicians as Nazi sympathisers (accusations which have also been levelled at KISS over the years, for much the same reason), on the rather flimsy basis that their name and logo bore a vague resemblance to the title of a German workers' paper from the 1920's (hardly the most obvious source of inspiration for some teenagers from Manchester). Fortunately, this gratuitous mudslinging exercise appears to have failed miserably, and the lads emerged unscathed from this hopelessly contrived piece of media sensationalism. In due course, they were ushered into the studio by their label and (at long last) allowed to capture some of their material in its intended form. The first release was the »No Fun After Midnight« single, issued in both 7" and 12" forms (the latter on rather spiffing red vinyl), and it finally allowed the public to hear how capable these musicians actually were. The main track was a cracking effort (despite some lyrics that truly beggar belief), and "Treason" (which was selected for inclusion on Phonogram's »NWOBHM '79 Revisited« compilation a decade later) wasn't far behind in terms of potential. "Valhalla Force", on the other hand, was a more adventurous number with vague similarities to DEF LEPPARD, and was the song which apparently (if you believe the claims of the lads themselves) went down best of all in some parts of the world, notably Scandinavia.

However, there was soon to be a bit of friction in the A II Z camp, and internal difficulties culminated in a parting of the ways later in the year, with the Owens brothers being forced to bring in a couple of new musicians in order to continue their recording and touring activities. Before long, they had roped in drummer Simon Wright (ex-TORA TORA) and bassist Tony Backhouse, after which the revised line-up released another single towards the end of 1981. Surprisingly, however, this marked a fairly unexpected shift towards more commercial territory, something that the band leaders freely admitted was the whole intention, as Gary Owens confirmed: 'Well, I've always tried to put melody into my songs like BOSTON cos I think loads of these new bands are just churning out riffs that were done better by the old bands anyhow. I'd like us to be like a RAINBOW/STYX cross, but with more energy and power.' (Ref: ibid.) Certainly, "I'm The One Who Loves You" (a Russ Ballard composition, which also featured guest keyboards from THE SWEET's Gary Moberley) was firmly in the RAINBOW/BOSTON mould (it had, apparently, been offered to RAINBOW themselves, who were actually on the same label as A II Z), and was, even at the time, classed as little more than a second-rate version of "Since You Been Gone". The reverse ("Ringside Seat") was an A II Z original, and far closer to the material on their first single, although the contrast between the two sides was just too extreme, and few fans acknowledged their new direction with any sense of approval whatsoever.

The band were still a going concern in the early months of 1982, at which point they announced plans for further recording sessions and live outings both within the UK and elsewhere (they had apparently completed several successful gigs in Europe, and hoped to return for a more extensive series of appearances in due course). Sadly, however, their latest single had died something of a death, which, coupled with virtually non-existent promotion and support from Polydor, resulted in the disintegration of A II Z within a surprisingly short space of time. Gary Owens was the first to jump ship, having accepted a lucrative offer to hook up with the emerging TYTAN (mind you, the guitarist was to enjoy a fairly brief stint with that particular outfit), although he was replaced in A II Z by new recruit Duncan Ferguson in the short term. Before much longer, though, vocalist Dave Owens concluded that it would probably be a good idea to lay the band's original identity to rest and reinvent the outfit as something of a brand-new proposition, whereupon the heavy entity known as AURORA (see separate entry) finally came into existence in the second half of that year.

The frontman was joined in this 'new' venture by the loyal pairing of Backhouse and Ferguson, and he was additionally able to rope in former cohort Simon Wright (who had now also defected to the ranks of TYTAN) on a part-time basis. In order to promote themselves to the masses, the foursome recorded a self-financed 7" single within a matter of weeks, but swiftly concluded that they were fighting a losing battle (having formed the collective opinion that the media had already written them off, permanently damaging their chances of success), and elected to throw in the towel before their vinyl debut had even made it into the shops in noteworthy quantities. The musicians kept an extremely low profile thereafter (although Simon Wright picked up a fair bit of additional employment in numerous acts), and Dave Owens later restricted himself to rather more peripheral involvement with the music scene, dabbling in production work later in the decade and helping out little-known local hopefuls such as MARQUESA.

LP's
»The Witch Of Berkeley« Polydor 1980
[Live album]

12" EP's
»No Fun After Midnight« Polydor 1981
[Limited edition issued on red vinyl, A-side different to album version, both "Treason" and "Valhalla Force" non-LP]

7" Singles
»No Fun After Midnight« Polydor 1981
[A-side different to album version, B-side "Treason" non-LP]
»I'm The One Who Loves You« Polydor 1981
[Both tracks non-LP]

CD's
»The Witch Of Berkeley« Reborn Classics 1993
[Bootleg release, includes debut album and material from »No Fun After Midnight« EP, also features four demo tracks by JAGUAR]

Compilation Appearances
"I'm The One Who Loves You" on »A Little Bit Of Light Relief« LP Polydor 1982
"Treason" on »NWOBHM '79 Revisited« Do-CD Phonogram 1990
"Danger UXB" on »NWOBHM Vol.3« Bootleg CD 1992
"No Fun After Midnight" on »NWOBHM Vol.4« Bootleg CD 1992
[Different to album version]

AURORA

Dave Owens (v)
Duncan Ferguson (g)
Tony Backhouse (b)
Simon Wright (d)

The incredibly short-lived AURORA's only vinyl legacy was their extremely scarce »I'll Be Your Fantasy« single (the A-side of which turned up on the »NWOBHM Vol.1« bootleg), a self-financed effort which was released (primarily as a promotional device) towards the end of 1982. With the outfit having formed from the ashes of Manchester's popular A II Z (who had struggled to keep things going after founder member Gary Owens defected to TYTAN), there was certainly a highly-similar commercial edge to AURORA's own material, although the outfit they resembled most closely would probably have been THIN LIZZY, particularly with respect to the flipside ("If I Really Knew Her"), with MEANSTREAK and ENERGY undoubtedly being the group's closest musical neighbours in the NWOBHM field. The single was pressed mainly to introduce AURORA's name to the general public, and the outfit were under no illusions that it would take the world by storm. Even so, the whole episode turned out to be a bit of an unmitigated disaster, and the ambitious project pretty much fell apart before it even got going at all.

Although an AURORA album was apparently being planned at a fairly early stage, this venture was rapidly shelved in the wake of (perceived) overwhelming disinterest in their activities. In fact, by the time the single was reviewed in 'Kerrang' early in 1983, it was revealed that the participants had already decided to go their separate ways, supposedly utterly disenchanted with the complete lack of public reaction and support throughout the North West. To be honest, this was slightly unfair to the fans and media, who were probably entirely unaware of the ensemble's existence up until that point. It was all very strange, and the musicians had seemingly failed to give themselves a sporting chance, although they kept their options open, intimating that they would be quite happy to reform at some future juncture if there was enough belated interest in their single to warrant a further attempt at cracking the market. However, with the two-tracker having been promoted very poorly in the first instance, and with no live appearances with which to boost the quartet's appeal, sales were understandably scant, with the end result being that the one-off AURORA record (never issued in a picture sleeve) failed to make any impression whatsoever upon either the fans or record companies. Consequently, the 7" is seldom sighted these days, and tends to command a very hefty price tag on the few occasions that it is offered for sale. Another of the great missed opportunities of the era!

7" Singles
»I'll Be Your Fantasy« Private 1982

Compilation Appearances
"I'll Be Your Fantasy" on »NWOBHM Vol.1« Bootleg CD 1992

AVALANCHE

Davidson
Wragg
Brook
Everett
Rush

Not to be confused either with numerous overseas namesakes or with the raunchy Scottish act who featured on the »It's Unheard Of!« and »Overtone 3-The Rock Album« compilations, the earlier version of AVALANCHE are a real mystery at present. Their only known release, a horrendously scarce two-tracker from 1980, has turned up in utterly minimal quantities over the years, and the absence of a picture sleeve means that there's precious little to report in terms of useful information. Still, the single is a pretty weighty effort, although it's fair to say that the pair of numbers on display occasionally suffer from slightly clumsy arrangements as well as a pretty limited vocal performance. A-side "The Preacher" is the worst culprit, and this track (lying somewhere between DEEP SWITCH and FUGITIVE) works best during the upbeat, instrumental sections, given that the more 'atmospheric' vocal parts don't really work particularly well. Flipside "Mean Lady", on the other hand, is a rather more conventional, mid-paced effort (it soon runs out of steam, though, after which it well and truly outstays its welcome) in the style of GOLDSMITH or FAIR WARNING.

Overall, this wasn't exactly a disastrous way for a small-time bunch of hopefuls to open their account, but »The Preacher« was very much a release of its time (if truth be told, it hasn't really aged too gracefully in the interim), although its sheer rarity will no doubt have a few avid collectors foaming at the mouth. The record itself is a pretty spartan affair in terms of presentation, the monochrome label (which features a suitably metal-looking skull at the top) crediting only surnames (plus a mystery chap called Bob Hockley, who evidently produced the whole shebang) and providing no information whatsoever as to where it might have been recorded. Given that I've never seen any mention of this bunch in any of the relevant periodicals of the time, I guess they were probably a fly-by-night act whose musical career (possibly consisting of a one-off visit to the recording studio) was soon being brushed under the carpet by those involved. Still, if anyone actually remembers this version of AVALANCHE, please do get in touch and spill the beans.

7" Singles
»The Preacher« Childers Records 1980

AVALON

Line-up unknown

There's no doubt that AVALON was a vastly overused name all over the world in the 80's, with several bands of that identity (the best-known being a Dutch concern) releasing vinyl of their own at one point or another. There has long been rumoured to be a British version from the NWOBHM era, although the 7" in question was originally believed to be called »Going Through« (see, for example, 'Heavy Metal-The Vinyl Years' by John Allinson). Hence, the arrival on the scene of a hitherto-undocumented, sleeveless oddity entitled »Embers« (B-side "Flags") on the outlandishly-named Flying Stilton Club Records (GONG would have been proud of that one) has thrown things into semi-confusion. It does indeed appear to be British (the record was manufactured here, although I supsect AVALON weren't English), in spite of the complete lack of writing credits or studio details, and it falls into the grey area between prog and metal. Both tracks are pretty substantial, despite the fairly technical and unusual arrangements (slightly reminiscent of KRAKEN), and feature the sort of vocal phrasing (utilised by the likes of THE COVENANT and SHERWOOD) that sounds more European than British in style. Nevertheless, the material is strong enough to justify AVALON's inclusion in this book, so keep an eye out for »Embers« (issued at some point in 1984) if you're not put off by the semi-prog tag. I'd like to clear up the mystery of the other single, though, so if anyone's actually got a copy, or has any information regarding the mystery bunch under discussion here (I'll happily eat humble pie if they turn out to be non-Brits, but SCRATCH fooled a lot of people too, remember), you know who to contact.

7" Singles
»Embers« Flying Stilton Club Records 1984

AVENGER

Brian Ross (v)
Steve Bird (g)
Mick Moore (b)
Gary Young (d)

For many dedicated NWOBHM enthusiasts, the exalted triumvirate of BLITZKRIEG, AVENGER and SATAN will forever be inextricably linked, and it's fair to say that they shared not only a common vocalist (Brian Ross) at various times, but also a highly-similar musical outlook (each used the other bands' compositions quite regularly, just to confound matters). Tyneside's AVENGER (not to be confused with numerous overseas namesakes, notably the German ensemble who would later become RAGE) came into existence in the second half of 1982, following the initial collapse of the much-loved BLITZKRIEG, whereupon the duo of Brian Ross and Mick Moore relocated permanently to the North East and duly linked up with a couple of new associates (Steve Bird and Gary Young, supposedly both veterans of a minor act called HORST) to form their latest musical vision. Before long, AVENGER had laid down a demo tape, featuring "The Space Traveller", "Too Wild To Tame" (two numbers salvaged from the BLITZKRIEG days, the latter having originally been earmarked as the intended follow-up to their »Buried Alive« single), "Hunt You Down" (later reworked by SATAN), "Love's Too Late" and "Hot'n'Heavy Express". Of these, the last-mentioned was chosen to appear on Neat's »One Take No Dubs« 12" EP, and the public were soon being won over by AVENGER's no-nonsense brand of powerful, upbeat metal, with many fans hailing the new outfit as the natural successors to BLITZKRIEG, whom most assumed would never be resurrected.

Following their instant approval by the metal community of the day, AVENGER were invited to lay down a single for Neat, and they obliged by basing it around their own version of "Too Wild To Tame" (b/w "On The Rocks"), by which time new guitarist John Brownless had been drafted in to take the place of Steve Bird. The single was a triumph, and went some way towards restoring Neat as a reliable source of new metal (the public hadn't been too enamoured of the releases from EMERSON, VALHALLA, JESS COX and so forth), so it was no surprise that a full album was commissioned in due course. By this time, however, AVENGER had (just to confuse everyone completely) swapped vocalists with SATAN, which meant that Brain Ross had handed over the AVENGER mike stand to Ian Davison Swift, although the newcomer proved to be a perfectly capable replacement. Furthermore, the group had already gigged successfully throughout the North for much of 1983, and had additionally recruited a second guitarist, Les Cheetham, to help out in the live environment. Towards the end of the year, however, John Brownless decided to pack his bags, so the outfit were reduced to a quartet once again, and it was this line-up which would enter the studio in the early months of 1984 (after a brief jaunt in Europe, where they were steadily developing a cult following) to record the tracks which would eventually comprise their debut full-length effort.

The »Blood Sports« set emerged in the second half of 1984, and proved to be a high-quality release in the best BLITZKRIEG tradition (the new vocalist being an extremely capable frontman, although lacking the range of his predecessor), with stand-out numbers in the form of "Enforcer", "You'll Never Take Me (Alive)" and "Death Race 2000". It was reasonably varied, however, and "Warfare" saw the lads attempting a rather more sedate style, whereas their unexpected choice of cover version (MONTROSE's "Matriarch") may have taken quite a few people by surprise, although it wasn't at all out of place. The album was instantly elevated to the status of 'classic' throughout mainland Europe, although the jaded UK reviewers tended to be rather less gushing in their write-ups at the time. Nevertheless, the band were soon out on the road once again, touring throughout the continent (occasionally utilising another second guitarist, this time a certain Ginger, the future QUIREBOYS/WILDHEARTS stalwart) with great success. Eventually, however, Les Cheetham decided to move on to pastures new (he helped out as second guitarist on VENOM's subsequent tour of the States in 1985), and American import

Greg Reiter was drafted in to fill the gap. Before long, AVENGER were being encouraged to lay down another full album (Mick Moore had, in the meantime, been moonlighting on BLITZKRIEG's »A Time Of Changes« long-player), so they rapidly ensconced themselves in the studio once again.

The second full-length AVENGER effort (»Killer Elite«) turned out to be a slightly confusing album, veering from proto-thrash to traditional metal and back again, with catchy choruses being thrown in to add a more memorable touch to many of the otherwise unremarkable songs. It was a difficult style for the lads to have attempted (all credit to them for not churning out an exact replica of their debut), although it was later carried off with slightly more finesse by the likes of GRIM REAPER and ONSLAUGHT. Nevertheless, there were still some decent numbers included, and the likes of "Revenge Attack", "Under The Hammer" and "Dangerous Games" come across as pretty respectable (albeit rather concise and unadventurous) efforts. Even so, something of an unforeseen AVENGER backlash was instigated almost immediately, with hardliners complaining that they had deserted their roots, while others merely dismissed them as making an incompetent and half-hearted attempt to pass themselves off as a thrash outfit. Inevitably, the hardworking lads were soon back out on tour to promote the new album, although they sensed that their original levels of popularity were beginning to cool off a bit, and the individual members soon began to doubt that they were actually heading in the right direction after all.

Things finally came to a head after AVENGER's ill-fated tour of the States in 1986 (which they undertook with a new drummer, Darren Kurland), which appears to have represented nothing less than a complete and utter disaster. Strangely, the blame for the outfit's transatlantic failure was laid squarely at the feet of new guitarist Greg Reiter (although I'm not entirely sure how his behaviour caused everything to go pear-shaped), and the dejected group decided to disband almost immediately upon their return to the UK. Ian Davison Swift rapidly teamed up with emerging heavy hopefuls ATOMKRAFT (it's entirely possible that Darren Kurland also joined in the fun under the assumed identity of DC Rage), the frontman having originally been approached to hook up with them several months earlier, although the remaining members of AVENGER (with the exception of original drummer Gary Young, who went on to play an important role in the fortunes of the revived

BLITZKRIEG) soon went to ground permanently. Mick Moore, by the way, later moved back to the Midlands and hooked up with a short-lived REBEL offshoot called BIG HEAT, although this particular venture ultimately failed to amount to much.

LP's
»Blood Sports« Neat 1984/Roadrunner 1984
[UK/Dutch issue]
»Killer Elite« Neat 1985/Roadrunner 1985
[UK/Dutch issue]
»Blood Sports/Killer Elite« Neat 1985
[Italian double album set in gatefold sleeve]

7" Singles
»Too Wild To Tame« Neat 1983
[A-side non-LP, B-side "On The Rocks" different to album version]

Exclusive Compilation Appearances
"Hot'n'Heavy Express" on »One Take No Dubs« 12" EP Neat 1982

Compilation Appearances
"Too Wild To Tame" on »Axe Attack« LP M Port 1985/Mausoleum 1986 + »Metal Masters« 4-CD Box Castle Communications 1993
"Yesterday's Heroes" on »Heavy Metal Collection 2« CD X-Tra Collection 1993
"Steel On Steel" on »Heavy Metal Collection 3« CD X-Tra Collection 1993
"(Fight For The) Right To Rock" on »Heavy Metal Collection 4« CD X-Tra Collection 1993

AVENUE

Valerie Cowell (v,g)
Anthony Cowell (v,g,k)
Stuart Woodley (b)
Bob Atkinson (d)

To be brutally honest, we're back in the same dubious territory as WARRIOR's »Troublemaker« long-player here; a record on which a minority of tracks just about conspire to elevate a band from mere pub rock status into the realm of semi-NWOBHM contenders. In the main, the selections on AVENUE's seldom-seen »Ill Cheers« LP are uneventful boogie/blues/MOR chimeras which tend to pass by almost unnoticed (apart from the hopeless "I Found A Life", which is genuinely *annoying*), with mouthpiece Anthony Cowell generally failing to make a particularly good impression. Mind you, almost without exception, on the relatively few occasions where his more talented sister (Valerie) is allowed to assume vocal duties, the standard of the quartet's material is lifted considerably. Indeed, enjoyable numbers such as "I'm Not Afraid Of Dying", "Cruel, Cruel Woman" and "He's Gone" are all raunchy rockers which showcase a powerful, assertive vocal performance, which, although not exactly rivalling ROCK GODDESS in terms of intensity, was undeniably comparable to the likes of AMAZON or AFTER HOURS, so it's a pity that Ms Cowell wasn't permitted to be their full-time vocalist.

AVENUE gigged around their native London like proverbial workhorses throughout the early 80's, and one side of the album was recorded at one of these many shindigs (with a certain Bas Smith, presumably the ex-KILLING FLOOR man, credited as drummer). Unfortunately, it's strictly amateur-hour in terms of production values, which tends to spoil things slightly, but I suppose it cut down on the amount of time they had to spend in the studio. Although the outfit apparently recorded a grand total of three albums (this one being the third), it looks as though the first two (»First Avenue«, predictably enough, and »Savage Amusement«, a title later used by the SCORPIONS) were cassette-only issues (and both were supposedly in a more mainstream vein), but were widely distributed by the mighty Pinnacle label. It also appears that AVENUE were just one of several projects which featured the American-born Cowells (part of a large musical family), and that they toured extensively throughout Europe with considerable success (particularly in Belgium, for some strange reason) over the years. »Ill Cheers« is a pretty rare record, all the same, but it's another one that doesn't deserve to be in the premier division in terms of value.

The original incarnation of AVENUE came to an end when the Cowells decided to go their separate ways in terms of musical projects, although Anthony himself later resurrected the group (now titled ANTZ AVENUE) in the mid-80's, employing a series of accomplices (including erstwhile AVENUE drummer Bob Atkinson, amongst others), in due course and, as a self-styled *'rock and blues trio'*) issuing further cassette-only releases including a well-received live album. Valerie, meanwhile, persevered in the music business for many years, eking out a successful career as a session vocalist/musician (she actually contributed backing vocals on the PRAYING MANTIS album »A Cry For The New World«), and also teamed up with guitarist Richard Hayes (a veteran of numerous minor boogie/blues acts) in the mid-80's. The eventual fruit of this liaison was a duo called BAD INFLUENCE (which took a few years to get going properly), another bluesy rock concern (featuring an anonymous selection of backing musicians) who did their utmost to get themselves noticed with a never-ending series of shows throughout the capital. In fact, after securing support slots with the likes of DUMPY'S RUSTY NUTS and SAMSON at around the turn of the decade, they were even featured on the seldom-seen »Metal For Muthas '92« compilation CD with the track "Life Goes On". How appropriate.

LP's
»III Cheers« Boulevard Records 198?

AXIS

Neil Grafton (v)
Mick Tucker (g)
Dave Little (g)
John Cunningham (b)
Paul McGuire (k)
Marty Day (d)

Little-known Cleveland outfit AXIS (a surprisingly common name both in the UK and the rest of the world in the 70's/80's) were, in 1980, afforded the honour of releasing the first product on Neat's short-lived (and rather baffling) Metal Minded subsidiary (also home to BADGE), although nothing much seems to be known about the band's history prior to that point. In any case, their debut single, coupling "Lady" with "Messiah" (the last-mentioned later put in an appearance on Neat's »Lead Weight« compilation, incidentally), represented a fairly interesting NWOBHM variation of mid-paced, heavy music with progressive/technical undertones, overall suggesting a mixture of WHITE SPIRIT, CHEMICAL ALICE and MARQUIS DE SADE. It was a decent enough start, and the band were retained by their sponsors, who clearly viewed AXIS as an outfit with a fair amount of potential. Matters became slightly confused the following year, however, when the sextet's follow-up 7" was scheduled to appear on the 'normal' Neat label, suggesting that the ill-fated Metal Minded concern had already been laid to rest (for reasons unknown) after a mere two singles. In any case, a pair of freshly-penned compositions ("You Got It" and "One Step Ahead") were duly recorded and pencilled in to be released (a catalogue number, Neat13, was even assigned) at the tail end of 1981, but the two-tracker appears to have been cancelled at more or less the last minute, with VENOM's »Bloodlust« subsequently taking its place. Bit of a mystery, that.

I believe, however, that the unfortunate AXIS were enduring a few internal problems at the time, with various members coming and going and casting the outfit's future into doubt, which may well have prompted Neat to conclude that they weren't prepared to take a chance and release their second two-tracker after all. Nevertheless, the persevering group had managed to get their act together again within a matter of months, although the only new AXIS composition to be made available to the public by Neat was "Flame Burns On", an effort included on both their »60 Minutes Plus« cassette and the European-only »All Hell Let Loose« LP a year or so later. By this time, however, the lads had clearly undergone a few reshuffles, with two recently-acquired members (vocalist Sam Blewitt and former WHITE SPIRIT bassist Phil Brady) having become established in the ranks. Furthermore, the group's original, progressively-inclined style had now become a rather more straightforward variation on the melodic rock theme (their keyboard player had also flown the coop, incidentally), although "Flame Burns On" was still a strong enough contribution to the sampler. Intriguingly, both of the outfit's compilation efforts subsequently appeared on early volumes of the famous Japanese series of bootleg CD's, and NWOBHM devotees GORGON have recently covered "Flame Burns On", so it looks as though they've got some loyal fans in the Far East!

Sadly, the all-new AXIS seems not to have won the hearts of the listening public, and it looks as though the participants no longer had the will to continue in the face of complete and utter disinterest from the nation's rock fans. The dejected musicians, having ultimately failed to make a lasting impression in either of their musical incarnations, seem to have gone their separate ways at some point in the latter half of 1982, although most of those involved with the last line-up proceeded to find gainful employment elsewhere. Vocalist Sam Blewitt, for example, moved over to the emerging EMERSON (later working with acts as diverse as SAMSON and YA YA), while drummer Marty Day joined forces with HOLLAND (later HAMMER) within a fairly short space of time. The guitarists also remained active on the scene, with Dave Little playing a role in the fortunes of the critically-ignored PAULINE GILLAN

BAND, while Mick Tucker, after a relatively brief stint with the rapidly-declining WHITE SPIRIT, ended up in one of the many incarnations of TANK. The first bassist (John Cunningham), on the other hand, teamed up with MASS (see separate entry), an obscure local bunch of melodic hopefuls who released a one-off single entitled »Rebel With A Cause« before evolving into an act called CHASE, who recorded an 'Into The Music' session but seem not to have made it to the vinyl stage.

Incidentally, it's possibly worth mentioning (as something of a cautionary tale) the fact that you might encounter a couple of fairly scarce singles by certain other (apparently British) versions of AXIS, these having absolutely no connection with the bunch under discussion here. First of all, there's the entirely disposable, lightweight pop of the »Wedding Bell« 7" (with some truly sickening lyrics for all the confirmed misogamists among us), and then there's an obscure two-tracker entitled »When You Hold Me«, both of which appear to have surfaced sometime in the early 80's. Neither of these records should be touched with an extendable barge-pole, no matter the asking price, and no matter how promising they might initially look. Indeed, »When You Hold Me« comes in one of the most metal-looking picture sleeves I've ever seen (a bright red effort depicting an axe-wielding savage and a suitable logo), although this eight-piece (!) proposition deliver nothing more than a passable impersonation of EARTH, WIND & FIRE. Be warned!

7" Singles
»**Lady**« Metal Minded 1980

Exclusive Compilation Appearances
"**Flame Burns On**" on »60 Minutes Plus« Cassette Neat 1982/CD Teichiku 1992 + »All Hell Let Loose« LP Neat 1983 + »NWOBHM Vol.3« Bootleg CD 1992

Compilation Appearances
"**Messiah**" on »Lead Weight« LP Neat 1981/CD Teichiku 1992 + »NWOBHM Vol.2« Bootleg CD 1992

BABY TUCKOO

Rob Armitage (v)
Neil Saxton (g)
Paul Smith (b)
Tony Sugden (d)

Yorkshire's strangely-monikered BABY TUCKOO (their name being taken from the utterly bonkers writings of James Joyce) started out as long ago as 1981, following the demise of various amateur-hour outfits (Tony Sugden, for example, was in a little-known act called EIGA, alongside MENDES PREY's Mark Sutcliffe), but took a fair old while before getting to the vinyl stage. Their early activities (as a quartet) were mainly dominated by minor club gigs and the occasional trip to the studio, but, as they freely admitted themselves, they didn't really think their flirtation with the music business would actually come to much. By the early months of 1984, however, it transpired that not only were these small-time hopefuls still together, but they had also somehow (much to their own amazement) managed to wangle a deal with the erratic Ultra Noise label (see also MARSEILLE), leading them to the inevitable conclusion that there might be a bit of mileage in this old rock and metal lark after all.

The outfit's debut album (»First Born«) hit the streets with little or no advance publicity, although word soon spread through the grapevine that the emergent BABY TUCKOO actually represented quite a decent prospect. Featuring a highly talented frontman in Rob Armitage (who, contrary to popular opinion, only sounded like David Coverdale on an occasional basis), the band were operating within the parameters of a fairly robust kind of melodic metal, with general comparisons to the likes of STAGEFRIGHT, AFTER DARK and SAPPHIRE (not to mention quite a bit of mid-period UFO) being fairly appropriate for the most part. It's also worth mentioning, incidentally, that Andy Barrott (formerly a member of local metal merchants GEDDES AXE) didn't actually contribute to the »First Born« sessions, as he wasn't recruited (as a full-time second guitarist/keyboard player) until after the whole affair had been recorded. He was, nevertheless, given both a place in the group photo and a co-writing credit on all the tracks featured, which is a bit odd. In fact, it would appear that one of JOHN VERITY's many associates (presumably Andy Wells, later of VOYAGER UK) supplied guest keyboards on the album (which was, incidentally, recorded at Verity's own studio), although there's no specific credit on the sleeve.

The band issued a single to promote the release, featuring the oft-recorded rock'n'roll standard "Mony Mony" (GASKIN got there first, lads) and "Baby's Rockin' Tonight", both taken from the newly-released album. Shortly thereafter, they were invited to record a session for the

'Friday Rock Show', and the recently-expanded quintet were only too happy to oblige. First broadcast on the 20th of April 1984, this confident performance showcased "A.W.O.L.", "Hot Wheels" and "Holdin' On", all taken from the album, plus the never-released "Baby Let The Good Times Roll". It was a warmly-received transmission at the time, and no doubt won them some new fans, but sales of BABY TUCKOO's debut long-player weren't quite as abundant as Ultra Noise had anticipated, with the upshot being that the label failed to promote the young group particularly effectively. Without the company's financial backing, the lads found it virtually impossible to get out and about, with any prospects of latching onto a major tour having now gone right out of the window. Nevertheless, they persevered, finally (in the wake of an aborted second single, »I'm Your Man«, and a much-postponed follow-up album) severing their links with their rather ineffectual label (which, in any case, went bust shortly afterwards) in 1985 and eventually (after several months spent trying to sell themselves to practically every company in the land) winning the hearts of Music For Nations, a label who were always looking for talented young outfits to add to their already-extensive roster.

After a bit of hectic studio activity, a second BABY TUCKOO album (»Force Majeure«) appeared in the early months of 1986, and this was soon winning extremely high praise from the fastidious 'Kerrang'. The generous recording budget seemed to have suited them, and the lads had delivered a more diverse and memorable set of compositions. The long-player was an extremely accomplished and confident effort (although it was occasionally slightly too keyboard-dominated and accessible), certainly, but it hardly led to an overnight change of fortunes for the members. Nevertheless, they continued to play live whenever they could, and the album finally began racking up a few sales as a result. Subsequently, the ludicrously-titled "Rock (Rock)" was trotted out as the lead track on a 12" EP, backed with the upbeat "Shoot On Sight" and the non-LP "Rock'n'Roll Hero", but sales were modest. The lads were lucky enough to support regional megastars SAXON at a local gig or two in the following months, but couldn't afford to pay their way for an entire tour either with Biff's mob or with any of the other big-name acts of the day, as Rob Armitage ruefully explained: 'We really wanted to move up a rung. We'd been around all the clubs and it felt like we were flogging a dead horse. So we tried to get on a bigger tour, like the MAGNUM tour and the SAXON tour, but they were just asking ridiculous prices; MAGNUM wanted fifteen thousand pounds from their support band.' (Ref: Kerrang No.139, February 1987).

Although the band had initially signed to Music For Nations for three years, there were, to quote the musicians themselves, 'plenty of get-out clauses', which appears to have worked more in their label's favour than to their own benefit. First, they were shunted off to the Fun After All subsidiary, then informed that they had just one more chance to deliver a hit single. In a last-ditch attempt to storm the charts, the lads prepared a single (issued in both 7" and 12" formats) featuring a cover of the well-worn SMO-

KEY ROBINSON AND THE MIRACLES classic "The Tears Of A Clown", a number which didn't suit their style particularly well, but it had reached the stage where they were prepared to try almost anything. Needless to say, it failed to reverse their fortunes, and the hapless outfit were released from contract as a matter of course. Refusing to give up the ghost, the lads took matters into their own hands and arranged a lengthy series of gigs with the affable CHROME MOLLY in the early months of 1987, which was initially conceived as a three-band tour, but Southern representatives CHARIOT pulled out due to outside commitments at short notice. The self-organised jaunt proved to be something of a success, and rumours were soon circulating that BABY TUCKOO had landed themselves a new deal with an influential American concern (whose identity was never actually revealed) as a direct result. Their third album was apparently all set to be recorded, with a batch of new songs having already been composed throughout the previous year, although their initial confidence and enthusiasm was eventually shattered in no uncertain terms when it became apparent that these mysterious benefactors wouldn't actually be financing a new album after all.

The group continued, hoping forlornly that a miracle might come their way eventually, but it was ultimately to fall apart before the end of 1987, when frontman Rob Armitage jumped ship after a lucrative offer to join ACCEPT (although this proved to be an extremely unproductive relationship) came out of the blue. His departure, however, effected an almost instant collapse of the BABY TUCKOO project, whereupon Andy Barrott subsequently moved over to CHROME MOLLY, reprising his previous role in BABY TUCKOO by contributing some additional guitar and keyboard work to the latter's studio and live activities. After he had finally parted company with ACCEPT (having failed to play a single gig or to take part in any recording sessions whatsoever), Armitage returned to Blighty, where he rapidly found gainful employment in Myke Gray's troubled JAGGED EDGE project, later fronting an unsuccessful offshoot called PASSION after the original group splintered within a year or so. The remaining musicians from the last incarnation of BABY TUCKOO, meanwhile, were snapped up as a job lot towards the end of the decade (bassist Paul Smith had also enjoyed a relatively brief stint with local lightweights VOYAGER UK in the interim) to act as a makeshift backing ensemble in a short-lived solo vehicle for erstwhile STATETROOPER frontman Gary Barden, although this proved to be a famously unsuccessful arrangement.

LP's
»**First Born**« Ultra Noise 1984
»**Force Majeure**« Music For Nations 1986
»**First Born**« Castle Communications 1986 *[Reissue]*

12" EP's
»**Rock (Rock)**« Music For Nations 1986 *["Rock'n'Roll Hero" non-LP]*
»**The Tears Of A Clown**« Fun After All 1986 *[A-side non-LP]*

7" Singles
»**Mony Mony**« Ultra Noise 1984
»**The Tears Of A Clown**« Fun After All 1986 *[A-side non-LP]*

Promotional Releases
»**Rock (Rock)**« Music For Nations 1986 *[DJ promo 7" with radio version, B-side "Shoot On Sight"]*

CD's
»**First Born**« Line Records 1988

Compilation Appearances
"**Broken Heart**" on »The Best Of British« LP Zebra 1985
"**Rock (Rock)**" on »Music For Nations-The Singles Album« Do-LP Music For Nations 1986
"**Over You**" on »Beyond Metal Zone« Do-LP Music For Nations 1986

BACKLASH

David Roper

The small Gargoyle label seems to have made a bit of a name for itself in the early 80's, releasing a fair few records by little-known Home Counties bands, the majority of whom appear to have been operating in a somewhat progressive style. One of the very first to be issued (in the heady days of 1980) was a four track EP (entitled »Off With His Head«) by BACKLASH, a popular outfit from Hertfordshire who gigged prolifically in their local area at the time. The material on display tends to come across as a blend of CHEMICAL ALICE and CRACKED MIRROR, with some capable guitar soloing, strong keyboard sections and typically complex, progressively-inclined arrangements. The two selections on the A-side ("Captain Pratt" and "Jackass") are the more enjoyable pair, these being considerably heavier than "Chess Game" and "Battle", the latter suggesting a lightweight sound more along the general lines of LIAISON or EARTHBOUND. Not bad, all things considered (although it clearly failed to raise BACKLASH above the level of small-time crowd pleasers), and definitely one to seek out if you like things slightly proggy. Issued in a plain, stickered sleeve, this EP (as with virtually everything else on Gargoyle) is seldom encountered these days, suggesting that the original pressings were all extremely limited. In other words, you'll need quite a bit of luck on your side if you go in search of this one.

7" EP's
»**Off With His Head**« Gargoyle Records 1980

BADGE

Graham Waudby (v)
Tony Dixon (g)
Stuart McLean (rg)

Mike Cooper (b)
Rob Zipfel (d)

The logic behind the creation of the ill-fated Metal Minded subsidiary by Neat Records in 1980 remains rather perplexing, to say the least, as it was a remarkably short-lived operation with, it would appear, no particularly strong underlying concept. The fairly obscure pair of hopefuls featured on the brace of singles in question (BADGE and AXIS), while talented enough in their own right, weren't exactly of sufficiently outstanding potential (or operating in such an original style) that a separate label was warranted to promote them effectively, so it's all a bit of a mystery. In any case, Humberside's BADGE (possibly inspired by the CREAM song, but they weren't operating in a remotely similar style to Clapton's mob) were (if their one-off single's anything to go by) a reasonably decent proposition, and the two-tracker showcased a group who might well have been able to develop into a pretty capable metal unit if they had been given the breaks. Their "Silver Woman", for example, is very much in the mid-paced MARZ scheme of things, with the merest hint of MYTHRA thrown in for good measure, whereas flipside "Something I've Lost" is a fairly powerful semi-ballad, although it's not a particularly accomplished piece of songwriting.

While the aforementioned AXIS were subsequently afforded the enviable opportunity to record a freshly-penned contribution for Neat's »60 Minutes Plus« cassette sampler in 1982, however, poor old BADGE (who were, nevertheless, fortunate enough to win a few precious support slots with regional amphibian heroes ETHEL THE FROG in their time) weren't given another chance to shine, and it looks as though most of the participants simply went back to their day jobs shortly thereafter. It transpires, however, that bassist Mike Cooper went on to play a part in the fortunes of emergent local favourites BLADE RUNNER (see separate entry), so at least one of them managed to earn a crust from rock music for a few more years. One thing's for sure, the BADGE lads certainly enjoyed the odd drop of local ale, as evidenced by the prominent acknowledgement at the base of the sleeve: *'Thanks to Scottish and Newcastle breweries for providing energy.'* I reckon someone in the area should have organised a drinking competition between BADGE and the A.R.C. ROCK BAND...

7" Singles
»Silver Woman« Metal Minded 1981

Compilation Appearances
"Silver Woman" on »NWOBHM Vol.2« Bootleg CD 1992

BADGER

Badger Bell (v)
Roy Baird (g)
Davey Hoyle (g)
Mogga Moon (b)
Gary Jones (d)

The worst thing about compiling a reference source of this type is surely *'the curse of the duplicate name',* an affliction which appears to have been utterly rampant during the NWOBHM period. We're already familiar with the proliferation of groups called WARRIOR, RAW DEAL, ROUGH JUSTICE *etc.*, but we're always coming up against sticky questions along the lines of *'was band X who appeared on a certain compilation related to band Y who issued their own single?'* Quite often, details concerning line-ups and home towns are so infuriatingly sketchy that it's impossible to give an unequivocal answer, but an educated guess can generally be imparted on the basis of musical similarity, if nothing else. Mind you, there are exceptions to every rule, and some changed direction dramatically within a couple of years (DRAGONSLAYER, to name but one), while certain awkward groups (notably TURBO) contrived to replace almost their entire line-up in a comparable timescale whilst retaining a virtually identical sound. After much consideration (well, a good few minutes, anyway), however, I've been unable either to prove or disprove the existence of a link between the Lancashire version of BADGER who were featured (with "The Traveller") on Ebony's »Metal Plated« album back in 1983, and the BADGER (also based in the North West) who offered the world the »Over The Wall« EP several years later. Musically, the twin-guitar sound and song structures are similar, although it's certainly a different frontman, given that the chap on the LP sounds like SHY's Tony Mills, whereas his counterpart on the 7" possesses a much deeper and rougher voice in the A.R.C. ROCK BAND vein.

Mind you, I'm beginning to suspect that they were unrelated, given that it transpires that the later bunch had actually issued a seldom-seen single under the identity of the BADGER BELL BAND a year or two earlier, but I'm leaving the

door open for someone to prove that the »Metal Plated« BADGER were indeed an antecedent after all. The two-tracker in question (issued on the band's own Noize Gate label at some point in the mid-80's) coupled "Nothing Left" and the ludicrously-titled "Rock The Vicar", these numbers apparently revealing the ensemble to be a rough'n'ready bunch of crowd-pleasers with a vague MOTÖRHEAD fixation. Still, it would appear that this sleeveless effort performed inauspiciously upon its release, suggesting that the lads probably failed to promote either themselves or their vinyl debut particularly effectively. The musicians presumably retreated to the pubs and clubs of the North for a couple of years in order to work on their sound and image, although they eventually returned (under the abbreviated moniker of BADGER) with a markedly more accomplished 7" EP. The record, produced by the capable Gordon Rowley of NIGHTWING, was a pretty solid slice of metal which resembled a mixture of WOLF, KARRIER and (particularly) CRUCIFIXION, with title track "Over The Wall" being very much along the lines of the latter's "The Fox". The forgettable "Faceless Gang", on the other hand, is a disappointingly weak effort, although "Runaway" (recorded live in North Wales) rounds things off quite nicely. For this final offering, we're back in CRUCIFIXION territory again (notably, their "On The Run") for another capably-written selection with strong guitar work.

The three-tracker isn't dated explicitly, but it looks as though it was probably issued towards the end of 1986 or early the following year, as there don't seem to be any reviews prior to this point. Mind you, it confirmed that BADGER had now become semi-serious contenders (they duly won a few mentions in some of the smaller fanzines, most of which were encouraging), although they had clearly missed the boat in terms of hitching a ride on the NWOBHM bandwagon (now there's a mixed metaphor). In the end, however, the momentum seems to have drained away fairly rapidly, and the musicians simply abandoned their ambitious programme of vinyl releases and concentrated on small-time fame on the club circuit. It would appear that BADGER (who had nothing to do with yet another identically-named outfit from the early 70's, by the way) remained on the scene and continued gigging throughout their locality until more or less the end of the decade, but eventually decided to pack it all in and go back to their day jobs. All in all, their »Over The Wall« effort is a deserving addition to any NWOBHM collection (as is their first single, but it's practically impossible to find nowadays), and it's worth mentioning that the record's monochrome cartoon sleeve, depicting a prison wall about to be scaled from within, actually shows more than just the band name. Wonders never cease.

7" Singles
»Nothing Left« Noize Gate Records 1985?
[As the BADGER BELL BAND]

7" EP's
»Over The Wall« Noize Gate Records 1986?

BASELINE

Mick Sollitt (v,b)
Kev Harton (g)
Martyn Long (d)

I hate to be prejudicial, but I've often voiced the concern that, had certain musically-ambiguous, NWOBHM-era singles actually been issued in picture covers with a group image, the musicians might not always look as *'metal'* as you might have been led to believe. Yorkshire's BASELINE certainly elicited this response with their crossover style, and, when a rare sleeved copy of their one-off 7" (from 1981) was finally uncovered (the front of which appears a bit arty and stylised compared with most metal releases of the time), they did indeed turn out to look distressingly normal in their photo. Mind you, it's always the music that counts, not the fact that the band members wear sensible jumpers and have short hair, and it's actually pretty good in this case. The two *'blink and you'll miss them'* slices of poppy punk/mod/metal/whatever are reasonably solid on the guitar front, and both hurtle along in a similar fashion to the FALSE IDOLS or SHADOWFAX, for example. I'd say that "Suspended Animation" is the stronger of the pair, with decent vocals and a fairly heavy riff, whereas "Truth About The Lies", while competent enough, sounds disturbingly close to the theme song to the TV show 'Whatever Happened to the Likely Lads' (that's one for the British readers, I guess), particularly the entertaining cover version that the punk-as-you-like SNUFF recorded a few years ago. The BASELINE two-tracker (nothing else appears to have been released) is well worth looking for, though, and it provides a salutary lesson that even the scary punk/mod sections in shops or at record fairs may actually harbour some vinyl to tickle your auditory fancy if you're willing to take a chance with your hard-earned cash.

7" Singles
»Suspended Animation« Extra Bit Records 1981

BASHFUL ALLEY

Dave Slamen (v)
Rob Tidd (g)
Ian 'Truff' Threlfall (b)
Donkey (d)

Although Rob Tidd and Ian 'Truff' Threlfall, the founder members of the bafflingly-named BASHFUL ALLEY, were both natives of the county of Staffordshire (having cut their teeth with a variety of small-time Midlands acts during the late 70's), it transpires that the original incarnation of their own outfit actually came together while the pair were studying at Lancaster University. After scouring their adopted home for some likely accomplices, the erudite duo hooked up, in the first instance, with vocalist Dave Slamen and the judiciously-named Donkey (maybe he had big ears or something) on drums, whereupon they started putting in a bit of practice in between lectures. Things seemed to work out pretty well, and so it wasn't very long before the newly-formed ensemble ventured into the studio, whereupon they recorded the original version of their first demo (featuring "Running Blind", "My My My" and "She Only Wants Me For My Body"), after which the lads proceeded to tour with reasonable success throughout their local area. There was no meteoric rise to stardom for BASHFUL ALLEY,

however, and the questionable 'highlight' of their spell up North was a one-off event supporting THE SWEET at their own college, as Rob Tidd later explained: 'That was a joke, hardly anyone turned up. The band that were supposed to support didn't show, so we were called in because of our previous connections with the University. We thought it would be our big break but we ended up playing to less people than at our own gigs.' (Ref: Kerrang No.13, April 1982).

Returning to their native county some time after finishing those all-important studies, Tidd and Truff soon recruited new drummer Robin Baxter and resumed as a trio, with Tidd now taking over the vocal responsibilities. Their aforementioned three track demo was subsequently re-recorded at Saccen Studios in Stourport, with the pairing of "Running Blind" and "My My My" being selected from the resulting tape for imminent release as a 7" single. With their excellent two-tracker being issued as a relatively modest pressing on the small-time Ellie Jay concern (with two slightly different sleeve colours), the compositions featured were catchy, mid-paced offerings (as was the unused track from their original demo) in the general manner of OMEN SEARCHER or LYADRIVE, which seemed to strike exactly the right chord with a high proportion of metal aficionados at the time. Crucially, it also won the seal of approval from the influential Geoff Barton, and a favourable write-up in the notoriously fickle 'Singles' section of 'Kerrang' attracted a great amount of fan interest within the UK. Indeed, such was the remarkable success of the single (a huge number of orders additionally arrived from fans in Holland after a glowing review in 'Aardschok' magazine) that a re-pressing was eventually called for (this time on the group's own Graffiti label), issued in a yellow version of the original picture sleeve, which showed hand-drawn images of the band members.

By this time, BASHFUL ALLEY seemed to have everything going for them, and they capitalised on the success of their single by getting back out on the road once more. Having wasted no time re-establishing themselves as a popular live attraction (they also found time to enter Switch Studios and demo rauncher selections such as "Rescue Me" and "Light It Up" along the way), the lads subsequently went on to play numerous gigs with emergent hopefuls throughout the Midlands, even sharing a stage with a virtually-unrecognisable WOLFSBANE at one point. Nevertheless, very little label interest came their way, and the band ultimately concluded that they needed to make a few changes if they were to win over the influential companies. In 1984, newcomer Anthony Jones was added as a second guitarist, and the lads, rather than sticking to a tried and tested formula, bravely attempted to steer their sound towards a twin-axe direction more along the lines of THIN LIZZY. Within just a year, however, things had already run their natural course, and the well-liked bunch disbanded in the wake of a cruel lack of attention from the movers and shakers. They obviously still had a desire to remain involved with the music business, though, with Truff ultimately joining SLEAZE BROTHERS INC. (a bluesy covers band, where he took to the stage alongside various ageing rockers), whereas Tidd moved to London and hooked up with the long-forgotten LINE OF FIRE (he subsequently enjoyed a modicum of media recognition with DOLLFACE in the 90's), while Robin Baxter proceeded to lend his services to a punk-influenced outfit called the BEACH PISTOLS.

7" Singles
»Running Blind« Ellie Jay 1982
[Original issue, initially in white sleeve, later cream sleeve]
»Running Blind« Graffiti Records 1982
[Second issue, yellow sleeve]

Compilation Appearances
"Running Blind" on »NWOBHM Vol.1« Bootleg CD 1992

BATTLEAXE

Dave King (v)
Steve Hardy (g)
Brian Smith (b)
Ian Thompson (d)

Wearside heavyweights BATTLEAXE got going in around 1980, and were soon making rock fans happy throughout the North East with their no-frills brand of metal, the band taking their lead from acts such as RAVEN, TANK and MOTÖRHEAD. At an early stage, they were given a useful piece of exposure after laying down a session for their local station, Radio Tees, and it wasn't long before their activities in the live environment attracted the attention of Guardian Records, who just happened to be putting together another one of their rock compilations. The BATTLEAXE lads duly took their turn in the studio, laying down "Burn This Town" and their "Battleaxe" anthem at the beginning of 1982, and they soon saw this pair of tracks featured on the resultant »Roxcalibur« compilation. Not only that, the label was so enamoured of these recordings that they saw fit to release them as a 7" single (no sleeve issued) shortly afterwards, a move which must have been even more beneficial to the band's fortunes. It looks as though it was quite an extensive pressing, too, and there have always been sufficient copies in circulation to prevent the asking price from rising above fairly nominal levels, as is the case with the MYTHRA 7" on the same label.

With BATTLEAXE having been given a considerable boost by the patronage of Guardian, the lads were soon back in the same studio facility to record another eight numbers, bringing them up to strength for a full LP release. In the event, however, the album didn't actually appear on Guardian, the group having been lured away by a more tempting deal from the emergent Music For Nations label in the interim. The debut longplayer, again titled »Burn This Town«, appeared at the start of 1983 (in a legendarily-awful sleeve), and this followed fairly unashamedly in the energetic (but rather unambitious) style of their earlier single. For the undemanding metal fan, though, it was a satisfactory release (tracks such as "Star Maker" and "Overdrive" were, admittedly, quite listenable), and the quartet were soon enjoying airplay throughout most of the rock-loving world. Within a few months, the lads were invited to record a session for the 'Friday Rock Show', by which time they had recruited former SATAN drummer Ian McCormack to the fold (Ian Thompson, meanwhile, moved on to DARK HEART). Broadcast on the 13th of May 1983, the enjoyable session saw the group showcasing "Ready To Deliver" and "Running Out Of Time" from the album, plus the new pairing of "Shout It Out" and "Mean Machine". A couple of weeks later, the lads were joining the likes of ANVIL, GIRLSCHOOL, TWISTED SISTER and SAXON onstage at a major rock festival in Leeds, so it was certainly all going BATTLEAXE's way at that point in time.

The debut album was a sufficiently good seller for their label to commission a sequel, and, following a spot of further touring alongside the mighty SAXON, BATTLEAXE were soon hard at work in the studio once again. 1984's »Power From The Universe« (the original title was the hackneyed »Licensed To Rock«) was an altogether more varied set of compositions (there were even a few keyboard contributions from former MAGNUM/ALASKA man Richard Bailey), although there was also something of an aggressive edge this time, suggesting that the

61

outfit might have taken on board a few influences from some of the more prominent European acts of the day. Tracks such as the lengthy "Fortune Lady", on the other hand, showed a markedly more thoughtful and mature aspect to the group's songwriting skills, and the album (supposedly featuring backing vocals from Chris and Tino Troy of PRAYING MANTIS, although I'm not sure how significant their contribution might have been) was a far more substantial effort than their debut set. Inevitably, therefore, it was something of a flop in terms of sales, and the BATTLEAXE lads were soon being given their freedom by Music For Nations, who saw little future in the act. Nevertheless, they remained a going concern, and eventually demoed an entire album's worth of novel material in the latter half of 1985, the intention being to release their third long-player (tentatively titled »Metal Edge«) as soon as the offers started coming their way in the new year.

Sadly, however, BATTLEAXE's initial optimism appears to have been completely wide of the mark, and the labels of the day were, in fact, extremely reluctant to take a chance on a selection of traditional British metal of the variety on offer. The despondent lads seem to have called it a day after being cruelly rejected at every opportunity, meaning that the fans were never able to appreciate new numbers such as "Scarlet Woman", "Demon Queen", "Mean Machine" and "Out In The Night". Strangely, however, King, Smith and McCormack (who were presumably still quite confident that the world was crying out for a third album) subsequently tried to re-establish the BATTLEAXE name in 1988, employing the services of John Stormont (ex-JESS COX) and Mick Percy as twin guitarists. It appears that this line-up even got as far as recording a three track demo soon after, although it presumably met with unanimous label indifference yet again, and the project was rapidly put on ice once more. Ian McCormack, incidentally, turned up in the most recent incarnation of PARIAH (having additionally lent a hand in the CRONOS venture from time to time), so it's nice to see that at least one of them still seems to be working.

LP's
»**Burn This Town**« Music For Nations 1983/Roadrunner 1983
[UK/Dutch issue]
»**Burn This Town**« Bernett 1983

[French issue with different sleeve]
»Power From The Universe« Music For Nations 1984/Roadrunner 1984
[UK/Dutch issue]

7" Singles
»Burn This Town« Guardian 1982

CD's
»Burn This Town« Pony Canyon 1994
[Japanese issue]
»Power From The Universe« Pony Canyon 1994
[Japanese issue]

Compilation Appearances
"Burn This Town" on »Roxcalibur« LP Guardian 1982/CD British Steel 1998
"Battleaxe" on »Roxcalibur« LP Guardian 1982/CD British Steel 1998
"Ready To Deliver" on »Metal Battle« LP Neat 1983/Roadrunner 1983 + »Hell On Earth« LP Music For Nations 1983
"Running Out Of Time" on »Metal Hammer« LP Roadrunner 1984
"Chopper Attack" on »Welcome To The Metal Zone« Do-LP Music For Nations 1985

BATTLEZONE

Paul Dianno (v)
Daran Aldridge (g)
John Hurley (g)
Charles Hurley (b)
Bob Falck (d)

After the unmitigated commercial disaster that was the DIANNO project (which finally fell apart in the early months of 1985), Paul Dianno decided that it would be a better idea to return to his roots and assemble a down-to-earth, heavy band instead of a contrived AOR proposition. He wasted little time getting his latest outfit together (although it might be wise to gloss over his involvement with GOGMAGOG), recruiting an entirely new set of musicians in the summer of that year. Joining him in this venture were guitarists John Hurley (ex-TOUCHSTONE) and Daran Aldridge (previously with obscure East End hopefuls GANDALF WIZARDRY), plus drummer Bob Falck (ex-PENTAGON), all three of whom had latterly been working together in an unsuccessful act called SHANGHAI TYGER. The all-new outfit (initially completed by bassist Lawrence Kessler, previously with Swedish unknowns SORCERER, although the chap was soon ousted in favour of former NEON GODDESS member Charles Hurley) was swiftly christened BATTLEZONE, and the experienced ensemble made their live debut in the capital a mere couple of months later, unveiling original numbers such as "Welfare Warriors", "I'll Make You Pay" and "In The Darkness". This time, however, there was a minimal number of IRON MAIDEN tracks in the setlist (and there was certainly no temptation to play any of those DIANNO shockers); you paid to see a BATTLEZONE show and that's entirely what you got, a selection of traditional British metal in the style of MILLENNIUM, SEDUCER or DEALER, for example.

In the early months of 1986, the unsettled Charles Hurley and Daran Aldridge flew the coop, the pair being replaced by Pete West and John Wiggins, respectively. Wiggins, who had just parted company with TOKYO BLADE, had previously been involved with Dianno's LONEWOLF, the outfit who eventually became DIANNO, so there was no need for long introductions. Before long, the group had wangled a deal with Raw Power Records, and their »Fighting Back« debut (the sleeve announcing the band to be *'Paul Dianno's BATTLEZONE'*, although this was never their official identity) appeared shortly thereafter, giving a wider range of fans the opportunity to hear the material that the musicians had been cultivating and performing live over the preceding period. All the live favourites were present (although a few of their early efforts had been kicked into touch by this stage), such as the epic "The Land God Gave To Caine", "Welcome To The Battlezone" and "Running Blind". The long-player unquestionably served to satisfy Dianno's many fans, who overwhelmingly hailed the album as a long-awaited return to form. The group toured extensively to promote the release (including a prestigious appearance at the Dynamo Festival, although they were actually only filling in for LAAZ ROCKIT), ending up in the States (where their debut set had been issued on a different label, Shatter) in the early months of 1987, delighting the crowds on the other side of the Atlantic with an eventful series of shows, a couple of which were spent supporting none other than STRYPER.

The American gigs were to prove somewhat stressful, however, and a *'lack of professionalism'* shown by various participants resulted in Bob Falck and John Hurley being given the order of the boot upon completion of the tour. Falck was left to fend for himself in the States (he soon found work with OVER KILL, where he took to calling himself *'Sid'*, given that there were two other *'Bobs'* in the outfit already), whi-

63

le Hurley (who later resurfaced in London also-rans L.O. GIRLS) was at least given the courtesy of a flight home before being sacked upon the plane's touchdown in the UK. Dianno seldom had much trouble in attracting new blood to his musical projects (well, he's a bit hard, you see), and so there wasn't any great delay before Graham Bath (g) and the much-travelled Steve Hopgood (d) stepped in to fill the gaps. Both had latterly been working with PERSIAN RISK, although the long-drawn-out demise of this popular outfit had left the pair at a loose end for a while. Understandably, they jumped at their chance to join another successful venture, and the revised BATTLEZONE were soon back in the studio, recording their follow-up album for new sponsors Powerstation Records (who had already issued material by the likes of TOKYO BLADE and MAINEEAXE), a release which would see the light later in the year. »Children Of Madness«, as it was titled, was a marked progression from the debut, something which took many people by surprise at the time.

The second BATTLEZONE album suggested that the group had assimilated a few new ideas and influences from their Stateside trip, with the whole affair being far more slickly-produced and ambitious than before, with Dianno demonstrating that, contrary to popular opinion, he could actually sing properly when he wanted to. The general feeling was more along the lines of bands such as FATES WARNING and (particularly) QUEENSRYCHE, especially on "Rip It Up", "Whispered Rage" and the title track itself. Reviews at the time tended to be mixed, and the majority of fans remained slightly unconvinced by this new direction. The album was regarded as something of a failure after the much-anticipated debut, although the band continued to tour (without Graham Bath, who had expressed serious doubts as to the strength of the latest material, his immediate replacement being a Dane called Alf Batz) throughout Europe to promote the release. Tours followed in 1988 and 1989, although the lads were struggling to maintain interest in their activities by this time. In due course, virtually the entire line-up would be replaced, with new recruits to the fold including such minor personalities as Eddie Davidson (b) and Chris Bennett (d), plus guitarists Randy Scott and Dave Harman. A very limited compilation release (the material taken mostly from the first two albums) by Powerstation, titled »Warchild-The Best Of«, brought BATTLEZONE back into the limelight for a short while, and they subsequently had a newer number (a reasonable effort entitled "Drawn Under") included on the relatively obscure »Elementals« compilation.

In the end, however, the members of BATTLEZONE drifted apart in the early part of 1990 (by which stage they had no European deal, and their option to deliver a further album for the Shatter label appears to have been an empty promise), the group having completed a final tour of Europe in the latter months of 1989. Dianno soon became involved with the activities of PRAYING MANTIS and the disappointing ALL STARS project (not to mention singing on all those godawful cash-ins like »The Original Iron Men«, »She Won't Rock« and »Hard As Iron«, to name but a handful), before finally returning to the fore with an entirely new outfit called KILLERS. Recruiting such scenesters as Nick Burr (ex-IDOL RICH), Gavin Cooper and his erstwhile colleague Steve Hopgood (all three of whom had latterly been working together in the ill-starred PASSION), the line-up was completed by occasional TANK guitarist Cliff Evans. The outfit's own material was in a considerably more harsh and forceful style than BATTLEZONE's power metal had been (although they also reworked various older compositions in the live environment), and their swift rise in popularity certainly reflected the fact that Dianno had his finger firmly on the pulse of current musical trends.

After two well-received studio albums and a pair of live releases (recorded on their numerous tours of Europe and the Americas), however, the KILLERS project was put on hold once again (Evans and Hopgood immediately busied themselves with the reformed TANK), only for Dianno to reform (yes, you guessed it) BATTLEZONE in 1998! The revised version of the band (once again featuring John Wiggins, plus two of the latter's colleagues from the latest TOKYO BLADE reunion, Colin Riggs and Mark Angel, and also former GANGLAND guitarist Paulo Turin) swiftly recorded a brand-new album for the benefit of Zoom Club Records (who had already reissued the original brace of Raw Power/Powerstation releases on CD), and »Feel My Pain« saw the revamped outfit attempting a fairly original, metallic style with some quirky, unpredictable arrangements. The outfit have been touring once more, mostly outside the UK, but it remains to be seen whether or not Dianno will persevere or simply move on to pastures new (word has it that he has already become involved with a fairly punky act called the ALMIGHTY INBREDZ) yet again.

LP's

»Fighting Back« Raw Power Records 1986

[UK issue]
»**Fighting Back**« Shatter Records 1986
[US release with different song order]
»**Children Of Madness**« Powerstation 1987
[UK issue]
»**Children Of Madness**« Shatter Records 1987
[US release with different song order]

CD's
»**Warchild-The Best Of**« Powerstation 1988
[Features material from »Fighting Back« and »Children Of Madness« albums, plus two non-LP tracks]
»**Fighting Back**« Zoom Club Records 1997
»**Children Of Madness**« Zoom Club Records 1997
»**Feel My Pain**« Zoom Club Records 1998

Exclusive Compilation Appearances
"**Drawn Under**" on »Elementals« LP Master Records 1989

Compilation Appearances
"**Rising Star**" on »Megalomania« LP Powerstation 1986 + »Metal Killers Kollection« CD Castle Communications 1991
"**Voice On The Radio**" on »Megalomania« LP Powerstation 1986

BEG TO DIFFER

Ray Berry (v)
Colin Riggs (g)
Pete Langford (b)
Russ Poole (d)

A later release, but one very much in the true NWOBHM spirit, comes courtesy of the little-known BEG TO DIFFER, an unrenowned four-piece who may well have originated from the Berkshire area (either that or from nearby Wiltshire), but I can't be positive at this stage. Their double A-sided single, issued in 1985, is certainly one of the most professionally-presented of the era, and is housed within a large, fold-out picture sleeve, one side of which portrays a magnificently clichéd fantasy landscape with two figures on horseback, the other featuring photos, recording details, lyrics and so forth. The ensemble's lyrics themselves are far removed from the usual prosaic nonsense, however, as the following representative extract from "The Singer And The Artist" reveals:
'In the night
The singer sings his favourite song
And no-one seems to hear him
As he dreams away

And in the night
The artist hangs a masterpiece
There's no-one there to see it
As he dreams away.'

Shades of "Eleanor Rigby", perhaps, but the music is very much to our NWOBHM tastes, with the emotive vocals (courtesy of Ray Berry) and changing tempos bringing the likes of BLEAK HOUSE to mind at times. "Movin' Away", however, is a more basic, upbeat number in the mould of OMEN SEARCHER or BASHFUL ALLEY, but it's an equally enjoyable effort all the same. Nothing much seems to be known about this particular bunch, to be honest (they don't

appear to have been active on the live scene, for example, and probably came and went within a relatively short space of time), but this would appear to be their only release. It's well worth seeking out, mind you, but you'll swiftly find that there don't seem to be many copies in circulation nowadays. Guitarist Colin Riggs re-emerged several years after the single's release, this time playing bass in the 90's incarnation of TOKYO BLADE (having previously been involved with the short-lived MR ICE project), and has, more recently, been helping out a certain Paul Dianno in his revitalised BATTLEZONE project.

7" Singles
»**The Singer And The Artist**« Micro Records 1985

BERLIN RITZ

Spooner
Smith

A total mystery, to be honest, is the recently-discovered single by the utterly unknown BERLIN RITZ (strange name for a British ensemble, that), an act who could have been based pretty much anywhere in the UK. Coupling "Crazy Nights" with "You're Where I Belong", the rather anonymous-looking two-tracker is a fairly pedestrian (but entirely inoffensive) offering, the laid-back numbers coming across as lying somewhere between PANZA DIVISION, H.G.B. and SLENDER THREAD (with a mere hint of BOULEVARD thrown in), suggesting a healthy respect for the hard-rocking 70's (the B-side also indicating a tendency towards American acts of the period) in terms of their heavy influences. It's nothing out of the ordinary, to be honest, and I'm sure the tracks would have been considerably more listenable if the musicians had livened things up a bit by trying faster arrangements and employing less rudimentary production values. Issued (at some point in 1980, as far as we know, without a picture sleeve, I reckon the only way this unassuming record will become a particularly sought-after artefact will be if the 'Spooner' credited on the label turns out to have been Mal Spooner in his pre-DEMON days (which is entirely possible, given that it's not a common surname, and since DEMON didn't form until late 1980), so the majority of collectors can easily get by without a copy. Nevertheless, any further information would be appreciated and acknowledged fully in due course.

7" Singles
»Crazy Nights« Big Muff Records 1980

BIG DAISY

Mervyn 'Spam' Spence (v,b)
Roger Fox (g)
Deg Newman (d)

The horrendously complex metal scene which established itself in Staffordshire in the early 80's is a real nightmare to document, and I'm indebted to musician/roadie/engineer/general scenester Dave 'Shaky' Shakespeare (who also co-produced BASHFUL ALLEY's »Running Blind« single, incidentally) for helping to make any sort of sense of the 'incestuous' (to use his own description) goings-on amongst local acts such as the aforementioned BASHFUL ALLEY, BIG DAISY and STEEL. Formed at more or less the turn of the decade, the peculiarly-named BIG DAISY wasted little time before commencing their assault on the rock world, and promptly ensconced themselves in Woodbine St. Studios in Leamington Spa, whereupon they proceeded to lay down a representative batch of demo compositions in an attempt to draw a

modicum of interest from the record companies. Sadly, they were cruelly overlooked at first, but the trio duly concluded that their material was already worthy of a place on vinyl, and so a double A-sided 7" (featuring "Footprints On The Water" and "Fever") was arranged through the Ellie Jay label even before the end of 1980. With regard to NWOBHM comparisons, you'd be looking at LIMELIGHT, SHIVA or SPITZBROOK for reference points, but, in more general terms, we're talking RUSH (and RUSH in a *big* way), with the enjoyable "Fever", in particular, coming across as immensely similar to the unsurpassable "Temples Of Syrinx". Fair enough, if you're going to imitate anyone, ensure it's one of the all-time greats in the first place!

BIG DAISY were, by all accounts, a remarkably popular act in the burgeoning Midlands NWOBHM scene, and the trio delighted many a local crowd with their enviable repertoire of self-penned numbers (which included never-released efforts such as "U.F.O.", "Gypsy Queen", "Day Of The Damned" and "Look To The East", some of which were even demoed during their trips to the Woodbine St. facility) over the following couple of years. Things went pretty much according to plan for a while, before the inevitable spectre of personnel instability finally reared its ugly head. Guitarist Roger Fox (brother of original STEEL bassist John Fox) flew the coop at fairly short notice, although he was soon replaced by Tim Rowe (an individual who had latterly been earning a crust with a small-time bunch of local hopefuls called VENOM, which makes you wonder just how much attention some people actually paid to the music press), so there was every possibility that BIG DAISY might get back on track before long. As it turned out, however, the revitalised line-up ultimately chose to reinvent themselves as JURY within a relatively short timescale, and began drifting into rather more accessible, raunchy territory soon after. The outfit (re)introduced themselves to the public by contributing the listenable "Don't Go" to Ebony's »Metallic Storm« set, and intended to follow up this initial exposure by issuing a single based around "Having A Party", but this seems not to have come to fruition in the long term.

Sadly, JURY never really managed to achieve the goals they had initially set themselves, and, for some reason, failed to cultivate the same level of local adulation that BIG DAISY had originally boasted. As all the NWOBHM-related hysteria finally began to peter out, the luckless musicians decided to call it a day (by 1984 at the very latest), having seen their chance come and go in the interim. The BIG DAISY 7", meanwhile, issued with a flimsy monochrome sleeve with a mirthsome 'picture postcard' illustration of an amply-proportioned lady, is a seriously rare, big-money item these days, and examples don't exactly come onto the market on a regular basis. The founder members of BIG DAISY could barely have had more disparate fates in later years, with Fox and Newman maintaining only a peripheral role in the music business (occasionally working as part-time club entertainers, for example), whereas the gregarious Spam Spence subsequently offered his vocal services to practically anyone who would have him, including the resurrected TRAPEZE, WISHBONE ASH, PHENOMENA, U.S.I., SILENT WITNESS and an unnamed, late 80's 'supergroup' who also included SOLDIER's Nick Lashley, MOTÖRHEAD's Philthy Taylor, GIRLSCHOOL's Kim McAuliffe and Beki Bond from the BOMBSHELLS. He now apparently owns a controlling share in a successful record company called Parachute Music, and is still firmly involved in the recording side of things too.

7" Singles
»Footprints On The Water« Ellie Jay 1980

Compilation Appearances
"Footprints On The Water" on »NWOBHM Vol.5« Bootleg CD 1992

BILL THE MURDERER

Pete Downes

It's always very tempting (especially if you're a shady record dealer trying to shift unsaleable records to trusting aficionados of the genre) to 'push the envelope' in terms of dates, so that the NWOBHM era actually started as long ago as 1977 (or earlier, if you're feeling particularly audacious). In most cases, this tends to result in lightweight rock/pop drivel such as MAINLAND, RUNNER or STRAIGHT EIGHT being foisted upon us, although, very occasionally, a genuine contender for the rather contrived title of 'obscure early NWOBHM' (a classic antilogy, to be perfectly honest) does indeed turn up. One notable example was released by the enigmatic BILL THE MURDERER, about whom absolutely nothing is known as yet. Admittedly, the feeble name would surely deter the vast majority of NWOBHM collectors from taking a chance with their cash, but this two-tracker (no picture sleeve known) isn't too bad at all. The A-side, the ominously-titled "I'd Find You", is a hybrid of 70's rock (particularly DEEP PURPLE, with a heavy organ sound) and 80's NWOBHM dynamics, with vocals slightly in the SPARTA vein. The B-side, "Spring Rain", is considerably less interesting, the group delivering a competent, but rather dull, ballad in the style of WHITEFIRE's "Suzanne".

Indeed, some might point to the existence of groups such as BILL THE MURDERER, WHITEFIRE, TERRA COTTA, the South Coast RAW DEAL (all of whom swam against the punk flow and issued a private rock 7" as far back 1978) etc. as concrete evidence of a 'missing link' between traditional 70's rock and NWOBHM, although, to be frank, vinyl offerings from such bands (most of whom were merely unambitious throwbacks with few aspirations of breaking out of the clubs) are few and far between. There were certainly far more metal outfits who evolved from the post-punk scene, as well as the multitudes who took their influences from heavier 70's acts such as JUDAS PRIEST, MOTÖRHEAD or BLACK SABBATH, so I think the notion of an overnight transition from heavy rock crowd-pleasers to NWOBHM revolutionaries at some unspecified point in 1978 is a bit of a non-starter. In conclusion, however, it might be worth considering buying privately-issued 'metal' singles from as far back as 1977 if you're a NWOBHM fan; after all, weighty combos such as QUARTZ, IRON MAIDEN, MARSEILLE,

MYTHRA, JAMESON RAID etc. were already active by that time...

7" Singles
»I'd Find You« SRT 1978

BITCHES SIN

Alan 'Cocky' Cockburn (v)
Ian Toomey (g)
Pete Toomey (g)
Perry 'Pez' Hodder (b)
Bill Knowles (d)

Cumbria's tactfully-named BITCHES SIN set off on their quest for stardom in the early months of 1980, having assembled themselves from the smoking remains of several amateur-hour club bands. From a very early stage, the quintet appear to have made a concerted effort to spread their music to the masses, although the outfit primarily concentrated on cassette releases as opposed to taking part in the lottery system of the live circuit, where they would have to slog their guts out alongside numerous other hopefuls and attempt to stand out from the crowd. In fact, BITCHES SIN appear to have been fairly reluctant to play live at all (the lads made a handful of local appearances, although their best-attended gigs were actually in Holland), and were never to participate in any particularly noteworthy events at home, which might have hindered their progress quite considerably. Nevertheless, they first came to prominence with their quirkily-titled »12 Pounds And No Kinks« demo, where the protagonists showcased such original compositions as "Bitches Sin", "Two Of A Kind" and "White Lady". Before long, the tape was selling in respectable numbers and gaining airplay in the North West, and a piece of luck was to come the band's way when Neat Records stepped in with an offer to sponsor their first two-tracker in the early months of 1981.

The single, coupling "Always Ready" and "Sign Of The Times", was a capable enough debut, revealing the lads to be operating in quite a powerful, driving style with similarities to the likes of BUFFALO, SPARTA and BATTLEAXE, and the record was soon selling in healthy quantities. In due course, BITCHES SIN would benefit from a further piece of handy exposure when one of their original demo compositions, "Down The Road", was featured on Neat's »Lead Weight« sampler. This strong contribution was an even more upbeat and energetic effort, and the band seemed to be making a good job of setting out their stall for a full album deal. As it turned out, the ambitious bunch viewed Neat as more of a stepping stone than a permanent home, and soon jumped ship to arch-rivals Heavy Metal, for whom they debuted with "Strangers On The Shore", a contribution to the label's »Heavy Metal Heroes« compilation. It looked as though an album would follow without too many problems, but it soon became apparent that the central duo of Ian and Pete Toomey were less-than-happy with the musical abilities of their compatriots, particularly vocalist Alan Cockburn (foreign readers will be disappointed to discover that this surname is, in fact, pronounced 'coeburn'), and the brothers soon decided to start all over again (original bassist Pez Hodder, meanwhile, was busy establishing his GOLDSMITH venture) with the assistance of Tony Tomkinson (v), Dave Newsham (b) and Tony Leece (d). BITCHES SIN Mk.II recorded an all-new demo (entitled »Your Place Or Mine«) to show off their collective talents, and the album-length tape was soon finding its way into the clutches of numerous NWOBHM fans and media personalities alike.

If Heavy Metal were still wavering as to whether or not a BITCHES SIN album would actually be a good idea, they were won over in no uncertain terms when the lads delivered a cracking session for the 'Friday Rock Show'. Broadcast on the 16th of October 1981, the session featured reworkings of "Strangers On The Shore" and "Down The Road", plus the previously-unheard "Hold On To Love" and "Fallen Star". With the tracks being received rapturously by the station's listeners, their label was left in no doubt as to the outfit's potential as a money-making act, and work on the debut album began in the early months of 1982. Still, however, the hard-to-please Toomeys weren't quite satisfied with the latest version of the band, and a new rhythm section was soon recruited, with both Martin Orum (b) and Mark Biddiscombe (d) being unceremoniously plundered from the ranks of the unfortunate CHAINSAW. Eventually, after various setbacks, the long-awaited album (»Predator«) finally emerged in mid-1982, but turned out to be something of a damp squib, disappointing fans and reviewers alike. In spite of the presence of a couple of reasonably decent, pacey numbers ("Runaway" and "Fallen Star", for example), most of the others (e.g. "April Fool", "Dirty Women", "Riding High") were so utterly forgettable and rudimentary in their construction (tinges of both TANK and CHAIN-

SAW themselves) that many observers formed the cruel-but-accurate opinion that the best thing about the entire record was its splendid cover.

It was all a great pity, especially as the group had been developing a genuinely fanatical following in some parts of the world, particularly Holland (they were even inspired to write two songs especially for the nation, namely "Haneka" and "Aardschok", dedicated to a well-respected DJ and magazine, respectively) and many BITCHES SIN fans had been anticipating a considerably more substantial album. In all honesty, I've absolutely no idea how the outfit contrived to come up with such a mundane long-player (which received a particularly vicious slating in 'Kerrang'), although the lads themselves (rather uncharitably, it must be said) blamed their hapless label for this substandard product, as Ian Toomey later insisted: *'I think the reason our recent stuff hasn't sounded so good is due to the difference between Neat and Heavy Metal Records. Paul Birch, who runs HMR, is a very good businessman and highly ambitious. He pushes bands to the limit, and certainly knows how to promote 'em. Our album got tremendous advertising back-up. In this respect he's got the edge on Neat. But, on the recording front, it's Neat who come out better. They've got their own studios, and can afford to give a band almost limitless time to get a proper sound, whereas with Heavy Metal, everything is much more 'rush rush'. I think this comes through in the final product.'* (Ref: Kerrang No.38, March 1983). Clearly, things needed to change pretty dramatically if BITCHES SIN were ever to regain the ground they had now lost in such major fashion.

Inevitably, the Toomeys' response to the adverse publicity was to hire yet another set of accomplices, although one of them was actually an old friend, original drummer Bill Knowles. Making up the numbers this time were vocalist Frank Qeugan and bassist Mike Frazer, the lads attempted to get things back on track in the first half of 1983, when they circulated a demo tape of freshly-penned material. The »Out Of My Mind« cassette featured such numbers as "Ain't Life A Bitch", "Day In Day Out", "No More Chances" and "Overnight", and signified something of a return to form, although it wasn't enough to persuade Heavy Metal to pick up on their option of a second album. Undeterred by their former label's apathy, BITCHES SIN announced that both Neat and Bullet were supposedly taking an interest in their affairs, although it looks as though neither of these companies put a firm offer on the table in the long term, leaving the

band to go it alone. The next vinyl offering from BITCHES SIN came in the shape of a three track EP, where they reworked "No More Chances" and "Overnight" from their latest tape, and rounded things off with one of their earliest compositions, the subtle "Ice Angels". The privately-pressed 12" was a huge improvement on their album, particularly the lively arrangement of "No More Chances", the lads showcasing some highly capable musicianship throughout.

Incredible as it may have seemed, BITCHES SIN were well and truly back with a bang, and were, before long, actively looking for a label who would be prepared to release their second long-player. Sadly, however, no particular interest came the group's way in the wake of their strong comeback EP, and the musicians struggled to remain particularly enthusiastic with regard to their collective future. By 1985, they were already keeping a worryingly low profile (their "Ain't Life A Bitch" effort was featured on Roadrunner's overlooked »12" Commandments In Metal« compilation, but that's about it), although BITCHES SIN finally came out of hiding to make one last-ditch attempt to resurrect their foundering career by recording a brand-new demo tape. The latest cassette featured a couple of novel compositions ("Dawn Of Destruction" and "Roundabout") in addition to a handful of reworked older numbers, but this selection of material still had the desired effect of attracting label interest within a matter of months. Strangely, however, the company in question was an unrenowned American concern, King Klassic Records, although the 'any old port in a storm' adage was evidently coming into play by this juncture.

The lads duly recorded their second album, »Invaders«, at the beginning of 1986, the new long-player being predominantly comprised of recycled material (e.g. "No More Chances", "Out Of My Mind", "Ain't Life A Bitch") which had earlier appeared on their various demo releases. Even so, it was the LP that BITCHES SIN should have been striving to make in the first instance, and conclusively showed them to be a class act after all. It was an immensely confident, powerful and varied set of compositions, and finally demonstrated the outfit's much-debated ability to deliver heavy music of the highest order, the band effortlessly slotting into a vacant space between JAMESON RAID and TRIDENT whenever they really hit their stride. Ironically, therefore, rather than being the record which finally propelled BITCHES SIN into the realms of metal stardom, it was to be their swansong. With their American sponsors exerting little or no influence in the global market, few fans were able to get hold of (or even hear about) the group's second LP. Given that there was no prospect of a UK or European licensing deal in the pipeline, the dejected outfit began to fall apart, and finally disintegrated towards the end of the year, whereupon the Toomeys proceeded to form FLASHPOINT (see separate entry) and vocalist Frank Quegan went on to front a Christian rock act called REACH.

It wasn't quite the end of the story as far as BITCHES SIN were concerned, though, as G.I. Records ultimately picked up the rights to their last batch of studio recordings and expressed a serious interest in giving the long-forgotten »Invaders« set an official UK release at last. In fact, the upshot was that the whole shebang was actually re-recorded (although I'm not sure when, exactly), by which time the Toomeys had realised, to their horror, that they hadn't quite exhausted every possible drummer in Britain, whereupon they were compelled to draft in Paul Smith to help out in the studio. Not only that, they also tried out a keyboard player (Dave Osbeldiston) for the first time, although this didn't signify a wholesale wimp-out by any means. Once the album was in the bag (again), G.I. kept their end of the bargain and repackaged the LP (now featuring three alternate numbers and a completely different cover) towards the end of 1988. In fact, this all-new version of »Invaders« turned out to be even more enjoyable than the American original, especially when one of the replacement tracks (the utterly superb "Destroyer") constituted a true classic of the genre which could surely have given any of the major NWOBHM players a run for their money if it had been released at the height of the movement. Ah, such sweet irony. The success or failure of the re-promoted LP was ultimately of little consequence (sadly, it was a failure), though, as there was never any serious talk of getting the band back together on a permanent basis. I guess the entire BITCHES SIN episode just goes to prove how difficult it is to retrieve the situation if you start off your career with a really awful album...

LP's
»Predator« Heavy Metal 1982
[Initial quantities with textured cover]
»Invaders« King Klassic Records 1986
[Original US issue]
»Invaders« G.I. Records 1988
[Re-recorded UK issue with different cover and three alternate tracks]

12" EP's
»No More Chances« Q.T. Records 1983
["Overnight" non-LP, both "No More Chances" and "Ice Angels" different to album versions]

7" Singles
»Always Ready« Neat 1981
[A few copies also pressed on yellow vinyl, both tracks non-LP]

Exclusive Compilation Appearances
"Down The Road" on »Lead Weight« LP Neat 1981/CD Teichiku 1992

Compilation Appearances
"Strangers On The Shore" on »Heavy Metal Heroes« LP Heavy Metal 1981 *[Issued in two different sleeves]* + »Heavy Metal Heroes Vol.I&II« CD British Steel 1996
[Different to album version]
"Ain't Life A Bitch" on »12 Commandments In Metal« LP Roadrunner 1985
"Ice Angels" on »NWOBHM Vol.1« Bootleg CD 1992

BLACK AXE

Chris English (v)
Simon Sparkes (g)
Bill Keir (g)
Stewart Richardson (b)
Mike Thorburn (d)

The original version of Cumbria's excellent BLACK AXE first took shape as far back as 1977 (initially based around the pairing of schoolfriends Chris English and Simon Sparkes), the lads starting off under the imposing name of LEVIATHAN. After spending a couple of years gigging fairly unobtrusively throughout the North West, during which time a stable line-up was established, the quintet (having now adopted their more familiar identity) finally made it into the studio to lay down a selection of originals such as "Head Contact", "Red Lights", "Highway Rider", "Shock Treatment" and "Too Close For Comfort". The major labels seemed nonplussed, but the lads were perfectly happy to go it alone, and it wasn't long before the group managed to get their debut single into the shops, a low-budget (but high-energy) offering (in a distinctive yellow sleeve) featuring "Highway Rider" and "Red Lights", which was unleashed upon an unsuspecting public in the second half of 1980. The two-tracker (bringing to mind acts such as WEAPON, LE GRIFFE and TRAITORS GATE) sold in huge quantities locally, with many further units being shifted through distribution deals with the likes of Bullet Records, and, with an abundance of copies being in circulation ever since, the record still can be picked up incredibly cheaply, so add it to MYTHRA's EP on Guardian and TURBO's »Charged For Glory« on your *'essential NWOBHM shopping list'* if you don't already own these items!

By early 1981, word of this talented young combo had reached those in charge of programming at BBC Radio, and it wasn't long before a 'Friday Rock Show' session was commissioned. Broadcast on the 6th of March 1981, this truly superb performance featured old favourites "Shock Treatment" and "Too Close For Comfort" alongside newer compositions "Night From The Blue" and "Edge Of The World", and the whole thing was rapturously received by the station's listeners. Some specially-recorded tracks were also broadcast on the smaller Capital Radio at around the same time, including "Head Contact" and the never-released classic "Lazer Blind". Furthermore, "Edge Of The World" was eventually included on one of the two albums compiled by BBC Records to immortalise various tracks taken from some of the most popular 'Rock Show' sessions. The lads must have thought the gods were smiling on them even more benevolently when they were plucked from relative obscurity and thrust into the public spotlight with a generous two-page feature in the first ever issue of 'Kerrang'. Asked about their affiliation with the all-powerful NWOBHM movement, drummer Mike Thorburn was quick to offer his own opinion: *'Yeah, the phrase 'heavy metal' does tend to get people's backs up. Everybody's searching for a new name for it. JUDAS PRIEST tried 'British Steel', MORE are calling their music 'Atomic Rock'-and we've got our own category too, 'Head Contact Rock'n'Roll', like in the song title. For us, I think that description's perfect.'* (Ref: Kerrang No.1, June 1981).

Sadly, things took a turn for the worse when BLACK AXE were picked up by the much larger Chrysalis label, who immediately insisted that they were to change their name to the overused WOLF (see separate entry), for no good reason whatsoever. With that, the hapless outfit seemingly developed something of a *'Samson Complex'*, where the removal of part of their essential identity had a deleterious effect on their overall personality or physical presence. As a result, their later big-budget vinyl offerings turned out to be a mere shadow of their humble »Highway Rider« two-tracker in terms of sheer energy and enthusiasm. However, it seems that the legacy of the outfit, in their original BLACK AXE incarnation, was considerable, as evidenced by the observation that their "Red Lights" effort successfully made it through the tough selection process to be included on Phonogram's prestigious NWOBHM commemorative set (compiled by Lars Ulrich towards the end of the decade), confirming that the outfit remained an extremely highly-regarded act in some quarters.

7" Singles
»**Highway Rider**« Metal Recording 1980
[Both tracks later appeared on »Edge Of The World« LP by WOLF]

Exclusive Compilation Appearances
"**Edge Of The World**" on »The Friday Rock Show« LP BBC Records 1981
[Different version later appeared as title track of WOLF album]

Compilation Appearances
"**Red Lights**" on »NWOBHM '79 Revisited« Do-CD Phonogram 1990
"**Highway Rider**" on »NWOBHM Vol.1« Bootleg CD 1992

BLACKMAYNE

Tim Cooke (v)
Phil McDermott (g)
Richard Mathews (g)
Julian 'Sack' Sackett (b)
Andy Terry (d)

I don't know where Ebony dredged up some of their NWOBHM-period artists from (particularly when it came to assembling their many samplers), but the enigmatic BLACKMAYNE (a little-known quintet who originated from the county of Kent) were surely one of their most obscure signings. Materialising out of nowhere (no previous compilation appearances or anything) in 1985 with their one and only album, an eponymous effort on the short-lived Criminal Response subsidiary, the ensemble turned in a fairly standard performance in terms of straightforward, mid-80's British metal as churned out by acts of the time such as CHARIOT, SAXON and ZENITH. It's all pretty samey, and nothing really stands out as particularly impressive, although punchier numbers such as "Hot Blooded Woman" tend to work slightly better than the lengthier compositions, where the combo's songwriting limitations tend to be exposed to a

71

greater extent. The publicity-shy outfit appear to have gone into hiding shortly after this release (drummer Andy Terry flew the coop towards the end of the year and the remaining members don't seem to have continued for very long without him), and none of the musicians appear to have resurfaced at a later date, so it looks as though details of their early history and subsequent activities on the rock scene must remain sketchy for the time being. It's well worth picking up the BLACKMAYNE album if you see it cheaply enough, though; let's face it, if they had released an obscure private single instead of a relatively common LP on Ebony, you'd probably all be falling over yourselves to get your hands on it...

LP's
»Blackmayne« Criminal Response Records 1985

BLACKOUT

Sandy Black (v)
Douglas Herd (g)
Allan Burns (b)
Shad (k)
Ian Wallace (d)

Although lagging a bit behind the industrious men of Wales in terms of the number of utterly obscure private pressings which have surfaced in recent years, there are still a respectable number of Scottish rarities lurking around out there. Joining the ranks are BLACKOUT (not to be confused with Dutch or American namesakes), who released the largely-unknown »Is There Anything?« single in 1984. The A-side (dealing with the heavy concept of life after death) shows the outfit to have been a fairly weighty proposition who used keyboards strategically, as did the likes of LYADRIVE, STORMCHILD and SKITZOFRENIK, in order to create a bit more of an atmospheric effect. Indeed, the overall sound is undeniably similar to the aforementioned acts, with a convincing vocal effort and strong guitar work throughout. On the reverse, "All I Needed" turns out to be a rather more lightweight semi-ballad, which comes as a slight disappointment after the capable A-side, but not a complete disaster by any means. There's also a vaguely progressive feel, but I suspect that this is probably a consequence of the keyboards rather than the arrangement of the material. A pretty good effort, all things considered, but the BLACKOUT lads don't really seem to have made much of a name for themselves at any stage, which is a bit of a shame, as they had potential. You might like to keep an eye out for the single, the cover of which shows the quintet looking a bit mystical around a bright source of light.

7" Singles
»Is There Anything?« Private 1984

BLACK ROSE

Steve Bardsley (v,g)
Kenny Nicholson (g)
Marty Rahn (b)
Charlie MacKenzie (d)

The founder members of Cleveland's BLACK ROSE were all remarkably youthful when the outfit first came together way back in 1978, and it looks as though the fledgling band represented little more than some post-school tomfoolery at the outset. In fact, it had all started to get a bit serious when hot-shot guitarist Kenny Nicholson was invited to join local small-time outfit ICE, who soon disposed of their original drummer and drafted in capable sticksman Charlie MacKenzie. After the obligatory groundwork on the local club circuit, the lads eventually decided to adopt the more interesting identity of BLACK ROSE (I strongly suspect that a recently-released THIN LIZZY album might have had something to do with this choice), whereupon they rapidly began building up a highly enviable reputation as regional crowd-pleasers. By late 1980, the emergent foursome had finally established themselves to the requisite extent, and the lads were soon able to venture into the recording studio, where some of their own numbers could be captured on tape for posterity. Nevertheless, the developing BLACK ROSE were still treading extremely familiar ground with their rudimentary rock/metal compositions such as "Fire", "I'm A Biker" and "Love Shock", and it took them another year or two to evolve into an act with a rather more distinctive personality of their own.

By the latter half of 1981, however, the band were beginning to undergo some fairly radical restructuring, with the unsettled Charlie MacKenzie defecting to local rivals TAURUS (the sticksman later played with EMERSON and SAMSON), while Kenny Nicholson, who felt severely constrained by the small-time aspirations of BLACK ROSE, went off to audition for WHITE SPIRIT, who had just lost the services of

Janick Gers. The talented axeman didn't get the gig, unfortunately, but eventually decided that it would be more constructive to start his own outfit, whereupon he embarked on a lengthy career with the likes of HOLLAND, HAMMER and FAST KUTZ (see separate entries). The remaining nucleus of Marty Rahn and Steve Bardsley soon regrouped with new members Chris Watson (g) and Malla Smith (d), and the revamped version of BLACK ROSE set about writing the sort of material that would hopefully elevate them to the status of NWOBHM superstars. Still, with there being no significant label interest coming their way at that time, it looked as though the outfit would have to follow the well-worn path of self-funded releases in the first instance. With precious little in the way of savings with which to finance that elusive private 7", though, the lads relied on local benefactors to come to their rescue in order to get to the vinyl stage. Fortunately, their luck was in, and their first real opportunity came with an offer to contribute a pair of tracks to Guardian's »Roxcalibur« sampler at the beginning of 1982.

BLACK ROSE contributed two very capable, mid-tempo numbers to the patchy compilation, namely "No Point Runnin'" and "Ridin' Higher", compositions which showed them to be operating in quite similar territory to JAGUAR and »Spellbound«-era TYGERS OF PAN TANG, this material being far more consistent with their stated influences (IRON MAIDEN and VAN HALEN) than their earlier studio recordings. Sadly, however, there was to be no follow-up single or album for Guardian, although the lads were soon to see their first 7" released on the little-known Teesbeat label. The double A-sided single (housed in a cheap paste-on sleeve) featured "No Point Runnin'" (again) and the energetic "Sucker For Your Love", and it proved to be a very popular purchase among metal fans of the day, instantly propelling the outfit to the status of local (and, to some extent, national) heroes. By all accounts, 1982 was definitely the year that things started happening for the outfit, and they were soon getting a bit of well-deserved recognition in various sections of the media. Still, the lads had to endure the departure of bassist Marty Rahn soon after the single appeared (he later resurfaced in PANAMA), although they were lucky enough to attract the services of Mick Thompson to plug the gap. With things back on track, a promotional video for "No Point Runnin'" was commissioned by 'Check It Out', a local TV programme, and the band were subsequently featured in the 'Armed And Ready' section of 'Kerrang', by which time they had successfully completed gigs with the likes of VARDIS and RAVEN, in addition to a prestigious Gateshead Festival appearance alongside such metal dignitaries as LIMELIGHT, BUDGIE and TRUST.

Towards the end of the year, having demoed some strong new material such as "Love On The Line", "Take Me Away" and "Red Light Lady", the group were invited to contribute a track to Neat's »One Take No Dubs« compilation EP, and they duly obliged with the excellent "Knocked Out". For some peculiar reason, however, the label didn't feel compelled to offer BLACK ROSE a deal at that stage, and the lads were forced to wait until 1983 before another offer finally came their way. Bullet Records were the company who encouraged BLACK ROSE to sign on the dotted line, but not before they had demoed yet more material, which included the likes of "We're Gonna Rock You" and "Burn Me Blind", tracks which suggested a tentative move into marginally more commercial territory with a vague feel of TOKYO BLADE or DIAMOND HEAD. The outfit's first release for Bullet was their »We're Gonna Rock You« EP, a four-tracker which utilised recordings from various studio sessions. It was well up to the usual standard, and such confident efforts as the excellent "Used And Abused" clearly demonstrated how Steve Bardsley's vocal performance was becoming more commanding with every trip to the studio. A full album, entitled »Boys Will Be Boys«, followed in 1984, although there was a distinct paucity of new material on display. "We're Gonna Rock You" and "Stand Your Ground", for example, were recycled from the first EP, while a version of "Knocked Out" was included again and perennial favourite "No Point Runnin'" was trundled out for the third (yes, third) time. There were, admittedly, a couple of decent newer numbers, particularly "Fun And Games" and "Baby Believe Me", but, strangely, it was the unremarkable title track that Bullet elected to issue as a 7" single (although relatively few copies appear to have been pressed), backing it with the non-LP cut "Liar".

BLACK ROSE's latter pair of releases had failed to satisfy Bullet in terms of sales figures, however, and the two parties were soon to sever all ties, only for the band (who had developed something of a cult following in Europe, where they had played some rapturously-received gigs) to reopen their relationship with Neat Records a short time later. In fact, they had been using the latter's Impulse Studios while under contract to Bullet, and had obviously maintained strong links with the company, so it came as little surprise when the outfit's next vinyl appeared on Neat in due course. This took the form of another four track EP, this time featuring all-new material, namely "Nightmare", "Need A Lot Of Lovin'", "Rock Me Hard" and "Breakaway". The release was of a consistently high calibre, although it saw a move towards even more polished, commercial material of the kind that was being churned out by numerous UK acts in the mid-80's. Towards the end of 1985, BLACK ROSE recorded a 'Friday Rock Show' session to try to establish themselves as serious contenders for the melodic rock crown, and the session (transmitted on the 17th of January 1986) was, admittedly, a competent display of their collective ability, as the outfit showcased "Need A Lot Of Lovin'" from the latest EP, plus the novel trio of "Easy Lovin' You", "Get Off Your High Horse" and "Go For The Throat".

Nevertheless, it was to be over a year before BLACK ROSE would deliver their next vinyl offering, by which time the group had experienced some serious internal turmoil, presumably over their future direction. Long-time drummer Malla Smith defected to local rivals STONEHEART, and guitarist Chris Watson soon packed his bags too, leaving the remaining nucleus of Bardsley and Thompson with no option but to bring in a pair of suitable replacements. A revised line-up was established in due course (the band eventually being augmented by a keyboard player, former HOT BLOODED member Gary Todd) *via* the recruitment of Pat O'Neill (g) and Barry Youll (d), and the persevering BLACK ROSE swiftly set about writing the material that would finally turn them into world-beaters. They returned to the fore in 1987, having kept an unusually low profile on the live front in the preceding months, with their second full-length album, the dismally-titled »Walk It How You Talk It« effort. Predictably, however, this record completed the group's metamorphosis into a chart-friendly act with mainstream pretensions, and was, in general (the likes of "Bright Lights Burnin'" and the title track weren't actually all that atrocious), a million miles away from their early recordings in terms of sheer songwriting averageness. It was all very sad, although this seemed to be a style of pop/rock that many once-respectable NWOBHM outfits (ENERGY, MENDES PREY, EXPORT, HEAVY PETTIN etc.) were inexorably drawn towards if they had somehow survived into the second half of the decade.

All things considered, »Walk It How You Talk It« was nothing short of a commercial disaster for both group and label, and the lads subsequently had to make a hasty decision as to whether they really had any future in the rock world at all. In fact, they decided to stick it out for a while longer, and continued to play occasionally in the North East with the likes of WARFARE (which would, on the face of it, have see-

med like a bit of a serious mismatch) throughout the remainder of 1987. The following year, however, saw the combo attempting to come up with a range of new compositions that would appeal to their established fan base, and they toured fairly extensively towards the end of that year in order to try out their latest repertoire in the live environment. Sadly, however, it would appear that the fans had already turned their backs on BLACK ROSE by this time, leaving the dejected quintet (now featuring former FAST KUTZ drummer Paul Fowler) to give up the ghost (at some point in 1989) in the wake of this massive loss of popularity and enthusiasm. Understandably, their earliest releases are now regarded as their most collectable and highly-valued output, with their scarce debut 7" quite rightly being the pick of the bunch.

LP's
»**Boys Will Be Boys**« Bullet 1984
»**Walk It How You Talk It**« Neat 1987/K-Tel 1987
[UK/US issue]

12" EP's
»**We're Gonna Rock You**« Bullet 1983
["We're Gonna Rock You" and "Stand Your Ground" different to album versions, "Used And Abused" and "Red Light Lady" non-LP]
»**Nightmare**« Neat 1985
[All four tracks non-LP]

7" Singles
»**No Point Runnin'**« Teesbeat 1982
[A-side different to album version, B-side "Sucker For Your Love" non-LP]
»**Boys Will Be Boys**« Bullet 1984
[B-side "Liar" non-LP]

CD's
»**Walk It How You Talk It**« K-Tel 1987
[US release]

Exclusive Compilation Appearances
"**Ridin' Higher**" on »Roxcalibur« LP Guardian 1982/CD British Steel 1998

Compilation Appearances
"**Knocked Out**" on »One Take No Dubs« 12" EP Neat 1982
[Different to album version]
"**No Point Runnin'**" on »Roxcalibur« LP Guardian 1982/CD British Steel 1998
[Different to album or single version]
"**Sucker For Your Love**" on »NWOBHM Vol.1« Bootleg CD 1992
"**Nightmare**" on »Metal Masters« 4-CD Box Castle Communications 1993
"**California USA**" on »Heavy Metal Collection 2« CD X-Tra Collection 1993
"**Don't Fall In Love**" on »Heavy Metal Collection 3« CD X-Tra Collection 1993
"**Walk It How You Talk It**" on »Heavy Metal Collection 4« CD X-Tra Collection 1993

BLACKWYCH

Ciaran James (v)
Declan James (g)
Bobby Tierney (g)
Niall James (b)
Chris Andralinus (d)

First coming to public attention with two unremarkable tracks on the scrappy »Green Metal« sampler of Irish rock talent in 1985, BLACKWYCH were held up as something of a major prospect by those responsible for assembling the album, who claimed in the sleeve notes that *'When the first demo tape from Kildare's BLACKWYCH circulated around Dublin, it scared the life out of the capital's contenders!'* This was certainly hyping the young outfit to an unnecessary extent, although their "Metal Mania" and "Out Of Control" offerings were vaguely passable slices of metal in the style of FAIR WARNING, Ebony-era DEALER or the original SATANIC RITES, although the rather flat vocals were a bit of a serious drawback. Even so, the lads were picked up for a full album in due course (although why the excellent ASSASSIN were left behind is a mystery), and both of the aforementioned compositions were subsequently recycled (in slightly different form) on the band's debut long-player, once again recorded for Crashed Records and licensed by Metal Masters.

While the ensemble doubtless had the potential to come up with something reasonably listenable if they had really managed to get their collective act together, »Out Of Control« (issued in a superbly clichéd sleeve) turned out to be a bit of a damp squib, unfortunately. Some of the featured tracks resemble little more than a souped-up THIN LIZZY, whereas others are distinctly heavier, although the group's compulsion to use over-intricate riffing and drum fills tends to reduce the power of individual numbers (although, given that it transpires that BLACKWYCH didn't actually write their own songs, you can forgive the band members themselves). Furthermore, over the course of a full album, the vocal performance of Ciaran James is really called into question, and several compositions suffer from his all-too-obvious lack of range. The semi-capable "Man Hunt" would probably be the pick of the bunch, but elsewhere it's all remarkably average and totally uninspiring. Sales can't have amounted to all that much (it's not at all easy to locate a copy nowadays), and I suspect that they must have called it a day soon afterwards, a move which probably didn't break too many hearts.

LP's
»Out Of Control« Metal Masters 1986

Compilation Appearances
"Metal Mania" on »Green Metal« LP Metal Masters 1985
[Different to album version]
"Out Of Control" on »Green Metal« LP Metal Masters 1985
[Different to album version]

BLADE RUNNER

Steve MacKay (v)
Gary Jones (g)
Mark Wilde (rg)
Mick Cooper (b)
Greg Ellis (d)

Forming from the ashes of unsuccessful Humberside bands BADGE (from whence came Mick Cooper) and SAVAGE ROSE (from whence came Gary Jones) the foundations of BLADE RUNNER were initially laid towards the end of 1983. After a bit of regional searching, the original duo of Jones and Cooper roped in a few former members of STALLION (a local act who had contributed the track "Don't Wait Too Long" to Ebony's »Metal Plated« compilation before eventually calling it a day) in order to make up the required numbers, and so the lads were soon plying their brand of metal to appreciative crowds throughout the region. Before long, they began dreaming of global domination, although the musicians had to endure a fair amount of disappointment before anything much happened for them. Certainly, BLADE RUNNER's rise to prominence didn't go entirely according to plan (as was the case with so many other young hopefuls with abundant hopes and dreams but strictly limited resources and influence), but it has to be stated that their vacillations were largely a consequence of a level of self-confidence

which, according to reliable sources, practically bordered on arrogance. Nevertheless, they still had a pretty good stab at making it big, and ultimately achieved a considerably greater level of public recognition than the long-forgotten STALLION had ever managed.

By the early months of 1984, the emergent group had already recruited a management team to handle their affairs, after which they began to make the odd pilgrimage to the recording studio, so it wasn't long before they actually had a spanking demo tape to circulate among the movers and shakers in the music business. However, their humble cassette met with the usual frosty response from most of the larger record companies of the day (which wasn't to say that they were no-hopers, they just weren't what the major labels were looking for at that time), and the ambitious quintet were reluctant to wait for further cruel (but entirely justified) rejection. After a period of serious soul-searching, therefore, the lads finally concluded that their best (indeed, *only*) chance to get some vinyl product into the shops in the short term would be to accept an offer which had recently come their way from the ever-dependable Ebony Records concern. Admittedly, it wasn't an ideal arrangement, and BLADE RUNNER pretty much viewed this as a mere stop-gap while they waited for that big-money offer from one of the influential labels. Before long, the musicians were hard at work in the studio (laying down a full album, which was promoted by a single featuring the listenable "Back Street Lady" and "Too Far Too Late"), although the lads were soon confronted with the harsh reality of the situation, namely the low-budget production values resulting from the lack of resources available to independent labels such as Ebony.

Nevertheless, a period of hectic activity led to the debut BLADE RUNNER long-player (»Hunted«) being completed on schedule, and copies began making their way into the shops towards the end of 1984. The first album was a perfectly adequate Ebony release (highlights would include the enjoyable duo of "The Stealer" and "Dogs Of War"), the developing group hardly pushing the musical boundaries in any sense, but still coming up with a reasonably listenable selection of catchy, substantial compositions with a few similarities to early TOBRUK or HEAVY PETTIN. Mind you, it's fair to suggest that their overall style possibly fell between two extremes (not quite powerful enough for fans of GRIM REAPER and SAMURAI, yet not sufficiently accessible to suggest that the band might ultimately be able to cross over to the mainstream), so it was entirely conceivable that there wouldn't exactly be a huge market for BLADE RUNNER's music. As it turned out, however, the record proceeded to sell in eminently respectable quantities upon its release (helped along by some favourable reviews in the music press), although the self-critical individuals soon formed the collective opinion that much of the recently-penned material (all attributed, at that time, to the songwriting partnership of Gary Jones and Steve MacKay) had failed to do them justice on vinyl. The lads were keen to distance themselves from those acts with all-too-apparent mainstream aspirations, and soon set about informing the world that they were, at heart, an unashamedly powerful unit who weren't content to follow the well-worn path towards chart-friendly melodic rock.

With this statement of intent, BLADE RUNNER effectively signed their own death warrant as far as major label deals were concerned, as most of the companies in question had pretty much formed an utter distrust of any band lacking a keyboard player. Still, good old Ebony kept the faith, deciding that a follow-up album would be a worthwhile investment, and the musicians were only too keen to deliver another batch of selections for their original sponsors. By the time the second LP was being assembled in the early months of 1986 (much of the previous year had been spent on the road and trying out freshly-penned material), the ensemble had made a concerted attempt to rectify their debut's failings, and had slimmed down to a quartet by disposing of the unfortunate Mark Wilde, while bassist Mick Cooper was now making his presence felt on the songwriting front. This change of heart manifested itself as a return to a fairly solid and dependable metal sound, and the group's sophomore »Warriors Of Rock« opus clearly set out to win over a few aficionados of the heavy stuff. Ironically, however, the sands of time had already shifted in the interim, and the lads now found themselves in the post-NWOBHM nuclear wasteland of 1986, when 'true metal' was being shunned in favour of either melodic rock or thrash. In fact, BLADE RUNNER (along with once-potent outfits such as SAVAGE or TOKYO BLADE) were now regarded as something of an anachronism, and were ill-prepared to mount much of a challenge to the young upstarts of the Bay Area scene or the influx of BON JOVI clones. Mind you, their traditionally straightforward, stoically British approach to metal probably found favour with a significant proportion of the loyal fans throughout mainland Europe.

It was evident that BLADE RUNNER were now pulling out all the stops in an attempt to reinvent themselves, and had been keen to try out a few novel ideas (the odd bit of twin-guitar riffing and some rather more subtle interludes) on their second album, but it still didn't constitute a total success by any stretch of the imagination. Nevertheless, there was some pretty decent musicianship on display, and one or two of the more substantial efforts (boasting suitably heroic titles such as "Wings Of Fear" and "Where Eagles Dare") would probably go down reasonably well with followers of DRAGONSLAYER, TYRANT, GRIM REAPER and so forth. Generally speaking, however, the wholesale conversion of BLADE RUNNER into a power metal proposition wasn't entirely suited to their collective abilities (Steve MacKay's vocal performance, in particular, seems unconvincing at times), with their original energy and enthusiasm having pretty much dropped off the scale. It's worth noting that the lads were allocated a mere five days to record the whole shebang, though, so it's quite possible that the rudimentary production may have contributed to the overall feeling of apathy. Whatever the explanation, you have to feel some degree of pity for a band who got things so spectacularly wrong; eschewing the melodic stuff just as the style was about to come into vogue in the UK, and then recording a power metal album at precisely the wrong time. Bad luck, that. In any case, the hapless bunch actually started to fall apart (after a couple of members elected to go back to their day jobs) soon after the second LP finally surfaced, and so the name of BLADE RUNNER was presumably laid to rest almost immediately.

With BLADE RUNNER having already bitten the proverbial dust by 1987, original guitarists Gary Jones and Mark Wilde reunited and joined forces with drummer Dave Dufort (ex-TYTAN), bassist Tom Prince (ex-TREDEGAR) and vocalist Jan Stevens (ex-FLARE) in a supposed 'post-NWOBHM supergroup' named PHANTASM. Although the much-vaunted outfit's live outings were apparently quite well-received (as evidenced by regular reviews in the rock press of the day), their somewhat unhealthy reliance on recycling numerous old TYTAN and BLADE RUNNER efforts failed to disguise the rather worrying fact that they actually had precious little self-penned material of the same standard, and the ill-fated project was to suffer from a few bouts of personnel instability (Mark Wilde was the first to decide that his heart just wasn't in it any more) before splitting towards the end of the decade without ever having reached the vinyl stage. Erstwhile BLADE RUNNER bassist Mick Cooper, meanwhile, collaborated with Paul Gaskin on some of the latter's early 90's studio endeavours, the fruits of which appeared on GASKIN's »Stand Or Fall« set comparatively recently, having gathered dust for several years.

LP's
»Hunted« Ebony 1984
»Warriors Of Rock« Ebony 1986

7" Singles
»Back Street Lady« Ebony 1984

BLAZER BLAZER

Ged Milne (v,g)
Derek O'Neil (g)
Steve Barnacle (b)
Simon Fox (d)

Although the quirky and oft-reshuffled outfit who came to be known as BLAZER BLAZER established themselves in London towards the end of the 70's, there's semi-reliable evidence to suggest that their humble roots actually lay in a long-forgotten bunch who were originally based in Canada way back in the temporal mists. To be honest, though, it's probably a pretty tenuous connection (maybe their frontman was of Canadian extraction or something), as a couple of the others (Simon Fox was previously in HACKENSACK and BE-BOP DELUXE, for instance) were familiar faces. Whatever the story, it's known that the ensemble utilised the services of a certain guitarist called Adrian Smith at some unspecified point in time (it's entirely possible that the busy chap was simultaneously in the ranks of URCHIN and merely acting in a guest capacity), although he made little or no contribution to BLAZER BLAZER's sole »Cecil B. Devine« 7", a slice of vinyl recorded for the Logo label in 1979. Somehow, in spite of the fact that the quartet were a small-time bunch of wannabes (with an extremely silly name) at that stage, it came to pass that the eminent Tom Allom (most famous among metal fans for his work with the likes of JUDAS PRIEST and PAT TRAVERS) was somehow roped in to oversee the production of their debut three-tracker, and the capable gent certainly made a pretty good fist of it. Mind you, we weren't exactly talking heads-down thrash here.

As it turned out, the title track of BLAZER BLAZER's first EP was a surprisingly mainstream effort (it bore virtually zero resemblance to the NWOBHM archetype) which veered perilously close to a typical WINGS composition on occasion, although the odd piece of vaguely substantial guitar work livened things up a tad. It was an off-the-wall combination, the outfit creating something which can only adequately be described as a pop/rock hybrid (see also BOMBAY, T34 and GOGMAGOG, for example), which, despite being pretty distinctive, was likely to appeal to few metal aficionados. Mind you, matters improved on the flipside, and both "Warsaw" and "Six O'Clock In The Morning" represented rather more conventional and catchy examples of proto-NWOBHM (reminiscent of SINGAPORE and the NEXT BAND, for instance), each being fairly typical of the transitional, post-punk period in question. Taking the group's alleged transatlantic background into account, however, it's entirely feasible that a major part of BLAZER BLAZER's oddball style had developed from the AOR and art-rock scenes rather than from anything more quintessentially British, and their open flirtation with such chart-friendly material (not to mention the rather homoerotic and suggestive sleeve which adorns the EP) would probably have distanced them considerably from the testosterone-charged rock community at the time. Nevertheless, some suspiciously-prestigious support slots (with the likes of NAZARETH, URIAH HEEP and AC/DC) and a trip or two to the Marquee at the turn of the decade doubtless helped to raise their profile among the British fans, although it appears to have been an ultimately fruitless exercise, with no further recordings ever seeing the light of day.

It would appear that BLAZER BLAZER had drifted apart well before the end of 1980 (although it was hardly a monumental event when they finally called it a day), with the last incarnation of the band evolving into the short-lived BROADWAY BRATS venture. Vocalist Ged Milne (aka Jeb Million) was the brains behind the operation once again, and his accomplices included drummer Ian Richardson and bassist Steve Wells (both of whom were apparently BLAZER BLAZER veterans themselves), plus journeyman guitarist Andy Barnett, who later collaborated with Adrian Smith in his ASAP project. Incidentally, the future IRON MAIDEN connection goes even deeper than you might think, as it transpires that the much-travelled Nicko McBrain may also have enjoyed a fleeting stint at the BLAZER BLAZER drumkit during his pre-TRUST days, although he certainly made no contribution to the songwriting side of things. It's also worth mentioning the fact that the excellently-named bassist Steve Barnacle also (after parting company with BLAZER BLAZER) proceeded to find his way into a great deal of session work and subsequent involvement with a variety of not-remotely-credible (in a metal sense, at least) acts, with the likes of JACK GREEN (the one-time PRETTY THINGS bassist), RICK WAKEMAN, VISAGE (where he worked alongside the aforementioned Andy Barnett) and SPEAR OF DESTINY being prime examples. Barnacle later collaborated with erstwhile colleague Jeb Million after the vocalist had (rather implausibly) formed an alliance with the Stock, Aitken and Waterman production team (responsible for countless pop disasters over the years), this partnership resulting in a couple of ill-advised JEB MILLION solo singles (the scarcely-sighted »Second Time Around« and »Speed Up My Heartbeat«), which hit the record shops (to calamitous public disinterest) in 1986.

7" EP's
»Cecil B. Devine« Logo 1979

BLEAK HOUSE

Graham Shaw (v)
Bob Bonshor (g)
Graham Killin (g)
Gez Turner (b)
Roy Reed (d)

Looking at the decidedly non-youthful photo of Hertfordshire's BLEAK HOUSE (a moniker taken from a literary classic by Charles Dickens, for those of you who regularly slept through English lessons at school) on the reverse of their »Lions In Winter« EP from 1982, it's clear that this wasn't exactly a bunch of starry-eyed youngsters doing the old *'teenage rebellion'* thing, so it's perhaps slightly fortuitous that this, er, *'mature'* concern ever came to be associated with the NWOBHM movement. Indeed, bassist Gez Turner's musical legacy actually extends back as far as the psychedelic 60's, having played with the legendary outfit PUSSY (cat lovers, evidently), who originally issued their extremely rare and highly-valued »Pussy Plays« LP on the Morgan Bluetown label in 1969. No doubt one or two of the other grizzled BLEAK HOUSE stalwarts have similarly chequered pasts, but I'm always open to bribes (no coins, just notes) to keep such potentially scandalous information to myself...

With the Home Counties being a notable breeding ground for rock acts at the time, BLEAK HOUSE came into existence in around 1978, playing numerous gigs at such venues as St. Albans City Hall and garnering a healthy following along the way. The lads failed to attract a massive amount of record company attention, however, although a close friend called Peter (affectionately known as *'the old buzzard'*) personally financed the release of their first EP (»Rainbow Warrior« in the summer of 1980, with the *'Buzzard Records'* label being a tribute to his generosity. With regional sales having been fairly modest at the time, the tracks from their debut (periously few copies of which appear to have been issued with the unremarkable picture sleeve) were heard only by a privileged few until a couple were plundered for inclusion on the Japanese series of bootleg CD's in the early 90's, before unsold copies began to come onto the market *via* the band members a year or two later. The music itself (the record was completed by "Inquisition", which I'm sure nobody expected, and the almost unpronounceable "Isandhlwana") was a very classy, melodic type of heavy rock (with what seems like a discernible semi-folk influence, although this is more detectable on vinyl than on live recordings) with relatively few direct comparisons in the NWOBHM field (their nearest musical allies would, without question, be Jersey's LEGEND), although the likes of LIMELIGHT, CRYER and EAZY STREET also come reasonably close.

The following eighteen months or so were evidently quite eventful for these experienced musicians, who proceeded to make many new fans and contacts at plentiful local gigs with the likes of CLIENTELLE, HIGH TREASON and TOAD THE WET SPROCKET (they even appeared live at one of the famous Radio Caroline rock roadshows in nearby Dunstable), where they unveiled a selection of original material including "Lost Fortunes", "The Darkest Night", "Arise With The Prince" and "To The Gods". Surprisingly, the band were a considerably heavier proposition in the live environment, with much of their own material coming across as quite similar to the likes of PHOENIX RISING or even OMEGA, so it's interesting that this bunch actually managed to deliver such subtle material on vinyl. To capitalise on their considerable popularity, the lads eventually concluded that another vinyl offering would probably be a good idea, and so a second EP was recorded at Quest Studios in Luton in November 1981. Again magnanimously financed by *'the old buzzard'* (what a nice chap), BLEAK HOUSE's »Lions In Winter« four-tracker was unleashed (housed in another minimalist sleeve with two inserts) the following year, and this release proved to be another big hit with the local fans. More importantly, though, a few copies actually made it slightly further afield this time, so there was every chance that the band would become familiar to the broader rock community. Displaying a markedly heavier and more metallic style (still not quite portraying the outfit at their most powerful, though), the all-new BLEAK HOUSE offering was rather more reminiscent of bands such as OVERKILL or SLEDGEHAMMER, and was undoubtedly the sort of thing which should have gone down an absolute storm with the nation's headbangers at the time. All things considered, the featured compositions (particularly "Chase The Wind" and "Down To Zero") are far more in keeping with the NWOBHM ethos, and the EP (completed by "No Reply" and the well-constructed instrumental "Flight Of The Salamander") is highly prized by collectors today. Even so, this strong release seems not to have turned BLEAK HOUSE into national heroes after all, and they were soon having second thoughts about their collective future. In the event, the group didn't actually hang around for too long afterwards (drummer Roy Reed subsequently had a stint with long-lived South Coast outfit the ENGLISH ROGUES, but the others more or less vanished from the music scene almost immediately), and all of the original members have long since returned to rather more sedentary, middle-aged activities such as running village pubs. Surprisingly, they seem, variously, to be either totally amazed or utterly nonplussed at their former outfit's belated adulation.

7" EP's
»Rainbow Warrior« Buzzard Records 1980
»Lions In Winter« Buzzard Records 1982

Compilation Appearances
"Rainbow Warrior" on »NWOBHM Vol.1« Bootleg CD 1992
"Inquisition" on »NWOBHM Vol.3« Bootleg CD 1992 *[Miscredited as "Isandhlwana"]*
"Down To Zero" on »NWOBHM Vol.5« Bootleg CD 1992

BLITZ, THE

Phil Long

Not to be confused with various punk/oi outfits who adopted a similar name, the horrendously obscure rock/metal band who went by the identity of THE BLITZ are known only by virtue of their monumentally scarce »The Border« single (b/w "I Love Myself"), released on their own Bitch label back in 1979. The tracks are quite heavy, sleazy efforts in the general style of the STOOGES or the NEW YORK DOLLS, with punk undertones in places and some reasonably strong guitar work throughout. There's also a slight affiliation with the NWOBHM archetype (although the 7" hardly constitutes a prime example of the style), the main similarity being to the punk/metal crossover conceived by the LIGHTNING RAIDERS, although I wouldn't be the first person to suggest that there's more than a hint of GUNS'N'ROSES in there too! Sadly, nothing else is known about the group at present; there's no handy sleeve to provide any details of personnel or geographical origin, and I haven't the remotest notion who this Phil Long character might have been. As with so many of these hopelessly rare and staggeringly uninformative singles, we can only hope that a copy eventually turns up with either a promo letter or helpful biography, or that somebody actually writes in to tell us more about the band in question. You might want to add this one to your wants list if you're a completist, but I wouldn't really hold out too much hope of procuring a copy, especially if you're not in the regular habit of paying huge prices for your acquisitions.

7" Singles
»The Border« Bitch Records 1979

BLITZKRIEG

Brian Ross (v)
Jim Sirotto (g)
Ian Jones (rg)
Steve English (b)
Steve Abbey (d)

Truly one of the most popular and enduring bands from the entire NWOBHM era, Leicestershire's much-loved BLITZKRIEG (not to be confused with either their British punk namesakes or American metal ones) nevertheless struggled against adversity for much of their career, and many devotees of the genre have expressed the opinion that they would undoubtedly have had a serious chance at major-label stardom had they managed to keep it together in the first instance. It's a commonly-made claim, admittedly, but I reckon there's actually a fair bit of evidence to support such assertions in this particular case. In spite of the fact that the BLITZKRIEG story has supposedly been established in minute detail (having been rehashed by numerous writers over the years), their history (especially the official biography) tends to gloss over a few important details, and some oft-repeated tales frequently present the same false information and draw an equivalent range of incorrect conclusions. There's little doubt that the outfit first came together in late 1980 (a precursor of the band had earlier been operating as SPLIT IMAGE, although the recruitment of vocalist Brian Ross swiftly led to the adoption of more forceful BLITZKRIEG name), but it's truly remarkable just how quickly they entered the studio to lay down their first demo. Within only a few weeks of formation (early November), the debut three-tracker (featuring the original compositions "Inferno", "Blitzkrieg" and "Armageddon") was recorded at Humbucker Studios in Leicester, and the tape was soon winging its way to various interested parties, getting the best response from those nice chaps at Neat Records.

Neat were immensely keen to feature BLITZKRIEG on their first compilation, the »Lead Weight« sampler, and were more than happy to use one of the tracks from the band's demo to save a bit of time and money. "Inferno" was the lucky number chosen, and it served admirably to introduce the listening public to the group's heavy interpretation of the NWOBHM style, being very much along the lines of the material that popular acts such as ANGEL WITCH and HOLOCAUST were already endeavouring to master. Following on from this initial exposure, Neat swiftly commissioned a single, so BLITZKRIEG were soon back in the studio to lay down "Buried Alive" and "Blitzkrieg" for imminent release in 7" form. This record turned out to be a sure-fire money-spinner for Neat, and the initial pressing was soon being snapped up with extraordinary fervour. It was, without any shadow of a doubt, a capable and memorable debut, although frontman Brian Ross (who was already developing an impressive range) hadn't quite hit his peak in terms of vocal performance just yet. Still, the BLITZKRIEG fans saw to it that the record sold out pretty quickly, rendering this the most collectable of all Neat's early singles. Everything was happening very quickly for the lucky quintet (a feature in the 'Armed And Ready' section of the second issue of 'Kerrang' gave them even more exposure), and they scarcely had time to make much of an impression of the live scene before they were being invited to make further trips to the recording studio for the benefit of various labels.

Even by this stage (the spring of 1981), BLITZKRIEG had a fairly impressive repertoire at their disposal, and the outfit first recorded such numbers as "Take A Look Around", "Calming The Savage Beast" and "Saviour" at around this juncture, although they appear to have decided to keep the master tapes under wraps for the time being, electing to concentrate on writing additional material and becoming more of a cohesive unit before offering any new recordings to the world. Shortly thereafter, BLITZKRIEG began to experience the dreaded personnel instability which afflicted so many unfortunate hopefuls at the time, and they were reduced to three permanent members after the departure of guitarist Ian Jones (who later formed his own act, DEAD

EASY) and bassist Steve English, who joined forces with the Leicestershire version of RAW DEAL (see separate entry), a raunchy and long-lived act whose greatest achievement was a single of their own on Neat. Happily, a suitable pair of replacements were soon identified, with axeman John Antcliffe being recruited from local rivals ELECTRIC SAVAGE, while unknown bassist Mick Moore made up the numbers. After the new pupils had done their homework and learnt their parts, the lads burst forth onto the scene once again, and recorded their second official demo, the »Blitzed Alive« effort. This was a live affair, the band having been captured in action while supporting TRUST at a gig in Newcastle, and the tape showcased five of their own numbers ("Blitzkrieg", "Inferno", "Armageddon", "Take A Look Around" and "Saviour"), plus a cover of DEEP PURPLE's "Highway Star". It was a very appealing tape, in spite of the ludicrously over-the-top crowd noises dubbed in to make the soundboard tape more listenable, and it didn't do BLITZKRIEG's chances any harm whatsoever.

In fact, the band began spending more and more of their time in the North East, and there was even talk of releasing a second single (based around "Too Wild To Tame", a track which was later recycled as the A-side of AVENGER's first 7") on Neat, although the notion was finally rejected in favour of recording a full album. Contrary to popular opinion, however, the long-player was never unequivocally scheduled to appear on Neat; the lads were in negotiations with several labels at the time (including such high-profile concerns as Carrere), and Neat was only one of many options for the finished product. The recording sessions for the debut album took place late in 1981 as intended, and the group eventually captured around an hour's worth of material, including such unfamiliar compositions as "The Space Traveller", "A Time Of Changes" (the anticipated title track), "Hell To Pay" and "Vikings", in addition to numerous favourites from the earlier part of their career. Everything seemed to be going according to plan until a couple of the participants expressed serious doubts as to the strength of these latest recordings, whereupon they swiftly decided to throw in their hands. Suddenly, the hapless BLITZKRIEG were on the path to oblivion. The rapidity of their demise was truly staggering, and it's utterly baffling as to why they couldn't simply have persevered with a revised line-up. Sadly, however, they hastily made the decision to call it a day, the upshot being that the album never got to the pressing stage in its original form (a tantalising rough mix made it out into limited circulation, showing just how worthy the release would have been), and the fate of the master tape remains something of a mystery, even to this day.

By the end of 1981, BLITZKRIEG were no more. Jim Sirotto and Steve Abbey returned to their day jobs down South, while John Antcliffe started all over again with the recently-established CHROME MOLLY. Mick Moore and Brian Ross were at a bit of a loose end for a while, and soon began infiltrating various bands in the North East, where they had decided to remain. Moore had a brief stint with the little-known MARAUDER (who feature on Guardian's »Roxcalibur« compilation) before moving on to UNTER DEN LINDEN (who also appear on the same album), where he was fleetingly joined by Brian Ross. Within a matter of months, however, the duo had come to the conclusion that they deserved a second crack at fame in an outfit of their own, and formed the relatively popular and successful AVENGER (see separate entry), who proceeded to utilise some of the defunct BLITZKRIEG's compositions (notably "Too Wild To Tame" and "The Space Traveller") in their own repertoire. After a relatively short spell fronting AVENGER, however, Ross was traded to fellow premier league outfit SATAN in return for Ian Davison Swift, although his involvement with SATAN also proved to be a short-lived affair. After parting company with the latter outfit, Ross shacked up with regional nonentities LONE WOLF (see separate entry), who had already recorded a single for Guardian but who were now struggling to maintain any interest in their activities. The well-travelled frontman gave them a much-needed boost, and soon took over as both manager and vocalist, singing on the outfit's »Nobody's Move« EP for Neat later in the year.

By 1985, however, Ross had developed seriously itchy feet once more, and abandoned his involvement with LONE WOLF in order to get his beloved BLITZKRIEG off the ground again. 'If you can get the album recorded, we'll release it' (or words to that effect) said Neat, and so the search was on for some suitable accomplices with which to re-record the whole shebang. Mick Moore was happy to oblige (although he was still very much a major part of AVENGER), and Jim Sirotto was soon coaxed out of retirement, but the trio were forced to borrow SATAN drummer Sean Taylor and well-travelled guitarist Mick Procter (NATO, JESS COX, TYGERS OF PAN TANG etc.) to bring them up to full strength. The outfit's second attempt at »A Time Of Changes« was captured on tape in due course, and the long-awaited album soon benefitted from a belated release on both Neat and Roadrunner. It was an excellent effort all round, and the fans were finally able to hear those mythical tracks such as "A Time Of Changes", "Hell To Pay", "Vikings" and "Saviour", in addition to listenable versions of old favourites such as "Blitzkrieg", "Armageddon" and "Inferno". The album also contained a reworking of SATAN's original demo composition "Pull The Trigger", which was all part of the jokey interchange of numbers between BLITZKRIEG, AVENGER and

SATAN, each of whom had immense fun reworking their rivals' songs. Not only that, the track also featured guest appearances from SATAN's Russ Tippins and AVENGER's Ian Davison Swift, so they certainly believed in keeping it in the family.

The album (which also featured selected contributions from keyboard player Ian Boddy, whose solo recordings also featured occasional vocals from Brian Ross, incidentally) went on to sell in extremely impressive quantities throughout many parts of the world, notably Europe (in particular), America and Japan, where the group had now developed something of a cult following. Not only that, the general public's interest in their activities had been piqued by METALLICA's recent patronage of the outfit (and their "Blitzkrieg" track in particular, which had appeared on the »Creeping Death« EP some months previously), so there seemed to be quite a market for further BLITZKRIEG vinyl. This put mainman Brian Ross at something of a disadvantage, however, as there was no way he could organise any lengthy tours (although a version of BLITZKRIEG, based around Ross, Moore and Procter, played a few gigs to promote the release, assisted by guitarist Gavin Taylor and erstwhile CHROME MOLLY sticksman Chris Green), collaborate on new material or undertake further recording sessions due to the numerous outside commitments of the various musicians who had played on the album. In the end, he decided to start again from scratch, and began attempting to assemble a fully-functioning version of BLITZKRIEG in the latter half of 1986. This took quite a while to achieve, although a revitalised incarnation of the outfit ultimately resurfaced the following year, when Ross was joined by relative unknowns Chris Beard (g), Darren Parnaby (b), Sean Wilkinson (d) and former MANDORA guitarist JD Binnie. The five-piece even got as far as recording a four track demo, but soon realised that they weren't a particularly effective unit, leaving Ross to dissolve the ensemble once again.

The next version of BLITZKRIEG was slightly more successful, their indefatigable vocalist enlisting the help of an equally-obscure set of musicians, namely Glenn Howes (g), Steve Robertson (g), Kyle Gibson (d) and bassist Robbie Robertson (not the one from THE BAND, needless to say). This time they had a nibble of record company interest after recording a two track tape, but most of the new members became disillusioned with the venture and flew the coop in 1989 (Kyle Gibson resurfaced in SMASH ALLEY), leaving Ross and Howes to soldier on alone. Fortunately, they were eventually able to find some considerably more dependable cohorts in the shape of erstwhile AVENGER sticksman Gary Young, guitarist Tony Liddle (who had previously manned the microphone in SEARGENT, the TYGERS OF PAN TANG offshoot), plus bassist Glen Carey. Towards the end of 1989, the lads took the unusual step of recording a semi-professional video of themselves in action at a gig in Sunderland, and subsequently used the tape as part of their master plan to get BLITZKRIEG back into the public eye at last. Fortunately, their luck was in, and, after getting back into the swing of things throughout 1990, came to an arrangement with Neat and Roadrunner (under the auspices of their American franchise, Roadracer) to get a comeback mini-album into the shops the following year.

It had now been a whole decade since BLITZKRIEG's original inception, and the group took full advantage of this observation (coupled with a handy bit of NWOBHM nostalgia inspired by Lars Ulrich's »NWOBHM '79 Revisited« compilation, which gave pride of place to old favourite "Blitzkrieg"), recording three new tracks and revamping the numbers from their original single to comprise the functionally-titled »Ten Years Of Blitzkrieg« mini-LP. Brian Ross was happy to give his opinion on the whole METALLICA thing at the time of the release: *'In actual fact, "Blitzkrieg" should have been the A-side of our single, but it wasn't commercial enough for Neat, so "Buried Alive" became the A-side instead. Nevertheless, I think it's great that METALLICA covered the song, I really like their version.'* (Ref: Iron Pages No.16, 1991). Not commercial enough for Neat?! How the hell did VENOM ever get any singles released? Bizarre revelations aside, their »Ten Years Of Blitzkrieg« was a highly listenable affair, and the new offerings ("The Sentinel", "Night Howl" and "Nocturnal Vision") were all well up to scratch, in a sort of heavy-but-melodic way. It was reassuring to find that BLITZKRIEG hadn't followed SATAN's ill-fated attempts to metamorphose into a thrash concern, although the reworked "Blitzkrieg" and "Buried Alive" were certainly a bit more frenzied this time around.

Sales were pretty healthy, and there seemed to be plenty of room for BLITZKRIEG in the traditional power metal niche market, so Ross and his associates (several of whom would come and go over the coming years) set about laying down a genuine album of predominantly-new material. »Unholy Trinity«, the second proper BLITZKRIEG long-player, was initially recorded in 1992, although various business-related wranglings meant that it went unreleased at the time. Neat, while no doubt eager to help out in such circumstances, were already in dire financial straits themselves, while Roadrunner, for understandable reasons, weren't prepared to commit to a perceived 'NWOBHM revival' on a long-term basis. Added to the fact that power metal really *was* a niche market in the early 90's (grunge has a lot to answer for), and you can surely appreciate the problems that BLITZKRIEG initially had in attracting any interest to their activities. Still, things came full circle in 1995, when Neat reinvented themselves as Neat Metal and started out on a generous programme of reissues and new releases, one of the first being »Unholy Trinity«. With the CD containing a massive seventeen tracks (including old chestnuts "Take A Look Around" and "Calming The Savage Beast", plus a cover of VENOM's "Countess Bathory", for no apparent reason), fans were soon familiarising themselves with a variety of strong numbers such as "After Dark", "House Of Pleasure", "Hair Trigger" and "Struck By Lightning". BLITZKRIEG were back!

With sales being encouragingly strong from the outset, the group soon capitalised on their Neat-induced revitalisation by going out on tour for the first time in several years. Wisely, they only used the UK for the unimportant warm-up gigs (given that BLITZKRIEG were no longer flavour of the month at home), electing to concentrate on the NWOBHM-friendly territories of Germany and Greece for the real thing. The shows in Germany (towards the end of 1996) were particularly well-received and successful, and the band were even interviewed and filmed in action for a cable television programme at one of these events. In the wake of this burst of popularity, the lads then decided to repackage the »Ten Years Of Blitzkrieg« set (which was now long out-of-print and rapidly becoming a sought-after piece), electing to supplement the original five tracks with five newer efforts and create a more substantial CD. This emerged in 1997 under the confusing title of »Ten« (ten tracks as opposed to ten years, this time), and provided listeners with the first chance to hear numbers such as "Fighting All The Way To The Top", "The Power Of The King" and the completely bonkers "Court In The Act", a track whose lyrics are based almost entirely (apart from one or two BLITZKRIEG and AVENGER originals) around a number of SATAN song titles! You certainly can't claim these guys are lacking in the humour or irony departments...

By this stage, the unstable outfit had actually reorganised once again, with the nucleus of Brian Ross and Tony Liddle now being augmented by bassist Steve Ireland (yet another MARAUDER veteran), guitarist Phil Miller and drummer Paul White, although BLITZKRIEG's followers were now well aware that the overall sound wasn't critically dependent on whichever musicians happened to be backing Brian Ross at any particular point in time. In fact, there was to be a further reshuffle before much longer, when Ross brought back guitarist Glenn Howes (who also now has a new group of his own called EARTH ROD, incidentally) and drafted in yet another rhythm section consisting of Martin Richardson (b) and Mark Hancock (d). This particular bunch recorded their first full album together in 1998, and »The Mists Of Avalon« has been warmly received by a great many fans since its release. BLITZKRIEG have followed up this spate of recording activity with some more high-profile live appearances, including a slot at the Wacken Festival of 1998 and their first ever dates in America early in 1999. I suspect that further CD's are in the offing, given the prolific group's proven ability to come up with new material, and let's all hope that the latest version of BLITZKRIEG finally achieve the recognition they have long deserved.

LP's
»A Time Of Changes« Neat 1985/Roadrunner 1985
[UK/Dutch issue]

Mini-LP's
»Ten Years Of Blitzkrieg« Roadracer 1991
[Features a mixture of new and re-recorded older material]

7" Singles
»Buried Alive« Neat 1981
[A-side non-LP and B-side "Blitzkrieg" different to album version, re-recorded versions of both tracks included on »Ten Years Of Blitzkrieg« and »Ten« releases]

Promotional Releases
»Pull The Trigger« New Records 1985
[Split 7" flexi given free with 'Enfer' magazine, other track "Bursting Out" by VENOM]

CD's
»A Time Of Changes« Castle Communications 1992
[UK issue with one bonus track]
»A Time Of Changes« Roadrunner 1992
[Japanese issue with two bonus tracks]
»Unholy Trinity« Neat Metal 1995
[UK issue]
»Unholy Trinity« Pony Canyon 1995

[Japanese issue with one bonus track]
»Ten« Neat Metal 1997
[UK issue, includes material from »Ten Years Of Blitzkrieg« mini-album]
»Ten« Pony Canyon 1997
[Japanese issue with two bonus tracks]
»The Mists Of Avalon« Neat Metal 1998

Mini-CD's
»Ten Years Of Blitzkrieg« Roadracer 1991
[Features a mixture of new and older material]

Compilation Appearances
"Inferno" on »Lead Weight« LP Neat 1981/CD Teichiku 1992 + »NWOBHM Vol.3« Bootleg CD 1992 *[Different to album version]*
"Blitzkrieg" on »NWOBHM '79 Revisited« Do-LP/Do-CD Phonogram 1990 + »Deeper Into The Vault« CD Music For Nations 1991 + »The Metal Box« 3-CD Box Castle Communications 1993 + »The Metallic-Era« CD Neat Metal 1996
"Buried Alive" on »Metal Masters« 4-CD Box Castle Communications 1993 + »Metal Mania« CD Castle Communications 1994
"A Time Of Changes" on »Heavy Metal Collection 1« CD X-Tra Collection 1993
"Vikings" on »Heavy Metal Collection 4« CD X-Tra Collection 1993
"Hair Trigger" on »Neat Metal« CD Neat Metal 1995
"Unholy Trinity" on »Neat Metal« CD Neat Metal 1995
"Power Of The King" (live) on »Unbroken Metal« CD Private 1997
[Exclusive live version]
"Yesterday (Hope For The Future)" on »Hard Roxx Taster Vol.6« CD Private 1999 (Free with 'Hard Roxx' magazine)

BLOOD MONEY

Danny Foxx (v)
Gramie Dee (g)
Dale Lee (b)
Bret Avok (d)

Arriving at the tail end of the NWOBHM, Manchester's BLOOD MONEY appear to have been one of those dreaded *'love them or hate them'* outfits. Sadly, the majority of metal fans seem to adhere to the latter opinion, although the chances are that the lads might have developed a rather more substantial following had they actually got around to releasing their first album a few years earlier. In fact, the quartet's early history is poorly documented, not helped by their remarkable and inexplicable reluctance to play any gigs whatsoever. We can surmise, however, that they probably got together in around 1984 (bassist Dale Lee had, incidentally, guested on the ARAGORN single, although none of the others were familiar faces), circulated a speculative demo at some stage and eventually attracted the attention of the obliging Ebony concern. BLOOD MONEY's first productive recording session yielded the »Red Raw And Bleeding« album in 1986, an effort which was to show the group attempting a fast (sometimes *too* damn fast) brand of post-NWOBHM in the general manner of RAVEN or late 80's JUDAS PRIEST, with the powerful, soaring vocals of capable frontman Danny Foxx lying somewhere between Billy Downs of DAMASCUS and BLITZKRIEG's Brian Ross.

Ebony tried valiantly to pass the band off as, variously, either a speed metal or thrash outfit (not quite as ludicrous as their assertion that COBRA were death metal, mind you), but this ambitious (nay, fraudulent) sales pitch failed to convince many punters. Fast metal, yes, but not really speed or thrash in a purist's opinion. There are some listenable moments, admittedly, such as on "Gor", "Lazarus" and "Stormer", although the tracks on display were severely lacking in variety (all very similarly structured and virtually identical in terms of pace and riffing), and it's extremely trebly throughout, the excessive speed meaning that any heaviness tended to go straight out of the window. Oh, and it had a bloody offal cover (sorry, folks, I had to get that one in). Nevertheless, the BLOOD MONEY lads (who also saw their "Metalyzed" effort being featured on one of Ebony's multifarious compilations as something of a *'bonus'*) were rapidly encouraged to lay down a follow-up album, whereupon they duly obliged with the »Battlescarred« set, released the following year. This time, the band members were pictured on the sleeve, attempting to look as mean and menacing as humanly possible (well, their collection of facial hair certainly scares *me*), with bullet belts, spikes, swords and, er, a chainsaw (something of a fixation, it would appear), which wasn't silly at all.

Ludicrous posturing aside, had there been much of a musical progression in the interim? Hardly. The second BLOOD MONEY album basically starts from where its vinyl predecessor left off, with precisely nothing in the way of new ideas thrown in at any stage. If anything, it's even less enjoyable than their debut release, and there's no particular evidence to suggest that there was any conviction or enthusiasm coming from the musicians themselves. The critics were generally unimpressed with BLOOD MONEY's pair of formulaic albums (the outfit's apparent preoccupation with fantasy/mythological lyrics didn't do them any favours, either), and most reviews tended to hail either LP as an unmissable release. Notwithstanding a general state of public apathy towards their music, however, the plucky foursome still somehow managed to convince those at the BBC that they would be able to deliver a top-quality session for the 'Friday Rock Show'. In the event, though, the lads merely ran through a mundane selection of their album cuts (the session was originally broadcast on the 1st of May 1987), namely "The Third Wish", "Caligula", "Battlescarred" and "Shape Shifter", and few (if any) additional fans were won over as a result.

BLOOD MONEY came to an end in the latter months of 1987, after vocalist Danny Foxx had reached a decision to join a more ambitious outfit, as he later explained: *'I left the band because they refused to gig. The thing with BLOOD MONEY was that it was all thrash and very boring. So I set about putting a new band together by advertising in 'Kerrang' and various music shops in Manchester.'* (Ref: Metal Forces No.41, July 1989). His initial attempt came with the short-lived BISON, in which he was joined by former colleague Bret Avok (whose replacement in BLOOD MONEY, Ade Dorsett, later joined local also-rans CIRCUS), although he soon started over with FOXX, teaming up with ex-WHITEFIRE (not the bunch responsible for the »Suzanne« 7") personnel to create something more closely resembling his intended musical vision. The new act recorded a well-received demo and 'Friday Rock Show' session (in a broadly similar style to CLOVEN HOOF) before the end of 1988, but soon decided to reinvent themselves, first as the absurdly-named ZIONOIZ (who were even reported to have signed a deal with Noise Records at one point) and then as SACRASANCT, although none of these ventures managed to reach the vinyl stage. Danny Foxx got slightly further with the more accessible CHINA BEACH (who released a self-financed EP or two in around 1992), but this bunch also failed to get their breakthrough in the long term. The vocalist's current activities are unknown (as are those of the remaining BLOOD MONEY characters, although Bret Avok had a very brief tenure with the long-forgotten VERRA CRUZ in the early months of 1988), but it's worth mentioning that one of his erstwhile colleagues in FOXX/CHINA BEACH (guitarist Mark Mynett) recently surfaced in the much-touted KILL II THIS.

LP's

»**Red Raw And Bleeding**« Ebony 1986
»**Battlescarred**« Ebony 1987

Compilation Appearances

"**Metalyzed**" on »The Metal Collection Vol.I« LP Ebony 1986

BLOODSHOT EYES

George Whitter (v,g)
Hanif Bulbulia (rg)
Matthew Russell (b)
William Hayter (d)

After London's SHADER (see separate entry) had finally called it a day in around 1983, frontman George Whitter remained out of the limelight for a relatively short space of time before returning to the fore with an act called BAD BLOOD, where he was joined by the unrenowned trio of Hanif Bulbulia (rg), Matthew Russell (b) and William Hayter (d). The newly-formed quartet began composing their own material with great haste, and offered the world their first demo cassette before the end of the year, the five-tracker showcasing a selection of fairly laid-back (almost rootsy) rock material with an occasional nod towards the 70's-style musings of CRACKED MIRROR and Derbyshire's WARRIOR. It certainly wasn't typical NWOBHM-era material, although he likes of "I Get Lonely" and "Burning Up For You" (with some semi-decent guitar work) are listenable enough (considerably more accomplished than SHADER's ramshackle concoctions), even if the more bluesy and uninspiring "I'm On My Knees" and "Deep Down I'm Crying" let the side down a bit. It looks as though the tape failed to make all that much of an impression on the rock community, however, and so the name of BAD BLOOD was quietly laid to rest at some point in mid-1984, allowing the members to pursue new interests.

Towards the end of that year, the duo of George Whitter and William Hayter proceeded to throw another new ensemble together, this time roping in Euan (g) and John Prim (b), whereupon they cunningly reinvented themselves as BLOODSHOT EYES. This quartet were keen to get their name known as quickly as possible, and hastily assembled a full-length album, which they duly issued on their own Flat Bee label with minimal delay. Bizarrely, however, the

»On My Knees« long-player was actually comprised of two sets of demo recordings, the first five tracks being taken from the aforementioned BAD BLOOD tape, while the remaining three dated back to an even earlier SHADER demo from 1982! Mind you, none of this was actually mentioned on the record itself, which happily identified all selections as BLOODSHOT EYES originals, although it was indeed revealed that they came from different recording sessions, each featuring a markedly different line-up. In truth, the handful of SHADER compositions were far more enjoyable than the other tracks on display, with the energetic "Lightning Man" being the pick of the bunch.

To be honest, few people really knew what to make of the debut BLOODSHOT EYES long-player at the time, as it was a chaotic release in every sense, an album which featured a baffling change of musical direction halfway through, and which came packaged in an extremely rudimentary, handmade sleeve which makes the cover of »Kent Rocks« look overly-elaborate. Still, the ensemble went on to enjoy a limited amount of coverage in minor fanzines such as 'High Octane', and mail-order sales of their long-player were solicited through the pages of 'Kerrang', although it looks as though remarkably few units were shifted at the time. A further demo was apparently in the pipeline for 1985, which the foursome intended to use in a concerted effort to win a proper deal, but I reckon the lads must have acknowledged the fact that they were fighting a losing battle by that stage. BLOODSHOT EYES appear to have called it a day by 1986 at the very latest, with none of the members going on to enjoy success in any act of note, and their one-off foray into the vinyl world remains a monumentally scarce (and largely-unknown) item today.

LP's
»On My Knees« Flat Bee Records 1984

BLUE BLUD

Mark Sutcliffe (v,g,k)
Dave Crawte (b)
Paul Sutcliffe (d)

Formed towards the end of 1986 by Mark Sutcliffe, Paul Sutcliffe and Dave Crawte, three of the founder members of East Anglia's legendary TRESPASS, the outfit known (initially) as BLUE BLUD burst onto the scene early the following year with some showcase gigs at London's Marquee, all of which soon set tongues wagging about this talented 'new' band. Remarkably, few cottoned on to the TRESPASS connection at first, and simply took the group at face value, which must have come as an unexpected bonus for the lads. Now basing themselves in North London as opposed to their native county, they duly recorded their first demo, a four track affair featuring "Real Live Love", "The Girl Is Hot", "Beat Of The Night" and the meteorologically-inaccurate "It Never Rains In England", memorable and classy numbers which revealed BLUE BLUD to be operating in a melodic, fairly powerful rock style with occasional similarities to contemporaries such as CHROME MOLLY, TARGET UK or BABY TUCKOO. Mind you, they still managed to retain something of a British identity, unlike countless other home-grown hopefuls of the day who shamelessly attempted to ape various American imports.

Following an extensive and overwhelmingly successful summer tour with the TYGERS OF PAN TANG, the lads recorded a five track mini-album featuring "Real Live Love", "The Girl Is Hot" and "It Never Rains In England" (all taken from the demo), plus "Get Rich Bitch" and the punningly-titled "Liquor'n'Poker", which served as the title track. Issued on their own label (Blud Donor Discs), the debut record was a capable enough release, and it soon became a popular purchase for melodic rock fans of the day. It has to be said, however, that Mark Sutcliffe's rather gruff vocal style didn't particularly complement the material, and it wasn't long before the possibility of recruiting a dedicated singer was raised. Shortly thereafter, Rob Ariss was drafted in as full-time keyboard player, while new frontman Phil Kane was snatched from his position as drummer (!) in a small-time rock act and promoted to vocalist at the behest of Mark Sutcliffe himself. Phil's first gig was a baptism of fire, with BLUE BLUD supporting WHITE LION at the Marquee, although the talented outfit still emerged from the nerve-racking experience with flying colours. In fact, such was their rapport with the difficult-to-please London audience, that they more or less became instant favourites as the Marquee's support band of choice, leading to slots throughout 1988 with the likes of FAITH NO MORE, SHY and THE GRIP.

Towards the end of the year, the lads (who were now being referred to, rather inaccurately, as 'the band formerly known as TRESPASS' on a regular basis) signed a coveted three-album deal with Music For Nations, and rapidly installed themselves in the studio in order to lay the groundwork for their debut offering. In the event, it was the best part of a year before the long-player (»The Big Noise«) appeared, thanks to various technical hitches and remixes, although they had managed to get »Running Back« issued as a single a few months earlier, following the completion of a summer jaunt with TIGERTAILZ. Prior to the LP's release, there had evidently been a battle of wills between the musicians (who wanted to include heavier material) and their label (who sought to issue as commercial an album as possible), so the final product was something of a compromise. On balance, though, I reckon this collection of melodic numbers (more in the manner of TOBRUK, JOKERS WILD or IDOL RICH than before) met with considerably more approval from the sponsors than the members of BLUE BLUD. Although the likes of "Love Grows Wild" and "Night Time City" were vaguely redolent of their mini-album material, the remainder of the long-player was basically comprised of the undemanding brand of overly-produced AOR mediocrity which was being churned out with truly monotonous regularity by numerous wannabes (in Britain and beyond) of the period. It's a sad state of affairs when the album's stand out track is the reworked "It Never Rains In England", but the record still won over some of the more easily-impressed rock fans and journalists of the day, and the lads duly capitalised on the LP's (limited) success by trawling around the UK in support of LIZZY BORDEN in the spring of 1990.

The outfit obviously weren't too happy with the way their first long-player had worked out, and album number two, 1991's »Universal Language«, saw a minor name change (to BLUE BLOOD) and a more drastic shift in image and direction. The record showed the unit to have drifted towards a raunchier, Americanised sound with a bit more in the way of attitude and personality. That said, there was nothing particularly ground-breaking about this all-new set of compositions, which had now taken the lads to a radio-friendly area lying somewhere between TESLA, EXTREME and BON JOVI. Sadly, BLUE BLOOD failed to emulate any of their peers from across the Atlantic, although they developed something of a cult following in Japan, doubtless helped along by that good old NWOBHM connection. In the end, however, the lads opted out of their contract to deliver a third album, electing instead to resurrect the TRESPASS name, first compiling a retrospective (»The Works«), and subsequently issuing the disarmingly-heavy »Head« set in 1993, showing that their AOR days were now firmly in the past. Asked, at around this time, how he now felt about their involvement with the melodic rock scene, Mark Sutcliffe offered a refreshingly honest opinion: *'BLUE BLUD was initially a three-piece, whose music wasn't actually all that different to TRESPASS. Sadly, we left that behind and new members gradually came in, including a keyboard player, which was certainly our biggest mistake, there's no doubt about that! Our really grave error was when we started listening to what other people wanted us to do. When you, as a recording act, begin to place too much importance on those outside influences, it's basically the kiss of death for everyone.'* (Ref: Iron Pages No.24, 1993). I guess, therefore, that this piece of musical experimentation is yet another which belongs in the *'well, it seemed like a good idea at the time'* file.

LP's
»The Big Noise« Music For Nations 1989
»Universal Language« Music For Nations 1991
[Under the name of BLUE BLOOD]

Mini-LP's
»Liquor'n'Poker« Blud Donor Discs 1987

12" EP's
»Running Back« Music For Nations 1989

7" Singles
»Running Back« Music For Nations 1989

CD's
»The Big Noise« Music For Nations 1989
[UK issue]
»The Big Noise« Pony Canyon 1989
[Japanese issue]
»Universal Language« Music For Nations 1991
[UK issue, under the name of BLUE BLOOD]
»Universal Language« Pony Canyon 1991
[Japanese issue with one extra track]

CD Singles
»Say A Prayer« Pony Canyon 1991
[Japanese-only release]

BOLLWEEVIL

Barry Oaten (v)
Steve Spencer (g)
Kevin Bezant (rg)
Brian Reid (b)
John Cope (d)

One of the more esoteric classics of the NWOBHM era was released on the prolific Ellie Jay label (back in the heady days of 1981) by a long-forgotten bunch of Surrey hopefuls named BOLLWEEVIL, whose small-time activities on Britain's flourishing metal scene were (almost inevitably) not documented in any great detail at the time. Mind you, STATIC mainman Noel Jones is known to have auditioned for the vacant position of singer at the outset, his refined tones ultimately losing out to the rough'n'ready voice of Barry Oaten. After establishing themselves as a stable unit, the quintet swiftly began thinking about getting a humble vinyl offering into the shops, and their sole single (recorded at the local Ark Studios facility in Kingston) was pressed up (in very modest quantities) within a matter of months. Indeed, the lads didn't even go through the formality of recording a speculative demo in the first instance, suggesting that their aspirations of long-term success were fairly realistic, and that BOLLWEEVIL were merely doing their thing for the benefit of local fans, enjoying all the attention while it lasted.

Given that so few copies were pressed in the first place, it's understandable that hardly any BOLLWEEVIL singles have come out of the woodwork in recent years, and this two-tracker still remains unfamiliar to the majority of collectors at the present time. Even so, I reckon that keen-eyed NWOBHM aficionados would certainly be extremely unlikely to pass it by if they were lucky enough to come across a copy on their travels, especially since most were housed within a metal-as-you-like monochrome sleeve depicting a severed, shrunken, human head! Musically speaking, this is top-notch stuff (although the production leaves a lot to be desired), with "Rock Solid" careering along at a rip-roaring pace in a distinctly HIGH TREASON mode, the chorus affirming the band's unbridled enthusiasm for, er, 'rock', as evidenced by the following extract:
'I wanna rock solid now, where the music takes me
I wanna rock, till the rhythm breaks me.'
My sentiments exactly, sir. The contrasting B-side ("Sands Of Time"), meanwhile, is a slightly more sedate composition which captures the musicians in a contemplative mood, bringing to mind CYNIC's excellent »Suicide« single. Clearly, there was more than one string to BOLLWEEVIL's bow, and, on the basis of this superb, down-to-earth debut, they should have had a pretty healthy future ahead of them. As it turned out, though, the lads went to ground within a fairly short space of time, possibly having concluded that there was just too much like-minded competition with which to contend. In fact, this bunch had a lot to offer the world, so it's a great pity that they didn't stick it out a bit longer and make their presence known, as they're another of those outfits (like the wondrous REINCARNATE) who might well have benefitted from a handy piece of METALLICA patronage in years to come. In short, you *need* this excellent 7" in your collection if you call yourself a big NWOBHM fan, although, yet again, it's likely to be a wallet-emptier, as there were only a few hundred examples manufactured in the first instance. Start checking out those second-hand record shops now!

7" Singles
»Rock Solid« Ellie Jay 1981

BOMBAY

Jon Willoughby (v,g)
Jim (b)
Steve Rodford (k,d)

Issued on the same label (well, subsidiary) as GOGMAGOG's »I Will Be There« EP, BOMBAY's sole »Breaking The Rules« single doesn't quite compare in terms of collectability (or even musical merit), which means that it hardly constitutes an essential purchase for the average NWOBHM fan. Formed as something of a one-off project by skin-beater (and part-time keyboard player) Steve Rodford and vocalist (and part-time guitarist) Jon Willoughby in the early part of 1984 (the pair having worked together in one of the later incarnations of THE SWEET in the preceding year or two), the duo wasted little time before making their intentions known to the world. Aided and abetted by the mysterious 'Jim' on bass duties (most likely to have been Jim Rodford, one of John Verity's cohorts from his PHOENIX days, and apparently Steve's old man), the unit recorded "Breaking The Rules" and "Save Me" in October of that year, after which the resultant 7" emerged on the Food For Thought label a few months later. Narrowly avoiding the 'out and out AOR' label which would have excluded BOMBAY from this book altogether, the music is, nevertheless, extraordinarily lightweight, suggesting facile comparisons with ensembles such as TUXEDO, IDLE FLOWERS and BLAZER BLAZER. Still, with melodic rock beginning to gain a fairly secure foothold in the British market, the musicians must have been cautiously optimistic of a warm reception from the national music press.

The two-tracker, however, failed to strike the right chord with either the fans or the media, and was utterly savaged in 'Kerrang', with the reviewer memorably commenting on its 'vomit-inducing effect', which can't exactly have made the record sound particularly appealing to the rock community of the day. Hardly surprisingly, sales were modest, to say the least, although the characters behind the project put on a brave face and assured everyone that they would soon conquer the world. It transpired, incidentally, that Rodford and Willoughby may have had rather more help in the recording process than they originally claimed, and that BOMBAY wasn't actually a self-contained unit after all. In fact, it appears that they utilised the services of several more session musicians (including guitarist Dave Kilminster, one of Steve Rodford's old colleagues from DUCHESS, where he had enjoyed a fleeting stint at the drumstool) than were credited on their debut record's sleeve. Strange, that. Anyway, the BOMBAY name itself seems to have been quite short-lived, although they were supposedly commissioned to record a full album for the Music For Nations concern (the parent company of Food For Thought) to follow up their first single. By this stage, Jon Willoughby was now calling himself Jon Neil (for reasons which were never made clear), and the duo subsequently reinvented themselves as RIO, perhaps trying to distance themselves from the critical mauling that BOMBAY had received.

The lads began writing a generous selection of new material with little delay (they also managed to carry on working as an integral part of the JOHN VERITY backing ensemble at the same time), and soon set about recording their latest opus with the help of session faces (although none were officially credited this time) once again. Even more blatantly commercial than BOMBAY (so much so that they're not actually worth including in this volume), RIO proceeded to issue two unspectacular albums (1985's »Borderland« and the tackily-presented »Sex Crimes« from a year later) plus a couple of mediocre singles for their label before (after a handful of showcase gigs in their native Hertfordshire) drifting back into obscurity. Interestingly, the inseparable duo of Willoughby (yes, he had gone back to his original identity) and Rodford later teamed up again in the little-known TINA EGAN BAND in the early 90's (which appears to have been a relatively short-lived venture) as well as helping out former TEN YEARS AFTER stalwart Leo Lyons with some of the latter's solo material. The BOMBAY two-tracker, incidentally, was issued in an unusually colourful and professionally-drawn picture sleeve, and, although it's seldom offered for sale these days, you'd be unwise to pay more than a few quid for it.

7" Singles
»Breaking The Rules« Food For Thought 1984

BOULEVARD

Geoff Ford (v)
Dave Fudge (g)
Phil Evans (b)
Steve Byrne (d)

Formed at the height of the NWOBHM explosion from the ashes of various small-time local hopefuls, Avon's BOULEVARD (not to be confused with the Canadian AOR bunch) first came into existence as a four-piece outfit in the summer of 1980. After barely six months together (most of which was spent rehearsing and taking a few tentative steps in the live environment), the quartet laid down their debut demo at the famous Loco Studios in South Wales, the tape featuring "Dawn Raid", "Take It Or Leave It", "Somebody Like You" (a relatively obscure TRIGGER cover) and "Boulevard Nights". The four-tracker immediately drew the attention of such publications as Howard Johnson's 'Phoenix' fanzine, among others, where the emergent group were praised for their fairly original approach to heavy rock, which supposedly included a variety of North American influences such as STYX, REO SPEEDWAGON and SAGA. 'Phoenix' were clearly quite smitten with these youngsters, and the lads subsequently benefitted from an extremely generous two-page feature, where the protagonists were grilled on various aspects of their music and general philosophy. On the prospects of gaining a record deal, frontman Geoff Ford was keen to bring everyone up to date: *'Everything's going quite well on the demo and gig front. We've had an offer from Neat Records but we didn't go with them because we feel we'd be thrown in with the basic Neat sound which we didn't want. We're looking for a deal which suits us.'* (Ref: Phoenix, Issue 3, 1981). There's confidence for you.

BOULEVARD continued to tour reasonably successfully, and their first demo turned out to be quite a well-received affair in general, with "Take It Or Leave It" even making an impact on the 'Sounds' Heavy Metal Charts, a pretty reliable indicator of a rock/metal act's popularity in the dark days before 'Kerrang'. As their vocalist revealed in the aforementioned interview, the group had a refreshingly realistic attitude to their chances of getting a big break: *'We'll play anywhere in order to get noticed and to show off our music to the people. I mean, with a demo you can only appeal to a certain number of business people, not to the average punter. We would have loved to have played at the Manchester HM festival at UMIST. We think we go about our job in a professional way.'* (Ref: *ibid.*) Even so, the big deal (or the small deal, for that matter) repeatedly failed to materialise, and so the outfit eventually decided to release a private single (the picture sleeve featuring a photo of the band looking a right bunch of miserable gits) comprising "Dawn Raid" and the highly-regarded "Take It Or Leave It", the recordings both being taken directly from their original demo cassette. At around this time, the group decided to augment their sound by recruiting Jon Rodd, a keyboard player, with the express intention of moving towards a yet more melodic style (he's credited and pictured on the 7", but didn't actually play on it), so there was something of an anomaly in releasing material which may even have been slightly unrepresentative by this juncture.

Well, I'll make no bones about it, I just don't like the BOULEVARD two-tracker much at all, sorry. I realise that a lot of people seem to enjoy it (for reasons unbeknownst to myself), but the lazy, monotonous vocals just ruin the otherwise decent guitar work, especially on the A-side, and the attempted semi-ballad on the reverse is just awful. Furthermore, the earlier comparisons with STYX or REO SPEEDWAGON seem to be way off the mark, so I've no idea how BOULEVARD's music came to be tarred with the same brush. With a decent vocalist and a souped-up rhythm section, I suppose they might almost have been up there with bands such as SHYWOLF or HELLANBACH, but I'm not remotely surprised that this bunch never made it in the long run. They appear to have persevered for around a year after their single was released, trying out an alternate keyboard player (a chap called Rob Wilsher) in the process, but it looks as though a continued lack of label interest eventually killed off their chances in the long term. Drummer Steve Byrne (quite a well-travelled musician) and the aforementioned Rob Wilsher managed to inveigle their way into the ranks of Welsh act MULTI-STORY shortly thereafter, a band who issued of a couple of LP's and singles on the FM label, but who ultimately failed to achieve a great deal of critical success either.

7" Singles
»Dawn Raid« SRT 1981

Compilation Appearances
"Dawn Raid" on »NWOBHM Vol.8« Bootleg CD 1996

BRIAR

Kevin Griffiths (v,b)
Dave Fletcher (g)
Darren Underwood (g)
Dean Cook (d)

Birmingham's likeable BRIAR were, as with EXCALIBUR and VIRTUE, yet another of those ridiculously precocious bunches of musicians who initially began playing while still at school, and who were fortunate enough to get a few breaks at an early stage. Having started out in around 1981, they recorded their first demo a year or so later, and were one of a handful of Midlands acts (other notable inclusions being TROUBLE and DIAMOND HEAD) who soon found themselves being played in session on daytime Radio One, courtesy of Peter Powell, one of the BBC's more eclectic broadcasters. In due course (after numerous local gigs with the likes of CRYER), a single was recorded for the ever-popular Happy Face label, and this came in the shape of 1983's »Rainbow (To The Skies)« 7" (B-side "Crying In The Rain"), a remarkably capable debut for such a young outfit. Having said that, the catchy and energetic A-side (with distinct similarities to early DEF LEPPARD and EXCALIBUR) was considerably more listenable than the fairly pedestrian semi-ballad on the reverse. Very few copies of the single appear to have been issued in a picture sleeve (showing a band photo, their logo and, would you believe, a monochrome rainbow), and the tiny number of examples which have surfaced in recent years have been known to fetch reasonably high prices.

It came as little surprise when, a year or so later, BRIAR were picked up by that bastion of Midlands rock talent, Heavy Metal Records, and the quartet (who had impressed the label with a new demo containing such numbers as "Freedom" and "Send Me A Cure") were soon ensconced in a local studio for the purposes of recording a full-length effort. The four scamps finally emerged with their appositely-titled »Too Young« long-player, a capable enough set which hit the shops in the second half of 1985. The LP revealed the group to be moving towards a more chart-friendly style on the majority of the tracks featured (the likes of "Phone Me" and "Two Hearts" are just a bit too commercial for their own good), although there were still a few numbers (notably "Push It To The Limit", "A Day In A Life" and "Prisoner") which served to remind everyone that the combo could shift into a more powerful mode (with seemingly little effort) whenever the fancy took them. A promotional single, coupling "One More Chance" and "Feelings", was also pressed to coincide with the album's appearance in the shops, although most (if not all) copies were given free with the LP itself, and this 7" doesn't appear to have been commercially issued in its own right. A fair bit of touring helped to promote the full-length release, both in the shape of headlining gigs and some support dates with the TYGERS OF PAN TANG, and BRIAR seemed to be heading in the right direction at this stage.

Unfortunately, fate soon dealt them a poor hand, and it came in the form of the much-ridiculed Jonathan King, who (tragically) hadn't yet given up on his dreams of rock-based world domination after the laughable failure of his GOGMAGOG vision. The lads had been beavering away quite happily during 1986, and were busily recording material for their second album, tentatively entitled »Back To The Wild Days«, when King graciously deigned to take them under his wing and transform BRIAR into global superstars. As you do. So, the follow-up was put on hold while the bewildered youngsters were gradually remoulded into what basically amounted to a glorified version of the BAY CITY ROLLERS. By early 1987, the fearsome transfiguration

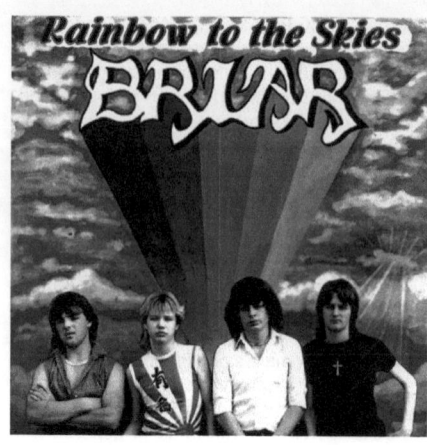

was complete, and the first glimpse of the all-new BRIAR came with the release (on the modest PRT pressing service) of a single featuring "Edge Of A Broken Heart", an obscure BON JOVI B-side (setting a precedent for an unhealthy dependency upon cover versions), as its main focus of attention. Surprisingly, this chart-friendly effort got the thumbs-up from someone or other, and so, following a brief jaunt with STRYPER, a full-scale deal with UK Records (licensed by Columbia in the States) came about as a result. An album was in the pipeline from an early stage, but another fluffy single was trundled out first (presumably in an attempt to garner some airplay), based around an utterly laughable version of SISTER SLEDGE's nauseatingly twee "Frankie" shocker. For the first time, the public became worried about BRIAR, and with good reason.

The quartet's second long-player (although it was, at least in the States, promoted as their debut, with some creative press releases announcing that, miraculously enough, their average age was still twenty) finally appeared in the early months of 1988, although it turned out to be a bit of an abomination. »Crown Of Thorns« featured a mere four BRIAR originals, the remaining compositions being a mixture of chart-oriented piffle (good old "Frankie" and the pitiful "La Bamba", most famously recorded by RITCHIE VALENS), marginally more rocking covers (THIN LIZZY's "The Boys Are Back In Town" and the Russ Ballard-penned "Just Another Day (In The Life Of A Fool)", also covered by CHEVY and VERITY) plus some obscure numbers composed by various mainstream songwriters ("One Foot Back In Your Door" and the obligatory ballad "Empty Words"). All in all, it was an utterly horrendous album, and even the group's self-penned compositions (with the exception of the semi-reasonable title track), such as "Back And Wild" and "Everyone's Going Crazy", had suffered a serious dip in quality. Things were summed up pretty succinctly by the outro, a two-second piece with the descriptive title of "Fart". With the outfit rapidly becoming a laughing stock in Britain, coupled with their failure to crack the American market in any shape or form, it came as no surprise that the hapless BRIAR were released from contract with little or no delay.

Inexplicably, though, they remained loyal to their musical guru Jonathan King, who somehow wangled a one-off deal with the mighty A&M label, which culminated in the release of another single, featuring the pop-rock of the ludicrously-titled "One Monkey Don't Stop No Show" (another BRIAR non-original) as well as the King-penned "It's Illegal, It's Immoral, It's Unhealthy But It's Fun", which had already died a death on the GOGMAGOG EP and was to receive exactly the same response here. The single was an unmitigated disaster, even by BRIAR's standards, and there was never any talk of further releases on A&M. It looked as though it could be the final nail in their coffin, but the band managed to soldier on, although it proved to be the end of an era in one important respect. Dave Fletcher had grown weary of the music business after the failure of »Crown Of Thorns« and its follow-up single, and elected to part company with his long-time friends in 1989. Nevertheless, the remaining members plugged away as a three-piece, issuing (in between fairly long periods of virtual inactivity) a further couple of unremarkable singles in more of a rockier DEF LEPPARD style (»Gimme All You Got« and »All She Wants«) on their own Shotgun Charlie label, although the almost-forgotten (not to mention besmirched) name of BRIAR was finally laid to rest in 1993 or thereabouts. The multi-talented Dean Cook, however, continues to record for the Shotgun Charlie label in the form of a more introspective solo project entitled TEN (not to be confused with a prominent and identically-named AOR outfit), with several releases having appeared in cassette and CD formats over the past few years.

LP's
»**Too Young**« Heavy Metal 1985
[Some copies with poster and free single featuring "One More Chance" and "Feelings"]
»**Crown Of Thorns**« UK Records 1988
[UK issue]
»**Crown Of Thorns**« Columbia 1988
[US issue with different cover artwork]

12" EP's
»**Edge Of A Broken Heart**« PRT 1987
[Includes two mixes of A-side]
»**Frankie**« UK Records 1987
»**One Monkey Don't Stop No Show**« A&M 1988
[All three tracks non-LP]

7" Singles
»**Rainbow (To The Skies)**« Happy Face Records 1983
[Both tracks non-LP]
»**One More Chance**« FM Records 1985
[Free with some copies of »Too Young« album, B-side "Feelings" non-LP]
»**Edge Of A Broken Heart**« PRT 1987
[Both tracks non-LP]
»**Frankie**« UK Records 1987
»**One Monkey Don't Stop No Show**« A&M 1988
[Both tracks non-LP]
»**Gimme All You Got**« Shotgun Charlie Records 1989
[Both tracks non-LP]
»**All She Wants**« Shotgun Charlie Records 1992
[Both tracks non-LP]

Shaped Picture Discs
»**Edge Of A Broken Heart**« PRT 1987

Promotional Releases
»**Frankie**« Columbia 1988
[US radio station promo 7"]

BRONZ

Chris Goulstone (v,g)
Simon Thomas (b)
Chris Giles (d)

After a couple of false starts with unsuccessful, amateur-hour outfits in the West Country, the founder members of Wiltshire's melodic metallers BRONZ finally got together at around the turn of the decade. In the first instance, the newly-formed ensemble operated quite happily as a three-piece, although it's fair to say that the only permanent fixture was talented guitarist Chris Goulstone (who originally acted as vocalist), who waded through several accomplices while searching for the ideal line-up. The trio's early exploits (where Goulstone was assisted by bassist Simon Thomas and drummer Chris Giles, the latter having ousted a certain Andy Wells, who later became involved with MEATLOAF's touring activities) centred mainly around the obligatory batch of small-time gigs on the regional club/free festival circuit, where BRONZ shared a stage with emerging NWOBHM hopefuls such as JAGUAR (plus such varied acts as the PINK FAIRIES and the HUMAN LEAGUE) every now and again. As they grew ever more confident of their own abilities, however, the group began venturing slightly further afield, and were soon able to make the pilgrimage to the nation's capital for some well-attended shows with the likes of ANGEL WITCH. At some point in 1981, the chaps decided to expand to a quartet via the recruitment of full-time frontman Paul Webb, allowing Chris Goulstone to concentrate on guitar (he also began tinkering with keyboards in due course), the resulting formation constituting a somewhat more favourable arrangement. It was then back to the grind in the live environment, the musicians penning a continually-expanding repertoire of original numbers as they went along.

Nothing much happened in the short term, admittedly (having said that, the lads were now garnering regular support slots at venues such as the Marquee and Music Machine), but BRONZ seemed happy enough to wait for the right offer to come along. Even so, the protagonists appear to have lost their way somewhat during 1982, their musical activities becoming more and more sporadic as time passed. In the event, they retreated from the spotlight for a while, whereupon the central characters decided to regroup with a new line-up. Joining Chris and Paul (who now also assumed bass duties) were second guitarist Shaun Kirkpatrick and former LAUTREC drummer Clive Deamer, and BRONZ Mk.II duly emerged with a greater sense of conviction. After re-establishing themselves on the scene towards the end of 1982, the foursome finally made a productive trip to the studio early the following year, laying down a representative demo which showcased a handful of original numbers including stand-out effort "Send Down An Angel", a track which was soon getting a few A&R representatives a bit hot under the proverbial collar. Furthermore, glowing live reviews revealed that the musicians were now realising their full potential (gigs with old stagers such as MAGNUM had helped to hone their stage presence), so it was plain for all to see that BRONZ had become ripe for picking. Before long, a small-scale bidding war was in full swing, and the lucky ensemble ultimately landed a deal with the, er, Bronze concern, which was slightly peculiar, but there you go. Still, it certainly wasn't merely a stunt which involved a publicity-conscious record company signing (manufacturing?) an almost identically-named act (they had, oddly enough, rejected BRONZ twice in their early days), but it may have felt somewhat contrived to the punters.

With Bronze now sensing that they had struck gold (sorry), an album was soon in the pipeline (the lads were, nevertheless, compelled to draft in new sticksman Carl Matthews after Clive Deamer went off to work with HAWKWIND), although their sponsors tactfully hinted that recruiting a dedicated frontman might be beneficial in the long term, whereupon former MOBY DICK singer Max Bacon was lured away from a comparatively cushy position in NIGHTWING to join in the fun. After being enrolled towards the end of 1983, Bacon swiftly found himself making his live debut when the lads hitched a ride on HAWKWIND's lengthy UK tour, and the combo proceeded to delight the crowds at some well-attended gigs. With these obligations honoured, BRONZ finally got around to recording their debut album at long last, and the resultant LP found its way into the shops within a remarkably short space of time. The »Taken By Storm« set was a capable enough stab at semi-commercial rock/metal, the outfit generating some highly polished compositions with undeniable similarities to the likes of WILDFIRE (Mausoleum version), LIONHEART and GRAND PRIX. Max Bacon's vocal contribution was as commanding as ever, and such tuneful inclusions as "Heat Of The Night", "Nightrunner" and "Sweet Lady" were all listenable enough, even if things became slightly too radio-friendly at times, the musicians having been encouraged to write in a more accessible style than they might have preferred, in the main. Moreover, the slick, over-the-top production wasn't to the band's taste at all, rendering one or two perfectly respectable songs as little more than functional melodic interludes, something which no doubt surprised all the metalheads who had already witnessed the power of a BRONZ live show. Overall, it's fair to suggest that there were more than a few parallels with the LIONHEART situation.

The debut long-player failed to set too many pulses racing in the group's homeland (even after BRONZ were fortunate enough to win a high-profile slot on the BBC's prestigious 'In Concert' radio programme), although it soon became perfectly clear that those ambitious sponsors had already pinned most of their hopes on promoting their latest discovery as a mainstream concern in order to crack the lucrative American market. Indeed, a rather different LP appeared in the States (repackaged with new sleeve artwork, alternate track order, remixes, you name it), although their unflattering reworking of NEW ENGLAND's "Don't Ever Wanna Lose Ya" probably did more harm than good in the circumstances. Still, Britain hadn't quite been written off just yet, so a tie-in single based around the lightweight "Send Down An Angel" was trundled out (in both 7" and 12" formats) to see if anyone at home was remotely interested in the fortunes of BRONZ, and the overall sales figures were passable (helped along by occasional airplay on Radio One), if not exactly staggering. After that, Bronze pretty much concentrated on turning their new protégés into chartbusting Stateside rockers (following in the well-worn footsteps of DEF LEPPARD), and went out of their way to promote BRONZ as the next big thing, allowing an album cut ("Loneliness Is Mine") to be included on the »British Steel« showcase sampler of the nation's latest talent. The remixed version of "Send Down An Angel" duly emerged as a single, primarily for the benefit of the American market (there was even a proper promo video, aired by MTV on a number of occasions), although it was also reissued in the UK (in an alternate cover), all of which appears to have been a fruitless exercise. By all accounts, things just weren't going according to plan, and the situation rapidly deteriorated for both outfit and label, who were clearly pulling in opposite directions.

Following a final round of last-ditch gigging (including an overly-ambitious, three month trawl around most of North America with high-profile touring partners such as RATT) in a misguided attempt to bulldoze their way into the hearts of the listening public, both Chris Goulstone and Carl Matthews elected to leave (amidst internal friction and label hassles), and the unsettled duo had packed their bags by the beginning of 1985. After that, things would never be the same again, and the whole project was soon crumbling in a most embarrassing manner. Before long, BRONZ had lost the services of virtually all of their key members, and the last straw seemed to be the much-anticipated departure of Max Bacon a few months later. Despite the fact that BRONZ now seemed to exist in name only, their management/label remained stoically determined to keep the project afloat (rumour has it that Bronze Records even turned down the chance to sign METALLICA back then, such was their devotion to the cause), and made valiant (not to mention desperate) attempts to rebuild the foundering act around an increasingly-unstable nucleus of musicians. It was all very messy, although Bronze (who were now practically in the process of calling in the liquidators) made repeated assertions that a second LP would definitely be recorded before the year was out, something which seems to have been a case of nothing more than wishful thinking. During this period of musical inactivity, the group would become virtually unrecognisable, as a procession of stand-ins, sundry guests and temporary members arrived and left with truly bewildering haste, with a few of the more prominent BRONZ associates being vocalists Ian Baker (later of BLUEPRINT, JAGGED EDGE and JOKERS WILD) and Paul Quigley (HELL'S BELLES), renowned guitarist Scott Gorham (of THIN LIZZY fame), bassists Lee Reddings (LYADRIVE) and Charlie McCracken (FASTWAY), plus seasoned drummers Clive Edwards and Steve Hopgood. Bit on the confusing side, that.

In the end, the once-proud name of BRONZ became indelibly tarnished by the fact that a consistent line-up never seemed to be retained for more than five minutes, and even their resolute sponsors duly concluded that enough was enough, after which the whole sorry episode was quietly laid to rest, not that too many hearts were broken in the process. In the immediate aftermath of the BRONZ collapse, only Max Bacon remained in the limelight as far as the rock scene was concerned, playing a pivotal role in the fortunes of the GTR and PHENOMENA ventures in later years, as well as undertaking some lighthearted appearances with his occasional knockabout club act MAX AND THE PROFESSIONALS. More recently, he has been carving out a successful solo career (his name has graced various respected AOR samplers and melodic rock compilations of late), and now appears to be setting the stage for some widely-anticipated releases of his own in the not-too-distant future. Chris Goulstone, meanwhile, having established a critically-ignored concern called HEADMASTER (where he again worked with Clive Deamer) after leaving BRONZ behind, ended up becoming a respected composer of music for television and film, having been responsible for countless CD's over the years, his recent credits including some high-profile collaborations with the WCW wrestling organisation. Intriguingly, however, three of the protagonists (Goulstone, Kirkpatrick and Matthews) have now reunited, spurred on by the NWOBHM revival and fond memories of their 80's exploits, and are currently making preparations for one or two low-key reunion gigs at their old haunts, as well as compiling a celebratory CD of unissued archive material with the very apt title of »Unfinished Business«. Once again, watch this space...

95

LP's

»Taken By Storm« Bronze 1984
[UK issue, cassette format has extra track]
»Taken By Storm« Bronze 1984
[Remixed US issue with different sleeve]
»Taken By Storm« Victor 1984
[Japanese issue]

12" EP's

»Send Down An Angel« Bronze 1984
[Original issue, "Stranded" non-LP]
»Send Down An Angel« Bronze 1984
[Second issue with 'USA mix' in different sleeve]

12" Singles

»Send Down An Angel« Bronze 1984
[US release, B-side "Nightrunner"]

7" Singles

»Send Down An Angel« Bronze 1984
[Original issue, B-side "Tiger"]
»Send Down An Angel« Bronze 1984
[Second issue with 'USA mix' in different sleeve, B-side "The Cold Truth"]

Promotional Releases

»Taken By Storm« Bronze 1984
[Split promo 7" flexi, also features MOTÖRHEAD]
»Send Down An Angel« Bronze 1984
[DJ promo 7" with two versions]
»Stranded« Bronze 1984
[US radio station promo 12"]

Compilation Appearances

"Loneliness Is Mine" on »British Steel« LP M Port Records 1984/Steel Trax 1986
"Send Down An Angel" on »The Bronze Story« Do-CD Essential 2000

BROOKLYN

Danny Willson (v,g)
Barry Coughlin (g)
Rick Willson (b)
Gordon Taylor (d)

Midlands-based BROOKLYN were one of Rondelet's more inexplicable signings, since they offered little or no potential crossover appeal to the punk market, something which the label generally seemed to bear in mind when looking for talent. In contrast to WITCHFYNDE, HERITAGE and GASKIN (the only other metal acts who went with Rondelet), the BROOKLYN lads delivered an extremely lightweight (almost poppy) brand of rock, more closely related to the likes of MAYDAY, ORION and VALHALLA (Neat version) than anything fundamentally heavier. Indeed, their first offering for the label came in the shape of an entirely unremarkable single, the two-tracker coupling the quirky "I Wanna Be A Detective" with the easy-going "Two Wheels". Despite appearing at the very peak of NWOBHM activity in 1980, it was hardly representative of the movement at all, and there was little reason to anticipate that Rondelet would persevere with this act. Nevertheless, a full LP was indeed commissioned, and emerged the following year in an extremely garish orange sleeve. »You Never Know What You'll Find« was a fairly uninspiring selection of rockers with a distinct 70's influence (the laid-back type of material also churned out by URCHIN and TRADER, for example), none of which leave much of an impression. The label attempted to promote the release with a further single, the atrocious »Hollywood« (b/w "Late Again"), although it once again failed to make an impression among the discerning rock fans of the day.

Whether or not we would ever have been subjected to further BROOKLYN vinyl is open to debate, as their label was to collapse under the weight of inescapable financial pressure the following year, leaving the aforementioned clutch of metal outfits to fend for themselves. In the main, they didn't fare too well on their own, and only WITCHFYNDE lasted the distance, consigning BROOKLYN (who had, along the way, developed a far smaller following than either HERITAGE or GASKIN, who also found it hard to survive in the big bad world) to the status of long-lost NWOBHM also-rans for all eternity. Needless to say, when British Steel acquired the rights to the Rondelet back catalogue a few years ago, they astutely concluded that there would be little, if any, demand for a CD reissue of BROOKLYN's one and only long-player.

LP's

»You Never Know What You'll Find« Rondelet 1981

7" Singles

»I Wanna Be A Detective« Rondelet 1980
»Hollywood« Rondelet 1981

BRUNEL

Line-up unknown

Another real obscurity, believed to have been pressed in truly minute quantities, is the 1982 single from Berkshire's BRUNEL (as in Isembard Kingdom Brunel, a man primarily famous for having a preposterously silly name, but also for designing the odd bridge and tunnel). As with bands such as MEANSTREAK and TUXEDO, this bunch (who were regularly to be found playing live in London at the start of the decade) seem to have suffered from a severe case of Americanitis, with both compositions being highly melodic pieces of keyboard-filled rock with rather basic arrangements, the type of material that was, on the whole, much better suited to transatlantic audiences of the day (with sincere apologies to all those astute Yanks who *did* get into the weightier stuff at the time). Nevertheless, "Astral Lady" is a very catchy (albeit immensely repetitive) little ditty with slightly phased vocals that you'll be humming for the rest of the day after hearing it just once, while "Southside Susie" is slightly closer to NWOBHM territory, bringing to mind BLACK ROSE or TOKYO BLADE at their most commercial. Not a bad effort at all (it was, incidentally, produced by PROCOL HARUM's Matthew Fisher, who also handled the PALI GAP single, for example), but I reckon you could almost certainly uncover a similar standard of material on any number of (considerably less expensive) AOR albums. Again, no picture sleeve, but the label on one side carries the band's attractive logo, complete with sword and chains, so they presumably regarded themselves as a genuine metal proposition!

7" Singles
»Astral Lady« I.K.B. Records 1982

BUFFALO

Paul Starkie (v)
Mick Priestley (g)
Rick Brent (rg)
Andy 'Tommy' Thompson (b)
Dave 'Duggie' Dugdale (d)

Sharing their name with a heavy Australian band who issued some highly-regarded albums in the early 70's, Lancashire's BUFFALO came into existence towards the end of the same decade after the demise of guitarist Mick Priestley's previous small-time outfit, TANGLEFOOT. Operating as a five-piece in the first instance, the lads got their act together pretty quickly, and laid down their inaugural demo (featuring a batch of original numbers such as "Broken Hill", "Pictures Of Dorian Grey" and "Rock Circus") as far back as 1978, a capable statement of intent which was soon attracting the attention of various influential parties in the music business. Among those who rapidly identified a great deal of potential in BUFFALO's repertoire was a part-time journalist called Nigel Burnham, an individual who eventually decided to assemble the legendary »New Electric Warriors« sampler (for my money, still just about the best introduction to the obscure end of the genre) in order to showcase some of the nation's emerging talent. It was this compilation album (released by Logo in the autumn of 1980), therefore, which was to give BUFFALO (who, by this stage, had already recruited new vocalist John Ralphs and guitarist Paul Kitchen, the latter replacing Rick Brent) their first significant exposure.

The outfit's solid contribution, "Battle Torn Heroes", was a fairly primitive, yet highly energetic number (some of their other compositions from this period included "Making It Back To You", "Long Gone" and "Lady Jane") in the style of SLEDGEHAMMER, BATTLEAXE or future labelmates DRAGSTER, but it ultimately failed to shine in the company of some rather more innovative acts such as DAWNWATCHER and OXYM. Nevertheless, BUFFALO (having recently triumphed in a national *'Battle Of The Bands'* competition and taken part in the *'New Electric Warriors Tour'*, where Priestley and Ralphs were temporarily augmented by Richard Boyd on guitar, Jez Brett on bass and Chris Thomson on drums) were subsequently picked up by the emergent Heavy Metal Records, and their "Battle Torn Heroes" number was duly recycled as part of a double A-sided single (coupled with the highly-similar "Women Of The Night") the following year. By this juncture, however, the main duo of John Ralphs and Mick Priestley had recruited yet another new set of accomplices in the form of Mike Bailey (g), Tom Reid (b) and Pete West (d), which must surely have given the public some cause for concern, given that there seemed to be a completely different line-up every few months. Nevertheless, the debut two-tracker was generally well-received, and the popular outfit, having already been allocated some high-profile support slots with the likes of MOTÖRHEAD and GILLAN, further established themselves as a force to be reckoned with by laying down the new track "Cold As Night" for the first »Heavy Metal Heroes« compilation.

Enjoying their new-found public approval (making an impact in the Heavy Metal Charts in prominent music publications such as 'Sounds'),

97

the lads embarked on a series of promotional gigs, including a prestigious one-off show in London with WITCHFINDER GENERAL, the latter making one of their incredibly scarce live appearances. In due course, further support slots with the likes of DEMON and Y&T would come their way, and it wasn't long before the musicians were back in the studio to lay down the tracks for a follow-up release, also scheduled to appear on Heavy Metal. In the event, their second single, featuring "Mean Machine" and the "Highway Star"-soundalike "The Rumour" (a vast improvement on their debut, with a move towards powerful, catchy tracks in the style of early SPARTAN WARRIOR), didn't appear until mid-1982, by which time the latest incarnation of BUFFALO considered the material to be somewhat unrepresentative, having now established yet another revised line-up (they must have been running out of local musicians by then) of Priestley, Bailey (now additionally taking on vocal duties), Gary Short on bass and ex-STREETFIGHTER sticksman Gary Taylor (who, bizarrely, replaced another drummer from the same outfit, Paul Milek, who was involved with BUFFALO only fleetingly). Previous singer John Ralphs had, incidentally, left to join none other than BUDGIE, but he enjoyed a very brief stint in their ranks.

This new, slimline version of BUFFALO (who were soon to be featured in the 'Armed And Ready' section of 'Kerrang') recorded a five track cassette for Heavy Metal, unveiling "In The Flesh", "Take It To The Limit", "Back To The Wall", "Detroit Motor City" and a cover of "Gimme Some Lovin", the old SPENCER DAVIS GROUP chestnut (later covered by RAVEN) from 1966. Although this marked a significant musical progression for the band (who had, all this time, been gigging successfully in their area and beyond), their fickle label rejected the material (one of several questionable decisions made by Heavy Metal over the years), and plans which had already been outlined for a full-length release were rapidly shelved. Refusing to accept this knockback, the lads tried a few other companies, but with much the same result, as Mick Priestley explained at the time: *'We were very pleased with the demo and sent it off to twelve different A&R departments with high hopes. So far we've heard nothing. They haven't even had the decency to return the tape. It seems to me that if you don't mention devil worship and that kind of demonism in your songs, then you can't get anywhere!'* (Ref: Kerrang No.20, July 1982). Understandably, with the luckless combo finding continual rejection increasingly difficult to take, it wasn't long before part one of BUFFALO's history drew to a natural close, the musicians eventually going their separate ways towards the end of 1983. Although most of them drifted away from the scene thereafter, Gary Taylor later found employment in TANK, playing on their self-titled set in 1987, while Mike Bailey joined forces with ex-TROJAN personnel to form SWEET SIN, who released an overlooked eponymous album towards the end of the decade.

That basically seemed to be the end of the road as far as BUFFALO were concerned, although things eventually started to happen again in the early 90's, following a lengthy period of musical inactivity from the various protagonists. A resurrected version of the outfit suddenly emerged out of the blue, boasting a revised (naturally) line-up of the ever-present Mick Priestley, erstwhile OXYM stalwart Tolly Talbot (b), former BAD TO THE BONE frontman Kris Webber (v,g) and the unknown Matt Tymon (d). Once the lads had got back into the swing of things again, a highly impressive hour-long demo was circulated in 1994, showcasing an entirely novel repertoire of self-penned material (much of which was considerably more mature and subtle than the band's straight ahead, NWOBHM-period style) such as the excellent

"Why In Hell", "Water Into Wine", "River Of Life" and "So Long". Over the next few years, the songs evolved naturally (as did the ever-changing line-up, with new bassist Steve Yates and drummer Phil Earnshaw taking a brief turn as the group's rhythm section), and many of them subsequently appeared, in re-recorded form, as part of an official, ten track promotional cassette which did the rounds in 1998. Alongside their earlier material, newer compositions such as "Bad Whiskey", "She's Got No Heart" and "One-sided Story" were also aired in order to gauge the reaction of the selected few who were allocated a copy of the demo.

Following an overwhelmingly favourable response to the tape (and to an even-more-limited promo CD-R), the veteran group (now featuring yet another rhythm section of Roger Cook on bass and Bob Hargreaves on drums) took the brave step of financing their own full-length CD release, a retrospective gathering of tracks spanning BUFFALO's twenty year history, simply entitled »The Best Of Buffalo«. From one of the band's very earliest compositions, the never-before-heard "Plastic Companion", through those prime-era recordings for Heavy Metal, to some of the more contemporary numbers from their 90's demos, the highly-listenable set paints a picture of a talented, diverse ensemble with a definite musical progression running throughout the course of their eventful and lengthy career. Early indications are that the release is selling pretty respectably, and, with the revitalised version of BUFFALO actually playing the clubs once more (now utilising the services of much-travelled vocalist Frank Knight, whose many past credits include the likes of the SAVAGES and CIRCUS) and even going so far as to develop their own comprehensive website in order to promote themselves internationally, there's no telling where it might all lead. Welcome back, lads.

7" Singles
»**Battle Torn Heroes**« Heavy Metal 1981
[Issued with two different label colours: blue copies identify the correct tracks, brown copies have the sides reversed]
»**Mean Machine**« Heavy Metal 1982

CD's
»**Best Of Buffalo**« Buffalo Music 1999
[Compilation of mostly unreleased studio material]

Compilation Appearances
"**Battle Torn Heroes**" on »New Electric Warriors« LP Logo 1980/CD British Steel 1997 + »N.W.O.B.H.M.« LP/CD Heavy Metal 1991 + »Heavy Metal Records Singles Collection Vol.1« CD British Steel 1996
"**Cold As Night**" on »Heavy Metal Heroes« LP Heavy Metal 1981 *[Issued in two different sleeves]* + »Heavy Metal Heroes Vol.I&II« CD British Steel 1996
"**Mean Machine**" on »NWOBHM Vol.1« Bootleg CD 1992
"**Why In Hell**" on »Mind Over Metal« CD Vivid Records 1995
"**Women Of The Night**" on »Heavy Metal Records Singles Collection Vol.1« CD British Steel 1996

BUZZARD

Dave Boswell (v)
Dave Comber (g)
Mick Comber (b)
Paul Norton (k)
Rob Rose (d)

As with London's utterly bonkers HELLRAZER, the English version of BUZZARD (not to be confused with their Belgian counterparts) appear to have something of a skeleton in their closet (although nowhere as embarrassing as SPIDER's), which I believe should be revealed at the earliest possible opportunity. While their »Catch Me Alone« 7" from 1985 has now become fairly well-known amongst collectors, an extremely scarce two-tracker exists from as early as 1981, which, although sorely lacking in writing credits, could well be a precursor to this later effort, so we'll assume for the moment that the same bunch were responsible for both. The group's history hasn't been documented in great detail (I'm pretty sure they were a product of the burgeoning Staffordshire music scene, although they appear to have based themselves in Surrey towards the end of their existence, for some unfathomable reason), and they failed to win a vast amount of press coverage at any stage, but it seems likely that they represented a long-lived concern with numerous line-up changes (there are suggestions that their original bassist resurfaced in the ranks of local eccentrics GOLGOTHA), splits and reformations occurring during the course of their chequered existence.

Returning to the 1981 single, however, the privately-issued »I'm Still Falling« release (B-side "Looking For A Ride") is in slightly more of a laid-back, 70's heavy rock style (the A-side is, to be frank, a bit too close to 10 CC for comfort), although the reverse has a reasonable guitar break, atmospheric keyboards and a decent vocal performance. By the time the »Catch Me Alone« two-tracker was released several years later, however, the group (who may well have featured an almost entirely different line-up by this stage) had evidently added more of a distinct metal edge to their sound, with the guitars now being rather more prominent in the mix. On this occasion, the nominated A-side is a fairly restrained number in the general manner of the first BLEAK HOUSE 7" (with a fairly memorable chorus, admittedly, which drew praise from the 'Kerrang' reviewers), but the real surprise comes with the excellent "Raven Eyed Queen" on the reverse, a full-on metal assault featuring a galloping riff which is, both lyrically and musically, highly analogous to DESOLATION ANGELS material from the same period. Neither single (both quite collectable pieces nowadays) seems to have been issued in a picture sleeve at any stage, but it's worth noting that the labels on each feature the image of a buzzard.

The only other vinyl appearances by this particular outfit (who were seldom, if ever, mentioned in the context of the live environment, although such activities may have been restricted to small-time local events) are to be found on two volumes of an extremely obscure, late 80's compilation entitled »The Academy Record Collection« (released by the Academy label itself, a non-illustrious concern who elected to promote Southern acts pretty exclusively), on which BUZZARD perform GOLDEN EARRING's "Radar Love" (sorry lads, Kent's DEUCE got it down on vinyl first, and MARSEILLE used to cover it live even earlier) and one of their own original compositions, the sensitively-titled "Deep Lust". Neither of these tracks were particularly enthralling examples of songwriting expertise, however, and I would imagine that the group had finally thrown in the proverbial towel and returned home before the end of the decade, but if anyone has additional information on their activities throughout the 80's, do please let us know. Any advance on two singles?

7" Singles
»**I'm Still Falling**« Private 1981
»**Catch Me Alone**« PTO Records 1985

Exclusive Compilation Appearances
"**Radar Love**" on »The Academy Record Collection Vol.1« LP Academy Records 1987
"**Deep Lust**" on »The Academy Record Collection Vol.2« LP Academy Records 1987?

CAGEY BEE

Clyde Ward (v,b)
Ben King (g)
Anthony Marchi (g)
Chris Pope (d)

At first sight, this little-known 7" appears to be yet another one from the 'complete and utter unknowns' file, although the unrenowned name of CAGEY BEE does, in fact, appear to represent an earlier incarnation of Hampshire's MASAI, evidently predating their 1982 album by at least a year (possibly even dating back to the late 70's), and I'm compelled to assume, in the absence of any contradictory evidence, that the two acts were identical in terms of personnel. Well, let's be charitable from the outset and forgive CAGEY BEE the truly awful pun in their name (work it out for yourself), shall we? Their NWOBHM-era »April Fooled« EP, recorded at Arny's Shack Studios in Poole (as with MASAI's own releases and CHINATOWN's 7", among others), is in an unassuming, good-time style (on the whole, indistinguishable from MASAI's more lightweight material), bringing to mind certain accessible acts such as TRADER, URCHIN and the GUNSLINGERS, with a whisky-soaked vocal performance from Clyde Ward which actually sounds uncannily like BRYAN ADAMS at times. The guitars are quite heavy in places, but I'd say that the overall sound is just a bit too restrained and Americanised, for the most part, to satisfy the whims of the average NWOBHM enthusiast. It's a pity, as the song titles, including "Rock Machine", "Talk Of The Devil" and "Into The Night" (the latter pair would be reworked on the MASAI long-player, incidentally), initially looked pretty promising. This EP, apparently issued without a picture sleeve, has turned up in minimal quantities in recent years, but can quite comfortably be left off most wants lists.

7" EP's
»**April Fooled**« Arny's Shack Records 19??
[Different versions of "Talk Of The Devil" and "Into The Night" later appeared on »Good Boys Never Grumble« LP by MASAI]

CAMARGUE

Charlie Bradley (v)
Phil Lovell (g)
Kim Todd (b)
Chris Stubley (k)
Ged Lineham (d)

This is about as rare as it gets! The »Howl Of The Pack« single from CAMARGUE, issued on the small Clubland label (who released some very collectable records in both the metal and punk fields, and were also responsible for pressing DESTROYER's »Evil Place« single) in 1983, is known to exist in truly minimal quantities, with only a handful of copies having come out of the woodwork in recent memory. Most likely to have been from the Home Counties, but not excluding London itself, this particular outfit were a hopelessly obscure act even at the time, and are still utterly unknown to the vast majority of NWOBHM collectors. Their 7" (a minority of which were issued in a picture sleeve showing the musicians and a metal-looking logo) couples "Howl Of The Pack" with "Someone Just

Like You", a pair of contrasting CAMARGUE originals. The former is a mid-paced composition which is very much in the early SEVENTH SON vein, albeit with a few keyboards chucked in for good measure. The ballad on the reverse, however, is an extraordinarily soppy piece not a million miles away from THE BEATLES' "Let It Be" crossed with any one of ELTON JOHN's numerous 'moving' efforts. Don't get me wrong, I enjoy a good, manipulative tearjerker as much as the next person, but they surely belong on albums by HARRY NILSSON or RANDY EDELMAN, not on prime-era NWOBHM singles. In any case, this record truly justifies the description of 'ultra rare' (record dealers take note, anything released on Ebony, Neat, Heavy Metal etc. is unlikely to be genuinely 'rare' by the standards of the genre) and, unless a box of unplayed copies miraculously comes out of the woodwork, most of us are highly unlikely ever to get our grubby mitts on one.

7" Singles
»Howl Of The Pack« Clubland Records 1983

CANIS MAJOR

Jackie Bodimead (v)
Tony Bodimead (v,g)
Mick Groves (g)
Terry Cooper (b)
John Pepe (k)
Gary Wise (d)

Although they may not be the heaviest band you'll ever hear, I think the exclusion of London's CANIS MAJOR from earlier NWOBHM volumes on the basis that their musical direction was allegedly 'pomp rock' (although I know where that particular description originated, and it provides a salutary lesson that you shouldn't believe everything you read) was grossly unfair. Formed in the late 70's by the musical partnership of Tony and Jackie Bodimead (brother and sister), their general manner may have been a bit restrained (and, admittedly, they featured a keyboard player), but they hardly conjure up images of STARCASTLE or TRILLION (to me, at least). Their debut album from 1980 (which seems to have been issued in remarkably limited quantities, leading to various unsubstantiated rumours that it was withdrawn or even unreleased, although the latter is patently untrue), lumbered with the rather fey title of »Butterfly Queen«, features material that runs the gamut of pop, rock and prog throughout its course, and represents an unusually varied selection. Indeed, while the title track and "This Painted Smile" veer perilously close to T'PAU territory at times, "Sorcerer Stays" and "Returning" suggest a more technical, progressive inclination towards the likes of WHITE LIGHTNING or even BLEAK HOUSE. Other featured compositions are, in the main, straightforward heavy fare, the best of these undoubtedly being "Freeway Rock", issued as a single in its own right and backed with the non-LP track "Fire". Coming across as a combination of THIN END OF THE WEDGE, SHE and AVENUE, "Freeway Rock" is, to be perfectly frank, the kind of uncomplicated material that would probably have been better-received by some of the less demanding rock fans of the time.

All things considered, the album wasn't a great success in commercial terms (understandable, since hardly any copies made it into circulation), and few observers were kind enough to offer any particularly sincere words of encouragement. Even so, CANIS MAJOR kept things going for a while, and the outfit recorded a great deal of music (favouring quite a few seven minute epics) during their time together, some of which is still to be found languishing on tape. It's a great pity that a second LP wasn't issued, since tracks such as "Judge Of Light", "General" and the excellent "Modern Mind Falls" all rival their vinyl counterparts in terms of quality. It would appear that the group persevered into the early 80's (supporting such dubious acts as NEW MUSIK and STEELEYE SPAN during the course of their career), eventually trying out another singer (Andy Sears, later of TWELFTH NIGHT), although the move to male-vocal mediocrity seems to have been their undoing. The departed Ms. Bodimead, meanwhile, subsequently had a very busy time of it, lending her talents to outfits such as SHE, GIRLSCHOOL, FUTURE GAMES, HARMONIC 228 and IF ONLY, and I guess she's probably still out there performing in the clubs somewhere. You could certainly do a lot worse than to check out CANIS MAJOR if you like melodic female vocals and/or a slightly progressive and thoughtful aspect to your music.

LP's
»Butterfly Queen« Gem 1980

7" Singles
»Freeway Rock« Gem 1980
[B-side "Fire" non-LP]

CATCH 22 (I)

Gareth Piper (v,g)
Derek Moles (g)
Simon Howard (b)
Andy Kimber (k)
Mark Wiggett (d)

Undoubtedly the weaker of the two UK bands currently known to have adopted the name CATCH 22 at approximately the same time (curiously, there was also a CATCH 23, although I'm not sure if they were metal or not), the obscure Essex version released an extremely lightweight, double A-sided 7" in 1986 which creates a kind of progressive/folky atmosphere vaguely reminiscent of outfits such as DORCAS, LOST FAMOUS or SHERWOOD. While "Freeway To Paradise" is more of a dreary semi-ballad than anything else (it reminds me somewhat of the feeble GOLDSMITH offshoot SMALL IN A BIG WAY, which isn't a recommendation in any sense), the reverse ("Truth Conquers All") is slightly (but only just) more upbeat and rocking,

although the vocal performance is generally pretty atrocious, with frontman Gareth Piper clearly being an honorary graduate of the PARALEX/MITHRANDIR school of 'singing'. I really can't recommend this record to any great extent, so if you ever see a copy (in its unremarkable picture sleeve showing the band's logo, the reverse cover revealing that they weren't exactly the most photogenic ensemble), you might (unless it's extremely inexpensive) do well to save your money for something more worthwhile, like the single released by the Yorkshire band of the same name, for instance (vide infra).

7" Singles
»Freeway To Paradise« Plankton Records 1986

CATCH 22 (II)

Dave Malt (v)
Jeff Ryan (g)
Kevin Hill (b)
Roy Hannam (d)

As stated in the preceding entry, the Yorkshire version of CATCH 22 were a considerably more attractive (in more ways than one) proposition than their uninspiring namesakes from Essex, and their football-related single (calm down, Matthias!) from 1985 fares rather better in the NWOBHM stakes. I'm not in a position to be able to reveal any details about the band's early history, although it would appear that they really were a genuine bunch of hopefuls as opposed to a project merely thrown together for the purposes of recording a one-off 'novelty' single. Anyway, "The Bantam Anthem" was a lighthearted tribute to their local team (Bradford City, who are actually enjoying something of a renaissance these days), and this brain-dead effort basically sounds exactly like every other lyrically-hackneyed, singalong, sport-connected track you've ever heard, with a distinct STATUS QUO/SPIDER influence creeping into its (very basic) arrangement. Things perk up a bit on the reverse, however, as "Who's Sorry Now" turns out to be a considerably heavier and more metallic effort in the general style of DARK STAR or BLACK AXE. This 7" was, incidentally, issued in a fairly colourful (albeit rather unimaginatively-designed) sleeve, which gives little away as to the manner of music contained within.

This record was, unsurprisingly, included on the playlist of one of the contributors to the local 'High Octane' fanzine shortly after its release, although I suspect that more copies were probably shifted to sports fans than metal enthusiasts at the time. As with FRENZY's »Blackburn Rovers« single (these two releases would appear to constitute the complete extent of the NWOBHM/footy crossover, as it seems that punk bands had a near monopoly on the subject matter), very few copies have come onto the market in recent years, which means that there might just be an example or two lurking in the comedy/novelty/sport sections of second-hand shops in the local area. It looks as though this was the group's only claim to fame, however, and they called it a day within a couple of years, although capable vocalist Dave Malt later resurfaced in the slightly more commercial (and long-lived) outfit FOUL PLAY, who released the perfectly respectable »Gimme Some More« two-tracker in 1989, sharing exactly the same production and studio credits as the CATCH 22 release.

7" Singles
»The Bantam Anthem« 22 Records 1985

CEFFYL PREN

Gareth Morlais (v)
Tosh Stuart (g)
Wyn Lewis Jones (b)
Tim Lewis (d)

Another contribution to the rapidly-growing Welsh-language pile is a little-known single (their only confirmed vinyl offering at present, although there are suggestions that there may have been even earlier releases on obliging labels such as Sain) by CEFFYL PREN ('Wooden Horse'), issued by the relatively obscure Anthem concern in 1984. It's an odd one, this, and it has the distinct feel of a short-lived project rather than representing a genuine act, although it's worth noting that the sleeve (optimistically, in my opinion) quotes a fan club address in Glamorgan. Anyway, the unknown outfit (who seem to have used a session musician or two to bring them up to full strength on this occasion) offer the extremely tasteful "Collasant Eu Gwaed" ("Spilling Their Blood") as the A-side, although the musical contents scarcely live up to this sanguinary song title, and the ensemble manage to deliver little more substantial than a mediocre, lightweight effort with some quirky guitars and a few keyboards aimlessly floating about in the background. Very poor, really, and this dreary composition just never really gets going at all.

It looks as though CEFFYL PREN were, on the evidence of this thoroughly average number (in spite of a vague similarity to the considerably more proficient BLACKOUT), much more attuned to the mundane, semi-folky rock style of fellow countrymen DORCAS, LOST FAMOUS and TRYDAN than anything more inspiring or energetic, so I reckon they're never going to be held up as one of the NWOBHM pioneers from the area. Worse is to come on the B-side, however, as their "Roc Ar Y Radio" turns out to be an absolutely dismal cover of "Bedside Radio" by KROKUS (never the best track in the first place), and it's hard to imagine even the most humble of amateur-hour club acts delivering a more laughable performance of the original. All extraordinarily disappointing, especially when you consider that those responsible for this particular release had even gone to the effort of preparing a reasonably professional-looking full-colour gatefold sleeve picturing the protagonists posing with crossbows and tunics (and very scary they look, too) in a scrapyard for effect. A scarcely-sighted rarity, but it's definitely only for completists.

7" Singles
»Collasant Eu Gwaed« Anthem Records 1984

CENTURION

McRae
Yorke

Although this humble two-tracker was very much an unknown entity until a significant quantity of unplayed copies mysteriously came out of the woodwork in the early 90's, CENTURION's »Two Wheels« single from 1982 is a prime example of unsophisticated biker rock in the general style of contemporaries such as SHADER, ROADSTER, EAZIE RYDER or NO FAITH. If you happen to be partial to any of the aforementioned acts, therefore, you're bound to appreciate CENTURION, especially as they possessed one of the more capable vocalists of the sub-genre. The Humberside hopefuls proceed to ram the biker message home on the anthemic "Two Wheels", with authentic sound effects (a revving engine) at the start and finish of the track, whereas the delicately-titled "Bitch" is a bit of a throwback to the rough and ready 60's, suggesting a tangible influence from upstarts such as THE

103

WHO or the SMALL FACES. Although we're certainly treading highly familiar ground in terms of both lyrics and musicianship, this one-off single (never issued in a picture sleeve) remains a sought-after, mid-priced item today. It's quite likely that each area of Britain had its *'own'* biker rock heroes at the time, and CENTURION (not to be confused with the unrelated outfit, who might well have been Scottish, who appeared on Ebony's »The Metal Collection Vol.II« in 1987) no doubt served their county well in the live environment (including a fairly wide-ranging tour in the spring of 1983) before finally riding off into the sunset for the last time.

7" Singles
»Two Wheels« SRT 1982

CHAINSAW (I)

Ian Heys (v,g)
Brian Evans (b)
Mark Biddiscombe (d)

Not to be confused with either the identically-monikered German combo or their Yorkshire namesakes (*vide infra*), the Midlands version of CHAINSAW first got going in around 1979, featuring ex-members of various small-time outfits such as SCORE, MAINLINE and SCHARNHORST. Gigging prolifically around the Birmingham area and beyond from their earliest days, the band soon became a popular live act, and had, by 1980, issued a modest five track demo, the latter featuring "Juggernaut", "Hole In The Road", "City Life", "Police And Politicians" and "April In Somerset". However, with the majority of their original material (with the exception of the reggae-tinged "City Life") tending to come across as rather unsubtle, boogie-inclined biker rock in the primitive manner of SHADER or CENTURION, the record companies predictably failed to take any notice of CHAINSAW whatsoever. Undeterred, the lads set about promoting themselves to the masses, printing their own T-shirts, stickers *etc.* and selling them at gigs, after which they eventually negotiated a single deal with the local Square Records concern (not to be confused with HORSEPOWER's identically-titled London home). Featuring re-recorded versions of their anthemic (but pretty tuneless, all the same) "Police And Politicians" (the anti-establishment subject matter not really lending itself to the knockabout musical style) and the heavier "Hole In The Road", the two-tracker (issued in a sleeve depicting their trademark biker logo) sold well at the time, and is seldom seen these days, so expect to pay a fair bit for a copy.

Featured in the 'Armed And Ready' section of the very first issue of 'Kerrang' in June 1981, the group announced the recent replacement of Brian Evans (he of the extremely impressive axe-shaped bass) with Martin Orum (ex-WITHERED MAN, a bunch briefly signed to Heavy Metal Records), and they were fully expected to return to the fore in the next few months. However, things went ominously quiet after a handful of summer appearances around the Midlands, whereupon Orum and Biddiscombe subsequently defected to Cumbrian rivals BITCHES SIN, leading to widespread speculation that we'd probably seen the last of CHAINSAW. However, after a couple of years of inactivity, a rearranged version of the band popped up entirely unexpectedly in 1984, their all-new line-up consisting of Heys, drummer Rich Carroll and troublesome bassist *'Tribble'* (who was actually none other than the returning Brian Evans after all), and the threesome duly set about the task of recapturing lost ground. With the combo issuing a 12" EP entitled »Massacre« (with a truly abysmal cover, even by the standards of the genre) on the inconsistent Thunderbolt label soon after, it became apparent that the resurrected outfit were now attempting some marginally more adventurous arrangements, although the very weak opener "Devil's Daughter" (vocals provided by Tribble) was certainly nothing to write home about. "Ballad Of Mean Street" and "Rock'n'Roll Gambler", on the other hand, were slightly more capable numbers with a vague similarity to ETHEL THE FROG, while "Accident Victim" represented a semi-decent stab at something melodic, although the saxophone backing was totally uncalled for. In any case, the comeback release failed to spark the public's imagination to any great extent, and the commercial failure of the EP seems to have signalled the end of CHAINSAW, for the time being, at least.

12" EP's
»Massacre« Thunderbolt 1984

7" Singles
»Police And Politicians« Square Records 1981
[Actually pressed on very dark purple vinyl]

Compilation Appearances
"Devil's Daughter" on »A Bolt From The Black« LP Thunderbolt 1984

CHAINSAW (II)

Boddy
Fern
Philpotts

In spite of the observation that all the CHAINSAW releases from the UK are often lumped together in various books and catalogues, it's been an established fact for some time that there were two identically-named bands operating simultaneously in the NWOBHM era. In truth, however, the outfit who issued the »Lonely Without You« and »Long Legged Woman« singles were a strictly amateur-hour pub concern from Yorkshire, who probably had few aspirations of world domination and who were presumably blissfully unaware of the fact that they had namesakes in the Midlands who were doing quite well for themselves. In any case, the Yorkshire version were perfectly content to do their own thing for appreciative, modest crowds at various hostelries throughout their locality, and eventually brought out their first vinyl offering in 1980, basically to give the lads something to sell as a souvenir and to bring in some extra beer money in the process. Both "Lonely Without You" and "On The Highway" are, in terms of both musical content and the rather sparse production, a bit of a throwback to the 70's (bringing to mind acts such as CREAM, CHRIS SPEDDING or the TOM ROBINSON BAND), so it certainly wasn't NWOBHM in its truest sense, but it's still just about heavy enough to appeal to fans of the genre.

After that, it was back to the pub circuit for a few years, and it initially looked as though the highlight of CHAINSAW's career may have come with their first slice of vinyl, although they eventually returned with a second release. In fact, their »Long Legged Woman« 'follow-up' effort (which didn't appear until as late as 1984) was actually a slight improvement, the A-side representing a raunchy, upbeat rocker in the style of TERRAPLANE or TRUX, whereas the flipside ("Midnight Blue") is a rather less hurried, bluesy number, although the inclusion of saxophones on both tracks is, as ever, both a criminal offence and detrimental to the music in general. This ended CHAINSAW's modest programme of vinyl releases, and the lads presumably retired to the clubs, where they no doubt played until the very end, assuming they're not still at it. Neither single was issued in a picture sleeve, and, to be perfectly honest, you can easily live without them, especially since the dealers seem to think they're worth silly money. Still, I'm sure the former members would be in absolute hysterics if they found out that their records had ever changed hands for more than a couple of quid...

7" Singles
»**Lonely Without You**« Pot Belly Records 1980
»**Long Legged Woman**« GMC Records 1984

CHALLENGER

Norman Lee Ward (v)
John Wakefield (g)
Martin Keighley (b)
Peter Whitford (k)
Alistair Wiseman (d)

Not much to work with if you pick up a standard issue of this obscure band's one and only 7" from 1981; no picture cover, no writing/production credits and no studio details whatsoever. If you're fortunate enough to locate one of the handful of promo sleeves, however, then slightly more is revealed. Yorkshire's CHALLENGER (not to be confused with French counterparts from the early 80's) were one of those relatively rare outfits (in fact, there have been repeated suggestions that this was possibly a side-project from members of an act not traditionally associated with the rock/metal scene) from the NWOBHM period who probably drew as much musical influence from combos such as THE DAMNED as they did from the likes of ANGEL WITCH. With prominent, doomy keyboards utilised throughout, coupled with heavy guitars and vaguely theatrical vocals (don't worry, we're not quite talking 'The Rocky Horror Picture Show' here), the sound created on "So Sure Of Yourself" and "Out To Kill" is more akin to groups such as PHYNE THANQUZ and SCORPIO than anyone else from the NWOBHM era, although it's worth noting that there are subtle hints of the likes of HELL in there, too.

Something of an acquired taste, perhaps, but this one-off single certainly won't be at all out of place if you decide to add it to your NWOBHM collection. The extraordinarily rare sleeve is basically a variation of the record's label, and you should, in either case, be looking for a distinctive design depicting a suitably anonymous, hooded figure and a lightning bolt. At this point in time, I'm not sure whether or not this actually *was* a side-project of another act, and I'm not even convinced that all of the participants were using their real names, although the fact that two of the surnames quoted (Wakefield and Keighley) are actually towns in Yorkshire is enough to raise a small amount of suspicion. On the other hand, keyboard player Peter Whitford was certainly a fairly well-known musician (he turned up in regional melodic rock hopefuls FKM a few years later), so I guess we had better record an *'open verdict'* on this oddity for the moment. Anyone got any ideas?

7" Singles
»So Sure Of Yourself« CMC Records 1981

CHARGER

Colin Bell (v,b)
Baz Cummins (g)
Steve Hall (d)

Although CHARGER's outstanding »Desperadoes« 7" has often been described in various dealers' catalogues as dating from as early as 1984 (it's always nice to hike the asking price up as high as possible, isn't it?), we can clear up the mystery of this undated masterpiece without too much effort. First, it was reviewed (in remarkab-

ly favourable terms) in the hallowed pages of 'Kerrang' fairly late in 1987, which suggests that it's highly unlikely to have been pressed any earlier than one year previously. Secondly, a bit of thorough research into the group's history suggests that they probably didn't even exist prior to 1986. CHARGER's mainman Colin Bell was, until

around mid-1985, a full-time member of DARK HEART, after which (following a stint in one of the many British outfits called ROULETTE) he joined the embryonic HOLOSADE. At the time of CHARGER's vinyl debut on Ebony's »The Metal Collection Vol.I« (with the inventively-titled "Rock"), Bell was apparently still involved with HOLOSADE (who also appeared on the same disc with "Cries In The Night"), suggesting that CHARGER (who were, in fact, based in North Yorkshire) was more of a side-project at the time. By mid-1987, however, 'Kerrang' announced his departure from HOLOSADE in order to *'pursue other activities'*, presumably referring to CHARGER. Concentrating on one project at a time was probably a wise move; if nothing else, it would cut down on the amount of time spent travelling between Yorkshire and HOLOSADE's Durham base.

Recorded at Teesbeat Studios in Cleveland, CHARGER's single (featuring "Desperadoes" and "Are You Out There") is a fantastic, albeit belated, contribution to the NWOBHM genre (still well worth including on the basis of musical merit, though), although it's unquestionably a tad more polished and professional than most of the shoddily-presented private releases which had been churned out in the previous part of the decade. The catchy A-side is an incredibly energetic effort, with an immensely charismatic performance from Bell, the trio sounding like a souped-up CHARIOT (with more raunchy, powerful vocals) or a variation on RICOCHET's "Off The Rails". The flipside is a bit closer to traditional rock territory, however, and the singalong lyrics, suggesting that the lads are headlining in front of several thousand devoted fans in a large stadium, are somewhat ironic, considering that they were probably far more accustomed to playing for the benefit of three punters and a sleeping dog in a dingy Yorkshire pub. In spite of its relatively tardy arrival on the scene, the record (issued in an excellent picture sleeve with an illustration of a bizarre horse/dragon chimera) is regarded as a top-ranking NWOBHM rarity in the present collecting climate. Incidentally, the mysterious »TNT« two-tracker, apparently issued by a British bunch called CHARGER as early as 1983 (as reported in 'Heavy Metal-The Vinyl Years' by John Allinson, for example), seems to be an entirely unrelated release.

A high-profile support slot at a TYGERS OF PAN TANG gig in Durham in the spring of 1987 can't have done CHARGER's reputation any harm whatsoever, and 'Kerrang' subsequently reviewed a short set by the talented trio at Dingwalls in London (never the most appreciative of crowds) in front of a sparse and disinterested audience early in 1988. With the lads showcasing a selection of newer numbers such as "Tiger", their latest material failed to elicit much of a response from those in attendance, although the journalist in question was quite complimentary in terms of the group's musical skills. Sadly, the band appear to have drifted apart towards the end of the decade (Col Bell remained in the music business, and has collaborated with local guitarist Steve Williams of BLUES DELUXE on some of the latter's solo material in the 90's), and their story has a slightly bizarre end, to say the least. In a last-gasp attempt to promote CHARGER in their area, copies of the single were apparently given away free with purchases made at a local fish and chip shop! I wonder just how many copies are still sitting unplayed in the council houses of Northallerton…

7" Singles
»Desperadoes« Private 1987?

Exclusive Compilation Appearances
"Rock" on »The Metal Collection Vol.I« LP Ebony 1986

CHARIOT

Pete Franklin (v)
Scott Biaggi (g)
John Smith (b)
Jeff Braithwaite (d)

London's long-lived CHARIOT were a band who tended to split the rock community right down the middle; some felt they were little more than no-hopers who merely jumped on the NWOBHM bandwagon to get some recognition, while others regarded them as genuine and sincere contenders. I'm sure that the same accusations could be levelled at countless other outfits, though, so I've no idea why CHARIOT were singled out for particular scrutiny. In any case, the youthful foursome formed at the height of the NWOBHM influx (Scott Biaggi and Jeff Braithwaite had earlier worked together in an unsuccessful act called N.16), and they managed to demo some material as early as 1982, including future favourites such as "Love Or Leave Me" and "Don't Forget". In general, however, it tended to be the heavier compositions which remained in their repertoire, and many of

the tracks from their formative years (some of which were more in the THIN LIZZY vein than anything else) were rapidly dropped or completely rewritten. It wasn't long before the lads had found their niche (various personnel changes occurred in the early days, although the eventual line-up turned out to be virtually identical to the original one), a fairly forceful kind of metal which married the down-to-earth attitude of the East End bands (IRON MAIDEN, ANGEL WITCH, DEEP MACHINE etc.) with the dynamics of early DIAMOND HEAD, creating a style shared by relatively few British acts, the best-known of which would probably be SAVAGE.

CHARIOT were soon making something of a name for themselves in the live environment, playing numerous shows throughout the capital, and it wasn't long before they successfully developed a pretty fervent following, with their fans ultimately becoming known as the 'Toothbrush Klan', for reasons which have never been explained in any great detail. By 1984, however, the quartet had an enviable level of support but still no prospect of a record deal, and so it came as something of a relief when the benevolent management of 'Shades' (a specialist rock/metal record shop in London) offered to set up a new label purely for the purposes of releasing the group's debut album. CHARIOT jumped at the chance, and were soon laying down their first record at Old Barn Studios in Croydon, with the talented Matthew Fisher (who also worked with PALI GAP and BRUNEL, for example) at the production helm. The resultant long-player, entitled »The Warrior«, was released to widespread critical acclaim soon afterwards, after which it was reissued by a variety of European companies, including an extremely handy pressing on the well-distributed Mausoleum label. Sales were, in general, eminently respectable, and tracks such as "When The Moon Shines", "Vigilante" and "Warriors" all stood out as effortlessly catchy, memorable numbers which came across just as impressively on vinyl as they had done on stage. Before long, the lads were invited to lay down a selection of tracks for the 'Friday Rock Show', and their session (broadcast on the 29th of June 1984) showcased the trio of "Vigilante", "Love Or Leave Me" and "When The Moon Shines", the listeners additionally being introduced to a new number, "Heartless".

In spite of the fact that their vinyl debut had performed admirably in terms of sales, however, CHARIOT weren't exactly inundated with offers of better deals, and elected to stay with the Shades label until something more appealing came their way. In 1985, they issued an EP based around the recently-penned "All Alone Again", which also featured remixed versions of "Run With The Pack" and "Warriors". It was something of a stop-gap release, designed to keep CHARIOT's name in the public's consciousness, although it was hard to avoid them, thanks to their relentless touring schedule, which now saw them travelling all over the UK and even venturing into Europe on occasion. The lads were also observed on the legendary 'E.C.T.' television programme, running through an enthusiastic performance of "When The Moon Shines" and "Vigilante" in front of an appreciative audience. Later in the year, the band were involved in further live activity, when they were selected to open for VENOM at a handful of the latter's much-anticipated British gigs, although ATOMKRAFT got the shout for the subsequent European dates. Soon, however, their thoughts turned to that second album, and they eventually (after going so far as to record an official video at a well-attended outing at London's Marquee in the early months of 1986) retired to the studio in order to lay down their long-promised follow-up to »The Warrior«, to be released on the ever-dependable Shades Records once again.

CHARIOT's second full-length effort, »Burning Ambition«, was very much in the style of their debut, although it contained its fair share of cracking numbers such as opener "Screams The Night" (with a slight ELIXIR feel), "Burning" and "Strangers". Clearly, the musicians were understandably reluctant to change a winning formula, and the record was to prove another big hit in Europe. Back home, however, CHARIOT were harshly criticised for their failure to adapt to the more typical metal sounds of the day, and were brushed off as representing the unacceptable face of British metal, the band being cruelly accused of purveying nothing more than 'hackneyed old twaddle'. It was a great pity, although they were hardly the only unfortunate outfit to be ridiculed in their homeland while still maintaining a significant following in other parts of the globe. It was to signal the end of their alliance with Shades, however, and 1987 saw CHARIOT being left to fend for themselves. Nevertheless, they were still able to attract a fair old crowd to their live appearances wherever they played, and, in addition to numerous headlining gigs of their own, they were soon to hitch a ride on MANOWAR's European tour and complete a similar jaunt with VULCAIN. CHARIOT also proved to be one of the more warmly-received acts at that year's Reading Festival (which wasn't a metal-dominated event at all by that stage), and had a new composition ("Life On The Line") included on a promotional EP given free with 'Metal Hammer' magazine, so it wasn't as if they dropped off the face of the earth overnight.

1988 proved to be a more testing year for the fortunes of CHARIOT, although reports from their live outings still tended to be replete with superlatives. At one point, the band announced that they would soon be back on top form with a privately-issued single entitled »Firing Line«, although these plans appear to have been slightly flimsy in their construction, and the release was eventually cancelled without much in the way of explanation. Pete Franklin was, by this time, beginning to tire of the baggage associated with the CHARIOT name, and, in due course, decided that it might be best to disband the project and start again under a new identity, recruiting new accomplices to the fold if necessary. At first, he and Scott Biaggi formed an outfit called CHARGE, where they collaborated with former DEEP SWITCH drummer Simon De Montford and bassist Tony Newton. There was very little change in musical direction, though, and the reinvented outfit operated under their *alter ego* for a year or two before evolving into OUTLAND, who were, in truth, almost indistinguishable from their original incarnation as CHARGE. Surprisingly, however, OUTLAND lasted a relatively short time before reverting back to (yes, you guessed it) CHARIOT! Franklin had evidently decided to resurrect their original identity (perhaps in the wake of the NWOBHM revival spearheaded by Lars Ulrich's activities) in the hope of appealing to a new generation of fans as well as some of those who fondly remembered the group from their early days. The rejuvenated CHARIOT gigged around the UK during the early 90's, playing mostly new material which, although just as strong as their original batch of compositions, failed to find a place in the hearts of all that many rock fans.

The second incarnation of CHARIOT was finally laid to rest in around 1992, only for Franklin and Newton to form yet another outfit, this time known as DIRTY DEEDS. Roping in former BRITISH LION axeman Barry Fitzgibbon, plus drummer Simon Dawson (who, as it turns out, had masqueraded as good old Simon De Montford in a previous existence), the four-piece duly set about modernising the basic CHARIOT sound, and they were soon touting around a demo tape featuring brand-new material such as "Facing The Enemy" and "Ruled By The Gun". It was indeed a slightly heavier and more contemporary sound than CHARIOT had once

Exclusive Compilation Appearances

"Life On The Line" on »The 2nd Wave Of New British Metal« 7" EP Private 1987 (Free with 'Metal Hammer' magazine)

Compilation Appearances

"Screams The Night" (live) on »Just In Power« LP Just In 1987
[Exclusive live version]

CHARLIE 'UNGRY

J. Gibbs
T. Sando

represented, although the tape was widely ignored by many of the labels and magazines who received a copy out of the blue. Nevertheless, the lads persevered, working their way up from small club gigs to better-attended appearances, eventually (after recruiting a new drummer, former GANGLAND sticksman Dave Cavill) tagging along with the likes of UFO and IRON MAIDEN on various UK and European gigs in the past couple of years. Eventually, their hard work and sheer determination was rewarded by a deal with Beast Records (owned by IRON MAIDEN bassist Steve Harris), which culminated in the release (originally in Japan) of an album entitled »Danger Of Infection« in 1998. Predictably, it met with utter indifference within the UK, but won the approval of many overseas fans, as did its follow-up (»Real World«) so we can only wait to see whether or not the central characters consider the project to be one worth developing in years to come.

Yes, I know. That's a shockingly bad name, isn't it? I can't fathom where some people got their inspiration from, but it surely wouldn't have done any harm for certain outfits to adopt a slightly more representative (or, at least, more sensible) identity. Feeble monikers aside, Middlesex also-rans CHARLIE 'UNGRY were yet another utterly obscure bunch of hopefuls from the NWOBHM era, and their only vinyl legacy seems to be a self-financed three-tracker from the heady days of 1980. Musically speaking, it's all quite peculiar, and suggests that the outfit had harvested quite a few influences from certain rock and pop acts of the 70's (and, on occasion, the 60's) to create a very unusual (but not always staggeringly listenable) concoction. The pair of lightweight efforts which comprise side one undeniably reveal a few similarities to the likes of BLAZER BLAZER, URCHIN, STATIC and early SAMSON, being very much the variety of proto-NWOBHM which leant rather too heavily on chart-oriented acts for comfort. Still, "House On Chester Road" is an extremely catchy piece which can't be disliked with any great vigour, whereas "Preacher" is a more moody affair with a semi-acoustic feel, but it doesn't really work in the way it was intended, if you ask my humble opinion.

Things actually get rather more promising on the reverse, though, and "Who Is My Killer" features some very substantial guitar work indeed, although the outfit seem intent on chucking in as many quirky ideas as humanly possible in order to dazzle the casual observer with their stunning originality. Even so, there's nothing here that hadn't been tried by the likes of LED ZEPPELIN, PINK FLOYD and QUEEN in the previous decade, and the BYRDS-style mid-section is a complete disaster, but the track is just about

LP's

»The Warrior« Shades Records 1984
[UK issue, cassette version contains extra track]
»The Warrior« Mausoleum 1984
[Belgian issue, alternate tracklisting]
»The Warriors« Axe Killer Records 1984
[Same album, French issue in different cover]
»Burning Ambition« Shades Records 1986
[UK issue]
»Burning Ambition« Dream Records 1986
[French issue]
»The Warrior« Woodstock Records 1987
[Brazilian reissue with different cover and one extra track]

12" EP's

»All Alone Again« Shades Records 1985
[A-side absent from UK pressing of »The Warrior«, also features remixed versions of "Run With The Pack" and "The Warrior"]

passable as a whole. Clearly, CHARLIE 'UNGRY were one of the more left-field groups of the early NWOBHM period, and would probably only have been happy sharing bills with similarly-minded oddballs such as ORION, MARQUIS DE SADE or CHEMICAL ALICE, assuming that most of their gigs took place in and around the capital itself. Their seldom-seen EP (housed within a generic, monochrome sleeve with precious few details) was sold through the pages of some of the music weeklies (where, confusingly enough, they were identified as CHARLIE'S 'UNGRY BAND), but the ensemble don't seem to have made a particularly favourable impression on the rock community at the time, and I wouldn't imagine that they managed to outlast the NWOBHM boom.

7" EP's
»House On Chester Road« SRT 1980

CHASAR

Alec Pollock (v,g)
Peter Marshall (b)
Jim Marshall (d)

Having formed as early as 1980, CHASAR (based in the NWOBHM wasteland of Central Scotland) didn't exactly rush to get to the vinyl stage, and the trio (comprising frontman Alec Pollock and a rhythm section handled by the Marshall brothers, Peter and Jim) were happy to record demos, play small-time gigs and be rewarded with the occasional bit of exposure on local radio during their formative years. They recorded some speculative demo material in around 1982 (including such early compositions as "The Wizard" and "Underground"), which saw them developing a rather technical style of metal with occasional similarities to OMEGA, SACRED ALIEN or KRAKEN, although their arrangements weren't usually as quirky as those of the last-mentioned, for example. Still, it was weighty stuff, extremely competently played throughout, and the lads soon developed a taste for fairly lengthy compositions with extended instrumental breaks, which drew additional comparisons with the likes of BLEAK HOUSE and Jersey's LEGEND. By the end of the year, the trio had already been invited to provide a session for the 'Friday Rock Show', and they duly obliged by laying down versions of "Underground", "Devil's Revenge", "Visions Of Time" and "Destiny". The session was broadcast on the 10th of December 1982, and this confident display immediately set CHASAR apart as being rather more of a talented proposition than many of their NWOBHM-era contemporaries. It was a healthy start, but it didn't lead to a deal at that point, unfortunately.

Although CHASAR were playing live and making studio visits from a relatively early stage, the record companies took little notice of their activities (given that most of the influential concerns were based down South, it wasn't entirely surprising), and the lads eventually concluded that they would be best-served by financing their own releases until a better offer came along. With their compositions being fairly lengthy on the whole, a 7" single seemed an inappropriate choice, so the trio recorded an album's worth of material towards the end of 1983 and prepared to release an official cassette in a limited edition of a couple of thousand copies. CHASAR's eponymous debut featured a mere seven tracks, although the average running time per number was over six minutes, so the listening public certainly weren't being short-changed in any sense. The album was a satisfyingly heavy affair all round, with the chugging riffs of "Destiny" and the NO QUARTER-style "Deceiver" standing out as particularly strong efforts. Even the semi-instrumental compositions failed to come across as the kind of ponderous and indulgent efforts favoured by many rock dinosaurs, so I reckon the release was undoubtedly something of a triumph.

Although the album was initially issued as a cassette-only release in the early months of 1984, it subsequently appeared on vinyl the following year, the band having been picked up by the confusingly-named American Phonograph label (also responsible for VENOM's »Official Bootleg« album, among others) in the interim. In due course, the set was additionally licensed by Mausoleum (retitled »Gypsy Roller« and repackaged with new cover artwork), giving the outfit an inroad into the lucrative European market, and their cause was helped by the fact that the LP even gained a favourable review in 'Kerrang'. By this stage, however, these particular tracks were fast becoming somewhat unrepresentative of the trio's style, and CHASAR were soon making a few radical changes to their line-up and musical direction. Although Alec Pollock was the proud possessor of a powerful and commanding voice, he struggled to perform night after night in the live environment, and eventually decided to hand over the reins to a dedicated frontman so that he could enjoy a well-earned rest and concentrate on his guitar playing. By this time, the musicians were beginning to tire of time-consuming, complex arrangements, and sought to simplify matters slightly once they had recruited a suitable vocalist. Their original choice, Gary Danza, lasted a very short time, but his successor, former BLIND ALLEY frontman Peter Scanlan, fared slightly better, and he was able to deliver the goods both live (the lads picked up a few support slots with the likes of PALLAS and went out on their own on other occasions) and in the studio.

Towards the end of 1985, the revised line-up demoed some new material, which included "Heartache", "Playing The Game" and "Out Of Touch", compositions which showed an uninhibited move towards a more straightforward, melodic style not a million miles away from the likes of BABY TUCKOO or early LIONHEART. The material was still reasonably strong, though, but it constituted a fairly unexpected departure from the early days. In the event, Peter Scanlan failed to last the distance, and new vocalist Ian Tait (who also dabbled in keyboard work) had been drafted in by 1986. Before long, he was soon permitted to show the world his ability when the outfit demoed a batch of unfamiliar material including "Good Times Bad Times", "Thrill Of The Crime", "Lost In Love" and "Tear It Apart". These recently-penned efforts were something of a return to form, suggesting that the lads had worked the semi-AOR experimentation out of their system, with the more ambitious arrangements now suggesting fairly close comparisons with WHITE LIGHTNING. In due course, CHASAR were given exposure in 'Mega Metal Kerrang', where the protagonists were cruelly mocked for daring to speak in a Scottish accent (let's face it, there's no excuse whatsoever for not sounding like a cockney barrow-boy), and the interview was transcribed phonetically for comic effect, distracting the reader from the fact that CHASAR were attempting to expound their recent decision to move into more accessible waters. Nevertheless, it let the general public know that they were still a going concern, since their gigging activities were now largely concentrated in Scotland once again.

Sadly, however, no significant record company attention came CHASAR's way in the wake of their latest material being touted around the various labels of the day, although the lads continued to play locally for most of 1987, a year which would also see the group performing at the Kelvingrove Rock Festival in Glasgow, a popular annual event sponsored by Radio Clyde. By 1988, however, things had already gone ominously quiet, and the CHASAR name was soon

being laid to rest for good. The industrious Alec Pollock later became involved with a couple of small-time outfits called MONITOR LIZARD and EXIT (he also spent some of his spare time teaching aspiring guitarists how to play properly), although he harboured a fairly strong desire to get CHASAR off the ground again at some stage in the future. Tragically, however, bassist Peter Marshall lost his life in a road accident in the early 90's, permanently ending any tentative notions of reassembling the band in its original form. Still, there's an official CHASAR website up and running nowadays, and fans should be able to keep abreast of any future developments, including Pollock's latest musical venture, a rock covers concern operating under the name of NO DICE.

LP's
»**Chasar**« American Phonograph 1985
[Original UK issue]
»**Gypsy Roller**« Mausoleum 1985
[European reissue of »Chasar« with different title and cover]

CD's
»**Gypsy Roller**« Mausoleum Classix 1994
[Unofficial release]

Compilation Appearances
"**Destiny**" on »War On The Planet« LP CP Records 1986?
"**Deceiver**" on »War On The Planet« LP CP Records 1986?

CHASE

Kevin Hamblett (v)
Abbz Abberley (g)
Kevin Harris (b)
Karl Wilcox (d)

One of at least three British groups to adopt the name (not to mention yet another minor bunch called THE CHASE), West Midlands-based CHASE (who featured the services of former REQUIEM drummer Karl Wilcox, who eventually cropped up in the 90's incarnation of DIAMOND HEAD) issued an intriguing single in 1983 which is certainly a strong contender for the *'least interesting sleeve'* award for its dingy black cover with the single word *'Chase'* on the front and absolutely *nothing* on the reverse. Why bother? Anyway, the music itself is in more of a progressive style than many of their regional contemporaries might have been tempted to try, particularly with regard to the slightly odd arrangements and keyboard accompaniment, with "Evensong" suggesting elements of various borderline rock/metal acts such as CHEMICAL ALICE, LIAISON and HAZE. The B-side, meanwhile, an instrumental entitled "Evermore Part II", is in much the same style, but is really a bit too lengthy for its own good. Amazingly, the single earned a favourable review in 'Kerrang', with complimentary comparisons to RUSH, LED ZEPPELIN and MARILLION being tossed around fairly shamelessly by the journalist in question. Quite an enjoyable bit of listening in store for those who don't object to the 'prog' label, I would think, but slightly tedious for many others. By the way, lads, calling your record label 'The Corduroy Mouse Wax Co.' is nearly as preposterous as AVALON's 'Flying Stilton Club Records'. Were the drugs really that bad in those days, or were prog-heads just a bit, er, *different*?

7" Singles
»Evensong« Corduroy Mouse Wax Co. 1983

CHASER

Steve Baker
Clive Richardson
Kevin Rogers
Adam Shelswell
Kevin Clark

The early 80's must have been an exhausting time, with numerous bands, obsessed with the concept of 'pursuit', naming themselves CHASE, CHASER, CHASAR, THE CHASE etc. or writing songs about the activity (people would apparently chase anything in those days, particularly dragons, storms, dreams and the night). Anyway, to get back to the point, this specific CHASER (there were several others operating in the UK throughout the 70's and 80's) came from Suffolk, and they got as far as issuing a one-off private single in 1984, the latter comprising the tracks "Raiders" and "Final Stand". Sounding, as do quite a few releases of the time, as though it features a different group on each side, the record nevertheless reveals the quintet to have been a competent bunch of musicians with a few good ideas up their collective sleeves. "Final Stand" is the heavier of the pair, with a charging riff and memorable twin-guitar parts, the overall effect coming across as a highly enjoyable amalgam of DESTROYER and DESOLATION

ANGELS. "Raiders", on the other hand, is a somewhat more catchy offering, bringing to mind the exalted musical duo of HIGH TREASON's "Waste My Love" and ENERGY's "Fight For Your Freedom", particularly with regard to the individualistic guitar arrangements.

This outfit appear to have gone through the typical NWOBHM sequence of formation/demo/label disinterest/private single/more label disinterest/disillusionment/split within a relatively brief space of time (they don't seem to have benefitted from a massive amount of media attention, for some peculiar reason, and were never exactly a high-profile act on the regional club circuit), and, as was the case for so many of their initially-enthusiastic contemporaries, presumably didn't survive long into the second half of the decade, which is a bit of a shame. Furthermore, none of the musicians seem to have maintained any particularly strong links with the local rock scene thereafter, suggesting that the participants simply went back to their day jobs following their fleeting moment of glory. Inevitably, the CHASER single is a very scarce and highly-priced relic nowadays (it was pressed in modest quantities), although it wasn't issued with a picture sleeve, so look out for a label with an image of a guitar-wielding horseman (I had no idea the guitar was ever used in combat) and you might just get lucky.

7" Singles
»Raiders« SRT 1984

CHATEAUX

Alec Houston (v,b)
Andre Baylis (v,d)
Tim Broughton (g)

Although the Gloucestershire-based trio known as CHATEAUX were another awkward bunch who chose to adopt a French identity for no good reason, they evidently didn't cause the same amount of consternation as LE GRIFFE (see separate entry), and their true nationality appears not to have been disputed by thicko music journalists at any stage. The three-piece (who had evolved from an earlier act called STEALER) established themselves in the metal-friendly West Midlands in around 1981, and they soon came to the attention of the talent-hungry Ebony label, who (after generously including their "Young Blood" effort on one of their many compilations, namely »Metal Maniaxe«) initially tested the water with an unassuming 7" single which coupled "Young Blood" (again) and "Fight To The Last". It was a heavy, powerful debut, bringing forth some fairly strong comparisons with outfits such as HELL and GRIM REAPER (for reasons which will rapidly become evident), and it was obviously sufficiently well-received at the time for their label to commission a full-length release. As a consequence, the first CHATEAUX long-player was being recorded within a matter of months, and this effort ultimately appeared as »Chained And Desperate« early the following year.

Their full-length debut showed the outfit to have mastered an impressively technical style of metal which alternated between fairly traditional territory (the title track and "Straight To The Heart", for example) and more epic pieces (such as "The Dawn Surrendered" and "Shine On Forever"), the overall impression being of acts such as JAGUAR, BLACK ROSE, TYGERS OF PAN TANG or the aforementioned GRIM REAPER. The latter comparison was hardly surprising, though, given that the talented Steve Grimmett (who was, at that juncture, yet to make his vinyl debut with his own new outfit) had sneakily been drafted in to supply a few vocals (and, as many people have speculated, he *'contributed'* rather a lot) to the set. In fact, all was not as it originally seemed, and it transpires that Grimmett really *was* the group's vocalist at the time (that's him on the single, too), although CHATEAUX (who had apparently tried in vain to recruit a suitable frontman on a permanent basis) attempted to play down his involvement, crediting him as nothing more than a *'guest musician'*. Even so, the album was a very capable effort, and, given the previously-stated comparisons with other powerful, heavyweight acts, it was equally predictable that CHATEAUX immediately achieved something resembling cult status among the metal fans of Europe. Those in Britain, meanwhile, merely shivered, muttered *'ooh, that's a bit heavy for my liking'*, and went back to their VAN HALEN albums. Nevertheless, the first CHATEAUX long-player stands up extremely well even after all this time, and the novel arrangements on tracks such as "Baton Rouge" and "Son Of Seattle" (pre-empting the grunge movement in more ways than one) actually have quite a contemporary edge.

It was a healthy start, and the band were soon preparing the groundwork for a follow-up, although they were to undergo some fairly radical rearrangement before returning to the studio. Tim Broughton later denounced the first album with brutal honesty and revealed the reasons behind the collapse of the original line-up: *'I wasn't at all happy with the results. It was all too rushed and had minimal input from most of the group at the time. There was an awful lot of apathy in the band and this began to affect me.'* (Ref: Kerrang No.81, November 1984). Out went Alec Houston and Andre Baylis (who had ostensibly shared the vocal duties when they weren't utilising the handy services of Steve Grimmett), and in came a couple of replacements from further afield, namely former SAM THUNDER/ARAGORN sticksman Chris Dadson and erstwhile CONFESSOR bassist/vocalist Krys Mason. CHATEAUX album number two, »Firepower«, appeared with almost indecent haste, and revealed the lads to be moving in more of a straight-ahead direction, with upbeat, high-energy compositions (a few tinges of BLITZKRIEG and DRAGONFLY creeping in from time to time) making up most of the featured selections. It was all quite listenable, although (with the notable exception of the excellent "Eyes Of Stone" and "White Steel"), the individual tracks tended to be rather less memorable than before. Nevertheless, the revised line-up had apparently gelled pretty convincingly, and there was every possibility that CHATEAUX might yet return with a cracking third LP (which seemed to be the theoretical maximum for Ebony) at some unspecified point in the future.

Again, the public didn't have all that long to wait in order to find out, as that *'difficult third album'* appeared a mere year later, this time under the title of »Highly Strung« (the original title of »Eastern Promise« had been eschewed in favour of a truly *hilarious* pun for guitar players). Sadly, however, it turned out to be another largely unremarkable record, and the occasional semi-highlight (such as "First Strike") failed to hide a fairly chronic lack of originality or progression. The musicianship was competent enough, and the album was better than many of Ebony's mid-period releases, but it failed, once again, to live up to the promise of the band's debut. CHATEAUX were in serious decline after the release of »Highly Strung«, and there was essentially no prospect of them being retained by Ebony. The label had failed to promote the outfit particularly strongly, and they were yet another of those Ebony signings (see also TYGA MYRA and SAMURAI, for example) who would almost certainly have benefitted quite considerably from a European tour or two. Having said that, they didn't even gig particularly prolifically in the UK (although they made it over to London on occasion), and failed to build up much of a fan base outside their own local area. It had fallen apart for the outfit within a year or two of their last release (Krys Mason was forced to leave, for reasons unrelated to music, in the early months of 1986), and the musicians involved seem to have drifted away from the scene in the long term. Nevertheless, they remain a highly-regarded act by many of today's fans and musicians, notably a bunch of Greek metalheads who operate under the suspiciously-familiar name of CHAINED AND DESPERATE...

LP's
»Chained And Desperate« Ebony 1983
»Firepower« Ebony 1984
»Highly Strung« Ebony 1985

7" Singles
»Young Blood« Ebony 1982
[Both tracks non-LP]

Compilation Appearances
"Young Blood" on »Metal Maniaxe« LP Ebony 1982

CHEEKY

Lyons

It would appear that, at the end of the 70's, several bands were definitely struggling with something of an identity crisis; the temptation to jump on the lucrative NWOBHM bandwagon must have been considerable, but some outfits were clearly reluctant to sever all ties with the punk movement. Recorded at Woodbine St. Studios in Leamington Spa and issued on the label of the same name (as was the EVERYONE ELSE 7", for example), CHEEKY's »Don't Mess Me Around« single (B-side "Get Outa My 'Ouse") from 1980 is a typical example of a hopelessly confused release which displays the same general shortcomings as the CLIENTELLE two-tracker viz. capable guitar work spoiled by comedy punk/SMALL FACES vocals and feeble lyrics. To be honest, the A-side isn't actually too bad, with the archetypal (metamorphosed/accelerated "Breadfan") NWOBHM riff leading into a reasonably metallic effort, vaguely similar to STRAY's "This One's For You". The reverse, however, is a blatant take on "Lazy Sunday Afternoon" with its supposedly 'hilarious' lyrics and 'chirpy cockney' phrasing, is actually about as funny as pancreatic cancer. Rather a waste of good vinyl, and one (with no picture sleeve) for completists only, especially considering the outrageous asking price which many dealers seem to think is currently justified. Needless to say, these CHEEKY chappies were never heard from again, having failed to convince the metalheads that they meant business, so hopefully the participants were all jailed for crimes against music shortly afterwards.

7" Singles
»Don't Mess Me Around« Woodbine St. Records 1980

CHEMICAL ALICE

Andy Grant (v)
Dave Weston (g)
Jack Grigor (b)
Mark Kelly (k)
Richard Crighton (d)

Formed in Essex back in 1980 (from the ashes of a long-forgotten, hard-rocking bunch called TYRANT), at a point in musical history when virtually all East End hopefuls aspired to be either IRON MAIDEN or ANGEL WITCH, the quirky CHEMICAL ALICE decided to try something a bit different, starting off with their less-than-metal name. Over the course of the following year or so, they went through the usual round of personnel changes (vocalist Tim Kelly and sticksman Phil Stubbs didn't last long), but managed to develop a consistent, original style along the way. Before long, the lads had an enviable repertoire at their disposal, and soon began drawing a modicum of attention from the music press. Citing a few dubious influences such as PINK FLOYD and YES, the thick-skinned quintet clearly weren't overly-concerned by the dreaded 'prog revivalists' tag which would almost inevitably be levelled at them by hostile journalists, at a time when such an outmoded direction was about as fashionable as skiffle. Founder member Dave Weston later outlined the combo's musical philosophy as follows: 'All of us have a say in the songs; everyone does about twenty per cent of the writing. If you have a band of five people and only two of them are allowed to put what they want into the music, then it's not a very good band.' (Ref: Kerrang No.10, March 1982). It all sounded commendable in theory, and, once the musicians had tried out some self-penned efforts in the live environment, the public didn't have to wait particularly long before discovering whether or not the group could deliver the goods in the studio.

Within a year of their formation, the outfit had

issued a private 12" EP, housed in an inadvisably psychedelic-looking sleeve (ahem, Lewis Carroll's 'Alice' taking a major hit off a large bong while sitting on an oversized mushroom) which seemed to be aimed squarely at the didgeridoo-playing, dog-on-a-string, hippy-dippy community. Certainly, this doesn't exactly bode well in terms of their relevance to the NWOBHM community, and, given that the first cut ("Goodnight Vienna") opens with a decidedly MARILLION-tinged, widdly keyboard passage, the unfortunate EP threatens to hurtle towards the filing cabinet marked 'prog' at great velocity. Happily, most of the music on display turns out to be rather heavier than the intro would suggest, and is often more in the WHITE SPIRIT scheme of things than anything else, although the PINK FLOYD influence is certainly there too. Mind you, "The Judge" is slightly dull and overlong, but "Henry The King" is a real cracker, very much in the mould of WHITE SPIRIT's remarkable "Red Skies" effort. The only real disappointment comes with the closer ("Lands Of Home"), which is a very lazy HAWKWIND rip-off with spaced-out vocals and phased guitars, which spoils an otherwise enjoyable piece of vinyl. Overall, it's easy to see why the adaptable group subsequently managed to get gigs with the likes of the CARDIACS, though.

It's fair to say that CHEMICAL ALICE were never the most stable unit, and endured a number of line-up changes throughout their relatively short lifespan, the most notable of which was the shameless pilfering of talented keyboard player Mark Kelly by prog legends MARILLION themselves, after which the relatively-unknown Steve Leigh was brought in as a replacement. The revised ensemble were soon doing their own thing in the live environment, and the lads proceeded to issue an official live tape (entitled »Taking Control«) in the early part of 1982, this well-recorded and generous offering featuring mostly non-EP material such as "The Beginning", "Across The Water" and "Autumn" (actually one of their oldest efforts), some of which was extremely listenable if you happened to be in the right frame of mind. Sadly, however, the unfortunate CHEMICAL ALICE appear not to have established a major following either amongst the headbangers or prog devotees, eventually being supplanted in the latter scene by emergent acts such as PENDRAGON, IQ and PALLAS. In fact, it transpires that the protagonists had already called it a day by the summer of 1982, having given it their best shot for a couple of eventful years without achieving a massive amount of recognition. It's a shame, really, as this bunch evidently had plenty of potential which never fully surfaced in the short term.

Nevertheless, all of the participants from the last line-up wasted little or no time before redistributing themselves, and the triumvirate of Andy Grant, Steve Leigh and Richard Crighton were soon lining up in the similarly-inclined TAMARISK, who got as far as issuing some well-received demo tapes. The duo of Jack Grigor and Dave Weston (the original nucleus of CHEMICAL ALICE), meanwhile, hooked up again within a matter of months, and (with the assistance of various musical associates) tried again under the abbreviated identity of ALICE. In fact, this ensemble were to remain operational until the middle of the decade, playing some memorable gigs and circulating a few cassette-only releases along the way. After ALICE drew to a natural conclusion, however, the pair went their separate ways, with Dave Weston establishing a range of projects (some more noteworthy than others) including SLARTIBARTFAST and OSIRIS, and is still tinkering away with his latest vision, BOX OF RAIN. Jack Grigor, on the other hand, went on to enjoy a brief stint with regional part-timers TOUCHSTONE before eventually re-emerging in a psychedelic/progressive band called TEA FOR THE WICKED, who currently have a couple of full-length CD releases under their belts.

12" EP's
»Goodnight Vienna« Acidic Records 1981

CHEVY

Martin Cure (v)
Paul Shanahan (g)
Steve Walwyn (g)
Bob Poole (b)
Andy Chaplin (d)

Although it's a fairly well-established fact that Warwickshire act CHEVY had something of a dodgy past as a mid-70's cabaret band before reinventing themselves as full-on NWOBHM heroes, I reckon their origins stretch back even further, with at least some of those involved having been musically active in the late 60's. As with certain members of BLEAK HOUSE, LIMELIGHT, QUARTZ and the LIGHTNING RAIDERS, for example, band leader Martin Cure appears to have been quite a prolific character throughout the psychedelic era, lending his weight to such flower-power combos as MARTIN CURE

AND THE PEEPS and THE RAINBOWS. This might all be a completely bizarre coincidence, but Martin Cure isn't exactly a common name and these earlier outfits tie in geographically, so I reckon it's probably all true, you know. And I'll bet you thought that STATUS QUO were the original inspiration for the colourful musical history of SPINAL TAP...

CHEVY's rise to prominence towards the end of the 70's seems to have been facilitated almost entirely by the inception of the NWOBHM movement, and there's little evidence to suggest that they were a particularly ambitious outfit prior to this piece of good fortune. Nevertheless, the lads saw their chance and jumped at it, landing a deal with Avatar Records and becoming a reasonably prolific recording act at the turn of the decade. Their debut LP, »The Taker«, was laid down in the summer of 1980, and proved to be a popular purchase for rock fans of the day. In truth, they had hit the nail pretty firmly on the head in terms of capturing the NWOBHM mentality (particularly on tracks such as "The Taker" and "Skybird"), and their classy, melodic rock/metal variation in the vein of PRAYING MANTIS or TRESPASS (with an occasional nod towards old stagers RAINBOW and BAD COMPANY, particularly on side two) was just the sort of thing that appealed to a considerable proportion of those who followed the fortunes of the movement. The album was promoted by two tie-in singles (»Too Much Loving« and »The Taker«, each with non-album B-sides), both of which served to further the outfit's cause, as did the appearance of an alternate take of the band's "Chevy" anthem on EMI's second »Metal For Muthas« compilation the same year. CHEVY proceeded to support fellow Avatar recording act ALVIN LEE in November 1980, before winning themselves a coveted (if slightly mismatched) series of gigs with HAWKWIND early the following year, by which time the lads had successfully developed a fairly serious fan base of their own.

Immediately after this jaunt with HAWKWIND, the group were offered the chance to tour the UK with APRIL WINE, although they eventually turned down this opportunity on the grounds that they would have been playing many of the same venues too soon after their last round of gigs. DIAMOND HEAD, on the other hand, were delighted to step in at short notice and pick up the lucrative support slot. CHEVY, meanwhile, were featured on the BBC's 'In Concert' programme in February 1981 (appearing alongside the TYGERS OF PAN TANG), where a half-hour live set was transmitted for the nation's delectation. In due course, a third single was issued, this time based around a Russ Ballard original, "Just Another Day" (b/w "Rock On", taken from the album), a song with a rather more commercial outlook (it later became part of the VERITY setlist, and was also recorded by BRIAR on their »Crown Of Thorns« album) than the group's own material generally tended to reflect. By the end of the year, the hard-working combo had also gigged extensively with labelmates LIMELIGHT and DARK STAR, and there was widespread anticipation that CHEVY would soon be recording a follow-up album for Avatar. Nevertheless, various obstacles were soon blocking the outfit's progress, a situation which culminated in Steve Walwyn and Andy Chaplin leaving the fold towards the end of 1981 (Walwyn eventually returned to his club roots with the persevering DR FEELGOOD), throwing a spanner in the works. New drummer Ted Duggan and guitarist Barry Eardly were swiftly recruited to restore CHEVY to their former status, and, at that stage, the outfit still intended to deliver another album for Avatar. In mid-1982, however, the quintet were to part company with their label in less-than-amicable circumstances, and this signalled the beginning of a period of instability for the hapless outfit.

The members were interviewed in 'Kerrang' some time later, where they announced that a second album (»Take A Chance«) would certainly appear at some point, although it would probably (in view of their ill-judged unwillingness to sign with any of the companies who had shown an interest in their activities) have to be a self-financed effort. In fact, this initial abundance of confidence and independence seemed to wane pretty rapidly, and, by the early months of 1983, the lads were once again reduced to touting around a three track demo in a pride-swallowing attempt to win favour with one or more of the influential labels. They were somewhat unlucky to miss out on the GARY MOORE tour (which eventually went to STAMPEDE), although they were fortunate to be awarded another slot on the 'In Concert' programme (alongside ROCK GODDESS) a couple of months later, where they were able to showcase a variety of new material. Sadly, the fat cats kept their money firmly inside their wallets, and the big deal never came CHEVY's way. By 1984, it was all over for the group, although three members (Martin Cure, Paul Shanahan and Rob Poole) later resurfaced in around 1987, forming the highly-tipped AOR combo RED ON RED, who, like many of their contemporaries, fell by the wayside before getting the chance to prove themselves on vinyl. Is the phoenix-like Martin Cure still reinventing himself every few years, we ask ourselves? Who knows, maybe he'll re-emerge in some trendy techno outfit (ever wondered why so many of them wear masks?) any day now…

LP's
»**Chevy**« Avatar 1980
[UK issue in single sleeve]
»**Chevy**« Bellaphon 1981
[German issue in gatefold sleeve]

7" Singles
»**Too Much Loving**« Avatar 1980
[UK issue in company sleeve, B-side "See The Light" non-LP]
»**Too Much Loving**« Bellaphon 1981
[German issue in picture sleeve]
»**The Taker**« Avatar 1981
[B-side "Life On The Run" non-LP]
»**Just Another Day**« Avatar 1981
[A-side non-LP]

Compilation Appearances
"Chevy" on »Metal For Muthas Vol.2« LP EMI 1980/CD Airraid Records 2000 + »The Bible Of Hard Rock« CD Toshiba 1990
[Different to album version]
"Skybird" on »NWOBHM Vol.3« Bootleg CD 1992

CHINA DOLL

Peter Fitch
Gary Gahan
John Lister
Nick Williams

As with STRUTZ, this name's caused a bit of confusion over the years, with the only *'common'* CHINA DOLL release being an awful pseudo-oriental pop debacle on the Graduate label. However, the real thing for NWOBHM collectors is a monumentally rare single recorded by a mystery South Coast band at Telecomms Studios in Portsmouth and issued on the small (predominantly punk-biased) Wessex label at the height of the metal explosion in 1980. The A-side ("Oysters And Wine") is a heavy, mid-paced affair with slightly peculiar vocals (a bit like a more refined version of SACRED ALIEN's Sean Canning), sounding overall like an amalgam of BUZZARD and HAMMERHEAD. The lyrical concept, dealing with a sort of 'Pygmalion' scenario, is pretty off-the-wall, too (for a metal outfit, at least), so I guess this quartet were pretty keen to express their individuality. On the reverse, meanwhile, "Past Tense", turns out to be a slower, atmospheric composition which starts off in the manner of ANGEL WITCH's "Devil's Tower" instrumental, before evolving into a weighty variant which is slightly reminiscent of ARC's "Ice Cream Theme". Not at all bad, I suppose, but it represented a one-off piece of exposure, and failed to set CHINA DOLL on the road to success.

I would imagine that this particular outfit were probably a fly-by-night concern, and that they made comparatively little effort to get out and about to promote themselves further, with the result that very few copies of their two-tracker ever made it into circulation. Still, it was a fairly interesting single (the sleeve depicting an arty-but-crap drawing of a classical Venus figure and a bottle), and, given the minimal quantities that have surfaced thus far (a tiny handful of copies have been unearthed in Hampshire and Dorset), one which ranks amongst the upper echelons of NWOBHM collectables. As to how long CHINA DOLL were around and what ultimately happened to them: your guess is as good as mine, as I've never met anyone (and I lived in what I assume to be the relevant area for a number of years) who had the remotest recollection of them.

7" Singles
»**Oysters And Wine**« Wessex Records 1980

CHINATOWN

Steve Prangnell (v)
Danny Gwilym (g)

Pat Shayler (g)
John Barr (b)
Steve Hopgood (d)

The popular bunch known as CHINATOWN evolved from the last line-up of long-forgotten Hampshire part-timers JODEY (see separate entry), the transmutation more or less coinciding with the recruitment of new frontman Steve Prangnell in the early months of 1980. In due course, keyboard player Adrian Chase made way for a second guitarist (Danny Gwilym, who had previously plied his trade with such unknown hopefuls as LYNX and FAT CHANCE, and who jumped at the opportunity to join forces with an act who seemed to be going places) as the group began to toughen up their sound somewhat. The final piece of the jigsaw slotted into place when original sticksman Russell Payne defected to South Coast rivals HIGH RISK, his successor being Steve Hopgood, formerly with local covers outfit SHY (who also featured future WHITE SPIRIT vocalist Brian Howe, incidentally), and the metamorphosis into an all-new NWOBHM proposition was a reality. Mind you, they didn't actually start all over again from scratch, and CHINATOWN retained a fair percentage of material from the JODEY set, which was (after a few musical reworkings and lyrical alterations) integrated into their ever-expanding repertoire. Although the five-piece were based on the South Coast, where a high proportion of their live activities were centred, they were frequent visitors to London, and soon became regular fixtures on the live scene in the capital, finding their way onto rock bills with relative ease and establishing a firm following of their own. In due course, CHINATOWN began to venture further afield, and ultimately identified various rock-friendly communities (notably Oxford) where they would always be guaranteed a warm reception from the locals.

After numerous well-attended gigs (which saw them taking in small-time events in their locality in addition to support slots with such luminaries as ANGEL WITCH and GIRLSCHOOL), the outfit managed to win their first proper deal in the early months of 1981, the offer having come from one of the champions of South Coast metal, Airship Records (also responsible for the likes of VOLTZ, PARADYNE and HIGH RISK, for example). CHINATOWN's vinyl debut came with an unassuming 7" single, coupling "Short And Sweet" and "How Many Times", the record being issued in a flimsy monochrome sleeve depicting an oriental dragon. Unsurprisingly, the group's musical style wasn't actually a million miles away from JODEY's, although the latter's lengthy, semi-progressive compositions had now been honed down to more instantly-memorable and dynamic efforts, the featured numbers being fairly enjoyable compositions with occasional similarities to acts such as GRAND PRIX, LIMELIGHT or STAMPEDE, although neither really did justice to the power generated in the live environment. The two-tracker sold in respectable quantities, and their label soon concluded that a full album would bolster the band's growing reputation in no uncertain terms, although it rapidly became apparent that Airship envisaged the long-player as a live affair, something that even a talented outfit such as CHINATOWN might find quite difficult to pull off particularly convincingly.

Nevertheless, the recording of a small-time gig in Surrey went ahead as planned, and the album duly appeared as the oddly-titled »Play It To The Death« set a few months later, the cover inadvisably showing the musicians all dressed up like rejects from a second-rate glam act. The long-player featured a decent enough recording of the outfit in action, and it sold in pretty remarkable quantities throughout mainland Europe (they had become immensely popular in places such as Holland), but in the UK they remained very much a 'love them or hate them' kind of group, with many rock fans being unconvinced by their collective ability to deliver something new and exciting. With hindsight, I suspect that Steve Prangnell's distinctive voice may have had something to do with it (personally, I'm not an admirer of the frontman's grating, high-pitched vocals), although there was no doubting the quintet's musical ability as a whole, particularly evident on strong numbers such as "No Time To Kill", "It Could Happen To You" and "Rock And Roll Legend". Another interesting inclusion was the epic power ballad "Time Will Tell", which was recycled several years later on the first SHOGUN album. Oddly, fewer copies of the CHINATOWN LP seem to be in circulation than the single, although at least twice as many were pressed, and the long-player remains a very highly-valued piece in the current collecting scene, whereas the single appears to have stabilised at a more realistic level.

Over the next twelve months or so, the band concentrated on building themselves up as a potential headlining act for some of the bigger clubs, while taking in a few support slots whenever the possibility arose. Their live appearances were used to try out a great deal of new material, and the ever-expanding set now included such favourites as "Hell Or High Water",

"Giving Your Love Away" and "Lady Love", plus the obligatory cover of LED ZEPPELIN's "Whole Lotta Love", a track which went down especially well with the majority of fans. In the spring of 1982, the combo were invited to record a session for the 'Friday Rock Show', and the musicians hoped to attract the attention of some of the major labels by showcasing four newer numbers, namely "Caught On The Wrong Side", "I Wanna See You Tonight", "Back On The Streets" and "City Woman". The session, broadcast on the 25th of June 1982, was a fairly strong effort, although it met with disinterest from the record companies, so there was little option but to return to the live circuit once again. However, a big break was to come their way a couple of months later, when the lads were added to the bill of the Reading Festival, and CHINATOWN grasped this welcome and unexpected chance to display their wares in front of a massive crowd, warming up the fans for acts such as MARILLION, Y&T and MSG. In due course, something of a bonus came their way when two tracks from their set ("Caught On The Wrong Side" and "I Wanna See You Tonight") were included on the double live album issued by Mean Records to commemorate the event.

Still, however, a deal failed to materialise, and the strain began to show within a couple of months, when unsettled guitarist Pat Shayler threw in his hand and went in search of a new outfit, initially joining up with a little-known Hampshire bunch called 1ST OFFENCE (not to be confused with the group who recorded an album for the Metalother label), and he still apparently plays with various local rock acts nowadays. Undeterred, the remaining members elected to continue as a four-piece, and the optimistic quartet were evidently putting on a brave face when interviewed by 'Kerrang' towards the end of the year, as John Barr insisted: *'A deal's gonna happen, it's just a case of which company we'll go with. The problem is that a lot of labels have been put off hard rock bands by the glut of acts who were signed up a couple of years back and did absolutely nothing. I'm talking about the likes of FIST and WHITE SPIRIT. We've now played Reading, done a session for the BBC Rock Show and are one of the biggest crowd-pullers at the Marquee-fact! So we've done everything to warrant a deal and a support tour, we hope to have everything signed and sealed by the end of the year.'* (Ref: Kerrang No.30, December 1982). Well, the support slot soon materialised in the form of some end-of-year gigs with BUDGIE, but that elusive deal proved rather more difficult to come by…

By the early months of 1983, things had already reached crisis point for the luckless CHINATOWN, who were experiencing acute personnel problems by this juncture, and the departure of John Barr himself (he later moved on to the restructuring LAST FLIGHT) led to widespread speculation that the freefalling band would soon be a thing of the past. Surprisingly, however, they continued to plug away, in a variety of guises, for another full year, utilising the services of new guitarists (including former TYTAN stalwart Stevie Gibbs and future MAMMATH axeman James Rees) as well as a replacement bassist (Dave Mandy, later of SEDUCER) in a desperate attempt to keep things going. Remarkably enough, CHINATOWN remained an active and determined unit in the face of severe adversity, somehow managing to attract the attention of none other than the mighty EMI (for whom they demoed some new material) in the process, and there was a very real possibility of a deal being proffered by the giant company if the lads could just achieve and maintain a stable line-up. Eventually, though, their position became untenable due to this constant instability and reshuffling, leading to the collapse of the projected EMI deal towards the end of 1983 and the ultimate fragmentation of CHINATOWN early the following year.

Original guitarist Danny Gwilym swiftly moved over to the ranks of Gloucestershire's TYRANT (eventually becoming part of the SHOGUN and MR ICE ventures), while in-demand drummer Steve Hopgood subsequently lent his skills to myriad recording acts, starting off with PERSIAN RISK before hooking up with the likes of BATTLEZONE, LIONHEART, WILD!, JAGGED EDGE, PASSION, KILLERS and TANK. Apart from those two, however, there appears to have been little mention of any of the former CHINATOWN members over the years, although most of the central characters remain in contact and it's not beyond the realms of possibility that we'll be hearing more from one or two of these talented individuals in years to come. Incidentally, devotees of the band have now been afforded the opportunity to pick up their scarce live album on CD format (complete with bonus tracks) courtesy of Vinyl Tap's reissue programme, saving themselves a vast amount of money and fruitless searching for the original vinyl in the process.

LP's
»**Play It To The Death**« Airship 1981
[Live album]

7" Singles
»**Short And Sweet**« Airship 1981

[Both tracks different to album versions]

CD's
»Play It To The Death« Vinyl Tap Records 1997 *[With four bonus tracks taken from »Short And Sweet« 7" and »Reading Rock Vol.1« compilation]*
»Play It To The Death« Soundholic 1998 *[Japanese issue]*

Compilation Appearances
"I Wanna See You Tonight" (live) on »Reading Rock Vol.1« Do-LP Mean Records 1982 *[Different to album version]*
"Caught On The Wrong Side" (live) on »Reading Rock Vol.1« Do-LP Mean Records 1982 *[Different to album version]*
"No Time To Kill" (live) on »Noise Level Critical« CD Hallmark 1997

CHINAWITE

Brian Glaves (v)
Al Thompson (g)
Ian von Coolburger (g)
Gary North (b)
Kevin Oxley (d)

Yorkshire's CHINAWITE (the mis-spelling was consistent, even if it wasn't necessarily intentional, but at least it served to dissociate the ensemble from various global acts called CHINA WHITE) had, after forming in around 1981, gone through the usual machinations of attaining recognition by gigging locally and recording a low-budget demo tape, and they first came to public attention *via* airplay on their local station, Radio Hallam. In due course, they were to debut with a single for Doncaster's eclectic Future Earth label (see also LIMELIGHT and FACTORY, for example), having been signed up towards the end of 1982. The deal resulted in "Blood On The Streets" and "Ready To Satisfy" being pressed up as the band's debut release, issued in a rather basic sleeve featuring a photo of the five members. Sadly, it was a lot nearer to the mediocrity of FACTORY than the classy compositions of LIMELIGHT, with CHINAWITE delivering a fairly average slice of unassuming rock/metal lying somewhere between PRAYING MANTIS, LIONHEART and BOULEVARD. Nevertheless, a full LP deal came about a year later, following on from negotiations with the influential Mausoleum concern (the Belgian label having tested the water by reissuing the two single tracks on its not-terribly-interesting »Metal Prisoners« compilation), who represented Future Earth in the European market.

The result of a concerted recording session at Vibrasound Studios in Sheffield in July 1984 was the quintet's »Run For Cover« long-player, an album which, sad to say, barely even lived up to the promise of CHINAWITE's unremarkable debut single. With the featured selection of lightweight, rudimentary compositions all being extraordinarily similar to one another in terms of pace and construction, absolutely none shone out as being remotely enjoyable, innovative or memorable. The majority of reviewers (those who even bothered to devote valuable magazine space to it, that is) concurred that the whole exercise amounted to little more than a scandalous waste of vinyl, and CHINAWITE's fate was probably sealed without much more ado. »Run For Cover« was, all things considered, an immensely disappointing effort, the outfit showing no sense of conviction or enthusiasm whatsoever (they look a pretty miserable bunch in their photo, too), and it's entirely possible that, despite having a fair bit of experience under their collective belts, the lads just weren't ready for a full-length release at that stage. The end must have come soon afterwards, following several months of spectacularly poor sales throughout Europe (they certainly made no impression whatsoever in the UK), and I imagine there was never any serious talk of a follow-up at any point.

LP's
»Run For Cover« Mausoleum 1984

7" Singles
»Blood On The Streets« Future Earth Records 1983 *[Both tracks non-LP]*

Compilation Appearances
"Blood On The Streets" on »Metal Prisoners« LP Mausoleum 1983
"Ready To Satisfy" on »Metal Prisoners« LP Mausoleum 1983

CHROME MOLLY

Steve Hawkins (v)
John Antcliffe (g)
Nick Wastell (b)
Chris Green (d)

Leicestershire's quirkily-named CHROME MOLLY (something to do with bike frames, apparently) initially gravitated together towards the end of 1982, following the usual demise of various less-successful local hopefuls. Steve Hawkins, for example, had earlier manned the mike stand for the little-remembered MEAN ARENA, while John Antcliffe had previously played a part in the fortunes of both BLITZKRIEG and ELECTRIC SAVAGE, the latter unit also featuring future CHROME MOLLY drummer Chris Green. It took the outfit a little over a year to get their act together well enough to record a humble demo and establish themselves on the regional live circuit, but they eventually concluded that the time was now right to have a crack at finding fame and fortune. Their vinyl debut was facilitated by the somewhat inconsistent Bullet Records, whose signings tended to vary considerably in terms of their vinyl-worthiness. Nevertheless, CHROME MOLLY turned out to be one of their better tips for the top, and the group duly delivered a 12" EP featuring "You Said", "When The Lights Go Down" and "One At A Time", the tracks representing a powerful concoction of melodic, heavy rock/metal in the general style of early HEAVY PETTIN or TOBRUK. Having said that, CHROME MOLLY had a rather harder edge, and were capable of jazzing up their offerings with more adventurous and quirky arrangements than many of their rivals, with "When The Lights Go Down" being a prime example of their originality.

It was a decent enough debut to propel CHROME MOLLY's name into circulation, and they apparently drafted in former ALIEN guitarist Chris O'Shaughnessy to bolster their sound in the wake of the EP's release, although it would appear that he was used in moderation, possibly only at live appearances, and it looks as though he was only there for a few months, making little or no contribution to the songwriting or recording side of things. Moving in 1985, interest in the band (now featuring new bloke Mark Godfrey in place of Chris Green, who went on to help out in BLITZKRIEG) was given a fillip when they were provided with the opportunity to lay down a few numbers for the 'Friday Rock Show'. The session, broadcast on the 8th of February 1985, allowed the lads to showcase "Lonely", "Too Far Gone", "Don't Fight Dirty" and "Lose Again", and their energetic, exuberant presentation, coupled with the memorable nature of the songs, yielded one of the most highly-praised performances of the year. In due course, CHROME MOLLY signed a deal with the Powerstation label, and were soon back in business with a new EP. It was apparent, however, that the lads obviously held their debut release in low regard, given that they were soon announcing their »Take It Or Leave It« three-tracker to be 'their first serious 12" EP'. Nevertheless, the new record was another strong outing, and a full album duly followed as a matter of course.

The lengthily-titled »You Can't Have It All…Or Can You?« was, in spite of its off-putting and tacky sleeve, a capable collection of songs, with session favourites such as "Too Far Gone" and "Don't Fight Dirty" coming across particularly well on vinyl, although there was something of a move towards the kind of anthemic, post-NWOBHM power metal personified by the likes of MARSHALL LAW and WRAITH, for example, especially on compositions such as opener "Thanks For The Angst". The album sold reasonably well, and the band were retained by Powerstation, who permitted them to assemble a follow-up set in due course. In the interim, the outfit released an upbeat single entitled »I Want To Find Out« (in both 7" and 12" formats), the last-mentioned including an energetic reworking of GARY MOORE's "Nuclear Attack". Album number two (they supposedly recorded a grand total of three for Powerstation, but one apparently failed to reach the pressing stage), »Stick It Out«, was released (in another tawdry sleeve) in 1987 (the year in which the band famously embarked on a self-organised, co-headlining tour with BABY TUCKOO), but it turned out to be a poor sequel, unfortunately. For some reason, the lads seemed intent on showing the world how moody and edgy they could be when they wanted, and the long-player was filled with fairly nondescript, heavier compositions with little or no enthusiasm shining through at any stage. It was all largely forgettable (the album is a cold and unrewarding listening experience, not helped by a pretty spartan production), although "Stand Proud" was an exception, and Powerstation soon washed their hands of the band, choosing not to promote the album with any singles, and the lads were soon being encouraged to seek out a new label.

In spite of the disappointment of their sophomore album's failure and their subsequent parting from Powerstation, CHROME MOLLY landed on their feet in no uncertain terms, and an offer duly came their way from I.R.S. Records, a powerful company who handled the affairs of outfits such as R.E.M., THE ALARM and THE CRAMPS. After a support slot with heavyweight labelmates BLACK SABBATH in the early months of 1988, the lads (now featuring new guitarist Tim Read in place of John Antcliffe) recorded a new LP, which appeared in due course as »Angst«. Bizarrely, however, the latest CHROME MOLLY set consisted almost entirely of pointless reworkings of many of their original numbers from early singles and their first album, the only exception being their cover of SQUEEZE's "Take Me I'm Yours" (featuring Jools Holland himself on keyboards), and even this was an old track, having appeared on the patchy »Megalomania« compilation two years previously. The outfit attempted to justify this cynical rehashing of well-worn songs on the basis of their new label's financial superiority, which meant that they could finally do justice to their favourite material with proper studio facilities and a decent recording budget. Hmmm. It was a pretty pointless exercise all round, and the set certainly wasn't promoted as a *'greatest hits'* affair, so it's hard to comprehend exactly what the musicians might have been thinking at this time.

In any case, CHROME MOLLY were soon out on tour with ALICE COOPER to promote their *'new'* LP, and they were joined, in due course, by second guitarist Andy Barrott (who also provided the occasional bit of keyboard work), who had now become available following the recent (but much-anticipated) demise of touring partners BABY TUCKOO. Two tie-in singles (»Take Me I'm Yours« and »Thanx For The Angst«) had already been issued (with reasonable success) to promote the latest album, and the group entered the studios later in the year to record a further vinyl offering. The commercially-inclined »Shooting Me Down« single was recorded with the assistance of SLADE bassist Jim Lea (in the production helm, and this unashamed, anthemic, BON JOVI-style effort consolidated CHROME MOLLY's position as back-on-form rock contenders, albeit slightly more accessible than before. Strangely, however, the outfit failed to capitalise on their resurrected popularity, and soon found themselves parting company with both the unsettled Andy Barrott (who proceeded to establish his SWAMPWALK venture, an act who signed to the Bleeding Hearts label and saw a couple of their releases make it into the shops) and the dissatisfied I.R.S. Records. Things didn't look particularly promising for the group, given that they were now evidently struggling to cope with label indifference and personnel changes.

CHROME MOLLY kept a disconcertingly low profile throughout 1989, and many observers assumed, quite reasonably, that they had finally called in the receivers. In fact, the lads reappeared in 1990 with an unheralded album for Music For Nations, the title of which (»Slaphead«) reflecting the fact that two of the band's members had been relieved of their splendidly impressive mullets in the interim. It was a patchy and inconsistent affair, though, with only a handful of tracks (such as "Shotgun" and "Caught With The Bottle Again") bearing any relation to their previous work, and their flirtation with semi-punky, sleazy compositions (in the GUNS'N'ROSES or FASTER PUSSYCAT vein) was an ill-conceived move. Elsewhere, there were some staggeringly mediocre numbers on display (particularly on side two, where they seem to have run out of ideas completely), and the outfit were clearly struggling to maintain either their direction or image at this point. This time, however, it really was to be the end of the road for the long-lived CHROME MOLLY, and the participants appear to have called it quits soon after. Definitely a case of *'one album too many'*, methinks.

LP's

»You Can't Have It All...Or Can You?« Powerstation 1985
»Stick It Out« Powerstation 1987
[Cassette version contains exclusive bonus track "Let Go"]
»Angst« I.R.S. Records 1988
[Consists of re-recordings of material originally recorded for Powerstation]
»Slaphead« Music For Nations 1990

12" EP's

»You Said« Bullet 1984
["When The Lights Go Down" non-LP, "You Said" later reworked as "Living A Lie" on first album, "One At A Time" different to album version]
»Take It Or Leave It« Powerstation 1985
[A-side and "Don't Let Go" different to album versions, "Lonely" non-LP]
»I Want To Find Out« Powerstation 1986
[Extended A-side different to album version, "Nuclear Attack" non-LP]
»Take Me I'm Yours« I.R.S. Records 1988
[Some as advance DJ promos in plain covers, both "Don't Fight Dirty" and "Lose Again" different to album versions]
»Thanx For The Angst« I.R.S. Records 1988
[Some as advance DJ promos in plain covers, "One At A Time" different to album version]
»Shooting Me Down« I.R.S. Records 1988
[Some as advance DJ promos in plain covers, both "Shooting Me Down" and "Led Heavy" non-LP, also features remixes of "Shooting Me Down" and "Thanx For The Angst"]

7" Singles

»I Want To Find Out« Powerstation 1986

[Both tracks different to album versions]
»Take Me I'm Yours« I.R.S. Records 1988
[Both tracks different to album versions]
»Thanx For The Angst« I.R.S. Records 1988
»Shooting Me Down« I.R.S. Records 1988
[Both tracks non-LP]

Shaped Picture Discs
»Take Me I'm Yours« I.R.S. Records 1988

CD's
»Angst« I.R.S. Records 1988
»Slaphead« Music For Nations 1990
[With two bonus tracks]

Compilation Appearances
"Thanx For The Angst" on »Metal Killers Kollection I« Do-LP Castle Communications 1985
"Take Me I'm Yours" on »Megalomania« LP Powerstation 1986
[Different to album version]
"Lonely" on »Megalomania« LP Powerstation 1986
"Set Me Free" on »Megalomania« LP Powerstation 1986
"Something Special" on »Metal Killers Kollection III« Do-LP Castle Communications 1988

CLIENTELLE

Rik Taylor (v,g,k)
Roy Powell (v,rg)
Steve Trudgett (b)
Phil Goodfellow (d)

Forming in the musically-verdant Home Counties at some point in the mid-to-late 70's, the oddly-monikered CLIENTELLE's initial activities on the region's rock scene were not documented in any great detail (they didn't get a vast amount of media attention, for some strange reason), although it seems perfectly reasonable to assume that they were probably entertaining local audiences from a comparatively early stage, given that their area boasted a pretty healthy music scene. Their first vinyl foray, however, came in the shape of a double A-sided 7" from 1979 (CLIENTELLE were one of the first heavy bands to organise such a release), the latter having been recorded during a trip to the busy Quest Studios facility in Luton. The weak "Can't Forget" is a somewhat uneasy mixture of metal and SMALL FACES-type snottiness, which really doesn't hold together too well, whereas "Skyflier", with its SKYCLAD-patented riffing, is a far better effort which comes considerably closer to traditional NWOBHM territory. Issued in a slightly drab picture sleeve showing individual images of the band members, the debut two-tracker (pressed in a modest quantity of only a few hundred copies) is a scarcely-encountered rarity, and is an item which appears on an extremely high proportion of wants lists nowadays.

After a couple of years of solid gigging, including numerous local appearances with the likes of TOAD THE WET SPROCKET, BLEAK HOUSE, VALHALLA and HIGH TREASON, the quartet proceeded to issue a full-length effort entitled »Destination Unknown« (on the tiny Banana label) at some point in 1981, on which the two tracks from their debut single were also included in their original form. On the remaining compositions, a surprisingly wide range of musical styles is apparent, ranging from the upbeat opener "Play To Win" (tinges of BOLLWEEVIL and early DEF LEPPARD at times) and "Nice Girl", to the atmospheric, PHOENIX RISING-tinged title track, whereas the hard-rocking "Missing Persons" and "Bike" are rather more traditional and unadventurous heavy fare. There's a tangible late 60's/early 70's influence in places, although it's weighty stuff (with some excellent and original guitar work) throughout, but it's fair to say that the CLIENTELLE long-player certainly isn't the mythical classic that certain individuals tend to make it out to be. It's a very scarce (and highly-valued) piece that unquestionably deserves to take its place in any serious NWOBHM collection, but »Destination Unknown« is probably a relatively poor return for the amount of cash you need to hand over to get hold of a copy these days.

Unsettled drummer Phil Goodfellow apparently flew the coop shortly after the album sessions were completed (something which seems to have destabilised the outfit to some extent), and they never really capitalised upon their full-length release, so the name of CLIENTELLE swiftly began to lose any sort of relevance. Nevertheless, the ensemble certainly persevered, in one form or another, until at least 1984, in spite of the observation that they still hadn't progressed beyond small-time, local gigs (it's not even certain that they managed to secure any significant appearances in London itself) and were playing exactly the same old circuit of venues at which newer heroes such as LYADRIVE and LIAISON were now establishing a staunch following. It looks as though poor old CLIENTELLE eventually called it a day without ever becoming anything more than minor regional favourites (it would also appear that nobody had the heart to point out that they'd spelled their name incorrectly all these years), although the semi-legendary status afforded to their rare vinyl releases (undoubtedly helped by their fortuitous inclusion in the NWOBHM supplement assembled by 'Kerrang' back in 1989) ensures that both the 7" and LP will probably remain extremely pricey, sought-after items for the foreseeable future.

LP's
»Destination Unknown« Banana Records 1981

7" Singles
»Can't Forget« Quest Records 1979

CLOVEN HOOF

David 'Water' Potter (v)
Steve 'Fire' Rounds (g)
Lee 'Air' Payne (b)
Kevin 'Earth' Pountney (d)

The origins of legendary Midlands outfit CLOVEN HOOF appear to go back to around 1979, when the embryonic band first took shape as NIGHTSTALKER, although their activities were strictly low-key at the outset. By 1981, however, things had become slightly more serious, and the young lads finally made it into the studio to lay down their first proper demo tape. Early compositions such as "Nightstalker" and "Return Of The Passover" showed the group to be operating in a fairly ambitious, semi-epic and technical style with an emphasis on sci-fi and fantasy lyrics, bringing to mind a combination of GRIM REAPER, TREDEGAR, SARACEN and early MOURNBLADE. By 1982, the lads had dispensed with their original moniker, settling instead on the more individualistic CLOVEN HOOF, and were soon showcasing some impressive new material such as "Road Of Eagles", "A Piece Of The Action" and "That's The Way It Goes". Associated with the grand lyrical concepts was a much-ridiculed image which involved identifying each member with one of nature's elemental forces (earth, air, fire and water) and wearing some monumentally silly costumes and ill-advised make-up to complete the overall effect. I'm sure none of these activities had the *remotest* influence on the makers of 'This Is Spinal Tap' whatsoever...
There was little doubt that CLOVEN HOOF were a talented enough bunch of musicians with some highly original ideas up their sleeves, but their early appearances (and there were only a handful, admittedly) around the clubs of the Midlands had left many audiences feeling slightly bemused, the visual impact and over-the-top theatrics being far better suited to bigger venues and (perhaps) to the less cynical overseas market. In due course, the musicians decided to spread their name with a self-financed slice of vinyl, although they went one better than many of their contemporaries by issuing a well-produced four track EP in an admirably-presented cover. »The Opening Ritual« featured some of the more popular numbers from their early live set (others, such as "Ready To Raise The Roof" and "Still Falls The Rain", would never be recorded officially), namely "The Gates Of Gehenna", "Stormrider", "Back In The U.S.A." and "Starship Sentinel", all equally strong and heavy efforts which quickly allowed the name of CLOVEN HOOF to become quite highly-regarded in many parts of the world, if not in the UK itself. In fact, demand outstripped supply at the time, and this situation persists in the current NWOBHM collecting climate, with the EP (despite all four tracks having been made available on a bootleg CD in the 90's) tending to nudge the three figure mark at times.
The press soon cottoned on to the band's activities, and 'Kerrang' were one of the first publications to give the lads some much-needed coverage. Asked to elaborate on the outfit's general philosophy, their breezy bassist was keen to offer an insight into the world of CLOVEN HOOF, and to defend the outfit against accusations that they might actually look a bit silly: 'What we're trying to do is sort of escapist. We wanna go one stage further than KISS ever have. And, I'd also just like to say that we don't regard ourselves as glam rockers like WRATHCHILD or ROX. We're an all-out British HM band. To us the so-called glam/metal groups play heavy 'petal' music. CLOVEN HOOF are VERY heavy indeed!' (Ref: Kerrang No.28, November 1982). In order to promote themselves as champions of 'real metal', therefore, and to further distance the name of CLOVEN HOOF from that shameful glam movement, the valiant quartet's next move was to put in an appearance at (ahem) the Salford Glamfest alongside the likes of, er, WRATHCHILD. Hmmm. No doubt this was actually a calculated and cunning ploy to subvert the glam world from within, or something. Within a matter of months, however, the lads were making their first assault on a national audience, having laid down a session for the 'Friday Rock Show'. Broadcast on the 10th of June 1983, the session showcased "Crack The Whip", "Return Of The Passover", "Road Of Eagles" and the excellent

"Laying Down The Law" (the latter showing a slightly more accessible style), four powerful efforts which did their chances no harm whatsoever. Further gigs followed, including their first shows in London, and CLOVEN HOOF now appeared to be ripe for plucking.

In 1984, a decent offer finally came the group's way, and they wasted little time before agreeing to deliver their first long-player for the benefit of Neat Records. The eponymous album was completed fairly rapidly, and CLOVEN HOOF's much-anticipated debut was soon hitting the shops, although it was largely to be overlooked by metal fans within the UK once again. In spite of the fact that much of the material featured was now two or three years old, the-

re were a couple of more recent efforts (notably "Laying Down The Law" and "Crack The Whip" from their session) to bring things up to date. In any case, there had been very little change in the band's songwriting since their inception, so even the older selections were still pretty representative of their general style. Undeterred by the lack of public approval in their homeland, CLOVEN HOOF merely hopped across the English Channel and performed some well-received shows (including the odd festival appearance) for the benefit of their more discerning followers in mainland Europe, all of which seems to have worked to their advantage in the long term. After returning to the UK in buoyant mood towards the end of the year, the protagonists wasted little time before announcing plans to commence work on their second LP almost immediately. This came as something of a surprise, especially to Neat, who (following relatively modest sales of the debut) hadn't actually been intending to commission a follow-up anyway.

Nevertheless, CLOVEN HOOF gave short shrift to such minor setbacks, and informed the world (as early as the first half of 1985, by which point they had sworn in additional guitarist Mick Grafton) that work on their second long-player was now underway as planned. Their original intention was to issue an album with the excruciatingly self-parodying title of »Heavy Metal Men Of Steel« (Dr Irony was a complete stranger, by the looks of things), although things seem to have gone a bit pear-shaped while they made preparations for this epic sequel. In fact, the whole thing appears to have ground to a halt when vocalist David 'Water' Potter elected to depart for pastures new, whereupon he trickled over to France and joined forces with the popular H-BOMB. The affairs of CLOVEN HOOF were thrown into disarray for a while, and their future was uncertain at first, although they eventually located a replacement in the form of erstwhile CHAIN REACTION frontman Derek Hodd, and things got going again for a brief period. It soon became apparent, however, that a further 'change of water' was called for, and the unlucky Hodd was soon out on his ear (later resurfacing in PANIK ATTAK) in favour of the well-travelled Rob Kendrick, whose considerable talents had been put to good use by the likes of TRAPEZE and BUDGIE in days gone by. With the ensemble having been restored to operational status once more (Mick Grafton was also to leave at around this time, later working with SHOCK PROMISE and DUMPY'S RUSTY NUTS), the revamped quartet finally started to lay the foundations for their sophomore effort.

For some inexplicable reason, however, CLOVEN HOOF's second album (released on the non-illustrious Moondancer label) emerged in the form of a pseudo-live affair (possibly trying to cover up a botched production job?), although it was patently obvious that these were all-new studio recordings with Budokan-style crowd noises dubbed in at strategic intervals. The whole thing really was an utterly pointless charade (why wasn't poor old David Potter credited as vocalist, if these recordings had genuinely been captured on their 'tour' of Europe?), especially when you consider that few (if any) of these tracks had actually been in the band's live repertoire up until this point. Nevertheless, »Fighting Back« was, in spite of its irritatingly fraudulent packaging, an extremely enjoyable album, even if the outfit's move towards accessible power metal with strong guitar leads was something of an unexpected surprise. It has to be said, though, that some of their latest material was truly stunning, especially the wonderful

"Reach For The Sky", "The Fugitive" and "Raised On Rock", all of which showcased Kendrick's powerful-but-melodic delivery, their latest frontman being the possessor of a resonant voice with distinct similarities to the likes of Jeff Scott Soto. In fact, bands such as RISING FORCE or IMPELLITERI would be a pretty good reference point for CLOVEN HOOF's material from this period, and there certainly weren't too many home-grown acts who even *attempted* this style of metal (HOLOGRAM were slightly more experimental, but the two outfits shared a few common ideas), let alone any who could carry it off with such conviction. It wasn't perfect, though, as a couple of tracks (notably the disappointing "Could This Be Love?") are a bit too melodic, while the confused "Daughter Of Darkness" doesn't work at all, and "Heavy Metal Men Of Steel" is, as you would expect, sub-MANOWAR drivel. Even so, it was still a solid effort overall.

Sadly, the new-look CLOVEN HOOF never really captured the public's imagination (I suppose »Fighting Back« might have been a bit overly-melodic for their original fan base), and the lads played remarkably few shows to promote themselves, which didn't help matters. In 1987, they once again experimented with a second guitarist (a chap called Paul Goodwin), although this move failed to reverse their fortunes. By the early part of 1988, the latest version of CLOVEN HOOF had fragmented pretty catastrophically, leaving bassist Lee 'Air' Payne on his own, although the plucky individual swiftly set about assembling another set of musicians to assist him in his future activities. Vocalist Russ North and guitarist Andrew Wood were hurriedly recruited from the ailing TREDEGAR, and unknown drummer Jon Brown was drafted in to restore CLOVEN HOOF to their familiar four-member status, although they had wisely dispensed with the pseudonyms, costumes and theatrics by this juncture. A convenient deal with the diversifying Heavy Metal label followed with almost indecent haste, and the lads were soon laying down their next long-player for the company. »Dominator« was more along the lines of the first album, with a hint of BLOOD MONEY thrown in for good measure, and a return to their early lyrical themes was clearly apparent on numbers such as "Warrior Of The Wasteland" and "Nova Battlestar", for example. Elsewhere, there were reworked versions of "Reach For The Sky" and "The Fugitive", alongside old favourite "Road Of Eagles", and it was all perfectly acceptable, although Russ North failed to shine quite as brightly as his predecessor.

Nevertheless, the album was a much better-received effort than the transitionary »Fighting Back«, and CLOVEN HOOF seemed to be recapturing some of their former glory by this stage. A follow-up set was soon commissioned, and the lads even started putting in a few appearances on the live circuit once more. 1989 saw the foursome making a return visit to the recording studio, and they eventually emerged with an album entitled »A Sultan's Ransom« (original title »Forgotten Heroes« was soon rejected), a rather less impressive affair than »Dominator«. This time, the tracks were slightly more commercial and polished in general, but the majority were fairly unmemorable in their construction. There were a few decent efforts, notably "D.V.R." and "Silver Surfer", although many others were a bit too anonymous for their own good. The album failed to perform particularly well, and the outfit's future looked a bit shaky, although they continued in the short term, recruiting a second guitarist yet again (they just couldn't resist trying this strategy, could they?). This time, the fifth member was a certain Lee Jones, yet another TREDEGAR veteran, and the revamped outfit were soon being featured on the 'Friday Rock Show' once more. Broadcast on the 21st of October 1989, CLOVEN HOOF's second session allowed the lads to perform "Astral Rider", "Mad Mad World" and "Mistress Of The Forest", three unremarkable numbers from their most recent album, plus a cover of THE SWEET's "Fox On The Run" (another cunning ruse to distance themselves from the glam community, presumably).

Sadly, the latest session failed to convince anyone (most importantly, Heavy Metal Records) that there was any mileage left in CLOVEN HOOF, especially as they seemed to be metamorphosing into TREDEGAR (a band who had never been a particularly highly-regarded entity themselves) at a fairly rapid rate. »A Sultan's Ransom« had painted a convincing picture of a talented group who could still come up with the occasional good idea, but who were now losing touch with their roots and the metal scene in general, and even their fanatical following throughout Europe had largely decided to abandon their one-time heroes. In fact, the end of CLOVEN HOOF appears to have come about through mutual agreement at some point in the early 90's (Russ North had already moved on to HOPE AND GLORY by 1991), and no further (official) releases ever appeared, although a naughty bootleg CD featuring the first EP and album was pressed up by the Reborn Classics label a couple of years after their demise, no doubt bringing a smile to the faces of many diehard fans.

LP's
»**Cloven Hoof**« Neat 1984
»**Fighting Back**« Moondancer Records 1986
['Live' album]
»**Dominator**« Heavy Metal 1988
[Also issued as limited edition picture disc]
»**A Sultan's Ransom**« Heavy Metal 1989

12" EP's
»**The Opening Ritual**« Elemental Music 1982
["Stormrider", "Back In The U.S.A." and "Starship Sentinel" all non-LP, "The Gates Of Gehenna" different to album version]

CD's
»**Dominator**« Heavy Metal 1988
»**A Sultan's Ransom**« Heavy Metal 1989
»**The Opening Ritual**« Reborn Classics 1993
[Bootleg release featuring first album and EP]

Compilation Appearances
"**Crack The Whip**" on »Metal Hammer« LP Roadrunner 1984 + »Metal Masters« 4-CD Box Castle Communications 1993
"**Laying Down The Law**" on »Metal Inferno« LP Castle Communications 1985
"**Gates Of Gehenna**" on »Metal Inferno« LP Castle Communications 1985

COBRA (I)

Nigel Boyd (v)
Glen Crawford (g)
Keith Sewell (g)
Mikey Thompson (b)
Nigel Hamilton (d)

As with the likes of NO SWEAT (see separate entry), for example, the relatively obscure Irish version of COBRA were one of the very first acts to be signed to the Rip Off label back in 1978, and the quintet were subsequently afforded the opportunity to lay down their debut single for the ambitious company. Issued in a picture sleeve with a truly abysmal front cover (featuring an atrociously-drawn gravestone, snake and ghost) and a practically illegible reverse, the two-tracker certainly let the band down pretty badly in terms of presentation. Unfortunately, the musical contents hardly compensated for this visual disaster, with both "Lookin' For A Lady" and "Graveyard Boogie" coming across as undeniably primitive, low-budget recordings with a variety of influences harvested from the rock'n'roll, punk and boogie camps. Certainly not in the same league as the likes of ROKKA, 100% PROOF or VARDIS, for example, and it's extremely unlikely that this exercise did all that much to improve COBRA's fortunes in years to come. To be honest, I'd give this one a miss if I were you, especially considering the preposterous price tag which has been attached to it with all-too-familiar arbitrariness. The two tracks were later recycled, incidentally, on the label's patchy »Belfast Rocks« compilation, but I reckon that COBRA had probably acknowledged their limited chances of achieving success by this stage, and presumably called it a day sooner rather than later. Sticksman Nigel Hamilton, incidentally, swiftly moved over to regional indie also-rans the TEARJERKERS, but the others seem to have disappeared from the scene completely.

7" Singles
»**Lookin' For A Lady**« Rip Off Records 1978

Compilation Appearances
"**Lookin' For A Lady**" on »Belfast Rocks« LP Rip Off Records 1979
"**Graveyard Boogie**" on »Belfast Rocks« LP Rip Off Records 1979

COBRA (II)

Paul Edmondson (v)
Steve Hughes (g)
Ian Beck (g,k)
Shaun Parker (b)
Chris Greer (d)

The best-known of all the home-grown acts (there were at least four) to have adopted the name COBRA (there were also several overseas equivalents, notably the melodic American outfit) were based in Lancashire, an area of considerable musical activity throughout the late 70's and the whole of the 80's. Having come together in the early part of the decade (originally as TALON, although they evolved into COBRA after recruiting new frontman Paul Edmondson and second axeman Ian Beck), the band's activities failed to raise too many eyebrows, and they seemed set to vanish into obscurity before long. However, the obliging Ebony concern offered them a lifeline in 1985, although the label had begun to lose its way somewhat in the years following the original NWOBHM explosion, and were handing out contracts rather haphazardly by the mid-80's, failing to take much notice of the development of the music scene and letting many of their acts down in terms of promotion and guidance. Nevertheless, COBRA happily signed on the dotted line and were soon recording their debut set for Ebony's rather pointless Criminal Response subsidiary, which eventually appeared in the form of the promisingly-titled »Warriors Of The Dead« long-player. It turned out to be a fairly curious slice of vinyl, featuring several heroic compositions in the general style of DRAGONSLAYER, TRIDENT or labelmates BLADE RUNNER (on their second album, anyway), although numbers such as "On My Knees" and "Wildest Dreams" also displayed a more down-to-earth, catchy type of material. It was a pretty good performance all round, although their offhand tendency to switch between styles might have been a tad confusing for the fans.

The lads didn't waste too much time before recording their follow-up (which emerged on Ebony itself this time, the company having apparently dispensed with the redundant Criminal Response by now), and the »Back From The Dead« set (laughably, promoted as a 'total death metal' release in the advertising of the day) made its way into the shops within a year of their debut. With COBRA now ostensibly featuring the services of a certain 'Stan' (before he teamed up with Kyle, Cartman and Kenny, presumably) on bass guitar (although I reckon it was probably still Shaun Parker all along), the group had developed a more consistent sound and were clearly attempting to make a move into decidedly GRIM REAPER-influenced territory on this slice of vinyl. While there are a couple of instances when the combo threatened to hit top form, such as "Devil's Daughter" and "Longest Night", the tracks were probably all a bit too similar to each other to win over some of the more 'middle ground' fans (the same fate befell BLADE RUNNER, whose flirtation with the power metal genre also went down like a lead balloon), which is a shame, as there were moments, such as on the keyboard-tinged "Life's Door" and the acoustic intro to "Night Creatures", where COBRA tried something slightly different.

Things went downhill for the COBRA boys after the release of their second long-playing effort, and (as with various ill-fated labelmates of the period such as BLOOD MONEY, RANKELSON, FAST KUTZ and TYGA MYRA) their activities had basically tailed off by the end of 1987, when the unsettled Chris Greer departed for pastures new. Nevertheless, a revised version of COBRA was to be found gigging again by the summer of 1988, the outfit now featuring replacement drummer Jason Lamb (recruited from local strugglers WITCHHUNT) and dedicated keyboard player Andy Hoyle. They were still fighting a losing battle, though, and the band seem to have called it a day within a relatively short space of time, having failed to attract any significant media or label interest in the interim. Most of the participants appear to have drifted away from the music scene altogether, although original drummer Chris Greer later resurfaced in the ranks of a Liverpool-based, melodic rock proposition called STADIUM. As with so many hopefuls who attempted to jump on the AOR bandwagon at this time, however, this keyboard-heavy quintet failed to make an impression on the British public in the long term. Erstwhile COBRA frontman Paul Edmondson, meanwhile, went on to lend a hand (as drummer!) in the TOUCHED offshoot known as the OUTSIDERS, and is probably still involved with the latter act on some level.

LP's
»**Warriors Of The Dead**« Criminal Response Records 1985
»**Back From The Dead**« Ebony 1986

COVENANT, THE

Stephen Thomas Hall (v,k)
Steven Perkins (g)
Michael Dennison (b)
Paul Turrell (d)

Scraping in at the tail end of the NWOBHM, the little-remembered Cheshire quartet who operated under the identity of THE COVENANT pressed up their sole two-tracker in such tiny quantities (back in 1986) that its existence was, until recently, a fairly well-kept secret. This is prog/metal territory (come back, it's not that bad), although I'm pleased to say that it's a bit heavier than the likes of HAZE or EARTHBOUND, for example. The competent A-side ("Stations") has clear, distinctively-phrased vocals and an unusual arrangement which is immensely similar to the material featured on the one-off single released by AVALON (another group who were partial to one-word song titles) two years previously. Flipside "Look At Us Now", on the other hand, is more of a power ballad with a widdly keyboard interlude, the overall sound coming across as an enjoyable combination of DAWNWATCHER and CHEMICAL ALICE. Both selections are quite long (hence the need for a 12" single) and proficiently written, with the record benefitting from an impressive production courtesy of London's Peppermint Place Studios (who obviously had a bad hair day when it came to producing EXOCET). THE COVENANT were never the most high-profile act doing the rounds in the mid-80's, however, and seem to have been a minor cult rather than genuine contenders for full-scale fame and fortune.

The band were still playing the odd gig a year or two after their single's release, but things seem to have gone relatively quiet shortly thereafter. However, as with such progressively-inclined acts as HAZE, GRACE, PALLAS etc., THE COVENANT actually remained a going concern, operating in decidedly low-profile mode for the remainder of the decade (occasionally contributing to cassette-only compilations) and eventually resurfacing (with a new drummer, the implausibly-named Baron Von Brown) with a CD entitled »Spectres At The Feast«, released at some point in the mid-90's. By this juncture, however, they were being touted as prime exponents of the 'neo-prog' (whatever the hell that means) style as epitomised by IQ and PENDRAGON, so the lads seem to have been angling for the lucrative prog market in no uncertain terms. I assume that additional releases could well surface in future, so you might want to check out the specialist dealers from time to time if your interest is sufficiently piqued. Confusingly, however, there's at least one other prog act currently utilising the COVENANT name (a one-man project), not to mention a black metal version (although I reckon they're now THE KOVENANT), so be careful! There's no connection, incidentally, with the much heavier (Bristol?) COVENANT who were operational at the time of their original release and who appeared on the »Metal Collection Vol.III« LP on Ebony. Keep an eye out for the »Stations« 12" (which comes in a slightly unusual picture sleeve) if you fancy something a bit out of the ordinary, but you might be searching for a very long time before you find a copy.

12" Singles
»Stations« Tree Frog Records 1986

CD's
»Spectres At The Feast« Private 1994?

CRACKED MIRROR

Jozef Rytlewski (v,g)
Michael Dixon (v,b)
Jackie Hazel (k)
Paul Harbin (d)

The once-neglected name of CRACKED MIRROR was yet another to be hauled back from the brink of utter obscurity in the early 90's, when a bevy of excitable NWOBHM collectors, tantalised by a few tales of long-lost classic albums, began clamouring for their extremely scarce, eponymous long-player. The record in question had originally been made available to local fans as a private pressing in 1983, and had long since been forgotten by virtually all those who had once encountered the band, especially since so few copies had been manufactured and sold in the first instance. Having initially formed as far back as 1978 in East Sussex, the outfit's appeal was based mainly on their live appearances, and the unit toured successfully throughout the whole of the South of England during their six year existence (performing a well-received repertoire of unassuming heavy fare), including two notable occasions where the quartet appeared as special guests at the 'Kent Custom Bike Show'. Well, when the Hells Angels invite you to provide some light entertainment at one of their exclusive soirées, you can hardly refuse…

CRACKED MIRROR's seldom-seen LP was pressed in a quantity of just a few hundred copies at the time, and this nine-tracker has subsequently become regarded as something of a high-ranking collectable amongst fans of the 70's-style, guitar-based end of the NWOBHM market (see also PHOENIX RISING, HIGH RISK and VOLTZ, for example). In fact, the selection of compositions on display serve to provide another exemplary demonstration that, even at the very height of the NWOBHM movement, not everyone in Britain had adopted the post-punk aggression and dynamic arrangements of the genre's flagship acts. Indeed, certain acts (CRACKED MIRROR and the Derbyshire version of WARRIOR, for instance) still clung pretty resiliently to the framework of 'old school' influences such as DEEP PURPLE and WISHBONE ASH, an outlook which (although alienating both the younger fans and record companies, reducing their chances of commercial success to a pretty nominal level) endeared them to their region's traditional rock devotees, who still revered some of the pioneering ensembles from the previous decade. In particular, inclusions such as "Waitin' For The Man" or "We Shall Not Forget" portrayed CRACKED MIRROR at their most retroactive, these unashamed efforts even going so far as to make the good old Hammond organ a prime focus of attention, something which the likes of

WHITE SPIRIT and BILL THE MURDERER also used to their advantage from time to time.

With the group being quite realistic about their chances of making it big (approximately zero) and the number of records they could sell at their gigs (a few dozen), they didn't go overboard in terms of the quantity pressed, and it seems that they were probably quite happy just to do their thing for the benefit of a modest number of loyal supporters on the South Coast. Although CRACKED MIRROR themselves had run their course and fragmented within a year or so of the album's release, band mainman Jozef Rytlewski has maintained a significant level of involvement with the music business, and has, most recently, been playing for his own enjoyment with a group called the PULLBACKS. If there's any justice, he will have been suitably rewarded for releasing some unsold copies of the CRACKED MIRROR LP (issued in a colourful sleeve depicting a guitar crashing through a mirror) onto the market in the past decade. The asking price is still quite high, though, but you might want to consider saving up for a copy if you're partial to a bit of heavy guitar material with something of a 70's feel.

LP's
»Cracked Mirror« Private 1983

CRAZY BLAZE

Dave Stockwell (v,g)
Paul Wayman (b,k)
Paul Caboche (d)
Dave Bowler (sx)

They often say you should never judge a book by its cover (or, by inference, a record by its sleeve), although, with a handful of exceptions such as SHADOWFAX and BASELINE, this axiom tends to be critically flawed in the case of metal singles and albums, which tend to stand out a mile and can usually be quite easily separated from punk, mod, pop *etc.* purely on the basis of cover design and song titles. Just to throw a weighty spanner in the works, though, here's another exception to the rule: CRAZY BLAZE. Even the name sounds a bit questionable, and to look at the four TEARDROP EXPLODES/SPARKS rejects pictured on the cover of their 1986 single, your expectations of finding an undiscovered NWOBHM masterpiece lurking within would, understandably, be pretty low. Mind you, the badly-drawn skull and Flying V on the rever-

se looks rather more promising. Then again, there's a disconcerting credit for a saxophone player...oh dear. Fortunately, the dreaded sax is restricted to the A-side, a fairly standard ballad of the type offered by acts of the time such as STATETROOPER or US. Nothing to get excited about, in other words.

The real surprise, however, comes on the reverse, and their "No Peace For The Wicked" effort is actually a bit of a cracker. This comes across as a kind of upbeat mixture of STAGEFRIGHT and ZENITH, with a capable guitar break and a strong vocal effort, so I reckon it's probably well worth buying for this track alone. It's a pity that so many bands felt obliged to feature a ballad (presumably to showcase their ability to diversify) as part of their singles when the fans of the time (and of the present day) would, more often than not, have preferred a pair of faster and heavier numbers. The general consensus of opinion is that more sedate and *'meaningful'* compositions tend to work best within the context of a full LP, although, to be fair, I suppose that very few part-timers had the resources for such a project. Certainly, CRAZY BLAZE failed to go on to greater things in later years, and had presumably called time on their quest for major-label status before the end of the decade. Still, they remain a mystery with regard to their origins, and I've never seen any mention of them in publications of the time, so I guess we may never know their story. To conclude, however, the CRAZY BLAZE oddity is a pretty respectable single and you might just want to consider adding it to your ever-expanding wants lists.

7" Singles
»Broken Dream« Short Records 1986

CRUCIFIXION

Glyn Morgan (v,g)
Pete Morgan (rg)
Paul Drinkwater (b)
Geoff Ford (d)

One of many outfits around the world to have adopted the name at one stage or another, the British version of CRUCIFIXION were based in Essex, and would appear to have formed towards the end of 1979, rapidly establishing a strong following throughout the county (including all the usual East End haunts) as one of the region's more energetic and powerful NWOBHM acts. By the second half of 1980, following numerous live appearances in the South East, the quartet had managed to organise a 7" release through the little-known Miramar label, which ultimately saw "The Fox" and "Death Sentence" being unleashed upon an unsuspecting public. It was a cracking debut, featuring a pair of aggressive, upbeat bruisers in the general manner of DEMOLITION, TANK or RICOCHET, the gravel-throated vocals of Glyn Morgan being the perfect foil for the musical accompaniment provided by the three-piece rhythm section. It was an excellent start, although it was an extremely limited pressing, and one which (despite its availability from national outlets such as Bullet Records) didn't really sell in huge quantities outwith their own area, so it was back to local gigging for another year or two until a somewhat bigger break finally came CRUCIFIXION's way.

In 1982, the group (now featuring new bassist Chris Mann) hooked up with Neat Records, and were soon re-recording "The Fox" (a truly scorching version) for the label's »60 Minutes Plus« compilation. In due course, they laid down their own vinyl two-tracker, a release which coupled "Take It Or Leave It" (featuring high-range vocals from their new recruit) and "On The Run", a far better number which saw the outfit operating in their original style. It was a pretty good way to begin their association with Neat, although it would appear that the label weren't swayed in favour of commissioning a full album at that stage, presumably reflecting the fact that the single had performed acceptably, but not outstandingly (a critical drubbing in 'Kerrang' didn't help matters), in terms of sales. In fact, the lads didn't actually release a follow-up until 1984, when the »Green Eyes« 12" EP was issued (in another superbly clichéd sleeve) by Neat. It saw a move towards a rather more accessible style of semi-power metal in the EXCALIBUR or BLITZKRIEG vein, with the title track being the stand-out effort by a long way. Mind you, the ending's a bit close to TYTAN's "Blind Men And Fools" for comfort, although we'll be charitable and forgive them. The other tracks featured ("Moon Rising" and the lyrically-dubious "Jailbait") were pretty disposable, to be honest, and the wisdom of including the lyrics to all three songs was slightly questionable, given that they hardly push the boundaries of literary credibility (the words to "Green Eyes" are truly remarkable, given that they barely rhyme, scan or make any sense whatsoever) in any way.

It sounded as though CRUCIFIXION had decided to recruit yet another new vocalist along the way (their latest line-up wasn't credited this time), as the singer on the EP seemed rather more capable and professional than either Morgan or Mann, so it would appear that the band might just have been struggling to maintain their personnel by this time. Nevertheless, their new, polished material and change in musical inclination was insufficient to reverse their fortunes, and this latest release failed to propel them into the big-time yet again. Almost certainly, the lads had finally called it a day within a year or two of their last vinyl offering, and none of the musicians appear to have resurfaced in any acts of note. It was a great pity, as the outfit certainly deserved their share of recognition for being one of the original exponents of the true NWOBHM archetype. Nowadays, all three of CRUCIFIXION's vinyl releases are regarded as highly collectable, with their seldom-seen debut (never issued in a picture sleeve) tending to fetch three-figure prices on the few occasions that it comes up for sale.

12" EP's
»**Green Eyes**« Neat 1984
[Labels identify tracks in wrong order, also released as limited edition on purple vinyl, a few marbled]

7" Singles
»**The Fox**« Miramar Records 1980
»**Take It Or Leave It**« Neat 1982

Compilation Appearances
"**The Fox**" on »60 Minutes Plus« Cassette Neat 1982/CD Teichiku 1992 + »All Hell Let Loose« LP Neat 1983
[Different to single version]
"**Green Eyes**" on »Metal Inferno« LP Castle Communications 1985 + »Metal Masters« 4-CD Box Castle Communications 1993
"**On The Run**" on »NWOBHM Vol.2« Bootleg CD 1992

CRY

Dave Pearsall (v,b)
Steve Clifford (g)
Andy Young (g)
Ian 'Len' Parkin (d)

Emerging from the ashes of Yorkshire's ill-fated LOTUS CRUISE (see separate entry), the musical entity known as CRY (boasting new guitarist Steve Clifford and with original vocalist Dave Pearsall assuming bass duties) came into existence towards the end of 1985. Discovering

POISON, MÖTLEY CRÜE, GUNS'N'ROSES et al., investing in hairspray/sunglasses/hats and cultivating a rather sleazier image, the revamped outfit burst onto the scene with a less-than-prestigious showcase gig at the not-remotely-legendary Hot Tub Club in Doncaster, this being followed by a recording session (in the latter half of 1986) which yielded an appearance on Ebony's »The Metal Collection Vol.III« album with "Party After Dark". The latter was subsequently recycled as part of an introductory single (B-side "Crazy Days, Crazy Nights"), which emerged as a self-financed 7" early the following year, copies of which were soon being snapped up by regional devotees of 'big hair' rock. The public reaction was, to say the least, mixed; the local press tended to heap praise upon CRY at every opportunity, but the wider community was, generally speaking, less-than-impressed with their sundry antics. In particular, a disastrous gig at the Royal Standard in Walthamstow, at which approximately fifteen people (few of whom were paying customers) were present, was reviewed in 'Kerrang', which can hardly have helped their reputation.

Nonetheless, the group were invited to support WOLFSBANE in due course, and even developed a loyal group of fans called 'The Salad Cream Team', who gleefully followed their heroes to many an eventful outing. A second two-tracker, the supposedly-risqué »Give Her An Ice-cream And Watch Her Melt« (the B-side had the rather more concise title "Star") was unleashed upon the public later in the year, by which time the ensemble had firmly taken their place as part of Britain's burgeoning glam/sleaze scene, incorporating raunchy-as-you-like interpretations of POISON's "Talk Dirty To Me" and ROD STEWART's "Hot Legs" in their ever-expanding live repertoire. All the while, the lads continued to benefit from some suspiciously-favourable coverage in the ever-obliging 'Kerrang' (friends in high places, perhaps?), including a remarkably generous full-page feature which allowed outspoken frontman Dave Pearsall to impart his rather opinionated views on why the sleazy ones were apparently so phenomenally unpopular in their native town of Barnsley: 'Cos we're different. We're not SAXON, we're not SEVENTH SON, we're not Heavy Metal and I don't think they can handle it. The last three times we've played there, there was so much trouble it was bringin' us down.' (Ref: Kerrang No.182, April 1988). If you say so, Dave…

The increasingly self-assured quartet, clearly confident of their collective ability, happily predicted that they would go from strength to strength, and both singles eventually went on to shift well in excess of a thousand copies. However, despite numerous support slots as well as their own headlining tours in 1987 and 1988, things evidently went a bit pear-shaped (various additional vinyl releases were occasionally outlined but always failed to materialise), which ultimately resulted in the group parting company with their original drummer and utilising the services of TREASON bloke Sean Kelley as a stand-in for a short time. However, the long-term problems continued to plague CRY, and, notwithstanding the extremely 'charitable' patronage of 'Kerrang', the members were forced to go their separate ways in late 1988. Dave Pearsall and Andy Young formed the short-lived ALLEYCATS in a last-ditch attempt to establish a heavier combo, while Steve Clifford joined one of the later incarnations of SEVENTH SON, whereas their hard-working original drummer, Len Parkin (who had also apparently played with the aforementioned SEVENTH SON at one time) eventually ended up in the glam outfit RICH RAGS. Incidentally, both of the CRY singles were issued with promo-only picture sleeves, although these are far less commonly encountered (and considerably more expensive) than the standard sleeveless versions.

7" Singles
»**Party After Dark**« Crazy Flowerpot Records 1987
»**Give Her An Ice-cream And Watch Her Melt**« Crazy Flowerpot Records 1987

Compilation Appearances
"**Party After Dark**" on »The Metal Collection Vol.III« LP Ebony 1987

CRYER

Graham Careless (v)
Gary Chapman (g)
Stu Clarke (g)
Fez Ferriday (b)
Mick Billingham (k)
Roger Whitehouse (d)

Emerging from that heaving metropolis known as Birmingham in the late 70's, CRYER (not to be confused with some obscure American namesakes) endured numerous line-up changes in their formative years, during which time their musical direction became pretty firmly established as a heavy, progressive style with more than a hint of BLACK SABBATH. By late 1978, they had started to get their act together properly, and were often to be found on the road with GILLAN, an outfit who apparently took quite a shine to the lads at an early stage. Nevertheless, a few changes were in store during 1979 (unlikely as it may seem, future STARFIGHTERS mainman Steve Burton actually fronted them for a short while at around this time), when internal dissatisfaction concerning their original stance resulted in a further rearrangement in personnel and direction, the most stable line-up being born later in that year. With a six-piece presence, featuring two guitarists and a keyboard player, CRYER became a forceful proposition, especially with the more dynamic, accessible style that they were rapidly mastering. In the spring of 1980, their debut release appeared on the Happy Face label (also connected to both DIAMOND HEAD and BRIAR in their early days), a two-tracker coupling "The Single" and "Hesitate". It was a strong way to introduce the outfit to the general public, the epic feel of the tracks bringing forth comparisons with the likes of LIMELIGHT, DAWNWATCHER, DAMASCUS and Kent's LEGEND. It wasn't a particularly common style in the UK at the time, however, although the likes of QUEENSRYCHE would soon be mastering a highly-similar variety of metal on the other side of the Atlantic.

There was a certain kind of logic behind calling one of their tracks "The Single", as it tied in with a competition for one lucky fan to win an electric guitar by suggesting the best original title for that number. History doesn't record who that fortuitous individual was, although the song subsequently became known as "The Visionary", and rapidly established itself as a firm favourite in the group's live set (by all accounts, CRYER gigs were memorable events, with the obligatory light show and pyrotechnics) for several years to come. Their 7" (issued in a slightly impressionistic, monochrome picture sleeve) shifted a respectable number of units at the time, and remains a fairly highly-valued commodity in the NWOBHM collector's market. Mind you, many examples still retain the original competition insert, so it looks as though relatively few punters bothered to enter the contest at the time. The band's next vinyl appearance came after they had been plucked from semi-obscurity to be included on MCA's »Brute Force« sampler of emerging talent, this worthy compilation being issued in the second half of the year. CRYER's "Day To Day" was another well-crafted composition, the excellent vocals of Graham Careless lending an air of authority to the proceedings, and the self-assured ensemble acquitted themselves admirably in the company of some rather more high-profile acts such as DIAMOND HEAD, FIST and RAVEN.

Long-serving keyboard player Mick Billingham was to depart towards the end of the year, however (defecting to chart-toppers DEXY'S MIDNIGHT RUNNERS, no less), but a suitable replacement was duly found in the form of erstwhile LIQUID MIRRORS stalwart Pete Wayne. The ensemble's fortunes were to pick up significantly in the new year, as the lads were invited to lay down a session for the 'Friday Rock Show'. Broadcast on the 23rd of January 1981, the revised act showcased "The Visionary", "Spaces", "Footsteps Through Time" and "Cyclone", the latter trio being a fine set of compositions in their now-established style. The session was an excellent effort all round, and the outfit were surely deserving of a place on one of the BBC's two tie-in compilations, although they were one of many outfits to be overlooked when it came down to the nitty gritty of the selection process. At this juncture, there was wide public speculation that it was only a matter of time before CRYER signed to one label or another and delivered an excellent debut album. Strangely, however, it proved not to be the case, and the group's activities over the next couple of years appear to have been largely restricted to the same old circuit of small-time, regional club shows alongside other local hopefuls such as DEMOLITION, BRIAR and the STARFIGHTERS. One of their well-attended appearances (at the legendary Railway Inn), towards the end of 1982, was reviewed in 'Kerrang', with the following assurance coming from Wayne Perkins: *'I still firmly believe that they can make it, if only they would get out of Birmingham. My argument is based on the sheer quality of their songs.'* (Ref: Kerrang No.31, December 1982).

In spite of this generous seal of approval, part one of the outfit's story appears to have drawn to a natural close shortly thereafter, although it's worth mentioning that their respected name was often bandied about as a prime influence by the emergent MARSHALL LAW in later years. It wasn't quite the end of the road, however, as the CRYER lads regrouped for yet another attempt to storm the rock world in 1984, this time operating as FORCE (see separate entry) and more or less promoting themselves as an all-new proposition. Under their new identity, they finally managed to get around to giving the fans that long-awaited full album, an extremely enjoyable set which featured a considerable number of CRYER originals. Sadly, however, times had clearly changed; their once-loyal followers had moved on in search of new musical stimuli and the record (despite being an eminently proficient effort) wasn't actually received quite as well as the musicians might have anticipated, leaving the dejected ensemble to go to ground once more.

7" Singles
»The Single« Happy Face 1980
[B-side "Hesitate" later appeared in different form on »Set Me Free…« LP by FORCE]

Exclusive Compilation Appearances
"Day To Day" on »Brute Force« LP MCA 1980 + »NWOBHM Vol.3« Bootleg CD 1992
[Later appeared in different form on »Set Me Free…« LP by FORCE]

CRYS

Liam Forde (v,rg)
Alun Morgan (g)
Scott Forde (b)
Nicky Samuel (d)

You wouldn't honestly expect great things from a band whose name literally translates as *'Shirt'* (I suppose *'Pants'* might have been worse, but not much), but this relatively obscure bunch were actually a pretty good advertisement for the early 80's Welsh metal scene. Their earliest known release, the »Lan Yn Y Gogledd« (something along the lines of »Shores Of The North«, I reckon) single (produced by Richard Morris of fellow hopefuls TROBWLL), is a pretty good stab at NWOBHM, although the unremarkable, mid-paced A-side pales somewhat beside "Cadw Symud" ("Keep Moving"?) on the reverse, this being a cracking, upbeat number in the style of BLACK AXE or LE GRIFFE. With their debut (issued on the tiny Click label in 1980) having attracted the attention of some more prominent record companies, the emergent CRYS were picked up by the much larger Sain concern, and duly issued their first album (again sung entirely in their native tongue) a year later. The »Rhyfelwr« (»Warrior«) LP suggested that the group's usual style was closer to "Lan Yn Y Gogledd" than the more energetic "Cadw Symud", the set being comprised mainly of competent (but fairly unmemorable) mid-paced rockers which occasionally bring to mind certain aspects of MARZ, GEDDES AXE or STAGEFRIGHT, but which tend to stop just short of *'out and out NWOBHM'*. It was, after their introductory two-tracker, slightly disappointing, although not a complete disaster, and highlights would include the heavier "Cân Lis", "Dyma'r Band Cymraeg" ("We're A Welsh Band", perhaps inspired by a certain GRAND FUNK RAILROAD number?) as well as the atmospheric title track, all of which show that the quartet were more than capable of pleasing the headbangers.

The lads were retained by Sain, so sales of the album must have been pretty respectable, and CRYS continued to make regular trips to the studio throughout 1982, the fruits of which emerged in the shape of a second long-playing effort, this time entitled »Tymor Yr Heliwr« (»Season Of The Hunter«). It saw them sticking pretty closely to their original direction, and the LP contained a selection of numbers which basically oscillated between semi-NWOBHM and semi-boogie without threatening to become especially interesting. It had a few enjoyable moments, admittedly, notably "Cwrdd A Gofid" ("Welcome To Sorrow", or something), the lengthy "Gwilth Y Bore" (a more ambitious affair in the NO QUARTER mould) and "Barod Am Roc" ("Ready To Rock"), which actually took pride of place as the title track of an obscure Sain Records sampler two years later. Although CRYS were rapidly becoming a familiar name on the local scene, they hardly went out on a limb to make themselves known further afield, and subsequently kept a fairly low profile until early the following year, whereupon they were invited to lay down four tracks for a 'Friday Rock Show' session, broadcast on the 28th of January 1983. Comprising "Pendoncwyr", "Merched Gwillt A Gwin" (both taken from their latest album) and two (shock horror) selections sung in English viz. "It's About Time" and "Rockin' Along" (a Welsh-language version of which had appeared on »Tymor Yr Heliwr«, revealing some shameless "Whole Lotta Rosie" pilferage), the slot suggested that the group might finally have been attempting to break away from their small-time roots and widen their potential audience.

In spite of their best efforts to cross over to a broader fan base, however, things didn't actually work out particularly well for the protagonists in the wake of this English-language experimentation. Not only did this exercise fail miserably to propel them to national prominence, it might even have led to them being ostracised by their local communities in the long term, and it seems unlikely that they were able to keep things going in the face of public disapproval. There appears to be little evidence to suggest that CRYS ever managed to play any shows outside Wales, so maybe they just didn't feel confident enough to abandon their roots and portray themselves as a full-scale English-language proposition. None of the lads appear to have resurfaced in other bands of note (I reckon Nicky Samuel assisted the feebly-monikered SWITCHY AND THE CIRCUIT BREAKERS, but that's about it), so they probably either retreated to the relative safety of the small-time club circuit or returned to their day jobs thereafter. Whatever the story, only these three releases are known to exist at present, the 7" (in its rather dull yellow sleeve picturing the musicians) being a relatively recent discovery (which would no doubt fetch a hefty price) due to its extreme scarcity, although the albums (»Tymor Yr Heliwr« had a pretty unremarkable cover, whereas its predecessor came in a Black Metal-looking sleeve with gothic lettering and a heroic, Norse-type warrior on horseback) are marginally easier to locate, particularly if you have friends in Wales!

LP's
»Rhyfelwr« Sain Records 1981
»Tymor Yr Heliwr« Sain Records 1982

7" Singles
»Lan Yn Y Gogledd« Click Records 1980
[Both tracks non-LP]

Compilation Appearances
"Barod Am Roc" on »Barod Am Roc 1« LP Sain Records 1984

CYNIC

Tony Eyres (v)
Sean Grant (g)
Dominic Heptinstall (g)
Raymond 'Baz' Pedlingham (b)
Tim Batkin (d)

No, I haven't gone completely bonkers (well, I have, but it's hardly a major revelation) and started including American techno-thrash propositions in this volume; the original version of CYNIC were, in truth, one of the NWOBHM movement's best-kept secrets. The influence of early British outfits on the likes of METALLICA, MEGADETH *etc.* has been comprehensively (some sceptics might say *excessively*) documented over the years, but how about the reverse situation? Certainly, atypically powerful ensembles such as JJ'S POWERHOUSE, WHITE HEAT, TYRANT and SALEM deviated significantly from the archetypal NWOBHM sound, possibly assimilating a few influences from heavier American and European acts of the period rather than merely retreading the familiar path travelled by all the feeble THIN LIZZY and BAD COMPANY copyists. Worcestershire's little-remembered CYNIC are yet another addition to the growing list, given that their self-financed »Suicide« two-tracker from 1983 contained a cracking pair of numbers that could practically be passed off as genuine »Master Of Puppets« out-takes to some of METALLICA's more gullible followers. The group's rise to non-stardom failed to make too many headlines at the time, although they appear to have started out a year or two earlier, and, like so many of their regional contemporaries (TYRANT, IDOL RICH, ARC, VIRGIN STAR *etc.*) decided to get themselves noticed by releasing a slice of vinyl rather than relying on the usual round of minor club appearances.

Having concluded that their only chance to break out of the small-but-enthusiastic local scene was to stump up the cash for a private single, CYNIC delivered their humble vinyl debut in due course, although it appears to have been such a modest pressing that relatively few copies probably made it into more widespread circulation after all. Anyway, the A-side itself is an extremely impressive number in the mould of METALLICA's "Fade To Black" or "Sanitarium", with a melancholic opening, multiple tempo changes and even a Hetfield-style vocal performance, spoiled only by some truly execrable lyrics (notably the laughable *'you really must not take your life'* and the bewilderingly-inept *'nothing's always what it seems'*), although it's all hugely enjoyable nonetheless. On the flipside, meanwhile, "No Time At All" is a faster, more straightforward composition which chugs along quite happily in the same vein as JJ'S POWERHOUSE's "Blackrods" or BLITZKRIEG's "Inferno", and, if we're sticking to the METALLICA comparisons, this effort is probably slightly more attuned to some of their earliest material. Top quality stuff all round, and there's no doubt that this sleeveless (and fairly unremarkable-looking) 7" should be placed at the very highest level in the hierarchy of ultra-rare, genre-defining collectables, sharing the company of the likes of RICOCHET, HOLLOW GROUND, JJ'S POWERHOUSE and HIGH TREASON. It was an impeccable start, but metal fans outwith the immediate area failed to get wind of this talented proposition, and CYNIC ultimately failed to achieve further recognition or to capitalise on their debut offering.

Although the ensemble began to fragment

within a year or so of releasing their first single (a couple of members defected to the emergent TYGA MYRA project along the way, but only bassist Baz Pedlingham lasted the distance, adopting the dubious *alter ego* of Randy Lingham), CYNIC kept going for some time thereafter. In fact, they continually evolved in terms of musical direction and personnel and remained a feature of the British metal scene until at least 1987, when the live reviews section in 'Kerrang' briefly mentioned their inauspicious appearance at a local multi-band event (alongside one or two long-forgotten minor hopefuls), although the publicity hardly revitalised their career. With the journalist in question objecting to the fact that the hapless CYNIC vocalist took to the stage wearing a dinner jacket (!), their newer material (although apparently covering an unusually wide range of styles) was dismissed as rather uninspiring, so it looks as though they had completely lost the plot by this time. C'est la vie.

7" Singles
»Suicide« SRT 1983

DAMASCUS

Billy Downs (v)
Dave Bridge (g)
Kevin Duncalf (b)
Paul Ryan (d)

Originally rising from the ashes of the recently-demised THIN END OF THE WEDGE (see separate entry), Merseyside's DAMASCUS first came into being in around 1983, having been formed by guitarist Dave Bridge and drummer Bill Campion. In fact, Campion stayed only a relatively short time before being succeeded by newcomer Paul Ryan, and the revised line-up (completed by bassist Kevin Duncalf and charismatic vocalist Billy Downs) didn't waste much time before getting their »Open Your Eyes« EP pressed up and into the shops the following year. Issued (twice) in a garish green sleeve featuring a demonic image of the frontman in full-blown 'Possessed' mode, the record is certainly a major departure from THIN END OF THE WEDGE's raunchy rockers. The material was quite weighty, although Billy Downs' distinctive vocals (an exaggerated version of a style utilised, on occasion, by EXPORT's Harry Shaw) are undoubtedly an acquired taste (they irritated me immensely on the first couple of listens). The title track and

"Something On My Mind", for example, are mid-paced numbers which reflect certain aspects of outfits such as BLEAK HOUSE, ORIGINAL SIN and BLOOD MONEY, while retaining a fairly unique identity. On the reverse, "Cold Horizon" is a very powerful ballad with highly original, double-tracked vocal passages, before "Midnight Train" (whose main riff is highly similar to BLEAK HOUSE's "Chase The Wind") rounds things off in energetic mode once again. A very enjoyable EP, it certainly wasn't what I was expecting, having trusted a rather unreliable source's assertion that it was by *'one of the really heavy bands'*...

DAMASCUS, having at least an album's worth of self-penned material at their disposal, laid down a considerable number of representative examples for demonstration purposes, including a highly capable six track cassette featuring such never-released selections as "Fight Or Flight", "Goodbye Harry", "This Is It", "Another Rainy Day", "Predator" and "Women In Black". With the group displaying an uncanny knack of writing memorable, powerful compositions, the musicianship was particularly impressive on the heavier tracks such as "Fight Or Flight" and "Predator", although the cassette was an excellent representation of their abilities throughout, even if a couple of numbers seem unnecessarily long. In view of all these regular trips to the studio, it originally looked as though DAMASCUS might have been preparing the ground for a full-length release, although the lads never seem to have expressed any serious intentions of going it alone and issuing another self-financed record. To be honest, I reckon their only hope would have been to sell themselves to someone like Ebony, but the observation that they didn't exactly go overboard with live appearances was probably their undoing, and the lads almost certainly lost their way within a year or so, after which they presumably returned to their day jobs (which, in Dave Bridge's case, is teaching the guitar) before long.

Strangely, none of the one-time members of DAMASCUS appear to have resurfaced in other rock acts of note, which really is a scandalous waste of talent, although they were hardly the only decent band who failed to last the distance. Billy Downs, it has to be stated, could probably have made a good living belting out MICHAEL BOLTON-style power ballads to middle-aged divorcees in later years, but seems to have decided against it, fortunately. The »Open Your Eyes« EP remains an extremely popular item amongst serious NWOBHM collectors (in spite of the fact that a reasonable quantity of copies were prised out of the former members a few years back), and one whose asking price usually hovers around the dreaded three-figure mark on most dealers' lists. If you ever see a playable copy at a knock-down price, therefore, don't hesitate to pick it up. It's also well worth mentioning that the record's production is, especially for a small-budget independent release of the early 80's, truly exceptional (although it's strange that nobody even got a credit for their troubles), with incredible clarity and separation of instruments. Well done, whoever was responsible!

12" EP's
»Open Your Eyes« Private 1984
[Original issue with different reverse sleeve]
»Open Your Eyes« Private 1984
[Second issue with insert, sleeve same both sides]

Compilation Appearances
"Open Your Eyes" on »NWOBHM Vol.2« Bootleg CD 1992

DARK HEART

Phil Brown (v)
Alan Clark (g)
Steve Small (rg)
Colin Bell (b)
Ian Thompson (d)

The history of DARK HEART, an act from County Durham, seems to be rather convoluted, although it would appear that they may well have evolved from the version of TOKYO ROSE who were featured on Guardian's »Pure Overkill« compilation in 1983 (as opposed to the bunch that released the shockingly-bad »Dry Your Eyes« single). The aforementioned outfit are certainly known to have contributed personnel to HOLOSADE in later years (as did DARK HEART), and the vocalist sounds extremely similar in both cases, so it looks as though TOKYO ROSE were indeed probably something of a DARK HEART forerunner, although the line-ups certainly wouldn't have been identical. In any case, DARK HEART (featuring former BATTLEAXE drummer Ian Thompson) appear to have come into existence in the early months of 1984 (vocalist Phil Brown shouldn't be confused with the identically-named individual who sang on the SHEER KHAN single), after which they somehow (as with SPARTAN WARRIOR) drew the attention of Roadrunner Records in Europe, presumably as a result of their involvement with Guardian in the first instance. The upshot was that DARK HEART were offered a coveted opportunity to record a full album for release throughout mainland Europe, and the lads jumped at the chance to get their own long-player into the shops.

Their »Shadows Of The Night« opus emerged (in an irrelevant and poorly-drawn sleeve) as a matter of course, and this showed the quintet to be a fairly powerful proposition with something of a MYTHRA-influenced vocalist, the overall sound being quite reminiscent of acts such as SAVAGE, SPARTA, CHARIOT or early SATAN. There was some pretty respectable musicianship and a few creative ideas on display throughout, particularly on the likes of "Don't Break The Circle" (no prizes for originality on the title front, though), "No Time For Turning" and the complex "Turn Of The Tide", the group probably winning over a number of metal fans by virtue of the fact that they didn't rely on any over-the-top riffing or super-fast arrangements to conceal a fundamental lack of talent or innovation. Nevertheless, there was a hell of a lot of competition in the semi-power field at the time, and the hapless DARK HEART were largely lost in the deluge of new outfits who were constantly materialising around them. As with the likes of JAGUAR and the aforementioned SPARTAN WARRIOR, DARK HEART's debut for Roadrunner failed to sell in particularly impressive quantities, and none of these three bands were ever invited to deliver a follow-up release.

By the middle of 1985, DARK HEART had already undergone a few changes (abandoning plans to record a second long-player entitled »Chase The Dawn«), with Colin Bell going off to do his own thing with other bands such as ROULETTE and CHARGER (see separate entry), while Phil Brown, having left towards the end of 1984, spent a short time with a German outfit called REBEL. Nevertheless, guitarist Alan Clark kept DARK HEART going (they briefly changed their name to ARENA, but elected to revert to their original moniker within a matter of weeks), whereupon the revised outfit (the identity of the new members was never fully established, although it's known that they tried out a couple of new drummers in Dave Hudson and Mark Burley) were featured on Ebony's »The Metal Collection Volume I« with the forgettable "Stone Cold Hearted". After that, the group proceeded to record an EP called »Straight From The Heart« (which was advertised for sale through the pages of 'Kerrang') towards the end of that year, although this would appear to have been their last notable piece of studio activity, the faltering band apparently ceasing all operations at some point in 1987. In fact, I've never heard of a vinyl copy of »Straight From The Heart« being offered for sale in recent times, which is a bit odd, and I suspect that it might actually have been a cassette-only release. If anyone knows differently, be sure to let us know!

That wasn't quite the end of the story, though, as the ex-DARK HEART duo of Colin Bell and Phil Brown had linked up again by the end of 1985 to form HOLOSADE (Brown adopting the alias of 'Philip de Sade' and wearing a silly mask from an early stage), the pair recruiting former TOKYO ROSE guitarist Gary Thomas, ex-PHANTOM axeman Jack Hammer (aka Simon Jones, later of SABBAT) and drummer Mick Allen (aka Damian Lee) to complete the line-up. The newly-established HOLOSADE were also duly featured (immediately after DARK HEART, as it happens) on the aforementioned »The Metal Collection Volume I« (as, bizarrely, were Colin Bell's other band, CHARGER!) with "Cries In The Night", a fairly accessible and melodic effort, although they were soon to develop into rather more of a powerful, speed-oriented outfit. HOLOSADE went on to record a reasonably successful album called »Hellhouse« for Powerstation in 1988 (by which time Colin Bell had left to pursue his career with CHARGER on a full-time basis), before the group eventually drifted apart in the wake of personnel instability and label rejection in the early 90's. After that, there were a few attempts to bring together former members of HOLOSADE and SARACEN in a new ensemble called DOMINION, but little seems to have come of this initial plan.

LP's
»Shadows Of The Night« Roadrunner 1984

Exclusive Compilation Appearances
"Stone Cold Hearted" on »The Metal Collection Vol.I« LP Ebony 1986

Compilation Appearances
"Don't Break The Circle" on »The Metal Machine« LP Roadrunner 1984

DARK STAR

Rik Staines (v,k)
Dave Harrison (g)
Bob Key (g)
Chris Causton (b)
Steve Atkins (d)

As with so many other outfits, the origins of Midlands heroes DARK STAR lie in the 70's rock scene, with most, if not all, of the original line-up having played in various small-time acts for a number of years before finally coming together, initially as BERLIN, in around 1979. The outfit was formed by the Harrison brothers, Dave and Rik (although the latter elected to use the unfortunate surname Staines, for some unfathomable reason), with former NIGHTRIDE (a popular rock covers outfit who had recently called it a day) members Chris Causton and Bob Key being

drafted in pretty swiftly, the outfit eventually reaching quorate status *via* the recruitment of drummer Steve Atkins. Original material was demoed fairly rapidly, and BERLIN's first proper tape soon came to the attention of EMI, who duly requested their "Lady Of Mars" for use on the second »Metal For Muthas« compilation in the spring of 1980. However, the label helpfully pointed out that at least one other outfit had already registered the name, so the more distinctive DARK STAR was adopted at short notice. Their SAPPHIRE-like track (featuring a rather more subtle mid-section in the manner of LIMELIGHT or SHIVA) was one of the highlights of the LP, and it wasn't long before the lads were encouraged by their management to give up their day jobs and get some product of their own on the market, which was to be the beginning of a rather sad and frustrating experience (through no fault of their own) for the DARK STAR lads.

By the summer of 1980, the musicians had laid down another two tracks, namely "Rock'n'Romancin'" and "Renegade", and were in the process of issuing a self-financed EP (with "Lady Of

Mars" as the main focus of attention) on their own Steel Strike label. At the eleventh hour, however, a certain unscrupulous individual (whom the group had trusted to organise the whole affair) did a runner with the cash, supposedly leaving the lads with nothing but sleeves and labels to show for their efforts. Press releases were rapidly circulated, announcing the cancellation of both the EP and the tie-in series of promotional gigs that had already been arranged, although it transpires that a few finished copies (nothing like the intended quantity, though) *were* manufactured after all. Only a handful have ever surfaced, however, and it's virtually impossible to find one with an original picture sleeve (with a pretty basic design, admittedly) at any price. This item, should you ever encounter a copy, is one of the very few rarities which genuinely warrants the *'mega rare'* tag, and you might have to hand over a large percentage of your life savings to get hold of one. Nevertheless, this ludicrous episode wasn't a complete disaster after all, as the kindly Avatar label stepped in with a timely offer to press »Lady Of Mars« as a 7" single (omitting "Renegade"), after which the company helped to get the band back on their feet once more by sponsoring their live activities. The series of shows, which had now been drastically reduced in size, went under the banner of *'The Metallical Mystery Tour'*, and saw DARK STAR taking to the road with a variety of accomplices such as WHITE SPIRIT and ANGEL WITCH.

The *'reissued'* single was an instant hit, and sold in quite staggering quantities at the time, making its way into virtually every Heavy Metal chart that was going. The B-side, admittedly, was something of a throwback to their 70's roots, but it still featured some strong guitar work, and it was only a matter of time before the lads were offered the opportunity to record a full album for Avatar. By the end of 1980, however, original bassist Chris Causton had decided to leave the DARK STAR fold, and so the lads were forced to break in new recruit Mark Oseland before finally undertaking the album sessions in the new year. Fortunately, their new line-up worked out just fine, and so a landmark, eponymous album was delivered as a matter of routine. The group clearly had their fingers firmly on the NWOBHM pulse, and the majority of tracks featured were capable, catchy efforts with more than a hint of DIAMOND HEAD and early DEF LEPPARD, a combination which many fans seem to regard as nothing less than a definitive example of the NWOBHM archetype. I wouldn't quite go that far, but it was certainly one of the more significant releases of the era, and one which is still held in particularly high esteem nowadays. The outfit's talents are shown to greatest effect on the energetic opening pair of "Kaptain Amerika" and "Backstreet Killer", although the semi-acoustic "The Musician" is a bit of a shocker, and "Green Peace" drags on a bit, so it's not a flawless opus by any means.

The lads toured the UK with labelmates LIMELIGHT and CHEVY over the coming months, and later embarked on a brief series of European gigs (supporting the likes of BUDGIE and MAGNUM) in an attempt to make their activities known to a considerably wider audience. For some reason, however, their second single (»Kaptain Amerika«) was only released in Spain, a nation which had been privileged enough to see a picture sleeve version of »Lady Of Mars« (with a different B-side), whereas the standard UK issue had merely been presented in an Avatar company sleeve. Sadly, however, things fell apart for DARK STAR at some point in 1982, at a time when, were it not for the unfortunate collapse of their mismanaged record label, they should have been conquering every part of the globe with their excellently-crafted and well-played compositions. The reasons which lay behind the ultimate failure of the original incarnation of DARK STAR were never actually made particularly clear, mind you, so I guess it was just one of those unavoidable things. Their fans, however, were given something of a treat in the 90's, when a Japanese CD pressing of the first album was released with six bonus tracks, including previously-unheard demo compositions and single B-sides.

It was, to say the least, something of a surprise when a version of DARK STAR reappeared in the second half of the 80's (various members of the original line-up had apparently been acting as part of MAGNUM's roadcrew and backing ensemble in the interim), the project having initially been reactivated, with minimal publicity, towards the end of 1985. After a low-key series of shows supporting ROBIN GEORGE, the members decided that they had still had something to offer the world, and duly set out to win themselves a new recording deal. In fact, it transpired that DARK STAR now consisted of a nucleus of Dave Harrison, Rik Staines and Bob Key, with session musicians being drafted in for recording and touring purposes. Within a year or so, the revamped outfit had wangled a deal with FM Records, and the all-new DARK STAR delivered a comeback album in 1987 (»Real To Reel«) which took almost everyone by complete surprise. Sadly, it attracted attention for all the wrong reasons, as it was a staggeringly lightweight and commercially-motivated collection of songs (all written and recorded within an unfeasibly short space of time), which seemed cynically manufactured to appeal to the American AOR market (titles such as "Voice Of America" and "Homicide On First And Last" were a bit of a giveaway as to their state of mind at the time) and nothing else. In terms of British comparisons, we would certainly be talking JOKERS WILD, VOYAGER UK or WINTER'S REIGN, although the album really was in a league of its own in terms of shameless inoffensiveness.

Tracks such as "Spy Zone" (a blatant HALL & OATES rip-off) and the quirky "Sad Day In London Town" (which borrows heavily from ABC) additionally make some major concessions to the pop market, so the LP as a whole was really nothing to do with the heavyweight DARK STAR of old. There were precious few moments of genuine musical merit, although the catchy "Goin' Nowhere" was an undeniably decent effort. The long-player, incidentally, featured contributions from original members Steve Atkins and Chris Causton (who supplied backing vocals), plus former STEEL drummer Simon Atkins (no relation to his predecessor), keyboard player Paul Hodson (who later joined PERFECT STRANGER and HARD RAIN) and bassist Dave Keates, just in case you were wondering who else was involved in this ill-advised exercise. In any case, the comeback album was regarded as an unmitigated disaster by all but the most tolerant of AOR fans, and their reformation was to be a mercifully short-lived affair, with Bob Key jumping ship to embark on other projects soon after. Rik Staines, incidentally, later turned his hand to the odd bit of production work, which involved helping out a variety of no-hopers such as the long-forgotten BITCHES BRUE. By the way, the DARK STAR identity has now been adopted by a completely unrelated act (a rather spacey LEVITATION offshoot), so don't get too excited if you see their name in the gig guides again.

LP's
»**Dark Star**« Avatar 1981
[UK issue]
»**Dark Star**« Avatar 1981
[French issue with different sleeve design]
»**Dark Star**« Avatar 1981
[Japanese issue with insert]
»**Real To Reel**« FM Records 1987

12" EP's
»**Lady Of Mars**« Steel Strike Records 1980
[Aborted release, very few copies in general circulation, both "Rock'n'Romancin'" and "Renegade" non-LP]

7" Singles
»**Lady Of Mars**« Avatar 1980
[UK issue in company sleeve, B-side "Rock'n'Romancin'" non-LP]
»**Lady Of Mars**« Avatar 1981
[Spanish issue in picture sleeve, B-side "Louisa"]
»**Kaptain Amerika**« Avatar 1982
[Spanish-only release in picture sleeve, B-side "Louisa"]

CD's
»**Dark Star**« Pony Canyon 1993
[Japanese release with six bonus tracks]

Compilation Appearances
"**Lady Of Mars**" on »Metal For Muthas Vol.2« LP EMI 1980/CD Airraid Records 2000 + »The Bible Of Hard Rock« CD Toshiba 1990
"**Kaptain Amerika**" on »HM Killers« LP Lark 1984
"**Voice Of America**" on »Coast To Coast« LP/CD FM Records 1987
"**Rock'N'Romancin'**" on »NWOBHM Vol.2« Bootleg CD 1992

DAWN TRADER

Mick Preston (v)
Wayne Vizard (g)
Chris Allard (g)
Ric Evans (b)
Keith White (d)

Although DAWN TRADER will be a familiar name to many, the extreme scarcity of their various releases decrees that relatively few collectors will actually have heard any of this Nottinghamshire band's output. Formed at the very height of the NWOBHM explosion and getting in on the old *'let's throw together a private EP'* lark at a comparatively early stage, the outfit issued their own four track 7" (produced by Graham Neale of Radio Trent) in 1980, to an overwhelmingly enthusiastic response throughout the rock-friendly Midlands. To be frank, though, the record is actually quite firmly rooted in the 70's, and there's only a tiny hint of true NWOBHM spirit shining through every now and again. In that respect, the music (especially on "Orphan" and "Dawn Trader") is generally reminiscent of the kind of proto-NWOBHM performed by the NEXT BAND, ANGEL STREET or

SINGAPORE, for example, although "No One Gonna Better Me" and "You On My Mind" also suggest some slightly heavier outfits such as TRACK 4 and the Essex version of WARRIOR. Issued in a red sleeve adorned by the band logo, this particular slice of vinyl is seldom seen for sale these days, and the normal asking price is a bit shocking, especially considering the mediocre musical content.

Although DAWN TRADER rapidly became a familiar name to the headbangers in their locality, the rest of the country remained blissfully unaware of their existence, so the lads were forced to make slightly more of an effort to promote themselves. After spending the best part of two years playing to a selection of appreciative audiences throughout the Midlands and beyond, the musicians were finally rewarded with a feature in the 'Armed And Ready' section of 'Kerrang' early in 1982. With the band having, by this time, replaced guitarist Chris Allard with new boy Steve Humphreys and played alongside DEF LEPPARD, MAGNUM, KROKUS and THE SWEET (in addition to extensive successful gigging on their own), DAWN TRADER were back in business with a newly-recorded demo. Featuring the unfamiliar numbers "Roller", "Whole Lotta Trouble", "Angel" and "Flash In The Sky", the four-tracker won approval from the magazine, who compared the outfit to PRAYING MANTIS (in between numerous jocular references to Robin Hood, Sherwood Forest and the Sheriff of Nottingham), which wasn't too far off the mark. A further cassette, issued within a matter of months (by which time they had recruited a new drummer, former SAVAGE sticksman Dave Lindley), featured selections such as "Good To Be Back Home" and "Running For Your Life", and this batch of material confirmed an overwhelmingly confident move towards the type of accomplished, melodic rock/metal purveyed by the likes of BASHFUL ALLEY, FRENZY and DRAGONFLY.

One of the outfit's other notable mentions in the annals of 'Kerrang' came with a review of a one-off gig organised by Radio Trent at Nottingham's Rock City in June 1982. Sandwiched between openers SARACEN and headliners DIAMOND HEAD, the *'local heroes'* (with ex-NOEL REDDING BAND trouper Andy Keeley having already been substituted for the luckless Steve Humphreys) proceeded to belt out the most warmly-received set of the evening; so much so, in fact, that the bustling crowd (a couple of thousand strong) were apparently still cheering for yet another encore when the mighty DIAMOND HEAD finally took to the stage! In spite of such massive local popularity, however, and notwithstanding the fact that a recording session for a full-length album (due to feature various crowd-pleasers such as "Poser" and "Take The Money And Run") was in the offing towards the end of the year, the band actually played what proved to be their farewell gig over the festive period, again at their spiritual home of Rock City. As reported in 'Kerrang' at the time, highlights included a bit of guitar smashing from Keeley and an extended jam with long-time friend Bernie Marsden (who had just terminated his ill-fated S.O.S. project), featuring many an old classic. Still, it came as something of a surprise that DAWN TRADER had decided to call it a day so suddenly, especially as the members failed to offer any particularly convincing explanations.

That wasn't quite the end of the story, however: at some point in their later history, DAWN TRADER had (apparently as a quartet) recorded a session or two for broadcast on Radio Trent, and one of their featured tracks was subsequently salvaged from the archives and posthumously included on the station's »Castle Rock Compilation«, the latter being compiled and produced by their old mucker Graham Neale and issued as a private pressing in 1984. Their capable contribution ("Homebreaker") was, once again, considerably more metal-sounding than their EP, so it's a great pity the group couldn't find the strength to persevere and set about finding a label to sponsor further releases. Only a thousand (numbered) copies of the compilation were supposedly pressed, but the rest of the artists featured are pretty much unspeakably awful, so I wouldn't go mad trying to locate a copy if I were you. Incidentally, it looks as though various members of DAWN TRADER might even have been lured out of retirement for the occasional impromptu live outing in later years, but there has never, as far as I'm aware, been a full-scale reformation of this much-missed act.

7" EP's
»**No One Gonna Better Me**« Private 1980

Exclusive Compilation Appearances
"**Homebreaker**" on »Castle Rock Compilation« LP Private 1984

DAWNWATCHER

Billy Barton (v)
Craig Richardson (g)

John Bootle (b)
Peter Darley (k)
Pete Kaberry (d)

Although Yorkshire's outstanding and superbly-named DAWNWATCHER were generally regarded as an extremely popular local attraction in the early days of the NWOBHM influx, the outfit's slightly *'progressive'* leanings (with regard to their prominent reliance on keyboards, abstract lyrical concepts and some rather grandiose vocal performances) might well have alienated some of the more *'straight ahead'* rock fans of the period. This is a great pity, as their use of synthesizers was, in the main, highly original, with jarring, almost disharmonic chords being used in strategic places to create an ominous atmosphere within songs, actually strengthening individual tracks as opposed to making them more accessible. In that respect, the quintet were utilising synth technology in much the same sense as TRIARCHY and MARQUIS DE SADE, for example, rather than all the keyboard-flavoured AOR wannabes. DAWNWATCHER appear to have started out at the height of the NWOBHM movement, and swiftly established themselves as a supremely confident act who could deliver the goods both in the live arena and in the recording studio. Within a comparatively short space of time, the lads had a highly impressive armoury of self-penned compositions at their disposal, and duly demoed some strong numbers in the early months of 1980.

DAWNWATCHER were one of numerous acts who dispensed with the notion of setting out to attract the attention of major labels, preferring to go it alone from an early stage, and some of their material was soon to be made available on a couple of slices of vinyl. The group's first offering of their own was an incredibly scarce, double A-sided 7" (never issued with a picture sleeve) featuring "Spellbound" and "Hall Of Mirrors" (the latter being included on the »NWOBHM Vol.4« bootleg), released as a private pressing in the second half of 1980. Although there are certainly comparisons to more progressive outfits such as THE COVENANT and TUTCH, the technical rhythms are more in the vein of KRAKEN and the vocals slightly comparable to ELIXIR's Paul Taylor. Excellent stuff throughout, and this particular single remains a seldom-seen rarity which comes with a pretty formidable price tag for the modern collector. Further useful exposure came the quintet's way when they were selected for inclusion on the influential »New Electric Warriors« LP at around the same time, their contribution coming in the shape of "Firing On All Eight", another extremely worthy example (although heartlessly described by Howard Johnson as *'banal'* in his 'Phoenix' fanzine review) in a largely similar style, outshone on the compilation only by TAROT's wondrous "Feel The Power" (now *there's* a band who deserved a deal).

Although the outfit were a regular attraction at many of the nation's rock clubs in the early part of the decade (typically doing the rounds with other local hopefuls such as RHABSTALLION), DAWNWATCHER never seem to have been invited to support any of the better-known outfits who were playing the live circuit at the time, possibly a reflection of the fact that they didn't really fit into any convenient musical pigeonhole. In fact, the pinnacle of their relatively brief career was, perhaps, their appearance at a charity festival which took place at their local Victoria Park in Keighley in July 1981. With the event being organised in support of the International Year Of The Disabled, the festival featured an eclectic bill, including acts such as NEW MODEL ARMY, AGONY COLUMN and SURFACE TENSION, so it presumably exposed the DAWNWATCHER lads to a far wider and more varied audience than they had become accustomed to thus far, having spent most of their formative years in the pubs and working men's clubs of Yorkshire and its environs. By now, their enviable repertoire included such weighty compositions as "Attitudes" and "Children Of The Night", as well as a reworked and extended version of the immensely popular "Hall Of Mirrors", and it's refreshing to note that there was little or no dependence upon the usual range of cover versions in their live set.

Moving into 1982, it soon became apparent that the talented band were more than happy to continue with their programme of self-financed vinyl releases, recorded mainly for the benefit of their fans rather than as a means of spreading their name further afield. To this end, DAWNWATCHER issued their second double A-sided single, coupling "Backlash" with "Salvador's Dream", this time in an excellent and colourful picture sleeve. Although this record (which achieved a remarkably high placing in the 'Top 30 Kuts' chart in 'Kerrang' upon its release) is a far more common (thanks to the band members releasing a quantity of unsold copies onto the market in the early 90's) and realistically-priced item than its predecessor, the musical contents are truly remarkable, with some disconcertingly heavy powerchords emanating from the keyboard of Peter Darley and a strong, emotional effort coming from frontman Billy Barton, particularly on "Salvador's Dream". "Backlash", on the other hand, isn't quite as heavy, although the vocal performance is extremely accomplished once again. Fantastic stuff. All in all, an essential piece of listening for those who appreciate groups who aren't *'three chord wonders'* and who like to try something a bit different.

I don't know whether DAWNWATCHER eventually bowed out with a bang or a whimper, as there doesn't seem to be any mention of their demise in any of the more prominent publications of the day, so it's possible that they just quit while they were on a high after the second single's release. Vocalist Billy Barton went on to enjoy a brief residency in one of several acts named ANTIGUA (I reckon Paul Dianno has a lot to answer for), where he was supported by various former EAST TO WEST members, although the luckless frontman had actually been replaced by the time the ensemble adopted their more familiar moniker of ARENA. Guitarist Craig Richardson, meanwhile, finally resurfaced towards the end of the decade, collaborating with ex-CYRKA stalwart Tony Green in an obscure outfit called KRAKATOA. After gigging around their locality for a few years (with Green taking responsibility for bass and vocals), the quartet (completed by drummer Gordon Steele and implausibly-named keyboard player Irvin P. Ratt) finally got around to issuing a limited edition full-length CD in 1992, which appeared in the shape of »Building Bridges« on the little-known Intrusion label. This album saw the ex-NWOBHM characters making a move towards a more accessible type of semi-AOR material which, nevertheless, retained a progressively-inclined outlook at times, but it doesn't really seem to have sold in staggering quantities upon its release.

7" Singles
»Spellbound« Private 1980
»Backlash« Private 1982

Exclusive Compilation Appearances
"Firing On All Eight" on »New Electric Warriors« LP Logo 1980/CD British Steel 1997

Compilation Appearances
"Hall Of Mirrors" on »NWOBHM Vol.4« Bootleg CD 1992

DEADLY ATLANTIC RUN

Line-up unknown

A rather quirky outfit operating under an equally peculiar name, Birmingham's long-forgotten DEADLY ATLANTIC RUN (actually given as 'Deady' on their one-off record's label, but this makes even less sense) were presumably trying something a bit different on their double A-sided single from 1985, but their musical style ended up being rather chaotic as a result. It's by no means easy to give any meaningful description of their intended direction, suffice to say that it was a somewhat distorted type of melodic heavy rock with elements of new wave punk thrown in for a bit of variation. Ordinarily, both "Put Me Down" and "Billy" would be fairly unremarkable numbers in the style of JOKERS WILD or LOTUS CRUISE, were it not for their confusing inclusion of instruments such as the trumpet, saxophone and piano, which results in the two compositions sounding something like a more metal version of DEXY'S MIDNIGHT RUNNERS, if you can imagine such an absurd thing. The nearest reference point in the NWOBHM field would probably be the unpredictable T34, although there are additional minor similarities to various other left-field acts such as FOUR WHEEL DRIVE, IDLE FLOWERS or the totally bonkers TOAD THE WET SPROCKET in their very early days. Certainly not one for the purists, and a single (no picture sleeve issued, by the looks of things) which will probably only appeal to a fairly select number of modern-day NWOBHM enthusiasts.

7" Singles
»Put Me Down« D.A.M. Records 1985

DEALER

Trev Short (v,rg)
Steve Tarrant (g)
Pete Gentil (b)
Andy Jones (d)

Originally one of the many bands operating under the identity of LONE WOLF in the NWOBHM era, Gloucestershire's DEALER came into existence in around 1981, initially featuring the services of Mark Grimmett (brother of GRIM REAPER's Steve) on vocals and Malc Hanselman on drums. Within a matter of months, however, the pair had been superseded by Trev Short and Andy Jones, respectively, whereupon their departed frontman went on to play a part in the fortunes of acts such as BLACK DOG, RAIDER and CRYWOLF. In fact, Steve Tarrant and Trev Short (experienced veterans of the West Midlands rock/metal scene) were old mates, the duo having played together in an outfit called AXE VICTIMS in the late 70's. The multi-talented Pete Gentil joined after the position of bassist became vacant, as he explained a short time later: *'I've known Trev for quite a while and when he told me that the band he was in needed a bass player I decided to switch from lead guitar to bass.'* (Ref: Kerrang No.17, June 1982). First coming to public attention with the nine track »Boogie, Booze And Birds« cassette (featuring such original compositions as "Lone Wolf" and "At Your Mercy"), the outfit subsequently received an honourable mention in the 'Armed And Ready' section (devoted to unsigned hopefuls) of 'Kerrang', something which can't have done their chances any harm whatsoever, and the general public were soon anticipating some vinyl product from DEALER.

Happily, the fans didn't have all that long to wait, and, after a fair bit of productive touring, predominantly in their immediate vicinity, the group's debut 7" (recorded at Windrush Studios) was released the following year. Both of the numbers on display ("Better Things To Do" and "Suspected Foul Play") are excellent, archetypal NWOBHM offerings in the vein of GEDDES AXE or early DEF LEPPARD, and this pairing certainly saw the outfit laying firm foundations for a successful career. The two-tracker (issued in an uninspiring band-image sleeve) sold in healthy quantities at the time, although the former members were still able to release a significant number of unsold copies in the early 90's, allowing the once-bonkers asking price to fall to slightly more sensible levels in recent times. It soon became apparent, however, that the outfit's debut release wasn't merely a one-off display of their collective ability, and another well-received demo tape (recorded a year or so after their single made its way into the shops) featured a selection of new tracks which also augured extremely well for the future. The epic "The Final Conflict", for example, was an amazing piece of songwriting (lasting almost ten minutes without seeming remotely excessive), featuring some excellent, powerful vocals and strong guitar work, the end result suggesting a possible move towards a rather harder style with distinct similarities to local rivals TYRANT. "Money Is Your Passport", on the other hand, was a somewhat more basic, upbeat rocker, whereas "Looking For A Reason", although slightly more akin to their earlier compositions, still represented a very proficient track nonetheless.

DEALER, with their newer material, deservedly garnered an album deal with the Ebony concern, which *should* have produced a true classic of the genre, but something went seriously awry along the way. Sadly, by the time the »First Strike« set emerged in 1986, the album sleeve revealed the ensemble (now featuring new drummer Andy Powell and second guitarist Ashley Jon Limer) to have become devotees of *'big hair and spandex'* outfits. Mind you, the new image didn't quite herald a complete wimp-out, but it wasn't the DEALER of old. While tracks such as "When Midnight Comes" and "Choose Your Weapon" aren't exactly awful, they tend to come across as a poor man's SAVAGE, although there's also a bit of an early American power metal feel (the likes of ANVIL CHORUS and AVATAR) which, for some peculiar reason, just doesn't work too well in this context. Elsewhere, "Son Of A Bitch" and "Bring The Walls Down" (the latter also turned up on Ebony's »The Metal Collection Vol.II« sampler) are merely frivolous rockers with an unhealthy dependency on backing chants. The LP's saving graces, however, came with the lengthy "Epitaph" (borrowing heavily from DIAMOND HEAD's "Sucking My Love") and the revamped (abridged) "Final Conflict". As I say, it's not the unmitigated disaster some people make it out to be (it's far more commendable than most of Ebony's later releases), and some of the tracks grow on you after repeated listens, but I get the distinct impression that it could have been a hell of a lot better.

Contrary to popular opinion, DEALER (whose greatest claim to fame seems to have been some prestigious support slots with the likes of MOTÖRHEAD, SPIDER and GARY MOORE)

DEDRINGER

Johnny 'JJ' Hoyle (v)
Neil Hudson (g)
Al Scott (g)
Lee Flaxington (b)
Kenny Jones (d)

The Yorkshire act known as DEDRINGER (the phonetic spelling being adopted at an early stage to differentiate between numerous other hopefuls called DEAD RINGER) were conceived in the late 70's as little more than a covers outfit, but gradually surprised their audiences by becoming more of a stand-alone band in their own right, working an increasingly-significant quantity of original compositions into their regular live set as time progressed. By 1980, the ensemble's relentless efforts were rewarded by a handy deal with the unassuming Dindisc label, a company who were rather more accustomed to furthering the careers of borderline pop/indie concerns such as ORCHESTRAL MANOEUVRES IN THE DARK. Nevertheless, DEDRINGER's undeniably lightweight debut single (coupling the singalong "Sunday Drivers" with "We Don't Mind") duly appeared in the latter half of 1980, the lads delivering a fairly basic, good-time boogie/blues amalgam lying somewhere between SPIDER and DUMPY'S RUSTY NUTS, no doubt going down a storm at numerous rock discos of the day. Moreover, the five-piece were soon able to get out on the road to promote their introductory release, as they managed to tag along on a series of gigs with PRAYING MANTIS and TRIUMPH towards the end of the year.

In due course, the group would pick up further support slots with such acts as GILLAN, GIRLSCHOOL and MSG, before offering the world their debut long-player in the early months of 1981. Their »Direct Line« set was a pretty rudimentary collection of rockers, although it was an inoffensive album as a whole. The band's roots as a 70's club act were quite clearly audible, and it's fair to say that this rather uninspiring debut was only skirting around the periphery of the NWOBHM genre. There was quite a high level of energy on display, though, and self-assured efforts such as "Maxine" and "She's Not Ready" (the latter being a short, upbeat number with a passing similarity to BLACK AXE) showed that they might be capable of moving in the right direction eventually. An edited version of "Maxine" was subsequently used as the basis of a tie-in single, issued as a (supposedly) limited edition double pack (pad-

didn't just give up the ghost completely after their nightmarish Ebony experience, but ultimately metamorphosed into the out-and-out AOR ensemble VANDAMNE in late 1987. Under this name, a few CD's have sneaked out on small labels, although the number of ex-DEALER personnel involved (drummer Andy Powell jumped ship at a very early stage) seems to have dwindled gradually along the way. For example, 1994's »Night Crimes« featured Short, Limer and Gentil, but, by the time »To The Bone« was issued a year later, Trev Short was the only remaining ex-DEALER representative. I'm led to believe that VANDAMNE, having been relatively quiet for several years now, have also called it a day, although it remains to be seen whether or not any of their former members return to the fore with new outfits in years to come.

LP's
»**First Strike**« Ebony 1986

7" Singles
»**Better Things To Do**« Windrush Records 1983
[Both tracks non-LP]

Compilation Appearances
"**Bring The Walls Down**" on »The Metal Collection Vol.II« LP Ebony 1987
"**Better Things To Do**" on »NWOBHM Vol.4« Bootleg CD 1992

ded out with unreleased live and studio compositions), and this was duly followed up by the rather more mundane »Direct Line« two-tracker a couple of months later. Before long, a handy piece of national exposure came DEDRINGER's way, when the lads were invited to contribute a prestigious session to the 'Friday Rock Show'. Broadcast on the 1st of May 1981, the showcase saw the quintet running through versions of "Maxine", "Took A Long Time", "So Still" and "Innocent Til Proven Guilty", allowing the station's listeners to digest a representative bunch of tracks from their back catalogue.

As it turned out, the album managed reasonably acceptable sales, with a competent distribution meaning that it ultimately reached some far-flung corners of the globe, but the lads still weren't happy with the way they had been promoted, as Neil Hudson later explained: *'The record company just didn't understand our music. I'm sure that a lot of other bands say that, but Dindisc really had no idea how they should market us. Basically, they were a hindrance to our career.'* (Ref: Kerrang No.33, January 1983). In fact, the band's eventual departure from Dindisc came primarily in the aftermath of a car accident which seriously injured both Al Scott and Neil Hudson, something which forced the group to take something of an enforced break while the luckless duo recuperated. By the time they returned, in the latter half of 1982, they had actually recruited a new bassist (Chris Graham) and frontman (Neil Garfitt), their predecessors having already flown the coop in fairly mysterious circumstances. Nevertheless, the revamped version of DEDRINGER were soon back on track with a brand-new deal, having been picked up by none other than Neat Records in the interim. Their first output for the respected company consisted of a freshly-penned contribution ("Lucy") to the »60 Minutes Plus« promotional cassette, followed shortly thereafter by a single featuring "Hot Lady" and "Hot Licks And Rock'n'Roll", the latter release suggesting that DEDRINGER were now moving into markedly more metal territory.

The outfit's capable new vocalist was certainly something of a find (possessing a more conventional rock style than his somewhat throaty predecessor), and the group appeared to have reinvented themselves slightly following his recruitment, the general impression being that DEDRINGER had now become a genuine hard-rocking proposition with less of a tendency towards boogie-influenced compositions. Recording sessions for another full LP followed in due course, and the appropriately-titled »Second Arising« appeared in the early months of 1983, by which time Mick Kremastoules was identified as a surprise replacement for long-standing guitarist Al Scott. Nevertheless, Scott had contributed both to the writing and recording side of things as the record was being assembled, so it looks as though this little-known newcomer had stepped in as a post-album substitute. The comeback LP contained a reasonably strong collection of not-particularly-heavy, bluesy rock numbers with a slight hint of TERRAPLANE, some listenable efforts coming in the form of "Sold Me Lonely", "Never Gonna Lose It" and "The Eagle Never Falls". Inevitably, however, the record largely failed to appeal to the majority of metal fans who still associated the likes of BLITZKRIEG, JAGUAR and RAVEN with the definitive *'Neat sound'*, and it appears to have been one of the company's less spectacular releases of the period in terms of worldwide sales figures.

Nevertheless, DEDRINGER were lucky enough to be retained by their understanding label, although they failed to make much of an effort to come up with new material thereafter. Still, the musicians were reported to be back in the studios in mid-1984, supposedly recording a cover of "Lazy Sunday Afternoon" by the SMALL FACES (a popular inclusion in their live set since their very earliest days) for subsequent issue as a new single. Sadly, however, this scheduled release seems to have been shelved in the long run, as do the outfit's activities as a whole, and the name of DEDRINGER finally passed into disuse around the middle of the decade, with none of their assorted members going on to resurface in any recording acts of note.

LP's
»**Direct Line**« Dindisc 1981/Ariola 1981
[UK/German issue]
»**Direct Line**« Victor 1981
[Japanese issue with insert]
»**Second Arising**« Neat 1983

7" Singles
»**Sunday Drivers**« Dindisc 1980
[A-side different to album version, B-side "We Don't Mind" non-LP]
»**Maxine**« Dindisc 1981
[A-side different to album version, B-side "Innocent Til Proven Guilty" (live) non-LP. Limited edition in gatefold sleeve with free single featuring "Took A Long Time" and "We Don't Mind", both non-LP. "We Don't Mind" different to version on »Sunday Drivers« single]
»**Direct Line**« Dindisc 1981
»**Hot Lady**« Neat 1982
[Both tracks non-LP]

Exclusive Compilation Appearances
"**Lucy**" on »60 Minutes Plus« Cassette Neat 1982/CD Teichiku 1992

Compilation Appearances
"**Sunday Drivers**" on »Dindisc 1980« LP Dindisc 1980
"**Direct Line**" on »Hammer« LP Ariola 1981
"**Comin' Out Fighting**" on »Axe Attack« LP M Port 1985/Mausoleum 1986
"**Rock Night**" on »Heavy Metal Collection 1« CD X-Tra Collection 1993
"**The Eagle Never Falls**" on »Heavy Metal Collection 3« CD X-Tra Collection 1993

DEEP SWITCH

The Duke (v)
Reverend Nice (g)
Old Nick (g)
Andy The Tank Engine (b)
Simon The Bishop (d)

I don't know what they were putting in East Anglia's water supply in the early 80's, but the outlandish DEEP SWITCH were certainly an extremely warped set of individuals! First attracting a bit of press attention with their wacky appearance (eat your hearts out, SLIPKNOT), bizarre aliases and the infamous »Pigfeeder« and »Time Machine« demo tapes in around 1985, the unhinged quintet immediately drew a fair amount of praise for their original, heavy music, particularly from fanzines such as the equally odd 'Organ' (appearing on the occasional cassette-only compilation put together by the magazine) and the more conventional 'High Octane'. Their choice of image was subsequently discussed in the latter publication by the Reverend Nice: *'At our first few gigs we experimented wildly with clothes & make-up, dressing in drag & rags and plastering fearsome designs on our faces.'* (Ref: High Octane, Issue 2, 1985). The ensemble's music was, itself, quite varied, ranging from heavy material in a WARFARE or VENOM vein, through theatrical proto-thrash in the style of HELL or SABBAT, to more melodic pieces with fluid guitar work, bringing to mind acts such as CLOVEN HOOF or MOURNBLADE (bands, incidentally, with a not dissimilar image). Clearly, there was more to DEEP SWITCH than just the over-the-top visuals…

All but one ("Silver Bullet") of the tracks comprising the two aforementioned demos ended up on the group's sole LP, which rejoiced under the unseemly title of »Nine Inches Of God«, housed in a rather perverted sleeve (it's worth noting, in passing, that CRADLE OF FILTH are from the same neck of the woods…) depicting a partially-clothed nun with a candle (stop me if any of this sounds familiar). Predictably, it was a self-financed affair, as I reckon they would have waited a hell of a long time before the major labels came knocking. By this stage, however, the outfit had evidently slimmed down to a four-piece (second guitarist Old Nick had been given the boot) and either adopted new pseudonyms or replaced a couple of members (their vocalist was now known as *'Jinx'* and the bassist as *'Gander'*), so it looks as though DEEP SWITCH were keen to change more than just their image from time to time. With familiar selections such as "Time Machine", "The Poison Lake", "Lovers Of The Dream" and "Spinning On The Wheel" taking their place alongside newer compositions such as "The Dark Angel" and the title track, the album served to perplex reviewers as to exactly what style of music these lunatics were attempting to deliver. As the lads themselves claimed on the record sleeve, however, *'This record contains awesome heavy metal, no artificial preservatives, and no ingredients. If you are not satisfied for any reason, return your copy, (stating where and when purchased), to DEEP SWITCH, and we guarantee that you will be tracked down and killed.' Charming.

The oddball outfit's confrontational image and uninhibited lyrical stance seems ultimately to have backfired, however, with the record-buying public failing to take much notice of the album at the time, rendering it a fairly collectable (and quite pricey) piece nowadays. The lads (who were never exactly the most hard-touring of acts) appear to have lost the will to continue within a fairly short timescale (concluding that the similarly-inclined ROGUE MALE, who enjoyed far more success with their over-the-top image and forceful music, had largely stolen their thunder), and there was never serious talk of a follow-up, given that they had probably spent all their pennies on the first record. After the group's eventual demise (within a year or so of their LP hitting the shops), drummer Simon The Bishop (aka Simon De Montford) got together (ooer) with LISA DOMINIQUE for a while before briefly hooking up with Pete Franklin and Scott Biaggi in a short-lived, late 80's CHARIOT offshoot called CHARGE. No doubt the one-time members of DEEP SWITCH later took their place in 'respectable' society; just think, one of these reprobates could now be your bank manager, solicitor or accountant…

LP's
»Nine Inches Of God« Switch Records 1986

DEF LEPPARD

Joe Elliott (v)
Pete Willis (g)
Steve Clark (g)
Rick Savage (b)
Tony Kenning (d)

Obscure Yorkshire band who failed to live up to the promise of their debut release. Oh, you want the full-length version, do you? Ho hum. Well, it all started back in 1977, when a bunch of young Sheffield lads began getting a few ideas about rock'n'roll stardom, and started to gravitate together with the intention of making it big in the music business. The first vehicle for the talents of Rick Savage, Pete Willis and Tony Kenning was ATOMIC MASS, who, after a few personnel reshuffles, established a semi-stable line-up and set out to play a few cover versions and the odd self-penned number. Their original vocalist, however, failed to last the distance, whereupon an acquaintance named Joe Elliott was invited to try out for the position. The frontman impressed the lads to a sufficient extent that he was immediately allowed to join in the fun, although the quartet soon decided that their original name had to go. Elliott had always dreamed of fronting his own band, and (for reasons best known to himself) had become slightly obsessed with the notion of calling his future outfit DEAF LEOPARD. Strange as it may seem, his colleagues happily went along with this bizarre idea, although they ultimately adopted a phonetic spelling to make it sound marginally more heavy metal. It may have been an extremely silly name indeed, but, as the lads themselves later pointed out in a memorable interview, it was a hell of a lot better than EPILEPTIC DONKEY…

The outfit were soon rehearsing like mad, but swiftly came to the conclusion that a second guitarist would be a considerable benefit in the long term, whereupon another likely character, Steve Clark, was auditioned for the role. The charismatic axeman got the job without too much difficulty, and the newly-expanded quintet were soon immersed in the task of building up a fairly rudimentary repertoire of covers and self-penned efforts. Their musical allegiances lay very much in the heavy rock/metal sound of the earlier part of the decade, their style leaning heavily towards the likes of LED ZEPPELIN, THIN LIZZY and (particularly) UFO, although they managed to infuse a bit of their own identity into the music from a very early stage. Their live debut came with a couple of extremely inauspicious events in the summer of 1978, and they completed only a tiny handful of shows before the year was out. Nevertheless, they soon decided to go out on a limb and record their own slice of vinyl, and started preparing the ground for their imminent visit to the studio. Three numbers were duly chosen to be captured on tape, although there was a moment of uncertainty when the lads suddenly decided to part company with Tony Kenning (for reasons which never became particularly clear) before undertaking the studio session. There was no time to audition for a replacement, however, but Frank Noon, affable drummer in local rivals the NEXT BAND, was happy to step in at short notice and deputise at the drumstool. The outfit entered the Fairview facility in Hull at the end of 1978, and laid down those fateful songs which would start off DEF LEPPARD's utterly phenomenal rise to superstar status.

The functionally-titled »Def Leppard EP« was unleashed upon an unsuspecting public at the beginning of 1979, and the limited pressing (the first few hundred with a picture sleeve and signed lyric insert) was soon causing a bit of a major stir in the rock underground, with fans clamouring for copies of this elusive item from the very moment it hit the shelves. It was a cracking debut, and it pretty much stood alone in terms of pre-empting the whole NWOBHM phenomenon, given that there weren't all that many acts outside London who were thinking in terms of self-financed metal (as opposed to glorified pub rock) releases in the early part of 1979. The featured tracks were, although quite heavily influenced by some of the big guns from the 70's rock scene, surprisingly upbeat and powerful, and it's fair to say that it took most UK acts a couple of years to catch up with LEPPARD's ground-breaking approach. "Ride Into The Sun" and "Getcha Rocks Off" were catchy-but-heavy efforts, while the lengthy "Overture" turned out to be a rather more epic and varied affair, showing more than one aspect to the group's abilities. In anyone's books, it was a huge success, and the original pressing was exhausted within a very short time, whereupon a more generous second issue (without the picture sleeve and with a yellow label to distinguish it from the red-label original) was organised as a matter of course. By this stage, they had also found a full-time drummer, Rick Allen (who had previously been involved with minor hopefuls such as RAMPANT and SMOKEY BLUE in his youth), and so the lads were able to get out into the live environment once more.

Before long, however, the youngsters were being encouraged by their ambitious management to come up with an entire album's worth of original compositions, and so embryonic versions of some of their latest material (such as "Answer To The Master", "Glad I'm Alive", "Wasted" and "Sorrow Is A Woman") were soon being captured on tape so that everyone concerned could form some sort of impression as to whether or not the outfit were actually ready for a full LP. In the event, the band members themselves decided that they needed a few more months to hone their material, and the proposed long-player was scrapped for the time being. Sadly, it didn't prevent their original management from utilising the tapes at a much later date (1985, in fact), when the unauthorised »First Strike« collection was hastily assembled from the results of these early studio visits. Entirely predictably, the musicians weren't remotely impressed with this shameless attempt to cash in on their recent success, and the album was withdrawn from sale with great rapidity, rendering it a collectable rarity, although this item has itself been counterfeited on at least one occasion in subsequent years. We'd better get back to 1979, though. Things were soon moving for DEF LEPPARD, and, before long, the lads were being swamped with requests for interviews and radio appearances, their first piece of useful exposure coming with a session for Piccadilly Radio, which was soon followed up by some recordings for the Andy Peebles show on Radio One, where they ran through numbers such as "Wasted" and "Sorrow Is A Woman". It was all very helpful to their cause, as was a generous booking for the BBC's 'In Concert' programme, where the outfit recorded a set of live material for subsequent broadcast for the nation.

By now, word was getting out in a big way, and Geoff Barton of 'Sounds' was keen to identify DEF LEPPARD as one of the acts who were spearheading this *'new metal'* explosion, citing them in the same context as IRON MAIDEN, SAMSON and ANGEL WITCH. To be honest, the LEPPARD lads never really felt all that strongly affiliated with all these NWOBHM machinations (which initially seemed to be centred around the promotion of a handful of East End hopefuls), although the publicity hardly did them any harm. Indeed, it was only a matter of time before one label or another committed themselves to putting a lucrative offer on the table, and the company in question were Vertigo. With a freshly-printed contract in their hands, the lads were freed from the uncertainty of the preceding months, and they were now finally able to ditch their small-time aspirations for good. Next up, however, were some increasingly high-profile appearances in the capital, the lads starting off with a support slot alongside SAMMY HAGAR, and swiftly progressing to activities with the likes of AC/DC. Their new sponsors subsequently decided that a good way to rake in some ready cash would be to reissue the »Def Leppard EP« (again), this time in a considerably greater volume, with an alternate running order and a silver label. This seemed to keep the fans happy while the group got on with their latest recording and touring activities, and the EP sold in impressive quantities yet again. Another big break soon came with the group's invitation to record their first session for the already-legendary 'Friday Rock Show', where they laid down "Satellite", "Wasted", "Rock Brigade" and "Good Morning Freedom" for transmission on the 26th of October 1979. The rapturously-received session was timed to perfection, and the broadcast set the stage nicely for the first instalment of DEF LEPPARD's forthcoming release programme.

Before the year was out, the lads saw their first *'proper'* Vertigo product hitting the shops, a single based around live favourite "Wasted" (backed with the prophetically-titled "Hello America"), which actually achieved a humble-but-significant placing in the mainstream charts. By the early months of 1980, the five-piece had already completed work on their debut long-player, and »On Through The Night« proved to be an extremely popular purchase among the rock/metal fans of the day. It was very much an upbeat NWOBHM release in the main, with some highly capable efforts on display, notably "Rock Brigade", "It Could Be You" and the cracking "Answer To The Master", although, on the basis of numbers such as "It Don't Matter", there were already signs that DEF LEPPARD might be contemplating the possibility of moving into more commercial waters at some point. The record achieved an immensely respectable 'Top 20' placing in the UK, and a couple of singles (»Hello America« and »Rock Brigade«) were soon being trundled out to rake in some further ready cash for Vertigo. The band then undertook a short series of British dates before heading off to the States for several memorable shows with PAT TRAVERS and JUDAS PRIEST, the majority of which were received pretty ecstatically on both sides of the Atlantic. Still, the lads were to receive a healthy dose of reality upon their return to the UK, when their appearance at the 1980 Reading Festival was marred by a seriously hostile reaction from many of those in attendance, some of whom objected quite vehemently to the very fact that DEF LEPPARD had even *dared* to attempt to make something of themselves in the States, as if this somehow made them any less relevant to the British rock scene. Strange sense of logic, some people.

Fortunately, the band took this minor setback with a pinch of salt, and eventually returned to the studio to lay down their follow-up album. »High'n'Dry« was a considerably more polished affair which benefitted from a rather more generous recording budget, although it retained a fair proportion of their debut album's energy nonetheless. The likes of "Another Hit And Run", "Let It Go" and the title track itself were all pretty decent efforts, although there were, in addition, some rather more restrained and commercially-motivated compositions such as "Bringin' On The Heartbreak" and the enjoyable "Lady Strange" to balance things out a bit, so there should, in theory, have been something for everyone. For some reason, however, it failed to emulate the extraordinary success of »On Through The Night« (in the UK, at least, although it did considerably better in the States),

and so the lads were soon left scratching their heads as to how they could reverse the downward trend. Still, there was a fair bit of touring to attend to first, during which time they also saw »Let It Go« and »Bringin' On The Heartbreak« released as singles, although neither performed particularly well. DEF LEPPARD dutifully promoted their new album with a European jaunt alongside RAINBOW, followed by some UK gigs and then some end-of-year headlining shows in the States once more. It rapidly became apparent that the group had a rosy future across the Atlantic if they continued to drift into more accessible waters, whereas the UK was almost certainly a lost cause unless they returned to their down-to-earth roots. In the end, it wasn't a particularly difficult decision for the musicians to make: IRON MAIDEN clearly ruled the roost in Britain, and LEPPARD weren't content to settle for second best, so they more or less decided that their big chance lay in the States. Consequently, there was a conscious decision to start writing material with a more radio-friendly approach when it came to the *'difficult third album'*.

1982 wasn't to be a particularly easy year for the outfit, as they soon had to cope with the delicate situation of Pete Willis going off the rails in major fashion, and they eventually concluded that he couldn't remain part of the LEPPARD set-up unless he cleaned up his act considerably. In the event, he was invited to leave mid-way through the recording sessions for their third LP (later resurfacing in GOGMAGOG, NIGHTRUN and ROADHOUSE), after which the search was soon on for a suitable replacement. Fortunately, they were ultimately able to secure the services of close friend Phil Collen, who was easily lured away from the struggling GIRL (at the second attempt, apparently, since he had originally been approached way back in the early days) to help the outfit to complete work on the album. It took quite a long time to finish all the necessary overdubs, re-tracking and post-production, though, and the long-player didn't actually see the light of day until the beginning of 1983. »Pyromania« was, as anticipated, a fairly wholehearted move into a variation on the theme of semi-anthemic rock/metal; not the complete sell-out that many claimed it to be, but still very much a statement of intent. The newer material was generally well-written and competently-performed, however, and numbers such as "Action! Not Words", "Photograph" and "Rock Of Ages" were soon winning the hearts of many of their more tolerant British fans, as well as prompting an extraordinary response in the States, where the album almost hit the top of the mainstream charts (and they would have made it too, if it hadn't been for that pesky MICHAEL JACKSON). Even in the UK, though, there was a pretty healthy reaction to the latest long-player, which duly emulated the 'Top 20' success of »On Through The Night«, no doubt helped by the fact that various melodic rock hopefuls were now beginning to break through at the expense of many of the original NWOBHM stalwarts. Vertigo made good use of the album in terms of singles, releasing »Photograph« (twice), »Rock Of Ages« and »Too Late For Love«, even if sales were slightly disappointing compared with those of the LP itself. They were soon out on tour, though, with the British and European dates (adequately-attended, but no more) merely setting the stage for their triumphant appearances in North America, where they played with BILLY SQUIER as well as headlining some rapturously-received shows of their own.

After conquering America, it was back down to earth for some end-of-year gigs in Europe, while the early part of 1984 took the lads yet further afield, including such far-flung corners of the globe as Australia and the Far East. The latter jaunt appears to have lost LEPPARD quite a bit of money overall, but I guess they were merely sniffing around to see how much demand there would be for their music elsewhere. Their world tour was finally over, and the lads looked forward to having a bit of a rest, although they were soon being forced to think about delivering yet another album. Tragedy was to strike cruelly at the end of that year, however, when Rick Allen lost control of his car and suffered horrific injuries in the resultant crash. Although the sticksman was extraordinarily lucky to survive, he was relieved of an arm in the accident (something of a necessity for a drummer), and he was not expected to return to music thereafter. Unfazed by this slight setback, however, Allen subsequently announced, in the grand old tradition of the quintessentially-British 'it's only a scratch' mentality, that he would indeed remain involved with LEPPARD, and the other members went along with this insanity for the time being. The original notion was that they could recruit a second sticksman and utilise three arms simultaneously on two separate kits, but Allen came up with the idea of an electronic kit which could be operated single-handedly (as it were) via a novel combination of arm/foot activity. Remarkably, the scheme was put into implementation, and, after a great deal of practice, it all came together as planned. Amazing what you can do when you put your mind to it.

By 1985, things were beginning to get back on schedule with regard to the fourth album, although it turned out to be a truly ludicrously-protracted affair, the whole thing famously taking a mammoth three years to complete. The group was keen to play down the tortuous nature of the studio sessions, suggesting that it just took a long time to get the production exactly right and to put all the overdubs in place. Fair enough, but three years? In reality, it transpires that many of those involved with the project were experiencing some pretty fundamental problems (the whole album was recorded at least twice, for one thing) at the time, and difficulties seemed to rise up at every opportunity: material was rejected on a regular basis, the drum technology didn't work quite as smoothly as it might have done, and there were clashes in terms of just how accessible the finished product should be. In the end, everyone resolved their differences and banished the associated problems, and »Hysteria« was eventually unleashed in the summer of 1987 amidst a veritable whirlwind of pre-publicity and media hype. Everywhere you looked, LEPPARD were in the public eye, and anticipation of the album (on both sides of the Atlantic) reached fever pitch before a single note of the material had even been heard. Before long, though, it was in the shops, and the new record (the band had now taken to stamping their own personality on every release by having them issued on the self-contained Bludgeon Riffola subsidiary of parent company Vertigo, taking them back to their roots in one sense) completed LEPPARD's metamorphosis into an accessible pop/rock outfit with mainstream aspirations, the over-produced and slickly-presented album bearing not the slightest resemblance to their original musical direction. Still, the rockers all went for it in a big way (given that *'real metal'* was now in a critical condition and melodic rock was currently flavour of the month), sending it to the top of the charts in the States and a 'Top 3' placing in the UK. Suddenly, LEPPARD apparently had fans everywhere they turned, and their newer material seemed to have tapped into the public's consciousness in major fashion. It really was a dream come true for their label, who proceeded to release a grand total of six singles from the latest set, all of which managed to achieve an impressive 'Top 30' placing in the mainstream charts, which was a notable feat in anyone's books.

The band organised an extremely lengthy tour to promote the latest offering, and took to the road for a whole year, taking in some pretty capacious venues in the UK, Europe, North America and even Japan, and, when they finally managed to take a break in the second half of 1988, it was revealed that »Hysteria« had now sold several million copies around the globe. Which was nice. Work on LEPPARD's next long-player was due to begin in the new year, but once again the project was beset with problems, some of which were associated with their choice of material and some of which revolved around Steve Clark, who was beginning to give serious cause for concern, having been living the rock'n'roll lifestyle to excess for some time. They managed to get him into the studio for a few sessions, but he was soon on the slippery slope to self-destruction, and the inevitable result was a fatal overdose of a drink/drugs combination in the early days of 1991. Clearly, the lads were knocked for six, but there was never any serious talk of calling it a day, and they duly began looking for a replacement, whereupon the much-travelled Vivian Campbell (who, since his humble beginnings in SWEET SAVAGE, had earned a crust with DIO, WHITESNAKE, RIVER DOGS and SHADOW KING) was given the shout. With a suitable line-up established once more, it was now a case of getting the much-delayed album recorded as soon as humanly possible, and »Adrenalize« made it into the shops in the spring of 1992. It was very much in the style of »Hysteria«, if not even poppier, but it managed the almost unprecedented feat of topping the charts on both sides of the Atlantic, so they had obviously hit upon a winning formula which they saw little or no reason to alter just to gain a bit of media credibility. As it was, the press had a field day with such ludicrous self-parody as "Let's Get Rocked" (with the infamous *'I suppose a rock's out of the question'* line), but the band seemed to be immune to any facile criticism of their mass appeal. A handful of singles made it into the shops to tie in with the release, although there was hardly the sort of multi-release overkill which had surrounded the whole »Hysteria« episode, and it seemed as though LEPPARD were now rather more in control of their destiny.

As usual, they were soon out on tour to spread their name even further (if that was actually possible), and much of the next year was occupied by their commitment to playing some huge gigs around the world. In the second half of 1993, however, they sanctioned the release of the »Retro-Active« anthology, which saw the lads making available various recordings of some of their less-familiar material (mostly culled from obscure B-sides and the like), which nevertheless sold pretty well for a compilation release. After that, they kept something of a low profile for a couple of years (although a single or two sneaked out to maintain some level of LEPPARD-related interest in the music press), but another album was on the cards before much longer. First, though, they took the surprising decision to allow another retrospective (»Vault«) to hit the shops, this time more of a *'greatest hits'* affair, although most of the material featured had, predictably enough, been plucked from the two most recent studio albums at the expense of their early 80's offerings. Once again, however, it sold in droves, and the musicians seemed assured of a healthy response to their next official album. This finally appeared as the »Slang« set in the spring of 1996, heralded by some slightly optimistic (and equally misleading) claims that it represented something of a turning point for the long-lived outfit, with some fanciful reports even assuring everyone that *'DEF LEPPARD go grunge!'* on their new long-player. In fact, it wasn't really a major shift in direction at all, although it was, admittedly, slightly more substantial and contemporary than much of their more recent work. The fans weren't as impressed as they might have been, though (possibly perturbed by the advance publicity), and sales were considerably down on »Adrenalize«, particularly in the States. Oh dear. Were LEPPARD losing the plot by this stage?

Well, it looks as though the relative failure of the latest long-player had something of an impact on the musicians (who, in previous years, could barely do wrong in the eyes of their fans), and LEPPARD's collective response was to go into hiding once more, keeping a low profile for the usual couple of years while they attempted to establish a consistent style and compose the kind of material which would still be relevant to a significant proportion of rock fans in the late 90's. Well, at least grunge was no longer the force it had been, so would LEPPARD attempt to jump on another convenient bandwagon or go back to what they did best, namely radio-friendly rock? Or, perhaps, might they revert to their metal roots and really surprise everyone? Hmmm, I reckon the latter was always an unlikely option, to be honest. In fact, they returned to the fore in 1999 with »Euphoria«, an album which largely (in the absence of the usual media hype which surrounded their every move in previous years) failed to make much of an impression on the general rock audience, and which sorely lacked the energy and spontaneity of their 80's heyday. By now, the lads may have been older and wiser, but they no longer seemed to know exactly which market they were aiming for, their latest batch of compositions attempting to cover too many bases with the slushy ballads, mediocre rockers and the occasional upbeat reminder of their undisputed songwriting ability. They still seem to be a going concern, although I reckon the next album could be the make-or-break release, and, if it dies a death, I doubt they'll want to prolong their existence unnecessarily. They've achieved a hell of a lot, triumphed in the face of severe adversity and broken free of the NWOBHM shackles in a way that no other act has ever managed. Even if they did *'sell out'* to get there, I can assure you that thousands of young hopefuls from the early 80's would (no matter what they may claim) have done exactly the same to enjoy a mere fraction of their success.

LP's
»**On Through The Night**« Vertigo 1980
»**High'n'Dry**« Vertigo 1981
»**Pyromania**« Vertigo 1983
»**First Strike**« Flash Records 1985
[Unofficial compilation of early demos, withdrawn but later counterfeited]
»**Hysteria**« Bludgeon Riffola 1987
[Also released as limited edition picture disc]
»**Adrenalize**« Bludgeon Riffola 1992
[Limited edition issued as picture disc]

12" EP's
»**Bringin' On The Heartbreak**« Vertigo 1981
["Me And My Wine" non-LP]

»**Photograph**« Vertigo 1983
[Original issue, includes "Mirror Mirror"]
»**Too Late For Love**« Vertigo 1983
»**Photograph**« Vertigo 1984
[Second issue in different sleeve, includes "No No No"]
»**Animal**« Bludgeon Riffola 1987
[With two versions of "Animal", "Tear It Down" non-LP]
»**Pour Some Sugar On Me**« Bludgeon Riffola 1987
[With two versions of "Pour Some Sugar On Me", "I Wanna Be Your Hero" non-LP, also released as limited edition picture disc]
»**Hysteria**« Bludgeon Riffola 1987
["Ride Into The Sun" different to version on first EP, also includes live version of "Love And Affection", issued in special 'Hysteria box set' cover with poster]
»**Armageddon It**« Bludgeon Riffola 1988
[With two versions of "Armageddon It", "Ring Of Fire" non-LP]
»**Love Bites**« Bludgeon Riffola 1988
[Includes live version of "Billy's Got A Gun" and remixed version of "Excitable", also issued as part of 'Hysteria box set']
»**Rocket**« Bludgeon Riffola 1988
[Also issued as limited edition picture disc]
»**Let's Get Rocked**« Bludgeon Riffola 1992
[Limited edition issued as picture disc]
»**Make Love Like A Man**« Bludgeon Riffola 1992
[Limited edition issued as picture disc]
»**Have You Ever Needed Someone So Bad**« Bludgeon Riffola 1992
[Limited edition issued as picture disc]
»**Heaven Is**« Bludgeon Riffola 1993
[Limited edition issued as picture disc]
»**Tonight**« Bludgeon Riffola 1993
[Limited edition issued as picture disc]

12" Singles
»**Rock Of Ages**« Vertigo 1983
»**Bringin' On The Heartbreak**« Vertigo 1984
[Both tracks remixed, B-side "Me And My Wine" non-LP]

7" EP's
»**The Def Leppard EP**« Bludgeon Riffola 1978
[First issue with SRT matrix, red label, most with picture sleeve, some with signed lyric insert, recently counterfeited with reproduction picture sleeve and off-white labels. "Ride Into The Sun" non-LP, "Overture" and "Rocks Off" different to album versions]
»**The Def Leppard EP**« Bludgeon Riffola 1979
[Second issue with yellow label, no sleeve]
»**The Def Leppard EP**« Vertigo 1979
[Reissue with silver label, no sleeve]

7" Singles

»Wasted« Vertigo 1979
»Hello America« Vertigo 1980
[B-side "Good Morning Freedom" non-LP]
»Let It Go« Vertigo 1981
»Bringin' On The Heartbreak« Vertigo 1981
[B-side "Me And My Wine" non-LP]
»Photograph« Vertigo 1983
[Also issued as limited edition in fold-out sleeve]
»Rock Of Ages« Vertigo 1983
[Also issued as limited edition in fold-out sleeve]
»Too Late For Love« Vertigo 1983
»Photograph« Vertigo 1984
[Second issue in alternate gatefold sleeve]
»Animal« Bludgeon Riffola 1987
[B-side "Tear It Down" non-LP]
»Pour Some Sugar On Me« Bludgeon Riffola 1987
[B-side "I Wanna Be Your Hero" non-LP]
»Hysteria« Bludgeon Riffola 1987
[B-side "Ride Into The Sun" different to version on first EP]
»Armageddon It« Bludgeon Riffola 1988
[B-side "Ring Of Fire" non-LP, also issued as limited edition in poster sleeve]
»Love Bites« Bludgeon Riffola 1988
[Includes live version of "Billy's Got A Gun"]
»Rocket« Bludgeon Riffola 1988
»Let's Get Rocked« Bludgeon Riffola 1992
»Make Love Like A Man« Bludgeon Riffola 1992
»Have You Ever Needed Someone So Bad« Bludgeon Riffola 1992
»Heaven Is« Bludgeon Riffola 1993
»Tonight« Bludgeon Riffola 1993
»Two Steps Behind« Bludgeon Riffola 1993
»Action« Bludgeon Riffola 1994

Shaped Picture Discs

»Rock Of Ages« Vertigo 1983
»Pour Some Sugar On Me« Bludgeon Riffola 1987

Selected Promotional Releases

»Too Late For Love« Vertigo 1983
[DJ promo 7" in 'football team' cover]
»Women« Vertigo 1987
[US-only DJ promo 12"]
»Stumpus Maximus And The Good Ol'Boys« Vertigo 1989
[Promo-only 12", features exclusive versions of "Please Release Me" and "Rock Of Ages"]

CD's

»Hysteria« Bludgeon Riffola 1987
»On Through The Night« Bludgeon Riffola 1991
»High'n'Dry« Bludgeon Riffola 1991
[With two bonus tracks]
»Pyromania« Bludgeon Riffola 1991

»First Strike« Bootleg 1992
[Unofficial reissue of withdrawn album]
»Adrenalize« Bludgeon Riffola 1992
»Retro-Active« Bludgeon Riffola 1993
[Compilation release, includes various recordings of old B-side material]
»Greatest Hits-Vault« Bludgeon Riffola 1995
[Compilation release, limited edition with bonus live CD]
»Slang« Bludgeon Riffola 1996
[Also released as limited edition with bonus live CD]
»Euphoria« Bludgeon Riffola 1999

CD Singles

»Animal« Bludgeon Riffola 1987
»Pour Some Sugar On Me« Bludgeon Riffola 1987
»Hysteria« Bludgeon Riffola 1987
»Armageddon It« Bludgeon Riffola 1988
[Also issued as limited edition in poster sleeve]
»Love Bites« Bludgeon Riffola 1988
»Rocket« Bludgeon Riffola 1988
»Let's Get Rocked« Bludgeon Riffola 1992
»Make Love Like A Man« Bludgeon Riffola 1992
»Have You Ever Needed Someone So Bad« Bludgeon Riffola 1992
»Heaven Is« Bludgeon Riffola 1993
»Tonight« Bludgeon Riffola 1993
»Two Steps Behind« Bludgeon Riffola 1993
»Action« Bludgeon Riffola 1994
»When Love And Hate Collide« Bludgeon Riffola 1995
»Slang« Bludgeon Riffola 1996
»Work It Out« Bludgeon Riffola 1996
»All I Want Is Everything« Bludgeon Riffola 1996
»Breathe A Sigh« Bludgeon Riffola 1996
»Promises« Bludgeon Riffola 1999
»Goodbye« Bludgeon Riffola 1999

Selected Compilation Appearances

"Satellite" on »Living Legends« LP Vertigo 1980
"Getcha Rocks Off" on »Living Legends« LP Vertigo 1980 + »Heavy« LP Vertigo 1980
"Rock Brigade" on »Axe Attack Vol.II« LP K-Tel 1981
"Getcha Rocks Off" on »NWOBHM '79 Revisited« Do-LP/Do-CD Phonogram 1990
[Different to album version]
"Wasted" (live) on »NWOBHM-The Days On Stage« Bootleg CD Taurus Records 1993

DEMOLITION

John Cadden (v)
Phil Guy (g)
Lita Panisar (b)

Ray Horton (d)

A very heavy concern from Britain's second city of Birmingham, DEMOLITION were yet another entry on the never-ending list of long-forgotten local heroes until one of their tracks was given a bit of belated exposure on the Japanese series of bootleg CD's. The number in question, "Hooker Hater", came from the outfit's lone single, released way back in 1981, which few collectors are privileged enough to possess nowadays. Issued in a monochrome sleeve depicting a silhouetted city skyline, both the A-side and "Axeman" are straight ahead, no-frills metal in the style of MOTÖRHEAD, SHOCK TREATMENT or the A.R.C. ROCK BAND, the gruff vocal style suiting the material admirably and accentuating the ominous lyrics to great effect. I'd say that there might be a bit of a North American influence at work in terms of the intensity of the tracks as well as the lyrical sentiments (indeed, the word 'hooker' is only commonly used in the UK to refer to a position on the rugby field). The foursome, having come from an area of considerable musical innovation over the years, are certainly yet another feather in the cap of Midlands metal, the latter being a hugely productive region which could always be relied upon to deliver heavyweight acts of the highest calibre. Other studio recordings from around the time of the single's release, such as "Hustling Around", "My Direction" and "No", were all in much the same mode, their uncompromising style reflecting the fact that appealing to the commercial rock market just wasn't DEMOLITION's intention at all.

Although DEMOLITION (who also featured ex-RICOCHET guitarist Dave Gough in place of Phil Guy at one point) were a popular enough live attraction on the regional rock scene of the day, the lads don't really seem to have achieved much, if any, success outwith their local area (a story which is becoming depressingly familiar), although they occasionally ventured a bit further afield, including a co-headlining gig with CRYER in Lowestoft in March 1981. Furthermore, the sheer commercial inaccessibility of their material (not to mention their 'in your face' attitude) probably alienated many rock journalists of the day, and I don't imagine they ever gained much airplay. Some of their other live favourites, incidentally, included the likes of "On Top Of The World", "No Time To Die" and the exquisitely-titled "See You Down In Hell", and it looks as though they had quite a strong biker following throughout the Midlands. Gravel-throated vocalist John Cadden subsequently spent some time

Hooker Hater
Axeman
SINGLE AVAILABLE NOW

in Germany (as did quite a few NWOBHM scenesters) and was briefly involved with some heavy outfits, including DAMIEN (a project which enlisted the services of a fair number of British musicians), VANDAL and the brutal EXUMER, but the much-travelled individual eventually returned to Blighty when his flirtation with the music business finally ran its course. It goes without saying that the DEMOLITION single is an immensely rare piece by anyone's standards, and is very seldom offered for sale. Keep your fingers, toes, arms and legs crossed and you might get lucky...

7" Singles
»Hooker Hater« Demolition Rock Records 1981

Compilation Appearances
"Hooker Hater" on »NWOBHM Vol.5« Bootleg CD 1992

DEMON

Dave Hill (v)
Mal Spooner (g)
Clive Cook (g)
Paul Riley (b)
John Wright (d)

The heavyweight proposition known as DEMON was conceived in the county of Staffordshire during the second half of 1980, the main protagonists in the venture (vocalist Dave Hill and guitarist Mal Spooner) having been involved with various amateur-hour club acts for some years beforehand. The duo rapidly assembled a five-piece unit around themselves, and had barely completed their first batch of rehearsals when they somehow obtained a one-off single deal with local label Clay, whereupon they laid down "Liar" and "Wild Woman" for imminent release. Their collective experience in the clubs had evidently served them well, and they managed to capture two (very brief) raunchy rockers with a nod towards the likes of CHEVY, MORE and FIST, nothing too spectacular at that stage, but, nevertheless, an impressive debut for an ensemble who were still finding their feet in the music business. The single sold well (helped, no doubt, by its excellent sleeve and some fetching red vinyl), and Clay were soon coming to an amicable agreement with the powerful Carrere Records (home of SAXON and RAGE) to sponsor DEMON's future activities in a joint capacity. Even before the lads had a chance to draw breath, they were being gently ushered into the studio at the beginning of 1981, the expectation being that these industrious types should be able to deliver a pretty competent long-player in no time at all.

To their credit, the DEMON lads wasted little time before getting down to business, and soon began assembling a set which largely revolved around various lyrical notions which had been floating around in the Hill/Spooner consciousness for some time. The resultant album, »Night Of The Demon«, emerged a few months later, and represented a semi-conceptual piece, with one side containing four tracks (and an ominous intro) which delved into the darker side of life and death, and (thanks to the lyrics printed on the reverse cover) left the listener in no doubt as to DEMON's fondness for occult themes. It wasn't all doom and gloom, though, as the other side contained an upbeat selection of enjoyable rockers, balancing things out (although the band modestly insisted that they were merely 'hedging their bets' in case there was something of a backlash against the heavy stuff) quite nicely. There was barely a duff number on display at all, and DEMON were already demonstrating an uncanny ability to knock out memorable, powerful pieces with an innate sense of melody and dynamism. Stand-out numbers would have to include the excellent title track and "Into The Nightmare", plus the lighter "Ride The Wind" and "Fool To Play The Hard Way", and the release as a whole was soon (helped along by some extremely favourable reviews and features in the rock press) selling in impressive quantities. With the journalists sensing that DEMON might represent something a bit out of the ordinary, they were soon all looking to get the lowdown on these unholy black metal blasphemers, and the hacks must have been pretty disappointed to discover that they were actually quite nice people after all. Dave Hill was keen to put things into perspective at an early stage: *'We're not just using all this as a cheap, as you say, attention-grabber. We'd really like to develop what we're doing in a classy way-but keep it simple, on the lines of good and evil, without talking about the cults and all that. We've always been interested in black magic and all that, but obviously we don't go around practising it or anything.'* (Ref: Kerrang No.3, September 1981). Still, I bet that disconcerting sleeve upset a few sensibilities…

With the long-player in the shops (closely followed by two singles, namely »Ride The Wind« and »One Helluva Night«), the lads could finally turn their thoughts to promoting themselves with a few well-chosen appearances in the live environment, although they restricted themselves (in the first instance) to some low-profile activities in the minor pubs and clubs of the Midlands. Nevertheless, the response seemed to be overwhelmingly favourable, and there was no witch-hunt from the moral majority (thankfully), so DEMON just kept on doing as they pleased for the time being. Before much longer, however, they were invited to lay down their first session for the 'Friday Rock Show', whereupon the outfit captured four representative selections ("One Helluva Night", "Night Of The Demon", "Father Of Time" and "Decisions") from their recently-released LP. The session, transmitted on the 7th of August 1981, turned out to be one of the station's most popular broadcasts of the time ("One Helluva Night" deservedly made it onto the BBC's »The Friday Rock Show« sampler of session highlights), and it looked as though there would be no stopping the might of the DEMON (as it were). Still, it proved to be the end of the line as far as original members Paul Riley and Clive Cook were concerned, whereupon new recruits Chris Ellis (b) and Les Hunt (g) were welcomed into the ranks. After re-establishing themselves and penning a batch of novel material, the musicians were soon venturing into the studio once more, their collective intention being to come up with another full-length effort to capitalise on their apparently-soaring popularity.

After a few months spent casting their spells in the studio, DEMON re-emerged in mid-1982 with a new long-player, the rather spookily-titled »The Unexpected Guest«. It conclusively proved that they weren't one-album-wonders after all, and the release turned out to be an eminently worthy successor to »Night Of The Demon«, the lads basing the entire record around their favoured lyrical stance, the topics covered including the cycle of life, malevolent spirits, nasty smells (no, I made that one up) and all sorts of quasi-spiritual gobbledegook. Musically, however, it was all immensely enjoyable, although certain compositions veered off into surprisingly melodic and accessible territory (DEMON never really shook off their 70's rock roots completely, although they became synonymised with the NWOBHM phenomenon almost immediately after their vinyl debut hit the shops) at times, something which occasionally seemed to clash with the lyrical sentiments. Still, tracks such as the cracking "Don't Break The Circle" (reworked by BLIND GUARDIAN in later years), "The Spell" and "Deliver Us From Evil" represented some excellently-crafted inclusions, and the public began snapping up copies of the LP as soon as it hit the shelves, sending DEMON hurtling towards a mainstream chart placing for the first time. Just one single emerged to promote the release, although "Have We Been Here Before" appears to have been a relatively unpopular choice of A-side among the fans, and comparatively few units were shifted. Pity, I would have liked to have seen DEMON on 'Top Of The Pops'.

By this stage, DEMON were taking further steps in the live environment, creating a semi-theatrical atmosphere which involved their frontman (having adopted an unsettling *alter ego* by donning one of his costumes and/or masks) emerging from a makeshift grave in the middle of the stage. It might have been an intriguing and original way to start a show, but I gather that the whole event constituted a slightly surreal spectacle in some of the small pub venues they chose to frequent. After a while, it looks as though they began to have second thoughts about all their over-the-top lyrics and imagery, and, by the time the third long-player (»The Plague«) finally emerged in 1983, it seemed as though DEMON had finally exorcised themselves and managed to get all of the black magic mumbo-jumbo out of their system. »The Plague« represented the outfit's first album for Clay alone (Carrere appear to have pulled out of the deal after just two full-length releases), and this saw the lads making an unanticipated move into considerably more ambitious, semi-progressive waters, the latest record being based around another of DEMON's grand conceptual ideas, this time dealing with an impossibly bleak and nihilistic vision of some post-apocalyptic future (?) civilisation experiencing a complete societal collapse. It was all immensely depressing (the music being complemented by a booklet with lyrics and an accompanying selection of grim images), as the following excerpt from the atmospheric title track admirably illustrates:

'What price the future and Orwell's dream
All yours big brother
On twenty two inch screen
The tragedy we bleed human
Can't feed emotion to the zombie brain
And as the rat becomes exhausted
We stand to lose the game
Beware of the...Plague.'

Blimey, give me a ruddy rope and I'll hang myself now. Still, at least the music was listenable enough (alternating between upbeat and melancholy efforts), and inclusions such as "Blackheath" and "The Writings On The Wall" were particularly strong. The record followed »The Unexpected Guest« into the charts (not achieving quite such a high placing, though), and the title track was even plucked to form the basis of a single, although it was evident that none of the album's material had been specifically written with this in mind. The fans seemed happy enough to allow DEMON to experiment with new ideas, although it looked as though they would be coming back to earth for their next long-player, having expressed a high proportion of their high-concept ideas on their first triumvirate of albums.

The recording of album number four was beset by problems and tragedy, the band suffering from personnel instability (Les Hunt threw in the towel at an early stage, later turning his hand to a great deal of production work) and being forced to experience Mal Spooner's deteriorating condition (the poor chap certainly hadn't exactly enjoyed the best of health in previous years and was now in a really bad way) at close quarters. In all honesty, it was a miracle that the long-player was ever completed at all, the outfit having to bring in a guest bassist (Gavin Sutherland) when Chris Ellis flew the coop at short notice, and employing a stand-in axeman (John Waterhouse) once Spooner could no longer continue. Nevertheless, the studio sessions were completed in the latter part of

1984 (the lads were also utilising the keyboard services of Steve Watts this time, having employed the largely-uncredited Andy Richards on the previous two albums), only for Spooner to succumb to a fatal bout of pneumonia only days later. Even though his musical colleagues had been painfully aware of the seriousness of his condition, Spooner's untimely death came as a severe shock, although the remaining members of DEMON were determined to issue the album to serve as a lasting tribute to the great man's creativity. The long-player, »British Standard Approved« (with various dedications to their departed friend on the inner and outer sleeves), appeared at the end of 1984, and revealed the outfit to have been in a pretty sober and reflective state of mind while it was being written and recorded, which is understandable enough in the circumstances. To be honest, though, much of the material featured (especially on side one) is so utterly cold and unlistenable that it fails to leave a positive impression at all, which is hardly the way Mal Spooner deserved to be remembered. It was a very poor album indeed, saved only by the superb "Wonderland" (later covered by MENDES PREY), which was also trundled out as a single, although sales of both were pretty modest.

It wouldn't really have been a shock if DEMON had ceased to exist in the wake of the »British Standard Approved« debacle, but they elected to keep going for the time being, presumably in the belief that they deserved to bow out with a more capable album. Therefore, 'guest' musicians John Waterhouse and Gavin Sutherland were retained to help out on the next long-player, whereupon Dave Hill began penning new material himself, aided by recent recruit Steve Watts (who actually had an eponymous outfit of his own at one stage) on occasion. Fortunately, 1985's »Heart Of Our Time« turned out to be a huge improvement, the album as a whole being far more upbeat and cheerful than its predecessor, with the likes of "High Climber" and the title track (both of which surfaced on a rather peculiar 'sampler' of highlights from their three most recent LP's) being particularly enjoyable. Still, the rock press (in the UK, at least) now regarded DEMON as having overstayed their initial welcome in no uncertain terms, and intimated that the group's traditional, powerful brand of rock music had little or no place in the modern metal world. Unconvinced that they had suddenly become an irrelevance, the lads persevered, recruiting a new bassist (Andy Dale) in the early months of 1986, whereupon they tried to re-establish themselves on the live scene, having made comparatively few appearances during the previous couple of years. In fact, there seemed to be enough sustainable interest in DEMON's future activities to warrant yet another full-length release, and so album number six (»Breakout«) duly appeared the following year, although it wasn't a classic by any means. There were, inevitably, a couple of decent efforts, notably "Living In The Shadow" and "The Big Chance", although the capable selections were outnumbered by all the overly-commercial, mediocre numbers scattered throughout the remainder of the set. Once again, DEMON had delivered a bit of a ropy record, and were now running the risk of imminent disintegration, especially when several members started packing their bags.

Although they were now widely regarded as well past their prime, and, with a rapidly-dwindling fan base, DEMON ploughed on regardless, establishing a new line-up following the recruitment of drummer Scott Crawford, bassist Nick Bushell and second axeman Steve Brookes (originally just for live work), the latter pair being veterans (unlikely as it may seem) of local punk legends DISCHARGE. The revised outfit toured whenever they could (even taking in the odd European gig, where they discovered a pretty healthy respect for their music), but took their time getting to the stage of releasing another full album. DEMON had contrived to issue long-players at the rate of almost one per year since their initial formation, and it now seemed as though they were acknowledging the need for slightly more in the way of quality control. The band's future clearly rested on their ability to assemble a sufficient quantity of new compositions to create a worthwhile LP, as there was little or no point in just throwing together the first ideas that came into their heads, something that they seemed to have been doing for several years now. There was only one release (enough to keep the fans happy) during 1988, and this contained a grand total of one new number, the fairly unremarkable "Tonight (The Hero Is Back)", the remainder of the double-single set being padded out with alternate versions of "Hurricane" (from their most recent album), "Night Of The Demon" and "Don't Break The Circle". To be blunt, DEMON didn't seem to have much of a future at that point, given that they appeared to be celebrating past glories and continually failing to come up with anything of a remotely comparable standard.

Remarkably, however, DEMON subsequently managed to pull a decent album out of the fire with their all-new offering, the optimistically-titled »Taking The World By Storm«. Although it wasn't a flawless opus by any means, it did contain a markedly higher percentage of classy numbers, particularly the likes of "Commercial Dynamite", "Blue Skies In Red Square" (which duly received a fair bit of airplay on the 'Friday Rock Show') and the title track itself, and it looked as though the fortunate DEMON had managed to retrieve their once-proud reputation just when it appeared to be disappearing down the tubes for good. On the back of this new release, the outfit toured with considerably greater success than they had been enjoying for quite some time, and made it over to mainland Europe towards the end of 1989, experiencing a hero's welcome upon their arrival in Germany. After completing some rapturously-received gigs, they returned to the UK in truly buoyant mood, and were now convinced that they should definitely be sticking around for a bit longer. At around the turn of the decade, Clay Records metamorphosed into Sonic, and established a lucrative European arrangement with Flametrader, which would allow the band's future product to appear simultaneously on the continent, an extremely efficient distribution network meaning that their fans were now able to get hold of new releases with comparative ease. Much of 1990 was spent in the studio, although the name of DEMON retained a high media profile thanks to the release of their »One Helluva Night« double live set, which had been recorded on their last tour of Germany. It was an extremely listenable performance, with highlights coming from most of their best-loved albums (largely drawing a veil over »British Standard Approved« and »Heart Of Our Time«), and the set proceeded to sell in impressive quantities.

Towards the end of 1990, the lads sauntered off to Germany once again (taking TREDEGAR along to open the proceedings), where they entertained the masses with an assortment of classics from an abundant repertoire, additionally grasping the opportunity to showcase some of their most recently-penned compositions. Moving into 1991, the group were, on the strength of their latest batch of material, invited back into the BBC's studios to record their first 'Friday Rock Show' session for an entire decade, and the lads duly laid down "Commercial Dynamite", old chestnut "Don't Break The Circle" and two equally-capable newer numbers, "No More Hell On Earth" and "The Lion's Share". The session, broadcast on the 25th of January 1991, became another instant hit among the station's numerous listeners, many of whom must have wondered just what DEMON had been up to since their first appearance on the show, way back in 1981. The group's latest album followed a couple of months later, and »Hold On To The Dream« was a pretty fair representation of the all-new DEMON personality, with upbeat rockers such as the aforementioned "No More Hell On Earth" and "The Lion's Share" sitting quite comfortably alongside undeniably contrasting pieces such as the epic "Barons Of Darkness" and the restrained "Ivory Towers". Overall, though, the outfit were now a far more convincing and less erratic musical entity than they had been during the awkward mid-80's, and, with a burgeoning following throughout Europe, it looked as though there was still a fair bit of life in the old dogs yet. 1991 also saw the first DEMON retrospective to come onto the market, with the »Anthology« set compiling material from their first six albums, introducing some of the newcomers to a selection of compositions from DEMON's lengthy back catalogue.

By the time DEMON got around to delivering a follow-up to »Hold On To The Dream« in 1992, however, they had experienced a few personnel reshuffles, the first to have afflicted them for some time. Out went Steve Watts, Nick Bushell and Scott Crawford, leaving only a nucleus of Waterhouse (who also had his own side-project on the go by this juncture), Brookes and the ever-present Hill. Fortunately, however, the trio managed to identify a likely pair of accomplices, whereupon Mike Thomas (b) and Paul Ros-

scrow (d) were drafted in to make up the numbers. The lads clearly had a bit of a rethink in terms of their future musical direction, and the songwriting partnership of Hill and Brookes duly came up with an album's worth of stripped-down, keyboard-free material for the next set. The resultant long-player, »Blow-Out«, was a pretty solid offering (predictably, it didn't garner much press attention, but the fans generally seemed perfectly happy with the contents), although it proved to be DEMON's last studio LP (to date) as an ensemble, since the participants elected to go their separate ways after a brief round of touring in 1993. Dave Hill proceeded to record a solo set (»Welcome To The Real World«, on which the frontman was assisted by various guesting musicians) a year later, although this represented a major departure from the heavyweight DEMON mentality, and the album appears to have been a one-off venture (a long-harboured desire to try something slightly different, perhaps) as opposed to a *bona fide* attempt to instigate a productive career as a solo artist.

After a few years in the musical wilderness, however, DEMON finally regrouped and returned to the live environment in 1997, playing a handful of select European dates during the next couple of years, and there are now concrete plans for the revitalised unit (currently featuring the services of Hill, Dale, guitarist Ray Walmsley, drummer John Cotterill and keyboard player Duncan Hansell) to deliver a brand-new studio album within the next year or so. A further compilation release (»The Best Of Demon Volume One«, assembled by the little-known Spaced Out Music concern) has recently been made available, as has a respectful tribute album with the appropriate title of »Day Of The Demon«, a release to which (bizarrely enough) DEMON themselves actually contributed a pair of previously-unheard numbers. I suspect we haven't heard the last of DEMON just yet (they've been getting back into the swing of things with more high-profile appearances during the past few months, including a well-received slot at Wacken 2000), and I'm sure their countless devotees (who are fortunate to be served by a comprehensive, official website, which, you won't be remotely surprised to learn, is called *'the site of the DEMON'*) won't ever let them fade away unnoticed.

LP's
»**Night Of The Demon**« Carrere 1981
»**The Unexpected Guest**« Carrere 1982
[Original issue in gatefold sleeve]
»**The Plague**« Clay 1983
[With gatefold sleeve and attached booklet, also issued as limited edition picture disc]
»**The Plague**« Roadrunner 1983/Atlantic 1983
[Dutch/US issue]
»**British Standard Approved**« Clay 1984
»**Heart Of Our Time**« Clay 1985
»**Breakout**« Clay 1987
»**The Unexpected Guest**« Clay 1987
[Remastered reissue in single sleeve]
»**Night Of The Demon**« Clay 1988
[Reissue]
»**Taking The World By Storm**« Clay 1989
»**One Helluva Night**« Sonic Records 1990/Flametrader 1990
[UK/German issue, double live album]
»**Hold On To The Dream**« Sonic Records 1991
[UK issue]
»**Hold On To The Dream**« Flametrader 1991
[German issue, limited edition with free 12"]
»**Blow-Out**« Flametrader 1992

Mini-LP's
»**Demon**« Clay 1985
[Selection of tracks taken from »The Plague«, »British Standard Approved« and »Heart Of Our Time« albums]

12" EP's
»**Wonderland**« Clay 1984
[Features remixed versions of "Blackheath" and "Nowhere To Run"]

7" Singles
»**Liar**« Clay 1980
[Issued on red vinyl, A-side different to album version, B-side "Wild Woman" non-LP]
»**Ride The Wind**« Carrere 1981
[B-side "On The Road" non-LP]
»**One Helluva Night**« Carrere 1981
[Also released as limited edition picture disc]
»**Have We Been Here Before?**« Carrere 1982
[Both tracks different to album versions]
»**The Plague**« Clay 1983
[A-side different to album version]
»**Wonderland**« Clay 1984
[UK issue, A-side different to album version, B-side remixed version of "Blackheath"]
»**Wonderland**« RCA 1985
[German issue, B-side "The Link (Part 2)"]
»**Tonight (The Hero Is Back)**« Clay 1988
[A-side non-LP, B-side "Hurricane" different to album version, issued in gatefold sleeve with free single featuring remixed versions of "Night Of The Demon" and "Don't Break The Circle"]

CD's
»**The Plague**« Clay 1988

»Breakout« Clay 1988
[With one extra track]
»Night Of The Demon/The Unexpected Guest« ZYX Records 1989
[Two tracks omitted]
»British Standard Approved« ZYX Records 1989
»Heart Of Our Time« ZYX Records 1989
»Taking The World By Storm« Sonic Records 1990
»Night Of The Demon« Sonic Records 1990
»One Helluva Night« Sonic Records 1990/Flametrader 1990
[UK/German issue, double live disc]
»Hold On To The Dream« Sonic Records 1991/Flametrader 1991
[UK/German issue]
»Anthology« Clay 1991
[Compilation release]
»Blow-Out« Sonic Records 1992/Flametrader 1992
[UK/German issue]
»The Best Of Demon Volume One« Spaced Out Music 1999
[Compilation release]

Exclusive Compilation Appearances

"Tonight Won't Last Forever" on »Day Of The Demon« CD Private 1998
"Trick Of The Light" on »Day Of The Demon« CD Private 1998

Compilation Appearances

"One Helluva Night" on »The Friday Rock Show« LP BBC Records 1981
[Different to album version]
"Total Possession" on »Heavy Metal Thunder« LP Carrere 1982
"Liar" on »Heavy Metal Thunder« LP Carrere 1982
"Wonderland" on »Axe Attack« LP M Port 1985/Mausoleum 1986
"Don't Break The Circle" on »Metal Inferno« LP Castle Communications 1985
"Beyond The Gates" on »Metal Inferno« LP Castle Communications 1985

DEMON PACT

Donald Meckiffe (v)
Richard Dickerson (g)
Roy Bridle (b)
Iain Finlay (d)

The legendary DEMON PACT, yet another of Kent's numerous musical legacies of the early 80's, became something of an instant cult after their first exposé in the 'Armed And Ready' section of the second issue of 'Kerrang', although this probably had rather more to do with their questionable lyrical sentiments than anything else. Even today, there's little doubt that some of those famous stomach-churning extracts concerning the joy of cannibalism, such as the oft-quoted *'cutting off the rind'* and *'you chew but she's too tough'* (from "Eaten Alive"), would still incur the wrath of the censor in some parts of the globe. Not exactly as distasteful as your typical CANNIBAL CORPSE offering, perhaps, but it was pretty graphic stuff for 1981, all the same. Musically speaking, things were rather less edifying, and the outfit actually sounded quite peculiar on vinyl, particularly the distinctly non-tuneful vocals of Donald Meckiffe (strangely, the band members all seemed to have Scottish-sounding names). Nevertheless, the heavy music alone was probably just about sufficient to generate a modicum of sustained interest in the group, even among those who weren't *'fortunate'* enough to appreciate the lyrical sentiments to their fullest extent.

In any case, DEMON PACT's first vinyl exposure came with the generous offer to contribute a track of their choice (which came in the form of "Escape") to the regional »Kent Rocks« compilation assembled by White Witch Records in the early part of 1981. Their powerful effort started off quite capably with an acoustic guitar intro, although the number soon mutated into a fairly typical NWOBHM piece in the general style of SPARTA or a more technical SHOCK TREATMENT. The musicianship was pretty reasonable, and it was certainly heavy enough, although those gravelly vocals really were a serious liability. Following on from the relative success of the compilation, however, DEMON PACT were invited to record a single under the auspices of White Witch, eventually surfacing on the outfit's own (typically tasteful) label, Slime Records. The new pairing of "Eaten Alive" and "Raiders" was selected for this offering, and the 7" duly emerged in an endearingly-awful picture sleeve which absolutely typifies the NWOBHM mentality, showing a poorly-drawn she-devil with preposterously large wings. Despite both efforts being undeniably weighty (not to mention very brief) once more, it was still pretty simplistic stuff (not up to the standard of "Escape" at all), and these numbers are basically the sort of thing that the likes of VENOM or WARFARE could easily have knocked out in their sleep before deciding they weren't actually worth releasing after all. Nevertheless, with the single being distributed quite competently by both the White Witch and Pinnacle concerns, it sold in healthy quantities at the time, which is one of

1981 + »NWOBHM Vol.8« Bootleg CD 1996

the main reasons why you shouldn't have to pay a vast amount to own a copy these days, as they tend to come onto the market quite frequently.

Although there have been widely-circulated rumours that DEMON PACT recorded an entire album's worth of material during their relatively brief time together, which is just waiting for some enterprising individual to release, I reckon this probably isn't the case (or it stretches the truth considerably), as the quartet weren't remotely prolific in terms of either songwriting or visits to the studio. At least one demo (with three or four unreleased numbers) was indeed recorded, however, and it appears that a follow-up single was also planned at one point, the latter scheduled to feature "Demon Pact" (the band's theme song, one of their more popular live favourites) and "Escape". Although this release was again pencilled in for imminent release on the Slime imprint (paper labels were apparently printed up in readiness), the record doesn't even seem to have made it to the test pressing stage, which is a blow for any hopeful fans out there. It looks as though some misfortune or other (perhaps nothing more sinister than the collapse of White Witch) must have struck the outfit in the early months of 1982, leading to the sudden cancellation of the second single and a rapid disintegration of DEMON PACT as a whole. The musicians seem to have vanished off the surface of the earth, so it would appear that this was a one-off attempt to make it big in the rock world.

7" Singles
»Eaten Alive« Slime Records 1981

Exclusive Compilation Appearances
"Escape" on »Kent Rocks« LP White Witch Records

DENIGH

Jon Everett (v,b)
Phil Allchin (g)
Ian Devlin (g,k)
John Regan (d)

The excellently-named DENIGH were one of the first rock bands to establish themselves on Kent's fledgling scene as far back as 1978, pre-dating the region's primary explosion of young hopefuls by a couple of years. A stable line-up swiftly emerged, and the central trio of Jon Everett, Ian Devlin and Phil Allchin pretty much assumed joint responsibility for writing all the material, while drummer John Regan (who made up the numbers in the first instance) elected to stay in the background (in more ways than one). From the outset, the lads were composing their own songs, and, by the time they made their regional live debut in 1979, they were confident enough to eschew the traditional assortment of cover versions and bombard an unsuspecting public with their self-penned repertoire. This strategy appears to have worked fairly efficiently, and the lads were soon pulling in the crowds in their own right, the advantage of this approach being that they didn't have to rely on catching the occasional support slot with more successful acts of the day. When the band finally got around to recording a speculative demo cassette (an eight track effort featuring such numbers as "Bed Of Nails", "Burn The Sky" and "Falling Snow"), copies were made available to fans at gigs, and a considerable quantity were shifted as a result, spreading their name even further.

Moving into 1980, the lads were riding the crest of a wave, and they decided to capitalise on their new-found popularity by releasing their own single. At that stage, the musicians had no particular intentions of waiting for a major deal to materialise, and their previous experience of marketing their own cassette product led them to believe (quite rightly, as it turned out) that they would surely be capable of financing and selling their own vinyl without getting involved with big business. The two-tracker, released via the local Ace label (home of SPITZBROOK, for example), took the form of a double A-sided affair (never issued in a picture sleeve) featuring "Running" and "No Way", a pair of truly excellent, heavy numbers which bring forth a few handy comparisons with the likes of DEMOLITION, VIRGIN STAR and prime-era ANGEL WITCH. Sales were understandably brisk, with local shops doing a roaring trade, while national distribution made the record available to a significantly wider audience. In due course, the group were able to develop a healthy following elsewhere, especially in the Midlands, where (unlike certain parts of the country) the metalheads didn't shy away from the heavier side of things. Local radio appearances followed, with the group contributing a few interviews and sessions to the popular 'Kent Rocks' show, and the lads now seemed to be going from strength to strength.

Crucially, however, DENIGH were severely hindered in their subsequent activities by two major factors. Most importantly, they always tended to be a bit short of cash, which negated the possibility of releasing further vinyl until the necessary finances had been accrued. Furthermore, they were still going it alone in terms of management, and were finding it inordinately difficult to make their presence known to those involved on the promotion side of things. Eventually, however, the lads managed to inveigle their way onto a handful of rock bills featuring the likes of BUDGIE, GIRLSCHOOL, RAGE, SAXON and SAMSON, but it was to be a long, hard struggle over the following two years. Matters weren't helped when one third of their writing partnership (Ian Devlin) left the DENIGH fold (in a dispute over future direction) towards the end of 1981 (the year in which the lads undertook a rather ambitious tour of France), and, although they utilised the services of stand-in guitarist Martyn Harris (who later found a more permanent position in VIGILANTE) on occasion, their main activities saw them operating as a stripped-down trio from that point onwards. Still, DENIGH kept plugging away in the regional pubs and clubs, although it's fair to say that they never really achieved the level of success they deserved.

A further official demo was circulated in 1983, this being another generous eight-tracker entitled »Lean On 'Em Hard«. The tape featured mostly newer numbers penned by Jon and Phil, such as "Call Me Angel", "Savage", "Roulette" and "Ironclad". Again, local sales turned out to be highly impressive, and the band (who also employed replacement drummer Chris Daughters at some point) concluded that it was well worth continuing in their quest for fame. The following year, the lads recorded a full album's worth of original material, initially hoping that someone would stump up the necessary cash to get the thing pressed on vinyl. Sadly, however, no philanthropic individuals happened to be walking along the streets of Folkestone at that time of year, and DENIGH simply resigned themselves to the fact that »Fire From The Sky« (which included such numbers as "Synthetic Seduction", "Put My Neck On The Line" and "Sentinel") would have to be yet another cassette-only release. In fact, it looks as though comparatively few copies made it into circulation, as the group were beginning to lose heart by this time. Nevertheless, they still proceeded to complete a successful show supporting BERNIE TORMÉ, recording their performance for future release in one form or another. In true SPINAL TAP fashion, however, the master tape was destroyed in mysterious circumstances (C.I.A. involvement, no doubt), and things all went downhill from that point onwards.

DENIGH officially called it a day at some point in 1985 (there were, in fact, one or two low-key get-togethers and club appearances in later years), although the central characters always believed that they could have gone considerably further with a modicum of luck, money and guidance (the same goes for several thousand other long-forgotten NWOBHM hopefuls, chaps). Nevertheless, a renewed level of interest in the 90's (fuelled primarily by a rapidly-escalating asking price for their one-off single) prompted a spate of frenzied activity on the DENIGH front. A couple of hastily-arranged reformation gigs took place at small local venues, and erstwhile colleagues Jon Everett and Ian Devlin subsequently began rootling around in their respective tape collections to see whether or not any old material could be salvaged for future release. Happily, they managed to turn up a few usable recordings in due course, and duly touted them around various companies to see if anyone was particularly interested. Unfortunately, however, once-prolific labels such as Vinyl Tap and British Steel had pretty much started winding down their archive reissue programmes by this stage (although the latter were happy to include the tracks from DENIGH's single on one of their NWOBHM compilations), and the lads appeared to have missed their golden opportunity.

Undeterred by this apparent setback, however, the persistent duo of Everett and Devlin have, over the past couple of years or so, compiled a recordable CD's worth of DENIGH material (culled from demo tapes and live recordings) for demonstration purposes (it's also now being offered for sale through certain outlets), and it now looks as though they might just see a proper CD being commissioned at long last. Interestingly, however, the majority of the band's later material actually differs considerably from the rough'n'ready direction adopted on their single (some of it is quite polished at times, and is possibly more along the lines of BLEAK HOUSE or Jersey's LEGEND than anything), and, generally speaking, the demo selections are a bit classier than "Running" or "No Way". Nevertheless, it's all immensely satisfying to the NWOBHM palate, although it's fair to suggest that only the live recordings really do justice to the sheer power once exuded by these overlooked heavyweights. Whatever material eventually ends up being made available to the public, however, there's every chance that a significant number of collectors and enthusiasts would appreciate the chance to hear these long-lost compositions at some stage.

7" Singles
»Running« Ace Records 1980

CD's
»Denigh« Private 1998
[Official compilation CD-R with printed cover]

Compilation Appearances
"No Way" on »N.W.O.B.H.M. Metal Rarities Vol.3« CD British Steel 1997
"Running" on »N.W.O.B.H.M. Metal Rarities Vol.3« CD British Steel 1997

DESOLATION ANGELS

Dave Wall (v)
Keith Sharp (g)
Robin Brancher (g)
Joe Larner (b)
Brett Robertson (d)

The heavyweight bunch known as the DESOLATION ANGELS (their identity originally being inspired by the title of a BAD COMPANY album) first came together in the early months of 1981, their various members having already played a part in the fortunes of many long-forgotten hopefuls in the Essex area and beyond. From BLACKWATER FEVER came Keith Sharp and Robin Brancher, while Dave Wall and Joe Larner were recruited from the ranks of ROADRUNNER and WARLORD, respectively. The emergent outfit employed a never-ending series of drummers in best SPINAL TAP tradition, the most successful being former DREAMWEAVER sticksman Brett Robertson, although there would appear to have been at least a dozen other candidates over the years. The DESOLATION ANGELS soon developed an appealingly heavy brand of doomy metal with fairly melodic and accessible foundations, the main NWOBHM similarities being with acts such as DEMON, PAGAN ALTAR and PHOENIX RISING. Their early activities tended to centre around the usual circuit of local gigging (in time, they would become regular fixtures in the clubs of the East End, playing alongside acts such as CHARIOT, ELIXIR, DRIVESHAFT and CARRERA), although they managed to circulate an official live demo in around 1983, which allowed a representative selection of material to be exposed to a slightly wider audience. It's worth noting that these talented musicians were, from a very early stage, performing a repertoire of predominantly original compositions, several of which ("Hounds Of Hell", "Doomsday", "Satan's Child", "No Mercy" *etc.*) failed to make it to vinyl at any stage.

By the end of 1983, the outfit decided to go it alone and release a 7" single (issued in a superbly clichéd sleeve of an evil *'grim reaper'* figure on a winged horse), which coupled the epic "Valhalla" with the more restrained "Boadicea". The tracks were both fairly strong (remarkably, they even passed muster in 'Kerrang'), although the length of the band's own compositions (typically hovering around the six minute mark) tended to suggest that they might do better to forget about getting any airplay with singles and concentrate on albums in future. Nevertheless, the two-tracker sold reasonably well, and the group continued to build upon their rapidly-growing reputation as a powerful and entertaining outfit, even going so far as to produce their own promotional video at one stage. Reviews of the regular DESOLATION ANGELS live shows began to appear in the smaller fanzines, and the quintet soon became fairly regular fixtures on London's club scene, occasionally linking up with more successful acts (notably SAMSON, DIAMOND HEAD and TREDEGAR) for one-off appearances. By the second half of 1984, their collective ambition had reached the point whereby a full-length vinyl effort seemed like a valid option, and they were fortunate enough to be picked up by Bullet Records (who, for some reason, were trading as *'Bulleon'* by this stage) towards the end of the year. The group's debut long-player was recorded in due course and was scheduled for release in the early months of 1985, so everything seemed to be going entirely according to plan at that point.

Cruelly, however, Bullet/Bulleon ran into

serious problems (which were, in fact, mostly related to the sudden collapse of the Pinnacle distribution network) and consequently ceased all operations shortly thereafter, well and truly scuppering the imminent release of the DESOLATION ANGELS LP. Fortunately, the album

```
D.R. PRESENTS    DESOLATION    D.R. PRESENTS
MAKE IT HEAVY' AT ANGELS THE ROBIN HOOI
FUNCTION SUITE: 807, LONGBRIDGE RD, DAGENHAM, ESSEX
          26-9-87 BAR 8PM-1AM
       TICKETS £3·00 – ON THE DOOR.
              PLUS Armistice
          PLUS HEAVY METAL DISCO.
           NEAREST STATION - BARKING
```

eventually saw the light of day early the following year (whether or not it was actually re-recorded is open to debate, but I suspect that it wasn't), when it was issued on the little-known Thameside (it might even have been a self-financed effort) concern. Again, the much-delayed eponymous effort turned out to be a highly listenable experience (although it was, predictably enough, dismissed as 'tedious' in 'Kerrang'), especially for those of us who enjoy the heavier side of things from time to time. Mind you, it's fair to say that some of the compositions tend to drag on a bit, and a tad more variety and originality surely wouldn't have gone amiss, although stage favourites such as "Evil Possessor" and "Dance Of The Demons" come across as effective efforts all the same. Significantly, no drummer was credited on the cover this time, and the hand-drawn image of the group members merely included a skeleton (!) in place of their most recent sticksman (they had been working with a chap called Adam Palfrey in the previous few months, although erstwhile INTERNATIONAL HEROES character Dave Maile also enjoyed a brief stint). Hmmm, sounds a bit ominous to me…

The press reaction to the album had been mixed, and the band appear to have taken on board the oft-voiced criticisms that much of their material was simply too lengthy to hold the attention of the average listener. Having reassessed the situation, the lads ultimately resurfaced with a five track demo (»Fury«) in 1987, a selection of material (including the likes of "Scream All Night" and "Black Heart") which, although still based around the framework of their favoured 'melodic semi-doom' style, tended to show a definite shift towards shorter, punchier compositions. The group continued to gig locally to try to keep the momentum going, although the public were, by this stage, starting to turn their backs on the once-popular stalwarts of the UK's straight-ahead metal scene. A year or so later, the DESOLATION ANGELS signed a new management deal, the surprising result of which was that the ensemble (along with various characters from erstwhile gigging partners CARRERA) ended up relocating to Los Angeles to work on fresh material. Sadly, though, things don't appear to have worked out for either act on the other side of the pond, and so the name of DESOLATION ANGELS was finally laid to rest in the early 90's. They remain a highly-rated act by aficionados of the NWOBHM and doom genres, though, and both of their scarce vinyl releases have assumed the position of mid-priced and collectable pieces in the years since their demise.

LP's
»**Desolation Angels**« Thameside Records 1986
[Original UK issue]
»**Desolation Angels**« Rock Brigade Records 1987
[Brazilian reissue]

7" Singles
»**Valhalla**« Private 1983
[A-side different to album version, B-side "Boadicea" non-LP]

DESPERATE OATES

John Singing Rock (v,g)
John 'Piggy' Line (b)
Shaun 'E' Muff (d)

The little-known Lincolnshire threesome who, for reasons best known to themselves, chose to be identified by the extremely dodgy moniker of DESPERATE OATES (as you can see, the members' own pseudonyms/nicknames were pretty ridiculous too) were, all things considered, 'desperate to be VARDIS', since they appear to have represented an analogous (and, in all honesty, equally unremarkable) proposition who were perfectly content to operate in the facile biker/boogie mode. In fact, given that the reverse sleeve of their one-off 7" features a prominent instruction to 'boogie on down' (I'd rather not, if it's all the same to you) and an acknowledgement to good old Steve Zodiac himself, we're left in very little doubt as to what their musical intentions might be. Issued on the punningly-titled Heavy *Mental* label (ho bloody ho), their seldom-seen three-tracker opens with the mid-paced "Burning Alive", a number slightly more akin to ROADSTER or Coventry's CHAINSAW, although the pair of compositions on the flip ("Why You Do It" and the unashamedly-titled "Boogie Toon") are nothing more than straightforward, formulaic efforts in the VARDIS or ROKKA vein. All in all, therefore, a pretty disposable slice of vinyl and one that you shouldn't be losing sleep over unless you're a particularly obsessive completist. And there's nothing wrong with that, although you should probably think about leaving the house and talking to girls occasionally. Unless you are a girl, that is.

Although the record (issued in a pretty dire picture sleeve showing the lads posing, rather embarrassingly, with an oversized guitar) is certainly a NWOBHM-era release, the exact date remains something of a mystery at present, but I would suspect that 1982 or thereabouts wouldn't be too far from the truth. Little has been conclusively established about the band's history or studio activities (the three-tracker was recorded at a facility called F&S Recording Studios, wherever the hell that was), although the persevering DESPERATE OATES were actually given a mention in the hallowed pages of 'Kerrang' as late as 1985, when the musicians announced their plans to release a privately-issued long-player entitled »Up And Rising« at some unspecified point in the future. Almost certainly, however, this record failed to materialise in the long term, and the group presumably fell apart within a year or two of this non-event. As ever, any additional information on the activities of this bunch would be appreciated, but I don't imagine too many people will actually admit to having followed their fortunes at the time.

7" EP's
»Burning Alive« Heavy Mental Records 198?

DESTROYER

Rob Osborn (v)
Phil Skidmore (g)
Dave McAuliffe (b)
John Walsgrove (d)

DESTROYER, a quartet from North London, were a relatively short-lived band who assembled themselves in the early 80's, released a very strong debut single, played a few local, small-time gigs and then disappeared into obscurity forever. At some point in 1981, the talented bunch somehow came to the attention of the diverse Clubland label (kind of a lesser version of Ellie Jay, all things considered), and laid down the numbers "Evil Place" and "Stand And Deliver" for their one and only release, a single which would emerge under the guise of a pseudo-private release on the group's own Clean Kill Records. Both tracks feature some very heavy, PALI GAP-style guitar work, with excellent, demonic vocals (which vaguely resemble the kind of intensity reached by outfits such as HOLOCAUST, WITCHFINDER GENERAL or PHYNE THANQUZ) all adding to the overall effect. It was a cracking release all round, and one which certainly deserved to be followed up at the earliest opportunity, although, sadly, it was never to become a particularly likely eventuality.

As with numerous other small-time outfits, DESTROYER failed to capitalise on their debut release and take a chance on making it big in the rock world, which would have necessitated the lads giving up on their education, day jobs, outside commitments and so forth. In the event, they suffered a pretty major crisis of confidence soon after, which provided the inevitable spectre of personnel instability with the perfect opportunity to rear its ugly head once more. In fact, the outfit found itself in serious decline from 1982 onwards, especially once the similarly-named DESTROYA, a capable bunch from the East End, burst forth upon the scene with their MAIDEN-influenced brand of metal. The original DESTROYER (who shouldn't be confused with American namesakes from later in the decade) disappeared from the gig listings shortly thereafter, leaving only a solitary vinyl artefact to remind the world that it hadn't all been a dream after all. Nowadays, this particular item is a highly coveted piece for many collectors, even though it was never released with a picture sleeve, and has remained a fairly high-ranking rarity ever since the collecting boom first started.

7" Singles
»Evil Place« Clean Kill Records 1981

DEUCE (I)

Paul Belton (v,g)
Guy Marriot (g)
Terry Seymour (b)
Adrian Fowler (d)

Not to be confused either with their popular American namesakes (who later evolved into TENSION) or with the equally well-known Nottinghamshire bunch (*vide infra*) who were on the go at around the same time and who issued their own »Backs To The Wall« EP in 1986, Kent's own version of DEUCE, initially conceived at more or less the beginning of the 80's, first came to prominence *via* their assorted appearances on the extremely obscure and seldom-seen »Southern Comfort« series of local-act compilation albums, this batch of samplers being issued by the little-known Spectrum Records operation from 1983 onwards. All things considered, the persevering group (who no doubt had a strong regional following of their own, but who made virtually no impression whatsoever outside Kent itself during their formative years) experienced something of a bumpy ride throughout their existence, and often struggled to maintain anything resembling a stable line-up. Mind you, the nucleus of guitarist Paul Belton and drummer Adrian Fowler always remained intact, and the hardy pair even continued their alliance in the ST. HELLIER project after DEUCE's eventual demise in the second half of the decade.

The quartet's earliest vinyl appearance came on the first »Southern Comfort« LP (it's entirely possible that they had some sort of financial or managerial involvement with the project, and it seems likely that DEUCE feature on all four volumes, although number two is proving inexplicably difficult to locate), the tracks in question being "Mystery Lady" and "Sail Me Away". With Guy Marriot (g) and Terry Seymour (b) completing the line-up at this time, and with Paul Belton doubling as vocalist, the band delivered an enjoyable, catchy rock/metal style, incorporating elements of outfits such as TRAXX, LOTUS CRUISE and REINCARNATE. By the time the epic "Madhouse Parts 1/2" appeared on the third instalment of »Southern Comfort«, however, Terry Seymour had now flown the coop and Paul Belton had relinquished the microphone, with Jim Batchelor and Andy Furgenor being drafted in to act as *'guest'* vocalist and bassist, respectively. Although "Madhouse" is a considerably heavier number (vaguely reminiscent of CYNIC's "Suicide", but not quite as well-written or performed), and is based around a more ambitious arrangement, the track itself is ultimately fairly unmemorable, so it's hard to say that DEUCE had actually progressed musically. Their contribution to the fourth volume of the series, meanwhile, was tenuous, to say the least, with the innovatively-titled "Intro" being nothing more than a mercifully brief guitar solo, the latter coming courtesy of Paul Belton. A completely pointless exercise if you ask me; a case of contractual obligation, perhaps?

After cutting their collective teeth with this remarkably generous helping of compilation appearances, the ambitious DEUCE presumably returned to the live circuit for another couple of years while they honed their style and sorted out those niggling personnel problems, but they eventually got around to releasing a single of their own as late as 1986, having recently expanded into a quintet *via* the addition of Steve Barns (v), Mick McGovern (g) and Marty Siggery (b). Ade Fowler, meanwhile, was to retain his seat at the drumkit, whereas the ever-dependable Paul Belton was now concentrating solely on guitar work. The revamped group's debut two-tracker (issued in a rather spartan red cover depicting a functionally-drawn portcullis) featured a pretty dire rehashing of GOLDEN EARRING's "Radar Love" (I've always felt this to be a vastly overrated number and DEUCE certainly don't improve on the original) plus a self-penned effort ("Christine"), a ghastly mess of a track with no sense of identity whatsoever. Without wanting to appear too over-critical (just in case any of them happen to read this), Steve Barns wasn't exactly the most capable singer I've ever heard, either. All in all, the record was a bit of a disaster, and came as a severe disappointment from a group who were evidently capable of far greater things.

The early part of 1987 saw the band recruiting former WHITE HEAT bassist John Tucker as a replacement for Marty Siggery, who, in due course, went on to join the melodic hopefuls PANAMA and CHAYNED MAYLE (the latter bunch also featuring two of his former partners in crime, Steve Barns and Mick McGovern). In a last-ditch move to draw the attention of the record companies, DEUCE issued a nine track demo tape, featuring versions of previously-released numbers (which served only to illustrate how poor their newer material was in comparison) such as "Madhouse", "Sail Me Away", "Mystery Lady" and "Christine", alongside a selection of unfamiliar tracks such as "Breakin' Free", "Lone Rider", "Combat Zone" and "Mirror Mirror". The remaining effort, "Power Of The Realm" (by no means the strongest of their newer compositions), was subsequently selected to appear on yet another compilation (Metalother's »Metal Warriör« six-tracker) later in the year, although this belated exposure doesn't seem to have helped to further DEUCE's chances to any significant extent. Furthermore, the ill-fated *'Metal Warrior Tour'* that the lads organised for November 1987 (to tie in with the sampler's release) seems to have been pretty much their last attempt to promote themselves under the name of DEUCE.

As previously mentioned, the dejected members of the much-reshuffled outfit elected to call it a day at the end of 1987, their spirits having been crushed by the continual rejection of every batch of studio material. Having touted their wares around with little or no success for several years, you might well have expected the duo of Paul Belton and Adrian Fowler to give up the ghost completely, but this turned out not to be the case. The pair soon decided that they merely needed to look a bit harder for suitable musicians rather than taking the first people that came along, and they subsequently resorted to advertising in the national rock press to find individuals of appropriate ability. After the search had been undertaken, the duo regrouped in 1988 with an entirely novel set of accomplices (none of whom were particularly well-known at the time) in the form of ST. HELLIER, an outfit who enjoyed slightly more exposure in the shape of a full LP on the G.I. label, plus a 12" EP and various compilation appearances, and who continued to ply their trade well into the 90's before reluctantly conceding defeat.

7" Singles
»Radar Love« Madhouse Records 1986

Exclusive Compilation Appearances
"Mystery Lady" on »Southern Comfort« LP Spectrum Records 1983
"Sail Me Away" on »Southern Comfort« LP Spectrum Records 1983
"Madhouse Parts 1/2" on »Southern Comfort III« LP Spectrum Records 1984?
"Intro" on »Southern Comfort 4« LP Spectrum Records 1984?
[As PAUL BELTON-DEUCE]
"Power Of The Realm" on »Metal Warriör« LP Metalother Records 1987

DEUCE (II)

Punkie Richards (v)
Russ Richards (g)
Paul Wild (g)
Stevie Dickinson (b)
Emmy (d)

It's odd that so many bands elected to operate under the identity of DEUCE throughout the 80's, especially when few of them sounded particularly like KISS, so maybe they all took their inspiration from somewhere else. Anyhow, the better of the two Brit outfits of that name to get to the vinyl stage were the Nottinghamshire bunch, who seem to have taken their first steps in around 1983 (they hooked up with the likes of BLADE RUNNER and local heroes HELL for some early gigs), although nothing much came of these activities for a couple of years. By 1985, however, the outfit had begun to win a few more prestigious support slots with acts such as THE SWEET and SAVAGE, and the lads duly tried their luck with a lengthy eight track demo. This raised one or two eyebrows in the rock press, although the labels appear to have seen little potential in DEUCE's brand of heavy material, as it didn't really fit into any convenient pigeonhole. Their songs were a fairly odd mixture of post-NWOBHM power with a slight glam edge, the overall effect suggesting elements of TOKYO BLADE, RANKELSON and HELL'S BELLES, although it was a listenable enough style all the same. Early the following year, the reshuffled outfit (featuring new guitarist Dieter T. instead of Paul Wild) recorded another demo, featuring such compositions as "Killer", "Seven Years", "X-Rated" and "Backs To The Wall", and seemed to be developing a reputation as local crowd-pleasers, having hooked up with various emergent acts such as SABBAT and THUNDERCHILDE for well-attended regional gigs in recent times, although there was still little in the way of label interest.

By mid-1986, DEUCE finally took the bull by the horns and undertook the studio sessions which would yield their vinyl debut, a self-financed three track EP with "Backs To The Wall" as the main focus of attention. Making up the numbers were the enjoyable "Queen Of The Night" (another heavy, mid-paced effort quite similar to the main track) and "Jealousy", a surprisingly-listenable power ballad in the manner of "Parisienne Walkways". It was a capable debut release, although it seems to have made little or no impression outwith their locality (I'm sure they must have shifted a fair number at gigs, though), and the lads didn't go on to achieve greater things as a result. The record, issued (without a picture sleeve, although some were apparently livened up with a stickered cover) on the optimistically-named Powermetal label, is now a fairly collectable piece, in spite of its later date of issue, and you'll be lucky to find one cheaply. Shortly after the 7" came out, the notoriously unstable outfit (half the population of Nottinghamshire appears to have passed through the ranks of DEUCE at the outset and towards the end of their career) lost Dieter T. and Stevie Dickinson, although they soon roped in the new pairing of Ken Tilley (g) and Simon Ward (b), both recruited from local rivals ORION (not the Lost Moment bunch), and things settled down again for a while.

By mid-1987, however, things had really begun to fall apart in major fashion, with the two most recent acquisitions running off to establish a novel venture of their own (the little-known ESPRIT), and DEUCE were forced to bring in Rimmo (b) and Gregg Russell (g) to plug the gaps. In the end, it didn't work out in their favour, and (after some increasingly-chaotic reshuffling towards the end), the group split into various factions, with Punkie Richards (aka Punky Wayne) joining SLEEZEPATROL (who were better than their moniker might suggest), whereas Emmy and Gregg Russell teamed up with erstwhile colleague Stevie Dickinson to establish WRAITH, an act who have also enjoyed a colourful career with numerous personnel changes along the way. In fact, various other former members of DEUCE have cropped up in WRAITH (who are still on the go and who have released CD's on a range of labels) from time to time, including Rimmo and Ken Tilley, so it's very much a family affair, by the looks of things. Furthermore, yet another DEUCE veteran, vocalist Ian Dilley (aka Ian Sabre), who was presumably Punkie Richards' forerunner, maintained a strong presence in the Midlands rock scene throughout the remainder of the 80's, lending a hand to also-rans such as PERSIA, SABREDANZ and APB. No doubt there are countless other one-time DEUCE bods out there (don't call us, we'll call you), but we have to draw the line somewhere, especially when they came and went at such a rapid rate.

7" EP's
»Backs To The Wall« Powermetal Records 1986

DIAMOND HEAD

Sean Harris (v)
Brian Tatler (g)
Colin Kimberley (b)
Duncan Scott (d)

Possibly the most over-used and infuriating phrase now connected with the NWOBHM scene relates to those four talented chaps from the West Midlands, DIAMOND HEAD, the usual variation on the quote being along the lines of 'had they not existed, then neither would METALLICA'. Well, let's not get too bogged down in the intricacies of the Ulrich Causality Theorem, but being relegated to the status of 'the band who inspired METALLICA' is no more appropriate or acceptable than being described as 'LED ZEPPELIN clones'. Funny how nobody ever suggests that METALLICA have anything in common with LED ZEPPELIN, isn't it? In fact, DIAMOND HEAD were undoubtedly the greatest legacy of the NWOBHM movement (although they always felt constrained by the term, and were more content to identify themselves as a 'plain old rock band'): they may not have been the longest-lived or highest-grossing act of their time, but they pushed back the musical boundaries to an extraordinary extent, shaming all those bands (and I won't name any names) who emerged in the 70's or 80's, won a record deal almost immediately, and made a career out of releasing dozens of formulaic records over the ensuing years. As any reference book will tell you, it all started back in the spring of 1976, when the youthful Brian Tatler decided that his guitar skills deserved to be heard by a wider audience, and duly roped in schoolmate Duncan Scott to bang out a few rhythms on whatever implement came to hand (any references to 'biscuit tin drums' actually have a kernel of truth in this case) while he tried out a few of his patented heavy riffs and intriguing chord progressions. It wasn't long before another acquaintance from the local comprehensive, Sean Harris, was headhunted after famously delighting his fellow passengers on a lengthy coach trip with impromptu versions of some old rock'n'roll standards, and the singer's subsequent recruitment to the fold was officially notarised by the signing of a makeshift contract during one of their lessons. The legend had begun.

There was no name at first, just a few clichéd suggestions, some of which included WOLF, COBRA and FIREBIRD, but the lads eventually came to a mutual decision that DIAMOND HEAD (a term associated with volcanoes, but pilfered from the title of a PHIL MANZANERA solo album) would be a distinctive and representative choice for this new musical venture. The trio managed to operate without a permanent bassist until the end of 1977 (it hardly mattered, as their live outings were few and far between up until that point, and largely consisted of appearances at school dances and youth clubs), when another acquaintance, Colin Kimberley, was encouraged to try out, and the lanky individual was soon being enrolled as a full-time member. Unusually, DIAMOND HEAD shunned the usual facile route of incorporating plentiful cover versions in their repertoire, and rapidly developed a pretty formidable writing style of their own, absorbing influences from several of their (predominantly Midlands-based) heroes, notably JUDAS PRIEST, BLACK SABBATH and, er, the NEW YARDBIRDS (or whatever they were called) to create an immensely listenable style of heavy music. To condemn the quartet as being mere impersonators of any one band would be a truly monumental injustice, as they genuinely represented the complete package, combining the raunch of FREE/BAD COMPANY, the dynamics of JUDAS PRIEST/RUSH and the bluesy riffage of ZEPPELIN/LEAFHOUND, but also incorporating elements of acts as quirky and unconventional as QUEEN and FOCUS. Without wishing to overstate the significance of the situation, the emergence of DIAMOND HEAD almost amounted to a complete reinvention of heavy metal, and their rise to public prominence would almost certainly have happened whether or not they had been conveniently lumped in with the rest of the young hopefuls at the onset of the NWOBHM explosion.

Throughout the late 70's, the foursome continued to grow in stature, and were soon racking up the live appearances, sometimes as headliners at rock-friendly venues such as Bogart's in nearby Birmingham, and they also occasionally managed to hook up with some of the local favourites (such as SLADE and QUARTZ, for example) for slightly bigger gigs, increasing their stagecraft at every opportunity. With DIAMOND HEAD steadily cultivating a healthy following of their own, they finally decided to make some of their material (at least an album's worth had already been laid down for their own use) available to a wider audience, and sent out a few demo tapes (featuring the likes of "Am I Evil?", "Streets Of Gold" and "Shoot Out The Lights") to journalists and local radio stations. The response was unprecedented, with the tracks being regularly playlisted by such dignitaries as Geoff Barton of 'Sounds', and generous airplay on stations such as BRMB led to a considerable elevation of the DIAMOND HEAD name in the public's consciousness. Before long, people were running out of superlatives, and the fans clamoured for a piece of DIAMOND HEAD vinyl to call their own. The major labels somehow contrived to overlook the group when on their talent-spotting rounds in the immediate aftermath of the NWOBHM explosion, however, and so the lads were left with no option but to go it alone. After laying down "Shoot Out The Lights" and "Helpless" towards the end of 1979, the tracks were pressed up as a single on the local Happy Face label (which also gave BRIAR and CRYER their first break), a release which emerged early the following year.

1980 was the year that it all started happening for DIAMOND HEAD; their single sparked a feverish reaction among the nation's rock fans, and Happy Face were soon shifting as many units as they could press up. The two-tracker contained a pair of upbeat, energetic efforts featuring some substantial riffing and sterling musicianship all round, with an immensely charismatic performance from the capable frontman, whose still-maturing voice was already taking on some of its full potential. It was a cracking debut, admittedly, but it really only offered the fans the merest glimpse of what was yet to come. Still, the youngsters were soon riding the crest of a wave, winning two coveted support slots on the AC/DC tour and then following up this valuable exposure by playing a couple of numbers ("Streets Of Gold" and "Helpless") on a regional television programme called 'Look Hear'. After that, they supported IRON MAIDEN at one of their shows on the 'Metal For Muthas Tour' (where they were allocated a mere twenty minutes to strut their stuff, but still managed to blow the headliners off stage), and were soon hooking up with the likes of GIRL and ANGEL WITCH for increasingly-well-attended gigs in the capital. In the spring of 1980, the outfit decided to lay down a full album's worth of material at a local studio, their recently-acquired manager stumping up the cash for the recording session. The original plan had been to tout the tapes around to the highest bidder, but DIAMOND HEAD elected to raise the stakes by pressing up a thousand white-label copies of the long-player to send out as promotional devices and to sell to fans at gigs. Since they had raked in a bit of cash on the back of their first single, they had just enough money to press the initial batch, and the ambitious youngsters soon instigated their master plan for global domination.

With a few dozen promotional copies of the 'white label promo album' (as it would soon become known) being disseminated in the first instance, the lads were soon selling the remainder to fans, both at gigs and by mail order. The record was a no-frills affair in terms of presentation, a white-label record in a plain white sleeve, without even the extravagance of a helpful tracklisting! At least those who purchased the album at DIAMOND HEAD shows (which were already featuring numbers such as "Dead Reckoning", "Trick Or Treat" and "To Heaven From Hell") were in a better position to be able to identify the tracks, whereas those who received a copy through the post were usually greeted with a sleeve bearing the illegible signature of one of the band members and nothing else. Copies purchased at gigs were either completely blank or were (if you were extremely lucky) signed by all four members on the night, but the identity of the featured selections were soon revealed in a 'Sounds' article, leading to many fans annotating their sleeves and/or labels with a makeshift running order. Some went even further, decorating the cover with as much information as possible (often including the names of everyone involved, such as producers, road crew etc.), while a few talented individuals went the whole hog and customised their copies with unique artwork, some examples of which are actually remarkably proficient (dealers have been known to pass these off as 'proof sleeves', either intentionally or otherwise). Before long, the initial batch had been exhausted, but the band had now gleaned enough cash to finance a second pressing, so another thousand copies (in a plain cover once again, but with printed labels this time, citing the album title as »Lightning To The Nations«) were manufactured to meet demand.

Although it hadn't originally been intended as a commercial release (the lads later commented that they would have 'made a better job of it' if they had known how things would have turned out), the album was soon being reviewed, given airplay and sold as a proper DIAMOND HEAD product, but it didn't take long for the second batch to be exhausted either. It's not difficult to see why, as the record stood head and shoulders above most of the independently-produced (and much of the major-label tat) vinyl being churned out by amateur-hour combos, with short, punchy tracks such as "It's Electric" and "Sweet And Innocent" sitting happily alongside lengthier, more convoluted numbers such as "Am I Evil?" and "Sucking My Love". Occupying the middle ground were "The Prince" (seldom played live, any requests usually meeting with a curt 'we don't do that one' response) and the absolutely immense title track, prime examples of compositions which took the listener on a rollercoaster ride of changing rhythms, styles and tempos, dismantling the rules as to exactly what you can and can't do within the confines of a heavy metal number. Everyone had their own favourite, and the shorter numbers were equally as popular as those which took their time building to their, er, climax, since DIAMOND HEAD were able to write epic non-epics, compositions which effortlessly stretched out to seven or eight minutes without ever seeming self-indulgent or remotely tedious. Astonishing. It was all truly bewildering for many listeners, who could hardly make the connection between this tour de force of musicianship and the energetic-but-ramshackle type of material being churned out by the majority of their contemporaries. It's hard to say just why it was all so effective, but an astute (if commonly-offered) opinion of later years was 'DIAMOND HEAD were greater than the sum of their parts'. True, they had the most formidable vocalist of the NWOBHM genre (and the rock world in general), plus one of the most innovative and skilful guitarists, but the quietly-assured rhythm section appeared to be just as important to the bigger picture; any bassist or drummer worth their salt will happily inform you that there were some highly individualistic examples of musicianship going on at all levels. Even so, this wasn't an ASIA-style clash of egos all competing for attention; it was a collection of musicians whose abilities complemented each other perfectly, creating something which has rarely been seen either before or since.

The album was seen as a stepping stone to bigger things, and (in the wake of articles which famously included such gushing plaudits as 'more great riffs in a single song than SABBATH had on their first four albums' and such ill-advised statements as 'we're the natural successors to LED ZEPPELIN') the lads were soon attracting a fair bit of interest from labels such as MCA (for whom DIAMOND HEAD contributed "It's Electric" to the »Brute Force« sampler), Carrere and A&M, although the initial enthusiasm of the larger companies tended to wane quite suddenly, for some strange reason. Still, there seemed to be a glint of hope when local label Media Records offered to take them under their wing and allow the band to re-record some of their favourite material for future release. They started off by laying down new versions of "Sweet And Innocent" and "Streets Of Gold" with Robin George at the production helm, and duly saw the tracks being released as their latest single. It showed the more accessible side of the outfit, but the fans still bought the record in droves, and the lads soon had a bit more cash in their pockets, which was always handy for financing those massive treks around the country, The next step was to have been a re-recording of the »Lightning To The Nations« album (omitting a couple of unspecified numbers and including some stronger new material) with Robin George handling the production once again, although the deal with Media was to fall through with great rapidity, the members of DIAMOND HEAD later painting the company as the kind of employer who would promise you the world one minute and go back on their word at a moment's notice. Too bad. Undeterred, the group just went out on one of their endless tours once more, delighting the crowd with an ever-expanding repertoire which now included formative versions of continually-evolving tracks such as "Don't You Ever Leave Me" (*'our only concession to a love song'*, as they put it) and "Borrowed Time".

After the tour, the lads were invited to lay down a session for the 'Friday Rock Show', where they took the opportunity to showcase "Lightning To The Nations" and "Sweet And Innocent" from the album, plus the new pairing of "Borrowed Time" and "Don't You Ever Leave Me". Broadcast on the 28th of November 1980, the session won the hearts of a huge percentage of listeners, and the overwhelmingly favourable response led directly to the inclusion of the lengthy "Don't You Ever Leave Me" on the BBC's »The Friday Rock Show« album of session highlights the following year. Moving into 1981, it was all systems go when DIAMOND HEAD picked up on the APRIL WINE support slot at very short notice (after CHEVY had pulled out), whereupon they got out on the road for a successful series of high-profile and well-attended shows. Next up for the lads was another recording session, yielding the third DIAMOND HEAD single, the latter being released to coincide with a fairly extensive headlining tour in the

spring. The latest offering was a double A-sided affair, with the energetic "Play It Loud" (a live favourite, often trundled out as an encore) impressing far more than "Waited Too Long", a rather saccharine and ill-judged composition which surely stands as one of the poorest tracks ever committed to vinyl by this particular incarnation of DIAMOND HEAD. Nevertheless, sales of the single were of the usual high standard, and further ready cash was raked in when the outfit's management sold the rights to »Lightning To The Nations« to a German company (Woolfe Records), who proceeded to press up a few thousand copies (in a full-colour sleeve) and send the band *one* example for their own use. Needless to say, their management weren't too happy with this arrangement, and soon took steps to ensure that the record wasn't re-pressed without permission, but their attempts to retrieve the original master tapes (yes, in best comedy fashion, they had sent off the only top copy) met with continual failure. To this day, nobody seems to know where those recordings actually reside...

In the summer of 1981, DIAMOND HEAD were out on the road once again (with SILVERWING in tow), this time promoting their latest slice of vinyl, a self-financed 12" EP featuring three unfamiliar numbers ("Diamond Lights", "We Won't Be Back", "I Don't Got") and a remixed version of "It's Electric". The new pieces were an eclectic selection, with the bluesy "I Don't Got" firmly justifying the ZEPPELIN comparisons for once, while the heavy "We Won't Be Back" was a capable effort which was soon to become a popular live favourite. Having said that, "Diamond Lights" was a very poor song; a sparse, lightweight number which never made it into the live set. We all make mistakes. The summer tour saw DIAMOND HEAD well and truly making a name for themselves as a genuinely stunning live proposition, a famous meeting of minds coming at the Woolwich Odeon in London, when a certain Lars Ulrich took his place in a depleted audience, caused by a rather unfortunate piece of timing which led to the lads playing in the capital while the riots of Brixton *etc.* were in full swing on the other side of town. Neither the group nor their hardy followers seemed to care: *'there's riots and nuclear wars and things going on outside'* quipped Sean. The aural barrage *inside* the venue was only marginally less intense. According to metal folklore, Ulrich stepped onto the next available flight, jetted off to America and was playing DIAMOND HEAD covers within a matter of hours. It's all a complete fabrication, but it makes for a good story, and at least it provides METALLICA fans with something to talk about other than the state of James Hetfield's hair. The quartet were already introducing the fans to yet more unfamiliar compositions, two of the latest additions to the set being a pair of majestic numbers entitled "In The Heat Of The Night" and "To The Devil His Due". It was apparent that the lads were always pretty prolific in terms of penning new material, and they occasionally claimed to possess *'hundreds'* of finished tunes, many of which had been captured on tape. To be honest, I'm not entirely sure just how accurate these statements were. With the exception of "Wild On The Streets", all of the tracks they played live in the early 80's made it onto vinyl within a couple of years, so I suspect that some of these other *'compositions'* were really only half-finished ideas or a few riffs cobbled together. If there really was a huge archive of usable material in the vaults, surely some of it might have been made available by now.

The latest round of touring culminated with an extremely high-profile appearance at the *'Rock On The Tyne'* Festival in Gateshead, but it was to mark the end of DIAMOND HEAD's hectic touring activities for the best part of six months, during which time they were attending to a variety of financial difficulties and trying to win themselves that major-label deal at long last. Happily, things worked out in their favour when MCA finally put in a proper bid and managed to get the band on their books at the second attempt. Immediately, the lads had some money to spend once again, and were soon making plans to get back into the live circuit. Gigs followed as a matter of course (they were becoming increasingly lengthy affairs by now, some lasting the best part of two hours after the fans demanded numerous encores), and the punters were introduced to yet more unfamiliar compositions such as "Knight Of The Swords" and "Call Me", the latter being their most chart-friendly effort to date. Before long, the lads were recording their vinyl debut for MCA, which came in the shape of the »Four Cuts« EP, issued in both 7" and 12" formats. This saw a couple of stage favourites ("Trick Or Treat" and the heavy, inventive "Dead Reckoning") making an appearance on vinyl at long last, the record being padded out with "Call Me" (which, oddly enough, became one of the most popular numbers at their live shows) and a reworked version of "Shoot Out The Lights". After completing their gigging schedule by the early summer, it was finally time to deliver their first *'proper'* album (they would always refer to »Lightning To The Nations« as a vinyl demo), so the musicians immersed themselves in the studio for a couple of months, coming out of hiding only to deliver a session for Peter Powell's radio show (unveiling a barely-recognisable version of "One More Night" in the process), and then when they were added to the bill of the 1982 Reading Festival (appearing immediately before headliners BUDGIE) at the eleventh hour (after MANOWAR had been stopped at customs for being too hairy, or something), playing a top-notch set which had the massive crowd calling them back to deliver a hasty encore. A half-hour snippet of the set was transmitted on the 'Friday Rock Show' shortly thereafter, and the *'complete'* show (they somehow lost the encore) subsequently appeared as part of a disappointing CD called »The Friday Rock Show Sessions« a decade later.

At around this time, MCA encouraged the members of DIAMOND HEAD to participate in a truly ludicrous exercise, where the band were forced to play (well, mime) half a dozen tracks in front of a non-existent (but very appreciative) studio audience for no good reason whatsoever. Still, it got them a bit of publicity (well, notoriety), and five numbers were eventually broadcast on some regional TV stations as a half-hour chunk, the sixth ("To Heaven From Hell") being saved for transmission on the 'Old Grey Whistle Test'. With regard to the album, it didn't take the lads too long to complete the recording sessions, given that many of the tracks scheduled for inclusion had now been in their live repertoire for the best part of two years (some even longer), so the long-awaited LP was soon being readied for imminent release. It was preceded by a double-single release (there was also a 12" version) based around new(ish) number "In The Heat Of The Night", and backed with two recently-recorded live tracks plus (rather oddly) a lengthy radio interview. The album itself was issued to coincide with a comprehensive headlining tour (they also fitted in an appearance on the BBC's 'In Concert' programme, alongside the ELECTRIC GYPSIES) of substantial venues (TANK came along for the ride after TWISTED SISTER pulled out), most of which went with a bang, although the restless outfit were already desperate to try out material for the *next* album, with some lucky audiences even getting a taster of an embryonic "Makin' Music". The long-player itself, »Living On Borrowed Time«, was both a triumph and a disappointment, as it relied on several numbers which many of their fans were now almost sick to death of hearing. "Lightning To The Nations" and "Am I Evil?", for example, were recycled from the white label album (fair enough, the group had always stated their intention of reworking these efforts, but two full years had since passed), while "Call Me" was familiar from the »Four Cuts« EP and "Don't You Ever Leave Me" from the BBC compilation. The title track was also showing its age by this point, as were "To Heaven From Hell" and "In The Heat Of The Night", which had now been part of the live set for quite some time. In terms of *'exclusive'* material, therefore, it was a dead loss, but in

173

terms of execution, it was utterly unsurpassable.

The record signified the complete metamorphosis of DIAMOND HEAD into a world-challenging ensemble, the general standard of musicianship never having been higher, with Tatler carving out some incredible riffs and exquisite solos, while Harris was now the proud possessor of a richly-textured, luxuriant voice (surely the most soulful 'rock' frontman this side of JODY ST.'s Noel McCalla), and the material had never sounded better. "Am I Evil?" and "Lightning To The Nations" were colossal, while "Borrowed Time" and "In The Heat Of The

Night" were moody, atmospheric takes which showcased the prosodic lyrics and imaginative use of instrumentation. Surely the most remarkable inclusion, though, had to be the painfully moving version of "Don't You Ever Leave Me", whose sentiments would bring a tear to the proverbial glass eye. Genius. It wasn't the perfect record, though, as "To Heaven From Hell" was never the most coherent number the foursome ever penned, and the singalong "Call Me" stood out like a sore thumb, its presence being a pretty baffling matter, although I suspect that the lads might have been actively encouraged to show their diversity as a pointer to their future activities. If the whole affair was a slight letdown for the dedicated fans, the newly-captured DIAMOND HEAD audience went utterly bonkers for the release, and phenomenal sales of the long-player rapidly sent »Living On Borrowed Time« hurtling towards a 'Top 30' position in the mainstream charts. It looked as though DIAMOND HEAD would surely be the next big thing, and the lads were soon enjoying truly effusive reviews of both their live and studio work, even if the promotional side of things proved to be a bit hit-and-miss. There were, for example, very real plans to take DIAMOND HEAD to the States at one point, but MCA failed to stump up the necessary spondulicks. Furthermore, there were no additional singles to promote the group in the wake of the LP's release, although it's fair to say that none of the featured tracks (aside from the already-released "Call Me") really lent themselves to the task of storming the singles charts. In fact, DIAMOND HEAD were soon struggling to cope with the various demands of label and management, and found themselves being pulled in a dozen different directions at once.

After the utterly hectic touring/recording schedule of 1982, things cooled off in no uncertain terms throughout the early months of 1983, and there were no further sightings of the once-prolific DIAMOND HEAD in the live environment for the time being. Instead, the members were busily working on new material, their collective intention being to get another album into the shops before the year was out. Already, though, the cracks were now beginning to show, and minor niggles about future direction were soon being amplified into full-scale slanging matches between all of the parties involved. By the spring, however, things seemed to be working out, and plans for a new long-player (whose title oscillated between »Knight Of The Swords« and »Makin' Music« for several months before finally metamorphosing into »Canterbury«) were eventually announced. There was still no tour, although the lads began making a few festival appearances (including Kuusrock in Finland and Parkpop in Holland) to keep their name in the press, but things soon went awry when the long-standing line-up finally began to disintegrate. Duncan Scott was the first to depart (halfway through the recording sessions), the sticksman being unable to cope with the complexity of some of the new material, whereupon an unknown stand-in called Jamie Lane was drafted in to help out at short notice. Towards the end of the recording session, however, Colin Kimberley was also 'invited' to leave, having apparently been under criticism for his lack of commitment to the project. The remaining nucleus of Harris and Tatler were forced to assemble a new band around themselves, whereupon they brought in Robbie France (an Australian import who had latterly been working with such minor acts as BIG RED and ASH) and Merv Goldsworthy (a veteran of STREETFIGHTER), although the latter duo only contributed to "Makin' Music", the remainder of the album being in the can by this stage.

Given the recent addition of two brand-new

members to the ranks, therefore, it probably wasn't exactly the best moment for DIAMOND HEAD to land the biggest gig of their career, when they were invited to open the proceedings at the Monsters Of Rock Festival. Still, they took to the stage as intended, operating as a quintet after stand-in keyboard player 'Bob' (whose family were so poor they couldn't afford surnames) had been tempted away from his regular job in a local cabaret band to help out on the big day. To be honest, the lads put in a reasonable performance (it was still slated by many as their worst ever), although the pressure of the situation seems to have hit them pretty hard, and an unusually-nervous DIAMOND HEAD were more than happy to leave the stage at the end of it all. A month or so later, the lads picked up on a brief (well, curtailed) European slot with BLACK SABBATH, which took them to the continent for some eventful gigs, faring better at some than at others. Before long, though, they were back in the UK, and were soon out on tour (they had, by this time, recruited full-time keyboard player Josh Phillips-Gorse from the ranks of SPITZBROOK) to promote the long-awaited new record. »Canterbury« was an extraordinarily ambitious album which surprised a fair percentage of fans, although an equal number had almost certainly seen it coming after observing their musical development over the preceding couple of years. As an attempt to marry the music of two of their heroes (final score QUEEN 2 ZEPPELIN 3), it was something of a pretentious and overbearing disaster at times, but it still contained some genuinely stunning tracks. Live favourites "To The Devil His Due" and "Knight Of The Swords" were strong inclusions which harked back to the outfit's earlier vinyl outings, but compositions such as "Ishmael" (with its intriguing Eastern rhythms) and the individualistic "Out Of Phase" (which bore little resemblance to anything else in the rock sphere) served to demonstrate that DIAMOND HEAD were really striving to create something a bit out of the ordinary.

»Canterbury« was an album which excelled on some levels but which foundered dismally on others, and it was rather overly-hopeful of the outfit to assume that the world was full of broad-minded individuals who would embrace their latest experimentation with open arms. Nevertheless, enough units were shifted to send it chartwards once again, although it failed to emulate its predecessor (sales weren't exactly helped by a production fault which resulted in many thousands of mispressed copies hitting the shops in the first instance) in terms of commercial success. The reviewers didn't really know what to make of it all, and some of the less-tolerant critics had a field day tearing some of the more off-the-wall inclusions to shreds. To be honest, it wasn't really that bad, although "The Kingmaker" was a portentous piece of over-the-top nonsense, and the piano intro to "Canterbury" was pretty excruciating. Still, there were some cracking efforts too, notably the reworked "Makin' Music", while "One More Night" had been given a major overhaul, and was now based around an almost jazzy framework. The disarmingly-accessible "I Need Your Love", on the other hand, was another top-notch effort (admittedly, it was THE POLICE's "Don't Stand So Close To Me" revisited, but never mind), so it's fair to say that the album was undoubtedly an overall success, even if many commentators focused on its limitations and inadequacies. True, it was all a bit over-elaborate in terms of production, with several numbers being swamped by overdubs and harmonised vocals, but these tended to work a lot better when stripped down to the basics in the live environment. "Makin' Music", in particular, having already been trundled out as a single to precede the LP, was already becoming a live favourite, and the likes of "Out Of Phase" and "Ishmael" were soon being incorporated into the repertoire. Having said that, the UK tour (which saw DIAMOND HEAD taking to the road with TOBRUK and BUDGIE) was rather less of a success than originally envisaged, and involved the bands playing to decidedly non-full venues on occasion. More worrying, their latest single, »Out Of Phase«, failed to spark the public's imagination at all, and sales were extremely modest.

From that point onwards, it was all pretty much downhill for the luckless outfit, with Merv Goldsworthy being sacked towards the end of 1983 (allegedly after he auditioned for WHITESNAKE, although he resurfaced in SAMSON), who was hastily replaced by an unknown Scot called David Williamson, who didn't really look the part at all, but never mind. Moving into 1984, a further single, coupling "I Need Your Love" and "Ishmael", was planned, but ultimately failed to put in an appearance, so I've no idea if it even got to the test pressing stage. Still, the lads took to the road once more, and played a fairly lengthy tour to keep the flag flying, but were now failing to introduce any new material whatsoever, concentrating on rehashing some of their older compositions (making a real mess of them in the process) to vary things somewhat. The loyal fans remained faithful, but it was now apparent that the DIAMOND HEAD of old was now a thing of the past. The band even filmed a 'professional' video (I've seen better bootlegs) of themselves in action, the intention being to flog it to the adoring masses, but (even after roping in their massive fan club to help out) hardly anyone bought it. The lads kept a low profile until the summer, where they put in an appearance at the Marquee in London, the crowd being treated to a novel number at last, the utterly forgettable "Today". In fact, it transpired that the outfit had long since parted company with MCA (the power struggle between band, management and label having run into serious difficulties on virtually all fronts), but were nevertheless demoing new material for a further album (tentatively titled »Flight East«), including "Back In The Power Age", "A New Messiah", "Be Good", "Today" and "Someone Waiting". The record labels of the day, however, were nonplussed by these mediocre offerings (having heard four out of the five tracks, I can assure you that the various companies were absolutely correct in their judgement), leaving DIAMOND HEAD with no contract and no immediate hope of releasing another album.

After that, they struggled to carry on, with Josh Phillips-Gorse leaving towards the end of 1984 to pursue a solo career (although he ended up touring with BIG COUNTRY before eventually resurfacing in an early 90's act called HUGE BIG THING), and it was only a matter of time before the whole DIAMOND HEAD empire crumbled. There was never an official split, as they soon became fond of reminding everyone, but Tatler and Harris went off to do their own things in 1985 (as did the last rhythm section, with David Williamson electing to hook up with a minor bunch called FIRST HAND FURY, whereas Robbie France proceeded to lend a hand in acts such as UFO, WISHBONE ASH and, believe it or not, SKUNK ANANSIE), putting DIAMOND HEAD on the back burner for the time being. After pottering about in the studio for a while (Tatler found time to remix some early tracks for the pointless »Behold The Beginning« compilation, and also appeared on stage with old mates METALLICA at a gig in Birmingham), the musicians concluded that their immediate future lay in the world of stadium rock, and both set about creating new projects to express their creative natures once again. Tatler initially threw his weight behind the U2-influenced RADIO MOSCOW (who started off by including a few DIAMOND HEAD numbers in their live sets), an act who issued an interesting 12" EP in 1987 before ultimately saying goodbye to Tatler and transforming into an utterly average bluesy rock concern. Harris, meanwhile, began collaborating with long-time associate Robin George in 1986, a fertile relationship which eventually gave rise to the NOTORIOUS (in more ways than one) venture, which primarily involved recording a big-budget album of mainstream pop/rock over an extended period (something which necessitated pretty astronomical expenditure), which almost didn't get released at all, but finally saw a limited issue (to overwhelming public disinterest) towards the end of 1990. In the interim, FM Records had compiled an album of early DIAMOND HEAD demos and alternate takes (it was originally scheduled to feature some unreleased material from the »Flight East« sessions, but this notion was soon shelved), and issued them under the title of »Am I Evil«. To everyone's great surprise, sales were soon mounting up impressively, and provided a concrete indication that there were still numerous devotees out there.

The next piece of the jigsaw came when Lars Ulrich began raving (has he ever stopped?) about some of his original heroes from the British metal scene, and singled out DIAMOND HEAD for particular praise, his own band having covered the likes of "Am I Evil?", "It's Electric", "The Prince", "Sucking My Love" and "Helpless" in their rehearsals and live outings over the years. Ulrich was asked to contribute sleeve notes for a US reissue of »Behold The Beginning« on Metal Blade, and the name of DIAMOND HEAD was soon elevated to an even higher profile when "Helpless" turned up on METALLICA's »Garage Days« release ("Am I Evil?" had already taken pride of place on the »Creeping Death« EP) a short time later. By 1989, when Ulrich was busily compiling his NWOBHM retrospective (on which DIAMOND HEAD would be the only outfit afforded the honour of two tracks), there were rumblings in the press that there might be a reformation in the offing. It was all denied at first, of course, since Sean was steadfastly keeping up the pretence that NOTORIOUS was a going concern and would soon be taking on the world with some live appearances, which was never really on the cards at all. Mind you, Sean and Brian did collaborate (as THE MAGNETIC AKA) on a new track called "Who's That Man", which appeared on the soundtrack of 'Highlander II' (NOTORIOUS also contributed an exclusive number, incidentally), so maybe this was the start of a renewed working partnership after all. Sean was also observed on stage with MEGADETH at a Wembley Arena gig (although relatively few of those present actually recognised him), and so it seemed as though he might be developing a presence on the rock scene again. Eyebrows were next raised in the early months of 1991, when a mysterious act called DEAD RECKONING appeared out of the blue and played a few select gigs in minor rock clubs, performing a repertoire of unfamiliar material which nevertheless seemed a bit, well, evocative of a bygone age. What the hell was going on?

All was revealed in the spring of that year, when it became common knowledge that DEAD RECKONING were none other than DIAMOND HEAD themselves, Tatler and Harris having brought in a couple of unfamiliar associates, bassist Eddie Chaos (aka Eddie Moohan) and experienced sticksman Karl Wilcox, a veteran of numerous Midlands acts such as REQUIEM and CHASE. The lads went out on the road in the summer, taking in a few sizeable venues to a truly staggering level of public appreciation, and were unequivocally convinced that the time was right to do it all again. In time, they won a deal with the resurrected Bronze label, and their first product was a vinyl two-tracker which was released to coincide with an end-of-year tour. The 12" exposed the public to the newly-penned "I Can't Help Myself" and a rejigged version of old number "Wild On The Streets", the general impression being that they really were going about things the right way this time, even if the new number was slightly funky and Sean's vocals sounded a bit croaky on occasion. The tour saw the revamped band playing a selection of the more popular numbers from the DIAMOND HEAD back catalogue, although they also took the opportunity to introduce the fans to newer compositions such as "Run", "Let Me Down Easy", "Home" and "She Comes Down", some of which turned out to be surprisingly melodic and accessible. Whatever they played, though, the crowd reaction was pretty much the same, and the gigs were all good-humoured and enjoyable affairs, the musicians seeming genuinely happy to be on stage together once more. Unlike other enforced reformations, this wasn't primarily motivated by financial considerations or mere nostalgia, it represented far more than that. The group's next move was to have been to release a mini-LP (»Rising Up«) at some point in 1992, in order to make some of their more recent material available to the fans. In the event, however, the release was delayed and delayed again (there were never any particularly convincing explanations), and it was eventually scrapped, although most reference books (having all plagiarised each other shamelessly) include it as a genuine release, some even giving catalogue numbers and date of issue, which is very clever indeed.

After all the kerfuffle with the aborted mini-album had died down, the lads finally decided to enter the studio and record a proper long-player, and work duly began towards the end of 1992. By this time, Eddie Chaos had gone off to become a comic-book character (or something), and the band were now working with new bassist Pete Vuckovic, recruited from the ranks of BLACKOUT (who had supported DIAMOND HEAD on their mid-1991 jaunt), establishing themselves as a semi-stable proposition once again. The recording of the album turned out to be a protracted affair, with mixes, remixes and overdubs taking far longer than expected, and things all got a bit out of hand when Uncle Tom Cobleigh and all (Tony Iommi, Dave Mustaine) got involved with the project, co-writing and guesting on a couple of tracks. Still, it eventually all came together in the spring of 1993 (a notable event had occurred late the previous year, when all four original members of DIAMOND HEAD, including a self-conscious Colin and bewildered Duncan, took to the stage with METALLICA in Birmingham, whereupon the musicians belted out a couple of old classics together), and plans were made to release the new album to coincide with DIAMOND HEAD's appearance at the Milton Keynes all-dayer, a major event headlined by METALLICA themselves. By this time, Lars Ulrich was publicly referring to DIAMOND HEAD as 'a little side-project of mine', which really was monumentally offensive, but there you go. The event itself was a bit curious, with DIAMOND HEAD taking to the stage in high spirits (Sean being dressed as the grim reaper, for no tangible reason), but the assembled throng were (at best) perplexed and (at worst) quite hostile to these silly-looking interlopers. Nevertheless, the show was recorded for posterity, and selected highlights were even subsequently transmitted on Radio One's 'Rock Show'.

The album itself (»Death And Progress«) was quite a capable and varied effort, although the lads clearly erred on the side of caution and kept things on the right side of pretension this time, despite the ever-present temptation to go out on a limb and shock everyone with something totally unexpected. In fact, tracks such as "Starcrossed (Lovers Of The Night)" and "Calling Your Name" were pretty commensurate with their »Living On Borrowed Time«-period compositions, while the likes of "Truckin'" and "Paradise" were enjoyable efforts with more of a contemporary edge. Elsewhere, we had "Wild On The Streets" and "I Can't Help Myself" (again), plus "Damnation Street", something of an in-joke, in that it was basically a reworked "I Don't Got" from the old days. The remaining efforts, namely "Dust" (a revamped "She Comes Down"), "Home" and "Run", were, in comparison, perhaps a bit too commercial and lacking in personality, but it was still all eminently listenable. Reviews tended to be quite favourable on the whole, but the resurrected group found it difficult to sustain their new-found momentum, and it came as no particular surprise when they announced that they were calling it a day at the end of the year. As an epitaph, their live set from Milton Keynes, plus a raft of unused studio recordings from the 90's (including cover versions and tracks earmarked for the unissued mini-album), appeared on CD as »Evil Live«, a worthwhile release which celebrated a band who were living for the moment and not worrying too much about long-term aspirations.

Since the early 90's, the fans have been treated to (or fleeced by, depending on your point of view) a pretty wide range of retrospectives, reissues and compilations, although these are invariably generated from an extremely restricted basis set of early 80's compositions, some of which have been recycled even more frequently

than some parts of VENOM's back catalogue (and that's saying something). If you ask me, it's time to plunder those archives and finally give the die-hard fans something a bit special. No doubt there will be legal objections and copyright problems with some material, but *surely* there are a few usable tracks somewhere in the vaults. Anyway, I wouldn't hold out too many hopes for another reunion in the foreseeable future, as the members have all gone their separate ways once again, with Pete Vuckovic now establishing a solo career after the collapse of the popular 3 COLOURS RED venture, and Karl Wilcox having returned to small-time activities on the club circuit. What about the *'big two'*, you ask? Well, Brian has played with a couple of outfits since the demise of DIAMOND HEAD, including DIZZY LIZZY (a THIN LIZZY tribute band), and he has, more recently, been helping out in the long-lived QUILL, an established act with rather more of a folky celtic rock feel. Sean, on the other hand, is constantly at work in his home studio, having written a vast amount of new songs, and is often approached with a view to releasing a long-awaited solo collection. In the meantime, however, he's happy enough to wait until precisely the right circumstances manifest themselves, but I reckon we'll definitely be hearing more from that extraordinary voice in the not-too-distant future. End of unashamedly fawning entry. Do I get to do the official biography now?

LP's

»**The White Label Album**« Happy Face/DHM Records 1980
[Original white label version, plain white sleeve, some autographed]
»**Lightning To The Nations**« Happy Face/DHM Records 1980
[Later printed label version, plain white sleeve, some autographed]
»**Lightning To The Nations**« Woolfe Records 1981
[European reissue in picture cover]
»**Living On Borrowed Time**« MCA 1982
[Initially with gatefold sleeve and poster, later in single sleeve]
»**Canterbury**« MCA 1983
[Thousands of copies were mispressed and fail to play properly, some re-sold with free »Makin' Music« 12"]
»**Behold The Beginning**« Metal Masters 1986
[Featuring remixed material from debut album]
»**Behold The Beginning**« Metal Blade Records 1987
[US issue with different cover and extra track "Am I Evil?"]
»**Am I Evil**« FM Records 1987
[Compilation of early demos, also issued as limited edition picture disc]
»**Behold The Beginning**« Heavy Metal 1991
[Reissue with another different cover]
»**Death And Progress**« Bronze 1993

12" EP's

»**Diamond Lights**« DHM Records 1981
["Diamond Lights", "We Won't Be Back" and "I Don't Got" all non-LP, "It's Electric" different to album version]
»**Four Cuts**« MCA 1982

[Both "Dead Reckoning" and "Trick Or Treat" non-LP, "Shoot Out The Lights" different to single version, alternate cover to 7" format]

12" Singles

»**In The Heat Of The Night**« MCA 1982
[B-side "Play It Loud" (live), alternate cover to 7" format]
»**Makin' Music**« MCA 1983
[Extended version of "Makin' Music" different to album version, B-side extended Andy Peebles interview]
»**Sucking My Love**« (Live) MCA 1983
[More correctly, this should really be the »Out Of Phase« 12", although "Sucking My Love" is identified as the A-side]
»**Wild On The Streets**« Bronze 1991
[One-sided single with etched reverse]

7" EP's

»**Four Cuts**« MCA 1982
[Both "Dead Reckoning" and "Trick Or Treat" non-LP, "Shoot Out The Lights" different to single version, alternate cover to 12" format]

7" Singles

»**Shoot Out The Lights**« Happy Face Records 1980
[A-side non-LP, B-side "Helpless" different to album version]
»**Sweet & Innocent**« Media Records 1980
[A-side different to album version, B-side "Streets Of Gold" non-LP]
»**Waited Too Long**« DHM Records 1981
[Both tracks non-LP]
»**Call Me**« MCA 1982
[European-only commercial issue in picture sleeve]
»**In The Heat Of The Night**« MCA 1982
[A-side different to album version, B-side "Play It Loud" (live), issued in gatefold sleeve with free single featuring "Sweet & Innocent" (live) and Tommy Vance interview]
»**Makin' Music**« MCA 1983
[Some as DJ promos, edited A-side different to album version, B-side edited Andy Peebles interview]
»**Out Of Phase**« MCA 1983
[Also issued as limited edition picture disc]
»**Out Of Phase**« MCA 1983
[German issue with different sleeve]

Promotional Releases

»**Call Me**« MCA 1982
[UK promo-only 7" single, issued in company sleeve]
»**Makin' Music**« MCA 1983
[Promo-only DJ white label 12" single with long and short versions]
»**Four Track Sampler**« Bronze 1993

[Promo-only mini-CD for »Death And Progress« album in special cover]

CD's

»**Am I Evil**« FM Records 1987
[Compilation of early demos]
»**Behold The Beginning**« Metal Blade Records 1987
[With extra track "Am I Evil?"]
»**Sweet & Innocent**« Metal Masters 1988
[Same as »Behold The Beginning« album in alternate cover]
»**Am I Evil**« Teichiku 1990
[Japanese issue]
»**Makin' Music**« Black Ghost 1991
[Live bootleg from 1984, also features first RADIO MOSCOW EP]
»**Living On Borrowed Time**« MCA Japan 1992
[Japanese issue]
»**Canterbury**« MCA Japan 1992
[Japanese issue]
»**The Friday Rock Show Sessions**« Raw Fruit Records 1992
[Features live and session recordings]
»**Lightning To The Nations**« Metal Blade Records 1992
[US issue in different cover]
»**Singles**« MCA Japan 1992
[Japanese-only compilation]
»**Death And Progress**« Bronze 1993
[UK issue]
»**Death And Progress**« Victor 1993
[Japanese issue with extra track "Good Lovin' Gone Bad"]
»**Evil Live**« Bronze 1994
[Double disc with live and studio material]
»**Am I Evil**« Heavy Metal 1994
[Reissue with different back cover]
»**Behold The Beginning**« Heavy Metal 1994
[Reissue with yet another different cover]
»**Helpless**« Masonic Records 1995
[Compilation release]
»**Lightning To The Nations**« High Vaultage Records 1997
[With eight bonus single tracks, same cover as Woolfe LP]
»**The Best Of Diamond Head**« Half Moon 1999
[Compilation release]
»**Live In The Heat Of The Night**« Zoom Club Records 2000
[Live release, double disc]
»**Diamond Nights**« Metal Blade Records 2000
[Compilation release]

Mini-CD's

»**To Heaven From Hell**« Metal Blade Records 1997
[Compilation release]

Exclusive Compilation Appearances

"**Who's That Man-Part 1**" on »Highlander II-The Quickening« Soundtrack CD Bronze 1991
[Under the name of THE MAGNETIC AKA]

Compilation Appearances

"**It's Electric**" on »Brute Force« LP MCA 1980 + »NWOBHM '79 Revisited« Do-LP/Do-CD Phonogram 1990 + »The Metallic-Era Volume II« CD Neat Metal 1999
"**Don't You Ever Leave Me**" on »The Friday Rock Show« LP BBC Records 1981
[Different to album version]
"**In The Heat Of The Night**" on »Heavy« LP K-Tel 1983
"**Out Of Phase**" on »Metal Killers« LP Kastle Killers 1984
"**Am I Evil?**" on »Metal Killers Kollection I« Do-LP Castle Communications 1985 + »The Best Of Metal Blade Vol.3« Do-LP/CD Metal Blade 1988 + »The Metal Box« 3-CD Box Castle Communications 1993 + »Give 'Em Hell« CD Nectar Masters 1995 + »The Metallic-Era« CD Neat Metal 1996
"**Helpless**" on »NWOBHM '79 Revisited« Do-LP/Do-CD Phonogram 1990 + »The Metallic-Era« CD Neat Metal 1996
"**Diamond Lights**" on »NWOBHM Vol.1« Bootleg CD 1992
"**I Don't Got**" on »NWOBHM Vol.2« Bootleg CD 1992
"**Am I Evil? (live 82)**" on »NWOBHM-The Days On Stage« Bootleg CD Taurus Records 1993
"**Am I Evil? (live 93)**" on »Rock Legends« CD Castle Communications 1995
"**This Flight Tonight**" on »Monsters Of Rock« CD Castle Communications 1995
"**Sucking My Love**" on »The Metallic-Era« CD Neat Metal 1996
"**The Prince**" on »The Metallic-Era« CD Neat Metal 1996

DIANNO

Paul Dianno (v)
Lee Slater (g)
Paul 'PJ' Ward (g)
Kevin Browne (b)
Mark Venables (k)
Dave Irving (d)

Following his departure from IRON MAIDEN in the autumn of 1981, there was never much doubt that Paul Dianno would soon resurface with a new outfit of his own, and his immediate plans centred around the formation of LONEWOLF, a venture which he initially began piecing together towards the end of that year. After first recruiting guitarist Paul Ward (previously with the unsuccessful RITCH BITCH), Dianno subsequently scouted for further talent around his regular haunts such as the legendary Ruskin Arms. On one of these occasions, he spied a young bunch of hopefuls known as MINAS TIRITH, and he later managed to persuade three of their members (drummer Mark Stuart, bassist Kevin Browne and keyboard player Mark Venables) to join forces with him in this newly-created project. Having successfully assembled the bare bones of a new group, all that remained was the small matter of enticing John Wiggins away from DEEP MACHINE in order to complete the obligatory twin-guitar formation. In due course, the six-piece outfit began writing material and gigging around the capital, throwing in a few old MAIDEN numbers to keep the punters happy. In the spring of 1982, however, John Wiggins finally decided that LONEWOLF wasn't for him and flew the coop, initially rejoining DEEP MACHINE and later resurfacing in TOKYO BLADE. He was soon replaced by another former MINAS TIRITH member (you have to feel sorry for those left behind), a certain Lee Slater, and a fairly stable unit was finally established.

The outfit gigged successfully throughout the following two years (even winning themselves a valuable support slot with THIN LIZZY at an early stage), steadily expanding their repertoire (including original numbers such as "Lonewolf" and "Overdose Of Fear") and developing a healthy following in many parts of the country. Eventually, however, the sheer volume of hopefuls using the same (or highly-similar) name compelled the group to think of something more original. The rather obvious (yet sufficiently distinctive) choice was simply DIANNO, and the newly-christened outfit benefitted significantly from the fact that they were no longer confused with various minor nonentities. In due course, the lads demoed a handful of fairly commercial numbers for the benefit of various record companies, and they were subsequently offered the chance to record a full album for the inconsistent Heavy Metal label, whereupon DIANNO entered the studio and duly delivered the goods on their eponymous (originally retitled as the preposterous »Two Swimmers And A Bag Of Jockeys« in Japan, although it's still generally referred to as »Dianno« over here) long-playing effort, the latter being unleashed upon the rock world in mid-1984.

For many (*i.e.* those who had not previously

been exposed to the gradual development of LONEWOLF's own material), the DIANNO album came as something of a considerable shock, not to mention a major disappointment, especially for the multitudes who were anticipating something which evoked the intensity of early IRON MAIDEN. Instead, the LP was a surprisingly lightweight affair (even by the standards of mid-80's Britain, where the AOR genre was now gaining a fairly strong foothold), and the prominent incorporation of keyboards and backing vocals tended to suggest an affiliation with acts such as JOKERS WILD, V8 or MEANSTREAK. In terms of this particular brand of radio-friendly material (originally pioneered by the likes of BOSTON and TOTO on the other side of the Atlantic), it was a fairly competent (albeit immensely derivative and samey) effort: unfortunately, however, it just wasn't what the fans were looking for from Paul Dianno, and so sales were understandably mediocre. A single, coupling "Heartuser" and "Road Rat" (the latter, like "Lady Heartbreak", was one of the very few numbers which adhered to the original LONEWOLF style), was also issued at around the same time in the UK (the Japanese issue featured a different combination), but this attempt to promote the group further also seems to have failed miserably, with the two-tracker being largely ignored by the masses.

Although the luckless outfit had already lost their original drummer by the time their album was being assembled, they were nonetheless able to utilise the services of Dave Irving (later of AOR hopefuls VIRGINIA WOLF, not to be confused with the combo who recorded for Creole some years earlier) for the necessary recording sessions. Nevertheless, they found it inordinately difficult to keep hold of a permanent skin-beater thereafter, employing former SAD CAFE (an act with whom LONEWOLF had gigged in their early days) stalwart Dave Hadfield for a while before eventually recruiting journeyman drummer Frank Noon (previously with just about everyone!) for various studio work, including a prestigious 'Friday Rock Show' session towards the end of the year. Broadcast on the 5th of October 1984, the session allowed the outfit to showcase some of their album material, and they obliged by running through "Antigua", "Razor Edge" and "Flaming Heart", plus the otherwise-unissued "Spiritual Guidance", one of their earliest compositions from the LONEWOLF days. A short time later, DIANNO proceeded to record a live video at a specially-organised appearance at the Camden Palace in London, although it proved to be something of a farewell show.

Dejected with unflattering reviews and disappointing sales of the debut long-player, Paul Dianno eventually (although there had even been talk of a second album at one stage) concluded that there was no future for DIANNO the band, electing to disband the poorly-received project in the early months of 1985 (in fact, it transpires that both original guitarists had actually departed by this time, and former WHITE SPIRIT/GILLAN axeman Janick Gers had stepped in to help out towards the end), by which time their official video had finally made its way into the shops. Even so, this offering shifted a relatively modest number of units, which was predictable, under the circumstances. The erstwhile DIANNO pairing of Mark Venables and Kevin Browne subsequently worked together in the second incarnation of Laurie Mansworth's AIRRACE project in 1986, although this proved to be a fairly unproductive relationship. Inevitably, Dianno himself was to remain out of the limelight for a very short time, putting the all-new BATTLEZONE (see separate entry) ensemble together in the summer of 1985 (in the wake of the GOGMAGOG debacle) with a completely revised set of accomplices. It proved to be a group with far more to offer the fans and critics, and their two albums are regarded by many as Dianno's most important work to date.

In more recent years, the busy Paul Dianno has additionally become involved with such diverse musical activities as the ill-advised ALL STARS project, the heavyweight KILLERS venture and a reformed BATTLEZONE, not to mention all those incredibly nasty cash-in releases with Dennis Stratton (»The Original Iron Men« etc.), although it transpires that several of these releases emerged without his full permission (which still doesn't explain why the flipping things were ever recorded in the first place), and all are treated with healthy contempt by the man himself. The frontman was later invited to reflect on the musical worth of the infamous DIANNO long-player: *'Everyone, quite understandably, was expecting an album that sounded exactly like IRON MAIDEN. I just decided that I would do something different, and even disappeared off to the Caribbean to write the material. I sat there for three months and came up with all those dreadful songs; I never really liked them at all!'* (Ref: Interview, Matthias Mader, November 1994). Well, at least you have to give him credit for honesty, if not artistic integrity!

LP's
»Dianno« FM Records 1984
[Also issued as limited edition picture disc and on blue vinyl]

»Dianno« King Records 1984
[Japanese issue]

7" Singles
»Heartuser« FM Records 1984
[UK issue, A-side different to album version]
»Flaming Heart« King Records 1984
[Japanese-only issue, B-side "Don't Let Me Be Misunderstood" non-LP]

Compilation Appearances
"Here To Stay" on »Heavy Metal Records« LP Heavy Metal 1984
"Antigua" on »The Best Of British« LP Zebra 1985 + »Metal Killers Kollection I« Do-LP Castle Communications 1985
"Heartuser" on »Metal Killers Kollection II« Do-LP Castle Communications 1986

DIAWLED

Kevin Davies (v)
Aled Davies (g)
Geraint Williams (g)
Carwyn Davies (b)
Paul Phillips (d)

As with relatively minor hopefuls such as CRYS, DORCAS, TRYDAN, CEFFYL PREN and TROBWLL, all of whom elected to sing in Welsh, the outfit known as DIAWLED (*'The Devils'*) didn't manage to make much of a name for themselves outwith their own restricted area, but they were, as far as I know, the only one of these native-language acts to have been mentioned in the pages of 'Kerrang' at any stage. At the time of writing, the complete extent of the group's discography is unknown, given that their vinyl all seems to have emerged on the kind of small-time label who could only afford to press their records in absolutely tiny quantities, so other examples could easily turn up at some future date. Anyway, their earliest known recording appears to be "Shwt Mae Siapus?" (sorry, but I haven't an earthly what this one is about), which appeared on an incredibly obscure compilation EP in 1982 (issued on the small Fflach label) featuring a variety of local wannabes. The composition, however, shows the band to have been one of the heavier acts from their region, coming across as lying somewhere between DEALER and DENIGH in terms of general NWOBHM comparisons. A pretty good start, I'd say.

The following year, the talented outfit (having presumably been identified as the most promising act on the sampler EP, not that they were pitted against stiff competition) were given the enviable opportunity to record their own two-tracker for Fflach, which ultimately saw "S.O.S." (at least that one doesn't require a translation) and "Llinos Yn Y Lleder Du" (something along the lines of *'blackbirds spreading their wings'*, which is hardly the most metal title ever) being captured for posterity. Building on the solid framework of their "Shwt Mae Siapus?" effort, the band continued to demonstrate a pretty confident songwriting ability, all of which makes for an enjoyable enough listening experience. Admittedly, DIAWLED weren't quite in the same musical league as gifted countrymen PERSIAN RISK, STORMQUEEN or IONA, for example, but they were still a hell of a lot better than many of the more borderline chancers who were doing the rounds in Wales back then. Their debut two-tracker (the busy Richard Morris of TROBWLL was once again involved in the recording process) probably shifted a fair old number of units in their locality, but has turned up very infrequently in recent memory, and comes in an unusually colourful picture sleeve showing a futuristic interpretation of a female figure. Phwoar.

Towards the end of the year, DIAWLED, having now been picked up by the slightly larger Sain concern, issued a further single (which is almost as scarce as their debut) in the form of »Noson Y Blaidd« (»Night Of The Wolf«), which was fortunate enough to make the 'Singles' review section in 'Kerrang'. Strangely, the magazine characterized the release as *'a kinda folky/metal blend that unfortunately scores rather low on the Kerrangometer'*, which didn't really seem particularly consistent with their formative material, so you had to question the accuracy of this statement. Indeed, the latest record (issued in a picture sleeve featuring little more than their logo and a pair of lupine eyes staring out of the darkness) turned out to be virtually as substantial as the debut two-tracker, although DIAWLED had, by this time, recruited a new singer in the shape of Rhiannon Tomos (who had previously fronted her own eponymous project, who were featured, alongside the likes of CRYS, on Sain's diverse »Barod Am Roc« compilation), whose vocals tended to lend rather more of a WARLOCK-style feel to the proceedings. Neither the A-side nor "Dewch Gyda Ni" ("Come With Us", I reckon) sound remotely folky to me, though, so I've absolutely no idea how the added 'Kerrang' hack might have come up with that feeble description. In any case, no further DIAWLED releases appear to have surfaced as yet, suggesting that they may have called it a day shortly thereafter, although I wouldn't be remotely surprised if additional small-label obscurities come out of the woodwork at some point.

7" Singles
»S.O.S.« Fflach Records 1983
»Noson Y Blaidd« Sain Records 1983

Exclusive Compilation Appearances
"Shwt Mae Siapus?" on »Gyda Chymorth C.A.C.« 7" EP Fflach Records 1982

DICK SMITH BAND

Dave Barrett (v)
Paul Downes (g)
Paul Madden (g)
Steve Barrett (b)
Steve Swift (d)

Yet another product of Merseyside's burgeoning rock scene of the late 70's, the DICK SMITH BAND were a fairly curious proposition, a quintet known mainly to present-day NWOBHM aficionados through their double A-sided single from 1980. In fact, there's actually an even earlier release, a relatively obscure two-tracker issued on the Smile label (see also 100% PROOF and THE LAW, for example) the previous year. In this case, however, the single in question (coupling "Motorway Madness" and "Body Heat") is an incredibly nondescript record, portraying the group as a very rudimentary, lightweight rock outfit with vaguely progressive leanings (cf. EARTHBOUND and MITHRANDIR), although the vocals of Dave Barrett served virtually no purpose at all in this instance, being mixed way too low and merely wavering unconvincingly over the top of the backing track as opposed to carrying the tune with any real sense of conviction. Terrible stuff, on the whole, and this slice of vinyl (issued in a fairly uninspiring sleeve) might just as well have been an instrumental release. Certain individuals are in the habit of charging a pretty obscene price for this insipid effort, but it's not one that you should even consider buying unless it's incredibly inexpensive.

Fortunately, their follow-up single from a year later proved to represent a considerably more worthy and capable offering, the latter pairing "The Way Of The World" (a composition which would be included on the »NWOBHM Vol.5« bootleg a decade later) with "Giving The Game Away". The material on display is rather heavier and the vocals markedly more prominent than before, with "Giving The Game Away" being a fairly enjoyable number lying somewhere between VAGABOND and NO QUARTER in terms of style and intensity. On the reverse, though, "The Way Of The World" (the ridiculous lyrics to which are printed on the back sleeve) is a rather more commercial effort with twangy guitars and a funky bass line which occasionally sounds distressingly close to certain SIMPLE MINDS material ("Don't You Forget About Me", for example) for comfort. Nevertheless, the single has sold well to NWOBHM devotees as a mid-priced item for many years, no doubt helped by the presence of an excellent (but not entirely representative) picture sleeve showing a flaming, demonic creature. Copies tend to come out of the woodwork quite regularly, though, suggesting that a fair old quantity must have been shifted at the time.

This particular bunch don't seem to have been an especially long-lived or commercially successful outfit, although they were still a popular enough attraction in their locality (where most of their records were sold, predictably enough), occasionally gaining valuable support slots with touring acts such as DIAMOND HEAD, at which their performances were apparently a bit heavier and more intense than their vinyl offerings might have suggested. The one-time members don't appear to have resurfaced in any other bands of note, which is a bit unusual, considering that the North West rock scene was a bit of a musical merry-go-round, but never mind. Just one tiny, little, niggling detail continues to perplex me, lads: who the hell *was* Dick Smith?!

7" Singles
»Motorway Madness« Smile Records 1979
»The Way Of The World« Hol-o-gram Records 1980

Compilation Appearances
"The Way Of The World" on »NWOBHM Vol.5« Bootleg CD 1992

DIE LAUGHING

Mick Mepham (v,g)
Terry Corder (v,b)
Lol Cooksey (v,d)

Although a couple of other British acts adopted the name in later years (including a fairly prominent dark/goth outfit), I reckon the original version of DIE LAUGHING were this remarkably obscure trio from Sussex, who, by all accounts,

183

seem to have represented the type of parochially popular outfit who tended to remain well and truly unknown outwith their own region. They presumably got together at some point in the late 70's (their music certainly had something of a traditional heavy rock feel to it), and came to the fore at the height of the NWOBHM movement, releasing an extremely scarce single along the way. The double A-sided effort, from 1980, featured "You Got The Power" and "Hard Living Man" (the latter, if you choose to believe the sleeve notes, being inspired by tales of prohibition-era America), two slightly odd numbers which didn't really fit in with the general archetype. They were hefty enough, certainly (elements of SPARTA and PALI GAP at times), but the arrangements sorely lacked the NWOBHM dynamism, and tended to hark back to the hard rock of the mid-70's. A strange release all round, and they probably failed to appeal to fans of all this *'new metal'* that was suddenly coming out of the woodwork wherever you looked.

DIE LAUGHING persevered for a year or two after the debut single's release, playing quite extensively throughout the South of England (getting up to Berkshire and London on occasion, but not any further up North, by the looks of things), but appear to have eventually called it a day for good as the NWOBHM began to fizzle out. Guitarist Mick Mepham soon threw his weight behind a tuneful act called the SAVAGE HEARTS, who received a modicum of regional exposure but still ground to a halt before long. The persevering chap wasn't finished, though, and resurfaced at the tail end of the 80's in an obscure local bunch known as LUCIFER, although this promisingly-named ensemble failed to achieve much during the course of their fleeting existence. The DIE LAUGHING single, meanwhile, is a little-known rarity, and relatively few copies (in a flimsy, cartoon-style picture sleeve) have made it into circulation in recent memory. If you decide to make it your mission to search for one, therefore, it might take you a very long time before you have any success.

7" Singles
»You Got The Power« Ocean Records 1980

DISTRAINERS

Pete Banbury (v, g)
Phil Hammond (v, b)
Steve Taylor (d)

Leicestershire obscurities the DISTRAINERS (people who seize goods, according to my trusty dictionary) were conceived on the cusp of punk and metal, and consequently took a few influences from both camps, although they always claimed to be more closely affiliated with the rock scene. The outfit more or less evolved from a notoriously unstable amateur-hour concern called XENITH (who failed to achieve much apart from annoying the neighbours), although the youthful Steve Taylor was more than happy to hook up with new accomplices Pete Banbury and Phil Hammond (the pair handled vocal duties fairly democratically) to form rather more of a coherent and ambitious proposition. After the usual routine of local shows (believe it or not, they even shared a stage with WITCHFYNDE on at least one occasion), the trio managed to get a self-financed 7" onto the market, which sold in semi-respectable copies at small-time gigs. The nominated A-side ("Say Goodbye") turned out to be a tuneful (but fairly disposable) piece of rock (with a few vaguely new wave undertones) in the URCHIN, BLAZER BLAZER and TRADER scheme of things, whereas the reverse ("Spies In Your Eyes") was a decidedly more substantial and distinctive effort with similarities (in the guitar department, at least) to WIKKYD VIKKER and SPARTA, although the rather moody vocals were slightly out of place, perhaps.

Sadly, this 1979 offering (which wasn't issued in a picture sleeve) failed to win the hearts of many reviewers ('Sounds' were among those who didn't mince their words), and relatively modest sales figures meant that the threesome were unlikely to make much of an impact on the charts. Still, the undaunted group persevered for another year or so, trying out some new ideas after expanding to a quartet and then finally to a quintet, although this failed to make a huge difference to their collective fortunes. By late 1980, the last incarnation of the DISTRAINERS (Pete Banbury had already flown the coop and Phil Hammond had switched to guitar) had mutated into ALIEN, an act who developed considerably more of a genuine metal style and touted their wares around until the mid-80's (unsuccessfully, in the long run), circulating several critically-acclaimed demos along the way. Steve Taylor wouldn't remain involved with the reinvented bunch for very long, however, as he candidly explained in a recent chinwag: *'Me and Phil were always arguing about something, usually over women. In the end, he kicked me out of ALIEN. Yes, I was kicked out of my own band!'* (Ref: Private communication, October 1999). Taylor subsequently featured in a short-lived venture alongside former BLITZKRIEG axeman Ian Jones before moving on to pastures new, eventually relocating to nearby Northamptonshire and enjoying a few happy years with the talented and popular SOLDIER. The DISTRAINERS 7", meanwhile, is an incredibly scarce piece nowadays, although most collectors can survive without one.

7" Singles
»Say Goodbye« D.J. Records 1979

DORCAS

Colin Roberts (v)
Rhys Evans (g)
Deiniol Morris (b)
John Hywel Morris (b)
Peter Roberts (d)

Unlike the vast majority of their compatriots (in the metal genre, at least), DORCAS were one of the relatively few bands from Wales who elected to issue a single which is sung entirely in their native language, so all credit to them for having a bit of national pride. Like the earlier TROBWLL, TRYDAN, DIAWLED and CRYS releases, the sleeve credits *etc.* are also all in Welsh, so you'll forgive me if there are any glaring inaccuracies in what's written here (believe me, it's a genuinely tortuous language for a novice/thicko to translate). "Blwyddyn Arall" ("Another Year") is the heavier of the tracks, starting off with a very promising riff, although the composition rapidly mutates into a rather more restrained effort in the KNOCK UP vein. Indeed, the vocals have a slightly folky aspect to them, which almost conjures up the image of a more metal RUNRIG, especially when coupled with the arcane lyrics. The flipside, "Nyth Y Frân" (sorry, couldn't get a remotely meaningful translation for this), on the other hand, is a semi-ballad which is vaguely reminiscent of TRUFFLE's "Round Tower", but which doesn't exactly set the pulse racing. Featuring a different bassist on each track, suggesting either personnel problems or a delay between recordings, the single isn't too bad, although I suspect that speakers of the Welsh language might get a tad more enjoyment out of it. This humble slice of vinyl (a self-financed affair, needless to say), featuring a pretty basic monochrome sleeve with just the band logo and song titles, is the only known output from DORCAS (it emerged at some point in 1984), although I wouldn't be surprised if they also appeared on the odd obscure compilation or two in their time.

7" Singles
»Blwyddyn Arall« SRT 1984

DRAGONFLY

Rudi Riviere (v,g)
Stephan Heath (g)
Pete Cornell (b)
Nik Szymanek (d)

One of several British outfits to adopt the name over the years, the version of DRAGONFLY who caused most of a stir amongst NWOBHM fans were yet another group who formed on the outskirts of London towards the end of the 70's, regularly making live appearances in the capital itself and eventually establishing themselves as a bit of a minor cult at the famous Ruskin Arms in the East End. At some point in 1980, the ambitious quartet got themselves into the recording studios, whereupon they laid down four commendably-varied tracks for release as a 7" EP. "Silent Nights" opens the proceedings, a memorable, upbeat number (as featured on the »NWOBHM Vol.4« bootleg CD) which leads into the quirky "Mercy", an interesting composition with a distinctive bass line. On the reverse, "Spacebound" turns out to be a fairly unremarkable semi-ballad, albeit quite a heavy one, before the mid-tempo "Disappear From View", a number featuring some highly competent guitar work throughout, rounds things off in impressive fashion. Frontman Rudi Riviere's vocals were, on the whole, quite individualistic, although they occasionally bring forth a few comparisons with JODY ST.'s Noel McCalla. Nevertheless, DRAGONFLY were a metal outfit through and through, and their EP additionally suggests elements of a variety of heavy acts such as GOLDSMITH, SALEM or Leicestershire's VALHALLA.

DRAGONFLY had a well-received demo tape or two under their collective belts by the time their fairly brief existence had come to its natural conclusion (within around a year of their EP hitting the shops), with the likes of "No No No" and "High Talk" adhering pretty strictly to the style captured on their earlier vinyl offering, although tracks such as "Loser" suggested the occasional bit of experimentation with more commercial numbers. Sadly, however, no further releases emerged under the DRAGONFLY moniker, with the immensely talented Riviere soon finding his way into the ranks of SAPPHIRE (and, eventually, after a bit of part-time work with such also-rans as the NEW TORPEDOS and BLACK MAIL, a brief tenure with the considerably more successful TERRAPLANE), while erstwhile DRAGONFLY drummer Nik Szymanek shifted direction slightly and subsequently teamed up with the more progressively-inclined TRILOGY for a number of years. DRAGONFLY's humble four-tracker, meanwhile, issued as a white label record in a generic sleeve, was an extremely limited pressing, and has been known to fetch fairly stratospheric prices in recent times.

7" EP's
»Silent Nights« Private 1980

Compilation Appearances
"Silent Nights" on »NWOBHM Vol.4« Bootleg CD 1992

DRAGONSLAYER

Tony Mamwell (v)
Phil Odins (g)
Steve Morgan (b)
Dave Philips (d)

You may not be aware that the heavy outfit who eventually came to be known by the extremely valiant moniker of DRAGONSLAYER actually started out under the plain old SLAYER handle, before the emergence of a certain bunch of speedsters from across the Atlantic eventually compelled them to take drastic action on the name front. The British version of SLAYER first came together in Lancashire as long ago as 1980, originally playing the humdrum circuit of local pub gigs with a repertoire of cover versions which included many a classic from the likes of JUDAS PRIEST and BLACK SABBATH. Gradually, though, they began writing their own material (one of their earliest compositions was the shamelessly-titled "Calling The Devil"), and duly recorded a speculative five track demo towards the end of the year, this formative effort being laid down at the famous Cargo Studios, a facility used by numerous outfits from the North West, and which also famously hosted the recording sessions for DEMON's »Night Of The Demon« opus. The first SLAYER live appearance to feature some of their own material came at an open-air event held in Ashfield Valley in November 1980, where the youthful outfit nervously took to the stage in front of a couple of hundred expectant fans. Mind you, their performance seemed to go down pretty well, so it looked as though they were going about things the right way.

Shortly thereafter, the quartet teamed up with long-lived local crowd-pleasers TRACTOR for a gig at Rochdale College (not exactly Wembley Arena, but everyone has to start somewhere), where they successfully entertained a crowd of several hundred punters. Through sheer hard graft and commendable perseverance, SLAYER gradually earned themselves an enviable reputation as a proficient live act, and they ultimately progressed to regional headlining status, where they occasionally pushed the boat out and went the whole hog in terms of pyrotechnic effects, plus a huge light show and professional sound system. Fast-forwarding to 1983 (not much else happened in the interim, apart from the usual round of incessant gigging), the outfit had reached the crucial stage of organising their debut vinyl release, a three-tracker (recorded at Cavalier Studio in Stockport) featuring "I Want Your Life", "Satan Is Free" and "Broken Hearts". At this point, however, fate dealt them a cruel blow, as Tom Araya and Co. soon began making a rather big name for themselves with the worldwide release of »Show No Mercy«, throwing the immediate plans of their hapless British namesakes into chaos. The lads had, however, already pressed up their EP by this juncture (it seems likely that some advance copies had even made it to the shops and to radio stations), and so a contingency plan sprang into action with great haste.

As with the RED ALERT/WILDFIRE situation, the plucky group merely reinvented themselves (as DRAGONSLAYER) and then slapped a strategically-placed sticker on one side of the record to show people their newly-chosen identity. A cheap solution, perhaps, but (given that you could clearly see the original label under the flimsy sticker) it all looked pretty ridiculous, to tell you the truth. Anyway, the EP itself turned out to be a decent enough release, and also one which was significantly more 'true metal' (although the HARRIER-style power ballad, "Bro-

ken Hearts", was a slight let-down) in its conception than many of the private releases which were being churned out by their contemporaries. In particular, "I Want Your Life" and "Satan Is Free" suggested that DRAGONSLAYER could quite easily have fitted in with 'mini-power-metal' scene which spontaneously established itself in and around the West Midlands at approximately the same time (see, for example, TYRANT, CYNIC, DEALER, GRIM REAPER, ARC etc.), even if the material was probably a bit too, er, heroic for the general British market. The EP was, however, advertised for sale through the pages of 'Kerrang' at the time, and I would imagine that orders probably flooded in from mainland Europe and the States. In any case, there sure aren't many copies left in the UK, and the three-tracker (never issued with a picture sleeve) is a top-ranking rarity these days.

Following on from their record's release, DRAGONSLAYER attracted a fair bit of attention from various labels, and the lads waited patiently for a deal to materialise at some point during 1984. Sadly, it didn't happen for them in the short term, and so the musicians were compelled to go back to basics and set about recording yet more demos. The ensemble duly resurfaced a year later, brandishing a lengthy seven track effort featuring all-new material such as "Lies In Your Eyes", "Satan's Soldiers" and "The Battle Is On". It was, on the whole, a slightly more accessible, PRIEST/MAIDEN-influenced set, which pretty much stuck to the unimaginative, tried-and-tested formula of galloping riffs and secular/mythical lyrics. If, therefore, they had gone over to Europe and gigged with the likes of ACCEPT and HELLOWEEN at this point, they would now almost certainly be national heroes in places such as Germany and Greece. In Britain, however, they died a bit of a death. The first seeds of doubt were sown in the minds of the band members themselves, whereupon bassist Steve Morgan finally decided to fly the DRAGONSLAYER nest in 1986. He was soon replaced by former VOLTAGE member Marc Webb, however, and the group attempted to regain their footing by trying out a few more original ideas.

Some time later, Ebony threw the lads a lifeline, offering them one last opportunity to contribute a track to one of their sampler albums, and the outfit duly recorded some newly-penned numbers for this purpose. In the event, their "Rock The Radio" effort (a composition entirely lacking in references to swords, dragons or the devil himself) was selected for inclusion, this being a blatant attempt at considerably more commercial material, although it still failed to convince anyone that DRAGONSLAYER genuinely had the potential to pull off an album which would be remotely relevant in the late 80's. Within a few months, it was becoming only too apparent that the writing was on the wall for the luckless outfit, and so, after a couple of local farewell gigs, they finally called it a day for good in mid-1987. The ex-members appear not to have moved on to any other projects of note, and the revered name of DRAGONSLAYER subsequently passed into the realms of NWOBHM folklore. The tracks from their EP, however, recently appeared (legitimately) on a British Steel compilation, offering fans the opportunity to appreciate their material without forking out a small fortune for the original vinyl rarity.

7" EP's
»I Want Your Life« Cavalier Records 1983

Exclusive Compilation Appearances
"Rock The Radio" on »The Metal Collection Vol.II« LP Ebony 1987

Compilation Appearances

"I Want Your Life" on »N.W.O.B.H.M. Metal Rarities Vol.3« CD British Steel 1997
"Satan Is Free" on »N.W.O.B.H.M. Metal Rarities Vol.3« CD British Steel 1997
"Broken Hearts" on »N.W.O.B.H.M. Metal Rarities Vol.3« CD British Steel 1997

DRAGSTER

Garry Owen (v)
Andy Trafford (g)
Mike Stansfield (b)
Steve Grant (d)

DRAGSTER, from West Yorkshire, were one of the earliest lucky outfits to be snapped up by the fledgling Heavy Metal Records, and the label's inaugural »Heavy Metal Heroes« compilation was to feature the quartet's "Do It", their tasteful paean to the questionable delights of various S&M practices. Ouch. The track itself was a pretty basic example of mid-tempo rock/metal lying somewhere between TORTURE's "Last Post" and LIONHEART's early "Lionheart" number, but was, nevertheless, a reasonable enough effort for an emergent metal ensemble. Far more accomplished, however, is the group's »Ambitions« two-tracker (featuring the much improved vocals of one Derick Pickles, who actually seems to have been their first frontman), which is easily one of the strongest of Heavy Metal's early singles. Comparable, in some respects, to vinyl releases of the time such as the BOLLWEEVIL and CYNIC efforts, particularly with regard to the pacey A-side and the more sedate reverse ("Won't Bring You Back", in this case), both of the compositions featured were highly proficient and dynamic efforts, all of which seemed to pave the way for a healthy career in the music business.

Sadly, the outfit don't seem to have been able to capitalise on their initial exposure, and their activities gradually became less and less noteworthy as time progressed. Personnel problems began to mount up, and their vocalist (who, confusingly enough, has been credited as both Gary Owen and Garry Horne) went off to get married in best not-remotely-rock'n'roll fashion. In fact, it appears that the original DRAGSTER had been laid to rest by around 1983 (having run into identity problems in the wake of the anti-NWOBHM backlash), whereupon they were happy to allow some of their mates from the Manchester area to adopt the identity for a while, although the latter had themselves run into problems and evolved into an embryonic TOUCHED within a year or so. Still, the members of the Yorkshire DRAGSTER didn't just disappear off the face of the earth immediately, and proceeded to tinker about with small-time acts during the wilderness years. By the second half of the decade, however, drummer Steve Grant and guitarist Andy Trafford had met up by chance and soon began jamming together on an occasional basis. After a while, they concluded that it might be a bit of a laugh to get DRAGSTER off the ground once more, so they recruited a new set of accomplices in the shape of Darren Hirst (g), Glenn Whatmough (v) and Lennie Perrett (b), although the latter was soon replaced by a chap called Mark Caffrey, who was (oddly enough) a veteran of the aforementioned TOUCHED. The revitalised act began writing together and making a few trips to the recording studio, although their low-profile activity failed to raise too many eyebrows at the time.

Nevertheless, the lads began demoing new material at around the turn of the decade, and even contrived to record an entire album's worth of novel songs in due course (by which time Mark Caffrey had been succeeded by Colin Lee), after which they went back out on tour once again (taking in a few European dates in the process), although they found the task of touting the tapes around the labels something of an unrewarding imposition. The whole DRAGSTER thing began to be taken rather less seriously once more, and, consequently, the members started drifting apart and only collaborating on an occasional basis. Along the way, Steve Grant became acquainted with an emerging act called NIGHTMARE VISIONS, although he and Andy Trafford kept DRAGSTER on the back burner for a while, and their original outfit even got around to demoing some newer compositions towards the middle of the 90's. Within a year or so, however, the faithful DRAGSTER name was more or less laid to rest (again), whereupon the drummer concentrated on the fortunes of his more heavyweight NIGHTMARE VISIONS project. With his new employers winning themselves a recording deal in due course, Steve Grant came into contact with various individuals in the music business (some of whom had fond memories of his old metal bunch), and the eventual happy outcome was that a DRAGSTER 'retrospective' was hastily assembled by the dependable British Steel concern.

A CD entitled »The Very Best Of Dragster« (where do they get those titles?) has recently been unleashed upon an unsuspecting public, who have now been given the chance to hear a selection of material from the latter part of the persevering outfit's career, although the deliberately vague sleeve notes are a bit irritating, given that they tend to hint that the material might just have been recorded back in the NWOBHM era. Careful, lads, we don't want to set any unhealthy precedents for that sort of thing. Still, the material is remarkably listenable (apart from the pointless inclusion of four well-worn glam standards to pad out the running time), and the *'unreleased album'* compositions are actually some of the best melodic power metal I've heard in a long time, with occasional similarities to SWEET SAVAGE, TOKYO BLADE, EXCALIBUR, VIRTUE and mid-period CLOVEN HOOF. Certainly, the likes of "So This Is England", "Mirror Image" and "Running" all deserve to be heard by a considerably wider range of metal fans than is likely to be the case, so it's a pity they didn't get a deal with someone like SPV or Century Media at the time. I mean, NWOBHM nostalgia is all very well, but it's a minority audience compared to the huge power metal fan base. Mind you, »The Very Best Of Dragster« isn't exactly a perfect release in terms of quality control (I suspect that they succumbed to the temptation to bung on absolutely everything they had at their disposal), and it seems unnecessary to have included alternate versions of several of the featured numbers to make it look more substantial. All in all, though, it's certainly one of British Steel's more worthy offerings thus far.

As an epilogue, it's worth mentioning that the luckless members of DRAGSTER were extremely unfortunate not to have seen their classic "Ambitions" included on Heavy Metal's hurriedly-thrown-together »N.W.O.B.H.M.« commemorative compilation in 1991, as they were the unwitting victims of a legendary (and, on the face of it, inexplicable) cock-up while the selected numbers were being assembled. Although "Ambitions" is credited on the sleeve and record (not that the band received any royalties anyway), the track featured is actually "Captured City" by PRAYING MANTIS, an original which Heavy Metal never, at any stage, had the rights to use. As eagle-eyed reviewers noted at the time, however, both compositions had been featured on Phonogram's celebratory NWOBHM set from the previous year (quite an honour, in DRAGSTER's case, although it transpires that they were never actually asked), both as CD-bonus selections. Hmmm. Perhaps some lazy employee thought they would save a bit of time in looking out the master tapes and hit the wrong button on their CD player…

7" Singles
»**Ambitions**« Heavy Metal 1981
[Issued with either blue or brown labels]

CD's
»**The Very Best Of Dragster**« British Steel 2000
[Compilation of later unissued studio material]

Exclusive Compilation Appearances
"**Do It**" on »Heavy Metal Heroes« LP Heavy Metal 1981 *[Issued in two different sleeves]* + »Heavy Metal Heroes Vol.I&II« CD British Steel 1996

Compilation Appearances
"**Ambitions**" on »NWOBHM '79 Revisited« Do-CD Phonogram 1990 + »Heavy Metal Records Singles Collection Vol.1« CD British Steel 1996
"**Won't Bring You Back**" on »Heavy Metal Records Singles Collection Vol.1« CD British Steel 1996

DRIVESHAFT

Gerry Lane (v,g)
Jeremy Nagle (g)
Noel Murphy (b)
Mike Maher (d)

Proudly flying the flag for Irish metal, the little-remembered DRIVESHAFT initially infiltrated their local rock scene at more or less the height of the NWOBHM influx, and, over the following couple of years, began winning some coveted support slots with certain touring acts from the mainland, notably SAXON and DEF LEPPARD. Even so, they evidently found it quite hard to attract any major-label interest, and eventually went with a small-time local concern called Undercover Records, who sponsored the first slice of DRIVESHAFT vinyl (the obscure »Heartbreaker« single) in 1982, the latter issued in a hand-drawn cover depicting a defenceless pericardium being riven asunder by a cruel pair of hands. Ouch. The pair of tuneful rock/metal tracks on display (any composition called "Heartbreaker" tends to set the alarm bells ringing on the AOR front, but it's not actually that bad) are dominated by the raunchy, bluesy vocals of Gerry Lane, with the overall sound being quite similar in style to the likes of ORE, AFTER DARK or XERO, although the B-side ("Now That It's Over") also hints at a possible SPIDER influence at times. The single was yet another NWOBHM release to be slated unfairly in the pages of 'Kerrang', but you'll no doubt be aware that it's in very good company.

In spite of the adverse publicity, it still got DRIVESHAFT's name into the public eye, and the lads elected to keep plugging away in their quest for fame, although their activities on the live circuit still failed to generate too much label interest. The following year, however, they were ready to unleash another modest vinyl offering, and so the »Live Cutz« (let's ignore the fact that NUTZ had used precisely the same title for one of their albums in the 70's, shall we?) 12" EP was recorded and issued (in a generic, monochrome sleeve with the band logo) on the equally-unrenowned Revolving label in due course. The

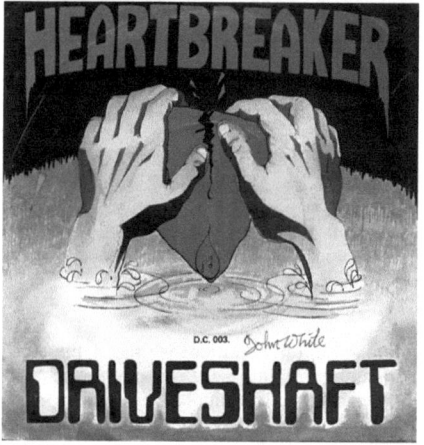

quartet's latest material suggested that they had recently added a slightly harder edge to their sound, with compositions such as "Let It Rock" and "Stepping Stone" eliciting comparisons with TRIDENT and fellow Irish heroes SWEET SAVAGE, for example. The slower and moodier "Take A Chance On Me" (as featured on the »NWOBHM Vol.7« bootleg CD), meanwhile, once again showcases Gerry Lane's impressively powerful vocal talents (not altogether dissimilar to Ronnie James Dio in places), and this extremely capable number additionally possesses a slight THIN LIZZY (predictably enough) tinge in the guitar department. Both the EP and the earlier single (few copies of which appear to have made it to the mainland at any point) are scarcely-seen pieces these days, even in Ireland itself, and each have been known to fetch correspondingly high prices among NWOBHM collectors in recent times.

At some point thereafter, probably in around 1985, Gerry Lane decided to try his luck in England, relocating to London (I reckon Mike Maher may have come with him at first, as a drummer with a suspiciously similar name later had stints with JEROD, LISA DOMINIQUE and VANDAMNE) and establishing an all-new version of DRIVESHAFT with an entirely different set of musicians *viz.* Graham Waxman (ex-LAST FLIGHT) on drums, bassist John Hennessey (ex-SLEDGEHAMMER/ORE) and Fred Avesque (ex-TROY) on guitar. Performing older compositions such as "Let It Rock", "Take A Chance On Me" and "Heartbreaker" alongside newer material such as "Run For Your Life", "Don't Walk Away" and "Dirty Work", the revised outfit won over many an appreciative audience in and around the capital (playing regularly with the likes of CHARIOT, for example) with their energetic and enthusiastic appearances, and it's possible that »Heartbreaker« was actually reissued as a single in 1987 or thereabouts (I seem to recall a review from around this time, although they might just have been repromoting the original release). The outfit won the approval of 'Kerrang' for their live performances, and there was serious talk that DRIVESHAFT might even get around to recording a full LP before much longer. Nevertheless, the luckless bunch ultimately failed to make their big breakthrough, and finally disintegrated in 1988 or thereabouts, with Fred Avesque going on to join ex-BLIND FURY vocalist Lou Taylor in the critically-acclaimed, but short-lived, TOUR DE FORCE.

12" EP's
»**Live Cutz**« Revolving Records 1983

7" Singles
»**Heartbreaker**« Undercover Records 1982

Compilation Appearances
"**Take A Chance On Me**" on »NWOBHM Vol.7« Bootleg CD 1996

DUCHESS

Martin Boyd (v)
Dave Kilminster (g)
Kym Dallaco (b)
Greg Wilson (d)

Thanks to a rather unfortunate piece of spelling, there have been quite a few question marks hanging over the DUCHESS story in the years since their demise. The fact that their one-off single, issued in 1981, consistently credits the band as 'Dutchess' on three separate places on the labels, has led to fairly widespread (but unsubstantiated) speculation that the hapless group might have been forced to alter the spelling of their name at the last minute in order to differentiate between themselves and some other bunch with the same identity. In fact, it would appear that the London quartet were the only outfit known to have laid claim to this particular moniker at the time (in Britain, at least), so all you collectors and enthusiasts shouldn't get too confused about the alternate spellings. The DUCHESS story itself, however, is rather more straightforward, the musicians involved in this ambitious (but short-lived) venture having been little more than minor personalities on the capital's burgeoning rock scene at the turn of the decade. These young hopefuls initially got together at the height of the NWOBHM explosion, recording the obligatory demo tape soon afterwards, although it was to meet with the usual fate of utter indifference from the nation's record companies, who were now being deluged with cassettes from hundreds of small-town nonentities on a weekly basis.

Undeterred, the band eventually scraped together enough cash to finance their own record, and their outstanding »Your Love« 7" was unleashed upon the public in the early part of 1981. The two-tracker represented a truly superb example of songwriting and musicianship, with the A-side (as featured on the »NWOBHM Vol.6« bootleg CD) being an innovatively-structured, atmospheric number reminiscent of GEDDES AXE (with a slight tendency towards heavier LYADRIVE or STAGEFRIGHT material), featuring a highly impressive vocal performance throughout. The upbeat "Dead And Gone", on the reverse, was just as enjoyable, this being a more intense number falling somewhere between PERSIAN RISK and JJ'S POWERHOUSE. All in all, this superb debut offering from DUCHESS acquitted itself impeccably, the single coming across as an extremely capable and distinctive release, revealing the talented outfit to have been operating in a challenging musical area into which few of their (British) contemporaries ventured. The two-tracker (definitely one for the wants list) was released without the extravagance of a picture sleeve, and has very seldom been offered for sale in recent memory, so you probably shouldn't expect to find a copy at a particularly modest price.

Sadly, the largely-overlooked group, who weren't exactly conspicuous in terms of live appearances (although they might well have been doing their thing at locally-publicised events), don't appear to have gone on to greater things (perhaps their material was regarded as slightly too adventurous for many fans of the rough'n'ready archetype), and it looks as though they struggled with personnel problems in the months following the release of their single. Much-travelled session drummer Steve Rodford eventually stepped in towards the end of the group's existence (they also briefly utilised the services of one Pete Martin, a sticksman who later hooked up with the long-lived ENGLISH ROGUES), although I suspect that the DUCHESS empire had pretty much crumbled even before the end of 1982. The majority of the participants appear to have left the scene completely, although the aforementioned Rodford was to continue working in acts such as THE SWEET and VERITY as well as forming the overly-melodic BOMBAY (see separate entry) project a couple of years later. Indeed, the multi-talented individual appears to have called upon one of his erstwhile colleagues (Dave Kilminster, a highly capable axeman) to help out in this rather lightweight venture from time to time, although the guitarist was never a permanent fixture in BOMBAY.

The aforementioned Kilminster, however, didn't stay in the background for too long, and subsequently teamed up with former McCOY vocalist Nikki Brooks in a competent melodic outfit called WILD! (not to be confused with Punky Mendoza's post-HEAVY PETTIN vehicle), who, after coming together in around 1986, persevered for a couple of years without ever achieving a massive amount of critical recognition. Nevertheless, the project (which involved Kilminster adopting the silly stage name 'Dave Wild' for effect) managed to win a 'Friday Rock Show' session along the way, before finally calling it a day at some point in 1988. Kilminster then attempted (in the early months of 1989) to get a revised version of his beloved DUCHESS off the ground once again, but appears to have experienced insurmountable difficulties in attracting any suitable accomplices to assist him in the pursuit of his musical vision, leading to the abandonment of this notion within a fairly short timescale. He now, however, plays in something of a self-styled supergroup called QANGO, the latter featuring certain ex-ASIA and E.L.P. members.

7" Singles
»**Your Love**« Blitzkrieg Waxworks 1981

Compilation Appearances

"Your Love" on »NWOBHM Vol.6« Bootleg CD 1996

DUMPY'S RUSTY NUTS

Graham 'Dumpy' Dunnell (v,g)
Malcolm McKenzie (b)
Chris Hussey (d)

It's fair to say that many bands have their own agenda in terms of the level of fame and fortune they seek to achieve, but it would appear that the long-lived DUMPY'S RUSTY NUTS never really set their sights much further than the humble status of eternal pub rock heroes. The trio were originally formed in mid-1981 by the utterly bonkers Graham 'Dumpy' Dunnell, erstwhile member of a knockabout punk act called THE RIVVETS, the well-travelled frontman (his musical exploits actually stretch back as far as the 60's) seeking to create more of a hard-rocking, lighthearted venture in order to appeal to straight-ahead rock fans and the biker community of the day. In fact, Dumpy had been fronting a bluesy club act called the DIRT BAND immediately prior to the inception of his RUSTY NUTS, so the transition to biker-friendly hard rock wasn't a particularly dramatic or contrived one. The certifiable vocalist was, in the first instance, assisted in the pursuit of his new musical vision by the duo of Chris Hussey (d) and Malcolm McKenzie (b), formerly the rhythm section of NUTHIN FANCY (see separate entry), who had defected immediately prior to the latter's evolution into TERRAPLANE.

After a few well-received jaunts around the pubs and clubs of the nation (initially in and around London, but soon venturing further afield), the first vinyl offering was recorded towards the end of the year, a single which featured the undemanding pairing of "Just For Kicks" and "Ride With Me". Issued on the small Cool King label, this was undoubtedly biker-friendly pub rock at its most unpretentious and rudimentary, although there was certainly something quite endearing about a group who made VARDIS sound like TANGERINE DREAM. After healthy sales of »Just For Kicks«, a second two-tracker was scheduled for release with indecent haste, although the RUSTY NUTS had already endured the first of countless personnel changes, with replacement bassist Jeff Brown (another well-kent personality from London's blues scene) stepping into the shoes of the departed McKenzie, who moved into the management side of things, famously handling the affairs of THUNDER after the demise of TERRAPLANE. The second single followed the blueprint of their debut to the letter, and featured "Boxhill Or Bust" (the title had something to do with biker rallies, apparently) and "It's Got To Be Blues". Famously, this particular single appeared under the name of DUMPY'S RUSTY BOLTS, amidst allegations that their debut had been blacklisted by radio stations because of their supposedly 'risqué' moniker. I've never heard such bollocks in my entire life.

Jeff Brown's tenure was a reasonably brief one, and he was lured away by an offer to join Paul Mario Day's WILDFIRE (see separate entry) in the second half of 1983. Founder member Chris Hussey was also soon on his way, and an all-new rhythm section had been permanently installed by the beginning of 1984. The new recruits were unknown bassist Kerry Langford and erstwhile TANK sticksman Mark Brabbs, and this line-up (which remained stable for almost three years) is generally regarded as the definitive incarnation of DUMPY'S RUSTY NUTS. Even before the end of 1983, however, the revised trio had captured one of their many live outings for posterity, and a deal with the newly-formed Landslide label allowed this show to appear as the »Somewhere In England« double album, the outfit having reverted back to their original moniker of DUMPY'S RUSTY NUTS by this time. This lengthy set was a pretty accurate representation of an energetic, self-effacing and humorous bunch who were just as happy to play a variety of crowd-pleasing covers (e.g. "Route 66", "Wild Thing" and "Tush") as their own repertoire of self-penned compositions. As well as being the year in which the band supported none other than VENOM (!) at the latter's debut British appearance, 1984 also saw the release of an EP (issued, for some inexplicable reason, under the abbreviated moniker of DUMPY) entitled »Rock The Nation«, which featured studio versions of some of the trio's more popular stage favourites. Sales were remarkably brisk, showing that you didn't necessarily have to be the most innovative combo on the face of the planet in order to cultivate a strong following. As Mark Brabbs later theorised, the bulk of the outfit's appeal was down to their non-starry aspirations: 'When I was with TANK, we got so sick and tired of going to see bands with spray-on jeans, permed hair down their backs and all the old HM poses that we used to rebel against it and put on a much more down-to-earth gig.' (Ref: Kerrang No.70, June 1984).

After the success of »Somewhere In England« (which was later reissued by the little-known Gas Music, who also released an EP called »Hot Lover« in 1985), the lads wisely concluded that they were best-suited to releases which were heavily based around live performances. Having said that, even the outfit's studio material had the feel of an impromptu jam-session, so it's not as though DUMPY'S RUSTY NUTS were a fundamentally different proposition the minute they stepped off stage. Nevertheless, their subsequent product (a couple of albums and a handful of official videos) were heavily biased in favour of live recordings, something which probably worked to their considerable advantage in the long term. The lads were soon to become national television stars, however, thanks to an ill-judged invitation to appear on the 'E.C.T.' show in mid-1985, where the assembled masses were treated to versions of "Hot Lover" and "Boxhill Or Bust", although I suspect that the majority of those present didn't really know how seriously they were supposed to take this troupe of loonies. In spite of this extremely high-profile appearance, however, the outfit rapidly began to fragment (Dumpy's *'interesting'* behaviour was cited as a contributory factor on more than one occasion), with the once-stable line-up of the preceding few years becoming increasingly discontinuous as time progressed, with numerous reshuffles (not to mention the odd guest appearance just to confuse everyone) occurring along the way.

By 1987, the crackpot frontman was being assisted by bassist Alan Fish and drummer Mick Kirton (Mark Brabbs had now departed for pastures new, some of his other credits including THE BLOOD, PAUL SAMSON'S EMPIRE and UK), both of whom had been recruited from the ranks of the GROUNDHOGS. Later that same year, their second long-player hit the shops (the incessant touring schedule included an eventful jaunt with strange bedfellows VOW WOW and TIGERTAILZ), this coming in the shape of another knockabout and humour-laden offering entitled »Get Out On The Road« (including a peculiar cover of "Hawkwind", where they were ably assisted by certain HAWKWIND personnel themselves), issued on the Metal Masters label. As usual, it sold to all the dedicated fans but made no threats to appeal to anything resembling a mass market, and that seemed to suit DUMPY'S RUSTY NUTS just fine. By 1988, however, yet another rhythm section had been assembled (I'm not suggesting that the increasingly-mad Dumpy, who even took to the stage in a wedding dress or fairy costume from time to time, was difficult to work with or anything), this time consisting of the relatively unknown duo of bass player Graham Le Mon and drummer Andy Smith (the departed Mick Kirton, incidentally, later worked with HAWKWIND, while Alan Fish formed the oddly-named AUTOLAND COMMAND, who eventually became EGYPT). Yet another live release, the punningly-titled »Firkin Well Live« LP, was duly trundled out for the Razor label, although the annual DUMPY'S RUSTY NUTS album now seemed to be coming as a matter of obligation.

By the turn of the decade, however, the persevering group (who had, in the interim, employed the services of another couple of short-term bassists, ex-MONTERREZ member Jim Houghton and HAWKWIND's guesting Alan Davey, plus erstwhile CLOVEN HOOF bod Mick Grafton in the unusual capacity of second guitarist) had long since passed their peak of popularity, and those fondly-remembered open-air appearances (notably the Kerrang Festival in 1984, where they were joined by HAWKWIND's Nik Turner, and the Reading Festival of 1987) and their well-attended national tours were now a thing of the past. Nevertheless, the lads carried on unabashed, and took the slightly surprising decision to release their first single in almost a decade, when they recorded a cover of "Run Run Run" (the popular JO JO GUNNE number from 1972) and their own "Rock City" for release on A Side Records in 1991. For reasons unknown, however, very few finished copies (either of the 7" or 12" version) actually made it into circulation, suggesting that some sort of major problem affected either the distribution or the pressing itself. Whatever the story, it was all a bit of an embarrassment, and it seems to have put an end to the outfit's programme of official releases. Surprisingly, DUMPY'S RUSTY NUTS are still a going concern on the club scene, regularly playing to small-but-appreciative audiences whenever the opportunity comes their way. I've no idea who else is actually in the group nowadays, and, aside from a couple of fairly obscure compilation appearances in the 90's, there has been precious little for their fans to spend their money on in recent times. Here's to the next twenty years...

LP's
»Somewhere In England« Landslide Records 1984
[Double live album, original issue in gatefold sleeve]
»Somewhere In England« Gas Music 1986
[Double live album, reissue in single sleeve]
»Get Out On The Road« Metal Masters 1987
»Firkin Well Live« Razor 1988
[Live album]

Mini-LP's
»Hot Lover« Gas Music 1985

12" EP's
»Rock The Nation« Landslide Records 1984
[Under the name of DUMPY]
»Run Run Run« A Side Records 1991
[With three versions of A-side, "Run Run Run" and "Rock City" both non-LP]

7" Singles
»Just For Kicks« Cool King 1982
»Box Hill Or Bust« Cool King 1982
[Under the name of DUMPY'S RUSTY BOLTS, first two singles later reissued as limited edition double pack]
»Run Run Run« A Side Records 1991
[Both tracks non-LP]

Exclusive Compilation Appearances
"Cowshit Under Me Wheels" on »Voice Of The Street« CD Pub City Royal 1995

Compilation Appearances
"Shnibob" on »Metal Killers Kollection III« Do-LP Castle Communications 1988
"Hot Lover" on »Metal Masters« 4-CD Box Castle Communications 1993
"Box Hill Or Bust" on »Metal Masters« 4-CD Box Castle Communications 1993

EARTHBOUND

Line-up unknown

A real obscurity, this, with no picture sleeve and a distinct paucity of information on the label itself. We're back in prog/metal territory here (see AVALON and CHEMICAL ALICE, for example), although it's certainly the type of music that would be of interest to a fair few NWOBHM enthusiasts. EARTHBOUND, having come out of nowhere before delivering a self-financed 7" at some point in 1984, are a complete mystery, although their single wasn't a bad effort at all. "The Prophet" gives rise to one of the most facile comparisons in this entire book, namely MARQUIS DE SADE's "Somewhere Up In The Mountains"; believe me, these tracks are very (and I repeat, *very*) similar, although EARTHBOUND are rather more melodic and catchy in their general approach. The lyrics, dealing with *'cosmic power'* and *'energy'* (we're on a SACRED ALIEN tip here, obviously) are undeniably repetitive and vacuous, but that's par for the course with this style of metal (*cf.* MARQUIS DE SADE and their grand universal plan of, er, going up a hill and listening to some records). "I Believe", on the other hand, is their attempt at something a bit epic, but which comes across as a fairly average combination of "A Whiter Shade Of Pale" and "Freebird". This is a rare single, admittedly, and few copies have ever surfaced, although I reckon most NWOBHM collectors would tend to go for something heavier, given the choice.

Clearly, EARTHBOUND's vinyl debut failed to turn them into superstars overnight, although this bunch were probably content to do their thing for small, appreciative audiences. The outfit certainly persevered for a good few years, sharing a stage with emergent hopefuls such as FULL MOON (the progressively-inclined group from Surrey, that is) in London as late as 1986, no doubt developing their own loyal following along the way. In the end, though, they possibly failed to match the luminaries of the prog scene in terms of creative ability or longevity, and presumably called it a day long before the end of the decade. It's also worth noting, in passing, that a group called EARTHBOUND was to be found gigging in the capital in the late 70's (they put out a single entitled »The Robot« in 1979), although it's extremely unlikely (given that the latter's style was quirky new wave with female vocals) that this might have been an earlier incarnation of the obscure outfit currently under discussion. In any case, »The Prophet« certainly isn't a record for the headbangers, but those of you who appreciate things slightly more restrained and cerebral may find a friend in EARTHBOUND.

7" Singles

»The Prophet« Private 1984

EAZIE RYDER

Geoff Bate (v,g)
Graham Wall (v,b)
Tony Bate (v,d)

One of the very first rock outfits to cotton on to the fact that sticking a picture of a motorbike on the cover of your single and penning basic ditties about the joy of cruising down the highway on two wheels was a surefire way of selling records, Midlands band EAZIE RYDER (if you don't know where that name comes from, kindly hang your head in shame) got in on the game as far back as 1978 (having formed only a short time earlier), predating the initial NWOBHM explosion to some degree. In this case, however, the threesome (who had more or less evolved from an unrenowned rock/pop proposition called the YOUNG ONES) didn't even pen the A-side themselves, electing instead to cover CHRIS SPEDDING's "Motorbikin'" (which was, incidentally, recorded by ROGUE MALE in later years), a popular chart hit (also invariably used in Public Information Films ever since, warning people about the mind-numbingly-obvious dangers of crashing into trees at high velocity) from 1975. EAZIE RYDER's version is, unsurprisingly, virtually identical to the original, so their 7" (the inaugural release on the diverse Graduate label, responsible for some real shockers in years to come) is one for the collection if you're remotely partial to the likes of CENTURION, ROADSTER, DUMPY'S RUSTY NUTS and their ilk, although it's interesting to note that the reverse ("City Lights") sees the trio attempting a slightly less flippant style, this being an upbeat, boogie-tinged number with a rather more polished vocal performance and a considerably better arrangement.

It's fair to say that EAZIE RYDER (not to be confused with the little-remembered EZY RYDER, a cosmopolitan act who released the seldom-seen »Power« album in the early 80's) were never the most high-profile combo on Britain's post-punk scene, although they were indeed a hard-working ensemble with their thoughts on the possibility of landing a major deal. Even so, well-received support slots with the GROUNDHOGS, SLADE and the ERIC BELL BAND (not to mention a successful appearance on a televised talent contest) failed to attract enough label interest to facilitate a follow-up to their vinyl debut. By the turn of the decade, the outfit had pretty much run its course, at which point the three protagonists went their own separate ways with little acrimony and few regrets, although it was only a couple of years before one of the lads resurfaced in a noteworthy metal concern, namely local stalwarts QUARTZ (restructuring in the aftermath of Mick Taylor's departure), who found themselves being fronted by Geoff Bate on their »Against All Odds« comeback LP. The multi-talented chap turned in a convincing enough performance on this occasion, showing his ability to adapt to more sophisticated material, but it still wasn't enough to save the struggling heavyweights from imminent demise, and they too were forced to hang up their boots within a matter of months.

Fortunately, though, that wasn't quite the end of the road for the persevering frontman, who wasn't yet ready to sever all links with the music business. After lying low for a few years, Geoff subsequently teamed up with new sidekick Colin Fidoe and resurrected the (correctly-spelled) EASY RIDER identity. Sad to say, however, this particular duo have nothing to do with rock or metal, and have been capitalising (immensely successfully, it must be stated) on the inexplicable popularity of country music in this part of the world, delivering numerous CD's purely for the benefit of the line-dancing community. Shocking. Even so, Geoff harbours a reassuring desire to remain involved with the rock scene on a fundamental level, and is preparing for a long-overdue return to live work even as we speak. Erstwhile friend and colleague Graham Wall, meanwhile, still takes to the stage with an easy-going covers concern called SPLINTER, whereas Tony Bate also continues to be engaged as a session drummer (recently assisting RAYMOND FROGGATT, for example), so it's unusual to be able to report that all of the original members of EAZIE RYDER are still musically active.

7" Singles

»Motorbikin'« Graduate Records 1978

EAZY STREET

Mick Castle (d)

Not to be confused with the not-remotely-interesting EASY STREET, a mainstream bunch whose main claim to notoriety was issuing an extraordinarily lightweight album of MOR called »Under The Glass« on the Polydor label in 1977, Yorkshire's little-remembered EAZY STREET unleashed a cracking 7" single sometime in the early/mid-80's that takes some beating in terms of anonymity. No picture sleeve, no date, no writing credits, no studio details, just the bare minimum of band name and song titles. Great, that sort of thing *really* makes my job easy. Never mind, the music more than compensates for the complete lack of information imparted by the record itself. The main focus of attention in this case is "Quest For Glory", an exceptionally classy and well-constructed slower number bringing to mind CRYER or BLEAK HOUSE, with an excellent vocal performance throughout and an anthemic chorus as a bonus. The poignant lyrics, dealing with the hopes and dreams of a young soldier, would surely bring a tear to a glass eye, and serve as a pleasant contrast to the typical NWOBHM subject matter (*i.e.* singing about lovely, saucy *'ladies'* or, alternatively, bad men doing naughty things with sharp objects in dark alleyways), so several bonus points are awarded for originality.

Meanwhile, the unabashed title of the flipside ("Let 'Em Rock") says it all, really, this equally-enjoyable composition representing a completely different style altogether. This one charges along at a hectic pace (musically speaking, somewhere between TORTURE and HIGH TREASON), with the *'isn't this jolly rock music thing really quite spiffing, actually'* sentiments almost making you want to put on some spandex trousers/patchy denim jacket/studded wristband/bullet belt (with apologies to those of you who dress like this on a daily basis) and have a good old-fashioned, fist-shaking *headbang*! A vastly underrated single, and one which can often be picked up considerably more inexpensively than some of the musically-inferior *'monsters'* whose price tags are now well into three figures. The critically-ignored EAZY STREET are known to have gone their separate ways at the beginning of 1986, suggesting that their one-off single had probably been released at some point in the previous couple of years, although the outfit's activities were never reported with any degree of comprehensiveness in the music press, so I guess they were never serious contenders. Drummer Mick Castle subsequently joined fellow Yorkshire obscurities VIXEN (no, not that lot), although the identity and fate of the other members remains a mystery for the time being.

7" Singles

»Quest For Glory« Private 198?

EF BAND

Pär Ericson (v,b)
Bengt Fischer (g)
Dave Dufort (d)

It would be extremely difficult to justify the exclusion of Sweden's EF BAND from this volume, as they became inextricably linked with the NWOBHM movement from an early stage, particularly when they began releasing their records on British labels and touring the UK in preference to their homeland. Their story goes back to the mid-70's, when mainmen Pär Ericson and Bengt Fischer were playing in a Gothenburg-based jazz-rock ensemble called EPIZOOTIC, an act who released just one record in their time, a seldom-seen effort entitled »Daybreak«. In around 1978, the duo parted company with their musical associates and set out to form a more hard-rocking venture of their own. The *'Ericson-Fischer Band'* (later abbreviated to the more familiar EF BAND) came into existence shortly thereafter, when they were joined by another local musician as a temporary drummer. In the early months of 1979, the trio began mounting a few reconnaissance missions to the UK mainland in order to check out the burgeoning metal scene, and duly became affiliated with the small-time Rok label (more familiar for their patronage of punk acts), who invited them to lay down a couple of numbers for future use. In the event, "Night Angel" and "Another Day Gone" were supplied, and the label kept their part of the bargain by issuing a split 7" (a device which pretty much became synonymous with Rok) which saw "Another Day Gone" coupled with "October Friday" by a little-known ensemble called SYNCHROMESH.

All things considered, the EF BAND's music (on the evidence provided by their early releases, at least) wasn't particularly representative of the NWOBHM ethos, being more of a traditional heavy rock variant, although it had a fair bit in common with other 70's-influenced acts of the time such as ETHEL THE FROG, SMOKIN ROADIE or QUARTZ. Nevertheless, their material went down like a lead balloon in their homeland, where the hefty stuff had yet to come into its element and where pop and jazz-rock still ruled the roost. Not only that, the treacherous musicians had committed the cardinal sin of not singing in their native tongue, which resulted in a pretty severe backlash at the time. With the citizens of Sweden having basically rejected the hapless EF BAND outright, it's fair to say that their vinyl debut failed to make front-page headlines at home. Undeterred, the lads concluded that they would stand a far greater chance of success in the UK, and were soon organising their first British tour. With an impressive lack of foresight, however, their occasional sticksman concluded that it wouldn't be worth making the trip, leaving Ericson and Fischer to come to London and seek out a new drummer to assist them in their quest for fame and fortune. Somewhat fortuitously, a likely candidate emerged in the form of the much-travelled Dave Dufort, a veteran of numerous recording and touring acts, dating back to the late 60's in the first instance.

With a stable unit having been established once more, the trio began gigging fairly extensively throughout the UK, and duly appointed a new manager who, apart from organising a fan club for the band, was soon helping to get the lads a proper deal. In due course, the offer came from the small Redball label (responsible for the first VARDIS EP, the UNDER THE SUN album and numerous punk/indie releases), and the EF BAND were soon hard at work in the studio once again. They were rewarded for their efforts with two singles, »Self Made Suicide« (b/w "Sister Syne") and »The Devil's Eye« (b/w "Comprende"), both of which sold in eminently respectable quantities by mail order and at gigs. For most of the following two years, the outfit were primarily based in England, and gigs with the likes of ANGEL WITCH saw the fans coming to regard them as *bona fide* members of the NWOBHM movement as time went on. Moving into 1980, the musicians finally realised that they had been accepted as honorary British scenesters when their activities came to the attention of EMI, who were seeking out new home-grown talent to feature on their first »Metal For Muthas« compilation. Within a short space of time, the threesome had laid down the freshly-penned "Fighting For Rock'n'Roll" at EMI's own studio facility, and the track was duly included on the album as promised. In due course, their »Night Angel« single (featuring the two numbers they had originally given to Rok) was issued by Aerco (it was even promoted with a prominent *'as featured on Metal For Muthas'* legend on the front cover), and, in spite of this being a fairly cynical cash-in which appeared without the band's permission, it performed pretty respectably.

With the EF BAND now having set out their musical stall in no uncertain terms, they were to get their just reward within a matter of months when the influential Mercury label stepped in with an offer to handle the outfit's affairs and subsidise the recording of a full album. The label's first move, however, was to reissue »The Devil's Eye« in repackaged form, before the lads were ushered into the studio to start work on their full-length debut. Before this could happen, however, they found themselves looking for another new drummer, as recent addition Dave Dufort had defected (at the end of 1980) to the ranks of ANGEL WITCH in the interim. In the wake of the sticksman's sudden departure, the central duo welcomed newcomer Dag Eliason (another Swede) to the fold, and the newly-established version of the EF BAND were soon laying down an album's worth of material (at home in Gothenburg) in the early months of 1981. The long-player emerged under the rather caustic title of »Last Laugh Is On You«, the lyrics to the opening lines of the title track leaving the listener in no doubt as to the band's attitude towards their many detractors:

'We been struggling for many a year
We been through a hell of a lot
People have turned us down in fear
But we never give up playing rock.'

Well, no points whatsoever for lyrical subtlety, but it got the message across pretty succinctly. Ironically, however, Sweden had now finally caught up with Britain in terms of its appreciation of heavy music (it even boasted a burgeoning rock scene of its own), and the EF BAND were now being received with open arms by a whole new generation of metalheads in their homeland. Funny how things turn out sometimes, isn't it? The outfit's debut set was, in spite of a slightly restricted distribution, something of a success throughout mainland Europe (»Last Laugh Is On You« was, in the main, a far more upbeat and listenable affair than might have been anticipated on the basis of their early recordings, although the stand-out cut was surely the lengthy "Anything For You"), and the EF BAND were even subsequently invited to support the mighty RAINBOW on their latest jaunt through Scandinavia. The times they were a-changin'…

In the early months of 1982, the lads were given further exposure in the 'Armed And Ready' section of 'Kerrang' (about three years too late, admittedly), and they were soon making a series of visits to the studio once again in order to prepare the groundwork for their second album. However, the members had come to a mutual decision that it might be an idea to experiment with a dedicated vocalist for the first time, and so new frontman John Ridge (an English exile who had latterly been performing with little success in Germany) was drafted in to do the honours. It seems to have worked out pretty well in the long run, and the result of several recording sessions undertaken over a period of five months (they didn't exactly hurry themselves, did they?) was the »Deep Cut« long-player, released on the Swedish-based Ewita label and distributed through Neon in the UK. Surprisingly, it saw something of a fairly dramatic shift towards more accessible and melodic numbers (including two Russ Ballard compositions, "Is Anybody There" and "Love Is A Game", the latter having already been interpreted by GIRL), and it has to be said that the vocal performance wasn't entirely convincing in places. It was a very patchy affair, veering from the capable ("Tonight's Alright" and "Trinity", occasionally reminiscent of JAMESON RAID or the TYGERS OF PAN TANG) to the dismal ("Sail Away", for example), and its poor reception from major sections of the listening public could easily have spelled the end for the EF BAND.

Nevertheless, the lads persevered, gigging furiously over the next couple of years and even winning a coveted support slot with SAXON in the process. By the second half of 1984, however, the outfit had undergone a further piece of rationalisation, with a variety of singers (whose names are now long-forgotten) having been tried out in the wake of John Ridge's decision to move on. Not only that, a handful of second guitarists (including such non-famous individuals as Tony Borg) came and went, bringing the average EF BAND membership up to five for the first time. In the end, though, experienced English frontman Roger Marsden (whose numerous former credits had included DEEP MACHINE, ANGEL WITCH, BORDELLO, KAMIKAZE and NEVADA FOXX) was given the shout, and the recruitment of talented second guitarist Anders Allhage brought a slightly greater level of stability to proceedings. Seemingly out of nowhere, a deal with Mausoleum came the outfit's way, and they wasted little time before locking themselves away in the studio yet again, before emerging with the »One Night Stand« album, housed in a sleeve which pictured the quintet as glammed-up leather boys (you can almost see the embarrassment in poor old Roger Marsden's eyes as one of his colleagues gropes his torso), a huge mistake which can hardly have projected the right image for these well-worn musicians.

Actually, it wasn't a complete abomination after all, with Marsden coming across as the group's most competent frontman to date, although the fairly primitive, semi-anthemic arrangements failed to showcase his capabilities to their full extent. It was also a very short album, suggesting that the lads might have been struggling to come up with all that many usable compositions by that stage, although efforts such as the energetic "Gimme Just A Little Rock'n'Roll", "Toll Of The Bell" and "Cold Heart Of The City" were probably as close as the outfit had ever come to the NWOBHM archetype. In spite of its off-putting cover, therefore, »One Night Stand« is probably the EF BAND album which can be most heartily recommended to the average NWOBHM fan. Sadly, however, things began to fall apart within a fairly short timescale, and the activities of the EF BAND became less and less prominent over the ensuing months. In the end, the inevitable split came around a year after their last album had been released, the band falling victim to internal difficulties and hassles with record companies which made further vinyl offerings a virtual impossibility. There have, nevertheless, been whisperings that there might be a get-together of the EF BAND (Roger Marsden officially gave up his musical career after a one-off DEEP MACHINE reunion in the late 80's) for a gig or two in the near future, so you might not have seen the last of them just yet.

LP's
»**Last Laugh Is On You**« Mercury 1981
»**Deep Cut**« Ewita 1982/Neon 1982
[Swedish/UK issue]
»**One Night Stand**« Mausoleum 1985

7" Singles
»**Another Day Gone**« Rok Records 1979
[Split single, B-side by SYNCHROMESH, "Another Day Gone" non-LP]
»**Self Made Suicide**« Redball Records 1979
[Both tracks non-LP]
»**The Devil's Eye**« Redball Records 1980
[Original UK issue, both tracks non-LP]
»**Night Angel**« Aerco Records 1980
[Both tracks non-LP]
»**The Devil's Eye**« Mercury 1980
[European reissue with different sleeve]

CD's
»**One Night Stand**« Mausoleum Classix 1994
[Unofficial release]

Exclusive Compilation Appearances
"**Fighting For Rock'n'Roll**" on »Metal For Muthas« LP EMI 1980/CD Airraid 2000 + »The Bible Of Hard Rock« CD Toshiba 1990

Compilation Appearances

"Night Angel" on »NWOBHM Vol.2« Bootleg CD 1992 + »N.W.O.B.H.M. Metal Rarities Vol.2« CD British Steel 1996
"Another Day Gone" on »N.W.O.B.H.M. Metal Rarities Vol.2« CD British Steel 1996

ELIXIR

Paul Taylor (v)
Norman Gordon (g)
Phil Denton (g)
Kevin Dobbs (b)
Nigel Dobbs (d)

London's ELIXIR, despite being relative latecomers to the music scene, were probably the last British band to have been hailed as a classic NWOBHM outfit, which is something of an honour. Initially conceived as far back as late 1983 by a trio of East End musicians *viz.* Phil Denton and the Dobbs brothers pairing of Kevin and Nigel, the fledgling outfit toyed with various dubious monikers (*e.g.* RITUAL and HELLFIRE) and personnel (including a female vocalist, one Sally Pike, in their early days), before settling on the excellent Paul Taylor, formerly the frontman in MIDAS (see separate entry), and guitarist Norman Gordon, an Irish import who, like most of his fellow countrymen, claimed to have been a member of SWEET SAVAGE in the dim and distant past. With the quintet becoming firmly established under the name of ELIXIR by the end of 1984, the lads set about delighting the audiences of London (and beyond) with compositions such as "Playing With Fire", "The Idol" and "Deal With The Devil", none of which would ever make it to the vinyl stage, such was their rapid turnover of material in this formative period. Developing an impressive, twin-guitar sound reminiscent of early TOKYO BLADE, VIRTUE or PROWLER, the youngsters rapidly assumed their rightful place in the capital's small-but-dedicated 'true metal' scene alongside CHARIOT, DESOLATION ANGELS, the relocated DRIVESHAFT and the resurrected ANGEL WITCH.

A speculative demo tape, featuring "Dead Man's Gold", "Deal With The Devil" and the never-officially-released "Born Loser", was circulated amongst journalists in due course, and copies also sold like proverbial hot cakes (I've often wondered why the world isn't full of *'hot cake shops'*, given that they're apparently in such universal demand) amongst the metal-loving public in the UK and Europe. Inevitably, the emerging ensemble were conveniently written off as *'IRON MAIDEN clones'* by certain lazy individuals, although it doesn't really seem to have hampered their progress too severely, as Phil Denton explained: *'CBS saw us a couple of times and Neat liked the tape but didn't want to sign us at the time and we didn't want to wait.'* (Ref: Mega Metal Kerrang No.3, 1986). With the outfit desperate to get some vinyl product onto the market, they ultimately decided to release

their own single, coupling "Treachery" with "Winds Of Time". This turned out to be an excellent offering (issued in a distinctive red picture cover with a medieval image) which, as Paul Miller pointed out in the aforementioned magazine article, owes a significant debt to the likes of DIO and RAINBOW with regard to the powerful-but-melodic arrangements. As you'll no doubt be aware if you're a serious collector of the genre, this piece of vinyl is a scarcely-seen, highly-valued commodity today.

On the basis of their single, the lucky outfit deservedly won the valuable patronage of Tommy Vance, and subsequently received the offer to record a session for the now-legendary 'Friday Rock Show'. With their truly excellent session being broadcast on the 28th of February 1986, the lads took the chance to showcase some newer material, and so "Hold High The Flame", "Pandora's Box", "Son Of Odin" and "Star Of Beshaan" were duly unleashed upon the nation's rock fans, most of whom registered their approval. Everything now seemed to be going according to plan, although there was, for some reason, still no record deal on the horizon, leaving the lads in something of a quandary. With the public response to the »Treachery« 7" and the recent radio session having been overwhelmingly positive (their single had also won a couple of beneficial mentions in 'Sounds'), however, the musicians ultimately decided to take the bull by the horns and, borrowing a great deal of money with which to finance the project, set about recording their debut album. The resulting LP (»The Son Of Odin«) appeared later in 1986, featuring all four session tracks plus "Treachery", "Children Of Tomorrow", "Trial By Fire" and "Starflight" (some of their stage favourites), and this capable record (housed in an excellent cover) turned out to be an immensely well-received effort, selling abundantly at the likes of 'Shades' and by mail order (the latter coordinated by their tireless manager, Seymour Mincer) from the outset. In fact, it seemed that nobody had a bad word to say against ELIXIR, which was a pretty remarkable state of affairs.

Moving into 1987, the lads were riding the crest of a wave, playing regular gigs to appreciative crowds around the country, running a fan club and being enthused over by Tommy Vance (who even played a new ELIXIR track, "Louise", from an acetate demo on his weekly show) and the rock press in general. Quizzed on the state of the state of the nation's metal scene, Paul Taylor was happy to offer his opinion: *'There seems to be a distinct lack of mainstream new talent. You've either got your 100mph thrash bands or your middle-of-the-road rock, so I think that we'd both agree that it's looking pretty unhealthy at the present time. A good few years back there seemed to be more of an opportunity for new acts, say for example when MAIDEN and SAXON were first picked up, but now things are pretty stagnant to say the least.'* (Ref: Metal Forces No.23, May 1987). Even so, ELIXIR went from strength to strength, and also saw two live tracks ("Pandora's Box" and "Son Of Odin", both recorded in Folkestone the previous year) featured on the impossible-to-find video compilation »The Power Cuts« (if anyone has this, by the way, I'd really like a copy), which was a perfectly good idea in theory, but turned out to be a project which ultimately failed to promote any of the featured bands to a significant extent. There's probably a stockpile of those tapes sitting in a junk shop somewhere...

With most, if not all, of the material scheduled for release on the outfit's second LP having been written by mid-1987, it was to come as a bit of a shock when internal difficulties within the ELIXIR camp eventually culminated in the departure of the Dobbs brothers, who later went on to form an ill-fated melodic outfit called SARATOGA. With an extended visit to the recording studio (to lay down the album demos) already on the cards for the ELIXIR lads, meanwhile, the remaining musicians drafted in replacement bassist Mark White (previously a member of JOKER and SCHUTT) and journeyman drummer Clive Burr (who hadn't been up to much lately) to restore ELIXIR to quorate status. The recording sessions were duly completed by mid-1988, although the luckless outfit were yet to find a suitable label to issue their LP, already tentatively titled »Sovereign Remedy«. In the event, it was a mind-boggling two years (during which time the outfit also parted company with their long-serving manager) before the Sonic label picked up the rights to the masters, and the album, retitled »Lethal Potion«, finally reached the shops. Strangely, the long-player featured a prominent sticker stating *'featuring Clive Burr ex-IRON MAIDEN'* (as if this was the major selling-point), although another ex-SWEET SAVAGE bloke, Stevie Hughes, had actually been appointed as full-time drummer by this stage.

Compared with the stellar debut LP, it was something of a comedown, although »Lethal Potion« was undeniably a respectable enough release in its own right. While the likes of "Sovereign Remedy", "Llagaeran" and "Light In Your Heart" certainly hark back to former glories, tuneful efforts such as "She's Got It" and "Louise" (the excellent riff from the latter seems to have inspired IN FLAMES, as evidenced by "Dead Eternity" from their »The Jester Race« masterpiece) suggested a slight tendency to experiment with rather more commercial numbers. It mattered not one jot, however, as the journalists decreed that, while this sort of musical and lyrical stance might have been perfectly acceptable in 1986, it was totally out of place in the cynical days of 1990. Sadly, the world had moved on in the interim, and ELIXIR were now regarded as an anachronism of the most despised kind. The group had already been stretched to breaking point by the monumental delay in getting the second album released, and were rightly irked by the realisation that their compositions hadn't stood the test of time too well. Utterly dejected, the lads called it quits shortly thereafter, and the various members all seem to have drifted away from the music scene since then. Never mind, lads, you'll always have a place in the heart of the true NWOBHM fan.

LP's
»The Son Of Odin« Elixir Records 1986
»Lethal Potion« Sonic Records 1990

7" Singles
»Treachery« Elixir Records 1985
[B-side "Winds Of Time" non-LP]

CD's
»**Lethal Potion**« Sonic Records 1990

Compilation Appearances
"**Treachery**" on »NWOBHM Vol.6« Bootleg CD 1992

EMERSON

Sam Blewitt (v)
Stu Emerson (g)
Bri Emerson (b)
Dru Irving (k)
Jon Sellers (d)

In spite of their rather inadvisable, semi-glam image, Tyneside's lightweight EMERSON (their handle, rather obviously, having been derived from the surname of two of the band's founder members) weren't quite such an awful outfit as most people seem to think, although they might have been an unusual choice to be snapped up (fairly soon after their formation, by the looks of things) by their local label, Neat Records. Certainly, the quintet deviated from the traditionally heavier 'Neat sound' quite considerably, and their debut single (coupling "Something Special" with "Stars In Hollywood") didn't exactly become a big seller for the label, but their melodic brand of rock (in the manner of BRUNEL, V8 or TUXEDO, for example) was quite capably written and performed, with some undeniably powerful vocals being supplied by erstwhile AXIS mouthpiece Sam Blewitt. With their Neat deal having been a one-off opportunity (drummer Jon Sellers had, incidentally, been replaced by former BLACK ROSE/TAURUS sticksman Charlie MacKenzie shortly after the recording session which yielded the single) to promote themselves to the masses, the lads were soon being left to fend for themselves, although, before long, they were getting plenty of offers to play at various rock venues.

As a direct result, EMERSON proceeded to undertake a fairly successful and widespread British tour in the opening months of 1984, after which they recorded a brand-new demo featuring "Maybe Someday", "Killer On The Line" and "Girl In My Dreams", which was soon drawing a limited amount of praise from various parties in the rock press. After this spate of activity, however, EMERSON gradually seemed to fade away in terms of their presence on the nation's club scene, and subsequently kept something of a low profile while contemplating their future. It's entirely possible that they relocated to London (given their later connections with certain bands from the capital, notably SAMSON) in order to seek out a life-saving deal, but it looks as though the lads met with limited success. Mind you, they turned up rather unexpectedly on a patchy Zebra compilation (entitled »The Best Of British«) in 1985, where the aforementioned "Maybe Someday" was trundled out for inspection. This unashamedly commercial contribution didn't fare too well in the company of better-known heavyweights such as PERSIAN RISK, JAGUAR, SAVAGE and LIMELIGHT, though, and this appears to have been EMERSON's last vinyl output.

Vocalist Sam Blewitt (aka Sam Blue) jumped ship relatively shortly thereafter (going on to join PAUL SAMSON'S EMPIRE), and was replaced by little-known newcomer Mick White, so it looks as though EMERSON probably struggled on valiantly for another year or two, without ever achieving a great deal of recognition. In the long term, however, I reckon the group must have collapsed at some point in 1987 or thereabouts, whereupon both Mick White and Charlie MacKenzie also proceeded to join forces (as it were) with Paul Samson (by this time, the latter's group had reverted back to their original SAMSON identity), meaning that White had (spookily enough) contrived to succeed Blewitt on two separate occasions! Undeterred, however, the aforementioned Blewitt moved over to a revived version of the more mainstream act YA YA (who went on to release a critically-ignored LP shortly thereafter), while obliging bassist Bri Emerson later helped out in one of the many line-ups of the legendary-but-faltering TYGERS OF PAN TANG, before teaming up with Jess Cox and Robb Weir in their ill-fated TYGER TYGER offshoot.

7" Singles
»**Something Special**« Neat 1983

Exclusive Compilation Appearances
"**Maybe Someday**" on »The Best Of British« LP Zebra 1985

ENERGY

Ian Wetherell
Steve Fulton
Mark Stewart
Boz Bosnic

You may find this quite hard to believe, but Northamptonshire's ENERGY (who shouldn't be confused with Ginger Baker's early 80's project of the same name, which, at one time, featured various future members of JODY ST.) were, in fact, one of NWOBHM's most prolific minor acts, with a grand total of five private releases under their collective belts. Indeed, their best-known track, the excellent "Fight For Your Freedom" (first brought to prominence on the »NWOBHM Vol.5« bootleg), is actually the B-side of their *third* 7", and isn't, in truth, particularly representative of the band's general direction of choice. With the participants having initially come together at the tail end of the 70's, ENERGY were a going concern for a relatively short space of time before they thought about making an impact on their regional rock community with a modest slice of vinyl. Their debut emerged in the heady days of 1980, and this extremely scarce offering took the form of a strictly limited 7" EP (»Energised«), the latter featuring the original selections "No-Go", "Don't Show Your Face", "Spoilt Child" and "Lovely Lady". At this stage, however, it's perfectly clear that the outfit (assisted, on the writing side of things, by a certain Bip Wetherell) were still attempting to find their musical feet, electing to open their account with a rudimentary, accessible bunch of rockers with a distinct 70's feel.

In general, the overwhelming influence in ENERGY's music at this specific juncture would undoubtedly have been THIN LIZZY, while their closest NWOBHM allies were certainly MEANSTREAK and AURORA. Still, it was very much the sort of thing that appealed to a fair proportion of the nation's rock fans, and it paved the way for the group to develop more of an individualistic style as they gradually progressed and grew in confidence. In fact, even by the time their second self-financed EP appeared (a mere year later), ENERGY's own compositions had already started to resemble more of a genuine NWOBHM style, with "Make It" and "Law Breaker" coming across as fairly analogous to TRESPASS or PRAYING MANTIS, whereas the heavier "Conquer The World" is more along the lines of DRAGONFLY's "Silent Nights". The quartet were, by this point, spreading themselves considerably wider in a concerted attempt to get their name known to the masses, regularly organising gigs throughout their home county, and taking in selected venues in nearby Cambridgeshire/Leicestershire (and, on occasion, further afield), grasping the opportunity to shift copies of their vinyl product to appreciative punters at these shindigs. ENERGY's first two EP's (both of which were originally pressed in pretty minimal quantities), meanwhile, are regarded as remarkably highly-valued pieces nowadays, and examples have been sighted on relatively few occasions in recent years.

Now we're getting to the *really* good stuff. In my extremely humble opinion, ENERGY's next two singles (both issued on their own Aros label) unquestionably contain the foursome's greatest moments, although, oddly enough, it turns out to be the B-side in each case that stands out as the highlight. Rather than just churning out a slice of vinyl on an annual basis, the lads took their time releasing their third 7", and it looks as though the extra period of studio experimentation made all the difference. Their »Nowhere To Hide« two-tracker from 1983 wins several bonus points for a fantastically clichéd title, the nominated A-side being a melodic and perfectly acceptable THIN LIZZY/BLEAK HOUSE mixture. The extraordinary "Fight For Your Freedom", on the other hand, with its quirky opening, unpredictable time changes and heartfelt, politically-motivated lyrics, is (with the possible exception of VIRGIN STAR's "When The Reds") quite unlike anything else from the NWOBHM era. Indeed, with its twin-vocal parts and incredible, er, *energy*, you can quite easily imagine the likes of EXTREME NOISE TERROR doing a hardcore version at some point. I mean, check out the opening lyrics:

'What do you think of this world today?
Is there something you think you should say?
Is there an answer to our trouble and strife?
Will we suffer the rest of our lives…NO!'

Inspiring stuff, lads. This one would certainly make an astute choice of cover version (OFFSPRING were already halfway there with "Smash", admittedly) for many of today's self-styled melodic punk outfits, so keep an eye out in future…

Moving into 1985 (the group presumably having continued to tour productively in the interim), ENERGY issued yet another 7", having clearly honed their writing style even further during the previous two years. »Too Good To Lose« possesses a disarmingly melodic A-side which is vaguely reminiscent of HIGH TREASON's "Waste My Love" (with something of an Americanised AOR influence in the vocals), while the truly outstanding "Cold Sweat" is an absolute cracker, a heavy (but incredibly catchy) number with highly original guitar work throughout. Comparisons with NWOBHM contemporaries are scant (LYADRIVE or IONA would, perhaps, be about the closest in terms of general musical similarity), so the best I can do is compare it to GARY MOORE/PHIL LYNOTT's superb "Out In The Fields", which is high praise indeed. Quite why this talented outfit didn't achieve world domination at this point is completely beyond my comprehension. Nevertheless, both »Nowhere To Hide« and »Too Good To Lose« are valued at around the three-figure mark (slightly more extensive pressings mean that rather more of each are still in circulation, compared with the scarce first pair of releases), and demand among collectors appears to be incredibly strong at the moment.

Sadly, ENERGY's last release (the only one to be issued in a picture sleeve) was an unmitigated disaster, with "Radio Radio" and "Rebel With A Cause" being a case of blatant sell-out, these sub-GO WEST pop offerings going way beyond the embarrassment of later commercial material issued by the likes of MENDES PREY and HEAVY PETTIN. Needless to say, the number of copies pressed far exceeded the quantity actually sold, and the lads decided not to persevere with further vinyl releases. It was a sad way to bow out, and it looks as though they just made too many concessions to the melodic rock market in a last-ditch attempt to win some more widespread recognition. However, the band, having remained a going concern until comparatively recently, are all still in contact with each other, and have an album's worth of mastered studio material at their disposal (an eponymous long-player was originally scheduled for release as far back as 1983), which may yet find its way onto the market *via* an official release. Let's hope so.

7" EP's
»**Energised**« Bips Records 1980
»**Conquer The World**« GRN Records 1981

7" Singles
»**Nowhere To Hide**« Aros Records 1983
»**Too Good To Lose**« Aros Records 1985
»**Radio Radio**« Aros Records 1986

Compilation Appearances
"**Fight For Your Freedom**" on »NWOBHM Vol.5« Bootleg CD 1992

ERIC BELL BAND

Eric Bell (v,g)
Dave Nilo (b)
David Donovan (d)

Unlike some of the more blatant, opportunistic cash-ins or all of those conveniently-timed *'reformations'* (TRACTOR, ENGLAND, STRAY, ATOMIC ROOSTER *etc.*) which various decomposing 70's acts inflicted upon us in the early 80's, the eponymous outfit formed by ex-THIN LIZZY guitarist Eric Bell (originally replaced in the aforementioned combo by Gary Moore) seems to have been a genuine proposition for the NWOBHM era. Picked up by the small-time Hobo label (who also sponsored MONEY's »Fast World« EP) in 1981, the threesome issued their »Lonely Man« 7" on two separate occasions, initially as a four track EP and later as a conventional single (only the former, possibly a promotional device, boasting a rare picture sleeve showing the main protagonists), for reasons which are still slightly unclear. Anyway, "Lonely Man" itself turned out to be a fairly slow, melancholic tune (incorporating, oddly enough, a snippet of the 'James Bond' theme) in the manner of ANTHEM's "England", while "Vampire Lady" is more like VOLTZ with bluesy guitar parts. On the reverse, "Anybody Seen My Baby" is out and out electric blues (real *'woke up this morning, thanked the Lord I was alive'* stuff), with the raunchy rocker "Deep End" (very much in the manner of DRIVESHAFT) rounding things off quite nicely. It wasn't exactly archetypal NWOBHM, but it still had the potential to appeal to a fair percentage of headbangers, and you would have expected the group (completed, in the first instance, by former PHOTOS bassist Dave Nilo and ex-WIZZO sticksman David Donovan) to develop a healthy following purely on the basis of the THIN LIZZY connection.

Strangely, however, the whole ERIC BELL BAND venture appears to have been something of a non-starter, and the trio were hardly an overwhelming success in their original incarnation, in spite of the fact that some high-profile gigs (most of which took place in and around the nation's capital) were timed to coincide with the record's initial release. I've no idea what may have prompted the reissue (which omitted "Vampire Lady" and "Deep End"), but the 7" appears to have suffered from rather incompetent promotion (selling in relatively modest quantities as a result), the upshot being that »Lonely Man« is very seldom mentioned in the context of Bell's musical activities over the years, even in otherwise comprehensive THIN LIZZY-related discographies. Nevertheless, the much-travelled frontman (who was, in his pre-LIZZY days, a member of Van Morrison's THEM, his many other credits including a stint with the NOEL REDDING BAND in the mid-70's) has now (following numerous club appearances under assumed identities such as ERIC BELL AND THE

SUNSETS) resurrected the original ERIC BELL BAND name. Joining forces with Tony Williams and Andy Golden in 1992, the trio have become a popular live act (including the odd THIN LIZZY number in their repertoire to keep the fans happy) in both mainland Europe and the blues clubs of the UK. Releases such as »Live Tonite« (recorded in Sweden in 1996) and the more recent »Irish Boy« have met with critical acclaim from many quarters, although the traditional material being performed nowadays can hardly be heralded as having any connection with the original NWOBHM spirit. The great man has, incidentally, also found time to front one of the 'reformed' versions of THIN LIZZY, who have been touring sporadically in recent times under the banner of 'Thin Lizzy-The Early Years'.

7" EP's
»Lonely Man« Hobo Records 1981
[Original issue with four tracks, some in picture sleeve]

7" Singles
»Lonely Man« Hobo Records 1981
[Second issue with two tracks, no picture sleeve]

E.S.P.

Montgomery
Collins

Quite an obscure one, this, just a plain sleeve with 'E.S.P.' and the tactful instructions 'To Play: 1. Bass Down 2. Volume Up' stamped thereon. Another Gargoyle Records release, suggesting a Home Counties (Hertfordshire/Bedfordshire) origin for the band in question (not to be confused with various namesakes including a BLUE ÖYSTER CULT offshoot), and probably the most 'metal' of the singles so far known on this small-time label. "Another Way" is a catchy tune with memorable guitar parts and soulful, bluesy vocals in the vein of ORE or XERO, which probably captures E.S.P. at their best. The same can't be said for the reverse, however, this being an ill-conceived track with the rather puzzling title of "The Poem". The latter consists of some extremely embarrassing and inconsequential lyrics (the group are playing in a pub, the landlord tells them to turn the volume down, the punters ask them to turn it back up again) spoken over a rudimentary instrumental backing. This is presumably supposed to render the listener in paroxysms of laughter, but it's simply neither a well-observed dichotomy nor a remotely funny situation. As with the similarly-inclined CHEEKY single (and, to a lesser extent, T34's debut), this is a truly wasted opportunity, and whoever first came up with the notion of the 'comedy B-side' should be utterly ashamed of themselves (or, alternatively, shot). Never mind, there are plenty of other records out there which don't cause the listener to cringe with embarrassment. Clearly, E.S.P. failed to progress to greater things after their 1981 debut, and the eventual fate of these small-town nonentities will have to remain a mystery for the time being.

7" Singles
»Another Way« Gargoyle Records 1981

ETHEL THE FROG

Doug Sheppard (v,g)
Paul Tognola (g)
Terry Hopkinson (b)
Paul Conyers (d)

Humberside's bizarrely-named ETHEL THE FROG (the moniker coming from a rather obscure 'Monty Python' song) first hopped onto the scene in around 1976, working their way up from initial obscurity to become one of the region's main rock attractions. The youthful quartet proceeded to lay down a couple of speculative demos in their early days, before they finally decided to grab the bull by the horns and do their own thing in the form of a privately-issued single. Their vinyl debut, released in 1978, was based around a cover of the well-worn BEATLES original "Eleanor Rigby" (not nearly as enjoyable as the JEDDAH version), plus a self-penned number, the excellent "Whatever Happened To Love". Despite the fact that a thousand copies (none of which were issued with a picture sleeve) of the 7" were supposedly pressed in the first instance, this item remains a seldom-sighted and highly-valued artefact nowadays. Even at that stage, it was apparent that the emergent outfit had already cultivated a heavy, melodic style of metal, with occasional similarities to the likes of ALKATRAZZ, MOTHER'S RUIN, LAST FLIGHT or some of the later QUARTZ output. Predictably, though, the two-tracker didn't turn the lads into superstars overnight, and it was soon back to the grind in the live environment. One of their more infamous appearances came at the Humberside Open Air Festival (I don't think that one ever really rivalled the Dynamo version), where the band's set was stopped by the police after just fifteen minutes, the local constabulary insisting that the noise levels emanating from the group and their many fans were upsetting the patients at a nearby hospital. A likely story.

A couple of years down the line, the lads eventually (having taken part, with fairly moderate success, in a rock competition organised by 'Melody Maker') managed to attract the attention of none other than EMI, who, under the auspices of Neal Kay, were looking for some promising young outfits to include on their first »Metal For Muthas« collection. Frontman Doug Sheppard was compelled to tell his local newspaper all about this monumental event, and enthused: *'Hopefully, EMI will be able to make use of our own recordings, but if they're not good enough, we'll have to go back into the studio in order to lay down a new version.'* As it turned out, the outfit's existing recordings were indeed of sufficiently high quality; not only was "Fight Back" included on the aforementioned sampler (the lads comfortably taking their place alongside such scene-stealers as ANGEL WITCH, IRON MAIDEN and SAMSON), therefore, but the label stepped in with a generous and well-timed offer to release a full album. The eponymous long-player (featuring a selection of tracks cobbled together from a variety of recording sessions) appeared in the early months of 1980, as did a reissued version of the »Eleanor Rigby« single (this time coupled with "Fight Back"), very few copies of which were issued in a picture sleeve, although it was basically the same image as the album cover itself.

The album wasn't quite the *tour de force* that the fans might have expected on the basis of their debut single (the vocals are occasionally a bit flat, and there were rather too many numbers which appeared to be firmly rooted in the 70's, which is when they were written, after all), although there were still some quality moments, notably "Apple Of Your Eye", the complex "Fire Bird" and the atmospheric "Bleeding Heart" (which bears more than a passing resemblance to HAMMERHEAD's "Lochinvar", incidentally). By this time, however, the success or failure of the long-player (recently reissued by British Steel, as it happens) was largely academic, as the group had practically ceased all activities by the time their latest product hit the shops. With no musicians remaining on the scene to promote the new releases, therefore, EMI wasted little in the way of finances in order to advertise or distribute the records particularly effectively, and sales hardly threatened to rival the likes of IRON MAIDEN (or ANGEL WITCH, for that matter). ETHEL THE FROG, on the other hand, had split into two separate factions within a remarkably short space of time (strangely, though, they got back together for a gig or two in the early months of 1981), with the duo of Conyers and Tognola proceeding to establish the highly-regarded SALEM (see separate entry), whereas the all-new outfit which Hopkinson and Sheppard intended to form appears not to have made it past the planning stage.

LP's
»Ethel The Frog« EMI 1980

7" Singles
»Eleanor Rigby« Best Records 1978
[Original issue, B-side "Whatever Happened To Love"]
»Eleanor Rigby« EMI 1980
[Second issue, B-side "Fight Back", some promotional copies with picture sleeve]

CD's
»Ethel The Frog« British Steel 1997

Compilation Appearances
"Fight Back" on »Metal For Muthas« LP EMI 1980/CD Airraid Records 2000 + »The Bible Of Hard Rock« CD Toshiba 1990

EVERYONE ELSE

Tim Hunter (v,g)
Keith Fennell (b)
Rick Collett (d)

Obscure Midlands trio EVERYONE ELSE (hopeless name, that) were one of many local outfits to frequent the Woodbine St. recording facility in Leamington Spa during the NWOBHM era, and, along with the likes of CHEEKY (see separate entry), these lads elected to issue their debut 7" on the studio's own label. Unleashed upon the listening public in 1979, the four-tracker is in more of a pub rock kind of proto-NWOBHM style than anything particularly more substantial, with the likes of "Schooldays", "Brainwashed", "Don't Call Us" and "Out Of My Mind" bringing forth comparisons with the likes of SINGAPORE, the NEXT BAND and MONEY. It's all pretty basic, knockabout stuff (reasonably typical of the period in question), and the overall sound profile is somewhat on the sparse side, so a bit of multi-tracking on the guitar front might have been a prudent idea. This particular project seems to have been a fairly short-lived affair, and none of the members appear to have resurfaced in any NWOBHM or post-NWOBHM outfits of note, so it looks as though it was merely a one-off attempt at finding fame and fortune. Nevertheless, the EVERYONE ELSE EP, issued in an uninspiring monochrome sleeve showing images of the trio, is still a fairly highly-valued piece today.

7" EP's
»Schooldays« Woodbine St. Records 1979

EXCALIBUR

Paul McBride (v)
Paul Solynskij (g)
Martin Hawthorn (b)
Stewart Meer (d)

Vying with the likes of VIRTUE and BRIAR for the coveted title of *'NWOBHM's most precocious young upstarts'* were Yorkshire's EXCALIBUR, who originally got together, while still in their early teens, way back in 1981. There's little evidence, however, to suggest that their valiant identity represented anything more than a *'bedroom project'* at the outset. That aside, the lads were certainly playing live on a fairly regular basis by the early months of 1983 (they even managed a small-time gig or two at the tail end of the previous year), although, thanks to various age-related legalities, such events were normally restricted to the local YMCA and youth clubs. Frequently-recalled stories of the members falling asleep during their school lessons, after having slogged their guts out in working men's clubs the night before, are likely to be apocryphal, although these almost certainly contain a kernel of truth. There was, however, comparatively little activity on the recording front prior to 1984, the year in which they replaced original drummer Stewart Meer with new boy Mick Dodson and released their first commercial demo (there was actually an earlier one, but it wasn't circulated), the »Back Before Dawn« effort featuring "Come On And Rock", "Haunted By The Shadows" and "Only Time Can Tell". Coming across as a melodic-but-heavy outfit with distinct similarities to the much-missed TURBO, as well as the likes of DEALER, GEDDES AXE and ELIXIR, the youngsters were already laying the foundations for a glittering career at this early stage.

By 1985, having been freed from the shackles of full-time education, the lads managed to wangle a deal with the somewhat inconsistent Conquest label, an arrangement which yielded just one solitary piece of vinyl, a mini-album entitled »The Bitter End«, housed in a suitably heroic sleeve. Featuring the three aforementioned demo compositions alongside "I'm Telling You", "Devil In Disguise" and the title track itself, this genuinely was an excellent (and remarkably mature) vinyl debut, which immediately drew praise from many quarters, the lads being held up as *'the next DEF LEPPARD'* by some, sentiments which were later to be echoed as the members of EXCALIBUR recorded their first session for the 'Friday Rock Show' while still all under the age of nineteen. With the session originally being broadcast on the 18th of July 1986, the group showcased "Hot For Love", "Death's Door", the excellent "Early In The Morning" and old favourite "Come On And Rock" to a national audience. This capable selection of original material was warmly received by many listeners, and it led directly to negotiations with Jet Records, who initially expressed a firm interest in releasing some EXCALIBUR product in due course. Sadly, however, the batch of material demoed for the aforementioned label didn't quite come up to scratch, and the original offer was soon withdrawn, leaving the musicians to have a bit of a rethink and to attempt to refine their songwriting style somewhat.

Nevertheless, the band members remained supremely confident of their own ability, and didn't let this minor setback prey on their minds for too long. Indeed, they felt so happy with their admirably-produced 'Friday Rock Show' recordings that they began looking into the possibility of using them again, and eventually organised a licensing deal with the BBC which resulted in the session being issued officially (not until 1988, though) as the »Hot For Love« 12" EP on the Clay label. By the time this record eventually appeared, however, the group had already finished a successful national tour (plus a handful of dates with the likes of VOW WOW and URIAH HEEP), broken in a new drummer (in the form of Dave Sykes) and recruited second guitarist (and occasional keyboard player) Steve Blades (previously with Scottish hopefuls ASSASIN), so they were barely recognisable as the same outfit. In this sense, therefore, their latest slice of vinyl was hardly representative of the state of EXCALIBUR in 1988, but it still shifted a worthwhile number of units. In fairness, the EP was regarded as something of a stop-gap release while the developing group searched for a proper deal, and it wasn't long before an acceptable offer came their way.

EXCALIBUR's relationship with the newly-established Active label began in 1989, the year in which they were to endure the departure of founder member Martin Hawthorn (who defected to the quirky LOUD! project), and it took a while for the musicians to settle down to business with their new bassist, Geoff Livermore. However, they managed to get their act together within a few months, and the result of some productive recording sessions at Ric Rac Studios in Leeds was 1990's »One Strange Night« album, an effort which received some extremely impressive reviews in the rock press, notably the opinion of 'Metal Forces' that it was *'an excellent release that no self-respecting rock fan can afford to miss.'* It was, indeed, a high-calibre, heavy offering, and it undoubtedly had something of a late 80's feel to it (comparable to the likes of FIRST OFFENCE or a harder and considerably more accomplished IDOL RICH in places), although it's fair to state that Paul McBride occasionally stretches his voice a bit too far on some of the featured numbers. Annoyingly, however, the track chosen to promote the long-player on a tie-in 12" EP was the BON JOVI-soundalike "Carole Ann", an entirely unrepresentative and inferior composition in every sense.

It transpires that EXCALIBUR were indeed retained by Active, following eminently respectable sales of the debut album (not to mention a series of well-received headlining gigs, plus a useful support slot with SAXON on their UK tour), and were encouraged to venture into the studio to prepare for a follow-up release at the earliest opportunity. It wasn't long, however, before yet another personnel change was forced upon the hapless outfit, when their most recent recruit, Geoff Livermore, announced that he didn't wish to stay any longer, compelling them to draft in ex-SLAMMER bassist Dean Wilson at short notice, whereupon they were able to complete their scheduled European gigs with VENGEANCE. In fact, it looks as though Wilson didn't actually become a full-time member, given that he was simultaneously lending a hand to certain other local acts such as CRIME INC., so this evidently represented a period of instability for EXCALIBUR. Moving into 1991, rehearsals for the second album were well underway when frontman Paul McBride began expressing serious dissatisfaction with the group's recent progress, and things soon began to look fairly bleak for the unsettled outfit.

Within a fairly short space of time, internal tension built up to an intolerable level and EXCALIBUR were eventually torn apart towards the end of that year, never to recover, although the members remained on pretty good terms and ultimately reunited for a farewell tour in the spring of 1992. It was another sad loss for the metal scene, but at least they gave the world a good run for its money for the best part of a decade. The pairing of Paul Solynskij and Martin Hawthorn (the latter had been working with a new concern called P.A.D.D. after the demise of LOUD!, but this particular bunch failed to make much of an impression) later reunited in a somewhat darker outfit called HARDWARE, who enjoyed a considerable amount of success in Europe (touring alongside the likes of AMORPHIS and THERION), and even released an emotionally-charged mini-CD called »Race, Religion And Hate« in 1996. Several of the former members of EXCALIBUR are also still involved with the club scene, by the way, and regularly take to the stage with various well-received covers outfits.

LP's
»**One Strange Night**« Active Records 1990

Mini-LP's
»**The Bitter End**« Conquest Records 1985

12" EP's
»**Hot For Love**« Clay 1988
[Four tracks taken from 1986 'Friday Rock Show' session, "Hot For Love" non-LP, all others different to album/mini album versions]
»**Carole Ann**« Active Records 1990
["Sick And Tired" only on CD version of album]

CD's
»**One Strange Night**« Active Records 1990
[With extra track "Sick And Tired"]

Compilation Appearances
"**Haunted By The Shadows**" on »Metal Masters« 4-CD Box Castle Communications 1993
"**I'm Telling You**" on »Metal Masters« 4-CD Box Castle Communications 1993
"**Come On And Rock**" on »Rock Out!« Do-CD Emporio 1996
"**Devil In Disguise**" on »Rock Out!« Do-CD Emporio 1996

EXOCET

Steven Slater (v)
Paul Wright (g)
Anthony Horsman (g)

Paul Hughes (b)
Lee Fryer (d)

The little-remembered EXOCET were very much a typical example of the kind of post-NWOBHM power metal concern which suddenly began cropping up in the UK from around 1984 onwards, although their only vinyl legacy would appear to be a seldom-seen 12" single from 1986. The two-tracker was recorded at the normally-reliable Peppermint Place facility in London (witness the admirable sound on THE COVENANT's 12" from the same year, for example), although the production job is utterly abysmal in this case, and sounds more like a particularly poor demo or even a rehearsal tape, if truth be told. Still, the powerful music is decent enough for a small-time outfit of this kind, and both "Stalemate" (the better of the pair) and "The Raven" (possibly a bit too lengthy for its own good) sit perfectly comfortably alongside the substantial, riff-dominated metal of ZENITH (in particular), PROWLER or the Tyneside version of WARRIOR, although it would have been nice to hear this quintet benefitting from a decent studio budget and a rather more flattering production. The record seems to have been well and truly overlooked upon its release, however, and barely managed to scrape a mention anywhere in the music press, which probably knocked the wind out of EXOCET's sails to a significant extent, and I expect that they probably called it a day sooner rather than later, which is a bit of a shame. Still, their one-off 12" is well worth keeping an eye out for (it comes in a nice-looking picture cover which retains the 'chess' theme) if you're a fan of the mid-80's metal style.

12" Singles
»Stalemate« Private 1986

EXPLORER

Bob Bruce (v)
Barry Kimber (g)
Gary Cole (b)
Chris May (k)
Rob Armstrong (d)

Hampshire semi-obscurities EXPLORER (not to be confused either with their Belgian namesakes or with America's EXXPLORER, both of whom were operational at more or less the same time) emerged from the ashes of a little-known act called CHARTREUSE towards the end of 1983 (vocalist Bob Bruce was swiftly brought in from SWITCHBACK to make up the numbers), and debuted with a humble demo tape early the following year, the cassette showcasing "Try To Lie" and "Lose Your Love". Within a remarkably short space of time, the lads had come to the attention of the local Rock Shop concern, a company which had pretty much taken over from where the original champions of South Coast rock/metal (the pioneering Airship and Arny's Shack labels) had left off. Unlike labelmates FRIENDS and WHITE HEAT, however, EXPLORER were lucky enough to be afforded the luxury of a full album, and their »Exploding«

debut turned out to be a fairly diverse affair, presenting a highly capable selection of pleasingly-heavy melodic rock/metal compositions (bringing to mind such disparate acts as TRESPASS, MONEY, GRAND PRIX and MASAI), with stand-out efforts including the excellent "Battle Cry" and "Down To The Ground". It's also worth noting the occasional flirtation with more progressive arrangements (particularly with regard to the group's shrewd use of keyboards from time to time), evoking similarities with the likes of SHERWOOD or local predecessors VOLTZ. The instrumental "Maginot Line", meanwhile, allowed the individual members the opportunity to turn in some virtuoso performances, and reveals a level of imagination which was sadly lacking in the music of so many of their post-NWOBHM contemporaries.

One of the outfit's frequent live outings (at the Kings Theatre in the Portsmouth suburb of Southsea) was reviewed in 'Kerrang' shortly after the album's release, and journalist Dave Dickson was keen to air his views on the evening's entertainment: 'I came away from this gig in two minds; on the one hand, I was impressed by the stageshow and the evident ease with which the band coped with the big stage. But on the other, I fear that here is a group with all the form but no substance.' (Ref: Kerrang No.79, October 1984). Hmmm, maybe he caught them on a bad night or something, as EXPLORER represented (on vinyl, at least) an entirely respectable and extremely capable prospect. Sadly, the lads don't appear to have capitalised upon their accomplished debut, and failed to maintain much of a presence on the national rock scene (although they remained an immensely popular act in their locality) from 1985 onwards. Bassist Gary Cole flew the coop in the end, although he was swiftly replaced by ex-HARD GRAFT man Martin Walls (who later went on to join AFTER HOURS), whereas keyboard player Chris May was keen to branch out and experiment with other outfits, notably ALIBI, although he still retained full involvement with EXPLORER. A final demo cassette, featuring the likes of "Shadow In The Dark" and "Open Road", was circulated in a last-ditch attempt to secure a follow-up release, but their efforts appear to have gone unrewarded, and it was all over for the luckless band by around 1986.

LP's
»**Exploding**« Rock Shop Records 1984
[With two sleeve variations, either predominantly black or red, black more common]

EXPORT

Harry Shaw (v)
Steve Morris (g)
Chris Alderman (b)
Lou Rosenthal (d)

A product of Merseyside's flourishing rock/metal scene of the late 70's (the North West possessed a truly enviable pool of talent back then, giving rise to a variety of pre-NWOBHM acts such as NUTZ, STRIFE, SPIDER, MARSEILLE *etc.*), the unremarkably-monikered EXPORT's early history hasn't been particularly well documented, and it's not even common knowledge among aficionados of the genre that the musically-experienced quartet briefly held a prestigious record deal with the huge Atlantic label (home of AC/DC, no less), although it would appear that the only product released through this collaboration was the seldom-seen »Julie Bitch« single (B-side "Nice To Know You") in 1979. Evidently, sales of this two-tracker were extremely disappointing, and it looks as though Atlantic, in their infinite wisdom, subsequently decided that MORE, with their somewhat more aggressive material, were a better proposition for the burgeoning NWOBHM market than the raunchy, 70's-rooted rock of EXPORT. Even so, the musicians remained largely unperturbed by this cruel rejection, and soon set about doing things their own way as the British metal scene began to evolve and restructure itself.

In the wake of being given their freedom, the foursome consequently released an eponymous LP (a connection with other local bands being maintained in that RAGE's John Mylett obliged with the photographic duties for the sleeve, a service he also provided for NIGHTWING) on their own label (the punningly-titled His Master's Vice) a year later. Listening to the long-player, it's apparent that EXPORT were yet another of those fortuitous combos who were swept up in the NWOBHM movement without being a particularly innovative or representative example of the style. Their general disposition was more in tune with bands such as NUTHIN FANCY, TRUX and MEANSTREAK than anything fundamentally heavier, and the pervasive influence of the aforementioned rock pioneers from their area is also readily detectable. The pick of the tracks featured would probably be "Fast Lane To Your Heart", "Light In The Dark" (Harry Shaw's vocal performance on this track providing a few hefty clues as to where Billy Downs from fellow Scousers DAMASCUS might have picked up his distinctive style) and "You're My Best Friend" (which sounds not entirely dissimilar to DEMON's "Into The Nightmare", incidentally), but the whole thing was a listenable enough affair. A single also escaped at around the same time (issued in a stamped, plain sleeve), featuring the non-LP "You Gotta Rock" and the upbeat "Wheeler Dealer" from the debut album. After a series of high-profile, nationwide dates supporting SLADE in March 1981, the lads were lucky enough to be featured, a few months later, on the 'In Concert' programme on BBC Radio (alongside WILD HORSES), giving them a further bit of valuable national exposure.

EXPORT's next move (after they had undertaken a further round of touring, this time alongside PRAYING MANTIS) was to throw themselves into the task of transmuting into a *bona fide* AOR outfit in a blatant attempt to crack the global rock market. They disappeared into the shadows for a couple of years, and ended up in the States, working on new material with a variety of co-writers, but were unwavering in their desire to become major contenders on the melodic rock scene. By 1984, EXPORT had apparently achieved their destiny, releasing first the largely-overlooked (and now incredibly difficult to locate) »Contraband« set (recorded for the benefit of the gargantuan Epic concern, no less), followed by their awkwardly-titled »Living In The Fear Of The Private Eye« effort on the same label two years later. While the group's shift towards mature, polished, accessible material (drafting in keyboard players and backing vocalists in

order to round out the sound even more) probably found a great many new admirers in the AOR field (some over-generous reviews in various music publications of the time no doubt helped their cause), it distanced them permanently from their quintessentially British roots (close comparisons with the DARK STAR story), and the lads never successfully recaptured their original, hard-rocking fan base. I'd imagine that material for a fourth album was probably being worked on by the time they decided to call it a day, which seems to have been in the summer of 1987 or thereabouts (there's evidence to suggest that some of those involved in the venture subsequently tried to get things going again under the name of CONTRABAND), although details of those final recording sessions remain sketchy.

In the immediate aftermath of the outfit's untimely demise, three-quarters of EXPORT (Shaw, Morris and Rosenthal) duly went looking for new employment, and the trio subsequently became part of Ian Gillan's backing ensemble on the GARTH ROCKETT AND THE MOONSHINERS tour a year or two later, lining up alongside a few regional stalwarts such as former RAGE bassist Keith Mulholland and ex-TOKYO keyboard player Mark Buckle. Drummer Lou Rosenthal also briefly held a post with 2AM, the pop/rock project conceived by former RAGE vocalist Dave Lloyd towards the end of the decade (although the sticksman now plays a rather more peripheral role in the music business), while Steve Morris subsequently turned his hand to production work, twiddling the knobs for yet another local outfit, TORINO, among others. Morris also proceeded to team up with the aforementioned Dave Lloyd in the revamped IAN GILLAN project at around the turn of the decade, and still continues to work alongside the aforementioned Gillan in his various musical endeavours to this day, including all those critically-acclaimed solo efforts and his occasionally-resurrected early outfit, the JAVELINS.

LP's
»**Export**« His Master's Vice 1980
[Original UK issue]
»**Export**« Ariola 1981
[Later German issue]
»**Contraband**« Epic 1984
»**Living In The Fear Of The Private Eye**« Epic 1986

7" Singles
»**Julie Bitch**« Atlantic 1979
[Both tracks non-LP]
»**You Gotta Rock**« His Master's Vice 1980
[A-side different to album version]

EXPOZER

Steve Byatt (v)
Tim Blackwood (g)
Kev Holmes (g)
Gary Marshall (b)
Tim Bedson (d)

By all accounts, Staffordshire's EXPOZER appear to have come and gone in a remarkably short space of time, but somehow managed to shift an impressive number of copies of their »Exposed At Last« 7" during their brief existence. Formed in the early months of 1980 by the trio of Tim Bedson, Steve Byatt and Tim Blackwood, all apparently ex-POZER (groan), the founder members swiftly recruited Kev Holmes and Gary Marshall to the fold. They didn't make much of an impression at first, but no doubt beavered away happily in the rehearsal rooms and local pubs (they might even have played a gig or two, for all I know) in the first instance, gradually honing their skills and developing a repertoire. In fact, within a mere six months of their formation, the youthful group concluded that they were now ready to record their debut single, although matters were complicated when the restless Kev Holmes decided to take a brief sabbatical. Hence, former MAYDAY guitarist Ian Morris was hurriedly drafted in for the relevant studio session, although it wasn't very long before the wayward Holmes returned to take up residence once more. Coupling "Rock Japan" with "On My Knees", EXPOZER's 7" illustrates a pretty energetic, slightly raunchy style of metal which brings forth occasional comparisons with likeminded contemporaries such as the HANDSOME BEASTS and ORE, with the effortlessly memorable arrangements and melodic backing vocals making for an enjoyable piece of listening.

The two track version of »Exposed At Last«, in its generic black and silver sleeve, was one of the first NWOBHM obscurities to turn up in notable quantities (having sold well nationally, and particularly so in the Midlands, where the outfit tended to play the majority of their gigs) at the start of the collecting boom, and its comparatively modest value today reflects the fact that a considerable number have been in circulation at one time or another. Far less commonly encountered, however, is the four track pressing, featuring two additional numbers (uncredited, for some reason, and your guess is as good as mine as to what those titles might actually be) and issued in a plain, stamped sleeve. As with the ERIC BELL BAND 7", the reason for the existence of these two variants is unclear, although the extreme scarcity of the EXPOZER four-tracker suggests that this may merely have been a strictly limited promotional device rather than a commercial issue. In any case, it may throw some light on the unusual logic of issuing their single under the »Exposed At Last« guise, when the more conventional (and considerably less confusing) scenario is to give titles only to EP's.

The single's A-side, "Rock Japan", was also featured on the first »Heavy Metal Heroes« compilation a year later, although it ultimately came too late to rescue EXPOZER from their inevitable fate. In fact, with the release of »Exposed At Last« having been delayed quite severely in the first instance, the luckless group struggled to make up lost ground (having lost both momentum and enthusiasm in the interim), resulting in the eventual departure of unsettled guitarist Tim Blackwood, after which the remaining members rapidly came to a mutual decision to put their activities on hold for a while. Strangely, their single continued to sell in reasonable quantities all the while, so they might have been rather hasty in their decision to take a break. As it turns out, although the outfit were fully expected to resume activities by the end of the year, there's no solid evidence to suggest that a reformation of EXPOZER actually took place at any point. The aforementioned Tim Blackwood subsequently joined the recently-established LE GRIFFE, who enjoyed considerable success in years to come, particularly throughout the Midlands, whereas bassist Gary Marshall went on to play with a fairly obscure act called ALLIED FORCES, while drummer Tim Bedson also teamed up with yet another local outfit, the long-lived NO FAVORS.

7" EP's
»Exposed At Last« Hit Hard Records 1980
[Four track version in stamped cover, relatively few copies in circulation]

7" Singles
»Exposed At Last« Hit Hard Records 1980
[Two track version in picture sleeve]

Compilation Appearances
"Rock Japan" on »Heavy Metal Heroes« LP Heavy Metal 1981 *[Issued in two different sleeves]* + »Heavy Metal Heroes Vol.I&II« CD British Steel 1996

EZY MEAT

Ivan Lavery (v,g,k)
Paul Lavery (v,b)
Ray McKenna (d)

One of the more innovative and forward-looking acts to emerge in Northern Ireland during the NWOBHM era, EZY MEAT were a three-piece who combined a healthy respect for the island's legendary musical heritage (THIN LIZZY, SKID ROW, RORY GALLAGHER, HORSLIPS *etc.*) with a style encompassing the attitude and dynamics of the flourishing NWOBHM movement. With the trio (featuring Ivan and Paul, the Lavery brothers, plus youthful stickman Ray McKenna) having become established as a stable unit by 1980, they started out as little more than an amateur-hour covers outfit who played at parties and sundry small-time events, although the rapidity with which their own compositions began to rival those of more established bands took everyone by surprise, not least the musicians themselves. The initial breakthrough came towards the end of that year, when the lads were approached by the Homespun Records concern (based in Belfast, where the trio rehearsed on a regular basis) to contribute a couple of original tracks to the label's forthcoming compilation of regional hopefuls. The lads jumped at the chance, and the cunning musicians elected to accept some additional free studio time instead of conventional payment for their efforts. With "Sexy Lady" and "Soho Escapade" having been laid down for the sampler, EZY MEAT also proceeded to record "Go", "D.A.Blues", "Get 'Em Off", "Ban The Bomb" and "Shot Down", combining the seven tracks to assemble their first demo tape, a release entitled »Makin' Noise«.

All things considered, the »Belfast« (clever title, that) compilation, released in 1981, didn't turn EZY MEAT (or any of the other hapless indie/pop nonentities featured, such as the long-forgotten REFLEX ACTION and STAGE B) into national heroes overnight, thanks mainly to its limited budget and distribution. Nevertheless, the lads had shown wisdom beyond their years in utilising the exercise to obtain a properly-recorded demo tape, and »Makin' Noise« was soon selling in impressive quantities at the band's increasingly well-attended gigs. In due course, EZY MEAT (who were, incidentally, once voted the most popular metal act in the whole of Northern Ireland) made further visits to the recording facility, laying down freshly-penned material as and when they could, and they always remained hopeful that an offer of further vinyl exposure would come their way. In the interim, the trio forged friendships with various other hopefuls from the area, notably SWEET SAVAGE, and, as time went on, they began to win a handful of coveted support slots with the relatively few rock acts (the likes of URIAH HEEP, ULI JON ROTH and MAGNUM) who actually bothered to play Irish dates. Crucially, however, EZY MEAT consistently failed to attract the attention of the labels (hardly surprising, given that they were unable to make it to the mainland to promote themselves), and were eventually forced to go it alone.

By the second half of 1983, former SWEET SAVAGE guitarist Vivian Campbell had completed work on his first album with DIO, and was back in Ireland preparing for the band's forthcoming tour of Britain. While he was there, he hooked up with his old chum Ivan Lavery and began talking about the quality of the EZY MEAT demos which he had been given over the years.

After a while (and a few pints of Guinness, no doubt), Campbell had convinced Lavery that the time was now right for EZY MEAT to record a full album of their own, and graciously offered to oversee the whole process himself as a testimony to his commitment and sincerity. In due course, the culmination of a rather hectic two days (!) in Slane Studios was a long-player's worth of usable recordings, and the EZY MEAT frontman was especially grateful for the experience in the recording facility: *'I learned a lot from him [Campbell], so much so that I was later able to produce our second album myself without any outside help. Vivian was a good friend of ours, he produced the album purely as a personal favour.'* (Ref: Singing Swords, Issue 2, 1996). All that remained was to get the record pressed up and arrange some sort of distribution deal, and EZY MEAT's debut set eventually appeared on the group's own Electric Storm label (published by S.R.S. Music, later responsible for the PURPLE HAZE single) the following year.

The descriptively-titled »Not For Wimps« was a surprisingly competent effort for a self-organised debut, and it showed EZY MEAT to be a talented bunch of musicians (with some especially strong guitar work in places) who could expertly switch from listenable, upbeat rockers such as "The Loner" to more complex and thoughtful pieces such as "Ban The Bomb", the latter being an epic composition in two parts, lasting around fifteen minutes in total. In the main, however, the group delivered an enjoyable brand of heavy NWOBHM with occasional similarities to the likes of HIGH TREASON, SEVENTH SON, HAMMERHEAD and (unsurprisingly) SWEET SAVAGE themselves, with particular highlights including "The Loner", "Get 'Em Off" and "Shoot Out In The City". A couple of the featured selections did, admittedly, suffer slightly from *'pilfered riff syndrome'*, notably the aforementioned "Get 'Em Off" and "Life And Death Of Pete", although the overall strength of the LP more than compensated for any minor shortcomings. The album performed admirably in terms of sales, and copies made it to mainland Britain (and, as it turns out, even further afield) in fairly substantial quantities, exposing the name of EZY MEAT to the broader metal community at long last. Additional gigs followed as a matter of course, and the lads finally sensed that they were making significant progress.

After a break of two years, spent trying out new material and attempting to introduce a few novel influences into their writing style, EZY MEAT re-emerged with a second self-financed long-player entitled »Rock Your Brains«, housed in an abysmal cover which did them no favours whatsoever. It was another heavy effort, although the overwhelming move was towards a more classy brand of guitar-oriented hard rock/metal with the occasional nod towards early MAMA'S BOYS or mid-period THIN LIZZY. Nevertheless, it was still (in spite of the fact that the tracks had now more or less been standardised at the five minute mark) quite a varied set of compositions (highlights including the powerful "I Gotta Run" and "Massacre"), all of which showcased the group's musical expertise pretty efficiently. Side two of the album, meanwhile, predominantly consisted of the twenty-minute "Alien Tale", a very ambitious, RUSH/ZEPPELIN-influenced epic which clearly revealed some of the influences which were now coming into play in EZY MEAT's latest batch of material. Ivan Lavery later elaborated upon his penchant for lengthy compositions: *'When I write songs, I like to tell a story, something that the listener can follow and understand, but I find it extremely difficult to express all my thoughts in short songs. Mind you, we've also written plenty of brief tracks; if someone demands a four minute song, then we could easily do it. For example, "Warrior", our track from »Rock Meets Metal«, the length of which was pretty much stipulated by Ebony. Personally, though, I prefer the long numbers!'* (Ref: Iron Pages No.50, September 1999).

Again, the new album proved to be a relatively successful affair, although it had drained the EZY MEAT coffers completely, and so there was little or no prospect of further self-financed records unless a particularly large windfall (or a proper deal) came their way. Nevertheless, 1987 saw the band featuring on a couple of compilations, with "Massacre" (not a THIN LIZZY cover, but a composition heavily influenced by Lynott's mob) appearing on Metalother's »Metal Warriör« six-tracker and the exclusive "Warrior" being recorded for Ebony's second »Rock Meets Metal« sampler. Sadly, however, a lack of public response, coupled with dwindling finances, meant that the lads finally had to call it a day a short time later, their farewell gig (ironically enough) being the best-attended of their entire career. Notwithstanding the fact that EZY MEAT has now been *'on hold'* for over a decade, however, the members are still in contact with one another and Ivan Lavery has been writing new material constantly since their demise. The outfit's two albums are worthy purchases for all fans of guitar-driven, heavy material, although the hefty asking price of recent years may well have frightened off a few buyers. Never fear, though, as it looks as though a CD reissue of both (with bonus tracks) is now on the cards. Even better, the good news is that there's a pretty significant chance that further brand-new EZY MEAT product will emerge at some stage.

LP's
»Not For Wimps« Electric Storm 1984
»Rock Your Brains« Electric Storm 1986

Exclusive Compilation Appearances
"Soho Escapade" on »Belfast« LP Homespun Records 1981
"Sexy Lady" on »Belfast« LP Homespun Records 1981
"Warrior" on »Rock Meets Metal II« LP Ebony 1987

Compilation Appearances
"Massacre" on »Metal Warriör« Mini-LP Metalother Records 1987

FACTORY

Ray Dodd

Prior to inking the deal for their one-off single with the Future Earth label (also home of LIMELIGHT and CHINAWITE) in 1982, the high-point of Yorkshire hopefuls FACTORY's career was probably a well-attended support appearance with the mighty DIAMOND HEAD at Tiffany's in Leeds a year previously. A popular local outfit who enjoyed considerable regional press and radio coverage in their time, FACTORY (who were, incidentally, entirely unrelated to the identically-named rock act from the late 60's/early 70's) chose to cover "You Are The Music" (a song originally performed by the 70's version of TRAPEZE, a power trio which featured the voice of Glenn Hughes) and make it the main focus of attention on their debut two-tracker. With their interpretation of the number apparently winning approval from the original composers (Mel and Tom Galley), the single (presented in a stickered, die-cut silver sleeve) was duly issued by the Doncaster-based label to the delight of the band's many loyal fans. Backed with the intriguingly-titled "The History Of The Turkey", the music has an undeniable 70's influence, and brings forth comparisons with the likes of DAWN TRADER and the NEXT BAND. Not typical NWOBHM fodder, and not something that you should be dreaming about at night, but it's still a passable effort.

As part of a long-standing arrangement between the Future Earth and Mausoleum labels

(which ultimately allowed LIMELIGHT and CHINAWITE to issue full albums on the continent, and which additionally gave helpful European exposure to a modest number of emergent British acts such as SEDUCER and SYAR), both tracks from the group's debut single were subsequently recycled on the unremarkable »Metal Prisoners« compilation, a peculiar record which, confusingly, featured four British bands in addition to Belgian heavyweights ACID. This would appear to have been the last vinyl outing for FACTORY (who also shouldn't be confused with the French bunch who recorded for labels such as Cobra at around the same time), however, as it looks as though the lads were never seriously considered (either by Mausoleum, Future Earth or anyone else) as particularly worthy candidates for a follow-up single or a full-length release of their own. I can't help but agree.

7" Singles
»You Are The Music« Future Earth Records 1982

Compilation Appearances
"You Are The Music" on »Metal Prisoners« LP Mausoleum 1983
"The History Of The Turkey" on »Metal Prisoners« LP Mausoleum 1983

FAIR WARNING

Steve Shearan (v)
Dean Cox (v,g)
Neil Farr (g)
John Eastaugh (b)
Danny Archer (d)

It's a pity that Wiltshire's FAIR WARNING (not to be confused with either the identically-named ZENO offshoot or some fairly obscure Australian namesakes, for example) didn't get around to making their vinyl debut until 1986, as their non-reconstructed style of metal would probably have been far more warmly received a couple of years earlier. There was, to be honest, little or no mention of the ensemble's activities in the years leading up to their grand entrance (although at least one of the participants, sticksman Danny

Archer, had apparently been involved with local part-timers WHEELZ beforehand), so I suspect that this was their chosen method of introducing themselves to an unsuspecting rock scene. Their opening gambit was an unassuming single, with the nominated A-side ("Dreamer") being a mid-paced number with a nice twin-guitar sound, bringing to mind such acts as STAMPEDE, WEAPON or BLACK AXE, whereas "Hold On" was a faster and heavier affair, with gruff vocals very much in the vein of CRUCIFIXION or BADGER. It wasn't a bad effort at all, although the consensus of opinion (from those who bothered to offer an opinion, that is), was that FAIR WARNING had missed the NWOBHM boat and were flogging a dead horse if they intended to plod ahead with such unfashionable and dated material.

Moving into 1987, however, it was suddenly all change on the FAIR WARNING front, and the unsettled group duly began to undergo a surprising number of personnel alterations within a period of only a few months, with newcomers Dean Martin (surely not) and Lee Jackson (if his nickname wasn't *'Python'* I'd be extremely surprised) eventually taking over on guitar, while Phil Peters assumed bass duties. With the revamped line-up came a more basic, commercial sound favoured by wannabes of the time such as CRY, as evidenced on their follow-up release, the laughably-titled »Rocking At The Speed Of Light« EP, unleashed in the second half of 1987. It was evident that FAIR WARNING were now embracing a rather conspicuous, new-found AC/DC influence (even attempting a *'risqué'* track in the form of "Tongue In Cheek"), which merely rendered their latest compositions instantly forgettable, and, in spite of a competent, if ultimately pointless, reworking of JUDAS PRIEST's oft-covered "Breakin' The Law", the three-tracker turned out to be a major disappointment. The fans failed to take much notice of the release, and few actually bothered to cough up for a copy. Incidentally, the EP, issued on the short-lived Areba concern, was produced by Andy Boulton of TOKYO BLADE (in fact, it was the latter's own label), who were pretty much the only other metal outfit of note to emanate from the county of Wiltshire during the NWOBHM era.

It's worth noting (well, almost) that the reverse sleeve of the EP announces the tracks to be taken from their soon-to-be-released album »First Public Warning«, although this seems to be more a case of wishful thinking than anything else. Nevertheless, there's solid evidence to suggest that the long-player was indeed recorded at around the same time, but it almost certainly wasn't mixed, let alone pressed up in any form. It's also fairly safe to assume that FAIR WARNING didn't survive for very long after their 12" was issued (they recruited new drummer Andy Griffiths towards the end of 1987, and were still playing the odd local gig as late as the spring of 1988, but things went ominously quiet soon after), and the various band members (with the exception of erstwhile guitarist Neil Farr, who was briefly involved with the dubiously-named DAWN TORPEDO in 1987, and original drummer Danny Archer, who later tried again with the popular-but-unsuccessful BARDICHE) don't seem to have turned up in other outfits, so that, as they say, is that.

12" EP's
»**Rocking At The Speed Of Light**« Areba Records 1987

7" Singles
»**Dreamer**« Wild Turkey Records 1986

FALSE IDOLS

Neil Templar (v)
Dave Percival (g)
Chris Widger (g)
Steve Kershaw (b)
Paul Bird (d)

The Avon-based quintet known as the FALSE IDOLS are certainly worthy of inclusion in this mighty tome by virtue of their »Ten Seconds To Midnight« two-tracker (released on the small-time Caveman label) from 1981, although it has long been suggested that this bunch might once have been responsible for a single or two of a somewhat more anarchic nature. This looks increasingly unlikely, however, with confusion seemingly having arisen due to the existence of an identically-named London combo who issued a couple of singles in the punk/new wave style at around the turn of the decade (and also because of the observation that Caveman wasn't exactly renowned for metal releases). In any case, "Ten Seconds To Midnight" itself is a cheerful, tuneful metal/punk crossover in the vein of SHADOWFAX, RED RAGE or (particularly) BASELINE, which undoubtedly borders on genuine NWOBHM territory. The guitar work is surprisingly capable for such an unrenowned act (distinctly evocative of early DIAMOND HEAD in places) but the effectiveness of the overall sound is, nonetheless, slightly diminished by the largely unconvincing vocals of Neil Templar. It's a great pity, really, as the FALSE IDOLS weren't actually all that far away from REINCARNATE or BOLLWEEVIL territory. Even taking the frontman's failings into account, however, both the A-side and the highly-similar reverse ("American Nightmare") are competent, mid-paced rockers that should put a smile on the face of any self-respecting NWOBHM fan.

The persevering FALSE IDOLS were, to be perfectly honest, never a particularly prominent name on the fertile West Country music scene, although the ensemble kept things going until at least 1983, at which point they were featured on 'Out West', a televised showcase for local talent which was broadcast in the Bristol area. Appearing alongside the mighty JAGUAR, no less (and the long-forgotten STREETS AHEAD), their contribution seems not to have been captured for posterity, which is unfortunate, but understandable. After their fifteen minutes of fame (well, ten minutes of mediocrity), however, the outfit probably failed to generate the same level of interest or to maintain their initial momentum, and presumably lost the will to continue in the long term. None of the members went on to greater things, as far as I'm aware, so I guess it was only a fleeting attempt at finding fame and fortune. Their one-off vinyl offering, incidentally, comes in a suitably metal-looking sleeve with the band logo and heraldic image of a knight's head, and you might, if you look hard enough (especially if someone has unwittingly placed it in their punk section), be able to find yourself a copy of this one at a pretty reasonable price.

7" Singles
»Ten Seconds To Midnight« Caveman Records 1981

FAST KUTZ

Keith Davison (v)
Kenny Nicholson (g)
Nev Percival (b)
Paul Fowler (d)

After failing to find a great deal of commercial success with either the HOLLAND or HAMMER (see separate entries) albums, the original members followed their own individual career paths from then on, although only Kenny Nicholson was to make a significant further impact on the metal scene. By 1986, the guitarist had parted company with the struggling HAMMER, and began negotiating with the latter's label, Ebony, to see if there was any chance of the company sanctioning a solo LP. Ebony seemed keen to give the talented chap a chance to do his own thing, and material was soon being penned for future release. Nicholson drafted in some local cohorts to help out on the recording side (drummer Paul Fowler, bassist Nev Percival and erstwhile WARRIOR vocalist Marty Clerkin), and eventually decided that the project would benefit from a 'proper' identity, whereupon FAST KUTZ was born. After a few months of rehearsals, the band seemed to have gelled pretty well, and the quartet soon convinced Ebony that financing a full album would indeed be a good idea. After some brief discussions, FAST KUTZ were initially afforded the opportunity to contribute a track to one of the label's series of samplers in order to test the water. Upon entering the studio for the first time, however, the group rapidly reached the conclusion that frontman Clerkin wasn't cutting the mustard, and the lads were therefore forced to look for a replacement pretty sharpish.

Luckily, a suitable candidate soon emerged in the form of ex-GYPO frontman Keith Davison, who was subsequently forced to learn the outfit's repertoire in a single week, but the plucky chap somehow managed to cope with these demands. Now that FAST KUTZ had finally managed to get their act together properly at the second attempt, the lads honoured their commitments to Ebony by laying down the strong "Midnight Love", which duly appeared on »The Metal Collection Vol.II« early in 1987, the substantial track confirming that FAST KUTZ certainly represented Nicholson's long-held desire to create a rather heavier beast than before. Following a generally-favourable public response to this effort, the group were swiftly snapped up for a full LP, which was duly recorded within a matter of days and rushed out with great haste (under the title of »Burnin'«) a couple of months later. It was, by anyone's standards, a far more enjoyable listening experience than either the HAMMER or HOLLAND albums had been, with mainman Nicholson (who had, incidentally, been the main songwriting force in both of his previous outfits) having now eschewed the raunchy rock of bygone years and established a somewhat more straight-ahead, powerful proposition.

It was, nonetheless, a distinctive release, with a strong vocal performance and some heavy guitar work suggesting a rather unusual combination of ELIXIR, SWEET SAVAGE and WOLFSBANE, with stand-out tracks including the excellent "Driving Me Crazy" (nice twin-guitar riffing) and "Fight To Be Free". In fact, at least one of the numbers featured ("Driving Me Crazy") actually dated back to the formative HOLLAND days (which shows just how capable the latter act might have become if they hadn't lost the plot at an early stage), so I suspect that this was the heavy album that Nicholson had striven to record all along. All in all, it was a highly impressive debut set, marred slightly by some hackneyed lyrics and song titles, not to mention a pretty dire cover. For some peculiar reason, however (I guess certain people associated 'Cleveland' with 'Ohio'), the British press of the day seemed to be under the impression that the band were American, and (knowing the mentality of certain reviewers) the lads would probably have received a somewhat easier ride if their true nationality had been established at an early stage. As it was, the reviews tended to be pretty lukewarm at the time, and sales were correspondingly average in the main, which is a pity.

Following the album's release (the group had, incidentally, won the approval of none other than Ozzy Osbourne, who praised "Fight To Be Free" in no uncertain terms while guesting on the 'Friday Rock Show'), the outfit soon found themselves parting company with bassist Nev Percival (Ian McLaughlan came in as a replacement), and they also proceeded to recruit ARIZONA member Ian Gillson as a permanent second guitarist. Still, Ozzy's kind patronage had clearly worked to their considerable advantage, and the reshuffled FAST KUTZ were soon being invited to contribute a prestigious session to the 'Friday Rock Show'. First broadcast on the 26th of June 1987, the session featured specially-recorded versions of "Looking For Love", "Midnight Love", "Playing With Fire" and "Driving Me Crazy", all taken from their vinyl debut. It was, by far, one of the more enjoyable showcases commissioned by Tommy Vance at the time, but it seems to have done little to promote the band or win them a new fan base. In spite of the fact that FAST KUTZ generally seemed to be faring rather more poorly than the musically-inferior HOLLAND/HAMMER had done, Ebony duly encouraged the musicians to lay down a second album (allocating them the same generous period of seven days to record the whole shebang once again), and it initially looked as though another FAST KUTZ long-player would be hitting the shops at some point in 1988.

In the event, however, the cash-strapped sponsors insisted that there was now little point in proceeding with the release, given that they

barely had sufficient funds to get the record pressed, let alone promote it particularly effectively, leaving the hapless bunch well and truly in the lurch. After a few more months of regional gigging to keep themselves busy while waiting for their situation to improve, internal friction began to build up, and the resentful members of FAST KUTZ were at each other's throats before long. Inevitably, the group disintegrated within a fairly short space of time, and Paul Fowler proceeded to join forces with the ailing BLACK ROSE for a year or so. Although the remaining musicians appear to have drifted away from the scene altogether in the short term, some of them are now getting back into the swing of things by playing in small-time pub acts. Paul Fowler and Keith Davison, for example, have appeared in various rock covers bands in the North East over the years, while Kenny Nicholson himself has recently teamed up with erstwhile HAMMER colleague Marty Wilkinson in a bunch of crowd-pleasers called OUTRAGEOUS WALLPAPER. Given the chance, however, he would jump at the opportunity to get his beloved FAST KUTZ going once more, and I'm sure that many fans of this outfit would be interested to hear that unreleased second LP (or, even better, some brand-new material) at some point in the future. I think the relevant phrase is 'watch this space'...

LP's
»Burnin'« Ebony 1987

Compilation Appearances
"Midnight Love" on »The Metal Collection Vol.II« LP Ebony 1987

FILTHY RICH

John Owen (v,g)
David Lewis (b)
Wyn Roberts (d)

Following the untimely demise of the immensely popular TRIDENT (see separate entry), band mainman John Owen decided that he would subsequently do his own thing, musically speaking. After a rather ambitious attempt to instigate a solo career with the assistance of various session musicians, Owen's conclusion was that the North Wales music scene was, in fact, crying out for a melodic rock trio to call their own. With the unknown duo of David Lewis and Wyn Roberts being drafted in to form a full-time outfit, FILTHY RICH (neither the first nor last bunch of heavy hopefuls to adopt the identity) was conceived in around 1986. After a bit of local gigging and rehearsing, the group released their inadvisably-titled »She's 17« (in your dreams, grandpa) single (b/w "Love Ain't A Fool") the following year, and hoped that this would set them well on their way to fame and fortune. Recorded at a very minor studio (The Cottage in Macclesfield), this tuneful slice of commercial rock/pop in the style of US or VIRGINIA WOLF didn't exactly set the world on fire, and, apart from the odd vocal nuance on the B-side (a fairly dull ballad), there's virtually nothing to remind us of TRIDENT's significant musical legacy.

Issued in a rather uninspiring monochrome sleeve picturing the three band members (who could hardly have looked more shifty if they had tried), the two-tracker didn't exactly sell by the bucketload, although I've no doubt that FILTHY RICH developed a significant following of their own (in the absence of a great deal of local competition, admittedly) on the back of this one-off release. The persevering trio were frequently to be found touting their wares around the humble music venues of Wales and the North West of England for the remainder of the decade, and gained the occasional mention in publications such as 'Kerrang' along the way, but presumably didn't have enough ready cash to finance any additional vinyl releases. As a result, they don't seem to have survived the vital transition into the 90's, and their ultimate demise failed to make front-page headlines. Too bad. How about a TRIDENT reformation, John?

7" Singles
»She's 17« JM Records 1987

FIREBIRD

Will Barker (v,g)
Jim Carter (rg)
Andy Rowe (b)
Steve Goodyear (k)
Steve Ricks (d)

Recorded in 1979 under the aegis of Ian Gillan at his Kingsway Studio facility, the only release from little-known Berkshire mob FIREBIRD was the »Change« two-tracker, which was unleashed upon an unsuspecting rock scene early the following year. This wasn't exactly prime-era NWOBHM, mind you, and there's certainly a bit of an early 70's influence in their music, particularly in the keyboard department, but it's a pretty good debut effort all the same. "Change" itself is an unusual number (too pedestrian for its own good at times) which alternates between vocal passages in the style of HAMMERHEAD's "Lochinvar" and faster, decidedly MAIDEN-ish, twin-guitar assaults. On the reverse, "Nightride", the quintet reveal that they desperately aspired to emulate BLUE ÖYSTER CULT, making a remarkably accomplished attempt at cloning "Don't Fear The Reaper", although they do manage to stamp some of their own identity on the track. FIREBIRD were one of the less prominent rock outfits of the day in terms of studio activities and live appearances, and it looks as though they never seriously considered themselves to have a genuine chance of making it big in the music business. They had certainly split by the mid-80's, possibly quite a bit earlier, and few of the musicians made any further impact on the music scene, although keyboard player Steve Goodyear subsequently formed a more AOR-influenced outfit called EAST NORTH EAST, an act who ultimately failed to make much of an impression in the long run.

It might be worth mentioning, in passing, that there could be an extremely tenuous DIAMOND HEAD connection here, in that FIREBIRD was one of the many names originally mooted for the Stourbridge lads, and it's possible (although it's difficult to imagine how the parties would have come into contact with one another) that they may subsequently have donated the rejected moniker to this bunch. The fact that there's a sleeve credit to 'Colin and Brian', possibly a reference to Messrs Kimberley and Tatler, adds weight to this conjecture, but I could be completely off the mark here, to be honest. The privately-issued FIREBIRD single does turn up from time to time, but only a tiny quantity of wrap-round picture sleeves (featuring a truly bizarre image) were ever fabricated, presumably for promotional purposes. Keep your fingers crossed!

7" Singles
»Change« Rat Records 1980

FIREBRAND

D. Sullivan

The excellently-named FIREBRAND appear to have been on the go for quite some time before getting to the vinyl stage (either that or there was more than one British act who shared the identity), since they seemed to be touting their wares around the Midlands and the West Country right at the start of the NWOBHM explosion. The band appear to have been based somewhere around this general area (their one-off 7" was released/sponsored/sold by a shop in Warwickshire, so this seems like a good bet), and they eventually got some product onto the market in 1985, when the minuscule What Records issued their debut two-tracker. Both "Never Felt This Way Before" and "I'm Leaving" turned out to be pretty unremarkable, pedestrian rockers with melodic arrangements, the overall effect being undeniably similar to such unrenowned contemporaries as US and FILTHY RICH. Flipside "I'm Leaving" is probably the stronger of the pair, and features some semi-reasonable vocals and guitar contributions, but it still falls well short of prime-era NWOBHM. No doubt the group were a rather more forceful proposition in the live environment, but this particular release presumably failed to cause a great deal of excitement at the time, and sales can hardly have amounted to all that much. The members of FIREBRAND had almost certainly called in the receivers within a couple of years, leaving only a seldom-seen single in their wake, a record which was issued in a picture sleeve showing a female figure in a state of disrobement, which was all very *'artistic'*, if you know what I mean.

7" Singles
»Never Felt This Way Before« What Records 1985

FIRECLOWN

Tony Dowler (v,g)
Gyp Nicholson (g)
Pete Dutton (b)
Graham Darbishire (d)

Manchester's excellently-named FIRECLOWN, who first established themselves in around 1980, were, when it came to their quest for a novel identity, one of several groups to have sought literary inspiration from the fantasy novelist Michael Moorcock (see also the TYGERS OF PAN TANG, MOURNBLADE and the numerous acts called STORMBRINGER, for example), and the ensemble initially came to prominence via a demo tape in early 1982 or thereabouts. With 'Kerrang' giving some useful exposure to the outfit a short time later in their 'Armed And Ready' section, it was revealed that bassist Pete Dutton once held the dubious distinction of playing alongside ex-BUDGIE stalwarts Ray Phillips and Tony Bourge in a little-known bunch called FREEZ, which was vaguely interesting, I suppose. To suggest that FIRECLOWN were an industrious live act would certainly be something of an understatement, although their somewhat contentious claim to have played over two hundred gigs within their first sixteen months of existence is surely enough to cause a few querulous eyebrows to be raised in suspicion. Their biggest moment of glory, however, must surely have been a prestigious appearance at the Monmore Festival in Wolverhampton during the spring of 1982, in the impressive company of acts such as TYTAN, LIMELIGHT and VARDIS.

With their quest for a deal drawing little response, the ambitious band subsequently resolved to lay down the tracks for their debut three-tracker at their own expense, and duly saw to it that the record would ultimately be issued in the form of a 10" EP, something of a novelty for NWOBHM releases of the era. Sadly, however, their collective finances didn't stretch to the manufacture of a picture sleeve, something which might well have helped to shift a few additional copies. In any case, the trio of songs featured, namely "Invasion" (an energetic and powerful opener), "Poor Man" and "Magic" (both slightly more raunchy and laid-back pieces, but still listenable enough), all conformed fairly broadly to the overwhelming style of the period, and they certainly draw a few comparisons with the likes of JAMESON RAID, SLENDER THREAD and SCORCHED EARTH. The one-off EP seems to have been the highlight of a fairly unsuccessful career, though, and FIRECLOWN appear to have made little progress after its initial release in 1983 (they played at the farewell gig of local legends ROX towards the end of 1985, although I suspect that this might actually have represented a one-off reunion for both outfits), although the record itself (which was commonly offered for sale at exorbitant prices at one stage, but has now dropped to a more affordable level) remains a reasonably popular item among NWOBHM aficionados.

10" EP's

»Invasion« Fireclown Records 1983

FIST

Keith Satchfield (v,g)
Dave Irwin (g)
John Wylie (b)
Harry Hill (d)

It has become a well-documented fact that the origins of Tyneside heroes FIST (not to be confused with their Canadian namesakes who operated as MYOFIST outside North America) can be traced back to a highly-regarded bunch of rockers called AXE, although it's not quite so well-known that the latter had themselves evolved from an obscure club outfit called WARBECK, who originally came into existence in the mid-70's. AXE, on the other hand, hit the scene a couple of years later, tirelessly slogging their guts out in the pubs and clubs of the North for quite some time (developing an enviable reputation along the way), although they ultimately failed to get their much-anticipated breakthrough in spite of considerable local popularity. Eventually, they decided to call it a day (laying the blame squarely at the feet of the dominant punk movement, which had distracted media attention away from the still-thriving rock scene) at some point in 1979, but regrouped (with a new bassist) early the following year under the revised identity of FIST, whereupon the lads soon found themselves at the forefront of the NWOBHM movement. Along with the new name (which they adopted to avoid confusion with the relatively successful American version of AXE) came something of a stylistic change, the band retaining much of their original material but coming up with shorter, faster arrangements with which to mount a concerted challenge for fame and fortune.

Things worked out well (a bit too well, if truth be told) for FIST, and they were allegedly snapped up by the emergent Neat Records immediately after their first gig. Following a swiftly-recorded demo to prove they were just as capable on tape, they were shepherded into the studio and encouraged to record a 7" single, and it would appear that this whirlwind of activity even took the quartet themselves by surprise. Nevertheless, the lads delivered the goods as requested, and the debut single did their chances no harm whatsoever, the pairing of "Name, Rank And Serial Number" and "You'll Never Get Me Up In One Of Those" giving rise to an extremely energetic (if slightly primitive) two-tracker with similarities to the upbeat, semi-raunchy material of MORE or the STARFIGHTERS. The all-new FIST were, without question, now widely regarded as part of the ubiquitous NWOBHM movement, but it's fair to say that they hadn't completely left the 70's behind (there was more than a hint of DEEP PURPLE or GILLAN in some of their early efforts) when they reinvented themselves. Asked about their direction at the time, the members collectively revealed: 'Well, we feel we've got the aggression of HM but we try to write songs that are not just based around simple riffs. They're not HM songs but we are still a sort of HM band and we play with the same sort of aggression. I'd rather not be hard rock, I'd much rather be HM than hard rock.' (Ref: Teenage Depression, Issue 13, 1980). So, not remotely confusing, then.

The single sold in impressive quantities, and the band were soon booked for a session on Capital Radio, which no doubt helped to expose them to the major players in London (as, apparently, did an ecstatically-received gig at the Ruskin Arms with SAMSON). In due course, Neat came to an arrangement with the much larger MCA concern (as in the case of the TYGERS OF PAN TANG and WHITE SPIRIT), which allowed FIST to benefit from the more abundant resources available to larger companies. Soon, after the label had hurriedly reissued their debut single, the lads were being ushered into the studio once again, this time to record a full album. The lads later insisted that they had been ill-prepared for all this activity, but they still managed to get through the recording sessions relatively unscathed, emerging with a full-length effort entitled »Turn The Hell On«. It wasn't, admittedly, the most memorable debut offering of all time, but it contained a few decent numbers, including "Forever Amber", "The Vamp" and "Terminus". Having said all that, it might have been advisable to have waited a few months longer so that the musicians had been given a chance to refine these compositions a bit and to work in some rather more distinctive arrangements. Two singles followed (as did an appearance on MCA's »Brute Force« sampler with "Brain Damage"), namely »Forever Amber« and the seldom-seen »Collision Course«, although neither seriously rivalled the success of their debut two-tracker.

The band remained in the public eye during the early months of 1981, touring the UK successfully in support of UFO, followed by a useful appearance on Neat's »Lead Weight« sampler with the otherwise-unavailable "Throwing In The Towel" (credited, with immense comic genius, as "Throwing In The *Trowel*" on quite a few copies). Strangely, this set also featured an old AXE favourite ("S.S. Giro") from 1978, a track which FIST would later resurrect themselves. Nevertheless, the group's activities tailed off over the ensuing months (a situation which wasn't helped by the fact that their label repeatedly refused to subsidise a European tour, cutting the group off from an important and expanding fan base), amid a great deal of dissatisfaction among various members of the outfit, and it eventually became clear that they would have to undergo a bit of restructuring in order to get back on the right track. In the event, frontman Keith Satchfield and bassist John Wylie departed in not-particularly-amicable circumstances, and a trio of new recruits were drafted in *viz.* vocalist Glen Coates (from HOLLOW GROUND), guitarist John Roach (from MYTHRA) and bassist Norman 'Pop' Appleby (from the less illustrious THRUST). It took a while for the new-look FIST to become accustomed to one another, but they emerged a stronger and (on the face of it) a more democratic outfit in the long term, with all of the members now contributing to the writing side of things.

By the early months of 1982, FIST were looking to the future with renewed optimism, although they were now a Neat-sponsored concern again, since MCA had understandably lost interest after the relatively poor performance of their unremarkable debut long-player. Nevertheless, their original label still had confidence in the lads, and FIST were soon laying down a second full-length effort at good old Impulse Studios. To be honest, the aptly-titled »Back With A Vengeance« is the album which should have put the group right back into contention, as it was a far more metal-oriented and capable effort than their debut set. In fact, it's a pity that they weren't able to deliver such a strong effort at the first attempt, as it would surely have turned FIST into a band who could have rivalled the likes of IRON MAIDEN and SAXON in the popularity stakes. The new musicians raised the standard of the material to a much higher level (especially the powerful vocals of Glen Coates), and tracks such as "Dog Soldier", "Devil Rise", "Too Hot" and "Turn The Hell On" (presumably having been left off their first album for some unknown reason) were right up there with such luminaries as DIAMOND HEAD and DEF LEPPARD in terms of songwriting, originality and musicianship. The reworked version of "S.S. Giro" was something of a triumph, too, and it's difficult to find a weak track at all, which is saying something when compared with the band's debut LP.

FIST continued to tout their wares around in an attempt to sell themselves to the masses, and gigged (including a support slot with the extremely popular Y&T) whenever the possibility arose, although they soon began to feel they had got their act together slightly too late, and the initial NWOBHM-fuelled buzz was now beginning to die down at precisely the wrong time. Still, they made a pretty good effort the second time around, and won their place on the 'Friday Rock Show' a short time later, where they ran through session versions of "Dog Soldier" and "Vamp", plus two new numbers in the form of "Lucy" and a cheerful cover of DION's "The Wanderer". The session, broadcast on the 30th of July 1982, turned out to be one of FIST's last productive visits to the studio, although they subsequently issued their fairly shocking interpretation of "The Wanderer" as a single in its own right. The fans and reviewers didn't get the joke (if, indeed, it really was intended as such), and began to wonder whether the band might be losing the plot. FIST were interviewed by 'Kerrang' towards the end of 1982, and were, by this stage, putting on a brave face and trying to convince the world that they were still a good bet for future success. As it transpired, the lads were living on borrowed time, and, although they apparently trundled on for another year or two (rather longer than they should have, if you ask me), the unit appears to have called it a day at some point in the early months of 1985. It was a pity that things had gone so badly wrong for FIST, as they had valiantly clawed their way back from critical disapproval to win over large sections of the rock community, and it would appear that they were just one of the unfortunate victims of the post-NWOBHM backlash that the media were bound to instigate sooner or later.

Several of the group's former members continued to play some sort of role in the music business thereafter, although none were to achieve any great level of success, and most have now returned to their day jobs. Drummer Harry Hill, for example, later teamed up with his erstwhile colleague John Roach (who is, incidentally, still playing for his own enjoyment and contemplating a return to the recording side of things at some stage) in a popular local rock covers outfit known as CENTREFOLD, although neither are now involved with the fortunes of this long-standing act. Dave Irwin, on the other hand, occasionally acted as a stand-in guitarist for VENOM (helping the evil ones to honour various live obligations during the mid-80's, notably their North American tour of 1985), although the axeman no longer enjoys such high-profile musical activities. I'm also pleased to report that Glen Coates (another one-time CENTREFOLD stalwart), meanwhile, is still putting his considerable talents to good use, and has apparently been in more or less constant employment ever since the unfortunate demise of FIST. His latest vocation, however, is entertaining the punters as a cabaret singer at a seaside holiday camp! How the mighty have fallen…

LP's
»Turn The Hell On« MCA 1980
»Back With A Vengeance« Neat 1982
[Also pressed in limited quantities on yellow vinyl]

7" Singles
»Name, Rank And Serial Number« Neat 1980
[Original issue, both tracks different to album versions]
»Name, Rank And Serial Number« MCA 1980
[Second issue in identical sleeve]
»Forever Amber« MCA 1980
[B-side "Brain Damage" non-LP]
»Collision Course« MCA 1980
[B-side "Law Of The Jungle" non-LP, very few copies in picture sleeve]
»The Wanderer« Neat 1982
[A-side non-LP]

CD's
»Turn The Hell On« MCA Japan 1992
[Japanese issue with two bonus tracks]
»Back With A Vengeance« Teichiku 1992
[Japanese issue]

Exclusive Compilation Appearances
"Throwing In The Towel" on »Lead Weight« LP Neat 1981/CD Teichiku 1992

Compilation Appearances
"Brain Damage" on »Brute Force« LP MCA 1980
"S.S. Giro" on »Lead Weight« LP Neat 1981/CD Teichiku 1992
[Under the name of AXE, different to album version]
"Lost And Found" on »60 Minutes Plus« Cassette Neat 1982/CD Teichiku 1992
"Turn The Hell On" on »Metal Killers Kollection II« Do-LP Castle Communications 1986 + »Metal Masters« 4-CD Box Castle Communications 1993 + »Heavy Metal Collection 1« CD X-Tra Collection 1993
"S.S. Giro" on »NWOBHM '79 Revisited« Do-CD Phonogram 1990
[Under the name of FIST]
"Forever Amber" on »NWOBHM Vol.3« Bootleg CD 1992
"Name, Rank And Serial Number" on »Give 'Em Hell« CD Nectar Masters 1995

5 A.M.

Green
Slater

By all accounts, the unremarkably-monikered 5 A.M. were hardly a household name during the NWOBHM era, and (on the evidence of their sole two-tracker) only skirted around the periphery of the energetic new metal sound with their fairly lightweight brand of inoffensively melodic material. They seem to have been a quartet (signed copies of their single credit Mark, Steve, Greg and Paz), and the consensus of opinion appears to be that they were based somewhere in the East Midlands, with a tacit suggestion coming from certain quarters that 5 A.M. might just have been pre-MARZ in some way. Admittedly, the vocalist does sound similar to the latter's Steve Farmer, and I suppose that the *'Mark'* might refer to Mark Lindley. *'Paz'*, on the other hand, *could* represent Ian Padgett, so there's a bit of corroboration, although the writing credits suggest the involvement of a couple of other individuals who had little or nothing to do with MARZ, so we'd better keep an open mind at the moment. Still, the music of 5 A.M. appears to have been considerably more accessible and 70's-influenced than the hard-rocking MARZ (and it had even less in common with the markedly heavier OVERDRIVE), so you shouldn't really get too excited in any case.

Whatever the story, the long-forgotten band's only known single was released (without a picture sleeve) in 1980, and few copies have surfaced in recent times. The self-financed, double A-sided effort couples "I Don't Believe It" (a very catchy affair with similarities to the likes of TRACK 4 or ISENGARD) with the less-impressive "Suzanne", which starts off like a COCKNEY REBEL-style singalong before losing the plot completely and meandering off into cod-reggae territory, so neither composition is exactly prime-era NWOBHM by any stretch of the imagination. It looks as though the general public were less-than-impressed by this modest opening gambit, though, and I don't imagine that the unremarkable ensemble remained a going concern for all that long thereafter. Still, at least if you pick up a cheap copy on your travels, you might (if the rumours are true) have something you can trade on (assuming there are any particularly fervent MARZ/OVERDRIVE fans out there) at some point in the future.

7" Singles
»I Don't Believe It« Terry Dactyl Records 1980

FLASH HARRY

Tony Jezzard (v,g)
Wayne Paulsen (b)
Bob Markham (b)
Charles Fellows (d)

Although the humble origins of the excellently-named FLASH HARRY (derived from a character in the famous 'St. Trinian's' series of films) practically date back to Victorian times (OK, maybe a slight exaggeration there), the unrenowned 'band' (essentially a solo vehicle for aspiring guitarist/vocalist Tony Jezzard, the latter being ably assisted by a handful of guest musicians) were certainly on the Midlands club scene right at the beginning of the NWOBHM. It's a tad surprising, therefore, that their one and only single, the portentously-titled »Turbulent Sea Of Emotion«, didn't appear until as late as 1985. Aided and abetted by two bassists (one on each track, that is) and a session drummer, Mr Jezzard offers us two slightly quirky rock/metal numbers (more of a cross between WOLFSBANE and THE CULT than anything else) with a distinctive punk/power pop (SIOUXSIE AND THE BANSHEES or the RAMONES) attitude also present. It was, as you can imagine, a fairly strange combination, and it hardly represents a typical NWOBHM sound by any means. The A-side was, to be honest, a bit overblown and repetitive, but the reverse (rejoicing under the award-winningly clichéd title of "No Place To Hide") turns out to be a listenable example of more straightforward, mid-paced rock/metal which is undeniably similar to some of WOLFSBANE's early material.

As evidenced by the photo on the picture sleeve (Jezzard himself sitting amongst an impressively varied collection of punk and rock records), the members of FLASH HARRY were clearly quite keen to embrace an unusually wide range of musical styles, and the sheer diversity of their assorted influences certainly comes across on vinyl. No doubt the group developed a local following of some description (assuming they managed to maintain a stable gigging line-up, that is), but there wasn't really much chance of Jezzard's off-the-wall ideas winning favour with the general rock press of the time, so I guess the project fizzled out within a couple of years. I've no idea what happened to the man himself after this single appeared, but it looks as though he and his cohorts only left this one (scarce, but not stunningly valuable) release for posterity.

7" Singles
»Turbulent Sea Of Emotion« SRT 1985

FLASHPOINT

Kev Graham (v,b)
Ian Toomey (g)
Pete Toomey (g)
Steve Turton (d)

With Cumbria's popular and long-lived BITCHES SIN having finally fragmented towards the end of 1986 after the initial failure of their second album in the American market (a re-recorded version was released 'posthumously' in the UK towards the end of 1988), it took a remarkably short time for the nucleus of Ian and Pete Toomey to form an all-new outfit called FLASHPOINT, an embryonic version coming together in January 1987. With the outfit having become a stable, serious proposition within a couple of months, local gigs followed throughout the North West, and their first tape, featuring "Grand Prix", "No More Love, No More Lies" and "Rock'n'Roll Heart", was circulated to journalists. Although the feedback was generally positive, the material wasn't regarded as sufficiently ground-breaking to attract record company interest, so the lads (the line-up being completed by drummer Steve Turton and vocalist Kev Graham) decided that it would be best to issue their own vinyl product. While their debut release was initially scheduled to be a single, this notion was rapidly scrapped and a full album was recorded at the Linden Sounds facility towards the end of the year.

The outfit's »No Point Of Reference« long-player hit the shops with a great deal of fanfare a couple of months later, the adverts playing unashamedly on the BITCHES SIN connection (as if that was really going to make much difference) and quoting some remarkably favourable reviews from the music press. Indeed, the likes of 'Metal Forces' and 'Kerrang' did the foursome a great service by offering commendatory opinions of the release as a whole, although most comparisons tended to be directed towards rather more commercial, lightweight outfits such as DOKKEN and RAINBOW. This wasn't actually too far from the truth at all, and FLASHPOINT's polished brand of melodic rock (the album featuring a few backing vocals from erstwhile BITCHES SIN compatriot Frank Quegan) sits quite happily alongside mid-80's LP releases from the likes of STRATUS, LIONHEART, TOBRUK and the TYGERS OF PAN TANG. Highlights would certainly include the upbeat "Blackjack", "Modern Lover" and "Grand Prix", although it has to be said that the vocal performance of Kev Graham is pretty average in places. Mind you, sales of the FLASHPOINT debut were reasonably brisk at the time, especially considering the fact that it was a self-financed effort, which must have been a genuine relief for the musicians involved with the venture. Nevertheless, it was quite a limited pressing (which sold out pretty quickly), and, since it was never re-pressed, the release remains a fairly expensive collectable these days.

FLASHPOINT was very much a one-off project, and there was little, if any, activity from the band members in the months following the album's release. A couple of years later, however, Pete Toomey was reunited with vocalist Frank Quegan in another studio concern called the PATRIOTS, an ensemble who originally came together to write material inspired by the Gulf War of the early 90's. Although the short-lived outfit (a couple of guest musicians helped out on the recording front) issued a couple of well-received tapes (material from which was even played to the British troops who were involved in the conflict) in a fairly analogous melodic rock style, the intended CD offering never actually came about (for reasons unknown), and Pete Toomey was soon turning his hand to other musical projects, such as an occasional live band with the highly questionable name of the BEARDED CLAMS. He also proceeded to set up a company called Green Man Products, which, in addition to promoting his own releases, also distributed a variety of 'new age' tapes and literature, mostly related to goings-on in the Lake District. He has also helped out, on the promotion side of things, with some of his former colleagues' subsequent projects, such as Frank Quegan's Christian rock outfit, REACH.

LP's
»No Point Of Reference« Private 1987

FLIGHT 77

Dave Sweet (v)
Paul Eustice (g)
Steve Cox (b,k)
Mike Tremethick (d)

The little-remembered FLIGHT 77, inhabitants of the NWOBHM desert known as Cornwall, are yet another of those small-time acts who seem to have made absolutely no impression on the national rock scene in the first instance, and were, it would appear, not even a particularly well-known ensemble in their locality at the time. Nevertheless, the quartet still managed to get to the vinyl stage back in 1982, delivering a self-financed two-tracker featuring "Looking For The Aliens" and "Stranger", a pair of very tuneful efforts with occasional similarities to the likes of LORELEI and the DICK SMITH BAND. It's not out-and-out metal, though, and it's certainly a bit on the poppy side at times, although the capable A-side (with some atypical-but-crap lyrics about visitors from space) is a listenable enough affair evoking a few comparisons with DIAMOND HEAD's "Makin' Music". The flipside, however, is a disturbingly funky (it practically has a latino feel in the mid-section) slice of rock which fails to do the outfit any favours whatsoever, and which would undoubtedly have alienated the vast majority of NWOBHM fans of the day. It looks as though this was the only vinyl offering from FLIGHT 77, who presumably went back into hiding almost immediately, and none of the members appear to have resurfaced elsewhere, which is perfectly understandable, given the lack of heavy talent in the region. Their one-off 7", meanwhile, might not be archetypal NWOBHM, but it's still worth picking up if you happen to spot it cheaply, so look out for a distinctive picture sleeve which incorporates their logo into a 'first contact' type of image.

7" Singles
»Looking For The Aliens« Private 1982

FORCE

Graham Careless (v)

Gary Chapman (g)
Stu Clarke (g)
Fez Ferriday (b)
Pete Wayne (k)
Roger Whitehouse (d)

It looked as though Birmingham's CRYER had, to all intents and purposes, bitten the dust completely by the end of 1982 (having lost their way and become disenchanted by media apathy), but it turned out not to be the case after all. Two years later, they resurfaced out of the blue, brandishing a new name (the rather overused FORCE) and a full album deal with the Heavy Metal label. How this all came about is open to speculation, although I get the impression that the group might actually have split and then reformed some time later, rather than just reinventing themselves at some point in 1983. In any case, they hardly went out of their way to promote themselves as a brand-new proposition, and most people picked up on the CRYER connection almost immediately. The long-player itself, entitled »Set Me Free…« (and issued in a pretty atrocious cover), appeared within a remarkably short space of time after the lads announced that they were back in business, and it featured a handful of numbers which would immediately be familiar to those who had heard CRYER's single or 'Friday Rock Show' session a few years previously.

Even so, there were plenty of new compositions of equal (if not greater) musical merit on display, all of which served to show that this was considerably more than a retrospective CRYER anthology. In general, the feeling was very much along the lines of their earlier material from around the turn of the decade, although there was a marginally less overblown and serious tone to the proceedings, the whole affair being carried off in an extremely polished and accomplished manner. With the familiar reference points of LIMELIGHT, DAMASCUS, SOLDIER and Kent's LEGEND coming to the fore, the album contains an exceptionally well-written set of compositions, ranging from intricate, proto-DREAM THEATER-style power/prog to catchy, RAINBOW-influenced efforts, the superb voice of Graham Careless lifting the material to an immensely enjoyable level. Stand-out tracks included "Time Is Right", "King's Fury", "Footsteps" and "Don't Throw My Love Away", all of which deserved to be heard by a far wider audience than was actually the case. Sadly, however, the record failed to set the world on fire at the time, and was probably slightly out of place in terms of the global rock consciousness of the day. Many offered the opinion that it would have fared better if the group hadn't wasted so much time before getting it released, although I suspect that it might actually have received better reviews if they had waited five years longer!

Although the original incarnation of FORCE appears to have disintegrated almost immediately after their album's release, a revised version, once again led by the unfortunately-named Graham Careless himself, actually attempted to establish themselves as a going concern in 1988. With the frontman now being assisted by a supporting cast comprised of various regional scenesters such as erstwhile BUCKSHEE man Vic Saul (g, k), one-time BORN LOSER stalwart Gary Morris (g), the economically-named Woody (b) and Andy Harper (d), the revamped outfit duly recorded a speculative demo (featuring "We Can Make It Last Forever", "We've Got Love", "Sleepin' Alone Tonight" and a peculiar cover of "Reach Out" by the FOUR TOPS), after which they made their collective intentions known through the rock press of the day. Inevitably, virtually no-one even noticed that FORCE had now 'reformed' (in spite of the outfit's insistence that an assortment of major labels were begging them to sign on a daily basis), and the increasingly-mainstream project was disbanded a short time later (after a few regional support slots with the likes of RADIO MOSCOW), with sticksman Andy Harper subsequently joining LOVE AND WAR, while the multi-talented Vic Saul tried again as part of a duo called BUILDING ROME. Mind you, I've absolutely no idea what former CRYER/FORCE frontman Graham Careless is up to nowadays, but it would be a tragedy if that commanding voice isn't being put to good use somewhere.

LP's
»Set Me Free…« Heavy Metal 1984
[Initial quantities in textured sleeve]

FORGER

Geoff Cornwall (v)
Steve Brooks (g)
Ian Busby (b)
Martin King (d)

Although Oxfordshire's FORGER were originally conceived as a straight-ahead rock/metal proposition in the spring of 1984, the members found themselves adopting an increasingly glammy image and writing style throughout their relatively brief existence, something which appears to have been their undoing in the long term. The quartet's early material, best-illustrated by a three track demo from later in the same year, employed an interesting blend of heavy guitars and melodic arrangements, coming across as a combination of early DEF LEPPARD and IDOL RICH, especially on the enjoyable "What You're Doing To Me" and "Wanted Lady". "Love In The City", meanwhile, is a bit of an obvious throwback (both lyrically and musically) to glam stalwarts ROX, but it's still a strong and memorable track all the same. Within a matter of months of their formation, the youthful outfit were receiving a fair bit of coverage in the local press, and soon began playing to appreciative crowds throughout the region, although no major support slots were ever forthcoming, limiting their chances to some extent.

Moving into 1985, the ensemble recruited new bassist Toby Pickford (whose brother, Tiff, was a member of another popular Oxford group, TRANZZZAM), adopted a series of truly ludicrous, MÖTLEY CRÜE-approved stage names (Tobe Roxx, Geoff Mega, Ringo Styxx and Steve Animal) and went the whole hog in terms of the glam image. Somehow, they attracted the attention of (wait for it) New Renaissance Records in the States, who were apparently so impressed with the lads (who hadn't a clue how the label had come into contact with their music in the first instance) that they were offered the opportunity of appearing on a compilation album, with the possibility of a full LP of their own if things worked out. Demos changed hands in due course, but this brief liaison never actually culminated in any exposure for the band, which is a bit of a shame. It's a truly bizarre story all round (although New Renaissance did, admittedly, promote some slightly more melodic outfits in its early days, before bringing us such heavyweights as POST MORTEM and DREAM DEATH), and it's rather difficult to imagine FORGER fitting in too well on the likes of »Speed Metal Hell«...

The summer of 1985 saw the band release their one and only single, the privately-pressed »She's A Liar«, housed in a picture sleeve showing the lads all dolled up in their full-scale glam regalia. It's a lot better than it looks, admittedly, although it's certainly a bit more commercial than the earlier material, this pair of FORGER originals bringing forth comparisons to the likes of STORYTELLER at times. The A-side was characterised by an excellent riff but a rather weak, singalong chorus, whereas the reverse ("Hot Love Tonight") represented a more balanced composition, but it still suffers from a slight case of 'heard it before' syndrome. Nevertheless, it was enthusiastic stuff, suggesting that the participants were merely enjoying themselves while it all lasted, and drummer Martin King (aka Ringo Styxx) fondly recalls his time in FORGER even now: 'I've got many great memories of those days, like so many other bands we all jacked our jobs in and went for it totally, we had some great gigs, and quite a bit of record company interest, but in the end we ended up putting out the single by funding it ourselves. We played many times at the Pennyfarthing and the Corn Dolly in Oxford, and pretty much all over Oxfordshire, there was a really good live circuit then and the punters were really into having a good time and supporting live rock, so it was a real joy to play.' (Ref: Private communication, March 1999).

FORGER were, perhaps, another bunch who were slightly out of step with the prevailing metal sound of the time, since the original British glam scene which had been established by ROX, SILVERWING etc. had petered out around a year previously (even the all-conquering WRATHCHILD were pretty much a spent force by 1985), and the 'second wave' of glam/sleaze outfits such as CRY and TIGERTAILZ didn't really establish themselves properly until later in the decade. You have to admire the lads for following their hearts and doing their own thing, though, and it can't have been particularly easy to compete with the emergence of all the thrash and AOR wannabes who sprang up practically overnight in the mid-80's. After becoming disillusioned with their apparent lack of progress and losing their way somewhat in the preceding months, the luckless FORGER had finally fallen apart for good by the beginning of 1986. Still, they gave it their best shot for a couple of years, entertained many a crowd and left one rare, mid-priced single for posterity. Martin King, meanwhile, having consigned his alter ego Ringo Styxx to the distant past, now plays in a rock covers band rejoicing under the name of SCOOBY DON'T.

7" Singles
»She's A Liar« Private 1985

FOUNDED

Line-up unknown

FOUNDED's »Looking For Love« single, the second offering to be issued through the short-lived Heroes concern back in 1982, is yet another of those infuriating records which sounds as though it actually features two entirely different bands. The B-side, "Run To Hell", is an absolute cracker, just the sort of fast and heavy, archetypal NWOBHM we crave, extremely similar in style to HAZZARD or early SPARTAN WARRIOR. The comparatively lacklustre A-side, on the other hand, starts off quite promisingly with a capable guitar attack, but soon degenerates into a lightweight semi-ballad reminiscent of VIRGIN's "Sitting In The Front Row" (which is hardly a high recommendation), albeit marginally more serious and less poppy. Another unfortunate example of the *'ill-advised slower number'*, I'm afraid! The Heroes singles were all (by the looks of things) issued without sleeves and with minimal information on the records themselves, so there's not much else to report about any of the mysterious groups who were involved with the label at this stage. Still, it seems safe to assume that FOUNDED were very much a fly-by-night concern who were incredibly lucky to be picked up by a small-time company, and who probably faced a comparatively bleak future once this kind sponsorship had ceased.

Clearly, none of those who kicked off their career with the label ever went on to greater things, so I guess this was really nothing more than a one-off chance for certain aspiring musicians to enjoy an incredibly brief spell in the limelight before going back to their day jobs for good. It's worth pointing out, by the way, that the inaugural release on Heroes Records (SPLIT IMAGE's »Now That We've Parted« single), often referred to (by deluded characters who haven't bothered to play it, presumably) as prime-era NWOBHM, isn't even rock, let alone metal! Sorry, folks, this two-tracker contains nothing more than lightweight *reggae* (and it's not even good reggae) with booming bass and feeble vocals, so keep your money firmly in your pockets if you ever see that one! Also, it's perhaps worth noting that, although the embryonic version of BLITZKRIEG had toyed with the name SPLIT IMAGE during their formative days, they're not associated with this particular bunch in any shape or form.

7" Singles
»Looking For Love« Heroes Records 1982

FOUR WHEEL DRIVE

Tony Dugdale (v,g)
Neil Dowling (v,b,d)

Although it has been established that the gradual disintegration of Surrey's STATIC (which had fallen apart for good by the summer of 1983) ultimately facilitated the formation of two completely new groups (vocalist Noel Jones putting together the critically-acclaimed WHITE LIGHTNING, while the remaining participants from the last, ill-fated STATIC line-up proceeded to form the overly-melodic SNOWBLIND concern), it's not common knowledge that two of their original members (guitarist Tony Dugdale and sticksman Neil Dowling) also remained in the music business after their departure from STATIC, coming together at some point to form the relatively unknown FOUR WHEEL DRIVE project. Given that both had been given their freedom by 1981 (Neil Dowling went on to enjoy a brief residency in L.A. HOOKER), I guess their new project was conceived within a year or so, but the pair hardly went out of their way to announce their intentions to the masses. Still, it was a fairly unusual venture, which saw the multi-talented duo following in the footsteps of the similarly-conceived STRATEGY and doing the whole thing themselves without any outside help. Whereas the latter was purely a studio-based concern who played instrumental music, however, FOUR WHEEL DRIVE resembled more of a traditional rock group, with Dugdale taking charge of guitar, Dowling serving as a one-man rhythm section and the pair sharing vocal duties.

In due course, they got around to demoing a few selections, and one of the duo's formative compositions ("Have You Ever Been In Love") was supposed to have appeared on the obscure »Dream Sequence« compilation in 1983, although the only copy I know of is completely mispressed with the wrong tracks, so this effort may or may not actually exist on vinyl. What is certain, however, is that FOUR WHEEL DRIVE managed to bung out a single coupling "Did You Have To" with "Give Me (What You Got)", a record which was probably issued in 1984. A curious release, the A-side is a fairly poppy, hard-rocking singalong somewhere between TEMPEST's "Hell Fire" and TOAD THE WET SPROCKET's "Pete's Punk Song", while the reverse is slightly reminiscent of early BUZZARD, with vocals very much in the vein of the RAMONES or JOE JACKSON as opposed to anything more metal-sounding. An odd mixture, and no mistake! The lads should be praised, at least, for not following trends and for doing their own thing, although the single (issued in a rather dull blue sleeve picturing the musicians ogling a distant female) seems to have been their only moment of glory (not that it sold all that many copies) and their ultimate fate is lost in the mists of time.

7" Singles
»Did You Have To« Triangle Records 1984?

Exclusive Compilation Appearances
"Have You Ever Been In Love" on »Dream Sequence« Do-LP 101 International Records 1983

FRAMED

Dave Parsons (v,g)
Enid Williams (v,b)
Barbara Spitz (g)
Gray Noon (k)
Ian Whitewood (d)

The ill-starred venture which would ultimately become known as FRAMED first got going within a remarkably short timescale after Enid Williams' hasty departure from GIRLSCHOOL in the spring of 1982, although her subsequent project actually started off under a slightly different guise. In the first instance, the bassist hooked up with unlikely associate Dave Parsons (a veteran of legendary punksters SHAM 69) and second guitarist Barbara Spitz (a one-time member of the theatrical SADISTA SISTERS ensemble), whereupon the newly-established trio duly began tinkering around under the unremarkable name of AVANTI. Before very much longer, however, the founder members had acquired a complete touring line-up (including veteran drummer Ian Whitewood and keyboard player Gray Noon, supposedly recruited from the ranks of the little-known ELGIN MARBLES) and adopted the novel identity of FRAMED, and so it seemed as though it would only be a matter of time before the ambitious five-piece (with Williams and Parsons sharing vocal duties for the most part) began playing some low-key shows in and around the capital. In fact, the publicity-shy outfit seemed to be inexplicably reluctant either to play live or to reveal too many details of their recording activities, and there was something of a hiatus before any further news escaped from the FRAMED camp.

At the tail end of 1982, however, the ensemble suddenly reappeared out of the blue with their debut vinyl release (an offering which emerged with virtually zero pre-publicity, and which came as a complete surprise to almost everyone in the rock world), a one-sided single (well, it wasn't a topological marvel, it had a completely blank track on the reverse) on the Thunderbay label (whoever they were), giving the public a chance to hear a grand total of one whole extract from their repertoire. "Into My Life" was the number in question, and this represented a fairly cheerful, upbeat attempt to marry the worlds of metal and melodic punk, although it's not a particularly memorable effort. Before long, however, this inauspicious debut was being brushed under the carpet, whereupon FRAMED tried again with another one-sided single (it's a total mystery why the band didn't just release a conventional two-tracker in the first instance) based around a composition called "Wonderland". It was an improvement on their initial offering, although it was, as 'Kerrang' pointed out in their review, 'messily arranged', even if the journo's additional gripes about excessive length and poor production were slightly harsh. Mind you, it was a highly confusing release which didn't really know whether to align itself with RAINBOW-style anthemic rock (as the intro would have suggested) or more of a punk/mod singalong in the vein of THE JAM or SECRET AFFAIR. In the event, it once again failed to generate much interest either from the rock or mainstream press, and, in the wake of media disinterest, the hapless outfit seemed to grind to a halt after a few more unsuccessful gigs during 1983.

Although the music press dutifully reported on a couple of the quintet's live outings in the capital, there seemed to be a peculiar reluctance to pass judgement on the outfit's material (or even to reveal any of their song titles), and so the general public remained unconvinced as to the long-term viability of the whole project. It had all started out with talk of albums and tours, but momentum began draining away from a very early stage, and even the musicians involved seemed to lose faith after the briefest of spells. Enid Williams eventually made her way back to GIRLSCHOOL (via the STRANGE GIRLS) in the early 90's, while Ian Whitewood later had a brief stint with TORMÉ before hooking up with Parsons in the revived SHAM 69. Each of the one-sided FRAMED singles sold in truly minuscule quantities at the time (they were definitely intended as commercial releases, though, not merely as promotional devices), and copies are very seldom seen these days. Even so, I reckon that even the most ardent GIRLSCHOOL fan could easily live without them. There were also, incidentally, a tiny handful of fold-round covers manufactured for at least one (and possibly both) of these records, which supplied a few additional details, but you'll wait a very long time before you see one of those little beauties.

7" Singles
»Into My Life« Thunderbay Records 1982
[One-sided single]
»Wonderland« Thunderbay Records 1982
[One-sided single]

FRENZY

Johnny Pawlowski (g)
Peter Pawlowski (b)
John O'Connor
Larry Layman
Dave Nixon

As many of you will be aware, Lancashire's tuneful FRENZY (not to be confused with a prominent British psychobilly bunch who famously issued EP's such as »Robot Riot« during the early 80's) have their origins in a three-piece ensemble with the not-very-metal moniker of ANNIVERSARY. Featuring future FRENZY mainmen Johnny and Peter Pawlowski alongside drummer Ian Maynard, the unsung trio toured pretty widely and even got as far as issuing a decidedly odd, four track 7" (entitled »Give Me A Smile«) on the diverse Aerco label back in 1978 before finally calling it a day. While this item is frequently touted around by certain characters as *'early NWOBHM'*, it actually represents an uneasy mixture of rock, punk, prog, new wave and general weirdness which doesn't make an essential (or particularly enjoyable) piece of listening for the typical NWOBHM enthusiast, so give it a wide berth unless it's incredibly cheap. Evolving into the five-piece FRENZY at the beginning of the 80's, the Pawlowskis' latest act duly set about releasing a grand total of three self-financed singles, two of which are quite well-known and respected within the NWOBHM community, while the remaining one (with very good reason) is not.

FRENZY wasted little energy faffing about in the studio or developing all that much of a live reputation before commencing their ludicrously intensive vinyl assault on an unsuspecting world, preferring to issue their own self-financed records at regular intervals rather than blindly following the usual route of recording a speculative cassette shortly after formation and waiting for all the major labels to beat a path to their door. Well, it probably saved them a fair bit of time and heartbreak in the long run, and certain other hopefuls might have been well-advised to adopt the same approach. The quintet's first release, issued at more or less the beginning of 1981, coupled "This Is The Last Time" (as featured on the »NWOBHM Vol.7« bootleg) with "Gypsy Dancer", both compositions being extremely catchy slices of commercialised rock/metal in the general manner of MOTHER'S RUIN, with shades of some of the more accessible material penned by IONA or HOLLOW GROUND from time to time. It was far removed from the rough'n'ready NWOBHM archetype, admittedly, but it was all eminently listenable, even if the utterly cringeworthy lyrics on the flipside (*e.g. 'My mother said-I never should, play with the gypsies in the woods'*) tend to provoke a bit of infantile sniggering. Rest easy, lads, I can't imagine that TOKYO BLADE's shocking "Five Inch Catwalk" will *ever* be beaten in terms of nauseatingly embarrassing lyrics.

The other FRENZY single which very occasionally surfaces is their »Without You« 7" (B-side "Thanx For Nothing"), which was evidently recorded within a matter of months of their debut, and which was already being offered for sale by the summer of that year. As it turned out, this was practically identical to their first effort, the tuneful ensemble having obviously seen little or no reason to change a winning formula (not in such a short interval, anyway) just yet. Both releases proceeded to perform admirably in terms of sales, with numerous copies being shifted by distributors such as Bullet Records, who identified the lads as a *'powerful Northern outfit'*. Still, the musicians failed to build upon this initial success, and they hardly made any great efforts to get out and about to promote themselves thereafter, so the general public soon concluded that FRENZY had probably ceased all operations and gone back to their day jobs. That was surely the end of the story, or so everyone thought, until years of painstaking analysis of the respective 7" catalogue numbers (*'Frenzy1'* and *'Frenzy3'*) by some of the world's top scientists eventually led to conjecture that *'Frenzy2'* might also be out there somewhere. And indeed it was. Contrary to popular belief, the group's second single had indeed been recorded and issued, and it actually turns out to be a not-terribly-serious football (I refuse to call it soccer, sorry) anthem dedicated to their beloved local team (see also CATCH 22 and their Bradford City tribute), although this particular release appears not to have been circulated widely at the time.

Based around the singalong "Blackburn Rovers" (backed, rather pointlessly, with the almost identical "On The Rovers"), the two-tracker was a very limited pressing for the benefit of local supporters (it features a label design which is supposed to represent a football), and it's virtually unknown for copies to come onto the open market. You're not missing much, to be honest, as this was basic, knockabout stuff (this sort of thing was all the rage at the time, although it wasn't common subject matter for metal outfits), with assorted references to all the goings-on *'down at Ewood Park'*, which would probably go down a storm on the terraces, but which is otherwise laughably awful. It's quite difficult to rationalise the prolificacy of these industrious Lancastrians, although I suspect that they may well have recorded a hefty batch of material during one visit to the studio, as it's unlikely that they made a pilgrimage to their local facility on a monthly basis. In the aftermath of FRENZY's all-too-rapid demise, the one-time members all appear to have drifted away from the rock scene, having steadfastly failed to resurface in any acts of note later in the decade, which is a bit baffling. None of the low-budget singles were ever issued with a picture sleeve, and (with the exception of the slightly more commonly-encountered »Without You«) tend to come up for sale on remarkably few occasions nowadays. If you ever see them at a reasonable price, snap them up, but beware of that dodgy second one unless you're a completist or (rather more implausibly) a Blackburn fan!

7" Singles
»This Is The Last Time« Private 1981
»Blackburn Rovers« Private 1981
»Without You« Private 1981

Compilation Appearances
"This Is The Last Time" on »NWOBHM Vol.7« Bootleg CD 1996

FRIENDS

Mark Russell (v)
Dave Russell

A relatively obscure and long-forgotten outfit from Hampshire, FRIENDS (there have been a fair few namesakes over the years) were formed in the early 80's by the ambitious musical brothers Mark and Dave Russell, who roped in a few unknown accomplices to assist them in their quest for fame and fortune. After playing numerous small-time gigs in their locality and then circulating a six track demo tape, the rapidly-developing band gradually won favour with their energetic brand of rock, with Mark Russell's, er, *distinctive* vocals going down particularly well with fans of Robert Plant, which isn't to say that this ensemble represented little more than a glorified ZEPPELIN tribute act, though. Their first vinyl exposure appears to have come fairly swiftly, when FRIENDS took their place on one of those extremely scarce local-band compilations (the charmingly-titled »Spit'n'Finish«), the latter being assembled by the Toucan label early in 1983. Their chosen contribution, "Pyramid Blue", was an enjoyable slice of rock/metal with an undeniable LED ZEPPELIN influence, but which also hints at NWOBHM-era STRAY. All things considered, it was a good enough way to start off their career.

The aforementioned compilation also featured a band called THE DODGERS, featuring one Rick Le Page (who went on to form his own label called Rock Shop Records, based in a local music shop), an individual who would do his utmost to promote several lucky Hampshire hopefuls in the coming years. Picked up by this nice chap's newly-established label (who would later issue material by the likes of EXPLORER and WHITE HEAT), FRIENDS were offered the opportunity to record their own single. As a direct result, a thousand copies of »Night Walker« (B-side "Wasted Time") were pressed, a large proportion of which were sold locally. The A-side itself is a fairly restrained affair, very much in the LED ZEPPELIN or RUSH mould, although the reverse (which apparently went down slightly better with the majority of their fan base) turned out to be a considerably pacier piece which was, on the whole, far closer to the kind of *bona fide* NWOBHM as typified by the likes of JAMESON RAID or HORSEPOWER. As with the other small-time acts signed to the label (not all of whom were rock/metal, incidentally, so be warned), however, the record was a one-off experience, and it looks as though FRIENDS probably started to lose enthusiasm before too long, and had pretty much faded into nothingness within a couple of years. Nevertheless, the single, which wasn't issued with a picture sleeve, is now a scarce, mid-priced item for today's NWOBHM collector.

7" Singles
»Night Walker« Rock Shop Records 1983

Exclusive Compilation Appearances
"Pyramid Blue" on »Spit'n'Finish« LP Toucan

Records 1983
[Issued on red vinyl]

FUGITIVE

Bernie Clark (v,g)
Lenny Lembo (v,rg)
Keith Robinson (b)
Rick Berry (d)

Nottinghamshire's FUGITIVE first got the metal bug at some point in 1980, and, after the obligatory personnel changes and temper tantrums concerning their musical direction of choice, finally established themselves on the local scene towards the end of the year. Following a modest number of gigs over the course of the next year or so, at which the response was generally favourable, the musicians were given some useful exposure on Radio Hallam, who were happy to playlist a selection of demo compositions to see how the public reacted to the music of FUGITIVE. Once again, they seem to have been given an overwhelming vote of confidence, whereupon the lads were duly invited to lay down a

few exclusive session tracks for immediate broadcast. Peculiarly enough, it transpires that FUGITIVE didn't seem to have one main vocalist, instead taking turns to sing (the guitarists being favoured for the most part), which was an unusually democratic arrangement, especially for a rock band. Not entirely surprisingly, however, the members weren't all equally talented on the vocal front, rendering some of the session material ("Destination Unknown", "On The Run") weaker than tracks such as "Changes", "Children Of The Street", "Live Now, Live Today" and "Hey You", all of which are excellent contributions to the genre in the style of HOLLOW GROUND or early DEF LEPPARD.

Even so, it was a perfectly decent demonstration of their collective talent, and it came as no surprise when the members of FUGITIVE decided to get a slice of vinyl into the shops as soon as humanly possible. The two-tracker was duly recorded at the end of 1981, and issued as a self-financed affair (with no picture sleeve) shortly thereafter. Against all odds, however, the lads contrived to select practically their weakest pair of numbers for inclusion, rendering the single as a considerable disappointment. On this particular release, the quartet appear to have been aiming for a more forceful style along the general lines of JJ'S POWERHOUSE, but, for various intangible reasons, the tracks on display fail to come across nearly as effectively. As an example, A-side "Need My Freedom" (which subsequently came to semi-prominence on the »NWOBHM Vol.7« bootleg CD) starts off strongly enough, but the dynamics of the song are compromised by some ill-advised time changes which ultimately don't work very well at all. Moreover, the repetitive *'need my freedom'* refrain towards the end is pretty annoying, and really calls the band's musical judgement into question. On the reverse ("Don't Tell Me I'm Crazy"), the vocals get a bit odd, vaguely reminiscent of THE SWEET's "Blockbuster", which certainly doesn't help the otherwise decent tune at all. Overall, therefore, this was a respectable slice of vinyl (a fair number of copies of which were obtained from the band in the early 90's, reducing the asking price quite dramatically) which could, with a more thoughtful approach, have been a lot better.

Despite the continued patronage of kindly radio stations such as Hallam, the lads began to lose their way somewhat during 1982, and their much-anticipated breakthrough failed to happen in the short term. Nevertheless, FUGITIVE kept plugging away in the live environment, where they were always assured of a warm reception by the regional fan base, although sales of the debut single appear to have been slightly disappointing, in the main. Predictably, the major labels kept their distance, and even the minor record companies failed to identify any serious potential in FUGITIVE's music, which was a great shame, especially when it was clear that they had some decent material in their repertoire all along. Disillusioned with the overall response to their 7", the lads disbanded a year later, but subsequently reformed under the name TORONTO RUN, apparently making several further radio appearances under this guise. Since then, nothing, so it looks as though their scarcely-sighted single was both the zenith and nadir of their career. There was, incidentally, a melodic rock duo who operated as FUGITI-

VE in the early 90's (releasing an EP entitled »Foundation« in 1993), and who also appear to have been based in the Midlands, although there seems to be absolutely no connection with the original bunch.

7" Singles
»Need My Freedom« SRT 1981

Compilation Appearances
"Need My Freedom" on »NWOBHM Vol.7« Bootleg CD 1996

FULL MOON

Tony Trott (v, rg)
Debbie Boner (bv)
Gary Boner (g)
Bill Hobley (b)
Steve Parsons (d)

Not to be confused with Surrey's HAWKWIND-influenced outfit from the late 80's or some relatively obscure American namesakes, the original FULL MOON were, in all probability, from London itself, but they don't seem to have made much of a name for themselves at any stage, having presumably started out at some point in the latter half of the 70's. Nevertheless, the quintet's only known single, the privately-issued »Stand Up« effort from 1979, is a perfectly adequate stab at the early NWOBHM ethos, being fairly firmly rooted in the rudimentary, 70's-influenced style of heavy rock/metal inhabited by the likes of DAWN TRADER, SLENDER THREAD and (particularly) the Essex version of WARRIOR. Indeed, the mid-tempo A-side could quite easily have fitted on to the latter's »Don't Let It Show« EP without seeming remotely out of place. On the reverse, meanwhile, "Fly Away" turns out to be a slightly more laid-back semi-ballad, although it's a reasonably weighty track nonetheless. A fairly respectable vinyl debut, all things considered, but it looks as though this bunch (as with so many others who had high aspirations in the beginning) had given up the ghost by the time the main period of NWOBHM activity had fizzled out. FULL MOON's one-off release, incidentally, comes in a not-remotely-subtle picture sleeve showing a drawing of an unclothed posterior, suggesting that the band's name might not have been taken from a lunar phenomenon after all. Remarkably, I've also somehow managed to get through this particular outfit's entry without drawing attention to the fact that two of the, er, members rejoiced under the mirthsome and extremely unfortunate surname of 'Boner'. Oh bugger.

7" Singles
»Stand Up« SRT 1979

FURY

Bill Padley (v)
Mark Owers (g)
Steve Owers (b)
Rob Drayson (k)
John Martin (d)

Hampshire quintet FURY (another vastly-oversubscribed identity) originally got going as far back as 1980, although the line-up was notoriously unstable in their formative days, during which time they nevertheless established themselves on the South Coast rock scene and famously won a regional support slot with none other than AC/DC in the process. By early 1982, however, they had achieved stability, with drummer John Martin being recruited from local rivals LONE WOLF to assist the Owers twins, keyboard player Rob Drayson (who didn't let the minor irritation of being deaf stop him) and talented singer Bill Padley. Before long, they had a proper demo tape to their name, and a selection of melodic rock tracks such as "Broken All The Rules" and "Lyin' To Me" were soon attracting a fair bit of attention from a number of record labels and magazines. Later in the year, the youthful ensemble received a welcome piece of additional publicity when they were featured in the 'Armed And Ready' section of 'Kerrang', who benevolently tipped FURY for big things in years to come.

In the early part of 1983, FURY signed to Anchor Records, a short-lived subsidiary of the influential Jet concern, and a debut single was hurriedly assembled within a matter of weeks. The A-side was an energetic reworking of IKE AND TINA TURNER's "River Deep Mountain High", the band coming across as a highly capable, raunchy rock/metal proposition in the general manner of BABY TUCKOO or TERRAPLANE. Flipside "Helpless", on the other hand, with its traditional keyboard backing, had slightly more in common with WHITE SPIRIT at their most PURPLE-influenced, although it was still an equally listenable effort. The label were keen to promote the emergent act as representing something a bit out of the ordinary, and tended to focus on some of the more obvious reference points (their *'Beethoven-like'* keyboard player, the almost *'telepathic'* Owers twins and a drummer with, er, *'personality problems'*) to drum up a bit of media attention. Sadly, it was all in vain, and the FURY 7" (no sleeve issued) failed to sell in particularly noteworthy quantities upon its release, after which the outfit were soon thinking about making a few changes.

Even by the early months of 1984, FURY had already mutated into an act called XS following the appointment of a replacement vocalist (erstwhile LOADED DICE frontman John Francis), and the revamped outfit (an extremely similar proposition to FURY, in all honesty) persevered for a few years, attracting the attention of FM Records along the way (and appearing on their »Coast To Coast« compilation in 1987) before eventually reinventing themselves once again. In the first instance, they became the hopelessly-monikered LOVE ATTACK, but subsequently had second thoughts and became the slightly less embarrassing AFTER HOURS, who ultimately released a highly-regarded (but widely-ignored) album or two of derivative AOR material at around the turn of the decade. The Owers brothers had already flown the coop by this stage, though, and were now (having originally wandered off in around 1985 to form an abortive venture called POLARIS) tinkering around in TOUCHÉ, a project instigated by former IDOL RICH frontman Mark Thompson-Smith. The latter's new act never really got anywhere, though, and the backing musicians were all subsequently poached by Steve Grimmett, who, in around 1989, was in the process of assembling his LIONSHEART concern. The Owers brothers enjoyed a fair bit of success with their new employers in the early 90's, while their erstwhile colleague John Francis went on to have a very brief stint with SHY (while they were calling themselves BLACKCAT), among others, so it's fair to say that a few well-respected musicians owe at least part of their success to their humble beginnings in FURY.

7" Singles
»River Deep Mountain High« Anchor Records 1983

GARBO

Boh Hamilton (v,g)
Billy Colvin (b)
Andi Steele (d)

Although London's JANINE (see separate entry) now seem to be quite a popular and collectable act among NWOBHM aficionados, it's not particularly common knowledge that several of their former members found further employment in the rock scene after the latter's disintegration, which is understandable in view of the small-time nature of these outfits. In addition to their contribution of personnel to the relatively unsuccessful DEEP MACHINE and BORDELLO, however, a third act also emerged from the ashes, and this obscure bunch even managed to get to the vinyl stage. The little-known GARBO were conceived at the tail end of 1981 by former JANINE vocalist Boh Hamilton, and he was soon joined by bassist Billy Colvin, a veteran of Hamilton's earlier outfit, NECROMANCER. By the early part of 1982, the final piece of the jigsaw slotted into place when drummer Andi Steele, a former colleague from both JANINE and NECROMANCER, decided to join in the fun. The group somehow wangled a deal with the tiny Rarn label from the West Country within a remarkably short space of time, and proceeded to lay down their debut 7" for release in the second half of that year. The three-tracker featured some fairly distinctive material which bore only a passing similarity to the semi-glam anthems of JANINE, with "The Dancing Strange", in particular, being a tuneful, semi-acoustic affair which had a considerable amount in common with the quirky HARLEQUYN style. "Why Don't You Call Me?", on the other hand, is a rather less impressive number, its highly confusing structure bringing forth comparisons with ORION and early MARSEILLE, whereas "Everyday Hallucinations" has a bit of a SWEET/BOLAN feel to it, but still fails to leave all that much of an impression.

Clearly, GARBO were intent on doing something a bit out of the ordinary, and the trio certainly set out their stall on their debut vinyl release. Promotional copies of the EP were circulated to the music press of the day, and the record even managed to win favour with the merciless reviewers in 'Kerrang', who must have been feeling uncharacteristically charitable on that occasion. Strangely, however, few examples of the finished product seem to have made it into the shops, although there were reports that GARBO would soon be mounting a concerted challenge on the rock world by expanding to a permanent five-piece *via* the recruitment of a keyboard player and guitarist, whereupon they would take the nation by storm on their extensive tour of 1983. In reality, the whole venture seems to have fallen through before it ever really got going properly, and the name of GARBO swiftly disappeared from the pages of the music weeklies, leading to the inevitable conclusion that they had already succumbed to the usual hurdles of personnel instability, financial shortcomings and major-label disinterest. Their one-off EP was issued in an uninspiring sleeve picturing the band members, and is certainly not an item you're likely to encounter on a regular basis.

7" EP's
»The Dancing Strange« Rarn Records 1982

GASKIN

Paul Gaskin (v,g)
Stef Prokopczuk (b)
Dave Norman (d)

The origins of the highly-regarded GASKIN stretch back to the late 70's, when the group was put together by Dave Norman and band leader Paul Gaskin after the demise of an obscure East Yorkshire outfit named SCEPTRE. With a stable line-up finally being achieved in January 1980 following the addition of bassist Stef Prokopczuk, the trio rehearsed and gigged for several months before venturing into the studio to lay down their first tape, featuring "Sweet Dream Maker", "End Of The World", "I'm No Fool" and "Despiser". Barely days later, the lads were offered a deal by Mansfield's Rondelet label, but were discouraged from signing at that stage by none other than NWOBHM guru Neal Kay. With the outfit subsequently deciding to base themselves in Nottingham itself, they secured many gigs throughout the region, including some valuable support slots with local heroes WITCHFYNDE. At the beginning of 1981, however, the threesome came to the conclusion that their overall sound was lacking that certain something, and briefly experimented as a quartet (their ranks being swelled by second guitarist David Screen), delivering a session for Radio Trent before having second thoughts and reverting to the three-piece line-up we're now so familiar with. With GASKIN's following becoming ever more fervent, and with live appearances now taking them as far afield as London, a second offer from Rondelet met with the band's collective approval.

In the spring of 1981, GASKIN's vinyl debut appeared in the form of the »I'm No Fool« single (B-side "Sweet Dream Maker"), a highly capable effort (quite a bit classier than much of the material being churned out by the majority of their NWOBHM-era contemporaries) which was closely followed by the trio's full-length »End Of The World« opus, the latter housed in an elaborate gatefold sleeve. Helped along by the kind patronage of 'Kerrang', the first album became a firm favourite among many of the genre's more adventurous fans, although the vocalist was keen to distance his outfit from the whole NWOBHM explosion: *'I don't really want us to be labelled an HM band. We're into heavy rock and we want to expand and develop the medium. We're anxious to avoid many of the classic clichés and pave the way with eighties-style stage presentation.'* (Ref: Kerrang No.4, October 1981). Clearly peeved by certain early references to RUSH and WISHBONE ASH, however, the musicians seemed equally determined to convince the nation's rock cognoscenti that they had now managed to cultivate a rather more individualistic sound of their own. In all fairness, this was an entirely justified assertion, as their »End Of The World« release displayed a wide range of styles and influences, marking GASKIN out as one of the more thoughtful and subtle acts of the era, alongside the likes of SHIVA, PRAYING MANTIS and LIMELIGHT, although some of the featured compositions (notably the title track itself) demonstrated that the trio could rock out with the best of the NWOBHM hopefuls.

Following the first LP's release, GASKIN were quite keen to experiment with new ideas, and duly entertained the notion of a dedicated vocalist for a while. After auditioning a few hopefuls, former ESCAPE (no, not Clive Burr's bunch) frontman Mick Clarke was given the shout, although his recruitment ultimately caused more problems than it solved. After internal tension had built up over the ensuing weeks, Stef Prokopczuk made the decision to defect, taking Mick Clarke with him, whereupon the duo proceeded to establish their own ACE LANE (see separate entry) project. The departed bassist was soon replaced by a certain *'Baggy'* (whose real name is known only to his mother and the F.B.I.), and it wasn't too long before GASKIN once more expanded to a four-piece, after they managed to recruit the powerful lungs of Bren Spencer. Stepping up the level of activity on the live front, 1982 saw the hard-working bunch taking to the road in support of the EF BAND and (ironically enough) WISHBONE ASH, as well as playing numerous headlining gigs of their own. That same year, their follow-up LP appeared (as did a single based around the old standard "Mony Mony", also covered by BABY TUCKOO, amongst others) in the shape of »No Way Out«, a far less pretentious and overbearing recording which, nevertheless, failed to elicit the same general level of enthusiasm among the nation's rock fans of the day. Again, the pick of the bunch would be the title track, a fairly energetic composition with some true NWOBHM spirit, although Bren Spencer's vocals were, more often than not, decidedly less charismatic than those of his talented predecessor.

Sadly, things were to go wrong for the lads within a fairly short timescale (in spite of some well-received gigs supporting the likes of GIRLSCHOOL, VARDIS and PRAYING MANTIS), the outfit having run into a few internal difficulties in the wake of the critical dismissal of their latest set. In fact, early in 1983, 'Kerrang' announced that GASKIN had recently split in half, with the surviving nucleus of Paul Gaskin and Bren Spencer vowing to recruit a new rhythm section and set about recording the third album, tentatively titled »Aftermath«. In the event, however, the revamped version of GASKIN (originally completed by drummer Dave Wagstaff and bassist Mark McKenzie, although the latter actually made way for Dave Gugelot after only one or two rehearsals) just never really managed to get off the ground at all (by this time, Rondelet had ceased to exist and so the luckless outfit no longer had any financial support whatsoever), and it wasn't long before Bren Spencer too was on his way, the singer subsequently forming CHEROKEE before joining forces with various heavyweight acts in the North West, notably KAMARG and SPYYTE. After that, there was little hope of mainman Paul Gaskin maintaining any serious level of interest in the project (although some original material was indeed demoed), and the central character elected to call it a day sooner rather than later, whereupon he proceeded to lend a hand in such minor local hopefuls as HARD CORE and MOSCOW. Fly-by-night bassist Mark McKenzie, on the other hand, soon inveigled his way into the ranks of SOLDIER, however, while Dave Gugelot had a stint with CHINA ROGUE and sticksman Dave Wagstaff hooked up with the more progressively-inclined QUASAR.

GASKIN have, nevertheless, always retained something of a cult following, particularly in mainland Europe and Japan, and interest in the outfit in these areas was sufficient to inspire some dastardly individual to release a bootleg edition of »End Of The World« on CD in the early 90's. This was enough to show the legitimate labels that GASKIN still had a bit of mileage in them, and so both of their albums were officially issued on CD by the Pony Canyon concern a short time later. At around this juncture, Paul Gaskin's enthusiasm for the project was renewed, and he began tinkering around in the recording studio once again, eventually laying down a selection of new material (pretty much on his own, although erstwhile BADGE/BLADE RUNNER bassist Mick Cooper and local guitarist Rick Maybury helped out on a couple of numbers) for possible release. In the event, the master tapes were left to gather dust for quite a few years, although they finally came to light once again when the rights to the GASKIN back catalogue passed on to British Steel, who duly reissued both of the original albums on a single CD in 1996, a release which went on to shift an impressive number of units.

Subsequently, Neat Metal expressed a serious interest in the unreleased recordings from the early 90's, and plans were duly made to issue them in the shape of the »Stand Or Fall« set, which has appeared on the Edgy imprint comparatively recently. It's not a flawless opus by any means, but still contains some excellent, well-crafted, classy metal numbers (notably "The Man Is Back", "City Of Lights" and "Only The Brave"), and it has definitely been worth all the effort in bringing the release to fruition at long last. Not only that, but GASKIN have also become a going concern once more, with the mainman working alongside a new set of accomplices, namely Andy Soloman (g), Tony Ilkiw (b) and Dave Pick (d), all of whom have proven themselves in the club scene over the years. Incredibly enough, one of the outfit's comeback shows came at a low-key European event called, er, Wacken 2000. Blimey, talk about being thrown in at the deep end. Still, they emerged victorious, and things look good for the future at this stage. Here's hoping it's not one of those dreaded fly-by-night reunions, and that these talented chaps achieve the recognition they surely deserve.

LP's
»**End Of The World**« Rondelet 1981
[Gatefold sleeve]
»**No Way Out**« Rondelet 1982

7" Singles
»**I'm No Fool**« Rondelet 1981
[Both tracks different to album versions]
»**Mony Mony**« Rondelet 1982
[A-side non-LP]

CD's
»**End Of The World**« Bootleg 1992
[Unofficial issue with two bonus tracks]
»**End Of The World**« Pony Canyon 1993
[Japanese issue]
»**No Way Out**« Pony Canyon 1993
[Japanese issue]
»**End Of The World/No Way Out**« British Steel 1996
»**Stand Or Fall**« Edgy 2000
[Features unreleased studio recordings from early 90's]

Compilation Appearances
"**I'm No Fool**" on »NWOBHM '79 Revisited« Do-LP/Do-CD Phonogram 1990
[Different to album version]
"**Sweet Dream Maker**" on »NWOBHM Vol.1« Bootleg CD 1992
[Different to album version]
"**Mony Mony**" on »N.W.O.B.H.M. Metal Rarities Vol.1« CD British Steel 1996
"**Queen Of Flames**" on »N.W.O.B.H.M. Metal Rarities Vol.1« CD British Steel 1996
"**Burning Alive**" on »Rock Out!« Do-CD Emporio 1996
"**End Of The World**" on »Rock Out!« Do-CD Emporio 1996

GEDDES AXE

Andy Millard (v)
Martin Wilson (g)
Andy Barrott (g)
Mick Peace (b)
Dave Clayton (d)

The excellent GEDDES AXE (who, as we're all now aware, took their name from a book about economic reform rather than anything more heroic) first got the metal bug in 1979, one of numerous acts to have been inspired to form in the wake of the phenomenal success achieved by local Yorkshire luminaries DEF LEPPARD and SAXON. In fact, the youthful five-piece managed to win quite a few support slots with both of the aforementioned acts during their formative years on the regional club circuit, something which couldn't have done them any harm whatsoever in terms of musical development. The lads got to the vinyl stage pretty rapidly (although, given that there was no real label interest, they had to go it alone), recording a three track EP in the summer of 1980, although, for some reason, it wasn't actually issued until early the following year. It was an excellent (belated) start, and showed the group to be operating in quite a powerful, semi-epic style reminiscent of DUCHESS or MILLENNIUM, for example. "Return Of The Gods" was the strongest track on display (the others being "Wildfire" and "Aftermath"), the following excerpt providing a representative example of their lyrical approach at the time:

'When the lords have to go there's tremors from below,
We take to the lands as if there's no tomorrow,
The heat builds around but we can't hear a sound,
We rise to the air for the siege on the new born.'

Relatively few copies of the EP were issued in a picture sleeve (a very basic one, nevertheless), and fewer still have retained the lyric insert, rendering such examples of the three-tracker as highly prized collectables. Following on from this undeniably impressive debut (which, incidentally, received the coveted accolade of a number one position in the Heavy Metal Charts in both 'Sounds' and 'Melody Maker'), the band were featured in the very first issue of 'Kerrang', taking pride of place in their 'Armed And Ready' section of up-and-coming young outfits, with references to RUSH and JUDAS PRIEST being offered in the way of a handy description of the GEDDES AXE sound. Around this time, the quintet also found their way onto a lucrative rock bill at the Rainbow in London, sharing a stage with A II Z and MORE for a memorable experience.

The band continued to gig far and wide over the following year (delighting the audience with

GEDDES AXE

SHARPEN YOUR WITS
C/W
ROCK AND ROLL IS THE WAY

NEW SINGLE OUT ON STEEL RECORDS

★ Not available in twelve inch form
★ Not available as a picture disc
★ No patches, Flying V's, PA systems or lighting rigs are given away with this single

THE MUSIC IS WHAT COUNTS
DISTRIBUTED BY PINNACLE (0689) 73146

---

numbers such as "Sharpen Your Wits", "Valley Of The Kings", "Six-Six-Six" and an ever-popular cover of "Detroit Rock City" by KISS), although they were to lose a couple of members during 1982. Dave Clayton and Andy Barrott departed for pastures new (the latter eventually resurfaced in BABY TUCKOO and CHROME MOLLY), with new members Nick Brown and John Burke eventually being enlisted for guitar and drum duties, respectively. Around the middle of the year, the lads released their second 7", a two-tracker (issued in a cartoon-style sleeve) featuring "Sharpen Your Wits" and "Rock And Roll Is The Way", a pair of popular numbers from their live repertoire. In contrast to their somewhat grandiose debut, however, this release was in more of a brash, straightforward rock style with an undeniable DEF LEPPARD influence, particularly on the B-side. It was another very strong effort, nonetheless, and was to sell in impressive quantities (as had its vinyl predecessor) as soon as copies made their way into the nation's record shops. Surprisingly, however, It proved to be vocalist Andy Millard's last contribution to the proceedings, as he had been replaced by new man Tony Rose within a matter of months. Rose slotted into the line-up with consummate ease, though, and the band resumed a successful bout of touring to promote their latest release.

In the early months of 1983, the ambitious young outfit were happy to outline their musical philosophy in a high-profile 'Kerrang' interview, with guitarist Martin Wilson elaborating on the reasons behind the various changes in personnel which had seriously affected the stability of GEDDES AXE throughout the previous year: 'The problem was that some of the band weren't taking the music or the band seriously enough, so they had to go. Unfortunately, replacing them wasn't as easy as we thought. Auditioning people isn't a cheap business, what with the cost of hiring rehearsal rooms, and playing a more complicated form of rock, a lot of the people who came along simply weren't good enough. So instead of it taking a couple of weeks as we'd originally thought, it ended up taking three or four months, which is a hell of a long time to be out of circulation in the rock business.' (Ref: Kerrang No.35, February 1983). Evidently, the lads weren't merely content to take the first musicians who offered their services, and their music was obviously a bit too complex for many young hopefuls to cope with. Nevertheless, it became apparent that the group had indeed found just the right combination of musicians in the long run, and it was only a matter of months before they were afforded a further chance to shine on vinyl, as an offer to record an EP for Bullet Records came their way a short time later.

Issued in 12" form, the »Escape From New York« three-tracker (benefitting from a considerably more accomplished production) was the first release to showcase the imposing, powerful vocal talents of Tony Rose, whose style was very much in the manner of TYTAN's Kal Swan. The songs featured (two of which had been part of the outfit's repertoire for some time) were something of a return to basics, with the title track and "Six-Six-Six" (the latter featuring some serious copyright infringement on certain DIAMOND HEAD-patented guitar parts) being fairly complex and interestingly-structured affairs, whereas "The Day The Wells Ran Dry" was a slightly more accessible and less convoluted effort. The EP managed (amazingly enough) to make it through a hazardous 'Kerrang' review relatively unscathed, and it looked as though this might have been the point at which GEDDES AXE finally broke away from their humble beginnings to become a forceful rock proposition. Sadly, however, it all seems to have fallen apart for the lads within the space of a year or so (most of the one-time members disappeared from the scene, although John Burke went on to have a fairly brief stint with Neal Kay's VENTURE), for reasons which aren't entirely clear, but you can surmise that the old chestnuts of musical differences and personnel instability probably had something to do with it. A great shame, really, and it would have been nice to hear a properly-produced, full-length effort from these talented Tykes.

12" EP's
»Escape From New York« Bullet 1983

7" EP's
»Return Of The Gods« A.C.S. Records 1981

7" Singles
»Sharpen Your Wits« Steel City Records 1982

Compilation Appearances
"Six-Six-Six" on »NWOBHM Vol.6« Bootleg CD 1992

GEMAGE

B. Gemage

An odd kettle of fish and no mistake! Lancashire's curiously-named GEMAGE (which, as you can see, actually appears to be the band leader's surname) issued a seldom-seen (but musically ambiguous) single in 1980 which has, in recent years, attracted the attention of a fair number of NWOBHM collectors. "The Story So Far", on the A-side, starts with an unusual, *staccato* riff (the closest comparison would perhaps be with RICOCHET's "Midas Light") and charges along quite happily in a fairly metal manner, although the vocals are more new wave punk than new wave metal. Overall, if you can grasp the rather abstract concept of a sound resembling early TYGERS OF PAN TANG (the fact that they had an identically-titled song is an unfortunate coincidence) crossed with ADAM AND THE ANTS, then you have some idea of what's going on musically. The cheerfully-titled "Bring Me Death", on the reverse, is an extremely unremarkable slower number that drags on far too long and which doesn't warrant a detailed analysis. This seems to have been the band's only output, and I get the feeling that, had this single come in a picture sleeve and had the protagonists been shown, they might not have looked like typical metallers. Certainly, GEMAGE weren't exactly a prominent name on the live circuit, and I suspect they probably came and went within a matter of months, but do let us know if you have any information to the contrary. Pick this up if you happen to see it cheaply, but steer well clear of it if the asking price is nudging towards three figures.

7" Singles
»The Story So Far« Private 1980

GENERAL WOLF

Les Maull (v)
Ron Hales (g)
Dave Ritchie (b,k)
Pete Edwards (d)

Another piece of melodic rock, sneaking in at the denouement of the NWOBHM era, comes courtesy of Humberside's GENERAL WOLF, who, having presumably started off a couple of years earlier, offered the world their sole slice of vinyl in 1986. Recorded at their local Fairview Studios facility in Hull, both "I Believe In Love" and "Take A Dream" represented quite listenable, keyboard-heavy compositions in the style of MOSELLE (the vocalist is, in places, suspiciously similar, so I wouldn't be at all surprised if this was a later incarnation of the aforementioned outfit) or SHOGUN, the B-side being additionally evocative of more lightweight bands from the period such as TUXEDO or even the pop/rock of VENDETTA. It wasn't a bad effort, and it sold in reasonable quantities at the time, although it ultimately failed to propel their name to national prominence. Although frequently to be found making up the numbers on local rock bills of the day, GENERAL WOLF, faced with increasing media and public disinterest, seem to have called it a day towards the end of the 80's, with Ron Hales (a veteran of such acts as MARINO THE BAND, among others, on an occasional basis) taking his place as one of the many associates of LISA DOMINIQUE before recording a solo LP entitled »The Resurrection«, which may or may not have been released on vinyl (although Hales has certainly turned up on a *'guitar hero'* set or two in recent years). GENERAL WOLF's lone 7" (which was apparently financed by the novel method of selling shares to the band's fans), housed in a nice monochrome sleeve with its heraldic illustration of a wolf's head, can still be found fairly cheaply today, and it's well worth picking up if you're a fan of the more melodic end of the market.

7" Singles
»I Believe In Love« 3-45 Records 1986

GENGHIS KHAN

Alan Marsh (v)
Ray Dismore (g)
Andy Boulton (g)
Andy Robbins (b)
Steve Pierce (d)

The origins of the immensely popular TOKYO BLADE lie, as we all know by now, in a small-time bunch of Wiltshire hopefuls called KILLER, who formed way back in 1980 and successfully plied their trade around the South of England for over two years (releasing a brace of well-received demo tapes in the process) before the emergence of a couple of European namesakes eventually forced an identity change upon them. At the beginning of 1983, therefore, the lads burst forth upon the scene with a recently-recorded five track cassette (which soon aroused a fair bit of interest from certain sections of the rock press) and a snappy new moniker, GENGHIS KHAN, presumably inspired by a certain number on IRON MAIDEN's »Killers« album. Shortly thereafter, the quintet took the unusual step of issuing their first two singles (financed by a local music shop, Rod Records in Salisbury) as a double pack (this weighty offering appeared under the appropriate guise of »Double Dealin«), which necessitated the pair of records being housed within a fairly bulky picture sleeve. With the tracks "If Heaven Is Hell", "Highway Passion", "Midnight Rendezvous" and "Mean Streak" (recorded at Cave Studios in Bristol) all coming across as professionally-written and capably-performed numbers with more than a hint of IRON MAIDEN and JUDAS PRIEST about them, the release garnered a remarkably favourable review in 'Kerrang', and this should really have set the boys on course for stardom at that point.

No sooner had the musicians circulated a few promotional copies and begun selling their records locally, however, than they discovered that one or two other acts had also elected to adopt the GENGHIS KHAN moniker, whereupon the Wiltshire lads reached the conclusion that they should reinvent themselves as something more distinctive. Their initial choice was TOKYO BLADE (at least one other British group shared this identity as well, so it wasn't really unique after all), and the transformation more or less occurred as they dispensed with unlucky guitarist Ray Dismore and recruited former DEEP MACHINE stalwart John Wiggins to the fold. The newly-christened TOKYO BLADE proceeded to withdraw the »Double Dealin« set almost immediately, although the singles were reissued shortly thereafter (with TOKYO BLADE labels cunningly plastered over the original GENGHIS KHAN ones) as individual items in new sleeves, and these proceeded to sell rather well locally. Contrary to certain ill-conceived rumours, however, there's no basis in the assertion that IRON MAIDEN (who had famously gigged under the assumed name of GENGHIS KHAN on at least one occasion in their heyday) and their management somehow *'had the release removed from sale'* (simply having a song title of the same name hardly constitutes copyright infringement), and the whole identity change/withdrawn record scenario was purely a matter of personal choice on the outfit's behalf. To follow the rest of the TOKYO BLADE story from this point onwards, kindly move to their own separate entry.

With the original GENGHIS KHAN double-pack having only been on general sale for a matter of weeks in the first instance, it's fair to say that an extremely limited quantity ever made it into circulation, and this seldom-seen item was once regarded as one of the most highly-valued NWOBHM collectables. In recent years, however, some shameless blackguard cottoned on to the fact that there was money to be made from this ultra-rarity, and organised a surreptitious re-pressing without the band's consent, touting around the plain-label records as legitimate *'test pressings'* in supposedly *'original'* sleeves. Given that so many copies (several hundred, by the looks of things) were suddenly in circulation, however, the truth was established fairly quickly and relatively few collectors were swindled by this method. Nevertheless, many dealers continue to offer these unofficial re-pressings for sale at grossly inflated prices, given the quantity that are known to exist. Shame on you!

7" Singles
»Double Dealin« Private 1983
[Double single with four tracks, later reissued with new labels and sleeves as separate TOKYO BLADE singles. Also re-pressed in mid-90's as white label copies in original GENGHIS KHAN sleeve]

GIRL

Phil Lewis (v)
Phil Collen (g)

Gerry Laffy (g)
Simon Laffy (b)
Dave Gaynor (d)

If ever there was a prime example of a suspiciously-meteoric rise from utter obscurity to mass popularity, it came in the unlikely shape of that bunch of London-based hopefuls named GIRL. With the five protagonists in question having initially come together in mid-1979, and with none of them owning up to any previous musical convictions whatsoever, it should really have taken them a couple of years to get to the stage of even *thinking* about winning a record deal. Instead, they went straight into the studio, knocked up some ramshackle tunes, laid them down on tape without too much fuss and even made a rudimentary video of themselves in action, all before they had played their first show in the capital. In fact, this spate of frenzied activity took place within a matter of weeks rather than months, which really is a remarkably brief space of time. Either GIRL were the most audacious group ever to walk the surface of the earth, or (as many people have hinted) they might have had slightly more experience under their belts than they were actually admitting. Whatever their background, the story unfolded in almost fairy-tale manner, the band (fronted by serial celebrity-shagger Phil Lewis) supposedly being snapped up by the first company they approached (which happened to be Jet Records), purely on the basis of their first demo. Talk about being in the right place at the right time…

Jet had reached the rather bewildering conclusion that GIRL somehow represented the future of rock'n'roll with their rehashed musical concoction, which, according to all the pre-vinyl hype, included liberal helpings of various well-respected glam, rock and punk acts from days gone by, notably KISS, the NEW YORK DOLLS and AEROSMITH. Still, the label made a good job of selling GIRL to the masses, and duly pressed up their first single (more of an introductory piece than anything more commercially-motivated) within an incredibly short space of time. Armed with their newly-recorded debut (featuring two versions of "My Number") and some strategically-placed promotional photos, GIRL were finally ready to rock the nation with their inaugural gig, a near-hysterical outing at London's Music Machine. There was no doubt about it, the kids had gone wild for these bad boys of rock'n'roll. At this early stage, GIRL could do no wrong, and they were soon snapped up as UFO's support band of choice,

making their first forays into Europe alongside the old stagers even before 1979 was out. These dates were, by all accounts, a staggering success, with the young pretenders showing their more accomplished masters a trick or two, and the ambitious upstarts were ready to take on the world by the time they returned to the UK.

Even by the early months of 1980, GIRL's reputation preceded them, and countless offers of radio, television and live work were now coming their way with utterly indecent regularity. It all seemed far too much, too soon, and the almost unprecedented intensity of media attention which was now surrounding the band's every move surely threatened to herald an equally spectacular fall from grace before long. Undeterred, GIRL's next move was to record a session for the 'Friday Rock Show', broadcast on the 25th of January 1980, where they took the opportunity to showcase some of the material from their forthcoming album. "My Number" and "Lovely Lorraine" represented two of their own compositions, while the catchy "Do You Love Me" (a KISS original, later covered by GIRLSCHOOL) and the ever-dependable "You Really Got Me" (by THE KINKS), served to identify some of their not-remotely-obvious influences. The long-player appeared within a few weeks of the session being transmitted, by which time the group had undertaken several high-profile shows, having set out on the road with UFO once again, this time on the UK leg of their lengthy world tour. In fact, »Sheer Greed« turned out to be a surprisingly well-mannered album, and it largely failed to recapture the brashness GIRL exuded by the bucketload in the live arena, although it was a listenable enough effort on the whole, the lads coming across as one of the more accessible and melodic semi-NWOBHM acts (with little to offer the hardline glam fans) in the general style of DEF LEPPARD, JANINE or SMART.

Although not quite evoking the spirit of their live shows, the first GIRL album proceeded to sell in remarkably impressive quantities, denting the mainstream charts in the process, and the publicity machine rolled on relentlessly. Another single, »Do You Love Me«, was trotted out to promote the outfit further, and the majority of reviews for both album and single were overwhelmingly positive. At this stage, GIRL could do no wrong in the public's rose-tinted view, and the quintet proceeded to flaunt themselves whenever and wherever possible, starting off with a prestigious half-hour live appearance on BBC Radio's 'In Concert' programme, followed by a visit to the studios of the legendary 'Old

Grey Whistle Test' a month or two later. In the spring of 1980, they were fortunate enough to be picked up by PAT TRAVERS, whereupon they went out on tour once again, releasing the »Hollywood Tease« EP to rake in a few more sales on the back of these high-profile appearances. By the summer, things had finally calmed down a bit, although it came as something of a surprise when original drummer Dave Gaynor was given the order of the boot (the ever-dependable *'musical differences'* chestnut rearing its ugly head), whereupon experienced replacement sticksman (although he was an equally capable bassist) Bryson 'Brillo' Graham (a veteran of numerous acts such as SPOOKY TOOTH, the ALVIN LEE BAND and PETER FRAMPTON) was brought in at short notice. Before long, the latest recruit was being exposed to the full spectacle of a GIRL gig with some low-key appearances in the capital, although the newcomer seemed to take it in his stride.

Within a few weeks of breaking in their new member, GIRL were lucky enough to be added to the bill of the 1980 Reading Festival, where they would appear well up in the running order, setting the stage for the likes of DEF LEPPARD and WHITESNAKE. By all accounts, both the warm-up gig at the Marquee (where they were joined by none other than Ritchie Blackmore for the encore) and the festival appearance itself went swimmingly, and the lads looked forward to wowing the fans with a follow-up album before too much longer. In the meantime, however, the band's devotees had to make do with another single, the A-side of which was the Russ Ballard-penned "Love Is A Game" (later covered by the EF BAND), an unremarkable number which hardly showed the group at their best, but never mind. After a few more gigs in the capital towards the end of the year (including some ill-fated shows with KISS), the knackered musicians finally put their feet up for a while, but soon turned their thoughts to that important second album as they entered 1981. With the outfit being such a success story at the time, they decided to capitalise on their popularity by going back into the studio without much delay, the intention being to get another long-player into the shops by the summer. Whereas their first collection had been written and recorded in a matter of weeks, however, the follow-up proved to be a much more time-intensive venture, and the lads immersed themselves in studio work for the best part of six months before any news of their activities started to filter out.

The protracted studio sessions had taken their toll on the band, though, and drummer Brillo Graham had flown the coop at a fairly early stage, so the latest version of GIRL now featured Pete Barnacle (formerly with GILLAN and BROKEN HOME, the latter being an act who had supported GIRL in their early days) at the recently-vacated drumstool. With the new album having finally been laid down in its entirety, it looked as though it would be rushed out with indecent haste, as had its immensely-successful predecessor. Strangely, however, the long-player consistently failed to materialise, although the public were given a sneaky glimpse of the outfit's latest activities when the »Thru The Twilite« single was finally issued (in the second half of 1981) as something of a taster for the much-anticipated album. Again, the record remained under wraps for the time being, much to the frustration and confusion of the fans, and even the members of GIRL seemed to have little knowledge of what was actually going on. Still, they began to put in a few appearances in the live environment once again, and assured the paying public that there would indeed be another full-length release at some stage. In the end, though, it wasn't until the early months of 1982 (by which time they had undertaken yet more gigs with the ever-dependable UFO) that album number two finally hit the shops.

By the time »Wasted Youth« was eventually made available to the general public, the hysteria surrounding the group's initial emergence had died down considerably, and there was no way on earth that GIRL were going to enjoy such an easy ride this time. If the new long-player wasn't an absolute scorcher, there would surely be hell to pay. In fact, there had been advance warnings that the protagonists intended to move away from *'heavy metal'* (and they barely qualified for such a tag in the first instance) on their sophomore effort, and this was pretty much evident on »Wasted Youth«, which contained a selection of nondescript and formulaic rockers that failed to set many pulses racing. It would probably have been a perfectly adequate release for many melodic rock hopefuls of the period, but people's expectations of GIRL were, in the wake of their astoundingly successful debut, almost unattainably high. It certainly wasn't a bad record by any means, but sales were well down on the stellar performance of »Sheer Greed«, and the seeds of doubt rapidly began germinating in the fertile minds of GIRL and Jet Records. This time, only one single was released to promote the record, and the »Old Dogs« 7" appears to have sold in very limited quantities indeed. Although many spectators likened the apparent demise of GIRL to the phenomenon of a particularly bright star which burned itself out with great speed, it was more a case of the public coming to terms with the fact that GIRL weren't all that special after all, the massive hype and media saturation which surrounded their early releases having given way to a dose of harsh reality.

In spite of the disappointment of the relative failure of their second album, it soon became apparent that the band already had sufficient material to fill a third, and they tentatively outlined plans to get another full-length effort into the shops before the end of the year. Their label, however, was far from convinced that this would be a worthwhile investment, and refused to give the lads any commitment towards releasing further vinyl in the short term. This left GIRL to go back to the clubs and try to claw back a few fans, although their appearances on the live circuit (including a short residency at the Marquee in the spring of 1982) appear to have dwindled away to nothing by the second half of the year. Nevertheless, the recording sessions for the next album went ahead as intended, and »Naughty Boyz« was laid down over the summer months. Sadly, the outfit's record label, sensing yet another commercial flop, flatly refused to give the project their blessing, and the future of GIRL was immediately thrown into doubt. Although the band (who parted company with Jet shortly thereafter) remained keen to get the long-player into the shops, its release was eventually shelved amidst contractual wrangling and personnel reshuffles, and the master tape was duly left to languish in the vaults.

By the second half of 1982, GIRL were on the danger list, having been moved onto a life-support machine in the aftermath of their acrimonious split from their record company. Even worse was to come, however, when star guitarist Phil Collen (who had, apparently, rejected offers to join both DEF LEPPARD and IRON MAIDEN in the band's early days!) finally defected to the ranks of DEF LEPPARD (having been acquainted with the Sheffield lads for some time, occasionally jamming together under the guise of DEF GIRL in the past), leaving the Londoners hanging by a rather tenuous thread. As a short-term measure, the remaining members brought in former BRAND X guitarist Pete Bonus as a replacement while they considered their future, and the new recruit deputised quite successfully on the outfit's end-of-year tour of the Far East. In fact, this series of dates went spectacularly well, the group realising that they actually had something of a fanatical following in countries such as Japan and Hong Kong, and it looked as though this boost to their rapidly-shrinking egos might just be enough to persuade them to carry on, if only for the benefit of the oriental market. In the end, however, it had all fallen apart for good even before 1982 was out, the musicians concluding that they had already made more than enough compromises in their quest for fame, as Phil Lewis explained several years later: *'We walked into a record company off the street with a demo; we never expected to get a record deal, I mean, we couldn't even play! We were all just doing it for a laugh. All of a sudden it became incredibly serious-they wanted image, albums-we were gettin' pushed in so many directions. What set out at a romp got serious and heavy. I hated it and started to rebel against it, cos we were being asked to conform and the whole thing lost its spirit.'* (Ref: Kerrang No.175, February 1988).

In the wake of GIRL's rapid demise, the various members scattered and joined up with new outfits, although it transpires that some of the musicians were, in fact, contractually barred (a nasty legacy from their Jet experience) from recording with any other major-label act for a period of several years. Phil Lewis had a busy time of it, nonetheless, and had stints with many outfits, notably SOLDIER, the NEW TORPEDOES, TORMÉ and the much-vaunted LONDON COWBOYS project (a venture to which Gerry Laffy also briefly lent his weight), before eventually jetting off to the States and joining the relatively successful L.A. GUNS, a prolific recording act (who even included a version of "Hollywood Tease" on their first album) who have (apart from a brief period when Lewis went off to form the ill-fated FILTHY LUCRE venture) been on the go for many years now. Gerry Laffy, meanwhile, became involved with film production and soundtrack work immediately after GIRL's demise, although he eventually returned to the rock scene with some critically-acclaimed solo albums (a programme of releases which is still underway as we speak), as well as the short-lived SHEER GREED project, where he was joined by erstwhile colleagues Simon Laffy (his brother) and Pete Barnacle (plus unknown guitarist Neil Gabbitas) for a couple of seldom-seen Japanese albums. Simon Laffy, incidentally, had also worked with a minor act called ATLANTIS immediately after GIRL, whilst former stand-ins Brillo Graham (later of BLACKFOX) and Pete Bonus had both played a part in the fortunes of the ill-fated ZEN ATTACK ensemble.

With Phil Lewis and Gerry Laffy still being extremely active in the recording sense, the notion of a GIRL reunion remains a distinct possibility, although it seems a fairly remote one at the moment. Intriguingly, though, Phil Collen (while still very much a part of the DEF LEPPARD set-up) seems to be surprisingly keen on the idea of further GIRL activity, as he revealed a few years ago: *'I've recently spoken to Simon, Gerry and Phil about it, and there still seems to be studio material in the vaults. After listening to the tracks once again, we discussed whether or not it might be possible to release another album sometime.'* (Ref: Interview, Matthias Mader, October 1996). As it turns out, interest in the original band appears to have picked up shortly after these statements were made, and that long-lost third album has recently been exhumed and issued belatedly (in Japan only, for the time being), the set having now been retitled »Killing Time«. Whether or not this totally puts the kibosh on a full-scale GIRL reunion (either for recording or touring purposes) is open to debate, however, so I guess we'll just have to wait and see what happens.

LP's
»**Sheer Greed**« Jet Records 1980
»**Wasted Youth**« Jet Records 1982

10" Singles
»**Love Is A Game**« Jet Records 1980
[Issued on white vinyl, A-side non-LP]

7" EP's
»**Hollywood Tease**« Jet Records 1980
["You Really Got Me" non-LP, also issued in limited edition poster sleeve]

7" Singles
»**My Number**« Jet Records 1979
[Includes two versions of "My Number", most copies issued on clear vinyl, demos on black vinyl]
»**Do You Love Me**« Jet Records 1980
»**Hollywood Tease**« CBS 1980
[Japanese two track issue, B-side "My Number"]
»**Love Is A Game**« Jet Records 1980
[Issued on white vinyl, A-side non-LP]
»**Love Is A Game**« Jet Records 1980
[Japanese issue in different sleeve]
»**Heartbreak America**« Jet Records 1980
[Japanese-only issue]
»**Thru The Twilite**« Jet Records 1981
[Also issued as limited edition picture disc]
»**Old Dogs**« Jet Records 1982

CD's
»**Sheer Greed**« Jet 1994
[UK issue]
»**Wasted Youth**« Jet 1994

[UK issue]
»**Sheer Greed**« Nippon Crown 1998
[Japanese issue]
»**Wasted Youth**« Nippon Crown 1998
[Japanese issue]
»**Killing Time**« Nippon Crown 1998
[Japanese-only issue, includes unreleased studio recordings for aborted »Naughty Boyz« album]
»**Sheer Greed**« Receiver 1999
»**Wasted Youth**« Receiver 1999

Compilation Appearances
"**Hollywood Tease**" on »Metal Treasures And Vinyl Heavies« LP Action Replay Records 1984

GIRLSCHOOL

Kim McAuliffe (v, g)
Kelly Johnson (v, g)
Enid Williams (v, b)
Denise Dufort (d)

If there's one thing that really annoyed me at the time of the original NWOBHM explosion (and which continues to rankle in terms of the modern-day appreciation of the genre), it was the widely-held belief that it was music *for* overgrown adolescent males, *played* by overgrown adolescent males. Now, I've no objection to being identified as a very sad case indeed (sorry, but I've been enjoying this immensely juvenile music for twenty-odd years, and still have absolutely no desire to trade it all in for jazz and classical albums), but I resent the suggestion that (a) females were all far too mature and sensible to enjoy the heavy stuff themselves and (b) the all-girl bands and female-fronted outfits of the era were mere novelties who played an entirely peripheral part in the development of the scene. Nothing could be further from the truth. The ladies were instrumental in giving the NWOBHM (and the rock world in general) a much-needed kick in the pants, and some of them (particularly the members of the high-profile and stupendously successful GIRLSCHOOL and, to a lesser extent, ROCK GODDESS) succeeded in permanently wresting the power away from the dominant (or, at least, more plentiful) males of the metal kingdom. Sure, there were contemporaries in other genres who exhibited plenty of *'girl power'* (notably the RUNAWAYS, the GO-GO'S, the SLITS and BLONDIE), although the success of these acts seemed to be critically dependent on visual appearance and image. The aforementioned GIRLSCHOOL and

ROCK GODDESS, on the other hand, pulled off the highly impressive feat of infiltrating the world of metal, the last great bastion of maleness, and they achieved their destiny purely (well, mainly) by virtue of their collective musical talents.

For GIRLSCHOOL, it had all started back in the spring of 1978, when Kim McAuliffe and Enid Williams (two founder members of the little-known PAINTED LADY, who also featured guitarist Kathy Valentine, later of the GO-GO'S) decided to knock their original band on the head (after a year's worth of fruitless gigging on the capital's club scene) and attempt to establish a rather more forceful proposition to challenge the giants of the rock world. With the addition of Kelly Johnson and Denise Dufort (whose elder brother, the much-travelled Dave, had passed on his drumming skills some years earlier), the revamped outfit swiftly metamorphosed into GIRLSCHOOL, who spent the next six months steadily making a name for themselves on London's notoriously arduous live circuit. If they had been a bunch of talentless dolly birds, they wouldn't have lasted five minutes, so the fact that they were still on the go at the end of the year was a healthy sign. Not only that, the thriving act had also managed to attract the attention of City Records in the interim, after which the company hurriedly snapped them up for a one-off single deal. GIRLSCHOOL's vinyl debut, recorded at the tail end of 1978, hit the shops in the new year, and »Take It All Away« (b/w "It Could Be Better") showed them to be (at that stage) a moderately heavy proposition who were merely taking some VARDIS-style, good time rock'n'roll and infusing it with the merest hint of RAMONES-influenced snottiness. It was, to be perfectly frank, a fairly inauspicious debut, although it proceeded to sell a grand total of several thousand copies within a matter of weeks (and this was before the main NWOBHM influx, remember), so it looked as though they were certainly doing something right.

The two-tracker also opened a few doors for the girls, who swiftly formed a long-standing alliance (all perfectly legal and above board, I'm sure) with MOTÖRHEAD, who invited GIRLSCHOOL to join them on their UK tour in the spring. Undaunted by the very tangible prospect of possible humiliation at the hands of Lemmy's leather-clad following, the quartet matched the old stagers every step of the way (including the post-gig drinking sessions, by all accounts), and were soon being heralded as the *'next big thing'* in the world of metal. Next up, though, was some early exposure to the European live circuit, when they accompanied TED NUGENT on a series of well-attended dates, one of which was actually taped and later bootlegged as the »Live At Appeldoorn« LP. In spite of Kim McAuliffe's subsequent claims that the album in fact contained a recording of a PAINTED LADY gig (strange, considering the latter didn't even make it out of London), however, it really is a *bona fide* GIRLSCHOOL show, albeit a pretty early one with a largely-unfamiliar set list (including numerous covers such as AC/DC's "Live Wire" and "Let's Spend The Night Together" by the ROLLING STONES). Funny how your memory plays tricks on you sometimes, isn't it? Anyway, the foursome returned to the UK in high spirits, and continued to delight the crowds with their ever-improving live repertoire, ditching the obligatory cover versions and writing strong material of their own. By the second half of the year, their developing friendship with MOTÖRHEAD led to a tentative deal with Bronze, who offered them the chance to show what they could do with a one-off single. Released at the beginning of 1980, by which time the NWOBHM had really taken off in a big way, their »Emergency« offering (b/w the oddly-titled "Furniture Fire") was the record which really broke GIRLSCHOOL, showing that they had introduced some rather more substantial riffing into their own compositions and were now ready to take their place at the very forefront of the NWOBHM explosion. It looks as though some rather more forceful acts were particularly fond of "Emergency", too, as it was later covered by both INFA RIOT and RYKER'S…

With a full album deal following as a matter of course, the rock world looked forward to the first GIRLSCHOOL long-player, although the studio work had to wait until the hard-gigging group had completed yet another tour, having gone out on the road with URIAH HEEP to further hone their skills. Before long, though, they were immersing themselves in the studio, emerging with a debut set entitled »Demolition«, released in the spring of 1980. It was, without any doubt, a cracking way to make their mark on the metal scene, and capable numbers such as "Demolition Boys", "Not For Sale", "Midnight Ride" and "Deadline" all demonstrated an uncanny knack for creating catchy, anthemic songs with heavy arrangements, just the sort of thing that would go down a storm with a high percentage of rock fans. It wasn't a perfect album by any means ("Breakdown" and "Baby Doll" were quite weak), and GIRLSCHOOL still had a lot to learn about songwriting, but the record proceeded to sell in hugely impressive quantities, making a significant impression on the mainstream album charts and thrusting the girls into the limelight in no uncertain terms. Bronze soon brought out a couple of singles, »Nothing To Lose« and »Race With The Devil«, the latter being based upon a song by 60's heavyweights GUN, although the new version, while listenable enough, wasn't a patch on the bonkers 1968 original. Still, the singles were to shift a great many units, and GIRLSCHOOL soon went out on the road yet again (with BLACK SABBATH, this time) to promote their debut album.

Even after completing a hectic series of dates, however, the tireless four-piece still weren't able to take a break, and went back out on tour with MOTÖRHEAD again, before they subsequently entered the BBC's studios to lay down their first session for the 'Friday Rock Show'. Broadcast on the 1st of August 1980, the session showcased "Demolition Boys", "Take It All Away", "Nothing To Lose" and "Breakdown", the energetic performance introducing the talented outfit to anyone who had somehow contrived to miss out on GIRLSCHOOL's meteoric rise to prominence. Towards the end of the year, the group began work on their second album (after a few headlining gigs with A II Z in tow, one of which was even recorded for the BBC's 'In Concert' programme), and gave the fans a taster for things to come with the »Yeah Right« single (B-side "The Hunter"), a powerful pairing which went a long way towards capturing the aggression (and, in the case of "Yeah Right", the humour) of a GIRLSCHOOL live show. The album was in the can by the end of January 1981, and the band celebrated by recording a session for the 'Richard Skinner Show' (a midweek music programme covering a wide range of acts, but hardly a renowned sponsor of rock music), where they showcased some of the material from the forthcoming long-player. However, the LP was kept under wraps for a good few months, during which time GIRLSCHOOL teamed up with labelmates (and long-time drinking partners) MOTÖRHEAD for a release which many still regard as the highlight of both acts' lengthy careers. The musicians all hooked up to form HEADGIRL (aka MOTÖRSCHOOL), a one-off studio get-together, and recorded a storming version of "Please Don't Touch", a fairly obscure JOHNNY KIDD AND THE PIRATES original from 1959. Then, GIRLSCHOOL laid down a version of MOTÖRHEAD's "Bomber", while MOTÖRHEAD returned the compliment by taking on "Emergency", and the whole unruly shebang was issued as the »St. Valentine's Day Massacre« EP (released, appropriately enough, on February 14th, in both 7" and 10" forms). It was a truly phenomenal success, achieving an astonishing 'Top 5' placing in the mainstream charts and leading to several appearances on a variety of televised music programmes (including 'Top Of The Pops') in both the UK and Europe, the end result being that GIRLSCHOOL's popularity swiftly reached an all-time high.

With the name of GIRLSCHOOL now well and truly on everyone's lips, studio album number two (»Hit And Run«) was finally readied for release in the spring of 1981, coinciding with the group's first ever headlining national tour. It was a far more rounded, polished and consistent effort than their debut long-player had been, and new numbers such as "(I'm Your) Victim", "Following The Crowd" and "Watch Your Step" were all extremely listenable. There were only a couple of poor numbers, namely the peculiar "Back To Start", and their cover of ZZ TOP's "Tush", an entirely average track (a staple of their live repertoire since the earliest days) which the TYGERS OF PAN TANG also felt compelled to immortalise on vinyl, for some unfathomable reason. If there had originally been any residual fears that the fans might not take to the newer GIRLSCHOOL material, however, these were soon dispelled when the album rocketed into the mainstream charts and ultimately achieved a highly commendable 'Top 5' placing, elevating the outfit to the status of *bona fide* rock giants, the act now selling roughly the same number of LP's as national institutions such as IRON MAIDEN and MOTÖRHEAD, for example. »Hit And Run« was duly trundled out as a successful single, and followed up by a three-tracker based around "C'mon Let's Go", with some energetic live material from their recent tour being used to complete the EP. With GIRLSCHOOL already riding the crest of a wave, the icing on the cake came with an offer to headline the Reading Festival, where the feisty lasses proceeded to delight the assembled throng with a lengthy performance of unbridled enthusiasm. They weren't finished yet, though, and went on to undertake a gruelling schedule of global gigging before the end of the year, taking in Canada (where they had already developed a truly fanatical following), the UK (including a show at Bristol which went out live on BBC Radio) and mainland Europe, followed by a brief sojourn to Japan in the early weeks of 1982.

Upon their eventual return to the UK in order to start work on their third album, however, Enid Williams finally announced her plans to quit the band in order to establish her own outfit, and the bassist was soon wending her way to the ill-fated FRAMED project (see separate entry), which barely lasted a couple of years before ending up in complete disarray. The remaining members of GIRLSCHOOL hadn't experienced personnel problems prior to this juncture, and didn't really know who to approach to act as a replacement bassist, so they turned to their old mate Lemmy, who soon introduced one of his, er, 'friends', Ghislaine 'Gil' Weston (formerly with the KILLJOYS), who was soon enrolled after proving her mettle at a few low-key gigs. The outfit were soon hard at work on their next album, and work was completed within the usual couple of months, leaving GIRLSCHOOL free to get out on the road once again. They made their first trip to the States, playing a handful of well-chosen dates on their own (remarkably successful affairs, by all accounts), before returning to the UK in the spring for an extensive tour which saw RAVEN opening the proceedings. It was then back to the States for a series of dates with IRON MAIDEN in the summer, topped off with another 'In Concert' appearance on BBC Radio, this time alongside STAMPEDE. Their album had reached the shops in the interim, and »Screaming Blue Murder« was a real 'in your face' affair, with a 'live'-sounding production and some considerably heavier material in places (which came as a surprise after the accessibility of »Hit And Run«), some of which seemed to be borrowing from TANK (a few of those song titles looked pretty familiar,

too) and MOTÖRHEAD themselves, although it was all undeniably listenable as a whole. The obligatory cover version came in the shape of "Live With Me", a relatively obscure ROLLING STONES original from the »Let It Bleed« album, while the only 7" to materialise this time was the »Wildlife« EP, using one of the LP's more commercial numbers as its main focus of attention.

The observation that sales were well down on »Hit And Run« (they were, indeed, highly similar to sales of the musically-analogous »Demolition«) may well have given GIRLSCHOOL and their label something to think about when it came to recording the next long-player, but they were to be allowed a fairly generous period to recover from the exertions of the preceding few months, only emerging for a European jaunt with RAINBOW later in the year. Moving into 1983, however, confirmed sightings of GIRLSCHOOL seemed to be increasingly rare events, and the musicians began to express serious doubts as to the sincerity and dedication of their label, as Kim McAuliffe revealed: *'Sometimes I wonder if Bronze have any interest in us any more. On occasions they seem like a bunch of twits up there. For example, they never released any of the tracks from »Screaming Blue Murder« set as singles, although lots of people said there were a few hit singles on there. And if your record company shows no interest in you, it doesn't exactly help. They also didn't seem to put any effort or enthusiasm into promoting the album either.'* (Ref: Kerrang No.33, January 1983). Still, they attempted to keep up their touring presence with the usual round of gigs (not nearly as many as before, though), both in the UK (including a major festival in Leeds, where the likes of TWISTED SISTER, ANVIL and SAXON also appeared) and the States, before eventually beginning work on album number four in the summer of 1983.

The full-length record was preceded by an EP featuring the anthemic "1-2-3-4 Rock And Roll" (penned by a transatlantic songwriting conglomerate whose past credits included FIONA and JOAN JETT AND THE BLACKHEARTS) as its main focus of attention, along with the omnipresent "Tush" (once was bad enough, surely) and a re-recorded version of "Don't Call It Love". Strangely, the record had a not-terribly-convincing *'apology'* printed on the sleeve, concerning the delay in getting the new album into the shops (the message feebly claimed that it was simply a result of their relentless touring schedule, although it actually had a lot more to do with a dire lack of decent material, continued label problems and a severe difficulty in persuading anyone to produce their latest output at a reasonable price). To be honest, it wasn't a particularly plausible excuse, and intentionally drawing attention to their plight wasn't a good idea at all. Still, they seem to have been genuinely disappointed by their recent period of relative inactivity, and appear to have rushed out the single with little or no regard to quality control. Interestingly, it was the first GIRLSCHOOL 7" to fail to make an impression on the charts for quite a long time, which didn't augur particularly well for the fate of the forthcoming album. Still, »Play Dirty« (produced by Noddy Holder and Jim Lea of SLADE) soon appeared as intended, and was promoted with yet another European tour. The latest record continued the peculiar pattern of alternating heavy/lightweight albums, although this was clearly GIRLSCHOOL's most commercially-oriented offering so far.

»Play Dirty« took GIRLSCHOOL into the world of pop/rock for the first time, and it was apparent that they were now making major concessions to the mainstream market in an attempt to get their music across to as many potential fans as possible. In spite of the fact that the longplayer represented a very well-played collection of melodic rock, however, they had now gone overboard in terms of accessibility, diminishing their original power to a huge extent. It was, to be honest, a frustratingly lightweight experiment, although sporadic flashes of the more traditional GIRLSCHOOL sound (on numbers such as "Breakout", "Running For Cover" and the title track itself) suggested that they hadn't (despite coming perilously close on occasion) quite lost the plot completely. Sadly, the LP met with a predictably frosty reception from reviewers and hardline fans alike, and it only skirted around the lower reaches of the charts, its modest performance contrasting markedly with the stellar success of their first three albums. In addition to the constitutional cover version ("20th Century Boy" by T. REX), the LP actually included two lesser-known SLADE compositions ("High And Dry" and "Burning In The Heat (Of Love)", the latter being released as a 7"/12" in due course, as was a single based around the aforementioned "20th Century Boy", although neither made the remotest impression on the charts. After a tour of North America to promote the album in the early months of 1984, however, GIRLSCHOOL subsequently decided to take a sabbatical, and the members seemed to go into hiding for the rest of that year.

Before long, however, it became apparent that the outfit had actually lost the services of founder member Kelly Johnson, with the unsettled individual having departed to pursue an ill-starred solo career long before GIRLSCHOOL had even begun thinking about recording their next album. Undeterred, the gals brought in new guitarist Cris Bonacci (originally with Australian group SWEET JAYNE, and also a veteran of SHE, the outfit formed by Tracey Lamb of ROCK GODDESS) to plug the gap, and the situation was rapidly salvaged without too much difficulty. Mind you, there were still a few further troubles in store, and the musicians ultimately parted company with Bronze (who, in any case, went into liquidation soon afterwards) as a direct consequence of the poor sales of their most recent album. With the persevering group trying out a few new ideas while attempting to negotiate a deal somewhere or other, they experimented by bringing in a dedicated singer, Jackie Bodimead (the former CANIS MAJOR singer, and yet another veteran of SHE), and matters seemed to improve with this injection of new blood. The newest GIRLSCHOOL recruits were soon being introduced to the British fans at a handful of shows in the autumn, and the revamped line-up later made a good impression at some selective European showcase gigs towards the end of 1984, the upshot being that the girls were soon being courted by none other than Phonogram, who offered them a very welcome album deal in the spring of 1985. After a few low-key gigs in North America (some of which were supporting DEEP PURPLE), the public were given a sneak preview of some new material when GIRLSCHOOL put in an appearance on the 'E.C.T.' television programme, where they performed "Running Wild" and "I Want You Back", a confident pair of raunchy tracks which seemed more in line with the most recent ROCK GODDESS album than their own lightweight compositions from the »Play Dirty« era.

The album (»Running Wild«) emerged a few months later, but it was to appear only in selected overseas countries on Phonogram (also linked with labels such as Mercury and Vertigo), although the group still remained confident that it would be licensed by a British concern sooner or later. It wasn't a bad album (which included a version of "Do You Love Me" by KISS, already covered by GIRL some years previously), with Ms Bodimead putting in a fairly charismatic performance on compositions such as "Let Me Go" and the catchy title track itself, although Kim McAuliffe later denounced the whole thing as a substandard offering, the recording and release of which took place in rather bizarre circumstances: *'We completely lost our minds. There were a few good songs on the album, but they* weren't representative of GIRLSCHOOL, what with the line-up changes and all that-we should have renamed ourselves. The record company had paid us a lot of money upfront, but then we were completely cut off from the person who originally signed us, so we had virtually no contact with our label, Phonogram in New York. Then there were a few financial problems; we tried calling them but nobody even knew who GIRLSCHOOL were by that stage!' (Ref: Interview, Matthias Mader, March 1996). With their ineffectual label having seemingly lost interest in the album shortly after the recording session, therefore, it's a miracle that copies made it into the shops at all, but it meant that negotiations for a UK release never really got off the ground. As a result, a minimal number of examples made it to their homeland as expensive imports, and, as a direct consequence, few fans were lucky enough to get their grubby mitts on a copy. Still, the outfit went ahead and toured the UK anyway (releasing a live video as a substitute for the intended album), hitching a ride with MAGNUM towards the end of the year and entertaining the crowds with a wide variety of material from throughout their career.

Clearly, however, the capable Jackie Bodimead was unhappy with her new-found role in GIRLSCHOOL, and departed after just one album, whereupon she reunited with brother Tony (they had worked together in the CANIS MAJOR days) in the short-lived HARMONIC 228 project (she also played a part in the fortunes of fly-by-night minor outfits FUTURE GAMES and IF ONLY), leaving GIRLSCHOOL to revert to their original four-piece design. After a couple of months, largely spent getting some fresh material together, they were to benefit from a well-timed offer from the recently-formed GWR label, the latest home of their old chums in MOTÖRHEAD. Within a remarkably short timescale, a brand-new LP had successfully been recorded, and this appeared in mid-1986 as »Nightmare At Maple Cross«, a record which, at times, seemed to be attempting to recapture the pop/rock style of the »Play Dirty« set. The likes of "You Got Me", for example, were enjoyable enough numbers, but the girls let themselves down on singalong efforts such as their cover of MUD's "Tiger Feet" shocker, and worse was to come when they teamed up with GARY GLITTER (the full implications of the words 'Gary Glitter', 'Girls' and 'School' being in any way connected now hardly bear contemplation) for an utterly chronic rehashing of his "I'm The Leader Of The Gang" monstrosity, the track being released as their new single (with accompanying promo video) to hoots of public derision. The move into anthemic glam rock territory wasn't exactly the sort of thing their dwindling fan base was hoping for, and sales of both album and single were pitifully poor.

Still, the hapless outfit tried everything to get back on the public's good side once again, recording another 'Friday Rock Show' session later in the year, where they showcased "Never Too Late", "All Day All Night", "Play With Fire" and "Turn It Up". Broadcast on the 14th of November 1986, the session was a pretty mediocre affair, but at least it showed everyone that

Photo: Tobias Thiem

GIRLSCHOOL were still a going concern, and the hard-gigging musicians soon went out on tour yet again, playing European dates towards the end of 1986 and returning for some UK shows early the following year. After completing these obligations, however, Gil Weston threw in her hand for no apparent reason (since she had recently become Mrs Gil Weston-Jones, it was probably a classic case of 'pipe and slippers syndrome'), although GIRLSCHOOL were now able to bring in a more-than-worthy replacement in the shape of former ROCK GODDESS bassist Tracey Lamb, whose promising SHE venture had collapsed some time previously, leaving the individual (who had latterly been involved with a small-time act called the PERFECT MOTHERS) at a bit of a loose end. GIRLSCHOOL, meanwhile, were still signed to GWR, with the option of another album (friends in high places, obviously), but they decided to bide their time before returning to the fray with yet another full-length effort. In fact, Kim McAuliffe took time off later in the year, whereupon she lent her services to an extremely ill-conceived (and unnamed) project which also featured such individuals as Beki Bond (from the BOMBSHELLS), Philthy Taylor (from MOTÖRHEAD) and erstwhile SOLDIER axeman Nick Lashley, who (in spite of a rather blatant gender flaw) had actually been helping out as extra guitarist on some of GIRLSCHOOL's recent touring activities. This particular venture came to nothing in the long term, however, and, with McAuliffe ultimately returning to the ranks of GIRLSCHOOL, the ladies soon got the touring bug yet again (well, since it had been a whole six months since their last major outing, this was understandable), whereupon they hooked up with those ever-accommodating labelmates MOTÖRHEAD once more, making their way over to Europe for some end-of-year gigs, followed by a further support slot on the UK leg of their tour.

Within a few months, however, it was back to the studio for another attempt at finding a winning formula, although GIRLSCHOOL were now struggling to find a genuine sense of identity in the thrash and glam-obsessed late 80's. Still, they duly delivered their »Take A Bite« offering as planned, a slight improvement on the preceding long-player, perhaps, but still weakened by space-filling inclusions such as "Fox On The Run" (originally by THE SWEET, and also covered by CLOVEN HOOF, believe it or not). One of the stronger numbers, "Head Over Heels", was subsequently used as the A-side for the one and only single to be taken from the album, but few people noticed. With the LP being utterly ignored by the public and the rock press, the luckless GIRLSCHOOL now seemed to be dead in the water, and a dismal European tour in the latter months of 1988 (playing alongside GARY GLITTER) confirmed the widely-held belief that they were flogging a dead horse. To their credit, the girls called it a day the following year, and went off to work on other projects. In fact, the members appear to have been quite fond of extra-curricular activities, with the duo of Kim McAuliffe and Cris Bonacci proceeding to join up with the misguided ALL STARS venture in the early 90's, before the pair hooked up with erstwhile colleague Enid Williams (who, after the failure of FRAMED, had turned her attention to treading the boards in more serious musical productions) and briefly worked together as the STRANGE GIRLS.

By the second half of 1991, however, the temptation to have another go as GIRLSCHOOL proved irresistible, and the faithful trio of Denise Dufort, Kim McAuliffe and Cris Bonacci regrouped with the intention of penning some novel material. Tracey Lamb couldn't be persuaded to re-enlist, however, and so new bassist Jackie Carrera joined in the fun. They got back into the swing of things with (you guessed it) an end-of-year European jaunt (did they time these activities to coincide with their Christmas shopping or something?), before returning to the UK to look for yet another label who would be prepared to sponsor their future career. In the end, it would be Communiqué (home of SAMSON and GOLGOTHA) who leapt in with a timely offer to release the next GIRLSCHOOL opus, and they duly started work a few months later. By this stage, however, Castle Communications had acquired the lucrative rights to the Bronze Age GIRLSCHOOL material, and had begun to issue the first of numerous cash-in compilations and shoddily-packaged retrospectives, much to the chagrin of the band themselves, as Kim McAuliffe revealed: 'Believe it or not, we sold over two and a half million records in our career, and got nothing out of it. Our early label, Bronze, sold all the rights to Castle and now they keep bringing out all the same tracks on compilations, each with a different cover and running order.' (Ref: Iron Pages No.37, 1996). Welcome to the cut-throat world of big business, ladies...

The all-new GIRLSCHOOL revealed some of their latest studio material with yet another session for the 'Friday Rock Show', transmitted on the 22nd of May 1992. In fact, "Can't Keep A Good Girl Down" (I wouldn't know about that sort of thing), "One More" and "We Came" were some of the strongest GIRLSCHOOL compositions for many a year, and there was every chance that they might actually pull it off with their comeback LP. The imaginatively-titled »Girlschool« did indeed represent a healthy selection of tunes, and, had there been any justice whatsoever, the press would have afforded them the dignity of a favourable review or two. Sadly, the release was cruelly ignored, leaving the girls with no option to go back to the incessant and gruelling round of live appearances, and the quartet subsequently took it upon themselves to get gigs wherever they could (even taking in some well-received appearances in Eastern Europe) in order to get a bit of recognition. Fortunately, there was still enough interest in their activities to keep the momentum going, and, after a few years of low-profile touring, the group returned with a live album based around both old and new songs (partly to give the fans the official live release that they wanted, and partly to claw back some of the money that was now being syphoned off by Castle's relentless programme of compilations).

By this time, though, not only had old mucker Tracey Lamb finally been persuaded to join in the fun, but Denise Dufort and Kim McAuliffe were also now being assisted by none other than the returning Kelly Johnson, who had ultimately been welcomed back into the GIRLSCHOOL fold (in the spring of 1993) after several years of mildly-successful musical experimentation on the other side of the Atlantic. The album (recorded, at the second attempt, at a small venue in a place called Wokingham on the outskirts of London) was warmly received by an increasingly-widespread fan base, and this paved the way for yet more touring activities in recent years. Although no new studio material has been delivered for quite some time now (a further full album has been *'in the pipeline'* for a couple of years, though), a touring version of GIRLSCHOOL is still wowing the fans sporadically in the live environment (including an appearance at the 1999 Wacken Festival alongside the likes of JAGUAR and the TYGERS OF PAN TANG), and the lasses have even been sighted in the UK of late, occasionally playing alongside fellow old-timers such as TANK and SAXON. Long may they continue.

LP's

»Demolition« Bronze 1980
»Hit And Run« Bronze 1981
[Also released as limited edition on red vinyl]
»Screaming Blue Murder« Bronze 1982
»Play Dirty« Bronze 1983
»Running Wild« Mercury/Phonogram 1985
»Nightmare At Maple Cross« GWR 1986
[UK issue with ten tracks]
»Nightmare At Maple Cross« GWR 1986
[US issue with extra track "I'm The Leader Of The Gang"]
»Race With The Devil« Raw Power 1986
[Compilation release, double album]
»Take A Bite« GWR 1988
»Cheers You Lot!« Razor Records 1989
[Compilation release]
»Live At Appeldoorn« Bootleg 198?
[Unofficial red vinyl release featuring live material from 1979, aka »To All Headbangers«]

Mini-LP's

»Motorschool« Victor 1981
[Japanese-only issue, with MOTÖRHEAD, inclu- des »*St. Valentine's Day Massacre*« *EP plus three extra tracks]*
»Live And More« Victor 1982
[Japanese-only issue]

12" EP's

»Stay Clean« Bronze 1981
[With MOTÖRHEAD, "Please Don't Touch" non-LP, also features live version of "Demolition Boys"]
»Don't Call It Love« Bronze 1982
[German issue of »*Wildlife*« *EP, "Don't Stop" non-LP]*
»1-2-3-4 Rock And Roll« Bronze 1983
[A-side non-LP, "Don't Call It Love" different to album version]
»20th Century Boy« Bronze 1983
["Like It Like That" non-LP]
»Burning In The Heat« Bronze 1983
»I'm The Leader Of The Gang« GWR 1986
[With GARY GLITTER, extended A-side non-LP in UK]

10" EP's

»St. Valentine's Day Massacre« Bronze 1981
[As HEADGIRL, A-side with MOTÖRHEAD non-LP, "Bomber" non-LP, also features "Emergency" by MOTÖRHEAD]
»C'mon Let's Go« Bronze 1981
[Features live versions of "Tonight" and "Demolition Boys"]
»Hit And Run« Bronze 1981
["Tonight" non-LP]

7" EP's

»St. Valentine's Day Massacre« Bronze 1981
[As HEADGIRL, A-side with MOTÖRHEAD non-LP, "Bomber" non-LP, also features "Emergency" by MOTÖRHEAD]
»C'mon Let's Go« Bronze 1981
[UK three track issue, "C'mon Let's Go" different to album version, also features live versions of "Tonight" and "Demolition Boys"]
»Wildlife« Bronze 1982
["Don't Stop" non-LP, also issued as limited edition on red vinyl]
»Wildlife« Victor 1982
[Japanese version in different sleeve]
»1-2-3-4 Rock And Roll« Bronze 1983
["Don't Call It Love" different to LP version]

7" Singles

»Take It All Away« City 1979
[A-side different to album version, B-side "It Could Be Better" non-LP]
»Take It All Away« City 1979
[French issue in different sleeve, also issued as limited edition on both red and blue vinyl]
»Take It All The Way« Mulligan 1979

[Irish issue with incorrect title, limited edition on red vinyl]
»Emergency« Bronze 1980
[B-side "Furniture Fire" non-LP]
»Nothing To Lose« Bronze 1980
[A-side different to album version, B-side live version of "Baby Doll"]
»Race With The Devil« Bronze 1980
»Yeah Right« Bronze 1980
»Hit And Run« Bronze 1981
[UK issue, B-side "Tonight" non-LP]
»Hit And Run« Victor 1981
[Japanese issue in different sleeve, B-side "Yeah Right"]
»C'mon Let's Go« Victor 1981
[Japanese two track issue in different sleeve, B-side "Kick It Down"]
»C'mon Let's Go« Bronze 1981
[Spanish two track issue, B-side "Hit And Run"]
»20th Century Boy« Bronze 1983
»Burning In The Heat« Bronze 1983
[A-side different to album version]
»I'm The Leader Of The Gang« GWR 1986
[With GARY GLITTER, edited A-side non-LP in UK]
»Head Over Heels« GWR 1988

Promotional Releases
»Running Wild« Mercury 1985
[US radio promo 12"]
»Head Over Heels« GWR 1988
[Promo-only DJ 12"]
»Head Over Heels« Enigma 1988
[US radio promo CD single]

CD's
»Take A Bite« GWR 1988
»Motorhead vs. Girlschool« Victor 1989
[Japanese-only issue]
»Demolition« Teichiku 1990
[Japanese issue with two bonus tracks]
»Hit And Run« Teichiku 1990
[Japanese issue]
»Screaming Blue Murder« Teichiku 1990
[Japanese issue]
»Demolition/Hit And Run« DoJo 1991
»Screaming Blue Murder/Play Dirty« DoJo 1991
»Cheers You Lot!« Metal Masters 1991
[Compilation release]
»The Collection« Castle Communications 1991
[Compilation release]
»Girlschool« Communiqué Records 1992
»Nightmare At Maple Cross/Take A Bite« DoJo 1994
»The Best Of Girlschool« DoJo 1994
[Compilation release]
»From The Vaults« Sequel 1994
[Compilation release]

»Live« Communiqué Records 1995
[Live release]
»Emergency« Snapper 1997
[Double compilation release of material from first two albums]
»In Concert 1984« King Biscuit 1997
[Live release]
»Can't Keep A Good Girl Down« Delta Music 1999
[Compilation release, material taken from »Girlschool« and »Live« sets]

Compilation Appearances
"Race With The Devil" on »Axe Attack« LP K-Tel 1980 + »A Quiet Night In« LP Bronze 1981 + »Leather And Lace« LP Dino 1990 + »Rock Legends« Cassette Music Club 1991 + »Rock Legends Volume 3« CD Castle Communications 1992 + »The Metal Box« 3-CD Box Castle Communications 1993 + »Giants Of Rock« Cassette Castle Communications 1993 + »Metal Mania« Do-CD Duet 1995 + »The Metal Box« 3-CD Box Kaz Records 1995
"Please Don't Touch" on »A Quiet Night In« LP Bronze 1981 + »The Metal Box« 3-CD Box Castle Communications 1993 + »The Metal Box« 3-CD Box Kaz Records 1995 + »The Bronze Story« Do-CD Essential 2000
[Under the name of HEADGIRL]
"Hit And Run" on »A Quiet Night In« LP Bronze 1981 + »Hammer« LP Ariola 1981 + »Rock Legends Volume 1« CD Castle Communications 1992 + »Metal Mania« Do-CD Duet 1995 + »The Metal Box« 3-CD Box Kaz Records 1995
"Don't Call It Love" on »A Little Bit Of Light Relief« LP Polydor 1982 + »Heavy« LP K-Tel 1983
"Demolition Boys" on »Metal Killers Kollection I« Do-LP Castle Communications 1985 + »NWOBHM '79 Revisited« Do-LP/Do-CD Phonogram 1990 + »Metal Killers Kollection« CD Castle Communications 1991
"Not For Sale" on »Metal Killers« LP Raw Power 1986 + »Metal Masters« 4-CD Box Castle Communications 1993 + »Rock Out!« Do-CD Emporio 1996
"Nowhere To Run" on »Reform School Girls« Soundtrack LP Rhino Records 1986
"Head Over Heels" on »Iron Brew« LP/CD Legacy Records 1990
"I'm The Leader Of The Gang" on »Iron Brew« LP/CD Legacy Records 1990
"Following The Crowd" on »Giants Of Rock-The Metal Decade Vol.1« Do-CD Teldec 1990
"Tonight" on »Rock Legends Volume 2« CD Castle Communications 1992
"(I'm Your) Victim" on »Rock Legends Volume 3« CD Castle Communications 1992
"Flesh And Blood" on »Rock Legends Volume

4« CD Castle Communications 1992
"Watch Your Step" (live) »NWOBHM-The Days On Stage« Bootleg CD Taurus Records 1993
"Hellrazor" on on »Metal Killers« CD Castle Communciations 1993
"Kick It Down" on »Metal Masters« 4-CD Box Castle Communications 1993 + »Metal Mania« CD Castle Communications 1994
"Take It All Away" on »Give 'Em Hell« CD Nectar Masters 1995 + »Rock Out!« Do-CD Emporio 1996 + »N.W.O.B.H.M. Metal Rarities Vol.3« CD British Steel 1997 + »The Best Of Indie Metal« CD Emporio 1998
"Nothing To Lose" on »Rock Out!« Do-CD Emporio 1996
"It Could Be Better" on »N.W.O.B.H.M. Metal Rarities Vol.3« CD British Steel 1997 + »The Best Of Indie Metal« CD Emporio 1998
"C'mon Let's Go" (live) on »NWOBHM Live« CD Emporio 1997
"Emergency" (live) on »NWOBHM Live« CD Emporio 1997
"Take It All Away" (live) on »NWOBHM Live« CD Emporio 1997
"Screaming Blue Murder" (live) on »The Best Of British Metal« CD Delta Music 1999
"Wild At Heart" on »The Best Of British Metal« CD Delta Music 1999
"C'mon Let's Go" on »The Bronze Story« Do-CD Essential 2000

GLASGOW

Mick Boyle (v)
Archie Dickson (g)
Neil Russell (b)
Joe Kilna (d)

Scotland's melodic rock/metal hopefuls GLASGOW (named, with a monumentally dull lack of imagination, after their home city), were another of the handful of NWOBHM-era bands who managed to win a coveted 'Friday Rock Show' session before releasing any vinyl. Having formed at pretty much the height of the explosion (initially as the rather more straight-ahead HEAVEN), word of the foursome's studio and live activities (including early support slots with the likes of NAZARETH) must have filtered through to the show's producers (most likely *via* their local patrons at Radio Clyde), and the BBC recordings duly took place at the end of 1983. With the session finally being broadcast on the 6th of January 1984, the enjoyable selection of "Heat Of The Night", "Shine On Me", "No Way Out" and "Stranded" were thrust upon the station's many listeners. Irrespective of the reaction of the general public, however, it didn't take long for Neat Records to get wind of GLASGOW, and two of the session tracks ("Stranded" and "Heat Of The Night") were subsequently re-recorded and issued as the group's impressive vinyl debut. Oddly, however, the lads were less-than-ecstatic with the end result, as vocalist Mick Boyle later revealed: *'The Neat single! We risked life and limb to record that cos we had a car crash on the way to the studios. I'd never heard a record like it, they left a whole guitar track off the pressing. We were offered an album with them, imagine a whole album with that sound, I'd have killed myself.'* (Ref: Metal Hammer Vol.3 No. 14, July 1988).

As was the case with so many other emergent hopefuls of the era, however, GLASGOW's earliest material turned out to be their heaviest, and it wasn't long before these upbeat compositions (initially in the style of SOLDIER or PERSIAN RISK) were rapidly metamorphosing into considerably more radio-friendly offerings along the lines of TOBRUK or regional favourites HEAVY PETTIN. Even by the end of that year, when the quartet released a self-financed, three track EP (»Miles Better«, the title mocking a cheesy slogan which had been coined to entice tourists to the city of Glasgow at the time) with the assistance of Radio Clyde, there was evidence that some of the rough edges were already being smoothed out, although both "Searching For Glory" and "After Midnight" were still pretty powerful, and not entirely dissimilar to later ELIXIR material. On the other hand, "Under The Lights" clearly pointed to the future, with its melodic chorus and more accessible arrangement suggesting that the band eventually wanted to move in a more commercial direction. With a precious publishing deal having come GLASGOW's way in the wake of their initial exposure, it looked as though the public would be hearing a full album sooner rather than later, although it's worth pointing out that only Neat had actually put an offer on the table by this juncture.

In spite of this early boost to their career, however, the group's desire to progress and record new material was severely hampered by the utter disinterest of the big record labels, and, unlike some of the more prominent Northern outfits, GLASGOW were unable to benefit from relocation to London to get themselves known to the movers and shakers. As a result, the lads had little option but to busy themselves in the live environment and write as much new material as possible, hoping that someone influential would somehow notice them eventually. In fact, their existence was largely overlooked for the best part of three years, and it wasn't until as late as 1987 (by which time new drummer Paul McManus had been recruited to the fold) that the group's debut LP finally appeared, another self-financed effort entitled »Zero Four One« (after the telephone code for the Glasgow area) on the (wait for it) Zero 4 1 label. By now, the lads had become firm advocates of the use of keyboards, although, at that stage, they still relied on session musicians to provide this backing to their increasingly-lightweight compositions. Featuring a vastly more chart-friendly version of "Under The Lights" alongside such unfamiliar numbers as "We Will Rock", "Back On The Run" and "Meet Me Halfway" (most of which, to be honest, were unnecessarily long and repetitive), the album was a fairly inoffensive (but highly derivative) example of mid-to-late 80's melodic rock, with only the occasional fleeting glimpse of a heavier style on tracks such as album closer "Breakout", for example.

A clutch of singles were unleashed to promote the album's release over the next couple of years, the most successful of these being based around the group's interpretation of the Chris Thompson original (penned by the singer after he had left MANFRED MANN to pursue a solo career) "Secrets In The Dark" (a number which totally outclassed most of the outfit's own compositions), with the subsequent »Under The Lights« and »Will You Be Mine« efforts both failing to sell in notable quantities. Nevertheless, GLASGOW persevered (their fortunes picking up briefly when their debut album belatedly benefitted from some overseas licensing), ultimately recruiting a full-time keyboard player in the form of ex-LA PAZ member Andy Mason (his predecessor, Brian Cartwright, originally brought in as a second guitarist, didn't last long), and they were still achieving some fairly high-profile support slots in Glasgow as late as 1989 (including further gigs in the company of NAZARETH, and also with such disparate headliners as URIAH HEEP and CELTIC FROST). However, the end came amicably a short time later, as the lads agreed they'd given the world a good run for its money and finally abandoned their rock'n'roll dream for good.

LP's
»**Zero Four One**« Zero 4 1 Records 1987

12" EP's
»**Miles Better**« Clyde Records 1984

["Under The Lights" different to album version, both "Searching For Glory" and "After Midnight" non-LP]

7" Singles
»**Stranded**« Neat 1984
[Both tracks non-LP]
»**Secrets In The Dark**« Zero 4 1 Records 1987
»**Under The Lights**« Zero 4 1 Records 1988
»**Will You Be Mine**« Zero 4 1 Records 1988
[A-side non-LP]

CD's
»**Zero Four One**« Sonet 1988
[Japanese issue with different cover artwork]

GOGMAGOG

Paul Dianno (v)
Janick Gers (g)
Pete Willis (g)
Neil Murray (b)
Clive Burr (d)

That self-styled *'guru'* of all things musical, Jonathan King, has got a hell of a lot to answer for. Not content with single-handedly killing off the promising career of BRIAR (see separate entry) by sucking all the life from the youngsters and ultimately turning a talented melodic rock band into a bland pop outfit, he was also the genius behind the GOGMAGOG fiasco, one of the most infamous episodes of the entire NWOBHM era. It all started when the publicity-hungry scoundrel witnessed the sheer spectacle of some mid-80's metal concerts in the States and instantly started seeing dollar signs materialising in front of his very eyes. His vision was to assemble a supergroup of British musicians, arrange for some catchy material to be written for the project, send them out on the road with a preposterously theatrical stage show and wait for the money to roll in. In practice, it turned out to be a rather more complicated process than he had expected, although the promise of freshly-printed money was (in the first instance) sufficiently tempting to lure several well-respected musicians (and Paul Dianno) to the conference table in order to thrash out a possible contract.

In the event, however, obligations elsewhere (I think that was a tactful way of saying they wouldn't touch it with a ten foot barge-pole) in the music business disqualified two of King's initial choices, John Entwistle (of THE WHO) and

Cozy Powell (of RAINBOW, WHITESNAKE et al.), leaving him to bring together a revised line-up consisting of vocalist Paul Dianno (whose past credits included IRON MAIDEN, LONEWOLF and the recent DIANNO flop), guitarists Pete Willis (ex-DEF LEPPARD) and Janick Gers (formerly with WHITE SPIRIT and GILLAN), bassist Neil Murray (best-known for his work with BERNIE MARSDEN, GARY MOORE and WHITESNAKE) and workaholic drummer Clive Burr (numerous previous convictions, notably IRON MAIDEN, SAMSON, TRUST, CLIVE BURR'S ESCAPE and STRATUS). Armed with some original songs (which had been hurriedly co-written with the assistance of the legendary Russ Ballard) and an underlying grand concept of (literally) biblical proportions, King duly sold the whole idea like a true professional, and so the GOGMAGOG project was finally brought one step closer.

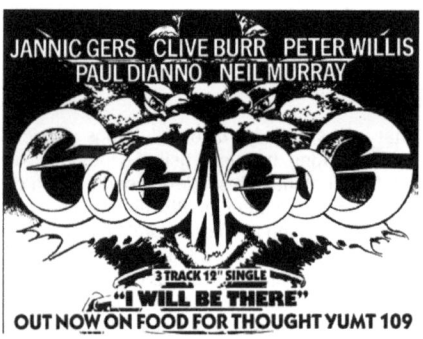

At some point in 1985, the musicians assembled themselves in the studio and proceeded to belt out three disappointingly pop-inclined rock numbers with vague similarities to the likes of BLAZER BLAZER, BOMBAY and T34, namely "I Will Be There" (a track which, incidentally, also appeared on Russ Ballard's own »Into The Fire« solo album), the offensively-titled "Living In A F••king Time Warp" and the far-too-many-words-for-my-liking "It's Illegal, It's Immoral, It's Unhealthy, But It's Fun" (I've no idea what that one's about, officer). All things considered, King seemed to be utterly delighted with the results (mind you, he also thought it was a good idea to wander around London in a rainbow-coloured afro wig on occasion) and proceeded to tout his new outfit around to various promoters and anyone from a record company who would listen. Inevitably, however, his sheer greed (asking for a million dollar advance just to get the show on the road is hardly the way to win friends and influence people) was his undoing, and he was unceremoniously shown the door at every opportunity. Chortle.

Nevertheless, the thick-skinned King refused to concede defeat, and ultimately decided to squeeze something out of the time and money he had already invested in this ill-fated venture. He eventually managed to interest a record label (the Music For Nations-related Food For Thought) in the rough studio recordings he now had in his possession, and secured their release in the form of a 12" EP, housed within an admirably-presented cover featuring a piece of already-commissioned artwork. Rather than admitting that this was a shameless cash-in, however, the self-congratulatory insert gave an extremely implausible version of events: how the original project would surely have been the saviour of metal, how the material would have worked to greatest effect in the live environment and how the whole thing had only been thwarted by sheer misfortune. Bollocks. It was an ill-conceived idea, poorly implemented by a complete halfwit and ultimately destroyed by financial avarice. The fans, to their credit, ignored the feeble record in droves (in spite of King's fanciful claims that it was being feverishly anticipated by the masses), deciding that, while GOGMAGOG might have represented certain people's blinkered conception of metal, it undoubtedly deviated from anything remotely credible or particularly viable in the commercial sense.

The musicians involved in the project later denounced the whole affair as a bit of a shambles (Paul Dianno refuses, point blank, to comment on it), with Pete Willis subsequently recalling the studio session in not-very-fond terms: *'I really wasn't sure what to do after LEPPARD, but I had some strange offers. Do you remember that project that Jonathan King was trying to put together? This must have been around 1984. He enrolled me, Paul Dianno and Janick Gers to play on these songs. Frankly, they were terrible. We all stood around in this studio for a day trying to make the best of it. The whole thing was pretty disastrous.'* (Ref: Metal Forces No.69, February 1992). Nevertheless, each member soon put the regrettable experience behind them and moved on to pastures new. Neil Murray, for example, found employment with the likes of MGM, PHENOMENA, VOW WOW, BLACK SABBATH and DAVE SHARMAN, while Pete Willis later tried again with NIGHTRUN and ROADHOUSE. Janick Gers, on the other hand, eventually found fame and fortune in IRON MAIDEN, whereas Clive Burr subsequently lent his talents to the likes of ELIXIR and DESPERADO. Paul Dianno, meanwhile (and I was only kidding about the 'well-respected' bit, mate) later enjoyed considerable success with BATTLEZONE and KILLERS, and is still going strong with various musical projects these days. The dastardly Jonathan King, on the other hand, later (after hijacking BRIAR and encouraging them to record some truly execrable, poppy cover versions and a totally pointless reworking of "It's Illegal, It's Immoral, It's Unhealthy, But It's Fun") turned his hand to overseeing the selection of British entries for the Eurovision Song Contest, a task much more suited to his very special 'skills'. Let's just hope he stays far away from the metal scene from now on.

12" EP's
»I Will Be There« Food For Thought 1985

GOLDSMITH

Perry 'Pez' Hodder (v, g)
Glen Milligan (b)
Mike Henderson (d)

Expeditiously assembled after his sudden departure from BITCHES SIN, Pez Hodder's GOLDSMITH initially appeared on the scene with little or no fanfare towards the end of 1981. Within a remarkably short space of time, the newly-established three-piece (contrary to assertions elsewhere, Hodder's former colleague Alan Cockburn was never involved with the group) were brandishing an extremely confident demo featuring "No Way Out", "Everybody Needs A Little Love", "Give Me Your Love" (all with Hodder at the mike stand) and the epic ballad "Evil Woman", showcasing the alternate vocal talents of drummer Mike Henderson. Purveying a heavy-but-melodic style of metal in the general vein of DRAGONFLY, GEDDES AXE or even TYTAN, the ambitious trio duly attracted the attention of none other than Neat Records (the original home of BITCHES SIN), and their aforementioned "Give Me Your Love" would subsequently be lifted for inclusion on the label's promotional »60 Minutes Plus« cassette, although GOLDSMITH were slightly unfortunate in that theirs was one of the four tracks omitted from the vinyl »All Hell Let Loose« pressing. Their material was soon drawing a fair bit of interest from various fanzines, though, and some useful airplay on stations such as Piccadilly Radio can't have harmed their chances at all.

The Cumbrian hopefuls must have been fairly optimistic in terms of landing a proper deal with Neat (indeed, they intimated that a single might even appear on the label in the second half of 1982), but, in the end, it just wasn't to happen. Instead, the independently-minded outfit (who drafted in a fourth member, a certain Pete Adams, to act in the capacity of second guitarist) simply immortalised two numbers ("Life Is Killing Me" and "Music Man") at Impulse Studios, and then issued the pair in the form of a self-financed 7" (which came in a remarkably drab picture sleeve featuring a reproduction of a record, the printers having contrived to mess up the colour scheme completely) on their own Bedlam label later in the year. With the newer material coming across as a tad more upbeat and energetic than their formative demo offerings, and with a markedly better vocal performance on display, the A-side was a perfectly adequate number in the style of FUGITIVE or ZENITH, whereas the reverse turned out to be an excellent, upbeat affair revolving around the NWOBHM riff (you know the one, later duplicated note for note by BLACKSTAR on the track "Instrumental" from their NWOBHM-tinged »Barbed Wire Soul« album), similar to that utilised by HOLLOW GROUND on "Warlord", for example. I've always been indebted to a certain rock/metal journalist for explaining the concept of the spiralling arpeggio riff (compulsory throughout the early 80's) in terms of either IRON MAIDEN's "Phantom Of The Opera" or, alternatively, the 'Dr Who' theme. Genius.

The two-tracker appears to have sold quite modestly at the outset, but no doubt won favour with a significant percentage of local fans, all of which presumably encouraged the ensemble to keep going for the time being. Things picked up after their 7" won the accolade of 'rock single of the week' in 'Sounds' and gained some much-needed airplay thanks to Tommy Vance, so the original pressing more or less sold out as a result. Although a follow-up EP (featuring such efforts as "Fly Away" and "Please Don't") was subsequently scheduled for release at some point in 1983 (in fact, with an abundance of material at their disposal, the outfit had already expressed their intention to release a full album), this idea was eventually shelved (it got to the acetate stage), which was a pity. In fact, following the demise of GOLDSMITH after the release of just one single (which was, inevitably, slated mercilessly in the pages of 'Kerrang'), Pez subsequently lost the plot in fairly major fashion, teaming up with an unrenowned accomplice called John Duffin and forming a quirky synth-pop duo called SMALL IN A BIG WAY. Astoundingly, this ill-conceived endeavour even made it to the vinyl stage themselves, releasing their »Katies Lips« 7" (to overwhelming public disinterest) at some point in 1984. Again produced by Keith Nichol at Impulse Studios and issued on Hodder's Bedlam imprint, this debacle (sorry Pez) apparently sold about three copies and is truly one of the most incompetent releases I've ever heard (which, believe me, is saying something). Following the lack of response to this disappointing effort, though, Pez and the other one-time members of GOLDSMITH have been keeping a very low profile indeed.

7" Singles
»Life Is Killing Me« Bedlam Records 1982

Exclusive Compilation Appearances
"Give Me Your Love" on »60 Minutes Plus« Cassette Neat 1982/CD Teichiku 1992

GOLGOTHA

Karl 'The Preacher' Foster (v, g)
Andrew French (b)
Dave Hickman (d)

Staffordshire's quirky GOLGOTHA were something of an anomaly in the NWOBHM era, failing to follow any of the more obvious musical trends of the time and steadfastly going about their business with little or no regard for those who failed to see the point in their off-the-wall experimentation. The outfit, essentially the brainchild of frontman Karl 'The Preacher' Foster, started out in earnest in around 1982 (although the bonkers vocalist had initially formed an alliance with drummer Dave Hickman as early as 1979, the duo having additionally played together in a small-time club act called the SULTANS in the dim and distant past), noodling around in the studio for the next couple of years and occasionally chucking out a limited cassette-only release. From the outset, though, highly individualistic compositions such as "Warlord" and "Treason" marked GOLGOTHA out as something of a peculiar proposition, their material tending to be pretty heavy on the guitar front, whilst still retaining a rather progressive outlook in terms of lyrics and complex arrangements. The overall effect combined elements of CLOVEN HOOF, Jersey's LEGEND, MARQUIS DE SADE and early MOURNBLADE, although it might all have seemed a bit over-the-top and inaccessible to the average rocker of the time.

Nevertheless, their fan base soon swelled to a respectable figure, something which can only really be attributed to word-of-mouth and tape sales, as the outfit seldom got out and about in their early days, not helped by their lack of a permanent bassist (a friend called Andrew French helped out on their early studio sessions) in the first instance. GOLGOTHA's »After The Curfew« release (showcasing a selection of compositions such as "Leather Julie", "Dangerous Games" and "Moondog"), which materialised in the early months of 1984, was the first cassette release to sell in notable quantities, and steady regional sales were boosted by mail-order adverts in the rock press. Even so, the outfit's live activities were still severely hindered by the impermanency of their latest line-up, although the central characters soon began looking for a full-time bassist, whereupon the enigmatic 'Jonah' (a veteran of local nonentities BUZZARD) joined in the fun in the spring of that year. The revitalised band gelled pretty quickly, and so the lads were soon able to make a far greater number of appearances in their locality, although their highly ambitious and diverse material must surely have been somewhat bewildering for many casual observers. With an encouraging response coming from a significant percentage of those who purchased their early tapes, though, GOLGOTHA started formulating plans for a vinyl assault on an unsuspecting world.

By the end of 1984, the time had finally come for the trio to try their luck with a vinyl offering, and this came in the shape of a self-financed 7" EP featuring some typically varied and offbeat titles. The proceedings get underway with "Dangerous Games", which opens with a folky, semi-acoustic passage before the 'proper' guitars burst in after a minute or so, livening things up somewhat, although it still comes worryingly close to JETHRO TULL territory at times. Next up is another semi-folky composition entitled "Old England's Dream" (a fairly passionate ballad), whereas the flipside opens with "Air", a heavyish (but mercifully brief) interpretation of Bach's "Air On A G String", a technically-proficient but pointless inclusion nonetheless. The four-tracker's saving grace, however, is undoubtedly "The Great Divide", a considerably more metallic affair (with some extremely flashy guitar work) than the preceding efforts, although the EP was, overall, a rather disappointing release for those who might have been anticipating a more immediately-accessible and NWOBHM-inclined offering. Having said that, the record was supposedly manufactured in tiny quantities (only a few hundred at most), so it looks as though GOLGOTHA were being fairly realistic about potential sales figures from the outset. The EP, which was never released with a picture sleeve, is currently valued remarkably highly by most dealers, although I'd be inclined to say that the musical contents fail to justify the price-tag.

Over the next few years, Foster and his cohorts continued to record a fair bit of new material (largely, it would seem, for their own pleasure), occasionally issuing the odd tape release for the benefit of their die-hard fans, notably the »Orchestral Stab« cassette album, released in 1988. By this stage, however, GOLGOTHA had metamorphosed into more of a solo project, with the aforementioned mainman only utilising the services of backing musicians from time to time. Predictably enough, the activities of GOLGOTHA were largely ignored by the mainstream rock press, although the quirky outfit were just the sort of act who would, in due course, win the patronage of the bonkers 'Organ' fanzine, who praised the venture in no uncertain terms and introduced them to an entirely new audience on the periphery of the rock scene. They contributed a typically-complex number called "Golgotha" (one of their most listenable compositions) to Reaction's »Full Force« sampler in 1989, which may have exposed their talents to a slightly wider audience, but they were still clearly looking for that big break. Eventually, GOLGOTHA abandoned their small-time roots after being picked up by the influential Communiqué label, who were brave enough to encourage Foster to deliver an entire album for future release. Assisted by long-time associate Dave Hickman (also a veteran of long-forgotten local acts such as NITELIFE, BROADSWORD and the STEVE WATTS BAND, incidentally), the frontman disappeared into the studio and emerged in 1990 with the debut GOLGOTHA long-player.

The grandiloquent »Unmaker Of Worlds« showed a progression towards an extraordinarily ambitious (not to mention pretentious and rather overbearing) montage of progressive rock (occasionally reminiscent of GENESIS or PINK FLOYD) and classical music (both Wagner-style symphonic sections and more traditionally-styled, extended instrumental passages), all of which was just a bit too *'different'* for its own good. With only four (excessively lengthy and hopelessly complicated) tracks featured ("Counter State Directive", "Unmaker Of Worlds", "Another Sunny Christmas" and "Raining On Still Waters"), this was a considerable departure from the norm as far as early 90's music was concerned, and very few reviewers of the period (either in the mainstream rock or progressive camps) knew exactly what to make of it all. Indeed, Foster's own biography proffered the opinion that his music was reminiscent of *'The London Philharmonic Orchestra on acid'*, as if this absurd statement would somehow put things into context. In general, therefore, the rock press tended to be rather non-committal about the debut album, coming up with vague, mediocre reviews and referring to the great originality of GOLGOTHA's work, without actually going so far as to recommend it to the general public. To be honest, it's hard to see exactly who might originally have been tempted to buy this type of material on the basis of the reviews that were handed out at the time, although I suppose it might now appeal to one or two easily-pleased dark metal fans.

Nevertheless, it looks as though the record must have sold in sufficiently substantial quantities to warrant a follow-up, although it took a further three years for »Symphony In Extremis« to hit the streets, this time in CD format only. By now, however, it was a genuine solo effort, with Foster himself supplying all vocals, effects and instrumental parts, and it was an even more pretentious affair than before, with the individual tracks (four of them once again) divided into 'movements', each comprised of two parts with subtitles of their own. Good grief. Coupled with some monumentally overblown and self-satisfying lyrics (which, although motivated by political and social concerns, are couched in such abstract and prosodic terms that any underlying concept is pretty much obliterated), and you have an extremely difficult listening experience in store. You will already have gathered that GOLGOTHA had now left their original rock roots well and truly behind, and, given that many people find DIAMOND HEAD's »Canterbury« LP (in fact, if you were to put the intro from "The Kingmaker" on tape loop for forty minutes, you'd have a pretty good simulation of a GOLGOTHA album) to be far too experimental and flamboyant, I suspect that very few NWOBHM fans (unless they have an equal fondness for prog rock, symphonic black metal or some of MEKONG DELTA's more classically-influenced material, for example) will be particularly smitten by any of Foster's studio recordings. The project finally appears to have been laid to rest in recent years, although I imagine that the ultimate demise of GOLGOTHA failed to break many hearts.

LP's
»Unmaker Of Worlds« Communiqué Records 1990

7" EP's
»Dangerous Games« Goth Records 1984
[All four tracks non-LP]

CD's
»Unmaker Of Worlds« Communiqué Records 1990
»Symphony In Extremis« Communiqué Records 1993

Exclusive Compilation Appearances
"Golgotha" on »Full Force« LP Reaction 1989

GRAND PRIX

Bernie Shaw (v)
Michael O'Donoghue (g)
Ralph Hood (b)
Phil Lanzon (k)
Andy Beirne (d)

The origins of GRAND PRIX date back to around 1978, when a minor outfit called PARIS (assembled by a variety of well-travelled rock musicians) began making something of a name for themselves in the pubs and clubs of the capital, gradually winning support slots with touring acts such as SAD CAFE and GILLAN. By 1980, the band had become GRAND PRIX, and were one of the first acts to be picked up by a major label (RCA, in this case) in the wake of the initial NWOBHM explosion. Featuring former DIRTY TRICKS drummer Andy Beirne and talented Canadian frontman Bernie Shaw in their ranks, the group also incorporated the duo of Ralph Hood and Michael O'Donoghue, formerly with small-time club band RAW DEAL, the line-up being completed by experienced keyboard player Phil Lanzon, who had latterly been working alongside future WILD HORSES guitarist Neil Carter. The quintet duly signed to RCA in the summer of 1980, and were rapidly encouraged to come up with a full album, taking time off to play at the Reading Festival, where, remarkably enough, they appeared just below IRON MAIDEN and UFO in the running order. After what seems to have been an overwhelmingly-successful festival appearance, the debut album was prepared for release, and the eponymous long-player hit the shops a couple of months later.

Their debut release was very much an AOR-inclined affair, featuring influences ranging from TOTO ("Waiting For The Night") to the EAGLES ("Mama Sayes"), the general effect being along the lines of lightweight UK acts such as SNOWBLIND, STRATUS, TRADER or LIONHEART, for example, none of whom enjoyed a particularly significant amount of success in their home country. Predictably, therefore, the long-player failed to make much of an impression on the public, most of whom had been anticipating a rather more substantial debut. A couple of singles (»Thinking Of You« and the horrendously overblown »Which Way Did The Wind Blow«) were soon trundled out, although neither of them performed particularly well in terms of sales. There were, however, distinct parallels with the first pair of ALKATRAZZ singles (also released on RCA), where the same B-side ("Feels Good", in this instance) was used twice, this particular flipside being by far the better track on each occasion! All things considered, GRAND PRIX had contrived to make a fairly inauspicious start, and it soon became apparent that their early material just wasn't going to last the distance. Aside from "Westwind" and the aforementioned "Feels Good", few of their original compositions would remain in the live set for very long, being replaced fairly swiftly by tracks with more of a forceful personality.

Undeterred by a lukewarm reaction to their first batch of releases, though, the band set about touring the UK, promoting themselves with a series of fairly well-attended outings (Phil Lanzon also found time to appear on CHRIS SPEDDING's »I'm Not Like Anybody Else« album) throughout the country. In due course, they would also make their way across the English Channel for a handy European jaunt with MANFRED MANN, although 1981 turned out to be a relatively quiet year, most of which was apparently spent writing new material for that make-or-break second album, which had already been commissioned by RCA. The fact that Bernie Shaw elected to leave for pastures new (PRAYING MANTIS, in the first instance) in the latter part of the year appeared to throw a spanner into the works, but help was soon at hand: Robin McAuley, yet another former member of the aforementioned RAW DEAL, was drafted in at short notice to team up with his old chums Ralph and Michael, and his recruitment proved to represent something of a turning point for the group's fortunes. Things seemed to work out better for the revised line-up, the lads being quite keen to showcase the talents of their new frontman, and another single was hastily rushed out, coupling the excellent "Keep On Believing" with the exclusive "Life On The Line". Incredibly, it entered the British singles charts (sharing the famous *'honour'* of a 'Number 75' placing with »Sweet Danger« by ANGEL WITCH), an extremely significant achievement for a group who were hardly a household name at the time.

Moving into 1982, the lads started to show the world that GRAND PRIX now constituted a serious rock proposition, starting off with a live broadcast on BBC Radio, where a half-hour set from the Hammersmith Odeon was presented to the nation, and the group happily took the opportunity to showcase some newly-penned material. Before long, this was followed up by their addition to the SAMMY HAGAR tour, plus yet more European activity, including an appearance on East German television, an achievement to which very few NWOBHM bands (with the notable exception of ANGEL WITCH) can lay claim! When the second long-player (»There For None To See«) finally hit the shops, though, it confirmed that GRAND PRIX had indeed moved somewhat closer to the NWOBHM archetype, but were still residing at the more lightweight end of the genre, the lads now operating in an area inhabited by the likes of KOOGA, MOTHER'S RUIN and labelmates ALKATRAZZ. It was a far stronger set than their debut, admittedly, particularly with such memorable tracks such as "Take A Chance", "Relay" and "Taking Your Life Away", any one of which would have served as a suitable choice for a tie-in 7". Strangely, however, no singles were released to coincide with the album's appearance; indeed, it seems that a fair old bit of tension existed between the musicians and their label at the time, and so it wasn't long before the two parties terminated their relationship. Ralph Hood subsequently explained the chain of events: *'By the end of the SAMMY HAGAR tour we were getting the right sort of reaction for the first time, and I think we'd adjusted to being more positive as a live band. We were going to do the BLACKFOOT tour but the record company didn't see the point in paying for it; as a direct result of that we changed management. We were soon dropped, it was inevitable really, I suppose. It was a bit of a lifesaver too, in fact, because as you can imagine we had a large debt hanging over us by that time.'* (Ref: Kerrang No.44, June 1983).

Undeterred by this recent spate of misfortune, however, GRAND PRIX made another successful appearance at the Reading Festival (well down in the running order, for some inexplicable reason), setting the stage for the TYGERS OF PAN TANG, BLACKFOOT and IRON MAIDEN. This high-profile shindig was followed by yet more exhaustive touring, before the musicians finally got back to the important task of finding a new label to release their third LP, the material for which had already been written while on the

road. In the event, Chrysalis (who had just dumped WOLF in an unceremonious manner) stepped in with an offer to come to the rescue. The latest album took a while to lay down, however (it was apparently remixed on three separate occasions), and the group fitted the studio sessions around their relentless touring schedule (including a memorable series of dates with IRON MAIDEN) in the spring of 1983. The new long-player (»Samurai«), when it eventually appeared, turned out to represent a fairly varied set of compositions, ranging from vaguely MAGNUM-tinged pomp ("Give Me What's Mine" and "Freedom") to more raunchy, TERRAPLANE-style material on tracks such as "Shout" and "High Time", whereas the likes of "50/50" and "Here We Go Again" are, in all honesty, a bit too sedate for their own good.

Unfortunately, however, the public weren't exactly blown away by the group's latest selection of material, and the brace of singles which were issued by Chrysalis to promote the album (»Give Me What's Mine« and »Shout«) failed to match the stellar performance of »Keep On Believing«. The quintet fully intended to release yet another long-player (inevitably, copious amounts of new material had already been written well in advance), but further GRAND PRIX releases failed to materialise, much to the disappointment of their loyal fan base. The reasons for their post-»Samurai« inactivity are not fully understood (they were scheduled to release a new single entitled »Angel« in the early part of 1984, but it never materialised), and it may have been a conscious decision on the part of the band not to take things further, rather than their label's reluctance to finance a fourth long-player. In any case, it was all over by the second half of 1984 (Andy Beirne had left at the tail end of 1983, and the much-travelled Clive Edwards stepped in as a replacement for their increasingly scarce gigs the following year), after which the individual members wasted little time in seeking out new musical careers for themselves.

In the aftermath of the disintegration of GRAND PRIX, Ralph Hood went on to enjoy a spell with Spanish-based outfit TARZEN, while Andy Beirne soon teamed up with SCORCHED EARTH for a while before having a brief stint with LIONHEART, where he was actually joined by another ex-GRAND PRIX member, Phil Lanzon. The latter also collaborated with his former colleagues Robin McAuley and Mick O'Donoghue in a largely-overlooked outfit (also featuring such experienced stalwarts as Phil Taylor, Chris Glen and Brian Robertson) called OPERATOR, who eventually (after a few personnel reshuffles and a name change to GMT) released an EP or two in around 1986. Lanzon subsequently moved on to URIAH HEEP and THE SWEET, and McAuley famously (as well as releasing the odd solo effort and working with the critically-despised FAR CORPORATION) formed the MCAULEY SCHENKER GROUP with some little-known German guitarist.

LP's
»Grand Prix« RCA 1980
[UK issue]
»Grand Prix« RCA 1980
[Japanese issue in different sleeve with insert]
»There For None To See« RCA 1982
»Samurai« Chrysalis 1983

12" EP's
»Shout« Chrysalis 1983
[Includes live versions of "Keep On Believing" and "Feels Good"]

7" Singles
»Thinking Of You« RCA 1980
[B-side "Feels Good" non-LP]
»Which Way Did The Wind Blow« RCA 1980
[A-side different to album version, B-side "Feels Good" non-LP]
»Feel Like I Do« RCA 1980
[Japanese-only issue, B-side "Thinking Of You"]
»Keep On Believing« RCA 1981
[Also issued as limited edition picture disc, A-side different to album version, B-side "Life On The Line" non-LP]
»Give Me What's Mine« Chrysalis 1983
[B-side "One Five Five" non-LP]
»Shout« Chrysalis 1983
[Also issued as limited edition picture disc, B-side live version of "Keep On Believing"]

Promotional Releases
»Which Way Did The Wind Blow« RCA 1980
[DJ promo 7" with two versions]
»Samurai Sampler« Chrysalis 1983
[One-sided flexi with excerpts from »Samurai« LP]

CD's
»Samurai« Zoom Club Records 2000
»Grand Prix« Zoom Club Records 2000
»There For None To See« Zoom Club Records 2000

Compilation Appearances
"Keep On Believing" (live) on »Reading Rock Vol.1« Do-LP Mean Records 1982
[Different to album and single version, also appears as B-side of »Shout« single]
"Relay" on »Hot Shower« LP RCA 1982

"Taking Your Life Away" on »Hot Shower« LP
RCA 1982

GRIM REAPER

Paul de Mercado (v)
Nick Bowcott (g)
Adrian Jacques (b,d)

It might initially have taken the legendary GRIM REAPER a couple of attempts to get going properly, but, when the Worcestershire lads eventually made their breakthrough, they were rapidly hailed as national heroes whose vinyl releases were eagerly anticipated by many. Well, maybe not in the UK itself, but certainly in some parts of the world. It had all started back in the heady days of 1979, when a barely-recognisable version of the band were brought together by the songwriting partnership of Nick Bowcott (g) and Paul de Mercado (v), two individuals possessed by a fundamental desire to play some of this new-fangled heavy metal stuff. GRIM REAPER failed to make much of a name for themselves at first (not helped by the usual merry-go-round of personnel reshuffles, which appears to have been particularly exaggerated in this case), and their early steps in the live environment were largely restricted to small-time events in front of modest local audiences. Towards the end of 1980, however, something resembling a stable line-up had finally emerged, by which time the deal-hungry hopefuls were now thinking of recording their first demo tape.

GRIM REAPER's first official cassette (on which the main duo were assisted by Adrian Jacques, a drummer who also contributed the necessary bass parts on this occasion), the lengthy »Bleed 'Em Dry« effort, was circulated in the early months of 1981, the tape showcasing virtually an entire album's worth of material. It wasn't, in all honesty, a particularly memorable or original selection of compositions (a couple of them were truly abysmal), although one or two ("Street Lady" and "The Reaper") shone out as a herald of greater things to come. The outfit's sound was already quite heavy, perhaps more along the lines of SOLDIER at this time, although the flat vocals of Paul de Mercado might have been something of a weak link. Nevertheless, the tape rapidly went on to shift several hundred copies, and gradually spread the group's name through both word-of-mouth and the occasional bit of airplay on regional stations. In due course, they felt able to venture further afield for gigs (recruiting full-time bassist Phil Matthews in the process), and the music of GRIM REAPER was soon winning new fans in areas such as Yorkshire and the North West. Furthermore, the demo also attracted the attention of the Heavy Metal concern, who duly allowed the lads to contribute a re-recorded version of "The Reaper" to their first »Heavy Metal Heroes« compilation. The possibility of a single (»Can't Take Any More«) was mooted at around this time, but it looks as though GRIM REAPER held out for a better offer.

By the end of 1981, having now got their first demo and vinyl appearance under their belts, it looked as though things were finally moving in the right direction for GRIM REAPER, and an enthusiastic write-up in the 'Armed And Ready' section of 'Kerrang' must have been the icing on the cake. Within a matter of months, however, it was revealed that they had gone into the garage for a complete overhaul, with only Nick Bowcott remaining from the original line-up. Joining him in the revamped version of GRIM REAPER were bassist Dave Wanklin (I'm not touching that one with a ten foot barge-pole) and drummer Lee Harris, the Mk.II line-up being completed in the spring of 1982 when erstwhile MEDUSA vocalist Steve Grimmett was successfully recruited into the ranks. With the revitalised line-up came an almost entirely novel set of compositions, with most of their early efforts being ditched with immense haste thereafter. The lads swiftly demoed some freshly-penned material (having recently been rewarded for their exploits in a *Battle Of The Bands'* contest with some free studio time) such as "All Hell Let Loose", "Liar" and "Loser In Love", and these efforts represented a move towards more metal-oriented and powerful songs, with Grimmett's soaring vocals coming across far more convincingly than those of the departed Paul de Mercado. Their new direction certainly seemed to appeal to one or two of the more noteworthy labels of the day, and the lads eventually formed a friendly alliance with the recently-established Ebony.

Although GRIM REAPER appear to have been added to Ebony's roster quite early in 1983, the sequence of events which followed is slightly odd. Rather than commissioning a GRIM REAPER album straight away, the label allowed (or perhaps encouraged) Steve Grimmett to lend his vocal talents to local hopefuls CHATEAUX (see separate entry), who were then in the process of recording their first long-player. In fact, it emerged that Grimmett had actually also appeared on the young band's earlier single as a personal favour, although he was never officially acknowledged as such. This pretence was continued on the CHATEAUX album itself, where the singer was merely credited as an additional 'guest musician'. Questionable though this semi-deception may have been, the long-player was completed with considerable haste, allowing GRIM REAPER to begin their own vinyl career in earnest. In fact, there was some talk of starting them off with a single (indeed, certain people claim to have seen such a relic, but it certainly didn't materialise as an official pressing, and it's pretty hard to imagine where it might have fitted into the Ebony discography), although the idea appears to have been shelved fairly quickly. After successfully showcasing some new material such as "See You In Hell" and "Now Or Never" (two GRIM REAPER demos are commercially available on the unofficial »NWOBHM Demo Tapes« CD, incidentally), their label became well and truly convinced of the band's full potential, and the lads were soon being encouraged to deliver a full LP.

GRIM REAPER's »See You In Hell« album eventually appeared fairly late in 1983, suggesting that there might have been quite a bit of tinkering around in the studio (indeed, they even tried to make use of a keyboard player, Andy Thomas, but eventually realised that it wasn't working out) to get the final product just right. Nevertheless, it was worth the wait, and cuts such as "Wrath Of The Ripper", "Dead On Arrival" and "Run For Your Life" (as well as reworked versions of "Liar" and "All Hell Let Loose", for example) showed a confident style which bordered on power metal (tinges of JUDAS PRIEST and DIO), although there was generally a pretty melodic edge to the proceedings. Overall, the band were now operating in a similar musical area to the likes of CLOVEN HOOF, TYRANT or DRAGONSLAYER, and they appear to have been the prototype for what would eventually become known as the 'Ebony sound' (e.g. BLADE RUNNER, SAMURAI, CHATEAUX, TYGA MYRA, PREYER). At the time, however, it was a reasonably good stab at something a little bit out of the ordinary, and it represented an immeasurable progression from their wishy-washy first demo. Significantly, it's worth noting that the lyrics had now shifted into more conventional (i.e. heroic and superbly clichéd) metal territory, and the absence of power ballads ("The Show Must Go On" came uncomfortably close, admittedly) was a very wise move, assuming that GRIM REAPER wanted to endear themselves unto the 'real metal' communities of the world.

After some remarkably healthy sales on both sides of the Atlantic, it came as little surprise that an offer to represent the group outside the UK soon came to the attention of the bosses at Ebony. The influential RCA concern had thrown their rather weighty hat into the ring (their interest having been sparked after news of this hot new act had spread like wildfire through the metal underground), and Ebony would have been fools to ignore this timely cash bonanza. As a result, »See You In Hell« received a full-scale reissue and re-promotion in 1984, predominantly for the benefit of the American market. It certainly can't be said that RCA went about things half-heartedly, and they really went to town with the promotional releases in an attempt to introduce GRIM REAPER to the music-buying public and radio stations. Their efforts paid off immediately, and the album was soon selling in quite astonishing quantities. The lads were flown over to the States for some hastily-arranged live performances (playing with the likes of DEUCE), and they also received real 'star treatment' when RCA financed a specially-shot promo video for "See You In Hell". With the release of »The Show Must Go On« (b/w "Dead On Arrival") as a single rounding things off, the first phase of the operation was complete, and it really had been an unequivocal and phenomenal success.

The lads returned to the UK in jubilant mood, but were soon forced to look for a new drummer when Lee Harris packed his bags at fairly short notice. Fortunately, a local replacement was swiftly identified in the shape of VIRGIN STAR's Mark Simon, who became a full-time member of GRIM REAPER in the early months of 1985. RCA had been sufficiently overjoyed with the group's debut album that a follow-up was commissioned with minimal delay, but the outfit (unlike SHY, who defected permanently to RCA at the first opportunity) remained loyal to Ebony in the first instance, agreeing to deliver the next album for the benefit of both labels once again. »Fear No Evil« really saw GRIM REAPER hitting their stride with ease, and this selection of freshly-penned material was a worthy sequel to their debut album. Compositions such as "Never Coming Back", "A Matter Of Time" and "Lay It On The Line" were all supremely capable efforts, the band skirting around the edges of ELIXIR territory at times, although many tracks were, perhaps, slightly too similar in construction. There were also a couple of low-points in the form of the singalong "Rock And Roll Tonight" (leave that sort of thing to WRATHCHILD) and the ridiculous intro to "Final Scream", but these were relatively minor distractions. The album performed spectacularly in the States once again, selling into the hundreds of thousands, and the lads were soon making more trips across the Atlantic, which culminated (after support slots with the likes of EXCITER and SANTERS) with a prestigious appearance at the legendary Texxas Jam, where they played alongside DEEP PURPLE for the benefit of some eighty thousand fans.

Unsurprisingly, the dollar signs were lighting up in front of RCA's eyes, and a further album was a foregone conclusion. It took a while to come about, though, as the band had begun having a few problems with Ebony, who seemed to be letting GRIM REAPER down in terms of European promotion and recording facilities. In fact, things came to a head after various technical shortcomings necessitated the third long-player having to be recorded twice, as Grimmett later explained: *'We originally recorded it at Ebony studios with Darryl Johnston producing and to be honest it sounded like shit. The tapes were sent over to RCA America and rejected on 'technical inadequacy'. I'll tell you how bad the Ebony recordings were, when our management asked for a master tape of the album to be sent over they rang back and said 'You've sent the wrong tape, these are rough demos!' RCA paid for us to re-record the entire thing with Max Norman which gave us that professional touch we'd always lacked.'* (Ref: Metal Forces No.30, August 1988). Clearly, the original version of the album never saw the light of day, and, although the masters have apparently survived, I don't expect that you'll ever get to hear the Ebony recordings. After their second attempt to capture the required sound with an experienced producer in the more lavish American studio environment, the lads essentially severed all ties with Ebony (and the UK in general), electing to remain in the States for recording, promotional and touring activities.

By mid-1987, GRIM REAPER's third album finally appeared (on RCA only, meaning that their hapless European fans had to track down elusive import copies) in the form of »Rock You To Hell«, although it transpired that the unfortunately-named bassist Dave Wanklin had actually thrown in his hand after the completion of the recording sessions. Nevertheless, their latest (slickly-produced) long-player was a fairly adept mixture of old (indeed, the dubiously-titled "Suck It And See" was a left-over from the »See You In Hell« sessions, while "Waysted Love", with its Paul de Mercado co-credit, was clearly of an even earlier vintage) and new, with inclusions such as "Lust For Freedom", "I Want More" and "When Heaven Comes Down" being rather more accessible efforts (with some pretty flashy guitar work) designed to appeal to the MTV generation. Overall, though, it was all very listenable once again, and the lads were now being hailed as genuine superstars in North America, although it was a pity to observe that their unfortunate European fans (who would surely have paid dearly just for one glimpse of their heroes in the live environment) were now being sidelined and ignored just a bit too readily. Back in the States, however, the musicians were soon out on the road once more (with IDOL RICH bassist Jeff Curtis now stepping in to fill the vacant position), this time out as part of a three-band package (their partners in crime being ARMORED SAINT and HELLOWEEN) which was promoted under the banner of the *'Hell On Wheels Tour'*. It was all a great success, and one of the shows (in Minneapolis) was even filmed professionally and later broadcast on MTV. There seemed to be no limits to GRIM REAPER's potential, but things were to go pear-shaped fairly rapidly.

A fourth GRIM REAPER album (again, for RCA) was being worked on in 1988, by which time new bassist Benjie Brittain (another ex-VIRGIN STAR bloke) had joined the fold, where he found himself teaming up with his erstwhile colleague Mark Simon. Things seemed to be going quite well at first, and a handful of new tracks such as "Shakedown" and "Get Out Of My Face" (the latter supposedly inspired by their volatile relationship with Ebony) were played live at around this time, but it looks as though these were never officially recorded. For some unknown reason, however, the group began to suffer a few internal problems over the ensuing months, and many casual observers speculated that they would soon succumb to *'victims of their own success syndrome'*. Towards the end of the year, the cynics were proved right, with Grimmett suddenly jumping ship after being lured away by a tempting offer to join ONSLAUGHT, resulting in the immediate demise of GRIM REAPER. The split was, in the end, fairly amicable, and Nick Bowcott elected to remain in the States, eventually attempting to generate some interest in his new project entitled BARFLY. Sadly, however, the outfit, despite signing an album deal with (you guessed it) RCA and recording a full-length effort entitled »No Place Like Home« in 1990, were actually dropped by the label before the finished product had even made it to the vinyl stage.

Most of the former members of GRIM REAPER appear to have gone to ground in recent years (mind you, something of a one-off reunion was organised for Wacken 2000, much to the surprise of many people), although Steve Grimmett, having worked his notice with ONSLAUGHT, is still keeping pretty busy with his LIONSHEART project, as well as making various other recording appearances, notably by helping out in MARSHALL LAW and singing on a recent IRON MAIDEN tribute album. GRIM REAPER have somehow maintained an astonishingly high level of interest among metal aficionados and NWOBHM collectors, particularly throughout the States and Japan, which has resulted in their albums being made available (both officially and unofficially) on CD in the 90's. As for future releases of exclusive material, Steve Grimmett remains doubtful: 'We just don't have anything in the way of single B-sides, you see. We once had a cover version of BLUE ÖYSTER CULT's "Don't Fear The Reaper" in demo form, but it would probably be impossible to find it! As for the live show recorded by MTV, there's also no chance of an official release now, as they've wiped their video archive in the interval.' (Ref: Iron Pages No.31, 1995). So, what should we consider to be GRIM REAPER's greatest legacy? Album sales of approximately three-quarters of a million in America alone, perhaps? No, I reckon we should revere them most for being one of the few NWOBHM bands to have been afforded the ultimate accolade of having one of their video clips ridiculed by those cartoon connoisseurs of taste, 'Beavis And Butthead'…

LP's
»See You In Hell« Ebony 1983
[Original UK issue]
»See You In Hell« RCA 1984
[Later US issue]
»Fear No Evil« Ebony 1985
[UK issue]
»Fear No Evil« RCA 1985
[US issue, different reverse cover]
»Rock You To Hell« RCA 1987

7" Singles
»The Show Must Go On« RCA 1984
[US-only issue, A-side different to album version]

Promotional Releases
»See You In Hell« RCA 1984
[One-sided 7" flexi with album excerpts]
»The Show Must Go On« RCA 1984
[US radio promo 12" with two mixes, some with press pack]
»Fear No Evil« RCA 1985
[US radio promo red vinyl 12" in picture sleeve]
»Rock You To Hell« RCA 1987
[One-sided 7" flexi with album excerpts]
»Rock You To Hell« RCA 1987
[US radio promo 12" in stickered company sleeve]

CD's
»Rock You To Hell« RCA 1987
»See You In Hell« Black Ghost 1992
[Bootleg release of first two albums on one CD]
»See You In Hell« Pony Canyon 1993
[Japanese issue]
»Fear No Evil« Pony Canyon 1993
[Japanese issue]
»Rock You To Hell« Pony Canyon 1993
[Japanese issue]
»The Best Of Grim Reaper« RCA 1999
[Compilation release]

Exclusive Compilation Appearances
"The Reaper" on »Heavy Metal Heroes« LP Heavy Metal 1981 *[Issued in two different sleeves]* + »N.W.O.B.H.M.« LP/CD Heavy Metal 1991 + »Heavy Metal Heroes Vol.I&II« CD British Steel 1996
"Loser In Love" on »NWOBHM Demo Tapes« Bootleg CD 1992

Compilation Appearances
"Final Scream" on »Let Them Eat Rock« LP RCA 1986
"Fear No Evil" on »Metal Forces« LP K-Tel 1987
"Entrance/All Hell Let Loose" on »NWOBHM Demo Tapes« Bootleg CD 1992
[With exclusive "Entrance" intro and main track different to album version]
"Liar" on »NWOBHM Demo Tapes« Bootleg CD 1992
[Different to album version]
"See You In Hell" on »NWOBHM Demo Tapes« Bootleg CD 1992
[Different to album version]
"Suck It And See" on »NWOBHM Demo Tapes« Bootleg CD 1992
[Different to album version]
"Now Or Never" on »NWOBHM Demo Tapes« Bootleg CD 1992
[Different to album version]

GROUND ATTACK

Tom Atkinson (v, g)
Mel Collins (v, b)
Tab (d)

For reasons best known to themselves, the three hirsute members of GROUND ATTACK have, on one side of the charmingly-presented gatefold sleeve which houses their »Red Lion« single from 1981, chosen to expose their rather unattractive backsides in all their naked glory (calm down, girls). On the inside cover, meanwhile, a motley horde of decidedly non-photogenic headbangers dragged out of the local hostelry (as you might imagine, the Red Lion of the title) pose for the benefit of the camera. Just in case you haven't quite grasped the blindingly obvious message yet, the knockabout GROUND ATTACK were a not-terribly-serious proposition (analogous to the ubiquitous DUMPY'S RUSTY NUTS on more than one level) who catered primarily for the inevitable biker following. Low on musical ability and originality they may have been, but GROUND ATTACK were equally abundant in terms of energy and high spirits. To their credit, they purveyed utterly unpretentious music, delivered without recourse to the kind of cynical media hype, excessive recording budgets, television appearances or blanket radio exposure which surrounded every piece of recording activity undertaken by certain high-profile acts of the time. This unrenowned act represented (either consciously or, in all probability, unconsciously) the NWOBHM at its most fundamental level: grass-roots music which stood a million miles from major labels and their fiscally-motivated activities.

Whether or not GROUND ATTACK ever actually constituted a particularly genuine attempt either to establish themselves as biker rock heroes or to jump on the passing NWOBHM bandwagon is open to debate, however, as at least one of their members (Mel Collins, best-known for his work with the BYRON BAND) was quite a familiar face on the club scene. Whatever the story, however, it's probably best to take GROUND ATTACK at face value and assume that they were a *bona fide* musical venture and not a jokey side-project after all. With their one-off single being recorded in Luton at the height of the influx, the tracks "Red Lion" (with an anthemic backing from their many fans) and "Every Mother's Son" are raw, good-time semi-NWOBHM, conveying the kind of down-to-earth attitude which must have been virtually a prerequisite for pleasing the type of provincial rock crowd attracted to *'do-it-yourself'* gigs in the early 80's. Unsophisticated material, perhaps, but there's little doubt that GROUND ATTACK must have blown away a few cobwebs and upset a few elderly residents of the Home Counties during their brief time on the music scene. Their one and only single (copies with sleeves are part of a sought-after minority) is now a prized artefact among many of today's NWOBHM collectors, and you're unlikely to find one particularly cheaply.

7" Singles
»Red Lion« Ground Attack Music 1981

GUNSLINGERS

James 'Scooter' Campbell (v)
Wilf Woods (g)
John Hall (rg)
Teddy Shermer (b)
Paul Hornby (d)

In true rock'n'roll fashion, the founder members of the rather sleazy GUNSLINGERS originally gravitated together as drinking partners in some of the more notorious pubs and clubs of London, before deciding (towards the end of 1982) to try their luck as a hard-rocking proposition with the world at their feet. Inspired by such legendary, raunchy hellraisers as MOTT THE HOOPLE, the ROLLING STONES and THE FACES (Rod Stewart's outfit from the early 70's), the newly-created five-piece (the brainchild of guitarist Wilf Woods, who was previously involved with an obscure combo called ZOOM CLUB) swiftly allied themselves with various like-minded hopefuls such as the DOGS D'AMOUR, the BABYSITTERS and the IDLE FLOWERS, originally merely basking in the reflected glory of HANOI ROCKS and AEROSMITH, but eventually, through sheer hard graft and numerous lively gigs throughout the capital, making a name for themselves in their own right. Throughout the following couple of years, the group would enjoy regular club appearances, ranging from small-time shindigs alongside the likes of the DOGS D'AMOUR, MARIONETTE and the infamous AUNT MAY, to markedly more prestigious support slots with crowd-pleasers such as GIRLSCHOOL and MOTÖRHEAD, usually going down well with their repertoire of original compositions, interspersed with a few carefully-selected cover versions from some of their influences.

As a result of various trips to the recording studio, a full album's worth of GUNSLINGERS material was laid down on tape over a period of several months, which drew a fair bit of attention from certain influential parties in due course, but which was never seriously considered suitable for release in its original form. Nevertheless, the plucky ensemble finally made it to the vinyl stage in the latter half of 1984, releasing their one and only single on their own label, coupling "Never A Dull Moment" (which, in spite of the fact that its title was taken from an early ROD STEWART album, wasn't a cover version) with their reworking of "Shake Some Action", originally recorded by the FLAMIN' GROOVIES in 1976. With the B-side having been captured live at Ronnie Scott's Club (a venue more noted for showcasing jazz acts, it must be said) in London a few months previously, the record comes across as a fairly representative snapshot of the UK's sleaze scene in its relatively early days, and quite happily sits alongside studio offerings of the time from outfits such as TARA ZARA and the DOGS D'AMOUR. Reviews of the single were mixed, with most journalists resorting to the facile use of ROLLING STONES comparisons, but the band themselves were pleased enough with the finished product.

In fact, original drummer Paul Hornby had defected to the aforementioned DOGS D'AMOUR (although he held a comparatively brief tenure) shortly after the tracks for the »Never A Dull Moment« 7" had been recorded, and, consequently, isn't pictured or credited on the seriously rare, fold-round sleeve which was manufactured in extraordinarily limited quantities and came with a handful of promotional copies only. His eventual replacement (after a couple of unsuitable candidates had been rejected) was a certain Bron Buick, an affable character whose vivid memories of his time with the GUNSLINGERS are mostly happy ones: *'The gig at Dingwalls [with GIRLSCHOOL] was funny. Our manager pulled a lovely little scam by 'leaking to the press' that the gig was being filmed as part of a big rock and roll movie, and anyone who wanted to be in the film should just turn up. We broke every attendance record known to man that night, there were people queuing right round the block! Of course, the film story was a complete lie, but we held that record for ages!'* (Ref: Interview, Pete Davis, July 1999). Sneaky. Towards the end of the year, a selection of new material was laid down in the studio in order to keep things ticking over, and the general response seems to have been favourable, although tentative plans for a follow-up single never came to fruition.

Moving into 1985, the GUNSLINGERS were to benefit from the occasional honourable mention in the likes of 'Kerrang' for their debauched live performances, and their management team pulled off yet another coup when a coveted appearance on the 'Friday Rock Show' was arranged. With the broadcast originally taking place on the 26th of April 1985, the tracks featured were "Monster", "There Must Be Something We Ain't Tried", "Lies All Lies" and "She Got Me Covered", the session being engineered, much to the outfit's delight, by erstwhile MOTT THE HOOPLE sticksman Dale Griffin. In spite of the group's initial enthusiasm, however, the post-production apparently left a lot to be desired, rendering the material considerably weaker than would have been anticipated from the original mix. Boo. A month later, however, the lads were able to make amends *via* a television appearance on the legendary 'E.C.T.' programme, an experimental series of shows commissioned by Channel 4 in the spring/summer of 1985, and which allowed four rock/metal bands to play two or three songs live (and it really *was* live!) in the course of each episode. Appearing alongside VENOM, LEE AARON and the TORPEDOS (who?), the GUNSLINGERS raced through versions of "Shake Some Action" and "I Laughed", much to the delight of the assembled masses. Later in the year, the lads were back in the studio once more, this time with the intention of laying down four new tracks to be released as an EP. In the event, however, the latest batch of recordings weren't thought to be up to scratch, and plans for this second slice of vinyl were eventually shelved.

Things had more or less ground to a halt for the original GUNSLINGERS (confusingly, a couple of other British outfits also adopted the same identity during the latter half of the 80's) by the end of 1986 (apart from the occasional ad hoc jam session with other hopefuls in the capital), as the erstwhile friends had, despite a coveted publishing deal having come their way in the interim, started to lose interest in their original quest for fame, feeling that they were now being left behind by the DOGS D'AMOUR, QUIREBOYS and newer imports such as GUNS'N'ROSES and FASTER PUSSYCAT. Oddly, there was one last attempt at reviving their dwindling career in 1988, when a new track ("Fuelling The Fire") was recorded especially for the obscure »Song And Legend« compilation, although only Woods and Hall now remained from the original line-up, the other faces being given as (and here come some dubious names) Phalvis Warner (b), Karim Khan (v) and John O'Liary (d). Mind you, given that Hall and Warner also seem to have been involved with an act called the LONDON GYPSIES at the time, it's more likely that this was simply a one-off reunion, rather than a full-scale reformation. In any case, the one-time members would drift apart completely as their cherished sleaze movement disintegrated towards the end of the decade, at which point many of the scenesters of the day took the opportunity to relocate to the West Coast of America, where they could live the hedonistic lifestyle for a few years longer. A reformation seems unlikely, but you never know...

7" Singles
»Never A Dull Moment« Ego Records 1984

Exclusive Compilation Appearances
"Fuelling The Fire" on »Song And Legend« Do-LP Abstract Records 1988

GYPP

Martin Newell (v)
Ian Peppercorn (g)
Tony Phillips (b)
Brian Rudd (k)
John Butters (d)

Another early and hopelessly obscure release comes courtesy of the largely unknown and atrociously-monikered GYPP, an act who inhabited the county of Suffolk. Their curiously-titled »Yaah!« EP from the pre-explosion days of 1978 is an odd mixture of rock with widdly keyboards, a confusing concoction which brings to mind the musical direction adopted, with fairly limited success, by bands such as the MOVIE STARS and LÉARGO. The tracks featured are quite varied in their construction, with "Marigoldz" being the most straightforward, in the MEANSTREAK or BILL THE MURDERER vein, while "Titania" is a more progressive number, occasionally reminiscent of OXYM. Rounding things off is the lengthy "Sister Darling", a melodic and restrained effort more in the style of CHEMICAL ALICE than anything else. As an example of proto-NWOBHM, it was reasonably worthy, although it's plain for all to see that GYPP were, like many, struggling to find a particularly stable musical stance at that juncture. The EP was issued in a picture sleeve showing a hand-drawn image of two fighter planes engaged in a dogfight, and very few copies are known to have surfaced, although it's unlikely ever to become a major-league rarity. This outfit appears to have been a going concern for a good few years (still gigging locally until at least 1981), taking in much of the South East of England in terms of their live appearances, but they don't seem to have lasted particularly long into the 80's. As with most progressively-inclined outfits of the era, only a one-off vinyl release reminds us of their existence and none of the members appear to have re-emerged in other bands of note. A better name might have helped a bit, lads...

7" EP's
»Yaah!« Shy Talk Records 1978

HAMMER

Marty 'The Dog' Wilkinson (v,k)
Bob Henman (g)
Kenny Nicholson (g)
Graeme Hutchinson (b)
Marty Day (d)

Cleveland's HAMMER adopted their new identity at the beginning of 1985, having previously issued a hard-rocking LP under the name of HOLLAND (see separate entry) before running into a few legal problems over the rights to the moniker. The quintet's rapid metamorphosis into HAMMER occurred under duress, though, and it's worth noting that the back sleeve of their debut album for Ebony includes the pithy 'Very special thanks to HOLLAND and their road crew' statement. In any case, HAMMER's »Contract With Hell« long-player, despite effectively being the second HOLLAND effort, saw the lads attempting to cultivate something of a more 'metal' image, with a heroic sleeve and logo, plus lyrics which occasionally went beyond the 'ooh baby, just look at the sheer size of this bulge in my trousers' mentality. In fact, the most detectable difference between the two incarnations of the group was the fact that the lads were now augmenting their sound with keyboards on occasion, used to the greatest effect on numbers such as "Caution To The Wind" and "Satellite".

Elsewhere, there were several strong compositions on display (notably "Across The Line", "Prayer Of A Soldier" and the title track itself), and these efforts definitely showed something of a progression in terms of songwriting. Mind you, the likes of "Try It", "Hey You" and "Hard Hittin' Woman", for example, were simply throwbacks to those raunchy rock roots (indeed a version of "Hard Hittin' Woman" had originally been demoed by HOLLAND as far back as 1982), and these could quite happily have taken their place on the critically-ignored »Early Warning« set. All things considered, though, »Contract With Hell« was a markedly more diverse and accomplished album than these characters had managed to deliver under their previous guise, but, in spite of some encouragingly positive feedback from the rock press, it proved not to be the turning point the lads had hoped for. Indeed, the cracks started appearing as early as 1986, when head honcho Kenny Nicholson made it quite clear that he would only remain involved if they all agreed to move in a substantially heavier direction. The guitarist's vision for HAMMER's future path was diametrically opposed to vocalist Marty Wilkinson's, however, who desired to steer the band into increasingly chart-friendly waters. There was no hope of resolving the situation, and Nicholson rapidly took off to do his own thing and write his preferred type of material, which eventually led to the formation of FAST KUTZ (see separate entry), a highly capable proposition who also proceeded to record an enjoyable album for Ebony.

Nicholson's departure didn't quite spell the immediate end of HAMMER, though, and the lads soldiered on with new guitarist Arthur Fixter, recording several more demos over the next couple of years, each taking the band progressively closer to mainstream territory. The persevering outfit still remained under contract to Ebony, however, who (for reasons best known to themselves) refused to sanction a name change to anything more representative of their increasingly-lightweight musical direction. A follow-up album was on the cards for a while, although the label expressed serious and continual doubts as to whether HAMMER's latest studio efforts were really the sort of thing that would appeal to the general public. With the group torn between their own desires to write mainstream material and their label's insistence that they toughen up their act once again, things started falling apart, and the hapless bunch were to lose the services of both Arthur Fixter and Graeme Hutchinson before much longer. By this stage, the remaining members were finding it almost impossible to carry on, and, in the wake of Ebony's inevitable decision to abandon any hopes of ever getting another HAMMER album into the shops, the disintegrating outfit finally called it a day towards the end of the decade. Bob Henman, incidentally, still plays in a small-time local pub act, while vocalist Marty Wilkinson has recently reconciled his differences with Kenny Nicholson, and the duo are now playing together once again in a covers band called (wait for it) OUTRAGEOUS WALLPAPER. How's that for a metal name?

LP's
»Contract With Hell« Ebony 1985

HAMMERHEAD

Brian Hodgson (v,g)
Graeme 'Buzz' Elliott (v,g)
Steve Archer (b)
Baz Ellwood (d)

Cumbria's HAMMERHEAD (not to be confused with Dutch or American namesakes) were one of the more talented minor NWOBHM ensembles, and came together at the turn of the decade after the demise of various small-time nonentities such as JUDAS, BITTER HARVEST and 8 HERTZ. Initially centred around the nucleus of Brian Hodgson and Steve Archer, the band happily operated as a trio at first, with sticksman Maurice Reay making up the numbers. Before long, though, they underwent a period of restructuring, whereupon new drummer Baz Ellwood joined in the fun, closely followed by second guitarist Buzz Elliott. After a few tentative appearances on the regional club scene during 1981, the group first came to public attention via a well-received demo tape which featured a range of recently-penned material, exposing the world to the quartet's contemporary take on the heavy rock/metal sound. In due course, selections from the cassette (notably crowd-pleaser "Time Will Tell") even made it into one or two national Heavy Metal charts, so it looked as though HAMMERHEAD stood a pretty good chance of attracting a bit of label interest before long. Nevertheless, with the response from local fans and music press having been overwhelmingly encouraging, these ambitious characters decided to take the bull by the horns and record a self-financed single, the latter being laid down towards the end of the same year at the nearby Linden Sounds facility and subsequently issued on the label of the same name.

Pressed in the regulation quantity of a thousand copies (a tiny number of which supposedly contained a poster, but even the group appear to have no knowledge of this), the single coupled the upbeat, twin-guitar attack of "Time Will Tell" with the more restrained "Lonely Man", both featuring catchy arrangements and memorable guitar work redolent of outfits such as CRUCIFIXION, BASHFUL ALLEY and OMEN SEARCHER. It genuinely was an excellent way to open their account, and HAMMERHEAD's two-tracker (issued in a monochrome picture sleeve showing individual images of the musicians) has long been regarded as one of the more impressive mementos from the NWOBHM period. Quite rightly, the »Time Will Tell« 7" has been a mainstay of the collecting scene virtually from the beginning, and still commands a hefty price. Following on from their single's release, the developing outfit began to venture further afield (up to Scotland on occasion) and picked up a few regional support slots with the likes of BUDGIE. Even so, the labels generally failed to acknowledge their existence (the lads subsequently circulated an official live cassette in the hope that someone might take the bait, but this didn't open any doors in the short term), leaving HAMMERHEAD to soldier on alone and attempt to make themselves known through sheer hard graft in the pubs and clubs.

Sadly, things didn't really improve for the luckless band, and, beset with financial problems and creeping disillusionment, the central characters had elected to call time on the venture by 1984. Buzz Elliott went off to lend a hand in local acts such as THE REBELS and THE RAIN, while Steve Archer and Brian Hodgson hooked up with new skin-beater Frank Hall, who had latterly been a member of the excellently-monikered NECROMANTIS. The new trio gelled pretty quickly, and (adopting the functional name of the FRANK HALL BAND) duly laid down a couple of tracks to get their name into circulation. Oddly enough, neither were originals, as "Don't Look Back" was salvaged from the NECROMANTIS repertoire, while "Lochinvar" dated back to Brian Hodgson's BITTER HARVEST days. The lads briefly entertained the notion of releasing the tracks in the form of a 7" single, although this idea had to be shelved on financial grounds. Nevertheless, their tape duly won favour with the Sane Records concern in Wales, who proceeded to include "Lochinvar" on their scarcely-seen »It's Unheard Of!« compilation. By now, however, the lads had elected to resurrect the original HAMMERHEAD identity, so nobody was any the wiser that the lads had been tinkering around under a different name in the interim.

The track itself (which, incidentally, later turned up on the »NWOBHM Vol.6« bootleg CD) was slightly removed from the material on the group's »Time Will Tell« single, and revealed a heavier, more atmospheric direction which was, perhaps, more in the OVERDRIVE or CYNIC scheme of things. Mind you, it's still a cracking effort (albeit uncannily similar to ETHEL THE FROG's "Bleeding Heart"), although, given that it wasn't a HAMMERHEAD original, it's hard to say whether or not it was representative of their new direction. Having got the music bug once again, the dedicated musicians continued to ply their trade in the pubs and clubs of the North for a few years after the sampler's release (keyboard player David Taylor was even drafted in to add a pinch of variety at one point), but HAMMERHEAD ultimately fragmented (again) towards the end of the decade (although they apparently got back together for the occasional special appearance in the 90's) after giving it their best shot for many years. Mainman Brian Hodgson has, by the way, since been involved in one or two post-HAMMERHEAD musical projects, such as the more progressively-inclined PLATEAU, although none of these appear to have advanced beyond the demo stage.

7" Singles
»Time Will Tell« Linden Sounds 1981

Exclusive Compilation Appearances
"Lochinvar" on »It's Unheard Of!« LP Sane Records 1984 + »NWOBHM Vol.6« Bootleg CD 1992

Compilation Appearances
"Time Will Tell" on »NWOBHM Vol.4« Bootleg CD 1992

HANDSOME BEASTS

Gary Dallaway (v)
Phil Aston (g)
Steven Hough (b)
Pete Malbasa (d)

It's unfortunate that the majority of press attention received by the Midlands-based HANDSOME BEASTS tended to focus on the remarkable size of their frontman, Gary Dallaway, as they were a pretty talented bunch in their own right. The aforementioned vocalist was the possessor of a soulful, bluesy voice, and he was backed by a highly capable group of musicians, so it was hardly surprising that they developed something of a cult following almost immediately, having pretty much formed at the very height of the NWOBHM explosion. The sarcastically-named quartet soon established themselves as a popular, crowd-pleasing act in the pubs and clubs of the region, and actually chose to incorporate Dallaway's girth as an integral part of the group's image and identity rather than trying to avoid the issue, pre-empting (with some degree of success) all the drunken halfwits who would take great pleasure in shouting 'you fat bastard' (which he may have been, but that's not the point) at every available opportunity. According to local folklore, the frontman's expansive gut was even miked up on occasion and utilised as the basis of a unique musical interlude, the legendary 'tum solo'!

By the end of 1980, the band decided that it was time to get some product on the market, and, with no record company interest on the horizon, their management team elected to form the Heavy Metal label as a means of releasing some HANDSOME BEASTS vinyl. They debuted with a 7" single (the cover of which depicted the members in gruesome masks, although their own features were almost as scary) featuring "All Riot Now" and "The Mark Of The Beast", two numbers which showed the lads to be operating in a similar musical area to that inhabited by the likes of LAUTREC, XERO, EXPOZER or the Essex version of WARRIOR. It was, generally speaking, a well-received release, and so it wasn't long before a follow-up was on the cards. Their second effort was an unusual three-tracker (released in 1981), featuring "Breaker" as the main focus of attention, with a double-grooved B-side which played one of two selections, either "Crazy" or "One In A Crowd". It was an interesting gimmick, although they were hardly the first or last outfit to employ the device, and at least it wasn't used as a particularly blatant sales ploy. In due course, the Heavy Metal concern branched out into signing other acts, and soon assembled their first »Heavy Metal Heroes« compilation, where (naturally enough) the HANDSOME BEASTS took pride of place with their "Local Heroes" composition.

On the basis of their early vinyl appearances, the lads were duly invited to record a 'Friday Rock Show' session, which gave them some valuable national exposure, and the featured tracks "David's Song", "Sweeties", "Another Day" and "Local Heroes" were enthusiastically received by the station's listeners when they were initially broadcast on the 10th of July 1981. By the second half of the year, Heavy Metal decided that they would be entirely justified in releasing a full HANDSOME BEASTS album, and so the tastefully-titled »Beastiality« (the cover of which famously showed a virtually-naked Dallaway posing with a bewildered pig, the frontman's modesty covered largely by his overhanging belly) appeared as a matter of course. Disappointingly, perhaps, the LP (featuring second axeman Paul Robins) recycled many previously-released numbers, and unfamiliar songs were few and far between. Nevertheless, the likes of "High Speed" and "Tearing Me Apart" were capable enough inclusions which were well up to the usual standard. The band's lyrics tended to be rather gritty, to say the least, and their apparent fascination with various aspects of social inadequacy and misanthropic behaviour was often rather disconcerting, especially on the odious "Sweeties", a track which should never have been committed to vinyl. Sadly, the latter was even released as a single (b/w "You're On Your Own"), although the publicity attracted as a result of this vile offering and its equally objectionable cover (sorry, but if you think paedophilia is remotely amusing then you really need your head examined) was undeniably detrimental to their cause. Nevertheless, "Sweeties" eventually made it into the 'Top 30 Kuts' chart in 'Kerrang' in the early months of 1982, so it must have shifted a fair number of copies at the time.

The band continued to gig during 1982 (by which time Paul Robins had taken over the guitar duties completely, Phil Aston later moving on to the ROGUE MALE venture before teaming up with local hopefuls TANTRUM), but their activities tailed off slightly as their label decided to concentrate on the promotion of various up-and-coming new outfits, leaving the HANDSOME BEASTS to fend for themselves. In fact, it looked as though they might have disappeared into the wilderness by the mid-80's, judging by their apparent lack of studio and live work, although it transpires that they were still a going concern at this time. Perhaps they were busily writing new material, or maybe Dallaway had finally received a government grant to develop his stomach to its fullest potential. Whatever the story, the BEASTS came out of hibernation in around 1987, swiftly grabbing some useful support slots with acts such as the dwindling TYGERS OF PAN TANG, although it became apparent that only Dallaway and Steven Hough now remained from the original incarnation, with new recruits Marjusz Mitrenko (g) and Ray Richman (d) having recently been drafted in to make up the requisite numbers. The revitalised outfit offered little or no indication that they would be having another crack at finding fame and fortune, however, and they were soon to fade into the background once again. It was something of a surprise, therefore, when they re-emerged, completely out of the blue, with a brand-new album (and another bassist, Mark Wright) in 1990, supposedly as a celebration of their decade-long existence.

The advertising blurb for »The Beast Within« (housed within another inadvisably-presented sleeve) suggested, rather oddly, that the album had been 'ten years in the making', although this was clearly nothing more than hyperbole, as the songs were almost certainly recent compositions which had been thrown together at relatively short notice. The long-player was, unfortunately, a fairly uninspiring affair, veering from simple, upbeat rockers to LED ZEPPELIN-influenced, semi-bluesy numbers, few of which ("Chain Gang" wasn't bad, admittedly, while the lengthy title track showed some promise) had any real panache or personality of their own. As a celebration of their career, however, it was something of a damp squib, and it's no surprise that the lads decided to go back into hiding fairly shortly after its release. Still, they actually got as far as recording a third LP (»Little Sister«) with the assistance of ex-RICOCHET stalwart The Finn, although this album has yet to see an official release. Faced with various label-related problems, the HANDSOME BEASTS empire slowly began to crumble, and finally fell apart in the mid-90's, after one last round of gigging throughout the Midlands. Apart from their imposing mouthpiece (who now fronts the resurrected BUCKSHEE), none of the participants appear to have resurfaced (no, I'm not suggesting that Dallaway could possibly have eaten them) in later years, so it looks as though the supporting cast more or less took their leave of the rock scene for good. Even so, their »Beastiality« set has been excavated for a CD reissue in recent times, so maybe some modern-day fans are rediscovering the band's music even as we speak.

LP's
»Beastiality« Heavy Metal 1981
»The Beast Within« Heavy Metal 1990

7" EP's
»Breaker« Heavy Metal 1981
[Double-grooved B-side plays either "One In A Crowd" or "Crazy", records have either blue or silver labels]

7" Singles
»All Riot Now« Heavy Metal 1980
[Both tracks non-LP]
»Sweeties« Heavy Metal 1981
[B-side "You're On Your Own" non-LP, also issued as part of »Munsters Of Rock« singles pack]

CD's
»The Beast Within« Heavy Metal 1990
»Beastiality« British Steel 1996
[With four bonus tracks]

Compilation Appearances
"Local Heroes" on »Heavy Metal Heroes« LP Heavy Metal 1981 *[Issued in two different sleeves]* + »Heavy Metal Heroes Vol.I&II« CD British Steel 1996
"The Beast Within" on »Heavy Metal Heroes Vol.III« LP/CD Heavy Metal 1990
"The Sixth Day" on »Heavy Metal Heroes Vol.III« LP/CD Heavy Metal 1990
"All Riot Now" on »N.W.O.B.H.M.« LP/CD Heavy Metal 1991 + »Heavy Metal Records Singles Collection Vol.1« CD British Steel 1996
"Mark Of The Beast" on »Heavy Metal Records Singles Collection Vol.1« CD British Steel 1996
"Breaker" on »Heavy Metal Records Singles Collection Vol.1« CD British Steel 1996
"Crazy" on »Heavy Metal Records Singles Collection Vol.1« CD British Steel 1996
"One In A Crowd" on »Heavy Metal Records Singles Collection Vol.1« CD British Steel 1996

HARD, THE

Bernie Tormé (v, g)
Phil Spalding (b)

It's fair to say that the gifted Bernie Tormé has kept himself pretty busy over the past twenty-odd years, and there have been numerous vehicles (some more roadworthy than others) for his musical talents. Most of these are relatively familiar, notably GILLAN, TORMÉ and a brief stint with OZZY OSBOURNE, but there are also a few earlier projects which failed to set the world ablaze. It pretty much started back in 1976 with THE URGE, a rowdy bunch of upstarts who operated in his native Ireland, which led neatly to SCRAPYARD in England, where he collaborated with John McCoy. After that, the BERNIE TORMÉ BAND enjoyed a modicum of success for a year or two, releasing a couple of singles and making the odd compilation appearance to promote themselves further, before he placed the project on hold and hooked up with GILLAN in 1979. A short time beforehand, however, the axeman became involved with a fly-by-night studio venture which masqueraded as THE HARD, who even made it to the vinyl stage, unlikely as it may seem. The whole episode was slightly baffling, and even the participants have precious little recollection either of the recording session itself or the original motivation behind the project, but the story revolves around a handful of mysterious characters, namely Riff Regan, Kenny Young and Andy Miller, who penned a couple of cheery tunes ("The Hottest

Woman In Town" and "I Know") and duly captured each track on tape, before concluding that it might be worth experimenting by bringing in a few scenesters to see if they could do any better.

It came to pass, therefore, that Bernie Tormé, bassist Phil Spalding and, er, *'the third man'* (nobody recalls who acted as drummer on this particular occasion) got together and proceeded to immortalise an alternate version of "The Hottest Woman In Town" in the early months of 1979. Before long, the latter was paired with the original take of "I Know" and pressed up as a single by the little-known CM Records, who presumably issued the unassuming 7" sometime thereafter, although it appears that an utterly minimal quantity ever made in into circulation, and are horrendously scarce nowadays. In fact, it looks as though the prominent *'featuring Bernie Tormé'* credit and a typically flashy guitar solo failed to draw in the punters, so this ill-starred venture was soon laid to rest. It was a slightly odd release, mind you, and coupled a catchy, knockabout A-side (not a million miles away from some of Bernie's own efforts) with a rather more commercial number (complete with melodious keyboards), and "I Know" (a capable enough composition, admittedly) was actually far more attuned to the likes of JOURNEY and BOSTON (largely pre-empting the emergence of LIONHEART and their ilk) than you might imagine. Neither track was particularly representative of the NWOBHM ethos, but the (sleeveless) single is still a worthwhile addition to this volume, and you'd be well-advised to snap up a copy if you ever happen to see one.

As you'll no doubt be aware, Bernie Tormé went on to enjoy a fruitful spell with GILLAN before getting his own, eponymous project (where he teamed up with Phil Spalding at one point) off the ground once more, after which he operated, variously, under the guises of ELECTRIC GYPSIES and TORMÉ before spreading himself wider and assisting in Dee Snider's short-lived DESPERADO concern. He's still doing his own thing, however, and is rightly regarded as one of our more capable (not to mention prolific), home-grown guitarists. Spalding, meanwhile, after collaborating with MIKE OLDFIELD for a while, had a productive stint with the overly-commercial GTR venture during the late 80's, but has been maintaining more of a low profile in recent times. Surprisingly, however, "The Hottest Woman In Town" actually came back to haunt the protagonists in 1984, when the track was exhumed and included (in slightly different form) on the »Metal Killers« compilation, much to the bemusement of metal fans, who were completely baffled by the involvement of Bernie Tormé, and who tended to assume that this must have been a brand-new recording. At least the truth has finally been established...

7" Singles
»The Hottest Woman In Town« CM Records 1979

Compilation Appearances
"The Hottest Woman In Town" on »Metal Killers« LP Kastle Killers 1984
[Different to single version]

HARLEQUYN

Paul Mother (v,g)
Titus Walker (g)
Phil Sargent (b,k)
Dave Wood (d)

Not to be confused with the earlier, transatlantic outfit called HARLEQUIN (whose »One False Move« album was eventually reissued through the Heavy Metal America label, for example), Yorkshire's HARLEQUYN initially formed in 1984 and (after numerous gigs with emerging regional hopefuls such as EXCALIBUR) soon began winning the hearts of Britain's rock-loving public. Some two years after their inception, the lads burst onto an unsuspecting music scene with their first foray into the world of vinyl, which came in the unlikely shape of the quirky »Burn« single, issued in a rather arty, abstract and slightly psychedelic sleeve. It was an odd-looking release, although the lads themselves had an equally unusual image (lying somewhere between SACRED ALIEN and T.REX), and I would imagine that the good people of Yorkshire might well have given these upstarts something of a hard time over their glam-influenced dandyism. To digress for a moment, it's worth mentioning the fact that there's a popular misconception/urban myth that this bunch were a pseudonymous (I mean, just look at those preposterous names) early incarnation of TERRORVISION in their pre-SPOILT BRATZ days. Nope. Right city (Bradford), wrong band. Two members of TERRORVISION were, in fact, in dodgy glam failures MASQUERADE, which is an embarrassing enough revelation on its own, but I've even got the pictures with which to engineer a subtle blackmail scheme at some future juncture.

Getting back to HARLEQUYN, the tracks from the debut single ("Burn" and "Experience Revolver") were really unlike anything else from the general NWOBHM era (the closest reference point, given that comparatively few of you will be familiar with the music of GARBO, would be the SHOTGUN BRIDES, an outfit with whom HARLEQUYN actually shared a stage in later years), and their own definition of being *'Northern space rockers'*, conjuring up images of HAWKWIND with a black pudding fixation, is fairly inaccurate too. The best I can do in NWOBHM-related terms is to suggest that if SACRED ALIEN and MITHRANDIR went slightly glammy, listened to a bit of EARTHBOUND and crossed swords with LOTUS CRUISE, they *might* sound a bit like HARLEQUYN. Confusing, huh? Incidentally, drummer Dave Wood also helped out in VOYAGER UK (playing on the latter's single at approximately the same time as HARLEQUYN's debut), but was never a full-time member of the AOR wannabes, with Rick Smith taking over from him soon after the record was released. To follow up their extraordinary first two-tracker, HARLEQUYN proceeded to record a lengthy demo (»One Incantation«) the following year, which exposed the listener to such intriguing self-penned efforts as "Sebastian Silhouette", "Finding A Place" and "Whirlpool World", most of which were immensely listenable (almost comparable to MOTHER LOVE BONE), even if they did drift off into semi-glam territory (on "Rock Revolution", for example) at times.

All things considered, HARLEQUYN's off-kilter music was a highly original concoction for the transitional post-NWOBHM period in question, and their next vinyl appearance, a number ("The Fragrancer") on the seldom-seen »Thwak« EP (one of those patchy local-band affairs, designed to showcase some of the more deserving acts from the region) in 1988, was just as impressive as their two-tracker and recent demo, standing out a mile from the other indie/punk nonentities featured. By this time, the lads had wisely dropped their previous glam/quirky image and looked considerably more like a *bona fide* rock proposition (they also now had a reasonably successful fan club in operation, a pretty impressive achievement for an act of this stature), which was an encouraging sign. Moving into 1989, the foursome issued another well-received demo, this time featuring "Oversoul", "Enchantment Child" and "Ghost", three selections which subsequently formed the B-side to their debut LP (»The Order Of The Golden Dawn«), the latter being recorded for the little-known Voltage label. With "Glass Island", "Love Leaves" and "Catch" completing an outstanding album, the outfit had progressed considerably, with the compositions including an excellent and highly imaginative use of rhythm, melody and instrumentation. The mystical and poetic lyrics are far removed from the NWOBHM norm, too, but aren't excessively pretentious.

Sadly, the band don't seem to have been anything more than a minor cult in the UK (despite rave reviews from the astute Dave Shack of 'Metal Forces' and the odd live review in 'Kerrang'), which is a desperately unfair situation, as they could easily have rivalled some of the more original overseas outfits of the late 80's/early 90's such as WARRIOR SOUL, MARY MY HOPE or KING OF KINGS. Truly a group who were years ahead of their time and who deserve a bit of belated adulation, if you ask me. After a few personnel reshuffles, HARLEQUYN finally metamorphosed into a quintet called ARCHITECT (Paul Mother, Titus Walker and Dave Wood being the main protagonists in this venture) at some point in 1991, releasing an introductory 12" EP entitled »More Than Before« shortly thereafter. In spite of the observation that the participants were now pushing something of a goth/metal image, their music had actually changed very little, and they followed up this debut with an extremely enjoyable album called »Poets & Thieves« (which even saw them reworking one or two of their old HARLEQUYN originals) in 1992. Once again, however, it looks as though the outfit never found any great success in their new incarnation, and must have called it a day for good within a further couple of years.

LP's
»**The Order Of The Golden Dawn**« Voltage Records 1989

7" Singles
»**Burn**« Starlight Records 1986
[Both tracks non-LP]

Exclusive Compilation Appearances
"**The Fragrancer**" on »Thwak-Four Kicks In The Right Direction« 7" EP Far North Music 1988

HARRIER

Phil Sheldon (v)
Lydon Ryles (g)
Dave Deakin (b)
Paul Farrington (k)
Paddy O'Rourke (d)

Staffordshire's short-lived and little-remembered HARRIER were, in a sense, a direct descendant of the outstanding REINCARNATE (see separate entry), although it's worth pointing out that the only member connecting the two acts was keyboard player Paul Farrington, who had previously served as bassist in his former outfit. HARRIER, however, were a completely different kettle of fish altogether (their post-NWOBHM music bearing no resemblance whatsoever to REINCARNATE's frenzied guitar assaults), and they appear to have formed fairly soon after the latter's demise in the middle of 1983 or thereabouts. HARRIER's activities failed to attract too much media attention at first, though, and it was only after the ensemble had forged a friendly relationship with the local Bullet Records concern that people started taking any particular notice of these new additions to the rock scene. Even before the end of the year, HARRIER's debut EP had already been recorded for the label, although it was eventually to emerge a few months later on *'Black Horse Records'*, one of the rather odd aliases that Bullet elected to use from time to time, for reasons best known to themselves.

Sadly, the quintet's three-tracker (there was, incidentally, also an extremely limited pressing of a 7" single, although these were manufactured purely for promotional purposes and seldom come up for sale nowadays) turned out to be a very limp effort indeed, the overly-long and under-produced numbers failing to leave much of a favourable impression at all. Both "Out On The Street" and "Nickels And Dimes" come across as pretty unremarkable, mid-paced rockers with distinct similarities to some of the more peripheral and inconsistent acts of the time, notably the quirky DICK SMITH BAND, although there are hints of obscurities such as LORELEI and CAMARGUE in there too. The lengthy "Shine On", on the other hand, seems to have been HARRIER's ill-advised attempt at an epic power ballad, although the track just never goes anywhere (in spite of some semi-capable guitar interludes) and drags on for an absolute eternity. Understandably enough, the record was on the receiving end of a typically wretched review in 'Kerrang', and little else was heard from HARRIER thereafter, although they evidently kept things going for a while, and even delivered another incredibly dreary effort called "Leave Me Now" for a local-band compilation (»To Boldly Go...«) a couple of years later. Again, few eyebrows were raised, and the dejected musicians finally appear to have realised (in view of continued public disinterest and widespread critical disapproval) that they were flogging a dead horse, and presumably ceased all activities within a remarkably short space of time.

12" EP's
»Out On The Street« Black Horse Records 1984

Promotional Releases
»Out On The Street« Black Horse Records 1984
[Promo 7" single, a few copies only, no picture sleeve]

Exclusive Compilation Appearances
"Leave Me Now" on »To Boldly Go...« LP Rats Kart Records 1986

HAZE

Paul McMahon (v,g)
Chris McMahon (v,b)
Michael Powell (k)
Andy McNaughten (d)

Along with the likes of LIAISON and CHEMICAL ALICE, Yorkshire's HAZE are one of relatively few bands who have managed the almost incredible feat of appealing to a highly significant proportion of NWOBHM fans, while still having their feet firmly planted in the progressive genre. It's difficult to ascertain why so few prog-influenced outfits from the era are currently favoured, but I suspect it's more a case of lack of familiarity than anything else, and it might only be a matter of time before some of the more open-minded NWOBHM aficionados eventually start checking out the likes of AIRBRIDGE, PALLAS or PENDRAGON. Mind you, it helps a bit in the first place if the outfit in question doesn't rely *too* heavily on widdly keyboards and occasionally rocks out a bit more (which is why we're not including the likes of MARILLION or IQ, for example), so that NWOBHM fans can establish some sort of connection with more familiar groups such as DAWNWATCHER, WHITE SPIRIT, SARACEN or SHERWOOD.

HAZE first got the music bug in 1978, when the main pairing of Paul and Chris McMahon teamed up with drummer Andy McNaughten and keyboard player Michael Powell, and started doing their own thing in the rehearsal rooms. Powell, however, was only to be a fixture for the first year or so, after which the others carried on as a stripped-down trio, with Chris taking over any necessary keyboard parts. By

1981, HAZE had already developed a sufficient local following that a trip to the recording studio (Input Studio in Sheffield) was in order, the end product of these sessions being an unusually lengthy, privately-issued single featuring "The Night" and "Dig Them Mushrooms", a reasonable enough debut release with occasional hints of DAWNWATCHER or TRIARCHY. Mind you, it was to be the outfit's only vinyl release of their own for quite some time, although they became extremely prolific in terms of issuing cassette-only releases (several of which were recorded specifically for their devoted fan club members) and appearing on local band/progressive compilations in years to come. The next few years were to see the trio getting through a wide variety of drummers in best SPINAL TAP tradition (although there's no firm evidence that either Dave Kirkham or Arthur Deas actually exploded on stage), before settling on what proved to be a permanent member in the form of Paul Chisnell.

The next vinyl offering was to be a full LP entitled »C'est La Vie«, issued on the band's own Gabadon label, the lads having failed to attract any significant interest from the major record companies of the day. This was followed fairly rapidly by a 12" EP featuring "The Ember", "The Ceiling's Coming Down", "Freedom Road" and "Mountain", the group apparently developing a style which paired the elaborate arrangements of PINK FLOYD with some forceful guitar parts, the heaviest material coming in the form of "Freedom Road", a track which wouldn't have seemed out of place on SARACEN's »Heroes, Saints And Fools« opus. Certainly a couple of releases to check out if you're partial to CHEMICAL ALICE, LIAISON, CHASE and so forth. Next up was the »Tunnel Vision« single (the entertaining back sleeve of which consists of a collage of rejection letters from record companies), which again featured a mix of fairly traditional, lightweight prog on the A-side and a more ambitious, heavier composition on flipside "Shadows". In 1987, HAZE got around to releasing their second LP, entitled »Stoat And Bottle« (no doubt the name of a local pub close to their hearts), but things evidently weren't going quite as swimmingly for the outfit by this time, and, despite the pleas of their many fans, HAZE elected to disband in early 1988 so that the members could move on to other projects.

At this point, the HAZE family tree becomes immensely complex, with short-lived side-projects, ambient/instrumental recordings and solo efforts being released by numerous offshoots (mostly with very silly names indeed) on a wide range of formats, some of the more notable ones being SYDNEY BRIDGE & THE HARBOUR, RODENTS OF UNUSUAL SIZE, BAD ASS MOTHERS and WINSTON'N'GOBOLA. During this extremely frenzied period of late 80's activity, there was even a very brief HAZE reunion with new members Andy Feeney and Alen Shaw (Paul Chisnell having moved on), although no further releases would eventuate from this short-lived get-together. More side-projects followed, mostly centred around Chris McMahon, including the experimental VON DANIKEN (who still record from time to time), the BASTARD

CUSTARD BAND (good grief) and the ALEN SHAW QUARTET. By mid-1989, however, the McMahon duo had reunited with Alen Shaw, recruited drummer Nick Beesley and adopted the name WORLD TURTLE, which was very much a revamped version of HAZE. This was, once again, to be a fairly transient project, although it was resurrected as a full-time concern in early 1993 (following on from yet further projects in the form of ALIEN SHORE and GROOVE TABOO; I'm not making any of this up, you know), when the Cyclops label approached the outfit to re-record some old HAZE/WORLD TURTLE compositions for a CD release. By this time this came about, however, a HAZE retrospective had also become available on the obscure Kinesis label, and matters were to be complicated enormously when the new WORLD TURTLE CD appeared under the title of (wait for it) »Haze«. Confusion was abound, especially as Cyclops subsequently advertised the set as »World Turtle« by HAZE. Duh.

Although HAZE seems finally to have bitten the dust as a separate recording entity (the band continue to run an extremely comprehensive website documenting the members' various current activities, and also still make most of their earlier cassette and CD releases available to fans), WORLD TURTLE remains a going concern, and the venture (now basically consisting of the McMahon brothers, aided and abetted by a variety of stand-in session musicians) recently issued their first CD proper in the form of »Wilderness In Eden«. Meanwhile, HAZE continue to play the occasional festival gig, and a live reunion appearance from 1998 was subsequently released as the »20th Anniversary Show« CD. Not content with the ongoing VON DANIKEN and WORLD TURTLE outfits, however, the workaholic Chris McMahon has also thrown his weight behind a couple of other local groups, SATSUMA and STRONGHEART. Does this man never get tired?

LP's
»C'est La Vie« Gabadon Records 1984
»Stoat And Bottle« Gabadon Records 1987
[Cassette version has one extra track]

12" EP's
»The Ember« Gabadon Records 1985
[All four tracks originally non-LP, all later appeared on CD reissue of »C'est La Vie«]

7" Singles
»The Night« Mushroom Records 1981
[Both tracks non-LP]
»Tunnel Vision« Gabadon Records 1986
[A-side different to album version, B-side "Shadows" only on cassette version of LP]

CD's
»In The End:1978-1988« Kinesis 1993
[Compilation release]
»Haze« Cyclops 1994
[Under the name of WORLD TURTLE]
»C'est La Vie/The Ember« Cyclops 1996
[Reissue with bonus tracks from »The Ember« EP]
»Wilderness In Eden« Cyclops 1997
[Under the name of WORLD TURTLE]
»20th Anniversary Show« Cyclops 1998
[Live release]

Exclusive Compilation Appearances
"Turn Around" on »Breakaway« LP Private 1983

Compilation Appearances
"Shadows" on »Fire In Harmony« LP Elusive Records 1985
[Different to single version]
"In The End" on »Double Exposure« Do-LP Private 1986
[Different to album version]
"The Ember" on »Sampler 1« CD Cyclops 1994
[Credited to HAZE, but is actually WORLD TURTLE version]
"Ophelia" on »Kinesis Sampler« CD Kinesis 1995

HAZZARD

John Reilly (v,g)
Gordon Muirhead (g)
Geordie King (b)
Arthur Cook (d)

The talented HAZZARD (not to be confused with German namesakes who later recorded for the Mausoleum label) were one of the minor players on the Scottish NWOBHM scene, always doing their best in terms of organising their own live appearances and attempting to share some of the glory afforded to the nation's musical heroes, but failing to achieve the same level of recognition as the more prominent HOLOCAUST or HEAVY PETTIN, for example. The foursome, based on the outskirts of Edinburgh, appear to have formed at the height of the NWOBHM explosion, deciding that they could compete quite strongly with all these English types who were suddenly the toast of the music press. Inevitably, however, their small-time activities and gigs in front of small local crowds failed to make headlines further afield, and so the ambitious members of HAZZARD were seemingly left with no option but to release a self-financed two-tracker in order to give their loyal fans something to spend their money on and (hopefully) spread their name a bit wider in the process.

HAZZARD's cheap and cheerful debut single emerged in 1981, coupling two energetic and heavy numbers in "Snake In The Grass" and "Kicked To The Ground", both bringing forth comparisons to the likes of PALI GAP, DESTROYER or the PENETRATIONS, although the slightly unconvincing vocal performance lets the side down a tad. Nevertheless, this one-off release, never issued in a picture sleeve, remains a very scarce and sought-after rarity these days, although it's also worth noting that the A-side has recently been included on the »NWOBHM Vol.7« bootleg, allowing fans to hear an example of the band's material without shelling out a fortune for the original vinyl. Clearly, the two-tracker failed to propel HAZZARD into the big league of NWOBHM hopefuls, and the disheartened bunch appear finally to have called it a day within a couple of years, much to the disappointment of their small-but-loyal fan base. Guitarist Gordon Muirhead later joined forces with an established and long-lived rock act called ASSASIN (the very same ensemble who contributed axeman Steve Blades to EXCALIBUR, incidentally), although whether or not this was the same ASSASIN who had earlier appeared on Ebony's »Metal Fatigue« compilation (with the weak "Lonely Southern Road" effort) remains open to debate.

7" Singles
»Snake In The Grass« Rammy Records 1981

Compilation Appearances
"Snake In The Grass" on »NWOBHM Vol.7« Bootleg CD 1996

HEADBANGERS

Peter French (v)
Jeff Summers (g)

Included purely for reasons of completeness, and because of the involvement of WEAPON/WILDFIRE personality Jeff Summers, the HEADBANGERS project was a hastily-assembled cash-in, a cynical ploy by the famous disco producer Biddu to make a bit of ready cash out of the NWOBHM phenomenon and the perceived rock/metal revival in general. Enlisting the vocal services of the much-travelled and extraordinarily talented Peter French (LEAFHOUND, CACTUS, ATOMIC ROOSTER etc.), two utterly unremarkable tracks were penned in about three nanoseconds and slapped down on a 7" piece of vinyl (released on the Magnet label, who were never the most credible record company) with minimal delay. The *'wittily'*-titled "Status Rock" (oh, my aching sides), on the A-side, turned out to be an entirely superfluous STATUS QUO medley (much along the lines of the similarly-conceived SPITFIRE project and their forgettable "Spitfire Boogie" effort), whereas "Headbang Boogie" was nothing more than a functional instrumental affair, performed with no sense of enthusiasm whatsoever. Fortunately, however, the movers behind the ill-conceived HEADBANGERS venture decided never to reprise this rather pointless and shambolic exercise, and the record itself has been cluttering up the bargain boxes in second-hand shops and at record fairs ever since.

7" Singles
»Status Rock« Magnet 1981

HEAVY PETTIN

Stevie 'Hamie' Hayman (v)
Punky Mendoza (g)
Gordon Bonnar (g)
Brian Waugh (b)
Gary Moat (d)

Possibly the most successful band to have emerged from Scotland during the NWOBHM era were the pride of Glasgow known as HEAVY PETTIN, a youthful act who came together in the first half of 1981 after the demise of a less-impressive bunch called WEEPER, who failed to achieve a great deal of recognition during their brief existence. HEAVY PETTIN, however, were a different matter entirely, and their first demo, recorded within a mere couple of months after their official formation, revealed them to be an extremely capable proposition with an ear for melody as well as the power which would undoubtedly be required for them to be lumped in with the rest of the NWOBHM hopefuls. In their favour, there really wasn't a great deal of serious heavy competition in Scotland at the time, although this double-edged sword also dictated that the young outfit would tend to find it extremely difficult to get gigs with other bands of a similar musical inclination, often resorting to sharing a bill with punk/indie nonentities until they were eventually able to secure headlining appearances of their own. Fortunately, however, it didn't take all that long for the promoters to be convinced, and their well-circulated demo (featuring "Love Times Love", "Hell Is Beautiful" and "Speed Kills") was soon finding its way into the hands of various influential individuals.

The group's first big break came in the spring of 1982, when their faithful demo won them the chance to record a prestigious session for the 'Friday Rock Show', with the ambitious members of HEAVY PETTIN taking their opportunity to lay down new versions of "Love Times Love", "Hell Is Beautiful", "Roll The Dice" and "Shout It Out". The session was broadcast for the first time on the 11th of June 1982, and swiftly established the precocious bunch as one of the more genuine and naturally-talented acts of the period, with their melodic brand of heavy rock/metal coming across as being in the general manner of SAXON, DEF LEPPARD or early TOBRUK. Within a remarkably short space of time, the lads were snapped up by the expanding Neat Records, who proceeded to issue the first HEAVY PETTIN single, an enjoyable affair which coupled specially-recorded versions of two of their most popular tracks, "Roll The Dice" and "Love Times Love". It turned out to be a pretty good seller for the label (who were, by this stage, starting to give their blessing to some rather more melodic acts than before), and there was every chance that the developing outfit would sign up for a full album deal in due course. Mind you, such possibilities became increasingly improbable once the major labels started waving their chequebooks under the group's collective noses.

The best offer came from Polydor, whose first two signings from the initial NWOBHM boom (A II Z and STAMPEDE) had hardly broken sales records with any of their releases, although it had at least given the label the chance to learn from their mistakes (like not skimping on studio costs by issuing shoddy live albums) and to get things right the third time around. In due course, the lads were ushered into the studio (their influential label roping in the walking perm himself, QUEEN's Brian May, to help out on the production side) to lay down extensive parts of their ever-expanding repertoire on tape, and it was soon time for the fruits of their labours to be unleashed upon the public. HEAVY PETTIN's debut album, »Lettin Loose«, was released in Europe in 1983 (an eponymous American version appeared the following year), and it represented a fairly noticeable shift towards some semi-anthemic singalongs (particularly "Rock Me" and "Love Times Love") at the expense of their more straight-ahead efforts of yore, although there were still a couple of decent, heavier inclusions, notably the upbeat "Victims Of The Night" and the well-worn "Hell Is Beautiful", whereas "Devil In Her Eyes", a top-notch example of melodic hard rock, should also be singled out for a modicum of flattery. Nevertheless, it was the more frivolous and instant tracks which tended to be trundled out as singles (»In And Out Of Love«, »Rock Me« and »Love Times Love«

all appeared in 7" and 12" forms over the ensuing months), and each of these records seem to have won favour with a considerable number of rock fans, whereupon high chart placings began coming the band's way with monotonous regularity.

All things considered, Polydor appear to have made quite a proficient job of promoting HEAVY PETTIN, and the Jocks went on to enjoy an extraordinary sequence of touring activities while signed to the label. By 1985, they had enjoyed plentiful gigs on both sides of the Atlantic with the likes of SAXON, ACCEPT, KISS and OZZY OSBOURNE, as well as taking in an extremely high-profile appearance at the Reading Festival in 1983. Eventually, however, the important matter of a second album needed to be addressed, and so the lads were soon hard at work in the studio once again. In fact, these sessions took place over a lengthy period of some six months, spanning October 1984 to April 1985, so it looks as though they might have been writing and trying out a considerable amount of fresh material all the while. »Rock Ain't Dead«, their much-anticipated follow-up to »Lettin Loose«, turned out to be a fairly polished and commercial affair, with more than a passing similarity to »Blackhearts«-era TOKYO BLADE in the main part. It was hardly an unforeseen progression for the band, and the huge chart success of the likes of EUROPE and BON JOVI (not to ignore the emergence of DEF LEPPARD as a mainstream group) made it all the more tempting for many metal acts to turn their backs on the heavier stuff and deliver something a bit more palatable for the borderline rock fans of the day. The tracks themselves tended to have little personality of their own, however, although the main exception was the excellent "Sole Survivor", the only effort from the long-player which actually made it out as a single this time around.

The new album and single were quite well-received releases, although the lads were forced to endure the inevitable 'sell-out' accusations from many of their original followers. Nevertheless, it appeared that they now had something of a brand-new fan base for which to cater, and their next move was to issue an official live video of an energetic London performance (a show which, incredibly enough, also appears to have been broadcast on British television on one or two occasions over the years) which had taken place in the summer of 1984. In the wake of the immediate promotion and touring activities which surrounded their latest album's release, however (including an appearance at the Lorelei Festival, bootlegged as the seldom-seen »Rock

Into Dead« LP), the increasingly-shy outfit appear to have gone into hiding for quite some time, leading to speculation that they might have called it a day. In due course, however, it emerged that HEAVY PETTIN were alive and well and recording another album for Polydor after all. Their much-anticipated 'comeback' gigs at the beginning of 1987 were centred around a successful series of appearances alongside the perennial MAGNUM, and details of the forthcoming third long-player swiftly began filtering through, as did worrying reports that the lads were actually giving serious thought to entering the Eurovision Song Contest! Surely not. The first evidence of their recent studio activities came with "Heaven Sent", a track included on an EP given free with 'Metal Hammer' magazine, and this was swiftly followed by the announcement that a new single, entitled »Romeo«, would soon be in the shops.

Incredibly, however, it transpired that those scurrilous rumours about Eurovision had been true after all, and the band were soon being trundled out on national television to perform their dismal "Romeo" offering at every possible opportunity. Sadly (well, maybe not), however, this monumentally bland and saccharine ballad failed to make it to the finals, although the release of the accompanying single still went ahead as planned. By this stage, however, the general public had now formed the overwhelming opinion that HEAVY PETTIN were something of a joke outfit who bore little resemblance to their earlier incarnation as a genuine rock proposition, and it was no surprise that their label began suffering a major crisis of confidence, eventually deciding not to release the third set after all. This came as a crippling blow to the lads, who rapidly concluded that there was little or no chance of regaining their previous position of much-loved rockers, and things started falling apart even before the end of the year. Punky Mendoza was particularly keen to break free, and soon went off to do his own thing in an ill-fated act called WILD, although HEAVY PETTIN continued (in name only) for a few months, drafting in new guitarist Alex Dickson to restore them to full status.

In the early months of 1988, however, it became apparent that the HEAVY PETTIN dream had finally ended, and the lads played an emotional farewell show in front of a local audience before calling it a day for good. By this stage, however, the outfit had also now lost the services of original bassist Brian Waugh, and were utilising RANSOM member Dave Leslie to plug the gap. Indeed, the fact that the classic line-up couldn't even be tempted back to play one last gig together suggested that there might have been a fair bit of acrimony among the protagonists at the time, which is a shame. In the wake of HEAVY PETTIN's split, their name disappeared (understandably enough) from the pages of the music press almost immediately, and, contrary to widespread expectations, there proved to be little or no mention of future projects from any of the former members. Nevertheless, 1989 saw the scrapped third album receiving a posthumous release *via* the FM label, who picked up the rights to the dusty master tapes and duly issued »Big Bang« (with little or no fanfare) to a largely disinterested public. Sales of the set hardly amounted to much (although I suspect that it probably made a few die-hard fans quite happy), and it was a predictably lightweight and patchy affair (more along the lines of LIONHEART than anything else), with hefty doses of poppy keyboards (courtesy of Gordon Bonnar) distancing the band even further from their heavy roots. In the end, however, the success or failure of the long-delayed album was essentially academic, given that there were (at that stage) no particularly serious moves to establish a fully-operational version of HEAVY PETTIN again.

Intriguingly, though, undaunted vocalist Hamie took himself off to the States in the early 90's, fuelling speculation that he might just be planning to resurrect his fortunes over there. Although these initial rumours of a HEAVY PETTIN Mk.II seemed to be based on flimsy foundations, however, there have indeed been genuine attempts to start over again, culminating in the release of the fairly obscure »Demos 98« sampler disc, where the central figure has evidently been assisted in the studio by some mystery associates. It's a considerable departure from the direction of old, mind you, and efforts such as "Shake", "No Substitute" and "Lie To Me" are in more of a post-grunge WARRANT/MÖTLEY CRÜE vibe (shamelessly tailored to the American market) than anything else, the frontman unveiling his best Axl Rose impersonation at times. Where they go from here is anyone's guess (there wasn't, in all honesty, a massive response to the new demos), and, since Hamie is clearly the one calling the shots these days, I guess the ball is in his court. Still, I'll only believe that the recent studio activity genuinely represents the next phase of HEAVY PETTIN's career when I see them releasing another proper album and taking to the stage once again.

LP's
»**Lettin Loose**« Polydor 1983
[Original UK issue]
»**Heavy Pettin**« Polydor 1984
[US issue of »Lettin Loose« with different title and cover]
»**Rock Ain't Dead**« Polydor 1985
[Initial copies with free songbook]
»**Big Bang**« FM Records 1989
»**Rock Into Dead**« Steel Blade Records 198?
[Live bootleg from 1985]

12" EP's
»**In And Out Of Love**« Polydor 1983
[Includes session version of non-LP track "Roll The Dice"]
»**Rock Me**« Polydor 1983
[With two versions of "Rock Me", "Shadows Of The Night" non-LP]
»**Love Times Love**« Polydor 1984
[Includes session version of "Hell Is Beautiful"]
»**Sole Survivor**« Polydor 1985
[A-side different to album version, "Crazy" only on CD version of album]
»**Romeo**« Polydor 1987
["City Girl" non-LP]

7" Singles
»**Roll The Dice**« Neat 1982
[A-side non-LP, B-side "Love Times Love" different to album version]
»**In And Out Of Love**« Polydor 1983
[A-side different to album version]
»**Rock Me**« Polydor 1983
[A-side different to album version, B-side "Shadows Of The Night" non-LP]
»**Love Times Love**« Polydor 1984
»**Sole Survivor**« Polydor 1985
[A-side different to album version, B-side "Crazy" only on CD version of album]
»**Romeo**« Polydor 1987
[A-side different to album version]

Shaped Picture Discs
»**Love Times Love**« Polydor 1984

Promotional Releases
»**In And Out Of Love**« Polydor 1984
[US radio promo 12" in special sleeve]

CD's
»**Heavy Pettin**« Polydor 198?
[US-only release of first album]
»**Rock Ain't Dead**« Polydor 1985
[With extra track "Crazy"]
»**Big Bang**« FM Records 1989

Mini-CD's
»**Demos 98**« Struggler Music 1998

Compilation Appearances
"Heaven Sent" on »The 2nd Wave Of New British Metal« 7" EP Private 1987
[Free with 'Metal Hammer' magazine]

HELL

Dave Halliday (v, g)
Kev Bower (g, k)
Tony Speakman (b)
Tim Bowler (d)

Anyone who would seek to chronicle the development of black metal and sundry occult dabblings in the UK's music scene would have little problem in finding a suitable starting point (BLACK SABBATH, BLACK WIDOW), and would no doubt make the transition to good old VENOM with little or no effort, although they might be left scratching their heads a bit after that. Could it be that VENOM (and, to a lesser extent, WITCHFYNDE) really were the only British recording artists with a genuinely nigrescent outlook during the early 80's? Well, no. Fair enough, the likes of ANGEL WITCH, DEMON, WITCHFINDER GENERAL and the DESOLATION ANGELS (to name but a few) all flirted with the dark side, but there were a handful of other small-time acts with somewhat more pronounced leanings towards such unholy naughtiness, notably PAGAN ALTAR, ROBESPIERRE, WIDOW (the Merseyside mob as opposed to the fly-by-night Surrey group) and the godawful STORMCRY (none of whom got to the vinyl stage originally), plus Nottinghamshire's own HELL, a hugely popular regional attraction who initially gravitated together at the beginning of 1982, following the recent demise of frontman Dave Halliday's previous outfit, RACE AGAINST TIME. Whereas the latter had been rather more of a traditional and unremarkable metal proposition, however, the impenitent name of HELL represented an ensemble with an altogether different lyrical outlook and musical direction.

Halliday was able to attract a supporting cast of regional scenesters to the project, including erstwhile PARALEX guitarist Kev Bower, one-time OVERDRIVE sticksman Tim Bowler and capable bassist Tony Speakman, who, in addition to a fleeting stint with the aforementioned PARALEX, had also worked with one of the many varieties of TOKYO ROSE. The group quickly established themselves on the Midlands rock scene, and soon got in on the act as far as live appearances were concerned, sharing bills with other local hopefuls such as RADIUM and winning over many an audience with their theatrical image and quirky, heavyweight material. Within a matter of months, they had already amassed a fairly impressive collection of self-penned compositions, the majority of which (for

example, "The Disposer Supreme", "Blasphemy And The Master" and "Macbeth") exposed a fundamental connection with the occult, historical unpleasantness and sundry goings-on 'downstairs'. In due course, selected numbers were demoed, and the likes of "Where Angels Fear To Tread" and "Intense Is The Sense Of Doom" were pretty representative examples of the band's music, their forte being the creation of lengthy, technical and slightly disturbing tracks with more than a hint of MERCYFUL FATE (with equivalent vocal contortions), and some occasional similarities to British acts such as MARQUIS DE SADE, DEEP SWITCH and KRAKEN. Frankly, however, the probability of getting a major label deal with this kind of music was exactly zero, and even the likes of Neat and Ebony failed to see any particular reason to sign HELL, leaving the lads with no option but to go it alone by releasing a self-financed single in the second half of 1983.

Notwithstanding Ebony's lack of commitment in terms of a proper deal, however, the quartet's debut single was recorded at the label's own studio facility, with experienced producer Darryl Johnston lending a hand on the knob-twiddling front. Wisely, the members of HELL had apparently made a conscious decision to chop some of their numbers down to size by this time, and neither of the featured tracks were to exceed the five minute mark. Having said that, the material wasn't the strongest they had to offer, and the inclusion of an instrumental ("Deathsquad") as part of a double A-sided single was a pretty pointless exercise, despite being a proficiently-played composition (with some interesting and atmospheric keyboard sections in the best traditions of WHITE SPIRIT) in its own right. The reverse was a slightly more worthy effort, however, the lengthily-titled "Save Us From Those Who Would Save Us" representing a bitter and frenzied tirade against various self-styled guardians of morality, who have, since time immemorial, sought to control the populace through censorship and religious persecution. In spite of the inevitable savaging from 'Kerrang' ('hilariously inept amateur hour demonic ramblings'), the record (never issued in a picture sleeve) proceeded to sell in eminently respectable quantities at the time (the first batch had been pretty much snapped up by their local following within a couple of months, and so it went to a second pressing almost immediately), and HELL's two-tracker is now regarded as a highly-valued rarity by NWOBHM collectors. It was a pretty decent start, and the lads proceeded to capitalise on their initial success by assembling a promotional video in an ambitious attempt to spread their name even further.

After the band had touted around their single and demo tapes to the labels (in between further periods of regional gigging), HELL finally appeared to have made a breakthrough towards the end of 1984, when the outfit were reported as having signed an album contract with Mausoleum. For some reason, however, this projected deal never yielded any vinyl product whatsoever, the explanation probably lying in the label's financial problems, not to mention the band's subsequent difficulties in maintaining a stable line-up. Whatever the story, HELL certainly began to lose their way during 1985 (despite some useful support slots with the likes of URIAH HEEP), and were forced to endure the departure of axeman Kev Bower (another unwitting victim of female sophistry) early the following year. Still, the remaining members deduced that a replacement was unnecessary, and proceeded to market themselves as a trio from that point onwards. A variety of new material was showcased for whichever labels showed any interest, and the likes of "Plague And Fire" and "Land Of The Living Dead" showed a move towards slightly more accessible and less dramatic material, all quite similar to early DEMON at times. Sadly, it appeared that the vicissitudes of time were no longer favouring the activities of HELL, and the lads struggled to find the strength to continue. Significantly, however, an emergent bunch of youngsters, heavily influenced by HELL from an early stage, were now establishing themselves on the rock scene. That group was SABBAT, and it soon became apparent that they were both willing and capable of taking over the mantle of regional *'occult metal heroes'*, should their idols ever decide to discard it.

Even by 1986, the precocious SABBAT were gaining ground at a remarkable pace, and it looked as though the newcomers would soon supersede the fading HELL, whose chance appeared to have disappeared completely by this stage. In fact, both acts actually appeared together at a large local concert a few months later, sharing the bill with DEUCE and THUNDERCHILDE. In spite of this event being one of the most prestigious appearances in HELL's career, it was also one of their last. Things were now falling apart pretty dramatically, and the departure of bassist Tony Speakman to join forces with the offbeat S.Y.Z. (see separate entry) must have been the final straw. Although various members of the band subsequently went on to other projects (including the melodic LIFE AFTER), the end of HELL came in tragic circumstances at the beginning of 1987, when Dave Halliday took his own life, setting a chilling precedent for black metal suicides. I'll leave the last word to SABBAT's Andy Sneap, speaking after a charity gig organised in honour of the late Halliday: *'We are heavily influenced by HELL and don't mind admitting it. The singer even taught me how to play guitar! We're not a deliberate copycat of HELL in any way though. They were a great band and it's a mystery to me why they never got anywhere. To be compared to them we don't mind in the least, we would take it more as an honour than anything.'* (Ref: Metal Forces No.25, 1987).

7" Singles

»Save Us From Those Who Would Save Us«
Deadly Weapon Records 1983

HELLANBACH

Jimmy Brash (v)
Dave Patton (g)
Kev Charlton (b)
Steve Walker (d)

Tyneside's popular HELLANBACH first started touting their wares around the North East at the tail end of the 70's, and rapidly established themselves as ever-dependable crowd-pleasers. In due course, media attention would focus on their alleged fascination with VAN HALEN, and snide comments along these lines (the band often being referred to as *'Halen-bach'*) would become *de rigueur* in articles of the day. In all honesty, though, this was grossly unfair and did the likeable group a great disservice. Aside from some overly-flashy guitar work, there was little to connect the foursome with the Californians, so their name (which is, rather obviously, a corruption of *'hell and back'*) might have been something of a liability in retrospect. As with various outfits in the region, HELLANBACH took advantage of the recording and pressing facilities at Guardian Studios in Durham, and it wasn't long before they had a 7" EP in their hands, pressed in fairly small quantities (comparatively few with the band-photo picture sleeve) to sell and distribute for promotional purposes. The four-tracker was a very effective debut, with "Out To Get You" and "Let's Get This Show On The Road" being upbeat, hard-rocking efforts, while "Nobody's Fool" and "Light Of The World" were more restrained offerings. In general, there was more than a hint of local heroes (and label-mates) MYTHRA and HOLLOW GROUND, although there were additional comparisons with acts such as SHYWOLF, HIGH TREASON or SAM THUNDER. Nowadays, their vinyl debut is a highly collectable piece (either with or without the sleeve), although not quite in the same league as HOLLOW GROUND or SATAN.

Hot on the heels of this early release, the lads set about writing new material (a fair proportion of which would be demoed throughout 1981) and reinforcing their growing status in the live environment. In the event, it wasn't until 1982 that some further vinyl exposure came about (HELLANBACH bassist Kev Charlton was, by this time, earning a bit of ready cash on the side by acting as one of FIST's roadies), when the quartet began a long-lasting relationship with Neat Records. First, the outfit contributed the energetic "All Systems Go" (not a million miles away from SWEET SAVAGE's "Killing Time") to the label's »One Take No Dubs« sampler EP, following it up with an appearance on the »60 Minutes Plus« cassette, this time with "All The Way". This brace of new compositions was sufficient to convince Neat that the band had genuine potential, and they were rapidly herded into the studio to lay down an album's worth of material. Recorded at the tail end of 1982 and issued early the following year, »Now Hear This« was a confident enough debut LP (some of their earlier material had clearly been given a major overhaul), featuring a handful of memorable, catchy numbers in the form of "Dancin'" and "Kick It Out", although I imagine that a few fans were perplexed by the inclusion of the group's interpretation of "Everybody Wants To Be A Cat" from Disney's 'The Aristocats' film! Strange sense of humour, some people.

Numerous HELLANBACH gigs followed on the back of the album's release, including well-attended support slots with the likes of the immensely-popular RAVEN, plus many headlining appearances of their own. With their debut long-player having been a successful release in terms of sales figures and public reaction, a follow-up was a foregone conclusion. Mind you, there was a fair old wait for the second LP, and the lads certainly took their time before going back into the studio. Still their second full-length effort finally put in an appearance in late 1984, this being the first piece of HELLANBACH vinyl to feature the talents of recently-recruited drummer Barry Hopper, formerly with now-deceased local favourites MYTHRA. »The Big H« consisted of a markedly more accessible and relaxed set of compositions in the general manner of ACE LANE or TARGET UK, although the likes of "When All Is Said And Done" and "Bandits Run" were highly enjoyable efforts all the same. This time, the cover version came in the form of ELTON JOHN's ever-popular "Saturday Night's All Right For Fighting", while the band displayed their quirky, irreverent side once again with the STRAY CATS-influenced "Daddy Dig Those Cats", a track which isn't to be taken too seriously…I hope.

Sadly, the latest vinyl release didn't manage to elevate the persevering bunch from their perpetual standing of local heroes to widespread national popularity, and it would appear that the lads soon began to grow weary of their humble status. The split was something of an inevitability, and the musicians seem to have drifted apart for good by the second half of the decade, having finally realised that their big chance had now surely gone for ever. Most of HELLANBACH's ex-members have, however, maintained some level of involvement in the North East club scene, with Kev Charlton, Dave Patton and Barry Hopper all having played, at one time or another, in the still-functioning BESSIE AND THE ZINC BUCKETS, a knockabout bunch of utter lunatics (with mercifully few aspirations of global domination) formed by erstwhile MYTHRA stalwart Maurice Bates. Dave Patton was also a key character in the highly-touted HOLY COW venture of the early 90's, a female-fronted bunch who performed a traditional brand of raunchy rock, although the latter seem to have ground to a sudden halt after releasing just one mini-album in 1994.

LP's
»Now Hear This« Neat 1983
[UK issue in black sleeve]
»Now Hear This« Roadrunner 1983
[Dutch issue in white sleeve]
»The Big H« Neat 1984

7" EP's
»Out To Get You« Guardian 1980
["Out To Get You" non-LP, "Let's Get This Show On The Road" different to album version, "Light Of The World" reworked as "Look At Me" on »Now Hear This«. "Nobody's Fool" reworked as "Little Darlin'" on »The Big H«, although labels still credit latter track as "Nobody's Fool"]

Compilation Appearances
"All Systems Go" on »One Take No Dubs« 12" EP Neat 1982
[Different to album version]
"All The Way" on »60 Minutes Plus« Cassette Neat 1982/CD Teichiku 1992 + »All Hell Let Loose« LP Neat 1983
[Different to album version]
"Dancin'" on »Metal Battle« LP Neat 1983/Roadrunner 1983
"All Systems Go" on »Metal Masters« 4-CD Box Castle Communications 1993

HELLRAZER

Norm Piechura (v,g)
Bonkka Bailey (b)
Nick Mullaney (d)

London's HELLRAZER are best known to collectors through their »Made of Metal« 7" from 1987, which would probably have been considered too late an issue to warrant inclusion in this volume, were it not for the fact that a considerably earlier (and much scarcer) single also exists. Mention has been made elsewhere that JAGUAR's Paul Merrell established a 'glam band' called HELLRAZER (who were believed to have made it to the vinyl stage) after the former's disintegration, although this pattern of events isn't totally accurate. Merrell was indeed briefly involved (he didn't form the outfit, though) after parting company with his earlier STORMTROOPER venture,

although he doesn't seem to have appeared on their double A-sided effort from 1981. Whether or not Merrell contributed to the four track demo tape released in the same year is, however, unknown at this time. The frontman later explained the situation in a taped conversation: 'In 1981 I joined a band in London called HELLRAZER, but they were more into the glam and make-up stuff, and I wasn't into that. I was with them for about three months and when I left, the guitarist pulled a knife on me, which was quite frightening, but I managed to get out all right!' (Ref: Private interview, 1984). I'm sure he felt far more at home with the peace-loving members of JAGUAR...

HELLRAZER's aforementioned debut two-tracker from 1981 (for which no picture sleeve is currently known to exist), coupling "The Devil's Got The Deeds To Rock And Roll" (which must surely go down as one of the most unwieldy song titles in this entire book) and "Glam Girl", is certainly something of an oddity, the former effort combining fairly normal guitar/vocal sections with some bizarre, squawking vocal emanations that wouldn't seem out of place in a 'Monty Python' sketch, while the latter is just a completely tuneless and unsynchronised mess. Overall, a bit of an unmitigated disaster, really. I

guess 'glam' would almost be a semi-appropriate label for this utter shambles, probably more SACRED ALIEN than SILVERWING, although nowhere near as competent as either. I reckon it might have been a better idea to learn how to play those instruments and write a few vaguely coherent tracks before bothering to lay down a single, lads. A minimal number of copies of this vinyl shocker have ever surfaced, although, as you can probably gather, it's not exactly an essential item for the majority of NWOBHM collectors.

Perhaps unwisely, the persevering trio continued to produce demo tapes into the mid-80's (by which time they had adopted the regulation glam aliases, namely Punky Puchino, Nikki Ritz and Linzy Rox), although tracks such as "Shout Hey" and "Space Girl" represented little more than sub-WRATHCHILD piffle. Evidently, the outfit subsequently decided that their image required to be toughened up a bit, and so, by the time »Made Of Metal« (B-side "Hooligan") was unleashed upon the public (six full years after their first vinyl foray), they had adopted a full-scale 'leather and studs' persona (fraudulently promoting the record as being their debut release and hoping nobody would rumble them), with a harsher metal sound (comically over-emphasised on the sleeve by a large Union Jack flag emblazoned with the slogan 'British Metal') to accompany their new-found identity. It was certainly a slight improvement, vaguely reminiscent of a more lightweight WARFARE, but it still offered nothing original enough to raise HELLRAZER above the massed ranks of hopeful metal bands of the period, and they probably (wisely) decided to call it a day after acknowledging the growing popularisation of the thrash movement in the UK in the late 80's.

7" Singles
»The Devil's Got The Deeds To Rock And Roll« Alias Smith and Jones Records 1981
»Made Of Metal« Speed Machine Records 1987

Compilation Appearances
"Made Of Metal" on »The Metal Collection Vol.I« LP Ebony 1986

HELL'S BELLES

Paul Quigley (v)
Pooch Purtill (g)
Gareth Holder (b)
Spiv (d)

The largely-overlooked HELL'S BELLES project (not to be confused with a later MADAM X offshoot) initially got off the ground in the early months of 1984, with the band soon finding their way into the gig guides, which saw them making many trips to various popular rock venues in the capital. Even so, it wasn't until late the following year that their sheer hard graft and a well-worn demo tape (featuring such original compositions as "Long Legs", "Hell's Belles" and "If It Don't Make Your Ears Bleed") finally won the quartet a deal with the Raw Power label, a subsidiary of Castle whose speciality seemed to be reissuing material from the back catalogues of rather more high-profile outfits. With HELL'S BELLES featuring a quirky hotchpotch of scenesters from both the rock and punk camps (notably Pooch Purtill, one of many axemen who had passed through the ranks of DISCHARGE, and vocalist Paul Quigley, a fly-by-night veteran of BRONZ), casual observers might reasonably have anticipated a rather raucous hybrid of the two styles, possibly evoking memories of the long-departed LIGHTNING RAIDERS. In fact, this wasn't an entirely safe assumption after all, as a fanzine review of a small-time gig at The Wellington in London subsequently intimated that their material of choice wasn't particularly innovative: *'Four black clad men took to the boards and proceeded to blast out a set of fast, powerful and uninspired heavy metal.'* (Ref: A Dose Of The Heavies, Issue 2, May 1986). Hmmm, all that talk of dull metal from *'men in black'* sounds strangely familiar…

With the group having recorded a fair bit of material for the benefit of Raw Power by the beginning of 1986 (a couple of their earliest efforts also appeared on two of Castle's myriad compilations), their label had to decide how best to sell their new acquisitions to the public, and they chose to start off by introducing HELL'S BELLES with a three track EP. This slice of vinyl represented a fairly strong debut, featuring a couple of relatively capable and memorable compositions in the shape of "Barricades" and "Storm Break Loose" (which would both appear on their forthcoming album), in addition to the exclusive (not to mention lengthily-titled) "If It Don't Make Your Ears Bleed (It Ain't Rock'n'Roll)". Reviews were decidedly mixed (people soon latched on to the quartet's quirky image, and offered some not-terribly-accurate comparisons with ROGUE MALE), but the full-length release went ahead as planned, the eponymous LP hitting the shops a short time later. While it was a competent enough effort in terms of both songwriting and musicianship (along the general lines of mid-period TOKYO BLADE or MAINEEAXE), »Hell's Belles« wasn't a ground-breaking release by any means, and the majority of tracks were enjoyable enough without being the most memorable selections ever committed to vinyl. Still, it wasn't formulaic by any means, and there was a fair bit of variety on display, although it's hard to tell whether this was a genuine show of diversity, or merely a desperate attempt to please as many punters as possible.

In any case, the group's inclinations veered erratically from the powerful (notably the energetic pairing of "Overload" and "Storm Break Loose") to the mindless, anthemic singalongs of "Strangelove" and "Dirty Girls", something which may have been just too much of a contrast for many fans. Occupying the middle ground were well-written efforts such as the superb "Looks Like Love", "Long Legs" and "Screaming For Mercy", highly listenable numbers (despite the hackneyed titles) which, to their credit, didn't try too hard to be especially heavy or original. HELL'S BELLES had also been prepared to experiment with some strategic keyboard sections (courtesy of much-travelled guest musician Lyndsey Bridgewater, who had worked with both BUDGIE and OZZY OSBOURNE in the past) on the long-player, although these weren't particularly prominent or overpowering. The intrepid outfit had clearly set out to develop a distinctive brand of raunchy metal (some of their ideas worked better than others, admittedly), and they made a pretty good fist at beefing up some of their tuneful selections with unexpectedly substantial riffs (a device also employed by RANKELSON and Nottinghamshire's DEUCE, for example), although these ambitious attempts to marry the worlds of melodic rock and power metal appear largely to have flown over the heads of the listening public.

All things considered, the plucky HELL'S BELLES gave the world a pretty good run for its money, although their valiant attempts to win the hearts of the rock community seem to have gone unrewarded in terms of media attention and record sales in the first instance, and it looks as though the project ground to a halt within a relatively short space of time. To be truthful, there seemed to be a pretty major conflict between the outfit's semi-glam image (which, as DEALER and RANKELSON also found to their cost, served to alienate many of the straight-ahead metal fans) and their forceful musical style, so a couple of sessions with the image consultants might have been a prudent idea. Mind you, if the metalheads were antagonised by their look, then the rapidly-dwindling clique of traditional glam enthusiasts would have been equally unimpressed by the music itself, so the group probably failed to appeal directly to any significant section of the rock community. It clearly wasn't what people were looking for in 1986, but matters probably wouldn't have improved even if they had decided to stick it out, as they would soon have found themselves competing against all the thrash upstarts and sleazy wannabes, so it would have necessitated a major change in style merely to keep up with the pack. If there was ever a definitive example of built-in obsolescence, therefore, it undoubtedly came in the shape of the ill-fated HELL'S BELLES.

LP's
»Hell's Belles« Raw Power 1986

12" EP's
»Barricades« Raw Power 1986
["If It Don't Make Your Ears Bleed (It Ain't Rock'n'Roll)" non-LP]

Exclusive Compilation Appearances
"Wastin' Away" on »Metal Killers Kollection II« Do-LP Castle Communications 1986

Compilation Appearances
"Hell's Belles" on »Metal Killers Kollection I« Do-LP Castle Communications 1985 + »Metal Killers Kollection« CD Castle Communications 1991
"If It Don't Make Your Ears Bleed (It Ain't Rock'n'Roll)" on »Rock Legends Volume 2« CD Castle Communications 1992
"Long Legs" on »Rock Legends Volume 4« CD Castle Communications 1992

HERETIC

Dave Clarke (v)
Karl Bruce (g)
Steve Macdougall (g)
Martin Andrew (b, k)
Paul Thurlston (d)

First brought to public attention *via* the inclusion of their excellent "In Time" offering on an obscure compilation called »The Bridge Album«, the latter featuring bands who regularly frequented Bridge Studios on the outskirts of London, Surrey's HERETIC (not to be confused with the later American outfit who recorded for the Metal Blade label) were a group who (initially, at least) showed a great deal of potential. Their aforementioned composition, a heavy, atmospheric number slightly reminiscent of some of ANGEL WITCH's Killerwatt-era offerings, was undoubtedly (even in the company of the likes of ROUGH CUT, TAKEAWAY, NORTH STAR and the pre-LYADRIVE act known as TEMPEST RIDE) one of the stand-out contributions to the sampler, and this surely set the stage for a pretty healthy future. Mind you, up until this point, the quintet had apparently struggled to maintain a particularly stable line-up, although the lads had still managed to tour with considerable success, developing an especially strong following around London and the Midlands.

After this compilation appearance (sadly, HERETIC weren't offered the chance to emulate NORTH STAR and LYADRIVE by laying down their own single for Bridge Records) came the obligatory deal-seeking demo (circulated to various parties in the industry at some point in 1983), which was swiftly followed by an offer (from the diverse Thunderbolt label) to sponsor HERETIC's first proper vinyl release. In due course, their »Burnt At The Stake« four-tracker was recorded and pressed up (in a rather fetching sleeve), by which time the group featured yet another revised line-up consisting of Martin Andrew (b,v), Karl Bruce (g), Stu Hurwood (g) and Spick Taylor (d). Martin Andrew's vocals, sadly, turned out to be rather more limited than those of his capable predecessor, although "Water Of Vice" was still a fairly strong opener in the vein of some of DEALER's later material. On the other hand, "Keep On Telling Those Lies" is a bizarre singalong effort (strongly evocative of SLADE's "Cum On Feel The Noize") which seems hopelessly out of context here. Matters become even more confused over on side two, and the passable "Fever Of Love" has a distinct SPIDER/VARDIS-style boogie tinge to it, whereas "Watch Me Grow" is merely an average melodic rocker which fails to leave all that much of an impression. To be honest, this was a pretty bizarre EP which enjoyed only a marginal relationship with the NWOBHM archetype.

All things considered, the HERETIC 12" was a hopelessly perplexing release in every sense, and the group did themselves no favours whatsoever by flitting constantly between unrelated musical styles. Furthermore, the outfit's sacrilegious moniker and the EP's inexplicably gruesome »Burnt At The Stake« title were completely at odds with the musical contents, so I suspect that a few unsuspecting fans got a surprise when they shelled out for a copy of this one. It's a shame that such a talented group deserted their earlier direction in favour of this shambles (no doubt all those constant personnel changes played a major part in their downfall), and I suspect that the record-buying public studiously avoided the EP in droves, leaving the dejected members of HERETIC with no option but to call it a day within a year or so. Guitarist Stu Hurwood, incidentally, went on to join forces with the relocated SPIDER in the wake of Sniffa's post-»Raise The Banner« departure in the second half of 1986, although it would appear that his contribution to the rapidly-disintegrating act was pretty minimal.

12" EP's
»Burnt At The Stake« Thunderbolt 1984

Exclusive Compilation Appearances
"In Time" on »The Bridge Album« LP Bridge Records 1982

Compilation Appearances
"Watch Me Grow" on »A Bolt From The Black« LP Thunderbolt 1984

HERITAGE

Darryl Cheswick (v)
Jeff Birkby (g)
Steve Johnson (g)
Tony Hynd (b)
Phil Gilbert (d)

Following in the well-worn footsteps of fellow hopefuls such as WITCHFYNDE, BROOKLYN and GASKIN, ambitious Yorkshire five-piece HERITAGE wasted little or no time dithering around before coming to the conclusion that Mansfield's Rondelet Records would stand a pretty good chance of turning them into global superstars. After recording a suitably-impressive demo and beating a path to the aforementioned company's welcoming door, the ensemble were soon being groomed for success, their label initially testing the water with a one-off single (issued at the height of the NWOBHM influx in 1981) to gauge the public's reaction to the music of their new signings. The HERITAGE boys debuted with a very strong 7" release (featuring an impressive twin-guitar attack) coupling the aggressive "Misunderstood" with the rather more restrained "Strange Place To Be", evoking such acts as FUGITIVE, TORTURE, SOLDIER and early DEF LEPPARD. Realising they were onto a good thing, Rondelet immediately stumped up the readies for the lads to record a full-length effort, something which was to prove a somewhat protracted process due to the subsequent comings and goings in the HERITAGE camp.

Indeed, such was the extent of these personnel reshuffles that, by the time their »Remorse Code« (a clever title, but the DESPERATE BICYCLES got there first) long-player appeared the following year, only guitarist Steve Johnson now remained from the original line-up. Joining him in the revamped outfit were Paul 'Fasker' Johnson on bass (Steve's brother, roped in to help out at short notice), drummer Pete Halliday and guitarist Steve Barratt (although some have speculated that this was actually former GEDDES AXE stalwart Andy Barrott, either miscredited or using a pseudonym). With the three guitarists now sharing vocal duties, the band's style had moved into rather more commercial territory, and there's more than a hint of the likes of TRESPASS and PRAYING MANTIS present in some numbers. It's a patchy album, but good in parts, such as the SAVAGE-soundalike "Attack Attack" and the reasonably heavy "Need You Today". Elsewhere, however, there are far too many lightweight inclusions and what appear to be semi-finished compositions fleshed out with lengthy guitar solos; all in all, an extraordinarily disappointing effort from a group who were capable of much greater things. Not only was HERITAGE's sole album a rather unmemorable performance, it also proved to be their final release. With Rondelet foundering under the weight of severe financial liabilities, the label eventually went into liquidation, and their dwindling roster (BROOKLYN had almost certainly given up the ghost beforehand) were left to fend for themselves.

While WITCHFYNDE successfully moved to a new European home, however, GASKIN and HERITAGE didn't last the distance, and both had more or less called it a day by the tail end of 1983. Pete Halliday later re-emerged in a venture called NIGHTRUN (alongside former DEF LEPPARD guitarist Pete Willis), a quintet who managed to release a single entitled »Crime Of Passion« in 1987 before evolving into the relatively successful ROADHOUSE. The Johnson brothers, meanwhile, teamed up with Gary Barden in the initial version of STATETROOPER, but both were soon to be made redundant in favour of various ex-WILDFIRE personnel when the new project was undergoing a period of restructuring. Fasker then proceeded to hook up with the mighty SAXON (replacing Steve Dawson) for a year or two, before eventually reuniting with his brother in the much-fêted U.S.I. project, a melodic rock outfit who recorded a popular session for the 'Friday Rock Show' in 1989 but split in the early 90's without ever having made it to the vinyl stage. There were, incidentally, a couple of local HERITAGE reunion shows at around this time, but details of the participants are extremely sketchy. As with much of Rondelet's back catalogue, HERITAGE's album recently benefitted from a CD reissue at the hands of British Steel, available for around half the price of the scarce vinyl original.

LP's
»Remorse Code« Rondelet 1982

7" Singles
»Strange Place To Be« Rondelet 1981
[A-side different to album version, B-side "Misunderstood" non-LP]

CD's
»Remorse Code« British Steel 1996
[With two bonus tracks]

Compilation Appearances
"Misunderstood" on »NWOBHM Vol.2« Bootleg CD 1992 + »N.W.O.B.H.M. Metal Rarities Vol.1« CD British Steel 1996
"Strange Place To Be" on »N.W.O.B.H.M. Metal Rarities Vol.1« CD British Steel 1996
"Attack Attack" on »Rock Out!« Do-CD Emporio 1996
"Remorse Code" on »Rock Out!« Do-CD Emporio 1996

H.G.B.

Henry Gorman (v, g)
Ronnie Garrity (b)
Danny Gisbey (k)
John Grant (d)

Resplendent in its rather pointless fold-out sleeve picturing the group members, the »Chase The Night Away« 7" by H.G.B. (the HENRY GORMAN BAND, to give them their full title) is a catchy piece of rock which happily fits in to the more melodic end of the NWOBHM spectrum inhabited by hopefuls such as TRADER, ANGEL STREET and TRACK 4, each of whom probably owed a far greater musical debt to the likes of BAD COMPANY and the EAGLES than to BLACK SABBATH and JUDAS PRIEST. Nevertheless, the nominated A-side is immensely listenable, although I *defy* you to hear it all the way through without once thinking of the theme to 'The Rockford Files', since the keyboard work is absolutely identical (all we need now is a NWOBHM version of the theme to 'The Flashing Blade' and I could die happy). Sadly, the reverse (the *'wittily'*-titled "Keep Off The Grass") is a much more lightweight affair, although you might enjoy it if you're a fan of the DOOBIE BROTHERS. I suspect that this particular ensemble were almost certainly from the West of Scotland (a reasonable amount of supporting evidence comes in the shape of the members' names, the fact that they regularly played in Glasgow in the early 80's and the observation that most known copies of the single have turned up North of the border), but I suppose they could have been from elsewhere. Even so, they stood very little chance of breaking through and achieving widespread popularity when pitted against the more energetic upstarts of the NWOBHM influx, so I guess these musicians probably called it a day within a couple of years, although they may have maintained some links with the small-time regional club scene in order to pay the bills. This unassuming vinyl artefact certainly doesn't rank among the upper echelons of NWOBHM collectables, but it's worth picking up if it's a cheapie.

7" Singles
»Chase The Night Away« Backshop Records 1981?

HIGH RISK

Steve Gibbs (v)
Malcolm MacDonald (g)
Forbes Cook (b)
Nick Beel (k)
Russell Payne (d)

The Sussex-based five-piece known as HIGH RISK were hardly one of the more prominent names on the South Cost rock scene at the outset, having started out in around 1980, although they soon (after a few personnel reshuffles, including the recruitment of one-time JODEY sticksman Russell Payne) managed to swing a deal with the local Airship label, leading to the release of a three track EP in 1981. The record itself is quite strongly affiliated with certain heavy acts from the 70's, notably LED ZEPPELIN, THIN LIZZY and CREAM, although the music is performed with something of an original edge, bringing forth a few handy comparisons with NWOBHM-era contemporaries such as CRACKED MIRROR, PHOENIX RISING or labelmates VOLTZ. "Must Be Crazy" is the most capable of the numbers on display, although the highly distinctive vocal style of Steve Gibbs is something you'll either love or hate (probably the latter option), while "I Go To Pieces" and "Rich Kid" were fairly unmemorable, mid-paced efforts, even if the last-mentioned does have some reasonable guitar work and a decent DAWNWATCHER-style keyboard section. The three-tracker was pressed in pretty small quantities (and there wasn't a picture sleeve), but sales appear to have been quite disappointing, even although the band were a reasonably popular local attraction.

Since their debut release was overlooked by the majority of the nation's rock fans, the protagonists ultimately decided that they needed to spice up their act somewhat, and HIGH RISK soon focused their attention on developing a rather theatrical image and over-the-top stage show, presumably trying to muscle in on THUNDERSTICK's territory. By their own admission, they took their lead from the likes of ALICE COOPER and the TUBES, bringing in the odd chainsaw, electric chair and spot of fake blood to liven things up, which, predictably, led to a number of venues refusing to book the outfit. Undeterred, they still managed to get onto a few bills by operating under assumed identities (some of these including CONTRABAND, MUSE and PTARMIGAN), and further attracted a bit of publicity by hiring up to three dancers/backing singers (female, needless to say) in order to increase the visual impact of their debauched performances. Along the way, they broke in a new drummer, Kev Robey, who had previously bashed the skins for indie nonentities ALL THAT'S FICTION, an act who had contributed a couple of numbers to Airship's »Seaside Rock« compilation. With HIGH RISK now back in business, they began sending out new demo tapes (in rather more of an accessible style) and hoping for some favourable press coverage.

Remarkably, their efforts seemed to have been rewarded by around 1983, when they started to win a few mentions in the likes of 'Kerrang', who reviewed a HIGH RISK gig in fairly praiseworthy terms and who also featured the outfit in their 'Armed And Ready' section, where the quintet were identified as a group to watch. They also received an offer to appear on local television, where the band took the opportunity to showcase a newer effort entitled "Finger On The Pulse". Nevertheless, the anticipated major-label interest ultimately failed to materialise in the long term, and the dejected ensemble (who had recently undertaken a handful of regional support slots with popular acts such as GIRLSCHOOL, and were starting to venture further afield in their quest for gigs and coverage) began to lose heart. By the middle of the decade, after a couple of earlier threats to call it a day had failed to come to anything, HIGH RISK finally threw in the towel for good, with bassist Forbes Cook moving over to the unsuccessful TRUFFLE offshoot known as NO FIXED ABODE. Apart from that, however, it was the last anyone heard from any of these particular musicians, who left just the one (very scarce, but not highly-rated at the time of writing) slice of vinyl as their legacy.

7" EP's
»**Must Be Crazy**« Airship Records 1981

HIGH TREASON

Barry Fearon (v)
John Pritchard (g)
Malcolm Scott (g)
Larry Barbato (b)
Gary Scarbrow (d)

The excellent HIGH TREASON were yet another product of the fertile rock/metal scene which sprang up almost overnight in the Home Counties in the late 70's, and the outfit soon established themselves as firm local favourites, sharing many a stage with other established acts such

as BLEAK HOUSE, CLIENTELLE and TOAD THE WET SPROCKET, for example. By 1980, after the obligatory series of small-time, regional gigs, the band had already made up their minds to get in on the NWOBHM explosion, and soon got around to issuing their own two-tracker on the Burlington label, a subsidiary of the folk-dominated concern known as Plant Life Records. As most serious collectors will surely be aware, this release represents a true classic of the genre, with "Saturday Night Special" (also featured on the »NWOBHM Vol.2« bootleg CD) being an incredibly energetic and catchy number in the general style of RICOCHET or BOLLWEEVIL, with a decidedly THIN LIZZY edge to the compelling guitar work. "Waste My Love", on the flipside, isn't quite as intense, and is slightly more in the AURORA or ENERGY scheme of things, but it still stands head and shoulders above the vast majority of independent rock/metal efforts of the period. Only a handful of copies of the single were issued with that elusive sleeve depicting a hangman's noose, and examples of the latter have been known to fetch extraordinarily high prices on the very few occasions that they've come up for sale in recent times. The sleeveless issue commands a considerably lower price, especially with the group having released a quantity of unsold copies onto the market in the early 90's.

Their vinyl debut set the aspiring band well on the road to success, and it was then back to the clubs to promote themselves further while they planned their next move. With the musicians making good use of Quest Studios in Luton (as did a great number of emergent hopefuls from the area), they were subsequently to benefit from inclusion on the little-known and seriously rare »Quest Tapes« sampler of local acts, released by Quest Records themselves in 1982. Annoyingly, however, HIGH TREASON seemed to represent the region's metal contingent in its entirety on this occasion, and the remaining obscurities featured were all sorely lacking in talent, the record therefore being pretty disposable as a whole. Nevertheless, the brace of HIGH TREASON (by this stage, newcomer Mark Taylor had replaced original axeman John Pritchard, who went off to carve out a solo career, but didn't really get much further than contributing a track to the seldom-seen »Guitar Exploration« compilation) numbers were well up to their usual standard, and both "The Siren Song" (a rather more restrained performance which even features a few TRIARCHY-style synthesizer sections) and the intriguingly-titled "Cake" served to showcase a couple of further strong examples from the outfit's impressive repertoire.

Strangely, however, the lads ultimately failed to make any further impression on the rock scene at the time (in spite of being one of the more capable minor acts of the period), and appear not to have committed any additional material to vinyl. Interestingly, however, a version of the group remained a going concern for the remainder of the decade and beyond (confusingly, a second HIGH TREASON, from nearby Cambridgeshire, was operating simultaneously by the late 80's), although they appear to have abandoned plans to make it big in the world of metal within a couple of years of their last vinyl appearance. Instead, their subsequent activities (as more of a mainstream cabaret/covers outfit) saw them gigging in modest local venues and playing the lucrative Air Force Base circuit in best SPINAL TAP tradition. Careful with those radio mikes, lads.

7" Singles
»Saturday Night Special« Burlington Records 1980

Exclusive Compilation Appearances
"Cake" On »The Quest Tapes« LP Quest Records 1982
"The Siren Song" On »The Quest Tapes« LP Quest Records 1982

Compilation Appearances
"Saturday Night Special" on »NWOBHM Vol.2« Bootleg CD 1992

HOGGS

Richie Galloni (v)
Gregg Harris (g)
Robert Margertson (g)
Steve Taylor (b)
John Lloyd (d)

The unremarkably-named HOGGS, a long-forgotten quintet from the fertile Glamorgan area, were, to be brutally honest, one of the less innovative acts to emerge from the South Wales rock scene, preferring to take their inspiration from a variety of familiar 70's heroes, notably LED ZEPPELIN. As it turns out, their roots actually date back to a similar period, with frontman Richie Galloni having taken his first musical steps with an early 70's bunch called QUEST, who boasted future BUDGIE participants Steve Williams and Myf Isaac in their ranks. After the collapse of the aforementioned band, Galloni drifted from one musical project to another, eventually finding himself fronting the JAMES HOGG BAND in the late 70's, which would appear to have evolved into HOGGS following the inevitable round of personnel changes. By the turn of the decade or thereabouts, the ensemble seem to have made a conscious decision to jump on the new metal bandwagon, and duly began making dastardly plans to promote themselves as *bona fide* NWOBHM contenders. Before long, the lads had managed to wangle a modest deal for themselves, and oversaw the release of their humble vinyl debut shortly thereafter.

The resultant offering, the »See It Now« two-tracker from 1980, pairs a semi-raunchy A-side (shades of FRIENDS, WHITEFIRE and LORELEI, with a very Plant-like vocal performance indeed) with a lengthy, more sedate flipside, the latter ("Time On The Line") being a rather dull effort in comparison. It's a pity that the group felt compelled to commit such a mundane and restrained number to vinyl, as HOGGS were certainly getting the right idea on the A-side (nevertheless, it's a mystery why "See It Now" is clumsily edited after around three minutes, while the reverse drags on for twice as long), and clearly weren't too far removed from genuine NWOBHM status. Even so, I suspect that this bunch probably failed to adapt to the new metal climate at the time, and were soon overtaken by more energetic and raucous upstarts from their locality. The one-off (presumably) HOGGS offering, issued (in a monochrome picture sleeve featuring the band name painted onto a brick wall) by the tiny Now label, is a little-known and seldom-seen item these days, but shouldn't really be at the top of any wants lists. Incidentally, Richie Galloni is still plugging away on the local club circuit like the trouper he undoubtedly is, and now fronts a small-time rock act called THE HAILERS.

7" Singles
»See It Now« Now Records 1980

HOLLAND

Marty 'Doggy' Wilkinson (v)
Bob Henman (g)
Kenny Nicholson (g)
Graeme Hutchinson (b)
Marty Day (d)

Formed towards the end of 1982 from the ashes of various local bands, Cleveland's HOLLAND (strange name for a British outfit, that) were the brainchild of original BLACK ROSE guitarist Kenny Nicholson, who had grown weary of his role in the aforementioned outfit, deciding that the only way to express his musical ideas properly would be to form an entirely novel project. Assisting in this venture were former AXIS drummer Marty Day, erstwhile ANVIL (no, not them) guitarist Bob Henman and one-time LAZY DOG bassist Graeme Hutchinson. The final piece of the jigsaw slotted into place when the members of HOLLAND (after unsuccessfully scouring much of the country for a suitable vocalist) observed an individual named Marty 'Doggy' Wilkinson fronting a little-known bunch of Tyneside hopefuls called RED DOG (from whence came the chap's canine nickname, allegedly), whom they eventually persuaded to join their own outfit. With HOLLAND now boasting a full complement of musicians at last, the lads proceeded to write and record some of their own material, a proportion of which was captured on tape in an attempt to generate a bit of interest. In fact, most of these early compositions ("Illusion", "The Lowdown" and "Driving Me Crazy", for example) were eventually consigned to the *'reject'* bin, and the group were soon forced to concede that they needed another few months together before they could mount a concerted challenge on the rock world.

After plying their trade with little success or recognition for the best part of two years, however, a second demo tape (laid down at the end of 1983) finally began drawing the attention of some notable record companies. By this time, though, the lads had moved into more commercially-acceptable territory, abandoning the rough'n'ready NWOBHM (their earlier demo had been an enjoyable affair, on the whole, with occasional flashes of THIN LIZZY and DIAMOND HEAD coming to the fore) which represented their first forays into the recording studios. HOLLAND's new material ("Liar" and "Second Time Casualty", to name but a couple of eminently representative examples) was very much the type of polished, chart-friendly, raunchy rock which had been churned out by the likes of EXPORT, TERRAPLANE and the WILD

HORSES over the years, and it comes as something of a surprise, therefore, to discover that the best two offers emanated from such unlikely sources as Roadrunner and Ebony. After carefully weighing up the situation, HOLLAND concluded that their favoured option was to go with a British company, and signed their lives away to the Ebony label soon afterwards, whereupon the lads swiftly set about laying down their debut album. After a fairly *'eventful'* recording session at Ebony's *'studio facility'* (the source of much mirth for the protagonists, who had been expecting a grand location, not a converted council house), the work was completed by the spring of 1984, and the LP eventually appeared a couple of months later under the title of »Early Warning«.

It's certainly fair to say that HOLLAND (like SHY before them) weren't a particularly obvious choice for the inconsistent label to have picked up on, and their melodic interpretation of the NWOBHM ethos deviated considerably from the predominantly power metal style that became virtually synonymous with the Ebony name in the mid-80's. Instead, the hopeful musicians delivered a competent enough (but somewhat uninspiring at times) album of material from the BAD COMPANY school of thought, bringing forth fairly unavoidable comparisons with the likes of ACE LANE, AFTER DARK and Leice-

stershire's RAW DEAL. The individual compositions were mostly fairly interchangeable, although a couple of semi-highlights came in the form of "I Need" and "No Chance", both of which have slightly more of a sense of identity. The band gigged in various smaller venues to promote the release, and secured the odd appearance at better-attended shows with MAGNUM, winning a few favourable mentions in the rock press and the occasional placing in the heavy charts of the time. The long-player sold in sufficiently high quantities for Ebony to commission a follow-up, although the group hit a slight problem when some transatlantic namesakes threatened to sue the pants off them for copyright infringement. In the end, the Brits gave way and soon reinvented themselves as HAMMER (see separate entry) and adopted a slightly different lyrical viewpoint and image, if not a fundamentally disparate musical style.

LP's
»**Early Warning**« Ebony 1984

HOLLOW GROUND

Glen Coates (v)
Martin Metcalf (g)
Brian Rickman (b)
Jon Lockney (d)

Right from day one in the NWOBHM collecting scene, the famous HOLLOW GROUND EP (one of the very few artefacts from the period which even the majority of non-specialist dealers would be able to identify as a top-ranking rarity) has been regarded as one of the most illustrious and sought-after releases of the era. Even now that all four of the featured selections have officially appeared on CD courtesy of British Steel (on their »N.W.O.B.H.M. Metal Rarities Vol.1« set), the sheer reverence afforded to the original vinyl article is a testimony to its importance to the NWOBHM community today, with a handful of collectors still being prepared to pay a pretty extortionate price for the few copies (a significant number of which were issued without the coveted picture sleeve) which occasionally come up for sale. Mind you, given that several dozen examples have actually been offered to the public by various dealers over the past decade or so, it seems truly remarkable that the potential market hasn't dried up completely, but I guess it just goes to show that we're dealing with a very special record here.

The background to this story goes back to November 1980 (the youthful outfit having started out around a year earlier), when a trio of relatively unknown North Eastern groups *viz.* SARACEN (nothing to do with the Midlands ensemble who recorded for the Nucleus/Neat labels), SAMURAI (not to be confused with the Welsh or Essex acts) and HOLLOW GROUND installed themselves in Guardian Studios in Durham, each recording a number of tracks for future vinyl release. In the event, all of these hopefuls were allowed to contribute a very generous four compositions to the legendary »Roksnax« sampler in due course. While the other two groups (even with BLIND FURY's Lou Taylor lending his considerable talents to SARACEN, a group which, at one time, also featured MYTHRA's John Roach, albeit extremely fleetingly) faded into total obscurity soon after, however, it's little surprise that HOLLOW GROUND were identified as the pick of the bunch. With "Rock On", "Fight With The Devil" (which would, in time, become one of the more obscure inclusions on Lars Ulrich's »NWOBHM '79 Revisited« celebratory compilation), the colossal "Flying High" (a superb track which single-handedly defines the entire genre) and "The Holy One" all combining excellent guitar work with some extremely impressive vocals, the talented quartet managed to encapsulate all the best elements of BLITZKRIEG, DEF LEPPARD, DIAMOND HEAD and the TYGERS OF PAN TANG to create a distinctive and immensely enjoyable brand of melodic, powerful metal.

With the band having captured the public's imagination in no uncertain terms, the canny Terry Gavaghan subsequently offered HOLLOW GROUND the enviable opportunity to deliver an EP of their own, a notion which met with enthusiasm from the musicians. Re-using "Rock On" and "Flying High" from the sampler, the group duly added "Warlord" and "Don't Chase The Dragon" (presumably also recorded during the original studio sessions) to create a classic four-tracker, the EP being issued (in the early months of 1981) in a suitably naff hand-drawn sleeve depicting a gun-toting guerilla (or possibly *gorilla*, it's quite difficult to tell). With the debut record instantly becoming a firm favourite at such outlets as Bullet Records (who memorably described the release as *'explosive'*) and selling well locally, the outfit looked certain to become one of Guardian's major success stories before all that much longer. However, it would appear that the lads failed to capitalise on the release in the short term, with the result that they never really broke out of the North East, although they were rightly regarded as one of the region's more talented acts of the period. In fact, it transpires that HOLLOW GROUND remained a going concern for a remarkably short space of time after their EP hit the shops (they demoed a final batch of more accessible material, including "Promised Land", "Rock To Love", "Easy Action" and "Loser"), although this was mainly a consequence of the unforeseen defection of Glen Coates to local rivals FIST, the vocalist having been headhunted to replace the recently-departed Keith Satchfield.

Following this shameless piece of pilferage, the remaining members of HOLLOW GROUND found it impossible to carry on, and elected to disband sooner rather than later. By the tail end of 1981, Glen Coates had well and truly become an integral part of the FIST set-up, although it was rather uncharitable of his new employers to offer the opinion (in a 'Kerrang' interview) that the vocalist had actually been HOLLOW GROUND's only saving grace. In due course, Coates appeared on the second FIST long-player, their 'Friday Rock Show' session and their final single, which saw them take the slightly unusual step of covering DION's "The Wanderer" (which, incidentally, isn't a patch on the magnificent "Runaround Sue"), so it's fair to say that he had a productive spell with his new compatriots. Apart from that, though, there's not much to report on the post-HOLLOW GROUND activities of the one-time members, although Coates (after a stint in a small-time covers concern called CENTREFOLD) is apparently still earning a crust as a cabaret singer in holiday camps (!), while guitarist Martin Metcalf was last heard of playing with an outfit called POWERAGE (who, unsurprisingly, featured a great deal of AC/DC material in their set). As for that legendary EP, is it worth the money? Well, I find it hard to accept that all but the very best and most horrendously obscure releases are worth anything like *half* the amount in question, but I guess it must be a realistic figure if some people are prepared to pay it.

7" EP's
»Flying High« Guardian 1981

Exclusive Compilation Appearances
"The Holy One" on »Roksnax« LP Guardian 1980
"Fight With The Devil" on »Roksnax« LP Guardian 1980 + »NWOBHM '79 Revisited« Do-LP/Do-CD Phonogram 1990

Compilation Appearances
"Flying High" on »Roksnax« LP Guardian 1980

+ »NWOBHM Vol.3« Bootleg CD 1992 +
»N.W.O.B.H.M. Metal Rarities Vol.1« CD British Steel 1996
"Rock On" on »Roksnax« LP Guardian 1980 + »N.W.O.B.H.M. Metal Rarities Vol.1« CD British Steel 1996
"Warlord" on »N.W.O.B.H.M. Metal Rarities Vol.1« CD British Steel 1996
"Don't Chase The Dragon" on »N.W.O.B.H.M. Metal Rarities Vol.1« CD British Steel 1996

HOLOCAUST

Gary Lettice (v)
John Mortimer (g)
Ed Dudley (g)
Robin Begg (b)
Paul Collins (d)

The pride of Scottish NWOBHM, Edinburgh's HOLOCAUST originally came together as far back as 1977, initially representing a bit of after-school fun for some teenage hopefuls, the lads getting through a few names in the early days, notably BUZZARD, APOLLO and (wait for it) PREYING MANTIS (nah, that would have been a hopeless choice), before settling on the identity of HOLOCAUST, a name which now seems glaringly insensitive in view of certain events of the twentieth century, but which was originally chosen (much like BLITZKRIEG) to represent a cataclysmic musical force rather than anything more sinister. Their awkward fumblings in the early days soon progressed to a more professional-sounding style, and, before long, the unit were being invited to support some of the more established outfits (in particular, SAMSON, VARDIS and the TYGERS OF PAN TANG) who ventured North of the border from time to time. Still, there was so sign of a record deal on the horizon, and HOLOCAUST began to feel that they might be cruelly overlooked in favour of some of the equally-talented acts who were doing the rounds down South, in full view of the influential record companies. A piece of luck was to come their way, however, when excellently-named vocalist Gary Lettice (he should have teamed up with old Steve Cabbage from SKITZOFRENIK) started working in a local record emporium, and his benevolent employer rapidly offered to sign the HOLOCAUST boys to his own label, Phoenix Records.

The first HOLOCAUST release to emerge on this newly-founded label (whose only other signing of note was a feeble indie act called the PERSIAN RUGS) was their unashamed »Heavy Metal Mania« effort, released as both a 7" single and three track 12" EP in mid-1980. Issued in a metal-as-you-like sleeve (an unfortunate phoenix with a sword shoved through its skull), the record was hardly the ground-breaking classic that many now seem to think, the youthful outfit's attempts at anthemic, heavy compositions coming across as extremely pedestrian and rudimentary in their construction, with the strained, tuneless vocals of Gary Lettice (which were passable enough in the live environment, admittedly) being exposed as a real limiting factor. Neither "Heavy Metal Mania" (later covered by GAMMA RAY) nor the flipside ("Only As Young As You Feel") were anywhere near as capable as "Loves Power" (the bonus track on the 12"), but at least the latter showed a bit of promise. Still, the record sold in pretty healthy quantities nationwide (I've no idea how their small-time label managed to distribute their releases quite so efficiently), and there was obviously enough demand to warrant a follow-up. Their »Smokin' Valves« single appeared towards the end of that year (issued in both 7" and 12" forms once again, but the former was an extremely limited issue, for some reason), and constituted a markedly less frustrating listening experience, as HOLOCAUST had now upped the tempo a bit. Mind you, the featured tracks were still pretty uninspiring, and the A-side was highly derivative (as was the 12" bonus, "Friend Or Foe"), although "Out My Book" was a reasonable enough effort.

Now, if you had cornered me at the time and asked whether or not the HOLOCAUST lads had any genuine potential, I would almost certainly have assured you that they did not, and it would have been no great surprise if the group had quietly gone to ground after their first two releases. Their label, however, had other ideas, and soon stumped up the readies for a full album, which was recorded in the early part of 1981 and ultimately saw the light of day in the spring of that year. To give a modicum of credit where it's due, »The Nightcomers« was a hell of a lot more listenable than their formative vinyl offerings had been, the album showing a considerably greater musical flair, a rather more impressive variety of compositions, and even (thanks to a bit of studio trickery to enhance Lettice's delivery) a capable vocal performance. It wasn't perfect, mind you, and a couple of the tracks featured should have been consigned to the 'pub rock rejects' pile at the earliest opportunity, but HOLOCAUST still shone through on the upbeat "Death Or Glory" and "Cryin Shame', plus the heavier "Mavrock" and "The Nightcomers". It was a major progression, that's for sure, and some of the band's stronger and heavier material now bore occasional similarities to BLITZKRIEG and early SATAN, although a greater percentage of HOLOCAUST's own compositions were probably more along the lines of OVERDRIVE and TURBO. The release proceeded to shift a remarkably impressive number of units (helped, this time, by a licensing deal with Lark Records in Europe), and HOLOCAUST were soon the toast of the town in many parts of the globe.

With a bit of overdue media attention finally coming in the outfit's direction, the musicians were given valuable exposure *via* an 'Armed And Ready' feature in 'Kerrang' later in the year (by which time they had broken in a new drummer, Nicky Arkless), although the magazine's writers weren't particularly effusive about the merits of the debut album. Nevertheless, HOLOCAUST were now developing an elaborate strategy for global domination, and they soon hit upon a cunning plan to capture themselves playing one of their frenzied live shows. Not content with traditional audio recording technology, however, the over-ambitious bunch proceeded to rope in a video production company to film the event as well. The dates were duly organised, and HOLOCAUST were soon announcing the imminent filming and recording of a home-town gig in September 1981, inviting their numerous fans to turn out *en masse* and make the whole occasion look really impressive. In fact, the publicity-shy inhabitants of Edinburgh appear to have been inexplicably reluctant to show their faces on camera, and it apparently took a fair old while to get a decent-sized crowd inside the venue, the situation finally helped by a few roadies going out into the streets and (with the promise of a few quid in their hands for a job well done) *'encouraging'* some metal-looking individuals to *'come and jump around and look as though you're enjoying yourselves'* (with sincere apologies to all the musicians if these libellous accusations are not entirely true, although they came from someone who was actually present at the gig). How embarrassing.

Producing an official video was an extremely expensive and ambitious project for a minor band to undertake at the time, and very few of their fans could actually afford the end product, a fifteen track tape featuring a selection of numbers from their earlier works, plus a handful of newies such as "Long The Bell Will Toll", "Bridge Of Impressions" and "The Small Hours". Still, the canny outfit intended to make full and good use of their live recordings, and subsequently pressed a four track EP featuring some of the shorter numbers from the set. The snappily-titled »Live From The Raw Loud'n'Live Tour« (*Tour*? What tour?) 7" hit the shops at the end of 1981, and was soon selling in healthy quantities, the featured tracks (with the exception of "Death Or Glory") all being exclusive to this release. The sound quality wasn't exactly state-of-the-art, but it was still sufficiently listenable to be able to appreciate the fact that HOLOCAUST were continually improving, with "Lovin Feelin Danger", "No Nonsense" and "Forcedown Breakdown" all reaffirming that these Jocks were worthy inclusions in the NWOBHM movement. With the

youngsters apparently becoming more confident and capable with every vinyl release, it looked as though they had a healthy future in the music business, but things were to go wrong before much longer, when main songwriting force John Mortimer packed his bags and left in the early months of 1982.

Mortimer's surprise departure came completely out of the blue, and was undoubtedly a major blow for the outfit, although they elected to soldier on without him in the short term. It was also to prove the end of the road for the recently-recruited Nicky Arkless, though, who was soon on his way to pastures new, whereupon the rapidly-disintegrating HOLOCAUST drafted in Ray Marciano in an attempt to salvage the situation. It seemed to do the trick, and the four-piece version of the band were soon back in the studios once more, laying the foundations for a second album by recording three new tracks for Phoenix to release as a taster. The »Coming Through« 12" appeared in mid-1982, and this turned out to be a rather atypical release with regard to their earlier output, the lads attempting to break into more commercial territory which didn't really suit their collective abilities too well. There was nothing fundamentally wrong with the trio of songs featured (the title track was augmented by "Don't Wanna Be (A Loser)" and "Good Thing Going"), each of which bore occasional similarities to the likes of A II Z and the TYGERS OF PAN TANG, but the outfit were once again let down by Lettice's flat vocal delivery, which simply wasn't up to the job in this case. With the public failing to take much notice of the EP and sales being correspondingly poor, the writing was on the wall for the hapless bunch, and the end came within a matter of months.

In the wake of HOLOCAUST's unfortunate demise, guitarist Ed Dudley went off to do his own thing in the form of HOLOGRAM (see separate entry), a side-project which had been waiting for a chance to break through for a while. However, since he took his erstwhile colleague Ray Marciano with him, Phoenix Records soon decided to offer the lads an album deal, as long as they were able to promote their outfit as *'the new HOLOCAUST'*. It wasn't really the case, but the deal-hungry group went along with this suggestion, and delivered the ambitious (but largely overlooked) »Steal The Stars« long-player towards the end of the year. With the HOLOGRAM venture failing to make a great deal of money for Phoenix Records, the label decided to squeeze the last possible vinyl offering from their stockpile of HOLOCAUST recordings, and proceeded to issue the »Live (Hot Curry And Wine)« album in 1983, the material again being taken from that legendary live show in September 1981. It was something of a shameless cash-in, given that the group no longer existed in its original form, although the record was a reasonable enough souvenir of a HOLOCAUST live outing. Two of the numbers from the live EP ("No Nonsense" and "Forcedown Breakdown") were recycled, and the fans were treated (in addition to energetic versions of old favourites such as "Smokin' Valves" and "Heavy Metal Mania") to a few curiosities such as "Long The Bell Will Toll", "The Small Hours" and the instrumental "Jirmakenyerut" (the apparently impenetrable title roughly translates as *'is your mother aware that you are not at home this evening?'*).

Perversely, the album went on to become a fairly high-selling item, although sales were largely restricted to the UK, as the licensing deal with Lark seems to have fallen through by this stage.

With the live album having been an unforeseen success, it became apparent that there were still HOLOCAUST fans out there, and presumably a market for further product if Phoenix could just persuade the lads to get back together again. In the end, John Mortimer was coaxed out of exile and permitted to assemble a brand-new incarnation of HOLOCAUST around himself, the guitarist taking over vocal duties himself and bringing in drummer Steve Cowen to help out. I've absolutely no idea who was contributing bass parts at the time (their only release failed to credit the rhythm section at all), but I reckon it was probably a session musician. In 1984, the outfit finally delivered a studio album called »No Mans Land«, a truly horrendous record which saw the lads churning out the kind of mid-tempo, unambitious NWOBHM that hundreds of tenth-rate demo outfits could quite comfortably have written in their sleep. If it had been a young act's vinyl debut for a minor label, it would have been an unremarkable enough effort; for experienced musicians of this stature, however, it was just plain embarrassing. In spite of the generous inclusion of eleven (mercifully-brief) tracks, it's impossible even to pick out anything vaguely resembling a *'highlight'*, as the standard of songwriting and musicianship was consistently dreadful. Unsurprisingly, few reviewers of the time were charitable enough to give the record any praise whatsoever, and the fans rightly ignored the release completely. In the aftermath of the critical panning afforded to »No Mans Land«, HOLOCAUST elected to lie low for a while, and had probably given up the ghost completely by 1985, when they finally realised that there was no easy way to salvage the situation. They were, of course, entirely unaware of the helping hand which lay just around the corner...

METALLICA's self-styled *'saviour of NWOBHM'*, Lars Ulrich, had been a fan of HOLOCAUST since their earliest days, and his own band decided to pay tribute to them on the »Garage Days Re-revisited« EP in 1987, where the Yanks delivered their own heavy interpretation of the sludgy "The Small Hours". Needless to say, many purchasers soon wanted to know all about these horrendously obscure NWOBHM outfits who had inspired their heroes in the first instance. Suddenly, the name of HOLOCAUST was being bandied about once again, much to the amazement of the band members themselves, who hadn't the slightest inkling that their music had made such an impression on METALLICA. Still, there's no such thing as bad publicity, and John Mortimer eventually realised that there might be a bit of mileage in getting his old outfit off the ground yet again. To this end, he roped in Steve Cowen once more (bringing in Graham Hall to act in the capacity of bassist) in the early months of 1988, and (again taking full responsibility for vocals and guitar himself) began writing new material for the first time in several years. Before long, the revamped HOLOCAUST were making some low-key appearances in Edinburgh, and the loyal crowds were rather surprised to discover that the trio weren't merely content to plough through a selection of favourites from their expansive back catalogue after all. No, Mortimer and his latest cohorts had something a bit more innovative up their sleeves...

After re-establishing themselves on the live scene once more and creating a minor media buzz amongst some of the journalists who had long memories and fond recollections of HOLOCAUST's glory days, the group burst forth with a mini-album entitled »The Sound Of Souls«, issued on the small Chrome label in 1989. The record came as a complete shock for both the reviewers and fans, and was (both lyrically and musically) far removed from their traditional NWOBHM roots. Instead, this was an extremely confident move into semi-industrial, technical thrash (I suspect that an album called »Dimension Hatross« had made a huge impression on John Mortimer some months previously), with occasional glimpses of acts such as VOIVOD (as every single reviewer pertinently pointed out) or BLOODSTAR (and even GODFLESH, when they really got going). Tracks such as opening trio "This Annihilation", "I Smash The Void" and "Dance Into The Vortex" were all very impressive and listenable pieces, although the outfit seemed to be struggling a bit by the time "Curious" and the overly-long "Three Ways To Die" put in an appearance. Still, it was a truly excellent way for HOLOCAUST to return to credible metal prominence, and the press heaped praise upon their new direction at every opportunity. The group played a handful of comeback gigs to promote the release, although the mixture of old and new material was an uneasy experience for the audiences, who found the extreme contrast between styles quite difficult to come to terms with. After the initial enthusiasm for »The Sound Of Souls« had finally worn off, the lads went back into hiding once more, and nobody really knew if HOLOCAUST were ever intending to return in yet another guise.

In fact, a version of the band (Mortimer and Cowen now being joined by bassist David Rosie) rematerialised in 1992, having now recorded a full album on their own label, Taurus Moon Records. The new set, the quirkily-titled »Hypnosis Of Birds«, saw a more intermediate style coming into play, considerably less extreme and experimental than »The Sound Of Souls«, but still a lot more ambitious than the rudimentary metal of their early days. Sadly, however, the individual compositions were, in spite of some quite unusual and (occasionally) innovative ideas, very laborious and rather dull in their execution. There were a few semi-listenable efforts, notably "Mortal Mother", "Caledonia" and "Into Lebanon", although many of the featured tracks were just too depressing and stretched-out (some of them actually resemble an unusually heavy amalgamation of ULTRAVOX and PINK FLOYD, which is a very odd combination indeed) to make any sort of favourable impression. To be honest, I reckon the outfit barely had enough new material to fill a whole album particularly efficiently, and resorted to chucking in several fillers (no less than three instrumentals, as well as a rehashed version of "The Small Hours") to boost the running time. The long-player was quite a limited pressing, but there wasn't really all that much demand for »Hypnosis Of Birds« anyway, the loyal fans (including DEATH's Chuck Schuldiner, who had taken to wearing an original HOLOCAUST T-shirt at many of his band's own gigs) having been warned in advance by some less-than-commendatory reviews that the latest HOLOCAUST effort was a bit of a turkey.

Nevertheless, the band proceeded to bring out a mini-CD to follow their latest release, including two versions (old and new) of old chestnut "Heavy Metal Mania", plus re-recorded takes of "Death Or Glory" and "The Small Hours". Again, this turned out to be an extremely limited pressing (with an equally restricted distribution), although it fared slightly better than the album, with a fair number of copies being shifted by mail order and some even making their way over to mainland Europe. In fact, the four-tracker was sufficiently well-received (particularly in Germany) that HOLOCAUST were invited to play at the 1993 Wacken Open Air Festival (with TRESPASS), and this appearance turned out to be so successful that the lads even managed to undertake a brief-but-productive tour of Germany in the spring of 1994, enjoying the welcome attention (including various requests for interviews) that came their way during this jaunt. The next couple of years were relatively quiet, although the reactivated Neat Metal label eventually identified the potential of reissuing »Hypnosis Of Birds« in 1996, making the set available to a considerably wider market as a result. Cunningly, it was issued under the guise of »Spirits Fly« (and promoted, to all intents and purposes, as a brand-new release), the label changing the packaging and running sequence, adding the reworked "Heavy Metal Mania" and "Death Or Glory", and rounding things off with HOLOCAUST's interpretation of "Master Of Puppets", a selection which had originally been recorded for a METALLICA tribute album, which brought things full circle, in a way.

Despite Neat's best intentions, I don't get the impression that the re-promoted album has sold in particularly noteworthy quantities at all, although it's nice that the loyal fans (not to mention a few of the latecomers who have only recently been made aware of HOLOCAUST's contribution to the metal scene over the years) are now able to acquire this CD with minimal effort, since the original pressing on Taurus Moon was exhausted a long time ago. Hoping to capitalise on this new-found interest, the band released a follow-up set (the quirky »Covenant«), although this also seems to have enjoyed relatively modest sales, despite favourable reviews coming from certain quarters. Surprisingly, though, the musicians seem to have abandoned plans to undertake additional touring (as far as I'm aware, the last time they were observed in the live environment was at a one-off European event towards the end of 1997), leading to speculation that HOLOCAUST were winding down their activities. Indeed, they kept a very low profile for a while, finally coming out of the woodwork in 2000 with another typically-offbeat album called »The Courage To Be«, which contains some distinctive, heavy numbers but (in my humble opinion) strives just a bit too hard to be different. It remains to be seen how long John Mortimer decides to keep the HOLOCAUST name alive, and, given that their small-but-dedicated fan base lies almost entirely outwith the UK these days, it can't be an easy situation to assess. Nevertheless, another live set (using recordings from the German tour of 1994, featuring a mixture of old and new material) remains a possibility, but the question of additional studio albums appearing at some future juncture is a different matter entirely.

LP's

»**The Nightcomers**« Phoenix Records 1981
[UK issue with black/blue sleeve]
»**The Nightcomers**« Lark 1981
[Belgian issue with black/red sleeve]
»**Live (Hot Curry And Wine)**« Phoenix Records 1983
[Live album in gatefold sleeve]
»**No Mans Land**« Phoenix Records 1984

Mini-LP's

»**The Sound Of Souls**« Chrome Records 1989

12" EP's

»**Heavy Metal Mania**« Phoenix Records 1980
[A-side different to album version, both "Only As Young As You Feel" and "Loves Power" non-LP]
»**Smokin' Valves**« Phoenix Records 1980
[Both "Friend Or Foe" and "Out My Book" non-LP]
»**Coming Through**« Phoenix Records 1982/Lark 1982
[UK/Belgian issue, all three tracks non-LP]

7" EP's

»**Live From The Raw Loud'n'Live Tour**« Phoenix Records 1981
[Features four live tracks, "Lovin' Feelin' Danger" and "Death Or Glory" not included on live album]

7" Singles

»**Heavy Metal Mania**« Phoenix Records 1980
[A-side different to album version, B-side "Only As Young As You Feel" non-LP]
»**Smokin' Valves**« Phoenix Records 1980
[Original UK issue without picture sleeve, B-side "Out My Book" non-LP]
»**Smokin' Valves**« DiscAZ 1981
[French reissue in picture sleeve, same cover artwork as »The Nightcomers« album, B-side "Out My Book" non-LP]

CD's

»**The Nightcomers**« Bootleg 1992
[Unofficial release, includes first album and eight

bonus tracks from early singles]
»Hypnosis Of Birds« Taurus Moon Records 1992
»Spirits Fly« Neat Metal 1996
[Repackaged »Hypnosis Of Birds« album with different cover and title, plus three extra tracks]
»Spirits Fly« Pony Canyon 1996
[Japanese issue with one bonus track]
»Covenant« Neat Metal 1997
[UK issue]
»Covenant« Pony Canyon 1997
[Japanese issue with one bonus track]
»The Nightcomers« Edgy 2000
[With three bonus tracks from »Heavy Metal Mania« 12"]
»Live (Hot Curry And Wine)« Edgy 2000
[With two bonus tracks from live 7"]
»The Courage To Be« Edgy 2000

Mini-CD's
»The Sound Of Souls« Chrome Records 1989
»Heavy Metal Mania '93« Taurus Moon Records 1993
[Features re-recordings of older material]

Compilation Appearances
"Death Or Glory" on »NWOBHM '79 Revisited« Do-LP/Do-CD Phonogram 1990
"Heavy Metal Mania" on »NWOBHM Vol.2« Bootleg CD 1992
"The Small Hours" on »The Metallic-Era« CD Neat Metal 1996
"Master Of Puppets" on »A Tribute To Metallica II« CD Tribute Records 1996 + »The Metallic-Era Volume II« CD Neat Metal 1999
"War In Heaven" on »Unbroken Metal« CD Private 1997
"The Small Hours" (live) on »The Metallic-Era Volume II« CD Neat Metal 1999

HOLOGRAM

Gordon Band (v)
Ed Dudley (g)
Nelson (b)
Ray Marciano (d)

'HOLOCAUST are now HOLOGRAM', proclaimed the promotional blurb which accompanied the debut release of axeman Ed Dudley's post-HOLOCAUST venture in 1982, in a calculated move which was surely designed to draw in a few fans of the original Edinburgh heroes. Actually, it was a pretty fraudulent (well, misleading) piece of advertising, given that this was essentially an entirely novel project and not a particularly natural progression after all. In fact, of the three auxiliary participants, only sticksman Ray Marciano (the other characters involved being talented vocalist Gordon Band and economically-named bassist *'Nelson'*) had been a paid-up member of HOLOCAUST towards the end of their existence. However, the similar-sounding moniker and a virtually identical logo largely failed to disguise the fact that HOLOGRAM were very much a distant relative in terms of talent and musical direction. To be honest, I very much doubt (said he putting on his Sherlock Holmes deerstalker) that they were ever conceived as a *bona fide* follow-up to HOLOCAUST at all, given that everything seemed to happen so incredibly quickly after the collapse of the original bunch, and I strongly suspect (given that HOLOGRAM's own material turned out to be quite so polished, confident and well-written) that Dudley had almost certainly been tinkering around with a few formative compositions at least a year earlier.

In any case, HOLOGRAM's debut »Steal The Stars« LP (issued towards the end of 1982 on the small-but-dependable Phoenix label once again) revealed that the four-piece had clearly been cocking an ear to some of the more popular chart music of the day, with the result being that their own efforts encompassed a pretty wide range of styles. You can, depending on your mood, either take the view that it represents an eclectic mixture of influences, or a hopelessly confused hotchpotch of material without any underlying stability. In truth, it's an album which takes quite a few spins to come to terms with, something which pretty much explains the dismissive attitude of many music journalists (who, let's face it, probably gave it the most cursory of listens) at the time. While there are a couple of fairly traditional rockers in the form of "Can't Live With You Any More" and "Lost In Love" (their frontman's distinctive and powerful vocals lifting the standard of the material quite considerably), contrasting tracks such as "Expected To" and "African" are rather more suggestive of THE POLICE and U2. The likes of "Shoot The Moon" and "Vigilante Man", meanwhile, are in an extremely unusual style for the period in question, and would probably appeal to fans of some of the more left-field outfits of recent times, notably DAMN THE MACHINE and INTO ANOTHER. There are moments, admittedly, where things get a bit over-ambitious and confusing, although the overall standard of musicianship and songwriting is remarkably high.

There's little doubt that the one-off HOLOGRAM long-player was regarded as a bit of a commercial disaster at the time (as with DIAMOND HEAD's »Canterbury«, for example, it was just too *'different'* when compared with the relative accessibility and familiarity of the original HOLOCAUST material), and the re-emergence of HOLOCAUST, a mere year or so later, was welcomed with open arms by both the fans and journalists. To be frank, HOLOGRAM hardly constituted a genuine NWOBHM act at all, and it appears to have been an extremely unwise move for their label representatives to have attempted to pass them off as *'the new HOLOCAUST'*, who were probably just *'resting'* while a few of the central characters immersed themselves in a brief spell of extra-curricular experimentation. I'd suggest that the long-forgotten »Steal The Stars« set deserves to be heard and reappraised by a far wider audience, and it would be nice, therefore, if some of you dug out your dusty old copies and gave them another spin. It might not have made all that much sense to you at the time, but I reckon it's one of those very rare vintages which actually improves with age.

LP's
»Steal The Stars« Phoenix Records 1982/Lark 1982 *[UK/Belgian issue]*

HORIZON

Gilligan
Durrant
Fairweather

The horrendously obscure UK version of HORIZON have often been confused with their considerably more successful namesakes from Holland, something which becomes entirely understandable as soon as you lend an ear to their one-off single from 1981, given that it doesn't really sound remotely British in any sense. The vocal phrasing and lyrics seem rather stilted, in the main, although the writing credits tend to suggest that this was indeed a home-grown (possibly Irish) act. Still, HORIZON remain something of a mystery outfit at present (again, matters aren't helped by the fact that no picture sleeve appears to exist), and no additional details of personnel, geographical location or history have been conclusively established thus far, so we're still searching for a breakthrough on this effort. Musically speaking, it's quite an odd one, with "Stage Struck" being a catchy enough number in the general SMOKIN ROADIE or TEMPEST vein, although the structure is pretty off-the-wall, and it's fair to say that this was a rather atypical style (remarkably similar to early EF BAND material) for a British ensemble to have attempted at the time. The nondescript "Remember The Bad Boys", on the other hand, is a semi-progressive (hints of FOCUS) and largely-instrumental affair which might have been the sort of thing TOAD THE WET SPROCKET tinkered around with in their early days, but which fails to make all that much of an impact. Despite being one of the better-distributed releases of the day (sold through the likes of Bullet Records, for example), few copies of »Stage Struck« appear to have made it into general circulation and are very seldom offered for sale these days. Any further information?

7" Singles
»Stage Struck« SRT 1981

HORSEPOWER

Mike Kennedy

Although the relatively obscure outfit known as HORSEPOWER (who were, in all probability, based in the nation's capital) were evidently a somewhat short-lived affair, they still managed to chalk up some notable successes during their time together, such as being chosen to open the proceedings at a prestigious *'Battle Of The Bands'* event at London's Lyceum in June 1980, appearing in the company of the illustrious DIAMOND HEAD, TYGERS OF PAN TANG and ANGEL WITCH. Furthermore, HORSEPOWER's earliest vinyl exposure came in the shape of the fairly raunchy "She Gives Me Candy", an enviable inclusion on EMI's second »Metal For Muthas« sampler, where the group took pride of place alongside the likes of TRESPASS, WHITE SPIRIT and DARK STAR. As with many of the other outfits promoted by EMI on their early compilations, this appearance led directly to a record deal, albeit with a rather small label, Square Records (a completely different company to the one who released CHAINSAW's debut), so it was something of a success story in that sense.

In terms of their musical approach, HORSEPOWER surely had a reasonably good chance of making the big time with their raw, traditional, hard rock disposition (this worked for the rather more classy TERRAPLANE and BABY TUCKOO, for instance), the band featuring a frontman who valiantly tried his utmost to emulate the revered vocal histrionics of David Coverdale, a chap whose own outfit was very much in vogue at that time. On their one and only single (a release, issued in a pretty irritating picture sleeve, which has never, for some peculiar reason, been regarded as a particularly coveted item), both "Outrageous" and "Highway Robbery" see HORSEPOWER coming across as a rather more energetic meeting of JAMESON RAID and FRIENDS, although the record-buying public appears to have been utterly nonplussed by its issue at the time, leaving the band members scratching their heads and wondering exactly what might have gone wrong in this instance, before giving up the ghost completely within a remarkably short timescale. Such is life.

7" Singles
»Outrageous« Square Records 1981

Exclusive Compilation Appearances
"She Gives Me Candy" on »Metal For Muthas Vol.2« LP EMI 1980/CD Airraid Records 2000

IDLE FLOWERS

René Berg (v,g)
Froze Garcia (b)
Kevin 'Smash' O'Neill (d)

A fairly unusual entry comes courtesy of the IDLE FLOWERS, a name which conjures up the depressing image of some indie miserablists dressed entirely in black, although the outfit in question were actually markedly more cheerful than this initial preconception might have suggested. Featuring an ex-HONEYDRIPPERS personality (drummer Smash O'Neill) in their ranks, the trio took their first faltering steps in the live environment by playing a handful of introductory shows at various small London clubs in 1981, but it was all pretty low-key at first. They didn't become an overnight sensation, admittedly, and many audiences tended to be slightly confused by the nature of the outfit's material. Indeed, when one of their shindigs in the capital came to be reviewed in 'Kerrang' a year or so later, journalist Dave Dickson struggled to find an adequate description of the set, which included compositions such as "True Love" and "When We Were Young". Settling in the end for the not-particularly-helpful tag of

'heavy pop', the bewildered individual duly commented that 'The IDLE FLOWERS have yet to find their niche but all they really need is a hit single and a little patience.' (Ref: Kerrang No.22, August 1982).

Well, the single appeared a couple of years later (after numerous small-time gigs and a few successful support slots with the KINKS and HANOI ROCKS, by which time the trio had extended their repertoire to feature original compositions such as "Head Over Heels" and "Without Your Love"), and I can empathise with Dickson's original difficulty in pigeonholing the outfit's music. Incorporating a pretty wide variety of musical influences, the IDLE FLOWERS created a melodic, slightly raunchy sound (not quite as overtly sleazy as some of their emergent contemporaries, two prime examples being the DOGS D'AMOUR and the GUNSLINGERS) which didn't become properly established (or particularly popular, for that matter) in the UK until slightly later in the decade. With the vocal inclinations of frontman René Berg being very much in the Harris/Plant vein, the A-side of their two-tracker comes across as a listenable piece of tuneful rock/pop in the general style of DIAMOND HEAD's "One More Night", which, despite being far removed from the NWOBHM archetype, is almost impossible to dislike. The B-side ("Fizz Music"), however, is a bit more of a mess, with Berg going into full-scale 'Percy' mode on occasion, and the track briefly threatens to mutate into something of a "Black Dog" pastiche before regaining its bearings.

In spite of the solid backing of See For Miles Records and a prestigious EMI publishing credit, the single obviously sold poorly, and is very seldom encountered these days, which probably means that the majority were either destroyed or are now merely gathering dust in a disused warehouse. There don't seem to have been any other releases by the IDLE FLOWERS in later years, and their name was never a particularly revered one in the pages of the rock press, so it looks as though they called it quits soon afterwards. Berg (having been a part of various non-illustrious projects such as the SUICIDE TWINS and the GANGBANG BAND in the interim) and O'Neill eventually resurfaced in 1987, teaming up with Tom Fox and Nasty Suicide (ex-HANOI ROCKS, a group in which Berg also allegedly deputised at one point), in the ill-fated glam outfit WEST END CENTRAL (later SOHO VULTURES), who recycled some of the numbers (e.g. "Head Over Heels") from the early IDLE FLOWERS days. After a few years in the wilderness, Berg finally released a solo set entitled »The

Leather...The Loneliness...And Your Dark Eyes« (featuring a guest appearance from Bernie Tormé) on Communiqué in 1992, but it doesn't appear to have broken any sales records. As for the IDLE FLOWERS 7", meanwhile, look out for a predominantly monochrome sleeve with a picture of the band, there are copies out there somewhere...

7" Singles
»All I Want Is You« See For Miles Records 1984

IDOL RICH

Lee Silver (v)
Nick Burr (g)
Tim Jones (g)
Jeff Curtis (b)
Mike Fisher (d)

For a relatively unknown group, it's remarkable just how many NWOBHM scenesters passed through the ranks of IDOL RICH (almost unbelievably, they shared their name with a pop/rock outfit from the North West, who emerged from the ashes of punk also-rans THE STIFFS and released a lightweight two-tracker entitled »Blaze Of Love« in the course of their fairly brief existence. Initially forming in Gloucestershire in the early months of 1984, the lads did their utmost to make themselves known to the local metalheads by playing live wherever and whenever they could (while trying to maintain a stable line-up), and it wasn't too long before the lads started thinking about issuing some vinyl product of their own. IDOL RICH duly released their self-financed »Working Girls« EP the following year (the regulation one thousand copies being manufactured), and the four-tracker soon found its way into the hands of many appreciative fans. On vinyl, the quintet delivered the sort of well-crafted, heavy-but-melodic rock of the variety peddled by British acts of the time such as CHROME MOLLY, HEAVY PETTIN and TOBRUK, and they certainly seemed to stand a pretty good chance of being catapulted to comparable prominence in due course. The excellent "Dirty Dreams", with its memorable guitar work and highly dubious lyrical sentiments, is undoubtedly the pick of the bunch, with "Paint Your Face", "Wind Up" and "City Streets" all being slightly more commercial, but still eminently listenable, in comparison. The EP was an extremely capable effort (which received a truly enthusiastic response from the reviewers at

'Kerrang'), and it proceeded to sell in respectable quantities from the outset.

Furthermore, the record immediately attracted the attention of Mick Wall from 'Kerrang', who duly cornered the lads in the once-famous Wellington venue in Shepherds Bush to ascertain the outfit's history and ambitions. Clearly disenchanted with local reaction, guitarist Nick Burr revealed: *'The Gloucester scene, if such a thing exists, is so out of the way it's very difficult for a band in our position to break out, unless you get some muscle, some cash behind you. And now that we've got our first record released, we're only too happy to come down to London and play as many gigs as possible.'* (Ref: Mega Metal Kerrang No.1, 1986). Affirming their intentions of getting a major record deal and citing a range of musical influences (with some, such as Y&T and DEF LEPPARD, being considerably more apparent than ACCEPT and the SCORPIONS), the musicians obviously had high aspirations. By all accounts, however, they appear to have acquitted themselves favourably in the live environment, so it looks as though their collective expectations were entirely justified. As time went on, though, IDOL RICH started to experience numerous line-up changes, significantly affecting the stability (if not the basic sound) of the outfit. First to depart was hapless vocalist Lee Silver (allegedly for not being sufficiently attractive!), who, after forming the unsuccessful SHOCK PROMISE, eventually resurfaced in LOVE AND WAR, whose sole »Touch Of Class« 7" presently fetches an absurdly high price, given that it wasn't issued until 1989, although the fact that the record is undated and *looks* just like a NWOBHM-era release unquestionably contributes to this anomaly. Silver's immediate replacement was one Mark Thompson-Smith, an unknown quantity at the time, but who later (after experimenting with some ill-fated outfits down South such as TOUCHÉ and FLIGHT 19, the latter appearing on the seldom-seen »Metal For Muthas '92« set) ended up as one of the oft-reshuffled vocalists in the resurrected PRAYING MANTIS venture.

The band's next output was an official cassette featuring the tracks "High Heaven", "Boys Are Missing Out", "All For Your Love", "Without Love" and "Fire Fire". This material comes across as significantly weaker, the outfit having sacrificed energy and spontaneity for a more polished, accessible sound. Nonetheless, the lads continued to tour relentlessly, and both their vinyl and tape releases proceeded to sell in impressive quantities at these outings. Moving into 1987, the line-up changes continued apace; first to go was bassist Jeff Curtis (who later had a very brief spell with GRIM REAPER), who was soon replaced by ex-PERSIAN RISK stalwart Nick Hughes. Next, Thompson-Smith flew the coop, only to be succeeded by the ex-TOBRUK voice, Stuart 'Snake' Neill, whose throaty vocals fitted the group's semi-raunchy style much more appositely, to be honest. As Nick Burr explained upon the latter's appointment: *'As soon as Snake joined the band you could tell there was a difference.'* (Ref: Metal Hammer Vol.2 No.9, September 1987). Back on track, the lads recorded a 'Friday Rock Show' session, broadcast on the 14th of August 1987, featuring "Dirty Dreams", "I.O.U.", "First Time" and "Just When I Thought I Had It All" (a heavily-reworked "Boys Are Missing Out"). The material was strong and the session well-received in general, but the personnel problems continued; Mike Fisher (who had previously been involved with TYRANT in a management/production capacity) left a couple of months later, whereupon he was replaced by Eddie Fincher (another ex-TOBRUK veteran), who had been occupying the drumstool in NO SWEAT for the previous few months, and who would also subsequently deputise in JAGGED EDGE.

Undeterred by all these enforced reshufflings, the outfit continued to tour with well-liked bands such as BLUE BLUD, TILT and CHROME MOLLY until mid-1988, even including the occasional TOBRUK number in their repertoire, and they were to enjoy fairly regular gig reviews in 'Kerrang' at this point in their career. Eventually, however, Snake and Fincher decided that enough was enough and left for pastures new (MIDNIGHT BLUE, in Fincher's case, while Snake actually held an extremely brief tenure with the fledgling WILDHEARTS), effectively resulting in the immediate demise of the luckless IDOL RICH. Too bad. Their sole EP (issued in a generic picture sleeve) is a worthwhile investment, however, and can often still be located at a reasonable price if you shop around. Incidentally, the working partnership of Nick Burr and Tim Jones proceeded to collaborate with Rob Armitage (ex-BABY TUCKOO) and the hugely experienced Steve Hopgood (ex-pretty much everyone) in PASSION, the outfit which rose from the ashes of the original JAGGED EDGE, with Burr subsequently going on to lend his services to Paul Dianno's KILLERS and Steve Grimmett's LIONSHEART in the 90's.

12" EP's
»Working Girls« SRT 1985

INCUBUS

Dave Crawford (v,g)
Ken Crawford (g)
Colin Evans (b)
Steve Crawford (d)

The four-piece concern who chose to be known by the occult name of INCUBUS (not to be confused with numerous overseas outfits from later years or the rather more obscure English bunch who contributed to the »It's Unheard Of!« compilation) were yet another of those small-time acts from the North East who were subsequently unearthed by Guardian back in the label's heyday. After initially being featured on the swiftly-assembled »Pure Overkill« sampler in 1983 (alongside the likes of MILLENNIUM and SPARTAN WARRIOR), the INCUBUS lads (three musical brothers and one of their mates) eventually signed a full album deal, their debut long-player being recorded without too much of a delay and appearing early the following year. On the basis of their two contributions to the aforementioned sampler *viz.* "Ain't Runnin' For You" and "Caught Red Handed", it looked as though the group were in their element when performing an entirely unremarkable, semi-bluesy, melodic rock style of the variety peddled by the likes of AFTER DARK and SHEER KHAN; INCUBUS, therefore, seemed a surprisingly lightweight act for Guardian to have taken under their wing.

By the time their »To The Devil A Daughter« long-player hit the shops, however, the INCUBUS lads showed that they were more than capable of toughening up their act on occasion (with nice twin-guitar work in places), with certain featured compositions suggesting comparisons with the likes of PRAYING MANTIS, MIDAS or pre-vinyl GRIM REAPER. The lads really hit top form on the stand-out effort "Tight Fisted", but elsewhere, unfortunately, there's often a tendency to revert back to overly-melodic, almost mainstream AOR material, shown to greatest (well, worst) effect on the interminable and extraordinarily soppy ballad "You've Taken My Love", which really hammers the final nail into the INCUBUS coffin. All in all, the album represented an extremely inconsistent mish-mash of styles, ranging from metal to semi-pop, and it's frustrating to see an emergent outfit (especially one with a fair bit of potential lurking just beneath the surface) completely failing to make up their mind as to where their true vocation might actually lie.

It's also rather baffling as to why the reclusive

quartet (whose extra-studio activities appear to have been virtually non-existent) adopted such an unrepresentative name, issued their lone album in a sleeve which bristles with satanic imagery and employed song titles (notably "Life Beyond The Grave", "Night Of Vengeance" and the not-entirely-original "Highway To Hell") which suggested to prospective buyers that they were very much of the WITCHFYNDE or PAGAN ALTAR school of thought. All in all, it's a disappointing album that most fans of the genre can easily live without, and a corresponding verdict of 'could have done much better' on the INCUBUS report card. There was, incidentally, a strong suggestion that a second long-player (tentatively titled »Seance«) might actually have been in the pipeline for 1985, but it looks as though this particular release was eventually shelved (along with the FALCON and CRUCIBLE efforts) in the wake of the financial crisis which gripped their label at the time. A lucky escape, perhaps…

LP's
»To The Devil A Daughter« Guardian 1984

Exclusive Compilation Appearances
"Ain't Runnin' For You" on »Pure Overkill« LP Guardian 1983
"Caught Red Handed" on »Pure Overkill« LP Guardian 1983

INFLUENCE

R. Brown
G. Ross
A. Gordon
K. Reach

The unremarkably-named INFLUENCE (nothing to do with the outfit of the same identity who feature way back in the IRON MAIDEN family tree) were something of a mystery, emerging in 1983 with a one-off single and then disappearing back into utter obscurity without ever making a name for themselves at all. The outfit's two-tracker features a prominent credit for 'Chrysalis Music' (something which has caused collectors a bit of confusion over the years), but it seems to be unrelated to the major label after all, since the release is almost certainly a private affair and would have featured a 'RCA Music' credit if, like the WOLF and GRAND PRIX releases, it had really been connected with Chrysalis Records. Anyway, it's a pretty curious effort, with quite unusual arrangements and vocals, although it's certainly a heavy enough release, with both "No Survivors" and "Queen Of Madness" coming across as mid-paced metal lying somewhere between BLACKWYCH and MEGATON. The vocals are a bit odd, and the music generally sounds more European than British, but I'm pretty sure they were a UK outfit after all. A couple of the members' names look typically Scottish, so I'd imagine they might well have been from either North of the border or from Ireland. The record is a scarce one nowadays, and was issued in an unusually-colourful sleeve with a metal-looking logo and a lot of clouds, while the reverse cover features the very silly lyrics to both tracks. If anyone happens to know anything about this bunch, drop us a line…

7" Singles
»No Survivors« Private 1983

INTERNATIONAL HEROES

Ricci Wright (v)
Gary Wallace (g)
Paul Douglas (b)
Roger Periam (k)
Dave Maile (d)

With their rather ambitious name being taken from an album track by MOTT THE HOOPLE offshoot the BRITISH LIONS, Cambridgeshire's INTERNATIONAL HEROES were certainly quite happy to be affiliated with the sleazy sounds of the 70's, rather than being one of the many hopefuls who shamelessly jumped on the NWOBHM bandwagon at the earliest opportunity. Indeed, with the five-piece apparently being big fans of Ian Hunter's music in general, you might have expected their output to be fairly raunchy rock of the early 70's variety. In fact, it transpired that they undoubtedly had more in common with some of the hard-rocking material churned out by DAWN TRADER or VARDIS than with fellow MOTT-worshippers such as the GUNSLINGERS. Their debut single, issued in the first half of 1982, coupled the mid-tempo (but pretty forgettable) "Strange Situation" with the slower, semi-acoustic "Silent Dreams", the latter also being an unremarkable effort, despite a reasonably heavy mid-section. Issued (without the extravagance of a picture sleeve) on the tantalisingly-named Heavy Leather label, the 7" wasn't exactly the sort of thing the boisterous metal community was clamouring for, and evidently sold in modest quantities at the time. As a direct result, »Strange Situation« is a scarcely sighted memento these days, but isn't considered a particularly collectable release as yet.

Even so, the musicians seemed to regard their introductory release as a success of some description, and began formulating plans for the next stage of their career. Later in the year, the group decided to spread themselves considerably wider than they had attempted thus far, and proceeded to hit the road for their *'Great British Blood'n'Thunder Tour'*, a lengthy trek which would ultimately take in numerous rock-friendly venues throughout the country. Although this series of outings was originally intended to promote the second INTERNATIONAL HEROES single, due to feature "Good Times" and a track also entitled "International Heroes" (in all probability, the BRITISH LIONS effort mentioned previously), nobody actually seems to possess this release, suggesting that, in the end, it probably failed to reach the pressing stage. You never know, though, an example could still surface even after all this time, so I guess we'll just have to wait and see. By 1983, the lads had recruited a new vocalist in the form of Mickie Shaw, continuing to do their own thing in the live environment whenever the circumstances were propitious. Another new single, featuring an interpretation of MOTT THE HOOPLE's "All The Young Dudes" (a more glaringly obvious choice for this particular bunch would be impossible to imagine), was subsequently scheduled for release, although, yet again, it looks as though the outfit's attempts to get the record pressed were ultimately unsuccessful.

The band's repeated failure to keep the promises that they were so fond of making in the press, coupled with their apparent inability to deliver a follow-up to their first single, seems to have led to their downfall in the long term. By the end of 1983, no less than four members (already frustrated by the band's failure to release any further product) departed *en masse* (having clashed over the outfit's future direction), leaving drummer Dave Maile to write new material (with original vocalist Ricci Wright) and try to recruit a new set of accomplices. Although an advert was placed in 'Kerrang' in the opening weeks of 1984 in an attempt to facilitate this process (with some rather unsubstantiated plans for a full LP release being outlined as an incentive), it looks as though the struggling group never managed to achieve a suitably stable revitalised line-up after all. Predictably, this meant that those involved with the venture wouldn't get a second chance to deliver the goods, and no further INTERNATIONAL HEROES recordings ever materialised. By 1985, having decided to throw his weight behind a more established act, mainman Dave Maile had become the latest sticksman to take part in the great DESOLATION ANGELS personnel lottery, although his tenure appears to have been predictably brief.

7" Singles
»Strange Situation« Heavy Leather Records 1982

IONA

Geoff Smith (v)
Andy Berry (g)
Wayne Williams (g)
Adrian Jenkins (b)
Lloyd Davies (d)

Originally forming under the rather overused name of GBH as far back as 1977, this particular bunch of Gwent-based metalheads further helped to establish Welsh music as a real force to be reckoned with in the NWOBHM era. While still operating as GBH, the lads rapidly won over many a crowd in South Wales and the West of England with their energetic live shows and wide-ranging repertoire of exclusively original material, which must have come as a welcome contrast to all those hopefuls who were perfectly content to trundle out the predictable cover versions at every available opportunity. Featuring a menacing three-guitar attack at one point, but subsequently reverting to a more manageable five-piece, the outfit eventually made it into a nearby recording facility towards the end of 1980, capturing eight *'live in the studio'* numbers for posterity. With self-penned compositions such as "A Million Miles", "666" (blimey, how metal can you get?), "Evil Woman" and "Rock And Roll Hero" coming across, in places, as a rather less sophisticated version of DAMASCUS (with a bit of a 70's influence in the guitar department), the band were, at that time, happily operating in a reasonably heavy style, albeit quite melodic and accessible.

Having decided upon a name change to the somewhat ethereal IONA (a handle utilised by local legends LONE STAR in their early days, incidentally, and shared with numerous folk and progressive ensembles over the years) in 1981, the lads subsequently recorded a proper demo featuring the recently-penned "Can It Be Me" and "Don't Need You Honey". Clearly, associated with their revised identity was a definite shift towards slightly harder material, this capable pair of compositions being much more in line with the overwhelming NWOBHM sound of the day. Within a year, their »Don't Cry For The Innocent« (not nearly as pompous as it sounds, fortunately) single was released to an overwhelmingly favourable response (both locally and further afield), the two-tracker even making the number two position (a remarkable achievement for such a little-known outfit) in the 'Melody Maker' Heavy Metal Chart in September of that year. It's a cracking release, with both the A-side and "You Ain't A Lady" being immensely similar to certain MENDES PREY material from the same period (with a bit of LYADRIVE thrown in for good measure), each combining substantial riffs and excellent vocals with memorable, catchy choruses to great effect. Issued without the extravagance of a picture sleeve (and, to be honest, featuring a very dull label design), this highly-prized item should, in my extremely humble opinion, be on every serious NWOBHM wants list.

Former GBH bassist Colwyn Knight returned to the fold later in the year, and yet more tracks were duly laid down for future use at the famous Loco Studios in Usk. Rejected, sadly, by Virgin Records (who were apparently quite interested at one stage), but undeterred, the persevering band continued to delight audiences until late 1984, when the sudden and untimely death of drummer Lloyd Davies effectively signalled the end of IONA. The remaining members struggled on valiantly for a few months, but eventually decided to call it a day, given that they no longer had the heart to continue. It was a sad end for an act who deserved to have got much further in the music business, but at least they enjoyed a reasonable amount of local adulation during their time together. Guitarist Andy Berry, incidentally, later compiled an unofficial GBH/IONA anthology tape which serves both as a tribute and as *'a reminder of a band who were at their best when they played loud and live!'* I'll drink to that.

7" Singles
»Don't Cry For The Innocent« Loco Records 1982

IPANEMA KATZ

Paul Taylor (v)
Russell Simon (g)
Paul Stutt (b)
Paul Nichols (d)

After releasing just one single in 1984, Worcestershire's VIRGIN STAR (see separate entry) ran into a few personnel problems, some of which were caused by losing their drummer to GRIM REAPER, and the act decided to reinvent themselves completely after a period of enforced restructuring. With the surviving nucleus of Russell Simon and Paul Taylor recruiting a new rhythm section (bassist Paul Stutt and drummer Paul Nichols) in the spring of 1985, it didn't take the newly-established quartet (who were now calling themselves the IPANEMA KATZ) all that long to pen some original compositions and begin thinking about their first vinyl release. Indeed, there were early reports that the debut single would be based around a number entitled "Coral Bar", although this seems to have been shelved in favour of a two-tracker (issued on their original label, Official Records) coupling "Night Kixx" and "Out Of Reach". After the blistering VIRGIN STAR 7", however, this was a major step backwards, and the outfit seemed to be reverting to an unremarkable brand of sub-HANOI ROCKS nonsense. Sure, it was sleazy enough, but carried off with very little conviction, and "Night Kixx" was an undeniably dreary semi-ballad, although the flipside was marginally more listenable, with elements of CRY, the GUNSLINGERS or the IDLE FLOWERS coming through from time to time. The release of the debut IPANEMA KATZ offering failed to make front page headlines, and the outfit more or less went back into hiding straight away, possibly having concluded that they might have been in too much of a hurry to get some product onto the market.

Still, they kept plugging away, and returned in 1987 with another two-tracker, this time featuring "Sister Resister" and "Hot Tonight". It was a considerably more upbeat and convincing affair, which seemed to show that the IPANEMA KATZ were heading in the right direction at last, and it soon won the hearts of the reviewers at 'Kerrang', who tipped the band as a bunch to watch from that point onwards. This latest 7" had actually identified the tracks as having been taken from their forthcoming »Summers In Saigon« long-player, also scheduled to be released on Official Records before the year was out, although I suspect that this particular album never made it to the pressing stage. I could be wrong, and there's a pretty good chance that it was actually recorded at some point, but I've never seen a copy or heard of one being offered for sale, so it looks as though the lads might even have called it a day before the LP's intended release date. In any case, there was little or no mention of the IPANEMA KATZ in the music press thereafter, so the hapless ensemble probably went under as the UK sleaze scene began to disintegrate towards the end of the decade. It's not inconceivable that other singles were released along the way (there are several Official catalogue numbers which haven't been accounted for as yet), so kindly let us know if you're aware of any additional releases. The efforts described here were issued in quite unusual and colourful picture sleeves, but don't seem to have been pressed in huge quantities, so you probably won't see them too often.

7" Singles
»Night Kixx« Official Records 1985
»Sister Resister« Official Records 1987

IRON MAIDEN

Paul Dianno (v)
Dave Murray (g)
Steve Harris (b)
Doug Sampson (d)

If any of you die-hard MAIDEN fans have turned straight to this entry in the hope of discovering a few exclusive snippets of information about your heroes, you're probably in for a bit of a disappointment. The band's story has been told and retold in obsessive detail by their official (and unofficial) biographers, and we can hardly hope to compete with such comprehensive tomes within the confines of a dozen or so pages. Still, if you're just looking for the bare bones of their history and development, then this is probably as good a place as any. The musical origins of IRON MAIDEN can be traced back a long way, as far as the late 60's in the case of one or two members, but the common thread is that most, if not all, of the musicians involved over the years, have been experienced players on London's rock scene. Several of these individuals first gravitated together towards the end of 1975 to form a barely-recognisable incarnation of MAIDEN, the band originally assembling itself around bassist Steve Harris, who had initially stated his intentions with the little-known GYPSY'S KISS (who formed in around 1973 but failed to progress beyond the usual small-time aspirations during their relatively brief existence) before moving on to the slightly more successful SMILER, an act who also gave up the ghost without ever achieving any great level of recognition. Joining him in the IRON MAIDEN (famously taken from the name of a medieval torture device) ranks in the first instance were a ridiculously youthful vocalist called Paul Mario Day, unconvincingly-named drummer Ron Rebel (aka Ron Matthews), plus the guitar pairing of Dave Sullivan and Terry Rance (the latter played with acts such as LIZARD in later years). Not much happened at first, although the lads were happy to wait until the moment was exactly right before mounting their challenge on the rock world, so the still-developing outfit began penning a suitable repertoire of covers and originals with which to storm an unsuspecting live circuit.

The lads made an inauspicious debut at a minor pub venue in the summer of 1976, but few casual observers saw a great deal of potential in an outfit who, in defiance of the overwhelming punk influx, were content to churn out a set which owed a great deal to bands (SABBATH, PRIEST, PURPLE) who had now lost much of their original appeal. Still, MAIDEN seemed to know what they were doing, and plodded along (without receiving a great deal of media attention) for another couple of years, during which time they endured numerous personnel changes. Paul Mario Day (who later had better luck with MORE and WILDFIRE) was ousted after only a few live appearances, whereupon he was succeeded by Dennis Wilcock (another SMILER veteran), who seemed to fit in slightly better. The first-choice guitarists also failed to make the grade in the long run, and so new blood was soon being brought in, with Bob Sawyer (aka Rob Angelo) and Dave Murray getting their big chance to play a role in the group's fortunes. As it turned out, Murray was to take his leave of MAIDEN after a short time, having had a few disagreements with Dennis Wilcock, and he hooked up with East End rivals URCHIN (see separate entry) while things sorted themselves out in the MAIDEN camp. Bob Sawyer also failed to last the distance and was soon on his way, later joining forces with PRAYING MANTIS, whereupon stand-in guitarist Terry Wapram was utilised to keep things going. Next up was a change in drummer, with Ron Rebel going off to do his own thing with acts such as McCOY and the ELECTRIC GYPSIES, whereupon Barry Purkis came in as a replacement. Strangely, the lads also tried out a keyboard player (Tony Moore) instead of a second guitarist as something of an experiment, but things didn't really work out at all for this incarnation, and the luckless Moore was soon out on his ear, although he later resurfaced in SHOGUN.

By now, it was late 1977, and there were already signs that the whole punk thing was beginning to self-destruct, and early indicators of a possible rock resurgence (some major acts were still more than capable of selling out lengthy UK tours) seemed to suggest that IRON MAIDEN were heading in the right direction, but the band were still struggling with personnel problems. Soon, Dennis Wilcock was to depart (forming an unsuccessful act called V1 with former colleague Terry Wapram), which paved the way for Dave Murray to return to the fold, and Barry Purkis (later of SAMSON) was tactfully invited to leave in order to make way for another of Steve Harris' former chums from SMILER, Doug Sampson. By early 1978, they had apparently weathered the worst of the storm, and things were showing signs of settling down at last, apart from the glaring absence of a suitable frontman, although the situation improved immeasurably when the members of MAIDEN discovered the gravel-throated Paul Dianno fronting an obscure bunch called BIRD OF PREY, and swiftly persuaded him to join in the fun. At the umpteenth attempt, MAIDEN finally seemed to have established a plateau of stability, and were soon reinforcing their reputation as local contenders by playing an exhaustive series of gigs around the capital, plugging in their equipment at whichever shabby dive would have them. Before long, they had won over many a crowd, and were to become firm favourites at several minor venues, notably the Ruskin Arms in the East End. By the end of the year, though, it was finally time to hit the studio with a vengeance, and the lads made the pilgrimage to Spaceward in Cambridge to lay down their first official tape, capturing versions of "Prowler", "Invasion", "Iron Maiden" and "Strange World". The four-tracker would soon be making a bit of an impact in the early part of 1979…

The cassette was never really recorded with the intention of selling to the general public, and only a relatively small quantity were manufactured in the first instance. One of several individuals to be strategically targeted to receive a copy was Neal Kay, DJ at the Heavy Metal Soundhouse, who was soon playing the contents to a rapturous reception at his rock discos. Kay rapidly identified the potential of this developing metal scene, and duly rounded up two of his other 'discoveries', ANGEL WITCH and SAMSON, before sending the three acts out on the road for a series of gigs entitled the 'Metal Crusade', most of which were a resounding triumph. Before long, more copies of the demo were being manufactured, and there were soon a pretty sizeable number in circulation. The tracks became mainstays of the rock charts for months on

end, and MAIDEN were now practically a household name, for fans in the capital, at least. Further exposure was yet to come, with *the* article in 'Sounds' and a well-received slot supporting MOTÖRHEAD at a secret gig, and the members finally came to the conclusion that they should get some vinyl out. Still, they had little or no cash, so the ever-dependable demo tape was salvaged for use once again. In fact, they didn't even have the studio masters by this stage, and had to resort to low-generation copies, which is one of the reasons their first slice of vinyl will never win any prizes for sound quality or be held up as a prime example of an accomplished production. MAIDEN used three of the numbers from the tape (omitting "Strange World"), and pressed up five thousand copies of »The Soundhouse Tapes«, most of which had already been sold to rabid metalheads within a fortnight. The general public was now able to hear MAIDEN's contemporary take on the heavy rock style, and it's fair to say that there were certainly elements of some of the great British heavyweights of the 70's in the melting pot, particularly on "Iron Maiden" and the excellent "Prowler". Mind you, "Invasion" was a bit of an odd one, and it's not at all easy to see where that quirky style might have come from.

The group had certainly managed to create something highly listenable, raw and exciting, though, and certain sections of the music press were soon intimating that MAIDEN might even have evolved from a more punk-oriented concern in the first instance, something which the members were at pains to deny from stage one. The outfit had always been exponents of the rock style, and had developed an energetic approach over the years, so I suspect that the main comparison was drawn from the vocal characteristics of Paul Dianno, who wasn't a rock frontman in the traditional sense, but who wasn't consciously trying to bridge the gap between punk and metal either. These brief attempts to tar MAIDEN with the punk brush failed to hamper their progress at all, and the lads were soon playing showcase gigs for major labels and laying down their first session for the 'Friday Rock Show', where they were joined by second guitarist Tony Parsons, who (like Paul Cairns and Paul Todd, his direct predecessors in the position) was to enjoy an extremely brief spell in the ranks of the MAIDEN army. The lads laid down versions of "Iron Maiden", "Running Free", "Transylvania" and "Sanctuary", the legendary first broadcast occurring on the 14th of December 1979 and setting the stage for MAIDEN's subsequent programme of world domination. They were rapidly snapped up by EMI, who afforded them the opportunity of contributing two tracks to their »Metal For Muthas« sampler, so the pairing of "Sanctuary" and "Wrathchild" was captured for posterity in due course. By the time the album appeared, however, Tony Parsons had been supplanted by the immensely experienced Dennis Stratton (formerly with UNITED, REMUS DOWN BOULEVARD et al.), while drummer Doug Sampson had given way to Clive Burr, recruited from the SAMSON fold. Still, the record showed MAIDEN to be one of the more promising metal acts of the period, and their contributions stood out as particularly capable efforts. On the basis of the selection of material submitted for use on the sampler, EMI gave a few bands the chance to release their own vinyl, but more or less pinned all their hopes on IRON MAIDEN, who were identified as the label's tip for the top at a fairly early stage. Whereas ANGEL WITCH, SAMSON and ETHEL THE FROG all fell by the wayside after just one or two releases on EMI, MAIDEN were to endure a far greater level of longevity, and began their career in earnest with a humble 7" single.

That single, released in the early part of 1980, coupled "Running Free" with "Burning Ambition", two tracks which caught the public's imagination in no uncertain terms, and the record was soon hurtling into the 'Top 40', winning the lads the chance to strut their stuff on 'Top Of The Pops', a programme which was far more at home with mainstream pop acts. Still, MAIDEN put in a sterling performance of "Running Free", having refused to mime as requested, showing everyone that they could deliver the goods without any sort of studio trickery. Next up was the brief 'Metal For Muthas Tour', which saw MAIDEN gigging with a selection of hopefuls such as PRAYING MANTIS, SLEDGEHAMMER and old muckers ANGEL WITCH, before they returned to the studio to lay down their full-length debut for EMI. The album was recorded in stages, in between further touring activity (supporting JUDAS PRIEST on a lengthy UK tour), and was rushed out within a matter of weeks. The eponymous long-player reworked several favourites from the demo and session, but introduced the fans to storming numbers such as "Charlotte The Harlot", "Phantom Of The Opera" and the instrumental "Transylvania", the latter two showing the band to be developing their trademark twin-guitar framework and skilful interplay between the two axemen. Admittedly, MAIDEN were hardly the first act to employ two guitarists, but they certainly did their utmost to turn the duelling style into an art form. The record was a phenomenal success, rocketing into the mainstream charts at the outset, and achieving an almost unprecedented 'Top 5' placing in the process. There was no doubt about it: MAIDEN had now arrived in major fashion, and capitalised on staggering album sales with an extensive headlining tour with PRAYING MANTIS in tow, the whole series of shows confirming their reputation as an exceptionally capable metal proposition.

Along the way, another 7" appeared, a three-tracker based around a brand-new recording of »Metal For Muthas« favourite "Sanctuary". The lads were soon courting controversy, however, with the sleeve initially depicting the British Prime Minister, Maggie Thatcher (who was hardly the flavour of the month at the time), meeting a sticky end at the hands of their ever-present mascot and sleeve character, good old Eddie. Some people regarded this as a politically-motivated act of defiance which struck a blow for the unemployed and disenchanted, while others took the more plausible and less sensationalistic view that this was just a tongue-in-cheek indication that the 'true' IRON MAIDEN was more than a match for this similarly-nicknamed figure of derision. Either way, the powers-that-be decreed that this sort of thing just wasn't on, and so the subsequent pressing was issued in a modified cover which obscured the offensive (in more ways than one) visage. Next up for the naughty scamps was a prestigious appearance at the 1980 Reading Festival, where several leading figures of the NWOBHM explosion (notably ANGEL WITCH and SAMSON) had been added to the bill. True to form, MAIDEN delivered a typically stunning performance, and delighted the massive crowd in no uncertain terms, something which largely stole much of the limelight from bewildered headliners UFO. The lads then hopped onto a European jaunt with strange bedfellows KISS, although it seems to have worked out quite well for the Londoners in the long run. It was to be the end of the road for the unsettled Dennis Stratton, though, and the guitarist soon stormed off in a huff and established his own LIONHEART (see separate entry) venture with erstwhile TYGERS OF PAN TANG frontman Jess Cox.

MAIDEN soon found a suitable replacement in the shape of Adrian Smith, recruited from the ranks of the struggling URCHIN, and the new axeman was soon being paraded in front of the fans at some end-of-year gigs, one of which was famously filmed and issued (in abridged form) as the »Live At The Rainbow« video. There was also another vinyl offering for the fans to add to their rapidly-expanding collections, another single (issued in both 7" and 12" formats) based around the newly-recorded number "Women In Uniform", a little-known track originally penned by Aussie obscurists SKYHOOKS. It made a brief appearance in the charts (as had »Sanctuary«), but it was more a case of breaking in new member Adrian Smith than anything more serious. Moving into 1981, the all-conquering outfit were soon ensconced in the studio once more, and proceeded to lay down their second album without making too much of a song and dance about it. »Killers« hit the shops a month or two later, and was rapidly to make an impression on the charts, although the reaction of the press (and, to a lesser extent, the fans) was slightly less effusive than in the case of their debut. Indeed, it turned out to be their least successful studio album of all, but it undoubtedly had its moments, notably old favourite "Wrathchild", "Purgatory" and "Twilight Zone" (an archetypal NWOBHM offering), although it's certainly fair to say that some of the other material on display was comparatively weak, and the whole thing had possibly been thrown together just a bit too hastily for comfort. Still, »Twilight Zone« and »Purgatory« were trundled out as singles, and both dented the charts as usual, the lads having gone out on the road for a lengthy series of headlining dates by this stage. First up were the UK shows, then a comprehensive tour of Europe, and finally a brief Japanese jaunt, the latter being celebrated by the release of their »Maiden Japan« live EP.

There was little respite once these headlining shows had been completed, however, and the quintet were soon jetting off to the States for some support gigs with JUDAS PRIEST, where they took the opportunity to showcase a selection of their material to some extremely receptive audiences. Mind you, things weren't going entirely according to plan in terms of the band's delicate relationship with their unhappy frontman, Paul Dianno, and the latter was soon experiencing a fair bit of personal strife which distracted him from the day-to-day activities of performing in a successful metal group. He managed to get through the American gigs and a few more European shows, but eventually decided that his priorities lay elsewhere, and took his leave of IRON MAIDEN, later forming LONEWOLF after getting his head together. There was no chance whatsoever of MAIDEN calling it a day, though, and they were soon scouting around for local talent, concluding that the right man for the job was a certain Bruce Dickinson (aka Bruce Bruce), who had put in a pretty sterling performance on the last two SAMSON albums. Dickinson was swiftly lured into the ranks of MAIDEN, and was soon learning an entirely new repertoire, the frontman getting a first taste of his role as MAIDEN figurehead at some low-key gigs in Italy towards the end of the year, after which the outfit returned to Blighty to round off 1981 with a couple of shows in London. As usual, they kicked off the new year by entering the studios to record an album, and the sessions for that *'difficult'* third LP occupied their time for the next couple of months.

The Dickinson-fronted IRON MAIDEN burst forth with a long-player entitled »The Number Of The Beast«, a record which dwarfed its patchy predecessor in terms of intensity and musical ability. This truly remarkable offering represented a new era in MAIDEN's history, with Dickinson's *'air-raid siren'* vocals (as they would soon become universally known) elevating the latest material to the highest standards of the power metal (which hadn't even been invented at the time) genre. Tracks such as "Children Of The Damned", "22 Acacia Avenue", "The Number Of The Beast", "Run To The Hills" and "Hallowed Be Thy Name" were all instant classics, and virtually the entire selection of featured compositions would swiftly find their way into the band's live repertoire. The whole performance was virtually faultless, the charging guitars and soaring vocals creating a perfect blend of melody and intensity which tapped into the metal psyche in no uncertain terms, with stratospheric sales of the long-player taking MAIDEN to the very top of the mainstream album charts for the first time. It's hard to convey just how highly-regarded the lads actually became in the wake of this release, as even the extraordinary distinction of a British 'Number One' album barely justifies their level of adulation. To say that the Londoners were a popular act at this stage of their career would be the understatement of the decade. DEF LEPPARD were popular, IRON MAIDEN were *huge*. Before long, they were out on tour once more, rapidly cultivating a deserved reputation as one of the hardest-gigging and most entertaining acts of the period. Their tour took them all around the UK and Europe once more, at major venues this time, and the reception experienced at every port of call was nothing short of ecstatic. More singles followed as a matter of routine, and »Run To The Hills« saw the lads hitting the 'Top 10' for the very first time, although its successor (»The Number Of The Beast«) didn't quite emulate this phenomenal success.

The MAIDEN lads were riding the crest of a wave once more, and early suggestions that they might initially have struggled to maintain their popularity after Dianno's departure were soon being treated with the contempt they deserved. It was off to the States next, playing a few well-attended shows with a couple of more established headlining acts, first the immensely well-liked RAINBOW, and then with the SCORPIONS. It was all a huge success, but it was soon back to the UK for a prestigious headlining slot at the 1982 Reading Festival, where MAIDEN delivered one of the most memorable performances of their entire career, exhausting the rabid crowd with a lengthy selection of material which had already become firm favourites among a huge percentage of rock fans. Within a mere couple of weeks of this triumphal appearance, the lads were back in the States for more shows alongside JUDAS PRIEST, and the year was rounded off with frenzied gigs in Japan and Australia, after which the group finally allowed themselves a bit of a breather (for a day or two) in order to recover. In fact, it wasn't all that long before the workaholic musicians were making plans to go back into the studio to undertake the obligatory new-year album recordings, although there was now an important matter to which they had to attend. At the beginning of 1983, the lads came to a mutual decision that Clive Burr (who had been accused of all sorts of irresponsible behaviour during the previous few months) was becoming something of a liability, whereupon the poor chap was given the grand order of the boot. A new sticksman was soon identified in the form of the dependable and experienced Nicko McBrain, whom the lads had known for some time. McBrain had played with the likes of

the STREETWALKERS and PAT TRAVERS in the past, and had latterly been lending a hand to French rockers TRUST, with whom (oddly enough) Clive Burr had a brief spell after MAIDEN sent him packing in the first instance. With the reshuffle complete, long-player number four was soon on the cards, and MAIDEN were soon beavering away in the studio to create the much-anticipated follow-up to their chart-topping »The Number Of The Beast« opus.

MAIDEN's »Piece Of Mind«, which appeared in the spring of 1983, wasn't an instant album in the sense that its predecessor had been, and the new record was a considerably more complex and less vocal-dominated affair which gave all the musicians ample opportunity to show off their skills. It may not have hit the top spot in the album charts this time (it got to number three), but it still contained some extremely respectable compositions, with stand-out numbers including "Where Eagles Dare", "The Trooper" and "Quest For Fire". Both »Flight Of Icarus« and »The Trooper« were released as singles to promote the group further, and each achieved a healthy placing in the charts once more. After that, the lads undertook an incredibly lengthy touring schedule which lasted until the end of the year, taking in the UK, Europe and North America (playing alongside SAXON at some major stadia), before returning to Europe for yet more gigs (where their famous mascot was now becoming something of a pivotal feature). After that, it's hardly surprising that they took several months off while they reflected on their achievements thus far. It was, on the face of it, all going swimmingly for MAIDEN at this time, but would they be able to maintain their status as national heroes? After all, the initial NWOBHM explosion had now dwindled to a major extent, and 99% of their contemporaries from the heady days of 1980 had faded away into total insignificance. Well, since they're still going strong today, I reckon it's fair to say that they well and truly transcended their humble NWOBHM beginnings to become something far more acceptable to the general rock fan. MAIDEN still took a fair bit of stick for their lyrics at times (especially the type of hackneyed sci-fi/fantasy/horror/heroic nonsense which perpetuates the widespread notion that all heavy metal fans are overgrown adolescent males with a tenuous grasp of reality and a pathological fear of women), but they somehow always managed to get away with it.

Album number five, »Powerslave«, emerged in the summer of 1984, and turned out to be something of a return to the kind of upbeat and memorable (but not overly-ambitious) material which had been performed with such great aplomb on »The Number Of The Beast«. It was all immensely listenable, with catchy, driving compositions such as "Aces High", "Flash Of The Blade" and "Back In The Village" contrasting nicely with the atmospheric title track and the epic "Rime Of The Ancient Mariner", based around a literary work by Coleridge, a famous romantic junkie poet. The new long-player made its customary impact on the charts, and it seemed as though MAIDEN were now assured of a 'Top 3' placing with every release by this stage. »Aces High« and »2 Minutes To Midnight« were the chosen singles this time, and their massive fan base continued to snap up every available piece of vinyl, which were now being issued in multiple formats such as 12" EP, picture discs, coloured vinyl and shaped discs. By now, MAIDEN were also becoming quite generous with their B-sides, treating their fans to exclusive tracks, live versions and well-chosen covers rather than the endless stream of remixes and fillers employed by certain other acts in more or less the same position. The inevitable world tour was an unfeasibly demanding year-long series of shindigs which took the lads even further afield than before, including (in addition to the relatively mundane British jaunt, although they were rapidly running out of venues big enough to hold all their followers) Eastern Europe, virtually the whole of North America (some with TWISTED SISTER), Brazil (for the Rock In Rio Festival), Japan and Australia, the lads working solidly from the summer of 1984 until the summer of 1985 with barely any period of respite along the way. Sheer lunacy, but it seemed to pay off in terms of the virtually unprecedented level of adulation which the lads were now experiencing.

Instead of taking six months off after the tour before thinking about their next record, however, the band decided that the time was right to deliver a live album, and they certainly had no shortage of material to choose from by this juncture. In the event, the double »Live After Death« set was predominantly taken from recordings made in California, and the fans were soon able to purchase an official MAIDEN live release (the bootleggers had been doing a roaring trade up until then) to call their own. There was no suggestion that the live album was a cop-out which

Photo: Dirk Lehberger

saved the outfit from having to deliver a new studio long-player, and the quality of the release was sufficiently high that the record was soon selling in equivalently impressive quantities as their more conventional studio releases. In fact, it was more or less treated as MAIDEN's regular annual LP, even to the extent that two live singles (»Run To The Hills« and »Running Free«) were released to coincide with the main product. The members of MAIDEN, meanwhile, were taking an extremely well-deserved break from the demands of the music business for the time being. Before long, however, they inevitably bowed to pressure to come up with another full-length effort, so they trooped back into the studio (it no doubt helped that their facility of choice was situated in the Bahamas) in the spring of 1986. »Somewhere In Time«, which emerged in the autumn, saw the lads broadening their horizons and experimenting with synthesizer effects to add a new dimension to the MAIDEN sound, and, even if it didn't represent a full-scale wimp-out in any sense, it certainly brought a more polished style to the fore. Even if there were a few minor concessions to the increasingly-popular melodic rock market, MAIDEN really needn't have bothered; they were never about fashion or trends, and their loyal fans would have bought their albums no matter what they put on them. At least we didn't get "Jazz Odyssey"...

»Somewhere In Time« was a mature album, but it still had some high-calibre numbers, notably "Wasted Years", "Heaven Can Wait" and "Deja-Vu", and it soon occupied the inevitable 'Top 3' placing in the charts as usual. »Wasted Years« and »Stranger In A Strange Land« constituted the standard two singles, and then it was out on tour once more. To be honest, it all seemed to be getting rather predictable, the lads releasing a successful album and two singles every year, before going out on a ludicrously extensive world tour to promote themselves further. This sort of routine might be a record company's wet dream, but it can often stifle a group's artistic creativity if they can do no wrong in the eyes of the fans and media. Would it all get too much to bear, or would MAIDEN just continue to plod along in the same manner until the end of time? Their latest tour was the expected year-long slog, taking them all over the world as usual, although there were now precious few parts of the globe left to conquer. In one respect, however, such activities were quite beneficial, as it was now impossible to deliver a full album on a yearly basis, given that their punishing touring schedule now occupied their time for such extended periods. By this point, therefore, the fans were only likely to see a new record every couple of years, giving the musicians slightly more of an opportunity to come up with a suitably strong selection of novel material. Work on album number seven finally began at the tail end of 1987, but the whole recording process turned out to be quite a relaxed and unhurried affair, which must have come as a welcome relief after their recent global jaunt.

The long-player, »Seventh Son Of A Seventh Son«, appeared in the spring of 1988, and signified MAIDEN's first real attempt to issue a concept album based around some mystical themes. It wasn't too embarrassing or pretentious, fortunately, and it just seems to have been a notion they couldn't resist toying with at the time. Musically, it was all a bit less intense than before, and the dynamic arrangements with duelling guitars seemed to be largely a thing of the past, with MAIDEN now apparently having considerably more in common with certain emerging acts who were once mere imitators, particularly the likes of QUEENSRYCHE and HELLOWEEN. Nevertheless, strong efforts as the memorable "Can I Play With Madness" and "The Evil That Men Do" were supremely-accomplished and well-crafted numbers, while heavier sections of the title track and "Only The Good Die Young", for example, illustrated that the lads were more than capable of returning to a more powerful writing style if the fans rejected their latest direction. In fact, the fans went absolutely crazy-ape-bonkers for it, and MAIDEN soon had their first number one album since »The Number Of The Beast«. Sales were truly astronomical, and EMI decided to cash in on a huge wave of interest by issuing no less than four singles from the album. »Can I Play With Madness«, »The Evil That Men Do«, »The Clairvoyant« and »Infinite Dreams« were all trotted out over a period of several months, and each one followed its predecessor into the 'Top 10', achieving the band's highest collective chart placings in the process. This time, the mammoth world tour started out in North America (by now, they were more than capable of headlining the enormodomes themselves), although MAIDEN returned to the UK in time to headline the 1988 Monsters Of Rock Festival, where a huge Donington crowd lapped up a legendary performance from an outfit who could still deliver the goods on both vinyl and in the live arena. After that, it was off to Europe for another lengthy trek before finally terminating their exhaustive schedule with a series of UK dates, the majority of which came in the shape of multiple nights at some of the most capacious venues in the land.

The outfit took a bit of a well-deserved sabbatical during 1989, during which time Adrian Smith went off to do his own thing (Bruce Dickinson also took time out to record a solo album, but he soon returned to the MAIDEN fold), which duly became known as the A.S.A.P. project, where he joined forces with various old chums and session faces to create something a bit different. Sadly, the lightweight album which resulted (»Silver And Gold«) was a bit *too* different for the majority of MAIDEN fans, and the LP died a complete and utter death in spite of some increasingly-desperate hype and promotional activities as the release date approached. Still,

Smith seems to have enjoyed his freedom more than he originally anticipated, and decided that he was in no great hurry to return to the MAIDEN ranks. With Smith out of the picture for the time being, the lads recruited Janick Gers, a veteran of such acts as WHITE SPIRIT, GILLAN and the ill-fated GOGMAGOG, and the newly-rearranged outfit eventually began work on their next album, scheduled for release at some point in the latter half of 1990 (by which time the lads had observed the re-release of all of their early singles on a ten-part series of limited EP's). The new MAIDEN album (»No Prayer For The Dying«) subsequently appeared as planned, and this much-anticipated record saw the lads delivering a rather more down-to-earth set of compositions (an intriguing title was "Fates Warning", perhaps in honour of some famous clones?) which, although still tuneful and accessible enough, weren't quite as blatantly chart-friendly as those featured on »Seventh Son Of A Seventh Son«. It was ironic, therefore, that the new record didn't quite take them to the very top of the album charts this time, giving some rather mixed messages about the sort of material that their followers now wanted to hear. Still, the energetic long-player seemed to please the vast majority of their fan base, and »Holy Smoke« turned out to be an extremely successful single, although the latter's performance paled into insignificance compared to its follow-up. The ludicrously-titled »Bring Your Daughter To The Slaughter« finally saw the MAIDEN lads achieving their ultimate ambition, a 'Number One' single, although it was (if we're being brutally honest) orchestrated *via* some rather cynical marketing chicanery, whereby the single was simultaneously released on a wide variety of formats, with many fans shelling out for multiple copies just to get hold of all those exclusive picture discs and the extremely limited variations in packaging and presentation. The upshot was that the single immediately entered the highest chart position as planned, and dropped completely out of sight the week after. Mission accomplished.

The lads were out on the road before long, although the UK leg of their tour saw them returning to slightly less auspicious venues, presumably out of choice as opposed to suggesting that they couldn't actually fill the bigger arenas nowadays. After that, it was Europe, the States and then Japan, although there were nowhere near as many dates as there had been in the past. Were they starting to tire of it all, perhaps? Anyway, MAIDEN's latest trek occupied most of their time until around the summer of 1991, but the lads didn't make any immediate recording plans in the wake of their worldwide jaunt. Instead, the various members seemed to be coming to the conclusion that there was indeed life outside MAIDEN, and it looked as though there might be something of a hiatus while certain individuals went off to do their own thing for a while. In the event, there were only a couple of semi-serious side-projects to cope with, and nothing much came of all the anticipated extra-curricular activity in the short term. By early 1992, the lads had regrouped and were now working on yet another album, which appeared in the spring as »Fear Of The Dark«. It was the kind of record the public had now come to expect from MAIDEN, hardly pushing the musical boundaries any more, but still keeping their countless fans happy, something reflected by its rise to the very top of the album charts. It featured some highly listenable material, and two of the stronger numbers ("Be Quick Or Be Dead" and "From Here To Eternity") were selected to form the basis of the traditional pair of singles, although the latter failed to perform all that impressively. The inevitable world tour wasn't quite as punishing as it had been in days of yore, although it still took them to North America, South America, Japan, Australia and Mexico by the end of the year. Along the way, the lads managed to fit in their second headlining appearance at the Monsters Of Rock Festival, which represented another consummately professional performance, although the masses in attendance seemed to be giving the newer material a rather cooler reception than the much-loved classics from their back catalogue.

In the spring of 1993, it was announced that Bruce Dickinson was finally leaving MAIDEN, after months (if not years) of media speculation. The frontman was keen to go off and do his own thing, which predominantly involved writing some embarrassingly puerile novels, flashing his fencing blade, appearing on the odd television programme, presenting his own radio show and, most importantly, carving out a proper solo career for himself, which ultimately yielded a handful of albums whose reception by the fans varied erratically. Still, he didn't jump ship overnight, and remained with MAIDEN for several months while they completed their latest touring activities. There would soon be a new live album or two which needed to be promoted, for example, the first of these being »A Real Live One«, which featured recordings of more recent compositions. To coincide with the release, the lads went back out on tour, and were soon doing their thing all over Europe as they had done so many times before. There was even a live single based around "Fear Of The Dark", which again made it into the charts, so there was definitely no loss of popularity in the immediate aftermath of Dickinson's decision to quit. Their touring schedule was rounded off with a special show in London, appropriately enough (although it's fair to say that the British leg of the farewell tour hadn't been particularly comprehensive), with highlights from this theatrical finale even being broadcast on national television at the time. After that, he was gone, although the live albums continued to appear, the next being »A Real Dead One«, which featured older material. Strangely, it sold considerably more poorly than its predecessor, so I guess you can never take anything for granted. Mind you, the accompanying live single, »Hallowed Be Thy Name«, dented the 'Top 10' once more, whereupon EMI took the truly bewildering decision to issue yet another live offering, the triple-album »Live At Donington« (from the 1992 appearance) set, although all the parties involved were keen to deflect facile accusations of desperate sales tactics by making sure the release was a fairly limited pressing, insisting it was merely a 'reward' for the loyal fans rather than a last-ditch attempt to screw some more cash out of the Dickinson era. Hmmm.

Photo: Tobias Thiem

Before long, names were readily being bandied about as to who Bruce's successor might be, and, for a while, it appeared that anyone who had ever been in a remotely MAIDEN-influenced act might just be in the running for the position. In the event, the outfit took their time before approaching anyone in particular, and the chosen one turned out to be Blaze Bayley from WOLFSBANE, an act who had supported MAIDEN during their 1990 tour. In fact, the latter outfit had been on the brink of a widely-anticipated comeback after a couple of years in the wilderness, but Bayley's shock defection signified an immediate collapse of the WOLFSBANE project, which was harsh on the other musicians involved. Still, Bayley was soon being groomed to take over the mantle of MAIDEN vocalist, although the public had to wait over a year to hear the first fruits of this new partnership. The band returned in the latter half of 1995 with an album entitled »The X Factor«, and the long-player showed Bayley to be making a reasonable stab at emulating Dickinson, having successfully developed his vocal range beyond the original nasal whine that had dominated much of WOLFSBANE's recorded output. Musically, it was the same old MAIDEN, with strong tracks such as "Lord Of The Flies" and "Man On The Edge" being perfectly in line with the material on the previous long-player. It hit the 'Top 10', but only just, and represented their worst-selling studio album since »Killers«, so there was obviously quite a bit of ground to make up before the band recaptured their one-time popularity. Still, »Man On The Edge« turned out to be a reasonably successful single, and the lads were soon out on the road as usual (taking in a fair number of European venues before the year was out), venturing further afield (with a brief North American jaunt) in the new year. Things seemed to be working out OK with Blaze.

In the second half of 1996, the outfit compiled a mammoth retrospective which covered their entire history, and the huge quadruple album set was issued under the title of »Best Of The Beast«. A surprisingly large number of fans shelled out for the release, which included a new track called "Virus" (which tied in with a computer game) as something of an incentive. Mind you, »Virus« also appeared as a single, so the fans were able to hear the track anyway without going to the effort of buying the latest album set. The group then kept a remarkably low profile for much of 1997, but returned in the spring of 1998 with a new studio effort, the »Virtual XI« (the

technology-friendly outfit were engaged in all sorts of strange multimedia projects at around this time, culminating in the release of their second computer game, 'Ed Hunter') long-player. This time, however, the public and press reaction was considerably less charitable, and their latest offering only managed a lowly 'Top 20' placing, making it the least successful MAIDEN studio album of all time. Clearly, drastic action was called for, and so the unfortunate Bayley was soon being given his freedom (he has recently resurfaced with a new venture known simply as BLAZE), whereupon things finally came full circle when both Bruce Dickinson (whose recent solo material hadn't exactly won the hearts of the public) and Adrian Smith (whose activities with PSYCHO MOTEL and the UNTOUCHABLES hadn't amounted to much) were persuaded to rejoin the MAIDEN army (news which was met with near hysteria when first announced in early 1999), bringing them up to a six-member format for the first time.

With three guitarists now in residence, the possibilities are truly mind-boggling, and the resurrected troupe, after a few select shows to get back into the swing of things, have finally unleashed a brand-new studio album entitled »Brave New World«, this comeback opus being preceded by yet another 'Top 10' single based around a highly enjoyable number called "The Wicker Man". Early indications are that an overwhelming percentage of fans have heralded the new MAIDEN long-player as a major return to form (not quite up to the standard of »The Number Of The Beast«, perhaps, but certainly comparable to »Powerslave«), so things look remarkably promising at this stage. They've been pretty cagey in terms of appearances in the live environment thus far, although they'll doubtless soon be announcing unfeasibly massive tours on an annual basis once more. I strongly suspect that the re-emergence of MAIDEN will be greeted with the same kind of phenomenal adulation which surrounded the recent batch of BLACK SABBATH reunions, and I imagine the lads will soon be taking on the young upstarts of the rock world once more. Death to false metal, and all that.

LP's

»Iron Maiden« EMI 1980
»Killers« EMI 1981
»The Number Of The Beast« EMI 1982
[Also released as limited edition picture disc]
»Piece Of Mind« EMI 1983
[Also released as limited edition picture disc]
»Powerslave« EMI 1984
[Also released as limited edition picture disc]
»Live After Death« EMI 1985
[Double live album]
»Somewhere In Time« EMI 1986
»Seventh Son Of A Seventh Son« EMI 1988
[Also released as limited edition picture disc]
»No Prayer For The Dying« EMI 1990
[Also released as limited edition picture disc]
»Fear Of The Dark« EMI 1992
[Double album]
»A Real Live One« EMI 1993
[Live album]
»A Real Dead One« EMI 1993
[Live Album]
»Live At Donington« EMI 1993
[Triple live album]
»The X Factor« EMI 1995
[Double album, limited edition issued on clear vinyl]
»Best Of The Beast« EMI 1996
[Compilation release, quadruple album]
»Virtual XI« EMI 1998
[Limited edition issued as picture disc]
»Brave New World« EMI 2000
[Double album, limited edition issued as picture disc]

12" EP's

»Women In Uniform« EMI 1980
[German issue, includes live versions of "Drifter" and "Phantom Of The Opera"]
»Live + One« EMI Japan 1980
[Japanese issue, "Women In Uniform" non-LP, also includes live versions of "Sanctuary", "Prowler" and "Phantom Of The Opera"]
»Women In Uniform« EMI 1980
[UK issue, both "Women In Uniform" and "Invasion" non-LP, also includes live version of "Phantom Of The Opera"]
»Maiden Japan« EMI 1981
[Live release]
»2 Minutes To Midnight« EMI 1984
[Issued as limited edition picture disc, both "Rainbow's Gold" and "Mission From 'Arry" non-LP]

»Aces High« EMI 1984
[Also pressed as limited edition picture disc, "King Of Twilight" non-LP, also includes live version of "The Number Of The Beast"]
»Running Free« (live) EMI 1985
[Also issued as limited edition picture disc, also includes live versions of "Sanctuary" and "Murders In The Rue Morgue"]
»Run To The Hills« (live) EMI 1985
[Also issued as limited edition picture disc, also includes live versions of "Phantom Of The Opera" and "Losfer Words"]
»Wasted Years« EMI 1986
[Both "Reach Out" and "Sheriff Of Huddersfield" non-LP]
»Stranger In A Strange Land« EMI 1986
[Also issued as limited edition picture disc, both "That Girl" and "Juanita" non-LP]
»Can I Play With Madness« EMI 1988
[Both "Black Bart Blues" and "Massacre" non-LP]
»The Evil That Men Do« EMI 1988
[Both "Prowler 88" and "Charlotte The Harlot 88" different to album versions]
»The Clairvoyant« (live) EMI 1988
[Also issued as limited edition picture disc, also includes live versions of "The Prisoner" and "Heaven Can Wait"]
»Infinite Dreams« (live) EMI 1989
[Also includes live versions of "Killers" and "Still Life"]
»Holy Smoke« EMI 1990
[Also issued as limited edition picture disc, both "All In Your Mind" and "Kill Me Ce Soir" non-LP]
»Bring Your Daughter To The Slaughter« EMI 1990
[Limited edition with calendar, also issued as limited edition picture disc, both "I'm A Mover" and "Communication Breakdown" non-LP]
»Be Quick Or Be Dead« EMI 1992
[Limited edition in gatefold sleeve, also issued as limited edition picture disc, both "Nodding Donkey Blues" and "Space Station No.5" non-LP]
»From Here To Eternity« EMI 1992
["Roll Over Vic Vella" non-LP, also features live version of "No Prayer For The Dying"]
»Hallowed Be Thy Name« (live) EMI 1993
[Limited edition issued as picture disc, also includes live versions of "Wrathchild", "The Trooper" and "Wasted Years"]
»Man On The Edge« EMI 1995
[Limited edition issued as picture disc, "I Live My Way" non-LP]
»Virus« EMI 1996
[Includes »Soundhouse Tapes« versions of "Invasion" and "Prowler"]
»The Wicker Man« EMI 2000
[Limited edition issued as picture disc, includes live versions of "Powerslave" and "Killers"]
»Out Of The Silent Planet« EMI 2000
[Limited edition issued as picture disc, includes live versions of "Aces High" and "Wasted Years"]

12" Singles
»Twilight Zone« EMI 1981
[German-only release, A-side non-LP]
»Run To The Hills« EMI 1982
[German-only release, B-side "Total Eclipse" non-LP]
»The Number Of The Beast« EMI 1982
[German-only release, B-side live version of "Remember Tomorrow"]
»Flight Of Icarus« EMI 1983
[German issue, B-side "I've Got The Fire" non-LP]
»Flight Of Icarus« EMI 1983
[UK picture disc issue, B-side "I've Got The Fire" non-LP]

7" EP's
»The Soundhouse Tapes« Rock Hard Records 1979
[Some with promo insert, "Invasion" non-LP, both "Iron Maiden" and "Prowler" different to album versions, original EP has been counterfeited, bootlegged and re-pressed unofficially on numerous occasions]
»Sanctuary« EMI 1980
[A-side non-LP, also includes live versions of "Drifter" and "I've Got The Fire". Originally with intact cover image, later censored]

7" Singles
»Running Free« EMI 1980
[A-side different to album version, B-side "Burning Ambition" non-LP]
»Prowler« EMI Japan 1980
[Japanese-only issue, B-side "Running Free"]
»Women In Uniform« EMI 1980
[Both tracks non-LP]
»Twilight Zone« EMI 1981
[Also issued on both red and clear vinyl, a handful mispressed on brown, A-side non-LP]
»Purgatory« EMI 1981
»Wrathchild« EMI Japan 1981
[Japanese-only issue, B-side "Genghis Khan"]
»Run To The Hills« EMI 1982
[Also issued as limited edition picture disc, B-side "Total Eclipse" non-LP]
»The Number Of The Beast« EMI 1982
[Also issued as limited edition on red vinyl, B-side live version of "Remember Tomorrow"]
»Flight Of Icarus« EMI 1983
[B-side "I've Got The Fire" non-LP]
»The Trooper« EMI 1983
[B-side "Cross Eyed Mary" non-LP]

»2 Minutes To Midnight« EMI 1984
[B-side "Rainbow's Gold" non-LP]
»Aces High« EMI 1984
[B-side "King Of Twilight" non-LP]
»Running Free« (live) EMI 1985
[B-side live version of "Sanctuary"]
»Run To The Hills« (live) EMI 1985
[B-side live version of "Phantom Of The Opera"]
»Wasted Years« EMI 1986
[B-side "Reach Out" non-LP]
»Stranger In A Strange Land« EMI 1986
[Also issued as limited edition poster sleeve, B-side "That Girl" non-LP]
»Can I Play With Madness« EMI 1988
[B-side "Black Bart Blues" non-LP]
»The Evil That Men Do« EMI 1988
[Also issued as limited edition in gatefold sleeve, B-side "Prowler 88" different to album version]
»The Clairvoyant« (live) EMI 1988
[Also issued as limited edition on clear vinyl, B-side live version of "The Prisoner"]
»Infinite Dreams« (live) EMI 1989
[B-side live version of "Killers"]
»Holy Smoke« EMI 1990
[B-side "All In Your Mind" non-LP]
»Bring Your Daughter To The Slaughter« EMI 1990
[Also issued as limited edition picture disc, B-side "I'm A Mover" non-LP]
»Be Quick Or Be Dead« EMI 1992
[B-side "Nodding Donkey Blues" non-LP]
»From Here To Eternity« EMI 1992
[B-side "Roll Over Vic Vella" non-LP]
»Fear Of The Dark« (live) EMI 1993
[B-side live version of "Tailgunner"]
»Hallowed Be Thy Name« (live) EMI 1993
[Limited edition issued on red vinyl, B-side live version of "Wrathchild"]
»The Angel And The Gambler« EMI 1998
[Limited edition issued as picture disc, B-side live version of "Blood On The World's Hands"]
»Out Of The Silent Planet« EMI 2000
[Limited edition issued on red vinyl in poster sleeve, includes live version of "Aces High"]

Shaped Picture Discs
»The Trooper« EMI 1983
»Wasted Years« EMI 1986
»Can I Play With Madness« EMI 1988
»The Evil That Men Do« EMI 1988
»The Clairvoyant« (live) EMI 1988
»Infinite Dreams« (live) EMI 1989
»From Here To Eternity« EMI 1992
[Includes exclusive track "I Can't See My Feelings"]
»Fear Of The Dark« (live) EMI 1993
[Some mispressed with wrong B-side, "Tailgunner" (live) instead of "Hooks In You" (live)]

CD's
»Live After Death« EMI 1985
[Live release]
»Somewhere In Time« EMI 1986
»Iron Maiden« EMI 1987
»Killers« EMI 1987
»The Number Of The Beast« EMI 1987
»Piece Of Mind« EMI 1987
»Powerslave« EMI 1987
»Seventh Son Of A Seventh Son« EMI 1988
»No Prayer For The Dying« EMI 1990
»Fear Of The Dark« EMI 1992
»A Real Live One« EMI 1993
[Live release]
»A Real Dead One« EMI 1993
[Live release]
»Live At Donington« EMI 1993
[Live release, double disc]
»Maiden England« EMI 1994
[Live release, issued as part of CD/video package]
»The X Factor« EMI 1995
»Best Of The Beast« EMI 1996
[Compilation release, double disc]
»Virtual XI« EMI 1998
»Ed Hunter« EMI 1999
[Double disc, compilation release, includes computer game]
»Brave New World« EMI 2000

CD Singles
»Infinite Dreams« EMI 1989
»Holy Smoke« EMI 1990
»Bring Your Daughter To The Slaughter« EMI 1990
»Be Quick Or Be Dead« EMI 1992
»From Here To Eternity« EMI 1992
»Wasting Love« EMI 1992
»Fear Of The Dark« (live) EMI 1993
»Hallowed Be Thy Name« (live) EMI 1993
»Man On The Edge« EMI 1995
[Two variations, issued as part of 2-CD set]
»Lord Of The Flies« EMI 1996
»Virus« EMI 1996
[Two variations, issued as part of 2-CD set]
»Futureal« EMI 1998
»The Angel And The Gambler« EMI 1998
»The Wicker Man« EMI 2000
[Two variations, issued as part of 2-CD set]
»Out Of The Silent Planet« EMI 2000

Selected Compilation Appearances
"Sanctuary" on »Metal For Muthas« LP EMI 1980/CD Airraid Records 2000
[Demo version]
"Wrathchild" on »Metal For Muthas« LP EMI

1980/CD Airraid Records 2000
[Demo version]
"Running Free" on »Axe Attack« LP K-Tel 1980
[Demo version appears on first pressing, album version on later pressing]
"Transylvania" on »Heavy Duty« LP Harvest Records 1980
"Sanctuary" on »Heavy Duty« LP Harvest Records 1980
"Murders In The Rue Morgue" on »Axe Attack Vol.II« LP K-Tel 1981
"The Number Of The Beast" on »Heavy« LP K-Tel 1983
"Aces High" on »Kerrang Kompilation« Do-LP EMI 1985
"The Trooper" on »Masters Of Metal« LP Powersaw Records 1986
"Run To The Hills" on »The Earthquake Album« LP Life Aid Records 1990
"Sanctuary" on »NWOBHM '79 Revisited« Do-LP/Do-CD Phonogram 1990
[Session version]
"Killers" on »Giants Of Rock-The Metal Decade Vol.1« Do-CD Teldec 1990
"Aces High" (live) on »Live'n'Loud« LP/CD EMI 1991
"The Ides Of March" (live) on »NWOBHM-The Days On Stage« Bootleg CD Taurus Records 1993
"Sanctuary" (live) on »NWOBHM-The Days On Stage« Bootleg CD Taurus Records 1993

ISENGARD

Johnson
Diffley
Gausden

Yet more valuable evidence for the *'NWOBHM bands got to all the best names at least a decade before the latest wave of Black Metal outfits arrived'* conspiracy theorists (see, for example, THE COVENANT, MAYHEM, GOLGOTHA, HOLOCAUST, WARRIOR *etc.*), here comes the original version of ISENGARD. Utterly unknown, but fear not, as it's hardly a freshly-discovered classic by any stretch of the imagination. Nay, in spite of the very promising moniker, the mystery outfit fail miserably to live up to expectations on their 1983 two-tracker, delivering an extremely chart-friendly (but moderately acceptable if you're in the right frame of mind) slice of melodic rock in the form of "Please Put Me On The Radio" (which I'm sure nobody did), a number which reveals the influence of various familiar 70's American acts, the group having a fair bit in common with lightweight NWOBHM-era hopefuls such as SMOKIN ROADIE, SINGAPORE and MEANSTREAK. The keyboard-tinged composition on the reverse (with the sickly title of "Love You Love Me") is more analogous to H.G.B. or KRUZA, but this effort does feature a reasonable guitar interlude. Not, as far as we know, issued in a picture sleeve, this single (a one-off release from a fly-by-night concern, I would imagine) is really only for the obsessive completists, and it just goes to show that there were probably almost as many *'borderline NWOBHM'* acts doing the rounds at the time as there were genuine *'out and out metal'* outfits. Hopefully we'll stop short of really sad barrel-scraping, I'd hate to think we'd eventually get to the stage when the likes of RACEY and the ARROWS are included in a NWOBHM reference book!

7" Singles
»Please Put Me On The Radio« Private 1983

JAGUAR

Rob Reiss (v)
Gary Pepperd (g)
Jeff Cox (b)
Chris Lovell (d)

Avon's much-loved JAGUAR were one of many NWOBHM-era outfits who flattered to deceive, in the respect that their early promise somehow deserted them in the long run, whereupon they transformed into a mediocre rock act with mainstream aspirations. Initially, however, it was an entirely different story, and this powerful, talented quartet, after their original inception towards the end of 1979, enjoyed a pretty meteoric rise to stardom (well, the kind of frenzied local popularity that was still remarkable for a young West Country act, anyway). Having been inspired to form by the sudden emergence of numerous fast'n'furious hopefuls in the preceding year or two (in particular, the members were all self-confessed admirers of IRON MAIDEN), JAGUAR soon set about establishing themselves as a hot new metal proposition to take on the world, and recorded their first demo in the spring of 1980. In spite of the tape's fairly limited circulation, it still served to introduce them to the organisers of a 'Melody Maker'-sponsored *'Battle Of The Bands'* competition, something which allowed the then-unknown JAGUAR to progress a fairly long way in a relatively short time, as drummer

Chris Lovell explained: 'We did rather well, getting to the South West regional finals, and finishing fourth out of seven. Since about seven hundred bands from our area entered in the first place, I suppose we can claim to have come fourth out of seven hundred! The regional final itself was actually our first gig, and to say my mouth went dry with tension is an understatement.' (Kerrang No.35, February 1983).

After cutting their teeth on the obligatory circuit of local pub and club appearances (occasionally playing alongside emergent hopefuls such as BRONZ), the lads made another trip to the studio in order to capture a few more tracks on tape, and duly combined the best numbers from their two sessions to create their first proper demo, a six track effort which they began selling towards the end of 1980. The cassette featured an intense selection of numbers, with "Stormchild", "Ain't No Fantasy", "War Machine", "Piledriver", "Feel The Heat" and "Battle Cry" (some of which would never see an official release on vinyl) coming across as quite heavily influenced by the likes of IRON MAIDEN, RAVEN and the TYGERS OF PAN TANG; so much so, in fact, that JAGUAR are often lumped in with the aforementioned acts as being one of the pioneering exponents of *'speed metal'*. Their demo went on to sell in quite astonishing quantities by mail order alone, with several hundred copies making their way to the four corners of the globe within a matter of months, and it became apparent that JAGUAR already had a significant fan base to build upon as they moved confidently into 1981. They received further valuable exposure when featured in the 'Armed And Ready' section of the very first 'Kerrang' later in the year, and word of their activities was soon reaching the sympathetic ears of the expanding Heavy Metal label, who promptly invited JAGUAR to contribute a track to their first »Heavy Metal Heroes« sampler. The outfit's "Stormchild" was a solid and energetic inclusion, and saw the youngsters shining brightly in the company of acts who would later become household names (well, in *my* household, at least).

As something of a reward for this sterling performance, the lads were offered the chance to lay down their own single for the label, and they wasted little time before capturing a couple of newer numbers, "Back Street Woman" and "Chasing The Dragon", for this purpose. It was a fairly blistering single, which was soon making a significant impact upon the rock charts of the day, and it sold in impressive numbers over the coming months. By the end of the year, the initial batch had already sold out, but, for some inexplicable reason, Heavy Metal refused to organise a re-pressing or offer JAGUAR any further opportunities to appear on vinyl, so it looked as though the hapless outfit would be left to fend for themselves by the beginning of 1982. Fortunately, it was to be a minor blip in JAGUAR's career, as they had already developed a sufficiently strong and loyal following throughout the nation's rock-loving community to be able to counteract this apparent lack of commitment from Heavy Metal. As well as winning the hearts of numerous rock fans at such venues as the legendary Granary club in Bristol, for example, the lads had worked hard to cultivate a healthy fan base in Europe (their music had been particularly well-received by the good people of Holland, where they would practically become regarded as national heroes), and the foursome played the first of many Dutch gigs towards the end of 1981, having made the pilgrimage to mainland Europe in order to share a stage with local favourites WELLS FARGO.

These gigs were to signal the end of the line for original vocalist Rob Reiss, however, whose apparent lack of dedication to JAGUAR's progress (particularly a reluctance to contribute on the songwriting front) had been causing the other members some considerable concern for several months. His departure came at a slightly inconvenient juncture, however, as the lads were already scheduled to headline a Dutch festival at the beginning of January, which left them a pitifully short time to recruit a suitable replacement. Remarkably, however, they managed to engage the services of Paul Merrell, a long-time associate from his days in local act STORMTROOPER, who had, more recently, been pursuing a rather unsuccessful career as stand-in singer for London-based oddballs HELLRAZER (see separate entry). Not only was Merrell expected to learn JAGUAR's entire repertoire in a mere five days (!), he would then be compelled to make his live debut in front of an expectant festival crowd in a foreign country. You wouldn't say that was a bit of a tall order, by any chance? Well, the talented and experienced frontman somehow managed to live up to the almost impossible expectations of his new colleagues, and the band's progress would continue with minimal loss of momentum over the coming months.

Before long, the contract-less JAGUAR were fortunate enough to be picked up by Neat, a company who were in a much stronger position to advance the career of heavy young bands (they messed up big time with BITCHES SIN, though), particularly those who had already demonstrated a proven ability to deliver the goods both on vinyl and in the live environment. Clearly, JAGUAR fitted the bill admirably, and the lads were soon hard at work on their first release for Neat, a single featuring "Axe Crazy" and "War Machine". It was another immensely capable and energetic release, one which even won praise from the barbarous 'Kerrang', and Paul Merrell seemed to be totally at home with

the material, where he was able to reveal a greater range and rather more powerful voice than had ever been on display in STORMTROOPER. "War Machine" also showed the outfit's ability to write more subtle and restrained compositions, disproving the cynics who had suggested that there was little substance to their 100 m.p.h. bluster. Once again, the single was to sell in spectacular quantities, leaving the public in no doubt that, this time, there really would be an album to follow. After various further gigs with touring acts such as THE RODS, STAMPEDE and the STARFIGHTERS, the ever-improving JAGUAR soon started making the necessary trips to the studio, initially laying down the exclusive "Dirty Tricks" (already showing clear evidence of a more melodic and accessible aspect to their music) for Neat's »60 Minutes Plus« cassette, and then undertaking the recordings for that vital first long-player towards the end of the year. The album was in the can by December, but its release was put on hold while JAGUAR made another trip to Holland, where they performed some headlining shows at various well-respected clubs, including the world-famous Dynamo in Eindhoven.

JAGUAR's »Power Games« album emerged in the early months of 1983, and featured several tracks which had already established themselves as popular live favourites, notably "Out Of Luck", "Prisoner", "Cold Heart", "Raw Deal" and the ubiquitous "Dutch Connection". The longplayer encompassed a variety of styles and tempos, from the frenzied guitar assaults of "Dutch Connection", "The Fox" and "Prisoner", for example, to more subtle, ambitious and interesting numbers such as "Master Game", "Ain't No Fantasy" and "Raw Deal". Overall, it came across as a supremely tight and accomplished affair, and it's fair to say that the entire album showcased the considerable musical talents of all four members. The LP hit the nail right on the head as far as many metal fans were concerned, and the record was soon doing brisk business for Neat throughout the UK and Europe, where it was assisted by a handy distribution deal with Roadrunner. The lads continued to promote themselves in the live environment, including more dates in Europe as well as widespread touring throughout the UK itself, and they also found time to fit in an appearance on a regional television programme, 'Out West', where they ran through upbeat versions of "Dutch Connection" and "Master Game" for the benefit of a lucky studio audience.

Nevertheless, just when everything seemed to be working out perfectly for JAGUAR, their collective ambition appears to have overwhelmed them, compelling the quartet to move into more and more lightweight and commercially-motivated territory. This isn't to say that the band were unprepared for a less-than-enthusiastic public reaction to this shift in direction, as the newer material was given an almost unanimous thumbs-down whenever it was tried out at their increasingly-scant live outings. It all became too much for Neat to handle, and the label soon offloaded the outfit to Roadrunner on a permanent basis. Obstinately undeterred by the public's utter indifference to their latest offerings, the lads eventually shut themselves away in the studio once again, and emerged with an album which pleased themselves, if nobody else. »This Time« saw JAGUAR being temporarily augmented by keyboard player Larry Dawson, whose inclusion probably gives some advance warning of the type of material on display. Disconcertingly, it also became apparent that the lads had undergone something of a makeover prior to the album's release, and the photos circulated at the time showed them to possess the appearance of a neatly-coiffed and nattily-dressed bunch of pop hopefuls. Sadly, their music now fitted the image quite appositely, and the album saw JAGUAR deserting their roots wholesale in order to concentrate on a nondescript type of semi-AOR/pop which bore precious little resemblance to their original direction.

If one were to be incredibly charitable, it might be worth mentioning a couple of the album's stronger efforts, notably the almost-enjoyable "Last Flight" (opens with a fairly substantial riff but meanders off into a lightweight chorus), "Another Lost Weekend" (ditto), "Stranger" (a semi-decent raunchy number) and "Streetwalker" (a capable melodic rocker). Elsewhere, however, it's all worrying close to the likes of MR MISTER, CUTTING CREW, IT BITES and their chart-friendly ilk. It's hard to comprehend the motives which lay behind JAGUAR's sudden decision to move in this particular direction, although I suspect that it might have been a more prudent idea to change their name if they were so utterly convinced that a complete alteration of image and musical style would be such a great wheeze. It's also difficult to accept that the two JAGUAR albums appeared within a mere year of each other, and the fans must have been completely bamboozled by the lightweight attitude adopted on the outfit's second longplayer. Quite understandably, global sales were way down compared with the debut set, and the group were soon trying out a few last-ditch ideas to rescue the situation. They had already recorded a session for the 'Friday Rock Show', but the listeners weren't exactly moved by JAGUAR's latest performance when "(Nights Of) Long Shadows", "This Time", "Last Flight" and "Stand Up (Tumble Down)" were finally broadcast on the 13th of April 1984.

Drummer Chris Lovell had already tired of the group's new direction by the time the second album hit the shops, although JAGUAR still managed to recruit a new member, Gary Davies, in order to keep things going in the short term (they also brought in keyboard player Gareth Johnson), which included a tour with headliners GIRLSCHOOL. In the event, however, the band's affairs were rapidly hurtling downhill (as was their previously-enviable reputation), and, in spite of the best attempts of the musicians, their management and their label to reverse JAGUAR's plummeting popularity, recapturing their once-fervent fan base ultimately proved to be a lost cause. They struggled on until 1985, trying out another drummer, erstwhile TOK-IO ROSE sticksman Les Foster (having utilised a stand-in, the implausibly-named Will Ng, for various studio and live work in the interim), although their activities failed to arouse much interest. By the end of the year, the original incarnation of JAGUAR had been laid to rest, the group's proud name having been tarnished irreparably by this ludicrously ill-advised and contrived piece of experimentation. In the wake of JAGUAR's demise, the members dispersed and joined up with new outfits or formed projects of their own, although few of these ever amounted to much. Paul Merrell, Gary Pepperd and Gareth Johnson, for example, teamed up in an AOR venture called THE ARENA, although this chapter drew to a

close after a couple of years, during which time they had achieved precious little in the way of recognition. Jeff Cox fared slightly better, however, and formed a productive alliance with guitarist Fred Hale to create a series of acts such as TARGA, ESCAPE and THE LOST BOYS, the last-mentioned even getting to the stage of releasing an obscure album (»Diamond Dust«) in 1991.

By the mid-90's, however, there were renewed rumblings in the underground which pointed to a possible get-together of JAGUAR for a one-off reunion gig. Although such rumours circulate quite regularly amongst some of the more excitable NWOBHM fans, and usually tend to be the product of overactive imaginations, they actually had some basis in truth on this occasion. In fact, things snowballed pretty quickly after the Neat Metal concern contacted the members in 1996, initially regarding the imminent CD reissue of »Power Games«. Coincidentally, one of the band's former roadies and associates, Lyndon Allen, had decided to set up an official JAGUAR website purely to pay tribute to his old friends, and this was soon generating a fair bit of interest among fans all over the world. Before long, Lyndon was making contact with most of the former

JAGUAR scenesters, and so his internet site actually became something of an ideal way to test the water and gauge how genuine and sustainable all this early interest might be. In the event, it turned out to be pretty substantial, resulting in a revived version of JAGUAR getting back together (original members Gary Pepperd and Jeff Cox duly hooked up with youthful vocalist Jamie Manton and new drummer Nathan Cox, who wasn't actually related to the bassist) for a bit of tomfoolery in the studio and the odd low-key gig to get back into the swing of things.

After keeping themselves to themselves for a short while, the revitalised JAGUAR even made it over to Europe in 1999 for an appearance at the Wacken Festival (alongside GIRLSCHOOL and the TYGERS OF PAN TANG), and subsequently announced plans for a comeback album on the Neat Metal label. Thankfully, the members of the group solemnly promised that it would be a tad heavier than »This Time«. True to their word, the lads delivered »Wake Me« in the early part of 2000, a release which certainly blew away a few cobwebs and consigned that mid-80's commerciality to the dustbin for good. In fact, the album was quite a varied affair, starting out with some fairly contemporary numbers with a semi-punk attitude, suggesting that the musicians may actually have been listening to acts such as 3 COLOURS RED and CECIL in recent times. As the record progresses, things move through some fairly groovy material with a bit of a MANSUN/REEF feel, but, by the time we reach the second half of the album, it's pretty much back to where the lads originally left off in 1982. With their trademark riffing and charging arrangements (and a convincingly powerful vocal effort from young Jamie), tracks such as "Power Games" (hmmm, good title, that), "Occasional Hell" and "Dawn Chorus" all successfully recapture the spirit of the glory days, but I'm happy to affirm that they've achieved the required level of intensity without merely resorting to making carbon copies of their early material. It's been an extremely pleasant experience to witness the re-emergence of JAGUAR (yet another of Ulrich's original faves, apparently), and I'm sure this bunch have plenty of surprises in store for their fans in years to come.

LP's
»**Power Games**« Neat 1983
[UK issue, also issued in limited quantities on purple vinyl]
»**Power Games**« Roadrunner 1983
[Dutch issue]
»**This Time**« Roadrunner 1984

7" Singles
»**Back Street Woman**« Heavy Metal 1981
[Both tracks non-LP]
»**Axe Crazy**« Neat 1982
[Both tracks non-LP]

CD's
»**Power Games**« Teichiku 1993
[Japanese issue with two bonus tracks]
»**Power Games**« Neat Metal 1998
[UK issue with three bonus tracks]
»**Wake Me**« Neat Metal 2000

Exclusive Compilation Appearances
"**Stormchild**" on »Heavy Metal Heroes« LP Heavy Metal 1981 *[Issued in two different sleeves]* + »NWOBHM Vol.3« Bootleg CD 1992 + »Heavy Metal Heroes Vol.I&II« CD British Steel 1996 + »The Metallic-Era Volume II« CD Neat Metal 1999
"**Dirty Tricks**" on »60 Minutes Plus« Cassette Neat 1982/CD Teichiku 1992 + »All Hell Let Loose« LP Neat 1983

Compilation Appearances
"**Run For Your Life**" on »Metal Battle« LP Neat 1983/Roadrunner 1983
"**Sleepwalker**" on »The Metal Machine« LP Roadrunner 1984
"**(Nights Of) Long Shadows**" on »The Best Of British« LP Zebra 1985
"**Axe Crazy**" on »Metal Concussion« LP Bandit 1986 + »Metal Masters« 4-CD Box Castle Communications 1993
"**Last Flight**" on »Metal Killers« LP Raw Power 1986
"**Back Street Woman**" on »NWOBHM '79 Revisited« Do-LP/Do-CD Phonogram 1990 + »N.W.O.B.H.M.« LP/CD Heavy Metal 1991 + »Give 'Em Hell« CD Nectar Masters 1995 + »N.W.O.B.H.M. Metal Rarities Vol.3« CD British Steel 1997
"**Cold Heart**" on »Heavy Metal Collection 1« CD X-Tra Collection 1993
"**Raw Deal**" on »Heavy Metal Collection 3« CD X-Tra Collection 1993
"**Chasing The Dragon**" on »N.W.O.B.H.M. Metal Rarities Vol.3« CD British Steel 1997

JAMESON RAID

Terry Dark (v)
Ian Smith (g)
John Ace (b)
Phil Kimberley (d)

The embryonic version of West Midlands metal heroes JAMESON RAID (an African uprising which preceded the Boer War, just in case you were wondering) first came together in the mid-70's under their original identity of NOTRE DAME, although this handle was ultimately shelved in around 1977, after which the musicians started making something of a name for themselves with numerous small-time shows around the Midlands. From a very early stage, JAMESON RAID's extensive repertoire consisted largely of their own material, which varied from sharp, punchy numbers to well-crafted, lengthy compositions in something of a semi-progressive style, many of which would remain in the set-list for a number of years. Among their formative efforts were such favourites as "Stop Looking At Me", "Bricks On The Wall" and the delicately-titled "Spit In Your Eye", as well as versions of certain tracks which would eventually make an appearance on vinyl. After several years of solid gigging (with local crowds rapidly warming to the quartet's unquenchable desire to incorporate long instrumentals and extended guitar freakouts into their set), the lads decided to issue their first slice of vinyl, a privately-pressed, three track 7" (released in 1979) featuring "Seven Days Of Splendour", "It's A Crime" and "Catcher In The Rye".

The combination of influences which had given birth to the band's overall sound was quite difficult to pin down, as there were elements of 70's rock/pop (particularly DAVID BOWIE and MOTT THE HOOPLE), heavier acts such as THIN LIZZY and the occasional nod towards punk snottiness. There were, in addition, slight similarities to the likes of BLEAK HOUSE and LIMELIGHT (groups with equivalently long musical histories), although JAMESON RAID appeared to be eminently capable of infusing rather more of a street-level attitude into their music, making it somewhat more palatable to the unpretentious rock fans of the day. Indeed, the outfit's debut EP seems to have sold in notable quantities at the time, and examples have come onto the second-hand market quite regularly ever since. The record was, incidentally, issued in a generic picture sleeve (with two colour variations, white being less common than black), although the real treat was the utterly ludicrous insert, which provided an entirely fictional (although certain individuals seem to have taken it at face value) account of JAMESON RAID's colourful history, including this particularly memorable statement: *'The music has progressed to its present form from versions of Swedish and Irish nursery rhymes, and Terry's influence of singing ballads while diving off wardrobes.'* Worth the price of the record alone.

It wasn't too long before rock fans were able to purchase a second JAMESON RAID 7", as the lads released another EP the following year, a four track offering in a picture sleeve which depicted an ominous-sounding poster, the latter stating *'JAMESON RAID story-end of part one'*. Indeed, it would appear that this was something of a farewell release, although it was to prove the end of the road only for long-serving members John Ace and Ian Smith. The EP itself was considerably more accessible than their debut, although most, if not all, of the tracks featured had been part of the band's live set for several years. There were slight similarities to the likes of RICOCHET, SLOWTRAIN and HOLLOW GROUND, particularly on "Getting Hotter" and "Straight From The Butchers", although "The Hypnotist" and "The Raid" weren't too far behind in terms of energy or intensity. As with its vinyl predecessor, the second JAMESON RAID EP became a sought-after collectable when interest in the genre was rekindled in the early 90's, and both items remain mid-priced pieces today. Before the end of 1980, the group would see their worthy track "Hard Lines" featured on the second »Metal For Muthas« compilation, but chose to be known by the name of THE RAID on this occasion. Perhaps it was a mark of deference for the departed members, but it wasn't actually all that long before the lads were once again gigging under their more familiar name, with new recruits Mike Darby (g) and Pete Green (b) making up the numbers.

Although the revised version of JAMESON RAID failed to produce further vinyl output, they remained on the scene for a couple of years, delighting audiences throughout the Midlands (showcasing newer numbers such as "Titanic" and the snappily-titled "Uncle Jim's Green And White Pick-up Truck") and even partaking of a short residency at the Railway Inn in Birmingham in the spring of 1982. Along the way, they tried out yet another guitarist, Jim Barrett, and demoed some original material such as "Electric Sun", "Run For Cover" and "Poor Little Rich Girl". In the end, however, it all fizzled out rather unspectacularly, with the outfit drifting apart in the wake of relentless label disinterest. Nevertheless, Pete Green tried (briefly) to get things going again in 1983, utilising the name of THE RAID once more and teaming up with Steve Makin (v,g) and Roger Simms (d), veterans of numerous small-time outfits. The resurrected venture failed to last the distance, however, and swiftly disintegrated yet again, with only Steve

Makin subsequently resurfacing in the ranks of such little-known hopefuls as JEKYLL and MISTRESS, the latter outfit even recording their own version of "Poor Little Rich Girl" at one stage.

7" EP's
»Seven Days Of Splendour« GBH Records 1979
[Issued in both black and white sleeves, black more common]
»The Hypnotist« Blackbird Music 1980

Exclusive Compilation Appearances
"Hard Lines" on »Metal For Muthas Vol.2« LP EMI 1980/CD Airraid Records 2000
[Under the name of THE RAID]

Compilation Appearances
"It's A Crime" on »NWOBHM Vol.2« Bootleg CD 1992

JANINE

Boh Hamilton (v)
Rick Gay (g)
Paul Smith (g)
Ross Landau (b)
Andi Steele (d)

The intriguing history of the unremarkably-named JANINE actually dates back to the late 70's and an obscure Scottish four-piece called NECROMANCER, who split fairly amicably after a couple of years so that their vocalist, Boh Hamilton, could establish a new venture more suited to his talents. The frontman's first move was to relocate to London (taking colleague Andi Steele with him) and to hook up with a variety of minor East End scenesters to create a quintet known as JANINE. After the usual routine of club gigs (the band having become established at the height of the NWOBHM movement), the somewhat glam-influenced bunch were ultimately driven to release a self-financed 7", and so the »Crazy On You« single (b/w "Candy") was hastily recorded and unleashed upon an unsuspecting public. Although they cultivated a slightly glammy image, their sound was, in fact, reasonably close to the NWOBHM archetype, albeit a fairly lightweight variant. At times, there were similarities to outfits such as MORE, MEANSTREAK and the EF BAND, but it was pretty listenable in general, with some capable guitar work on display throughout. The single, issued in a basic sleeve featuring little more than their logo, is a highly-priced rarity these days, although the tracks in question have now been made available to fans on one of British Steel's recent spate of compilations.

JANINE were to play a fair number of gigs in many parts of the country, opening for an eclectic range of headlining acts (including QUARTZ, DIAMOND HEAD, MARILLION, GIRL and MORE, for example), and they also recorded a studio demo or two during their time as a unit, but never really built upon the minor success of their debut single, which won them a coveted placing in the 'Sounds' Heavy Metal Chart at the time. Within a matter of months, the spectre of personnel instability had reared its ugly head, and drummer Andi Steele was one of the first to throw in his hand, although he was swiftly replaced by Symon Tomkins for a short period. By early 1982, however, the JANINE empire had finally fallen apart for good, whereupon vocalist Boh Hamilton proceeded to establish his ill-fated GARBO (see separate entry) venture, in which he resumed his working partnership with former colleague Andi Steele. Guitarist Paul Smith, on the other hand, hooked up with the legendary DEEP MACHINE after the latter had run into line-up trouble, although the axeman ultimately failed to make much of a difference to the dwindling group's fortunes. Ross Landau and Symon Tomkins, meanwhile, comprised the rhythm section in the short-lived BORDELLO (who, incidentally, retained a handful of JANINE numbers such as "Crazy On You" in their live set), before Tomkins moved on to various other projects such as AIRRACE and BAT. Landau later returned to session work, gradually becoming more involved with the production side of things, and ended up running his own company called Zeus Music.

7" Singles
»Crazy On You« Stiletto Records 1981

Compilation Appearances
"Crazy On You" on »N.W.O.B.H.M. Metal Rarities Vol.2« CD British Steel 1996
"Candy" on »N.W.O.B.H.M. Metal Rarities Vol.2« CD British Steel 1996

JEDDAH

Dean Salonga (v)
Dave Cook (g)
Quirk (g)
El Sid (b)

Paul Cooke (d)
Ron Emms (d)

The strangely-named JEDDAH were one of the many fly-by-night acts who cropped up in the Worcestershire and Gloucestershire areas during the NWOBHM era, and who disappeared after just a couple of recording sessions. Unlike so many of their contemporaries, however, this particular outfit managed to get to the vinyl stage, leaving a tangible reminder of their otherwise ephemeral existence. With this ensemble including both of the characters behind STRATEGY (see separate entry) in their ranks, it looks as though the project probably came together at some point in the early months of 1983, with JEDDAH's debut two-tracker appearing towards the end of that year on their own label, the sensitively-titled Death Records. Their reworking of "Eleanor Rigby" was rather more imaginative and enjoyable than ETHEL THE FROG's note-for-note interpretation, while the bizarre "Ghosts (Never Leave You Behind)" was an extraordinarily original slice of pop/metal, coming across as a mixture of ENERGY's "Fight For Your Freedom", MARQUIS DE SADE's "Somewhere Up In The Mountains" and the theme from 'Fame' (I kid you not, folks), a recipe for disaster which somehow actually yields an incredibly listenable piece of music! The singles reviewers in 'Kerrang' seem to have formed the same opinion, suggesting that *'if you're into something different, this is for you.'*

JEDDAH's one-off single, which has become a reasonably collectable item in recent times, wasn't issued in a picture sleeve, although some copies came with a fold-out insert with some decidedly non-serious comments about the group's history (such as the fact that their two sticksmen were selected from an original pool of five hundred candidates, and both were too shy to be photographed). Why they felt the need for two drummers isn't clear (I suppose it's always wise to have a back-up in case of any unforeseen spontaneous combustion episodes), although one of them (Paul Cooke) eventually resurfaced in one of the many line-ups of the melodic DEALER offshoot known as VANDAMNE, while the other (Ron Emms, aka Mark Emms) later teamed up with one-time WRATHCHILD/PERSIAN RISK stalwart Phil Vokins, initially in the ranks of the little-known FIREWORX, and then as a duo operating under the peculiar identity of ROGUE ISLAND. Given that their existence was apparently so fleeting, it seems highly probable that JEDDAH were, in fact, assembled specifically to release this two-tracker, and

there's no evidence to suggest that they ever actually played live. The single's well worth keeping an eye out for, though...

7" Singles
»Eleanor Rigby« Death Records 1983
[Some copies with poster insert]

JESS COX

Jess Cox (v)
Trevor Sewell (g)
Dave Donaldson (b)
Pete Rea (d)

Following on from his infamous stint with LIONHEART (see separate entry), former TYGERS OF PAN TANG vocalist Jess Cox wasted little time before cultivating a solo career for himself. By mid-1981, having spent several months working as a swimming pool attendant in Whitley Bay (possibly the least glamorous job description in the history of Western civilisation), he had already teamed up with one-time EROGENOUS ZONES guitarist Trevor Sewell and started composing material as a multi-instrumentalist duo. Shortly after this relationship had become established, Cox outlined his plans (which basically revolved around releasing a JESS COX single as quickly as possible) in a fanzine interview: *'I can't see myself in another band cos it's very frustrating having to rely on other people when you're in a band. I might release the single on my own label or on an independent one as that will cut out the huge record company profits.'* (Ref: Acne'n'Dandruff, Issue 4, 1981). In fact, the intended single didn't materialise quite as swiftly as anticipated, and the JESS COX project (initially little more than a piece of studio-based experimentation) gradually evolved into something more closely resembling a proper outfit, with a handful of guest musicians such as Dave Donaldson (b) and Pete Rea (d) being drafted in to provide a bit of musical support on their various trips to the recording facility.

As it happens, the first JESS COX composition to make it to the vinyl stage was their "Devil's Triangle", a number which was commissioned especially for the »Heavy Metal Heroes Vol.II« compilation towards the end of 1982. This track turned out to be a reasonably heavy, if unmemorable, effort not a million miles away from early TYGERS OF PAN TANG offerings, so it originally looked as though Cox wasn't going to be pushing the barriers too far with his latest material.

Nevertheless, the act was picked up by Neat shortly thereafter, and, by the time his debut album materialised towards the end of 1983 (having been preceded by a single coupling "Bridges" and the non-LP "Check It Out"), things had moved in a decidedly more accessible direction, with certain tracks featuring keyboards, saxophones (ugh) and piano sections. All things considered, »Third Step« (presumably referring to his third musical identity) wasn't a particularly good debut in terms of its appeal to the rock-loving public, and the vocals came in for the inevitable slating, which I've always found to be harsh; Cox might not have had a great range, but I've heard *far* worse performances in my time. It's somewhat ironic, however, that the best numbers are old LIONHEART compositions, namely "Piece Of The Action" and "Fallen Hero (Everyman)" (a third, "Bad Time Girl", appeared on the flipside of the »One In A Million« single, which emerged at around the same time as the LP), suggesting that Cox probably found it slightly more difficult to come up with his own material than he had originally anticipated.

Although the album had been recorded with the assistance of numerous session musicians and sundry scenesters from the North East (notably axeman Mick Procter, who served time with NATO, BLITZKRIEG and the TYGERS OF PAN TANG, bassist Dave Donaldson, who later had stints with the aforementioned TYGERS and TOKYO BLADE, and alternate guitarist John Stormont, who cropped up in an ill-fated BATTLEAXE reunion in the late 80's), the JESS COX band was also a touring concern, and gigs (including a successful tour with HEAVY PETTIN and a memorable outing at the Marquee, where they supported none other than METALLICA) took place on a fairly regular basis during 1983 and 1984 (drummer Geoff Nixon and second guitarist Neil Shepherd, later of WAYSTED and the TYGERS OF PAN TANG, were drafted in for this purpose), and it's hardly surprising to note that the setlists featured a mixture of JESS COX, TYGERS and LIONHEART compositions, just to keep everyone happy. Moving into 1985, Cox was busily penning a wide variety of new material in the hope of securing a second album, but tracks such as "Lost Without Trace", "Movin' Numbers" and "Breaking Through" (which saw the man attempting a more refined vocal style) were a bit too poppy and nondescript for the rock market. The labels weren't impressed, and the JESS COX project finally ground to a halt.

End of story? Not quite. It wasn't long before Cox had new goals in mind, and early in 1986 he teamed up with erstwhile TYGERS/SEARGENT guitarist Robb Weir, former EMERSON bassist Bri Emerson and mysterious drummer Mr Roland to form TYGER TYGER. The unit hastily recorded some newly-written material, and were lucky to have one of these compositions, "Small Town Flirt", included on Neat's TYGERS retrospective entitled »First Kill«. Musically speaking, this *'back to basics'* effort (with a more contemporary edge reminiscent of TRAXX) was a major return to form, and their full album (»On The Prowl«), due to be issued on Neat before the end of the year, was eagerly anticipated. Sadly, the TYGER TYGER thing never really got off the ground properly, despite several successful gigs, numerous trips to the studio and an abundance of material at their disposal, and it eventually died a natural death within a couple of years. Jess Cox, as I'm sure you're all aware, is now doing an excellent job of running the resurrected Neat Metal concern, and is constantly bombarded with *'when are the original TYGERS reforming?'* questions from fans. Well, a version of the group recently got back together for a European festival appearance, and if you're very, very good, there might be a few more surprises in store one of these days...

LP's
»Third Step« Neat 1983

7" Singles
»Bridges« Neat 1983
[B-side "Check It Out" non-LP]
»One In A Million« Neat 1983
[B-side "Bad Time Girl" non-LP]

Exclusive Compilation Appearances
"Devil's Triangle" on »Heavy Metal Heroes Vol.2« LP Heavy Metal 1982 + »Heavy Metal Heroes Vol.I&II« CD British Steel 1996

Compilation Appearances
"One In A Million" on »British Steel« LP M Port Records 1984/Steel Trax 1986
"Piece Of The Action" on »Heavy Metal Collection 4« CD X-Tra Collection 1993

JJ'S POWERHOUSE

Austin 'Ozzy' Davies (v)
Jon 'JJ' Cox (g)
Dave Gornall (b)
Mick Commons (d)

The name says it all! The four-man unit known as JJ'S POWERHOUSE delivered the sort of fast and heavy material which absolutely epitomises the term 'NWOBHM' for many, but which relatively few British hopefuls of the period actually attempted, if we're being brutally honest. The intriguing story surrounding the release of their one-off single goes back as far as the tail end of 1976, when an individual known as Jon 'JJ' Cox formed an outfit in his native Lancashire, initially taking the rather unpromising name of QUAD (although, given that they were a four-piece outfit, this choice had seemed like a good idea at the time) and attempting to create some heavy music which would ultimately revitalise a stagnant rock scene. The young guitarist had been influenced by an unusually wide variety of genres (from soul, Motown and r'n'b to more traditional heavy rock and metal territory) since taking up his instrument at an early age, and the chap was intent on playing innovative material which crossed boundaries and offered something new to the fans, many of whom had initially turned to punk in their quest for something energetic and exciting, but who now sought genuine musicianship to go with it. After gravitating together over a period of time, the embryonic group (initially completed by vocalist Austin 'Ozzy' Davies, bassist Chas Wilson and drummer Ted Barlow) set about making a name for themselves locally, and their individualistic brand of high-powered heavy fare went down a storm in the pubs and clubs of the North West, especially with the biker community.

After a comparatively short period of rehearsals and local gigging, QUAD's first proper visit to the recording studio came in the summer of 1977, where three of the outfit's own original compositions viz. "Thinking Of You", "Overlord" and "Saucers Of The Future" (you can't beat a good crockery-related number, can you?) were captured for posterity, although it proved to be the only session ever undertaken by their original line-up. Bassist Chas Wilson elected to chuck in the music business for personal reasons the following year, and was initially replaced by new bloke John Egerler, although the latter was himself eventually supplanted by a certain Mark Clegg. In due course, QUAD secured a healthy following throughout the North of England after fairly extensive (and, on occasion, eventful) gigging throughout the late 70's (including plentiful support slots with the likes of STRIFE, SAXON and THE TROGGS), effortlessly outlasting the punks and ultimately assuming their rightful place at the forefront of the NWOBHM explosion, as mainman Jon Cox recalls: *'I can remember sup-*

porting a punk rock band in the 70's and we completely burnt them into the ground with our raw power. I remember them being really nasty to us after the gig because what we did was exactly what they wanted to do but couldn't because fashion would not allow it. How sad!' (Ref: Private communication, February 2000). Things looked pretty rosy at that stage...

Cruelly, however, just when they should have been making plans for global domination, the extremely popular outfit began to fragment, with the supporting cast (who, after several years on the gritty club circuit, were now reluctant to partake of the incessant grind of touring) becoming increasingly disenchanted with the day to day activities of a rock band. Still, Cox and Davies kept things going themselves, penning new material and making a few further trips to the studio throughout the early 80's, utilising the services of stand-in rhythm sections as and when necessity demanded. By 1982, however, things had finally run their course, and (after recording two new tracks with bassist Dave Gornall and drummer Mick Commons) Cox decided to knock QUAD on the head for good. Undeterred, the guitarist decided that his musical vision deserved to live on in one form or another, and subsequently made the crucial decision to relocate to London in order to make more of an impression on the national rock scene and to expose his prodigious talents to as wide an audience as possible. Before doing so, however, Cox cunningly arranged for the two most recent QUAD recordings ("Running For The Line" and "Blackrods", recorded at Amazon Studios under the auspices of NIGHTWING's Gordon Rowley) to be pressed up on vinyl in order to give him something to hand out to various interested parties by way of an introduction to his music.

The original handful of white labels were exhausted in no time at all, however, whereupon a full-scale issue (pressed in the regulation quantity of a thousand copies) on the Sillysybin (as in the hallucinogenic *psilocybin* mushroom, one of which is, rather naughtily, pictured on the record) label was eventually initiated in 1983. The self-financed single (credited to JJ'S POWERHOUSE, an act who had never actually existed in their own right) benefitted from a remarkably favourable review in the hard-to-please 'Kerrang', with healthy comparisons to METALLICA (which was pretty accurate, particularly with respect to the heavy, chugging "Blackrods") being bandied about even then. On the other hand, the magnificent "Running For The Line" must be a prime contender for the accolade of *'ultimate*

NWOBHM classic', with its incredible, hyperspeed riffing (lend an ear to the mid-section and you'll discover an accelerated variation on DEMON's classic "Night Of The Demon" riff, recorded a full decade before IMPALED NAZARENE got in on the act), combined with the powerful, RAVEN-style vocals and catchy arrangement (slightly in the vein of early IRON MAIDEN) making you wish that all early 80's metal could have sounded like this. Astonishing.

Luckily for Lars Ulrich and Co., JJ'S POWERHOUSE weren't in any position to become the world's biggest band (given that they didn't actually exist) at this juncture, and it's only in recent years that fans have really become aware of the single, following its high-profile inclusion on the »NWOBHM Vol.8« bootleg CD. By mid-1983, however, Cox had relocated to the capital as planned (taking his stash of newly-pressed singles with him) and, after announcing the availability of his services to various interested parties, soon hooked up with a small-time metal proposition who would eventually evolve into WHITE HEAT (see separate entry). Not quite as, er, *powerful* as JJ'S POWERHOUSE, but another heavy (by British standards) outfit with strong guitars, this project had a fair bit of potential lurking beneath the surface but soon fell apart after releasing just one single (financed by selling the JJ'S POWERHOUSE 7" at their well-attended gigs in Europe) on the Rock Shop label. The genius of JJ Cox was notably absent from the British metal scene for a good few years thereafter, although the guitarist subsequently cropped up again after forming the PANIK ATTAK venture towards the end of the 80's (releasing a seldom-seen 12" in 1990) and is now working on brand-new material with former members of both QUAD and WHITE HEAT. Nowadays, the JJ'S POWERHOUSE 7" (never issued in a picture sleeve) is not only one of the genre's musical high-points, but also one of its rarest and most collectable pieces.

Just one final thought to keep you awake at night: *'Cox'* is hardly a common English surname, and it's truly mind-boggling that we had no less than three versions of *'J. Cox'* operating within the NWOBHM scene, namely guitarist Jon (JJ'S POWERHOUSE), vocalist Jess (TYGERS OF PAN TANG) and bassist Jeff (JAGUAR). Now, sparks would surely have flown if *that* particular trio had joined forces! Any drummers out there called Jim Cox interested in forming the ultimate post-NWOBHM supergroup?

7" Singles
»Running For The Line« Sillysybin Records 1983

Compilation Appearances
"Running For The Line" on »NWOBHM Vol.8« Bootleg CD 1996

JODEY

Stuart Southern (v)
Pat Shayler (g)
John Barr (b)
Adrian Chase (k)
Russell Payne (d)

It's funny how certain groups can be a bit, er, *'vague'* about their early career, isn't it? Numerous outfits have conveniently *'forgotten'* about their dubious minor-label releases, dodgy past identities, flirtation with other musical genres and so on. In some cases, such details are fairly irrelevant to their future activities, but for others it's occasionally worth exposing a few dark secrets. For example, how many of you knew that the outfit who eventually became known as CHINATOWN originally formed in the late 70's under the not-very-metal name of JODEY? Not many, I'll wager. Furthermore, hands up if you're also aware that the last-mentioned actually managed to issue their own two-tracker? Hmmm, I thought not. Well, it's all true, and I'm about to spill the beans, although there's really nothing too shameful about those early days. Their humble origins can be traced back to a small-time concern which initially took shape while the members were all studying at college in Hampshire, with their formative jam sessions paving the way for the emergence of JODEY at some point in 1978. As the months passed, the lads began to grow in stature as their musicianship and songwriting skills improved, and they were soon operating in a musical style which, to some extent, bridged the semi-progressive outlook of the 70's with the more down-to-earth NWOBHM mentality.

Within around a year of their formation, the increasingly-ambitious outfit decided to get in on the private single lark, whereupon the quintet duly laid down a couple of their favourite compositions for imminent release. Issued (without a picture sleeve, as far as we know) as a truly minuscule pressing on the renowned Ellie Jay label towards the end of 1979, the scarcely-sighted 7" couples "The Rocker" with "Frontman", two reasonable enough attempts in a fairly generalised rock/metal style with elements of LIMELIGHT or early GRAND PRIX. As you might expect, these numbers are very much in the mould of CHINATOWN (indeed, both were retained in the live set after the name change, along with the likes of "Time Will Tell", which eventually put in an appearance on both CHINATOWN's live LP and SHOGUN's debut set), although the distinctive, Jon Anderson-style vocal performance of Stuart Southern (especially when combined with the prominent keyboards) tends to evoke a metal version of YES. The nominated A-side is the more rocking (as its title might suggest) of the pair, with the epic flipside unquestionably being in a somewhat more progressive style. Hardly an embarrassment, lads, would it have been too much to ask that you might just have mentioned it in one of your interviews?

The continuation of the story can be found elsewhere in the CHINATOWN entry itself, the transformation apparently occurring in the early months of 1980 following the recruitment of vocalist Steve Prangnell, whereupon the outfit adopted their new oriental identity and made a real attempt to establish themselves as a genuine NWOBHM proposition. A further period of reconstruction would see the lads disposing of unlucky keyboard player Adrian Chase in favour of a second guitarist (Danny Gwilym, formerly with LYNX and FAT CHANCE), while original drummer Russell Payne (later of HIGH RISK) was ultimately superseded by Steve Hopgood (formerly with a small-time covers act called SHY). All things considered, however, JODEY's »The Rocker« is an excruciatingly rare piece today (Ellie Jay pressings aren't, as a whole, noted for their abundance, but this seems to be a particularly extreme example), and you'd better resign yourself to the fact that you might never *see* a copy, let alone *own* one.

7" Singles
»The Rocker« Ellie Jay 1979

JODY ST.

Noel McCalla (v)
John Mizarolli (g)
Henry Thomas (b)
Brett Morgan (d)

You can argue the toss over the inclusion of JODY ST. until the cows come home, but they were certainly an obscure and heavy act, and they satisfy the criterion of having released their own vinyl product at the height of the NWOBHM explosion, so I can't really comprehend why so many people seem to have a problem with them. Oh, I *see*. Brothers don't play heavy metal, right? Well, if you seriously believe that, you might as well start listening to some other kind of music. The band's story centres around immensely talented guitarist John Mizarolli, a childhood prodigy who was originally motivated to pick up his instrument after listening to various musical pioneers such as ELVIS PRESLEY and CHUCK BERRY, eventually becoming inspired by more heavyweight and innovative guitar maestros such as ERIC CLAPTON and (yes, you guessed it) JIMI HENDRIX. After spending several years in the States in the mid-to-late 70's (playing with such acts as THE PLATTERS), the axeman returned to Blighty and set about the task of locating a suitable vehicle to showcase his talents. Rather than attempting to establish a new outfit of his own, however, Mizarolli would initially team up with former CREAM drummer Ginger Baker in his short-lived GINGER BAKER'S ENERGY venture, a highly-regarded act who ended up playing in front of numerous appreciative audiences throughout Europe.

By the second half of 1980, however, Baker's band had ceased all operations for the time being, and Mizarolli duly turned his thoughts to the possibility of getting his own ambitious musical venture off the drawing board, in which he could attempt to fuse assorted influences from the worlds of rock, funk, jazz and soul. First of all, he enlisted the services of bassist (and erstwhile ENERGY colleague) Henry Thomas, a veteran of funky rockers FBI, and the seeds of JODY ST. were already being sown. The newly-recruited Thomas then collared one of his chums, former MOON vocalist Noel McCalla (who had additionally recorded as a solo artist at various times in the past), and invited him to join in the fun, while Mizarolli sought out another former acquaintance, Brett Morgan (the token honky), an experienced session drummer, to make up the numbers. With all the vital ingredients having now been assembled, the lads (resembling something of a modern-day version of the unfeasibly superb FOUNDATIONS) soon began a bit of studio-based experimentation to see just how well they could work together. Incredibly, it took the quartet only a couple of weeks to conclude that they had the right stuff, and the London-based ensemble proceeded to enter Morgan Studios even before the end of the year, whereupon they composed and recorded an entire album's worth of material for future use.

After several months of gigging in the capital, the lads eventually decided to do something with their master tape, and pressed up a tiny quantity of white-label albums (decorating the sleeves by simply stamping them with the band's boxed logo) in an attempt to get their name heard by those that mattered. The album's minimalist presentation was very much along the lines of DIAMOND HEAD's promotional issue of »Lightning To The Nations«, and, like the aforementioned LP, didn't even reveal any of the song titles. Very few people were fortunate enough to hear the eight-tracker in the first instance, which is a great pity, as it contained some stunning and original numbers, with elements of (in addition to the intended targets of HENDRIX and CREAM) acts as diverse as THIN LIZZY, PARLIAMENT and, as a few others have commented, VAN HALEN. The musicianship was exceptional, and Noel McCalla's exciting, soulful vocals identified the outfit as representing something entirely out of the ordinary. This wasn't NWOBHM in its purest form at all, but it would still be immensely listenable for the typical aficionado of the genre. In fact, the record's polished performance and innovative style was probably its undoing, as the labels of the day were generally happier to invest in groups who followed the usual route of rough'n'ready metal and didn't rock the boat too much.

The album was circulated in the spring of 1981, and the band sat back and waited for offers to come their way. Sadly, nothing much happened in the first instance, although things seemed to pick up in the summer when they were invited to go out on the road with THE KINKS, and the lads enjoyed a few more high-profile appearances as a result. Still, nothing came of their attempts to crack the rock market, and the dejected outfit finally called it a day within a matter of months. Their monumentally scarce LP rapidly passed into the realms of NWOBHM folklore, with rumour and counter-rumour surrounding its legendary musical contents. In spite of the fact that nobody seemed to be entirely sure just how good the album really was, NWOBHM fans (and a few aficionados of certain other genres) were, by the early 90's, foaming at the mouth at the prospect of any copies coming up for sale, and the theoretical value swiftly rocketed to astronomical levels. In fact, I reckon that only a couple of examples have come onto the market in recent times, which is probably quite a good thing, as I imagine that relatively few NWOBHM devotees would consider it to be worth half a month's salary after all. It's a capable LP, admittedly (you might even hear the odd reminder of acts such as DRAGONFLY or MEANSTREAK in places, and the wondrous "I Want Your Love" could *easily* pass for a DIAMOND HEAD composition), but I suspect that most collectors would demand a more metal-sounding release for this kind of money.

If you think the album is impossibly rare, however, I've got news for you. There's actually a single as well. At the risk of breaking a few hearts amongst avid collectors, I have to reveal that JODY ST. also issued a two-tracker (another white label with a stamped sleeve) featuring the twisting "Fight Back" (a heavy effort with a convoluted arrangement) and the preposterously-titled "Granny Did It" (a very catchy song nonetheless), the two opening selections from their album. Given that the titles were actually revealed on this pressing, however, I reckon the 7" was intended for radio play whereas the LP was circulated purely for promotional purposes. Whatever the story, the two-tracker seems to have been manufactured in truly minuscule quantities (a few dozen at most), and I don't imagine many will ever come out of the woodwork. The good news for NWOBHM enthusiasts, however, is that some enterprising individual got hold of a copy of the LP a few years back, and proceeded to press a few hundred bootleg CD's of the whole thing, including the promotional blurb and photo which came as part of the original package. It was a well-presented release, and the sound quality couldn't be faulted, although the fact that they've had to guess at the song titles (most of which are completely wrong) is a bit of a giveaway that this didn't come out with the group's approval. Nevertheless, it gives some of us the chance to hear the album without shelling out a small fortune.

In the wake of JODY ST.'s ultimate failure to break into the expansive rock market, the individual members acknowledged their limited chances of global domination, and set their sights a bit lower in later years. John Mizarolli fared pretty well, though, and secured a deal with Carrere Records in 1982, which soon led to the release of his »Message From The Fifth Stone« solo album. Although this was credited solely as a JOHN MIZAROLLI offering, however, you could practically view this as the second JODY ST. long-player, given that he enlisted the help of all three of his former colleagues to assist him in this venture. The in-demand Noel McCalla subsequently lent his services to PARTNERS IN CRIME, John Coghlan's post-STATUS QUO venture, before playing a part in the fortunes of the persevering MANFRED MANN. The workmanlike Mizarolli, meanwhile, has gone from project to project in recent years (he also guested on ATOMIC ROOSTER's »Headline News« album back in 1983), constantly reinventing himself and his music in a series of predominantly instrumental ventures such as MIZAROLLI MAGIC and the MIZAROLLI AXE PHENOMENON (some of which have, in fact, recorded a fair old bit of studio material), and you'll be intrigued to learn that he's still to be found playing live in various guises these days.

LP's
»Jody St.« Private 1981
[White label with stamped plain sleeve]

7" Singles
»Fight Back« Private 1981
[White label with stamped plain sleeve]

CD's
»Jody St.« JS Records 1996
[Unofficial reissue]

JOE LETHAL

Alan Aitken
Bigham

Predating the main NWOBHM explosion by a year or so, the utterly obscure JOE LETHAL (an unrenowned trio from Ayrshire in the West of Scotland) issued their own single in the latter part of 1978, this being a seldom-seen item which reveals the outfit to have been operating in a style which borrows from both the boogie and (to a lesser extent) punk camps. The A-side, "Don't Come Back", is a rudimentary, good-time rock'n'roll number in the general mode of ROKKA or PREDATÜR, while the reverse ("You Ain't Free") has more of a punky edge (which is understandable, as the band apparently started out at the height of the punk influx) and some reasonable guitar work, the overall effect being slightly more along the lines of VIRGIN STAR and their rowdy cohorts. Neither composition outstays its welcome, and there's nothing remotely out of the ordinary in terms of musicianship, but it all seems quite upbeat, cheerful and enthusiastic enough. No doubt they were their region's token boogie/pub rock act with the typical biker following, although it looks as though this bunch never managed to break into the big league as did VARDIS and SPIDER. The single was apparently issued without the extravagance of a picture sleeve, and there's not exactly a wealth of information on the record itself, so I guess we'll just have to be patient and wait for further details to become available at some point in the future.

7" Singles
»Don't Come Back« Lethal Records 1978

JOKER

Tony Ruhberg (v,b)
Mark White (g)
Bob Palfrey (d)

In retrospect, perhaps signing to the rather nondiscriminating label known as Lost Moment Records might have been rather a bad career move for JOKER (and, in all probability, the utterly bonkers ORION), as the company developed the unenviable habit of signing some astonishingly unworthy and untalented ensembles in years to come, earning themselves something of an undesirable reputation in the process. Even so, the aforementioned JOKER (who were apparently regarded as a fairly popular act throughout the Home Counties) still managed to throw together a semi-competent single in the form of »Back On The Road«, although both numbers rely rather too heavily on recycling old DEEP PURPLE and RAINBOW riffs and plastering a somewhat rudimentary song construction over the foundations. There's absolutely nothing here that hasn't been done far better by the likes of BLADE RUNNER or EXCALIBUR, and the lyrics on both tracks are (even by the standards of the genre) extraordinarily amateurish, especially on "Pusher", where the *'drugs are bad, kids'* message is rammed home with all the subtlety of a punch in the face. Awful. In all honesty, there are several outfits of this calibre on Ebony's early compilations, many of whom could probably have issued a more worthwhile single, given half a chance.

In spite of its shortcomings, the sole JOKER effort (issued in a fairly enticing sleeve) has remained a reasonably popular item among NWOBHM collectors over the years, even though certain avaricious characters were initially tempted to pass it off as an *'undiscovered classic'* for truly ludicrous amounts of money. Guitarist Mark White, incidentally, resurfaced a year later (by which time JOKER had almost certainly bitten the dust) in the atrociously-named SCHUTT, a band formed by musicians from various regional acts such as VALHALLA (who had issued two rather poor singles on Neat before calling it a day), TIGON and BLACK TIGER. The new outfit also came to the attention of Lost Moment, and there was, at one stage, a very real chance that they too would be invited to record a 7" for the label, although this prospect appears to have evaporated in the long term. Following on from the demise of SCHUTT, White moved over to ELIXIR, revealing his versatility by switching from guitar to bass in the process, and contributed to the latter's studio activities towards the end of their existence.

7" Singles
»Back On The Road« Lost Moment Records 1984

JOKERS WILD

Ian Baker (v)
Robin Yates (g)
Mark (b)
Kev (k)
Mick Ransome (d)

London's JOKERS WILD burst onto the capital's live scene in the early 80's, and, after several years of hard graft, eventually established themselves as highly-regarded exponents of tuneful rock/metal, although it transpires that a fair percentage of their earlier compositions were apparently quite firmly rooted in the NWOBHM ethos. With the driving force behind the group being capable songwriter/guitarist Robin Yates, the five-piece concern (featuring one-time PRAYING MANTIS drummer Mick Ransome) had few problems coming up with usable, original material, and they finally circulated a self-financed debut (no sleeve known) late in 1985, coupling "Don't Fall In Love" with "Rock And Roll Hearts". It revealed a confident prospect at the height of their powers, their well-crafted, American-influenced rockers bringing forth general comparisons with UK contemporaries such as SHOGUN, TOBRUK and SHY, with memorable, catchy arrangements on display all round. Although the two-tracker was well-received in certain quarters at the time, notably the easily-pleased 'High Octane' fanzine, it performed relatively poorly in terms of sales (the old melodic rock lark was always a hit-or-miss affair), and this opening gambit ultimately failed to raise the ensemble's profile to a significant extent.

Seemingly undeterred by this apparent lack of appreciation from the masses, JOKERS WILD continued to ply their trade in the live environment over the next year or so (the much-travelled Mick Ransome was replaced by the mysterious *'Tim'* along the way, although the original sticksman ultimately landed a rather more permanent position with the TATTOOED LOVE BOYS), with numerous enthusiastic performances (featuring self-penned selections such as "So Alone", "It's Only Heartbreak", "On Top Of The World" and "Break In The Clouds") going down an absolute storm with their ever-dependable following, particularly in the capital itself. Still, it makes you wonder why so few of them actually bothered to buy the band's first single. By 1987, however, the musicians had finally decided to try their luck with another modest vinyl offering, opting to re-release »Don't Fall In Love« (in a proper picture cover this time) through the small-time Bold Reprive (no prizes for spelling there, folks) label and pairing it with the unfamiliar "Where There's A Will", an unashamedly commercial cut which, for my money, isn't a patch on the original flipside, the excellent "Rock And Roll Hearts". Nevertheless, it was second time lucky for JOKERS WILD, and this particular release appears to have thrust them into the public spotlight at last, drawing some long-overdue attention from publications such as 'Kerrang', who proceeded to review one of the group's regular London gigs with great approval.

Unfortunately, JOKERS WILD struggled to maintain either a stable line-up or their enthusiasm thereafter, and were forced to bring in new vocalist Ian Baker (who had briefly taken Max Bacon's place in BRONZ after his defection to the GTR project, and who also enjoyed stints with BLUEPRINT and JAGGED EDGE) in an attempt to salvage a rapidly-declining situation. At first, it looked as though matters were steadily improving, although things subsequently seem to have fizzled out over a period of several months, despite the fact that a further single (»Simple Life«) was scheduled for release in the latter half of 1988. However, as far as we know, this only reached the test pressing stage (the commercial issue was ultimately scuppered by a severe lack of finances, although I reckon Bold Reprive came a cropper after throwing their weight behind the decidedly dodgy MESSIAH FORCE), and it looks as though JOKERS WILD called it a day not long after. In any case, the proposed 7" was far too commercial (sickeningly so, to be honest) for the rock market, and probably wouldn't have done their reputation any favours at all. Mainman Robin Yates, incidentally, tried his luck again in the early 90's with an unacclaimed outfit called CRAZY GANG, who failed to break through after organising an unspectacular self-financed release or two to introduce themselves.

7" Singles
»**Don't Fall In Love**« SRT 1985
[Original issue without picture sleeve, B-side "Rock And Roll Hearts"]
»**Don't Fall In Love**« Bold Reprive Records 1987
[Second issue in picture sleeve, B-side "Where There's A Will"]
»**Simple Life**« Bold Reprive Records 1988
[White label promos only]

JONAH

Dean Shepherd

Clearly, the handful of bands who originated from the Channel Islands struggled to make themselves known further afield, and the utterly obscure JONAH appear to have been overshadowed by fellow Jersey artists LEGEND and TRACER during their fleeting time on the regional rock scene. Mind you, they were a markedly more cheerful proposition than either of their aforementioned contemporaries, as evidenced by their sole vinyl offering, a double A-sided effort from 1985. Both numbers reveal the group to have been operating in an undeniably accessible style (a few similarities to MOSELLE, SHADOWLANDS and GENERAL WOLF), with "This Is Love" being a very classy semi-ballad which showcases a pretty impressive vocalist. The succinctly-titled "Tough", on the other hand, is rather more upbeat, and even includes some twin-guitar work at one point. All in all, however, this brand of melodic, keyboard-infused rock showed a reasonable amount of potential to the major labels, although I suspect that the lads would have found it difficult to attract a significant level of interest without relocating to the mainland. As a result, they seem to have been overlooked quite cruelly, and had presumably called it quits within a year or two. Apart from mainman Dean Shepherd (who additionally helped out in rival act TRACER when the latter ran into personnel problems, incidentally), however, the identity of the other conspirators is currently unknown, but I wouldn't be remotely surprised if this turns out to have been a predominantly solo venture. In any case, this sleeveless two-tracker is an extraordinarily rare item these days, and I would be very surprised indeed if more than a handful of examples ever surface.

7" Singles
»**This Is Love**« MW Records 1985

JUNO'S CLAW

Line-up unknown

The ludicrously obscure JUNO'S CLAW appear to have been active in the North West at the very inception of the NWOBHM movement, and were early exponents of a kind of technical, left-field style which later became associated with acts such as SACRED ALIEN and KRAKEN, who might even have been influenced by this bunch in the first instance, you never know. Anyway, nothing is currently known for sure about the outfit's personnel or history, but their only piece of vinyl appears to be a three track EP recorded at Smile Studios in Manchester way back in 1979. It's not the most competently-produced offering you'll ever hear, but it's a pretty sincere and enthusiastic affair, which, from time to time, also hints at acts such as NEON SPIRIT, TRACER and Hampshire's LONE WOLF. The lengthy "Barbara" starts things off, a pretty hefty stab at quirky NWOBHM in best SACRED ALIEN fashion, while "The Master" is a more technical and powerful number in the KRAKEN mould, the EP's stand-out cut without any shadow of doubt. The slower, more atmospheric "Big City" rounds off the three-tracker, and comes across as a slightly more cheerful (well, it wouldn't really be possible to be *less* cheerful) TRACER. Truly excellent stuff throughout, and it's just a pity that there's such a lack of useful information on the record, which doesn't seem to have been issued in a picture sleeve at any stage. It's a long shot, but if anyone has any further info, get in touch…

7" EP's
»Barbara« MPA Records 1979

KARRIER

Gary Garner (v)
Chris Clowsley (g)
Ian Hall (g)
Mark Fletcher (b)
Mick Suddens (d)

Midlands-based KARRIER didn't really get going until the initial NWOBHM explosion had died down considerably (if they had been operating for a few years beforehand, then they certainly didn't make themselves known to the masses), although their vinyl debut made a pretty good attempt at recapturing the original spirit of the early 80's. No doubt the group had dreamed of a multi-album deal with EMI at the outset, but, like most of their small-time rivals, ended up signing to a somewhat less illustrious company. The modest label in question were Unit Records, who sponsored the first slice of KARRIER vinyl (the »I'm Back« single), which hit the shops at the tail end of 1984. Unusually, it was released in both 7" and 12" forms (although the latter, boasting the extra track "Dreaming", is extremely scarce), with the A-side being an eminently capable, mid-paced effort reminiscent of BLACK AXE or MYTHRA. Flipside "Way Beyond The Night", on the other hand, is a rather more commercial number with a distinct feel of GRAND PRIX or STRUTZ in places, although it benefits from some highly enjoyable twin-guitar interplay throughout. After some healthy feedback from the rock community, a full LP followed within a relatively short timescale, the outfit recycling the selections from their earlier release (which had already won favour with publications such as 'Kerrang') and installing "Way Beyond The Night" as the title track.

Although the average NWOBHM aficionado might well find the fairly extreme variations in KARRIER's musical stance (veering from heavy, BLITZKRIEG-influenced riffing to considerably more melodic, even funky, material at times) slightly difficult to take in at first, »Way Beyond The Night« (again recorded for the Unit concern) is actually a very well-written and competently-performed set of compositions, particularly the aforementioned (and excellent) "Dreaming", which sounds not entirely dissimilar to "Loser" by ANGEL WITCH. Having said all that, it might be a release which, on balance, appeals more to the melodic rock fan than those whose allegiances lie with the likes of TANK or SATAN. In the aftermath of the long-player's release (the lads having tried in vain to attain some European exposure by offering the recordings to such labels as Noise Records in Germany), KARRIER toured fairly widely throughout the UK, occasionally supporting the likes of MAGNUM at bigger events. They consistently failed to attract the interest of any remotely influential companies, though, and the lads eventually went back to basics and recorded a second single for Unit. This appeared as the seldom-seen 1986 effort »Poor Little Rich Girl« (B-side "Endless Shadow"), but it constituted another fairly unsuccessful release which proved to be KARRIER's last vinyl output.

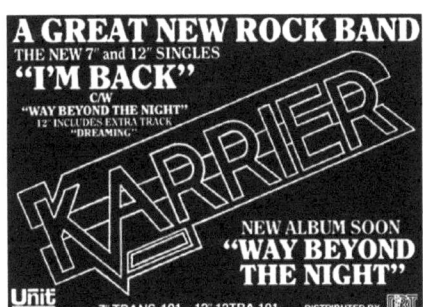

Personnel problems started to hamper the outfit's progress before long, and new vocalist Barry Thorne, recruited to the fold in 1987, failed to establish himself to any great extent. The latter was to leave after a few months (scuppering the outfit's tentative plans to lay down a second long-player) to join fellow Midlands hopefuls EXPRESS, an act who recorded a capable melodic rock single or two (e.g. »Crying To The Night«) for the Status label (winning the patronage of 'Kerrang' in the process) and also contributed members to the ever-changing RADIO

MOSCOW line-up along the way. It seems, however, that KARRIER stumbled on blindly for a while, and there are unconfirmed reports that the future DIAMOND HEAD rhythm section of Karl Wilcox (d) and Eddie Moohan (b) joined in for a brief spell towards the end of their existence, but it eventually all crumbled at some point in the late 80's. Original vocalist Gary Garner, meanwhile, sang on the tracks credited to the DIRT BOX BAND (but originally written and performed by DIAMOND HEAD themselves) on the seldom-seen »Midwest Rock« compilation in the early 90's.

LP's
»Way Beyond The Night« Unit Records 1985

12" EP's
»I'm Back« Unit Records 1984

7" Singles
»I'm Back« Unit Records 1984
»Poor Little Rich Girl« Unit Records 1986
[Both tracks non-LP]

KICK

Dave Fulcher (v)
Mole Naylor (v)
Ian Morris (g)
Dave Yardley (b)
Rob Bee (k)
Bob Naunton (d)

Apart from giving the flourishing NWOBHM movement an extremely valuable piece of early exposure with their renowned »Metal For Muthas« compilations, it's a well-known fact that the giant EMI corporation also took a few of the more promising acts under their wing at the time. Whereas IRON MAIDEN were unquestionably the company's success story, certain others enjoyed a markedly less illustrious period of major-label patronage, notably the inadvisably-named ETHEL THE FROG (who fragmented just as their debut long-player was hitting the shops, a move which was hardly conducive to commercial success), ANGEL WITCH (given the chance to record only one single before being given their freedom) and SAMSON (poached by rival concern Gem before their EMI debut had even been officially issued). In fact, it transpires that there were some even earlier rock acts on the company's books, one of whom recorded a 7" as far back as the beginning of 1979, so it looks as though EMI might have been scouting for heavy talent long before the metal explosion got underway, saving them from cruel accusations of bandwagon-jumping once the phenomenon was already firmly established.

In fact, it's more likely that the aforementioned hopefuls were picked up by EMI at around the same time as the rather more high-profile WILD HORSES, whose connection with established acts such as RAINBOW and THIN LIZZY would have assured their sponsors of a certain amount of commercial success even if their protégés weren't conveniently lumped in with the NWOBHM movement as time went on. Getting back to their more obscure signings of the pre-NWOBHM period, however, one of the unfamiliar names which crops up is KICK, whose activities on the rock scene currently remain something of a mystery. In any case, their one-off EP showcased three original tracks, whimsically divided into *'a bit of smooth stuff'* and *'a bit of rough stuff'*, which was possibly a slightly optimistic state of affairs. The *'smooth'* is represented by the unremarkable "Wrong For You", a hypnotic (in the sleep-inducing sense) semi-ballad which does, nevertheless, reveal a competent vocalist (quite why two are credited on the sleeve is confusing, mind you) to be part of the picture. The *'rough'*, on the other hand, comes in the shape of "Goggle Box (Whole Lot Better Than You)" and "The Writer", two markedly heavier rock tracks which are both undeniably similar to Gillan-era DEEP PURPLE, but which are perfectly acceptable to the NWOBHM palate.

Clearly, the band didn't exactly become a household name in the wake of this average release, and the observation that most, if not all, of the records actually emerged as demo issues (as with SAMSON's original version of »Vice Versa«) suggests that KICK weren't considered a particularly viable proposition at the time; indeed, it's entirely possible that the general issue may ultimately have been cancelled. Whatever the story, the three-tracker (issued in a green sleeve showing the musicians posing on some scaffolding) is seldom sighted these days, indicating a modest pressing. KICK presumably parted company with EMI shortly thereafter, although they certainly remained a going concern for at least another couple of years, playing to appreciative crowds in rock-friendly cities such as Oxford (although I suspect that they were actually based somewhere in the Midlands) until mid-1981 or thereabouts, whereupon things finally went rather quiet. I would imagine that KICK disbanded a short time later, but it's not impossible that they persevered in low-profile mode for a bit longer. Indeed, there was an identically-named British outfit who released a couple of singles in the mid-80's (not to mention an AOR band who are still on the go), but I reckon they were almost certainly unrelated to the original bunch.

7" EP's
»Rough'n'Smooth« EMI 1979

KNIGHTRIDER

Tam Toye (v,b)
Dave Marmion (g)
Billy McCready (g)
Jamie Cosgrove (d)

It's time to pay tribute to one of the original NWOBHM outfits that refused to die! First coming into existence (as the metal brainchild of band mainman Tam Toye) in 1982 or thereabouts, Strathclyde's KNIGHTRIDER recorded some truly excellent material in their formative years (an early pair of demos won considerable praise in the rock press), notably such memorable offerings as "Reflections", "Knightrider" and "MI5", but, for some reason, just didn't manage to make it to the vinyl stage until as late as 1987. Just for the sake of it, though, let's be inordinately charitable and include them here, shall we? Their debut single (the sleeveless »Shout Out Loud«) apparently sold pretty well at the time, particularly at gigs, although most of the outings evidently took place in England (the outfit appear to have been especially popular in the Midlands) as opposed to their native land. The A-side is, admittedly, a fairly unremarkable rocker in the mid-80's TERRAPLANE vein, although "Extra-terrestrial Girl" (another one of their older demo tracks) was a major improvement, this being a heavy-but-melodic number in the general manner of SAPPHIRE or STAGEFRIGHT. It wasn't a bad start at all, but it's a great pity it took so long to materialise.

Sadly, the two-tracker didn't receive a particularly good review in 'Kerrang' (as with so many other perfectly acceptable releases), with the production being marked out for a slice of hefty criticism, although I've heard far worse over the years. Strangely, though, the magazine reviewed »Shout Out Loud« again as late as 1992 (!), suggesting that it might even have been reissued or repromoted at some point. Following their initial vinyl foray, KNIGHTRIDER subsequently appeared on a relatively obscure local-band compilation (the little-known »Paisley Rock 500 Album«) at some point in 1988 (by which time Tam Toye was being assisted by axemen Paul McGuiness and Andy Fraser, plus sticksman John McLaughlan), their contribution coming in the shape of "Princess Patricia". Cast from the same mould as their single's B-side, but with a marginally more commercial edge, the lads were clearly intending to crack the lucrative melodic rock market, but just never seem to have made the big time in spite of all their efforts in the live environment. Mind you, I reckon that a couple of further releases are likely to have sneaked out (possibly only on CD format) during the 90's (a promotional CD-R or two certainly put in an appearance), although the pressings were presumably so minuscule that few second-hand copies have come onto the market thus far.

It's worth mentioning that KNIGHTRIDER also benefitted from an enviable amount of local radio exposure (not to mention the occasional appearance on Scottish television, some of which were later recycled to form the basis of an official video or two), and they were almost certainly featured on additional small-time compilations over the years. Furthermore, it's not inconceivable that the long-lived outfit might even still be in existence (in one form or another) today, having undergone numerous personnel variations along the way (including bassists Chuck MacGuire, Guz Adams and Grant Woolard, guitarists Alan Kinney, Paul Pelosi, Rob Wilson and Brian Russell, and drummers Rocky Jones, Brian Queen and Scott Antico, among countless others), and their familiar name has, in comparatively recent times, even graced the weekly gig guide pages of 'Kerrang'. Keep going, Tam, you might make it eventually; let's just hope that David Hasselhoff doesn't sue you for use of the name!

7" Singles
»Shout Out Loud« Omega Records 1987

Exclusive Compilation Appearances
"Princess Patricia" on »Paisley Rock 500 Album« LP SRT 1988

KNOCK UP

Paul Dixon

Another reasonably familiar two-tracker which was issued by a bit of a mystery group; KNOCK

UP (a name which has, er, a *variety* of connotations) released their »Telling Lies« single at the height of the NWOBHM, but don't seem to have made much of an impression on the headbangers at the time. It transpires that the ensemble were, in fact, based in the fertile region of Glamorgan, although they were one of the less outstanding representatives of a very healthy local metal scene, I'm afraid. To be honest, the music showcased on their one-off release is extraordinarily average, with a feeble production and weak vocal performance which tends to overshadow the otherwise passable riffing and general guitar work. "Telling Lies", the weaker of the numbers featured, is a fairly mediocre and haphazard cross between URCHIN and SHADER, while "Need Your Love", despite its improved guitar structure, is again let down by the unconvincing vocals, and occasionally brings to mind some of the less interesting CRACKED MIRROR or HIGH RISK material. The standard issue of this particular 7" (which, unsurprisingly, received a less-than-glowing review in 'Kerrang' upon its release in 1982) came with an uninformative label and plain sleeve, although a handful of examples came in a hand-written promotional cover, which still makes them only marginally more interesting. Although a reasonable number of copies have turned up of late, this is still a genuinely rare item, and is rapidly hurtling towards the three-figure mark as competition among the NWOBHM community hots up. As with SHADER, CHEEKY, WHITEFIRE and many others, however, it's simply not worth the money, not by a long chalk.

7" Singles
»Telling Lies« Movie Music 1982

KOOGA

Neville MacDonald (v,g)
David Howells (b)
Neil Garland (k)
Martin Williams (d)

The origins of Welsh heroes KOOGA lie in an obscure rock outfit named PREACHER, formed in the implausibly-named town of Ynysybwl (Vowels? We don't need no stinking vowels!) towards the end of 1981. The fledgling band featured the trio of Neville MacDonald, David Howells and Martin Williams, and their early activities on the local scene were notable only in the sense that they were utterly unremarkable.

Nevertheless, the lads completed numerous live appearances, purveying a slightly bland style of hard rock, but it was the recruitment of keyboard player Neil Garland in 1983 that was ultimately to prove the turning point in terms of the outfit's fortunes. Their newer material started to become considerably more dynamic and memorable, and the quartet began to draw attention from parties other than their local fan base. By mid-1984, they had become KOOGA, and a year later the outfit circulated a speculative demo entitled »Unleashed«, a three track affair featuring "Across The Water", "Lay Down Your Love" and the Byronic "She Walks In Beauty". Almost immediately, the cassette was attracting label interest, and a copy also found its way into the hands of those responsible for the 'Friday Rock Show'. Within a remarkably short space of time, the lads were ensconced in the studio and laying down their debut session, which was eventually broadcast on the 3rd of January 1986. The lads happily took the opportunity to showcase all three tracks from the recent demo, plus the previously-unheard "Gabrielle", this confident display helping their cause considerably.

On the basis of their demo and session, it looked as though KOOGA surely had a healthy future in front of them, their latest material lying somewhere between the raunchy style of TERRAPLANE and the semi-pomp of FORCE, LYADRIVE or GRAND PRIX. Nevertheless, there was also a distinct similarity to certain acts who wouldn't come to the fore until the second half of the decade, notably SHERWOOD, BLUE BLUD and VOYEUR. As had been widely anticipated, KOOGA were picked up a few months later, the offer coming from a slightly unusual source, namely the French label Black Dragon, a concern more commonly associated with powerful, chest-beating acts such as LIEGE LORD, HEIR APPARENT and the excellent MANILLA ROAD. Nevertheless, the company made an extremely good job of producing KOOGA's debut long-player, which hit the shops in mid-1986. »Across The Water« featured all four tracks from their BBC session, plus "Lifeline", "Fall From Grace", "Like I've Never Known" and the oddly-titled instrumental "Lockjaw". The album received almost universal praise, the critics mostly agreeing that it was unusual and pleasing to find such a classy British outfit who were bucking the trend towards thrash or American-influenced glam/pop. Sales were relatively healthy, although it appears to have been a one-off deal, leaving the group to seek a new label who would sponsor the follow-up. Incidentally, I'm sure there was a single released at this point (in an identical sleeve to the album), although I've only ever seen one copy, way back in the mists of time. Can anyone tell us exactly what that 7" was, and also why it's so mind-bogglingly scarce?

1987 proved to be a year of ups and downs for KOOGA, with possible deals with Warner Brothers and MCA falling through after initial interest, the upshot being that the musicians were forced to record some new demos (a six track effort featuring the likes of "Rain" and "Motion Lotion" failed to attract much attention) to tout around the majors. They did, however, expand to a five-piece by recruiting guitarist Gerwyn Howley (formerly with the awful 20/20 VISION), allowing Neville MacDonald to develop his vocal skills and stage presence even further, although he still retained some guitar duties. The revised outfit (after support slots with the likes of FM) contributed "Across The Water" and "She Walks In Beauty" (marginally different versions) to the patchy »The Vinyl Frontier« sampler, and appeared at the 1987 Reading Festival, where their reception from the bottle-throwing lunatics was, to say the least, mixed. Towards the end of the year, the founder members decided that a bit of reorganisation was now a necessary evil, and the end result was the departure of Neil Garland (who supposedly proceeded to help out in TOK-IO ROSE) and original bassist David Howells. The new line-up was completed by bassist Steve Colley (ex-TRAITORS GATE/IN PURSUIT) and much-travelled keyboard wizard Tony Lambert (an experienced scenester who had played with the RACING CARS and the SENSATIONAL ALEX HARVEY BAND), whereupon the band stepped up their touring activities once again.

As something of a stop-gap, the outfit chose to issue a privately-pressed two-tracker at the beginning of 1988, coupling new number "Don't Break My Heart" (a slightly more commercial offering than their album material) with a reworked version of old favourite "Lay Down Your Love". It might not have sold in outstanding quantities, but it showed the world that KOOGA were very much still a going concern. It wasn't long, however, before new boy Lambert was on his way, the band drafting in Lee Dallon as a swift replacement for their upcoming gigs with SAXON. With the outfit experiencing difficulties in obtaining and holding onto a genuine record deal (their much-touted affiliation with Beserkley Records turned out to be an 'on/off' relationship, although the company were at least responsible for a seldom-seen alternate issue of their »Don't Break My Heart« single), they chose to venture into the studio to prepare material for their second album, hoping that someone would step in with a suitable offer before long. In the event, though, there was remarkably little interest shown in KOOGA's activities, and it was only a matter of time before the disillusioned Howley and Colley handed in their letters of resignation. The remaining members concluded that they were fighting a losing battle, and had called it a day by the end of a decade (apparently altering their name to COUGAR towards the end, which made precisely zero difference) without making much of a fuss about it.

In around 1991, however, talented frontman Neville MacDonald was head-hunted by Myke Gray and Andy Robbins, who wanted to get their ailing JAGGED EDGE project (which had suffered chronically from personnel instability ever since its inception in 1986) off the ground once more. The singer jumped at the chance, and soon took his place in a four-piece unit who evolved from JAGGED EDGE to PHOENIX to BAD FOR GOOD to TASTE (the name changes occurred on an almost weekly basis), before finally ending up as the much more familiar SKIN, an act who enjoyed a considerable amount of press attention and mainstream chart success for the remainder of the decade. As a direct consequence, interest in KOOGA vinyl was briefly rekindled (surprisingly, the »Across The Water« set was also bootlegged on CD), although this ultimately failed to send the prices skyrocketing to any great extent, and, nowadays, it's only really the NWOBHM (and, to a lesser extent, AOR) fans who consistently maintain any sort of demand for these original vinyl artefacts.

LP's
»Across The Water« High Dragon Records 1986

7" Singles
»Don't Break My Heart« Kooga Records 1988
[A-side non-LP, B-side "Lay Down Your Love" different to album version]
»Don't Break My Heart« Beserkley Records 1988
[Alternate issue]

CD's
»Across The Water« Reborn Classics 1993
[Bootleg release, also features »Fleet Street« album by Canadian version of FIST]

Compilation Appearances
"Across The Water" on »The Vinyl Frontier« LP BB Records 1987
[Different to album version]

"She Walks In Beauty" on »The Vinyl Frontier« LP BB Records 1987
[Different to album version]

KOREA

Huw Lucas (g)
Fennell
Johnson
Clark

Birmingham's unrenowned KOREA appear to have emerged from the ashes of the popular TROUBLE, who must have called it a day at some point in the early months of 1984, presumably a short time after the defection of bassist Roy Davis to local rivals SHY. In all probability, guitarist Huw Lucas then formed the new group himself, hastily roping in a few unknown colleagues (I've no idea whether or not *'Fennell'* might have been one-time EVERYONE ELSE bassist Keith Fennell, but it's a distinct possibility), after which the musicians soon settled down to the unenviable task of writing some original material, which saw them adopting the kind of facile, melodic rock approach favoured by regional favourites SHY and BRIAR. At some point, they made it into the studio and laid down a pair of their own compositions ("I Don't Know" and "Deep In Your Heart"), which would be kept aside for future use. Before long, however, these tracks were pressed up on vinyl by the short-lived Romac label (also home to the original HELLFIRE CLUB), and the KOREA single was soon being circulated to various influential parties in the business.

It was an inoffensive enough stab at semi-AOR commercialism, with both selections bearing a fairly close similarity to chart-friendly acts of the time such as TUXEDO, JOKERS WILD and SHOGUN, but it was all carried off with consummate ease, the lads showing a fair bit of potential to the major labels. It was certainly a lot better than much of the drivel churned out by LIONHEART, for instance. Sadly, however, their collective efforts failed to win them all that many admirers, although the A-side put in a brief appearance in the 'Local Chart' section of 'Kerrang' some time later. In fact, it looks as though the two-tracker might only have been manufactured for promotional purposes, and there may not even have been a commercial issue at any stage, which would explain the record's extreme scarcity these days. In any case, the band appear to have gone under with great haste, and, with Huw Lucas going off to work with ROBIN GEORGE at the end of 1984 (later resurfacing in the UNTOUCHABLES), it seems unlikely that his colleagues carried on without him. The KOREA single wasn't issued with a picture sleeve, by the looks of things, and really is a genuinely rare piece by the standards of the genre, but it hardly qualifies as prime-era NWOBHM, so I reckon most of us can quite happily live without it.

7" Singles
»I Don't Know« Romac Records 1984

KRAKEN

Andy Hopkins (v,b)
Ian Leach (g)
Jim Connolly (d)

Not to be confused with either their later Canadian namesakes (who were, absurdly, featured on the »NWOBHM Demo Tapes« bootleg CD) or the later Merseyside group who contributed to the »It's Unheard Of!« compilation, the *'genuine'* NWOBHM version of KRAKEN are primarily known by virtue of their legendary three track EP from 1980. Mind you, the background is a bit perplexing, given that the trio supposedly evolved from a mainstream club act who were active in the North West at the tail end of the 70's. This is completely at odds with the observation that most of their touring activities in the early 80's were centred around the Midlands, so it looks as though their reinvention as a metal concern may have coincided with a relocation to a more southerly destination. Anyway, their one-off EP may have had the general appearance of a typical, no-frills private pressing, although it featured a selection of highly individualistic tracks, which came in the shape of "Fantasy Reality", "Deadmans Dreamland" and the grandiloquently-titled "Winged Bulls Of Ninevh". The talented band were operating in a highly technical, somewhat progressive style (very much in the manner of »Hemispheres«-period RUSH) with unpredictable, stop/start arrangements and quirky rhythm changes; all very impressive, certainly, but not a particularly easy piece of listening by any means. In addition, the extreme length of the compositions (the best part of twenty minutes between them) also manifests itself as being quite detrimental to sound quality (the 7" format was hardly designed for such material), and the skilful musicianship occasionally threatens to become a bit too clever for its own good.

If you're attempting to form a mental picture of KRAKEN's music, the most helpful comparison in the NWOBHM field would unquestionably be SACRED ALIEN (an act who also shared a similar lyrical viewpoint), with tinges of OXYM, JUNO'S CLAW and AVALON coming across here and there. Their highly-regarded EP, which was never issued in a picture sleeve, has been a mainstay of the collecting scene since its inception, and is still highly prized today. Nevertheless, both the production and content received an utter savaging in 'Sounds' at the time (*'how much longer must we tolerate music murder?'*), but I guess there's just no pleasing some folks. Still, there was talk of a full album at one point, and a demo from a year or so later (featuring freshly-penned numbers such as "Lord Of The Mountain", "Destroyer", "Take My Hand" and "Freakshow") saw a definite move towards marginally more accessible material, with shorter tracks and rather less convoluted arrangements, their latest compositions being more reminiscent of outfits such as Hampshire's LONE WOLF, although the distinctive vocals and instrumentation still characterised the group's overall sound. Sadly, in spite of the fact that the lads continued to trek around Britain on a regular basis (with extensive activity throughout the Midlands, as I say, although they made it over to London occasionally) in search of that big break, it looks as though they had bitten the dust by the tail end of 1982 or thereabouts. If anyone has any inside knowledge of KRAKEN's mysterious history, please get in touch!

7" EP's
»Fantasy Reality« Knave Records 1980

KRUZA

Gordon Apicella (v)
Donald MacLachlan (g)
Harry Rush (b)
Allan Scott (k)
Steve James (k)
Neil Cockayne (d)

Comparatively little is presently known about the hopelessly obscure KRUZA, whose undated EP (although it's very much turn-of-the-decade stuff) represents a fairly unusual mixture of styles which occasionally borders on NWOBHM. The sextet (featuring the services of two simultaneous keyboard players, for no tangible reason) would appear to have been based in the West of Scotland (two of the members, Donald MacLachlan and Neil Cockayne, were previously involved with the legendary IRON CLAW, whose early 70's recordings were eventually exhumed by the Audio Archives label and released as the weighty »Dismorphophobia« CD in the mid-90's), although this particular bunch can hardly claim to have represented a major presence on the local rock scene during the NWOBHM era. KRUZA's one-off foray into the vinyl world took the form of a humble four-tracker on Black Hole Records, which showcased a surprisingly lightweight and tuneful direction (a complete contrast to the proto-stoner musings of IRON CLAW), their keyboard-flavoured style of choice (lying squarely between mainstream material and melodic rock) bringing forth a few handy comparisons with similarly non-committal acts such as the MOVIE STARS, H.G.B., WHITEFIRE or SINGAPORE.

Side one begins with the widdly keyboard intro of "Movies In The Night", which soon shifts into a more comfortable, mid-paced rocker with vague similarities to the likes of TRACK 4 or TRADER, while "Sun In My Eyes" is a more laid-back affair, which, although inoffensive enough, is really only on the periphery of the NWOBHM genre. On the reverse, the utterly mediocre "Someone's There" barely scrapes a mention, given its uncanny similarity to MOR luminaries such as the EAGLES or STEELY DAN, although things pick up slightly on "All Stood Up", which occasionally shares a common thread with the BLAZER BLAZER scheme of things. All in all, though, this scarcely-sighted item (no picture sleeve, but there's a double-sided insert which provides some relevant info and pictures) shouldn't really be on too many wants lists, and I reckon KRUZA probably represented little more than a glorified cabaret outfit (they certainly weren't starry-eyed youngsters, that's for sure) who attempted to get a bit of much-needed media attention on the back of the NWOBHM boom.

7" EP's
»Movies In The Night« Black Hole Records 19??

LADY JANE

Line-up unknown

It's somewhat ironic that Humberside's talented LADY JANE didn't make it to the vinyl stage until after the NWOBHM had pretty much burnt itself

341

out completely, as they were bang on the money as far as the energetic, exuberant spirit of the original movement was concerned. The youthful quartet don't appear to have been in existence for too long before they got around to unleashing their initial vinyl assault, which emerged in the early months of 1984 as the aptly-titled »The Sheer Power Of Rock« EP. The material on display was very much in the manner of »Spellbound«-era TYGERS OF PAN TANG, with occasional glimpses of SAXON and MYTHRA thrown into the melting pot for good measure. The rough'n'ready "Out For The Count" was surely the pick of the bunch, closely followed by the slightly more refined "For You Tonight", although the closing cut ("Whiskey And Leather") was marginally less enjoyable, this anthemic effort being the only occasion where the lads live up to their claim of being a 'party rock' proposition. All things considered, though, it was an unusually confident debut for such an inexperienced bunch, but I suspect that relatively few metal fans of the time ever got to hear it, such was the excessively limited nature of the pressing. Still, the three-tracker ended up being reviewed (twice!) in 'Kerrang' (favourably in the first instance, not-so-glowingly the second time around), although it looks as though this failed to further their cause, leaving the dejected musicians to call it a day soon after. Their EP remains an extremely scarce item these days, and comparatively few NWOBHM collectors are lucky enough to own a copy, so it would be nice if a few were miraculously to come out of the woodwork at some point. Some examples, incidentally, were issued with a colourful (but inexplicably oversized) picture sleeve, although the members weren't credited anywhere, so please do let us know if you have any additional details of LADY JANE's personnel or activities on the regional rock scene.

7" EP's
»The Sheer Power Of Rock« Schizoid Records 1984

LAST FLIGHT

Bob Hawthorne (v)
Paul Murray (g)
John Sinfield (b)
Graham Waxman (d)

London-based foursome LAST FLIGHT (fronted by the talented Bob Hawthorne, a veteran of 70's rockers STRIDER) seemed to appear out of nowhere at the height of the NWOBHM influx, although it transpires that they had actually been on the scene since about 1977, at which time they operated under the identity of BUSINESS (not to be confused with the infamous oi outfit), their raunchy material winning a fair few fans and allowing them to appear at the Reading Festival in 1978. Mind you, they weren't regarded as worthy of a record contract back then, although that all changed once the lads had adopted their new identity and become part of Britain's new metal scene. LAST FLIGHT were one of the first acts to be picked up by the emergent Heavy Metal label in 1981, and it didn't take all that long for them to get their first single released. Both "Dance To The Music" and "I'm Ready", the tracks comprising the outfit's debut offering, were semi-raunchy, hard-rocking numbers in the general manner of ALKATRAZZ or ETHEL THE FROG, although these were let down in each case by rather weak and overly-melodic choruses. Even so, it was a decent enough way to kick off a career, and the classy metal sounds of LAST FLIGHT soon began to win over a considerable number of loyal supporters in the music press.

In due course, the experienced outfit started making a name for themselves in the live environment, and several of the major labels checked them out as a possible big-bucks signing. For some reason, though, that big deal would always remain tantalisingly out of reach. Even so, LAST FLIGHT kept plugging away regardless, and the group were also fortunate enough to gain some valuable national exposure by virtue of an appearance on the 'Friday Rock Show', originally broadcast on the 20th of March 1981. Alongside specially-recorded session versions of both numbers from their debut two-tracker, the newly-penned "Everybody Fight Some" and "Headlines" (both in a very similar vein) were showcased to the station's listeners. Later in the year, "Dance To The Music" was duly included on the BBC's »The Friday Rock Show« compilation, suggesting that LAST FLIGHT's session had been one of the better-received efforts of the previous few months. Although the quartet elected to maintain something of a low profile immediately after this initial burst of activity, they had risen to prominence once again by the spring of 1982, playing many a well-attended show throughout the capital and its environs, where they delighted the crowds with a range of self-penned compositions such as "Raid The Streets", "I Need Your Lovin' Tonight" and an ever-popular cover of "Tired Of

Waiting For You" by the KINKS.

Although Heavy Metal famously passed on their lucrative option of releasing a full LAST FLIGHT LP (deciding, at the time, that sponsoring the likes of BITCHES SIN and SPLIT BEAVER was a far better idea), the persevering band continued to record new demos, featuring such numbers as "Keeping Out Of Mischief" and "Sherry's On The Rocks", well-written pieces which might even have been a tad harder than their earlier material. Sadly, a new deal failed to come their way in the short term, and things were thrown into turmoil when vocalist Bob Hawthorne jumped ship to join BERNIE MARSDEN'S S.O.S. project, after which (following a very brief stint in LIONHEART and some collaborative work with Scott Gorham after the latter's departure from THIN LIZZY) he went on to play a major role in the fortunes of ALASKA as well as working in the studio with Laurence Archer on some of the well-travelled axeman's solo material. LAST FLIGHT, meanwhile, remained in limbo for several months while the remaining members assessed the situation (and took time off to help out VOW WOW guitarist KYOJI YAMAMOTO by playing on his »Electric Cinema« solo album), but it wasn't until early 1983 that a revamped version finally got going, after former CHINATOWN bassist John Barr had joined in the capacity of replacement vocalist.

With their new line-up having become established, it looked certain that LAST FLIGHT would indeed get a second bite of the cherry before long, and Barr himself was particularly keen to offer his opinion of the band's progress and to outline their future activities a few months later: *'Our management company, CBM, is stinking rich. In the last three weeks, they've given us fifteen hundred pounds just towards rehearsal costs. They're also paying for a high-quality demo and sending it to all the major companies. Things are looking good for us.'* (Ref: Forearm Smash, Issue 2, August 1983). In fact, things didn't work out quite as well as these hopeful musicians had originally anticipated, and they had more or less called it quits for good by early 1984, with John Barr moving to the States and joining forces with a long-forgotten bunch called TOKYO ROSE. Sticksman Graham Waxman, meanwhile, soon inveigled his way into the ranks of the recently-relocated DRIVESHAFT, but the others appear to have dropped off the face of the earth completely. All things considered, though, I'd suggest that LAST FLIGHT were clearly another of those *'one hit wonders'* who could, with a few lucky breaks, have progressed considerably further.

7" Singles
»Dance To The Music« Heavy Metal 1981

Compilation Appearances
"Dance To The Music" on »The Friday Rock Show« LP BBC Records 1981
[Different to single version]
"Dance To The Music" on »Heavy Metal Records Singles Collection Vol.1« CD British Steel 1996
"I'm Ready" on »Heavy Metal Records Singles Collection Vol.1« CD British Steel 1996

LAUTREC

Reuben Archer (v)
Laurence Archer (g)
Simon Ridler (b)
Steve Holbrook (k)
Steve Jones (d)

Formed by the father and stepson pairing of Reuben and Laurence Archer towards the end of the 70's, the quirkily-named LAUTREC (who originally operated under the name of THRILLER) tend to be regarded as the direct antecedent of STAMPEDE (an act which also featured the central Archer duo), although, as usual, the story isn't quite that straightforward. LAUTREC (whose greatest claim to fame was undoubtedly a couple of cherished support slots with SAXON and GIRLSCHOOL) appear to have had a fair few personnel reshuffles (interestingly, one of their alternate drummers, Clive Deamer, later enjoyed productive stints with the likes of BRONZ, HAWKWIND, HEADMASTER and trip-hop oddballs PORTISHEAD) throughout their relatively brief existence (starting out as a quartet and adding keyboards at a later date), although they eventually achieved a sufficiently stable line-up to be able to record a selection of original material, some of which was soon drawing the attention of the newly-established Street Tunes company. The LAUTREC lads, originally based in the West Country, where they developed a pretty loyal following, were subsequently given the opportunity to lay down two studio tracks at some point in 1980, which were then scheduled to be pressed up as the first single on the label.

In the event, however, it transpires that the whole LAUTREC episode was something of a non-starter, the upshot being that their projected 7" only appears to have reached the white-label stage, with a few of these being circulated to journalists and radio stations with minimal information (typically, nothing more than the band name on the label itself, although you would expect that these would have been embellished with a bit of promotional documentation in the first instance), none of which managed to yield any airplay or media attention whatsoever. It's not beyond the realms of possibility that a minimal quantity of finished copies or sleeves were indeed manufactured at some point, but it seems increasingly unlikely, given that nobody (least of all the band members) claims to have seen such an item. Understandably, only a tiny handful of these test pressings have surfaced in the years since they were originally manufactured, and these are rightly

regarded as an example of one of the very rarest of all releases from the NWOBHM era. The music of LAUTREC, incidentally, was actually in a considerably heavier and raunchier style (the keyboards weren't at all intrusive, I'm happy to say) than the Archers' later offerings as STAMPEDE, the tracks on the single bringing to mind contemporaries such as XERO (in particular) and SLEDGEHAMMER. It would almost certainly have sold in respectable quantities at the time, so it's a real pity that the commercial release never saw the light of day.

The reasons for the LAUTREC single's non-appearance remain slightly flimsy, and even the musicians themselves seem to have been somewhat bewildered by the reality of the situation. A full-scale release was indeed scheduled, but their label (who may well have been experiencing a few financial problems in their early days) just never got around to issuing it commercially. Mind you, the promotion of LAUTREC soon became irrelevant, given that the group was already beginning to fragment by the early months of 1981. First to go was vocalist Reuben Archer, lured away by what must have seemed like a tempting offer to replace the ousted Jess Cox in LIONHEART. After the failure of this brief relationship, however, Reuben joined forces with his stepson once more, this time in WILD HORSES, by which time LAUTREC was already becoming ancient history. After terminating their involvement with Jimmy Bain's struggling outfit after a remarkably short time, however, the duo eventually regrouped under the identity of STAMPEDE (see separate entry) towards the end of 1981, initially recruiting another one-time LAUTREC member, keyboard player Alan Nelson (later of STRATUS, JAGGED EDGE et al.), to the fold. Under their new name (and following a more melodic direction), the Archers enjoyed considerably more success, but this part of their story can readily be found elsewhere.

That wasn't quite the end of the road for LAUTREC, however, and it soon became apparent that the group hadn't been forgotten completely. In the summer of 1982, the single's proposed A-side ("Mean Gasoline") was licensed by Abstract Records and included on their eclectic »Steel Crazy« compilation (curiously, STAMPEDE were also featured on the same record), giving fans a belated opportunity to hear the defunct outfit on vinyl at last. What about the mysterious B-side, though? Well, although the track never appeared officially, this elusive composition eventually cropped up on the »NWOBHM Vol.8« bootleg CD in the mid-90's, where the title was identified as "Shoot Out The Lights" (now there's an original one), which was surprising (but correct), as I'd always assumed that "Someone To Kill" was probably its more likely identity. Nevertheless, at least you can now hear both of LAUTREC's most accomplished recordings without having to fork out a fortune for the original vinyl item!

7" Singles
»Mean Gasoline« Street Tunes 1980
[White label promos only]

Compilation Appearances
"**Mean Gasoline**" on »Steel Crazy« LP Abstract Records 1982
"**Shoot Out The Lights**" on »NWOBHM Vol.8« Bootleg CD 1996

LAW, THE

Line-up unknown

The only known vinyl release by an obscure, early outfit called THE LAW (not to be confused with Paul Rodgers' identically-named and somewhat short-lived project from the early

90's) is their »Be My Girl« three-tracker, captured at Smile Recording Studios in Manchester in mid-1979. Although nothing is currently known for certain about the group themselves, it seems safe to assume that they were from the North West, given that most of the rock bands who used the aforementioned facility (*e.g.* DICK SMITH BAND, 100% PROOF) tended to be reasonably local. In any case, their EP (never, as far as we know, issued in a picture sleeve), featuring "Be My Girl", "Dead City Kicks" and "I Just Want Your Body", is in a fairly rudimentary, slightly bluesy style, comparable at times to outfits such as NO FAITH, XERO and the HANDSOME BEASTS, although it's all quite energetic stuff with a powerful vocal contribution throughout. Assuming that THE LAW were indeed from the Lancashire/Merseyside area, they appear to have been yet another product of the bustling local rock scene which gave rise to a range of similarly-influenced outfits such as RAGE, EXPORT, NUTZ, NIGHTWING and the ALEC JOHNSON BAND, but who ultimately failed to last the distance in the aftermath of the post-NWOBHM return to normality. Not a bad effort at all, although it's not strictly classifiable as prime-era NWOBHM, and I suppose some of you might want to keep an eye out for it.

7" EP's
»Be My Girl« Smile Records 1979

LÉARGO

Alan Fullard (v,k)
Andy Ford (g)
Jules Burrowes (b)
Ray Fullard (d)

The strangely-named LÉARGO (sorry, I haven't a clue where this particular identity originates), from the West Midlands, were another of those ensembles who occupied a musical space lying somewhere between prog and melodic rock, possibly attempting to emulate the likes of RUSH or TRIUMPH, but not quite coming across with the same level of confidence, expertise or professionalism. Nevertheless, they were a popular enough bunch in their locality, and their »Played Out Angel« offering from 1979, issued on the Motor City Rhythm label (the original home of the STARFIGHTERS), evidently sold pretty well at the time. Both the A-side and "The Artist" are quite restrained attempts at a rock style, with the gentle keyboard backing serving to elicit a few comparisons with the kind of material favoured by the MOVIE STARS, DORCAS, LOST FAMOUS and GYPP, none of whom were able to achieve particularly significant levels of success at any stage, suggesting that this type of well-mannered outfit probably had a pretty limited appeal outwith their immediate areas. The »Played Out Angel« single is, however, quite a collectable and scarce item (some of which were issued in a prized picture sleeve with a comic-book illustration of some strange-looking characters) for aficionados of the NWOBHM and prog genres.

Although the single's insert claimed that a full album was just about to be issued, there seems to be little evidence to suggest that this was actually recorded after all. Furthermore, while at least one further LÉARGO single was also scheduled for release by M.C.R. (and there has been considerable speculation over the years that additional vinyl obscurities might possibly have emerged on some completely unrelated labels), it now looks increasingly likely that any planned follow-ups to »Played Out Angel« were never commercially issued. If finished copies had indeed been pressed, it would be extremely difficult to explain their remarkable reluctance to come out of the woodwork, as there appear to have been precisely zero confirmed sightings of such items over the years. A track entitled "Water" (a live favourite) was, however, played on local radio in the Midlands at the time, although this composition might actually have been taken from a tape, acetate, compilation or promo-only single rather than an official LÉARGO release. I'm sure we'll uncover the whole story in due course, but it's slightly frustrating, nevertheless, to be able neither to confirm nor deny the existence of any later singles at this stage.

What is definitely known, however, is that the ensemble (having recruited replacement bassist John Barry and enlisted a dedicated vocalist in the form of Adrian Lynden, veteran of a comparatively brief stint with TRESPASS) evolved into a tuneful project called the SUMO GIANTS towards the middle of the 80's, securing a cherished session for Tommy Vance's (ultimately unsuccessful) 'Into The Music' programme in 1985, and releasing a single entitled »Tower Of Babel« a couple of years later. The relaunched outfit (who also included a new version of "Water" in their live set) were a substantially more commercial proposition, and their brand of well-crafted melodic rock (on tracks such as "Wishing I Could Be", "Living On The Airwaves" and "Fe Fi Fo Fum", for example) came across with considerably more conviction than had been the case in their early days. Sadly, however, it looks as though the quintet, who received a generous amount of magazine coverage in their time, never managed to make it big in their revitalised incarnation, and folded towards the end of the decade after some well-received demos and a series of small-time gigs around the Midlands.

7" Singles
»Played Out Angel« Motor City Rhythm 1979

LEFT HAND DRIVE

Martin Harney (v)
Jack Swann (g)
John Brassett (b)
Tommy Kerr (d)

There once was a time when LEFT HAND DRIVE's »Who Said Rock & Roll Is Dead« oddity was quite commonly observed at provincial record fairs throughout the UK, invariably in sections devoted to punk singles. Predictably, few individuals took much notice of this unremarkable-looking effort, so the two-tracker seemed to have little future other than as an ashtray. At some stage, however, somebody actually bothered to play the thing, only to conclude *'blimey, it's metal!'*. Well, almost. It's fair to say that this little-remembered quartet were another of those turn-of-the-decade ensembles who hedged their bets somewhat in terms of their musical direction, and who clearly lifted a few ideas from more than one genre. The picture sleeve of the two-tracker in question (an old codger loitering in a hedge with a guitar) certainly doesn't look overly-metallic, and the music featured is by no means *'out and out NWOBHM'*. However, the A-side is an extremely energetic number which is *so* similar to SILVERWING's (you guessed it) "Rock & Roll Are Four Letter Words" it truly beggars belief, the perfect collision of snotty punk/glam which the likes of WRATHCHILD and ROX could only endeavour to imitate in years to come.

After that, flipside "I Know Where I Am" is something of a let-down, to be honest, the latter painting itself as more of a garage/punk effort, with twangy guitars and a decidedly 60's-influenced sound (*cf.* EDDIE COCHRAN's "C'mon Everybody"). So there you have it. Closet glam/sleaze fans (I know you're out there) should snap this one up at the earliest opportunity, but I reckon you're unlikely ever to play the B-side more than once. Interestingly, it transpires that there's a tenuous connection with some of Sean Tyla's cult outfits from the 70's, notably DUCKS DELUXE and the TYLA GANG (the latter, incidentally, also contributed personnel to the LIGHTNING RAIDERS), with ex-members of these projects supposedly appearing in a very early version of LEFT HAND DRIVE, although they had departed by the time »Who Said Rock & Roll Is Dead« saw the light of day at some point in 1978. There are, however, reliable indications that another LEFT HAND DRIVE single (»Jailbait«) was recorded a year or so earlier, although I'm not aware of anyone who possesses a copy. Even so, material from this release apparently cropped up on an obscure Japanese anthology, so it may well exist on vinyl, but I'd prefer to judge the musical merits of this offering (also sponsored by the Milton Keynes-based Bancrupt label) myself before including it in a NWOBHM volume such as this.

7" Singles
»Who Said Rock & Roll Is Dead« Bancrupt Records 1978

LEGEND (I)

Chris Thow (v)
Mark Dawson (g)
Jose Rodriguez (b)
Alan Tracy (d)

Kent's own version of LEGEND were a fairly short-lived concern, initially coming together in around 1980 and (in spite of the observation that they acquired something of a reputation in their locality) disbanding two or three years later. Nevertheless, the band gave it their best shot while they were active on the rock scene, and were (luckily enough) seldom confused with any of the other young hopefuls who chose to adopt the same identity. The four-piece were initially introduced to studio technology through their guitarist, Mark Dawson, who had worked on the production side of things in a full-time capacity prior to starting his own outfit, and it wasn't long before LEGEND were busily recording their first single. The self-financed effort, coupling "Hideaway" with "Heaven Sent", appeared at the beginning of 1981, and showed the group to be a reasonably original and capable proposition, the soaring vocals of frontman Chris Thow bringing forth some inevitable

JUDAS PRIEST comparisons from many quarters, although the band's general style was (at this stage) in rather more of a semi-progressive vein along the lines of CRYER, DAWNWATCHER or LIMELIGHT. The memorable "Heaven Sent" was also featured on the legendary »Kent Rocks« sampler assembled by White Witch the same year, and it really is extraordinarily difficult to listen to this track nowadays without immediately commenting on its uncanny resemblance to early QUEENSRYCHE material.

The lads persevered for a couple of years (getting through successive short-term bassists Gavin Matthews and Mark Griffiths in the process) in their quest for the breakthrough, but their big chance already seemed to have passed them by. The collapse of local sponsors White Witch came as a fairly major blow, and the constant accusations of being 'PRIEST wannabes' soon began to rankle. Mainman Mark Dawson later gave his honest opinion of all the JUDAS PRIEST associations: *'Well, I can understand the comparison, as Chris, our singer, always had a very distinctive voice, but with far more depth and power than Rob Halford. I often turned to watch him at concerts, and wondered how this guy could sing in such a fantastic way. Rob Halford just screams in a fixed pitch!'* (Ref: Iron Pages No.31, 1995). After numerous visits to the studio to lay down new material, LEGEND finally called it a day, with Mark Dawson returning (after a brief period of collaboration with some members of TRIARCHY) to his day job at Goldust Studios, while the resonant tones of Chris Thow were subsequently to be heard on the »Apocalypse« album, released by German metal merchants VIVA in 1984. After that, there was a hiatus of several years before the NWOBHM collecting scene took off, and the LEGEND single (issued in a live-action, monochrome sleeve) began to change hands for serious money. Once again, the dealers tracked down various former members in order to extract unsold copies, and these initial negotiations eventually led to a CD of largely-unissued studio recordings appearing on the Vinyl Tap label in 1994.

LEGEND's »A.D. 1980« CD (which, disappointingly, gives no details about the source or date of any of the featured tracks, and fails miserably to provide any useful information about the band whatsoever) was a fairly mediocre collection, to be honest, and it delivers a salutary lesson that there's often a very good reason why certain outfits didn't attract major label attention. There were, admittedly, a couple of half-decent moments, notably the likes of "Legend" and "Wooden Sword", but the remainder of the tracks featured were pretty much a selection of unremarkable and anonymous compositions, more in the general style of mid-80's TYGERS OF PAN TANG than anything too inspiring or original. There was no talk of a reunion or a follow-up release, so I reckon it was merely a one-off chance to disseminate some long-lost music to a (very) small-but-loyal group of fans. As such, it serves its purpose, but it's a release which has probably sold in relatively modest quantities in recent years.

7" Singles
»Hideaway« Private 1981

CD's
»A.D. 1980« Vinyl Tap Records 1994
[Compilation of mostly unreleased studio material]

Compilation Appearances
"Heaven Sent" on »Kent Rocks« LP White Witch Records 1981 + »N.W.O.B.H.M. Metal Rarities Vol.1« CD British Steel 1996
"Hideaway" on »NWOBHM Vol.3« Bootleg CD 1992 + »N.W.O.B.H.M. Metal Rarities Vol.1« CD British Steel 1996
"My Heart Is There" on »Noise Level Critical« CD Hallmark 1997

LEGEND (II)

Mike Lezala (v)
Peter Haworth (g)
Marco Morosino (g)
Eggy Aubert (b)
Dave Whitley (d)

To be honest, the Channel Islands have never been a particularly fecund source of musical talent, although they still managed to give rise to a handful of genuine NWOBHM outfits, namely TRACER, JONAH and LEGEND, all of whom originated on the isle of Jersey. The last-mentioned originally came into existence in the summer of 1980, and the group's early activities centred mainly around songwriting and rehearsing; the island boasted virtually no live music scene as such, and so the quintet were only able to play a tiny handful of gigs during the course of their existence. It wasn't going to be easy for LEGEND, and the odds seemed stacked against them from the outset. Nevertheless, word got around that there was now a talented rock proposition on Jersey, and, when the group finally made their live debut towards the end of that year, it turned out to be a sold-out affair which was nothing less than a resounding success for all concerned. Sensing a bit of mileage in the old music lark, the lads soon concluded that they might just be able to further their cause by issuing their own vinyl product, and, by the time the recording session came about, their collective finances actually stretched to a full LP rather than the conventional 7" single. LEGEND's eponymous debut was duly pressed up and released on their own Workshop label in 1981, unveiling seven lengthy compositions in a semi-progressive, heavy style with comparisons to the likes of BLEAK HOUSE, CHASAR, OMEGA or TRIARCHY.

It was an extremely capable opening gambit, and grim titles such as "Buried Alive" and "Torture" served to belie a complex and subtle range of original songs, with various individualistic and inventive aspects to LEGEND's music becoming apparent as the set progresses. The album had been pressed in modest quantities (it rapidly sold out completely), given that it was originally intended to satisfy local demand only, so it came as something of a surprise when a significant number of copies began making their way considerably further afield, with a handful even going abroad in the long term. In due course, selected tracks would be featured on the 'Friday Rock Show', and the band swiftly became something of a minor cult throughout the land. Further exposure came in the shape of a local support slot with none other than THIN LIZZY, and LEGEND's sudden rise to the status of serious contenders took practically everyone by surprise, including the protagonists themselves. Nevertheless, guitarist Marco Morosino remained unconvinced that the group had genuine potential after all, and was to quit later in the year in order to return to college. The other members attempted to find a replacement, but were ultimately unsuccessful, and they were compelled to operate as a slimmed-down quartet from that point onwards. With their debut release having constituted such an unexpected success, the lads swiftly decided that it would be prudent to get a follow-up into the shops as soon as possible (needless to say, they hadn't received any miraculous offers from major labels in the interim), and so another self-financed long-player was on the cards for the spring of 1982.

»Death In The Nursery«, the second LEGEND long-player, saw the outfit making a conscious move towards shorter, more upbeat songs (it has to be said, the first album isn't exactly the most uplifting of records) in a bid to appeal to a broader fan base. This slight shift in direction was carried out with great aplomb, and the resulting opus was a far more instant and accessible affair, although it was still a heavy set of compositions, with highlights including the excellent "Lazy Woman" (with some truly remarkable fretwork from Peter Haworth), "Why Don't You Kill Me?" and "Anthrax Attack". The latest record was fortunate enough to receive a considerable amount of airplay on various stations, and actually benefitted from a favourable review in 'Kerrang', with the lads being praised as much for their impassioned, atypical lyrics as their musical creativity. Not only that, an approving write-up of one of their infrequent live outings (in the local town of St. Helier) was even included in an issue of 'Sounds' at around the same time, so it's fair to say that the name of LEGEND was firmly lodging itself in the nation's consciousness by this juncture. Again, the new offering sold in impressive quantities from the word go (leading to an unprecedented amount of fan mail for the bewildered musicians to deal with), and copies were soon finding their way into the collections of various dedicated rock aficionados around the world.

Far from resting on their laurels, however, LEGEND continued the relentless vinyl assault with a limited edition EP featuring four brand-new selections, namely "Frontline", "Sabra & Chatila" (no, me neither), "Stormers Of Heaven" and "Open Up The Skies". The 12" was recorded towards the end of 1982 and issued early the following year, and it was soon garnering approval from numerous sources. Again, the new release was hailed almost universally as a worthwhile effort, with 'Kerrang' giving the lads an extremely encouraging review (and, quite rightly, singling out the truly excellent "Stormers Of Heaven" for particular praise), but it was to be LEGEND's last vinyl offering. A third album was supposedly in the pipeline at one stage, and half a dozen tracks were laid down in readiness later in the year, but it was all going wrong by this time. Bassist Eggy Aubert had already been compelled to quit the group through injury (forcing the sudden cancellation of an intended tour of the mainland), although the situation was swiftly remedied by the recruitment of Neil Haworth (brother of Pete) at relatively short notice, bringing the outfit up to full strength once again. Nevertheless, the group were now beginning to sense that their efforts were largely going unrewarded, and formed the opinion that they would never actually be picked up by a major label after all.

Resentment had gradually built up over a period of time, the musicians finding it increasingly difficult to watch helplessly as mediocre, London-based acts were being signed left, right and centre, while those in more isolated parts of the British Isles were overlooked purely as a consequence of geography. Eventually, vocalist Mike Lezala threw in his hand early in 1984, and, having failed to locate a suitable replacement (given that there weren't really all that many rock musicians available in their immediate locality), the remaining members elected to call it a day sooner rather than later. Lezala was persuaded to return for a farewell show (a prestigious appearance at London's Marquee), but LEGEND officially ceased to exist within a couple of months. It was a sad loss for the scene, but this came at a time when countless hopefuls from the NWOBHM explosion were beginning to lose heart and giving up the ghost for good. In the years following their untimely demise, however, the outfit's scarce records began to assume the status of highly-coveted rarities, with the asking prices reaching a peak in the early 90's. At around this time, the former members were approached to see if they had any spare copies lying around, and it transpired that the Haworth brothers were still actively involved in the business of making music. Peter had recorded a solo album entitled »The Business« in 1988 (released only on cassette), while Neil had gone one better and managed to issue an AOR-influenced solo set (»Call Me«), which was manufactured in both cassette and CD forms.

As a result of the interest being shown in their old group, the brothers began wondering whether or not there would be any mileage either in a reformation or in an official CD issue of some archive material. In fact, it took a few years for them to be convinced that the original interest in LEGEND wasn't simply going to disappear overnight (some well-attended internet pages provided conclusive evidence that many modern-day fans of their music really did want them to keep things going), and so mainman Peter Haworth was finally inspired to compile a promotional CD-R entitled »Retroshock 1981-1984« a couple of years ago, the latter featuring a selection of some of the more popular material from throughout their eventful career. Intriguingly, however, this set also included a previously-unheard number called "Questions And Answers" as something of an exclusive for their loyal followers, suggesting that there might just be a handful of unused tracks in the archives. The CD has been warmly received by those lucky souls who have been privileged enough to obtain a copy, and it remains to be seen whether or not it will be pressed officially or if LEGEND might finally reform after all. I guess it depends on how much positive feedback they get, so I'd encourage you to get in touch with them...

LP's
»Legend« Workshop Records 1981
»Death In The Nursery« Workshop Records 1982

12" EP's
»Limited Edition Four Track Single« Workshop Records 1982
[All four tracks non-LP]

CD's
»Retroshock 1981-1984« CiCD Interactive 1998
[Official compilation CD-R with printed cover]

LE GRIFFE

Chris Hatton (v, g)
Tim Blackwood (g)
Paul Wood (g)
Kev Collier (b)
Martin Allen (d)

Staffordshire's LE GRIFFE probably thought that it was a highly innovative idea to adopt a French name (*'The Claw'*) when they formed back in 1979, but it was to prove a bit confusing for certain dim-witted journalists at the time, with one memorable and xenophobic 'Kerrang' review announcing *'at least they have the decency to sing in English.'* Chortle. The emergent outfit (who featured former EXPOZER guitarist Tim Blackwood in their ranks) gradually progressed from their humble beginnings and small-time gigs to, er, marginally better-attended small-time gigs, and eventually circulated a live demo towards the end of 1981, featuring a variety of self-penned numbers such as "Who's Kidding Who", "Breathe Deeply" and "Silent Running". With a sound very much in the general style of SOLDIER, BLACK AXE or SEVENTH SON, it seemed fairly inevitable that LE GRIFFE, like many of their similarly-inclined contemporaries, would earn themselves a deal sooner or later. Sure enough, the newly-established Bullet Records label (which, like Reddingtons, started off as a company selling other people's records before deciding to get in on the act themselves) beat a path to their door the following year, and duly offered the lads the chance to release a 12" EP.

The band's vinyl debut for their local sponsors

was a three track affair (released at the beginning of 1983) featuring "Fast Bikes", "Where Are You Now" and "The Actor", all housed within a rather striking red sleeve. Almost immediately, this offering became regarded as something of a classic, a reputation which appears to have survived to the present day, with collectors still clamouring for any copies which come onto the market. Mind you, it turned out to be a pretty big seller at the time, thanks to a fervid local following and competent distribution, meaning that there's seldom been a shortage of copies in circulation. To be frank, though, I don't consider the EP to be an outstanding release at all; it's a decent enough effort, admittedly, but it hardly stood out as head and shoulders above the rest of the vinyl offerings of the day. Nevertheless, Bullet rightly sussed that LE GRIFFE had a bit of mileage in them, and proceeded to issue a couple of follow-up releases. First up was the »You're Killing Me« 12", recorded in the latter half of 1983 and issued early the following year. Rather pointlessly, this featured (in addition to "E.T.A.") two versions of the title track, one of these being the *'radio play'* edit, which seems to have been a somewhat ambitious (some might even say *conceited*) move, as I can't quite imagine all the radio stations being in complete turmoil and thinking *'oh my, we'd really like to play this LE GRIFFE track more often, but it's just too darn long.'* No doubt it received a limited amount of local airplay, but I don't recall the number making an appearance in the BBC's 'Top 40'. Maybe the monumentally tacky cover, which may well feature the very artwork originally rejected for SPINAL TAP's »Smell The Glove«, put off a few potential customers. Oink.

The second EP was rapidly followed by a mini-album, which, bizarrely enough, utilised "You're Killing Me" yet again, this old favourite appearing alongside "Breaking Strain" (the title track), "Breathe Deeply", "Silent Running" and "Movin' On". Strangely, most (if not all) of the featured titles dated back to the band's earliest days, and it seems a bit odd that they chose not to showcase any newer compositions. Indeed, it looks as though the LE GRIFFE lads weren't particularly productive in terms of extending their repertoire, and there's a very real possibility that the group chose to issue a mini-album simply because they barely had enough suitable material for a full-length effort. The new record was, however, considerably more convincing than their previous EP's, with the upbeat "Breaking Strain" and "Movin' On" coming across fairly strongly, as does the chugging "Silent Running". Notwithstanding the fact that LE GRIFFE were still recycling old material, however, it looked as though they might be capable of delivering something reasonably special in the next couple of years, assuming the musicians put their heads together and came up with some new tunes.

After the mini-LP had been recorded, however, Tim Blackwood flew the coop and was duly replaced by the extraordinarily-named Amos Sanfillipo, although this new line-up seems to have been a very short-lived affair, and no studio recordings appear to have materialised from the revised outfit. In fact, it looks as though the dwindling LE GRIFFE had finally called it a day for good by the end of 1984, the members going their separate ways shortly thereafter. Stand-in guitarist Sanfillipo apparently went on to spend a very short time with STATETROOPER (I'm not sure exactly when this might have been, though) before joining forces with Californian glamsters LONDON, although this proved to be yet another brief liaison. Paul Wood, on the other hand, elected to team up with local rock hopefuls OLE VERADI (a persevering but strictly amateur-hour bunch), while the major success story was undoubtedly that of Kev Collier, who subsequently found his way into the ranks of ROGUE MALE, whereupon he enjoyed several vinyl appearances and extensive touring activities with his new outfit over the ensuing years.

Mini-LP's
»Breaking Strain« Bullet 1984

12" EP's
»Fast Bikes« Bullet 1983
»You're Killing Me« Bullet 1984
[Includes two versions of "You're Killing Me"]

Compilation Appearances
"Where Are You Now" on »NWOBHM Vol.5« Bootleg CD 1992

LIAISON

Howard Rogers (v, b)
Keith Young (g)
Barry Connell (d)

The progressively-inclined LIAISON, a highly capable trio from Middlesex, gravitated together in 1980 or thereabouts, making their initial forays into the capital's live venues towards the end of that year. They were content to keep a relatively low profile on the recording front until early 1982, though, when their first official tape was laid down, a four track affair featuring "See In My Mind", "Sometimes A Woman", "Turn The Gun Around" and "Dear Gina". Before long, this release was shifting an impressive number of units at local gigs, and the lads soon decided to capitalise on their growing popularity by issuing their debut single. The two-tracker was duly assembled in the summer of that year, with the catchy "Play It With Passion" and "Caught In A Landslide" being immortalised at Pineapple Stu-

dios in Southall, the resulting 7" (which, curiously, was released with two different sleeve colours, showing the same split images representing the tracks featured on each side) appearing in the shops shortly thereafter. In musical terms, the band were clearly bedfellows of the likes of HAZE, SPITZBROOK and CHASE, sharing broadly similar influences and attempting to marry a melodic rock style with slightly more adventurous arrangements. It certainly struck the right chord with the fans, though, many of whom were soon snapping up copies at the earliest opportunity.

The lads kept plugging away in the live environment, but ultimately took the decision (in the summer of 1983) to round out their sound by expanding to a quartet, whereupon they recruited a combined bassist/keyboard player (Frank Keepfer), permitting mainman Howard Rogers to concentrate solely on vocals. Further original material was subsequently presented to the listening public in the form of another cassette, incorporating "Looking After Number One", "Who've You Been Seeing", "Only Heaven Knows" and "Ease The Pain Away", revealing occasional indications of a possible shift towards the type of elaborate compositions that the likes of CANIS MAJOR had striven to perfect during their existence. This early batch of vinyl and tape releases garnered LIAISON a healthy following, and regular jaunts throughout London and the Home Counties (where they frequently played with local hopefuls such as LYADRIVE and URBAN CLEARWAY, as well as sharing more progressive bills from time to time) tended to be relatively well-attended and enthusiastically-received events. Before much longer, though, the lads progressed to headliner status, playing to packed houses at the Marquee on quite a few occasions, as well as picking up some high-profile support slots with the likes of MARILLION. A second two-tracker appeared in 1984 (the year in which LIAISON were tipped as a 'band to watch' in the pages of 'Sounds'), the latter coupling "Only Heaven Knows" (by this time, a huge live favourite among their many fans) and "Ease The Pain Away", both numbers being taken from their most recent cassette. The latest offering, issued in a monochrome sleeve picturing the four protagonists, was well up to their usual standard, and the devotees were more than happy to add it to their collections once again.

With the single proceeding to sell in notable quantities at their well-attended gigs in and around the capital (the record somehow even managed to get through a perilous 'Kerrang' review relatively unscathed), the chaps continued to delight numerous appreciative audiences, where a highly impressive and extensive repertoire of self-penned compositions (including "Start The War Without Me", "Cut You Down" and "The Movie Of Your Life") would be performed with great aplomb. In fact, there was even a bit of major-label interest at around this time (they were apparently courted by the giant RCA corporation at one stage, as well as winning approval from Bronze Records), although the outfit, for reasons best known to themselves, chose not to pursue any of these options. The group kept a comparatively low profile after the end of 1984, although they subsequently contributed another new track to the progressive sampler »Fire In Harmony«, a fairly obscure release which appeared on Elusive Records, a subsidiary of EMI which had been set up by MARILLION's manager of the time. LIAISON's chosen composition (the lengthy "A Tale Of You"), while fairly lightweight and unsubstantial (compared to some of their earlier offerings), sat pretty well alongside the numbers offered by the likes of TRILOGY, SOLSTICE, PENDRAGON and QUASAR, and this must have seemed like a useful piece of exposure.

In the event, however, LIAISON's new-found association with some of the nation's more established progressive acts doesn't really seem to have helped their cause in the long term, and this proved to be their swansong appearance on vinyl. Things began to peter out within a remarkably short timescale, and their musical activities gradually wound down over the ensuing months (much to the disappointment of their many loyal fans), culminating in a farewell show at the Marquee in the summer of 1985. Both of the LIAISON singles, however, remain reasonably highly-valued and collectable pieces today, although a quantity (of the first one, at least) of unsold copies were obtained from the members in the early 90's. Sadly, bassist Frank Keepfer didn't enjoy the best of health after LIAISON's demise, and eventually passed away a few years back. The others, meanwhile, have maintained a bit of involvement in the music scene over the years, and guitarist Keith Young still takes to the stage with his latest outfit (a rock covers concern who go by the name of ACROSS THE TRACKS) on a regular basis.

7" Singles
»Play It With Passion« Catweazle Records 1982
[Issued in both grey and yellow sleeves]
»Only Heaven Knows« Liaison Records 1984

Exclusive Compilation Appearances
"A Tale Of You" on »Fire In Harmony« LP Elusive Records 1985

Compilation Appearances
"Only Heaven Knows" on »NWOBHM Vol.6« Bootleg CD 1992

LIGHTNING RAIDERS

Gass Wild (v)
John Hodge (g)
Andy Allan (g)
Duncan 'Sandy' Sanderson (b)
George Butler (d)

Although an early version of the LIGHTNING RAIDERS was originally conceived in West London as far back as 1977 (from the ashes of a group with the award-winningly-bad name of LAWNMOWER) by the guitar pairing of Andy Allan and John Hodge, it was very much a part-time operation at the outset. A stable line-up was, however, eventually achieved by around 1979, after the duo had recruited vocalist Gass Wild (previously employed by a small-time French outfit), bassist Sandy Sanderson (formerly with the legendary DEVIANTS and PINK FAIRIES) and drummer George Butler (a veteran session musician who had worked with the likes of IAN DURY and ALEX HARVEY), although Andy Allan himself was still finding time to help out in other musical projects, notably the SEX PISTOLS. Indeed, by the time the first LIGHTNING RAIDERS single (released on the large Arista label) came about in 1980, it turned out to be a bit of a SEX PISTOLS reunion, with Allan's former cohorts Steve Jones and Paul Cook lending their services to the unruly recording session. With the LIGHTNING RAIDERS having originally been brought together by the desire *'to play unpretentious rock and roll music'*, it was no surprise to find that the quintet delivered precisely that, with both "Psychedelic Musik" and "Views" bringing forth the kind of snotty punk/metal collision favoured by such acts as VIRGIN STAR, LEFT HAND DRIVE and the pre-metal incarnation of TOAD THE WET SPROCKET. They received further exposure, incidentally, via an exclusive live version of "Views", which made its way onto a seldom-seen sampler entitled »The Moonlight Tapes« the same year.

Soon after the debut release had made its way into the shops, however, founder member Andy Allan concluded that his work with the LIGHTNING RAIDERS was done, whereupon he subsequently jumped ship to hook up with his aforementioned SEX PISTOLS colleagues in an outfit called the PROFESSIONALS, before eventually forming a brand-new project known as FUTURE. Allan's replacement in the LIGHTNING RAIDERS was erstwhile TYLA GANG guitarist Bruce Irvine, and the outfit (who, for some peculiar reason, briefly chose to be known as THE RAIDERS before reverting to their original name) started writing slightly more metallic numbers and attempting to affiliate themselves with the NWOBHM scene rather than with their post-punk contemporaries. In early 1981, the lads managed to win some valuable support slots with the likes of MOTÖRHEAD and TANK, and soon set about the task of recording their follow-up release for the small Revenge label. The latest two-tracker, featuring "Criminal World" and "Citizens", was quite a bit heavier on the guitar front, but there was still an underlying similarity to more sleazy acts such as the NEW YORK DOLLS or the STOOGES rather than anything more representative of the NWOBHM movement as a whole. Nevertheless, the band were swiftly adopted as heroes by many a metal fan, and a licensing deal was soon signed with the influential Island concern, who proceeded to reissue »Criminal World« as a 12" single in Europe.

With this new-found backing from a major label, the group were able to enjoy some rather more high-profile activities, with numerous headlining gigs in the West End culminating in a well-received appearance at the Reading Festival in August 1981. By this stage, however, the outfit's debut full-length effort had been recorded and mixed (not only that, material was also being written in readiness for the follow-up album), and so it seemed only a matter of time before it was released throughout Europe. Indeed, a 12" sampler EP appeared towards the end of the year, showcasing tracks from their forthcoming »Sweet Revenge« long-player. While "Sweet Revenge", "Rowdies", "Addiction" and "Soul Rescue" were some of the most accomplished LIGHTNING RAIDERS compositions, however, the album never seems to have emerged in finished form (some books include it in discographies, and it's not inconceivable that the odd acetate or test pressing might exist), something which has always baffled those in the music industry. It's certainly not a simple case of the band splitting and cancelling the release, as they were still a going concern in 1982, with 'Kerrang' reviewing an impressive headlining show in London in February of that year, followed by a rather less memorable appearance at the Hackney Festival alongside MOTÖRHEAD and SAXON towards the end of July.

Whatever the story, the LIGHTNING RAIDERS appear to have called it a day towards the end of that year, with Bruce Irvine resurfacing shortly thereafter in an outfit called INFIDEL, who managed to get themselves an enviable support slot with TWISTED SISTER but who don't seem to have delivered any vinyl product of their own. Gass Wild, on the other hand, formed an ill-fated, glam-influenced act called the MANNISH BOYS (actually the name of an early DAVID BOWIE vehicle), although this bunch failed to make much of an impression with their live appearances in and around the capital, after which the frontman simply jetted off to the States and hooked up with various long-forgotten sleaze acts, none of whom achieved any recognition whatsoever. Sandy Sanderson, meanwhile, joined forces with some of his one-time colleagues (taking erstwhile LIGHTNING RAIDERS drummer George Butler with him) when Mick Farren decided to reform his beloved DEVIANTS a couple of years later, and the bassist additionally played on the »Kill 'Em And Eat 'Em« reunion LP released by the PINK FAIRIES in 1987. Intriguingly, there has, in recent years, been a fair bit of dialogue concerning the possibility of giving the unissued LIGHTNING RAIDERS album an official release, but this ambitious venture seems likely to be thwarted by matters of legality and expense. It's a pity, as such a (belated) release would undoubtedly show everyone that the group could, with the right promotion, image and timing, have become pretty serious contenders in the rock field.

12" Singles
»Criminal World« Island Records 1981
[European-only issue in alternate sleeve to 7" release]

7" Singles
»Psychedelic Musik« Arista 1980
[Commercial issue with 'adult version' of A-side, in picture sleeve]
»Criminal World« Revenge Records 1981
[UK issue, alternate sleeve to 12" format]

Promotional Releases
»Psychedelic Musik« Arista 1980
[DJ promo 7" with 'clean version' of A-side, no sleeve issued]
»Four Track Sampler« Revenge Records 1981
[Promotional 12" EP, exclusive selections from unissued »Sweet Revenge« album]

Compilation Appearances
"Views" (live) on »The Moonlight Tapes« LP Danceville 1980
[Exclusive live version]

LIMELIGHT

Mike Scrimshaw (v,b,k)
Glenn Scrimshaw (g)
Pat Coleman (d)

Nottinghamshire's LIMELIGHT were a bit of an oddity; one of the many bands who first came to prominence in the NWOBHM era, but whose musical heritage actually stretches back as far as the swinging 60's. Even before they had left school, in fact, Glenn and Mike Scrimshaw formed a long-standing writing partnership and played together in various small-time outfits. It wasn't until 1974, however, that they finally made a dedicated attempt to find fame, recruiting a permanent drummer in the form of Pat Coleman and adopting the name LIMELIGHT (confusingly, a couple of other UK acts with this identity had already issued singles by the mid-70's). Officially, Mike took sole responsibility for vocals, bass and keyboards, while Glenn provided all the guitar work and Pat supplied the drums. In truth, they often changed over in terms of instrumentation, particularly in the recording studio (which the trio had, rather ambitiously, built at the Scrimshaw family home), with Mike regularly contributing second guitar tracks, Glenn moving to keyboards (and mellotron!) and Pat getting in on the act by exercising his vocal cords on occasion. In the early days, it was very much a case of peddling their RUSH/ZEPPELIN-influenced material around the traditional circuit of endless shows in pubs and working men's clubs of the Midlands and the North of England (going down a storm, by all accounts), but the lads eventually became considerably more cosmopolitan, venturing not only to mainland Europe, but (incredible as it may seem) even as far as Australia!

These early exploits in the live environment paved the way for a productive career in the music business, and the lads edged ever closer to making their much-anticipated vinyl debut. With an uncanny sense of timing, LIMELIGHT contrived to lay down their first single just as the whole NWOBHM thing was really kicking off in a big way. They had already signed up with the fledgling Future Earth label in Doncaster (who would also issue vinyl from FACTORY and CHINAWITE, along with various indie nonentities) by this time, and their debut two-tracker emerged in 1980, coupling the quirky "Metal Man" with "Hold Me, Touch Me". Certainly, they had now developed a distinctive and accomplished style of heavy music which, to be honest, had comparatively little in common with many of the precocious young upstarts who were dominating the NWOBHM scene. Even so, LIMELIGHT still managed to win the hearts of a considerable number of metal fans of the day with upbeat efforts such as the appositely-titled "Metal Man" itself. Mind you, the group's more general inclination was, nevertheless, clearly biased towards semi-progressive, technical numbers lying somewhere between CRYER, SPITZBROOK and BLEAK HOUSE, something which was to become even more apparent as the musicians prepared to release their first full-length effort.

Recorded in the latter half of 1980, the band's eponymous debut long-player was laid down at Matrix Studios in London and released a couple of months later to coincide with LIMELIGHT's extensive winter tour in support of the mighty SAXON, a jaunt which took them the length and breadth of the country, climaxing in a couple of well-received shows at London's Hammersmith Odeon. It was a pretty confident debut, although several tracks are a bit too lengthy, and the inclusion of two epic numbers ("Man Of Colours" and "Don't Look Back") seems excessive. Nevertheless, within a fairly short space of time, LIMELIGHT began making a serious impact in the Heavy Metal charts of the day, selling a healthy quantity of albums and garnering an enviable collection of favourable reviews for both their studio and live activities. Around this time, the lads also became one of the very few minor acts who assembled their own video product, which supposedly featured alternate versions of various tracks from their album. Sadly, this seems to have been an immensely limited release (in all probability, it would have been for promotional purposes only, due to the huge expense of the medium in those days), and very few copies ever appear to have been circulated. Moving into 1981, their album was picked up by the more influential Avatar label, who promptly reissued the whole thing in a rather lurid green sleeve. The label's more widespread distribution network appears to have given sales of the record a considerable boost, and LIMELIGHT's affiliation with the company led directly to valuable touring exposure with labelmates DARK STAR and CHEVY over the following months.

Towards the end of 1981, the members of LIMELIGHT finally got around to recording their second single, which saw them unveiling the non-album track "Ashes To Ashes" (paired with a slightly more radio-friendly version of "Knife In Your Back"), something of a commercially-motivated cut which suggested that the band were now ready to move into slightly more accessible waters. Issued at the beginning of 1982, the two-tracker again made a considerable impression on the charts, and the lads set out on the road once more to promote the release, the highlight of the year undoubtedly being an appearance at the prestigious Monmore Festival alongside the likes of TYTAN, FIRECLOWN and VARDIS. Nevertheless, their activities tailed off slightly over the following couple of years (as in the case of labelmates DARK STAR and CHEVY, the rapid collapse of Avatar probably didn't help matters), although they continued to gig sporadically, including several well-attended outings at the Marquee in London, at which LIMELIGHT delighted the crowds with an extensive and impressive repertoire of self-penned compositions (including such gems as the unrecorded "Human Emotion", "Drowning", "Over The Wall" and "Red Light"), plus the ever-present cover of the JIMI HENDRIX classic "All Along The Watchtower" and the occasional extended guitar freakout thrown in for good measure.

Things started moving again in 1984, when an arrangement between Future Earth and their European counterparts at Mausoleum saw LIMELIGHT's debut set being reissued (again!), this time as a completely repackaged version with new artwork, an extra track and a novel title in »Ashes To Ashes«. If this undertaking was intended to break the outfit in Europe, however, it might have been a bit too late, as the lads were now writing some rather more commercial material than before, rendering their earlier compositions somewhat unrepresentative. The first evidence of these clandestine studio activities came with two numbers which had recently been commissioned for a (very) low-budget action film entitled 'White Fire'. LIMELIGHT delivered the extremely catchy (semi-pomp rock) title track plus "One Day At A Time", a schmaltzy effort (which played over the end credits) featuring a co-vocal from Vicky Browne (whoever the hell she was), both of which distanced the outfit quite considerably from their heavy roots. The track "White Fire" itself was subsequently featured on a reasonably obscure compilation or two (and, some years later, on the »NWOBHM Vol.4« bootleg CD), although it sounds marginally different from the version used on the soundtrack. However, despite various assertions to the contrary, I'm pretty certain that "White Fire" and "One Day At A Time" were never intended to be issued as a tie-in single.

Always hopeful that they might be given the opportunity to deliver a second album for one label or another, the persevering outfit undertook several further recording sessions throughout the mid-80's, basing themselves in Germany for the majority of these time-consuming and (generally-speaking) frustrating studio activities. In the end, however, assorted personality clashes and fundamental disagreements between the various band members and their refractory production team resulted in the sessions being curtailed before a complete album's worth of new material had actually been captured on tape to everyone's satisfaction. Upon returning to England, the disappointed LIMELIGHT lads briefly tried to get their act together once more, attempting to define that elusive sound and style that would finally bring them fame and fortune in the second half of the decade. There were a few suggestions that their second album would be re-recorded in due course, but these tentative plans appear to have been somewhat flimsy in their construction. Eventually, however, things petered out over a fairly long-drawn-out period of increasing inactivity, and the trio gradually accepted the fact that they had probably missed their golden opportunity.

Although the protagonists are all still on the best of terms and never officially decided to call time on the venture, there have been no 'proper' LIMELIGHT gigs since 1987, the year in which they played some comeback shows around the Midlands. Still, the Scrimshaw brothers continue to write and record new material both for their own use and (occasionally) for unrelated projects. They have also been known to take to the stage for low-key gigs around the Midlands (working, from time to time, as the STUMBLE BROTHERS) as part of larger ensembles (playing blues-influenced sets with former members of SAVAGE, among others), events which occur even to this day. Pat Coleman, on the other hand, spent several happy years assisting JIMMY JAMES AND THE VAGABONDS on the regional club circuit, while Glenn and Mike now combine their musical activities with successful day jobs (music technology lecturer and property developer, respectively). Intriguingly, though, it transpires that the original trio still occasionally get together to perform at private parties, and there's a very real possibility of a full-scale return to recording and touring activities (possibly involving expansion via the recruitment of a dedicated keyboard player and/or second guitarist) under the LIMELIGHT name in the not-too-distant future. We await further developments with anticipation…

LP's
»Limelight« Future Earth Records 1980
[Original issue with black sleeve]
»Limelight« Avatar 1981
[Second issue with green sleeve, also known as »Limited Limelight«]
»Ashes To Ashes« Mausoleum 1984
[Same album as »Limelight« with different cover and song order, plus extra track "Ashes To Ashes"]

7" Singles
»Metal Man« Future Earth Records 1980
[A-side different to album version, B-side "Hold Me, Touch Me" non-LP]
»Ashes To Ashes« Future Earth Records 1982
[A-side exclusive to Mausoleum version of LP, B-side "Knife In Your Back" different to album version]

CD's
»Limelight« Teichiku 1990
[Japanese issue with one bonus track]
»Ashes To Ashes« Mausoleum Classix 1994

[Unofficial release]
Exclusive Compilation Appearances
"White Fire" on »The Best Of British« LP Zebra 1985 + »Axe Attack« LP M Port 1985/Mausoleum 1986 + »NWOBHM Vol.4« Bootleg CD 1992

Compilation Appearances
"Metal Man" on »NWOBHM Vol.2« Bootleg CD 1992

LIONHEART

Jess Cox (v)
Dennis Stratton (g)
Steve Mann (g, k)
Rocky Newton (b)
Frank Noon (d)

The London-based LIONHEART project was conceived in the latter months of 1980 by former IRON MAIDEN guitarist Dennis Stratton, who had a dream of creating the very first 'NWOBHM supergroup' (or, at least, that's what the rather fanciful press releases announced). What followed was a near-legendary series of cock-ups, weekly personnel reshuffles and missed opportunities which largely reduced the hapless outfit to an utter laughing stock, which needn't have been the case at all. Stratton had experienced comparatively little difficulty in attracting an impressive array of seasoned musicians to his venture, initially hooking up with Jess Cox, the erstwhile TYGERS OF PAN TANG frontman (who also just happened to be looking for employment, having recently been given his freedom), and the pair soon enlisted Rocky Newton and Frank Noon from WILDFIRE (aka RED ALERT). The only vacancy which remained to be filled was that of second guitarist, a position which was duly occupied by none other than one-time LIAR axeman Steve Mann, who had actually auditioned for the very same role in the TYGERS OF PAN TANG (losing out to John Sykes), but who had made a sufficiently good impression on Jess Cox that the pair had kept in touch. Stratton's brainchild was complete, and the outfit immediately began composing original material with astonishing haste. Demos were recorded (although not officially released to the public) before the end of the year, featuring numbers such as "Piece Of The Action", "Stay With Me" and "Lionheart", the overall sound being not dissimilar to that of the TYGERS OF PAN TANG themselves.

In January 1981, LIONHEART played a much-vaunted headlining gig at the Marquee in London, a remarkable achievement for such a newly-established act. In spite of the fact that the crowd's response was essentially favourable, however, it proved to be the end of the road for Cox, whose unrefined vocal performance had failed to win favour with his colleagues. Added to the fact that the remaining members clearly wished to steer the outfit into more commercial waters, there was no room for compromise, so the unfortunate frontman was out on his ear (although he took some of his compositions with him and recorded them on his later solo efforts) before much longer. This set the pattern for an ever-changing series of vocalists who would come and go over the years (conservative estimates would suggest that there were at least eight), many of whom lasted for only one or two gigs (notably John Farnham, although he subsequently enjoyed considerably more success as a solo artist) before moving on to pastures new. The first serious contender was Reuben Archer, freshly plucked from the ranks of LAUTREC, but who was to leave after only a couple of months (taking Frank Noon with him) to join the restructuring WILD HORSES. Not to be outdone, ousted WILD HORSES drummer Clive Edwards immediately joined the ranks of LIONHEART! While various other frontmen came and went as a matter of routine, Stratton and Newton continued to share vocal duties on a semi-permanent basis, and the outfit eventually recorded a proper demo tape featuring newly-penned numbers such as "Changing Winds", "The Devil's In You" and "Thunder And Lightning", in addition to some reworked versions of their formative efforts.

The group successfully completed a series of high-profile gigs throughout 1981, playing alongside the likes of WHITESNAKE, VARDIS and DEF LEPPARD, after which they were fortunate enough to become last-minute additions to that year's Reading Festival, an appearance which must surely go down as LIONHEART's greatest achievement in their early days. Following on from this initial flurry of activity, however, 1982 turned out to be something of a comedown for the lads, with far fewer gigs (Rocky Newton taking the mike stand for most purposes) and a considerably more subdued public profile. It also saw yet more instability on the personnel front, following the recent departure of Clive Edwards (who went on to collaborate with former THIN LIZZY guitarist Scott Gorham), the outfit subsequently relying on TYTAN's Les Binks to assist them at the drumkit on occasion.

LIONHEART, meanwhile, were more than happy to return the favour by allowing Steve Mann to help out in the equivalently-unstable TYTAN. Nevertheless, it was to be the year when the lads successfully made their vinyl debut, as they were encouraged to contribute their "Lionheart" anthem to the second »Heavy Metal Heroes« compilation in the closing months of 1982. For the majority of fans, this was their first real chance to appreciate the outfit's talents, and this mid-tempo effort in the style of CHINAWITE or DRAGONFLY seemed to be a pretty decent starting point. However, it soon became apparent that those in control still fully intended the project to become even more of a lightweight proposition, as band spokesman Dennis Stratton revealed in a 'Metal Forces' interview when asked about his musical inspirations of the time, where he worryingly quoted FOREIGNER and STYX as his role models.

In due course, LIONHEART (having steadfastly held out for a contract which was commensurate with their collective talents) contrived to obtain a prestigious deal with the mighty CBS/Epic label, and so the lads soon turned their thoughts to assembling a worthy set of compositions for their full-length debut. They had, by 1984, finally acquired a suitable vocalist in the shape of the unknown Chad Brown (erstwhile LAST FLIGHT vocalist Bob Hawthorne had been tried out the previous year, but didn't last long), whereupon the members ensconced themselves in the studio in Los Angeles (aided by occasional session drummer Bob Jenkins), emerging towards the end of the year with a batch of material to take the world by storm. Well, that was the plan. For those fans who had been expecting a hard-rocking effort with heavy guitars, however, there was a shock in store on the eponymous long-player, as the lads had scrapped virtually their entire repertoire and started again from scratch, this time in a much more commercial vein. With prominent keyboards, harmonised vocals and a clean-cut, sanitised AOR sound in the style of TOTO or REO SPEEDWAGON, LIONHEART's new direction (with an unhealthy reliance on material written for other artists, including "Nightmare", penned by Colin Towns and originally performed by GILLAN) was hardly the sort of thing that was likely to appeal to the denim'n'leather brigade. Indeed, the rather overblown album (which was, admittedly, geared for the American market first and foremost) died a bit of a death upon its release in the UK, as did a tie-in single coupling "Die For Love" and "Dangerous Games" (one of their older numbers, and probably the album's strongest cut), although these two vinyl artefacts have subsequently attained something of a cult status amongst certain excitable AOR fanatics.

Undeterred by overwhelming public indifference, however, the persevering LIONHEART set about attempting to win the hearts of Britain's rock audience, and started off by laying down a 'Friday Rock Show' session. Broadcast on the 29th of March 1985, the band showcased "Wait For The Night", "Hot Tonight", "Towers Of Silver" and "Give Me The Light" (the latter being a non-LP cut), by which time they had expanded into a six-piece via the recruitment of former GRAND PRIX duo Andy Beirne (d) and Phil Lanzon (k). They followed up this valuable piece of radio exposure with a rather more visual appearance on the short-lived 'E.C.T.' television programme a couple of months later, where the lads ran through lively renditions of "Hot Tonight" and "Heartbeat Radio", another unreleased number. They were ultimately fighting a losing battle, however, and, after a few more gigs (and another couple of short-term drummers, including a certain Nicko McBrain), Chad Brown (the possessor of quite an impressive and soulful voice) left in order to pursue an ambitious solo career, although the extent of these activities appears to have been the release of just one seldom-seen single (entitled »I'm Sorry«, the A-side supposedly being entered for the Eurovision Song Contest!) in 1986. He later had a spell with THE SWEET (in one of their later incarnations), a group who seem to serve as the final resting place of numerous NWOBHM scenesters.

LIONHEART bravely soldiered on for a while, with a couple more hapless vocalists (including former AIRRACE frontman Keith Murrell, who subsequently moved over to MAMA'S BOYS) failing to last the distance, before the main songwriting partnership of Stratton, Newton and Mann finally decided to go their separate ways in around 1987. Newton and Mann subsequently had stints with the MCAULAY SCHENKER GROUP in the late 80's, while the pairing of Mann and Lanzon (the latter also becoming involved in the activities of URIAH HEEP from time to time) additionally helped out in one of the later revivals of THE SWEET. Stratton, on the other hand, became involved with the revived PRAYING MANTIS and the ALL STARS project in the early 90's, achieving a far greater level of success than he had done with his previous endeavour. As something of a postscript, the Japanese label Pony Canyon has been delving into the tape collections of various acts over the past few years, and recently came up with a veritable bounty for LIONHEART fans: a double CD set entitled »Raiders Of The Lost Archives«, featuring a wealth of studio material from throughout their entire history. Finally, the public are now able to hear a selection of works-in-progress (several of which are actually highly listenable), and can make up their own minds as to whether or not the outfit should have stuck to their original direction and tried to issue an album in 1982. Let's face it, they could hardly have come up with a more poorly-received effort than the one which eventually hit the shops. As a commercially-motivated concept, the whole LIONHEART episode was yet another case of *'severely misguided venture'*, I'm afraid…

LP's
»Hot Tonight« Epic 1984
[UK issue]
»Hot Tonight« CBS/Sony Japan 1984
[Japanese issue with poster]

7" Singles
»Die For Love« Epic 1984

CD's
»Hot Tonight« CBS/Sony Japan 1991
[Japanese issue]
»Raiders Of The Lost Archives« Pony Canyon 1998
[Japanese-only double disc, compilation of unreleased material]

Compilation Appearances
"Lionheart" on »Heavy Metal Heroes Vol.2« LP Heavy Metal 1982 + »Heavy Metal Heroes Vol.I&II« CD British Steel 1996 + »NWOBHM Vol.5« Bootleg CD 1992

LONELY HEARTS

Glenn Marples (v,g)
Rick Corcoran (g)
Andy Fisher (b)
Steve Mitchell (d)

Rising from the ashes of Yorkshire's much-loved PANZA DIVISION in around 1983, the LONELY HEARTS originally came into existence when founder members Glenn Marples and Rick Corcoran decided to try their hand at something a bit different. Their latest musical vision took a while to become properly established, though, and it would appear that former GEDDES AXE member Andy Barrott may have been involved at the outset, although the latter soon moved on to a more permanent role in BABY TUCKOO. After recruiting a new rhythm section in the form of Andy Fisher and Steve Mitchell (the latter had, in fact, appeared in the last version of PANZA DIVISION shortly before the split), the lads started penning a repertoire of original material with more of a commercial slant, and their debut release for the Tenacity label, a 7" single with a really cheap paste-on cover, gave pride of place to the radio-friendly (in more ways than one) "F.M. Fantasy", a track closely resembling either STATUS QUO or SPIDER (take your pick) at their mostly blatantly accessible. Mind you, the saving grace came on the reverse, as the somewhat heavier "Young Girl" turned out to be a fairly capable rocker, not a million miles away from the type of material that JESS COX was committing to vinyl at around the same time. It was a passable debut, and it seems to have sold quite respectably, although it didn't lead to greater things in the short term, and so it was back to the grind of the clubs for the next year or two until they had raked together enough cash to finance another slice of vinyl.

The quartet's follow-up release, the »Believe« 12" from 1986, was essentially more of the same, with both "You're The One" and "Run" being far too lightweight and nondescript for the majority of rock fans of the day. On the other hand, the title track is an incredibly dated effort, more like LINDISFARNE than anything else, although the SPIDER-like "She's A Rocker" isn't too bad. The general public didn't exactly go overboard in terms of praise, however, and this pretty much signified the end of their vinyl release programme. In spite of the observation that the lads persevered valiantly for several years afterwards, the LONELY HEARTS bequeathed just these two collectable (but not highly-valued) vinyl offerings (both produced by the renowned Pete Hinton, best-known for his work with SAXON) to the nation. The group evidently cultivated an enviable local following along the way, although they developed more of a reputation as club entertainers (in the vein of DUMPY'S RUSTY NUTS) than as genuine contenders for global superstar status. Nevertheless, they tried out a couple of alternate faces to see if it would reverse their fortunes, and 1987 saw them bringing in drummer Steve Spring and adding a full-time keyboard player in the shape of Mark Gordon. The expanded outfit continued to compose original material and play live to the very end, but they eventually had to admit that their chance had gone. Their farewell gig was supposed to be a local performance in 1989, although it's worth pointing out that the lads subsequently reunited a couple of times in the 90's for special occasions. By 1994, however, Glenn Marples had decided to take his talents over to mainland Europe, where, assisted by some unknown conspirators, he proceeded to *'delight'* an array of unsuspecting British holidaymakers in the pubs and clubs of Spain with a selection of old favourites and STATUS QUO covers. Since then, though, I reckon the LONELY HEARTS name has finally been laid to rest for good.

12" EP's
»**Believe**« Tenacity Records 1986

7" Singles
»**F.M. Fantasy**« Tenacity Records 1984

LONE WOLF (I)

Martin Johnson (v)
Colin Stickland (g)
Ian Bazant (b)
John Martin (d)

Not to be confused with their namesakes from the North East who ended up recording for the Guardian and Neat labels, Hampshire's version of LONE WOLF (a surprisingly popular identity which was also adopted by Paul Dianno's first ex-MAIDEN outfit and DEALER in their early days, among others) issued an exceptionally rare single (persistent rumours suggesting that as few as a hundred copies may have been manufactured, although this estimate seems phenomenally low, even by the minimalist standards of the genre) at the beginning of the decade, which remarkably few collectors have ever seen, and only a tiny minority actually possess. There was little or no build-up to this release, though, and the young quartet appear not to have made much of an attempt to develop a loyal following prior to making their vinyl debut, so perhaps it really was an introductory/promotional affair after all. It was a low-budget release, admittedly, although the musicians went as far as to design a picture cover, so it's fair to say that this self-financed two-tracker (issued in 1980) wasn't nearly as half-hearted as some of the ill-conceived, poorly-presented slices of vinyl churned out by various contemporaries, many of which did the groups no favours whatsoever.

Neither the quirky "Cash For Candy", with its unusual time signature and changes of pace, nor "Pipedream Mary" are exactly typical NWOBHM rockers, both coming across instead as somewhere between OXYM and a less technical KRAKEN, with vocals slightly in the vein of SAMSON-era Dickinson. Not at all bad, especially for an emergent bunch of hopefuls, but it's yet another of those singles which hardly justifies a massive asking price on musical merit alone. Once again, this humble offering came in a generic, monochrome picture sleeve, the majority of which seem to be hand-numbered, so it's entirely justifiable to assume that LONE WOLF didn't press all that many examples in the first

instance. All in all, a much-coveted little item, and, if you've got one, you should hold on to it very tightly indeed. If, on the other hand, you've got a box of unplayed copies stashed away in your garage, you can now afford to book that world cruise. Still, the group were evidently a fly-by-night concern, and had apparently given up the ghost within a year or so. Erstwhile drummer John Martin, incidentally, later cropped up in another relatively unrenowned Hampshire band, FURY (see separate entry), but the other members are missing, presumed lost.

7" Singles
»**Cash For Candy**« Wolf Music 1980

LONE WOLF (II)

Brian Ross (v)
Dave Johnson (g)
Dave Allan (b)
Steve Hutchinson (d)

Although the Tyneside version of LONE WOLF were, at one time, yet another vehicle for the considerable vocal talents of Brian Ross (of BLITZKRIEG, AVENGER, SATAN etc.), it transpires that this particular outfit weren't originally one of his musical projects after all. While the great man subsequently appeared on their »Nobody's Move« EP after finishing with SATAN (the busy chap had, in the past, also found time to lend his services to the ropy-as-you-like UNTER DEN LINDEN, who contributed to the »Roxcalibur« sampler), the first version of LONE WOLF had actually managed to reach the vinyl stage two years previously. With the act having initially been formed by guitarist Dave Johnson a relatively short time beforehand, the original incarnation (featuring an entirely different vocalist) recorded the »Leave Me Behind« two-tracker (B-side "High Class Hooker") for Guardian as early as 1982, showing LONE WOLF to be a competent, hard-rocking outfit in the manner of LAUTREC or SNAKEBITE. For some strange reason, though, their single (no sleeve issued) is very seldom sighted these days, although it doesn't rival HOLLOW GROUND or SATAN as one of the label's big collectables.

After a few reshuffles (the first single credited 'Morris' and 'Byrne' in addition to Johnson, incidentally, so it might have been a markedly different line-up), Brian Ross joined the crew (largely taking over the group as his own, admittedly), and it wasn't long before his old chums at Neat waded in with an offer for the outfit to record a one-off release. Ross takes up the story himself: 'I discovered LONE WOLF playing a gig at a very small venue. They asked me to manage them, so I agreed to do it. I got the band a recording deal with Neat Records and the band began rehearsing for the recording session. The singer that they had really wasn't very good, so the band fired him. They didn't have enough time to replace him before they went into the studio, so I stepped in and recorded the vocals on those songs for them. I stayed as vocalist for a while, as well as managing the band, and we did quite a few live shows, but as it got closer to the time for me to record the BLITZKRIEG album, I found that I couldn't give LONE WOLF the time that they should have from a manager, so I had to quit.' (Ref: Singing Swords No.3, June 1998). Very chivalrous.

LONE WOLF's aforementioned vinyl debut for Neat took the form of a 12" EP featuring "Nobody's Move", "Town To Town" and a rewritten (considerably shorter) version of "Leave Me Behind", showcasing their replacement vocalist's more metallic and less raunchy style. Unsurprisingly, the group's newer material had more than a hint of AVENGER and (particularly) BLITZKRIEG about it, although there are also a few tinges of ZENITH and SAVAGE in places. The title track ("Nobody's Move"), as featured on the »NWOBHM Vol.8« bootleg CD, is undoubtedly the stand-out number, and the EP as a whole should have allowed the band to capture a fair old proportion of BLITZKRIEG's enviable fan base. In the end, however, it just wasn't to work out for the luckless LONE WOLF, and, as we've already heard, Ross was ultimately lured away by the prospect of a possible BLITZKRIEG reformation (a project which has occupied his time ever since), leaving the dejected LONE WOLF to fold shortly thereafter.

12" EP's
»Nobody's Move« Neat 1984
["Leave Me Behind" different to version on 7" single]

7" Singles
»Leave Me Behind« Guardian 1982
[A-side different to version on »Nobody's Move« 12"]

Compilation Appearances
"Nobody's Move" on »NWOBHM Vol.8« Bootleg CD 1996

LORELEI

Roger Scott
Steve Christopher

LORELEI's hopelessly obscure »Can't Stand The Heat« single is a relatively recent discovery, and, as yet, few useful details of this unrenowned Berkshire outfit's career have been ascertained with any degree of confidence, given that the record itself gives precious little away. Unfortunately, as is the case with so many private releases of the time done *'on the cheap'*, there appears to be no picture sleeve to help us along either, so you'll have to make do with a bare minimum of information for now. However, the unremarkable-looking two-tracker, issued at some point in 1981, sees the combo delivering a cheerful piece of lightweight rock in the general style of FLIGHT 77, early PRAYING MANTIS or the DICK SMITH BAND, especially with regard to the distinctive (dare I say, *'funky'*) guitar sound of the latter. The nominated A-side is reasonably memorable, albeit undemanding on the ears, while flipside "Gold Digger" is simply more of the same, to be honest, with a vaguely BLUE ÖYSTER CULT feel in places. All in all, not the heaviest piece of vinyl you'll ever hear, and not in the *'big money'* league of NWOBHM rarities. I suppose LORELEI failed to last the distance and went back to their day jobs soon afterwards, but maybe we'll have some slightly more enlightening information next time around…

7" Singles
»Can't Stand The Heat« Siren Records 1981

LOST FAMOUS

Geraint Jones (v, g)
Terry Phillips (g)
Dread (b)
Porl Hackling (d)

Another contender for the increasingly-substantial *'difficult to categorise'* pile, the »Anywhere Else« single by the oddly-named Welsh quartet LOST FAMOUS (a release which hit the local shops at some point in 1982) is probably most adequately served by the *'prog/metal'* tag, being somewhat analogous in terms of general style and arrangement to similarly-minded groups such as AVALON and THE COVENANT. Both "Anywhere Else" and "A Warning" feature vaguely heavy-ish guitars in places, but also include some more sparse passages and rather faltering, miserable vocals in the TRACER manner. There are a couple of (uncredited) synthesizer moments, although not quite enough to warrant comparisons with more progressively-inclined acts such as EARTHBOUND or SHERWOOD, so I'm less happy with the *'prog'* description than I could be, but it'll have to do. Recorded at the oft-frequented (cheap and cheerful, apparently) Loco Studios facility, the one-off LOST FAMOUS single (the protagonists returning to the shadows almost immediately afterwards) was housed within a monochrome sleeve, depicting an endearingly simplistic line drawing of some birds and a human figure. Having presumably been sold only at regional gigs and through a couple of outlets, the two-tracker suffered from a particularly limited distribution, and has turned up in minimal quantities in recent times, although it's not a highly-valued item at present.

7" Singles
»Anywhere Else« Silent Records 1982

LOST PROPERTY

D. Connolly
J. Connolly
Cole
Irvin

As with SIAN (see separate entry), this band only just made it into the final draft, largely on the basis of some reasonably assertive (female) vocals and in view of the fact that the two-tracker in question was issued through the collectable Clubland concern, as with such highly-regarded obscurities as CAMARGUE, AIRBORNE (visitors from Sweden) and SPITEFUL CHILD. Mind you, if punk-influenced acts such as the largely-hopeless VERMILION and TOO MUCH can somehow become regarded as *bona fide* NWOBHM by the majority of modern collectors, then there shouldn't really be a huge fuss kicked up about these two entries. LOST PROPERTY were frequently to be found gigging in and around London in the early 80's, so it's not entirely surprising that, after developing a sufficiently strong following, the combo ultimately decided to proffer a modest single to their admirers. This effort (issued at some point in 1981) was an unspectacular affair, to be frank, with both "Persuasion" and flipside "Waste Of A Nation" turning out to be comparatively lightweight and sparse in terms of their guitar sound, although the passable vocals (in a kind of proto-T'PAU style) help to carry the material somewhat, as with AFTER HOURS or, to a lesser extent, CANIS MAJOR. "Waste Of A Nation" is the slightly punkier of the pair, the frontwoman taking some rather obvious influences from TOYAH, suggesting that, if this particular bunch were indeed affiliated with the metal scene in any way, then they were certainly on the periphery. Additional details are decidedly sketchy, however, with no helpful picture sleeve known to exist at this time. Mind you, Clubland singles were, more often than not, issued with a proper cover, and it's entirely conceivable that one may be unearthed at some point in the future. Any further info?

7" Singles
»Persuasion« Clubland Records 1981

LOTUS CRUISE

Dave Pearsall (v)

Carl Denton (g)
Andy Young (g)
Phil Langley (b)
Ian 'Len' Parkin (d)

Although Yorkshire's CRY (see separate entry) are comparatively familiar to metal collectors by virtue of their two privately-pressed singles from 1987, the story actually begins a few years earlier, their humble roots lying in an obscure outfit who went by the non-obvious name of LOTUS CRUISE (although I bet it's got something to do with cars or bikes) during the early part of the decade. By 1983, having already circulated a well-received demo or two, the ambitious unit had become sufficiently polished to start thinking about a vinyl release, whereupon they confidently took the bull by the horns and issued their own single, coupling "Billy's Got A Gun" (nothing to do with the DEF LEPPARD original) with "Tonight" (the latter brought to prominence on the »NWOBHM Vol.7« bootleg CD). The quintet's own music was, at that stage, considerably more metal-sounding than their subsequent offerings as CRY, but it's frustratingly difficult to compare them to any 'name' bands (I mean, how many people have actually heard the UK version of EUPHORIA?) of the period. There are hints of acts as disparate as TRAXX, DEMON and BLACK ROSE, but the overall sound is fairly original and accomplished, with only a vague suggestion of their later leanings towards POISON or WRATHCHILD. The LOTUS CRUISE single, issued without a picture sleeve, is an extremely rare item these days, suggesting that the original pressing was a relatively modest one, and you'll now be very lucky to locate one at any price.

Clearly, the LOTUS CRUISE two-tracker failed to capture the public's imagination in the intended manner, although the lads kept plugging away for another couple of years in an attempt to achieve more widespread recognition. The youthful outfit demoed a fair amount of additional material during their time together on the regional rock scene, penning highly capable numbers such as "Queen Of Broken Hearts" and "I Got A Feeling", for example. Indeed, one or two of these selections occasionally threaten to eclipse the standard of those efforts previously immortalised on vinyl, so it's a shame that they never got the chance to follow up their debut. Other sporadic LOTUS CRUISE recordings from the mid-80's, meanwhile, particularly "Heartache" and "Tokyo Blade", showed the lads at their heaviest, these even bringing to mind Killerwatt-era ANGEL WITCH at times. The young Tykes struggled to maintain their sense of identity after releasing that first single, though, and it appears that, towards the end of their existence, the rapidly-fading outfit even tried out a different vocalist (Tony Hewitt from OLYMPIA) in a last-ditch attempt to reverse their fortunes and break into the big league. Evidently, however, things didn't work out for the band in their original incarnation, and, after a few enforced reshuffles, the eventual metamorphosis into CRY (whose exploits are documented elsewhere) had occurred by the early part of 1986.

7" Singles
»Billy's Got A Gun« Armbury Records 1983

Compilation Appearances
"Tonight" on »NWOBHM Vol.7« Bootleg CD 1996

LYADRIVE

Nick John (v, k)
Steve Jones (g)
Barrie Flemming (g)
Steve Christiansen (b)
Lee Burrows (d)

The five-piece concern who eventually became known as LYADRIVE got together early in 1981 in the North London area, originally assuming the name TEMPEST RIDE. Under this guise, the outfit (comprising various scenesters from the original days of Neal Kay's Bandwagon, including one-time PRAYING MANTIS roadie Lee Burrows) took their first tentative steps in the music business by playing a few low-key gigs, after which they contributed a number entitled "Another Time, Another Place" to »The Bridge Album«, a scarcely-sighted sampler highlighting various acts who came from (or at least rehearsed in) the nation's capital. For such an inexperienced bunch, the composition (as featured on the »NWOBHM Vol.7« bootleg and, more recently, in slightly remixed form, on the, er, »Legends Of Progressive Rock« compilation, in the unlikely company of acts such as CARAVAN, RENAISSANCE and AMAZING BLONDEL!), with its changing tempos and rhythms, showed an incredible maturity in terms of songwriting ability and depth of musicianship. With occasional similarities to various melodic, powerful outfits such as HIGH TREASON, ENERGY and DEALER, the aforementioned effort was unquestionably the album's stand-out track, and instantly set these youngsters on the long and winding road to fame and fortune.

Moving into 1983, the band (having actually changed their identity to the unusual LYADRIVE, a corruption of *'Liars Drive'*, before the aforementioned sampler had been issued) recruited new bassist Den O'Leary and replaced Barrie Flemming with Charlie Green, before putting together the tracks "We've Got The Rock" and "Spinning The Wheel" for the benefit of Ebony, from which the former was chosen for inclusion on the label's »Metal Warriors« compilation. With their memorable contribution having been well-received by the masses, particularly in mainland Europe, the lads were soon invited back into Bridge Studios to record two further numbers for future release as a single. With "Anytime" and "White Dress" being captured for posterity in due course, the pair were issued as a double A-side on the Bridge label itself (they also put out a seldom-seen two-tracker by NORTH STAR, an act with whom LYADRIVE shared a stage on more than one occasion) several months later, which rapidly led to a fair bit of media exposure. Indeed, the band proceeded to enjoy mostly favourable reviews (although one memorably described them as *'a pub rock BLUE ÖYSTER CULT*') in the likes of 'Kerrang', 'N.M.E.' and 'Enfer', their single having revealed a move into slightly more classy and restrained territory in the STORMCHILD or BLACKOUT vein. It was still very listenable, though, and the catchy "Anytime", with its memorable keyboard passages, even made it onto the »NWOBHM Vol.7« bootleg CD a decade later.

Over the following year, the group toured constantly, mostly around London (taking in the famous Ruskin Arms and Dingwalls) and its environs, but occasionally venturing further afield (*e.g.* Slough, Milton Keynes and Southend). Showcasing material taken from a selection of impressive demo tracks such as "Lazerwind", "Young Lover", "Madame Guillotine", "Sign Of The Hunted" and the excellent "Steal Away The Night", the combo (now featuring Dave Collett in place of Charlie Green) continued to consolidate their well-earned reputation as a popular, energetic live act. Towards the end of 1984, LYADRIVE (having had a prospective deal with the mighty CBS label scuppered by personnel problems) duly negotiated an arrangement to have a three-tracker issued on the Loose label (who had, as Brickyard, infamously released the XERO 7"/12"). The lads (having

now replaced axeman Dave Collett with Graham Stuart and recruited replacement bassist Lee Reddings) proceeded to lay down "Young Lover" and "Here Comes The Night" (alongside a re-recorded version of live favourite "We've Got The Rock") for this project, but, with the shaky label beset with financial problems and eventually declaring bankruptcy, plans for this release were reluctantly shelved in the long term. With the group having had the stuffing knocked out of them by this major setback, they only continued for another six months or so (with new bassist Kevin Goodman, after Lee Reddings had been poached by BRONZ), before finally disbanding.

The untimely demise of LYADRIVE had come as a pretty severe disappointment for both the group and their many fans, although the erstwhile members were generally philosophical about their fate. Interestingly, however, several of them were to maintain a fairly high level of involvement with the business, as the garrulous Lee Burrows later revealed: *'Since LYADRIVE, I have played in a couple of bands, THE RAGGY DOLLZ (a sort of proto-BACKYARD BABIES) and TIGON (aka BEERHUNTER), a covers act with ever-evolving members, therefore an ever-changing set list! When I joined, they were mostly playing 70's/80's mainstream metal, but by the time I left, they were introducing more modern stuff. Guy Wilson still plays with them. Nick has also dabbled; after the collapse of LYADRIVE, he and Steve Jones did some demos for a band called DUST TO DUST, more poppy stuff, followed by some material for a background music company. In 1992, he released an instrumental cassette called »Capercaillies Wedding« with Mike Burdett and he later put a band together called MOSES WIGGINS, who issued a CD called »Box Of Tricks«, more rootsy stuff but still rocky. He and Keith Thompson also record in an occasional project called THE DEADWEIGHTS.'* (Ref: Private communication, July 1999). Clearly, these guys were just too talented to be kept out of the limelight for long, but, with the members all doing their own thing, it seemed as though the name of LYADRIVE would soon be little more than a distant memory...

By the mid-90's, however, a few lucky NWOBHM collectors had started turning up some copies of the rare (sleeveless, although a handful came with an insert giving details and a photo of the group) LYADRIVE 7", and the insatiable fans soon clamoured for more. With enterprising specialists such as Vinyl Tap tracking down certain ex-members and paying good money for unsold copies, interest in the outfit was rekindled, much to the amazement of the musicians themselves, as their genial sticksman revealed: *'I was aware of the Japanese interest, as my connection with PRAYING MANTIS meant that whenever I spotted their name, I would read with interest. However, I wasn't really aware of it until we had two phone calls within a week, from dealers on either side of the Atlantic, asking for copies of the single. To say that Nick and I were gobsmacked wouldn't be exaggerating.'* (Ref: ibid.) Things snowballed pretty rapidly, with the upshot being that an all-new version of LYADRIVE, comprising the central duo of Burrows and John, plus Keith Thompson (g), Paul 'Rhino' Ryan (g) and bassist Guy Wilson (the latter pair having been compatriots of Burrows in the aforementioned TIGON venture) was revived in around 1995. Although the lads had, by this stage, been offered the enviable opportunity to issue a CD of archive material, the revised outfit decided to take full advantage of modern studio technology, and proceeded to re-record the whole shebang, with a few musical and lyrical changes being incorporated along the way so that the new line-up felt more comfortable with the material.

After a few irritating hiccoughs and false starts with the various labels involved, a pair of previously-unissued LYADRIVE numbers surfaced on 1997's »Noise Level Critical« sampler, these being followed in due course by their full-length »Another Time, Another Place« CD, finally released in 1998 by the Minority One concern, a subsidiary of HTD Records. With the title track and "Anytime" having been given a major revamp, these new recordings of old favourites were highly enjoyable efforts (as are all the classic demo compositions featured), and the album (including the aborted EP as bonus selections) has sold quite respectably thus far, with considerable interest coming from fans outside the UK (isn't it always the case?), although I'm glad to say that they haven't been totally ignored in Blighty. A notable and somewhat surprising inclusion on the CD was the group's interpretation of the TRESPASS classic "One Of These Days", its presence explained by Lee Burrows himself: *'It's a relatively simple song, but it's very effective all the same. Tony from Vinyl Tap really thought that it would be a good idea to cover TRESPASS, simply because they were experiencing a bit of a revival in Japan. It may have been a minor detail, but every little helps!'* (Ref: Iron Pages No.47, January 1999). Further compilation appearances have also followed, the LYADRIVE name being featured on a couple of CD's issued by the likes of Hallmark and Delta Music, although I'm sure the fact that frontman Nick John was heavily involved with these releases is a total coincidence...

Far from resting on their laurels, the resurrected ensemble remain a going concern (attracting a fair amount of attention in some of the more discerning publications of the moment) with their sights on the future, rehearsing whenever the possibility arises (the fact that they all have day jobs makes things a bit tricky), writing brand-new material with a more contemporary edge and making vital inroads into the live scene (including a fairly recent outing in the slightly unusual company of the GROUNDHOGS) in order that their undoubted talent is exposed to as wide an audience as possible. It may have taken the best part of fifteen years for the members to reap the rewards of their early NWOBHM career, but it's heartwarming to see such genuinely nice people being given some belated recognition. Somehow I don't think we've seen the last of LYADRIVE, not just yet.

7" Singles
»**Anytime**« Bridge Records 1984
[Both tracks different to CD versions]

CD's
»**Another Time, Another Place**« Minority One Records 1998
[Features re-recordings of early studio material]

Compilation Appearances
"**Another Time, Another Place**" on »The Bridge Album« LP Bridge Records 1982 + »NWOBHM Vol.7« Bootleg CD 1996 + »Legends Of Progressive Rock« CD Hallmark 1998
[Under the name of TEMPEST RIDE, different to CD version]
"**We've Got The Rock (You're Gonna Roll)**" on »Metal Warriors« LP Ebony 1983
[Different to CD version]
"**Anytime**" on »NWOBHM Vol.6« Bootleg CD 1992
[Different to CD version]
"**Sign Of The Hunted**" on »Noise Level Critical« CD Hallmark 1997
"**Steal Away The Night**" on »Noise Level Critical« CD Hallmark 1997
"**Lazerwind**" on »Legends Of Progressive Rock« CD Hallmark 1998 + »Hard Roxx Taster Vol.4« CD Private 1998
[Free with 'Hard Roxx' magazine]
"**Another Time, Another Place**" on »The Best Of British Metal« CD Delta Music 1999
[Under the name of LYADRIVE]
"**White Dress**" on »The Best Of British Metal« CD Delta Music 1999

LYNX

Jon Keighley

It's not exactly a prime-era NWOBHM release by any stretch of the imagination, but the 1978 single from the completely obscure LYNX (nothing to do with Danny Gwilym's identically-named act from his pre-CHINATOWN days, incidentally) is still a listenable enough piece of crossover material, quite representative of the sort of quirky post-punk experimentation that was going on in many parts of the country in the late 70's. Their self-financed two-tracker (which appears to have been a one-off) couples the catchy "See The Light" and "C.I.A.", two numbers which combine the tuneful punk/metal collision of BASELINE or SHADOWFAX with the unusual keyboard backing of ZORRO or early TOAD THE WET SPROCKET. It's considerably more effective than it ought to be, mind you, given that the potential for a disastrous outcome is remarkably high. Still, even though the combination of punky metal and keyboards is hardly a marriage made in heaven, the band manage to carry it off quite admirably, although it's fair to say that they had very little chance of landing themselves a major-label deal with this particular brand of material. I've absolutely no idea who LYNX were, or what happened to them, and the fact that so many small-time outfits adopted the same identity throughout the 70's and 80's doesn't help matters, but their oddly-named label was based in Sheffield, so I guess they were yet another Yorkshire bunch. Any other ideas, anyone?

7" Singles
»**See The Light**« S.T. Roducts 1978

MAD DOG

Eddie Edmonds (v)
Tony M (g)
Busby (g)
Steve George (b)
Tonto (d)

The origins of Mid-Glamorgan's infamous MAD DOG apparently lie, as with so many others, in an amateur-hour band which began life as a bit of post-school mucking around for some young friends, in this case stretching back as far as 1976. Centred around the ever-present duo of

Steve George and Tony M (an unusual surname, it must be said), their musical associates came and went at a truly alarming rate in the early days, although things settled down a bit when utterly bonkers vocalist (and professional John McCoy lookalike) Eddie Edmonds joined the fold in 1978. Having finally achieved something resembling a stable line-up (completed by, ahem, drummer Tonto and second guitarist Busby) by 1979, the group took their first faltering steps in the recording field by contributing two tracks to the incredibly obscure »Is The War Over?« sampler, a self-styled *'Cardiff compilation'*, even though MAD DOG were actually based a bit further North. Both "Killer" and "Someone Here Must Like Me" saw the youthful outfit operating in a fairly rudimentary boogie/pub rock style (with occasional similarities to early GIRLSCHOOL) which featured a rather nasal, semi-punky vocal delivery from frontman Eddie Edmonds at that stage. Guitarist Busby, however, appears to have flown the nest shortly thereafter, and a new drummer (Viv Roberts) also joined up before the end of the year.

Had this new version of MAD DOG managed to issue a single within a year or two of this initial exposure, it would probably have done reasonably well, but it didn't happen. For some reason (possibly associated with Tony M taking time off to do a degree), the outfit became something of low-profile concern (in terms of studio activities) for quite some time, although they continued to gig sporadically in their locality. By 1984, however, the lads had finally sorted out whatever had been holding them back in the previous couple of years, and returned to the fray with a brand-new demo. A year later (having still not received a great deal of interest from the record labels), they elected to issue their debut single on their own Brainy label, the latter featuring "Sheriff" and "You're A Beautiful Sight". By now, the outfit had become a considerably more metal affair, and their vocalist had obviously been conditioning his voice to perfection by gargling with low-grade whisky on a regular basis, so that the MAD DOG two-tracker turned out to be a markedly more listenable offering than people might have expected on the evidence of their earlier sampler appearance. Coming across as somewhere between DUMPY'S RUSTY NUTS and »Honour And Blood«-era TANK, but with little or no punk influence now apparent, the lads were almost certainly angling for a slice of the biker market, and I suspect that the combination of image, humour and musical orientation probably hit precisely the right note. Incidentally, the recording session for the 7" (which is now a fairly rare and sought-after piece) saw journeyman drummer Kerry Loveluck (MAMMATH, ASHMATA, RANKELSON etc.) filling in for the unlucky Viv Roberts, who was actually recuperating from a broken leg at the time.

The single (which soon garnered the almost inevitable rave review from 'High Octane' fanzine) swiftly led to a proper deal with the Stud label (see also SEDUCER's »Eads Down-See You At The End« LP), a short-lived subsidiary of Castle Communications. An eponymous long-player (produced by none other than Martin Turner, the WISHBONE ASH mainman) duly appeared in 1986, featuring an all-new selection of material, the most impressive of which would include the blistering "Fallin" and "Johnny Cyclops", as well as the lengthy "Fortune Favours The Brave" and excellent closer "The Last Great Wilderness". In spite of the observation that certain uncharitable individuals have, over the years, been remarkably quick to dismiss the MAD DOG album as containing little more than a disposable selection of uninspiring boogie/blues material, it's actually nothing of the sort; the upbeat numbers, in particular, are extremely listenable, often coming across as a kind of proto-WILDHEARTS/QUIREBOYS mutant. All in all, it's an accomplished (and at times, genuinely surprising) set of compositions which, for some reason, tended to receive a rather bumpy ride ('Kerrang' were one of those who gave it a decent write-up) as it made its way through the reviews sections.

The band, however, were sufficiently happy with the album to make preparations for a follow-up release, and were still extremely active and ambitious when featured in the 'Welsh Metal Special' compiled by 'Kerrang' at the beginning of 1988. By this juncture, the lads had played literally hundreds of gigs (their modern repertoire including SEX PISTOLS and TED NUGENT covers) in their homeland over the years, and had made the pilgrimage to London's Marquee for no less than eight headlining appearances. Not only that, they had also gained British television exposure on two separate occasions, and had even made it over to Holland for a short sojourn. As Tony M explained at the time: *'We'll play anywhere. We have done before, and it was all our hard work that paid off then. I think someone is due to break through, it could be us.'* (Ref: Kerrang No.174, February 1988). Furthermore, since the release of their debut long-player, MAD DOG had evidently been receiving a great deal of fan mail, not only from mainland Europe (Germany, Spain, Italy etc.), but also from the likes of the USA and Brazil; all the more impressive when you consider that the album wasn't officially released in such territories! Curiously, though, a second single (»Smiling Stranger«), which was initially supposed to have been issued towards the end of 1987 (and again in the spring of 1988), doesn't appear to have made it into the shops, the reasons for this non-event being rather mysterious.

All the same, the quartet had already booked a generous slice of studio time in order to record their second album in February 1988, and were due to take to the road for a national tour a month or two later. Sadly, however, things seem to have gone a bit pear-shaped (although the majority of these shindigs almost certainly went ahead as scheduled) and their plans didn't work out exactly as anticipated. Whether or not the full-length follow-up was ever recorded is unclear (I'm not even sure if any labels had actually offered to release the album), although it certainly didn't get to the vinyl stage. It looks as though MAD DOG fell apart by the end of the decade, whereupon the musicians pretty much drifted away from the scene altogether. Steve George, for example, now earns a crust as a cartoonist, while the current whereabouts of the other members is a total mystery.

LP's
»Mad Dog« Stud Records 1986

7" Singles
»Sheriff« Brainy Records 1985
[Both tracks non-LP]

Exclusive Compilation Appearances
"Killer" on »Is The War Over?« LP Z Block Records 1979
"Someone Here Must Like Me" on »Is The War Over?« LP Z Block Records 1979

MADE IN ENGLAND

Tony Vassé (g)
Colin Malloy (g)
Stuart Dear (b)
Ken Gascoine (k)
Andy Scarlino (d)

Sad to say, this 1981 obscurity, on the increasingly-collectable Gargoyle label (see also E.S.P., BACKLASH, TUTCH etc.), promises considerably more than it actually delivers. Judging by the cover (a hand-drawn effort showing two animal visages, possibly lions) and metal-sounding song titles, this really should be a NWOBHM monster, but look a bit more closely. Keyboards. No vocalist. Oh dear, this could easily be another DAGABAND. Well, it's not quite that poor (it's probably one to covet if you enjoy the likes of STRATEGY), but these unassuming instrumentals aren't in the same league as BLEAK HOUSE's "Flight Of The Salamander", for instance. MADE IN ENGLAND, from Hertfordshire (an outfit of the same name apparently issued a single entitled »Prospects« in the mid-80's, although I suspect that this was an entirely unrelated project), offer two pleasant enough (keyboard-dominated) tracks, "Dance Of The Warriors" and "The Quest", which don't overstay

their welcome but don't really leave a lasting impression either. Not a major-league rarity, to be honest, and not the sort of thing that will sit easily beside the likes of DEMOLITION and SHOCK TREATMENT if you're more partial to the raucous stuff. If, on the other hand, EARTHBOUND or CANIS MAJOR are more your cup of tea, then it might be worth looking for a copy.

Interestingly (well, perhaps), the sleeve notes once again credit the little-remembered 'Make it Yourself' scheme (see also WARRIOR's »Don't Let It Show« 10" EP on the Rambert label, for example), which apparently helped young people to produce and market 'an artistic product' (I'm not entirely sure if this is what the organisers originally had in mind, though) themselves. This was all very noble, I'm sure you'll agree, although it's a great pity that some of the more deserving demo bands from around the country weren't able to benefit from similar projects. As a bonus, incidentally, the history-conscious group felt the need to include the following, incredibly informative, explanation of the A-side's underlying concept: 'In the fifteenth century, two goblets were discovered. The design of the goblets represented the images of two warriors dancing around a fire. It was found that they did this the night before a battle.' Ah, it all makes sense now.

7" Singles
»Dance Of The Warriors« Gargoyle Records 1981

MAINEEAXE

Mick Adamson (v)
Dave 'Zeff' Stewart (g)
I.J. Greensmith (b)
Doc Simpson (d)

The origins of Yorkshire's MAINEEAXE apparently lie in an ill-fated outfit called TRANS-AM, an act who formed at the start of the 80's but whose chequered history and numerous line-up changes prevented them from achieving much in their original incarnation, and it transpires that this venture (from whence came the rhythm section of Doc Simpson and I.J. Greensmith) bore absolutely no relation to the rather obscure TRANS AM (see separate entry) who released a NWOBHM-era 7". In any case, MAINEEAXE themselves came into existence towards the end of 1983, and had been active as a unit for a comparatively short time when Powerstation Records popped up and offered the lads an unexpected chance to lay down some vinyl at the earliest opportunity. The end result was the »Shout It Out« album, released in mid-1984, which revealed the musicians to be a talented bunch, with much of their material being in a melodic, semi-power style (featuring a capable vocal performance throughout) with occasional similarities to SALEM, TRAITORS GATE or MASTERSTROKE, some particular highlights being "Cold As Ice", "Rough Trade" and the superb "Run To The Angels". Elsewhere, there was a fair bit of variety on display, and the epic "Steel On Steel" was a powerful inclusion in the style of DAWNWATCHER or CRYER, while "Bad Boys" and "Shout It Out" were pretty straightforward (but perfectly listenable), hard-rocking numbers. All in all, it was an extremely competent debut, and a couple of singles (based around the soppy ballad "The Game" and the more upbeat "Gonna Make You Rock", the last-mentioned being particularly well-received by 'Kerrang') were trundled out to promote the release in due course.

With the record doing brisk business for Powerstation, they were understandably keen to commission a follow-up, although, by the time the next MAINEEAXE vinyl offering hit the shops (in the early months of 1985, neatly coinciding with their support slot on MAGNUM's British tour), it became apparent that the group had experienced a change in personnel, following the sudden departure of two original members late the previous year. Undeterred, the remaining nucleus of Mick Adamson and Zeff Stewart had quickly enticed three likely characters (Grant Kirkhope, Nigel Harrison and Roger Gibbons) away from local metallers SYAR (see

separate entry) to build a new line-up. The revamped, twin-guitar version of MAINEEAXE debuted with a 12" EP based around "Gimme Your Love" (the unfamiliar pairing of "Call Of The Wild" and "Lady From The Night" were also unveiled), which further consolidated the band's position as one of Powerstation's stronger acts. Within a matter of weeks, their second full-length effort (»Going For Gold«) was unleashed, revealing the lads to have contributed a decent album once again, with strong numbers including "The Score", "Ride The Storm" and "The Best Is Yet To Come", although it's not quite as consistent as their debut. Moreover, a few of the other tracks are in such a contrasting style that they could almost be cover versions (admittedly, "Get Up, Get Down", "Infatuation" and the power ballad "Alone Again" were actually salvaged from SYAR's live set), and I reckon the lads might have listened to a fair bit of RAVEN's back catalogue before going into the studio this time. Again, Mick Adamson (who had, in the past, featured in such obscure acts as FLIGHT and BULLDOG BREED) delivered an inspiring vocal performance, and surely qualifies as one of the NWOBHM's most talented and underrated frontmen.

In spite of the fact that MAINEEAXE were undoubtedly one of Powerstation's more profitable signings (with pressings of their releases being licensed to various labels in Canada, France, Germany, Spain *etc.*), they were never able to issue a third long-player. In fact, they bowed out with a disappointing mini-album, which featured three of their B-sides ("Call Of The Wild", "Lady From The Night" and "No Foolin'"), plus "The Hour Of Thunder" (the title track), "Spark To The Flame" and "Misgivings". It was a peculiar (rather pointless, in all honesty) release, and one which looks more like a contract-fulfiller or a cash-in than anything more creative. Perhaps the group wanted to move on to another label or start afresh in a different style, or maybe it was a case of Powerstation looking to squeeze out another release too quickly after the last album. Whatever the story, it wasn't a great success (a couple of the tracks saw the band attempting a style more along the lines of EXCALIBUR or TYTAN), and it was to be MAINEEAXE's last piece of vinyl. A great pity, really, and it suggested that, when it came to writing new material together, the revised unit didn't really cut the mustard. In that respect, it's unfortunate that they couldn't have hung on to their early line-up, as I'm convinced this bunch originally had the potential to develop into a hugely popular outfit.

By the beginning of 1987, the luckless MAINEEAXE had well and truly bitten the dust, having either lost their way or come to blows over future musical direction, although a couple of the protagonists retained some additional involvement with the rock scene for a few years. Both Grant Kirkhope and Nigel Harrison decided that their immediate future lay with more commercially-inclined acts, whereupon they joined local hopefuls NOUSSOMMES and ARENA (later BRAZIL), respectively. This pair of outfits persevered for a while, each getting a fair quota of favourable press attention and winning themselves a useful 'Friday Rock Show' session along the way. Even so, they were both to fall by the wayside in the early 90's (victims of the all-conquering grunge scene, basically) when that particular brand of semi-AOR banality suffered a massive loss in popularity among rock fans in the UK. Since then, precious little has been heard from any of the one-time MAINEEAXE conspirators.

LP's
»Shout It Out« Powerstation 1984/Banzai 1984/Bernett 1984
[UK/Canadian/French issue]
»Going For Gold« Powerstation 1985/Banzai 1985/Steamhammer 1985
[UK/Canadian/German issue]
»Shout It Out/Going For Gold« Powerstation 1985
[Cassette-only release with extra track]

Mini-LP's
»The Hour Of Thunder« Powerstation 1985

12" EP's
»Gimme Your Love« Powerstation 1985

7" Singles
»Gonna Make You Rock« Powerstation 1984
[UK issue, B-side "Snatch" comprises excerpts from »Shout It Out« LP]
»Gonna Make You Rock« Victoria 1984
[Spanish issue in different sleeve, B-side "Are You Ready"]
»The Game« Powerstation 1984

CD's
»Going For Gold« Steamhammer 1985
»Shout It Out« Powerstation 1986

Compilation Appearances
"No Foolin'" on »Wango Tango Vol.1« LP Bernett 1984
"Rock City" on »Axe« LP Banzai 1985
"The Game" on »Megalomania« LP Powerstation 1986

MAISON ROUGE

Paul Willis (v)
Philip Histon (g)
David Neal (b)
Greg Wall (d)

The NWOBHM explosion had well and truly evaporated by the time the little-known MAISON ROUGE began getting ideas about a self-financed release, although the fact that such small-time acts were still motivated to issue their own singles in the mid-80's suggests that the original *'do it yourself'* mentality continued to reverberate for quite some time afterwards. Recorded at the beginning of 1985, the quartet's introductory two-tracker turned out to be a somewhat quirky affair, with a peculiar mixture of styles and some off-the-wall lyrical sentiments coming into play at various stages. A-side "Questions" opens with a semi-folky intro with flutes and all sorts (very "Stairway To Heaven"), although the track itself is, in the main, a fairly substantial effort which, in addition to comparisons with semi-progressive acts such as AVALON and BACKLASH, also flirts with a markedly more rudimentary, DEDRINGER-style song construction at times. Prog-boogie, anyone? Fortunately, the light-hearted flipside is a considerably less perplexing composition, the preposterously-titled "The Devil Made Me Buy This Shirt" identifying itself as a more traditional heavy rocker with slight similarities to XERO or MASAI, although the unconventional structure is possibly more along the lines of a SWEET SAVAGE or RICOCHET offering.

All in all, it was an undeniably intriguing piece of post-NWOBHM experimentation (better than local rivals TITAN, that's for sure), although I suspect that the members of MAISON ROUGE were probably reassuringly realistic in terms of their chances of world domination. These lads were no doubt perfectly content to perform solely for the benefit of an appreciative provincial fan base, and I'm sure everyone enjoyed themselves immensely while it all lasted. It's pretty good-natured, and the humour also extends to the record's cartoon picture cover, featuring a particularly dilapidated dwelling. I'm not entirely sure where this mystery bunch were based, as they seem to be one of those fly-by-night acts who completely failed to make their presence known to the national rock press, although the fact that their two-tracker was recorded at Sheffield's non-illustrious Input Studios (where HAZE also laid down their debut single) tends to suggest a Yorkshire connection. None of the erstwhile members of MAISON ROUGE appear to have played a part in the fortunes of any other rock acts of note, however, and only a handful of copies of their single have surfaced in recent years, although it's not generally regarded as an outstandingly collectable item at the time of writing.

7" Singles
»Questions« Red Barn Records 1985

MALLET

Line-up unknown

Despite being issued at the height of the NWOBHM explosion, the unrenowned MALLET's one-off single only skirted around the very periphery of the genre, and was, quite evidently, aimed squarely at the nation's biker fraternity. Released on Merseyside's punk-dominated Rox label back in 1980, the two-tracker coupled a pair of well-worn r'n'b standards, namely "C.C. Rider" and "Route 66" (surely *'Route 666'* would have been considerably more metal), both of which were delivered with a fair degree of enthusiasm, but which ultimately failed to trouble any of the luminaries of the biker rock scene. It was very much along the lines of DUMPY'S RUSTY NUTS or EAZIE RYDER as opposed to SHADER or CENTURION, and the singalong, accessible nature of the songs (even featuring the dreaded saxophone) was surely seen as part of the record's charm. The single was issued in a highly predictable sleeve (a bike and a metal-looking logo), but it provided no information whatsoever (I'm sure it was deliberately vague) as to who might have been involved, and I wouldn't be surprised if the identity of MALLET concealed a one-off studio project rather than a proper touring band. Sales of the two-tracker can hardly have amounted to much in the first instance, though, rendering it a scarcely-sighted rarity these days, although the vast majority of collectors can safely live without a copy.

7" Singles
»C.C. Rider« Rox Records 1980

MAMA'S BOYS

John McManus (v,b)
Pat McManus (g)
Tommy McManus (d)

The colourful origins of Ireland's popular MAMA'S BOYS have been discussed with great alacrity by numerous journalists and music writers over the years, but I suppose it's quite understandable in the circumstances. Going back to the mid-70's, it all started when brothers Pat and John McManus (members of a large musical family, but not in the same league as the NOLANS) were encouraged by their well-meaning parents to take up some traditional Irish instruments (fiddle, pipes, bodhran *etc.*) and follow the well-worn path leading to the folk/celtic scene. The lads seemed quite happy to partake of the isle's rich musical heritage at first, but eventually began to rebel, turning to the devil's guitar to express their ideas more lucidly. By 1978, they were beginning to experiment with a sort of folk/rock crossover, although they remained slightly unsure as to where their allegiances truly lay. The critical point came when the pair attended a HORSLIPS (an act who combined a reasonably heavy rock style with a few traditional Irish influences) show at around the turn of the decade, which well and truly captured the energy and enthusiasm of rock music, conveniently showing them the way to go. With the duo roping in their youthful brother Tommy to act as a drummer, the threesome adopted the identity MAMA'S BOYS (which they may have been, but it wasn't exactly a rock'n'roll name) and began messing about by covering a selection of THIN LIZZY and BLACK SABBATH originals. When it came to penning their own compositions, however, the lads felt comfortable to include the odd reminder of their roots, with various quirky instrumental breaks forming part of their live appearances from an early stage. It wasn't long before the trio established a friendship with HORSLIPS themselves, leading to valuable touring experience and a management deal which helped to promote the developing band in their locality.

By 1980, the lads decided to spread their name by getting some product onto the market, electing to finance a vinyl release rather than the more conventional cassette offering, whereupon they captured an album's worth of their formative compositions in the studio and pressed up the rough'n'ready »Official Bootleg« long-player on the small-time Pussy label. Although the record had been intended predominantly as a promotional device, a fair old number were pressed, with quite a few getting into the shops, and the fans were soon snapping up any copies which appeared on the shelves of their local vinyl emporia. The early MAMA'S BOYS material was a self-assured amalgam of various influences, from heavy rock to boogie/blues, with the occasional glimpse of RORY GALLAGHER, THIN LIZZY or, at times, even a semi-folky interlude or undercurrent. Some of the tracks worked considerably more effectively than others, although MAMA'S BOYS managed to acquit themselves pretty well when they really hit their stride, and the trio quite happily found themselves inhabiting the sort of midtempo, semi-heavy NWOBHM style as purveyed by DEF LEPPARD and SAXON. Relatively few copies of the debut album made it to the mainland, however, and there was no particularly obvious way for the cash-strapped lads to fund their own tour of the UK, so it was back to the grind for the next year or two, with various singles (which have never really been documented with any great authority) escaping on several minor Irish labels (such as Pussy and Scoff) along the way. A useful break finally came towards the end of 1981, however, when the trio contrived to hitch a ride with HAWKWIND for their British tour, which took the youngsters to the mainland for the first time. It wasn't an astoundingly successful jaunt (HAWKWIND's support acts are notoriously poorly-received by their followers), but at least it allowed MAMA'S BOYS to introduce themselves.

It seems to have paid off, as the outfit were duly invited to supply a session for the 'Friday Rock Show' in the new year, although they chose to record the tracks in Ireland and ship the tape over rather than making an expensive trip to London merely for this purpose. Either way, the session (transmitted on the 19th of February 1982) proved to be a big hit with the listeners, who were treated to a quartet of strong numbers in the shape of "In The Heat Of The Night", "Straight Forward", "Runaway Dreams" and the poignant "Belfast City Blues". Within a matter of months, the lads had hooked up with WISHBONE ASH for another round of UK gigs, and subsequently inked a deal with Ultra Noise Records to ensure a British release for their next album. With the long-player being recorded a short time later, »Plug It In« appeared in due course, and the band's first *'proper'* album showed them to be coming along quite nicely, shining out on capable numbers such as the energetic "In The Heat Of The Night", "Reach For The Top" and "Runaway Dreams". The record proceeded to shift an extremely respectable number of units, and the lads soon saw »In The Heat Of The Night« and »Needle In The Groove« being trundled out as singles in a bid to rake in a bit more handy cash. Armed with their first royalty cheque, the jubilant MAMA'S BOYS made a brief sojourn to Europe, where they undertook a handful of select gigs at small clubs, wallowing in the warm reception they received during this early European exposure. After returning to their homeland, however, the trio gave serious consideration to the possibility of recruiting a dedicated frontman, and actually approached Dave King of local rivals STILWOOD to add his weight to the project. The frontman politely declined (he later got a better offer from FASTWAY), and the McManus brothers decided to continue as a three-piece concern, given that there was nothing fundamentally wrong with John's vocal prowess.

In 1983, MAMA'S BOYS finally realised they

had now hit the big-time when they were invited to open the proceedings on THIN LIZZY's farewell tours of the UK and Europe, a memorable and prestigious series of gigs which the lads undertook with immense enthusiasm. After recovering from their recent exertions, they managed to attract the attention of Spartan Records, who offered the trio a deal to handle their affairs for the next album. Work started within a matter of weeks, and MAMA'S BOYS soon had »Turn It Up« in the can, although it wasn't released straight away, for some reason. In fact, the lads were added to the bill of that year's Reading Festival while they were waiting for the new album to materialise, and their performance was sufficiently impressive to arouse the interest of various other record companies, several of whom wanted to snap up MAMA'S BOYS as soon as they were freed from their recently-signed contract with Spartan. They had to worry about the new album first, though, their attention turning to the promotion of »Turn It Up« when it hit the shops a couple of months later. The record saw a move towards markedly more commercial territory, but still contained a selection of pretty listenable material, notably raunchy efforts such as "Shake My Bones", "Gentleman Rogues" (interestingly, a track reworked by TOKYO BLADE during their rehearsal sessions, so it might not be completely out of order to point out the similarity between the latter's "Midnight Rendezvous" and the MAMA'S BOYS number "Late Night Rendezvous") and "Crazy Daisy's House Of Dreams". The band found a few new followers with their confident move into a more melodic style (they also undertook a productive headlining tour of medium-sized British venues to promote the release), and saw »Too Little Of You To Love« and »Midnight Promises« released as singles (the 12" pressing of »Too Little Of You To Love« was generously packaged with a truncated version of the »Official Bootleg« album) with considerable success.

MAMA'S BOYS enjoyed a remarkably brief relationship with Spartan, as they jumped ship as soon as their commitments to the label had been honoured, and swiftly signed to Jive, who (having disposed of the troublesome STARFIGHTERS) had been pursuing them since their triumphal appearance at Reading. Within an indecently short space of time, the trio delivered an eponymous long-player for the new label, although »Mama's Boys« was largely comprised of material from their previous two albums. In fact, "In The Heat Of The Night", "Straight Forward" and "Runaway Dreams" dated back to the »Plug It In« days, while "Midnight Promises", "Lonely Soul", "Crazy Daisy's House Of Dreams" and "Gentleman Rogues" had appeared on »Turn It Up« only a few months previously. It was all a bit disappointing for the fans, especially when there were only a couple of new recordings (one of which was a pointless cover of SLADE's "Mama Weer All Crazee Now", which formed the basis of an EP to promote the album) on display, but the record somehow seems to have shifted a reasonable number of copies, all the same. After a few gigs in the UK, the threesome jetted off to the States for their inaugural transatlantic gigs, where they played several shows with the likes of RATT and BON JOVI to get their name into the consciousness of North American rock fans. After completing their hectic schedule, however, it was back down to business once again, as MAMA'S BOYS were expected to deliver an album of novel material for Jive with minimal delay. After some frenzied studio activity in the early part of 1985, »Power And Passion« hit the shops, and showed a further move away from the heavier end of the market, with most of their newer compositions being based around a melodic rock framework with the occasional bit of keyboard backing (courtesy of producer Chris Tsangarides). Strangely, though, they were still recycling older numbers, which meant a third (!) outing for "Straight Forward" and a second sighting of "Needle In The Groove", which suggested either a lack of decent material or an inexplicable fondness for some of their original selections.

The album was a fairly well-received effort, nonetheless, slotting effortlessly into the kind of semi-AOR niche which was soon to become massively overpopulated by talentless copyists, although it was a fairly logical progression for MAMA'S BOYS, who had been gradually drifting into such tuneful waters as opposed to jumping on a convenient bandwagon at short notice. The lads toured the UK once again, re-releasing »Needle In The Groove« as a single to tie in with the album, before subsequently issuing an EP based around the unremarkable "Hard'n'Loud". Next up was an appearance on the 'E.C.T.' television programme, where the increasingly-popular outfit dutifully ran through versions of "Needle In The Groove" and "Power And Passion" for the benefit of the assembled masses. The group then enjoyed a high-profile appearance at the Knebworth Festival (alongside DEEP PURPLE), before touring the States once again, this time in the company of TWISTED SISTER and RUSH, before moving on to Japan for a brief jaunt with FOREIGNER. It was during this strenuous schedule, though, that the lads noticed a deterioration in young Tommy's health (the lad had been diagnosed with leukaemia at an early age but had been in remission for some time), whereupon the drummer was advised to take a break from the music business and undergo a course of medical treatment. The remaining duo drafted in Jimmy DeGrasso (of Y&T fame) to deputise for Tommy on their remaining live schedule (including some end-of-year dates supporting GARY MOORE in Europe), but the group was subsequently placed on hold while Tommy concentrated on getting better.

It had looked pretty ominous at the time, but 1986 saw a progressive improvement in the youngster's health, and the lads were soon making plans for a comeback. This time, however, they decided to go the whole hog and seek out a top-quality frontman, securing the services (after originally experimenting with one-time STEEL singer Rick Chase, later of GRAFFITI) of erstwhile AIRRACE vocalist Keith Murrell (who had earlier served time with MOONTIER and LIONHEART) before finally starting work on their long-awaited new album. There were a few suggestions that MAMA'S BOYS might even adopt an all-new identity at this point, but they had clearly grown fond of their infamously non-metal moniker, as Pat McManus himself commented: 'It's a crazy sort of name. It defies everything to do with heavy metal, and that's what we like about it. It contradicts everything. We don't want to be a DEATH anything, or an ANGEL anything or a BLOOD something.' (Ref: Metal Hammer Vol.2, No. 11, October 1987). The lads returned to the fore in the second half of 1987, unveiling their »Growing Up The Hard Way« LP to considerable critical acclaim and getting back into the swing of things by undertaking a few choice gigs (assisted by keyboard player Alan Nelson, a veteran of acts such as STRATUS and JAGGED EDGE) later in the year. The latest album represented a conscious migration into mainstream rock territory (Murrell's raunchy vocals lifting some of the more mediocre efforts quite effectively), with some of the band's most lightweight material thus far being laid out for inspection. Still, the record still featured some extremely well-crafted tracks, particularly the catchy "Waiting For A Miracle" and "Blacklisted", although their interpretation of STEVIE WONDER's "Higher Ground" (later covered by the nauseating RED HOT CHILI PEPPERS) might not have been such a great idea. Still, with favourable reviews and generous airplay coming their way, it seemed as though MAMA'S BOYS might be about to hit the big time at long last.

After a bit of further European touring in the spring of 1988, however, things began to fall apart quite badly, with Keith Murrell deciding that he didn't really want to be bothered with the touring activities of a semi-successful rock concern after all, whereupon the singer duly went off to get involved in stage musicals instead (as well as the PHENOMENA venture), leaving the McManus brothers at something of a loose end for the time being. Worse was to come when they parted company with Jive, although the lads continued to pen new material and send off demos to the influential labels, but the outfit quickly realised that they needed to find an equally-capable frontman to restore them to full strength. In 1989, they tried out local lad Connor McKeon, although the latter ultimately failed to make the grade after having been tested at some low-key Irish gigs. After a bit more searching, however, they finally got their man, when the little-known Mike Wilson joined up for action, and the lads were soon back in business with a very good chance of winning that elusive deal after all. Still, they kept an extraordinarily low profile for the best part of two years before finally getting back out on the road, but eventually resurfaced with a new long-player for Music For Nations. Surprisingly, however, it turned out to be a live affair, recorded on the most recent European tour with their latest frontman. »Live Tonite« was a slightly odd mixture of old, new and cover versions, but at least it proved that MAMA'S BOYS were still an active unit, even if the sales figures proved to be rather modest. After the usual round of touring towards the end of the year, the musicians began work on a proper full-length effort, but Music For Nations ultimately declined the offer to release it. Instead, 1992's chart-friendly »Relativity« escaped on the little-known CTM label, and, unfortunately, comparatively few fans were even aware that a new album had been released, with only a handful of journalists being lucky enough to obtain a copy for review purposes.

With the largely-overlooked »Relativity« having performed extremely poorly in terms of sales, things looked bleak for the band, although they put on a brave face and gigged sporadically for the next year or two, hoping to attract a bit of interest from some label or another. Eventually, however, their activities began to wind down again as Tommy began to succumb to another bout of serious ill-health. This time, however, there wasn't to be a happy ending, and the drummer passed away after contracting a life-threatening infection at the end of 1994. In the immediate aftermath of Tommy's death, his distraught brothers decided to quit the music business altogether, and the name of MAMA'S BOYS was soon being laid to rest as a mark of respect. However, Pat and John were eventually persuaded by friends and family that to abandon their beloved music would have been against their late brother's wishes, and so the duo subsequently started writing together once more. The mid-90's saw the pair forming a new act called CELTUS, a more reflective, emotionally-charged project with a strong inclination towards more traditional Irish music. With a couple of critically-acclaimed albums under their belts so far, it looks as though the McManus brothers will be on the music scene for several years to come.

LP's
»Official Bootleg« Pussy Records 1980
[Original issue with ten tracks]
»Plug It In« Pussy Records 1982
[Irish issue]
»Plug It In« Ultra Noise 1982
[UK issue in different sleeve]
»Plug It In« Line Records 198?
[Reissue on white vinyl with three extra tracks]
»Turn It Up« Spartan 1983
»Mama's Boys« Jive 1984
[UK issue]
»Mama's Boys« CBS Japan 1984
[Japanese issue]
»Power And Passion« Jive 1985
[Also issued as limited edition with free 12" picture disc featuring "One Last Chance" and interview]
»Plug It In« Castle Communications 1986
[Reissue in different sleeve]
»Growing Up The Hard Way« Jive 1987
»Live Tonite« Music For Nations 1991
[Live release]

12" EP's
»Needle In The Groove« Ultra Noise 1982
["Hard Headed Ways" non-LP]
»Too Little Of You To Love« Spartan 1983
[Also issued as limited edition with free eight track »Official Bootleg« LP]
»Midnight Promises« Spartan 1984
["High Energy Weekend" non-LP]
»Mama Weer All Crazee Now« Jive 1984
»Needle In The Groove« Jive 1985
["If The Kids Are United" non-LP]
»Hard'n'Loud« Jive 1985
["Without You" (live) non-LP, also features remixed version of "Lettin' Go"]
»Waiting For A Miracle« Jive 1987
["Lightning Strikes" non-LP]
»Higher Ground« Jive 1987

12" Singles
»One More Chance« Jive 1985
[Picture disc given free with some copies of »Power And Passion« album, A-side non-LP, B-side interview]

7" Singles
»Silence Is Out Of Fashion« Pussy Records 1980
»High Energy Weekend« Pussy Records 1980
[Both tracks non-LP]
»Telephone Teaser« Pussy Records 1982
»Belfast City Blues« Scoff Records 1982
»In The Heat Of The Night« Ultra Noise 1982
»Needle In The Groove« Ultra Noise 1982
[First issue, B-side "Hard Headed Ways"]
»Too Little Of You To Love« Spartan 1983
»Midnight Promises« Spartan 1984
»Mama Weer All Crazee Now« Jive 1984
[Also issued as limited edition in gatefold sleeve with free single]
»Mama Weer All Crazee Now« CBS Japan 1984
[Japanese issue in different sleeve]
»Needle In The Groove« Jive 1985
[Second issue, B-side "Don't Tell Mama"]
»Waiting For A Miracle« Jive 1987
[B-side "Lightning Strikes" non-LP, also issued as limited edition on red vinyl]
»Higher Ground« Jive 1987
[Also issued as limited edition in gatefold sleeve with free single]
»Higher Ground« Jive 1987
[Japanese issue in different sleeve]

Shaped Picture Discs
»Needle In The Groove« Jive 1985

Promotional Releases
»Lettin' Go« Virgin 1985
[Promo 6" flexi featuring 'speed remix', given free with 'Enfer' magazine]
»Three Track Flexi« Jive 1987
[7" flexi with excerpts from »Growing Up The Hard Way« LP, free with 'Kerrang' magazine, in picture cover]
»Waiting For A Miracle« Jive 1987
[Promo 12" single with long and short versions]

CD's
»Growing Up The Hard Way« Jive 1987
»Plug It In« Line Records 1988
[With three bonus tracks]
»Mama's Boys« Jive 198?
[UK issue]
»Mama's Boys« CBS Japan 198?
[Japanese issue]
»Power And Passion« Jive 198?

»Live Tonite« Music For Nations 1991
[Live release, with two bonus tracks]
»Relativity« CTM 1992
[With one bonus track]
»The Collection« Connoisseur Collection 2000
[Compilation release]

Mini-CD's
»Higher Ground« Jive 1987
»Laugh About It« CTM 1992

Compilation Appearances
"Straight Forward" on »Metal Treasures And Vinyl Heavies« LP Action Replay Records 1984
"Don't Tell Mama" on »Kerrang Kompilation« Do-LP EMI 1985
"In The Heat Of The Night" on »Metal Killers Kollection II« Do-LP Castle Communications 1986

MAMMATH

Tony Robson (v)
James Rees (g)
Bob Phillips (g)
Paul Kelly (b)
Kerry Loveluck (d)

The curiously-monikered MAMMATH (who shouldn't be confused with MAMMOTH, the *'we're fat and we don't give a toss'* unit from the late 80's), from Glamorgan, were undoubtedly one of Neat's more obscure and short-lived signings. They originally formed in the early months of 1984 (English import Tony Robson had previously worked with the version of STALLION who appeared on the »Metal Plated« compilation, while James Rees was apparently a veteran of the last CHINATOWN line-up), and soon came to the attention of the aforementioned label, for whom they demoed a few tracks ("Fool On The Run", "Rock Until You Drop" and "Are You Ready") at Impulse Studios. These initial efforts appear to have been rejected in their original form, although the outfit eventually recorded a two-tracker for Neat later in the year. With little or no fanfare, MAMMATH's »Rock Me« 7" (B-side "Rough'n'Ready", possibly a reworked "Are You Ready") was issued as part of a batch of more melodic efforts (along with product from EMERSON, SARACEN and VALHALLA), although the release failed to generate much interest among the record-buying public. It's easy to see why, to be honest, as both selections were fairly nondescript, anthemic rockers lying somewhere between SILVERWING and BADGER, with only a hint of the power and energy generated by fellow countrymen PERSIAN RISK and TOK-IO ROSE, for example. The messy production job didn't do them any favours either, and the group, having contrived to issue a single that appealed neither to the British nor overseas rock market of the period, were forced to have a bit of a rethink.

After playing a handful of shows with BRONZ towards the end of the year, the lads promoted themselves further by undertaking a couple of fairly extensive national tours in the early part of 1985 (bizarrely, some deluded individual even felt compelled to set up a MAMMATH fan club with both UK and European branches at around this time), and things seemed to be going reasonably well for the quintet at that stage. Even so, the musicians involved soon appeared to be suffering from something of a dramatic loss of confidence (Neat had offloaded them by this stage and nobody else really expressed much of an interest in sponsoring their future activities), after which the lads concluded that a period of

restructuring was a necessary evil, and so MAMMATH duly tried out a new vocalist (Ian Simmons) to see if this would get them back on track. Sadly, it didn't make a great deal of difference, and the major record companies continued to keep their distance, whereupon the dejected outfit ultimately decided to call it a day (Liverpudlian bassist Paul Kelly was the first to throw in his hand, and it looks as though the remaining members didn't really bother searching too hard for a replacement) within a remarkably short space of time.

After MAMMATH's demise, however, the majority (if not all) of its former members were soon able to find gainful employment in various other (mostly local) combos. Guitarist James Rees, for example, went on to join the up-and-coming PREYER, who released an EXCITER/JUDAS PRIEST-influenced LP of power metal on Ebony in 1986, while Bob Phillips and Ian Simmons proceeded to establish an ill-fated project of their own, which went by the identity of AIR-RADE. It also looks as though vocalist Tony Robson may have hooked up with the relatively obscure Yorkshire version of ROUGH JUSTICE (who won themselves a 'Friday Rock Show' session at one point), although it's entirely possible that this was just some other individual with an identical name. The intriguingly-named Kerry Loveluck, meanwhile, subsequently featured in the so-called *'supergroup'* ASHMATA (alongside the likes of STORMQUEEN's Paul Burnett) before going on to serve time as drummer in one of the later incarnations of RANKELSON, although they too were to give up the ghost towards the end of the decade. He also helped out on the MAD DOG single in 1985, incidentally, deputising for the unfortunate Viv Roberts, after the latter chose a particularly inopportune moment to break his leg.

7" Singles
»Rock Me« Neat 1984

MAMMOTH

Nicky Moore (v)
Kenny Cox (g)
John McCoy (b)
Vinnie Reed (d)

Behind the hefty name of MAMMOTH (not to be confused with the earlier Neat signings MAMMATH) lay a grand concept which was certainly stunning in its simplicity: assemble a collection of *'metabolically challenged'* (*i.e.* fat) stalwarts from the post-NWOBHM rock scene and create a brand new proposition to conquer the world. Heavy music by heavy musicians, you see. We laughed until our sides were sore. In all fairness, it was quite a novel gimmick (not a unique one though, as an outfit called GOLIATH later attempted to resurrect the idea in the 90's), albeit one lacking in terms of longevity. The project all started towards the end of 1986, when the heavyweight pairing of Nicky Moore (ex-SAMSON) and Kenny Cox (ex-MORE) got together with man-mountain bassist John McCoy of GILLAN (who had worked together with Moore on PAUL SAMSON's »Joint Forces« album a few months previously) and employed the services of a session drummer to record their first demo tape, showcasing the confrontational "Fatman", "All The Days" and "Dressed To Kill". The hefty trio then set about looking for a full-time fourth member and advertised for a skin-pounder through the pages of 'Kerrang'. The tone was set by their assurance that, although the ideal candidate would weigh in at more than twenty stone, they would *'accept anyone of eighteen stone if he is a top-class drummer.'* Very charitable, I'm sure. In the end, largely unknown quantity (and thoroughly nice bloke) 'Tubby' Vinnie Reed got the gig, and the quartet were soon in the studio recording in earnest, having wangled a deal with the Jive label in the interim.

By the time »Fatman« was released as their debut single in the summer of 1987, the outfit were already crediting Kenny Cox as a *'guest musician'*, alongside none other than Bernie Tormé (surely Gary Dallaway from the HANDSOME BEASTS would have been a more appropriate choice?), whose skinny frame must surely have breached the terms of MAMMOTH's contract in a major fashion. The lads were due to make their live debut at the Reading Festival a short time later, but eventually pulled out, quipping that the stage wasn't strong enough to hold them! It emerged in due course that Cox had been *'suspended'* from the outfit for having failed to pile on the pounds over the festive period (it's a good story, even if it's not strictly true), and the guitarist was ultimately replaced as a full-time member by Big Mac Baker, whose massive frame, er, *outweighed* the fact that he wasn't exactly a household name. After a high-profile live broadcast on BBC Radio towards the end of the year, two further single releases followed (the group employed occasional keyboard player Rob Fisher for some of their recording work, incidentally) in the form of »All The Days« and »Can't Take The Hurt«, the latter emerging towards the end of 1988 (let's face it, these guys weren't exactly prolific, but it's a miracle they could all fit in the studio at once), before a full-length eponymous effort finally (after a bit of last-minute remixing and some problems with the record label) made it into the shops a couple of months later.

»Mammoth« was a reasonable enough release, and featured a selection of tracks which, unsurprisingly, might not have been too dissimilar to the type of material that MORE would have been attempting (and which SAMSON certainly *were* attempting) by the second half of the 80's, had they managed to stay together. There was nothing outstandingly original, but it was high-calibre hard rock, if nothing else. Some of the more commercial numbers, such as "Bet You

Wish", failed to hit the mark at times, but it was still a considerably better debut than the cynics had predicted for this so-called *'novelty'* act. The album was, incidentally, promoted with a 'Friday Rock Show' session (broadcast on the 7th of April 1989, and featuring a second guitarist in the form of Colin Pincott, weight unknown) for their long-time advocate, Tommy Vance, which showcased "Long Time Coming", "Can't Take The Hurt", "Political Animal" and "Piggin' Out". In spite of some extremely charitable reviews, however, sales for the album were evidently pretty unspectacular, and the project finally elected to disband in mid-1990 (their last scheduled appearance was at the Mildenhall Festival in August of that year, but they didn't actually appear) in the wake of some lukewarm, sparsely-attended gigs around the country.

The trio of Moore, Cox and Baker eventually reunited in an obscure quintet called MORE'N'MORE, who also gained exposure *via* a helpful 'Friday Rock Show' session in 1991, before Moore went back to basics and started writing more bluesy material for his own enjoyment (which he still regularly plays to enthusiastic audiences throughout London). John McCoy, meanwhile, hooked up with Joey Belladonna from ANTHRAX in the short-lived BELLADONNA venture, but ultimately went back to doing his own thing. Vinnie Reed, incidentally, also dabbles in the music business to this day, and still hires out his services as a session drummer on occasion. Strangely, however, a release which was advertised as MAMMOTH's *'long-awaited second album'* appeared courtesy of new label Angel Air (see also the McCOY CD reissues, for example) a couple of years ago, although »XXXL« is basically a compilation of early material, alternate takes and the odd left-over song from the original recording sessions for the first album. As far as I'm aware, however, there wasn't (in spite of claims that it featured some brand-new numbers) another get-together of the musicians involved to record anything specifically for this CD-only release.

LP's
»Mammoth« Jive 1988

12" EP's
»Fatman« Jive 1987
[With remixed A-side, "Political Animal" non-LP]
»All The Days« Jive 1987
[Both "None But The Brave" and "Let Me Out" non-LP, also issued as extremely limited edition picture disc, possibly withdrawn]
»Can't Take The Hurt« Jive 1988
[Both "None But The Brave" and "Political Animal" non-LP]

7" Singles
»Fatman« Jive 1987
[B-side "Political Animal" non-LP]
»All The Days« Jive 1987
[B-side "Let Me Out" non-LP, also issued with limited edition poster sleeve]
»Can't Take The Hurt« Jive 1988
[B-side "None But The Brave" non-LP]

Promotional Releases
»Fatman/Bad Times« Jive 1987
[Split flexi given free with 'Metal Hammer' magazine, other track by SLAVE RAIDER]

CD's
»Mammoth« Jive 1988
»XXXL« Angel Air 1998
[Compilation of earlier material and unissued recordings]

Mini-CD's
»Fatman« Jive 1987

Compilation Appearances
"Fatman" on »Protect The Innocent« Do-LP/Do-CD Telstar 1989
"Bad Times" on »Pure Soft Metal« LP Stylus 1990
"Always And Forever" on »Angel Air Sampler« CD Angel Air 1998 + »The Gillan Family Album« CD Connoisseur 2000

MARIONETTE

Ray Zell (v)
Dave Veal (g)
Kevin 'KK' Matthew (b)
Adam 'Pig' Honey (d)

Although the UK's original glam/sleaze revival of the early 80's (as personified by the emergence of WRATHCHILD, ROX, SILVERWING *etc.*) had largely petered out by the mid-80's, there were always a few outfits who would try to keep the dwindling scene alive, particularly in London itself. One of the bands in question were the *'legendary'* (according to numerous tongue-in-cheek references in the pages of 'Kerrang') MARIONETTE, who first graced a stage in around 1982, sharing the limited sleaze market with a handful of like-minded hopefuls such as TARA ZARA, the IDLE FLOWERS, the GUNSLIN-

GERS and AUNT MAY, all of whom had, no doubt, originally been influenced by WRATHCHILD, HANOI ROCKS et al., but who were probably just as impressed with newer imports such as MÖTLEY CRÜE and their cohorts. In fact, the outfit claimed to have included HANOI ROCKS drummer Razzle among their alumni at one stage, and the glamsters were fortunate enough to be awarded a support slot with the ROCKS themselves on their UK tour of 1983. MARIONETTE were also given an early chance to display their wares on vinyl, and duly contributed "Too Far Gone" and "My Baby Sucks Real Bad" (count your blessings, sunshine) to Flicknife's largely-atrocious »Trash On Delivery« sampler of emergent sleaze hopefuls. It was, to be perfectly honest, nothing too out-of-the-ordinary, but it was an adequate enough way to start.

With the Heavy Metal label, meanwhile, having long since moved on from its rudimentary NWOBHM roots into the worlds of melodic rock and glam, MARIONETTE had arrived on the scene at just the right time to be featured on the latter's »Rock Pretty« sampler, a similarly-conceived release (featuring some of the label's new talent alongside some completely unknown hopefuls) which sold fairly dismally at the time. Nevertheless, a full album deal followed in due course, with the flamboyant »Blonde Secrets And Dark Bombshells« long-player hitting the shops (along with a 12" EP based around "On A Night Like This") in 1985. It was very much a raucous mixture of ramshackle rock'n'roll and snotty punk, a style which fundamentally distances MARIONETTE from the original NWOBHM orthodoxy, although they are a group whose inclusion here is justified entirely by their position (in the hypothetical 'NWOBHM family tree') as direct descendants of pioneers such as WRATHCHILD, THE BLITZ or even LEFT HAND DRIVE. Having said all this, the album appealed to relatively few metal aficionados back then, a situation which is more or less mirrored in the present collecting climate. Mind you, with the emergence of various retro-glam-punk (or whatever they call themselves) heroes such as BUCKCHERRY or the BACKYARD BABIES, maybe it's just a matter of time before the likes of MARIONETTE and VIRGIN STAR are held up as icons by some of today's metal fans…

Although MARIONETTE had, despite a few wild appearances in the capital in the previous couple of years (they occasionally utilised the services of a second guitarist named Tommy Dean), pretty much run out of steam as a semi-serious glam/sleaze proposition by 1986 (see also PET HATE, FORGER, PURPLE HAZE, the BABYSITTERS etc.), the odd reunion gig and jam session still took place later in the decade, when the lads would gleefully take to the stage with some of the more persevering and/or successful acts of the genre such as the DOGS D'AMOUR and the QUIREBOYS. In particular, this included a memorable event towards the end of 1988, when three of the original members (with journeyman drummer Mick Ransome standing in at short notice) had a much-publicised get-together in the capital. Guitarist Dave Veal later joined up with another group of sleazy hopefuls in the form of DANGEROUS TOYS (not to be confused with the WATCHTOWER offshoot of the same name), but ultimately failed to make much of an impression with any of his subsequent musical projects. Frontman Ray Zell, on the other hand, went on to draw lots of silly cartoons for 'Kerrang', and, thanks to his utterly merciless colleagues, has been forced to run the gauntlet of ridicule concerning his 'dodgy glam past' ever since.

LP's
»**Blonde Secrets And Dark Bombshells**«
Heavy Metal 1985

12" EP's
»**On A Night Like This**« FM Records 1985
["Little Johnny Rockstar" non-LP]

Compilation Appearances
"**My Baby Sucks Real Bad**" on »Trash On Delivery« LP Flicknife 1983
[Different to album version]
"**Too Far Gone**" on »Trash On Delivery« LP Flicknife 1983
[Different to album version]
"**Gettin' Sticky**" on »Rock Pretty« LP Heavy Metal 1984
"**You Better Believe It**" on »Rock Pretty« LP Heavy Metal 1984

MARQUIS DE SADE

Chris Gordelier (v)
Kevin Pope (g)
San Remo (g,k)
Pete Gordelier (b)
Gary Pope (d)

Not to be confused with an identically-named bunch who released the promisingly-titled (but apparently very poor indeed) »Crystal Grief« 7" in 1982, London's legendary MARQUIS DE SADE are another of those NWOBHM-era groups whose modern-day status as cult heroes has probably increased disproportionately in the years following their demise. There's nothing to suggest that this bunch were an overly-popular live act in the early 80's (although they did get out and about a fair deal), and their music is hardly archetypal, heads down NWOBHM, so what lies behind all this adulation? Hard to say, really, although their »Somewhere Up In The Mountains« single from 1981 is an extremely accomplished and well-produced piece of weighty prog/metal, although few aficionados had heard either track until the B-side ("Black Angel") turned up on the »NWOBHM Vol.4« bootleg in the early 90's. Actually the heavier number by far, "Black Angel" opens with an atmospheric keyboard intro and a heavy riff before Chris Gordelier's powerful, semi-operatic vocals appear, carrying the rest of the song admirably. There are a few technical twists and turns along the way, and the overall arrangement is undeniably original, particularly the mid-section, with the sound as a whole coming across as a combination of HELL, DAWNWATCHER and KRAKEN. After that, the A-side is a bit of a disappointment, being a somewhat mediocre semi-ballad with an attempt at an anthemic chorus, the largely nonsensical lyrics describing someone's ambition to go and live up a hill with their record collection and basically have a really mellow time, man. I can understand how London might have that sort of effect on people after a while.

Although MARQUIS DE SADE demoed a fair old bit of material, it wasn't widely circulated, and it's unlikely that most of us will ever get to hear unreleased compositions such as "Welcome To The Graveyard", "London Air" and "Living In The Ice Age", which is a real pity. The participants had probably gone their separate ways by the end of 1982, in good time for bassist Pete Gordelier to hook up with Kevin Heybourne, initially in the ill-starred BLIND FURY project and then in the mid-80's incarnation of ANGEL WITCH, where he happily remained until the end of the decade, although I'm led to believe that both he and his brother are now involved in running clubs as opposed to playing in them. As you're no doubt aware, the MARQUIS DE SADE single (issued in a rather functional picture sleeve with an insert featuring a group photo) is still regarded as one of the top-ranking NWOBHM rarities, with some collectors having paid an obscene amount of money for the slightly questionable privilege of owning a copy. Certainly, anyone who possesses the »NWOBHM Vol.4« CD has heard the stronger track already, and the A-side hardly justifies all that extra expenditure. To be honest, I'd resist temptation if I were in your shoes; spend the cash on a large household appliance or a holiday instead and you'll have a considerably better chance of maintaining domestic bliss.

7" Singles
»Somewhere Up In The Mountains« X-Pose Records 1981

Compilation Appearances
"Black Angel" on »NWOBHM Vol.4« Bootleg CD 1992

MARSEILLE

Paul Dale (v)
Neil Buchanan (g)
Andy Charters (g)
Steve Dinwoodie (b)
Keith Knowles (d)

Merseyside's popular MARSEILLE turned out to be a pretty prolific recording act once they finally got going properly, but they were actually old hands in the business by the time the NWOBHM thing really kicked off. There seems to be a fairly widely-held belief that the musicians were initially brought together to establish an outfit who would primarily be involved with composing music for film scores, but I suspect that comparatively little credence can be attached to such tales. In truth, the group was conceived in 1976 (emerging from the ashes of a schoolboy band rejoicing under the not-entirely-unique identity of AC/DC), and they did, admittedly, become associated with the French soundtrack company Varèse International the following year, supposedly having been commissioned to record some cheery songs for a ribald European film (which had, strangely enough, been completed a good two years previously) entitled 'The French Way'. In due course, the label threw together a seldom-seen 12" EP (housed within a very plain, stickered cover) featuring the title track (credited as "Do It The French Way"), "Not Tonight Josephine" and "She Gives Me Hell", three risqué rockers in the 70's-influenced style of PET HATE or URCHIN, with more than a hint of SLADE and the SMALL FACES to them. It wasn't NWOBHM by a long way, although the group would, like many others, be roped into the movement in years to come, more by serendipity than through playing any particularly strong role in its development.

In 1978, MARSEILLE (their debut was credited to MARSEILLES, although I suppose this might have been a mistake) were signed by the Mountain label (home of NAZARETH) after triumphing in a national talent contest, and so the lads were soon being groomed for promotion as the next big thing in the rock world. A couple of singles (»The French Way« and »Kiss Like Rock & Roll«) were duly trotted out as a taster for their forthcoming debut album, as was a limited white-label promo 12" which served to introduce the group to the DJ's and journalists of the day. The band were encouraged, supposedly by their label and management, to deliver a long-player in the general manner of their formative releases (Mountain tended not to acknowledge the existence of their debut 12", and pretty much presented themselves as their first label), although MARSEILLE were now tending to write somewhat heavier compositions with far less juvenile lyrics, and reports of their powerful live performances (supporting the likes of WISHBONE ASH, UFO and GILLAN) had already begun filtering down to a rapidly-expanding fan base. Nevertheless, the debut album (»Red, White And Slightly Blue«) was recorded and pressed up in due course, although the lads were less-than-satisfied with the outcome, and few copies actually made it into the shops as a result, as Paul Dale explained: 'We also had a bit of bad luck in a couple of studio sessions that we did. We made an album which was produced by Leo Lyons but it was so terrible that we scrapped it.' (Ref: Teenage Depression, Issue 10, 1979).

Now, withdrawing your first album is hardly the ideal way to kick off a career, but things weren't actually as bad as they originally seemed. In fact, the outfit wasted little time before attempting to salvage the situation, and were soon back in the studio to record an 'official' debut long-player. Sessions for MARSEILLE's first proper LP began in the early months of 1979, and the group hoped to have a finished product by the time they went on tour with JUDAS PRIEST, although things took considerably longer than they anticipated, and it was much later in the year before the eponymous long-player was ready to hit the shops. The release tied in with yet another series of gigs, a support slot with WHITESNAKE, and this novel collection of songs proved to be considerably more representative of the band's style. The album (many copies of which were, incidentally, presented with a free copy of the otherwise-unavailable »Red, White And Slightly Blue« set) saw MARSEILLE moving into more substantial territory, with some distinct similarities to the melodic rock/metal disposition of MOTHER'S RUIN, FRENZY and TOBRUK, and the record was soon selling in healthy quantities throughout the land. Tracks such as "Rock You Tonight", "Some Like It Hot" and "Armed And Ready" showed a confident move in the right direction, and the LP was promoted by further 7" releases in the shape of »Bring On The Dancing Girls« and »Over And Over«, both of which helped their cause by performing admirably throughout Europe.

Things now seemed to be going fairly well for MARSEILLE, and, after a further single (based around the offbeat "Kites", by SIMON DUPREE AND THE BIG SOUND) in the early months of 1980, their label finally stumped up the readies for an extensive tour of the States with BLACKFOOT and labelmates NAZARETH. Although the jaunt went swimmingly, however, the lads arrived back home to discover that Mountain Records had gone into liquidation while they were away! Needless to say, their already-made plans to record a further LP were immediately laid to waste; not only that, their equipment remained stranded in America and the musicians were unable to retrieve it, so this unfortunate chain of events was to prevent the band members from undertaking any further musical activities for a considerable time. In the event, they gradually drifted apart and began working with other local outfits (most notably, their vocalist established his own venture, the PAUL DALE BAND), although there was never a point at which MARSEILLE officially disbanded. By early 1982, however, it appeared that their financial and personal situations had now improved significantly, and the majority of the original members decided to have another crack at the big time. Neil Buchanan, Keith Knowles and Steve Dinwoodie drafted in new guitarist Mark Hay, and completed the line-up with vocalist Sav Pearse, formerly with local hopefuls SAVAGE LUCY. In due course, they hooked up with a different management company, and soon began to get their career back on track.

After getting back into the swing of things with some low-key gigs and a brand-new demo (featuring a selection of never-released material such as "Raise Hell", "Yesterday's Hero" and the unfeasibly superb "CC Riders", the latter illustrating a new-found ability to rock it up in best BLACK AXE or CRUCIFIXION fashion), MARSEILLE were scheduled to make their vinyl comeback with a much-heralded three track EP, due to be released in the early months of 1983 on Next Records, a label owned (conveniently enough) by their recently-acquired manager. The tracks selected for inclusion were the all-new "Till It's Gone", "Open Fire" and "We Got Rock'n'Roll", although, strangely enough, this release never actually came to fruition. In the long term, the outfit decided to hold out for a better deal, and the much-anticipated offer (from Ultra Noise) finally came their way in the early months of 1984, by which time Mark Hay had handed in his notice and been swiftly replaced by another former SAVAGE LUCY member, Mark Railton. Even before the group were able to start work on their comeback album, however, the ambitious Neil Buchanan had also flown the coop in order to move into television work (he's still there, incidentally, presenting a popular TV show for kids called 'Art Attack'), after which the MARSEILLE lads elected to continue as a slimmed-down quartet rather than waste any further time looking for a suitable replacement.

Their new album (»Touch The Night«) appeared a few months later, and saw the revived outfit operating in a highly competent and polished style of melodic rock, evoking comparisons with the likes of CHROME MOLLY, DEF LEPPARD and ALKATRAZZ, some stand-out tracks including excellent opener "Crazy", "After The Fall" and "Open Fire". Sadly, though, when it came to choosing a single to promote the release, Ultra Noise plumped for one of the album's weaker cuts, "Walking On A High Wire", and it failed to storm the charts in the manner they had anticipated. Within a fairly short space of time, therefore, MARSEILLE (who had recruited second guitarist Toby Martin before the end of the year) were released from contract (Ultra Noise actually went into liquidation in the spring of 1985) and vocalist Sav Pearse soon deserted the sinking ship, hooking up with Dutch act HIGHWAY CHILE for a short time. Although the remaining four members initially believed that they would be able to carry on without their departed frontman (they toyed with the notion of adopting a new identity and reinventing themselves as a musically-different proposition), the lads soon lost the will to continue, and MARSEILLE, having suffered more than their fair share of misfortune and disappointment over the years, finally called it a day for good, with none of the former members (with the exception of Toby Martin, who went on to join SHOGUN) making a significant further impression on Britain's rock scene at any stage thereafter.

LP's
»Red, White And Slightly Blue« Mountain Records 1978
[Very few copies issued in their own right, most given free with »Marseille« LP]
»Marseille« Mountain Records 1979
[Many sold with complementary copy of un-issued debut album]
»Touch The Night« Ultra Noise 1984

12" EP's
»Do It The French Way« Varèse International 1977
[Credited to MARSEILLES, all three tracks different to album versions]

7" EP's
»Over And Over« Mountain Records 1979
["Over And Over" and "Can Can" different to album versions]

7" Singles
»The French Way« Mountain Records 1978
[A-side different to album version, B-side "Cold Steel" non-LP]
»Kiss Like Rock & Roll« Mountain Records 1978
[A-side non-LP]
»Bring On The Dancing Girls« Mountain Records 1979
[Both tracks different to album versions]
»Kites« Mountain Records 1980
[A-side non-LP, B-side "Some Like It Hot" different to album version]
»Walking On A High Wire« Ultra Noise 1984
[A-side different to album version, also released as limited edition on silver vinyl]

Promotional Releases
»Special Sampler« Mountain Records 1978
[Four track white label 12" with stickered sleeve]

Compilation Appearances
"Walking On A High Wire" on »The Best Of British« LP Zebra 1985
"Gatecrashin'" on »Metallergy« LP Bandit Records 1985
"Open Fire" on »Metal Concussion« LP Bandit Records 1986

MARZ

Steve Farmer (v)
Dave Lamond (g)
Mark Lindley (g)
Russ Clough (b)

Ian Padgett (d)

As with so many minor NWOBHM outfits, comparatively few people had any knowledge of MARZ, a relatively obscure five-piece from Lincolnshire, until one of their early tracks was plundered for use on the infamous Japanese series of bootleg CD's in the early 90's. The band's one and only vinyl release, the privately-

issued »Lady Of The Night« EP from 1980, was originally pressed in very limited quantities indeed, and a minimal number of copies have been offered for sale in the years since the act finally called it a day. The quintet's music itself was fairly memorable, mid-paced rock/metal in the general manner of SOLDIER or TRESPASS, nothing spectacularly heavy or original, admittedly, but their one-off release showcases a competently-performed selection of NWOBHM, all the same. The title track is certainly the strongest MARZ composition to have been committed to vinyl, since both "On The Road To Freedom" and "Daydreamer" were, in comparison, a bit too pedestrian and unhurried for their own good. By all accounts, though, the record proved to be a fairly popular purchase among local rock fans of the period, and MARZ were soon developing a small-but-solid following throughout the East Midlands and its environs.

Within a year, however, talented vocalist Steve Farmer and drummer Ian Padgett were to be found lending their services to OVERDRIVE (see separate entry), another bunch of hopefuls from the same locality. The latter (considerably heavier) ensemble were already an established concern, and it transpires that the aforementioned duo were recruited by this outfit to replace some recently-departed members. Despite this undeniably cruel blow to the emerging MARZ, however, it would appear that the remaining characters soldiered on for a year or two with an alternate line-up (one of their roadies, a chap called 'Mole', subsequently made a stint at the mike stand, but I'm not sure who the replacement sticksman was), although the outfit ultimately failed to achieve any particular level of success in this later incarnation. By the early 90's, though, the ex-members eventually cottoned on to the fact that their long-forgotten EP (issued in an eye-catching, monochrome sleeve depicting a guitar-playing alien) was fetching silly prices (given that only a couple of examples had come out of the woodwork at the time), and, after selling their own spare copies, shamelessly harassed various ex-friends and roadies to part with the treasured 'gifts' they had once been given, purely in the interests of making a bit of ready cash from the NWOBHM fraternity. Absolutely disgraceful behaviour...

7" EP's
»Lady Of The Night« Frozen Owl Records 1980

Compilation Appearances
"Lady Of The Night" on »NWOBHM Vol.8« Bootleg CD 1996

MASAI

Clyde Ward (v,b)
Ben King (g)
Anthony Marchi (g)
Chris Pope (d)

Hmmm, it looks as though we've got another one of those spooky, unexplained name-change scenarios going on here, given that the reasonably familiar Hampshire rock hopefuls MASAI share at least three of their members with the rather more esoteric CAGEY BEE (see separate entry). In all likelihood, the two outfits were probably identical in terms of personnel, although you can never be completely sure about these things; it could theoretically be an APOCALYPSE-style 'let's ditch the crap drummer and reinvent ourselves' deal, but I seriously doubt it in this case. Whatever the story, it looks as though the ensemble's original CAGEY BEE identity had been laid to rest by around 1980, with MASAI taking over almost immediately, whereupon they set about having a proper stab at finding fame and fortune under their novel guise. Indeed, the *'new'* outfit (who, somewhat contentiously, claimed in their biography to have been voted the *'most popular Southern band'* in 1981, something which CHINATOWN would surely have been intrigued to discover) proceeded to enjoy a reasonable amount of commercial success and recognition after being snapped up by the small-time Turbo label a year or so later.

MASAI debuted with a full-length effort, which came in the shape of their »Good Boys Never Grumble« LP (the cover of which shows the lads looking a right bunch of pillocks in safari suits and pith helmets), recorded at Arny's Shack Studios in Poole at some point during 1982. The long-player contains a selection of tuneful, raunchy rockers, around half of which are in CAGEY BEE's more lightweight style (indeed, two tracks from their original EP are also included here), vaguely reminiscent of GRAND PRIX, TRADER or SINGAPORE. However, compositions such as "Nightmare", "Born Loser", "Thunder In The Sun" and "Lorelei" are markedly heavier, bringing to mind certain THIN LIZZY-influenced outfits of the time such as AURORA or ENERGY. To coincide with the LP's release, a single was also issued, the latter coupling "Stranger To Myself" (one of the more blatantly commercial cuts) with the non-LP "Lightning", a catchy, SPIDER-style singalong. It doesn't seem to have helped their cause, unfortunately, and the quartet appear to have gone into voluntary liquidation without releasing any further product under the MASAI name.

Although both the album and single (issued in virtually identical sleeves) are relatively scarce items nowadays, neither seem to be particularly sought-after by the majority of NWOBHM collectors. Mind you, I'd still rate »Good Boys Never Grumble« as a considerably superior purchase to WARRIOR's extortionately-priced »Troublemaker«, for example. After the commercial failure of the MASAI LP, the persevering group subsequently (presumably having listened to rather a lot of U2 and SIMPLE MINDS records in the interim) evolved into an even more obscure and overlooked proposition called THE STORM (nothing to do with the identically-named JOURNEY offshoot) a year or two later, this being more of a mainstream pop/rock venture in the RADIO MOSCOW vein. However, after just one release, the little-known »Malice In Wonderland« 12" in 1985, this project also seems to have fallen to pieces. End of story?

LP's
»**Good Boys Never Grumble**« Turbo Records 1982

7" Singles
»**Stranger To Myself**« Turbo Records 1982
[B-side "Lightning" non-LP]

MASS

Phil Harvey (v)
Mark Lathan (g)
Dave Steiman (g)
John Cunningham (b)
Mark Hall (k)
Mike King (d)

After parting company with Cleveland's talented AXIS following his appearance on the latter's »Lady« single in 1980, bassist John Cunningham's first port of call was local melodic hopefuls MASS (an identity shared with a couple of indie acts in the UK, and one or two metal outfits elsewhere), another sextet with a few decent tunes in their repertoire. Mind you, it's reasonable to say that MASS were slightly less ambitious in their overall approach, and seemed content to purvey an accessible brand of Americanised rock, as evidenced on their debut two-tracker from 1982. The self-financed effort coupled "Rebel With A Cause" and "Running From The Morning", a pair of tuneful selections which showed the ensemble to be perfectly capable of emulating major-label talent such as GRAND PRIX and STAMPEDE. It was a capable and classy way to kick off their career, and the single (which doesn't appear to have been issued in a picture sleeve) soon won a few friends at the likes of 'Kerrang', who identified MASS as worthy of attention. After that, it was presumably back to the regional club circuit while the participants waited for a few influential labels to make enquiries.

Sadly, however, it looks as though the hapless group were yet another of those outfits who were left on the shelf (see also contemporaries such as MEANSTREAK and V8, for example) when the record companies came scouting around for new talent, and the lads never really managed to capitalise on the warm reception afforded to their first slice of vinyl. Still, they kept things going for a while, becoming a semi-popular attraction throughout the North East, although they ultimately reinvented themselves as CHASE (an identity which was shared by even more outfits than their original choice) in around 1984, which pretty much involved slimming down to a more manageable quintet (Dave Steiman got the push) and recruiting new drummer Gary Hunt. The revamped group eventually won themselves a session for 'Into The Music' (the more melodic 'Friday Rock Show' offshoot) at the beginning of 1985, where the ensemble showcased unfamiliar material such as "Lies", "Stand Your Sins" and "Lost In Love", in addition to a reworked "Rebel With A Cause". It would appear, however, that this was very much a last-ditch attempt for these musicians to get themselves recognised in the rock world, after which CHASE ground to a halt within a matter of months. The protagonists all pretty much drifted away from the scene thereafter (a couple of them have actually shuffled off their mortal coils since then), leaving only a semi-collectable vinyl souvenir of their NWOBHM-period exploits.

7" Singles
»Rebel With A Cause« SRT 1982

MASTERSTROKE

Tomlinson
McMurray
McFarnell

It's somewhat ironic (and not a little irritating) that some of the most enjoyable NWOBHM releases are so utterly sparse in terms of useful information, and MASTERSTROKE's extraordinarily obscure »Prisoner Of Love« single is yet another example which fits that description admirably. This undated piece of vinyl contains two genuinely excellent examples of prime-era NWOBHM, very much in the forceful manner of DRIVESHAFT, SWEET SAVAGE or TRIDENT, with the energetic "Burning Heart", on the reverse, being a slightly more rocking number than the rather melodic (but still powerful) A-side. Issued without the extravagance of a picture sleeve and with virtually no information on the labels themselves (which are, strangely enough, completely different colours on each side), we're left with no option but to speculate wildly as to the origins of this curio. Given the very strong similarities (particularly in the vocal department) to DRIVESHAFT and SWEET SAVAGE, however, I wouldn't be remotely surprised if this bunch were Irish, and the writing credits seem to lend further weight to this hypothesis. As to the likely date of issue, your guess is as good as mine, although I wouldn't have thought (since DTS Records appear to have been operational since around the late 70's, sponsoring prog-flavoured singles by the equally-obscure WEATHER MAN, for instance) that 1981 or thereabouts would be a particularly rash estimate. Has the name of MASTERSTROKE jogged a few memories out there? If so, kindly enlighten us!

7" Singles
»Prisoner Of Love« DTS Records 198?

MAYDAY

Martin Smith (v)
Steve Warr (g)
Rob Ostler (b)
David Kovacevic (k)
Mick Burns (d)

Formed at some point in the late 70's, MAYDAY (not to be confused with the tuneful Americans who were signed to the A&M label at more or less the same time) were a comparatively mundane Midlands group who, despite their youthful naivety and relatively meagre experience in terms of studio recordings and live work, somehow managed to wangle a handy deal with Reddingtons Rare Records, a popular music shop in Birmingham who also ran their own label (home to PARALEX and, briefly, QUARTZ). A couple of tracks were captured on tape soon afterwards, and the »Day After Day« single (produced by Mick Hopkins of the aforementioned QUARTZ) hit the streets in due course. Certainly looking quite a peculiar bunch on the picture sleeve, the quintet offered a curious mixture of lightweight rock and mainstream material, with some unashamedly poppy keyboards underpinning the whole thing. Overall, this 7" doesn't quite know whether it wants to be accessible rock in the general style of TOTO or REO SPEEDWAGON, or something altogether more progressive along the lines of WHITE SPIRIT. Very confusing, really, and the excessively prominent keyboards (combined with practically inaudible guitars) suggest that the final mix may have been slightly botched. Still, enough units were shifted to make all the effort worthwhile, but it failed to propel MAYDAY into the realms of stardom.

The outfit also featured on the seldom-seen »Brum Beats« double LP, recorded as a souvenir of a week-long series of gigs promoting Midlands bands at Birmingham's Barrel Organ venue in June 1980. With the tracks "Moving In Time" and "Standing On The Edge Of The World" being taken from a set which also included the likes of "Love In The Spaceage" (the single's B-side) and "Out Of Reach", the MAYDAY lads managed to come across in a somewhat better light on this occasion. Happily, the keyboards were no longer the prime focus of attention, allowing the ensemble (who now featured Dave Silburn on guitar and Paul Hedges on drums) to cultivate a sound rather more in touch with contemporaries such as CHEMICAL ALICE. It was a move in the right direction, but it seems not to have saved the outfit from their inevitable fate, unfortunately. Although the compilation's sleeve notes suggested that the lads had already developed a strong local following by this juncture, it seems that they ultimately drifted apart (they were still playing live in the Midlands in 1981, though) without issuing any additional material. You might like to know that the Reddingtons shop exists to this day, and they'll be delighted to furnish you with one of the many unsold MAYDAY singles at a very reasonable price. Don't bother asking about PARALEX EP's, though, they're all *long* gone!

7" Singles
»Day After Day« Reddingtons Rare Records 1980

Exclusive Compilation Appearances
"Moving In Time" (live) on »Brum Beats-Live At The Barrel Organ« Do-LP Big Bear Records 1980
"Standing On The Edge Of The World" (live) on »Brum Beats-Live At The Barrel Organ« Do-LP Big Bear Records 1980

MAYHEM

Mick McGee (v)
Chris Hind (v,g)
Dead Cat (b)
Collo (d)

In the post-NWOBHM fallout of the mid-80's, some rather peculiar things were happening. Bands who had once adhered to the early 80's archetype were trying to move into more commercial waters, while various peripheral hard rock outfits were trying to regain their own sense of identity, having ridden on the coat-tails of the new metal explosion for several years. Strangest of all, though, certain punk groups, who were now in danger of falling into total anonymity, attempted to kick-start their careers by forming a rather tenuous affiliation with the metal scene. While the various members of WARFARE (most of whom had had a bit of a punky backgro-

und) managed this manoeuvre with enviable aptitude, the likes of London's ONSLAUGHT and THE BLOOD fared less well, as did Merseyside's MAYHEM, a rather fractious and politically-motivated outfit (not to be confused with some, er, *infamous* projects from overseas) who had originally recorded for the influential Riot City label in the early 80's. By 1985, however, they had come to the conclusion that their brand of noisy, high-speed, MOTÖRHEAD-style aggression might equally be acceptable to a significant proportion of metalheads, whereupon the quartet duly set about repromoting themselves with a new offering entitled »Bloodrush«, commonly only seen as a 12" EP (with a suitably lurid, metal-looking sleeve), although some 7" copies were also pressed up as promotional devices.

Featuring three tracks recorded in Manchester between 1983 and 1984, the MAYHEM EP is a heavy slice of vinyl, complete with a snotty vocal performance, interesting sound effects and pretty good guitar work, and each of the numbers featured ("Bloodrush", "Addictive Risk" and "I Defy (Part 1)", the latter omitted on the 7" version) are all sufficiently competent to appeal to fans of noisy metal outfits such as WARFARE (or even mid-period VENOM), for example. Mind you, this may not have been MAYHEM's original intention at all, and it's equally possible that they might have been attempting to associate themselves with some of the heavier punk/sleaze outfits who were breaking through at the time. Either way, their strategy doesn't seem to have gone according to plan, leaving the musicians to go back into hiding shortly thereafter, although at least one of them (the ludicrously-named Dead Cat) resurfaced when local punk legends BLITZKRIEG had one last crack at grabbing a modicum of notoriety towards the end of the decade. In truth, however, MAYHEM's *'reconstructed'* metal sound wasn't a million miles from their early 80's roots: if you particularly enjoy »Bloodrush«, therefore, it might be even be worth looking through the punk sections on occasion to see if you can pick up one or two of those Riot City releases (such as »Gentle Murder«, for example) at a reasonable price.

12" EP's
»Bloodrush« Vigillante Records 1985

7" Singles
»Bloodrush« Vigillante Records 1985
[Limited quantities circulated, issued with different sleeve design]

McCOY

Tony 'T-Bone' Rees (v)
Steve Linton (g)
John McCoy (b)
Colin Towns (k)
Liam Genockey (d)

The imposing figure of John McCoy had played a pivotal role in the fortunes of the extremely successful GILLAN (among various other more fleeting appearances elsewhere) for several years before the much-loved group eventually foundered towards the end of 1982, and the colossal bassist subsequently wasted little time in getting his own, eponymous outfit off the ground. He had, in the past, exerted a direct musical influence throughout the early days of SAMSON's career, co-writing the majority of the material on their »Survivors« debut set with mainman Paul Samson (a long-time acquaintance from the SCRAPYARD days of the mid-70's, and a colleague from the pre-SAMSON version of McCOY) and producing their first two singles (as well as various other vinyl releases of the period), even going so far as to contribute bass parts to "Telephone" and "Drivin' Music". As a result, his connections with SAMSON (and, of course, GILLAN), would come in particularly useful when he got around to establishing and developing his own outfits in years to come.

Centred around the writing talents of the bassist himself, the (revived) McCOY project also featured two of his erstwhile colleagues from GILLAN, namely keyboard player Colin Towns (yet another musician who had contributed to SAMSON's debut, and also a successful solo artist in his own right) and session drummer Liam Genockey. Completing the line-up in the first instance were relative unknowns Steve Linton (formerly of the imaginatively-named STEVE LINTON BAND) on guitar and the implausibly-named T-Bone Rees at the microphone. A three-track demo tape, featuring "Night Lights", "Because You Lied" and a cover of FLEETWOOD MAC's "Oh Well" (earlier reworked by NO FAITH), soon won the ensemble a deal with the influential Legacy label, and it wasn't too long before a glut of vinyl product started hitting the shops. As well as an eponymous mini-LP (featuring an utterly interminable take of the aforementioned "Oh Well"), the group saw fit to release two singles (both of which had escaped by the early months of 1984) to promote themselves further, so the public were given ample opportunity to voice their opinion on the music of McCOY. In fact, it was hardly a surprising revelation that the prolific quintet were content to operate in a style not a million miles away from the early, blues-infused, raunchy material of SAMSON's debut long-player, although, when the lads really cranked up the power (on tracks like "Night Lights" and "The Sound Of Thunder"), the McCOY mentality was even occasionally reminiscent of MORE or the HANDSOME BEASTS.

Mind you, the SAMSON influence was to become even more blatant when Paul Samson himself (who had, in fact, helped out on some of the earlier studio sessions) was drafted in to provide a few overdubs on the first full McCOY album, the »Think Hard« effort for the Mausoleum concern. The axeman certainly stamped his mark on the project from the outset, and some freshly-penned raunchy rockers were soon being captured for posterity. Much of the blues-tinged material laid down at this stage may have been regarded as having very little in common with the revolutionary spirit of the NWOBHM in its original form, but, even so, McCOY's musical attitude and direction was undeniably commensurate with the type of material that the likes of SAMSON and SCORCHED EARTH were attempting at around the same time. The new LP constituted another varied selection, and benefitted from the inclusion of such contrasting efforts as the energetic opener "Freemind" and the epic, anthemic "Jerusalem". Still, the majority of reviews were lukewarm, and it soon became apparent that the album wasn't going to break too many sales records, but it no doubt went down a treat with a percentage of the nation's traditional rock fans. Paul Samson's involvement with the McCOY venture became even more committed as time progressed (his own band having now been placed on hold for an unspecified period), and, with both Steve Linton and Liam Genockey having moved on to other projects by this time, the act soon became critically dependent on both the guitarist and one-time IRON MAIDEN/ELECTRIC GYPSIES drummer Ron Rebel (who had also helped on the »Think Hard« sessions), particularly when it came to live appearances.

Nevertheless, Paul Samson eventually got itchy feet (or fingers, perhaps) and once again went off to do his own thing (the »Joint Forces« album, in the first instance) at some point in the early months of 1985, after which Mark Keen from THE GRIP was brought in to take his place in the live environment. The fortunes of McCOY tended to fluctuate thereafter (they don't appear to have received much in the way of radio exposure, for example, although their gigs were evidently well-attended affairs on the whole), and further personnel instability was to manifest itself when vocalist T-Bone Rees decided to move on to pastures new at relatively short notice. Undeterred, John McCoy merely made a few phone calls, and a new singer was rapidly located in the capable form of the little-known Nikki Brooks, who was soon experiencing a fairly high-profile debut when McCOY were invited to appear on the infamous 'E.C.T.' television show a short time later. The revamped outfit duly took the opportunity to showcase powerful versions of "You're Mine" and "Ride The Night" to a national audience, and it looked likely that they would soon be announcing plans for further vinyl releases. Strangely, however, the name of McCOY rapidly disappeared from the pages of the rock press (the talented Nikki Brooks swiftly found a new role in the WILD! project, incidentally), suggesting that the revised line-up must have run into serious problems of one kind or another within a remarkably short timescale. In fact, it would appear that the original incarnation of McCOY had already ceased to exist by the beginning of 1986.

Even so, John McCoy subsequently contrived to keep the SAMSON connection going strong, as he swiftly teamed up with the latter's Nicky Moore (who had, in his time, also fronted his own eponymous project, an act who recorded for the small Street Tunes label) to establish the semi-serious MAMMOTH (see separate entry) entity, the central duo recruiting various other, er, 'carefully selected' musicians along the way. More recently, however, the McCOY name has been resurrected thanks to the Angel Air label, who have not only reissued the group's debut album and mini-LP on one CD, but have also allowed the man to oversee the release of (supposedly) a brand-new collection entitled »Brainstorm«, on which the bassist was ably assisted by experienced Yank session men Al Romano (v,g) and Mike Sciotto (d), a pair best known for their work with SUN RED SUN and FROM THE FIRE, respectively. In fact, I reckon this material was recorded in the States in the early 90's (and not, in the first instance, as a genuine follow-up to the original batch of McCOY releases), when the threesome played together in the short-lived BELLADONNA venture (formed by erstwhile ANTHRAX vocalist Joey Belladonna) and also recorded an album of their own entitled »Disillusioned«, which should have surfaced under the identity of the HEAVY METAL COWBOYS as long ago as 1993. An archive McCOY live set (recorded by the original version of the band in the heady days of 1977) has latterly been exhumed by Angel Air (several of the featured tracks would later show up on the first SAMSON album), meaning that three releases credited to McCOY (each featuring entirely different bands!) are now on the market, and it's additionally worth mentioning that some of John McCoy's work has also been featured as incidental music on various television shows in recent years, so you can't say he's taking things easy in his old age…

LP's
»**Think Hard**« Mausoleum 1985
[Cassette version features two extra tracks]

Mini-LP's
»**McCoy**« Legacy 1983

7" Singles
»**Oh Well**« Legacy 1983
[A-side different to version on mini-LP]
»**The Sound Of Thunder**« Legacy 1984

CD's
»**Think Hard Again**« Angel Air 1997
[Combined reissue of »Think Hard« and »McCoy« mini-album, with two extra tracks]
»**Brainstorm**« Angel Air 1998
[Features unissued studio material from early 90's]
»**Live 1977**« Angel Air 2000
[Live release from original incarnation of McCOY]

Compilation Appearances
"**Because You Lied**" on »Kiss Yer Skull Goodbye« LP Conifer Records 1987
"**Temporary Threshold Shift**" on »Kiss Yer Skull Goodbye« LP Conifer Records 1987
"**The Demon Rose**" on »Angel Air Sampler« CD Angel Air 1998
"**Heavy Metal Cowboy**" on »The Gillan Family Album« CD Connoisseur 2000

MEANSTREAK

Mark Hopkins (v)
Tony Lee (g)
Dave Williams (g)
Steve Hall (b)
Tim Friend (d)

Utilising another of the more over-subscribed names of the era, this particular NWOBHM proposition (from Sussex) shouldn't be confused with Ray Askew's ex-TORTURE project, the post-TUXEDO outfit or their heavier American counterparts (hey, this stuff is getting complicated) from later in the decade. The MEANSTREAK in question evolved from an amateur bunch who first started out while the members were studying together at college, although it transpires that their original choice of vocalist didn't hang around on the scene once his studies were completed. Undeterred, the remaining musicians swiftly brought in a new frontman, the youthful Mark Hopkins, and (after deciding to turn professional and renaming themselves MEANSTREAK) duly set about establishing themselves as serious rock contenders. It didn't take all that long for the combo to gain a decent reputation, thanks largely to numerous live appearances in the area (including residencies at various well-attended rock venues), and so the lads were soon turning their collective thoughts to getting some vinyl of their own into the shops, electing to save up their meagre pennies in order to finance a privately-issued record rather than waiting for a proper deal to come their way.

MEANSTREAK eventually issued their one and only 7" EP at some point in 1981, and, unsurprisingly, it sold in relatively healthy quantities locally but didn't (as with the vast majority of their contemporaries) propel them into the status of national heroes. With hindsight, it's relatively easy to judge why: they sounded too American. While the UK went bonkers for BON JOVI and MÖTLEY CRÜE a few years later, the wisdom of peddling Yank-style AOR to beer-swilling bikers in English pubs and clubs in 1981 was questionable, to say the least. There has always been a strange phenomenon afflicting Britain, with audiences being insufferably loyal to their local acts (no matter how poor their music was), while they could be equally hostile to *'outsiders'*, even if they outclassed their regional heroes completely. As such, MEANSTREAK might have been one of those bands who could do no wrong at their regular haunts, but who died a death whenever they ventured out of their particular locality. All three tracks featured on their EP are proficiently written and confidently performed, however, with "Played It Right", in spite of a severe case of copyright infringement (a strong, er, *'influence'* of BOSTON's "More Than A Feeling" and RAINBOW's "Since You Been Gone" here), acquitting itself particularly favourably. "You Took The Fire" and "I Know", meanwhile, are more of the same (the latter even bringing the J. GEILS BAND to mind), with a slight THIN LIZZY influence becoming apparent in the guitar department.

All things considered, this type of music would certainly have been far better received in the States in 1981 (or in the UK in 1986, assuming the lads had drafted in a keyboard player and fluffed up their hair a bit), so it's very much a case of *'another time, another place'* (with apologies to LYADRIVE). As with various other home-grown acts who were occasionally tempted to experiment with something of a LIZZY/BOSTON hybrid direction in their early days (LIONHEART, ENERGY and AURORA, to name but a handful), MEANSTREAK seemingly had precious little chance of attaining major-label status, and were soon coming to terms with this harsh reality. Despite being regulars on the Brighton Rock (sorry) scene throughout the early 80's, the quintet eventually fragmented (their unsettled vocalist was apparently the first to flee) and these well-educated musicians presumably returned to their day jobs, eventually filing away those fond memories of their youthful rock'n'roll lifestyle for good. I have a slight fondness for MEANSTREAK's record (now a scarcely-sighted item), however, so if you happen to see an inexpensive copy, housed in its striking red/purple sleeve, do me a favour and find a good home for it.

7" EP's
»Played It Right« SRT 1981

Compilation Appearances
"Played It Right" on »NWOBHM Vol.6« Bootleg CD 1992

MEGATON

J. Gartland
Nagle
Torlak

As you'll be only too aware, good old heavy metal has always been a particularly easy target of ridicule for those sections of the populace who are just too damn cool to wear bullet belts, grow their hair down to their arses and sing heroically about dragons and rainbows. To be honest, therefore, you really have to admire the sheer audacity of any bunch of aspiring musicians who have the nerve to lumber their debut two-tracker with the title of »Aluminium Lady« and immortalise such unashamedly ludicrous lyrics as the following:-

'She's the iron maid of Nuremberg,
Slams doors upon your scream,
She makes your heart a shish kebab,
She haunts each evil dream.
While she's driving home the rivets,
That entomb your love alive,
Cut through, cut loose, don't touch her,
Get out while you still survive.'

Cringe. The outfit in question were the slightly quirky quartet known as MEGATON (not to be confused with some heavy British namesakes from the early 70's), who would appear to have been based in or around the nation's capital, although surprisingly little is actually known about the ensemble. In fact, apart from the limited information given on the record itself, additional details of MEGATON's personnel or history never seem to have been established with any great degree of accuracy. Still, their one and only slice of vinyl was released by London's tiny Hot Metal concern in the summer of 1981, and showed the fly-by-night group to be followers of the METAL MIRROR, INFLUENCE or SCORPIO school of thought (in terms of the slightly ramshackle musicianship and also the unusual vocal style), particularly with regard to the flipside ("Diehard"), where certain guitar parts actually come a bit too close to METAL MIRROR for comfort.

All things considered, though, it's quite an odd-sounding release, and their frontman doesn't really come across like a native English speaker (I suppose the writing credit for *'Torlak'* might be implicated here), although he certainly puts in a very spirited attempt at impersonating Bruce Dickinson's infamous *'air raid siren'*-style vocals. The single was reviewed in 'Sounds', rather inaccurately, as *'pretty much run-of-the-mill MOTÖRHEAD stuff'*, although it's always been a comparatively popular, mid-ranking collectable among NWOBHM aficionados, and it comes in a bulky, handmade, monochrome sleeve depicting images of the four musicians. Peculiarly, nobody seems to have the remotest inkling as to what ultimately became of MEGATON (whose main claim to fame appears to have been a couple of London shows opening for the likes of LIMELIGHT), although there are suggestions that there may be a tenuous connection with WEAPON in one of their later incarnations. On balance, I think we'd better await confirmation of this theory before it becomes written in stone. Anyone know anything else about MEGATON?

7" Singles
»Aluminium Lady« Hot Metal Music 1981

MENDES PREY

John 'Jih' Seymour (v)
Steve Holt (g)
Phil Lawn (g)
Tony Boulton (b)
Martin Brough (d)

The humble origins of Yorkshire's popular MENDES PREY date back to the tail end of the 70's, when the nucleus of the band (Steve Holt, Martin Brough and Phil Lawn) gravitated together after the break-up of various long-forgotten minor hopefuls. It wasn't a full-time operation in the early days, though, particularly when their vocalist of choice, Jih Seymour, was prone to jetting off to Australia to be with his antipodean girlfriend on a fairly regular basis. Disgraceful. After he returned from one extended visit in 1980, however, the musicians finally decided to make a rather more serious attempt at becoming rock stars. Bassist Tony Boulton (who had played in VARDIS in their pre-vinyl days) was drafted in to complete the line-up, and the outfit soon set about the task of getting gigs (originally playing the obligatory array of cover versions) and composing their own material. Their first proper demo sneaked out the following year, the tape featuring "Take Me 'Cross The Water", "Losing Man", "The Sun Don't Shine", "Drifting" and "What The Hell's Going On". These inclusions all revealed the outfit to be a strong rock/metal proposition even at that stage, skilfully combining the classic influence of acts such as UFO with more contemporary inclinations along the lines of PERSIAN RISK, STAGEFRIGHT and IONA, the excellent vocals of Jih Seymour highlighting one of the most gifted frontmen of the entire genre. With the cassette drawing significant attention from the rock community, various selections even achieved some impressively high placings in the 'Sounds' and 'N.M.E.' Heavy Metal Charts around this time.

Original guitarist Phil Lawn decided to pack his bags after contributing to the first demo, however, although he was swiftly replaced by new arrival Richard Emsley. The revised line-up received valuable exposure in the 'Armed And Ready' section of 'Kerrang' towards the end of the year, but it wasn't long before Emsley himself was also on his way, having failed to impress his colleagues in the preceding few months. At this point, the more capable Mark Sutcliffe (who had come from a local concern called EIGA, and wasn't, contrary to popular misconception, the same guy who played in TRESPASS) entered the ranks, and a solid, stable quintet was finally established as a result. Although plans to release a four track EP were outlined at the beginning of 1982, this notion was originally shelved, and the group concentrated on getting ever-bigger gigs and writing new material. Numerous local appearances with the likes of DIAMOND HEAD didn't do their reputation any harm at all, and their thoughts soon returned to the possibility of releasing a self-financed single. As you're all no doubt aware, the classic »On To The Borderline« 7" (b/w "Running For You") was duly recorded and subsequently released towards the end of that year. Issued in its distinctive sleeve depicting a bird of prey clutching a guitar, the record became an instant favourite among fans at the time (no doubt helped by an airing or two on the 'Friday Rock Show'), and has found its way into the collections of numerous NWOBHM devotees throughout the world, who regard the two-tracker as one of the archetypal releases of the genre.

By this juncture, the activities of MENDES PREY had also attracted the attention of Heavy Metal Records, who not only included "What The Hell's Going On" on the »Heavy Metal Heroes Vol.II« compilation, but additionally offered the youngsters the enviable opportunity to record their own single in due course. Peculiarly, however, it transpires that the lads were expected to finance this endeavour themselves, and they politely declined the offer, feeling confident that the big deal was just around the corner. Early 1983 saw MENDES PREY making the pilgrimage to London's famous Marquee for memorable shows with both CHINATOWN and SARACEN, the latter coming about when they agreed to step in at the last minute after the original co-headliners pulled out at short notice. The gig with CHINATOWN, on the other hand, was subsequently reviewed in 'Kerrang', and MENDES PREY must surely have been delighted when Dave Ling referred to them as *'the best Marquee support band I've seen in quite a while'*. At around the same time, the lads also benefitted from a piece of remarkably good fortune, when a representative of Levi's jeans picked up on their "What The Hell's Going On" track, and arranged to use the number to promote their product on local radio stations. In turn, this eventually yielded a full-scale sponsorship deal, which (in addition to some free *'stagewear'*) allowed the group to arrange their own headlining tour (supported by the rather dubious choice of Chesterfield's self-indulgent progsters DAGA-BAND) of Northern venues, which appears to have been a resounding success. One of these gigs was even filmed by the BBC for their 'Bubbling Under' programme, and three tracks ("Red Alert", "On To The Borderline" and "Running For You") were subsequently broadcast to audiences in the North of England.

The live appearances continued throughout the remainder of that year, notably a fondly-remembered outing (where the lads shared a stage with the likes of TWELFTH NIGHT and TERRAPLANE) at a well-attended festival in Bicester. By this juncture, the outfit were delighting the masses with an impressive repertoire of self-penned numbers such as "Lone Survivor", "Tomorrow Today" and "Take It Or Leave It", in addition to a variety of familiar compositions from their earlier demo and single,

many of which were now becoming firm favourites. They were, however, always looking to the future, and the ambitious bunch constantly tried out novel ideas when writing material. To this end, a keyboard player was recruited in the form of Steve Allen, an associate member who contributed to the writing and recording side of things for a few months, but who never became fully assimilated into the ranks. By the autumn of 1983, founder member Steve Holt elected to depart in order to concentrate on other activities, and, following his last gig in September of that year, MENDES PREY were reduced to a four-piece. The remaining participants, however, swiftly concluded that they were more than capable of proceeding as a slimmed-down unit, and so the solid line-up of Brough, Seymour, Sutcliffe and Boulton was to remain intact for the duration of the group's existence.

The next couple of years were, on the face of it, fairly quiet in the MENDES PREY camp, with much of their time being spent in the studio penning new material (and tinkering around with various old favourites) as opposed to undertaking endless touring activities. Even so, the musicians remained extremely optimistic that an album deal would indeed materialise before much longer, and the outfit's latest batch of studio sessions were very much geared towards preparing themselves for this eventuality, as Tony Boulton explains: *'We always wanted to release an album, that was the whole point. We could have self-financed one but we wanted a proper deal. Some labels showed an interest, and they probably monitored our movements for a while, but no-one came forth with a firm commitment.'* (Ref: Private communication, September 1999). The first concrete evidence of all these clandestine activities finally emerged in 1985, when the lads contributed "Cry For The World" and the excellent "Red Alert" (two numbers which had, in fact, been a staple part of their live repertoire for a number of years) to the extremely scarce »Parkside Steelworks« set, where they appeared alongside a motley variety of fairly obscure Northern rock/metal hopefuls who frequented Parkside Studios in Leeds. Such was the severely restricted nature of this pressing, however, that it probably failed to garner the featured outfits all that much additional publicity at the time, although it has become a sought-after (and highly-priced) collectable in recent years, predominantly due to the inclusion of this otherwise-unavailable MENDES PREY material. Although gigs were still few and far between at this stage, the quartet continued to take to the stage on occasion, just to keep their hands in and to maintain some level of personal contact with the fans.

By this time, the group's affairs were now being handled by a new management/promotion team, who attempted to steer MENDES PREY towards more commercial waters, assuring them that this was the best route towards making the big time. In their quest for that elusive *'hit single'*, a phenomenal amount of time and effort was expended trying to write a song which would meet with the approval of those behind the venture. The band's own compositions were ruthlessly and repeatedly rejected, and it was eventually suggested (without a great deal of tact) that they might prefer to use DEMON's "Wonderland" instead. Reluctantly, the members of MENDES PREY capitulated, and their second single (issued in both 7" and 12" formats in a picture sleeve showing a photo of the band themselves) featured their reworking of the aforementioned classic, backed with their own new number "Can You Believe It". By the time the record was eventually issued, however, the songs had been remixed and reprocessed countless times, the ensemble realising too late that this particular material wasn't actually representative of their intended musical direction at all. The move towards slickly-presented, over-produced melodic rock/pop was accompanied by a change of image, which involved the lads sporting smart suits and shorter haircuts, and, to all intents and purposes, this period of (largely enforced) experimentation was an unmitigated disaster.

You won't be remotely surprised, therefore, to learn that the »Wonderland« debacle effectively signalled the end of MENDES PREY. After a bit of serious soul-searching, Jih finally decided to follow his heart and relocate to Australia on a permanent basis. Understandably, the remaining members felt unable to continue without him, and the trio had finally drifted apart for good by the end of 1986. Although the lads initially hooked up with various other local hopefuls (Mark Sutcliffe, for example, spent a year or two in the company of a more funk-based concern called SERLE), they ultimately abandoned any significant level of involvement with the rock/metal scene and simply returned to their day jobs. Jih, meanwhile, still maintains an interest in the music business, and now works for a regional radio station down under. The good news for the numerous fans of MENDES PREY, however, is that various ex-members have now been made aware of the huge amount of interest still being expressed in the NWOBHM phenomenon, and have taken the first steps towards developing an official and regularly-maintained website. Moreover, tentative plans have been outlined for a full-length CD (at last!), which would feature a high proportion of previously-unreleased tracks. Let's hope this venture comes to fruition within a reasonable timescale, eh?

12" Singles
»Wonderland« Wag Records 1986
[Includes extended version of "Wonderland"]

7" Singles
»On To The Borderline« M.P. Records 1982
»Wonderland« Wag Records 1986
[Includes edited version of "Wonderland"]

Exclusive Compilation Appearances
"What The Hell's Going On" on »Heavy Metal Heroes Vol.II« LP Heavy Metal 1982 + »Heavy Metal Heroes Vol.I&II« CD British Steel 1996
"Red Alert" on »Parkside Steelworks« LP LiL Records 1985
"Cry For The World" on »Parkside Steelworks« LP LiL Records 1985

Compilation Appearances
"On To The Borderline" on »NWOBHM Vol.4«

Bootleg CD 1992

METAL MIRROR

Cameron Vagges (v)
Paul Butterworth (g)
Chris Haggerty (g)
Ian Thomson (b)
Gary Hitchens (d)

In contrast to the Neat and Ebony labels, who tended to favour unknown, grass-roots level acts, the Midlands-based Heavy Metal Records frequently (particularly for use on their compilations) picked up on those who had previously released their own product. This was the case with London's METAL MIRROR, who, like EXPOZER, OVERKILL, NO FAITH and PERSIAN RISK (all of whom had issued a private single beforehand), were afforded the opportunity to lay down one of their numbers for use on the famous pair of »Heavy Metal Heroes« samplers. For the aforementioned METAL MIRROR, it had all started a year or two previously, when the young quintet recorded the snappily-titled "Rock & Roll Ain't Never Gonna Leave Us" and "English Booze", pressed them up as a 7" single on their own label and waited for the money to roll in. Well, as with most of their contemporaries, the record (issued in a nice, fantasy-style sleeve) didn't allow them to become an overnight sensation, but their brand of no-nonsense, straightforward metal no doubt went down a storm in the capital's rock clubs. The arrangements on both of the aforementioned compositions are fairly primitive, bringing to mind acts such as SCORPIO, Kent's RAW DEAL or early TYGERS OF PAN TANG, with the charismatic Cameron Vagges doing his utmost to promote himself as a more metal version of MARC BOLAN. Nevertheless, the record remains a rare and sought-after item, and has, in terms of value, now been in the *'three figure club'* for quite a long time.

The lads promoted their debut two-tracker with a series of gigs around the capital, one or two of which were even reviewed in the rock press, where numbers such as "Crazy" and "Never More" were identified as particularly capable efforts. In 1981, METAL MIRROR contributed their "Hard Life" effort to the aforementioned »Heavy Metal Heroes« LP, a composition which showed little or no deviation (or progression, for that matter) from their original musical direction. Although there's nothing fundamentally wrong with the track itself, it tends to pale somewhat in the company of JAGUAR, WITCHFINDER GENERAL, GRIM REAPER, BITCHES SIN *etc.*, all of whom delivered highly capable numbers and, consequently, went on to much greater things. In fact, it looks as though the only *'failures'* from the sampler were METAL MIRROR and EXPOZER, and it seems probable that both outfits ceased all activities shortly thereafter, although METAL MIRROR appear to have tried out a new drummer, Mick Green (who later worked with PALI GAP), towards the end of their existence. Frontman Cameron Vagges (aka Cameron Vegas) proceeded to carve out a solo career for himself (a small series of CAMERON VEGAS gigs took place around London and its environs in 1990), and his songwriting partnership with Paul Butterworth remained a going concern, yielding a couple of obscure privately-pressed CD's (the tasteful »Life's A Bitch And Then You Die« and »Live Rollin' In Greece«) in the early 90's. It's hard to believe that these represented anything other than vanity releases, though (the material really is extremely weak and even borders on mainstream pop nonsense at times), with few copies having been in circulation at any time since they were initially issued.

7" Singles
»Rock & Roll Ain't Never Gonna Leave Us«
M+M Records 1980

Exclusive Compilation Appearances
"Hard Life" on »Heavy Metal Heroes« LP Heavy Metal 1981 *[Issued in two different sleeves]* + »Heavy Metal Heroes Vol.I&II« CD British Steel 1996

METAL VIRGINS

Steve (v,g)
Gary (b)
Glenn (d)

Fair enough, a lot of extremely ropy acts managed to issue their own singles during the NWOBHM era, but privately-pressed LP's were a different kettle of fish entirely. You might suspect that any band prepared to go to the effort of laying down an album's worth of material must have been quite a capable proposition with some decent compositions of their own. Indeed, even by the mid-to-late 80's, the UK was still throwing up some pretty good post-NWOBHM outfits who got to the stage of releasing a self-financed long-player (you don't have to look much further than ELIXIR for conclusive evidence), but you'd be cruelly mistaken if you reckon that the sole album issued by the abysmally-named METAL VIRGINS in 1984 could be one of the undiscovered classics of the genre. This ill-conceived effort from a comically-untalented trio (based somewhere around the South East) is a pretty tortuous listening experience all round, and has virtually no redeeming features whatsoever. Taking the worst elements of punk (the *'we can't play a note and we're proud of it'* attitude) and free jazz (*'let's all just do our own thing and see what happens'*), the hapless combo managed to create an utterly horrible racket, which can hardly be recommended to anyone except one or two of the more tolerant and undemanding fans of noisy outfits such as THE BLOOD, MAYHEM, WARFARE and their ilk.

In all honesty, »Animal People« isn't really classifiable as a genuine metal effort at all (admittedly, the title track itself has a reasonably capable guitar interlude, probably more by chance than design), in spite of the trio's best efforts to convince us otherwise, the publicity-shy members even going so far as to issue it on their own *'Thrash Metal Records'* label to ram home the message. It's not beyond the realms of possibility that this was nothing more than a jokey release (not remotely funny for those who bought it, though) or a side-project by a better-known outfit, although these more often took the form of singles or EP's; stretching a jolly jape out as far as a full LP would surely have been a bit excessive. All in all, therefore, a criminal waste of good vinyl (quite rightly, 'Kerrang' ripped it to shreds) and an item that you'd be advised to steer well clear of, really.

LP's
»Animal People« Thrash Metal Records 1984

MIDAS

Paul Taylor (v)
Martin Wright (g)
Dave Hunt (g)
Richard Howard (b)
Bernie Désbléds (d)

Although the original version of MIDAS initially took shape in East London as early as 1980, it appears that things didn't go according to plan at first, and so the founder members came to a mutual decision to disband shortly afterwards. After getting back together in March 1982, however, the outfit (featuring the distinctive vocals of the talented Paul Taylor, who subsequently achieved much greater success in ELIXIR) went through the usual process of recording speculative demos and gigging exhaustively, before deciding to go it alone, whereupon the highly listenable »Can't Stop Loving You Now« single was issued (in a tiny

run of only a few hundred copies) in 1983. As featured on the »NWOBHM Vol.5« bootleg, the nominated A-side is a slightly poppy number with twangy guitars and a curiously-mechanical drum sound, which would probably have made a pretty good theme tune for a 70's soap opera on British TV. On the other hand, "Power In The Sky" is an absolute classic of the genre, with a superb vocal performance and standard of musicianship, very similar in style to the type of material that ELIXIR themselves later mastered. It's difficult to conceive why this track wasn't used on the bootleg as opposed to the A-side, unless the vinyl copy they were working with was unplayably damaged on the reverse. Who knows?

The talented band continued to tour frenetically, as the insert claims, *'from East End night clubs to motorcycle rallies, all to great acclaim'*, and must surely have anticipated that a big break would come their way sooner or later. Along the way, the ensemble also found time to assemble a video of themselves in action, a financially-demanding project at the time, and one which was usually reserved for more successful acts with a bit of major-label backing. You certainly can't say they went about things half-heartedly, so MIDAS surely deserved to be rewarded for their collective efforts. Inevitably, though, things didn't work out in the long term and, by the summer of 1984, Taylor had already decided to throw his weight behind the youthful ELIXIR, presumably effecting an almost immediate cessation of operations on the MIDAS front. With so few copies having been manufactured at the time, the »Can't Stop Loving You Now« 7" is, naturally, a scarce piece these days, and is likely to be a big-money item whenever it's offered for sale. Look out for a monochrome cover (although a significant percentage were actually issued without one) depicting a hand reaching for a microphone.

7" Singles
»Can't Stop Loving You Now« Small Run Records 1983

Compilation Appearances
"Can't Stop Loving You Now" on »NWOBHM Vol.5« Bootleg CD 1992

MILLENNIUM

Mark Duffy (v)
Dave Merrington (g)
Pete McArdle (g)
Dave Price (b)
Steve Mennell (d)

Cleveland's MILLENNIUM enjoyed a pretty rapid rise through the ranks, first coming to prominence (relatively shortly after their initial formation) after deservedly winning a place on Guardian's inconsistent »Pure Overkill« compilation in 1983. Afforded a very generous allowance of three whole tracks, the lucky quintet duly delivered "Steal Your Heart", "Rock Was Meant For Me" and "Magic Mirror" (miscredited as "Mirror Mirror" on the sleeve), a capable selection of numbers which stood out in the company of some less-than-inspiring competition. The talent-hungry label was clearly impressed with the cut of their jib, and soon stumped up the cash for a full album release. In fact, each of the aforementioned compositions would subsequently find their place on MILLENNIUM's eponymous debut (saving a bit of studio time, no doubt), which saw the light of day the following year. The LP, the recipient of a glowing review in 'Kerrang', contained a generous helping of mid-paced, powerful metal, occasionally reminiscent of NWOBHM outfits such as AVENGER or DUCHESS (or, at times, even certain later 80's combos like the DESOLATION ANGELS or BLACK RIDERS). The stand-out numbers would probably be opener "Gang War" and "Demons Of The Light", although a minor criticism of the album as a whole would be that, with the notable exception of the two slower compositions ("The Traveller" and the recycled "Rock Was Meant For Me"), the tracks are all a bit too samey and readily interchangeable.

After the surprise success of the LP, the band underwent a period of restructuring, replacing guitarist Dave Merrington with Mike Muskett (of former Guardian hopefuls SKITZOFRENIK), and they briefly chose (for reasons which defy logic) to be known by the utterly hopeless moniker of TYRONE POWER. Realising that naming yourself after a heroic actor wasn't actually a brilliant idea after all, the lads swiftly reverted to their original identity and set about recording some new demos. A seven track affair from early 1985 was enthused over in 'High Octane' fanzine (they also had a few fans at 'Metal Forces'), with recently-penned numbers such as "Caught In A Warzone" and "Princess Of Light" featuring a more prominent twin-guitar assault and melodic-but-powerful vocals, generally tending more towards European groups such as HELLOWEEN than most of the acts typically doing the rounds in the UK at the time. A further MILLENNIUM cassette, dating from around a year later, featuring such unfamiliar compositions as "Mutiny" and "Kill Or Be Killed", was perhaps slightly more in tune with their earlier direction, and the lads were soon on the receiving end of yet more encouraging reviews. Even so, the material seemed to give the distinct impression that the group were feeling a bit unsure of themselves at this point.

Sadly, MILLENNIUM's latest selection of compositions wasn't enough to impress those in the industry who really mattered, and the labels soon reached the conclusion that these hopefuls just weren't a big-money proposition after all, sending the dejected outfit into self-destruct mode, the musicians finally electing to go their separate ways in 1987. Mark Duffy's considerable vocal talents were soon in demand by some rather heavier outfits, though, and he subsequently lent his services to thrash wannabes MAJOR THREAT before finding considerable success with TORANAGA, stars of a 'Friday Rock Show' session in 1988 and veterans of a critically-acclaimed LP or two at around the turn of the decade. By the way, there's actually an AOR ensemble called MILLENIUM (one 'n') doing the rounds at the moment (oddly enough, quite a few AOR bands have unwittingly taken fairly similar identities to some of the acts featured in this volume), but you should be aware that they have absolutely no connection with the original NWOBHM version.

LP's
»Millennium« Guardian 1984

Compilation Appearances
"Steal Your Heart" on »Pure Overkill« LP Guardian 1983
"Rock Was Meant For Me" on »Pure Overkill« LP Guardian 1983
"Magic Mirror" on »Pure Overkill« LP Guardian 1983
[Miscredited as "Mirror Mirror"]

MITHRANDIR

Graham Gargiulo (v,b)
Paul Chester (g)
Keith Billson (d)

With the majority of privately-pressed NWOBHM releases, I guess you always have to take the rough with the smooth. In the case of Cambridgeshire's MITHRANDIR (the name coming from 'Lord Of The Rings', apparently),

the operative word is 'rough', proving that the self-issued single was often the only way that some outfits were *ever* going to make it to the vinyl stage. The group's second record (although how they ever got beyond one release is one for Mulder and Scully) has been widely pilloried for being rather, er, stylistically ambiguous, but their little-known debut, which few individuals have actually been 'privileged' enough to hear, is nothing short of *astonishingly* unworthy of release. Amazingly, however, some people actually seem to like it, but they're in a tiny minority. The trio's »Magick« EP, issued in the early months of 1982 (housed within a generic, monochrome sleeve), is almost *endearingly* awful; the stunning musical ineptitude on "Eyes Of The Madman", "All The Time" and "Call Of The Wild" and the utter lack of talent on display all round is phenomenal. The vocalist somehow manages to defy the law which states that you can only go so far out of tune before coming back into tune on a different octave, whereas the song arrangements are abysmal and the time-keeping non-existent. Remarkable.

In fact, it all sounds like a trio of awkward adolescents mucking about in a garage after school, and, to be fair, that's basically what it was. No doubt, some well-meaning parent decided to share their offspring's undisputable talent (presumably having been inspired by the fact that these ankle-biters had somehow achieved a modicum of success in a national 'Rockschool' contest a few months earlier) by financing a vinyl release, although I can't imagine that too many copies made it into the shops, which is one of the reasons behind the EP's monumental rarity today. Towards the end of the same year, MITHRANDIR (whose biography claimed, rather optimistically, that they were taking on board a range of influences such as LED ZEPPELIN, the YARDBIRDS, JIMI HENDRIX and RUSH) decided to inflict a second offering upon the world, which, funnily enough, is actually nowhere near as bad as their debut. The follow-up single, coupling "Dreamers Of Fortune" and "After Tomorrow", was a major improvement in terms of both instrumentation and arrangements (and it had a better sleeve), but the vocals remained as atrocious as ever. If you can imagine an outfit lying somewhere between SKITZOFRENIK and early BUDGIE, you're getting some idea of their attempted style, but I reckon a couple of extra years of intensive rehearsals might have been a good idea, lads.

The trio unwisely chose to send a promotional copy of their »Dreamers Of Fortune« effort to 'Kerrang', who (inevitably) slated the release mercilessly, the 'review' including a scathing attack on their hapless vocalist, so it's probably just as well the magazine never got a copy of the first EP or they would have had a field day. The band was laid to rest shortly afterwards, and the name of MITHRANDIR disappeared into utter obscurity until one or two examples of their vinyl releases came to light in the early 90's, driving collectors wild with anticipation that these might actually represent long-lost NWOBHM classics. They were wrong. Both records are extremely rare, admittedly, but you'll save a hell of a lot of money (not to mention some serious ear trauma) if you steer clear of them. Wisely, old Graham Gargiulo subsequently gave up the singing lark to train as a teacher, although he has resurfaced in a couple of recording acts in the 90's (playing guitar), namely indie twangers the CHARLOTTES and BAREFOOT CONTESSA, although neither of these outfits can exactly be recommended to metal fans.

7" EP's
»Magick« New Leaf Records 1982

7" Singles
»Dreamers Of Fortune« New Leaf Records 1982

MOBY DICK

Max Bacon (v)

Cheshire's short-lived MOBY DICK (sounds like a particularly nasty complaint) were an extremely capable outfit (although they were, apparently, perfectly content to bang out the usual batch of cover versions in the live environment) who took their first serious steps in the music business with their 1982 offering "Can't Have My Body Tonight", a track utilised both on Ebony's »Metallic Storm« sampler and as part of their double A-sided debut single (pairing it with "Nothing To Fear"), issued on the same label. With both selections coming across as accomplished, mid-paced numbers lying somewhere between FUGITIVE and a more down-to-earth TYTAN, the group left a collectable memento of their relatively fleeting existence, which, like most things on Ebony, can still be located at a fairly reasonable price these days. Given that the two-tracker (which was even afforded the signal honour of a favourable review in 'Kerrang') was issued without the extravagance of a picture sleeve, however, and, since Ebony's publicity machine was decidedly defective in its early days, the outfit's personnel remain something of a mystery even now, although it has become fairly common knowledge that they featured the vocal talents of Max Bacon, who subsequently went on to make quite a name for himself with his productive stints in acts such as NIGHTWING, BRONZ, PHENOMENA and GTR. Anyone care to fill in the gaps?

7" Singles
»Nothing To Fear« Ebony 1982

Compilation Appearances
"Can't Have My Body Tonight" on »Metallic Storm« LP Ebony 1982

MONEY

David West-Mullen (v)
John Overton (g)
Larry Phillips (b)
Tony Boden (d)

Not to be confused with the American act who released the »Trust Me« album in 1984, Midlands-based MONEY established themselves on the rock scene in the mid-to-late 70's, before finally inking a lucrative deal with the perennial Gull label (home to JUDAS PRIEST and NIGHTWING, among others, over the years). The first fruit of this partnership was the unremarkable »Searching« two-tracker, recorded late in 1978, followed shortly thereafter by the »First Investment« LP. Produced by the capable (and much in-demand in later years) Chris Tsangarides (who also contributed a few keyboard sections), the album is far from typical NWOBHM fodder, bringing forth comparisons with slightly quirky outfits such as the NEXT BAND, ORION and TUTCH. While there are certain instances, notably on excellent opener "Mari-Anna", where the quartet display a heavier style, other numbers (such as "Geneva" and "Statements And Demands") show a tendency to drift into more ambitious material in the oddball vein of QUEEN or even SPARKS. To be honest, it looks as though MONEY were swept along, rather adventitiously, by the momentum generated by the NWOBHM, without ever being *bona fide* exponents of its musical archetype. Their ambitious label, however, did their utmost to promote the group, and even saw to it that special pressings would be made available to the receptive Japanese market, for example.

The following year saw the outfit gaining further exposure courtesy of the magnanimous Tommy Vance at BBC Radio. A capable 'Friday Rock Show' session, initially broadcast on the 22nd of February 1980, showcased the newly-penned compositions "Man In A Subway", "Fast World" and "Another Case Of Suicide", these listenable efforts sharing centre stage with a rejigged version of long-time favourite "Leo The

Jester". With the band clearly having been boning up on NWOBHM riffs and song structures, their newer offerings were, reassuringly, much more in tune with the sound craved by rock fans of the day. Indeed, the session take of "Leo The Jester" was subsequently selected for inclusion on the first of two compilations issued by BBC Records themselves, each featuring some of the best-received numbers from 'Friday Rock Show' transmissions of the previous few months. The upbeat "Fast World" and epic "Another Case Of Suicide", meanwhile, also turned up (alongside the unfamiliar "Small Time Criminal") on a seldom-seen 7" EP, released by the tiny Hobo label (home of the ERIC BELL BAND) later in the year. This scarce item, issued in a generic picture sleeve, is easily the group's rarest and most highly-valued piece of vinyl.

Hoping to build on their new-found popularity, the MONEY lads organised a series of headlining dates at the beginning of 1981, with the express intention of trying out a selection of new material which they envisioned as forming the basis of their second LP. In the event, however, the tour wasn't a great success and, after a couple of support gigs with the PRETTY THINGS came their way some time later, the dejected outfit elected to cease all operations shortly afterwards. As with certain other outfits who had their roots in the traditional 70's rock scene, such as QUARTZ, NIGHTWING and RAGE, the NWOBHM might have thrown them a lifeline initially, but couldn't be expected to work miracles in the long term. Tony Boden, incidentally, later had a very brief stint at the drumstool of TYTAN after Dave Dufort and Les Binks had also failed to measure up to the aforementioned band's high standards of professionalism. He subsequently tried his luck a few years later with an experimental outfit called (wait for it) CATHEDRAL, but this bunch don't seem to have been a particularly long-lived operation.

LP's
»First Investment« Gull 1979
[UK issue]
»First Investment« Gull 1979
[Japanese issue with insert]

7" EP's
»Fast World« Hobo Records 1980
[All three tracks non-LP]

7" Singles
»(Aren't We All) Searching« Gull 1978
[UK issue in company sleeve, B-side "Where Have All The Dancers Gone?" non-LP]
»(Aren't We All) Searching« Gull 1979
[Japanese issue in picture sleeve, B-side "Mari-Anna"]

Compilation Appearances
"Leo The Jester" on »Metal Explosion« LP BBC Records 1980
[Different to LP version]

MORE

Paul Mario Day (v)
Kenny Cox (g)
Paul Todd (g)
Brian Day (b)
Frank Darch (d)

Originally coming together under the name of DEFENDER at the tail end of the 70's, the embryonic version of MORE included a kindly German bassist who helpfully arranged for the outfit to travel to his home country, whereupon they enjoyed a handful of small-time club gigs as well as a few early sessions in the recording studio. This experience was to serve the participants well, and, on returning to London at the height of the NWOBHM influx, the ensemble (who started off as more of a traditional, bluesy rock concern) soon began making a name for themselves as an emergent rock proposition. Even before they had organised a record deal, numerous live gigs and fanzine interviews were coming their way, with one memorable example concentrating on their collective opinion of this whole *'new wave heavy metal'* (sic) thing: *'Well, I tried to find out what it means and I was told that it meant less bass and more metallic, but that means losing the energy.'* (Ref: Teenage Depression, Issue 12, 1980). Clearly, the cynical members of MORE weren't exactly enamoured with all this media hype surrounding the latest metal renaissance, and were equally critical of the general apathy of record companies towards bands who favoured more of a *'classic'* rock style and who didn't try to conform to the new ideal.

By the spring of 1980, a stable MORE line-up had already been achieved, with vocalist Paul Mario Day (who had, at the tender age of sixteen, acted as IRON MAIDEN's original frontman) being joined by bassist Brian Day (no relation), guitarists Kenny Cox and Paul Todd (the latter having famously been a member of IRON MAIDEN for two whole days), plus drummer Frank Darch. Their activities on the rock scene swiftly attracted the attention of the 'Friday Rock

Show', and the lucky quintet were invited to lay down a session before they had even made it to the vinyl stage. The lads happily obliged, and an impressive selection of early compositions ("Atomic Rock", "Way Of The World", "Soldier" and "I Have No Answers") was broadcast to the nation on the 23rd of May 1980. In due course, their session version of "Soldier" would also be included on the BBC's »Metal Explosion« album, suggesting that the confident performance had been one of the more warmly-received and highly-regarded efforts of the time. Before long, the mighty Atlantic label (who had just disposed of the luckless EXPORT after only one single) came looking for a new act to add to their roster, and the fortunate MORE appear to have been in the right place at the right time, signing up for a full album deal without much delay. Before the lads were finally ready to enter the studio, however, they were forced to attend to the minor inconvenience of replacing Paul Todd, who had done a bunk at short notice. Fortunately, however, the band were able to recruit former OPHIDIAN guitarist Laurie Mansworth to the fold, and it was all systems go once again.

MORE's debut album was recorded towards the end of 1980, and the long-player appeared early the following year under the very metal-sounding title of »Warhead«. It was a highly listenable effort, featuring some well-crafted, upbeat numbers in the best NWOBHM tradition (such as "Warhead", "Way Of The World" and "I Have No Answers"), all of which were fairly similar to the likes of FIST, the STARFIGHTERS or the HANDSOME BEASTS. On the other hand, things were balanced out by the inclusion of some longer, heavier, raunchier efforts such as "Soldier", "Depression" and "Lord Of Twilight", which were rather more in keeping with XERO, QUARTZ and their ilk. It was a sterling effort all round, though, apart from the weak cover of "Fire" by THE CRAZY WORLD OF ARTHUR BROWN, which completely failed to do justice to the menacing and unhinged original. MORE wasted little time before they started to promote their album in earnest, although they had to endure another line-up change, with Andy John Burton being drafted in to replace departed sticksman Frank Darch. After successfully breaking in their latest recruit, the revised band were soon out on the road with KROKUS (in the UK) and IRON MAIDEN (in Europe), benefitting from an overwhelmingly positive reaction at almost every stopping-point.

The lads also saw their label utilise "We Are The Band", another strong album cut, as the basis of their first single (in both 7" and 12"

forms), the B-side in each case being the non-LP "Atomic Rock", which soon became a byword for MORE's musical philosophy, as they apparently wanted to distance themselves from both the NWOBHM and their traditional rock roots. They obviously enjoyed the touring side of things at least as much as their recording sessions, and Kenny Cox was happy to reflect on some of the band's recent live activities in a radio interview at the time: *'KROKUS were a good bunch, nice people, we got along very well with them. On the first day, they decided to have a laugh at our expense, we didn't really know*

GET YOUR **FREE** 'MORE' PATCH WITH OUR FIRST 12" SINGLE AT YOUR LOCAL RECORD STORE

"WE ARE THE BAND" K11561T

them and they didn't know us. To welcome us onto the tour, they hid all of our guitars. I mean, I play a very expensive custom Flying V, and so we got to the dressing room to prepare for the soundcheck and the guitars had gone. KROKUS, who had hidden them, just pretended they knew nothing about it. They brought them back later, though, it was their idea of a joke!' (Ref: Interview, Tony Jasper, BFBS Radio, 1981). Utterly hilarious, I'm sure. Those long hours on the tour bus must have just *flown* by.

MORE didn't content themselves with support slots, though, and were soon organising numerous headlining gigs of their own, the highlight of which being a series of shows (sponsored by 'Sounds' magazine) called the *'Atomic Rock Roadshow'*, where the lads played around Britain with support from various emergent hopefuls such as LIONHEART. The gigs became more and more (as it were) out of control as time went on, with many a night ending with half of the audience on stage as the set drew to a close, the whole scene resembling something of a

Bacchanalian orgy to the casual onlooker. MORE's reputation as high-spirited crowd-pleasers soon filtered through to the organisers of the newly-established Monsters Of Rock Festival, who secured the outfit as opening act for their forthcoming all-dayer. The group jumped at the chance, and delivered the goods in front of a massive crowd, warming things up nicely for the likes of BLACKFOOT, WHITESNAKE and AC/DC. Moving into 1982, there was no let-up on the gig front, the band even taking in a few festival gigs as far afield as Finland, where they warmed things up for headliners such as SLADE (who had also appeared at Donington the year before), and their growing reputation in Europe was soon the envy of several (supposedly) more successful British acts.

Eventually, however, the lads had to turn their backs on touring for a while and get down to the important business of recording that crucial second album. Guitarist Laurie Mansworth had already departed for pastures new (eventually resurfacing in the largely-overlooked AIRRACE) towards the end of 1981, but the remaining members concluded that they were more than capable of continuing as a quartet without any significant loss of quality. Things started out pretty well when the studio sessions finally got underway, although the situation rapidly went pear-shaped halfway through, when talented frontman Paul Mario Day clashed with his accomplices over some of the changes in direction they seemed to be adopting without sufficient prior consultation. As it turned out, this wasn't merely a minor disagreement, it grew into a stalemate which no amount of diplomatic mediation could realistically resolve, and so MORE were left without a vocalist. Clearly, this action threatened the stability of the outfit in no uncertain terms (it forced them to pull out of a lucrative support slot with BLACK SABBATH at the beginning of 1982), and there was little chance that they would resort to releasing an instrumental album, so it came as a rather good piece of fortune that the lads were able to recruit a suitable replacement, the unknown Mick Stratton, at relatively short notice.

In the first instance, the group's master plan was merely to re-record all the tracks which had already been laid down with their original vocalist, although it soon became apparent that the ambitious new frontman wanted to contribute slightly more to the project. As a consequence, much of their existing material was changed around, rewritten and given some completely novel lyrics at Stratton's behest, although they retained one number in its original form ("Traitors Gate"), for which Paul Mario Day was given full credit in due course. With the album in the can by the middle of the year, and, with the studio sessions having been completed more or less on schedule, there seemed to be no particular reasons why the LP's worldwide release shouldn't go ahead as originally planned. Indeed, Atlantic duly trundled out a 7" (featuring the catchy "Trickster" and a cover of the JIMI HENDRIX standard "Hey Joe", neither of which were scheduled to appear on the album) to keep things ticking over, although the label already seemed to be losing interest by this time. By all accounts, Atlantic were failing to promote MORE in an effective manner, mailing out half-hearted press releases featuring photos of outdated line-ups, and (ludicrous as it may seem) refusing to send out complimentary copies of albums and singles to magazines and radio stations, a situation which culminated in the bizarre scenario of the outfit having to buy extra records themselves and make their own haphazard attempts at self-promotion.

While waiting for their second long-player to materialise, the persevering group continued to make a few live appearances to keep some momentum going, including an unmemorable gig at the poorly-received Hackney Festival alongside the likes of SPIDER, MOTÖRHEAD and SAXON, although the lads must have wondered whether or not the new album would actually appear at all by this time. In the end, it did receive a limited release, most copies being pressed in Europe for the benefit of countries such as Germany, where MORE had developed something of a cult following in the preceding couple of years. Relatively few examples of »Blood And Thunder« made it to the UK, but it was a disappointing effort in any case, with Stratton's inelegant vocal performance failing to match that of the departed Day, who was now in the process of putting together his own venture (which would eventually become WILDFIRE). Sadly, the much-anticipated long-player was filled with an extremely anonymous selection of rock/metal hybrids in the general style of SNAKEBITE or CHAINSAW, few of which rose above the underlying level of mediocrity, although "Nightmare" was probably the pick of the bunch. Elsewhere, however, the likes of "Killer On The Prowl", "I've Been Waiting" and "I Wanna Take You" all come and go without leaving a lasting impression, so maybe it would have been better if the album had remained in the Atlantic vaults after all.

In view of Atlantic's lack of dedication to their cause, MORE elected to part company with the label, whereupon the lads proudly announced that they already had at least half an album's worth of fresh material at their disposal, and would be open to offers from any companies who wanted to negotiate for the rights to release their third opus. However, they were brought down to earth with a bump when few labels of any consequence expressed the remotest interest in their subsequent efforts, and the lads were soon coming to terms with the reality of the situation i.e. that it wouldn't be as laughably easy to get a deal the second time around. This applied to countless other hopefuls from the original NWOBHM explosion who now found themselves in precisely the same situation, but it seems to have hit MORE particularly hard, and they pretty much went into steady decline thereafter. It also became apparent that Brian Day had actually flown the coop (he proceeded to contribute to the early studio activities of WILDFIRE, but didn't become a full-time member) after laying down his bass parts for the »Blood And Thunder« disaster, and it appears that a suitable permanent replacement was never found at any point thereafter, with session musicians being recruited at disconcertingly short notice for the band's increasingly-scarce live appearances.

By 1983, the luckless ensemble had finally thrown in the towel, only for the indefatigable Kenny Cox to try again in 1985, recruiting an all-new set of accomplices in the shape of Barry Nicholls (b), Mel Jones (g), Paul George (d) and Ron Jackson (v), none of whom were particularly well-kent names on the rock scene. Sadly, but entirely predictably, the revamped version of MORE failed to attract any significant interest (either from labels or fans) the second time around, and this ill-fated reformation appears to have been laid to rest mercifully quickly. Kenny Cox remained unemployed for a relatively short time, however, as the talented guitarist was recruited into the ranks of MAMMOTH (see separate entry) within a year or two, a project which allowed him to share a stage with some equally *'imposing'* musicians. After the unexpectedly swift demise of this relatively high-profile outfit, however, it's not such common knowledge that he formed a spin-off with Nicky Moore called MORE'N'MORE (shouldn't that have been *'More'n'Moore'*, we ask ourselves?), a semi-serious act who even managed to win themselves a 'Friday Rock Show' session in the early 90's before Cox finally disappeared into the shadows once again.

LP's
»Warhead« Atlantic 1981

[UK issue]
»Warhead« Atlantic 1981
[US issue with slightly different layout, alternate tracklisting and omitting "Lord Of Twilight"]
»Blood And Thunder« Atlantic 1982

12" Singles
»We Are The Band« Atlantic 1981
[B-side "Atomic Rock" non-LP]

7" Singles
»We Are The Band« Atlantic 1981
[UK issue in company sleeve, B-side "Atomic Rock" non-LP]
»We Are The Band« Atlantic 1981
[Dutch issue with 'group image' picture sleeve]
»We Are The Band« Atlantic 1981
[Italian issue with 'logo' picture sleeve]
»Trickster« Atlantic 1982
[Both tracks non-LP]

Promotional Releases
»Sounds Atomic Rock Roadshow« Lyntone 1981
[7" flexi disc featuring "Way Of The World", given free with 'Sounds' magazine]

Compilation Appearances
"Soldier" on »Metal Explosion« LP BBC Records 1980
[Different to album version]
"We Are The Band" on »Rock The Nation« LP WEA 1981
"Warhead" on »Hard« LP WEA 1981

MOSELLE

J. Morelli

And still they keep coming. You can't honestly say we're not covering obscure enough acts in this mighty tome, can you? The oddly-named MOSELLE are a bit of a mystery at present, but were (in spite of their foreign-sounding identity and suspiciously-European writing credits) apparently a British ensemble, with mention of their recent visit to Hull's Fairview Studios being made in an advert for Ebony Records in 'Kerrang' towards the end of 1982. Presumably the result of the aforementioned recording session, their sole »Call Me« 7" from the following year turns out to have been a reasonable enough stab at tuneful rock/metal with slightly affected vocals (which, irritatingly, bring CHRIS DE BURGH to mind every time I hear them), the style being quite similar to that mastered by SHO-

GUN several years later. The A-side itself is a lightweight and commercial effort in the GRAND PRIX vein, featuring harmonised backing vocals and a curiously mechanical drum sound, whereas flipside "Rock Anthem" is a big improvement, although the title is somewhat misleading. This is a faster, straight ahead number with capable guitar parts and a memorable chorus with greater appeal to the average NWOBHM fan. The lyrics are of the fairly inconsequential, lovey-dovey kind that's best left to Eurovision Song Contest entries, so the band lose points for that, but this single (again, no sleeve appears to exist) certainly warrants its place in this book. MOSELLE could have been based pretty much anywhere, as the Ebony-owned studios were frequented by visitors from all over the country (and, on occasion, from overseas), so any further information would be greatly appreciated. Whatever the story, though, they seem to have gone under with great haste, and little was heard of them after their vinyl debut.

7" Singles
»Call Me« SRT 1983

MOTHER'S RUIN

Dale Nathan (v,k)
Phil Hunt (g)
Malcolm Jones (g)
Andy Brown (b)
Martin Bell (d)

All things considered, North London's MOTHER'S RUIN (not to be confused with the minor band from the West Country who appeared on Ebony's »The Metal Collection Vol.1« compilation several years later) weren't exactly the most high-profile act in terms of live appearances during the NWOBHM period, although they were quite prolific with their vinyl offerings once they got started. To be honest, little is known about how it all began for MOTHER'S RUIN, and none of the members appear to have been involved with other recording acts either before or since, so it's entirely possible that they were assembled mainly as a studio project in the first instance. Whatever the story, their first taste of the recording facility as an ensemble seems to have been in 1981, after they had signed to the little-known Spectra label with the intention of getting their first single into the shops. The »Streetfighter« 7" (b/w "Leaving You") appeared in due course, and this effort was soon selling in reasonable quantities thanks to their label's handy distribution deal through Pinnacle. It wasn't exactly the heaviest material you were ever likely to hear (especially the ballad on the B-side), although the record showcased some highly capable musicianship, suggesting that this might not have been an inexperienced bunch of youngsters after all. In any case, the A-side was a competently-played slice of melodic rock/metal, with some undeniably substantial guitar work thrown into the melting pot at times. In terms of NWOBHM contemporaries, you'd probably be looking at the likes of FRENZY, ALKATRAZZ or even MAMA'S BOYS, although MOTHER'S RUIN were hardly representative of the NWOBHM ethos in any sense.

The following year, Spectra Records commissioned a full LP, and the lads were more than happy to oblige, although personnel problems appear to have necessitated the use of a guest bassist, Andy Brown (possibly on loan from the MOVIE STARS, but I can't be totally sure), for the relevant studio sessions. Sadly, their »Road To Ruin« set turned out to be an extremely lightweight and disappointing selection of compositions (the occasional glimpse of guitar artistry largely failing to save the situation), the outfit trying their hardest to come across as an Americanised, chart-busting, pop/rock proposition, veering between semi-AOR (FOREIGNER, BOSTON) and even more melodic, mainstream material (the EAGLES, STEELY DAN), rendering the album as a purchase which can only really be recommended to fans of H.G.B., TRADER, ANGEL STREET and their easy-going ilk. Strangely, however, the long-player contained one truly stunning number, the immensely catchy and energetic "Turn Another Corner" (as included on the »NWOBHM Vol.2« bootleg CD), a track which stands out like a sore thumb amongst the shocking dross which comprises the rest of the set. Unfortunately, however, Spectra chose to issue a pair of truly unremarkable singles in the shape of »Say It's Not True« (b/w "It's Illogical") and »Streetlights« (where the aforementioned "Turn Another Corner" was criminally relegated to the B-side), although these appear to have fared slightly better than might have been expected, with "Streetlights" even making it into the 'Top 30 Kuts' listings in 'Kerrang' in April 1982. Interestingly, "Streetfighter" also put in an appearance in the same chart a couple of months later, suggesting that the first single might even have picked up a few extra sales on the back of the album release.

Even by 1983, however, the name of

MOTHER'S RUIN already seemed to be falling into disuse, and one can only assume that the venture had drawn to a close without any further visits to the studio becoming a reality. Their original vinyl releases, however, currently command fairly hefty prices amongst fervent NWOBHM collectors, something which is rather at odds with the outfit's unrepresentative style and lightweight tendencies, so it looks as though a few naughty individuals might have been spreading a few tales about the musical merit of MOTHER'S RUIN over the years. In any case, their long-player appears to be the most collectable of the bunch, while the »Say It's Not True« and »Streetlights« singles are valued significantly higher than the musically-superior »Streetfighter« effort, purely because of the fact that the later pair were issued with picture sleeves. It's a funny old world, you know.

LP's
»Road To Ruin« Spectra Records 1982

7" Singles
»Streetfighter« Spectra Records 1981
[Both tracks non-LP]
»Streetlights« Spectra Records 1982
»Say It's Not True« Spectra Records 1982

Compilation Appearances
"Turn Another Corner" on »NWOBHM Vol.2« Bootleg CD 1992

MOURNBLADE

Duncan 'Dunken' Mullett (v)
Rich Jones (g)
Clive Baxter (b)
Nigel Tubb (d)

Formed as long ago as 1982, Middlesex-based MOURNBLADE (another NWOBHM-era outfit who lifted their name from Michael Moorcock's writings) originally came together as a four-piece, and, in due course, took it upon themselves to compose a fairly original style of material with something of a fantasy/sci-fi basis. They first came to prominence with their »Servants Of Fate« cassette from 1984, featuring such numbers as "Anthem Of Chaos", "Eternal Champion", "Desolation", "Sidewinder", "Sorcerer" and the title track itself. This showed the group to be operating in a rather unique area of heavy, complex metal with progressive undertones, bringing forth tenuous comparisons with the likes of DEEP SWITCH, HELL and MARQUIS DE SADE. All in all, it was a highly competent offering, and it wasn't long before the musicians (who were now making regular trips to the studio in order to lay down their newly-penned selections) managed to swing a lucrative deal with the influential Flicknife concern. With the lads having plenty of material at their disposal, a mini-LP was swiftly assembled for their new sponsors, although they were already experiencing a few personnel problems. Having lost the services of Nigel Tubb before the year was out, MOURNBLADE duly broke in 'new' drummer Jeff Ward (who was actually only 'on loan' from WHITE LIGHTNING), before adding a keyboard player, Derek Jasnock, to create a more commanding musical presence. They also struggled to keep hold of a suitable bassist, and one or two of their subsequent studio sessions credited guest contributions from Richard Max Goddard, another individual who (after becoming a paid-up member for a short spell) was to play an important part in WHITE LIGHTNING's later activities.

Issued in the first half of 1985, the »Time's Running Out« mini-album saw the group building on their initial foundations (reworking some of their formative compositions in the process) by developing an even heavier sound with various effects thrown in (spoken sections, CHEMICAL ALICE-style spacey guitars and crashing keyboards) to liven things up a bit. It certainly made them stand out from the crowd, and, with the possible exception of GOLGOTHA (see separate entry), there weren't too many metal-oriented outfits attempting such ambitious material at the time. The six-tracker isn't a masterpiece by any means, however, and the band occasionally (as they were happy to admit in many of their subsequent interviews) veer slightly too close to HAWKWIND territory for comfort. The spoken intro to "Titanium Hero", for example, is a bit embarrassing, and the sound effects are a tad overpowering at times, but original, well-crafted tracks such as "Battlezone" and "In The Arms Of Morpheus" compensate for these minor shortcomings. Sadly, MOURNBLADE's first vinyl release was hit by serious distribution problems, which left the lads with little option but to sell the records themselves. Nevertheless, they still managed to shift a considerable number of units at gigs (unsurprising, given that they were one of the hardest-working live acts of the day) and through mail-order, although this experience led them to become wary of apparently-lucrative record deals.

Instead, the band (who had now located a permanent rhythm section in the form of one-time KILLERHURTZ bassist Paul White and erstwhile BLITZ drummer Garry Bowler) elected to concentrate on cassette releases such as »Ein Heldentraum« and »The Titanium Tapes« (primarily circulated amongst the many members of their thriving official fan club) for the next year or two. A couple of line-up changes occurred along the way, with Derek Jasnock being replaced by new recruit Peter Jon Lazenby in 1986,

before founder member Rich Jones decided to depart the following year in order to start his own offshoot called BLADEWITCH, a venture which (like its almost identical 90's equivalent, THUNDERBLADE) was to prove a somewhat short-lived and unsuccessful affair. A likely replacement was soon identified (former JIFFY BAG axeman Steve James, who was only too happy to join in the fun), and so MOURNBLADE briefly maintained something of a stable line-up once again. They continued to gig sporadically, winning generally favourable reviews in the rock press of the day, although it gradually became apparent that both their over-the-top musical direction and outdated image (the kind of theatrical, 'Mad Max'-influenced, post-apocalypse style favoured by the likes of ROGUE MALE and DEEP SWITCH) needed something of a kick up the backside to get things moving again.

In the end, Mullett more or less dissolved the original band in the winter of 1987, restructuring the project around himself over a period of several months (abandoning previously-announced plans to release a new single featuring "Red Hot Reputation" and "Good Enough To Eat" along the way) as he checked out minor acts in the live environment and attempted to persuade one or two of the more impressive musicians to join him in his own venture. By the latter half of 1988, Mullett was celebrating the fact that a novel line-up had finally been assembled, although, in truth, he had merely roped in erstwhile cohorts Paul White (who, having adopted the nickname of 'Blacken', had latterly been playing bass for the excellently-named GAY VICARS) and Steve James (who was now operating under the assumed identity of 'Steve Tallens'), the troupe being completed by enigmatic drummer Magpie (a Mancunian who was supposedly a former member of TORA TORA, but I've no idea how reliable this assertion actually was). Luckily, most people failed to appreciate the fact that this wasn't really an all-new MOURNBLADE after all, and a handy deal with the flourishing G.I. concern (a division of Plastic Head Music) came their way with little delay, whereupon a full-length effort was duly laid down over a period of several months. Issued at the beginning of 1989, the »Live Fast, Die Young« set was a more basic, stripped-down affair which saw the lads eschewing their previous grandiose musical constructions and contrived image for something rather more accessible. Asked about their progression as the long-player hit the shops, Dunken explained: *'You're bound to be pigeonholed, but we'd rather be compared to British bands than to American ones. I mean, people have compared us to the RAMONES and people who've seen us live often mention IGGY POP, but I reckon it's more of a cross between early DAMNED, »Machine Gun Etiquette« era, and »Bomber/Overkill« period MOTÖRHEAD. It's not all about synthesizers, drums taken from computers, that's bollocks!'* (Ref: Metal Forces No.38, April 1989).

In all honesty, it was a truly radical departure from their original material, and the reinvented MOURNBLADE should really be regarded as an entirely different proposition by this stage. Furthermore, the frontman's DAMNED/MOTÖRHEAD comparisons were fairly inaccurate (wishful thinking, perhaps), and I'd say that WOLFSBANE, ZODIAC MINDWARP or even good old TIGERTAILZ would be considerably nearer the mark. It's not a bad release (two of the better numbers being "Desdemona" and "American Dream"), but, if the fans had been expecting something closely resembling their vinyl debut, then this would have been a pretty major shock for them. On the back of their first full album, however, the lads were invited to lay down a session for the 'Friday Rock Show', and they grasped this opportunity with both hands. Initially broadcast on the 14th of July 1989, the outfit took the chance to showcase "If You Can't Be Good", "Red Hot Reputation" and "American Dream" from their latest collection, alongside the previously-unheard (unless you had the CD version of the album) "Whizzkid". It was a pretty decent performance, and plans were soon outlined to issue a single based around the aforementioned "Whizzkid" in the second half of 1989, but this offering simply didn't materialise in the long term. Nevertheless, MOURNBLADE announced their intention (literally a couple of months later) to release an EP to coincide with their winter tour in support of MOTÖRHEAD, so they were evidently keen to get some additional product onto the market. Again, however, this doesn't appear to have made it past the planning stage.

Clearly, all these cancelled releases and half-baked plans didn't exactly bode too well for the band's collective future, and things soon began to fall apart. MOURNBLADE finally ground to a halt in the spring of 1990, the members going their separate ways at fairly short notice and without giving much in the way of an explanation. In fact, it transpires that the unfortunately-named Mullett had decided that it was finally time to lay the name to rest and start again under a brand-new project. He joined forces with the WILDHEARTS for a very brief spell later in the year (former TOBRUK frontman Snake having flown the coop by this stage), although it would appear that this wasn't a particularly constructive relationship. No doubt Mullett tried to establish various other musical ventures of his own, although he appears to have given up on his quest for fame in the long run. Magpie and Blacken, on the other hand, announced semi-serious plans to collaborate together in a *'more nasty and loud'* act immediately following the MOURNBLADE split, and they subsequently demoed some material under the identity of MUTANT, although their enthusiasm for this project seems to have waned within a relatively short space of time.

LP's
»Live Fast, Die Young« G.I. Records 1988

Mini-LP's
»Time's Running Out« Flicknife Records 1985

Promotional Releases
»Live Fast, Die Young« G.I. Records 1988
[Promo album in black stickered sleeve with signed photo, one hundred copies only]

CD's
»Live Fast, Die Young« G.I. Records 1988
[With extra track "Whizzkid"]

Compilation Appearances
"If You Can't Be Good" on »Shooting From The Hip« LP G.I. Records 1989
"Red Hot Reputation" on »Shooting From The Hip« LP G.I. Records 1989

MOVIE STARS

Robbie Matthews (v)
Clive Wagerfield (g)
Andy Brown (b)
Larry Lamborne (k)
Mick Gardiner (d)

After the RADIO STARS and the TELEVISION PERSONALITIES, I suppose it was just a matter of time before a band named themselves the MOVIE STARS, although it seems a slightly unusual choice for the particular style of music involved in this case. Their sole »No Time To Kill« single from 1982 (the five-piece having apparently formed in 1980 or thereabouts) is a listenable enough example of prog/melodic rock crossover, with the nominated A-side (after a lengthy instrumental intro) coming across as a confident blend of SHERWOOD, CHASE and LIAISON. The less epic reverse, "Heroes", on the other hand, is somewhat more lightweight and unmemorable, apart from the distinctly QUEEN-like guitar passage towards the end. They were remarkably fortunate to be approached with regard to contributing a session to the 'Friday Rock Show' later in the year, with the selections "No Time To Kill" (again), "It's Your Life", "Waking Up" and "Eye Of The Storm" being broadcast to the nation on the 5th of November 1982. It seemed, on the face of it, as though the group had a few decent efforts in their repertoire, and might be capable of greater things in the future. Listening to these session recordings with a critical ear, however, their tendency to switch from progressively-inclined material to facile mainstream rock at a moment's notice (even within the same track) is quite distracting, and it smacks of indecisiveness rather than originality.

The overwhelming lack of public reaction to this particular slot (Tommy Vance gave it the thumbs-up, though) would tend to indicate that there just wasn't a mass market for this type of music at the time, and the group (along with similarly-minded acts such as CHEMICAL ALICE and MAYDAY) presumably disappeared into obscurity shortly afterwards. Their two-tracker was issued (without a picture sleeve) on the small Lancaster label, which, logically, would suggest that this bunch originated from the

North West of England, but not so. They were, in fact, from the prog-worshipping region of Buckinghamshire (the lads frequented the local club circuit and regularly played in thriving, rock-loving cities such as Oxford in their formative years), and it looks as though they were another example of a smaller outfit attempting to hang on to the coat-tails of a more successful regional act, in this case MARILLION. Whatever the motivation behind the creation of the MOVIE STARS, though, their one-off slice of vinyl certainly wasn't manufactured in particularly generous quantities, and hardly any examples have been offered for sale in recent memory.

7" Singles
»No Time To Kill« Lancaster Records 1982

MYTHRA

Vince High (v)
John Roach (g)
Maurice Bates (rg)
Pete Melsom (b)
Barry Hopper (d)

Possibly the best-known (and yet still rather mysterious until now) of the *'minor'* NWOBHM groups, the story of the legendary MYTHRA began in around 1975, when three Tyneside schoolfriends *viz.* John Roach, Pete Melsom and Maurice Bates, got together with the intention of forming a small-time covers band. Recruiting drummer Kenny Anderson after finding their feet in terms of the type of material they wanted to play, the outfit (then known as ZARATHUSTRA) started to play their first small gigs as a four-piece, with Maurice Bates contributing vocals at the time. With a repertoire including material by LED ZEPPELIN, BLACK SABBATH, HUMBLE PIE, UFO and RUSH, the lads managed to become a popular local rock/metal attraction a good two or three years before the major NWOBHM explosion, confounding all the cynics who assured everyone that heavy music was a spent force. Moving into 1977, they were forced to seek out a replacement drummer, whereupon Barry Hopper was invited to join in the fun, although it still seemed as though a vital piece of the jigsaw was missing. Before long, however, the central characters realised that a dedicated vocalist might enhance their sound somewhat, and so a young chap called Vince High was called up to the ranks to act as frontman, his recruitment convincing the musicians that they were finally heading in the right direction.

As the years went by, the lads became slightly more aware of their own potential, and slowly began penning a few original numbers in order to gauge the public reaction, which turned out to be overwhelmingly positive. Having now additionally decided to adopt the eminently more pronounceable name MYTHRA (for those interested in etymology, this stemmed from the Zoroastrian root *'Mithras'*, an identity which was itself utilised by at least one musical act), the group were ultimately to become extremely close associates of another emergent North East proposition, namely AXE (the forerunner of the famous FIST), embarking on a long-running relationship and regularly covering the latter's "Name, Rank And Serial Number" in their live set. Working the local club scene at a time when the likes of SON OF A BITCH (later SAXON), RAVEN and GEORDIE were also doing the rounds, the ensemble gradually became firm favourites in their region, eventually playing to appreciative audiences several times a week. Noticing that some of their younger followers often had difficulties getting into the licensed pubs and clubs, however, MYTHRA set about organising regular events of their own at modest venues (community centres and the like), hiring PA equipment and doing the promotion work themselves. With these gigs proving to be remarkably successful affairs, the musicians eventually ended up making a sufficiently substantial profit that a trip to the recording studio became a financial viability.

Following the astute advice of Terry Gavaghan, the boss of Guardian Records, the group decided to press some copies of a vinyl EP in order to get themselves known further afield, rather than merely concentrating on producing a somewhat anonymous cassette product as most hopefuls did. John Roach elaborates: *'The idea behind the EP was to attract media and record company interest and hence become incredibly rich and famous. At the time of the original Guardian issue there were only two hundred copies pressed-those that weren't given away sold very quickly but, as MYTHRA hadn't played outside of the North East at this time, they only sold locally. There were subsequent pressings of the EP, done quickly to try to meet demand, but no one will admit to how many. I remember "Death And Destiny" being number one in the 'Sounds' Heavy Metal Chart for over eleven weeks.'* (Ref: Private communication, June 1999). I wouldn't get too excited by the revelation that the initial pressing of the »Death And Destiny« EP was limited to a couple of hundred copies, though, as these are indistinguishable from later issues. As the above statement attests, it took the musicians no time at all to shift the first batch of records, sending a few dozen copies off for promotional purposes and selling the rest locally. It's easy to see why they all got snapped up so quickly: "Killer" (featuring *the* archetypal NWOBHM riff, although the lads vehemently deny nicking it from BUDGIE's "Breadfan"), "Overlord" and "UFO" (not to mention the esteemed title track itself) all represented absolutely superb examples of energetic, upbeat, heavy NWOBHM with a respectful nod towards early DIAMOND HEAD, although occasional similarities to the likes of HOLLOW GROUND, REINCARNATE, JJ'S POWERHOUSE and A II Z can also be glimpsed at times. Overall, therefore, it's no great surprise that MYTHRA are known to have had something of an influence on METALLICA's early sound…

After the initial run of EP's had been exhausted, Guardian soon set about the task of pressing the four-tracker in earnest. Several thousand copies were duly manufactured (no picture sleeve was ever issued at any stage, contrary to rumours and/or wishful thinking by some) and these proceeded to sell by the bucketload. Before long, the title track was featured on the BBC's 'Friday Rock Show', and the EP as a whole received generous airplay on their local station, Radio Metro. Some influential journalists were keen to register their approval of the release, with Geoff Barton of 'Sounds' (where "Death And Destiny" itself was to spend several months at the top of their Heavy Metal Chart) citing the EP as *'this year's »Getcha Rocks Off«'*, which was high praise indeed! While the original Guardian pressing found its way into the hands of many metal aficionados nationwide (having sold well at the likes of Bullet Records, who were, within a matter of months, already describing the release as *'legendary'*), MYTHRA's management deemed that there was sufficient demand for a more high-profile re-release, which resulted in the master tapes being passed to the influential Pinnacle label, who were to issue the EP in 1980 on their little-known Street Beat subsidiary in both 12" and 7" forms (the latter omitting "Overlord"), this time in a rather fetching picture sleeve which commands relatively high prices among collectors of the genre today. Again, sales were plentiful, although, unfairly, the band members never reaped the financial rewards themselves.

MYTHRA's original guitarist (and major writing force) John Roach was to leave the fold fairly amicably in the spring of 1980, the academic axeman having decided to return to his studies at college, although he later hooked up with his old amigos in FIST, playing on their »Back With A Vengeance« album and making a significant

contribution to the songwriting side of things. His place in MYTHRA was swiftly taken by the youthful Mick Rundle, and it wasn't long before the lads signed a new management deal, which resulted in them being added to the bill for the legendary *'Heavy Metal Barn Dance'*, held at the Bingley Hall in Stafford, alongside MOTÖRHEAD, SAXON, GIRLSCHOOL, ANGEL WITCH, VARDIS and WHITE SPIRIT, infamous for the post-gig festivities as much as the concert itself! Although the band received a mixed reception from the crowd, a good time was apparently had by all concerned, and the event was even reviewed in the music press of the day. The group should have received some additional exposure a couple of months later, although things swiftly went pear-shaped when a prestigious support slot with TED NUGENT collapsed before their very eyes. Although MYTHRA had originally been earmarked for Gonzo's European tour, the management of WILD HORSES stepped in with a more lucrative offer and the cash-strapped MYTHRA were forced to renege on the deal as a result. Towards the end of the year, the revised line-up recorded a couple of demo sessions (where tracks such as "Warrior Of Time", "Heaven Lies Above", "Together Forever" and "At Least I Tried" were captured on tape) at the Guardian facility in Durham, this venture having been financed by Street Beat with a view to issuing a follow-up EP. During these visits to the studio, however, Mick Rundle's lack of experience was to be put under the spotlight, and it became necessary to re-record some of the material at a later stage in order to achieve the desired effect.

Towards the end of their existence, MYTHRA tried out new guitarist Alex Perry in place of the recently-ousted Mick Rundle, which seems to have given them a rather better chance of making the grade, as the newcomer was, by all accounts, a considerably more capable musician. Not only that, but Perry was even able to contribute the occasional composition to their ever-expanding repertoire, which was a particularly valuable asset now that the prolific John Roach was no longer part of the picture. In the long term, however, the fickle Street Beat decided not to pursue their option to subsidise the outfit's second slice of vinyl (a grotesquely gauche decision, given the truly phenomenal success of their debut release), and the lads began to feel (with some justification, admittedly) that the odds were cruelly stacked against them. With rejection and disappointment seemingly lurking around every corner, therefore, the group as a whole began to lose heart, and the writing appeared to be on the wall. MYTHRA's promotional team subsequently suggested that they would benefit from a full-scale relocation to the nation's capital, but this met with disapproval from the individual members, who were all happily settled in the North East. By the end of 1981, the lads had finally called it a day.

After MYTHRA's demise, sticksman Barry Hopper eventually went on to join fellow hopefuls HELLANBACH (another outfit with links to FIST, as bassist Kev Charlton had been a roadie in the latter's »Back With A Vengeance« days) as a replacement for Steve Walker, whereupon he proceeded to play on their second album in 1984. Original guitarist John Roach, apart from his high-profile activities with FIST, was also involved in a less-serious covers concern called CENTREFOLD, where he took to the stage alongside a variety of regional scenesters such as Harry Hill (from FIST), Glen Coates (from HOLLOW GROUND/FIST) and a bassist called Pete Scott. Interestingly, a version of this long-running outfit is apparently still doing the rounds in the North East, although countless personnel changes along the way mean that none of the original members remain affiliated with the group. Maurice Bates and Barry Hopper have, in more recent times, been involved with a rockabilly-style (!) band going by the not-very-sensible name of BESSIE AND THE ZINC BUCKETS (or, rather more succinctly, just the BUCKETS), a project which has, in its day, also featured various ex-HELLANBACH personnel.

With interest in NWOBHM obscurities being rekindled towards the end of the 80's, MYTHRA were quite rightly featured in the '10th Anniversary' supplement compiled by 'Kerrang', with Geoff Barton once more singing the praises of their now-legendary EP and insisting that the title track would undoubtedly *'make a mega-magnificent METALLICA cover version'*. As it was, the lads were unlucky to miss out on being included on Lars Ulrich's NWOBHM compilation due to licensing difficulties, as the man himself explained: *'Actually, the only band that said no was MYTHRA. You see, the thing is, it's not just the band who have to say yes, it's who owns the song, and in the MYTHRA situation it was like the bass player's great uncle or something who had financed it, and he had taken control of the tapes and basically said he wasn't interested.'* (Ref: Metal Forces No.56, November 1990). In fact, it would appear that it was actually the band's former label who refused to release the material (for reasons best known to themselves), as John Roach later confirmed: *'If I had been contacted, I would have said yes. So would all of the other* guys. Lars was doing a great thing in acknowledging his influences-exposing the roots of METAL-LICA. I can only assume that Terry Gavaghan was contacted and said no. I understand Lars was told that the tracks were owned by the person who financed it-who was not in the band. The truth is, the five original members of MYTHRA own all of the rights and title to the »Death And Destiny« EP.' (Ref: Private Communication, June 1999). So there you go. In any case, it was a great injustice, if you ask me.

There had long been rumoured to be a fair amount of unissued MYTHRA material languishing on tape (a handful of tracks were in circulation among collectors, albeit in pretty poor quality), but it wasn't until the late 90's that (the now defunct) Guardian's archives were raided and some master tapes exhumed. As a result, the »Death And Destiny« CD (hardly the most original of titles) was assembled and released (without the knowledge or consent of the musicians, it must be stated) in 1998, the set featuring the EP and aforementioned demo tracks, plus several other unreleased takes, identified as "Paradise", "England", "The Age Of Machine", "Vicious Bastard" and "Blue Acid". With the latter few having evidently come from an unlabelled source tape, it subsequently became apparent that certain attributed titles were inaccurate ("Paradise", "The Death Of A Loved One" and "Blue Acid" should be "New Life", "Together Forever" and "W.A.S.A.", respectively), although a second pressing with more detailed sleeve notes and corrected versions may now be in the offing, given that certain ex-members of MYTHRA are now in contact with those responsible for the release. A full-scale band reformation is also something of a possibility at some stage, with the lads still living in close proximity and keeping in contact over the years. Certainly, interest in the CD (and the group in general) remains extremely strong, and it's nice to see such a talented outfit (who are still fondly remembered in their locality after all these years) being given a bit of exposure and recognition as we enter the new millennium.

12" EP's
»Death And Destiny« Street Beat Records 1980
[All four tracks included]

7" EP's
»Death And Destiny« Guardian 1979
[Original issue with four tracks]
»Death And Destiny« Street Beat Records 1980
[Second issue with three tracks]

CD's
»Death And Destiny« British Steel 1998
[Compilation of mostly unreleased studio material]

Compilation Appearances
"Killer" on »NWOBHM Vol.2« Bootleg CD 1992 + »N.W.O.B.H.M. Metal Rarities Vol.1« CD British Steel 1996
"Death And Destiny" on »N.W.O.B.H.M. Metal Rarities Vol.1« CD British Steel 1996
"UFO" on »N.W.O.B.H.M. Metal Rarities Vol.1« CD British Steel 1996
"Overlord" on »N.W.O.B.H.M. Metal Rarities Vol.1« CD British Steel 1996

NATIONAL GOLD

Dave Edwards (v)

Although the Essex combo known as NATIONAL GOLD actually turned out to be quite a long-lived musical concern, the highlight of their time on Britain's music scene appears to be a seldom-seen two-tracker which dates from as far back as 1981. Despite being quick off the blocks in terms of getting a self-financed slice of vinyl onto the market, this bunch (fronted by a certain Dave Edwards, possibly the ex-REMUS DOWN BOULEVARD stalwart) seem to have been well and truly overlooked in terms of media exposure at the time. In fact, they don't even seem to have attracted a significant following in the East End, suggesting that London's metalheads weren't too enamoured of their slightly dated sound. Still, their one-off single couples a pair of highly listenable numbers, both of which come across as capable, raunchy rockers in the general TERRAPLANE, BABY TUCKOO or TRUX vein. Admittedly, the peculiarly-titled "I Need Your Time" borrows quite heavily from the original BAD COMPANY design, although it's performed with great self-assurance, with some strong guitars and decent vocals on display throughout. Mind you, I'd say that flipside "I'm A Loner" (a marginally more energetic and memorable cut) would have made a better A-side, but it was still a perfectly respectable effort all round. Sadly, this inauspicious opening gambit (not issued in a picture sleeve, by the looks of things) was presumably swamped by the massive influx of vinyl releases at the time, and I suspect that relatively few copies ended up being shifted to the local rock fraternity in the months that followed.

You might reasonably expect, therefore, that NATIONAL GOLD's existence would (like so many of their contemporaries) have been a predictably fleeting one, the lads failing to last the distance as the NWOBHM movement finally began to fizzle out. In fact, the persevering bunch plugged away for the remainder of the decade and beyond, presumably delighting a hardcore following at small-time shows throughout the South East. Strangely enough, however, these musicians almost won themselves a prestigious deal in the early 90's, a reversal of fortunes which came about in utterly bizarre circumstances when an individual purporting to be none other than fallen FLEETWOOD MAC luminary Peter Green (who had kept his distance from the music scene for two decades) emerged from the shadows and offered his services. Needless to say, the lads were delighted to lay out the welcome mat, and were soon undertaking a few rehearsals. Whereas NATIONAL GOLD had always been a small-time proposition, 'NATIONAL GOLD featuring Peter Green' was a completely different kettle of fish, so the record companies duly began taking notice of their activities. In due course, a contract was indeed proffered, whereupon it came to light that this particular 'Peter Green' was a total impostor, all of which resulted in the deal being withdrawn with immense haste. With NATIONAL GOLD being reduced to a veritable laughing stock, there was very little to be gained from carrying on, and their good name was laid to rest shortly thereafter. Their lone single, however, is a remarkably scarce item these days, and is likely to be unearthed infrequently.

7" Singles
»I Need Your Time« K&M Records 1981

NATO

David Simpson (v,k)
Michael Procter (g)
Graham Brown (b)
John Ward (d)

Tyneside's enigmatic NATO hardly managed to make much of a name for themselves during their time together, and only a scarcely-sighted single now reminds us that they ever existed at all. The foursome were presumably on the go at the height of the NWOBHM explosion, but failed to get their name mentioned very often (if at all), which is a bit of a shame, as their one-off »Gangland« 7" showed a fair amount of potential. The A-side is quite hard to pin down in terms of easy comparisons, the snotty vocals and the energetic, hard-driving guitars sharing some common ground with the punk movement, and the general feeling (apart from the rather unusual chorus) is really more along the lines of VIRGIN STAR or TOAD THE WET SPROCKET than anything else. The flipside ("Tied Down"), on the other hand, is a somewhat more restrained piece, and has a very slight THIN LIZZY feel at times, although there's still something undeniably quirky (it's not out and out metal, but certainly fits in pretty well with the NWOBHM ethos) about the whole thing. To be frank, this doesn't scream 'early 80's' in the way that most rock and metal releases of the period tend to, and, given that it isn't dated explicitly, I would have assumed that it was released later in the decade.

Mind you, the modest mail-order price quoted on the reverse of the lurid orange sleeve (with a basic logo design) certainly seems appropriate for the period in question, and the general consensus of opinion now appears to be that the most likely date would perhaps be 1981, although it's somewhat bizarre that any emergent Tyneside outfit would release a song called "Gangland" within months of the famous TYGERS OF PAN TANG version. Time will tell, no doubt, but the NATO single is still a collectable enough piece to justify its inclusion here. The only name of interest in this fly-by-night venture is that of guitarist Mick Procter, who had a very busy time of it throughout the 80's, lending his services to the likes of JESS COX, BLITZKRIEG and the TYGERS OF PAN TANG themselves, usually as a session musician as opposed to a full-time touring member. Apart from Procter, however, there's very little to report on the post-NATO activities of any of his former colleagues, and I would imagine that the others had gone back to their day jobs by the middle of the decade.

7" Singles
»Gangland« D.V. Records 1981?

NEON SPIRIT

Kim Hooker (b)
Steve
Andy

Yet another of those hopelessly obscure and monumentally rare records from South Wales comes in the shape of the self-financed single issued by the long-forgotten (but excellently-named) NEON SPIRIT, an unrenowned act from the Glamorgan area. Although the unassuming record itself (there's no picture sleeve, needless to say) completely fails to enlighten us as to who was responsible for the music, it's been established that the driving force was actually none other than Kim Hooker in his pre-RANKELSON (and, obviously, pre-TIGERTAILZ) days. Issued as far back as 1982, the single is marred by an atrocious, tinny production (I've heard far better rehearsal tapes) with badly-tuned guitars, suggesting that the recording budget must have been absolutely microscopic, as the eminent Mal Skrines was evidently capable of considerably better results (see, for example, the expertly-produced TOK-IO ROSE 7"). Musically, however, it's quite an energetic effort in a semi-glam style, with elements of SACRED ALIEN, HELLRAZER and (occasionally) STORYTELLER coming across reasonably strongly. It has to be said, though, that the nominated A-side, "Loser", isn't quite as listenable as the reverse ("Cruisin' Into The Unknown"), the latter being a more upbeat composition with pretty impressive guitar work in places. It looks as though the band were a fairly short-lived affair, as RANKELSON came into being towards the end of 1984, although I suspect that few actually mourned the passing of NEON SPIRIT. Nevertheless, it's worth pondering (for a couple of seconds, at least) whether or not the lads would perhaps have been able to deliver the goods on a more generous studio budget. If you've got one of these, incidentally, I wouldn't part with it unless someone offers you a fair bit of dosh, as they really are phenomenally scarce these days.

7" Singles
»Loser« Private 1982

NEVER AMBER

I. Nicoll

OK, so this is hardly the place for socio-economic observations, but the sad fact remains that relatively few Scottish rock bands (particularly those outwith the main population centres) were in a position to finance their own vinyl releases in the late 70's and early 80's, especially when compared, for example, with all those lucky acts based in the more affluent South. In truth, the NWOBHM hopefuls in areas such as London, Kent, Essex etc. often had a much easier ride, given that they stood a greater chance either of being sponsored by small-time labels or being able to stump up the spondulicks themselves, given that rock gigs were a relatively common occurrence in these areas, and the outfits could rake in a bit of cash on the back of these events. This isn't to say that there wasn't a thriving scene in Scotland (or Wales, or Ireland, for that matter) in the NWOBHM era (it was a genuinely nationwide phenomenon), but it still seems likely that many young hopefuls never made it to the vinyl stage largely as a consequence of demographics. Mind you, I suppose all the punk, indie and mod acts from these 'poorer' areas were in precisely the same boat, and many of them managed to get something into the shops, so perhaps the metallers just got a particularly raw deal, for some strange reason.

One of the more obscure exceptions to the rule, however, is NEVER AMBER, a long-forgotten four-piece proposition who, having pretty much missed the original NWOBHM explosion, finally issued the unspectacular »Scene Of Surrender« two-tracker on (presumably their own label) Crunchy Recordz of Aberdeen in 1986. The A-side itself is, unfortunately, an interminably long and dreary ballad (explaining the need for a 12" pressing) which should undoubtedly have been chopped in half and hidden away on the flipside, while the band's arrangement of the nonsensically-titled "Renegade Is Love" (which appears, originally, to have been a somewhat obscure CURVED AIR composition) fares much better, with a heavier guitar sound and a catchy chorus which compensates for the unusual, ROXY MUSIC-style vocals throughout much of the song. Comparisons with better-known NWOBHM groups are few and far between, although, on the basis of the B-side, JAMESON RAID (and it's only a very faint similarity) would probably be about the nearest. Nice try, lads, but a 7" (preferably a tad heavier and a couple of years earlier) would have been a better idea. Needless to say, this appears to have been a one-off, and the musicians presumably went back into hiding soon after, but I can't see their 12" becoming one of the genre's major collectables in the near future.

12" Singles
»Scene Of Surrender« Crunchy Recordz 1986

NEXT BAND

Rocky Newton (v, b)

John Lockton (g)
Frank Noon (d)

Yorkshire's NEXT BAND (who actually relocated from Lincolnshire at an early stage) will, unfortunately, probably be remembered more for providing DEF LEPPARD with a stand-in drummer for their first EP than for anything they actually achieved themselves. To be honest, this is a bit of an injustice, as Frank Noon's early ensemble had managed to issue their own self-financed EP as far back as 1978, a record which more than deserves inclusion here. The outfit's musical inclinations were perhaps slightly unusual (overall, I reckon the closest comparison would be with MONEY), the musicians cultivating something of a proto-NWOBHM sound (with regard to the distinctive vocals) whilst still retaining a fairly conventional 70's framework in places. "Close Encounters" (with the appropriate film-intro) and "Too Many Losers" are undoubtedly the nearest to traditional NWOBHM territory, this capable pairing occasionally evoking the odd aspect of early TURBO or OVERDRIVE material. "Never On A Win", meanwhile, is a rather more laid-back inclusion, eliciting comparisons with DAWN TRADER or mid-period THIN LIZZY, while "Red Alert" has a detectable similarity to the likes of SLENDER THREAD at times. The selection of material was quite confusing, on the whole, and it tends to suggest that the young trio were possibly trying to come to terms with the musical revolution they sensed was just round the corner. With hindsight, I reckon the pairing of "Close Encounters" and "Too Many Losers" might have worked more effectively as a 7" single, and stretching things out as far as a four-tracker may have been slightly over-ambitious at that stage of their career. Mind you, the »Four By Three« EP (issued in a peculiar picture sleeve showing distorted images of the band members) should, in spite of its early date, be of interest to many NWOBHM fans, although it's not exactly an item which regularly turns up for sale.

The threesome certainly had potential, and were well on the way to developing a fairly energetic brand of heavy music (their EP had showcased some reasonably enjoyable guitar work, although it never really exploded into a full-on metal assault), but they failed to build on these foundations in the short term. Within around a year or so of the NEXT BAND's debut hitting the shops, however, the project evolved into one of the many varieties of RED ALERT (presumably named after the aforementioned EP track), before being forced to assume the new identity of WILDFIRE (see separate entry) to alleviate confusion with various other groups sharing the same moniker. All things considered, the NEXT BAND was, in retrospect, a bit of a nursery outfit for future NWOBHM scenesters: Rocky Newton subsequently went on to spend several turbulent years with LIONHEART before decamping to the MCAULEY SCHENKER GROUP towards the end of the decade, while John Lockton served time with the struggling WILD HORSES during the latter part of their existence, before collaborating (for a very short spell, admittedly) with John Sloman and Neil Murray in the ill-fated BADLANDS project after the departure of original guitarist John Sykes. Frank Noon's drumming skills, on the other hand, were evidently in high demand: after the eventual demise of WILDFIRE, he would later lend his services to the likes of LIONHEART, WILD HORSES, STAMPEDE, WAYSTED, DIANNO and the ELECTRIC GYPSIES, among others. Nice work if you can get it!

7" EP's
»**Four By Three**« Gannet Records 1978

NICKY MOORE BAND

Nicky Moore (v)
Leigh Highwood (g)
Pete Sinclair (b)
X-Ray (k)
Chris Sharley (d)

Having been a permanent fixture on the national club scene for much of the 70's (fronting traditional acts such as HACKENSACK and TIGER, for example), the logical next step for the capable Nicky Moore was to think about establishing a hard-rocking unit of his own, where (in theory) his songwriting creativity could be exploited to greatest effect. By the tail end of 1979, this musical vision, the functionally-named NICKY MOORE BAND, was finally being assembled, and various characters from London's bustling rock scene were swiftly drafted in to back up Moore's vocal talents. After finding their feet with some humble club appearances in and around the capital (they also hooked up with SAMSON for a few shows in due course), the quintet signed a deal with the emergent Street Tunes label, which (after some extended tinkering around in the studio) resulted in the combo releasing a three track EP to introduce themselves to the masses early in 1981. Oddly, however, the record was to boast just one original composition, a raunchy, singalong effort entitled "Year Of The Lie", which revealed that, contrary to widespread speculation, Moore had by no means severed his ties with the 70's scene and started afresh with an all-out NWOBHM assault. In fact, the outfit were perfectly content to operate in a similar mode to the likes of EXPORT, NUTZ and the WILD HORSES, and clearly felt no particular compulsion to jump on the metal bandwagon. Moreover, their debut's flipside contained reworkings of tracks originally penned by transatlantic luminaries of the previous decade, namely JOURNEY ("Walks Like A Lady") and BOSTON ("Smokin'"), both of which were listenable enough, but I reckon it would have been wiser to showcase another self-penned number. This isn't to say that the NICKY MOORE BAND lacked material of their own, as they were able to unveil a fairly comprehensive repertoire whenever they touted their wares around in the live environment, which saw them taking to the stage with the likes of the JACKIE LYNTON BAND in the months that followed. Before long, another 7" was on the cards, and so the lads delivered a pair of freshly-recorded efforts viz. the accessible "The Other Side" and yet another cover, namely BOSTON's "Long Time". They clearly had a particular fondness for the latter act, although it's fair to say that BOSTON never threatened to emulate their stellar North American success in the UK, so perhaps the NICKY MOORE BAND were slightly misguided in these attempts to become their British counterparts.

Still, the group's initial brace of Street Tunes releases were surely geared towards paving the way for a full album, and I suspect that such an undertaking was almost certainly in the offing at first, although it all became academic when frontman Nicky Moore was headhunted by SAMSON towards the end of 1981, following Bruce Dickinson's sudden decampment to IRON MAIDEN. Clearly, this pretty much signalled the end of the line as far as Moore's own venture was concerned, although he proceeded to enjoy a notable amount of success with the likes of SAMSON and MAMMOTH in years to come, so I don't imagine he ever regretted his decision to lay the NICKY MOORE BAND to rest. Most of his erstwhile colleagues seemingly vanished into anonymity in the immediate aftermath of the outfit's demise, and presumably went back to mundane session duties, although experienced sticksman Chris Sharley (who would work with the likes of HARD LINES and BAD INFLUENCE in years to come) was recruited to assist in the recording of the »Joint Forces« LP (credited to PAUL SAMSON) in 1986. Guitarist Leigh Highwood, on the other hand, eventually resurfaced with a club act called FLYING ANVIL (which supposedly featured ex-members of ALKATRAZZ) in the early 90's, although this venture failed to make all much of an impression. Both of the original NICKY MOORE BAND releases are surprisingly scarce items these days, incidentally, so pick them up (neither had a picture sleeve) if you ever happen to see a copy at a knock-down price.

7" EP's
»The Year Of The Lie« Street Tunes 1981

7" Singles
»The Other Side« Street Tunes 1981

NIGHT GAMES

Huw Williams (d)

Behind the ridiculously-obscure identity of NIGHT GAMES lay an extraordinarily short-lived studio project conceived by a young Welsh drummer named Huw Williams, who evidently assembled a few other citizens of Gwent to assist him in his musical quest for fame and fortune. Despite the observation that Williams wasn't exactly a high-profile name on the local rock scene, he clearly had a few good ideas up his sleeve, and so the participants were soon making a trip or two to the recording studio, although the only fruit of their labours was to be a one-sided promo single, the latter being circulated at some point in 1984. The chosen selection was "Searching For An Angel", a melodic and classy number which demonstrated a capable and confident writing style (elements of SHERWOOD and DAMASCUS on display throughout), with a few vaguely progressive undertones (in the manner of WHITE SPIRIT) coming across at times. It was all surprisingly coherent and polished for what must have been a thrown-together bunch of musicians, though, so there seemed to be plenty of potential in the first instance. Even so, it was a slightly strange decision to showcase just one tune from their repertoire.

Sadly, though, the record seems not to have caused all that much of a commotion in the media (to be honest, I suspect that few remotely influential individuals got a chance to hear it), and so there was no further activity on the NIGHT GAMES front thereafter. Williams soon abandoned the notion of spearheading a personal assault on the music scene, after which he moved on to a fair variety of other Welsh/West Country outfits such as OMEGA (not the well-known bunch who recorded for Rock Machine), COUNT SHOUT and DECEMBER ROSE, although none of these contrived to make an impact in the long term. History doesn't record who else was actually involved in the recording of the NIGHT GAMES release, but, given the immensely similar vocal performance, I would suspect that a few members of local heroes TRAITORS GATE might just have lent a hand. Since the record itself was pressed in minute quantities (dozens as opposed to hundreds), released only as a promotional device and issued as a white label in a plain sleeve, I wouldn't have thought that too many copies will ever turn up, so you might want to forget about adding this one to the collection…

7" Singles
»Searching For An Angel« Private 1984
[One-sided white label promo single]

NIGHTIME FLYER

Leighton John (v)
Roger Davies (g)
Neil Rogers (b)
Philip John (d)

Yet another band who emerged from the inexplicably fertile South Wales rock scene (there has been speculation that the collapse of the coal industry hit this area particularly hard, leading to a huge number of disenchanted working-class youths forming punk and metal outfits), Glamorgan's NIGHTIME FLYER were one of the first acts from the region to come to prominence in the NWOBHM era, with the self-financed »Out With A Vengeance« single from 1980 being the quartet's sole legacy to the collecting world. In fact, the 7" was actually recorded at the tail end of 1979 at the Spaceward facility in Cambridge, which can hardly have been the closest studio, but never mind. Mind you, this early contribution to the genre wasn't entirely representative of the rough'n'ready NWOBHM mentality in its purest sense, and the nominated A-side (with a discernable 70's rock influence in the guitar department) is rather more in keeping with the likes of SLEDGEHAMMER or TOAD THE WET SPROCKET than anything else, although the foursome still manage to deliver the track with a sincere sense of conviction. The unashamedly-titled "Heavy Metal Rules", on the flipside, is a considerably heavier offering, almost in the early QUARTZ or WITCHFINDER GENERAL mode, although the immensely clumsy attempt at an anthemic chorus was extraordinarily weak.

On the evidence of their debut release, it seems reasonable to surmise that NIGHTIME FLYER probably didn't have anything in their musical armoury which might ultimately have elevated them to the status of national metal heroes, although they no doubt developed something of a following at their oft-frequented live haunts. Given that the ensemble probably had relatively few like-minded contemporaries in their locality at that time, however, we should probably forgive them their musical limitations and view »Out With A Vengeance« as something of a pioneering release. Still, the two-tracker was on the end of some less-than-glowing reviews upon its release (including a real drubbing in 'Phoenix' fanzine, for example), so it evidently failed to strike the right chord with certain sections of the rock press. The single was, incidentally, issued in a sleeve featuring four individual photos (all very unconvincingly-posed) of the band members *'in action'*, and has turned up in significant quantities over the years (I think it actually went to a second pressing, so sales must have been pretty respectable), such that the asking price has never escalated to outlandish levels. Even so, the name of NIGHTIME FLYER seldom made it into the pages of the music weeklies (their major claim to fame being a couple of inclusions in the Heavy Metal Chart in 'Sounds' and a bafflingly high-ranking position in a Dutch metal poll), so it's possible that they didn't hang around for too long.

Following the extremely non-newsworthy demise of NIGHTIME FLYER sometime (we presume) in the early 80's, it's entirely possible (given the widespread *'recycling'* policy of the Welsh rock/metal establishment) that the various one-time members were eventually swallowed up by newer outfits. Having said that, the only one of the four who definitely made a further impact on the metal scene was drummer Philip John, who later managed productive spells with heavyweights PREYER (see separate entry) and TALAN, both of whom got to the vinyl stage in the second half of the decade. Frontman Leighton John, on the other hand, ultimately moved into management, and successfully handled KOOGA's affairs for a number of years. NIGHTIME FLYER, meanwhile, were privileged enough to warrant a posthumous mention in

Adrian T'Vell's one-off publication ('NWOBHM 79-81'), issued a few years ago, the author postulating that their "Heavy Metal Rules" effort could easily have become an ironic favourite in the rock clubs of the capital due to its *'unintentional humour'*. Had the good people of London already become so cynical by 1980?

7" Singles
»Out With A Vengeance« Red Eye Records 1980

NIGHTWING

Gordon Rowley (v, b)
Alec Johnson (g)
Eric Percival (g)
Kenny Newton (k)
Steve Bartley (d)

The origins of the prolific NIGHTWING lie in the 70's outfit STRIFE, a well-liked, hard-rocking (but fairly traditional) act who gigged exhaustively around the North West for most of the decade but ultimately delivered only a couple of moderately-successful albums for the Chrysalis and Gull labels during the course of their existence. Having been beset with contractual problems and personal misfortunes towards the end of 1978, the band elected to call it a day just as the whole rock genre was beginning to gain momentum once more, which seemed like pretty bad timing. Nevertheless, their mainman, Gordon Rowley, wasted little time before relocating to sunny California, where he was able to pick up some valuable experience in various recording facilities, lending his new-found production skills to many a studio session and collaborating on material with a few high-profile faces from the West Coast scene. It was a productive visit, by all accounts, and it well and truly rekindled the bassist's dwindling enthusiasm for rock music. Indeed, by the time he finally returned to the UK in the second half of 1979, Rowley was sufficiently motivated to commence the process of assembling a new group, and a handful of scenesters were soon attracted to his latest project, swiftly christened NIGHTWING. From the ALEC JOHNSON BAND came Steve Bartley and Alec Johnson himself, while Kenny Newton was best-known for his work with local heroes NUTZ. Eric Percival, meanwhile, wasn't quite such a prominent name, but he had still served time in various rock acts over the years.

NIGHTWING was initially conceived as a proposition with something of a political agenda, with Rowley being a staunch opponent of nuclear energy, global pollution and so forth. To promote the underlying message, their debut two-tracker (issued in the summer of 1980 by an American concern, Ovation Records) was based around the emotive "Barrel Of Pain", a composition which was written by one of Rowley's former associates, Graham Nash (of CROSBY, STILLS AND NASH fame), and which portrayed the potential consequences of environmental catastrophes. Lyrically, this was diametrically opposed to most of the puerile nonsense being churned out by the majority of NWOBHM hopefuls (it also showed up on GRAHAM NASH's »Earth & Sky« solo set the same year, incidentally), but, musically, it had quite a bit in common with the likes of RAGE, QUARTZ and MONEY, established outfits who now found themselves in the spotlight thanks to the recent rock/metal explosion. The subsequent long-player (»Something In The Air«), however, turned out to be something of a disappointment with its predisposition towards ponderous, lengthy compositions (it has the feel of a concept piece, but the tracks seem unrelated, and their interpretation of the SUPREMES classic "You Keep Me Hanging On" is disastrous), while the use of numerous session musicians (including three drummers) made it a rather impersonal affair. As a result, the band (who were utilising both Rowley and Newton as main vocalists at this stage) had a rethink and slimmed down to a quartet by disposing of Eric Percival, before setting about the task of penning some new material.

The outfit re-emerged in 1982 (having played at the previous year's Reading Festival, gigged productively in the States and supported GILLAN and BUDGIE towards the end of the year) with an album entitled »Black Summer«, having swung a deal with Gull and a valuable licensing arrangement with Intercord in Germany. The mood was considerably more upbeat and cheerful (with far better vocal performances, this time from Rowley and Johnson) than had been the case on their rather pedestrian debut, with elements of acts such as EXPORT, MASAI and (particularly) GRAND PRIX coming across pretty strongly. It still wasn't entirely representative of the NWOBHM archetype by any means, but it was slightly more in keeping with the stylistic tendencies of the day, and strong tracks such as "Evil Woman" (a bit of an overused title, that) indicated that there was good reason to be cautiously optimistic for the future. Rowley was to relinquish the microphone after this particular release, however, handing over the reins to new recruit Max Bacon, formerly of Cheshire hopefuls MOBY DICK. Fans were able to hear how the latter's vocal talents measured up the following year, when NIGHTWING unleashed their »Stand Up And Be Counted« long-player, promoted with the »Treading Water« single in both 7" and 12" formats.

The latest album was a significant further improvement, and saw the newly-established quintet extending their repertoire considerably, even moving into more raunchy, bluesy territory in the TERRAPLANE or TRUX vein on occasions. Their attempts at more AOR-influenced compositions, in the manner of mid-80's TYGERS OF PAN TANG, are generally quite competent too (the lads hitting top form on "Dressed To Kill" and the MEANSTREAK-style "Call Your Name"), and the whole set features an extremely confident vocal effort from new boy Bacon. Sadly, with NIGHTWING having only just found the ideal frontman, the young lad was soon to be lured away by an offer to join the BRONZ project, whereupon he departed for good towards the end of 1983. He had, however, laid down enough vocal tracks for NIGHTWING to squeeze out another full-length set, which appeared in the early months of 1984 under the title of »My Kingdom Come«. It was more of an AOR-tinged selection of compositions (occasionally reminiscent of SARACEN at their most commercial), a pretty limp affair marred by a very off-putting, multi-layered production, although "Back On The Streets" and "The Devil Walks Behind You" save it from being completely disposable. The only other track of note is "Cell 151", a number which had been recorded and issued as a single by the STEVE HACKETT BAND a year previously, the ex-GENESIS guitarist (who had contributed to the latest album in terms of production and guitar work, and who would also subsequently work with Max Bacon in GTR) being yet another of the gregarious Rowley's long-time associates. »Night Of Mystery« was trundled out as a single, again in two formats, but it was a fairly insipid choice.

With Bacon having flown the coop, and with a hectic touring schedule having already been lined up, NIGHTWING were compelled to recruit a new frontman, electing to call up relative unknown Dave Evans (previously with obscure act DAYS OF GRACE) for their intended live appearances. They successfully undertook a grand tour of Europe in the summer of 1984 (by which time Alec Johnson had also been replaced by former HARVEST MOON guitarist Glynn Porrino), recording some of the gigs for a subsequent live album. This emerged, in the early part of 1985, as the oddly-titled »A Night Of Mystery-Alive!Alive!« (most of the material being taken from their previous two long-players), and saw Evans mounting a valiant attempt to emulate Bacon's resonant vocal prowess. This offering was, incidentally, preceded by a limited edition double single, with one record featuring studio recordings (including the otherwise-unavailable "Strangers Are Welcome" and a new version of "Games To Play" which is virtually indistinguishable from the album take) and the other containing live numbers which would appear on the forthcoming full-length release. The revised line-up subsequently ventured into the studio to lay down some numbers for their fifth studio album, but, for reasons which are not entirely clear, this set was apparently pulled from global release at short notice, although it still appeared officially in Yugoslavia, of all places, a territory where NIGHTWING had toured successfully in the past.

Having decided not to persevere with further vinyl releases, and with personnel problems continuing relentlessly, NIGHTWING finally disbanded, although apparently not until as late as 1987, the lads having tried to salvage the situation by recruiting a new vocalist in the shape of erstwhile ANGEL WITCH frontman Dave Tattum. That was the end of the story, or so we all thought, with Rowley (having reformed STRIFE for a one-off gig towards the end of 1987) subsequently turning his hand to production work once again (he had already helped out with JJ'S POWERHOUSE, BADGER et al.), until the resurrected Neat Metal label finally dusted off the master tapes for the last studio album, mixed them properly and officially issued a posthumous NIGHTWING CD (it had now been retitled »Natural Survivors«) in 1996. It was a nice gesture, but sales figures hardly amounted to much, and, with no band around to promote or give any particular credibility to the release, it was to represent one of Neat's less successful ventures of recent years. The Zoom Club label has, more recently, made the remainder of the NIGHTWING back catalogue available on CD format for the first time, which suggests that interest in the group is pretty significant, but I still can't imagine that an official reunion is remotely likely.

LP's

»**Something In The Air**« Ovation Records 1980
»**Black Summer**« Gull 1982/Intercord 1982/Jugodisk 1982
[UK/German/Yugoslavian issue]
»**Stand Up And Be Counted**« Gull 1983
[UK issue, also released as limited edition picture disc]

»**Stand Up And Be Counted**« Intercord 1983/Jugodisk 1983
[German/Yugoslavian issue]
»**My Kingdom Come**« Gull 1984
»**A Night Of Mystery-Alive!Alive!**« Gull 1985
[Live album]
»**VI**« Jugodisk 1986
[Yugoslavian-only release]

12" EP's
»**Treading Water**« Gull 1983
[UK issue, limited edition on red vinyl]
»**Treading Water**« Intercord 1983
[German issue]
»**Night Of Mystery**« Gull 1984
["Edge Of A Knife" different to album version]

7" Singles
»**Barrel Of Pain**« Ovation Records 1980
»**Treading Water**« Gull 1983/Intercord 1983
[UK/German issue]
»**Night Of Mystery**« Gull 1984
»**Strangers Are Welcome**« Gull 1984
[A-side non-LP, B-side "Games To Play" different to album version, issued as limited edition in gatefold sleeve with free single featuring live versions of "The Devil Walks Behind You" and "Cell 151"]

CD's
»**Natural Survivors**« Neat Metal 1996
[UK reissue of »VI« album]
»**Natural Survivors**« Pony Canyon 1996
[Japanese issue with one extra track]
»**Something In The Air**« Zoom Club Records 1999
»**Black Summer**« Zoom Club Records 1999
»**Stand Up And Be Counted**« Zoom Club Records 2000
»**My Kingdom Come**« Zoom Club Records 2000
»**A Night Of Mystery-Alive!Alive!**« Zoom Club Records 2000

Compilation Appearances
"Black Summer" on »Metal Attack« LP Intercord 1982
"Searching" on »Metal Attack« LP Intercord 1982
"Back On The Streets" on »Axe Attack« LP M Port 1985/Mausoleum 1986
[Miscredited as "Out On The Streets"]
"Treading Water" on »Heavy Metal Monsters« Do-LP Cambra Records 1985
"Dressed To Kill" on »Heavy Metal Monsters« Do-LP Cambra Records 1985
"Let Me Be Your Lover" on »Heavy Metal Monsters« Do-LP Cambra Records 1985
"The Devil Walks Behind You" on »Heavy Metal Monsters« Do-LP Cambra Records 1985

NO FAITH

Tony Edwards (v,b)
Gary Edwards (g)
Ric Gibbs (d)

It's a little-known fact that, prior to inking the deal with Heavy Metal Records which allowed their cover of FLEETWOOD MAC's "Oh Well" to be included on the second »Heavy Metal Heroes« compilation, Midlands-based power trio NO FAITH actually managed to issue a private single in 1981, coupling "Double Trouble" with "Only The Good Die Young". While the record itself is marred by an atrociously murky production (and an equally ignominious live-action sleeve), the songs are quite energetic, straight ahead, bluesy rock of the variety peddled by bands of the era such as CENTURION or ROADSTER, probably going down a storm with the biker community. Their contribution to the aforementioned sampler LP, issued a year after their vinyl debut, is fairly representative of their general style, although the wisdom of covering an old chestnut like "Oh Well" (also recorded by McCOY in later years and subsequently incorporated in DIAMOND HEAD's live set in the 90's), when performing one of their own compositions would surely have been a better career move, is open to debate. In any case, the ensemble seems to have gone to ground within a fairly short space of time, although I suppose they might have kept plugging away in the clubs once the NWOBHM explosion had died down. The NO FAITH single is now an extraordinarily scarce item (although well worth keeping an eye out for), but, unless you have a keen-eyed contact who regularly scours all the second-hand shops and car boot sales throughout the Birmingham area, you're likely to end up disappointed.

7" Singles
»**Double Trouble**« Private 1981

Exclusive Compilation Appearances
"Oh Well" on »Heavy Metal Heroes Vol.II« LP Heavy Metal 1982 + »Heavy Metal Heroes Vol.I&II« CD British Steel 1996

NO QUARTER

Philip 'Snappi' Lyes (v)
Dave Young (g)

Griff (b)
Steve Chard (d)

One of the more individualistic acts to have emerged from Wales in the NWOBHM era, Gwent's ZEPPELIN-obsessed NO QUARTER initially formed in 1980, after which they gradually found their feet in the rock world and recorded their first cassette, the »Songs In Circles« five-tracker, the following year. With this selection of lengthy, adventurous compositions such as "Starbird", "Shine On" and "Light And Sound" being distributed by Neon Records, the tape went on to shift an incredible number of units (in excess of fifteen hundred copies), the outfit attracting customers from territories such as France, Germany and (remarkably enough) even Australia. Vitally, however, a copy also found its way into the hands of those responsible for the 'Friday Rock Show' at Radio One, who were continually seeking new heavy acts to promote via specially-recorded session appearances. The lads were in luck, as Dave Young later explained how the regular selection process operated: *'Tommy Vance and his producer Tony Wilson would start off by listening to around fifty tapes, whittle it down to twenty or so, start exchanging them and eventually select the best, one of which turned out to be ours. So, we had the opportunity to record a half-hour performance, which was very helpful for us. It was a good experience; you just go into the studio, plug the instruments in and start playing, all very spontaneous and with no overdubs.'* (Ref: Iron Pages No.31, March 1995).

On the fateful night of 16th of April 1982, NO QUARTER's session was broadcast for the first time, allowing the nation to cock an ear to "Power And The Key", "Racing For Home", "The Last Song" and "Calling". The set was warmly received by the station's many listeners, and was to benefit from a repeat transmission a few months later, all of which helped to familiarise the public with their name. Towards the end of that year, the group were to enjoy their first appearance on vinyl with the aforementioned "Power And The Key", this capable track having been selected for inclusion on the second »Heavy Metal Heroes« compilation. While LED ZEPPELIN (and, to a lesser extent, national institution LONE STAR) were undoubtedly the most obvious reference point for many casual observers, NO QUARTER considered their own material to be somewhat more contemporary in its conception, and they certainly had a few musical allies in the NWOBHM field, notably WHITEFIRE, FRIENDS and HARRIER. At the intimation of Neon Records, a second cassette offering was subsequently prepared, a seven track affair (»Uncertain Future«) featuring a selection of unfamiliar numbers including "Wildfire Woman", "C'mon" and "Can You Feel It?". It transpires, however, that relatively few examples were actually sent out, as the musicians rapidly decreed that the sound quality just wasn't up to scratch and ultimately prevented further copies from being distributed.

Moving into 1983, the lads found a new bassist in the form of Rob Palmer, and soon began giving serious thought as to how they might achieve further notoriety. By this stage, NO QUARTER had become firm favourites throughout South Wales, but were still virtually unknown in Britain's major population centres, and the members concluded that their cassettes weren't getting through to as many metal fans as intended. After this had finally dawned on them, it became apparent that a vinyl EP might actually be a more efficient method of disseminating their music to a wider audience. Another trip to the recording studio was arranged with great haste, and the self-financed »Survivors« 12" was soon being pressed up in a limited edition of a thousand copies, all issued in a large, fold-out sleeve. The three-tracker (featuring "Time And Space" and "Racing For Home" in addition to the title track) proved sufficiently popular ('Kerrang' didn't quite know what to make of the release, and couldn't really bring themselves to give it the thumbs-up) with the masses that the initial pressing was rapidly exhausted, and, following the intervention of good old Bullet Records (who were only too happy to act in a distribution capacity), a second issue was swiftly organised, allowing the lads to make a bit of ready cash at last. Gigs kept coming their way, taking the talented musicians ever further afield, and the rather questionable *'highlight'* of 1983 was their appearance at a *'prestigious'* all-dayer held at Broadmoor Hospital, a prison facility used for holding the criminally insane! Mind you, it was probably one of the very few occasions in NO QUARTER's history when the audience were on stronger *'medication'* than the band themselves…

Things seemed to be working out pretty well for NO QUARTER at this juncture, although they could not possibly have foreseen the piece of misfortune which was to strike at one of their well-attended regional gigs a year or so later. Completely out of the blue, vocalist Snappi collapsed halfway through the set, and the poorly frontman was subsequently advised to *'retire'* from such strenuous activities on health grounds. Although this came as a killer blow to the hapless outfit, it didn't immediately signal the end of their story, and the plucky group went ahead with the scheduled release of an EP entitled »Birds Of Prey« (this being heavy metal, you can guarantee that *'birds'* didn't refer to ornithological creatures), which had been in the pipeline as the much-anticipated follow-up to their successful vinyl debut. The lads had already finalised the tracklisting, and had laid down a tender ditty called "Broadmoor Blues" (although Chesterfield's WARRIOR got there first, having included a near-identical song title on their »Let Battle Commence« opus) as a musical memento of their brief spell *'behind bars'*. With the recordings safely in the bag, therefore, it was all systems go, and their second slice of vinyl should have hit the shops as a matter of routine. Sadly, however, the entire »Birds Of Prey« episode took the form of one disaster after another, and culminated in the record being released as a very *'limited edition'* indeed.

Having allegedly blown most of the production finances, in true SPINAL TAP style, by hiring an up-market glamour model to pose *'artistically'* for the cover, the mastering was carried out on a shoestring budget and the results turned out to be far from ideal. Then, after a considerable (and inexplicable) delay before the EP was finally pressed up, the group and their management had a slight, er, *'disagreement'* about something or other, with the end result being that the luckless members of NO QUARTER didn't actually take delivery of their records at all. Stories abound (which are suspiciously similar to DARK STAR's original »Lady Of Mars« fiasco) that the management team disappeared with virtually the entire consignment (and then attempted, with pitifully little success, to flog them by mail order after placing adverts in the music press), the upshot being that none of the band members even received a copy of the EP at the time! Whatever the truth of the matter, it's known that a handful of copies of »Birds Of Prey« did indeed make it into limited circulation, although virtually none have been offered for sale in recent memory; clearly, any examples which surface from now on would certainly be assured of making a healthy profit for some lucky individual. Hopefully not their old management team, though…

In a postscript which mimics the LYADRIVE experience pretty closely, however, interest in the group's early releases (from labels such as Vinyl Tap in the UK, for example) eventually led to a resurrected version of NO QUARTER coming together in 1992, initially just to muck around in the rehearsal rooms and to dust off a few favourites for old time's sake. In the end, however, the revised line-up of Snappi, Dave Young, Glenn Daniel (b) and Justyn Hook (d) even started writing new material and playing the odd low-key gig. The enterprising Vinyl Tap then compiled a CD's worth of unissued recordings from throughout their history (plus three *'bonus'* tracks taken from the now-collectable »Survivors« EP) and proceeded to issue a commemorative set, the questionably-titled »The Best Of No Quarter«. Although the lads were in high spirits when this retrospective effort first made its way into the shops, and duly assured everyone that a follow-up was pretty much a foregone conclusion, it proved to be a predictably short-lived reunion, and NO QUARTER were soon laid to rest once more. Nevertheless, »The Best Of No Quarter« is a worthy offering, and represents a fairly prudent purchase, given the ever-increasing price of their original vinyl.

12" EP's
»**Survivors**« Reel Records 1983
»**Birds Of Prey**« Bonzo Bear Records 1985
[Not commercially issued, very few copies in circulation]

CD's
»**The Best Of No Quarter**« Vinyl Tap Records 1994
[Compilation of mostly unreleased studio material]

Exclusive Compilation Appearances
"**Power And The Key**" on »Heavy Metal Heroes Vol.2« LP Heavy Metal 1981 + »Heavy Metal Heroes Vol.I&II« CD British Steel 1996

Compilation Appearances
"**Racing For Home**" on »NWOBHM Vol.5« Bootleg CD 1992
"**No Stopping It Now**" on »Noise Level Critical« CD Hallmark 1997

NORTH STAR

Bill Hayward (v)
Graham Collier (g)
Pete Hutchins (b)
Roger Kenyon (d)

The hard-rocking quartet known as NORTH STAR, based around the outskirts of London, first came to prominence as one of the acts to contribute to »The Bridge Album«, a showcase for some of the emergent hopefuls who rehearsed and recorded at the Bridge studio facility in Middlesex. Assembled in 1982, the compilation was to feature a self-penned number called "It's Only Money", a fairly decent effort which combined a healthy respect for the 70's with a rather more dynamic NWOBHM sound, the overall effect bringing forth comparisons with the likes of SPITFIRE, FULL MOON and the Essex version of WARRIOR. The sleeve notes mentioned that NORTH STAR were actually quite a recent addition to the bustling rock scene, and had yet to play a solitary gig, so this was clearly a useful piece of exposure for an extremely inexperienced bunch. Still, the lads were already formulating plans to hit the clubs of the capital, and it wasn't much longer before they became regulars on the live circuit, often sharing a stage with fellow veterans from »The Bridge Album« such as LYADRIVE and TAKEAWAY. After becoming slightly more confident in their own abilities, therefore, the foursome were able to win over a fair number of rock fans, and soon started thinking about delivering a vinyl release of their own.

At some point in 1983, NORTH STAR were fortunate enough to be offered the opportunity to lay down a modest two-tracker for the Bridge label itself (the company would later sponsor the debut LYADRIVE 7", although no additional releases seem to have materialised), whereupon "It's Only Money" was simply recycled and paired with the unfamiliar "Too Many Chances" to constitute a double A-sided single. The new composition was possibly a bit closer to the NWOBHM archetype, lying somewhere between VHF and SNAKEBITE's "Thin Ice", but the arrangement wasn't particularly flattering. Still, it was a perfectly respectable way for a new group to introduce themselves to the masses, but NORTH STAR's attempts to make it big appear to have been pretty fruitless in the long term (their lack of image was cited as something which worked against them), and the lads had called it quits within a couple of years, having played their hearts out to anyone who would listen. None of the participants appear to have resurfaced in any other recording acts of note, so I guess their flirtation with the rock industry was merely a passing fancy. Their one-off release (never issued in a picture sleeve), however, remains a collectable, seldom-seen rarity these days.

7" Singles
»Too Many Chances« Bridge Records 1983

Compilation Appearances
"It's Only Money" on »The Bridge Album« LP Bridge Records 1982

NO SWEAT

Clive Culbertson

The »Belfast Rocks« compilation, a local-band sampler issued by the dubiously-named Rip Off label back in 1979, is fairly well-known amongst collectors as a source of obscure rock and punk acts from Northern Ireland, and many NWOBHM enthusiasts will be aware that heavy hopefuls COBRA had actually seen their pair of contributions pressed up on a (hopelessly overrated) 7" single a year or so earlier. It's not such common knowledge, however, that NO SWEAT also received the same treatment from their label (who also issued numerous singles by the likes of BLUE STEAM, CRAMP and PRETTY BOY FLOYD AND THE GEMS, these being of fairly minimal interest to most NWOBHM fans), suggesting that their »Start All Over Again« offering was less-than-enthusiastically received by the general public, although it's a decent enough effort. The A-side is a highly catchy, American-sounding piece of melodic rock (with the obligatory THIN LIZZY influence that pervades so many Irish groups of the era), extremely similar to the type of material played by English rivals MEANSTREAK. On the upbeat flipside ("You Should Be So Lucky"), however, the trio attempt a heavier, faster style with an almost punky, singalong chorus, bringing to mind some of the more borderline acts such as CHEEKY, GROUND ATTACK or early CLIENTELLE.

Although it's not all that unusual to see such disparate styles on a two track release (remember, a number of groups saw their debut single as the stepping stone to a major album deal, and took the opportunity to reveal different aspects of their musical abilities), it's uncommon to see both numbers attempted with such confidence and enthusiasm. A very competent release (issued in a monochrome sleeve picturing the three band members) all round, and it's a pity that NO SWEAT didn't get any further (although mainman Clive Culbertson apparently released a solo 7" called »Time To Kill« a year or so after their eventual demise) in the cut-throat music business. There isn't, by the way, any connection with the identically-named six-piece THUNDER copyists who came out of Ireland a few years later (or, for that matter, the rather more obscure English outfit who issued the »Work On Her« 7" on the Eel Pie label in 1978), so don't get too confused by all the similarly-named groups in this case.

7" Singles
»Start All Over Again« Rip Off Records 1978

Compilation Appearances
"Start All Over Again" on »Belfast Rocks« LP Rip Off Records 1979
"You Should Be So Lucky" on »Belfast Rocks« LP Rip Off Records 1979

NUTHIN FANCY

Danny Bowes (v)
Luke Morley (g)
Malcolm 'Mac' McKenzie (b)
Chris Hussey (d)

The humble origins of the successful TERRAPLANE (and, ultimately, the immensely popular THUNDER) are relatively well-documented in many reference sources, and the name NUTHIN FANCY (which, in all likelihood, was shamelessly pilfered from a LYNYRD SKYNYRD long-player) will be familiar to many as the embryonic, NWOBHM-period incarnation of these South-Londoners, although it's a widely-held belief that no vinyl was ever issued under that particular guise. Guess what? A private single *did* indeed sneak out, presumably in the first few months of 1981, which perfectly fits the mould of a proto-TERRAPLANE offering. At this point, the main protagonists (Luke Morley and Danny Bowes) were being assisted by bassist Mac McKenzie (latterly THUNDER's manager) and sticksman Chris Hussey (currently residing in the *'where are they now?'* file), although they had been operational for a couple of years by the time they got around to making their debut. In fact, having initially got together in 1979 or thereabouts, the quartet initially adopted a glam rock image which (due to reassuringly practical reasons) wasn't retained after their first name change, as frontman Danny Bowes revealed at the time: *'I was getting a bit fed up with spandex trousers. Apart from anything else they make your balls itch.'* (Ref: Kerrang No.29, November 1982). A timely warning on the untold dangers of spandex, if you ask me.

Having gigged all over the capital and its environs (to a generally favourable response) for two eventful years, the lads decided to present the headbangers with a vinyl offering, which emerged through Dynamic Cat Publishing, responsible for various nonentities such as NO DICE. The two selections featured on the one and only NUTHIN FANCY single, "Lookin' For A Good Time" and "Too Much Rock And Roll", while undeniably primitive in terms of production, could quite easily pass for TERRAPLANE out-takes, and would certainly be of interest to THUNDER completists, assuming they could afford today's exorbitant asking price! Although the record was supposedly distributed by Spartan, the band evidently weren't exactly overwhelmed by demand from the nation's record-buying public, as Danny Bowes later elaborated: *'Oh yeah, you get people turning up with all sorts of scary remnants. We had a guy turn up with a NUTHIN FANCY single, which was the band we were in before TERRAPLANE! We only sold about fifty of 'em, and he'd paid two hundred quid for it!'* (Ref: Kerrang No.542, April 1995). Evidently, the subsequent change of name and personnel (McKenzie and Hussey had, by the summer of 1981, already defected to the ranks of DUMPY'S RUSTY NUTS) was an extremely good idea, with the reinvented TERRAPLANE (now featuring Gary James on drums and Nick Linden on bass, the pair having been recruited from the ranks of local amateurs MOONTIER and WHITE NOIZ) going from strength to strength in years to come. Given that only a few dozen copies of the NUTHIN FANCY two-tracker (issued in a distinctive blue sleeve picturing a wrench) allegedly made it into circulation, however, you probably shouldn't hold your breath waiting for one to fall into your hands...

7" Singles
»Lookin' For A Good Time« Dynamic Cat Records 1981

OMEGA

Nick Brent (v, g)
Steve Grainger (g, k)
Dave Robertson (b)
Graham Roberts (d)

London's OMEGA (not to be confused with a couple of identically-named hard rock acts from the 70's, one of them Hungarian) were a direct descendent of the equally heavy APOCALYPSE (see separate entry), who had run into minor personnel problems after recording just one cracking single for the Gate label in 1982. Having found a suitable new drummer in Graham Roberts (who had latterly been assisting London metallers G.B.H., and had, earlier still, been involved with Paul Dianno's legendary

BIRD OF PREY) and adopted their novel identity, OMEGA set about sending off demos (their first effort was entitled »Alpha«, and featured selections such as "Abandon Hope", "Blood Sacrifice" and "Heat Of The Night", but only a limited number were sent out before the master copy was accidentally wiped) to various parties in the record industry. Soon after, the band's first opportunity to appear on vinyl came with an offer from the ever-accommodating Ebony to contribute a track to one of their multitudinous metal compilations. And so it came to pass, dear brethren, that the grimly-titled "Blood Sacrifice" was included on the label's typically-patchy »Metal Warriors« sampler a few months later. While OMEGA's distinctive composition (the renamed group being very much in the APOCALYPSE mould, albeit a tad more technically-minded and ambitious) may have come across as a bit over-the-top and grandiose in terms of its structure and vocal performance, this confident effort was undoubtedly one of the highlights of the album.

Over the next twelve months or so, the band refined their writing style and continued to compose a great deal of material, culminating in a prospective deal with the aforementioned Gate label. While an entire album's worth of songs were laid down and demoed for the company, however, the deal appears to have fallen through at some stage, leaving OMEGA with no choice but to tout the tapes around and hope that another label would wade in with a suitable offer sooner or later. Fortunately, their collective luck was in, as the newly-established Rock Machine concern (a short-lived subsidiary of Metal Masters) provided the lads with the opportunity for which they had striven so valiantly. Their long-playing opus (»The Prophet«) finally materialised in 1985, and this supremely confident offering showcased an extremely tight, atmospheric brand of post-NWOBHM with progressive (quite reminiscent of early GENESIS at times) overtones, occasionally bearing some resemblance to contemporaries such as ARC, CHASAR, ANTHEM and Jersey's LEGEND. It certainly stood out as being far more ambitious and individualistic than much of the bog-standard metal being churned out by numerous identikit hopefuls at the time (which the majority of British rock fans seemed perfectly happy with, admittedly), although it's yet another example of an album which, on balance, would probably have been better suited to the overseas market.

A menacing and disconcerting opener ("The Dark") sets the tone for the selection of lengthy, doom-flavoured compositions which serve to comprise much of the record, and »The Prophet« gradually evolves into an extremely satisfying and consistently-enjoyable piece of listening. "Shadows Of The Night" continues the initial assault with its epic structure and towering riffs, which bring to mind none other than the deific DIAMOND HEAD in terms of their sheer scale and variety. Side one of the LP, which has the distinct feel of a conceptualised musical triptych, is completed by the title track itself, a restrained (not to mention lengthy) effort with rather more of a heavy PINK FLOYD feel. On the other hand, the mood lightens considerably on side two, with "Yesterdays Children" being a somewhat more upbeat and accessible effort, whereas "Drive Me Crazy" is fairly typical, accomplished NWOBHM (a bit of a DIAMOND HEAD feel again) with disappointingly hackneyed lyrics. Unfortunately, OMEGA then contrive to lose the plot in major fashion, deciding to spice things up with a mundane cover version, their rather perverse choice being "Day Tripper" (a particularly poor BEATLES number), the motivation for such an inclusion being virtually impossible to fathom. Fortunately, the quartet manage to recover from this silly interlude, and bow out with another heavy epic ("The Child"), a number which actually dates back to the original APOCALYPSE demo. All in all, though, it was an extremely ambitious and capable display of talent, with some sterling musicianship (top marks for guitar and vocals) on show throughout.

In spite of its considerable deviation from the accepted NWOBHM archetype, many modern enthusiasts consider »The Prophet« to be an extremely underrated album, although I'd stop short of heralding it as an undiscovered masterpiece. In fact, the record appears to have performed rather poorly in terms of sales upon its original release, suggesting that the hapless OMEGA might have been slightly ahead of their time. As a direct consequence, relatively few examples of the album (and its accompanying lyric sheet, which serves to provide some insight into Nick Brent's complex and disturbing vocal performance) have ever made it into circulation at any point, and the asking price has risen fairly steeply over the years. Sadly, the talented OMEGA never followed up this auspicious debut, having been disappointed by poor sales and a lukewarm media reception, and the outfit (who, in spite of fairly regular outings at London's minor venues in their early days, appear to have become rather less active on the live scene thereafter) finally fragmented towards the end of 1986. The much-travelled Graham Roberts soon moved on to pastures new in the form of the persevering DEEP MACHINE/BURN offshoot called STRUTT, an excellent and powerful melodic rock proposition (featuring the outstanding vocals of the charismatic Tony Smith) who were on the music scene for a good few years but never achieved the success they deserved.

LP's
»The Prophet« Rock Machine 1985

Exclusive Compilation Appearances
"Blood Sacrifice" on »Metal Warriors« LP Ebony 1983

OMEN SEARCHER

Alastair Boden (v)
Chris Hiley (g)
Andy Dobson (b)
Bob Beebe (d)

Derbyshire's little-remembered OMEN SEARCHER came and went over a fairly short timescale, and left just one solitary single as a souvenir of their fleeting existence. Issued privately in 1982, their 7" paired "Too Much" with "Teacher Of Sin" (it's difficult to determine which was the intended A-side, as the sleeve and labels give conflicting information), two decent enough, mid-tempo offerings in the general manner of DESTROYER or BASHFUL ALLEY, with the odd minor similarity to the likes of the more inventive BLEAK HOUSE or BEG TO DIFFER. The production is a bit murky, suggesting a severely limited recording budget, but it would surely have been a reasonable enough starting point for a productive career in the rock/metal business, had someone been benevolent enough to offer them a proper record deal. Inevitably, however, OMEN SEARCHER were another of those who vanished without trace as the NWOBHM burned itself out, having made little or no impression in the first instance, more's the pity. Nevertheless, their one-off single remains a highly-regarded item among NWOBHM collectors, and doesn't usually come particularly cheaply. If you're looking for it in the bargain boxes, keep an eye open for a monochrome picture sleeve featuring a distinctive, spiky logo design with 'OS' occupying the centre.

7" Singles
»Too Much« O.C.S. Records 1982

100% PROOF

Steve Wright (v, g)
Charlie Wilson (v, g)
Steve Harrison (b)
Phil Wright (d)

To their credit, Manchester's 100% PROOF never shied away from the fact that they adhered to the Christian faith (indeed, the musicians actually met each other through their membership of a local church), although their music, fortunately, wasn't quite as fundamentally righteous and didactic as some of their like-minded contemporaries in the rock field. Formed towards the end of the 70's from the vast pool of musical talent which existed in the North West at the time, the outfit's vinyl debut took the form of a humble four-tracker on the Smile label (see also the DICK SMITH BAND and THE LAW, for example), featuring the original numbers "New Way Of Livin'", "Lookin In", "What's The Cost" and "Resurrection". Generally speaking, it was something of a 'heavy boogie' variant, pretty much in the style of ROKKA, PREDATÜR or SPIDER, with the occasional hint of rather more intense outfits such as CHAINSAW, for example. Like most releases on Smile, the EP (issued in an unimaginative sleeve with photos of the band members) didn't benefit from a particularly extensive pressing, and is now a mid-range rarity.

Their eponymous debut LP, issued in 1981 on the small Myrrh label (a concern who actually specialised in Christian releases), featured a selection of reasonably listenable compositions in a predominantly-similar style (none of which really stood out as particularly remarkable), including an emotional number entitled "The Loner", dedicated to the memory of the recently-departed Bon Scott (appropriately enough, as it was often pointed out that the Mancunians bore slightly more than a passing resemblance to AC/DC in places), featuring some pretty heartfelt lyrics. Well, you're more than welcome to feel a modicum of sympathy for self-obsessed alcoholics if you like (ooh, little bit of controversy there), but count me out. Significantly, 1981 was also the year in which the 100% PROOF lads entered the national 'Battle Of The Bands' contest (sponsored by the giant RCA concern), an ambitious move which was to pay off in the long term, as the outfit eventually triumphed in their local heat and progressed to the televised grand final. Sadly, however, they didn't go all the way and win the competition itself, although the otherwise-unavailable "Bad Boy" was subsequently featured on the compilation album issued by RCA to commemorate the event.

The outfit's follow-up release surfaced a couple of years later in the shape of »Power And The Glory«, another small-label offering which saw 100% PROOF delivering a set which practically amounted to a carbon copy of their first album (although it was a rather more competently-produced affair this time), which was more than a little disappointing. In fact, it was plain for all to see that their newer material showed a crucial lack of musical progression or ingenuity, and most of the featured compositions were still severely limited by a monotonous vocal performance. The record was, however, fortunate to be given an overwhelmingly favourable review in 'Kerrang', with the excessively-charitable Xavier Russell likening much of the material to the kind of thing purveyed by one or two of his Southern Boogie heroes, although I can't imagine that too many other music journalists of the time gave it such an easy ride. Following on from this initial frenzy of vinyl activity, however, things went very quiet, and I imagine that 100% PROOF were no longer a going concern by the middle of the decade, although an obscure American issue of their second album apparently appeared as late as 1987. The more open-minded among you might care to check out their triumvirate of releases if they're ever offered for sale at a suitably affordable level, especially if you're partial to a bit of undemanding boogie in your spare time.

LP's
»100% Proof« Myrrh 1981
»Power And The Glory« S.B. Record Company 1983
[Original UK issue]
»Power And The Glory« Kosher Records 1987
[Later US issue on yellow vinyl]

7" EP's
»New Way Of Livin'« Smile 1980
[All four tracks non-LP]

Exclusive Compilation Appearances
"Bad Boy" on »Battle Of The Bands« LP RCA 1981

ONSLAUGHT

Neil (v)
Dale (v, g)
Tony (g)
Ian (b)
Buddy Reg (d)

Having nothing to do with the well-liked thrashers from the West Country, this particular ONSLAUGHT appear to have their origins in the punk movement and were, in all probability, based in or around the London area. With their two-tracker being recorded at Image Studios at some point in 1985, the quintet's unremarkable cover of THE WHO's "My Generation" (backed with their "Angel Of Mercy" original) is quite heavy and metallic, although there's certainly a tangible punk influence in there too. To be honest, the overall sound comes across as a slightly weird combination of WARFARE, DEEP SWITCH and TENPOLE TUDOR, so it's not exactly one for the dedicated metal fan. After issuing the single (in a monochrome, slightly punky-looking sleeve), the outfit (clearly a bit shy about revealing their surnames) probably fizzled out within a fairly short space of time, having ultimately failed to convince either the rock community or the record companies that they genuinely meant business. Furthermore, I would suggest that any earlier vinyl offerings by this bunch are almost certain to be out and out punk nonsense, so you should probably steer well clear of such items. Still, at least ONSLAUGHT score a few bonus points for one-upmanship by electing to cover "My Generation" several years before the likes of PEARL JAM and DIAMOND HEAD introduced it into their live repertoire!

7" Singles
»My Generation« 69 Records 1985

ORAL

Bev (v)
Monica (g)
Candy (b)
Dee (d)

In a cynical move which (on the face of it) was almost certainly calculated to titillate impressionable adolescents and incur the wrath of feminists everywhere, some unknown genius masterminded a project in the mid-80's which involved gathering together four obliging female wannabes, lumbering them with the rather unsubtle ORAL moniker and encouraging them to release a mini-LP with the even-less-subtle title of »Sex«. Oral sex, eh? What would the neighbours think? Just to ram the ever-so-dodgy message home (as it were), the cover features three of the *'young'* London lasses (strangely enough, the bassist allegedly did a runner immediately after the recording session) posing in skimpy leather outfits and wielding whips. Ah yes, chuck in a bit of S&M imagery, a liberal quantity of suggestive lyrics and it's bound (as it were) to sell like proverbial hot cakes, right? Unfortunately, no. Things might just have gone according to plan if the rock mentality conformed to such stereotypical misogyny (it still doesn't occur to some evolutionary throwbacks that one or two women actually listen to this type of music too), but this sordid package missed the mark completely, and the somewhat ill-conceived ORAL project fell flat on its face almost immediately.

When confronted with ORAL's monumentally tacky vinyl debut (issued on the Conquest label, EXCALIBUR's original home), the rock press unanimously decided that it was an utterly irrelevant release ('Kerrang' branded it *'pathetic'*), and merely denounced it outright. This was all perfectly understandable, but slightly harsh nonetheless. Sure, it's not a classic release by anyone's standards, and the embarrassingly puerile titles (such as "Love Pole" and "Pearl Necklace", for example) no doubt alienated many listeners, but it has to be said that the music (compared to the likes of METAL VIRGINS, anyway) wasn't *totally* worthless after all. ORAL certainly managed to acquit themselves pretty well on a couple of the featured tracks, notably "Black Leather", a SEX PISTOLS cover, no less. Having said that, the six songs are all extraordinarily primitive and far too similar in terms of their construction, and the band's self-confidence (arrogance, even) was severely misplaced in the context of the sheer averageness of their material. If you're searching for some straightforward musical comparisons, however, I suppose you don't really have to look all that far beyond the inevitable reference points of ROCK GODDESS and GIRLSCHOOL, although it's difficult to conceive that either of these ensembles would be particularly troubled by such unremarkable efforts as the laughably-titled "Gasmasks, Vicars And Priests", for example.

When it comes down to hard facts, though, the whole ORAL episode had a bit of a fishy smell about it, if you know what I mean. The unknown outfit were afforded a suspiciously-generous two-page feature in 'Kerrang' at around the time the mini-album was released, which should, at the very least, have *attempted* to provide the magazine's readership with some sort of plausible background as to how the project started and how they contrived to win themselves a deal. Intriguingly, however, the *'exposé'* artfully skirted round the group's musical history, although guitarist Monica claimed to have been taught how to play by none other than Lemmy (oh my, how convenient), concentrating instead on the sex lives, underwear and sundry non-musical activities of the band members. High-quality journalism at its best, eh? In fact, it transpired that the extremely dubious premise of ORAL was that these particular *'musicians'* all came together (as it were) in the first place because they just happened (yeah, sure) to be working in the sex industry (as glamour models, strippers *etc.*) and were duly encouraged to form a rock group (as you do) by some shadowy figure who was out to make a bit of extra cash from some of his employees. Hmmm.

In view of this flimsy and rather implausible version of events, and, given that ORAL never appear to have made any live appearances (nevertheless, their interview suggested that they were all experienced *'performers'*, but I guess that this might not have been in the musical sense) or followed up their debut at any stage, it's inevitable that speculation and rumour would become rife in subsequent years. Could it, perhaps, have been the case that the hapless specimens on the record's cover were merely *'glamour'* models (and not particularly attractive ones, at that) and that ORAL was actually a bit of a light-hearted prank by some of the better-known names in the rock business? Could be. Listen carefully and decide for yourselves…

Mini-LP's
»Sex« Conquest Records 1985

Compilation Appearances
"**Black Leather**" on »Metal Masters« 4-CD Box Castle Communications 1993
"**Head**" on »Metal Masters« 4-CD Box Castle Communications 1993

ORE

Gordon MacArthur (v)
Dean Howard (g)
Dave Boyce (b)
Andy Elphick (d)

Having formed at the beginning of the 80's with high hopes of being picked up by one of the influential labels, things got off to a pretty slow start for London's ORE, especially on the gig front, where they found it extraordinarily difficult to inveigle their way into the pubs and clubs. Mind you, having finally been noticed, they famously missed out on a coveted support slot with ANGEL WITCH when their luckless vocalist chose a particularly bad moment to get involved in a serious car crash! Nevertheless, the persevering outfit soon saw their fortunes improving, and, before much longer, their humble name was being added to numerous rock bills throughout the capital, whereupon ORE began to cultivate a healthy local following thanks to support slots with the likes of DIAMOND HEAD, TYTAN, GIRL, TANK and MARILLION. With the lads being featured in the 'Armed And Ready' section of 'Kerrang' some time later, bassist Dave Boyce fondly recounted the story of how their rather imposing frontman was recruited to the fold, and enthused over his talents: *'Not only was he the kind of singer we never dreamed we'd get, but he had us all in fits of laughter within a few seconds of walking through the door.'* (Ref: Kerrang No.13, April 1982).

The following few months were quite eventful for the outfit, who, nevertheless, finally got around to releasing their one and only single (a double A-side featuring "Your Time Will Come" and "Yellow Fever") in due course. With their effortlessly catchy arrangements and powerful, bluesy vocals, the tracks bring forth some facile comparisons with the likes of XERO, SLENDER THREAD and Nicky Moore-era SAMSON, and the record soon began making a few ripples in the metal community. The single, which was never issued in a picture sleeve, was given a fair bit of praise in a 'Kerrang' review upon its release, and it remains quite a high-priced rarity today. In August of 1982, the lads were fortunate enough to be added to the bill of that year's Reading Festival (probably the most *'metal'* one ever to be held), a prestigious appearance that was undoubtedly the pinnacle of ORE's career. Going on stage in mid-afternoon as a prelude to the headlining TYGERS OF PAN TANG and IRON MAIDEN, the foursome proceeded to delight an appreciative crowd with compositions such as "Don't Start To Get Rough", "She's So Permanent", "Take It As It Comes" and "Hot On Your Tail", these all being cracking numbers which confirmed that the quartet's repertoire and stage presence had been honed to a fine art by this time.

After numerous appearances in the capital and its environs, however, the original version of ORE fell apart at the beginning of 1983, despite rave concert reviews in 'Kerrang', with the band citing *'contractual problems'* as the critical factor. Axeman Dean Howard initially disappeared off to Australia and joined forces with a group called BLACK ALICE (who actually recorded for the Street Tunes label in Britain) for a short time, but returned to the UK before long. After re-establishing himself in London, he contacted his one-time colleagues (who had all been spectacularly unsuccessful in their attempts to form new outfits) to try to get the whole ORE venture going again. These negotiations ultimately resulted in MacArthur and Elphick returning to the fold, although Dave Boyce couldn't be tempted to re-enlist. Nevertheless, with the addition of erstwhile SLEDGEHAMMER bassist John J. Hennessey (aka John Jay, who had latterly been working with MacArthur in the ill-fated SPRINGHEEL JACK venture), the revitalised outfit got going again in the spring of 1984. Sadly, though, it wasn't to be a long-term success, and the lads called it a day (again) after only a handful of gigs in the capital (with hindsight, it might perhaps have been prudent to venture a bit further afield occasionally). Hennessey went on to join Gerry Lane's DRIVESHAFT, while Elphick later played in the minor rock outfits MORITZ and IF ONLY. Original bassist Dave Boyce, on the other hand, later resurfaced in a late 80's incarnation of SAMSON, but hasn't been sighted recently. Gordon MacArthur, meanwhile, is presumably out there somewhere, but hasn't been particularly active on the club scene since ORE's demise.

7" Singles
»Your Time Will Come« Bandit Records 1982

ORIGINAL SIN

Steve Daley (v)
Kev McGuinn (g)
Les Brunskill (g)
Paul Hollingsworth (b)
Alan Brunskill (d)

Although two separate all-girl groups subsequently adopted the identity later in the decade, the original (as it were) ORIGINAL SIN were a heavy (all-male) quintet from Merseyside, who, having initially formed in mid-1982, gradually developed into a hard-working outfit who gigged regularly throughout the rock-loving North West. In due course, the lads began picking up a handful of precious support slots with the likes of BUDGIE and MAMA'S BOYS, before they reached the important decision to go it alone and finance their own vinyl release. In the event, it took a bit of outside help (in the unlikely form of Tony Barwood, manager of those local indie stalwarts known as the ICICLE WORKS) to get this idea off the ground successfully, and, following a much-needed cash injection from the latter, the two chosen tracks were immortalised at the oft-frequented Amazon Studios in Liverpool at the tail end of 1983. The double A-sided 12" single, when it finally appeared in the early months of 1984, turned out to be a surprisingly competent and well-produced affair, the powerful vocals and heavy arrangements bringing forth comparisons with the likes of DAMASCUS, AVENGER and (to a lesser extent) BLOOD MONEY. Both "The Shadow" and the slightly more restrained "Salvation" were extremely well-crafted compositions, although it's unclear why the band felt the need to issue a 12", as the tracks aren't excessively lengthy.

The record was issued in a picture sleeve showing a hand-drawn, shadowy figure, and is rated as a collectable, mid-priced rarity these days, although a significant number of examples have come onto the market over the years, suggesting that sales of the single (helped by a well-organised distribution) may have been pretty respectable at the time. The group toured to promote the release (which received quite a favourable review in 'Kerrang'), recruiting a new drummer, Steve Ashton, along the way, although further glory was always to elude them. ORIGINAL SIN appear to have called it a day for good at some point in the second half of the decade (they tried out yet another sticksman, Brian Parry, in 1985, an individual who had supposedly played with both GRIM REAPER and WRATHCHILD during their formative years), and it looks as though the participants probably went back to their day jobs rather than teaming up with emergent regional hopefuls. In the absence of any further information, therefore, we're left with no option but to classify ORIGINAL SIN as yet another of those cruelly-overlooked, fly-by-night outfits who could have gone a lot further with a bit more luck.

12" Singles
»The Shadow« Private 1984

ORION

Mike Ryde (v, g)
Al Risk (g)
Jay Ryde (b)
Pete Andrews (d)

Self-confessed QUEEN fanatics from Middlesex, the quartet known as ORION (not to be confused with the melodic BOSTON offshoot who also became known as ORION THE HUNTER) were hardly a household name when they contrived to wangle a deal with Hertfordshire's oddball Lost Moment label (home of the fairly capable JOKER and a variety of, shall we say, more *'experimental'* outfits), which culminated in the release of the group's sole »Insane In Another World« single in 1984. The over-ambitious A-side is a bit of a disaster, to be honest, a clumsily-arranged song (with decidedly off-the-wall lyrics) which doesn't know whether it aspires to be early GENESIS-style prog or straightforward pop, and which ends up as neither. The semi-decent flipside ("Storm"), on the other hand, is a rather more convincing effort, a catchy, mid-tempo rocker with blindingly obvious QUEEN influences, particularly with respect to the grandiose, layered guitars and synthesizers (analogous to the similarly-conceived "The Battle" by fellow obscurities TUTCH), which owe a major debt to the 'Flash Gordon' soundtrack. Not bad, but far too over-the-top for most NWOBHM fans, if you ask me. Interestingly, a completely different (and, for my money, more enjoyable) version of "Storm" subsequently cropped up on Lost Moment's bizarrely-titled »Colours Of The Bastard Art« sampler, in the company of some astonishingly bad indie outfits.

With the members of the relatively short-lived ORION having apparently gone their separate ways even by the middle of the decade, bassist Jay Ryde subsequently teamed up with certain ex-FORTUNE personnel to form the melodic trio ZERO ONE FIVE in 1987, although this ill-starred project (in spite of some encouraging early reviews in the rock press) doesn't appear to have got off the ground properly at any stage. Apart from that, however, there seems to have been little or no additional musical activity from the one-time participants. Significantly, due to a substantial quantity of unsold ORION (and JOKER) singles having been obtained from their still-functioning label in the early 90's, the asking price for this once-expensive (and unjustifiably so) two-tracker has dropped quite considerably in recent years, and, accordingly, you should now be able to procure yourself a copy (which comes in a rather arty sleeve depicting a disintegrating face hovering over an otherworldly landscape) for a far more sensible figure, should you decide that you can't live without it.

7" Singles
»Insane In Another World« Lost Moment

Records 1984
Compilation Appearances
"Storm" on »Colours Of The Bastard Art« LP Lost Moment Records 1985?
[Different to single version]

OVERDRIVE

Steve Farmer (v)
Tracey Abbott (g, k)
Ian Hamilton (b, k)
Ian 'Scratch' Padgett (d)

It has become a fairly well-established fact that Lincolnshire's OVERDRIVE (not to be confused with their highly-regarded Swedish namesakes from the same musical period) shared a couple of their members with local rivals MARZ (see separate entry), leading to the widespread belief that they may have evolved directly from the latter, although this wasn't the case at all. In spite of the fact that vocalist Steve Farmer and drummer Ian Padgett flew the MARZ coop sometime after appearing on the »Lady Of The Night« EP in 1980, their departure certainly didn't signal the end of the line for MARZ, who soldiered on with a revised line-up for some time afterwards. Not only that, it transpires that they weren't founder members of OVERDRIVE, given that an operational version of the group was already in existence by this stage (they were certainly playing live in their locality by late 1980, at which time they employed future HELL sticksman Tim Bowler), so it's entirely likely that the two acts had coexisted quite happily for some time. It looks as though OVERDRIVE got through quite a few musicians over the years, with many regional scenesters lending a hand at one time or another, although most of these names are now lost in the temporal mists. Following the recruitment of Farmer and Padgett, however, they had become a rather more stable unit, and it's fair to suggest that the duo brought something of a MARZ feel to the proceedings.

OVERDRIVE's sole contribution to the vinyl world during the NWOBHM era was to be their »On The Run« three-tracker, a self-financed release which hit the shops at some point in 1981. The musical contents elicit some reasonably strong comparisons with cult heroes WITCHFINDER GENERAL or the West Midlands version of SCARAB, particularly on "Stonehenge" (I bet they nearly died of embarrassment when 'This Is Spinal Tap' was released) and the atmospheric "Nightmare", with Steve Farmer delivering his best OZZY OSBOURNE impersonation in places. The title track was also a capable enough effort, and this was included on the »NWOBHM Vol.5« CD a decade later, exposing the long-forgotten music of OVERDRIVE to a whole new generation of NWOBHM aficionados. The unit's vinyl debut immediately became an extraordinarily popular purchase for numerous headbangers throughout the Midlands and beyond, and swiftly found its way into both local and national rock charts. The weighty contents seemed to be perfectly attuned to those who frequented the pubs and clubs of the Midlands, and it looked as though OVERDRIVE would be elevated to the status of regional heroes before long. The EP (produced by Rick Woolgar of local contenders RED ALERT) seems to have been a fairly modest pressing, however, and remains a scarce and sought-after piece these days, particularly those (around half of the original run) which were issued in a striking picture sleeve featuring some semi-heraldic imagery.

With OVERDRIVE playing numerous well-attended gigs around the Midlands during the following couple of years (occasionally sharing a stage with the likes of SPARTA, as well as delighting the crowds as headliners), the ambitious outfit were clearly doing their utmost to promote themselves to the masses and to attract a modicum of label interest in the process. Strangely, however, the record companies kept their distance, leaving the lads with no option but to go back to basics and demo another batch of material for critical inspection. A peculiarly-titled cassette (»Shhh…It's Overdrive«) was circulated in late 1983, and I'm assuming, in the absence of any contradictory evidence, that this was indeed the same group (strangely enough, it was sold through a contact address in Norfolk), since it bore only a passing resemblance to the earlier material. Indeed, it was hardly the most accomplished of offerings, and had the feel of an act who were only just finding their feet. Sounding more like a ramshackle rehearsal tape than a properly-mastered studio demo, the ten compositions featured (including unfamiliar numbers such as "Back With A Vengeance", "Take Me Higher" and "Turn It Up") suggested a move towards a rather more upbeat style of metal in the vein of HOLOCAUST or TURBO. However, even overlooking the dreadful sound quality, it's fair to say that the ensemble (who may well have experienced personnel instability in the interim, and it certainly didn't sound like Steve Farmer on vocals) just didn't seem to be sufficiently cohesive or original enough to carry off the latest material with any real sense of authority or conviction. It comes as no surprise, therefore, to discover that OVERDRIVE failed to attract any significant label interest with this half-hearted offering.

I'm not entirely sure whether or not the outfit remained a going concern over the ensuing six years (I doubt that they did, given that they maintained no level of involvement in the live scene, but you never know), but a revamped version of OVERDRIVE unexpectedly popped up again in 1989, this time contributing an energetic effort called "Make Or Break" to the »Full Force Vol. III« sampler (which, oddly enough, sounded as though it featured Steve Farmer), and then returned the following year brandishing a full LP entitled »Dishonest Words«. With the ex-MARZ duo having flown the coop some time previously, the latest line-up had been assembled around the nucleus of Ian Hamilton (who assumed vocal duties) and guitarist Tracey Abbott, the central characters now being assisted by bassist Roger 'Wot' McKown and Richard 'Droop' Mulhall on drums. Their album had been recorded inconspicuously, and appeared with truly minimal publicity, the set revealing the foursome to have assembled a somewhat odd collection of songs, mainly in a melodic power metal style which occasionally verges on thrash. To be honest, this was nothing like the OVERDRIVE of old, and offbeat song titles such as "Your Greasy Boyfriend" and "The Bed With The Broken Springs" tended to suggest a move away from their more traditional metal roots. Having said that, tracks such as "All Dogs Have Their Day" and "Diamonds And Pearls" (not a PRINCE cover, thankfully) were reasonably listenable, and the long-player as a whole would probably appeal to fans of certain post-NWOBHM outfits such as DEEP SWITCH or even MARSHALL LAW. It seems to have been widely ignored at the time, however, and the failure of the album seems to have sent the lads back into hiding once again. Given that another decade has since expired, though, maybe we're due for another record any day now...

LP's
»Dishonest Words« Boring Grantham Records 1990

7" EP's
»On The Run« Boring Grantham Records 1981
[All three tracks non-LP]

Exclusive Compilation Appearances
"Make Or Break" on »Full Force Volume III« LP Reaction 1989

Compilation Appearances
"On The Run" on »NWOBHM Vol.5« Bootleg CD 1992

OVERKILL

Mick Fowler (v, g)
Shaun Kebby (v, g)
Paul Nicholson (b)
Randy Williams (d)

Not to be confused with their rather more successful American namesakes, Hampshire's version of OVERKILL are, nevertheless, still fondly remembered as having been one of the region's most highly-regarded acts during the NWOBHM era. With the musicians having initially gravitated together in 1979, the quartet duly set about honing their technical skills with extensive periods of rehearsing and gigging, and managed to amass a phenomenal tally of gigs (upwards of two hundred, including a headlining appearance at the Isle Of Wight Rock Festival, although this once-legendary event had become considerably less prestigious since the heady days of the early 70's) in their formative years. By 1981, the lads had already initiated a fan club and issued their own private single (apparently *'due to local demand'*, as the featured tracks had been recorded purely for demonstration purposes in the first instance), the latter release coupling "Elemental" with "On My Own". Both numbers are in something of a heavy-but-accessible style (the two guitarists sharing vocal duties) which elicits a few comparisons with weighty ensembles such as PALI GAP and QUARTZ, or even with some of WITCHFINDER GENERAL's later offerings. Issued without a picture sleeve, the two-tracker sold well at the time, but is seldom encountered these days, and is quite justifiably regarded as one of the genre's top collectables.

Bassist Paul Nicholson was to part company with the group sometime after their single's release (the foursome having been featured in the 'Armed And Ready' section of 'Kerrang' later on in 1981), and, after a suitable replacement had been found in the shape of Marcus Nason, the outfit continued to delight audiences, by this time taking in venues even further afield. On visits to London, they often unveiled more or less their full repertoire, including the epic composition "The Time Of Man", to appreciative crowds. In 1982, the quartet recorded a two track demo, featuring "Out Of My Head" and "Feels So Good", from which the former was selected by Heavy Metal Records to appear on the second »Heavy Metal Heroes« compilation. Their energetic, SLEDGEHAMMER-tinged contribution was one of the highlights of this rather lacklustre sequel, and the group's good fortune continued when they were booked as one of the openers at that year's Reading Festival (the organisers liked to include the odd minor/local outfit to get the crowds warmed up), where they played to a huge audience in the company of such luminaries as PRAYING MANTIS, STAMPEDE and TANK. With the lads having apparently gone down a storm (delivering a selection of novel compositions such as "A Thousand Miles Away" and "Hammer Strike"), plans for a follow-up single were hastily drawn up, its release scheduled for some time in the latter part of 1982. Sadly, this project never came to fruition (for reasons which never became all that clear), suggesting that some sort of intractable problem had beset the hapless ensemble after their festival appearance, and it looks as though OVERKILL had called it a day by fairly early in 1983, whereupon the musicians pretty much drifted away from the music scene.

7" Singles
»**Elemental**« Killer Records 1981

Exclusive Compilation Appearances
"**Out Of My Head**" on »Heavy Metal Heroes Vol.II« LP Heavy Metal 1982 + »Heavy Metal Heroes Vol.I&II« CD British Steel 1996

OXYM

Rob Rigby (v, g)
Phil Lord (g)
Ross Halliwell (b)
Mik Wilson (d)

The embryonic version of Lancashire's innovative OXYM was first put together by the youthful trio of Rob Rigby, Mik Wilson and Ross Halliwell as long ago as 1976, the outfit soon becoming a full-time project (permanent guitarist Phil Lord was recruited along the way) which grew in stature during the next couple of years. With the stabilised unit steadily developing a powerful, refined metal style *via* a never-ending series of well-attended local gigs, the quartet soon started giving serious thought to the possibility of issuing some vinyl of their own. Tragically, however, their original bassist (Ross Halliwell) was killed in a motorbike accident in May 1979, and the surviving members were subsequently forced to endure a lengthy period of intensive soul-searching while they reassessed the situation. Courageously, the lads decided to continue, and regrouped with new addition Nigel 'Tolly' Talbot (formerly of legendary local punksters SCHOOLGIRL BITCH) after a respectful interval. Within a year, however, the revitalised OXYM had gone from strength to strength, and they were soon ensconced in Cargo Studios in Rochdale, laying down tracks for their own postponed single (which would be dedicated to their departed friend) in the spring of 1980.

With OXYM's vinyl debut finally being issued (on the Cargo label itself) a couple of months later (in a rather odd-looking, Celtic-influenced sleeve which depicted their distinctive, rune-style logo), the tracks featured ("Music Power" and "Mind Key") appeared to be quite heavily influenced by early JUDAS PRIEST, although the technical, slightly progressive arrangements were additionally reminiscent of such innovators as BLEAK HOUSE, WHITE LIGHTNING and Hampshire's LONE WOLF, with Rob Rigby putting in an excellent vocal performance throughout. The single went down extremely well with the general metal community (surprising, really, given that it wasn't exactly a typical NWOBHM release in any sense), rapidly selling out of its initial edition of one thousand copies, with a repressing becoming a necessity merely to satisfy exceptional national demand. In fact, it looked as though OXYM might just have stood an outside chance of escaping the narrow confines of the NWOBHM genre and becoming a top-ranking technical outfit to mount a challenge on the likes of RUSH, but they would soon find themselves fending off talented new arrivals such as GASKIN and SHIVA. Still, with those much-anticipated OXYM live appearances apparently being completely *'over the top'* (to use the group's own description), the heady combination of impressive original material and some spectacular stage effects led to the ensemble becoming an extraordinarily popular attraction wherever they played.

Later in 1980, OXYM were to benefit from further exposure on the influential »New Electric Warriors« compilation, where they delivered the otherwise-unavailable composition "Hot Rain". With this excellent number being widely praised (in 'Phoenix' fanzine, among others) as one of the more worthy contributions to the LP, things should have been bright for the band's future.

Sadly, though, the musicians don't seem to have capitalised on their enviable early success in the months which followed, and were soon on a downhill slide, despite their loyal following, an embarrassment of individualistic compositions and considerable media interest. Still, popularity and talent only takes you so far, as I'm sure you realise, and the dejected unit presumably disbanded a year or two later, having consistently failed to win that coveted album contract in the interim. Drummer Mik Wilson resurfaced in a little-known mid-80's proposition called PARAGON, who ultimately failed to get off the blocks, while bassist Tolly later proceeded to help out in the original 90's incarnation of the rejuvenated BUFFALO, appearing on a highly impressive demo tape issued in around 1994. Since then, however, the OXYM lads have been keeping a distinctly low profile.

7" Singles
»Music Power« Cargo Records 1980

Exclusive Compilation Appearances
"Hot Rain" on »New Electric Warriors« LP Logo 1980/CD British Steel 1997

Compilation Appearances
"Music Power" on »NWOBHM Vol.2« Bootleg CD 1992

PAGAN ALTAR

Terry Jones (v)
Alan Jones (g)
Trevor Portch (b)
John Mizrahi (d)

There's little doubt that London heavyweights PAGAN ALTAR would truly epitomise the term *'cult'*, as their reputation among fans of the NWOBHM genre unquestionably belies the fact that the lads never actually made it to the vinyl stage in the first instance. They are, therefore, part of an utterly tiny minority of outfits from the era (along with DEEP MACHINE, for example) whose modern-day legacy is not built upon vinyl foundations, as it were. Why are they included in the book, you ask? Well, the circumstances are somewhat atypical in this case. The story dates back to 1978 or thereabouts, when a handful of aspiring musicians got together in the capital and took their first steps in the world of metal, gradually finding a weighty niche of their own and cultivating a style which was inspired largely by the imagery and sound of early BLACK SABBATH. It's fair to suggest that PAGAN ALTAR's musical direction and lyrical inclinations changed very little over the course of their eight year existence (during which time they plied their trade valiantly and saw numerous contenders fall by the wayside), but at least they remained true to their roots and didn't (unlike many of their contemporaries) degenerate into a facile melodic rock variant towards the mid-80's. Predictably, the very nature of their uncompromising music was sufficient to attract a dedicated following, and procuring gigs in and around the capital was never a problem, although the important matter of achieving their vinyl destiny proved to be rather more of a continual stumbling block.

Even so, the musicians were pretty serious in their quest for fame and fortune, and the central characters abandoned any notion of pursuing day jobs while PAGAN ALTAR remained a going concern. Furthermore, given that the ambitious bunch proceeded to construct their own studio facility, it became possible to immortalise a selection of original compositions as and when it suited them, and so a significant amount of material was duly captured for posterity over the years. As it turns out, the lads had initially outlined plans to issue a single as early as 1980, but this idea was ultimately scuppered by financial shortcomings, whereupon PAGAN ALTAR elected to concentrate on humble cassette releases until a *bona fide* record deal came their way. Sadly, however, that fabled offer never materialised, and so the whole project was reluctantly laid to rest in the mid-80's, by which time several other musicians had fleetingly passed through their ranks, notably sticksman Ivor Harper, bassist Glenn Robinson and guitarist Ron Neary, who also worked with the better-than-their-name-suggests L.A. HOOKER. The outfit's eventual unsung demise wasn't quite the end of the story, however, and the good name of PAGAN ALTAR steadfastly refused to die, the upshot being that their scarce demo recordings have continued to be traded around the metal underground ever since, making regular appearances in the playlists of magazine contributors throughout the globe and finding their way into the possession of various aficionados of heavy music.

By the mid-90's (a full decade after the group had given up the ghost for good), however, events took an unexpected twist, as some enterprising characters on the other side of the Atlantic (at Doom Records) decided to exhume a selection of these long-lost studio recordings and press them up as an extremely limited and not-remotely-official vinyl release. With the first pressing of around a hundred copies (housed within a pretty minimalistic white sleeve) being such a restricted issue, it looks as though the shady individuals responsible weren't primarily motivated (originally, at least) by financial concerns, but merely sought to make the material available to what they surmised would be an extremely limited set of enthusiasts. In the event, demand (even at a remarkably steep asking price) proved considerably greater than anticipated, after which a more extensive re-pressing (in a professionally-presented, black cover with a handful of group details) was rushed out within a matter of months. Showcasing such substantial, lengthy and ominously-titled compositions as "Reincarnation", "Black Mass" and "In The Wake Of Amadeus" (all dating from 1982), the self-titled PAGAN ALTAR bootleg confirms the unit to have been pioneering exponents of the post-SABBATH doom style, bringing forth some rather facile comparisons with like-minded NWOBHM contemporaries such as WITCHFINDER GENERAL, PHOENIX RISING, REQUIEM and APOCALYPSE, as well as the more theatrical BLACK WIDOW (responsible for the seminal »Come To The Sabbat« single of the early 70's) and HELL. Understandably, the sound quality is severely compromised by the fact that the album was assembled from low-generation cassette copies rather than from the original master tapes, although it still represented a fairly listenable collection for those who were able to overlook the shortcomings of the source material.

Remarkably, however, the one-time members of PAGAN ALTAR subsequently cottoned on to the fact that some of their music had been circulated by these naughty bootleggers, and have now set up a business to release their recordings officially (through Oracle Records) and provide fans with slightly more information about their personnel and history. Predictably, this revolves predominantly around the nigrescent image and occult leanings, the unholy ensemble spinning various tales about their activities (many of which were conveniently cursed by malevolent spirits and outside forces of evil) in the recording studio and on the live front, although I'd suggest that some of these revelations should be taken with a generous pinch of salt. Still, I suppose a bit of creative embellishment always helps to shift a few units, so the motivation is perfectly understandable, but I'm sure they weren't originally taking it nearly as seriously as they're now making out. Undoubtedly, though, PAGAN ALTAR would surely have given their eye teeth to have hitched a ride with any of the established touring concerns of the time (preferably those with a compatible image and an equal fondness for secular lyrics, such as WITCHFYNDE or DEMON), or even to have wangled a high-profile support slot with their eternal idols, the ever-present BLACK SABBATH. In reality, however, they tended (through necessity) to play on their own and to take whatever other openings came their way (including a show or two with SPIDER, who weren't exactly renowned for their black metal pretensions), usually (despite overly-ambitious plans to take their theatrical stage show to the States at one point) at pretty modest venues.

With the industrious PAGAN ALTAR having contrived to record so much of their original material throughout the early 80's, it transpires that the equivalent of five (yes, *five*) full-length albums (four studio efforts plus one live affair) survives in usable condition, and their collective intention is to oversee an official programme of remastered CD releases (the first of which, a repackaged version of the bootlegged album, has been drawing extremely high praise from both the NWOBHM and doom factions, and a follow-up set, »Lords Of Hypocrisy«, featuring alternate drummer Brian Cobbold, is in the pipeline) over the course of the coming years. It's good to see these musicians finally reaping the rewards of their original studio sessions, and we await further releases with considerable interest and optimism. I'll admit to being slightly concerned, however, that this frenzied spate of activity might inspire a few no-hopers from days of yore to *'discover'* a few recordings of their own, and this could, in theory, open the floodgates for a glut of so-called *'NWOBHM-era'* cash-ins which were actually knocked up in someone's garage in the past fortnight. I'm not suggesting that this has already happened, or that *any* of the outfits featured in this volume might be guilty of passing off brand-new studio recordings as *'archive material'* (although the recent DRAGSTER CD came disconcertingly close, thanks to its ambiguous sleeve notes), but it has already happened with other genres and will always remain a possibility whenever there's an opportunity for someone to make some ready cash.

Don't get me wrong, genuine *'archive releases'* are always extremely welcome, and I've absolutely no objections to long-forgotten groups getting back together, whatever their goals may be. Whether they just want to muck around and play reunion gigs or to go a bit further and either rework some of their original compositions or record a batch of brand-new material for future release, they should make their intentions perfectly clear; I heartily object to the very real prospect of NWOBHM devotees being targeted as gullible halfwits who will readily swallow half-baked stories about studio sessions which may or may not actually have taken place in the early 80's. The fans should be treated with respect (this applies to *all* the bands, labels and dealers who view the NWOBHM genre as a nice little earner), and don't deserve to be exploited by fraudulently-marketed products or misled by deliberately vague sleeve notes. Call me Captain Cynical if you want, but behind all this paranoia lies a mild warning that anyone tempted to churn out a few cash-in releases had better get their stories right (the PAGAN ALTAR situation is extraordinarily unusual, and very few bands of similar stature possess even *one* album's worth of usable material) or they'll be exposed in no time at all…

LP's
»Pagan Altar« Doom Records 1995
[Original unofficial pressing with white cover, very limited quantities]
»Pagan Altar« Doom Records 1996
[Second unofficial pressing with black cover, titles and band details]

CD's
»Pagan Altar-Volume One« Oracle Records 1998
[Official release with different cover]

PALI GAP

Ian Ellis (v, g)
Martyn Hawley (b)
Terry Grantham (d)

Taking their unusual name from a number featured on the »Rainbow Bridge« soundtrack album by JIMI HENDRIX, Essex trio PALI GAP formed in 1981 and soon won over local audiences (their energetic style wearing out a couple of drummers in the process) with their particular brand of heavy, accessible metal, which included such original selections as "Serpent's Eye", "Cities On Fire" and an epic set-closer, the implausibly-titled "Guitar Solo". Within around a year of their initial formation, the lads were already thinking about getting some vinyl into the shops, and so their debut single (produced by PROCOL HARUM's Matthew Fisher) was duly recorded at the tail end of 1982 and released a couple of months later to fairly widespread critical acclaim. A-side "Under The Sun" opens with a disarmingly-heavy, chugging riff which leads into the main body of the song, with the phased vocals lending a vaguely psychedelic feeling to the whole affair, whereas the upbeat reverse ("The Knives Are Out") is, after a widdly guitar intro, a more straightforward number, but is still played with considerable panache. It's fair to claim that PALI GAP were one of the weightier UK outfits of the day, with elements of ANGEL WITCH, DESTROYER and SCARAB (West Midlands version) coming across in their overall sound, although their general approach to metal was actually pretty individualistic. Despite the fact that it wasn't issued with a picture sleeve, their two-tracker (which even received a relatively favourable review in 'Kerrang', who had largely relinquished their patronage of NWOBHM outfits by this time) has been a consistently popular and pricey item for collectors over the years.

The group continued to release demos and promote themselves at every opportunity, and subsequently received a glowing write-up in the 'Armed And Ready' section of 'Kerrang', having recently submitted a demo with three newer tracks to the magazine. Towards the end of 1983, the lads recruited new vocalist Paul Thorpe to the fold (presumably allowing Ian Ellis to concentrate solely on guitar duties) and announced concrete plans to release a second single (to be entitled »Three Miles High«) within a matter of months. Sadly, this project never seems to have got further than the planning stage (matters weren't helped when Terry Grantham decided to hand in his notice fairly shortly after Thorpe joined the group), and it looks as though the revamped line-up didn't really gel in the long term. Nevertheless, PALI GAP were still a going concern as late as 1984, having recruited a replacement drummer (one-time METAL MIRROR stalwart Mick Green) and parted company with the luckless Paul Thorpe. With the band reverting to their original three-piece format, they again began planning their next assault on the rock world, although, inevitably, it appears to have fallen apart for good within a matter of months. PALI GAP had disappeared without trace by the mid-80's (having inspired a few regional hopefuls such as NO MERCY to form along the way) and the members faded into obscurity, leaving only a solitary, highly-regarded single in their wake.

7" Singles
»Under The Sun« Synister Records 1982

PANZA DIVISION

Glenn Marples (v, g)
Rick Corcoran (v, g)
Alan Edwards (b)
Andy 'Spider' Freeston (d)

The sudden demise of ROKKA in 1980 came as a disappointment for many of Yorkshire's headbangers, although it wasn't actually all that long before their former guitarist, Glenn Marples, returned with another bunch of hopefuls named PANZA DIVISION. Once again, this represented something of a boogie-influenced proposition, although the newly-established quartet turned out to be a rather heavier and more diverse ensemble than the down-to-earth ROKKA had been. The group's first vinyl exposure came with "Blitz" and the quirkily-titled "The Day Delta 4 Played Mars", their pair of contributions to the rare »Scene Of The Crime« compilation (which also featured the likes of SPARTA and SAVAGE), the aforementioned numbers revealing the outfit to be operating in a fairly raunchy style of rock/metal with similarities to such acts as SNAKEBITE, 100% PROOF and CHAINSAW. Around this time, the lads also demoed novel material such as "Good To Be Alive", "Hot Line For You" and "Standing On The Outside", tracks which soon became popular live favourites among an ever-expanding fan base and which received generous airplay on several local radio stations. The logical next step was to get some vinyl product into the shops, although the familiar story of major label disinterest was to hinder their progress considerably.

In the end, therefore, PANZA DIVISION were left with little option but to scrape together enough cash for a privately-issued single. Predictably, this proved to be a pretty intensive drain on their meagre finances, but the loyal fans stepped in to save the day, with three hundred benevolent souls placing advance orders to allow the pressing to go ahead in the first instance. The double A-sided effort, coupling "We'll Rock The World" and "Standing On The Outside", surfaced in the early months of 1982 (by which time they were employing the services of a keyboard player, Eugene Maloney), and was soon shifting an impressive number of units in their locality. Gigs further afield followed in due course, and the ensemble duly established something of a reputation as the perennial openers for the JACKIE LYNTON BAND (it helped PANZA DIVISION's cause enormously that they could bring several coachloads of their own fans with them) on many a jaunt around the capital. Before long, "Standing On The Outside" was making a regular appearance in the 'Top 30 Kuts' chart in 'Kerrang', and the magazine subsequently sent a reviewer (Dave Dickson) to check out the band in the live environment. The gig in question was a prestigious support slot with Y&T, and the journalist wasn't scared to compliment these emergent hopefuls: *'Opening for the Americans would not have been an easy task for any band, especially one as raw as PANZA, but Glenn Marples and his crew rose to the occasion with a creditable self-effacement that warmed them to the sardine-packed crowd.'* (Ref: Kerrang No.19, July 1982).

Further tracks were unveiled on their numerous sessions for Radio Hallam, and those live appearances continued to delight the fans, with new numbers such as "Rockin' People" and "Forty Days And Nights" being presented for the public's delectation. After a while, however, the temptation to move into more commercial waters started to influence the band's collective writing style, and, towards the end of their existence, the lads drafted in a new drummer in the form of Steve Mitchell (who, incidentally, also collaborated with erstwhile RAGE guitarist Mick Devonport in the short-lived FIELD FORCE) prior to trying out some more accessible numbers. In the end, however, the central characters ultimately elected to lay the much-loved PANZA DIVISION name to rest, before starting all over again under the revised identity of the LONELY HEARTS (see separate entry) at some point towards the end of 1983. Along with their more melodic direction came a change of bassist (new recruit Andy Fisher joined the fold, while the departed Alan Edwards proceeded to work with WITCHFYNDE), and the newly-christened outfit were soon enjoying a modest amount of regional success with their SPIDER-tinged repertoire, although their activities eventually petered out unspectacularly towards the end of the decade.

7" Singles
»We'll Rock The World« Panza Trax Records 1982

Exclusive Compilation Appearances
"Blitz" on »Scene Of The Crime« LP Suspect Records 1981
"The Day Delta 4 Played Mars" on »Scene Of The Crime« LP Suspect Records 1981

PARADYNE

Mark White

Hampshire's extraordinarily obscure PARADYNE were yet another of those outfits who never really achieved a great deal of critical approval or recognition outwith their local area (indeed, they seldom ventured particularly far afield for gigs), but can still count themselves fortunate in the respect that they actually made it to the vinyl stage at one point. Some time after their initial formation, the group were offered the enviable opportunity to lay down two original tracks for Airship Records, after which their debut single hit the local shops in 1982. This no-frills release (no picture sleeve, and with one label left blank for a sticker featuring the PARADYNE logo) coupled "Take Your Time" with "Down To Amsterdam", two fairly substantial efforts with some heavy riffing and decent guitar work, although deflated by the rather flat vocals. The band's "Take Your Time" effort is the stronger of the pair, and takes a few musical cues from BLITZKRIEG and ANGEL WITCH, while the reverse is a less inspiring number along the lines of SPARTA or OVERKILL. Even so, it's a lot better than many of their contemporaries managed to come up with, and it's a single which would sit happily in all NWOBHM collections, were it not for the fact that copies come onto the market once in a blue moon. Both of the featured compositions are quite lengthy (at around the six minute mark), though, and it would have been interesting to see if the outfit could have come up with a few punchier tracks, so it's a pity they didn't appear on any of the Airship compilations, as far as we know.

7" Singles
»Take Your Time« Airship Records 1982

PARALEX

Phil Ayling (v)
Mark Gibson (g)
Kev Bower (g)
Ian Dobbs (b)
Neil Bryan (d)

You know you must have made it as a true NWOBHM legend when the eminent Lars Ulrich includes one of your humble compositions on his celebratory compilation, citing you in the music press as *'an incredibly obscure band'* (forgive the poor lad for his youthful naivety) who had a profound influence on his own outfit, whose name temporarily escapes me. Nottinghamshire's PARALEX were the lucky ensemble in question, and, having formed at the tail end of the 70's, it didn't take the quintet all that long to arrange a deal with Reddingtons Rare

Records, an obliging label which was more than happy to promote Midlands bands irrespective of talent or commercial viability. The musicians duly recorded five studio tracks viz. "White Lightning", "Satan's Arrow", "Southern Star", "Black Widow" and "Travelling Man", before circulating a handful of cassette copies to various respected parties in an attempt to discern which numbers should ultimately make it to vinyl. In the event, "Satan's Arrow" and "Southern Star" (both in much the same general style) were omitted, and so the PARALEX three-tracker was pressed up on fetching green vinyl and housed within an excellent 'skull' sleeve (although I've also seen one or two examples with a plain white cover embellished with a sticker bearing the legend 'Satan's arrow strikes') in due course.

The admirably-presented PARALEX record sold in remarkably healthy quantities from the outset (unusually, for a Reddingtons release), and rapidly found its way into many a collection. It seemed to strike precisely the right chord with both the local and national metal communities, rendering the three-tracker as one of the very first bona fide collectables of the period. Even to this day, however, the sheer reverence afforded to this EP by NWOBHM aficionados is quite baffling, and, to be brutally honest, I completely fail to see what's supposedly so fantastic about it. Fair enough, the music itself is perfectly adequate, bringing to mind such eminently capable outfits as MYTHRA, Kent's RENEGADE and Cheshire's WOLF, so there's no major problem in that sense. However, in my humble opinion (and you may disagree as vehemently as you desire), the abysmal caterwauling of frontman Phil Ayling (whose surname is tragically apt) completely ruins the listening experience. Technically, it's quite an achievement for someone to sing out of tune so consistently (the statistical probability of hitting the right note every now and again is actually pretty high), even on "Black Widow", where the hapless chap attempts (and fails miserably) to reach a lower register. Surely a prime contender for the title of 'NWOBHM's least capable vocalist', although I reckon MITHRANDIR's Graham Gargiulo (at least they had the excuse of being very young) definitely has that one sewn up. I'm not saying I could do any better, though...

The group kept a fairly low profile after the EP's release, although, as part of the 'East Midlands Bands Cooperative', they gigged regularly with their chums in RADIUM, RACE AGAINST TIME and HELL (the latter featuring erstwhile PARALEX guitarist Kev Bower, who seems not to have been replaced at any stage, as well as fly-by-night PARALEX bassist Tony Speakman) over the ensuing months. By late 1982, however, things had ground to a bit of a halt, and there were to be no further PARALEX shows for around eighteen months. Whether or not the ensemble remained a going concern in the interim is open to debate, although it's worth noting that the central characters never announced an official split at any stage. Eventually, however, the outfit resurfaced with a markedly different line-up (Ayling and Gibson now being assisted by new guitarist Ian Johnson, bassist Dave Blundy and drummer Jez O'Donovan), and began playing the clubs again in the early months of 1984. PARALEX, having now got the music bug once more, finally circulated a demo of freshly-penned material the following year, presenting themselves (rather inaccurately) as an entirely 'new' band and hoping that people had short memories. Tracks such as "Dogfight" and "Crossing The Bridge" went down a storm in 'High Octane', for example, their latest selection of material supposedly veering towards a more thrashy sound in the vein of EXCITER or METAL CHURCH. Clearly, however, the revamped outfit didn't secure any record company interest and presumably elected to disband sooner rather than later.

Former PARALEX drummer Jez O'Donovan proceeded to join an obscure melodic outfit called APB (which also featured personnel from local favourites DEUCE), while guitarist Mark Gibson later reunited with one-time colleague Tony Speakman (who had now flown the HELL coop) in the rather jokey S.Y.Z. (see separate entry), the latter releasing one seldom-seen 7" (»Heavy Rider«) before disappearing. There's also a connection with the semi-mainstream late 80's project LIFE AFTER, who featured various ex-members of the 'E.M.B.C.', although I'm not exactly sure who was actually involved. Our friend Ayling, meanwhile, subsequently joined speed metal wannabes METAL MESSIAH, appearing on their first demo and on their 'Friday Rock Show' session in 1988. At this point, the aforementioned band perspicaciously noted that Ayling could not, in fact, hold a note to save his life and replaced him with the more competent Jim Aspinall of WICKED. METAL MESSIAH went on to record an LP, while Ayling (I'm sure he's a lovely chap really, so I hope he'll forgive the character assassination) presumably went on to the nearest unemployment bureau. Since then, none of the original PARALEX stalwarts appear to have been particularly active on the music scene.

12" EP's

»Travelling Man« Reddingtons Rare Records 1980
[Issued on green vinyl, most with printed sleeves, some with stickered white covers]

Compilation Appearances
"White Lightning" on »NWOBHM '79 Revisited« Do-LP/Do-CD Phonogram 1990 + »N.W.O.B.H.M. Metal Rarities Vol.2« CD British Steel 1996
"Travelling Man" on »NWOBHM Vol.4« Bootleg CD 1992 + »N.W.O.B.H.M. Metal Rarities Vol.2« CD British Steel 1996
"Black Widow" on »N.W.O.B.H.M. Metal Rarities Vol.2« CD British Steel 1996

PARIAH

Michael Jackson (v)
Russ Tippins (g)
Steve Ramsey (g)
Graeme English (b)
Sean Taylor (d)

Although a great many people seem to regard PARIAH as a simple continuation of the SATAN story, in the same way that the brief name change to BLIND FURY somehow represented a logical part of their musical progression, this is entirely at odds with the musicians' own thoughts on the matter. Whereas the members of SATAN were happy to condemn BLIND FURY as an ill-conceived piece of experimentation, their metamorphosis into PARIAH was a much more serious matter. By the end of 1987, the band had become well and truly sick of the limitations of such a deplorable moniker, in spite of the fact that they still had a substantial following in Europe, and the lads actually felt that they would be able to achieve far greater success if they were able to break free from the constraints of their original handle. As if by magic, their artistic creativity would suddenly soar into overdrive, and the world would welcome their new-found brilliance with open arms. Now that's what I call a cunning plan. So, after rapidly ditching the devilish identity which seemed to be holding them back so cruelly, the group briefly elected to reinvent themselves as THE KINDRED in the early months of 1988, and soon announced that an album was already scheduled for imminent release (on Steamhammer, once again), this being expected to emerge under the title of »For Justice«. Needless to say, things didn't quite go according to plan (do they ever?) for the newly-christened quintet, and it was subsequently agreed that *'The Kindred'* would make a better album title than a band name. This left the lads seeking yet another new handle, and they hastily decided to adopt the rather distasteful choice of PARIAH, an identity they would later share with an unremarkable American act.

The group's sympathetic label seemed to be quite happy to go along with all these name-related vacillations, however, and their debut album as PARIAH emerged on Steamhammer in due course, its title having been altered to »The Kindred« in the interim. Although the musicians had already intimated that they might be pursuing more of a classy, power metal-inspired direction from this point onwards, it turned out that they had actually mutated into a *bona fide* thrash proposition in the style of TESTAMENT, HOLY TERROR or even DEATH ANGEL, with frontman Michael Jackson screaming into the microphone like a man possessed and the rest of the musicians all racing each other to see who could get to the end of each track first. Blimey. It was all very intense, admittedly, and the songs still contained the same cynical, hate-filled lyrics (titles such as "Scapegoat", "Inhumane" and "Icons Of Hypocrisy" serve to illustrate the PARIAH mindset perfectly adequately) which had graced the outfit's earlier Steamhammer releases, but it's fair to say that the individual numbers had little or no personality of their own, something which PARIAH later blamed on a lack of time with which to write new material. Sales of »The Kindred« were evidently rather modest, although neither the band nor their label could figure out whether this was merely due to confusion about the name or whether it really was a bad album. I couldn't possibly comment.

Nevertheless, Steamhammer magnanimously decided to give the lads the benefit of the doubt, and duly commissioned a follow-up a year later. Their »Blaze Of Obscurity« effort seemed to paint a picture of a band who, after surveying the oversaturated thrash scene of the late 80's, had wisely concluded that they couldn't really hope to compete with the luminaries of the movement after all. Still, all was not lost, and the PARIAH lads were able to fall back upon what they knew best, good old power metal. The latest long-player was an immeasurably more listenable affair than its overly-intense predecessor, and the well-constructed compositions placed far greater emphasis on melody, variety and finesse. It was still sufficiently upbeat and powerful to keep their fans happy, but it wasn't as pointlessly over-the-top as »The Kindred« had been. Stand-out tracks such as "Missionary Of Mercy", "Blaze Of Obscurity" and "Hypochondriac" helped the LP to sell in markedly more impressive quantities, and the lads were soon receiving some encouragingly flattering reviews. Amazingly, however, much media attention was still being focused on their name change, although Russ Tippins was always happy to explain the circumstances surrounding the decision: *'We got fed up with being accused of being satanists. Every interview was the same and we have never been into the occult. We were still kids when we thought of the name and didn't know any better. Plus there wasn't any 'Death Metal' around at the time so it didn't matter.'* (Ref: Metal Forces No.41, July 1989). Poor old PARIAH, they had chosen to start over again in an attempt to deflect criticism away from their original identity, and somehow only succeeded in exacerbating the problem!

With the band having rescued their career from disappearing down the toilet, Steamhammer were more than happy to keep them on their books, and invited the lads to lay down a third LP in due course. First of all, though, PARIAH had to attend to the important task of promoting themselves in both Europe and the UK, and undertook some fairly successful touring towards the end of 1989. They had, in the previous few months, also appeared at some high-profile festivals and on German television (in addition to recording a live video of themselves in action), so things seemed to be going pretty well as they moved into 1990 and finally began working on their third long-player under the name of PARIAH. Out of nowhere, however, their unsettled frontman announced that he was about to hand in his notice, having become disillusioned with the whole music thing in the previous few months. The situation rapidly deteriorated when drummer Sean Taylor also threw in his hand and moved to the States, leaving the remaining nucleus of Ramsey, Tippins and English (a triumvirate which had been stable since the very inception of SATAN) to decide amongst themselves whether or not to soldier on. In the event, the decision was largely made for them when former SABBAT frontman Martin Walkyier approached Steve Ramsey and Graeme English to join him in his new SKYCLAD venture. The duo agreed, but promised their old chum Russ Tippins that they would eventually regroup as PARIAH and record that long-awaited third album as planned.

In fact, SKYCLAD turned out to be a phenomenally popular and prolific outfit (and still is), so English and Ramsey tended to have very little time to think about the well-intentioned promise they had made to Tippins all those years ago. Still, the trio kept in touch and continued to swap musical ideas, and they did eventually find a gap in SKYCLAD's hectic schedule to write and record that PARIAH long-player. This didn't happen until 1997, however, so it just goes to show how busy those SKYCLAD chaps had been during the previous seven years! Nevertheless, the central figures soon roped in two of their former colleagues in SATAN, namely stand-in vocalist Alan Hunter (whose own band, TYSONDOG, had fallen apart in the late 80's) and drummer Ian McCormack, who had (in the aftermath of an ill-fated BATTLEAXE reunion in 1988) latterly been helping out in CRONOS. The quintet had laid down an album's worth of fresh material by the end of that year, and, in the absence of any significant label interest, soon set about getting it released as a private CD. »Unity« finally appeared in the spring of 1998, and showed the lads to have been assimilating one or two contemporary influences in recent times (some distinct similarities to the likes of DREAM THEATER, ALICE IN CHAINS and IMPERIUM in places), the new album standing as a more-than-worthy successor to the first two PARIAH efforts.

In all honesty, the much-delayed third album was actually a lot better than it needed to be (excellent tracks such as "No Exit", "Walking Wounded" and "Mutual Street" genuinely deserve to be heard by a far wider audience), as there was little chance of this unassuming private release getting the stamp of approval from all that many rock journalists. Still, it sold in sufficient quantities to justify all the effort, and I'm pleased to report that they've received a fair amount of positive feedback thus far. I've no idea where (if anywhere) they'll go from here, but, on the evidence of the »Unity« set, there's certainly a hell of a lot of potential there. If SKYCLAD ever decide to call it a day and PARIAH choose to make another serious attempt to crack the rock market (although, given that Russ Tippins has now apparently established a brand-new act called NATIVE TONGUE, it's beginning to look increasingly unlikely), I reckon they'll have a serious chance of making it big.

LP's
»The Kindred« Steamhammer 1988
»Blaze Of Obscurity« Steamhammer 1989

CD's
»The Kindred« Steamhammer 1988

»Blaze Of Obscurity« Steamhammer 1989
»Unity« RTM 1998

Compilation Appearances
"Blaze Of Obscurity" on »The Future Of Metal Is Now« Do-LP/Do-CD Steamhammer 1990

PAUL DALE BAND

Paul Dale (v)
C.C. Frost (g)
Steve Skinner (b)
Robert Michael (k)
Shaun King (d)

I'm not quite sure of the whole story here, but it seems that vocalist Paul Dale didn't hang around too long after MARSEILLE's initial split (resulting from the entirely unforeseen collapse of the Mountain label) before forming his own, eponymous venture. Whether or not they ever represented anything more than a studio project is open to serious debate, however, as the two-tracker released in 1981 seems to be a one-off and the ensemble don't appear to have made many (if any) live appearances at the time. In any case, the act's unassuming »Alright On The Night« single couples two reasonable enough numbers, the A-side being not a million miles away from MARSEILLE's own material, with a slight inclination towards the more mainstream compositions that the likes of DIAMOND HEAD were attempting by the mid-80's. Flipside "Hold On", meanwhile, turned out to be a considerably weightier effort (still not metal in its true sense by any means, though), coming across as a melodic effort in the manner of some of TOAD THE WET SPROCKET's more lightweight output. It was an adequate release, I suppose, but hardly the sort of thing that threatened world domination for Dale and Co.

For some inexplicable reason, however, this unremarkable record seems to have sneaked out with utterly minimal publicity at the time; so much so, in fact, that I've encountered die-hard MARSEILLE devotees who had absolutely no inkling of the single's existence. In view of this baffling observation, it's certainly understandable why so few reference sources make mention of the PAUL DALE BAND either in relation to MARSEILLE or in their own right. Sales were evidently modest, and gave the mainman little or no encouragement to pursue his quest for global stardom, the end result being that he appears to have gone into self-imposed exile almost immediately. The quintet's two-tracker was issued on both black and clear vinyl, just to make it marginally more interesting, both versions being housed within an ostensibly 'live-action' picture cover (although, intriguingly, only Dale is actually shown), the extremely unconvincing nature of which adds weight to the theory that this was merely a short-lived studio experiment. In any case, the single can still be picked up fairly inexpensively, should you be remotely tempted to look for it.

7" Singles
»Alright On The Night« KA Records 1981
[Also issued as limited edition on clear vinyl]

PENETRATIONS

Line-up unknown

Not to be confused with the punk combo PENETRATION who featured guitarist Fred Purser in his pre-TYGERS OF PAN TANG days, the unpromisingly-named PENETRATIONS (based in Ayrshire, in the West of Scotland) offered the world their sole 7" single in 1980. In spite of their puzzlingly punky moniker, however, A-side "Coming To You" is a cracking, archetypal NWOBHM rocker in the style of SNAKEBITE, HAZZARD or OVERKILL. "Cheap Thrills", on the reverse, doesn't quite measure up to such high standards, suggesting more of an AC/DC or JESS COX influence, but it's still a pretty good effort, all the same. The quartet, having apparently materialised out of nowhere and issued yet another of those dreaded sleeveless records, were originally something of a mystery, with no writing credits on the label itself, and only the 'Jammy Music Publishing Ltd.' reference (shared with SO WHAT and BLACKOUT, for example) providing any indication of the Scottish connection. Their sole offering, meanwhile, has turned up in pretty minimal quantities over the years, and I suspect that few collectors are even aware of its existence.

In the absence of any additional information, I'm sure you would safely assume that the PENETRATIONS disappeared completely within a year or two of this one-off release hitting the local shops. It transpires, however, that the four-piece were actually something of a popular and long-lived (persevering until at least the late 80's) live attraction in their locality, and were often to be found gigging with other minor rock hopefuls, as well as obtaining the odd support slot with slightly more successful acts (notably TREDEGAR, who seem to have ventured up North on quite a number of occasions) from time to time. They also won a fair bit of valuable airplay on regional stations such as Radio Clyde in their early days, but it ultimately seems to have failed to make much of a difference in

terms of their chances of success, and the lads appear to have resigned themselves to their fate of becoming crowd-pleasers rather than world-beaters. You would do well to add this obscurity to your collection, however, so look out for a slightly cluttered, monochrome label featuring the Kik Records insignia and the distinctive 'Penetrations' logo with the 'P' having been superimposed on an axe. Good luck!

7" Singles
»Coming To You« Kik Records 1980

PERSIAN RISK

Carl Sentance (v)
Phil Campbell (g)
Alex Lohfink (rg)
Nick Hughes (b)
Razz Lemon (d)

Hailing from various parts of Glamorgan, but basing themselves in the Welsh capital of Cardiff, the superb PERSIAN RISK (which, if I remember correctly, was originally a nuclear war scenario) were unquestionably the nation's most accomplished and revered act of the entire NWOBHM period, imitated by many (notably those pretenders to the regional throne, TOK-IO ROSE and TRAITORS GATE) but surpassed by none. Formed at around the height of the NWOBHM explosion, it took the band a year or two to establish themselves on the local live circuit, struggling with ill-timed personnel changes at first (vocalist John Deverill and guitarist Dave Bell both defected to audition for the TYGERS OF PAN TANG in 1980, but only the former was successful), although they had well and truly made their mark by mid-1981, following a well-received demo tape, an appearance with BUDGIE in front of a couple of thousand rabid fans and valuable exposure on their local radio station's 'Red Dragon Rock Show'. Towards the end of that year, having already penned a wealth of original material (notable formative efforts included "Hang On", "Maybe I Could Change", "Streetwalker" and "Take A Trip"), the quintet (having been featured in the 'Armed And Ready' section of 'Kerrang') burst forth with their memorable debut single, a self-financed effort featuring "Calling For You" and "Chase The Dragon", a superb record which immediately came to be regarded as a classic of the genre.

The single, issued in a monochrome sleeve showing photos of the band members, was soon selling out of its original limited pressing, and it's not hard to see why, with "Calling For You", in particular, being a genre-defining moment, a powerful and melodic song which was right up there with the likes of IRON MAIDEN, MENDES PREY and the TYGERS OF PAN TANG in terms of sheer musical ability. "Chase The Dragon", on the other hand, had a slightly more quirky and heavy arrangement, but it was another cracking effort, especially from such an inexperienced act. As you'll be aware, the PERSIAN RISK debut is now, quite rightly, situated right at the top of the collectability scale, with a mammoth asking price reflecting the amount of competition which currently exists among NWOBHM collectors. Before too long, the larger labels came sniffing around, and the group, after dumping oddly-named rhythm guitarist Alex Lohfink and supplying a re-recorded version of "Calling For You" to the second »Heavy Metal Heroes« compilation, swiftly formed a productive relationship with Neat Records. Their first recording for the label was "50000 Stallions", a track which was included on the »60 Minutes Plus« cassette (later featured on the »NWOBHM Vol.3« bootleg

CD), and the band subsequently laid down the excellent "Ridin' High" (with a MAIDEN-style, galloping riff) and "Hurt You" for use as their first single for Neat. Again, it was an immensely strong record (it sold in healthy quantities and had a long-standing run in the 'Kerrang' singles chart) which stands out as one of their label's most impressive releases of the time.

Strangely, however, Neat completely failed to come up with an album offer, leaving the lads with no option but to demo a new selection of material (including the likes of "Night Prowler", "Sky's Falling Down" and "Dark Tower", slightly more classy and accessible numbers than before) and attempt to draw interest from one of the other rock-friendly record companies of the day. Fate was soon to deal them something of a cruel blow, however, when guitarist Phil Campbell was poached by MOTÖRHEAD (a group with whom PERSIAN RISK shared a stage on at least one occasion) in the latter half of 1983, and things took a further turn for the worse when drummer Razz also packed his bags before the year was out. Fortunately, however, the remaining duo of Carl Sentance and Nick Hughes were able to locate temporary replacements in the shape of ex-SPHINX guitarist Graham Bath and erstwhile LONE STAR/WILD HORSES sticksman Dixie Lee, so PERSIAN RISK were soon back on track. In due course, a more suitable drummer was found (former CHINATOWN stalwart Steve Hopgood), and the reversal of fortune was completed when Zebra Records eventually stepped in with an offer to sponsor an EP at the earliest opportunity. This emerged as a three track affair in mid-1984, the compositions featured being "Too Different", "Sky's Falling Down" and "Dark Tower", and these latest efforts confirmed that the lads were now moving into somewhat more melodic and commercial waters.

The new EP was a highly listenable slice of vinyl, although it was a considerable departure from their original heavy roots, and this shift in direction may have been a bit hard for many diehard fans to take, particularly the slightly soppy ballad "Sky's Falling Down", although the TYTAN-style "Dark Tower" was a much better effort altogether. Nevertheless, the record still put in an appearance in various charts of the day, and must have sold in sufficient quantities for Zebra to keep PERSIAN RISK on their books. Further material was demoed in due course, including "Once A King", "Out Of Control" and "Fugitive", and an additional single (to be followed by a full album) was tentatively scheduled for the early months of 1985. Sadly, these plans failed to come to fruition, although plenty of original compositions had already been laid down for future release, and it soon became apparent that Zebra were actually preparing to wash their hands of the luckless band after initially promising them several releases of their own. It was a great pity, although the lads continued to tour and circulate the odd cassette (an official live tape was issued in 1985, for example) in an attempt to keep the momentum going. After a while, they recruited a second guitarist, the much-travelled Phil Vokins (aka Phil Wrathchild, formerly with WRATHCHILD, CRASH K.O. and TYRANT), and the revamped outfit then tried to kickstart their dwindling career with an appearance on the 'E.C.T.' television show, where the lads demonstrated their ability to deliver the goods with energetic renditions of "Women In Rock", "Rise Up" and "Too Different".

By the early months of 1986, however, things were looking fairly bleak, with frontman Carl Sentance having already started to lend his considerable talents to various other projects such as TREDEGAR, the GEEZER BUTLER BAND and TOKYO BLADE (guesting on the latter's recent European tour dates at short notice), and bets were soon being placed as to when the beleaguered PERSIAN RISK would finally call in the receivers. Surprisingly, however, the situation flipped around pretty dramatically when the Metal Masters label unexpectedly waded in with an offer to pick up on their unreleased recordings for Zebra (much as they had done with

TYTAN's demos for Kamaflage) and issue a slightly belated long-player. This emerged in due course as »Rise Up«, an enjoyable set of compositions all round, with stand-out numbers including "Rip It Up", "Don't Turn Around" and the title track itself. The album received high praise almost universally, and the outfit were to promote the release with a session for the 'Friday Rock Show', eventually transmitted on the 11th of July 1986 (but recorded some time earlier). With the outfit being augmented by keyboard player Philip James on this occasion, PERSIAN RISK elected to showcase a fairly strong selection of material, namely "Jane", "Women In Rock", "Break Free" and the otherwise-unreleased "One Day One Night". At this point, it looked as though everything was finally working out for the plucky bunch, but, in fact, all was not as it seemed.

Although the advertising which surrounded the debut album's release suggested that the band were indeed a going concern, it soon emerged that they had virtually split in half by the time the record was making its way into general circulation, with only a semi-stable nucleus of Sentance, Hughes and Vokins (Hopgood and Bath having already been recruited to the ranks of BATTLEZONE in the interim) remaining from the last line-up. In the first instance, however, there were some speculative reports that the trio would attempt to keep things going by reinventing themselves as RISK, although this idea was actually rejected at a fairly early stage. Instead, the persevering PERSIAN RISK made repeated efforts to salvage the situation, although the surviving members were almost certainly fighting a losing battle by this time. Carl Sentance himself finally flew the coop later in the year (joining forces with local hopefuls MONRO and then helping out in TOK-IO ROSE), and, although the surviving duo tried out former BLIND FURY vocalist Lou Taylor for a short time, the inevitable demise was only postponed until early 1987, when Nick Hughes accepted an offer to join IDOL RICH, signifying the end of the line for PERSIAN RISK. Lou Taylor, on the other hand, wasted little time before forming his own TOUR DE FORCE venture, while Phil Vokins proceeded to work with BILL WARD and FIREWORX (later establishing the ROGUE ISLAND venture with one-time STRATEGY/JEDDAH sticksman Ron Emms), so it's reassuring that all these talented musicians didn't just disappear completely.

Intriguingly, though, that wasn't quite the end of the story, though, as Carl Sentance decided (after his unsuccessful stints with a couple of local outfits) to emigrate to the States in the early 90's to try his luck again. He later revealed that one of his old compositions had been put to good use by another heavy bunch in the wake of PERSIAN RISK's demise: *'Paul Dianno's BATTLEZONE used an old PERSIAN RISK song on their album, Paul had changed the lyrics a bit, but it was definitely my song. I was extremely surprised to hear a song of mine on the radio, although I was aware that Graham Bath and Steve Hopgood were playing in BATTLEZONE by that time.'* (Ref: Interview, Matthias Mader, April 1996). After moving to the States, the frontman took the strange decision to establish a brand-new touring band using the defunct PERSIAN RISK moniker, and this particular ensemble successfully played the American club circuit with a mixture of covers and original material, the latter comprising merely a third of their set. Unlikely as it may seem, it would appear that Sentance's erstwhile colleague, Phil Campbell, became aware of the outfit's existence while MOTÖRHEAD were touring North America some time later, and suggested that they might be able to get together for a bit of a reunion.

Sadly, MOTÖRHEAD's hectic touring schedule precluded any impromptu jam sessions at that juncture, although Carl Sentance (who subsequently began working on various musical projects on both sides of the Atlantic) was later able to organise a one-off PERSIAN RISK reformation show at a small London club in 1996. The frontman was joined by old muckers Steve Hopgood and Graham Bath (and, for the encore, by Paul Dianno) for a remarkably solid performance (especially considering their lack of practice) which included versions of old favourites such as "Women In Rock" and "Ridin' High", as well as some surprising cover versions (notably "Man In The Box" by ALICE IN CHAINS), showing that the frontman was keeping abreast of current musical trends. Sadly, however, this well-received, nostalgic get-together appears to have been an isolated appearance, and there now seems little chance of a repeat performance. PERSIAN RISK's long-deleted LP has, however, recently benefitted from a timely CD reissue courtesy of High Vaultage, giving modern-day NWOBHM enthusiasts the opportunity to appreciate their considerable talent.

LP's
»Rise Up« Metal Masters 1986

12" EP's
»**Too Different**« Zebra Records 1984
[A-side non-LP, "Sky's Falling Down" and "Dark

Tower" different to album versions]

7" Singles
»Calling For You« SRT 1981
[Both tracks non-LP]
»Ridin' High« Neat 1983
[Both tracks non-LP]

CD's
»Rise Up« High Vaultage 1997
[With three bonus tracks]

Exclusive Compilation Appearances
"50000 Stallions" on »60 Minutes Plus« Cassette Neat 1982/CD Teichiku 1992 + »All Hell Let Loose« LP Neat 1983 + »NWOBHM Vol.3« Bootleg CD 1992

Compilation Appearances
"Calling For You" on »Heavy Metal Heroes Vol.2« LP Heavy Metal 1982 + »N.W.O.B.H.M.« LP/CD Heavy Metal 1991 + »Heavy Metal Heroes Vol.I&II« CD British Steel 1996
[Different to single version]
"Too Different" on »The Best Of British« LP Zebra 1985 + »Axe Attack« LP M Port 1985/Mausoleum 1986 + »The Best Of Indie Metal« CD Emporio 1998
"Ridin' High" on »Heavy Metal Collection 2« CD X-Tra Collection 1993
"Jane" on »Rock Out!« Do-CD Emporio 1996

PET HATE

Alistair Terry (v, k)
Stuart MacFarlane (g)
Michael Parris (g)
Dave Roberts (b)
Steve Roberts (d)

It seemed a strange idea that, after five years spent building up a sizeable national following as SILVERWING (see separate entry), the Roberts brothers would suddenly dismantle the outfit and start again from scratch under the revised moniker of PET HATE. Nevertheless, Steve Roberts was soon at hand to proffer an explanation for their actions: 'SILVERWING ran its course. You know, the spandex, glitter, pyros and the stupid song titles. We simply reached a point where there was nowhere left to go with it. We had to reinvent ourselves, but because of all the baggage that was associated with SILVERWING, we changed the name.' (Ref: Metal Forces No.11, 1984). As it turned out, the central cadre of Dave and Steve Roberts reunited with erstwhile compatriots Alistair Terry and Stuart MacFarlane for this all-new venture, bolstering the line-up with the unknown Michael Parris as an additional guitarist. With Terry taking over the vocal position on a permanent basis, it was initially open to speculation as to whether there would indeed be a significant deviation from the SILVERWING sound of yore.

The public had a relatively short wait before finding out for themselves, as the revamped outfit debuted with a full LP on the Heavy Metal label early in 1984. PET HATE's »The Bride Wore Red« was a mediocre opening gambit, on the whole, with the vast majority of featured tracks being unmemorable rock/pop in the style of BLAZER BLAZER, MARSEILLE or BOMBAY, with only "Caught (Red Handed)" (a previously-unissued SILVERWING composition, as was "Wanting You") and the title track itself serving to remind us of anything approaching their original energy and attitude. Even their unremarkable cover of MOTT THE HOOPLE's "Roll Away The Stone" was an insipid effort, yet they still elected to issue it as the main focus of a tie-in 12" EP, the featured B-sides being "Caught (Red Handed)" and the otherwise-unavailable "Playing With My Heart", the latter being a reasonably listenable number. PET HATE's first batch of recordings had certainly come as a serious disappointment to the fans, and the lads were somewhat fortunate to be offered the chance to redeem themselves with a follow-up album. The studio sessions for their »Bad Publicity« release took place before the end of the year, although these were to signify Stuart MacFarlane's final involvement with the outfit, and he was eventually to be replaced by Jimmy Beatson after the LP appeared in the shops.

The latest album, produced by the esteemed Eddie Leonetti (famed for his work with the likes of ANGEL and LEGS DIAMOND), was a more restrained and moody affair (a discarded JAPAN long-player on the sleeve giving a pretty accurate representation of their mindset at this point) with far fewer concessions to the mainstream market. Tracks such as "Cry Of The Wild", "Dancing On My Heart" and "Stale Lipstick" show the band at their strongest, and their capable cover of "Street Fighting Man" by the ROLLING STONES (rather than any of the hackneyed glam anthems they had favoured in their youth) was a pretty appropriate choice in the circumstances. Having said that, there are a couple of stinkers too, notably "For Sex Sake" and the mercifully brief "Teenage Party" (so much for giving up the *'stupid song titles'*, eh?), so it's not exactly a flawless set of recordings by any means. PET

HATE's last vinyl output was a 7" single featuring "Girls Grow Up Too Fast" and the unremarkable "Wreck The Radio", issued in the early months of 1985. The upbeat A-side, despite being a highly listenable and catchy effort, had stuck out like a sore thumb on the long-player, as it was reminiscent of the kind of late 60's/early 70's pop purveyed by manufactured acts such as EDISON LIGHTHOUSE or WHITE PLAINS, and it appears to have failed miserably as a single, which is a bit of a shame.

The outfit's last known recordings comprised a session for the 'Friday Rock Show', broadcast on the 12th of April 1985. By this juncture, guitarist Michael Parris had been replaced by the implausibly-named James Page, and the band dutifully ran through versions of "Girls Grow Up Too Fast", "Wreck The Radio", "Cry Of The Wild" and "Love Me Madly". It appears to have been PET HATE's swansong (although the lads showed up on the 'E.C.T.' television programme a month later, where they performed "Wreck The Radio" and "Girls Grow Up Too Fast"), as there's no evidence to suggest that any additional studio visits took place in readiness for a third album. They could probably have delivered something quite impressive eventually, so it's a shame that they started off on the wrong foot by issuing such a run-of-the-mill debut. After formally disbanding PET HATE in the early months of 1986 (by which point Alistair Terry had already sauntered off to record a critically-ignored solo LP called »Yonge At Heart«, which was also released on FM Records), the Roberts brothers subsequently took a couple of years off prior to having yet another attempt at reviving the SILVERWING name (which again fell apart towards the end of the decade), after which Dave Roberts and James Page eventually teamed up again (with a publicity-shy drummer known only as *'Duncan'*) in an ill-fated early 90's venture called THE UNLOVED.

LP's
»The Bride Wore Red« Heavy Metal 1984
»Bad Publicity« Heavy Metal 1984
[Also released as limited edition on white vinyl]

12" EP's
»Roll Away The Stone« FM Records 1984
["Playing With My Heart" non-LP]

7" Singles
»Girls Grow Up Too Fast« FM Records 1985

Compilation Appearances
"Wreck The Radio" on »Heavy Metal Records« LP Heavy Metal 1984

PHASSLAYNE

Michael Maughan (v, g)
Paul Gago (b)
Andrew Stidolph (d)

Tyneside's curiously-monikered PHASSLAYNE (a rather pointless corruption of *'fast lane'*, I'll wager) were an unrenowned power trio who originally gravitated together in around 1982, the act centred around the songwriting duo of Michael Maughan and Paul Gago. Their small-time activities on the club circuit raised comparatively few eyebrows at the time, although they swiftly became good friends with numerous other heavy outfits who were doing the rounds locally. Musically, PHASSLAYNE skirted around the edges of the proto-speed metal scene which had established itself in the North East at the height of the NWOBHM, largely based around the pioneering work of RAVEN, plus the immortal SATAN/BLITZKRIEG/AVENGER triumvirate. In fact, it would appear that the ever-present duo of Maughan and Gago initially sought to expand their musical vision to a stable four-piece, although the search for a suitable vocalist was ultimately unsuccessful, leaving the guitarist to occupy the microphone himself for the duration. By mid-1984, the group were finally becoming slightly more ambitious, having established something of a semi-stable line-up *via* the recent recruitment of sticksman Andrew Stidolph. A demo tape, circulated a few months later, drew its fair share of label attention, although the lads eventually decided that their best option was probably to go with that ever-dependable local operation, Neat Records.

Issued in the early months of 1985, PHASSLAYNE's »Cut It Up« long-player was a hit-and-miss affair, their attempts to play raw metal at high speed occasionally resulting in the rhythm section losing track of the frontman's guitar histrionics. In addition, the primitive production is staggeringly bad for a Neat release, and the trio's decision to include a knockabout interpretation of ELVIS PRESLEY's "King Creole" merely lowers them to the status of pub rock crowd-pleasers. Nevertheless, the group deliver a few quality numbers, particularly when they lay off the gas pedal and attempt to create something more listenable, notably on "Don't Walk Away", "Run For Guns" and "Minute Man", when the similarity veers more towards acts such as SAVAGE and CHARIOT. Rock fans of the day remained largely nonplussed by the release, however (Neat didn't exactly go to town on the promotion front, either), and few of those who were unfamiliar with PHASSLAYNE (*i.e.* virtually everyone) were willing to take a chance on an album by a group with such a silly moniker, especially when it came in an utterly nondescript cover. The public might eventually have latched onto the trio when their LP's started appearing in the bargain bins of local record shops, but, by that time, it was too late: the luckless band had already gone to the wall.

PHASSLAYNE hung around for a remarkably short time after their debut set was completed (it's entirely possible that they had, in a bizarre ETHEL THE FROG-type scenario, split before it was even released), which certainly didn't help to promote or give credibility to the long-player in any way. To be honest, the record has the feel of a one-off studio get-together, and doesn't suggest that the ramshackle group were ever going to be held up as the *'next big thing'* by their sponsors. The partnership of Maughan and Gago appears to have dissolved completely in the wake of the album's commercial failure, while Andrew 'Stidi' Stidolph later went on to have a considerably better chance of finding fame and fortune when (after initially pottering around with minor regional hopefuls such as BROKEN ANGEL and GUNSLINGER) he was assimilated into the ranks of the WILDHEARTS (something of a retirement home for clapped-out old NWOBHM scenesters) in the early 90's. He ultimately ended up working with a happy-go-lucky bunch called WHATEVER, whose collective activities waned towards the end of the decade following a couple of unassuming releases on small indie labels.

LP's
»Cut It Up« Neat 1985
[UK issue]
»Cut It Up« Roadrunner 1985
[Dutch issue with reversed colour scheme on cover]

PHEETUS

P. Simpson
N. Hudson
C. Lawn
N. Holmes
G. Pearson

Another utterly abysmal name, although the punky-sounding PHEETUS actually conceals a pretty traditional (but rather obscure, all the same) boogie/metal act from the late 70's, whose one and only vinyl legacy appears to be a privately-issued two-tracker from way back in 1978. At times, the Yorkshire outfit come across as being very much in the VARDIS or DEDRINGER mould, and I reckon that a couple of future NWOBHM stalwarts (Gary Pearson and Neil Hudson, one member from each of the aforementioned acts) might just have been involved with this earlier bunch, although nobody seems to remember them well enough to be able either to confirm or disprove this notion with any great level of certainty. Maybe we'll find out in due course. Anyway, "Nomads" is a heavy, good-time number with a very slight punk tinge, quite reminiscent of ROKKA in that particular respect, but still considerably closer to the NWOBHM archetype than you might expect for a release as early as this. On the reverse, "Blind Man" is a somewhat more restrained affair, and this succinct effort captures PHEETUS in a rather different light (vaguely similar to LIMELIGHT or BLEAK HOUSE in some of their more reflective moments), showing that they clearly had more than one string to their bow. Nevertheless, this little-remembered ensemble seems to have constituted a very fleeting concern, and nothing else appears to have been committed to vinyl under that terrible name. Precious few playable copies of their two-tracker (no picture sleeve) have surfaced in recent times, with a considerable number of examples clearly (now warped beyond belief) having been stored in close proximity to a nuclear power station in the interim, by the looks of things.

7" Singles
»Nomads« Pollen Records 1978

PHOENIX RISING

Jack Bunker (v)
Pete Bangert (g)
Chris Hamilton (b)
Danny Spencer (d)

PHOENIX RISING were a fairly obscure metal bunch (loosely based around the productive South Yorkshire area) who initially came to prominence on the basis of a well-received demo and a couple of local radio appearances in mid-1982 or thereabouts. Indeed, such was the outfit's regional popularity that "Understanding", from their original cassette, actually managed a placing in the 'Local Chart' section in 'Kerrang' at the beginning of 1983. The lads were obviously doing something right, and swiftly concluded that they wouldn't bother waiting for a major-label deal to come along, whereupon they simply organised a private offering. The four selections (ignoring "'Av An 'Am", which is basically just a wacky outro taken from a well-known 'Muppet Show' song) which comprise the group's self-financed »Lonely Attack« 12" (issued towards the end of that year) certainly had more in common with heavier 70's outfits such as BUDGIE and NUTZ than most of their NWOBHM contemporaries, although they share quite a bit of common ground with the likes of CRACKED MIRROR and Derbyshire's WARRIOR, particularly in terms of the accomplished guitar work. The title track is probably the pick of the bunch, as it's undoubtedly the closest to traditional NWOBHM territory, whereas "The Minstrel" is a more restrained, progressively-inclined piece. Elsewhere, demo favourite "Understanding" illustrates an entirely disparate vocal technique, but is still a strong and heavy track all the same, while the doomy, atmospheric "Phoenix Rising" rounds things off in fine style.

A number of additional demo compositions were unveiled in the form of sessions for Radio Hallam at around this time, some of the more memorable inclusions being "About The Time", "See You Babe", "So Easy" and "Stormbringer". With these tracks all being in an equivalently heavy style to the EP (their talented vocalist sounding, on occasion, *uncannily* like TROUBLE's Eric Wagner, but completely dissimilar on other numbers), the general standard was consistently high, and I would imagine that, had this bunch ever managed to get around to recording a full LP, it would surely be held in particularly high esteem by those underground rock/metal devotees who appreciate weighty 60's/70's innovators such as BLUE CHEER, BANG, NECROMANDUS and LEAFHOUND. Sadly, however, it wasn't to be, and the protagonists appear to have drifted apart within a year or two of their excellent EP's release. Issued in an eye-catching cover, the record rightly remains a coveted item these days, and may yet become a cult classic. Drummer Danny Spencer, incidentally, went on to join the revamped SARACEN in time to play on the latter's »Change Of Heart« album for Neat, but none of the other PHOENIX RISING stalwarts appear to have remained in the music business.

12" EP's

»**Lonely Attack**« Rising Records 1983

PHYNE THANQUZ

Dr Death

Weird name for a band, huh? Don't go looking for any mystical significance, though, it's merely a particularly daft way of spelling *'fine thanks'* (those crazy kids!), although it still hardly represents the most metal of monikers. Mind you, just cast thy humble gaze upon that magnificently clichéd sleeve! A long-haired skull, a crucifix,

the obligatory gothic logo...it must be a good 'un, right? Added to the observation that both of the exquisitely-titled songs "Into The Sun" and "Curse Of The Gods" were ostensibly written by an individual calling himself *'Dr Death'*, this enigmatic outfit's two-tracker certainly *looks* like it should be a top rarity, and indeed it is. Only a tiny handful have ever come out of the woodwork, most of them emerging from a house clearance near Edinburgh a few years ago. Apart from the assertion that this utterly mysterious ensemble were apparently Scottish, nothing else is known for certain, and even the bloke who produced it has absolutely no recollection of the recording session, which is a bit spooky. No doubt the forces of evil were responsible for his memory loss, either that or the traditional post-recording celebrations in the local pub.

When it comes to pinning down details of the story behind this one-off release, there seems to be a dead end wherever you look. Matters aren't really helped by the fact that the record isn't dated explicitly (you can discount the earlier speculation from certain shady individuals that it emerged in 1983, as this was totally unfounded), there's no picture of the group and the members' names aren't revealed (furthermore, I have a sneaking suspicion that 'Dr Death' may also be a soubriquet, you know). The music, however, is pretty decent, a heavy garage/metal sound akin to certain semi-NWOBHM outfits such as SPEED or SCORPIO, with some doomy, DAMNED-style keyboards (particularly on the B-side) adding to the general atmosphere, much as they do on the CHALLENGER single. The vocals seem to be heavily influenced by HOLOCAUST, and it's entirely possible that the two acts were on the scene at the same time, although it's equally conceivable that this particular 7" could have been recorded any time from the mid-70's onwards. Information, anyone?

7" Singles
»Into The Sun« ERC Records 19??

PRAYING MANTIS

Tino Troy (v, g)
Pete Moore (v, rg)
Chris Troy (b)
Chris Hudson (d)

The lengthy and convoluted story of the London-based PRAYING MANTIS revolves around the nucleus of Tino and Chris Neophytou, two talented musical brothers of Mediterranean extraction, both of whom had been encouraged to master the traditional flamenco guitar technique from an early age, but who gradually developed an affiliation for somewhat more raucous musical styles. The first to pledge his allegiance to the gods of rock'n'roll was lead guitarist Tino, who formed his first semi-serious group, JUNCTION, while still at college in the early 70's, roping in his chum Pete Moore to write a few cheery tunes and play some well-chosen cover versions to get into the swing of things. After a year or so, brother Chris was finally persuaded to join in the fun, adroitly switching from guitar to bass in order to fill the relevant vacancy, the trio being assisted by several temporary drummers (plus fly-by-night vocalist Stan Cunningham at one point) while attempting to establish themselves on the capital's music scene. By 1975, they had evolved into a proper gigging band, their repertoire still consisting predominantly of covers, with their own numbers being heavily influenced by WISHBONE ASH, THIN LIZZY and STATUS QUO at that stage. Within a year or two, the lads had outgrown their rather nondescript moniker, and so the extremely metal-sounding PRAYING MANTIS was born, the group having also now attained something of a stable line-up after the recruitment of drummer (originally keyboard player) Chris Hudson. With Tino and Pete sharing vocal duties, the outfit began making a serious impact in the live environment, and were soon penning some highly capable material of their own, including formative compositions such as "Nightchild", "Golden Rainbow" and "Give Me A Reason". Before too much longer, the lads eventually decided that a proper demo was now well overdue.

For their first official demo tape, PRAYING MANTIS laid down "Captured City", "The Ripper" and "Johnny Cool", three tracks which largely pre-empted the NWOBHM explosion, having a lot more in common with some of their hard-rocking heroes from the early 70's (and it wasn't quintessentially British, either, there were definitely hints of the EAGLES and CREEDENCE CLEARWATER REVIVAL in the melting pot too) than the furious, upbeat mayhem which came to be associated with the term 'NWOBHM' in years to come. Nevertheless, PRAYING MANTIS would eventually become well and truly linked with the movement, their style becoming slightly heavier and rather more refined as time progressed, culminating in a brand of sophisticated, melodic metal as performed by the likes of TRESPASS and SOLDIER. Although the first PRAYING MANTIS tape was apparently doing the rounds as early as 1978, it failed to arouse much interest in a transitional music scene (punk had just blown itself out and nobody really knew what would take its place), but a piece of good

fortune finally came their way early the following year, when a copy found its way into the possession of Neal Kay, who ran the 'Heavy Metal Soundhouse' (pretty much the country's first rock disco) at the legendary Bandwagon venue. He agreed to play their demo once to see if it elicited any sort of response whatsoever, and the chap was so utterly flabbergasted by the (virtually unprecedented) hysterical public reaction that the songs went on to become a permanent fixture in his playlist for months to come. After being pestered for a while, the members were persuaded that it would be a prudent idea to utilise these rough'n'ready recordings to form the basis of their first vinyl release (as IRON MAIDEN had already done with their low-budget demos), and so an arrangement was expeditiously made with Harvest (although it emerged as a pseudo-private job on 'Ripper Records') to release »The Soundhouse Tapes Part 2« (just to ram home the Neal Kay connection) later in the year.

The release proved to be an instant hit with the fans, who were soon forking out ready cash to hear PRAYING MANTIS on vinyl (three tracks on the 12" version, the 7" omitting "The Ripper"), and sales rapidly went through the roof, causing a few eyebrows to be raised among the rock press and those in charge of radio programming, some of whom were lucky enough to receive a limited edition picture sleeve issue which credited the two-tracker as »Captured City«. Before long, the protagonists were being invited to provide a session for the 'Friday Rock Show', whereupon they proceeded (with an immense lack of imagination) to record almost identical versions of two of the numbers ("Captured City" and "Johnny Cool") which had appeared on their recent EP. Strange idea, that. Nevertheless, their session (transmitted on the 9th of November 1979) was warmly received by the station's listeners (the third track, the unfamiliar "Lovers To The Grade", was a worthy addition to their repertoire), the upshot being that the 'Rock Show' take of "Johnny Cool" made its way onto the BBC's »Metal Explosion« compilation of session highlights. Moving into 1980, the lads parted company with long-time drummer Chris Hudson (who more or less packed in the music business) and eventually recruited Mick Ransome to the fold. The latter proved to be a capable addition to the ranks, although the lads didn't manage to get hold of him until after they had been asked to contribute a track to the first »Metal For Muthas« sampler (where they used a session sticksman), the number in question being yet another re-recording of "Captured City", which must have left the public wondering whether or not PRAYING MANTIS actually had much more than a handful of songs in their repertoire. In truth, they had a veritable abundance of original material even at that stage, so it looks as though they were just particularly fond of these early classics.

On the back of the »Metal For Muthas« release came a support slot with fellow contributors IRON MAIDEN, which took PRAYING MANTIS around the country for a well-received series of gigs at many of the major rock venues of the day. By this juncture, they had already broken in new second guitarist Rob Angelo (aka Bob Sawyer, who had been an IRON MAIDEN member for a very brief spell in their pre-vinyl days), who stood in for Pete Moore at short notice after the latter elected to throw in his hand and start a new life overseas. The spring tour was an immense success in anyone's books, and it yielded a one-off single deal with Gem, which saw the rapid release of a 7" featuring "Praying Mantis" and "High Roller" (the latter being penned by new recruit Bob Angelo). It was also the first release to feature experienced sticksman Dave Potts (a veteran of numerous acts throughout the 70's, including the likes of TEN YEARS AFTER and LOVE AFFAIR), who had stepped in to plug the gap after the sudden departure of the unsettled Mick Ransome, who later found gainful employment with various minor hopefuls such as RITCH BITCH, TEXAS (no, not the famous lot), JOKERS WILD and the slightly more successful TATTOOED LOVE BOYS. By now, incidentally, the Neophytou brothers had come to the conclusion that their mouthful of a surname was 'a bit too European' (I hope you're not thinking the Brits are all xenophobes or something), and reinvented themselves as the brothers Troy. I'm sure it made an absolutely *huge* difference. Anyway, their latest single was a strong release (it didn't lead straight to an album deal, though, which was a bit of a shame), the outfit now showing signs that they might be moving into more of a heavy, driving, twin-guitar style than before (as evidenced on the A-side, at least) and taking their rightful place at the very forefront of the NWOBHM explosion.

Nevertheless, Bob Angelo never really gelled properly as part of the PRAYING MANTIS unit, and the luckless chap was soon tactfully shown the door (although he later resurfaced in a post-vinyl incarnation of WEAPON, and has actually been recording as a solo artist in recent times), whereupon new bloke Steve Carroll (formerly with punk/pop oddities LITTLE BO BITCH) was drafted in to see if he would fare any better. Happily, the latest axeman impressed his prospective employers at their next handful of live appearances (including a support slot with GIRLSCHOOL), so he was allowed to stay for the time being. Finally, they seemed to have located the ideal musicians for the job, establishing a stable line-up as a result, and this particular incarnation of PRAYING MANTIS is widely regarded by the majority of their fans as the definitive version. Anyway, the lads were soon out on the road once more, playing alongside IRON MAIDEN on another lengthy UK jaunt, followed by a prestigious appearance at the 1980 Reading Festival. PRAYING MANTIS played an absolute blinder on the big day, and were justly rewarded for their efforts with a lucrative deal to deliver a full album for Arista. Work commenced almost immediately, and the recording sessions had been completed by the end of the year, the fans getting a taster for the forthcoming full-length effort when Arista released the »Cheated« double single, which included the exclusive B-side "Thirty Pieces Of Silver" and two excellent live tracks, "Flirting With Suicide" and "Panic In The Streets". This vinyl bounty was rushed out to coincide with the band's end-of-year support slot with TRIUMPH, and it proved to be a huge success, even denting the mainstream charts after incredibly healthy sales. Clearly, the new PRAYING MANTIS material (a bit more upbeat and raunchy than before) was striking precisely the right chord with the rock community, and the LP was soon being anticipated feverishly.

The album, »Time Tells No Lies«, finally appeared in the early part of 1981, and caught the public's imagination in no uncertain terms, with strong, catchy numbers such as "Running For Tomorrow" and "Panic In The Streets" contrasting with equally-capable (but rather more subtle and reflective) compositions like "Children Of The Earth" and old favourite "Lovers To The Grave". Overall, it was a highly impressive debut, and demonstrated an unusually broad range of musicianship and a considerable depth of lyrical ingenuity. No *'lick my love pump'* stuff here, folks. Sales were hugely satisfying for such a comparatively unfamiliar act, with the album making an impression on the mainstream charts and receiving a fair bit of airplay on radio stations throughout the land. The quartet went out on tour with GAMMA to promote the long-player, and were soon to benefit from further exposure after their interpretation of the old KINKS standard "All Day And All Of The Night" was used to form the basis of another successful single. All in all, things seemed to be going according to plan. It was something of a surprise, therefore, when PRAYING MANTIS came to a mutual decision to recruit a dedicated vocalist fairly shortly after the immediate flurry of activity to promote »Time Tells No Lies«. The lucky chap in question was Tommy Jackson, previously with the Scottish version of TURBO, who proceeded to demonstrate his talents at a series of gigs throughout the summer of 1981. Sadly, however, the new recruit failed to make a good impression on the fans, and he was soon on his way (later hooking up with Bernie Marsden in the S.O.S. venture before taking up a short residency in the ranks of French hopefuls NIGHTMARE), being supplanted within a remarkably short space of time by erstwhile GRAND PRIX frontman Bernie Shaw, who proved to be a considerably more popular and effective choice.

Shaw's vocal prowess undoubtedly had the potential to take PRAYING MANTIS to the next rung of the proverbial ladder, and the lads were soon thinking about preparing the groundwork for their second album, so they upped sticks and moved over to Germany for a while, laying down a selection of novel material (Bernie Shaw didn't make the trip, but his vocals were later overdubbed on some of the finished tracks) for their follow-up. The recording sessions seemed to be going OK at first (compositions such as "The Story", "Battle Royal" and "Time Slipping Away" were all completed satisfactorily), but things began to go a bit pear-shaped towards the end of the year, when a variety of financial and contractual problems with their management and record label culminated in the whole project being shelved for the time being. Still, PRAYING MANTIS continued to do their thing in the live environment, touting their wares around in the early months of 1982 (by which time they had parted company with Steve Carroll and brought in keyboard player Jon Bavin, originally part of the outfit's entourage) in an attempt to secure some interest from another major company, but it wasn't until the summer that an offer came their way from Jet Records to finance an EP. To this end, the group recorded "Tell Me The Nightmare's Wrong" (which, you'll be utterly fascinated to learn, was penned by the same individual responsible for the theme to TV show 'Cheers'), the catchy "Turn The Tables", the instrumental "A Question Of Time" and old favourite "Give Me A Reason", the original intention being to release a generous four-tracker to coincide with their forthcoming appearance at the Reading Festival of 1982. In the event, "Give Me A Reason" was given the elbow (I'm not entirely sure why), and the remaining three efforts were pressed up in the form of a 7" EP, certain

examples of which were housed within an astonishingly amateurish picture sleeve.

PRAYING MANTIS proceeded to deliver the goods at Reading again (enjoying a pretty high billing this time), and it looked as though they would surely be riding the crest of a wave once more. Selected highlights from the show were broadcast on the 'Friday Rock Show' shortly thereafter, and there was good reason to assume that another LP would soon be forthcoming. In fact, the lads struggled to maintain their identity, direction and general enthusiasm for the venture as they moved into 1983 (their most recent piece of vinyl had illustrated a move into considerably more radio-friendly waters), and were soon reluctantly coming to terms with the fact that their big chance had apparently gone. By the spring, it was apparent that the deal with Jet had fallen through, and the musicians now found themselves aimlessly messing around in the studio to see if they could come up with anything that might be able to salvage their collective careers. Freshly-penned material such as "Enough Is Enough", "Nightmares" and "Raining In Kensington" came across as capable enough efforts, but it was too little, too late, and the band finally ground to a halt later in the year. Fortunately, they were only to remain inactive for a couple of months, whereupon erstwhile IRON MAIDEN drummer Clive Burr recruited the Troy brothers and Bernie Shaw (Dave Potts became their manager) to assist him in his new CLIVE BURR'S ESCAPE venture, which rapidly evolved into STRATUS (see separate entry), something which occupied the participants' time for the next couple of years.

By 1986, however, STRATUS had bitten the dust in the wake of very poor album sales and a lukewarm public reaction, neither of which were helped by the fact that their »Throwing Shapes« LP had received a ludicrously limited distribution, with pitifully few copies having reached the British PRAYING MANTIS fans, who were surely the ones most likely to buy it in the first place. The dejected members subsequently dispersed and kept a distinctly low profile for a while, but were eventually drawn back together after deciding to play a one-off PRAYING MANTIS reunion gig in London at the tail end of 1987. On this particular occasion, the Troys were rejoined by erstwhile colleagues Bernie Shaw and Dave Potts, with an old friend called Hugh Bestik stepping in to help out on second guitar. It was, by all accounts, a good-humoured and well-attended event which even raised a fair bit of passing interest in the rock press of the time, but it still wasn't enough to suggest that a full-scale reformation might actually be a viable proposition, so the members went their own separate ways once more. Bernie Shaw went off to carve out a new musical career (later enjoying a productive spell in URIAH HEEP), while Chris immersed himself in studio work for a couple of years and Tino messed around with various knockabout club acts including the WANDERING CRUTCHLEES and PADDY GOES TO HOLYHEAD. Good names, those, honestly.

By 1990, however, there was a bit of a mini-NWOBHM revival in progress, with various Ulrich-sanctioned activity surrounding the imminent release of Polygram's commemorative retrospective set. Several ex-scenesters decided to get back in on the action as a consequence, and a touring version of PRAYING MANTIS duly assembled themselves for a few Japanese shows, with the Troys playing the nostalgia card by teaming up with former IRON MAIDEN stalwarts Paul Dianno and Dennis Stratton, with much-travelled drummer Bruce Bisland (whose many credits included stints with WEAPON, WILDFIRE and STATETROOPER) making up the numbers. In spite of the observation that these performances were rather ramshackle affairs which included a variety of PRAYING MANTIS, IRON MAIDEN and even LIONHEART numbers in the set, the Japanese fans lived up to their reputation and went absolutely wild, and the general consensus of opinion was that there might actually be a bit of mileage in getting the outfit off the ground once more. The PRAYING MANTIS tour led to the ALL STARS project, which was rather less of a major success, but the Pony Canyon concern (who had released a live show from the 1990 tour on CD) went out of their way to persuade the lads to deliver a brand-new PRAYING MANTIS album after all these years. Unsurprisingly, the outfit were slightly taken aback, and they had precious little recently-penned material at their disposal, so it was a case of delving into the vaults and seeing what might be worth reworking to pad out the forthcoming release.

With Paul Dianno having already gone off to do his KILLERS thing in the interim, it was now down to the bare bones of the Troys, Stratton and Bisland, although the foursome managed to throw together an album (»Predator In Disguise«) of old and new, the 'old' coming in the shape of compositions such as "The Horn", "Time Slipping Away" and "Battle Royal", while newer numbers included such listenable efforts as "Still Want You", "This Time Girl" and "She's Hot". It was something of a move away from their thoughtful material of the early 80's into an undemanding, easy-going variation on the melodic rock style, although the outfit (with the Troys sharing vocal duties with Dennis Stratton) still managed to come across very effectively, and were soon winning over a huge number of new fans in the Far East. Back in the UK, where the group were signed to Under One Flag, barely anyone noticed that PRAYING MANTIS were back in business, but the band hardly cared by this stage. They were soon out on tour in Japan once again, bringing in erstwhile LA PAZ singer Dougie White and TOBRUK keyboard player Jem Davis (both of whom had latterly been employed by the failed MIDNIGHT BLUE) to bolster their sound in the live environment. Again, it was all a huge success, with gigs being recorded for television broadcasts, interviews aplenty and a pretty phenomenal level of reverence being afforded to their every move. Quite hard to understand, really, I guess they just struck exactly the right chord with the Japanese consciousness or something…

Dougie White had been acting purely in the capacity of locum for the most recent spate of touring activities, and he was soon moving on to pastures new (notably RAINBOW), although the lads soon identified a suitable full-time frontman in the shape of Colin Peel, a veteran of such melodic hopefuls as CANNES and OUTSIDE EDGE. The newcomer was gradually broken in, and made his debut on the »A Cry For The New World« set, issued in 1993. By this stage, they had abandoned the notion of using a permanent keyboard player on their albums (Jem Davis went on to work with FM and UFO), and had now committed themselves to delivering a brand of high-class AOR which bore very little resemblance to their once-heavy style of preference. Still, it was an extremely listenable (if slightly over-long) set of compositions, some of which could happily hold their own with the giants of the melodic rock world (the title track, in particular, was a supremely confident number), and Colin Peel's superb voice really carried the material in a way which had been sorely lacking in previous years. By this point in time, the lads had somehow broken free from the shackles of the 'NWOBHM' tag (which had handed them a lifeline in Japan but represented the kiss of death elsewhere), and were now just going about their business as a top-notch AOR proposition, with the group actually beginning to pick up a few additional melodic rock fans in other parts of the world, even including (shock horror) Britain itself. It was something of a disappointment, therefore, when their latest frontman decided not to commit himself on a permanent basis, and he was soon swanning off to a wide-ranging career which still includes a great deal of film and stage work.

Peel's immediate replacement was Mark Thompson-Smith, a vocalist who had served time in IDOL RICH, TOUCHÉ and FLIGHT 19, and he was introduced to the fans when PRAYING MANTIS released their »Only The Children Cry« EP (a mix of old and new material) later in the year. Once again, however, the newcomer failed to last the distance, and the luckless band were already looking for yet another frontman as they moved into 1994. Fortunately, they were swiftly brought back up to strength when Gary Barden (of MSG and STATETROOPER fame) offered his services, and he was soon taking his place as the latest contender in the grand PRAYING MANTIS vocal lottery. Having settled in quite nicely over the previous months, Barden made his first contribution to the studio side of things in 1995, when the lads laid down another set for Pony Canyon (the Under One Flag deal had fallen by the wayside by this stage), the slightly lacklustre »To The Power Of Ten« effort. The general consensus of opinion from the fans, however, was that it was something of a step backwards, the album failing to build upon the solid foundations of its predecessor. Still, there was always the chance to salvage the situation in the live environment, where the latest material would only feature to a limited extent. After learning the group's entire repertoire in a matter of weeks, the recently-recruited vocalist made his debut at some further shows in Japan, one or two of which were recorded and subsequently issued as the »Captured Alive in Tokyo City« set. This turned out to be another real winner, and it became evident that the outfit were more or less committing themselves to delivering material purely for the Far East market by this juncture, staying out in Japan for extended periods to undertake the necessary touring and promotional activities. Sadly, Gary Barden wasn't too keen on this side of things, and soon elected to part company with PRAYING MANTIS, meaning that the search was on for their umpteenth vocalist. This time, the lucky individual was a chap called Tony O'Hora, a much-travelled singer who had lent his services to such disparate acts as LARRIKIN, TORINO, HIGH WIRE and ONSLAUGHT in the previous decade.

Fortunately, PRAYING MANTIS appear to have found the right person for the job, and O'Hora seems to be a considerably more dedicated member than most of his fly-by-night predecessors. He made his debut on their »Forever In Time« album in 1998, which received an extremely encouraging response, and has now become a firm fixture in the set-up. The lads remain an extremely active unit, especially in the Far East, and are a prolific touring and recording operation, even if their British and European fans are privileged enough to observe them on very few occasions nowadays. In 1999, an 'original' PRAYING MANTIS (the Troys, Dave Potts and Steve Carroll) delighted the assembled throng at the Japanese '20th NWOBHM Anniversary' concert (alongside TANK, SAMSON and TRESPASS), and their devout following have now additionally been treated to legitimate reissues of the original »Time Tells No Lies« set, as well as the impressive »Demorabilia« retrospective of unreleased material from throughout their original career. A brand-new album called »Nowhere To Hide« has appeared (in Japan, needless to say) comparatively recently, and further offerings from the modern-day incarnation of PRAYING MANTIS are anticipated in the not-too-distant future, assuming they don't experience an inexplicable loss of popularity, which seems a safe bet. Sure, they may have had to go to the other side of the world to achieve the recognition and respect they surely deserved all along, but at least the lads got a second chance at finding fame and fortune eventually. Incidentally, their touring schedules, discography, interviews, general history and current recording activities are all now documented in phenomenal detail by the inimitable Jon Hinchliffe, who (in addition to being one of the nicest blokes on the face of the planet) runs a truly staggering website which contains far more information than mere mortals such as myself could ever hope to assimilate.

LP's
»**Time Tells No Lies**« Arista 1981
[UK issue]
»**Time Tells No Lies**« EMI Japan 1981
[Japanese issue]
»**Predator In Disguise**« Pony Canyon 1991
[Japanese-only vinyl issue]

12" EP's
»**The Soundhouse Tapes Part 2**« Ripper Records 1979
[All three tracks non-LP]

7" EP's
»**Turn The Tables**« Jet Records 1982
[All three tracks non-LP]

7" Singles
»**The Soundhouse Tapes Part 2**« Ripper Records 1979
[Both tracks non-LP, very limited quantities issued in »Captured City« picture sleeve]
»**Praying Mantis**« Gem 1980
[Both tracks non-LP, some with iron-on transfer]
»**Cheated**« Arista 1980
[A-side different to album version, B-side "Thirty Pieces Of Silver" non-LP, issued in gatefold sleeve with free single featuring live versions of "Flirting With Suicide" and "Panic In The Streets"]
»**All Day And All Of The Night**« Arista 1981
[B-side "Beads Of Ebony" different to album version]

Promotional Releases
»**This Time Girl**« Pony Canyon 1990
[Japanese four track promo CD]

CD's
»**Time Tells No Lies**« EMI Japan 199?
[Original Japanese issue]
»**Live At Last**« Pony Canyon 1990/Grand Slamm 1990
[Japanese/US live release]
»**Predator In Disguise**« Under One Flag 1991
[UK issue]
»**Predator In Disguise**« Pony Canyon 1991
[Japanese issue]
»**Cheated**« Manti 1991
[Bootleg release of early vinyl appearances]
»**Live And Singles**« Bootleg 1992
[Live bootleg from 1982 plus single recordings, two different covers]
»**A Cry For The New World**« Under One Flag 1993
[UK issue]
»**A Cry For The New World**« Pony Canyon 1993
[Japanese issue]
»**Play In The East**« Excalibur 1993
[Live bootleg release from 90's]
»**Marquee '79**« Nova 1994
[Live bootleg release of early recordings]
»**To The Power Of Ten**« Pony Canyon 1995
[Japanese-only issue]
»**Captured Alive In Tokyo City**« Pony Canyon 1996

[Japanese live release, also issued as limited edition double disc set]
»Time Tells No Lies« High Vaultage 1996
[With three bonus tracks]
»Time Tells No Lies« Pony Canyon 1997
[Japanese issue, remastered version with three bonus tracks]
»Forever In Time« Pony Canyon 1998
[Japanese issue]
»Demorabilia« Pony Canyon 1999
[Japanese-only double disc featuring unreleased archive studio material]
»Metal Crusade 99« Pony Canyon 1999
[Japanese-only live double CD set, shared with TANK, SAMSON and TRESPASS]
»Live At Last« Zoom Club Records 2000
[UK reissue]
»Captured Alive In Tokyo City« Zoom Club Records 2000
[Live release, UK reissue]
»Forever In Time« Zoom Club Records 2000
[UK reissue]
»Nowhere To Hide« Pony Canyon 2000
[Japanese-only issue]

Mini-CD's
»Only The Children Cry« Pony Canyon 1993
[Japanese-only issue]

Compilation Appearances
"Captured City" on »Metal For Muthas« LP 1980/CD Airraid Records 2000 + »The Bible Of Hard Rock« CD Toshiba 1990 + »NWOBHM '79 Revisited« Do-CD Phonogram 1990 + »N.W.O.B.H.M.« LP/CD Heavy Metal 1991
[Different to »Soundhouse Tapes« version, miscredited on »N.W.O.B.H.M.« as "Ambitions" by DRAGSTER]
"Johnny Cool" on »Metal Explosion« LP BBC Records 1980
[Different to »Soundhouse Tapes« version]
"Children Of The Earth" on »Hammer« LP Ariola 1981
"Running For Tomorrow" on »Steel Crazy« LP Abstract Records 1982
"Praying Mantis" on »NWOBHM Vol.1« Bootleg CD 1992 + »N.W.O.B.H.M. Metal Rarities Vol.1« CD British Steel 1996
"High Roller" on »N.W.O.B.H.M. Metal Rarities Vol.1« CD British Steel 1996

PREDATOR

Joey Lee Francisco (v)
Andy Trevelyan (g)
Shuff Salvadoro (b)
Gil Johnson (d)

Initially formed as early as 1982, Staffordshire's PREDATOR (not to be confused with the later American or Irish versions or with either of the UK outfits PREDATÜR or the PREDATORS) didn't take particularly long to establish themselves as a semi-popular local outfit. Their formative years, dominated by extensive gigging and personnel reshuffles, didn't allow the group much time to devote to studio exertions, and it wasn't until 1985 that things started motoring for the lads. At the beginning of that year, the quartet embarked on a successful tour covering fairly large parts of the country, and, in the spring, they proceeded to record the tracks "Don't Stop" and "Shotdown" (the latter being much the heavier number) for a double A-sided release on their own C.T.M. (Cool Tunes Music) label. With the majority of the one thousand copies pressed being issued in a generic picture sleeve, the resultant single (a pretty scarce item today) received mostly favourable reviews (especially from the local Radio Stoke and Radio Signal stations), the outfit being praised for their highly competent brand of melodic rock/metal in the general manner of STRUTZ or GRAND PRIX. The fans continued to follow PREDATOR throughout the remainder of that year (their activities including a full-length UK tour in the summer), the highlights of which must surely have included a prestigious headlining event at the *'Chopper Club Of Great Britain Festival'* (let's just assume it was something to do with motorbikes…) in Hertfordshire and a memorable one-off gig supporting MOTÖRHEAD in Southport. Everything looked pretty rosy for the future…

However, it looks as though the musicians failed to build upon their initial success during 1986, and presumably endured a crisis of confidence thereafter. By the early months of 1987, PREDATOR had inexplicably bitten the dust (the reasons for their failure were never divulged with any great degree of clarity), although the nucleus of Andy Trevelyan and Joey Lee Francisco were soon to be found amongst the seven-piece (!) local outfit DIRECT ACTION. While this particular venture originally started off as a realistic enough attempt at cracking the melodic rock market, things soon degenerated into sheer farce, with the band subsequently recruiting a popular glamour model (Natalie Banus, a lass not exactly known for her vocal talents) to the ranks and using her more as a prop than a genuine frontwoman. With this move having been laughed out of court by the rock establishment, Banus departed at the beginning of 1989 and the hapless group (who somehow even got to the stage of issuing a semi-professional video in addition to the usual demo tape or two) ultimately went their separate ways shortly thereafter.

7" Singles
»Don't Stop« C.T.M. Records 1985

PREDATÜR

M. 'Baz' Barry (v, rg)

The long-lived Berkshire outfit PREDATÜR have kindly helped us out by utilising a different spelling from the vast majority of their namesakes (*vide supra*), but have still occasionally been confused with some of the other similarly-named bands over the years. Presumably having formed at the beginning of the decade and winning the hearts of local audiences with their no-nonsense brand of affable, but rather unimaginative, boogie rock in the basic manner of SPIDER, 100% PROOF or ROKKA, the outfit finally got around to issuing a single (pairing "Take A Walk" and "Seen You Here" on the tiny local Quicksilver label (home of SCORPIO) in 1982. The jokey picture sleeve (a cartoon-style affair, quite similar to that presented by Ireland's PURPLE HAZE) and messages on the reverse suggest that the group weren't taking themselves too seriously, and it all seems as though they were merely having a good time in the music business without being overly ambitious. A number of unsold copies have surfaced in recent years, by the way, so you shouldn't have to re-mortgage your house in order to be able to afford this once-pricey item. The PREDATÜR two-tracker doesn't, unfortunately, credit any of the band members, although their guitarist looks remarkably like Mark Bickerstaffe (who also played with fellow part-timers TRACK 4), which would fit in with the general geography and chronology of events.

Predictably, the knockabout, good-time music of PREDATÜR was guaranteed to amuse the crowds who attended regional rock shows, where the lads took the opportunity to unveil a range of original material including "Over The Top", "Shadowplay" and "Need Your Love", all of which seems to have been received with considerable enthusiasm. Although the outfit didn't release any further vinyl product after their debut offering, it's surprising to note that mainman Baz Barry continued to keep the PREDATÜR name alive in later years, and various incarnations of the ensemble were to be found gigging around their vicinity (supporting the evergreen DUMPY'S RUSTY NUTS, among others) for the remainder of the decade (and possibly beyond), with local personality Larry Miller (who had his own eponymous outfit) joining them on stage from time to time. Furthermore, an unusually high-profile (and remarkably well-attended) show at the Rivermead Centre in Reading (cheekily advertised as a *'Mini Reading Festival'*) took place in October 1988 (where they played in the company of IRON HEART, BURMA and LOOSE TORNIQUET), which even managed to gain a review in both 'Kerrang' (who described PREDATÜR, with some degree of accuracy, as *'QUO meets MOTÖRHEAD'*) and 'Metal Hammer'. In fact, I guess it's not inconceivable that some of these characters are still active on the regional club scene, although there don't appear to have been many PREDATÜR reunions of late.

7" Singles
»Take A Walk« Quicksilver Records 1982

PRESENCE

Keogh

One of countless bands to adopt the name over the years, and one of at least three such recording acts in the UK alone, the only British PRESENCE to have reached the vinyl stage in the NWOBHM era appear to have been an extremely obscure bunch of hopefuls from the Home Counties. Their only known 7" was recorded very early in 1979 at Weemeenit Studio in Barnet and issued through the ever-obliging SRT pressing service a few months later. "No Reason", on the A-side, is vaguely acceptable to the NWOBHM palate due to some semi-heavy guitar work, although, if we're being brutally frank, it barely makes it out of the dreaded pub rock category. There are, admittedly, a few minor similarities to the likes of TRACK 4, DAWN TRADER and the ALEC JOHNSON BAND, but it's a pretty disposable effort in general. On the reverse, however, the soppily-titled "I Care For You" is an unmitigated disaster, and sees the mystery combo attempting a rather quirky and freeform kind of cod-reggae, which is so utterly devoid of both tunefulness and rhythm that even die-hard fans of CAPTAIN BEEFHEART would find it a virtually unlistenable experience. Hopeless stuff, and you should be well and truly convinced that this single (never issued in a picture sleeve, by the looks of things) just isn't worth picking up unless it's incredibly cheap, and even then it's only a borderline candidate for genuine proto-NWOBHM status.

7" Singles
»No Reason« SRT 1979

PREYER

Pete MacIntosh (v)
Craig Thomas (g)
Phil Scourfield (b)
Phil John (d)

The weighty Welsh entity known as PREYER first came together in Glamorgan in the autumn of 1984, following the demise of various small-time hopefuls (most notably, NIGHTIME FLYER, from whence came drummer Phil John), originally as a four-piece. Early the following year, the outfit set out their stall by unleashing their first demo tape (»On The Prowl«), featuring the heavy "No Mercy For The Wicked", the power metal of "Beware The Night" and the anthemic "Rock Crusader". From the outset, it was apparent that PREYER had considerably more in common with fast'n'furious outfits such as JUDAS PRIEST, FATES WARNING and EXCITER than the majority of their post-NWOBHM contemporaries, although it's certainly justifiable to say that their repertoire varied quite a bit, ranging from pretty traditional heavy metal to frenzied power/speed efforts with soaring vocals from Pete MacIntosh. Their second demo (»Fear The Dark«), from later in the year, was another three-tracker, featuring "Shout It Out", "Rifferama" and "The Preyer", and it proved to be a fairly logical progression from their first offering. By this time, the lads had added a second guitarist in the form of James Rees (who had just become available after the demise of his previous outfit, MAMMATH), and, if anything, the material evolved into an even heavier variant as a result, almost bordering on thrash in some instances. In terms of NWOBHM comparisons, the main ones would be RAVEN, GRIM REAPER, BLOOD MONEY and Newcastle's WARRIOR (in their »Breakout« phase), so it's probably the type of thing that went down better in Europe than the UK at the time.

Nevertheless, the band's demos had successfully attracted the attention of Ebony Records (who, unlike certain companies, weren't predisposed to signing the more insipid and melodic acts of the day), and it wasn't long before the quintet were ensconced in the studio, busily working on their debut long-player (Ebony having now abandoned their original notion of breaking in their acts with a 7" single) for future release. PREYER's »Terminator« album appeared in 1986, and, remarkably enough, swiftly proceeded to garner one or two decent reviews in the rock press. With the eight-tracker consisting of a selection of previously-recorded demo favourites plus some heavier numbers such as "Reserve The Right" and "Over The Top", the listener was left in no doubt whatsoever that PREYER were out to win themselves the dubious accolade of being the heaviest metal act from Wales, and they presumably welcomed the development of the British thrash scene with open arms. Still, in spite of the observation that their debut release performed acceptably upon its initial release, the PREYER lads made no secret of the fact that they considered it to be entirely substandard in terms of production, Craig Thomas memorably commenting in 'Kerrang' that Darryl Johnston *'couldn't mix a cake'* (ooh, you bitch). It transpired that their original choice of producer, Mal Skrines (who had previously worked with the likes of NEON SPIRIT and TOK-IO ROSE), had apparently been rejected for the job, something which had annoyed the musicians considerably, and which they sought to rectify as they prepared to record their follow-up release.

The band demoed some new material in 1987 (having enlisted Skrines, at the second attempt, to oversee things), eventually circulating a speculative three track demo featuring freshly-penned efforts such as "Raising Hell", "Machine Gun" and "Street Lethal", which clearly showed the musicians attempting to move into *bona fide* thrash territory. Towards the end of that year, however, drummer Phil John decided to pack his bags and join up with the youthful TALAN, leaving PREYER to draft in new recruit Lloyd Coates in his place. Back on track, their next step was to assemble an entire album's worth of new material with which to acquire another deal, having acrimoniously severed all ties with Ebony by this juncture. Given that they had received a generally favourable response to their debut from both magazines and fans worldwide, and, with live appearances going swimmingly, the lads didn't anticipate that they would experience too many problems in attracting a significant level of label interest thereafter. They were, however, completely misguided in their unflinching optimism. By early 1988, PREYER had even selected the numbers which would ultimately comprise their second album (announcing its *'imminent'* release at every opportunity thereafter), which was surely jumping the gun to an unnecessary extent.

The forthcoming LP, tentatively titled »Taste Of Sin«, was evidently due to feature the three aforementioned efforts from their latest demo, plus the unused numbers from their earlier tapes ("No Mercy For The Wicked" and "The Preyer"), in addition to "Warhead", "Nightmare" (going for the VENOM fan base, eh?) and the title track itself. Still, the record companies continued to keep their distance from PREYER, and things suddenly didn't look quite so rosy any more. Bassist Phil Scourfield eventually tired of waiting for the elusive deal to materialise, and, in the wake of his departure, the lads roped in new bassist Ian Bodenham (ex-KRUZER) while they continued to tout around their newer material (their live appearances at this time including some outings with the likes of the dwindling GRIM REAPER) to anyone who might take an interest. Shortly afterwards, desperation finally set in, and, as a last resort, the lads attempted to shift their writing style towards a rather more commercial direction. In the end, however, it was ultimately a lost cause, and PREYER appear to have ceased all activities at some point in 1989, with the members gradually drifting away from the rock scene thereafter, no doubt wondering where it all went wrong.

LP's
»**Terminator**« Ebony 1986

PROWLER (I)

Rob Philpotts (v, g)
Chris Vye (g)
Dave Challis (b)
Steve Philpotts (d)

Not to be confused with either the identically-named Essex outfit (who appeared on the »Brute Force« compilation and released the melodic »Heartbreaker« single several years later) or numerous overseas namesakes, Leicestershire's PROWLER originally issued forth from relative obscurity at some point in 1982, delighting those in attendance at local gigs and cultivating an impressive brand of metal based around powerful riffs (in the manner of JAMESON RAID or FIRECLOWN), the youngsters growing steadily in stature over a comparatively short timescale. Building upon the encouraging response which came their way, the group got around to issuing a private single the following year, an extremely limited pressing which coupled the lengthy "Forgotten Angel" (as featured on the »NWOBHM Vol.5« bootleg) and the more vibrant "Don't Let Go". Although ruthlessly condemned in the pages of 'Kerrang' as a hapless offering from substandard JUDAS PRIEST imitators, the

two-tracker (featuring a hand-drawn picture sleeve showing a peculiar-looking monster looming ominously over the unsuspecting band members) has become an extremely sought-after piece in recent years. In fact, I've been reliably informed that it's supposedly so rare that not even all of the outfit's former members actually possess a copy! In any case, the upbeat B-side is probably a more proficient number than the rather pedestrian "Forgotten Angel", although the guitar work is very effective throughout.

Presumably having taken criticism of their original vocalist on board, the ensemble reshuffled, with the luckless Dave Challis being given the push, Rob Philpotts relinquishing the mike stand and replacement bassist Ian Morrison assuming vocal duties. After getting their act together, the lads circulated a six track demo in 1984, showcasing some rather more varied and original numbers such as "Soldier Of Fortune", "Ready For Action" and "Fighting For The Nation". With a much-improved frontman now at the helm and some increasingly-tight musicianship in their armoury, this revamped incarnation of PROWLER appeared to stand a far greater chance of achieving significant success, although their latest tape failed to attract any sustained label interest in the short term. Eventually, the ambitious group took the decision to issue a second self-financed 7" (a double A-side featuring "Alcatraz" and "So Lonely"), which immediately drew praise from fanzines such as 'High Octane'. With both tracks building on the faster, twin-guitar direction of their more recent demo selections, the strong vocal performance helped to raise the quartet's material to a considerably higher standard, these intense efforts being more along the lines IRON MAIDEN or VIRTUE than before. Cracking stuff throughout, and a record worthy of inclusion in every NWOBHM collection. You'll be glad to know that this particular single, with its sleeve showing a wildcat savaging a guitar (I don't know where they got their artistic ideas from), is much easier to locate than the band's debut.

Just when PROWLER appeared to be about to make their long-awaited breakthrough, however, they appear to have had second thoughts about playing the old power metal game, and, noting the increasing popularity of melodic rock, came to a mutual decision to try something more accessible. They apparently tried out a few different name changes and shifts in direction, although nothing concrete (a three track demo from a year or so later, featuring markedly more commercial efforts such as "Take My Love" and "Fantasy", was about as far as they got) ever materialised out of this experimentation, and the band finally drifted apart in around 1987. Steve Philpotts and Chris Vye resurfaced shortly thereafter in PASSION (confusingly, one of several groups in the UK using the name simultaneously), a considerably more melodic five-piece (featuring a vocalist with a tendency to sing on an unnecessarily high octave) who were around on the local rock scene for a year or two, and who released the private »Time Of My Life« single in 1988. Steve Philpotts has subsequently been linked with a little-known outfit called LIAR (nothing to do with the late 70's bunch), who released a CD entitled »While The City Sleeps« a year or two ago (they seem to be involved with Neat Metal nowadays), while Chris Vye recorded an instrumental demo. Since then, all has been quiet.

7" Singles
»Forgotten Angel« Pirate Records 1983
»Alcatraz« SRT 1985

Compilation Appearances
"Forgotten Angel" on »NWOBHM Vol.5« Bootleg CD 1992

PROWLER (II)

Trev Pattenden (v, b)
Martin Burrows (g)
John Pattenden (g)
Mike Dowling (d)

If you've ever gazed wistfully out of your window, thinking *'I wonder whatever happened to the Essex band PROWLER after their appearance on the »Brute Force« sampler?'*, you've probably got far too much time on your hands. Nevertheless, there's a (rather complicated) story to be told, so here goes. The MCA compilation was an extremely well-received piece at the time of its release (tens of thousands were shifted in a comparatively short period), and PROWLER's "Gotta Get Back To You" contribution (an excellent, upbeat rocker in the manner of RICOCHET's "Off The Rails") didn't go unnoticed even in the illustrious company of such luminaries as DIAMOND HEAD, RAVEN and QUARTZ, making a strong impact on the 'Sounds' and 'Record Mirror' Heavy Metal Charts and securing the lucky quartet a handful of support slots with touring acts such as VARDIS, BUDGIE and ATOMIC ROOSTER. At some point, however, it must have dawned on the youngsters that they shared a name with an unnecessarily large number of outfits around the country, and so, after five happy years as PROWLER, they hastily reinvented themselves as (wait for it) SAMURAI. Oh dear, originality wasn't really your strong point, eh lads?

Under their newly-adopted moniker, the group were featured in session on Essex Radio's rock show in early 1982, showcasing a selection of newer material such as "Bad Child Running", "Lost Without Your Love" and "Prisoner", which were broadcast alongside the old PROWLER favourite "Gotta Get Back To You". On the basis of the three freshly-penned compositions, all of which were very much in the fast and heavy mould of early IRON MAIDEN, the future should have been very bright indeed for this talented ensemble. However, no vinyl output appears to have been forthcoming under the SAMURAI identity (their later Welsh namesakes turned out to be a considerably more prolific act) at any stage, which is a bit of a pity, especially when you consider some of the dross which was actually captured for posterity at the time. In fact, given that the outfit had ample opportunity to lay down the material of their choice (at their own studio, no less) as and when it suited them, the failure of SAMURAI to release any vinyl product tends to suggest total label disinterest and/or a critical lack of personal finances with which to organise a private single at that particular stage.

Here's where things get a bit strange. Over the next couple of years, it looks as though the increasingly-unstable outfit endured quite a few personnel alterations and shifts in musical outlook, with mainman Martin Burrows eventually recruiting an entirely new set of accomplices in the form of T. John (v, b), John James (g) and Bob Harding (d), and steering the project in a considerably more commercial direction. By late 1984, however, it transpires that the latter trio had gone off to do their own thing with the US (see separate entry) venture, leaving Burrows to resurrect the PROWLER identity by drafting in another batch of (presently unknown) cohorts. This revised line-up proceeded to release their double A-sided »Heartbreaker« (b/w "Victim Of The Night") 7" in 1985 (by which time their capable namesakes from Leicestershire had released a single or two of their own), which revealed the outfit now to be operating in a surprisingly melodic rock style (with both male and female vocals playing a part), their latest material being quite similar, at times, to the likes of SHOGUN, JOKERS WILD or BRIAR. By all accounts, the disappointing private two-tracker, for which no picture sleeve is currently known to exist, is an extraordinarily scarce item these days, suggesting that it probably enjoyed spectacularly poor sales at the time. Truly a wasted opportunity, given that this was apparently PROWLER's first and last attempt to make it big in the music business, so it's a tragedy that the majority of NWOBHM fans are unlikely ever to hear just how capable this bunch actually were at the outset.

7" Singles
»Heartbreaker« Jest Records 1985

Exclusive Compilation Appearances
"Gotta Get Back To You" on »Brute Force« LP MCA 1980

PURPLE HAZE

Stee V (v, b)
Jon Fleming (g)
Ray Mullins (d)

In spite of a rather obvious source for their moniker, there's not much of a JIMI HENDRIX influence on display here, folks. Ireland's PURPLE HAZE (there was, incidentally, also an obscure Belgian bunch from the era who elected to use the same identity) issued a curiously European-sounding two-tracker in 1985 (the youngsters having started off while still at school a couple of years earlier), coupling "Hear It On The Radio" with "Forever Lost". The former pilfers the riff from JOURNEY's "Don't Stop Believing" before turning into a peculiar 'heavy glam' variant, the material being along the general lines of contemporaries such as SHEER KHAN or FORGER. Sadly, however, in spite of some vaguely acceptable guitar work and a singalong chorus, the track itself is let down by a pretty awful performance from singer Stee V. The B-side, meanwhile, isn't really all that much of an improvement, unfortunately, with the sub-par vocals and dreary arrangement once again failing to leave a positive impression. It looks as though the single hit the wrong note with many reviewers at the time (perversely, the notoriously-hostile 'Kerrang' was one of the few publications who gave it the thumbs-up), with some hefty criticism of the frontman being delivered in the pages of 'High Octane' fanzine, for example. Nevertheless, it appears to have sold in sufficient quantities (mainly in their homeland) that a second pressing was called for, so the lads must have shifted a fair few copies at the time.

Within around a year of their vinyl debut hitting the shops, however, the band seemed to have heeded this warning concerning their liability of a frontman, and were soon making a few radical changes, reinventing themselves as the dubiously-monikered DIRTY FINGERS and replacing the unfortunate Stee V with vocalist Paul Purcell and bassist Robbie Dunphy. A three track demo (featuring compositions such as "Flyaway" and "Whisper On The Wind") went down slightly better with the reviewers and further vinyl output seems to have been forthcoming in the long term, so I guess they eventually just lost the will to continue. No great loss to the scene, to be honest, and »Hear It On The Radio« is a two-tracker (with a distinctive, cartoon-style sleeve) which should never command silly prices among the die-hard collectors. By the way, let's not get too bogged down in politics or pedantry, there's no compelling reason to exclude outfits from Eire in our discussion of the NWOBHM phenomenon, even if the 'British' bit of the description is somewhat amiss. Let's just unite the whole of the British Isles (including the Irish Republic and the Channel Islands) under this definition; I mean, we'd be just as happy to feature acts from the Isle Of Man, Orkney or Shetland Islands...

7" Singles
»Hear It On The Radio« S.R.S. Records 1985

PYRAMID

Coe
Gunstone
Barker
Bowden

This particular version of PYRAMID are certainly something of a mystery, and have no connection with the obscure Yorkshire group who contributed to the »It's Unheard Of!« compilation in 1984. There's very little information to help us out, and no picture sleeve in this instance, but the outfit's double A-sided effort from 1982 is a perfectly respectable stab at NWOBHM, with "Star" being the more impressive of the pair, coming across as a heavy, mid-paced number, the music being very much in the disposition of DESTROYER or PALI GAP. Flipside "Wasted Time", meanwhile, is a considerably more restrained affair which seems completely at odds with the powerful reverse, although this semi-ballad is still a listenable piece of lightweight rock with some capable guitar work on display. Whoever they were, PYRAMID presumably failed to make much of an impression on the scene at the time, and probably called it a day when the NWOBHM boom began to lose its momentum. I suspect they were from the Southern part of the country, but could easily be wrong, and any additional details would be greatly appreciated. In the meantime, keep an eye out for the single, which is currently known to exist in absolutely minuscule quantities.

7" Singles
»Star« Scorpion Records 1982

QUARTZ

Mick 'Taffy' Taylor (v)
Mick Hopkins (g)
Geoff Nicholls (g, k)
Derek Arnold (b)
Malcolm Cope (d)

It would be a severe understatement to suggest that the members of Birmingham-based QUARTZ were experienced and well-respected veterans of the Midlands music scene, their many previous credits including the likes of COPPERFIELD (a band in which Derek Arnold, Mick Hopkins and Malcolm Cope had originally recorded together in the late 60's), WAY OF LIFE (featuring future LED ZEPPELIN sticksman John Bonham) and IDLE RACE (Jeff Lynne's forerunner of the popular ELECTRIC LIGHT ORCHE-

STRA). The direct antecedent of QUARTZ, however, was the less weighty BANDYLEGS, purveyors of a rather uninspiring hard rock style, who first got going in around 1973. With the erstwhile COPPERFIELD triumvirate of Arnold, Cope and Hopkins being complemented by the powerful lungs of newly-acquired frontman Mick Taylor, the quartet delivered a handful of single releases for various respected labels, culminating in the »Bet You Can't Dance« 7" for Jet Records in 1976. Unlike the outfit's previous two sponsors, however, the latter ultimately decided that BANDYLEGS actually had a modicum of potential, and started grooming the lads for success by sending them out on tour with labelmates WIDOWMAKER, after which the group duly acquired some further valuable experience on the road when they hooked up with AC/DC for a memorable European jaunt.

The real turning point, however, came when BANDYLEGS formed an alliance with the pride of the Midlands, BLACK SABBATH, who took them under their wing and installed the group as a support act for some British dates in the early months of 1977. Inspired by the rapturous response garnered by the headliners' far heavier music, BANDYLEGS swiftly decided to beef up their image, penning some considerably more potent material, recruiting an additional guitarist (Geoff Nicholls, who also dabbled with keyboards) and reinventing themselves as QUARTZ (not a unique name by any means, but infinitely better than their original choice). The recently-expanded quintet were soon busying themselves in the studio, and the recording of their debut album for Jet was carried out under the watchful eye of none other than Tony Iommi himself. In spite of some distinctly SABBATH-like riffs (on "Mainline Riders", in particular), the eponymous record (which came in a bafflingly-nondescript sleeve) was a hit-and-miss affair, with only a couple of reasonably heavy efforts ("Street Fighting Lady" and "Pleasure Seekers") saving the day. In fact, much of the debut long-player was filled with compositions which clearly harked back to their original days on the club scene, notably the terrible trio of "Sugar Rain", "Hustler" and "Little Old Lady". Nevertheless, the outfit showed plenty of scope for development, and were clearly capable of delivering similar proto-NWOBHM material to the likes of ETHEL THE FROG, NIGHTWING or RAGE.

A three track 7", featuring the super-weak "Sugar Rain" as its main selling point (with the far better "Mainline Riders" and "Street Fighting Lady" on the reverse) was originally scheduled for release at around the same time as the album, although the EP was never officially issued in its intended form. Demo copies were pressed as a matter of routine (quite a lot of them, as it turns out), although it looks as though their label may have had second thoughts about the A-side, electing instead to press up a replacement single pairing "Street Fighting Lady" and "Mainline Riders". Sadly, it performed utterly dismally in terms of sales, and Jet were soon wondering if they had made an enormous mistake by putting their faith in QUARTZ. In fact, even a last-minute arrangement which saw the band being added to the bill of 1977's Reading Festival in place of WIDOWMAKER (they actually opened the whole event) failed to help their cause to any great extent, and their early offerings were soon littering the bargain bins of the nation. Undeterred, the lads continued to promote themselves at every possible opportunity, gigging in front of small-but-loyal crowds whenever they could and even making a couple of television appearances in 1978. QUARTZ were to endure considerable hardship at around this time (parting company with Jet, for example, and struggling to get gigs), though, something which they attributed to the recent emergence of the supposedly-dominant punk scene (a contentious claim, it must be said), but things started picking up again in the second half of 1979 (with the NWOBHM explosion now being in full swing), by which time Geoff Nicholls had packed his bags after being lured away by an offer to assist the mighty BLACK SABBATH in the live environment.

Soldiering on as a quartet, the lads soon found themselves signing a contract (of sorts) with Reddingtons Rare Records, the famous shop/label who briefly made a habit of giving a helping hand to some lucky Midlands acts, notably PARALEX and MAYDAY. Their sponsorship of QUARTZ was comparatively generous, though, extending as far as a single and a full album, the latter being a live effort (»Live Quartz«, tenderly subtitled *'Count Dracula And Other Love Songs'*) recorded at a local shindig, and featuring original compositions such as "Count Dracula" and "Belinda", plus (in addition to various numbers from their debut album) a couple of rock'n'roll standards in the form of "Good Time Tonight" and "Roll Over Beethoven". In all honesty, »Live Quartz« was hardly an earth-shattering release, although the performance was very good-natured and likeable, and, if nothing else, the LP served to associate QUARTZ with the huge resurgence in the popularity of heavy music. Their one-off single for Reddingtons (where the lads were temporarily augmented by keyboard player Alan Long) was, admittedly, a strange affair, as it featured the outfit's interpretation of MOUNTAIN's "Nantucket Sleighride", which had recently been picked up for use as the theme to 'Weekend World' (a monumentally dull current affairs programme of the day), as if this gave it any sense of credibility whatsoever. In truth, the upbeat B-side ("Wildfire") was a considerably more impressive number, and firmly suggested that QUARTZ might be moving in the right direction at last.

Before long, things started motoring for QUARTZ, and their live release benefitted from a more widespread circulation thanks to its timely reissue by Logo, who were also handling the affairs of VARDIS by that stage. Their new label also saw fit to sponsor a three track EP, featuring recent studio recordings of "Satan's Serenade" and "Bloody Fool", plus a remixed version of "Roll Over Beethoven" from their live album. On the basis of the group's own new material, they were moving a lot closer to the general NWOBHM archetype, with heavy, upbeat numbers which didn't (unlike many of their early efforts) overstay their welcome or veer off into more flimsy territory halfway through. The EP was released (in several different colour variations) to coincide with the band's latest tour, undertaken as guests of RUSH, and was probably the first QUARTZ record to sell in particularly healthy quantities. The busy outfit also found a gap in their schedule to contribute the exclusive "Back In The Band" to EMI's »Muthas Pride« sampler, and the lads barely had time to draw breath before the mighty MCA concern was waving a spanking new contract in front of them. It was around this time, however, that their original label decided to exploit the outfit's new-found semi-popularity, whereupon Jet hastily reissued the first QUARTZ album (under the acerbic title of »Deleted«, presented in a sleeve fashioned out of a grocery bag) and their »Street Fighting Lady« single (again, in brown paper packaging). I've never been entirely sure whether these were good-humoured releases, pressed merely to satisfy demand, or shoddily-packaged cash-ins, the intention being to bring the lads down to earth with a bump…

Whatever their motivation, Jet certainly got their money's worth, even going so far as to include *three* QUARTZ numbers on their shabby »Metallergy« compilation, but the band made little or no fuss about their former label's activities, and proceeded to immerse themselves in studio work before delivering their new long-player for MCA. The first evidence of these activities came in the shape of "Can't Say No To You", their contribution to MCA's »Brute Force« sampler, which set the stage nicely for the full album proper. Their »Stand Up And Fight« opus was released a couple of months later, and the record more or less completed the gradual transformation of QUARTZ into a raunchy, mid-tempo NWOBHM proposition along the lines of MORE or FIST, the outfit having largely abandoned their traditional roots and fondness for extended guitar workouts in favour of more accessible, down-to-earth numbers by this stage. It was a decent enough affair, with capable new versions of "Wildfire" and "Can't Say No To You", in addition to strong, unfamiliar efforts such as "Charlie Snow", "Stoking Up The Fires Of Hell" and the title track itself, but it was never the sort of thing which genuinely threatened global domination. »Stand Up And Fight« and »Stoking Up The Fires Of Hell« were duly trundled out as tie-in singles to help the album sales along, and the lads were soon out on the road once again, promoting themselves to the masses by embarking on a national tour with the headlining GILLAN.

Gradually, sales of the latest QUARTZ long-player began to pick up, further aided by a series of support appearances with SAGA in early 1981, although the lads were soon to fall victim to MCA's inevitable post-NWOBHM cull. Having picked up several emergent acts at the height of the explosion, MCA decided that most of them were sorely lacking in long-term potential, and swiftly axed the unfortunate trio of FIST, WHITE SPIRIT and QUARTZ, relying on DIAMOND HEAD and the TYGERS OF PAN TANG to carry the flag from that point onwards. Having worked their way through no less than four labels already, QUARTZ were suddenly faced with the unenviable task of looking for yet another new home, and they failed to attract all that much interest in the short term. Still, the plucky foursome struggled on until 1982, whereupon the abrupt departure of founder members Derek Arnold and Taffy Taylor threatened the integrity of the outfit in no uncertain terms. Nevertheless, a revamped version of QUARTZ was to rise by the end of the year, with little-known bassist Steve McLoughlin and former EAZIE RYDER frontman Geoff Bate having been drafted in to fill the gaps. In due course, they benefitted from a well-timed offer from Heavy Metal to release their next vinyl product, and work finally began on the fourth QUARTZ long-player in the early part of 1983.

The lads were temporarily rejoined by departed keyboard player Geoff Nicholls for the recording of »Against All Odds« (the title referring to all the unforeseen problems which had occurred during its assembly), although the latter was soon wending his way back to BLACK SABBATH once the studio sessions had been completed. The latest album (produced by Robin George) turned out to be a fairly blatant attempt to steer the outfit into more commercial waters, although it stopped well short of a full-scale wimp-out. It wasn't, in all honesty, a particularly radical departure from their early direction, although much of their newest material (particularly the likes of "Just Another Man", "Hard Road" and "Avalon", which could almost have passed for GRAND PRIX out-takes) seemed to be largely inconsistent with some of the markedly heavier compositions which had appeared on their »Stand Up And Fight« long-player only a couple of years previously. Still, the shamelessly melodic stuff was balanced, to some extent, by a handful of more substantial efforts such as "Madman", "(It's) Hell, Livin' Without You" and the excellent "Buried Alive", with sticksman Malcolm Cope later providing a glimpse of the rationale lying behind their musical shift: *'That one was a commercial record all right, something of a contrived release which came out after we'd gone through various line-up changes and management problems. We were basically suffering a chronic lack of finances after the collapse of the MCA deal, and we thought it would be a better policy to deliver a* selection of more commercial music in the hope of boosting our record sales.' (Ref: Interview, Matthias Mader, August 1996).

Sadly, this experimentation seems to have been something of a disaster, alienating their original followers and failing to win all that many new fans, and album sales never really amounted to much. Heavy Metal brought out a 7", »Tell Me Why« (b/w "Street Walker"), in an attempt to rake in a bit of extra cash, but both the band and their label were clearly fighting a losing battle, and the long-lived QUARTZ had finally thrown in the towel within a year or two. The members themselves soon drifted away from the scene, although their music lived on in the hearts of many fans, and the group enjoyed a very brief renaissance a few years back, when Neat Metal took it upon themselves to assemble a CD of hard-to-get QUARTZ recordings. The »Resurrection« set was, in many respects, a somewhat peculiar release, and the total absence of sleeve notes suggested that those responsible might have been slightly reluctant to reveal the true source of this supposedly 'exclusive material'. In fact, the album itself seems to have been hastily cobbled together from various concert recordings (a professionally-recorded show at the Hammersmith Odeon in 1980 and, cheekily, the original »Live Quartz« tapes from late 1979, to which Neat Metal had presumably acquired the rights in the interim), but it's all immensely clumsily edited and confusingly presented. In fact, there's very little in the way of genuinely 'exclusive' material at all, since most of the featured tracks are available (in one form or another) on the official releases. Nevertheless, we're treated to yet more cover versions (WISHBONE ASH's "Jailbait" and RARE BIRD's "Bird Man"), although there's one unreleased studio effort thrown in for good measure, the enjoyable "Born To Rock The Nation". It's fair to suggest that sales of »Resurrection« have been modest, to say the least, and this ill-conceived offering seems a pretty inappropriate way to commemorate the career of such a highly-regarded group.

LP's

»**Quartz**« Jet Records 1977
»**Live Quartz**« Reddingtons Rare Records 1980
[Live album, original issue, some in monochrome sleeve]
»**Live Quartz**« Logo 1980
[Second issue]
»**Deleted**« Jet Records 1980
[Reissue of »Quartz« LP in brown paper bag sleeve]
»**Stand Up And Fight**« MCA 1980
»**Against All Odds**« Heavy Metal 1983

[Also issued as limited edition picture disc and on blue vinyl]

12" EP's

»**Satan's Serenade**« Logo 1980
[Both "Satan's Serenade" and "Bloody Fool" non-LP, "Roll Over Beethoven" different to album version. Also issued in limited quantities on red and blue vinyl]

7" EP's

»**Sugar Rain**« Jet Records 1977
[General release cancelled, demo copies only, both "Sugar Rain" and "Street Fighting Lady" different to album versions]

7" Singles

»**Street Fighting Lady**« Jet Records 1977
[Original issue without picture sleeve]
»**Nantucket Sleighride**« Reddingtons Rare Records 1979
[A-side non-LP, B-side "Wildfire" different to album version, various combinations of sleeve and vinyl colour]
»**Street Fighting Lady**« Jet Records 1980
[Reissue in brown paper bag sleeve]
»**Stoking Up The Fires Of Hell**« MCA 1980
[B-side "Circles" non-LP]
»**Stand Up And Fight**« MCA 1980
»**Tell Me Why**« Heavy Metal 1983
[A-side different to album version, B-side "Street Walker" non-LP]

Promotional Releases

»**Satan's Serenade**« Logo 1980
[Three track promo 7" flexi]

CD's

»**Stand Up And Fight**« MCA Japan 1992
[Japanese issue with one bonus track]
»**Resurrection**« Neat Metal 1996
[UK issue]
»**Resurrection**« Pony Canyon 1996
[Japanese issue with two bonus tracks]

Exclusive Compilation Appearances

"Back In The Band" on »Muthas Pride« 12" EP EMI 1980 + »NWOBHM Vol.2« Bootleg CD 1992

Compilation Appearances

"Can't Say No To You" on »Brute Force« LP MCA 1980
[Different to album version]
"Street Fighting Lady" on »Metallergy« LP Jet Records 1980
"Devils Brew" on »Metallergy« LP Jet Records 1980
"Mainline Riders" on »Metallergy« LP Jet

Records 1980
"Satan's Serenade" on »Pop Rocky« LP Metronome 1981 + »NWOBHM Vol.1« Bootleg CD 1992
"Bloody Fool" on »Pop Rocky« LP Metronome 1981
"Charlie Snow" on »Double Hard« LP Ariola 1981
"Stoking Up The Fires Of Hell" on »Metal Killers« LP Kastle Killers 1984
"Buried Alive" on »N.W.O.B.H.M.« LP/CD Heavy Metal 1991 + »Give 'Em Hell« CD Nectar Masters 1995

RADAR

John Steane (v, g)
Andy Venters (b)
Chris Huddleston (d)

The three-piece unit known by the palindromic moniker of RADAR were one of the more obscure outfits from the era, but appear to have been close neighbours (geographical, if not musical) of MITHRANDIR, being based in the county of Cambridgeshire. Their one and only single, a double A-sided effort recorded at Miller Studios in Leicestershire (a facility favoured by local heroes PROWLER) and released in mid-1983, featured the tracks "Leave Her Alone" and "Reach For The Sky", the latter showing the trio at their most potent. The aforementioned "Leave Her Alone" turns out to be a rather awkward indie/metal hybrid (a peculiar style also attempted, with equally limited success, by the likes of ROLLIN' THUNDER) which has always reminded me of none other than BLUR, which probably isn't all that much of a recommendation to most NWOBHM fans. The semi-capable "Reach For The Sky", on the other hand, is a fairly substantial number with reference points such as TEMPEST or NIGHTIME FLYER, so I guess it's a passable release for the NWOBHM community. It's not a classic of the genre by any stretch of the imagination, though, and it would appear that the ensemble enjoyed relatively little success or media recognition either before or after its release.

RADAR appear to have come and gone within a comparatively short timescale (none of the members went on to greater things, as far as I know), and were, in all likelihood, only operating on the periphery of the rock scene, so they would probably be somewhat intrigued to discover that their one-off release is now regarded as a genuine NWOBHM collectable. Fortunately for the average enthusiast, however, the asking price for this obscurity (housed within an utterly abysmal picture sleeve, although you have to admire the sheer absurdity of the revelation that it's *'a bagpipe free record'* on the reverse, suggesting that one or two of those involved might originally have been of Scottish extraction) has never gone too far over the top, primarily due to a number of copies finding their way onto the market almost overnight during the early days of the NWOBHM collecting boom. Even taking into account its relatively unspectacular value, though, I reckon it's still a bit overpriced these days, given that it hardly qualifies as anything resembling an archetypal release.

7" Singles
»Leave Her Alone« House Of Wax Records 1983

RADIUM

Kevin Healey (v, g)
Andy Meehan (v, g)
John Vaites (v, b)
Adrian 'Tonka' Loosemore (d)

One of the founder members of the so-called *'East Midlands Bands Cooperative'* (alongside PARALEX, RACE AGAINST TIME and, latterly, HELL), an *'organisation'* which originally came into existence at the beginning of the 80's, Nottinghamshire's RADIUM were one of the heavier outfits to have emerged from the productive Midlands metal scene during the NWOBHM era. The aforementioned *'E.M.B.C.'* was a light-hearted tag adopted by the bands involved, referring to their habit of sharing equipment (and possibly musical ideas) and arranging gigs together, which seems to have been mutually beneficial to all the outfits concerned. PARALEX were quick off the mark in terms of getting some vinyl product into the shops, their debut three-tracker hitting the shelves even before the end of 1980, whereas the short-lived RACE AGAINST TIME were content with an appearance on the »New Electric Warriors« compilation. RADIUM, having developed an extensive repertoire (including such weighty offerings as "Satan's Hideaway" and "Into The Grave") which was proving popular with the local crowds, also decided to get in on the whole *'private release'* bandwagon, and duly issued their »Through The Smoke« EP in 1981, with one side recorded live and the other in the studio.

Sadly, the RADIUM three-tracker really lets itself down in terms of sound quality, and the live material sounds as though it was recorded on a cheap walkman, rendering "Angel Of Fear" (a heavy, mid-paced number evocative of REQUIEM and PARALEX) and "Dusty Road" (a slower and somewhat less interesting affair) a rather frustrating listening experience. On the *'studio side'*, meanwhile, "Making Changes" presents the group in a far more favourable light, this being a largely-instrumental, technical effort reminiscent of a more jazzy KRAKEN, although the vocal parts (when they finally arrive) are undeniably similar to yet another Midlands outfit, namely Derbyshire's WARRIOR. I don't believe for one minute that all these comparisons with other hopefuls from the area are entirely coincidental (furthermore, the "Angel Of Fear" riff is suspiciously similar to RACE AGAINST TIME's "Bedtime" from the »New Electric Warriors« compilation), so it looks as though RADIUM were quite adept at harvesting influences from a range of their parochial NWOBHM counterparts. Their three-tracker, issued (needless to say, in fairly modest quantities) in a rather lurid orange and black sleeve featuring some indistinct silhouettes of the band members, remains a very scarce and highly-prized artefact today.

RADIUM were evidently a short-lived affair, however, with Kevin Healey and John Vaites subsequently joining forces with drummer Steve Wright and forming JACKAL (not to be confused with the Middlesex concern who appeared on the »Shooting From The Hip« compilation towards the end of the decade) in 1982. With their first demo, featuring "Don't Look Back" (a fairly basic, mid-tempo rocker) and "Lords And Laymen" (a multifaceted epic in the style of SHIVA or BIG DAISY, but with lyrics straight out of the SPINAL TAP book), meeting with critical approval in the 'Armed And Ready' section of 'Kerrang', things looked bright for the trio, especially when "Lords And Laymen" found its way into the magazine's 'Local Chart' later in the year. However, JACKAL was also ultimately an unsuccessful operation, and the ex-RADIUM duo had, by 1985, become assimilated into the six-piece melodic rock outfit LIFE AFTER. With the latter bunch allegedly keeping the *'E.M.B.C.'* connection going strong (various one-time PARALEX and HELL members appear to have been involved), the group attracted a couple of favourable live reviews in 'Kerrang' in 1987, after which the lads made an ambitious attempt to crack the American market. Predictably, however, the project collapsed after they had failed to make a breakthrough on either side of the Atlantic, and Kevin Healey has, in more recent years, teamed up with Tony Speakman (ex-PARALEX/HELL/S.Y.Z.) in a STATUS QUO tribute band with the imaginative name of DOWN DOWN.

7" EP's
»Through The Smoke« Isotope Records 1981

Compilation Appearances
"Angel Of Fear" on »NWOBHM Vol.7« Bootleg CD 1996

RAGE

Dave Lloyd (v)
Mick Devonport (g)
Keith Mulholland (b)
John Mylett (d)

Merseyside hopefuls RAGE (not to be confused with their German namesakes) evolved from a popular quintet called NUTZ, a fairly traditional hard rock outfit who gigged around their locality for most of the 70's and released a grand total of four albums on the A&M label before falling by the wayside in the aftermath of the punk onslaught of 1977. By 1980, however, EMI had picked up on one of their last studio recordings (which had presumably been laid down a year or two earlier), a track called "Bootliggers", and this effort was subsequently featured on the label's »Metal For Muthas« compilation. This was enough to spur the lads into action once again, and they swiftly regrouped (keyboard player Kenny Newton, meanwhile, had already defected to NIGHTWING) for a second crack at making it big in the rock world, adopting the novel identity of RAGE and adding something of a harder edge (although NUTZ had occasionally shown their ability to rock out on numbers such as "Wallbanger" and "Bootliggers" itself) to their sound, in keeping with the general attitude of the NWOBHM era. Within a remarkably short timescale, the lads were being courted by the influential Carrere concern, who were currently assembling an impressive roster of rock and metal outfits, and the members of RAGE were soon in a position to showcase some of their newly-penned material.

RAGE kicked off with an unassuming single entitled »Money« (b/w "Thank That Woman"), showcasing a pair of enjoyably raunchy compositions which clearly demonstrated that the revamped unit were perfectly capable of delivering a heavy brand of rock lying somewhere between TERRAPLANE, BABY TUCKOO and QUARTZ, banishing all doubt that they would simply be a reheated version of NUTZ after all. They soon came up with a full album, »Out Of Control«, which proved to be a satisfyingly weighty collection (not quite fitting the NWOBHM archetype, but still significantly closer to metal territory than NUTZ had ever been) with a commanding vocal performance from Dave Lloyd and only an occasional hint of their original hard-rocking tendencies. In fact, the most lightweight number on display was the tuneful "Roll The Dice", an obscure COUCHOIS original which was also covered by CHARLIE at one stage. The debut long-player was promoted by two singles, namely »Out Of Control« and »Bootliggers«, the latter featuring a recently-recorded live version of the old »Metal For Muthas« favourite, and the name of RAGE was soon firmly established in the public's consciousness. Gigs followed the album's release, including one or two European treks, all of which helped to promote the outfit further, and their label encouraged them to deliver another full-length effort with minimal delay.

By the time »Nice'n'Dirty« appeared (in a slightly dubious sleeve, which no doubt went down a storm with female fans) in 1982, RAGE had recruited a second guitarist in the form of ex-THIN END OF THE WEDGE man Terry Steers, although this wasn't to suggest that they were going to be attempting some MAIDEN-style twin-axe riffing in future. Instead, the musicians unveiled a considerably more lightweight and accessible album, full of all the usual semi-AOR moves (it seems to be a legal requirement for most commercial outfits to have a song called "Heartbreaker"), but with none of the grittiness of their debut set. They again demonstrated their penchant for cover versions with FANDANGO's superb "Blame It On The Night", but it served only to exaggerate the mediocrity of their own compositions. It was a great pity, but it would appear that the RAGE lads had made up their minds that they ultimately desired to head in a chartbound direction, although the lone single (»Woman«) chosen to promote the latest album failed to elicit much of a response from the record-buying public. All in all, RAGE hadn't done themselves any favours by selling their souls to the gods of AOR, and the adverse publicity which resulted from their tacky sleeves was to haunt them for a lot longer than they might have anticipated.

After lying low for a while (their main claim to fame in the interim was a support slot with MEATLOAF), the lads attempted to make something of a comeback in 1983, drafting in EXPORT's Steve Morris as a co-writer in a concerted effort to get things back on track. The third RAGE album, »Run For The Night« (with another feminist-baiting cover, although the fact that they had actually eschewed the original title of »Hard Feeling« was probably a good thing), had more of a pomp/AOR feel, with some distinct leanings towards TOTO and RAINBOW in places, although it was certainly an improvement on their rather lacklustre second LP. In this case, however, the long-player started off quite strongly, but it ran out of steam well before the end, and there weren't enough songs of the calibre of "Rock Fever" and "Lady Killer", for example. The rock fans of the day weren't convinced that it represented a sufficiently dramatic return to form, and the lack of sales was extremely disappointing for both the musicians and their loyal label. After two final singles, »Never Before« and the MAGNUM-like »Cry From A Hill«, both parties concluded that it probably wasn't worth continuing after all. By the spring of 1984, RAGE had finally been laid to rest.

The various members soon began looking for other projects to join (Mick Devonport swiftly established an ill-fated venture called FIELD FORCE), but the sudden death of John Mylett in a car accident a few months later brought the surviving RAGE musicians back together for one final benefit gig, which helped to raise funds for the drummer's family. Subsequently, after brief stints with DIESEL and ULI JON ROTH, Dave Lloyd teamed up with guitarist Mark Thomas to form a chart-oriented, semi-AOR concern known as 2AM, who released a reasonably well-received album entitled »When Every Second Counts« for RCA in 1987. He has (as well as fronting none other than MARILLION on a one-off fan club date towards the end of 1988) also collaborated sporadically with IAN GILLAN on some of the latter's solo projects, where he occasionally finds himself reuniting with his one-time writing partner, Steve Morris from EXPORT. Keith Mulholland, on the other hand, initially had a fairly brief tenure in the unsuccessful ZEN MACHINE towards the end of the decade, before also finding lucrative employment with the aforementioned Mr Gillan, lining up alongside various former EXPORT/TOKYO members in the touring outfit known as GARTH ROCKETT AND THE MOONSHINERS. More recently, he has been keeping his hand in by helping out on DEMON frontman Dave Hill's »Welcome To The Real World« solo album, so it looks as though several of the ex-RAGE stalwarts are still in regular demand.

LP's

»**Out Of Control**« Carrere 1981
»**Nice'n'Dirty**« Carrere 1982
»**Run For The Night**« Carrere 1983

12" Singles

»**Money**« Carrere 1980
[Limited edition on red vinyl]
»**Out Of Control**« Carrere 1981
[Limited edition on yellow vinyl, B-side "Double Dealer" non-LP]

7" Singles

»**Money**« Carrere 1980
[B-side "Thank That Woman" different to album version]
»**Out Of Control**« Carrere 1981
[A-side different to album version, B-side "Double Dealer" non-LP]
»**Bootliggers (1981)**« Carrere 1981
[A-side non-LP, also issued as limited edition picture disc]
»**Woman**« Carrere 1982
»**Never Before**« Carrere 1983
»**Cry From A Hill**« Carrere 1983
[A-side different to album version]

Compilation Appearances

"Long Way From Home" on »Heavy Metal Thunder« LP Carrere 1982
"Thank That Woman" on »Heavy Metal Thunder« LP Carrere 1982

RAMPENT

Anne Stephenson (v)
Kevin Wildsmith (g)
P. Selby (g)
K. Owen (b)
Rich (d)

Another record which gives away very little in the way of useful information is the four track EP issued by the hopelessly obscure RAMPENT at some point in 1980. Musically speaking, it's not too bad at all, the unrenowned quintet being a female-fronted affair with a few similarities to the likes of SIEGE, OMEN SEARCHER and BASHFUL ALLEY, with the upbeat "Back Street Walker" and "Livin' In The Past" being the pick of the bunch on display. The entirely unremarkable "Fight Back", on the other hand, is slightly weaker, despite some reasonable guitar work, while the dull ballad "No Friend Of Mine" is completely disposable. To be honest, they may have been better-advised to ditch the dodgy pair and issue a two-tracker in the first instance. All in all, though, it represented a semi-decent release for a small-time act, who presumably failed to make any impression whatsoever with this particular offering. Nobody seems to recall this band at all, and few copies of their four-tracker have surfaced in recent times, although most appear to have been found in the Midlands. There are virtually no other details given on the record itself (once again, the absence of a picture sleeve doesn't exactly help), except for a couple of writing credits, plus an indication that all of the tracks were *'unpublished'* at that time, suggesting that this might even have represented little more than a vinyl demo, manufactured in tiny quantities *via* the SRT custom pressing service and touted around in the hope of drawing interest from a major label. The fact that a minimal number of copies appear to have survived would tend to support this conjecture, although it might have been a commercial release after all. Anyone got any ideas?

7" EP's

»**Back Street Walker**« SRT 1980

RANKELSON

Col 'Zack' Sergeant (v)
Fox (g)
Kim Hooker (b)
Ric Ferrar (k)
Dave Vincent (d)

Formed towards the end of 1984 by ex-NEON SPIRIT (see separate entry) bassist Kim Hooker, RANKELSON (it was actually supposed to be RAN-KELSON, but their name was almost invariably spelled without the hyphen) slotted neatly into the rock/metal scene in South Wales almost immediately, their over-the-top *'pretty boy'* image belying the fact that they were actually a pretty talented metal proposition as opposed to worthless glam wannabes. A four track demo was circulated to various promoters and labels a short time after their formation, and, while it didn't serve to garner the lads a great deal of useful attention in the first instance, it nevertheless allowed them to work their way up from humble beginnings to more prestigious support slots with the likes of BUDGIE and (ahem) GARY GLITTER. Another notable story concerns their participation in a regional 'mini-Live Aid' event shortly after the real thing, where they got up on stage with members of KOOGA and MAD DOG, treating the assembled masses to an impromptu jam session of old SAXON favourites. It was all good fun in the beginning, but the serious business of getting a proper record deal was always lurking in the back of their minds.

Eventually, the RANKELSON lads managed to convince Ebony that it would be worth taking a chance on their outfit, and so a full-length studio album was laid down towards the end of 1985, the set being released early the following year. Resplendent in a rather ill-advised sleeve depicting the musicians in their garish stage personas and glam regalia, »Hungry For Blood« was actually one of Ebony's better releases of the period, the band occasionally resembling a heavy-but melodic mixture of TYTAN, DEMON and TRAITORS GATE, with numbers such as "Break The Chains" and the title track being extremely strong compositions with an excellent level of musicianship and vocal ability. Even songs such as "Sex Slave" and "Abuser" were considerably better than their feeble and contentious titles would suggest, but I guess their inclusion was all part and parcel of their 'shock rock' ethos. There were a couple of occasions, such as on "Can't Stop Rockin'" and "Hot Tonite", where the ensemble displayed a rather more formulaic and rudimentary approach in terms of lyrics and songwriting, although there's nothing fundamentally objectionable (apart from certain song titles) about the album as a whole. It was an excellent start, and, after a hectic touring schedule to promote the LP, the lads were soon hard at work writing material for a follow-up release.

Before they finally got around to undertaking the recording sessions for the second LP, however, there was the small matter of finding a new drummer (the first significant personnel change in their entire history) to replace the departed Dave Vincent (aka Dave Evans), who had grown weary of RANKELSON in the early months of 1987 and drifted off to assemble a new outfit with the utterly ludicrous name of PRATS ON THE PROWL. Eventually, their new drummer was announced, the much-travelled Kerry Loveluck, veteran of such hopefuls as MAMMATH, MAD DOG and ASHMATA. With their revised line-up firmly established, the lads duly locked themselves away in the studio for a while before finally emerging with another satisfactory clutch of recordings. Their delicately-titled »The Bastards Of Rock'n'Roll« opus appeared (in spite of some serious objections from their label, who initially refused to issue the long-player unless it was retitled »The Bad Boys Of Rock'n'Roll«) in due course, and it turned out to be a slightly more commercial affair, falling somewhere between TOK-IO ROSE and mid-period PERSIAN RISK (bands from the same neck of the woods, incidentally). It was still very listenable, on the whole, with another textbook vocal performance, particularly on the likes of "Be Good For Me" and "White Fire". Asked about their future plans to promote the new release with further live appearances, axeman Fox recalled a memorable 'incident' from their past: 'There's not many places that'll let us play now. We played in one place and set the club on fire. Pyrotechnical error! When they went off the whole stand fell over, four Marshall cabinets went up in flames, and the audience have come to expect so much from us because the show is so over-the-top that the place was just burning down and they didn't move! They thought it was part of the show!' (Ref: Kerrang No.156, October 1987).

Nevertheless, the outfit received pretty decent reviews for the latest album, not only in the UK but also in mainland Europe, Japan and the States, something which almost led to a licensing deal with Warner Brothers at one point, although this arrangement ultimately fell through. The lads were subsequently included in the 'Welsh Metal Special' feature in 'Kerrang' early in 1988 (by which time they had wisely toned down their outlandish image a tad), at which point the confident musicians revealed that they were enjoying a significant amount of commercial success (having delivered two profit-making albums for Ebony), and it seemed a foregone conclusion that the group would surely go on to delight their many followers with additional full-length releases in due course. Sadly, however, it all fell apart later in the year when Kim Hooker was finally enticed away from his post to become the new vocalist in TIGERTAILZ (he had, apparently, played a part in an embryonic version of the outfit before RANKELSON were signed) after the sudden departure of the hairspray-heavy Steevi Jaimz. Whereas most acts would tend to regard the loss of a bassist as a somewhat trivial matter, the remaining members of RANKELSON formed the opinion that it would be practically impossible to carry on without their main songwriting force, and duly elected to disband almost immediately (Col Sergeant soon found himself fronting a more traditional glam act called HYPER VYPER, while Fox tried his luck with THE HAPPENING), leaving two extremely respectable albums as their vinyl legacy.

LP's

»**Hungry For Blood**« Ebony 1986
»**The Bastards Of Rock'n'Roll**« Ebony 1987

RAVEN

John Gallagher (v, b)
Mark Gallagher (g)
Paul Bowden (g)
Mick Kenworthy (d)

It's hard to believe that Tyneside legends RAVEN actually started out as early as 1974, although the group (always featuring the central duo of John and Mark, the original songwriting Gallagher brothers) were, in the early days, a fairly distant relative of the proto-speed monster that established itself at the height of the NWOBHM. In their formative years, RAVEN amassed a huge tally of guitarists and drummers, with gigs (the band's set comprised almost entirely of rock standards) being few and far between at that stage. By 1977, the first quasi-stable line-up established itself, and RAVEN (now featuring Paul Bowden and Mick Kenworthy) set about making a name for themselves on the club circuit. It was a long, hard slog, and their live outings didn't exactly pass without incident; tales of nerve-jangling altercations with Hells Angels and equipment-smashing frenzies have now become part of heavy metal folklore in the North East! Nevertheless, some music actually got played along the way, and the popular outfit were soon able to attract a healthy crowd to their shindigs, gradually working some of their own material into the repertoire as time went by. The lads were still a couple of years away from a truly stable line-up, though, and they reluctantly parted company with both Mick Kenworthy (replaced by Sean Taylor in 1978) and Paul Bowden (succeeded by Pete Shore a year later) in the short term. As it transpired, Sean Taylor also packed his bags before long (he later resurfaced in SATAN), and a new maniac, the aptly-named Rob 'Wacko' Hunter, was brought in as a replacement. A short time later, further adjustment was required (their new guitarist had failed to impress over the preceding few months), and the outfit elected to continue as a trio from that point onwards. It turned out to be a pretty shrewd decision, and it marked RAVEN's final evolution into the band that so many know and love.

By early 1980, the activities of RAVEN had now come to the attention of the emerging Neat label, who (after releasing some popular and high-grossing singles by the TYGERS OF PAN TANG, FIST and WHITE SPIRIT) had decided that heavy metal was the way to go. Without much further ado, the trio were being invited to record their own single, and so "Don't Need Your Money" and "Wiped Out" were duly captured for posterity at Impulse Studios. As soon as their record hit the shops, it was apparent that we were dealing with something a bit out of the ordinary. Unlike many of their contemporaries, who were either content to rehash musical ideas from the 70's (although quite a few managed to put a more high-powered spin on things), RAVEN really were pushing the envelope slightly further. It's hard to pinpoint exactly where this proto-speed metal style came from, especially when the group had cut their teeth on nothing more adventurous than STATUS QUO and DEEP PURPLE covers, but I guess they must have taken some inspiration from JUDAS PRIEST ('Sounds', in their infinite wisdom, concluded that they were, in fact, *'MONTROSE clones'*) and just stepped on the accelerator. Whatever the story, RAVEN contrived to innovate with their high-velocity, guitar-torturing compositions, the alternating gruff/shrieking vocals of John Gallagher accentuating their individuality to an even greater extent. Fortunately, the notoriously unpredictable and fickle rock fraternity took to RAVEN immediately, and the lads were soon being hailed as future all-conquering heroes. Talk about giving an emerging bunch some impossibly high aspirations…

On the back of their debut single (which surely paved the way for the likes of JAGUAR and SAVAGE to follow their example), RAVEN managed to pick up various support slots with the likes of IRON MAIDEN, WHITESNAKE and OZZY OSBOURNE, and they were (after contributing "Let It Rip" to MCA's »Brute Force« compilation) soon busying themselves in readiness for the recording of their first album. By the beginning of 1981, the trio were all set to start the laborious process of compiling a full-length effort, although it took them quite a long time (several months, in fact) to complete the studio work. Still, the finished product was in the can by the spring, and should have appeared within a matter of weeks. For some reason, though, it failed to materialise (a new track, "Inquisitor", appeared on Neat's »Lead Weight« sampler as something of a taster), although it was eventually scheduled for release in the summer (when the group were also featured in the 'Armed And Ready' section of the very first

'Kerrang'). Once again, however, it was put back a bit longer, but finally emerged in around October, by which time the headbangers must have been wondering if RAVEN (who had now been out of the limelight for an entire year) had actually been a figment of their imagination all along. The members gave a typically modest explanation of events, though: *'We delayed the release of the album a fraction just to let the rest of the metal/rock folks get their singles and albums underway etc. After all, it wouldn't be fair to others to release the album which would defeat all others. Well, it'll soon be heard from all angles of the world, even in territories not yet explored by man.'* (Ref: Neat News No.2, 1981). After subjecting everyone to such an interminable wait, it needed to be a *bloody* good album.

And it was. RAVEN proceeded to deliver a long-player (»Rock Until You Drop«, the cover of which showed the musicians to have completely destroyed a recording studio with the sheer power of metal, or something) which, from the very outset, identified them as a considerably more substantial proposition than many critics would give them credit for in years to come. Of course, there were a generous handful of upbeat bruisers, notably opener "Hard Ride", "Nobody's Hero", "Tyrant Of The Airways" and "Lambs To The Slaughter" (later covered by KREATOR, a band allegedly inspired to form after witnessing the spectacle of an early 80's RAVEN concert), although they were balanced by some musically-inventive efforts such as "Hell Patrol", the superb "For The Future" (even preceded by a *'hey nonny no'*-style folky interlude) and the quirky title track. The oddball medley of two numbers by THE SWEET ("Hellraiser" and "Action") was a peculiar notion though, being the sort of thing that was far better-suited to the live environment. Overall, however, it was a cracking, energetic and demonstrative way for any bunch of metal hopefuls to open their account, and certainly stood them in good stead for a productive career. »Hard Ride« (B-side "Crazy World") appeared as a single to help sales along, and was soon doing its job, as the debut long-player eventually made its way into the upper reaches of the mainstream charts. A massive achievement for Neat, and a huge boost to the fortunes of RAVEN, although they remained loyal to their employers, and resisted the temptation to jump ship to a major, as FIST, WHITE SPIRIT and the TYGERS OF PAN TANG had all done before them.

The RAVEN lads spent the latter months of 1981 headlining some medium-sized venues in Europe, but eventually returned to the UK to

Photo: Tobias Thiem

record their debut session for the 'Friday Rock Show'. Broadcast on the 29th of January 1982, the session (now available on the scarcely-seen »Radio Hell« CD) showcased "Hard Ride" and "Lambs To The Slaughter", plus two newer efforts, "Hold Back The Fire" and "Chainsaw", and represented a charismatic, energetic performance of *'athletic rock'* (to use their own silly term) which surely won the band many new fans. After that, it was over to Europe (again) for yet more touring, followed by a lengthy UK jaunt supporting GIRLSCHOOL in the spring, culminating in an appearance at the well-attended Wrexham Festival in the summer. It was then back into the studio with no delay, as Neat wanted a brand-new album to capitalise on the outfit's popularity, so »Wiped Out« was captured within a remarkably short space of time. Although there was a distinct possibility that RAVEN might not have had quite enough time to compose a particularly strong LP this time, the trio still managed to deliver some pretty decent numbers nonetheless. It wasn't quite as *'in your face'* or varied as the earlier set, and it seemed a bit too polished (compared with their rough'n'ready debut, anyway) at times, but strong, pacey compositions such as "Live At The Inferno", "Faster Than The Speed Of Light", "Firepower" and "Chainsaw" were still enough to set many pulses racing. Mind you, it failed to make the charts this time, suggesting that sales might have taken a dip in view of various emergent outfits competing for attention by operating in a vaguely similar style. Only one single was released at the time of the album's release, a 7"/12" offering based around the previously-unheard "Crash Bang Wallop", with quite a few fans being enticed to part with their hard-earned cash in view of the inclusion of exclusive material (supposedly *'leftovers'* from the album sessions).

The critics hadn't been quite as obliging with respect to RAVEN's second album, although the lads were happy enough to get out on the road and convince the punters of their capabilities by playing a fairly extensive series of dates, their activities including a series of transatlantic shows alongside ANVIL. There were also the obligatory European gigs later in the year, but it was eventually back to Blighty for yet another album. This time, the lads didn't hurry themselves, and immersed themselves in the studio for several months before finally emerging with »All For One«, the *'difficult third album'*. The latest RAVEN long-player benefitted from a more generous studio budget, although it was a fairly patchy affair, representing a move into more of a heavy, chugging, anthemic style of metal, with only a couple of their trademark upbeat efforts on display. Still, there were a few tracks with slightly more of a personality (the excellent "Run Silent, Run Deep" and "Hung, Drawn And Quartered", for example), which just about compensated for the interchangeable nature of several other inclusions. The lads had been assisted during the recording process by ACCEPT's Udo Dirkschneider, and the latter had collaborated on two numbers at the time *viz.* a reworking of "Inquisitor" and an utterly abysmal cover of STEPPENWOLF's perennial "Born To Be Wild" (believe it or not, the biker gods actually recorded one or two other songs during their career). These selections were released as a single in their own right, and also appeared as B-sides on the »Break The Chain« 12", so the group certainly made the most of them. The trio toured around the UK and Europe (including an appearance at the Aardschok Festival) to promote their latest album, and subsequently (after the LP had been released in the States through Megaforce) proceeded to play their first headlining gigs in North America, with support coming from METALLICA (yes, you read that correctly).

RAVEN's relentless touring activities continued into 1984, including European dates alongside JUDAS PRIEST and Stateside gigs with ANTHRAX, some of which were recorded for future use. In fact, RAVEN were in the midst of some contractual wrangling at this point, and so they released the »Live At The Inferno« set as something of a stop-gap release while waiting to enter the studio to start work on album number four. Nevertheless, the live release was a worthwhile offering, a well-recorded and energetic souvenir of a RAVEN performance, although stretching it out to fill a double album seemed a bit excessive. By 1985 (the year in which the Raw Power label released a retrospective set entitled »The Devil's Carrion«), the musicians had already arranged a new contract with the big boys at Atlantic Records, and were now largely basing themselves in the States for both recording and touring purposes, having received a particularly warm welcome at their North American gigs in the past. Their opening gambit for Atlantic came in the shape of the considerably more accessible »Stay Hard« album, a commercially-oriented release which single-handedly alienated virtually their entire fan base in the UK and Europe, but which brought them a whole new (and possibly even more bountiful) following throughout the States, helped along by some generous radio airplay and even the odd appearance on MTV. The latest version of RAVEN bore little or no resemblance to the band in their original incarnation, and it seemed that they were now being pushed very firmly into a kind of BON JOVI/VAN HALEN vibe, something which they weren't really able to pull off with any sense of conviction at all. Still, plenty of easily-pleased rockers were motivated to fork over their hard-earned cash, and, with »Stay Hard« turning out to be one of RAVEN's most successful releases to date, Atlantic soon saw dollar signs lighting up in front of their very eyes; if only they could get the group to do something yet more commercial, as John Gallagher explained: *'You have to realise, everybody was expecting us to be the next big thing. Atlantic wasn't looking at us for what we were, but for what they thought we could be. They wanted us to be KISS meets BON JOVI…not a good thing.'* (Ref: Metal Forces No.33, November 1988).

Although much of »Stay Hard« had been comprised of mundane, formulaic rockers (their reworking of "Hard Ride" merely served to exaggerate the weakness of the newer material), the album did contain one real gem, the intriguing and original "Pray For The Sun", a track (although possibly slightly too pedestrian for its own good) which sounds not dissimilar to some of the more sedate material penned by the impossibly godlike MIND OVER FOUR (and you don't get any higher praise than that in my book) over the years. Strangely, RAVEN chose to make this track the main feature of a 12" EP to promote their latest long-player, although it was (in view of the commercial material on the rest of the album) an odd choice which surely won them little additional airplay. The lads were, inevitably, soon out on tour once again, although it proved to be a remarkably short time before they actually began work on yet another opus for Atlantic. Would they give in to overwhelming market forces and label pressure to deliver a real radio-friendly effort? Well, not quite, but their »The Pack Is Back« set still veered perilously close to the SKID ROW and EXTREME mentality at times. It was, nevertheless, a routine demonstration of fairly tuneful and anthemic 'big hair' rock material (with some utterly brain-dead lyrics), based around raunchy riffs and accessible vocals, with the occasional quirky idea (and an unremarkable version of "Gimme Some Lovin'" by the SPENCER DAVIS GROUP, also covered by BUFFALO at one point) thrown in to liven things up a tad. As usual, the hapless trio were utterly pilloried by the British and European rock press for having apparently 'sold out' so blatantly, but the new record still hit the mark with their American fans, so the lads weren't too bothered about the frosty reception they were getting at home.

It was evident that RAVEN were now being steered towards chart-friendly waters at every opportunity, although they were still penning a few more substantial compositions from time to time, even if these didn't tend to make it onto their finished albums any longer. In fact, to prove that they were still capable of pleasing the true headbangers, the lads compiled a mini-LP of previously-unheard material from the »Stay Hard« sessions, and issued them under the title of »Mad«. It was reassuring to find that RAVEN hadn't completely lost touch with their roots, and high-powered tracks such as "Speed Of The Reflex" and "Gimme Just A Little" were virtually as strong as anything they had penned back in the early 80's. It remained to be seen, however, whether or not any similar compositions would feature on the next full-length effort. In the meantime, the hard-working outfit were out on the road once more, undertaking a hectic touring schedule which included another jaunt with JUDAS PRIEST. Needless to say, they didn't bother coming over to Europe. Towards the end of 1986, RAVEN began work on their sixth album, and »Life's A Bitch« (no arguments there, mate) appeared early the following year. It saw the band abandoning their chart-friendly material of recent times and returning to something approaching their former glory, with many of the tracks (still pretty anthemic at times) showing a far heavier and speedier style than of late. In spite of the fact that the new record saw RAVEN rediscovering their roots to a great extent, the European fans remained unimpressed by their latest offerings, which just goes to prove that you can't please all of the people all of the time. Interviewed shortly after the release of »Life's A Bitch«, the philosophical John Gallagher reflected on the fact that the group were now seen to be turning their backs on the fans in Europe and concentrating on cracking the American market: 'There are die-hard RAVEN fans and there is always a new audience coming up every four years so there's hope. The press over here though seems to be very schizophrenic. Why? What have we ever done wrong? Maybe we're different.' (Ref: Metal Forces No.24, 1987).

Nevertheless, the largely-overlooked »Life's A Bitch« long-player failed to win favour with their supposedly-loyal American fan base either, for some reason, so it was back to the drawing board after another round of gigs with W.A.S.P. and SLAYER. The outfit parted company with Atlantic soon after the release (and commercial failure) of the latest album, and they were soon also saying goodbye to long-time drummer Wacko Hunter (in the early months of 1988), who had become dejected with the amount of flak the group were taking every time they bothered to release a new record. Hunter went into production work at first, electing to stay out of the limelight for a few years, although it's worth noting that he has recently re-emerged with another act called JOHNNY FRANKENSTEIN. His immediate replacement in RAVEN, however, was a certain Joe Hasselvander (who had previously been involved with such heavy Stateside outfits as PENTAGRAM, PHANTOM LORD and DEVIL CHILDE), who had become friendly with the Gallaghers during their stay in New York. After spending much of 1988 composing a batch of new material and trying out a variety of musical ideas, the lads wangled a deal with Combat Records (licensed by Under One Flag in Europe), and delivered yet another album, »Nothing Exceeds Like Excess«. It was an odd affair, embracing a variety of styles from raunchy rock to semi-thrash (sometimes within the same song!), and was a bit directionless in the main, although it contained some strong, heavy numbers within the grooves. After a few gigs in the States with TESTAMENT (they had also played on the 'Ultimate Revenge Tour', and featured on the accompanying video and album), the lads finally took the plunge and returned to Europe for the first time in several years, where they were given a surprisingly warm reception at their gigs alongside none other than KREATOR, the fans acknowledging that some of RAVEN's latest material represented something of a return to form, which must have given the band some cause for optimism.

By 1990, the lads had parted company with Combat, and were actively seeking a new deal, although it took a while to attract the interest of any noteworthy companies. Towards the end of the year, however, RAVEN (who were now basing themselves in Europe once more) had won a deal with Steamhammer, and rapidly set about writing a new selection of world-beating songs. By the time their »Architect Of Fear« long-player finally materialised in the early months of 1991, the general consensus of opinion was that their latest record finally marked an overwhelmingly successful attempt to recapture the original early 80's spirit. Both the fans and the band themselves seemed to regard this 'back to basics' effort as RAVEN's strongest release for many a year, and the back-on-form outfit toured successfully throughout Europe (taking to the road with RUNNING WILD) to promote the new album. Following their return to the UK, RAVEN assembled another of their special mini-LP's (»Heads Up«), featuring a few unreleased tracks from the LP sessions plus some recently-recorded live material, and it proved to represent a popular purchase for a large proportion of their rapidly-recovering fan base. Unfortunately, however, the luckless trio subsequently became plagued by management hassles, personal misfortune and label worries, all of which culminated with RAVEN being left without a deal or adequate representation. With the group now feeling unable to maintain a particularly high profile on the rock scene, they went to ground for a couple of years (during which time Joe Hasselvander briefly helped out in the ranks of CATHEDRAL), although the Gallagher brothers continued to bounce a few ideas off each other in the interim.

In 1994, RAVEN came out of hiding and stormed the gates of a post-grunge rock scene with a new demo and some high-profile showcase gigs on either side of the Atlantic, attracting the attention of various minor labels such as Fresh Fruit (a division of SPV) and Zero, coming to an arrangement for a further album to be delivered for these concerns in due course. »Glow« turned out to be a deliberately varied affair, the group showing a few different aspects to their latest compositions, including some traditional rock

numbers, some subtle and restrained efforts, plus a few speedier and heavier tracks to keep the headbangers happy. It seems to have been a great success, and (after some gigs in the States with ANVIL) the lads were soon making their first ever pilgrimage to Japan, where they encountered a truly fanatical following, leading to the release of the »Destroy All Monsters« live

set the following year. A further album for Fresh Fruit seemed a formality, although it took the lads a couple of years to compile enough new material to produce a long-player of a suitably high standard, the end result being 1997's »Everything Louder«, another extremely well-received offering which was also promoted with a few choice gigs in Europe. Since then, the lads have seen their original Neat albums reissued on CD by the Neat Metal concern, plus a compilation entitled »Raw Tracks« on Zero, and have recently returned with another album (the confusingly-titled »One For All«) on the Massacre label, which has even been winning a bit of praise from the unpredictable rock press in the UK, which is an achievement in itself. The trio seem set to issue a further full-length effort in the next year or two, and there are still presumably a few secrets in the RAVEN vaults which may be exhumed and released officially in the not-too-distant future. With an enviable presence on the web, RAVEN are keen to maintain close contact with their many loyal fans, and it looks as though they'll be around for a good few years yet.

LP's
»Rock Until You Drop« Neat 1981
[Also issued as limited edition picture disc]
»Wiped Out« Neat 1982
[Some with poster and free 7" featuring "Crash Bang Wallop" and "Rock Hard", both non-LP]
»All For One« Neat 1983/Roadrunner 1983/Megaforce 1983/Banzai 1983
[UK/Dutch/US/Canadian issue]
»Live At The Inferno« Neat 1984/Megaforce 1984
[UK/US issue, double live album]
»The Devil's Carrion« Raw Power 1985
[Double compilation album]
»Stay Hard« Atlantic 1985
»The Pack Is Back« Atlantic 1986
»Life's A Bitch« Atlantic 1987
»Nothing Exceeds Like Excess« Music For Nations 1988/Combat 1988
[UK/US issue]
»Architect Of Fear« Steamhammer 1991

Mini-LP's
»Mad« Atlantic 1986
»Heads Up« Steamhammer 1992

12" EP's
»Crash Bang Wallop« Neat 1982
[Issued on multicoloured vinyl, "Crash Bang Wallop", "Rock Hard" and "Run Them Down" all non-LP]
»Break The Chain« Neat 1983
[Both "Born To Be Wild" and "Inquisitor" non-LP]
»Pray For The Sun« Atlantic 1985

7" Singles
»Don't Need Your Money« Neat 1980
[A-side different to album version, B-side "Wiped Out" non-LP]
»Hard Ride« Neat 1981
[B-side "Crazy World" non-LP]
»Crash Bang Wallop« Neat 1982
[Some given free with copies of »Wiped Out« LP, both tracks non-LP]
»Break The Chain« Neat 1983
[B-side "The Ballad Of Marshall Stack" non-LP]
»Born To Be Wild« Neat 1983
[As RAVEN AND UDO, issued as limited edition picture disc, both tracks non-LP]
»Gimme Some Lovin'« Atlantic 1986

Promotional Releases
»On And On« Atlantic 1985
[DJ promo single, issued in both 7" and 12" forms]
»Gimme Some Lovin'« Atlantic 1986
[DJ promo single, issued in both 7" and 12" forms]

CD's
»Stay Hard« Atlantic 1985
»The Pack Is Back« Atlantic 1986
»All For One« Neat/Roadrunner 1986
»Life's A Bitch« Atlantic 1987
»Nothing Exceeds Like Excess« Music For Nations 1988/Combat 1988
[UK/US issue, with one extra track]
»Live At The Inferno« Teichiku 1990
[Double live disc, Japanese issue]
»Unreleased Tracks« Teichiku 1990
[Japanese-only compilation release]
»Wiped Out« Pony Canyon 1990
[Japanese issue with one bonus track]
»All For One« Pony Canyon 1990
[Japanese issue with two bonus tracks]
»Architect Of Fear« Steamhammer 1991
[With two bonus tracks]
»Heads Up« Victor 1992
[Japanese issue]
»Rock Until You Drop« Castle Communications 1992
»Glow« Fresh Fruit 1995
»Destroy All Monsters« Fresh Fruit 1995
[Live release]
»Everything Louder« Fresh Fruit 1997
»Raw Tracks« Zero 1999
[Compilation release]
»All For One« Neat Metal 1999
[With three bonus tracks]
»Wiped Out« Neat Metal 1999
[With three bonus tracks]
»Rock Until You Drop« Neat Metal 1999
[With three bonus tracks]
»One For All« Massacre 1999
[US issue]
»One For All« Pony Canyon 1999
[Japanese issue with one extra track]

Compilation Appearances
"Let It Rip" on »Brute Force« LP MCA 1980
[Exclusive studio version, live version appears on »Live At The Inferno« set]
"Inquisitor" on »Lead Weight« LP Neat 1981/CD Teichiku 1992
[Different to EP version]
"Live At The Inferno" on »60 Minutes Plus« Cassette Neat 1982/CD Teichiku 1992 + »All Hell Let Loose« LP Neat 1983
"Mind Over Metal" on »Metal Battle« LP Neat 1983/Roadrunner 1983 + »Metal Hammer« LP Roadrunner 1984

"**Crash Bang Wallop**" on »Metallergy« LP Bandit Records 1985
"**Wiped Out**" on »Metal Killers Kollection I« Do-LP Castle Communications 1985 + »Metal Killers Kollection« CD Castle Communications 1991
"**Take It Away**" (live) on »From The Megavault« LP Megaforce 1986
[Exclusive live version]
"**Break The Chain**" on »Metal Killers Kollection II« Do-LP Castle Communications 1986 + »The Metal Box« 3-CD Box Castle Communications 1993 + »Metal Masters« 4-CD Box Castle Communications 1993 + »Metal Mania« CD Castle Communications 1994
"**Never Forgive**" on »Time To Rock« LP WEA 1987
"**The Savage And The Hungry**" on »Power Chords Volume 1« LP Atlantic 1987
"**All For One**" on »Metal Killers Kollection III« Do-LP Castle Communications 1988
"**Into The Jaws Of Death**" (live) on »Ultimate Revenge 2« LP/CD Combat 1989
[Exclusive live version]
"**Gimme A Break**" (live) on »Ultimate Revenge 2« LP/CD Combat 1989
[Exclusive live version]
"**Don't Need Your Money**" on »NWOBHM '79 Revisited« Do-LP/Do-CD Phonogram 1990 + »Give 'Em Hell« CD Nectar Masters 1995
[Different to album version]
"**Take It Away**" on »Deeper Into The Vault« CD Music For Nations 1991
"**Lambs To The Slaughter**" on »Radio Hell« CD Raw Fruit 1992
[Different to album version]
"**Hold Back The Fire**" on »Radio Hell« CD Raw Fruit 1992
[Different to album version]
"**Hard Ride**" on »Radio Hell« CD Raw Fruit 1992
[Different to album version]
"**Chainsaw**" on »Radio Hell« CD Raw Fruit 1992
[Different to album version]
"**Hell Raiser**" on »Heavy Metal Collection 1« CD X-Tra Collection 1993 + »Monsters Of Rock« CD Castle Communications 1995
"**Hell Patrol**" on »Heavy Metal Collection 2« CD X-Tra Collection 1993 + »Metal Killers« CD Castle Communications 1993
"**Take Control**" on »Heavy Metal Collection 3« CD X-Tra Collection 1993
"**Faster Than The Speed Of Light**" on »Heavy Metal Collection 4« CD X-Tra Collection 1993
"**Nobody's Hero**" on »Wild Thing« CD Kaz Records 1995
"**Rock Until You Drop**" on »Rock Legends« CD Castle Communications 1995
"**Faster Than The Speed Of Light**" (live 95) on »Fast« CD Zero 1996

RAW DEAL (I)

Rob Childs (v, g)
Paul Reynolds (g)
Brian Smith (rg)
Ade Jones (b)
Steve Richardson (d)

Kent's version of RAW DEAL were perhaps the ones most deserving of the 'HM' bit of the NWOBHM tag, as the Leicestershire bunch (*vide infra*) were, in all honesty, a bit too bluesy, while the little-known South Coast act (responsible for the proto-NWOBHM »Struck Down By Your Love« EP) are too firmly rooted in the 70's even to make it into this volume. The youthful quintet assembled themselves in 1978 or thereabouts, their members being the usual assortment of schoolfriends and aspiring musicians located *via* adverts placed in the weekly music press of the day. Inevitably, the combo's humble beginnings revolved mainly around small-time activities on the local club scene, although RAW DEAL's rise to popularity among the rock-loving community was relatively swift, the musicians capturing the hearts of many an audience with an unusually confident brand of high-powered metal. Even so, there seemed to be little chance of getting much further in the short term, given that RAW DEAL lacked the vital resources with which to record a proper demo tape or to venture to more remote music venues. It looked as though it would be necessary to acquire a skilful management team in order to open a few doors, although a stroke of luck was to come the band's way when the small-time White Witch label (actually just a local record shop which, as with the likes of Bullet and Reddingtons, had decided to start promoting unsigned talent) encouraged the ensemble to enter the studio and lay down a couple of selections for possible use on a forthcoming vinyl compilation.

Towards the end of 1980, the lads made the trip to a local recording facility and duly set about the task of immortalising a pair of RAW DEAL originals. In the event, two usable numbers were captured for posterity, and "Cut Above The Rest" was soon earmarked for the as-yet-untitled White Witch sampler. Even so, that hectic studio excursion had evidently been an eye-opening experience, as bassist Ade Jones reveals: *"The session was all a bit rushed because we could only afford a couple of hours on the graveyard shift, and since it was the band's first time in the studio, things weren't as polished as they could have been. We did lots of takes, and* there were quite a few cockups; one memorable disaster being when our drummer lost a stick, which then flew back and hit him in the throat, knocking him off his stool with an accompanying explosion of drums and cymbals, all of which sounded great on 24 track! The final take was a great relief, hence the cheer in the background at the end of the track!" (Ref: Private communication, November 2000). True to their word, White Witch subsequently included the cut on their soon-to-become-legendary »Kent Rocks« (a somewhat questionable title, given the presence of various atrocious indie hopefuls) compilation in the early months of 1981, where "Cut Above The Rest" was revealed to be an excellent, energetic rocker in the manner of early TYGERS OF PAN TANG, BOLLWEEVIL or EAZY STREET's "Let 'Em Rock". Admittedly, RAW DEAL's opening gambit may have been lacking in finesse, but it was certainly overflowing with youthful exuberance, and represented one of the patchy album's highlights.

Sales of the compilation were fairly brisk at the outlets which offered it for sale, and the general public throughout the South East voiced the opinion that RAW DEAL were undoubtedly an act who were worthy of further attention. To their considerable credit, White Witch duly agreed to sponsor the band's debut two-tracker (they had already issued RENEGADE's 12" single) within a matter of months, although a parting of the ways would occur before this came to pass. While most of the musicians were now convinced that they were going places and should throw all of their weight behind the project, bassist Ade Jones decided that it was too risky to pin all his hopes on RAW DEAL, whereupon he departed in order to undertake a college course. After that, the group restructured (Brian Smith switched from rhythm guitar to bass) and resumed as a four-piece, after which they finally got around to recording the tracks for their much-anticipated debut. In due course, the disc hit the shops, exposing the metalheads to a brace of freshly-penned RAW DEAL cuts. In fact, "Out Of My Head", the main focus of attention, was cast from the same mould as their contribution to the aforementioned sampler, suggesting that the minor personnel changes had affected the overall style very little. The flipside ("In The Mood"), however, is a bit of a curiosity, this being a lively boogie/blues workout which was actually a variation on the theme of GLENN MILLER's famous big band instrumental of the same name. Not the most obvious source of inspiration for a youthful heavy metal outfit, but there you go. Although the record (which was,

predictably enough, pressed in modest quantities) was soon snapped up by many of the devoted local fans, it failed to make much of an impact elsewhere, hence this capable 7" proved to be RAW DEAL's finest hour, rather than a stepping stone to greater things.

Having done its best to promote some of the area's NWOBHM talent, the White Witch label soon ceased to exist, after which the luckless RAW DEAL, like most of the Kent outfits who issued singles in the period (RENEGADE, LEGEND, DEMON PACT, SPITZBROOK, TRIARCHY, DENIGH, TORTURE etc.), were apparently to lose their way in major fashion. In fact, the majority of these heavy acts had pretty much bitten the dust (or, at least, wound down their activities to a major extent) within a couple of years, leaving the region with a severely-depleted metal presence. Strange that such a thriving scene (perhaps all trying to emulate the area's major success story, ALKATRAZZ) could have had such a relatively short lifespan, and, even though the likes of DEUCE and TNT came along to pick up the pieces towards the middle of the decade, it would never really be the same again. As it turns out, the main protagonists from the RAW DEAL venture seem to have drifted away from the music business altogether, although erstwhile stalwart Ade Jones maintained a noteworthy level of involvement with the scene, playing with pub legends STRANGE BREW for a while before becoming involved in a behind-the-scenes capacity as a respected sound engineer. The »Out Of My Head« two-tracker, a tiny handful of which apparently boasted a promo-only picture cover (although only one or two examples of the latter have ever come out of the woodwork, to my knowledge), is currently regarded as the greatest rarity on the collectable White Witch label, and the asking price (even for the standard, sleeveless version) now tends to be well into three figures.

7" Singles
»Out Of My Head« White Witch Records 1981

Exclusive Compilation Appearances
"Cut Above The Rest" on »Kent Rocks« LP White Witch Records 1981

RAW DEAL (II)

Des Horsfall (v)
Regan Cairns (g)
Steve English (b)

Kevin Thompson (d)

Although Leicestershire's RAW DEAL might not have won any points for originality on the name front (sharing the identity with at least a dozen small-time acts in the UK alone), it's unlikely that they could have persevered with their original moniker of ANVIL (and even that was shared with a band from the North East) for very long after their successful Canadian namesakes appeared on the scene! The outfit's one and only single (don't confuse the quartet with their Kent counterparts, who also got to the vinyl stage at around the same time) was issued on the Neat label back in 1981, and it reveals this particular RAW DEAL to have been a bunch of unashamed FREE copyists, from the opening "All Right Now"-cloned intro of "Lonewolf" through the BAD COMPANY-tinged flipside ("Take The Sky"), although additional similarities to a couple of prominent NWOBHM-era outfits (notably SLENDER THREAD and STREET LEGAL) are also evident. Given that the group deviated significantly from the fast and furious *'Neat sound'* to which so many hopefuls aspired and which so many fans expected, however, the 7" didn't exactly rival the likes of JAGUAR, BLITZKRIEG or VENOM in the sales stakes, and there was never any question of an album deal materialising. At some point thereafter, the band appears to have experienced a significant personnel defection, leaving only the central duo of Regan Cairns and Kevin Thompson to keep things going.

Gamely refusing to give up the ghost, however, the central characters subsequently recruited erstwhile TURBO vocalist Des Horsfall and ex-BLITZKRIEG bassist Steve English (a mystery duo, O. Youll and G. Youll, had been credited in their place on the earlier single), after which RAW DEAL returned to slogging their guts out in the live environment, playing plentiful gigs across the country (although the majority of their appearances seem to have focused on the Midlands) to anyone who would listen. The full extent of this particular line-up's recording activities, however (apart from a small handful of unremarkable demo tapes which were only made available to their fans at shows and which appear to have been circulated very poorly otherwise), seems to have been a one-off session appearance on 'Into The Music' (the short-lived 'Friday Rock Show' offshoot devoted to more tuneful acts), broadcast on the 31st of January 1985. On this occasion, the selections recorded were "Easy Lovin' Man", "Rollin' On", "A Little Understanding", "Your Love" and "Second Time Around", a representative batch of material which indicated that the band were now firmly rooted in the bluesy style of rock which clearly suited them down to the ground. The transmission hardly rocketed the combo to stardom overnight, however, and it would have been all too easy for people to predict a fairly rapid decline for RAW DEAL, culminating in eventual disillusionment and an inevitable split within a couple of years.

Unlikely as it may sound, therefore, it transpires that a version of RAW DEAL was apparently still active at the turn of the decade, with 'Kerrang' having generously afforded them an entry in their commemorative NWOBHM '10th Anniversary' supplement in 1989, making mention of the fact that the persevering group had now relocated to the nation's capital and were supposedly busy writing material for a potential album deal with the Atco label. Recording sessions eventually took place in Germany in 1992 (it's not remotely clear who, apart from the ever-present Regan Cairns, was actually involved with the band by this stage, though) as a result of their publishing contract, whereupon the group began laying down new versions of session favourites "Easy Lovin' Man" and "Second Time Around", alongside less-familiar material such as "Manufactured Love" and "Little Sister". Since then, however, all has been suspiciously quiet, so it looks as though the hapless outfit didn't get around to releasing their album as intended and the likes of THUNDER and SKIN ultimately beat them to ascend the vacant *'bluesy rock throwbacks'* throne. Incidentally, Des Horsfall (who has an occasional act of his own called the EARLY RIDERS) now appears to have largely abandoned his rock roots (traitor!) and is currently attempting to carve out a new career as a country music star (snigger), so be warned that his solo albums (for example, 1996's »Easy Road«) might not be quite what you would expect...

7" Singles
»**Lonewolf**« Neat 1981

RED

Mark Robbins (v, k)
Paul Newton (g)
Stephen Flood (rg)
Richard Edgington (b)
Pete Briggs-Fish (d)

With the notable exception of URCHIN's debut two-tracker, the earliest record to be featured in this particular tome is RED's »Rider In The Sky« EP from 1977. As such, it's far too early to have been a NWOBHM release in its own right, pre-dating the main period of activity by around two years, although the obscurity and musical merits of the release are just about sufficient to warrant its place as an item of interest to NWOBHM enthusiasts. The unrenowned five-piece, based in or around the capital, were one of those slightly off-kilter outfits who used the general rock framework as the basis for some technical experimentation, thus being entirely consistent with the manner of pre-NWOBHM activity that was going on throughout the nation, typified by the likes of GYPP, WHITEFIRE and BILL THE MURDERER. RED's one and only release, issued by the Electric Record Company (home of the utterly bonkers QUANTUM JUMP), was a heavy enough offering, with the deceptively-titled "Thrash" being the pick of the bunch, a concise, mid-tempo piece with a healthy nod in the direction of DEEP PURPLE, whereas "Going Going Gone" is a longer, more varied (slightly progressive) number with synthesizer sections, vaguely similar to TURBO's "Take My Life". On the reverse, "Rider In The Sky" is a rather unremarkable semi-ballad in the general style of CHEMICAL ALICE, although veering a bit close to PINK FLOYD territory at times.

So there you have it. An EP (with an extremely unremarkable *'live action'* picture sleeve) which tends to turn up for sale fairly infrequently (although it's not commonly regarded as a particularly valuable or coveted item), but an obscurity which would appeal to a considerable number of collectors nevertheless. The group appear to have gone back into hiding almost immediately after their record hit the shops, and were probably never even a particularly high-profile name on the club circuit, but I guess you have to give them a bit of credit for bucking the system and doing their own thing in those punk-favoured times. Incidentally, at least three British rock outfits (not to mention the typically offbeat bunch who later recorded for Lost Moment) chose to adopt the utterly nondescript identity of RED in the NWOBHM era (with typical irony, the best of the bunch failed to get past the demo stage), and it's worth stating that the little-known version who released an eponymous album of instrumental prog (boasting some monumentally silly song titles) on the Jigsaw label in 1983 were entirely unrelated to the band under discussion here.

7" EP's
»Rider In The Sky« Electric Record Company 1977

RED ALERT

Pat Devlin (v)
Dave Bilton (g)
Colin Moss (g)
Rick Woolgar (b)
Trevor Fearnley (d)

Oh gawd, not another one. Yes, folks, we now appear to have yet another heavy variety of RED ALERT to contend with, as if the situation wasn't confusing enough already. In fact, this bunch aren't actually all that much of a mystery after all, although there's no connection with either the Yorkshire version (later WILDFIRE) or the little-known bunch who appeared on »Metal For Muthas Vol.II«. Formed in Lincolnshire in around 1978 from the ashes of minor groups such as SCAPA FLOW, SF2 and SEAGULL, this particular ensemble originally adopted the nondescript name of PICTURES, but eventually, in a rather bad career move, settled on the vastly over-subscribed RED ALERT instead. After building up the obligatory local reputation, the quintet sent their demo tape to a variety of parties in the music business, getting the most favourable reaction from the small-time State Records. The label persuaded the lads to enter the *'Arctic Lite Rock Search 80'* competition, a *'Battle Of The Bands'*-style venture in which RED ALERT were ultimately to triumph as overall winners, leading to a substantial amount of prize money, equipment and a coveted recording deal.

It would appear, however, that the only vinyl to be released under this arrangement was their »Break The Rules« single (issued in a generic company sleeve), which shows the band to have been a fairly melodic rock proposition in the manner of GRAND PRIX or SINGAPORE, although the flipside, "What Do You Do For Laughs", was a considerably heavier and raunchier composition than the mediocre and disposable A-side. The record doesn't seem to have done much to expose the outfit to the rock world, unfortunately, although they were, nevertheless, invited to open the proceedings at 1980's Reading Festival, which was presumably their greatest claim to fame. History doesn't record how well their performance was received by the masses, although it looks as though the lads didn't go on to greater things, so perhaps they didn't fare too well among all the bottle-throwing delinquents who were waiting impatiently for KROKUS and GILLAN. I imagine they called it a day soon after (they were still gigging in 1981), but I suppose there could be later singles out there somewhere. Bassist Rick Woolgar, incidentally, went on to twiddle the knobs on the OVERDRIVE EP, and occasionally turned up in a production role in later years, overseeing RUNESTAFF's recordings for the FM label, for example. No more bands called RED ALERT, please!

7" Singles
»Break The Rules« State Records 1980

RED RAGE

Noggin (v, g)
Dave Pelling (b)
James Edmonds (d)

The forceful trio known as RED RAGE were apparently one of those troublesome outfits who simultaneously appealed to both the punk and metal communities of the day (this situation is pretty much mirrored on the modern-day collecting scene), but whose musical style is, nevertheless, rather poorly served by either of these categories. Alongside the likes of BASELINE, SHADOWFAX and the FALSE IDOLS (to name but a few), their upbeat, catchy brand of 'power pop' (as evidenced by their sole two-tracker from 1980) is, to my ears, more reminiscent of a souped-up version of the KINKS than anything else, with their "Total Control" effort, in particular, bearing a distinct similarity to the latter's "Lola", although the unusually-titled flipside ("I Give You...This") is a reasonably powerful and effective selection in its own right. Issued by the Flicknife label (notorious for releasing a wealth of material by various HAWKWIND offshoots, among others) in a slightly odd-looking picture sleeve, the RED RAGE 7" was, until comparatively recently, quite easy to locate at an affordable price, although competition between punk and NWOBHM collectors from the mid-90's onwards has started to drive the listed value considerably higher. It might make an interesting purchase for the affluent completist, admittedly, but those of us on a budget might want to spend our pennies on something slightly closer to traditional NWOBHM territory. The band, incidentally, were still to be found playing in and around the capital throughout 1981, but appear to have drifted apart within a fairly short space of time thereafter.

7" Singles
»Total Control« Flicknife 1980

Compilation Appearances
"Total Control" on »Flicknife Records-The Punk Collectors Series« CD Anagram 1995

REINCARNATE

Shane Barnett (v)
John Guest (g)
Paul Farrington (b)
Dave Tye (d)

All things considered, Staffordshire's outstanding REINCARNATE were unquestionably one of the comparatively few British outfits who genuinely epitomised the term 'NWOBHM' in its original and purest sense, so it really is a great tragedy that this long-forgotten bunch ultimately failed to become established as one of the genre's more prominent bands. Conceived, towards the end of 1980, in a geographical area possessing a considerable pool of musical talent, REINCARNATE (good name, that) started out as a quintet utilising a twin-guitar attack, the lads playing the usual circuit of small-time gigs at their local youth clubs and pubs to get them-

selves known to the masses. Initially bolstering their live set with well-received cover versions of old faithfuls such as "Paranoid" (along with virtually every other NWOBHM group who ever graced a stage) and MOTÖRHEAD's "No Class", the emergent outfit gradually incorporated more and more of their self-penned compositions into the repertoire as they began to grow in stature and confidence.

By mid-1981, however, the group found themselves suddenly being reduced to a quartet, following the unforeseen departure of one of their original guitarists. Although various hopefuls were apparently auditioned for the vacant slot over the ensuing months, a suitable replacement was never located, so the lads were compelled to soldier on as a four-piece from that point onwards. Mind you, such was the intensity of their overall sound, that you'd probably never have guessed that they were actually operating in something of a reduced capacity. The obligatory demo was recorded before long, and the cassette was duly circulated to a wide variety of prospective companies, although, sadly, the fabled major deal was always to elude them. Nevertheless, tracks from the tape were featured quite heavily on their local station, Radio Stoke, the favourable response to which culminated in the band recording a session for broadcast to the region's listeners later in the year. There was no let-up in the sheer quantity of shows in and around the pubs and clubs of the Midlands, either, but it looks as though the talented outfit were never fortunate enough to secure any support slots of note, and rarely managed to gig further afield, which is a great shame.

Having benefitted from the patronage of their local media, the quartet eventually decided that their considerable regional popularity warranted a further trip to the recording studio, but this time their ambitious intention was to lay down the tracks for a self-financed 7" single. Enlisting the help of Les Hunt of local heroes DEMON on the production side of things, "Take It Or Leave It" and "Metal In Disguise" were captured on tape in the summer of 1982, and the record duly appeared on the Zipp label (another local act, GRACE, recorded a seldom-seen offering for a similarly-named concern, although this may just be a bizarre coincidence) towards the end of the year. As most of you will surely now be aware (ever since the A-side took pride of place on the »NWOBHM Vol.5« bootleg, that is), REINCARNATE's modest-looking two-tracker is truly one of the undisputed classics of the genre, with both selections constituting incredibly catchy, powerful, energetic and memorable efforts in the general manner of a more metallic SHADOWFAX or a souped-up TURBO. Outstanding. It's highly unlikely that the members of METALLICA ever heard this particular slice of vinyl during their formative years (still, it would be nice to see a REINCARNATE original on the next »Garage Days« set), but the general similarities to numbers such as "Motorbreath" and "Four Horsemen" are quite astonishing nonetheless. Needless to say, the single received the inevitable drubbing from the perfidious 'Kerrang', although the fact that a DIANA ROSS record was considerably more warmly-received by the reviewer in question (yes, it's true) speaks volumes.

It would appear that the quartet persevered for a year or so after the single's release, trying out a few new ideas in the process, before the participants finally decided to knock it on the head and go their own separate ways. Bassist Paul Farrington made his way to HARRIER (see separate entry), occupying a place at the keyboard in what proved to be a markedly more lightweight project, while the others seem to have drifted away from the music scene. Nevertheless, the REINCARNATE single has long been regarded as one of the genre's most sought-after pieces, and its three-figure value reflects this observation. While the standard issue came without a picture sleeve, a handful of 'promotional' copies were livened up by hand-written versions with a colour photograph attached to the cover, these depicting the band in a variety of static poses and live-action shots. REINCARNATE were surely one of the finest of the numerous hopefuls to have been overlooked during the NWOBHM era, and it's a great pity that so little of their material is still available. To quote from their own biography, they were also 'a band whose Heavy Metal brand of music can give you nose bleeds.' Amen.

7" Singles
»Take It Or Leave It« Zipp Records 1982

Compilation Appearances
"Take It Or Leave It" on »NWOBHM Vol.5« Bootleg CD 1992

RENEGADE (I)

Paul Armfield (v)
Steve Welch (g)
Pete Smith (b)
Mark Cunningham (k)
Paul Smith (d)

One of the seemingly endless rock/metal propositions to have cropped up in the county of Kent in the early 80's, RENEGADE (not to be confused either with the later British bunch who recorded a two-tracker in 1984 or with numerous overseas namesakes, the best-known of which were Swedish and American) formed in the second half of 1980, the youthful members having previously been involved with various small-time rock acts such as S.T.2 and STARBURST. After a mere couple of months together, the quintet were rapidly snapped up by the local White Witch concern, who rewarded the lucky RENEGADE with the opportunity to record both a 12" single of their own (for some reason, all copies seem to have been issued in an unfinished, 'promotional' sleeve, so you shouldn't get overly-excited if you possess one of these) and a subsequent appearance on the legendary »Kent Rocks« compilation. The A-side of the aforementioned 12" (released towards the end of 1980), "Lonely Road", recounts the totally inconsequential story of someone making their way home by road (cf. NO QUARTER's "Racing For Home"), which suggests a few musical similarities to acts such as REQUIEM and ARC, with atmospheric keyboards in the style of SCORPIO or CHALLENGER.

It has to be said that the vocals of frontman Paul Armfield were a bit unconvincing and wavering, however, and occasionally threatened to wander off into PARALEX territory (not nearly as irritating, though) at times. Even so, the general standard of musicianship pretty much compensates for this minor quibble. The flipside ("Last Thought"), meanwhile, is a slower, more pensive composition which reflects at length on how the possibility of a large thermonuclear bomb going off in your neighbourhood could really, like, ruin your day completely. Check out this award-winning octet:

> "Idle days spent lazing under a gentle sun
> Listening to songs that will never be sung
> Dangling toes in a cool running stream
> Visions of the future in an intangible dream
> Drifting and sailing into a surrealistic sleep
> Dreams of golden fields and spirals so steep
> Pleasant views of a peaceful world
> without care
> Terrifyingly shattered in an atomic nightmare."

Ooer. Makes you think, doesn't it? Both tracks were reasonably heavy, nonetheless, and this particular 12" (an extremely scarce and highly-valued piece nowadays) was certainly a decent enough way to start off a fairly promising career. Their strongest of RENEGADE's numbers to have been committed to vinyl, however, was probably "Last Warrior", as featured on the »Kent Rocks« sampler the following year. With substantial guitars and an improved vocal performance, the latter composition is more reminiscent of outfits such as MARZ or PHYNE THANQUZ, so it's a pity it wasn't included on their original slice of vinyl.

The initial pressings of both the single and compilation were rapidly exhausted, with local shops tending to do a brisk trade in virtually any product either released or distributed by White Witch (DEMON PACT, RAW DEAL, LEGEND etc.), so RENEGADE's future looked pretty healthy at that stage. The outfit appeared set to go from strength to strength after their early exposure, playing live to numerous appreciative audiences in the region and swiftly developing an extensive repertoire of their own. Somehow, however, the hapless White Witch contrived to make some rather poor investments and were soon in serious financial arrears. With the inevitable collapse of the company coming shortly thereafter, the bands of Kent were left to fend for themselves; like most of their contemporaries, RENEGADE didn't last the distance. Vocalist Paul Armfield later formed a melodic rock outfit called DEJA VU (not to be confused with the rather quirky band who recorded for Berkshire's TVR Records in the mid-80's), who had a song entitled "Black Angel" included on an extremely obscure sampler EP called »Hands Off, Hands On« towards the end of the decade, and who also appeared on the seldom-seen »Full Force Vol.II« compilation with the track "Love Me Tonite".

12" Singles
»Lonely Road« White Witch Records 1980

Exclusive Compilation Appearances
"Last Warrior" on »Kent Rocks« LP White Witch Records 1981

Compilation Appearances
"Lonely Road" on »NWOBHM Vol.7« Bootleg CD 1996

RENEGADE (II)

Morrow
Boyd
Grattan

Aside from the well-known bunch from Kent (vide supra), there were evidently quite a number of outfits called RENEGADE doing the rounds throughout Britain in the 80's, notably small-time acts from Nottinghamshire, Leicestershire and Devon, although I suspect that the hopelessly obscure combo responsible for the »(I Don't Need) The Fighting Man« single from 1984 were actually an Irish ensemble. The surnames tend to suggest a connection with the Emerald Isle (there was certainly a Belfast bunch of that name doing the rounds a year or two earlier), as does the music itself, especially on the upbeat B-side, "Hysteria In America", which charges along in the best tradition of SWEET SAVAGE, EZY MEAT, STRYDER or DRIVESHAFT, and which outshines the nominated A-side in no uncertain terms. Even so, the awkwardly-titled "(I Don't Need) The Fighting Man" is an undeniably well-constructed, slower affair in the general manner of EAZY STREET's "Quest For Glory", which benefits from an extremely impressive vocal effort throughout. All things considered, a perfectly respectable debut for such an unrenowned act.

It seemed like a healthy enough start for an emergent band, although it looks as though the record companies failed to take note of RENEGADE's potential, concentrating instead on some of the more established acts from the mainland (the likes of KOOGA and TERRAPLANE, for example) when it came to snapping up a few classy, melodic hopefuls in the mid-80's. Once again, it would appear that yet another Irish concern lost out in the long term mainly as a result of their geographical isolation, which was a great shame. The group's sole two-tracker had been something of a no-frills affair, with no picture sleeve and precious little information on the label, and it has the feel of a promotional device (surprisingly, it was actually reviewed in Kerrang upon its release, although they ripped it to shreds) rather than an official product, especially since they appear to have forgotten to credit the ensemble in the first instance, necessitating the 'Renegade' name being stamped across the label as something of an afterthought. Even so, a minimal number of examples have come out of the woodwork thus far, and you're unlikely to locate one particularly cheaply.

7" Singles
»(I Don't Need) The Fighting Man« Strayed Records 1984

REQUIEM

Mike Reid (v)
Steve Slater (g)
Gordon Denny (b)
Karl Wilcox (d)

One of the heavier NWOBHM-era offerings comes from the Midlands-based proposition called REQUIEM (not to be confused with the later Italian group), a long-forgotten act (formed as the metal scene began to take shape) who issued the »Angel Of Sin« single at some point in 1980. Featuring the drumming skills of a very young Karl Wilcox (who eventually took his place in the reformed DIAMOND HEAD a decade later) and the guitar heroics of erstwhile ARC stalwart Steve Slater, this release is largely dominated by the mournful, doomy vocal performance of non-cheerful frontman Mike Reid, which would probably go down extremely well with many fans of the wrist-slashing genre today. Both "Angel Of Sin" and "Sacrificial Wanderer" (good titles, those) are epic compositions with satisfyingly heavy guitars and changing tempos, the overall sound bringing to mind ARC and TRACER (in particular), with a subtle hint of RENEGADE and APOCALYPSE also thrown in for good measure. Mind you, I'm not entirely convinced of the need for such lengthy tracks (both running over six minutes), especially when a bit of judicious editing (the guitar solo on the A-side, the intro on the reverse) might have allowed the songs to hold the listener's attention more efficiently. A respectable debut effort, all the same, but a bit too sorrowful and dreary for many NWOBHM fans, and I'll wager there wasn't a lot of merry dancing going on at any of REQUIEM's gigs at the time.

Although an outfit of the same name could be found touting their wares around the clubs during the late 80's (possibly the identically-monikered act who appeared on »The Whinging Album«), it would appear that they had nothing to do with the original bunch, who seem to have drifted apart (having lost the services of their first-choice vocalist quite soon after the single was released) by around 1982. Karl Wilcox subsequently went on to play with the more progressively-inclined CHASE (see separate entry) for a fairly short period, before eventually getting his prestigious call-up to the resurrected DIAMOND HEAD, while Steve Slater proceeded to join an obscure, Wolverhampton-based outfit called PREDATOR (not another one), who failed to achieve a great deal of recognition and who shouldn't be confused with any of the heavy recording acts who adopted this identity (or a similar one) over the years. The lone REQUIEM two-tracker, which is now almost impossibly rare (the one-time band members having been 'relieved' of their few remaining copies some years ago), was issued without a picture cover, but it has an extremely prominent logo in gothic script on the label, so you'd be unlikely to overlook it easily. Keep searching, folks…

7" Singles
»Angel Of Sin« Sacrificial Records 1980

RHABSTALLION

John Anderton (v)
Stuart Toddington (g)
Dave Thompson (g)

Graham Hooper (b)
Jack Himsworth (d)

The origins of Yorkshire's peculiarly-named RHABSTALLION lie, as with many others, in various hard rock outfits who established themselves in their locality from the mid-70's onwards, although RHABSTALLION themselves didn't emerge as a separate entity until the latter part of the decade. In 1979 or thereabouts, the group began writing their own powerful material and testing it out in the live environment, gradually making their way along the tried and tested path towards small-time popularity. The youngsters' first real opportunity to reach a somewhat wider audience came with the invitation to contribute a track to the legendary »New Electric Warriors« compilation in the summer of 1980 (the lads having already demoed a selection of original material earlier in the year), and RHABSTALLION duly obliged by supplying their energetic "Chain Reaction" effort. It might not have been the album's stand-out selection (local rivals DAWNWATCHER and TAROT get the nod in that respect), but it was still a pretty healthy way to lose their vinyl virginity, and the ensemble's eclectic combination of TURBO, DEALER and early SILVERWING looked sure to serve them well in their future activities.

Early the following year, RHABSTALLION (now featuring new drummer Mark Crowther in place of the departed Jack Himsworth) decided that it would probably be a fairly prudent idea to put out one of those self-financed single thingies that had suddenly become all the rage with heavy acts. With the band pairing "Day To Day" with "Breadline" and issuing the record in a monochrome sleeve showing a photo of the lads in action, the 7" (sponsored mainly by some obliging local benefactors, evidently) became a firm favourite among local fans, and copies were soon finding their way into numerous rock and metal collections. The single provided strong evidence that the outfit's songwriting ability was maturing at a considerable pace (a bit of a SALEM influence was now sneaking into the proceedings), and should really have attracted a bit of record company interest at the time. Sadly, it doesn't appear to have happened in the short term, and so the RHABSTALLION lads were therefore left to reflect upon whether or not they wanted to continue plugging away in the same style as before and hope that the vicissitudes of time would eventually work to their advantage.

It would appear that the outfit's writing team ultimately decided to try something a bit different in a concerted attempt to attract some of the media attention they certainly deserved, recruiting new vocalist Steve Ancliffe (the lucky possessor of an enviably impressive range) at some point thereafter, and moving towards more of a semi-power metal style with distinct similarities to the likes of TRAITORS GATE and PERSIAN RISK. A recording session for a proposed second single (again, this was envisaged as another self-organised affair) took place in the spring of 1982, when the band laid down "Stranger Stranger" and "Shock 'n' Roll" at Fairview Studios in Hull. Sadly, in spite of the fact that these well-crafted numbers totally eclipsed their earlier efforts, the single never actually reached the pressing stage, most likely due to a lack of finances on RHABSTALLION's behalf. From that point onwards, the outfit's activities failed to arouse a great deal of public or press interest, although a notable highlight of their later career was the filming of a gig (in February 1983) at Bradford University by none other than the BBC, who duly broadcast a couple of the featured tracks on their 'Bubbling Under' regional programme, an honour also bestowed upon MENDES PREY a short time later. By this stage, RHABSTALLION had now endured yet another personnel change, with Stuart Toddington having flown the coop and new recruit Andy Wood being drafted in as a permanent replacement.

In the early months of 1984, RHABSTALLION were back in the studio once again, the persevering bunch working on rather more melodic and sophisticated material (such as "I Could Not Believe My Eyes" and "Runaway") with a vaguely QUEENSRYCHE-type feel at times. Sadly, their recording activities appear to have failed to create much of a buzz in the music industry yet again, and it wasn't long before the dejected lads finally called it a day for good, having tried their utmost to get that elusive break for five long years. Mind you, several of the ensemble's erstwhile members proceeded to follow careers with other newly-founded outfits (Dave Thompson, for example, after a stint in Neal Kay's ill-fated VENTURE supergroup, made it to the vinyl stage with VOYAGER UK, while the extremely talented Steve Ancliffe spent time with a little-known melodic proposition called ANTIGUA), although there were to be no fairy-tale success stories for any of them in the short term. However, a couple of RHABSTALLION's founder members (Dave Thompson and Jack Himsworth) later cropped up in a rather more successful AOR concern called LOST WEEKEND, where they were joined by a handful of local scenesters from the likes of CYRKA and VOYAGER UK. After establishing themselves on the national rock scene, the new outfit began attracting interest from various quarters, and ultimately came to the attention of Vinyl Tap, who issued a full-length LOST WEEKEND album on CD in the early 90's. Consequently, the group became darlings of the AOR set, and are now (having been given the Now And Then stamp of approval) in great demand for live events.

Coincidentally, however, the emergence of LOST WEEKEND more or less occurred just as the NWOBHM collecting scene was taking off in a big way, and (after the best part of a decade's worth of total anonymity) the RHABSTALLION name was suddenly back in vogue, their long-lost single making an appearance on the wants list of many a NWOBHM fanatic. With the ever-enterprising dealers sensing a potential money-making opportunity, a limited quantity (enough to satisfy demand, meaning that the price has remained at reasonably sane levels) of unsold copies of their record were swiftly liberated for sale. As a result of the interest expressed in the outfit's original exploits in the NWOBHM era, however, the possibility of releasing some archive material on CD (as with TRIARCHY, LEGEND etc.) was tentatively raised, and the subsequent negotiations eventually yielded a full album in 1993. In fact, not only did this feature a generous selection of tracks spanning the band's entire history, plus comprehensive recording details and some fairly interesting (if slightly self-congratulatory) sleeve notes, it additionally featured two tracks which resulted from many of the group's assorted members getting back together (something that also happened for the NO QUARTER CD, for example) and mucking about in the studio at the time of release. Not only that, it would appear that they even got their act together just in time for a few low-key reunion gigs…

RHABSTALLION's fourteen track CD, simply entitled »Day To Day«, was one of the more impressive additions to the Vinyl Tap series of NWOBHM reissues, and finally saw justice being done by allowing fans to hear just what the record companies had failed to appreciate in years gone by. I reckon the reformation tracks are a bit out of place, though, and the simplistic, singalong nature of these efforts tends to tarnish the good impression made elsewhere. Dave Thompson, interviewed at around the time of the CDs release, offered an overview of the contents: *"The songs were recorded by various line-ups at different times, in certain cases they date from as far back as 1979. We just laid down the material as we went along, but you can certainly hear how the outfit changed direction over the years. We released the first single on our own label way back in 1981, after which »Stranger Stranger« should have appeared as a follow-up, but it was never pressed, unfortunately."* (Ref: Iron Pages No.29, 1994). The impromptu reformation turned out to be a relatively short-lived celebration of the life and times of RHABSTALLION, however, after which the participants either (in the case of Dave Thompson and Jack Himsworth) elected to focus on the flourishing LOST WEEKEND venture or simply went back to their day jobs. Even so, I reckon we were extremely privileged to be afforded the opportunity to appreciate quite so many of the band's NWOBHM-era compositions. Cheers, lads!

7" Singles
»Day To Day« Rhab Records 1981

CDs
»Day To Day« Vinyl Tap Records 1994
[Compilation of unreleased studio and live material]

Compilation Appearances
"Chain Reaction" on »New Electric Warriors« LP Logo 1980/CD British Steel 1997
[Different to CD version]
"Shock 'n' Roll" on »Noise Level Critical« CD Hallmark 1997

RICOCHET

Geoff Sewell (v)
Dave Gough (g)
Neil "The Finn" Finnegan (b)
Mick Collett (d)

In an ideal world, many more of the NWOBHM small-timers would surely have been elevated to the attention-grabbing status they deserved by virtue of their talent and sheer determination. In reality, though, youthful exuberance and an indefatigable sense of humour will only take you so far, as I'm sure the members of RICOCHET would be happy to confirm, as these lads possessed both qualities in abundance. This quartet of heavy hellraisers from the West Midlands (who evolved from a HAWKWIND-influenced group called THORAZIN, and who actually played their first local gig as early as 1977) were, predictably enough, an extremely popular regional attraction, but ultimately failed to achieve nationwide fame (or infamy, for that matter), so they were certainly in the same boat as countless others in that sense. Still, they did, at least, manage to issue a low-budget single before finally going their separate ways. The release in question, a *'double B-side'* from 1980, surfaced on the outfit's own label, the unashamedly naff Heavy Rock Records, featuring label artwork which shows a hapless metalhead meeting a sticky end under a weighty boulder. Superb. In terms of presentation, therefore, this good-natured effort couldn't be faulted, and the musical contents were more than a match for the packaging.

Their "Midas Light" (subtitled *'an arty pharty look at the weather'*) effort is an outstanding, upbeat number in the general style of CRUCIFIXION, GEDDES AXE or early DEF LEPPARD, with some incredible, jazzy guitar work which raises the whole piece to a standard seldom achieved by such minor NWOBHM hopefuls. On the reverse, meanwhile, "Off The Rails" is another genuine cracker, albeit a somewhat less intense affair, which features a raucous backing throughout, the suggestion (which some people seem to have swallowed hook, line and sinker) being that the track was indeed recorded as the musicians were *'enjoying'* themselves at a particularly rowdy party. As if. All things considered, the rare-as-you-like RICOCHET two-tracker, around half of which were issued in a hand-drawn picture sleeve depicting the members and an excellent logo, is truly one of the most highly-regarded and prized artefacts from the entire NWOBHM period. Mind you, it was an extremely restricted pressing, with only around five hundred examples being manufactured in the first instance, although this quantity seemed to suffice at the time. Most importantly, it gave them something to sell to their regional fans, and it ultimately facilitated a brief sojourn to mainland Europe, where RICOCHET beat a path to Germany in order to play the lucrative Air Force Base circuit. Before long, though, their initial enthusiasm for the project began to fizzle out, and the participants eventually started to lose faith in their collective abilities, resigning themselves to the fact that the British metal boom was now well past its peak.

It really is a great pity that no further RICOCHET output ever materialised, although they supposedly featured on local radio stations quite a bit at the time, possibly even recording a session or two before finally calling it a day. In any case, things appear to have fallen apart for the lads by early 1982, with guitarist Dave Gough going on to serve time with Brummie bruisers DEMOLITION, while enigmatic bassist *'The Finn'* put his passport to good use, relocating to Germany for a productive spell which culminated in the assembly of the DAMIEN project. Boasting an unlikely array of British expatriates (most of whom had links with the Midlands rock scene itself, including former DEMOLITION growler John Cadden and future MARSHALL LAW vocalist Andy Pyke) in their ranks during the course of their relatively short existence, the outfit managed to release a self-titled mini-LP on the Steamhammer label before packing their bags and returning to their homeland. The Finn actually enjoyed a brief stint with the persevering HANDSOME BEASTS upon his return to Blighty, although the latter called it quits before their third album saw the light of day. Intriguingly, however, the one-time members of RICOCHET have recently begun formulating dastardly plans to get back together (inspired by the sustained interest in their old band) and record some previously-unheard material for future release. Better late than never, I guess, so let's hope these characters manage to grab a bit of attention during their second spell on the music scene.

7" Singles
»Midas Light« Heavy Rock Records 1980

Compilation Appearances
"Midas Light" on »NWOBHM Vol.6« Bootleg CD 1992

ROADSTER

Malc Shipman (v, b)
Martyn Howes (g)
Gary Standing (d)

For some reason unbeknownst to myself, the majority of ROADSTER singles in circulation today have, at some point, been relieved of their original sleeves and/or *'dinked'* (*i.e.* the centre hole has been enlarged to permit their use in jukeboxes), so that it's now extraordinarily difficult (but not impossible) to locate a completely *'intact'* copy. Very strange. You would imagine that the jukebox market would account for only a tiny fraction of the total number of sales, but there you go. Anyway, the front of the scarce picture cover shows a photo of the band (not looking the happiest set of individuals, it must be said) and their metal-as-you-like logo, while the reverse depicts a mean-looking, hand-drawn biker astride his mighty chariot, which pretty much gives the game away as to the style of music involved. Yep, good old biker rock in its purest and simplest form. These Yorkshire lads clearly lived the two-wheeled lifestyle to the full (I've never seen the fascination, to be honest, and you don't have to be Sigmund flipping Freud to work out where all the *'feel the power between my legs'* nonsense comes from), with both "Fantasy" and "45 m.p.h." evoking, both musically and lyrically, similarly-minded hopefuls of the period such as CENTURION, EAZIE RYDER and, to some extent, VARDIS.

As with the majority of their biker-pleasing contemporaries, I suspect that ROADSTER accepted their musical limitations and were perfectly aware of the fact that they were never going to win a major-label deal and become wildly famous, but I guess it hardly mattered to them. They were, in all likelihood, probably just playing for the sheer hell of it, and the fact that they managed to entertain a few Yorkshire pub-dwellers along the way was something of a bonus. No doubt the unassuming trio went down an absolute storm with the down-to-earth rock community of the day (they actually persevered, in one form or another, until at least the mid-80's), and I'm sure their occasional outings at biker rallies would have been a bit 'eventful', but they failed to win many too mentions in the music press. This seems to have been their only vinyl offering, however, and it was evidently a pretty modest pressing, so playable copies very seldom crop up even in the sleeveless state. As a result, the asking price is creeping inexorably upwards, although it's not really an item you should be looking for unless you appreciate the biker rock style just as much as the archetypal NWOBHM releases.

7" Singles
»**Fantasy**« Mayhem Record Label 1981

ROCK GODDESS

Jody Turner (v, g)
Tracey Lamb (b)
Julie Turner (d)

From the amount of media scrutiny which surrounded the emergence of London combos GIRLSCHOOL and ROCK GODDESS, you would think that no female personages had ever picked up a guitar prior to that point in time. I suppose the fact that they were all young and attractive(ish) might have had a trouser-perturbing effect on certain impressionable male journalists of the time, but it's fair to say that neither act ever went out of their way to make a selling-point out of their gender or looks (quite the reverse, in truth), and it now seems pretty unthinkable that the perceived *'infiltration'* of heavy metal by the fairer sex could ever have caused so much of a commotion in the first place. Gender politics aside, the humble origins of ROCK GODDESS date back to the mid-70's, when two extremely youthful sisters (Jody and Julie Turner, the latter being four years younger than her sibling) were first encouraged (by their supportive father John, an individual with various interests in the music business) to express themselves musically. At first, this amounted to little more than making an unholy racket in their bedrooms after school, but things started taking shape properly in the early months of 1977, when another schoolfriend, Tracey Lamb, joined in the fun. With Jody assuming responsibility for guitar and vocals, Tracey supplying bass lines and Julie resident at the drumstool, ROCK GODDESS was finally born, although their early activities were severely hampered by their respective ages (Julie was a mere *nine* years old at this stage, well below the age at which she would legally be allowed to perform in pubs and clubs), so the trio had little option but to immerse themselves in rehearsals for a few years.

Up until the early months of 1981, the low-key activities of ROCK GODDESS (including a tiny handful of live appearances, usually with a stand-in drummer in tow) failed to raise too many eyebrows, although things started happening once Julie Turner hit the magical age of fourteen, whereupon the group could legally play together in clubs (and, more importantly, get paid for it). Nevertheless, all those misspent years of incessant rehearsing and songwriting (with constant supervision and encouragement from John Turner, whose involvement seems to have been motivated by a genuine belief in his daughters' ability, rather than sinister fame-seeking vicariousness or profiteering) had served them well, and the threesome now had an impressive armoury of well-worked compositions at their disposal. Before long, they had recorded their first official demo tape, and subsequently won a place on the diverse »Making Waves« compilation LP, released to showcase a number of female-dominated acts, mostly from the indie end of the music spectrum. Although ROCK GODDESS might just have felt a little out of place with their raunchy "Make My Night", they still benefitted from the associated exposure which resulted from sales of the album, and they soon went out on the road with the GYMSLIPS and the ANDROIDS OF MU (two of the other featured acts who had been instrumental in getting the project off the ground) to promote themselves further. Before long, 'Kerrang' picked up on the young ladies, and afforded them the honour of a full-page 'Armed And Ready' feature towards the end of 1981, where the metal-loving members (citing some pretty hefty influences, namely SABBATH, ZEPPELIN, MAIDEN, LEPPARD and KISS) duly announced their plans to take the rock world by storm.

Inevitably, sensation-seeking journalists soon latched on to the stunningly-obvious fact that there were now two extremely prominent all-female acts on the scene, and tried to instigate a *'friendly rivalry'* between ROCK GODDESS and the more popular and established GIRLSCHOOL at every possible opportunity, but both outfits (to their immense credit) steadfastly refused to take the bait, preferring to let the music speak for itself and not to get involved in any petty squabbles over who was *'best'*. Moving into 1982, the trio rapidly began making more lucrative and impressive inroads into the live scene, and were soon being offered the chance to play at clubs such as the Marquee on quite a regular basis. Naturally, certain reviewers couldn't resist making the odd disparaging remark about the effect these *'crowd pleasers'* were having on the excitable adolescent males in the crowds, although it would be grossly unfair to suggest that ROCK GODDESS ever pandered to the dirty mac brigade (eat your hearts out, GYPSY QUEEN) or attracted anything other than a cosmopolitan audience. It had, by this stage, become apparent that the group were operating in a considerably heavier and more raunchy style than the increasingly-accessible GIRLSCHOOL (or most of their female-fronted contemporaries such as CANIS MAJOR, AFTER HOURS or THIN END OF THE WEDGE), and it was by no means certain that any record company of note would be particularly willing to take a chance on signing such a no-nonsense bunch of wailing viragos. Sensing a possible re-enactment of the AMAZON (see separate entry) fiasco, the labels kept their chequebooks firmly in their pockets until they were absolutely convinced that there was a genuine market for ROCK GODDESS vinyl.

Crucially, however, the musicians were (after recording a new demo featuring "One Hot Night", "Heavy Metal Rock 'n' Roll", "Make My Night" and "My Angel") given an opportunity to prove themselves in front of a notoriously hostile crowd at the 1982 Reading Festival, and this appearance seems to have been such a resounding success that the record companies started beating a path to their door within a matter of days. The lucky winners in the near-hysterical bidding war were A&M, a company who flirted with semi-mainstream rockers (BUDGIE, NUTZ, SPIDER) from time to time, but were generally more accustomed to promoting chart acts such as THE POLICE than anything closer to real metal territory. Nevertheless, the band were tempted to sign by the offer of an overly-generous ten-album deal (!), and ROCK GODDESS were rapidly bundled off into the recording facility once again, where they busied themselves by laying down their debut album. Before the end of 1982, A&M decided to get their new signings known to the general public by releasing an introductory single, coupling the award-winningly-titled "Heavy Metal Rock 'n' Roll" and "Satisfied Then Crucified". It was a strong and assertive debut, the outfit taking the heavy music of GIRLSCHOOL and the RUNAWAYS one stage further, adding a touch of SLITS-style attitude and chucking in a healthy quantity of PMT-fuelled aggression, surely paving the way for the likes of L7, BABES IN TOYLAND and the LUNACHICKS in years to come.

The debut single finally pushed ROCK GODDESS firmly into the public eye, and the bewildered members were soon being bombarded with numerous requests for magazine features, radio interviews and even television appearances, which the ever-obliging lasses attempted to honour whenever possible. There was also a trip to the BBC's studios to lay down their debut session for the 'Friday Rock Show' (broadcast on the 26th of November 1982), where they grasped the opportunity to showcase "Satisfied Then Crucified", "Back To You", "Take Your Love Away", "To Be Betrayed" and "The Love Lingers Still", five numbers lifted from their forthcoming long-player. It was, considering their relative lack of studio experience, an impressively-delivered and varied set of original compositions, and this valuable piece of exposure set the stage nicely for their much-vaunted LP. The overworked band ended the year by undertaking their first proper club tour, including several venues outwith London for the first time, and steadily created a healthy level of interest in their various activities. At this stage, the forthcoming long-player was still tentatively titled »The Goddessa File« (a somewhat contrived play on words which appeared as the headline of an early article in 'Kerrang'), although, by the time the termagant triumvirate got around to releasing the set early the following year, it had reverted to an eponymous affair.

Nevertheless, »Rock Goddess« was an eminently listenable and highly capable effort all round, the powerful and uncompromising numbers (such as the excellent "Satisfied Then Crucified", "My Angel" and "Back To You", for example) being adroitly balanced by the rather more subtle (but still undeniably heavy) "Take Your Love Away", "To Be Betrayed" and "The Love Lingers Still", with Jody Turner putting in an excellent vocal performance throughout. It was also a refreshing change to hear a metal band delivering heartfelt lyrics from a uniquely female perspective, especially when many ROCK GODDESS songs centred around dragging unsuspecting blokes into their boudoirs and giving them a right good seeing-to (you know, I always had a sneaking suspicion that some shameless trollops actually enjoyed a bit of nookie), although it's a pity that some of their more explicit live favourites ("Give Me Sex" and "I Ain't Got A Man To Love", for example) were destined to remain unrecorded. The album proved to be an instant hit amongst rock fans of both genders, and proceeded to sell in surprisingly impressive quantities around the globe, whereupon even the most ardent sexist was forced to concede that these *'chromosomally-challenged'* individuals were a particularly worthy addition to the pitifully male-dominated rock world of the early 80's. The hard-touring lasses were soon hitting the road once again, taking in some rather more well-known and prestigious British venues in the process, but were back on BBC Radio before long, when they showed up on the celebrated 'In Concert' programme (alongside CHEVY), delivering a highly enjoyable half-hour live set for the benefit of a national audience.

In due course, the crowd-pleasing »My Angel« was trotted out as a single, which went on to shift a considerable number of units (denting the charts in the process), and the popular ROCK GODDESS were subsequently invited to open the proceedings on IRON MAIDEN's European tour in the spring of 1983. To bolster their sound in the live environment, the trio swiftly roped in second guitarist Kat Burbella, and this European trek seems to have gone extremely well for the newly-expanded outfit, although founder member Tracey Lamb was already beginning to express a level of dissatisfaction with her role in ROCK GODDESS. By the second half of the year, however, it was already time for the group to begin thinking about material for their second album, which A&M wanted to get into the shops with minimal delay. Shortly after the band had begun penning material for the follow-up LP, however, Tracey Lamb finally handed in her notice, and the bassist rapidly went off on her own to establish a new all-girl venture, who elected to adopt the over-subscribed name of SHE (not to be confused with their Neat-label namesakes, for instance). Within a comparatively short space of time, Kat Burbella was also enticed away to join forces with Lamb's emergent project, although it was ultimately a relatively unsuccessful act (who, contrary to popular opinion, didn't actually release any vinyl), plagued by constant personnel instability and a distinct lack of decent material. After touting their wares around London for a couple of years, SHE finally gave up the ghost, and Lamb later inveigled her way into the ranks of supposed *'arch-rivals'* GIRLSCHOOL.

With ROCK GODDESS having been reduced to the nucleus of the Turner sisters once again, people began expressing serious doubts about the band's future, although they hurriedly drafted in a new bassist, Dee O'Malley, and decided to remain a trio for the time being. After finding their feet once again, it was back into the studio to resume work on their second album, and the sessions for the long-player were hastily completed within a matter of weeks. »Hell Hath No Fury« was unleashed towards the end of 1983, the group promoting its release with a comprehensive series of dates with DEF LEPPARD (in Europe) and Y&T (in the UK), a show from the latter tour being recorded and used for their second appearance on the BBC's 'In Concert' programme. The album showed a slight progression from their debut, and the occasional use of keyboards (from Dee O'Malley) demonstrated the group's intention to branch out into more ambitious material. It was a polished performance all round, and live favourites such as "The Visitors Are Here", "Gotta Let Your Hair Down", "You Got Fire" and "God Be With You" stood out as particular highlights. The record went on to shift around the same number of units as their debut in the UK, and additionally benefitted from an American release, where the album was repackaged with a slightly different tracklisting. The girls were enjoying every minute of their success, but didn't let it go to their heads, as Jody Turner revealed: *"I'm no better and no worse than the fans out front. I'm just an ordinary human being. To me, the superstar bit is so ugly and I'd never get into that trip. When I go to gigs I just like to get off on the music like everyone else, not stand at the bar posing. In this band, the members are all determined to keep their feet on the ground."* (Ref: Kerrang No.55, November 1983).

Moving into 1984, things had finally cooled off a bit on the ROCK GODDESS front, although you can hardly have blamed the poor souls for wanting to take it a bit easier after all their hectic exertions of the previous two years. The busy outfit had already outlined plans to spend much of the year promoting themselves in America, although their Stateside activities (if they actually made it over the pond at all) seem to have been conducted with a great deal of discretion, with very little positive feedback emerging from the American market. Nevertheless, the group soon saw a new two-tracker released by A&M, which coupled a functional cover of GARY GLITTER's anthemic "I Didn't Know I Loved You (Til I Saw You Rock & Roll)" with "Hell Hath No Fury", two *'exclusive'* numbers which had actually been featured on the American pressing of the second long-player. The new record gave ROCK GODDESS their biggest chart hit to date, and the trio soon went out on the road once again (headlining some major venues in the process), playing throughout the UK (gaining their *third* slot on 'In Concert' along the way) and mainland Europe, where they took the opportunity to unveil a handful of novel compositions ("Here I Go Again" and a cover of CHER's "Bang Bang", for example) which were scheduled to appear on their next LP. Work on the *'difficult'* third long-player (for A&M, once again) began later in the year, although something appears to have gone seriously and irreversibly awry along the way, resulting in the band parting company with their label in rather mysterious circumstances before the sessions had really got going properly.

In the wake of their split from A&M, ROCK GODDESS kept a very low profile for some six months, although they resurfaced in mid-1985 with a comeback appearance on the 'E.C.T.' television programme, where the trio affirmed their intention to continue their quest for world domination by bludgeoning their way through an extremely intense version of "Satisfied Then Crucified", plus new numbers "So Much Love" and "Love Is A Bitch". Following this impressive return to the public eye, the musicians came to an arrangement with Paul Samson (and his producer friend Jo Julian) to begin collaborating on the aborted third album, adding one or two newer compositions and weeding out some of the weaker tracks which had originally been chosen to appear on the set. By the latter half of 1985, the recording sessions had been completed, although there was still no concrete offer from any of the major labels to issue this long-awaited slice of vinyl. Moving into 1986, valiant attempts were still being made to find ROCK GODDESS the deal they surely deserved, but the musicians themselves were beginning to lose heart with every rejection that came their way. Still, they forced themselves to go back out on the road in the spring, desperately trying to maintain a significant level of interest in their flagging career, and promising their dwindling fan base that the new long-player really would be in the shops within a matter of weeks. Sadly, it was to take a lot longer for anything to happen, and the lasses busied themselves by returning the favour to Paul Samson by appearing as backing vocalists on the guitarist's »Joint Forces« album.

Eventually, a small French company offered to press the album in limited quantities for a European release, and the band reluctantly agreed to this arrangement, just to make sure that the record actually appeared in its finished form somewhere in the world. Meanwhile, however, they had to endure the departure of the pregnant Dee O'Malley, the press releases announcing that the bassist had been intending to leave for some time in order to start a family. In truth, it was a totally unplanned bun/oven scenario, which really dropped the Turner sisters in the mire at short notice. Nevertheless, with that LP release just around the corner, the duo had to soldier on, and soon drafted in bassist Julia Longman (formerly with PDQ) as a replacement for O'Malley, before subsequently recruiting Becky Axten to act as a full-time keyboard player. In the early months of 1987, the »Young And Free« long-player finally hit the shops in some lucky parts of Europe (surprisingly, the label also issued a single to precede the album's release), and showed the outfit to have been moving into rather more accessible, refined territory at the time the sessions took place. It wasn't a bad effort at all (a bit well-mannered in comparison to their rough 'n' ready releases from 1983, perhaps), and some of the featured numbers were a bit anonymous and interchangeable, although the likes of "Streets Of The City", "So Much Love", "Sexy Eyes" and "Raiders" were all eminently listenable. Mind you, with a generous fourteen tracks included, none of which outstayed their welcome (only one of them actually broke the four-minute mark), you didn't have to endure the weaker selections for all that long before something a bit better would invariably come along.

With the band still hoping that a UK label would pick up on the release sooner or later, ROCK GODDESS continued to play live whenever possible, although the absence of big-money backing now dictated that they were largely restricted to travelling around Britain, playing new material to bewildered audiences who weren't even aware that a third album had already been released. In the end, the absurdity of the situation just became too much for the poor lasses to bear, and, with no prospect of a proper deal on the horizon, the frustrated members finally called it a day. By the second half of 1987, ROCK GODDESS were no more, although the outfit's former members were soon outlining plans to return with various revamped projects. In the event, however, only the Turner sisters appear to have carried this through with any conviction, resurfacing in 1988 as the JODY TURNER BAND, where they were ably assisted by unknown bassist Phil Manley-Reeve and guitarist Gavin Taylor, who held the rather dubious distinction of having played one whole gig with MAMMOTH as a stand-in for one of the regular fatties. In spite of a few high-profile live appearances over the following months, however, this latest vehicle for the talents of Jody Turner failed to get off the round convincingly, and the project was soon laid to rest, with Gavin Taylor going on to join the likes of GIGOLO, FIRST STRIKE and GENERAL DYNAMIX. Although nothing further has been heard from any of the original members of ROCK GODDESS from the 90's onwards, interest in the group was briefly rekindled in 1994, when the long-forgotten »Young And Free« set finally earned an official UK release, appearing in CD-only form on the Thunderbolt label. Surprisingly, A&M never got around to making the original albums available on disc, although both have finally received a belated reissue thanks to emergent labels such as Renaissance Records.

LP's
»**Rock Goddess**« A&M Records 1983
[Initially with free poster]
»**Rock Goddess**« Warners 1983
[Japanese issue with different sleeve]
»**Hell Hath No Fury**« A&M Records 1983
[UK issue]
»**Hell Hath No Fury**« A&M Records 1984
[US issue with different cover and alternate tracklisting]
»**Young And Free**« Just In 1987
[French-only release]

12" EP's
»**Heavy Metal Rock 'n' Roll**« A&M Records 1982
["One Hot Night" non-LP]
»**My Angel**« A&M Records 1983
[Both "In The Heat Of The Night" and "Our Love's Gone" non-LP, some copies with free 7" flexi and poster]
»**I Didn't Know I Loved You (Til I Saw You Rock & Roll)**« A&M Records 1984
[A-side non-LP, "Hell Hath No Fury" non-LP in UK]

7" Singles
»**Heavy Metal Rock 'n' Roll**« A&M Records 1982
[Issued as limited edition picture disc]
»**My Angel**« A&M Records 1983
[B-side "In The Heat Of The Night" non-LP]
»**I Didn't Know I Loved You (Til I Saw You Rock & Roll)**« A&M Records 1984
[A-side non-LP, B-side "Hell Hath No Fury" non-LP in UK]
»**Love Has Passed Me By**« Just In 1986
[French-only release, issued on blue vinyl]

Shaped Picture Discs
»**I Didn't Know I Loved You (Til I Saw You Rock & Roll)**« A&M Records 1984

Promotional Releases
»**Heavy Metal Rock And Roll**« A&M Records 1982
[DJ promo 7"]

CD's
»**Young And Free**« Thunderbolt 1994
»**Hell Hath No Fury**« Beartrack Records 199?
[German release]
»**Hell Hath No Fury**« Renaissance Records 1998
[US release, double disc, includes both albums and six bonus tracks]

Compilation Appearances
"**Make My Night**" on »Making Waves« LP Girlfriend Records 1982
[Different to album version]
"**Hell Hath No Fury**" on »Metal Fusion« LP A&M Records 1984
"**Turn Me Loose**" on »Noise Level Critical« CD Hallmark 1997
"**Streets Of The City**" on »Noise Level Critical« CD Hallmark 1997
"**The Party Never Ends**" on »The Best Of British Metal« CD Delta Music 1999
"**So Much Love**" on »The Best Of British Metal« CD Delta Music 1999

ROGUE MALE

Jim Lyttle (v, g)
Phil Aston (g)
Chris Aylmer (b)
Steve Kingsley (d)

The London-based creation known as ROGUE MALE was, in reality, only one of myriad musical visions conceived by frontman Jim Lyttle, who had been active in the British scene since at least 1977. From an early stage, the Irish-born vocalist knew that he would eventually be responsible for something a little bit out of the ordinary, although his first real band in the Emerald Isle was the unremarkable PRETTY BOY FLOYD AND THE GEMS, a somewhat punky bunch of individuals who recorded a couple of singles for the Rip Off label in the late 70's and appeared on the »Belfast Rocks« compilation alongside various other hopefuls such as COBRA and NO SWEAT. The outfit eventually relocated to London in their quest for fame and fortune, but fell apart within a fairly short space of time, whereby Lyttle set about establishing new musical ventures such as the little-known PICTURES and VISA (I suspect that there were others, but it appears that he only ever admitted to this pair), although none of these short-lived acts really matched his expectations in terms of the whole music/image/lyrics package. By around 1982, however, he had finally found his niche with an uncompromising metal/punk collision which became known as ROGUE MALE, and which threatened to deliver a confrontational slice of musical mayhem, the general intention being to shake up the rock scene in no uncertain terms.

Although material was being written (Lyttle alone was solely responsible for the music and lyrics) and recorded from an early stage, the additional personnel varied quite erratically in the first few months of the project's existence, although something resembling a stable line-up emerged in the early months of 1984, when Lyttle was joined by original HANDSOME BEASTS guitarist Phil Aston, one-time SAMSON bassist Chris Aylmer and erstwhile DEEP MACHINE drummer Steve Kingsley. If you had been expecting a post-NWOBHM supergroup to emerge from the meeting of these scenesters, however, you were in for something of a surprise! Demos were recorded and circulated in due course, and the much-anticipated offer soon came ROGUE MALE's way courtesy of Music For Nations (their records would be issued through Elektra in the States), who allowed the band to capture an album's worth of material on tape at their leisure. By the time ROGUE MALE were ready to lay down their debut long-player, however, the jittery outfit had already restructured themselves yet again (Aylmer and Aston had flown the coop, the former working with M-80 and then joining a fly-by-night act called HEAD OVER HEELS, while the latter would resurface in TANTRUM), having broken in new members John Fraser Binnie (the ex-DIRTY TRICKS guitarist, a long-time associate of the frontman) and unknown bassist Phillipe Clark to fill in the gaps for the time being. With things apparently back on track, the lads entered the studio towards the end of 1984, and their LP finally hit the shops several months later.

Few people had been privileged enough to hear the music of ROGUE MALE in the run-up to their vinyl debut (the group having *'controversially'* decided not to play live at all until people were familiarised with the material), and nobody really knew what the »First Visit« long-player held in store. With the majority of reviewers favouring the most facile comparisons available to their limited experience, the overwhelming press reaction was to denounce the group as *'MOTÖRHEAD clones'*, an opinion which was largely based on the simplicity and heaviness of straight-ahead numbers such as "Devastation" and "Crazy Motorcycle", although certain other tracks tended, from time to time, to have rather more in common with the likes of WARFARE, DEEP SWITCH, VENOM and MOURNBLADE. Although the rock press remained largely unconvinced by the LP, it wasn't too bad in places, and compositions such as "On The Line" and "All Over You" suggested that there was more to ROGUE MALE than a fundamental desire to play furious music and generally get up people's noses. The publicity-hungry Lyttle was soon being interviewed at every possible opportunity, where he attempted to pass off his latest brainchild as a politically-motivated entity, although his revolutionary stance basically seemed to revolve around the most naive and unconstructive anarcho-punk mentality imaginable, where everything remotely connected with notions of *'government'*, *'authority'* or the *'establishment'* was, by definition, *'bad'*, and anything which involved alcohol, sex, motorbikes or general work avoidance was somehow striking a major blow for the most oppressed sections of society. Like, heavy concepts, man.

Questionable manifestos aside, the outfit were now all set to promote their debut album, and were soon releasing »All Over You« as a 12" EP in a not-terribly-realistic attempt to storm the charts (including a *'radio edit'* doesn't really help when the objectionable lyrics alone preclude any sort of airplay). The lads were also one of the first acts to appear on the 'E.C.T.' television showcase, when the foursome (having now appointed a more permanent bassist in the form of ex-LE GRIFFE stalwart Kev Collier) ran through explosive versions of "Crazy Motorcycle" and "Dressed Incognito" before an audience who, on this particular occasion, actually looked marginally more preposterous than the musicians themselves. All things considered, ROGUE MALE's 'Mad Max'-influenced cyberpunk gear was quite distinctive, but it tended to become something of a serious liability as time went on. Nevertheless, the ensemble were soon making fairly regular appearances on the live circuit, including headlining gigs of their own in both the UK and mainland Europe (they developed a particularly strong following in France, for some unfathomable reason), plus the occasional support slot with dignitaries such as MOTÖRHEAD themselves. In due course, it was decreed that a transatlantic jaunt in the company of a rather more established act would be a prudent idea, although several headliners who were originally targeted as suitable candidates (MÖTLEY CRÜE, RATT and WAYSTED, for instance) repeatedly failed to welcome ROGUE MALE onto their tours with open arms.

Eventually, however, ROGUE MALE managed to get themselves onto a three-band package which saw them touring the States with ILLUSION and SAVATAGE, a poorly-promoted series of gigs which saw their fortunes varying quite considerably from town to town. On balance, however, it was a pretty valuable experience for a group whose previous exploits in the live environment had been somewhat thin on the ground. Before long, ROGUE MALE were back in Britain, and they soon found themselves recording their first session for the short-lived 'Friday Rock Show' offshoot known as 'Into The Music' (considering this show was conceived as a more lightweight alternative, the presence of ROGUE MALE seems utterly baffling), an appearance (broadcast on the 20th of September 1985) which saw the lads performing "On The Line", "Get Off My Back" and "Dressed Incognito" (all from their album), plus the non-LP "Rough Tough (Pretty Too)", the latter being a reworked PRETTY BOY FLOYD AND THE GEMS number which had originally appeared on the »Belfast Rocks« sampler. This more or less marked the final contribution of drummer Steve Kingsley, however, and he was to depart (later working, in a fairly limited capacity, with the rapidly-fading VARDIS) before the outfit had begun recording their second long-player in the early months of 1986. The sticksman's departure appears to have come as something of a surprise, though, leaving the remaining members with little option but to bring in session drummer Charlie Morgan (formerly with the TOM ROBINSON BAND) to assist with their studio activities.

The second ROGUE MALE album, »Animal Man«, appeared in the summer of 1986, the release being promoted by a semi-successful series of headlining UK gigs (by which time they had recruited another full-time drummer, European import Danny Fury). The long-player was slightly more varied and accessible than their debut had been, although the likes of "You're On Fire", "The Real Me" and "Animal Man" were heavy enough to allay any residual fears that the lads might be transmuting into a metal version of SIGUE SIGUE SPUTNIK. Once again, the pseudo-politics continued with the pairing of "Belfast" and "Job Centre", although these selections were sorely lacking in conviction, and seemed to be present only as a matter of obligation, the group (having painted themselves as a socially-conscious ensemble at the outset) being forced to maintain some semblance of political motivation. By this time, however, the initial novelty of the outfit had worn off quite dramatically, and the public failed to send ROGUE MALE hurtling towards the top of the album charts. Once again, a 12" EP was released, this time using "Belfast" as the main track (a version of "Rough Tough (Pretty Too)" finally put in an appearance as a B-side), although it proved to be another fairly disappointing performer in terms of sales.

By the beginning of 1987, Music For Nations had finally decided to reject their option of sponsoring any further ROGUE MALE material, although the plucky quartet remained confident of their own abilities and affirmed their intention to release a third set on one label or another, the prolific band supposedly having sufficient material for at least another two albums at their disposal. They returned to the fray a few months later, having taken time off to assess the situation, brandishing an all-new demo featuring such compositions as "Motorbikin'" (the well-worn CHRIS SPEDDING chestnut, covered by EAZIE RYDER back in 1978), "Rawhide" (based around the original TV show theme), "Rogue Male", "In The Dark" and "Fit To Drop". Clearly, ROGUE MALE weren't ready to give up the fight just yet, and appeared confident that the tape would attract a modicum of interest. In the event, however, it would appear that few record companies of the day saw any fiscal potential whatsoever in bankrolling the career of ROGUE MALE, and, after a few gigs alongside GIRLSCHOOL later in the year and some dismally-attended headlining shows in the spring of 1988 (at which the lads optimistically announced further details of their long-awaited 'comeback album', now tentatively entitled »Danger Zone«), the outfit finally appears to have bitten the dust, the members going their separate ways and rapidly drifting away from any prominent activities in the rock scene thereafter.

LP's
»**First Visit**« Music For Nations 1985/Elektra 1985
[UK/US issue]
»**Animal Man**« Music For Nations 1986/Elektra 1986
[UK/US issue]

12" EP's
»**All Over You**« Music For Nations 1985
[Includes two versions of "All Over You"]
»**Belfast**« Music For Nations 1986
["Rough Tough (Pretty Too)" non-LP]

Compilation Appearances
"**Crazy Motorcycle**" on »Metallergy« LP Bandit Records 1985 + »Welcome To The Metal Zone« Do-LP Music For Nations 1985 + »Metal Killers Kollection II« Do-LP Castle Communications 1986
"**All Over You**" on »Music For Nations-The Singles Album« Do-LP Music For Nations 1986
"**Belfast**" on »Music For Nations-The Singles Album« Do-LP Music For Nations 1986
"**The Passing**" on »Nightmare On Carnaby Street« Do-LP Music For Nations 1988

ROKKA

Glenn Marples (v, g)
Phil Casey (v, rg)
Tony West (g)
Pete Burgin (b)
Simon Freeston (d)

Although Yorkshire's PANZA DIVISION (and, to a lesser extent, the overly-melodic LONELY HEARTS) have become known to a significant proportion of modern-day NWOBHM devotees in recent years (their stories are told in separate entries), comparatively few are familiar with mainman Glenn Marples' earlier vehicle, a small-time bunch called ROKKA. Between 1978 and 1980, the latter were an extremely active unit in terms of live appearances in their locality (cutting their teeth at a selection of not-remotely-famous venues) and were regular fixtures in the pubs and clubs of Sheffield, sharing the limelight with various indie/new wave hopefuls such as PULP (which shows just how long Jarvis Cocker's mob have been on the go!) and ARTERY. They did make it down to London from time to time, however, mostly as a popular support act to the JACKIE LYNTON BAND (a working friendship which would extend well into the PANZA DIVISION days), and enjoyed quite a healthy following of local metalheads. ROKKA's musical direction of choice was a highly accessible mix of STATUS QUO/VARDIS-style boogie (very much tailored for the ubiquitous biker community) with the odd punky touch thrown in, as evidenced by the material featured on their sole 7" from 1980, a record which is now quite a collectable piece.

Having failed to win favour with any of the record labels of the day, the happy-go-lucky quintet decided to give the fans a souvenir to take home from their local gigs, and arranged for a modest, self-financed two-tracker (never issued in a picture sleeve) to be pressed up in fairly limited quantities. ROKKA's unassuming single coupled "Come Back" and "Touch And Go" (both very much in the general manner of PREDATÜR or PHEETUS), a pair of originals which weren't pushing the boundaries of musical or lyrical ingenuity in any sense, but which represented a pretty energetic, down-to-earth ensemble who could please the crowds with little or no effort. Relatively shortly after their debut single's release, however, the main protagonists in the ROKKA venture (Phil Casey and Glenn Marples) decided it was time for them to go their own separate ways, with Marples forming the similarly-inclined PANZA DIVISION (who evolved into the LONELY HEARTS), whereas Casey tried to keep his musical career afloat by hooking up with a couple of (ultimately unsuccessful) club acts. In recent years, though, Casey has been more active in a behind-the-scenes capacity, at one time masterminding Vinyl Tap's much-missed programme of archive NWOBHM reissues before moving over to work for a diverse and long-running label called Celtic Music.

7" Singles
»**Come Back**« Rock Trax Records 1980

ROLLIN' THUNDER

Ian Erics (v, b)
Robert Brown (g)
Ian Brown (d)

A bit of a weird one, this, a NWOBHM-era act who seem to have been attempting a kind of indie/rock crossover, which wasn't a particularly common style at the time. The band in question are the relatively obscure ROLLIN' THUNDER, a quirky bunch who were presumably based in Yorkshire (given that their contact address was in Sheffield), although most of their live activities seem to have taken place in the North West. Either they had namesakes in Merseyside, or they were inexplicably fond of touring in and around the Liverpool area. Anyway, the trio were active for much of the 80's, but took their time getting to the vinyl stage, and initially made their mark with a couple of unassuming releases on (presumably their own label) the very metal-sounding Hells Kitchen Records. The first of these was the »Too Loose« 7" from 1984, a curious concoction which brings to mind some of the more borderline or new wave-influenced groups of the period (such as T34, SKITZOFRENIK or the IDLE FLOWERS) without ever threatening to explode into a full-on metal assault. It's a passable effort if you're open to more restrained musings (if not, skip to the next entry forthwith), and the A-side represents a reasonably rocking, mid-paced number, while the reverse ("Devil May Care") has more of a laid-back, bluesy edge to it. You'll have gathered that this wasn't anything like a typical NWOBHM single (it even features my least favourite instrument, the dreaded saxophone, but in mercifully small doses), although the two-tracker is just about worth picking up (it came in an unremarkable picture sleeve featuring a blurry 'live action' shot) if you ever see a copy at a knock-down price.

The following year, the three-piece returned to the fore by releasing a mini-album on the same label, although this six track effort (»Lonesome«) was a patchy affair, to be honest, and failed to show the group in particularly favourable light. Side one was especially disappointing, with none of the featured selections really hitting the mark (too moody for their own good), although "Bloodstained Legends" was passable, I suppose. The reverse was markedly more upbeat and listenable, with inclusions such as "Wrecked Black Car" and "Street Of Lost Causes" bringing forth some tentative comparisons with the likes of GARBO and HARLEQUYN, but it's still slightly too restrained for comfort, and you get the distinct impression that the lads were just itching to throw caution to the wind and become a semi-sleazy proposition. To be frank, they would probably have been better-advised to transform themselves into a more overtly raunchy act in the manner of the GUNSLINGERS et al., as they really fell between two stools as far as their musical direction was concerned. It wasn't sufficiently indie to win favour with the HAPPY MONDAYS/STONE ROSES cro-wd, and too ambiguous to see them making inroads into the conventional rock scene, so it's hard to tell which market they were actually aiming to crack.

Nevertheless, the lads must have impressed a few influential parties in the music industry, and ultimately won a contract with none other than Flicknife, who had experimented with a number of semi-metal propositions (RED RAGE, UNDERGROUND ZERO et al.) over the years and had given MOURNBLADE their initial vinyl exposure, so they must have felt pretty confident of their ability to mould ROLLIN' THUNDER into a more coherent musical entity with which to take the world by storm. Along the way, the chaps brought in a fourth member, Nick Styran, who immediately assumed bass duties and allowed frontman Ian Erics to strum away on rhythm guitar to his heart's content. A full album hit the shops in 1987, although »Howl« showed little or no genuine progress, and it even recycled one or two of the better numbers from the mini-LP, which, sadly enough, tended to outclass the newer efforts completely. Overall, the band's general style was still far too polite and repressed (I suppose tracks like "Once…" had their moments, but most of you still wouldn't give this album the time of day), and it was now only too apparent that the participants were never going to rock out in major fashion after all. With the long-player dying a death in terms of sales, the Flicknife deal soon went up in flames, and ROLLIN' THUNDER eventually followed suit, although they plugged away until the end of the decade, for reasons best known to themselves.

LP's
»Howl« Flicknife 1987

Mini-LP's
»Lonesome« Hells Kitchen Records 1985

7" Singles
»Too Loose« Hells Kitchen Records 1984
[Both tracks non-LP]

ROUGH JUSTICE (I)

John Wallace (v, b)
Fudge Forsyth (g)
Richie Carlin (g)
Jim Wallace (d)

Some outfits had to struggle against considerable odds just to make their existence known amidst the massive influx of new acts at the height of the NWOBHM explosion, and those in remote parts of the country often had more difficulty than most. Well, you really don't get much more remote than the Outer Hebrides (yes, honestly), a sparsely-populated group of islands off the West Coast of Scotland. Understandably, this region has comparatively little in the way of musical heritage, and most of their home-grown talent (clearly, the greatest Hebridean success story was RUNRIG) would undoubtedly have been inclined towards traditional folky territory. Not so in the case of ROUGH JUSTICE, however, a four-piece who claim to have released the first (and probably the last) rock single from the area. Surprisingly, this was way back in 1979, so it's hard to believe that they were attempting to jump on the NWOBHM bandwagon, although it's always difficult to judge how far and how quickly word of this exciting new metal scene actually got around in the early days. Anyway, the outfit somehow managed to scrape together just enough cash to lay down a single (I haven't a clue where it might have been recorded or pressed, though), and their two-tracker was unleashed upon an unsuspecting (and, in all probability, utterly bewildered) local audience at some point thereafter.

To be honest, it's not exactly a ground-breaking example of accomplished musicianship, original ideas or the general NWOBHM archetype, but you have to cut them some slack just for getting the thing out in the first place. The A-side, "Black Knight" (subtitled *A Gothic Legend*), is a semi-listenable, mid-paced number with occasional similarities to SKITZOFRENIK, MITHRANDIR or OMEN SEARCHER, although it's all quite ramshackle for the most part. The reverse ("White Dove") is pretty poor, though, a slower effort which seems to drag on for an eternity without ever going anywhere or threatening to become interesting. I suspect that the single (no picture sleeve) was pressed in absolutely minuscule quantities, given that their local fan base presumably consisted of a few easily-entertained shepherds and several very confused sheep. If the quartet ever managed to play any gigs at all (it's quite possible that they might have relocated to the mainland at one point or another), I'd imagine that the attendance would have been pretty modest, but no doubt the musicians enjoyed themselves while it lasted. Amazingly, ROUGH JUSTICE did apparently receive a bit of airplay on remote stations and on Radio Scotland, so at least they had a very limited taste of success, even if stations further afield were rather less charitable in their patronage of these small-time hopefuls. Needless to say, you'll encounter this esoteric two-tracker once in a blue moon, and I shudder to think what price the dealers would attach to it.

7" Singles
»Black Knight« Croft Records 1979

ROUGH JUSTICE (II)

Biz Meir (v)
Jon Lacey (g)
Pete Lee (g)
Tim Lacey (b)
Gavin Watts (d)

Another bunch of hopefuls who adopted the vastly over-subscribed moniker of ROUGH JUSTICE were a young, female-fronted quintet from Buckinghamshire, who got in on the act towards the end of the NWOBHM boom. There appears to be little evidence of their activities on the regional scene before the end of 1984, so it seems likely that they didn't come into existence until earlier that year. In spite of their reasonably forceful-sounding name, however, they were one of the more lightweight propositions of Britain's rock scene at the time, operating in a fairly similar style to the likes of SHE and RUNESTAFF, for example. The band seem to have spent quite some time working the regional clubs in their formative days, no doubt building up a reputation as crowd-pleasers and secretly hoping that some influential record company executives might become aware of their existence before long. It looks as though the outfit suffered the usual label indifference for a year or two in the first instance, however, although they eventually took the bull by the horns and achieved their vinyl destiny with a self-financed three-tracker which probably hit the shops at some point in 1986, although I suppose it might possibly have materialised very late the previous year.

The ROUGH JUSTICE 7" contained three largely uninspiring and entirely unremarkable selections, to be honest, opening with the undeniably catchy semi-pop of "Million To One" before moving on to the marginally more impressive "Wandering Heartache", one of those compositions which begins promisingly enough but which soon turns into a rather lumpen attempt at something fairly anthemic. To its credit, this number featured a semi-competent instrumental section to break the monotony, although it still comes across as slightly clumsy in view of the group's rudimentary musicianship. On the reverse was "Broken Dreams", the kind of interminably long and dreary ballad which barely warrants space on *any* record, let alone a rock EP, so that was probably a mistake. All in all, it was an inoffensive release (compared to the likes of TOKYO ROSE and WITCHES BREW, for example), but one which failed to sell in particularly significant quantities. It's a rare piece nowadays, admittedly, but it appears to be utterly reviled by the majority of collectors, a situation which is slightly unfair, especially when there are *far* worse offerings from the same period. To be honest, I suspect that this is more of a backlash resulting from the incredibly high price which some dealers have attached to the record, proclaiming it to be a NWOBHM classic when it is nothing of the sort. If you want to vent your anger, blame the dealers, not the musicians!

The activities of this particular ROUGH JUSTICE had pretty much ground to a halt by the end of 1986, the members presumably having decided that there was little future for the band unless they reinvented themselves pretty drastically. Vocalist Biz Meir and guitarist Jon Lacey were eventually to be found lending their services to local rivals RUNAWAY STRAY, a fairly anonymous bunch who persevered for a couple of years but who never really had any serious prospects of getting anywhere. By the early 90's, all of the one-time members appear to have drifted away from the music scene for good, not that this was a massive loss to the nation, to be honest. If you're actively looking for a copy of the self-financed ROUGH JUSTICE 7", meanwhile, it was issued in an eye-catching red sleeve featuring the band's logo, and it's an item which you should, in all likelihood, be able to locate at a far more reasonable price than certain individuals are in the habit of charging.

7" EP's
»Million To One« Rough Justice Records 1986?

ROX

Mark Anthony (v)
Ian Burke (g)
Paul Hopwood (g)
Gary Maunsell (b)
Tony Fitzgerald (d)

Mancunian glamsters ROX (not to be confused with a pop act who were also recording in the early 80's) started out (originally under the name of, er, VENOM) at around the same time as their local contemporaries SILVERWING, and the two outfits rapidly established a close musical alliance which would continue for several years. After finding their feet by writing and gigging throughout 1980, VENOM recorded a demo tape early the following year, featuring "Loser", "City Streets", "Get Out" and "Are You Ready", tracks (very much in the SILVERWING vein, you won't be remotely surprised to hear) which would soon be given further exposure in the form of a session for the band's local station, Piccadilly Radio. In May 1981, the lucky outfit appeared at the U.M.I.S.T. Metal Festival, alongside SILVERWING, SACRED ALIEN, TORA TORA and DIAMOND HEAD, giving an impressive and confident performance even at this early stage. Shortly thereafter, drummer Tony Fitzgerald decided that glam just wasn't his bag after all, and left to form his own jazz-rock venture. *Nice*. In no time at all, however, the lads recruited Bernie Nuttall (previously with the ludicrously-named WIFFER) to the fold, but it soon became apparent that, with the proliferation of bands named VENOM, some drastic action was called for. Towards the end of the year, fed up with being asked to play "In League With Satan" at gigs (well, it's a good yarn, even if it wasn't strictly true), the outfit duly reinvented themselves as ROX (which wasn't a unique choice either, but never mind) and recruited a new vocalist, Kevin Read, who soon revealed himself to be a worthy occupant of the position of frontman.

Moving into 1982, the revamped group recorded a brand-new demo with the truly shameless title of »Ass-Kickin Krazies«, featuring a generous seven tracks, including newer compositions such as "Hot On Your Trax" and "Dressed To Kill". By this time, the outfit had gained enough of a reputation through their live activities that a vinyl offering had become a reality, although a severe lack of record company interest meant that this would have to be a self-financed affair. The first ROX 7" emerged as a three track EP, by which time the members had bowed to rigid glam convention and adopted some fairly embarrassing aliases: Kevin Read was now 'Kick-Ass Kev Kozak', Ian Burke was 'Red Hot Red', Bernie Nuttall was 'Bernie Emerald' and Paul Hopwood was 'Paul Diamond', while Gary Maunsell was now operating under the hilariously preposterous pseudonym of, er, 'Gary Maunsell'. Erm, bit of a cock-up there, lads. Never mind, the record (issued in an unremarkable sleeve with logo, titles and small individual photos) featured "Love Ya Like A Dia-

mond", "Hot Love In The City" and "Do Ya Feel Like Lovin'", three efforts which, although not quite as over-the-top as WRATHCHILD, were very much in the Brit-glam style of SILVERWING or FORGER. Happily, the EP proceeded to sell quite respectably, although ROX would never ascend to the same level of adulation as SILVERWING, for some reason.

By the end of the year, the group had already sacked bassist Gary Maunsell for his persistent inability to think up a suitably naff soubriquet, whereupon they invited new bloke Billy Beaman (whose own name was already sufficiently silly that he wasn't required to change it) to join in the fun and games. By the early months of 1983, the ROX lads had played a few more gigs with old mates SILVERWING, and eventually swung a deal (supposedly taking the form of a three year contract) with Music For Nations, who tested the water by allowing the outfit to record a 12" EP later in the year. The »Krazy Kutz« three-tracker immortalised "Sweet Sixteen" (easily the weakest of the three), "Sidewalk Strutter" and "Shock Rockin'", all of which were much in the vein of their earlier release. Again, their EP sold quite healthily, making it into various rock charts, although the ambitious outfit were now starting to wonder whether they might enjoy an even greater level of commercial success if they were to bring in a slightly less limited vocalist. In due course, therefore, Kozak was invited to leave (he later formed a short-lived electro-pop outfit called KOZAKADE, alongside SILVERWING's Stuart MacFarlane, who were, in all honesty, utterly abysmal), and original vocalist Mark Anthony (now reinvented as 'Mark Savage') was brought back into the ranks for a second bite at the cherry.

The 'new' frontman was given the opportunity to show the world his vocal talents on the group's first full-length effort (»Violent Breed«), recorded for the benefit of Music For Nations towards the end of that year. It turned out to be a surprisingly varied affair (more hard rock/metal than out-and-out glam on the majority of numbers featured), with something of a nod towards one or two of the more high-profile American scene-stealers of the day. "I Wanna Be A Hero", for example, could quite easily pass for an ALICE COOPER original, while "Wild And Crazy" even creeps into W.A.S.P. territory, whereas the genuinely excellent pairing of "Say Goodbye To Love" and "Daylight Robbery" (where ROX really hit their stride) are probably closer to »On Through The Night«-era DEF LEPPARD than most people would probably care to admit. Elsewhere, such effortlessly catchy efforts as the capable "Jailbait" and "Violation" (both quite individualistic compositions) were lifted considerably by the performance of their recently-acquired vocalist, making for a highly enjoyable listening experience throughout. All in all, the debut album was a significantly stronger and more consistent effort than many observers (working on the basis of their earlier releases) seem to have predicted the ROX lads would deliver.

While »Violent Breed« should have been the record which propelled ROX several rungs up the ladder of success, they struggled to retain any kind of momentum during 1984, despite hitching a ride on the QUIET RIOT tour, and they were to be one of the many victims of the great glam/sleaze famine of the mid-80's, where many acts of that ilk either sought to change their image (SILVERWING), lay low for a while (WRATHCHILD) or to call it a day for good (the GUNSLINGERS, the IDLE FLOWERS, FORGER and so forth). In the event, ROX drifted apart in the second half of 1985 (having struggled to continue after Paul Diamond's departure several months previously), their farewell local gig (where they performed alongside the long-forgotten FIRECLOWN) taking place towards the end of the year. Of the one-time members, only Paul Diamond (it looks as though he actually preferred his stage name) later resurfaced (his original intention of establishing an act called JAILBAIT appears to have fallen through pretty rapidly), this time in Liverpudlian AOR merchants TORINO (originally GRAN TORINO), although his new-found career didn't last beyond the recording of their second album.

LP's
»Violent Breed« Music For Nations

1983/Roadrunner 1983
[UK/Dutch issue]

12" EP's
»Hot Love In The City« Roadrunner 1983
[European reissue of debut 7" EP]
»Krazy Kutz« Music For Nations 1983
[All three tracks non-LP]

7" EP's
»Hot Love In The City« Teenteeze Records 1982
["Love Ya Like A Diamond" different to album version, both "Hot Love In The City" and "Do Ya Feel Like Lovin'" non-LP]

Compilation Appearances
"Love Ya Like A Diamond" on »Hell On Earth« LP Music For Nations 1983 + »British Steel« LP M Port Records 1984/Steel Trax 1986
"Daylight Robbery" on »British Steel« LP M Port Records 1984/Steel Trax 1986
"Sweet Sixteen" on »Music For Nations-The Singles Album« Do-LP Music For Nations 1986

RUNESTAFF

Joanne Syme (v)
Wayne Moyez (g)
Andy Page (g)
Jamie Durrant (b)
Kaust Rakhit (k)
Kevin Hunt (d)

East Anglia's RUNESTAFF initially got off the ground towards the end of 1982, when a bunch of local musicians came together with the hope of achieving something a bit special. Among their ranks was bassist Jamie Durrant, formerly of THE ANGELS (another long-forgotten rock/metal outfit from the same neck of the woods), an act who had not only shared a stage with IRON MAIDEN on more than one occasion, but who had additionally performed at the Reading Festival of 1982, although they ultimately failed to release any vinyl product of their own. With RUNESTAFF having already issued a brace of speculative demos of melodic semi-NWOBHM by the latter half of 1983, the youngsters duly attracted the attention of Sane Records in North Wales, who were assembling their own compilation of (predominantly local) hopefuls, and so the lucky outfit were invited to contribute to the scarcely-sighted »It's Unheard Of!« sampler in 1984. With its gentle-but-confident personality, "The Games You Play" (a number later featured on the »NWOBHM Vol.5« bootleg CD, incidentally) was a perfectly respectable addition to the album (vaguely reminiscent of LYADRIVE or IONA at their most lightweight), and the group certainly outshone several of the more forceful no-hopers featured.

Within a few months of this initial exposure, the band had been picked up by the Heavy Metal concern (who, like Ebony, had rather lost their sense of identity by this time), who arranged to issue RUNESTAFF's eponymous debut long-player (recorded at The Chapel in Lincolnshire and produced by RED ALERT's Rick Woolgar) shortly thereafter. By this juncture, however, a female vocalist had already been introduced into the ranks (the identity of her

predecessor is currently unknown, although the LP sleeve credits a 'former colleague' named 'Ade') in the form of one Joanne Syme, whose style was, to be frank, slightly at odds with the outfit's direction of choice. As a consequence, the album (which features a reworked version of "The Games You Play") is something of an oddity, grotesquely poppy in places (almost hitting TOKYO ROSE territory), more ethereal on selections such as the CANIS MAJOR-soundalike "Road To Ruin", and, with the possible exception of the reasonably listenable "Runestaff" itself, just plain dull elsewhere. A major anticlimax after the initial promise shown on their compilation appearance, but never mind. A couple of singles (featuring album tracks exclusively) were issued by the FM label in an attempt to help sales of the long-player along, although the stratagem appears to have misfired entirely.

Following on from several crushing reviews in the rock press (and from the tragic death of keyboard player Kaust Rakhit, who succumbed to a rare medical condition shortly after the album had been recorded), RUNESTAFF decided to take stock of the situation and make a last-ditch attempt at getting their career back on the rails. They duly tried out a few new ideas (having now recruited keyboard player Barry Godfrey) and toured sporadically throughout 1986 (by which time guitarist Andy Page had flown the coop to go back to college), although their activities were, evidently, constantly hampered by Joanne Syme's continual throat problems, which eventually required surgical intervention. Against all odds, however, RUNESTAFF persevered until 1987, whereupon they finally conceded that their quest for critical appreciation was now a lost cause. Drummer Kevin Hunt went on to join a somewhat unsuccessful project called ELYSIAN FIELDS, before working with another long-forgotten bunch called the THIEVING GYPSIES, while Jamie Durrant moved on to an unpromisingly-named venture known as SITTIN PRETTY (yes, they were a glam band), although the rest of their former associates appear to have quit the music scene altogether after a couple of abortive attempts to establish some new outfits and (oddly enough) instigate an ill-fated RUNESTAFF reformation in 1989.

LP's
»Runestaff« Heavy Metal 1985

7" Singles
»Road To Ruin« FM Records 1985
»Do It!« FM Records 1985

Compilation Appearances
"The Games You Play" on »It's Unheard Of!« LP Sane Records 1984 + »NWOBHM Vol.5« Bootleg CD 1992
[Different to LP version]

SABRE

Nick Pyatt (v)
Nick Fusco (g)
Alan Beschi (g)
Geoff Gillespie (b)
Allan Angold (d)

Surrey's excellent SABRE (one of several outfits to assume the name both in the UK and elsewhere, notably a Home Counties group who were on the go for most of the 80's) were fortunate enough to be picked up by the Neat label at the height of its powers, and were initially rewarded with an enviable opportunity to record a contribution to the »60 Minutes Plus« sampler towards the end of 1982. Prior to that, however, the outfit had been on the go (without a great deal of success or recognition) since late 1980, their first demo (featuring the vocals of a certain Nick Pyatt) having failed to solicit all that much interest from the record companies of the day. With the musicians eventually deciding that the problem lay with their unfortunate frontman, Pyatt received the grand order of the boot in the latter half of 1981 and was replaced by ex-PREACHER vocalist Rob Brown. Sadly, the latest singer didn't come up to scratch either, and was soon succeeded by John Ward (whose *curriculum vitae* included a stint with ANGEL WITCH, no less, although there seems little evidence to support this claim), who evidently fitted in much better. With the talented Ward lifting SABRE's material to a higher level, a brand-new demo was circulated, and, after two separate features in the 'Armed And Ready' section of 'Kerrang', the relationship with Neat came about in due course.

The capable "Cry To The Wind", SABRE's powerful contribution to Neat's aforementioned sampler, turned out to be a cracking effort with a solid vocal performance and duelling guitars (which would, inevitably, lead to facile IRON MAIDEN comparisons coming from many quarters), although the overall sound was actually more in tune with the likes of PERSIAN RISK, VIRTUE and early TYGERS OF PAN TANG. Following on from their debut appearance on this cassette-only release (although a slightly abridged version of the sampler also appeared on vinyl in Europe as the »All Hell Let Loose« set), the band (who were, by this time, already becoming something of a popular attraction in the rock-friendly clubs of London and Surrey) were given their own 7" release by the label, a record which appeared in the early part of 1983. Both "Miracle Man" and "On The Loose" were extremely energetic workouts with interesting, memorable riffing, although there appeared to be rather less of a reliance upon twin-guitar sections than before. In terms of Neat's patchy programme of 7" releases, however, it was certainly one of the company's strongest two-trackers of all time, and brisk sales reflected the fact that SABRE had plenty of potential which would surely shine through if they were given some gentle encouragement, allowed to develop at their own pace and ultimately deliver a full album.

As with so many metal outfits of the era, though, it looks as though SABRE had already run out of steam within a matter of months of their debut hitting the shops (a significant number of small-time hopefuls clearly assumed that a sole 7" single would almost certainly be the pinnacle of their career and suffered motivational problems thereafter), with bassist Geoff Gillespie soon deciding to move on to pastures new, whereupon SABRE ceased to exist more or less immediately. In the end, he joined up with vocalist Noel Jones in an ill-fated attempt to get a new version of the latter's STATIC off the ground before eventually starting his own project in the form of the overly-melodic SNOWBLIND (see separate entry). I reckon SABRE unquestionably had a lot more to offer the world, though, and feel slightly cheated by their all-too-rapid demise. Indeed, if they had made a concerted effort to hang onto a semi-decent vocalist and then somehow inveigled their way onto an ego-boosting tour alongside a more high-profile act, I've absolutely no doubt that these musicians could have achieved far greater success in the long term.

7" Singles
»Miracle Man« Neat 1983

Exclusive Compilation Appearances
"Cry To The Wind" on »60 Minutes Plus« Cassette Neat 1982/CD Teichiku 1992 + »All Hell Let Loose« LP Neat 1983

SACRED ALIEN

Sean Canning (v)
Martin Ainscow (g, k)
Dave Clowes (b)
Chris Lea (d)

Manchester's extraordinary SACRED ALIEN were a band far ahead of their time, a fact which, unfortunately, resulted in them being lumped in with the likes of SILVERWING, ROX etc. in the 'heavy glam' category. In fact, their own material was considerably more technical (the similarity to some aspects of the RUSH sound was identified at an early stage) and accomplished than this narrow-minded pigeonholing would suggest, their general direction being far better represented by tentative comparisons with KRAKEN (in particular), JUNO's CLAW, HELL or MARQUIS DE SADE. The youthful quartet originally came together in October 1980, based around the nucleus of Sean Canning and Chris Lea, two friends who had gravitated together at art college. The line-up was completed in the first instance by guitarist Martin Ainscow and bassist Dave Clowes, and the musicians ensured

that the name of SACRED ALIEN would rapidly become synonymous with adventurous music, a quirky image and energetic, semi-theatrical live appearances. Their first demo tape, issued in the early months of 1981, featured such intriguing numbers as "Portrait", "Eternal Flame", "Both Sides Of The Globe" and "Energy", these compositions going down particularly well with regional audiences and soon gaining useful airplay on their local station, Piccadilly Radio. In due course, the lads were added to the bill of the U.M.I.S.T. Metal Festival in their home town of Manchester, alongside DIAMOND HEAD, TORA TORA, SILVERWING and ROX (still known as VENOM in those days), and they successfully opened the day's proceedings on behalf of the better-known acts who followed.

Towards the end of the year, having been given some valuable early exposure in the 'Armed And Ready' section of 'Kerrang', the lads managed to get their debut vinyl release into the shops, an enjoyably-heavy 7" single (a self-financed affair, needless to say) which featured "Spiritual Planet" and old demo favourite "Energy". The technical, unpredictable arrangements, combined with the rather mystical/cosmic lyrical viewpoint and genuinely distinctive vocal performance from the precocious frontman all served to distinguish SACRED ALIEN as something far removed from the NWOBHM norm, and the fans were suitably impressed by their collective talents. The two-tracker, issued in an unassuming sleeve showing the musicians 'performing' on a suspiciously sparse-looking stage, sold in extremely impressive quantities (despite being severely hindered by an atrocious production job) throughout the North of England and beyond, suggesting that the lads had a lucrative musical career ahead of them. Unfortunately, however, their rhythm section jumped ship in the first half of 1982, the very point at which the group intended to capitalise on the success of their single with a wide-ranging tour. By the summer, however, things had rectified themselves following the recruitment of bassist Paul Davies and drummer Darren Wilcock, the group proceeding to gig sporadically and record new demos at various studio sessions.

Over the following months, the foursome well and truly got back into the swing of things, and had soon re-established their presence on the rock scene, whereupon several observers tipped SACRED ALIEN as a name to watch in future. They duly outlined their collective plans in an interview at the beginning of 1983, with frontman Sean Canning revealing their constant struggle to attract major label interest: "We have had a mild response, but nothing too great. Kamaflage Records are typical. They told us our music wasn't right, that bands like TANK are where it's at-all that denim and leather and a 'one of the lads' attitude." (Ref: Kerrang No.34, January 1983). Those live outings still continued apace, however, a notable inclusion being the group's memorable appearance at the Salford Glamfest a couple of months later, where the lads shared a hurriedly-assembled bill with the likes of SILVERWING, CLOVEN HOOF and the long-forgotten CHINA ROGUE. Despite the fact that such activities served merely to enforce the unfortunate *'glam'* stereotype from which they were initially keen to distance themselves, SACRED ALIEN continued to delight the assembled masses pretty much wherever they played (they began venturing further afield, making it down to London on occasion), continually adding to their extensive repertoire, which now included such varied compositions as "Nightmares In Paradise", "Attack" and "Do You See Me". The fans were treated to most of these new numbers in due course, as well as popular covers such as the ever-dependable "20th Century Boy" by T.REX and "Foxy Lady" by JIMI HENDRIX.

By mid-1983, however, the lads had more or less given up waiting for a record deal to materialise, and announced imminent plans to release their second single, scheduled to take the form of another self-financed affair. In the event, this never came about in its envisaged form, although the group (by this time featuring yet another rhythm section in the form of drummer Mark Robo and erstwhile TORA TORA bassist John Murney) subsequently featured on an unusual split 7" single (issued on the Heighway Robbery Wreckords label, which their long-serving manager had recently set up himself) alongside Yorkshire's decidedly dodgy glam/pop hopefuls VIRGIN (who, incidentally, also contributed to the rare »Parkside Steelworks« sampler but ultimately failed to release any vinyl product of their own), issued in a fold-open picture sleeve showing the pair of cosmetically-enhanced acts involved. SACRED ALIEN's contribution was the catchy "Legends", a fine effort which benefits considerably from an immeasurably more capable production than had been the case on their debut two-tracker. It's just a shame we're subjected to VIRGIN's awful number on the reverse, when another SACRED ALIEN original would surely have been a better idea…maybe VIRGIN stumped up half the recording costs?

It would appear that the ill-conceived split single (pretty much the only example of such an item from the NWOBHM era) didn't exactly change SACRED ALIEN's fortunes for the better, and, by the early months of 1984, the lads had finally drifted apart for good. Their second drummer, Darren Wilcock, later resurfaced in the ranks of the similarly-inclined TRAXX (see separate entry), while the talented Sean Canning wasted little time in getting his WHITE TRASH project of the ground, an act with rather more of a punky attitude and a RAMONES-influenced sound. The latter outfit persevered for a few years, gigging productively throughout the North of England and winning over a minority of rock fans in the process, but finally ground to a halt when bassist Johnny Vincent elected to join forces with former TIGERTAILZ frontman Steevi Jaimz in his predictably sleazy ST.JAIMZ venture towards the end of the decade. In the early 90's, however, there were reports that certain (unspecified) ex-SACRED ALIEN personnel had formed a brand-new act called COLD SHOT, who were scheduled to release a mini-album shortly thereafter, although nothing seems to have come of it in the long term. Both of SACRED ALIEN's scarce vinyl releases, meanwhile, are highly rated by NWOBHM connoisseurs, and have (deservedly) been viewed as collectable, mid-priced rarities for a considerable number of years.

7" Singles
»**Spiritual Planet**« Greenwood Music 1981
[Labels on wrong sides, most with stickered amendments]
»**Legends**« Heighway Robbery Wreckords 1983
[Split single, backed with "Sittin' In The Front Row" by VIRGIN]

SAIGON

Keys
McClelland

Although numerous outfits (mostly from overseas) opted for the handle SAIGON throughout the 80's, I reckon the only NWOBHM-era rock act from Britain (the Scottish bunch who recorded for the Ryme Tyme label, for example, operated in more of an electro-pop style) were the small-time Irish group who came out of nowhere and offered the world a private 7" in 1981. Issued on their own Heartbeat label (not to be confused with the established company from the West of England who were responsible for records by the likes of STORMTROOPER), the low-budget single (presented in an anonymous-looking sleeve and with equally functional labels) is an unremarkable offering, to be honest, and would probably only appeal to a fairly limited percentage of NWOBHM enthusiasts or collectors. "Times Like These" (labelled, a tad optimistically, as the 'fast side') is unquestionably the better of the pair, a mid-paced, melodic effort with occasional keyboard backing and reasonably competent guitar work in places, overall reminiscent of obscure contemporaries such as BILL THE MURDERER, WILDSMITH ST. or RED, although probably more in keeping with the musical mediocrity of the late 70's than with the more raucous NWOBHM mentality. On the other hand, "Rip It Up And Start Again" (you guessed it, the 'slow side') is an uninspiring and dismal semi-ballad which ultimately fails to leave a favourable impression, so I don't imagine that this introductory slice of vinyl opened too many doors for SAIGON.

Having said that, it transpires that the band remained on the regional rock scene for another year or two, the musicians presumably taking to the stage whenever the possibility arose, as well as contributing an exclusive studio session or two for some of their local radio stations. In fact, concrete evidence of such activities can be found on the scarce »Now In Session« compilation, assembled by Downtown Radio at some point in 1982. SAIGON's selection, a catchy affair entitled "Crackin' Up", was a decent enough effort, although failing to shine particularly brightly in the presence of strong local competition from SWEET SAVAGE, SPITTIN' IMAGE and PSYCHO. Still, it confirmed that the lads were happy enough to keep plugging away in their eternal quest for that elusive big break, although it looks as though predictably few major labels came knocking, leaving the various protagonists to go their separate ways thereafter. All in all, SAIGON's hopelessly obscure debut single (which has the look of a vinyl demo or a promo-only release, but which may indeed have represented a commercial issue) is really only for the fanatical completist, and probably wouldn't go very far towards justifying the huge price tag that most dealers would no doubt attach to it at the earliest opportunity.

7" Singles
»Times Like These« Heartbeat Records 1981

Exclusive Compilation Appearances
"Crackin' Up" on »Now In Session« LP Downtown Radio 1982

SALEM

Simon Saxby (v)
Paul Macnamara (g)
Mark Allison (g)
Adrian Jenkinson (b)
Paul Conyers (d)

With Humberside's ETHEL THE FROG having ultimately been little more than a tax write-off for the giant EMI label, high hopes were pinned on the follow-up project conceived by Paul Conyers and Paul Tognola. SALEM, as they were christened, having spent most of 1980 finding their feet and achieving a stable line-up (Tognola himself departed after a few months), laid down a demo tape in 1981 which featured the original efforts "Coming For You", "Cold As Steel", "Fool's Gold" and "Make The Grade". The compositions were, in the main, enjoyable examples of mid-paced NWOBHM (slightly heavier than most of ETHEL THE FROG's material,

perhaps, but a logical progression, nonetheless) in the general style of OMEN SEARCHER, BASHFUL ALLEY or REINCARNATE, and paved the way for what should have been a healthy career in the metal-friendly world of the early 80's. After some tentative gigging with other emergent hopefuls in their locality and throughout Yorkshire, the lads gradually built up an enviable repertoire of self-penned numbers, and must have been confident of garnering a record deal with one of the recently-established concerns such as Heavy Metal or Ebony, especially when they began to attract some favourable publicity in the rock press.

A full year later, however, despite having been promoted in the 'Armed And Ready' section of

'Kerrang' in the interim, the unlucky quintet had still received no firm offers, and so the plucky SALEM proceeded to issue an introductory single entitled »Reach To Eternity« (b/w "Cold As Steel"), an endeavour which they financed themselves and released on their own Hilton label. Having toughened up the sound quite a bit, the band now appeared to represent more of a power metal proposition, the twin-guitar interplay and soaring vocals on "Reach To Eternity" suggesting a style that tended to reflect certain heavier European groups such as H-BOMB, for example, rather than the sort of thing that most British-based outfits (with the notable exception of JUDAS PRIEST and IRON MAIDEN) were attempting at the time. For what it's worth, I'd say that "Cold As Steel" is a tad more powerful than the demo version, too, so it seems to have been a genuine move into more hard-hitting territory. Most copies of the single were issued without sleeves, incidentally, but a handful came wrapped in an oversized, fold-round jacket depicting a demonic visage and the band logo (which was reproduced, in miniature, on the label). Either way, the 7" (which earned a placing in the 'Local Chart' section of 'Kerrang' later that year) is a highly collectable and valuable rarity today.

After comparatively successful sales of the 7", the lads tried out some fresh ideas and kept their fingers crossed that a deal might yet come in their direction. A further SALEM demo surfaced in around 1983, featuring a selection of new numbers such as "Rock Fever", "Save The Night", "The Other Side Of Hell", "Hangman's Noose" and "The King (Part 3)". In spite of a couple of extremely promising song titles, however, the latest material actually turned out to be quite melodic and (compared with the considerably more forceful single) rather more in keeping with some of the outfit's early compositions. There were still some reasonably heavy moments, nevertheless, and the individual songs were all competently performed, although the overall sound now tended more towards acts such as RHABSTALLION, DEALER and MIDAS than anything more substantial. Sadly, this direction doesn't seem to have won the lads too many additional friends, although they were certainly more than deserving of a deal with their local Ebony label, for example, especially considering some of the dross that the company had on their books over the years. It seemed that SALEM had already missed their only chance to make a significant impression on the rock world, and were soon on the slippery slope to destruction.

With the disillusioned and critically-overlooked SALEM having presumably disbanded by the middle of the decade at the latest, Adrian Jenkinson shifted his alliances and formed the melodic rock proposition MAYFAIR in 1987, an accessible outfit who issued a five track mini-LP entitled »Roll Out The Dice« two years later. Mind you, apart from the fact that erstwhile SALEM vocalist Simon Saxby co-wrote one of the songs (he was originally a member of the new outfit, but had been replaced by John Lynas by the time their record was issued), however, there's little to connect this unashamedly commercial venture with the heavy music of SALEM, so you shouldn't be under any illusions that this was some sort of genuine follow-up. For some reason (friends in high places, perhaps), though, MAYFAIR received some remarkably kind reviews in the rock press, before being offered enviable studio time in the States and the opportunity to record a full album at their leisure, but it looks as though things just didn't work out for them in the long run, mirroring the SALEM situation pretty closely. It's a cruel world.

7" Singles
»Reach To Eternity« Hilton Records 1982

Compilation Appearances
"Reach To Eternity" on »NWOBHM Vol.6« Bootleg CD 1992

SAMSON

Paul Samson (v, g, k)
Chris Aylmer (b)
Clive Burr (d)

The lengthy and convoluted history of the much-loved SAMSON could fill a sizeable volume on its own, but you should be able to get the gist of things from this abridged version. The group were the metal vision of mainman Paul Samson, a talented guitarist who had first picked up his mighty axe at a ridiculously early age, and who finally started finding his way into proper bands in the mid-70's or thereabouts, forming a long-term alliance with the much-travelled (not to mention imposing) bassist John McCoy shortly thereafter. The multi-talented duo first dabbled together in a knockabout, bluesy act which had emerged from the earlier John McCoy/Bernie Tormé vehicle SCRAPYARD, whose small-time activities on the capital's music scene were largely swamped by the massive publicity overkill which surrounded the phenomenon of the rapidly-developing punk culture. By the spring of 1977, however, Samson and McCoy (ably assisted by drummer Roger Hunt) instigated something of a backlash against the all-conquering punk upstarts of the day, and (originally under the functional name of McCOY) began writing some heavy tunes (one of their first being "Big Brother") with a decidedly metal edge. Unbeknownst to the band members themselves, they were (along with the likes of IRON MAIDEN and URCHIN) actually sowing the seeds for a major musical development (and I'm sure you can't possibly guess which one I'm referring to) which wouldn't really burst forth until around two years later.

By the summer of that year, though, McCoy had already gone off to do his own thing (achieving greatest success with GILLAN), and his place was filled at short notice by one of the group's entourage, Chris Aylmer, a guitarist/roadie/soundman who actually had his own small-time act called MAYA, whose aspirations barely extended beyond entertaining the lively rabble at their local drinking establishment. To work with Paul Samson, therefore, must have seemed like a golden opportunity to jump a few rungs up the ladder of success, and so the lucky chap was soon practising his bass skills. The new line-up never really managed to get going properly, however, and the disenchanted Roger Hunt soon jacked it all in, whereupon Aylmer suggested that they bring in one of his former colleagues from MAYA, an unknown called Clive Burr. Happy to give the youngster his big break, Samson allowed the sticksman to join in the fun, whereupon the trio (the guitarist himself, in the absence of any suitable candidates for vocalist, taking charge of the mike stand) swiftly began building up a repertoire of self-penned compositions. Before their first gig, however, the lads reached a mutual decision that they should probably reinvent themselves just to make the public aware that this really was a brand-new rock proposition, and the frontman's own surname was regarded as sufficiently metal-sounding (I don't think AYLMER or BURR would have had quite the same impact) to fit the bill. SAMSON rapidly made an impression on the live scene, and had, by the early months of 1978, even begun to develop a healthy following. After some well-attended shows in the capital, therefore, the lads had raked together enough cash to enter the studio and lay down a couple of tracks.

With old buddy John McCoy taking his place at the production helm for the recording session, "Telephone" and "Leavin' You" were captured for posterity, and the tape soon found favour with Lightning Records, more commonly (but not exclusively) associated with its patronage of punk acts. With the label stumping up the readies for a limited pressing, the first SAMSON product emerged a couple of months later, the vinyl two-tracker coupling an unremarkable pair of numbers which were very much in the catchy, traditional rock vein personified by a variety of local hopefuls such as URCHIN, ANGEL STREET and REMUS DOWN BOULEVARD. Still, it proceeded to sell in sufficient quantities to warrant a follow-up, and so the trio were soon working on the kind of new material (showcasing a generous selection at their increasingly-numerous gigs) which might just take them one step further in their quest for fame. Before the end of the year, their second single was recorded for Lightning (the lads were also out on the road with GILLAN at around this time), and all the parties involved were pretty keen to see the next SAMSON effort in the shops as soon as possible. »Mr Rock And Roll« (b/w "Drivin' Music") appeared in the early weeks of 1979, and turned out to be a rather more forceful affair, the impressive riffing and dynamic arrangements having far more in common with the style which would eventually become associated with the term '*NWOBHM*'. In fact, many people now consider this particular single (along with the DEF LEPPARD EP, for example) to be one of the key releases which actually kicked the whole thing off.

The latest offering saw SAMSON making an impression on the various rock charts of the day (as had its vinyl predecessor), and the outfit, despite officially *'disbanding'* for a short period, primarily for financial reasons, kept things going and duly regrouped with experienced session drummer Barry Purkis in place of the departed Clive Burr, who had recently gone off to join IRON MAIDEN. Before long, SAMSON were rapidly establishing themselves as live heroes at local venues such as the legendary Bandwagon (especially when Purkis started messing around with a variety of stage personas, which culminated in his reinvention as the enigmatic and malevolent *'Thunderstick'* simply by pulling on an extremely scary balaclava), with the equally-legendary Neal Kay swiftly identifying them as an act to watch. Still, it was by no means certain that further SAMSON vinyl would be appearing in the foreseeable future (Lightning Records, being a relatively small-time concern, had hardly been in the position to subsidise a full-length effort), and the group now found themselves in the unenviable position of seeking out a new deal. Nevertheless, they began working on a full album in any case (bringing in John McCoy once again), and soon found themselves undertaking an immensely successful national tour (christened the 'Metal Crusade') in the spring of 1979 (with IRON MAIDEN and ANGEL WITCH co-headlining), the whole shebang having been hurriedly organised by the astute Neal Kay himself. With their debut album already in the can by this juncture (John McCoy had, as it turns out, supplied much of the bass work himself, and fellow GILLAN member Colin Towns also contributed a keyboard section or two), the musicians continued their hectic touring activities while their recently-acquired management began touting the tapes around, and it was something of a relief when a timely offer to release the full-length debut duly came from Laser Records.

At precisely this time, however, SAMSON were joined by a dedicated vocalist, Bruce 'Bruce' Dickinson, whom they had seen fronting a small-time Essex act called SHOTS some months earlier. In fact, they had approached him with a view to linking up at the time, although the erudite individual was just about to graduate from university at that point, and still needed a few months to revise for his finals. With his degree conferred, however, there was no stopping Dickinson when offered his big chance to hook up with a popular and established band, so he was soon swotting up on SAMSON songs rather than anything more academically demanding. The timing was all a bit odd, though, especially for the confused fans, some of whom saw a three-piece SAMSON one night and then a quartet the next! Still, the talented frontman, who had mucked about with various amateur-hour combos such as PARADOX, STYX (!) and SPEED in his youth, was a valuable addition to the fold, with his exciting vocal prowess changing the very nature of SAMSON in a fundamental manner. With the hectic touring schedule more or less complete by the summer, it was time to think about the long-awaited album, but the musicians were now faced with a dilemma: either release the LP in its original form, or get Bruce to lay down an entirely new vocal track. In the event, they ultimately concluded that they would be better off sticking to their guns and releasing the original mix (although re-recorded versions of five of the numbers, with Dickinson on vocals, were indeed later captured for posterity, but these remained in the vaults for a good few years), and so it was the early recordings which formed the basis of SAMSON's debut long-player.

Before the album appeared, however, Laser took the unusual decision to reissue »Mr Rock And Roll« as a single (featuring a Dickinson-free re-recording of the A-side and backed with the rather dull, semi-boogie of "Primrose Shuffle"), presumably as a means of introducing SAMSON to those who had somehow remained unaware of their existence until now. In any case, »Survivors« (which, confusingly, credited Dickinson as vocalist) hit the shops a relatively short time later, and the much-anticipated LP showed the ensemble to have matured into a more metal-oriented proposition with similarities to PRAYING MANTIS, CHEVY and AFTER DARK. Having said that, the upbeat openers ("It's Not As Easy As It Seems" and the not-remotely-pervy "I Wish I Was The Saddle Of A Schoolgirl's Bike") were slightly misleading, in that these soon gave way to considerably lengthier, semi-bluesy offerings (some of which dated back to the very inception of the outfit) which revealed a bit too much of SAMSON's roots, if you ask me. Still, it was a record which rapidly won many admirers, and Paul Samson's much-maligned vocals (although markedly different to his successor's) were actually pretty listenable on this particular occasion. Inevitably, the hard-working characters were soon back out on the road to promote their new release (initially sharing a stage with old muckers GILLAN once again) towards the end of the year, and the public reaction at every port of call seems to have been nothing short of fanatical. They also managed to find just enough time to lay down a useful session for the 'Friday Rock Show' (broadcast on the 2nd of November 1979), where the Dickinson-fronted version of SAMSON showcased "Big Brother" and "Six Foot Under", plus the so-far-unheard "Take It Like A Man" (which later appeared on the »Metal Explosion« album of session highlights) and "Hammerhead".

At the beginning of 1980, SAMSON were approached by EMI Records, whose Neal Kay-approved »Metal For Muthas« was being hastily assembled to introduce some of the new metal heroes to a wider audience, and the group happily contributed an edited version of "Tomorrow Or Yesterday" (with Paul on vocals) for the project. EMI were sufficiently smitten with SAMSON (who had been supporting ROBIN TROWER and RAINBOW in recent months) that they slapped a contract on the table, whereupon the lads expeditiously laid down "Hammerhead" and "Vice Versa" for release as their next vinyl offering. Several hundred demo-stamped copies were pressed up as promotional devices in readiness for the full-scale single and album to follow, although things soon went a bit pear-shaped (after a strike at the pressing plant threw the label's release programme into chaos), whereupon Gem Records (an RCA subsidiary) sneakily stepped in and poached the band from under their very noses. With SAMSON duly moving over to the Gem stable, therefore, the general EMI release was cancelled, rendering the promos as instant collectables. Almost immediately, the outfit's new label pressed up the two-tracker properly (even using the same artwork as the EMI original), and the group's heaviest slice of vinyl to date was hitting the shops before long. The double A-sided single proved to be an instant success, and was soon shifting a highly impressive number of units, so little time was wasted before the album was scheduled for imminent release. »Head On« was a highly enjoyable collection of down-to-earth NWOBHM, largely consigning the interminable blues-based workouts to the past, and the long-player made a healthy impact on the Heavy Metal charts from the outset. Even so, it still sounded very odd in places, which led to some drastic action in the first instance, as Bruce Dickinson recalls: *"There were about thirty thousand copies of »Head On« pressed up and they'd gone to the Americans or somebody who said the production sucks. Get it remixed. So they got Tony [Platt] to remix it, particularly "Hard Times" and he remixed the whole album. I forget how you can tell, it's got PP1 or something in the run-off groove."* (Ref: Survivors, Issue 1, 1995).

In spite of the original ropy production, the worldwide fan base appeared to be delighted with SAMSON's latest opus, and a single based around the remixed "Hard Times" proved to be another popular seller, although the outfit were soon to become embroiled in an acrimonious legal dispute with their management team, which severely restricted their touring activities for several months. Nevertheless, they contrived to put in an impressive appearance at the 1980 Reading Festival, where their mid-bill slot would set the stage nicely for the likes of IRON MAIDEN and UFO. With those tiresome contractual wranglings being more or less sorted out towards the end of the year, the industrious musicians (who had already penned enough new material for another LP) went out on tour with URIAH HEEP (stealing the show on many occasions), and the ambitious bunch were already thinking about album number three before much longer. Although Gem had once again been the intended recipients of the next SAMSON long-player, the group ultimately found themselves on the books of parent company RCA, a mixed blessing in terms of the finance/expectation ratio. The recording sessions took place in the early months of 1981, and the album (»Shock Tactics«) appeared a few months later without too many problems. It was a varied and ambitious affair, with a range of tempos, styles and influences on display, although it's generally the more energetic and upbeat numbers ("Bright Lights" and the Russ Ballard-penned "Riding With The Angels") which tend to come across most strongly. Dickinson was putting a lot of effort into his vocal performance by this stage, which was all very well, but I get the distinct impression (which many of you will disagree with) that he seemed to be carrying some of the slightly weaker material almost single-handedly, which wasn't a particularly good sign. In fact, their new set failed to spark the public's imagination in the same way that »Head On« had done (although many fans seem to regard it as their most accomplished LP), and sales were quite considerably lower.

Still, »Riding With The Angels« appeared as a single in due course, and it even scraped the mainstream charts, so it looked as though SAMSON had retained a significant number of fans, whom they proceeded to entertain during a headlining tour of the UK. The energetic performances confirmed that they hadn't lost their enviable live reputation, although comparatively few of their recently-recorded numbers seemed to be making an appearance in the set, the lads concentrating on delivering the crowd-pleasing numbers from earlier on in their career. Nevertheless, SAMSON were still a powerful and popular attraction (although they had now lost the services of old Thunderstick, who had gone off to establish an eponymous project), and they were to benefit from a late addition to the bill of 1981's Reading Festival, having made a favourable impression at the previous year's shindig. It turned out to be another enjoyable outing, with the lads (having now recruited erstwhile LIGHT OF THE WORLD sticksman Mel Gaynor) attaining a slightly higher billing this time. The gig was even recorded for future broadcast by BBC Radio, with half an hour of their set being transmitted on the 'Friday Rock Show' shortly thereafter, while the complete performance formed the basis of the functionally-titled »Live At Reading '81« release almost a decade later. The lads were to benefit from this spate of high-profile activity for a remarkably short time, however, when Bruce *'I didn't get where I am today without knowing a meal-ticket when I see one'* Dickinson was ultimately lured away by an offer to join an obscure bunch of East End chancers called IRON MAIDEN, leaving the remaining SAMSON members with no option but to look for a new frontman (either that or revert to a three-piece with Paul Samson himself at the helm), although they soon identified a likely candidate in the portly shape of Nicky Moore.

Moore was a veteran of numerous popular club acts, notably HACKENSACK and the bluesy-as-you-like TIGER (who recorded for a variety of major labels during the mid-to-late 70's), and had latterly been trying to get his own NICKY MOORE BAND (who briefly held a deal with Street Tunes) venture off the ground. He was yet another long-time associate of Paul Samson's (I'd hate to see the size of his address book), however, and it took comparatively little effort for the guitarist to coerce him into the studio to work on some new material. Before Moore knew what was happening, he had become the latest SAMSON vocalist, so everything seemed to be working in the band's favour once again. Moore was (and still is) the possessor of a very likeable, soulful voice, and proved to be a popular choice when he was introduced to the fans at some end-of-year gigs, although his involvement naturally led to widespread speculation that SAMSON might be returning to their roots with their next album. The rock world would have to wait quite a long while to find out, though, as work on the fourth long-player was delayed until the outfit had really established themselves on the live scene once again and written enough fresh material of a sufficiently high standard to justify a further LP. In any case, the lads no longer had a record deal, so that was something else to which they would have to attend in due course. By the early part of 1982, the musicians had installed former WILDLIFE drummer Pete Jupp in place of Mel Gaynor (who proceeded to enjoy a productive spell with the despicable SIMPLE MINDS), the latter having departed after the briefest of spells at the SAMSON drumkit. In spite of all this instability on the personnel front, though, the lads managed to keep the momentum going, and were soon wowing the fans when they hooked up with BLACKFOOT for a tour of capacious British venues.

By the summer of 1982, SAMSON had managed to swing a new deal with Polydor, and the first fruit of this affiliation came in the form of the »Losing My Grip« single, which appeared in both 7" and 12" forms, the latter additionally featuring two live numbers with Nicky Moore on vocals. It was a great success, and, with a full album now on the cards as hoped, the lads eventually (after a well-attended tour with ANGEL WITCH in tow, culminating with an attention-grabbing appearance at the Mildenhall Festival) immersed themselves in the studio for a couple of months to judge how well their latest efforts might come across on vinyl. SAMSON soon emerged with a usable set of compositions, and, before long, the long-player was being assembled for release. The lads whiled away the time by making their first trip to mainland Europe for some well-attended live events (including the obligatory festival appearances), and returned just in time to see »Before The Storm« (which had been preceded by the »Life On The Run« single, the double-pack version including material from their Mildenhall gig) hitting the shops. As anticipated, the album was an undeniably raunchy collection (sharing a fair bit of common ground with the likes of TERRAPLANE and BABY TUCKOO), although it stopped short of being an out-and-out bluesy rock release, something which must have come as a welcome relief to the headbangers. In fact, such newly-penned tracks as "Dangerzone", "Test Of Time" and "Turn Out The Lights" represented some of SAMSON's strongest efforts for quite a while, and healthy sales of »Before The Storm« reflected this return to form. The lads rounded off the year by touring alongside WHITESNAKE, although the release of a further single (coupling "Red Skies" with "Young Idea") from the latest album was ultimately cancelled in mysterious circumstances after promos had already been circulated.

Moving into 1983, the SAMSON lads undertook another round of European touring, and finally saw a belated release of their »Red Skies« single, although its flipside had now been replaced by "Living, Loving, Lying", a track featuring ROCK GODDESS as backing vocalists. After yet more gigging and a summer jaunt in Germany alongside ACCEPT, the group began thinking about their next record, and work began on schedule in the second half of 1983. In the event, however, the long-player consistently failed to appear in the shops, the outfit fighting a constant battle with Polydor (who had already disposed of all their other NWOBHM-era signings such as A II Z and STAMPEDE, and were now banking on more commercial acts such as HEAVY PETTIN) just to get the record pressed at all. It did eventually put in an appearance, but not until the early part of 1984, by which time SAMSON's long-standing bassist Chris Aylmer had tired of being messed about and had gone off to do his own thing, originally hooking up with ROGUE MALE for a brief period. Aylmer's replacement, lured away from the struggling DIAMOND HEAD at the end of 1983, was Merv Goldsworthy (a talented young musician who had earlier played in Lancashire favourites STREETFIGHTER at the height of the NWOBHM explosion), although the newly-recruited bassist wasn't credited on the fifth SAMSON album (which is fair enough, I suppose, given that he didn't actually play on it). Before long, the lads also decided to bolster their sound further by adding second guitarist Dave Colwell (a veteran of such minor hopefuls as HOTLINE, ANGEL STREET and 720), a highly talented individual who had successfully collaborated with various IRON MAIDEN members over the years.

While waiting patiently for the album to materialise, the lads recorded another session for the 'Friday Rock Show', where they showcased (on the 16th of March 1984) some strong numbers from the forthcoming opus. "Are You Ready", "Love Hungry", "Don't Get Mad-Get Even" and "Doctor Ice" were the chosen compositions, and the public were soon able to hear the vinyl versions when »Don't Get Mad-Get Even« hit the shops a short time later. It was a slightly more accessible offering (moving into ALASKA territory by this stage), although there were, nonetheless, some highly capable inclusions, notably "The Fight Goes On", "Doctor Ice" and "Bite On The Bullet". Mind you, it still wasn't nearly commercial enough for Polydor, who (after half-heartedly releasing the »Are You Ready« and »The Fight Goes On« singles to promote the LP) swiftly terminated SAMSON's contract. More or less immediately, Paul Samson brought chapter one of SAMSON's chequered history to a close, and went off to work with old buddy John McCoy on his self-titled McCOY project (see separate entry), while Pete Jupp and Merv Goldsworthy proceeded to establish FM from the ashes of the last WILDLIFE line-up. Dave Colwell, meanwhile, went back to regular session work and Nicky Moore lent his in-demand services to ELECTRIC SUN. Before too long, though, Samson and Moore began writing new material together, and rapidly decided to collaborate on a one-off album, with various musicians being drafted in to act in a guest capacity. The usual suspects were swiftly rounded up (Nicky Moore himself, John McCoy, Colin Towns, Jo Julian), and additional help was sought from drummers Edgar Patrik (from the German version of SINNER) and Chris Sharley (from the NICKY MOORE BAND) during the recording process. The studio sessions took place sporadically over a period of many months, however, and the long-player wouldn't be finished until the spring of 1985, by which time various other SAMSON-related vinyl was coming onto the market once again.

Some of SAMSON's early material, originally recorded for the benefit of Laser and Lightning, had passed into the possession of Thunderbolt Records by this stage, and the company had already utilised these recordings on two separate occasions (giving rise to the straight reissue of »Survivors« in a completely different sleeve, plus the »Last Rites« compilation, featuring various single tracks to pad things out). Furthermore, Metal Masters had offered to release a live set, and so »Thank You And Goodnight« was duly mixed and released in addition to the various reissues. Also, Capitol Records now owned the rights to the Gem/RCA albums, which meant that a repackaged long-player called »Head Tactics«, comprising a selection of material from the Dickinson era, was soon putting in an appearance, as was a tie-in 7"/12" coupling "Vice Versa" and "Losing My Grip", the latter being an exclusive version with Dickinson at the mike stand. By 1986, there was a glut of SAMSON vinyl on the market, which was unfortunate in one sense, given that their brand-new long-player (credited to PAUL SAMSON) finally made it into the shops and was swamped by all the reissues, belated issues, compilations and cash-ins which were now cluttering up the shelves. Still, »Joint Forces« (released by the rather unpopular Raw Power label) was a listenable, upbeat collection of semi-commercial rock (with ROCK GODDESS featuring on a couple of numbers again), although several of the tracks were throwaway efforts which lacked depth. It had its moments ("Russians", for example), but it was a record which confused the fans, especially as there was no tour to go with it. A single even escaped on a small French label, but it hardly made much difference to the album's fate, and the »Joint Forces« episode was soon forgotten.

With the musicians from the »Joint Forces« sessions all going their separate ways thereafter (Nicky Moore and John McCoy, for instance, were busy establishing their MAMMOTH project), Paul Samson was left to start again by piecing together a brand-new touring act. Dave Colwell was happy to lend a hand once more, and a tight rhythm section was soon found (bassist Kevin Riddles from ANGEL WITCH/TYTAN and drummer Mark Brabbs from TANK/DUMPY'S RUSTY NUTS), the line-up being completed following the recruitment of the little-known Sam Blue (aka Sam Blewitt), who had formerly fronted long-forgotten Tyneside lightweights EMERSON. The new venture was christened PAUL SAMSON'S EMPIRE, and they soon won themselves a session for the 'Friday Rock Show' (transmitted on the 6th of June 1986), where the lads introduced the public to four original compositions viz. "One Day Heroes", "Tomorrow", "A Matter Of Time" and "Turn On The Lights". It was a strong debut, and it seemed inevitable that Paul Samson would, before long, be returning to prominence with his latest outfit. The lads spent a few months composing material, and finally began attracting attention from various labels, although Sam Blue unexpectedly jumped ship (resurfacing in YA YA), whereupon he was succeeded by a chap called Mick White (who, ironically, had also replaced Blue in EMERSON!), who was chucked in at the deep end when the band hooked up with IRON MAIDEN for an eventful end-of-year tour. In the early months of 1987, things seemed to be going according to plan, and their enjoyable "One Day Heroes" was duly included on a promotional EP given free with 'Metal Hammer' at the time, although the luckless combo began to fragment shortly thereafter. It really was a great pity that no PAUL SAMSON'S EMPIRE releases emerged while the talented group were a going concern, although it's worth mentioning that their »Live At The Marquee« set has recently been made available on CD.

After a few months penning yet more material, it was time to reform SAMSON once again, and the guitarist (assisted by Mick White) set about assembling another revamped outfit, bringing in erstwhile ORE bassist Dave Boyce, former EMERSON drummer Charlie Mack (aka Charlie MacKenzie, also a veteran of BLACK ROSE and TAURUS) and keyboard player Toby Sadler (formerly a member of WHITE SPIRIT and AIRRACE). The revised version of SAMSON were content to bide their time, though, and they spent a couple of years playing live and developing a new repertoire. Their first vinyl exposure came with a mini-album entitled »And There It Is…«, issued by Metal Masters in 1988. It was, to all intents and purposes, a shameless example of a melodic rock style, and (although capable enough) was far too similar to dozens of other UK acts of the period to stand out from the crowd. It wasn't a great commercial success, although SAMSON persevered, returning in 1989 with a new vocalist (former MORITZ singer Peter Scallan), and duly recorded yet another 'Friday Rock Show' session, where (on the 11th of August 1989) they unveiled the numbers "State Of Emergency", "Look To The Future", "Love This Time" and "Someone To Turn To". It seemed to be enough to win the lads a deal with Communiqué, who snapped them up for a full album in due course, and »Refugee« (featuring the recent session tracks and reworked versions of several efforts from their mini-album) appeared the following year. It proceeded to sell in respectable quantities, and the group were subsequently retained for a further release, although they took their time recording it.

In contrast to the eventful, turbulent and prolific 80's, SAMSON haven't had such a high-profile presence on the rock scene in the 90's and beyond. Numerous reissues and compilations have burst forth on a truly bewildering variety of labels, although there has been little in the way of brand-new material, with the exception of 1993's generally-overlooked »Samson« release. Paul Samson himself has played with a wide range of musical projects throughout the decade, including a contribution to the ALL STARS debacle (where SAMSON were fronted by little-known vocalist Gary Owen), the short-lived PAUL SAMSON'S ROGUES venture (where he was ably assisted by drummer Tony Tuohy and bassist Gerry Sherwin, the latter being another MAYA veteran, having also played with the ENGLISH ROGUES and SLEDGEHAMMER), and various blues-based club acts such as METALLIC BLUE and the RICHARD BLACK PROJECT. The eponymous album, meanwhile, saw the axeman teaming up with old mate Chris Aylmer (who had pottered around with various long-forgotten hopefuls such as HEAD OVER HEELS in the wilderness years) for the first time in a decade (Tony Tuohy was retained from the ROGUES project), and so a reformation of the original (well, the most familiar) line-up seemed a distinct possibility at that stage.

In fact, the long-awaited SAMSON reunion eventually seemed to be on the cards by the late 90's, with both Thunderstick and Bruce Dickinson giving some serious consideration to the project after being approached by Paul Samson. In the event, however, Dickinson was unexpectedly recalled to the ranks of IRON MAIDEN at a particularly awkward moment, effectively eliminating him from the picture, although the remaining trio of Samson, Aylmer and Thunderstick finally gravitated together for a rapturously-received '20th NWOBHM Anniversary' show in Japan in 1999, and have elected to remain an active unit (recently being joined by Nicky Moore once again, the ensemble delighting the crowds at Wacken 2000) in an attempt to deliver a brand-new album after all these years. With SAMSON benefitting from some extremely well-maintained and informative pages on the internet (not to mention a dedicated fanzine, 'Survivors'), there seems very little chance that their many fans will lose touch with their heroes' future activities now.

LP's

»Survivors« Laser 1979
[Original issue]
»Head On« Gem 1980
[Released with two different mixes, originally with A1/B1 matrix, later with A2/B2]
»Shock Tactics« RCA 1981
»Before The Storm« Polydor 1982
»Survivors« Thunderbolt 1983
[Reissue in different sleeve]
»Last Rites« Thunderbolt 1984
[Compilation release, includes material from first album and early singles]
»Don't Get Mad – Get Even« Polydor 1984
»Thank You And Goodnight« Metal Masters 1985
[Live release]
»Head Tactics« Capitol Records 1986
[Material taken from »Head On« and »Shock Tactics« albums, with some alternate versions]
»Joint Forces« Raw Power 1986
[Under the name of PAUL SAMSON]
»Pillars Of Rock« Connoisseur Collection 1990
[Double album, compilation of live and studio material]
»Survivors« Repertoire 1990
[Reissue on white vinyl with five extra tracks]
»Head On« Repertoire 1990
[Reissue on red vinyl]
»Shock Tactics« Repertoire 1990
[Reissue on red vinyl]
»Live At Reading '81« Raw Fruit 1990
[Live release]
»Live At Reading '81« Repertoire 1990
[Alternate issue in different sleeve]
»Refugee« Communiqué Records 1990
»Samson« Communiqué Records 1993

Mini-LP's

»And There It Is…« Metal Masters 1988

12" EP's

»Losing My Grip« Polydor 1982
["Pyramid To The Stars" non-LP, also features live versions of "Tomorrow Or Yesterday" and "Mr Rock And Roll"]
»Red Skies« Polydor 1983
["Red Skies" different to album version, both "Living, Loving, Lying" and "Running Out Of Time" non-LP]
»Are You Ready« Polydor 1984
["La Grange" non-LP]
»Are You Ready« Polydor 1984
[Limited edition French tour issue in different sleeve]
»The Fight Goes On« Polydor 1984
["Riding With The Angels" different to album version, also features live version of "Vice Versa"]
»Mr Rock & Roll« Thunderbolt 1984
[Comprising material from earlier singles]

12" Singles

»Vice Versa« Capitol Records 1986
[Issued as limited edition picture disc, B-side "Losing My Grip" different to album version]

7" Singles

»Telephone« Lightning Records 1978
[Both tracks non-LP]
»Mr Rock And Roll« Lightning Records 1978
[Original issue, B-side "Drivin' Music", both tracks non-LP]
»Mr Rock And Roll« Laser Records 1979
[Second issue with re-recorded A-side, B-side "Primrose Shuffle", both tracks non-LP]
»Hammerhead« EMI 1980
[Original issue in purple sleeve, demo copies only]
»Hammerhead« Gem 1980
[Second issue in blue sleeve, B-side "Vice Versa" different to album version]
»Hard Times« Gem 1980
[Remixed A-side different to album version, B-side "Angel With A Machine Gun" non-LP]
»Riding With The Angels« RCA 1981
[A-side different to album version, B-side "Little Big Man" non-LP, most issued as picture discs, some on normal black vinyl]
»Life On The Run« Polydor 1982
[B-side "Drivin' With ZZ" non-LP, also issued as limited edition in gatefold sleeve with free live single featuring "Walking Out On You" and "Bright Lights"]
»Losing My Grip« Polydor 1982
[B-side "Pyramid To The Stars" non-LP, also issued as limited edition picture disc]
»Red Skies« Polydor 1983
[A-side different to album version, B-side "Living, Loving, Lying" non-LP, also issued as limited edition picture disc]
»Are You Ready« Polydor 1984
[A-side different to album version, also issued as limited edition picture disc]
»The Fight Goes On« Polydor 1984
[Both tracks different to album versions]
»Vice Versa« Capitol 1986
[B-side "Losing My Grip" different to album version]
»No Turning Back« Just In 1986
[French-only release, as PAUL SAMSON, issued

on blue vinyl]

Promotional Releases
»**Red Skies**« Polydor 1982
[Promo-only copies of cancelled 7" single, B-side "Young Idea"]
»**Red Skies**« Polydor 1983
[One-sided DJ promo 7"]

CD's
»**Pillars Of Rock**« Connoisseur 1990
[Compilation release]
»**Refugee**« Communiqué Records 1990
»**Survivors**« Grand Slamm 1990
[US reissue with five bonus tracks featuring Bruce Dickinson]
»**Live At Reading '81**« Raw Fruit 1990
[Live release]
»**Live At Reading '81**« Repertoire 1990
[German issue in different sleeve]
»**Survivors**« Repertoire 1990
[With five extra tracks]
»**Head On**« Repertoire 1991
[With part one of band interview]
»**Shock Tactics**« Repertoire 1991
[Should have featured part two of band interview, but includes part one again by mistake]
»**Joint Forces**« Repertoire 1992
[With one bonus track]
»**Thank You And Goodnight**« Magnum 1993
[Live release]
»**1988 (And There It Is)**« Razor 1993
[Reissue of »And There It Is…« mini-album with extra tracks]
»**Samson**« Communiqué Records 1993
»**Joint Forces**« Magnum 1994
[With one bonus track]
»**Live At The Marquee**« Magnum 1994
[Live album, under the name of PAUL SAMSON'S EMPIRE]
»**Refugee**« Magnum 1995
[With extra tracks]
»**1993 (Samson)**« Magnum 1995
[Reissue of »Samson« LP]
»**Burning Emotion-The Best Of 85-90**«
Magnum 1995
[Compilation release]
»**The BBC Sessions**« High Vaultage 1997
[Compilation of material recorded for radio]
»**Don't Get Mad-Get Even**« Samsonite 199?
[Unofficial reissue with six bonus tracks]
»**Before The Storm**« Samsonite 199?
[Unofficial reissue with seven bonus tracks]
»**Test Of Time**« Delta Music 1999
[Compilation release]
»**Past, Present And Future**« Zoom Club Records 1999

[Double disc, compilation release of live and studio material]
»**Metal Crusade 99**« Pony Canyon 1999
[Japanese-only live double CD set, shared with TANK, PRAYING MANTIS and TRESPASS]
»**Survivors**« Airraid Records 2000
[Reissue]
»**Head On**« Airraid Records 2000
[Reissue]
»**Shock Tactics**« Airraid Records 2000
[Reissue]
»**Live At Reading '81**« Airraid Records 2000
[Reissue]
»**Live In London 2000**« Zoom Club Records 2000
[Live release, double disc]

Mini-CD's
»**And There It Is…**« Metal Masters 1988

Exclusive Compilation Appearances
"**One Day Heroes**" on »The 2nd Wave Of New British Metal« 7" EP Private 1987 (Free with Metal Hammer magazine)
[Under the name of PAUL SAMSON'S EMPIRE]

Compilation Appearances
"**Tomorrow Or Yesterday**" on »Metal For Muthas« LP EMI 1980/CD Airraid Records 2000 + »The Bible Of Hard Rock« CD Toshiba 1990
[Different to album version]
"**Take It Like A Man**" on »Metal Explosion« LP BBC Records 1980
[Different to album version]
"**Earth Mother**" on »Axe Attack Vol.II« LP K-Tel 1981
"**Test Of Time**" on »A Little Bit Of Light Relief« LP Polydor 1982
"**I Wish I Was The Saddle Of A Schoolgirl's Bike**" on »Meer Thunderbolt Hard Rock« LP Thunderbolt 1984
"**Koz**" on »Meer Thunderbolt Hard Rock« LP Thunderbolt 1984
"**Losing My Grip**" on »Metal Treasures And Vinyl Heavies« LP Action Replay Records 1984 + »Rock Giants Vol.1« CD Mastertone 1994
"**Vice Versa**" on »NWOBHM '79 Revisited« Do-LP/Do-CD Phonogram 1990
"**Riding With The Angels**" on »Giants Of Rock-The Metal Decade Vol.1« Do-CD Teldec 1990 + »The Metal Box« 3-CD Box Castle Communications 1993
"**Hard Times**" (live) on »NWOBHM-The Days On Stage« Bootleg CD Taurus Records 1993
"**Telephone**" on »N.W.O.B.H.M. Metal Rarities Vol.2« CD British Steel 1996
"**Leavin' You**" on »N.W.O.B.H.M. Metal Rarities Vol.2« CD British Steel 1996

"**Mr Rock And Roll**" on »N.W.O.B.H.M. Metal Rarities Vol.2« CD British Steel 1996
"**Drivin' Music**" on »N.W.O.B.H.M. Metal Rarities Vol.2« CD British Steel 1996 + »The Gillan Family Album« CD Connoisseur 2000
"**Too Late**" on »Rock Out!« Do-CD Emporio 1996
"**The Silver Screen**" on »Rock Out!« Do-CD Emporio 1996
"**Losing My Grip**" **(live)** on »Noise Level Critical« CD Hallmark 1997
"**Vice Versa**" **(live)** on »Noise Level Critical« CD Hallmark 1997
"**Red Skies**" **(live)** on »NWOBHM Live« CD Emporio 1997
"**Drivin' With ZZ**" **(live)** on »NWOBHM Live« CD Emporio 1997
"**Riding With The Angels**" **(live)** on »NWOBHM Live« CD Emporio 1997
"**Turn Out The Lights**" **(live)** on »The Best Of British Metal« CD Delta Music 1999
"**Voodoo Chile (Slight Return)**" **(live)** on »The Best Of British Metal« CD Delta Music 1999

SAM THUNDER

Tex Barlow (v)
Eddie (g)
Steve Ferguson (g)
Rob Naylor (b)
Chris Dadson (d)

Having originally formed at the beginning of 1981, it didn't take the ambitious Mancunian quintet SAM THUNDER (not sure about that name, though) particularly long to install themselves in a local studio facility and set about the task of laying down their first demo, an undeniably capable three-tracker featuring "Always The Pretty One", "Hot Head" and "Yours For The Taking", the latter being a surprisingly enjoyable instrumental (it didn't overstay its welcome, which is always a good thing) with memorable twin-guitar sections. The two vocal-based tracks, meanwhile, suggested a reasonably melodic (vaguely ROX-influenced at times) and quite heavy style reminiscent of outfits such as HELLANBACH or FORGER, and these early compositions paved the way for the band to become a pretty decent proposition in the North West (once they actually got around to playing some gigs, that is) in years to come. This particular batch of studio recordings came under close scrutiny in the 'Armed And Ready' section of 'Kerrang' some time later, where comparisons with the mighty VAN HALEN were abound (which was perfectly reasonable, I suppose), the generally-favourable review serving to identify SAM THUNDER as a group with potential and a name to watch.

Within a couple of years, after having paid their dues in the live environment (including a valuable support slot with LEE AARON), the developing group had managed to wangle a deal with Bullet Records, with the first fruit of this liaison being the »Don't Take Forever« EP, issued in 1984. By this stage, though, the outfit had endured a few radical changes, with Nic Bennett having replaced the economically-named 'Eddie' on guitar, while Wilson Davies and Andy Chemney (both recruited from the ranks of THD, a popular outfit from the area who had failed to make their much-anticipated breakthrough) took over from Tex Barlow and Chris Dadson (the latter, in addition to helping out for a brief spell in ARAGORN, went on to join CHATEAUX in time to appear on their »Firepower« LP), respectively. The tracks featured on the SAM THUNDER 12" ("Don't Take Forever", "A Piece Of The Night" and "You Set My Heart On Fire") were all in a pretty similar vein to those on their first demo (marginally more commercial, perhaps, and with something of a mid-period TYGERS OF PAN TANG influence in the vocal department), although it's fair to say that this selection of originals wasn't exactly the most memorable batch of material ever committed to vinyl. One thing's for sure, SAM THUNDER certainly weren't a patch on the jewel in Bullet's crown, the wonderful TRAITORS GATE!

Still, the release must have sold in worthwhile quantities, and the autumn of 1984 saw the band recording a full LP (entitled »Manoeuvres«) for their label, the long-player being issued only in picture disc form (never a good move, either in terms of sound quality or sales figures). With the recently-expanded outfit now featuring keyboards from new recruit Mike Heppleston, SAM THUNDER were evidently moving into markedly more commercial territory in the style of GRAND PRIX or BOMBAY. Again, however, the tracks on display are all pretty samey and formulaic, with "Always Waiting" and the slightly heavier "Time After Time" probably constituting the sole highlights. Bullet Records, meanwhile, having seemingly reached the conclusion that they had signed a pretty unremarkable proposition after all, don't appear to have committed themselves to promoting SAM THUNDER to the masses, and basically cut their ties with the ensemble in the wake of this inauspicious release, so the disillusioned musicians probably decided to call it a day soon after. The duo of Andy Chemney and Rob Naylor, incidentally, resurfaced several years later in another overly-melodic concern known as A.O.K. (Naylor also featured in a fly-by-night venture called LANSON), while Wilson Davies (aka David Wilson Glover) tried his luck again with TURIN, neither of which seem to have made it past the demo stage.

LP's
»Manoeuvres« Bullet 1984
[Issued as limited edition picture disc]

12" EP's
»Don't Take Forever« Bullet 1984
[All three tracks non-LP]

SAMURAI

Len Williams (v)
Huw Lewis (g)
Craig Ridsdale (g)
Neil Rogers (b)
Mike Davies (d)

Forming at the beginning of 1983, Glamorgan's SAMURAI (not to be confused with an obscure outfit from the North East who appeared on the »Roksnax« compilation) continued the tradition of Welsh metal successes by signing to Ebony after releasing just one demo tape. In fact, they had been courted by no less than four of the more influential labels of the day *viz.* Ebony, Neat (who expected the musicians to pay for studio time themselves), Heavy Metal and Music For Nations, but they were eventually lured to Ebony by the offer of a multi-album deal. Mind you, their debut »Sacred Blade« offering (from 1984) demonstrated admirably what all the fuss had been about. Generally speaking, it was very much in the powerful style of many of Ebony's mid-80's signings (DEALER, GRIM REAPER, CHATEAUX, TYGA MYRA *etc.*), although the individual compositions were carried off with a level of enthusiasm and energy which was sorely lacking in certain other releases of the era. True, there were also a couple of more commercial and restrained numbers to lend an air of variety to the proceedings, although, when the quintet really hit the mark, on tracks such as "Fires Of Hell", "Attack", "Fire In Our Eyes" and "Gotta Rock Tonight" (a bit close to SAVAGE's "Ain't No Fit Place" for comfort, admittedly), the inevitable comparison would be with the godlike FIFTH ANGEL, something which earns SAMURAI an extremely favourable thumbs-up in my book. All things considered, it was an excellent start, and a strong single also emerged at around the same time, coupling "Fires Of Hell" with the otherwise-unavailable "Dreams Of The World", another extremely capable effort.

With the public and press response to SAMURAI's debut being overwhelmingly positive, it came as no surprise that they were invited to deliver a follow-up with minimal delay. As a result, most of 1985 was spent composing a selection of fresh material, trying it out in the live environment and paying regular visits to the recording studio. Their resulting long-player, »Weapon Master«, hit the streets in the early part of 1986, by which time the group claimed to have performed in excess of one hundred gigs as a unit, and they soon lined up a further national tour (with GRIM REAPER in tow on some occasions) to promote their latest opus. Interviewed at the time, bassist Neil Rogers elaborated on the outfit's stagecraft: *"We try hard in all aspects as well as the musicianship of playing instruments. We work out stage movements, train, exercise-all that sort of thing-so we can be more visual and keep the audience's attention. We try not to be boring. When we write songs we keep them as varied as possible, we don't go in for long riffy parts or very long guitar or drum solos-so things are kept sharp and interesting."* (Ref: A Dose Of The Heavies, Issue 2, May 1986). Sadly, in spite of this explicit assurance that their songs would always remain individualistic, »Weapon Master« saw a move away from SAMURAI's power metal roots towards a selection of more anthemic and catchy compositions lying somewhere between SAVAGE and mid-period TOKYO BLADE, most of which turned out to be pretty interchangeable. A great pity, really, but I'm sure the band members were happy enough at the time with their *'musical progression'*, especially as the record, like its predecessor, eventually went to a third pressing in order to meet demand.

Again, the outfit were keen to persevere in their quest for global domination, and dutifully set about the task of compiling that *'difficult third album'* for their ever-accommodating label. Mind you, their once-prolific studio activities appear to have tailed off dramatically in terms of frequency, and it looks as though the fruit of 1987's labours may have been a solitary two track demo (featuring the original pairing of "Show Me Your Love" and "Stay With Me Tonight"), which wasn't circulated particularly widely at the time. By the end of the year, though, the lads now claimed to have amassed a huge tally of well over three hundred gigs (I reckon the previous eighteen months must have been a bit hectic), latterly including an extended, financially-crippling sojourn in the States, plus British jaunts with such varied acts as GIRL-SCHOOL, MGM, LEE AARON and DUMPY'S RUSTY NUTS. Featured in the reasonably comprehensive 'Welsh Metal Special' article in 'Kerrang' in the early days of 1988, the SAMURAI lads made it perfectly clear that a third album was definitely on the cards, although they were yet to decide whether or not it should appear on Ebony this time.

In the event, however, things didn't really work out too well for the luckless SAMURAI, and they never actually got the chance to release any further vinyl product. Within only a few months of the aforementioned magazine going to print, guitarist Craig Ridsdale was hard at work with the recently-established TALAN project (also featuring the services of STORM-QUEEN's Paul Burnett and PREYER's Phil John), which almost certainly meant that SAMURAI had already bitten the dust, given that they were such a close-knit group. It's entirely possible that they might have been able to pull off a cracking return to form on their (hypothetical) third long-player, but I guess we'll never know for sure. It's just a pity that so many British acts suffered from the anti-metal backlash in the second half of the decade, and SAMURAI were certainly one of many once-potent outfits who failed to maintain their momentum or sense of identity in the face of the melodic rock onslaught.

LP's
»Sacred Blade« Ebony 1984
»Weapon Master« Ebony 1986

7" Singles
»Fires Of Hell« Ebony 1984
[B-side "Dreams Of The World" non-LP]

SAPPHIRE

Steve Gett (v)
Rudi Riviere (g)
Chris Boland (b)
Fred Zeppelin (d)

The original four-piece known as SAPPHIRE (not to be confused with the obscure Lancashire outfit who later appeared on the »It's Unheard Of!« compilation) were a bunch of scenesters who came together towards the end of 1981 at the behest of former DIRTY WHITE BOYS mainman (and part-time contributor to 'Kerrang' magazine) Steve Gett. Based in the Northern outskirts of the capital, Gett soon enlisted ex-DRAGONFLY guitarist Rudi Riviere and ex-STALLION bassist Chris Boland to the fold, completing the picture with drummer Fred Zeppelin (I'll bet), on the personal recommendation of GIRL's Phil Collen, no less. Within a mere couple of months, the group's first demo was being circulated, featuring the tracks "Black Cat", "Jealousy", "I Love Rock And Roll" (nothing to do with JOAN JETT, apparently) and "Don't Let Go". Following on from a predictably enthusiastic reception from Kerrang, who duly promoted the lads in their 'Armed And Ready' section, material for a private single was being recorded within a matter of weeks, and this offering emerged at around the time the band were enjoying enviable support slots with touring acts such as BLACKFOOT and ALICE COOPER.

Issued in a rather unimaginative, blue and white picture sleeve (just a logo and titles), the two-tracker featured the aforementioned "Jealousy" alongside the unfamiliar "Let It Burn", showing SAPPHIRE to be an extremely accomplished outfit, their catchy brand of melodic rock/metal evoking memories of similarly-minded outfits such as STAGEFRIGHT and BABY TUCKOO. Their debut single (which is now regarded as one of the highest-valued, top-ranking NWOBHM rarities) rapidly became a popular purchase among Britain's rock community of the day, and "Jealousy" itself even put in an appearance in the 'Top 30 Kuts' chart in 'Kerrang' a few months later, no doubt helped along by some energetic live appearances and their down-to-earth attitude, as personified by mainman Steve Gett: *"After all, it's only entertainment. Rock and roll is about having fun, not only for the band but also for the people who pay to come and see us. We like to entertain and at the same time enjoy ourselves."* (Ref: Kerrang No.7, January 1982). Nevertheless, SAPPHIRE were to enjoy a comparatively brief spell in the limelight, and had already gone their separate ways by the beginning of 1983. Axeman Rudi Riviere was (after stints with the NEW TORPEDOS and the confrontationally-named BLACK MAIL) eventually assimilated into the ranks of TERRAPLANE, while Steve Gett moved to the States, initially maintaining a role in the music business, but latterly turning his hand to running a wine store. To paraphrase the man himself, *"rock and roll really can drive you to drink".*

7" Singles

»**Jealousy**« Sapphire Rocks Records 1982

Compilation Appearances
"**Jealousy**" on »NWOBHM Vol.5« Bootleg CD 1992
"**Let It Burn**" on »NWOBHM Vol.6« Bootleg CD 1992

SARACEN

Steve Bettney (v)
Rob Bendelow (g)
Barry Yates (b)
Richard Lowe (k)
John Thorne (d)

The Derbyshire version of SARACEN (not to be confused with their »Roksnax« namesakes or the Australian bunch who also recorded under the alter ego of TRILOGY) came to prominence at the height of the NWOBHM explosion, although, in terms of musical style, they were really (as with regional favourites WARRIOR, who had already issued their »Let Battle Commence« opus by 1980) only on the periphery of the movement. Their first long-player (»Heroes, Saints And Fools«) appeared on the Nucleus label (the band's own company), without much in the way of hype, towards the end of 1981, and immediately found a loyal fan in Tommy Vance, who was to feature selections from the LP on his 'Friday Rock Show' for many years to come. The quintet tended to favour lengthy, semi-progressive compositions such as "Crusader", "Horsemen Of The Apocalypse" and "Ready To Fly", well-crafted, intriguing numbers which featured various elements of WHITE SPIRIT, OMEGA, DAMASCUS and DAWNWATCHER, without being particularly representative of the NWOBHM ethos. On the other hand, however, there was something of a conscious attempt to balance things out with some rather more accessible efforts, although it would appear that the striking contrast between the two styles was perhaps a bit too pronounced for some people's liking.

With the outfit having won the patronage of Tommy Vance at an early stage, it came as no surprise that they were offered the chance to record a 'Friday Rock Show' session within a remarkably short space of time. Eventually broadcast on the 15th of January 1982, the group chose to showcase only one number from the album ("Crusader"), making up the remainder of the session with "Flame Of Youth", "Jekyll And Hyde" and "Equinox". It was, by anyone's standards, a highly capable display, and it didn't do SARACEN's chances any harm whatsoever. In due course, the lads were given some additional useful exposure in the 'Armed And Ready' section of 'Kerrang', and it wasn't long before their debut single was appearing in the shops. The »No More Lonely Nights« two-tracker (B-side "Rock Of Ages") paired a couple of the more commercial compositions from their debut long-player, more along the lines of DEEP PURPLE than anything more complex, although the song structures were vaguely reminiscent of Max Bacon-era NIGHTWING. John Thorne explained the motivation for the single: *"»No More Lonely Nights« was written as a single, with fairly banal lyrics for SARACEN, with plenty of hooks to suit that market, and it's a useful direction to go in while still retaining our integrity. We are considering a slight reappraisal of our songs to attempt to improve on what we've already done."* (Ref: Kerrang No.21, July 1982). Well, if that wasn't a presage of impending wimp-out, then I don't know what is!

The lads toured successfully in the early months of 1983, before taking something of an extended break for the remainder of that year, during which time they broke in a couple of new members, namely bassist Jason Gardner and guitarist Haydn Conway. Before the year was out, however, it became apparent that a new deal had been wangled with Neat, whereupon the outfit hurriedly released a single featuring "We Have Arrived" and "A Face In The Crowd". Although many saw this as something of a sharp change in direction for SARACEN, it was basically only the culmination of their musical development over the preceding two years. A full album was recorded for Neat in the early months of 1984, and the title (»Change Of Heart«) was rapidly identified as something of a giveaway that the outfit had deserted their original musical orientation, although it's by no means clear that this was the band's actual intention. Nevertheless, the fairly blatant shift towards semi-pomp material (the pick of the bunch would be the aforementioned "Jekyll And Hyde", as featured on their session a couple of years previously) in the style of MAGNUM or SHERWOOD failed to win favour with many of their original fans, although it may have won a few converts to take their place. Having said that, it's their first long-player that NWOBHM aficionados tend to remember most fondly, not its rather bland sequel.

By the time the second SARACEN album finally appeared in the shops (it took quite a long time getting there, for some reason), the outfit had already recruited former PHOENIX RISING drummer Danny Spencer to the fold, and they continued to ply their trade for the remainder of that year, although their activities failed to create all that much of a stir in the wake of the widespread critical denouncement of »Change Of Heart«. Nevertheless, Tommy Vance invited them back to the BBC's studios at the beginning of 1985, whereupon the lads laid down another session for radio use. Tellingly, however, this batch of recordings was considered to be better-suited to the 'Into The Music' audience, this offshoot programme tending to feature considerably more lightweight and commercial material than the 'Friday Rock Show' itself. Broadcast on the 14th of February 1985, the musicians ran through efficient versions of "Cheatin'", "A Face In The Crowd", "Love On Sight" and the previously-unheard "It's Not Over". Sadly, however, the latter title proved to be a less-than-accurate representation of the group's future, and they appear to have disbanded within a few months of this particular appearance.

Of their various one-time members, only axeman Haydn Conway can be confirmed as having resurfaced in any heavy outfit of note (although Jason Gardner has been fairly active on the production front, and there was supposedly some level of SARACEN involvement in an early 90's bunch called DOMINION, who shouldn't be confused with the heavyweights who recorded for the Peaceville label), his first port of call being an act called WANTED, where he happily teamed up with erstwhile SAXON stalwarts Steve Dawson and Nigel Durham. Although this particular venture failed to amount to much in its original form, it gradually evolved into the rather more successful and familiar SON OF A BITCH as more ex-SAXON personnel (namely Graham Oliver and Pete Gill) joined in the fun, and this conglomeration of post-NWOBHM scenesters have undertaken various touring and recording activities in recent years, including the release of a CD or two of their own.

LP's
»Heroes, Saints And Fools« Nucleus Records 1981
[Issued with two slightly different colour schemes and with different sleeve details]
»Change Of Heart« Neat 1984/Roadrunner 1984
[UK/Dutch issue]

7" Singles
»No More Lonely Nights« Nucleus Records 1982
»We Have Arrived« Neat 1984
[Both tracks different to album versions]

CD's
»Heroes, Saints And Fools« TRC Records 1992
[With seven bonus tracks from second album]

Compilation Appearances
"We Have Arrived" on »Powertrax« Cassette Neat 1986 + »Heavy Metal Collection 2« CD X-Tra Collection 1993

SATAN

Trev Robinson (v)
Steve Ramsey (g)
Russ Tippins (g)
Graeme English (b)
Andy Reed (d)

With the seeds of Tyneside legends SATAN having been sown by some youthful friends towards the end of 1980, the band finally became a going concern early the following year, whereupon they joined in with the burgeoning local music scene, soon forming alliances with many of the other regional hopefuls. As their uncompromising moniker suggested, however, SATAN's interpretation of the NWOBHM ethos involved a rather heavier musical stance than most of their contemporaries, and they were one of the earliest outfits (along with ANGEL WITCH and WITCHFINDER GENERAL, for example) to take on board the weighty influences of JUDAS PRIEST, IRON MAIDEN and BLACK SABBATH, rather than merely retreading the familiar ground covered by the countless heavy acts who had set their sights on emulating the more accessible music of UFO, THIN LIZZY and LED ZEPPELIN. It took less than a year for the quintet to establish themselves as genuine contenders in the North East, and their first proper trip to the studio took them to the hallowed gates of Guardian Records, where the likes of MYTHRA, HELLANBACH and HOLLOW GROUND had all started out on the long and winding road to fame and fortune. SATAN proceeded to record four tracks at the facility, namely "The Executioner", "Oppression", "Kiss Of Death" and "Heads Will Roll" (no songs about fluffy bunny rabbits for these metal merchants), and these subsequently formed the basis of a promotional cassette which the lads would tout around the labels and radio stations in an attempt to get a bit of airplay and recognition.

The keen ear of Terry Gavaghan (Guardian's boss), however, had spotted some stars in the making, and he rapidly came up with bigger plans for SATAN, suggesting that the outfit might like to see some of their demo efforts appearing on vinyl. The ambitious band eventually capitulated to these requests and stumped up the necessary cash, with "Kiss Of Death" and "Heads Will Roll" being selected to comprise the

first SATAN 7", issued (in a functional-but-imposing picture sleeve) on the Guardian label in the early months of 1982. The sheer intensity of their debut release took many observers by complete surprise, although respectable sales throughout the country swiftly confirmed that there was indeed a genuine market for this kind of heavy-duty metal in Britain. Mind you, it rapidly became evident that an even greater level of interest from overseas (mainland Europe, in particular) would ultimately see demand massively outstripping supply as far as the meagre original pressing (a thousand copies) was concerned. The success of the single came as a shock to both label and band, and stocks of »Kiss Of Death« were swiftly exhausted, but the record was never re-pressed, for some strange reason, rendering it an extremely coveted and highly-valued piece nowadays. Still, the label subsequently decided to include both of SATAN's remaining demo selections, "The Executioner" and "Oppression", on their »Roxcalibur« compilation, allowing fans another chance to get their hands on some exclusive material. In all honesty, there were practically no other groups (with the notable exception of VENOM) in Britain performing such hard-hitting material at the time (even the likes of SHOCK TREATMENT and DEMOLITION generally had more in common with MOTÖRHEAD than BLACK SABBATH), and some of the astoundingly heavy riffing (on "The Executioner", in particular) was surely a source of inspiration for the likes of HELLHAMMER in years to come.

By mid-1982, the lads were riding the crest of a wave and enjoying their new-found popularity to the full, although they soon began contemplating their next move, and whether the current line-up was sufficiently strong to propel them into the realms of power metal immortality. In the event, they decided to ditch the limited vocal range of the unfortunate Trev Robinson (pity, I rather liked his distinctive style, later put to good use in a melodic act called NOTRE DAME), favouring the more powerful lungs of Ian Davison Swift instead. Around this time, they also parted company with drummer Andy Reed (who vanished off the face of the earth), replacing him with new blood in the shape of Ian McCormack, a long-time associate. The revamped outfit's master plan for world domination was now set in action, and the lads recorded their famous »Into The Fire« demo (as featured on the »NWOBHM Demo Tapes« bootleg) in an attempt to win themselves a lucrative deal. Fortunately, the tape was a very strong effort, and tracks such as "Trial By Fire", "Blades Of Steel" and "Pull The Trigger" (slightly more accessible, but still powerful) soon had the labels sniffing around. Unsurprisingly, one of the first to call round were Neat, and the lads seemed pretty happy to sign with their local company, especially when they had such a useful, money-spinning partnership with Roadrunner. Before the outfit's debut album was recorded, however, they had to endure a couple of further reshuffles. Drummer Ian McCormack defected to rival act BATTLEAXE, and new sticksman Sean Taylor (a veteran of an early incarnation of RAVEN) was drafted in to fill the gap. More surprisingly, SATAN then came to a fairly amicable agreement to swap vocalists with the recently-established AVENGER, which led to Brian Ross (who had formed AVENGER after the initial collapse of BLITZKRIEG) joining the SATAN camp.

With the latest version of SATAN (now featuring their third frontman in just over two years) being a fairly stable affair in the first instance (many regard this to be the definitive line-up, although it was actually quite short-lived), the band finally (after a few gigs to find their feet, including the first of many memorable trips to the legendary Dynamo club in Eindhoven) got around to entering the studio and laying down their punningly-titled »Court In The Act« longplayer. With the lads having had little time to write new material, the album was based largely around the numbers from their recent demo, although there were a few less-familiar compositions ("Broken Treaties", "Alone In The Dock" and "Hunt You Down", the latter originally penned by Ross during his time with AVENGER) to balance things out. It was a truly sterling performance all round (Brian Ross bringing a commanding presence to the mike stand and belting out the numbers with an impressive degree of conviction), although the inclusion of two consecutive instrumentals ("The Ritual" and "Dark Side Of Innocence") may have seemed slightly excessive. Having said that, the latter was only a brief interlude, and the former was such an inventive and competently-played affair (bonus points awarded for some razor-sharp riffing and an astonishingly tight rhythm section) that it's hard to come up with any particularly harsh criticism. It was, all in all, a substantial and self-assured release which appealed to a great many fans around the world, and copies were soon being snapped up wherever it was made available for sale. Mind you, the number of units ultimately shifted *via* the Roadrunner pressing far exceeded the fairly limited quantity sold by Neat (suggesting that the British weren't particularly enamoured of the combination of unashamedly forceful music and magnificently heroic lyrics, a fair proportion of which centred around the activities of rampaging hordes of valiant warriors), however, so the musicians elected to convert themselves into a full-time Roadrunner act from that point onwards.

The band wasted little time before going out on the road to promote the album, and the latter part of 1983 saw them venturing across to mainland Europe once more, where the lads undertook a lengthy headlining tour and delighted the crowds with a selection of material from throughout their history (and, more often than not, chucking in old chestnut "Blitzkrieg" as an encore). Upon their return to the UK, SATAN hurriedly entered the studio once again, whereupon they proceeded to record three numbers ("Break Free", "Pull The Trigger" and "Dynamo") for Roadrunner, their label's intention being to get a further slice of vinyl into the shops as rapidly as possible. The three-tracker was scheduled for release in the spring of 1984, although

SATAN's plans were thrown into turmoil when the restless Brian Ross unexpectedly announced his decision to go off and do his own thing again (this initially involved helping out in LONE WOLF, before he eventually decided to get BLITZKRIEG off the ground once more), leaving the members of SATAN to reassess the situation. With Ross no longer a part of the set-up, the remaining musicians certainly didn't want to release the EP in its intended form, although they gave serious consideration to the possibility of getting someone else in to re-record the vocals at short notice. Eventually, however, the whole idea was scrapped, and the master tapes were left to gather dust for a considerable number of years.

SATAN still has to address the problem of finding another new frontman, however, and the fact that they already had some additional European shows in the pipeline made it all the more urgent that they attempt to rectify the situation as quickly as possible. In fact, they were forced to use a stand-in for their forthcoming live commitments, the deputy vocalist taking the form of TYSONDOG guitarist Alan Hunter, who had actually guested on one of the tracks ("Break Free") on the band's debut album. With those important touring activities completed, Hunter was able to return to his own outfit, and SATAN began looking for a full-time replacement in earnest. Fortunately, they managed to identify a likely candidate, former MYTHRA roadie and SARACEN (»Roksnax« version) frontman, Lou Taylor, who had recently been earning a crust in BLIND FURY, Kevin Heybourne's post-ANGEL WITCH venture. With hindsight, inviting Taylor to join the party might have been a slightly unwise move, as he soon began taking over the outfit as his own, suggesting name changes and fairly major shifts in musical direction. After putting up a bit of initial resistance, the remaining members finally succumbed to the frontman's wishes, and the lads elected to sever all links with their heavy past by seeking out a brand-new identity. Their first suggestion was the utterly atrocious RASKALLE (which I'm pretty sure they pinched from a minor act they had once played alongside in Europe), but this proposal was eventually vetoed on the grounds that it was a monumentally hopeless choice. They subsequently flirted with the notion of calling themselves FIREFOX (a bit better), but this also seems to have fallen foul of someone-or-other. Fortunately, Kevin Heybourne's BLIND FURY venture had already ceased to exist by this stage, so the lads concluded that it would be perfectly acceptable to help themselves to the identity, causing a fair bit of consternation among rock fans, who wrongly assumed that the Northerners would now be playing a selection of Heybourne-penned originals. Let's get this straight once and for all, the two versions of BLIND FURY were completely separate acts, the only connection being Lou Taylor!

After a few months spent trying out some new material, the newly-christened BLIND FURY (who had relocated to London some time beforehand) went back into the studio towards the end of the year, whereupon they set about the task of laying down their next album for Roadrunner. »Out Of Reach« appeared in the spring of 1985 (by which stage sticksman Sean Taylor had already guested on both WARRIOR and BLITZKRIEG records in his spare time), and the long-player saw the group making a wholesale move into more commercial waters, although it stopped well short of becoming mainstream AOR. To be honest, the whole thing was more along the lines of mid-period CLOVEN HOOF than anything else (some of the more restrained efforts were, additionally, quite similar to HARRIER), although the individual numbers generally failed to come across particularly strongly. It wasn't, on the face of it, a total disaster (the title track and "Living On The Edge" were fairly listenable), although a few critical drubbings from the reviewers soon warned the fans that this sure wasn't the SATAN of old. In the same way that BATTLEZONE failed to pull off this kind of over-ambitious musical about-turn on their second album, BLIND FURY sold themselves down the river on this record, and the general public were far from impressed. Nevertheless, they tried to salvage the situation with a session for the 'Friday Rock Show', broadcast on the 31st of May 1985, where the lads took the opportunity to showcase versions of "Contact Rock 'n' Roll", "Back Inside", "Feel Just The Same" (which had originally been penned by Taylor way back in his SARACEN days) and "Hard Times", the latter pair being non-LP compositions. It failed to reverse their fortunes, however, and sales of the long-player were extremely poor. After a few, ill-fated gigs as BLIND FURY, where only new material was featured in the set, the whole thing was revealed to have been a massive mistake.

In the aftermath of its commercial failure (not to mention its unrepresentative musical content), »Out Of Reach« was soon being written off as an ill-conceived 'Lou Taylor project', and the luckless frontman was soon out on his ear, later joining up with the fragmenting PERSIAN RISK for about a week before forming his own TOUR

DE FORCE venture. Having disposed of their wayward vocalist, the lads soon reverted back to the SATAN identity and recruited new singer Michael Jackson (insert your own joke here, I can't be bothered), formerly with a minor club act called ROUGH EDGE. After getting things back on track, the band went into the studio to record the puzzlingly-titled »Dirt« demo, where they unveiled some rather more forceful compositions such as "The Ice Man" and "Key To Oblivion". Within a short space of time, they were being courted by Germany's Steamhammer label, and the four tracks from the »Dirt« demo (one of which is so rude that decency forbids me to reveal its title) were subsequently pressed up as the »Into The Future« 12" (marketed as a mini-LP, although four tracks only constitute an EP), a release which was to allow the outfit to recapture some of their original fan base. They also adopted a rather odd image at this time (which I'm positive they nicked from SLAVE RAIDER), which involved wearing some tattered garments and chucking a lot of mud (at least, I *hope* it was mud) over themselves. They were probably trying to make some sort of statement, but they still looked like tossers.

After a successful European tour towards the end of the year (with ANGEL WITCH in tow), the lads were soon back in the studio to record their *'proper'* second album. This finally emerged in 1987, under the title of »Suspended Sentence« (I don't know what lay behind their fascination with legal matters), and represented something of a return to form at last. SATAN were now operating in a semi-thrashy style (in the manner of ATOMKRAFT or ONSLAUGHT) at times, although many of the numbers were still quite similar in construction to the material featured on their weighty debut set, and it was enough to convince the European fans (the British public had long since given up on them) that SATAN were now back in business. Admittedly, novel tracks such as "Who Dies Wins", "11th Commandment" and "Calculated Execution" were all extremely powerful (both musically and lyrically), and the general standard of musicianship couldn't be faulted, although some of the numbers dragged on far too long and (with the notable exception of the emotionally-charged "Avalanche Of A Million Hearts"), much of the material on display was pretty interchangeable, so it wasn't a perfect record by any stretch of the imagination. Still, it met with the inevitable rapturous reception from Europe (their fan base now appeared to be primarily located in Germany), and the quintet went out there on tour (with labelmates RUNNING WILD) towards the end of the year. Whenever the lads went out on the road, though, they were invariably collared by someone or other and informed how influential they had been to many of the heavier acts of the day (EXODUS were particularly big fans, apparently), which must have been particularly rewarding for an outfit who were now regarded as *'tired old fogeys'* at home.

Although the lads now seemed to be regaining their original popularity in no uncertain terms, they began to question whether or not they really wanted to be ploughing on as SATAN when their music now bore only a passing resemblance to the type of material purveyed by the outfit in their original incarnation. Indeed, the fact that many casual observers failed to regard the ensemble as anything but a hackneyed bunch of ageing rejects from the NWOBHM explosion meant that it was a constant struggle just to maintain any significant level of interest in their activities. After a lengthy and turbulent career as SATAN, the quintet finally tired of both the NWOBHM millstone and the widespread assumption that they adhered to a demonic lyrical stance (which was never really the case), and, after receiving one ribbing too many about their *'hopelessly clichéd'* moniker, decided that enough was enough. In the end, the lads concluded that it was now time to start afresh once more, although they had no intentions of heading down the BLIND FURY route to tuneful oblivion this time. Within a matter of months, the lads started a new career as PARIAH (see separate entry), and the much-maligned name of SATAN was finally laid to rest. Their debut album, however, has recently been exhumed by those hard-working chaps at Neat Metal (having been issued as a bootleg CD some years previously to meet demand), and the long-lost tracks from the aborted Ross-era EP were generously included as bonus selections.

LP's
»**Court In The Act**« Neat 1983/Roadrunner 1983
[UK/Dutch issue]
»**Out Of Reach**« Roadrunner 1985
[Under the name of BLIND FURY]
»**Suspended Sentence**« Steamhammer 1987

12" EP's
»**Into The Future**« Steamhammer 1986
[All four tracks non-LP]

7" Singles
»**Kiss Of Death**« Guardian 1982
[Both tracks non-LP]

CD's

»Suspended Sentence/Into The Future«
Steamhammer 1987
»Court In The Act« Roadrunner 199?
[Japanese issue]
»Out Of Reach« Roadrunner 199?
[Under the name of BLIND FURY, Japanese issue]
»Court In The Act« Reborn Classics 1993
[Bootleg release, also includes SAVAGE's »Loose 'n' Lethal« album]
»Court In The Act« Neat Metal 1997
[With three bonus tracks]

Exclusive Compilation Appearances
"Oppression" on »Roxcalibur« LP Guardian 1982/CD British Steel 1998 + »12 Commandments In Metal« LP Roadrunner 1985 + »NWOBHM Vol.3« Bootleg CD 1992
"The Executioner" on »Roxcalibur« LP Guardian 1982/CD British Steel 1998
"Pull The Trigger" on »NWOBHM Demo Tapes« Bootleg CD 1992
[A different recording was featured on BLITZKRIEG's »A Time Of Changes« LP]

Compilation Appearances
"Hunt You Down" on »Metal Battle« LP Neat 1983/Roadrunner 1983
"No Turning Back" on »Metal Hammer« LP Roadrunner 1984
"Kiss Of Death" on »NWOBHM Vol.4« Bootleg CD 1992
"Heads Will Roll" on »NWOBHM Vol.6« Bootleg CD 1992
"Into The Fire/Trial By Fire" on »NWOBHM Demo Tapes« Bootleg CD 1992
[Different to album version]
"Blades Of Steel" on »NWOBHM Demo Tapes« Bootleg CD 1992
[Different to album version]
"No Turning Back" on »NWOBHM Demo Tapes« Bootleg CD 1992
[Different to album version]
"Break Free" on »NWOBHM Demo Tapes« Bootleg CD 1992
[Different to album version]
"The Ritual" on »NWOBHM Demo Tapes« Bootleg CD 1992
[Different to album version]

SATANIC RITES (I)

Patterson
Frankland

Call me a sceptic if you like, but I find it extremely difficult to accept that the particular version of SATANIC RITES who chose to unleash a heavy, straightforward, biker-friendly single at some point in 1981 subsequently evolved into a considerably more thoughtful and sophisticated rock outfit with accessible female vocals, tasteful keyboard backing and a completely different outlook towards life in general. It just seems a particularly unlikely course of events, and it's highly improbable that any band would lie dormant for a period of four whole years before resurfacing in such a dissimilar style (and, by the looks of things, with a completely different line-up) and releasing two full albums within a relatively short space of time. Admittedly, it's not completely impossible that the all of the SATANIC RITES releases were attributable to a project with some common lineage (witness the dubious musical progression of the Essex version of PROWLER between 1980 and 1985, for instance), although I reckon we should probably err on the side of caution and classify them as separate units until proven otherwise.

SATANIC RITES were unquestionably the most obscure outfit to have been given a vinyl release of their own by the Heavy Metal label, and even a full exposé on the group's personnel is impossible at this point in time, although they appear to have been a quintet, judging by the seldom-seen picture cover which accompanies their rare single. Both "Live To Ride" and "Hit And Run" are fairly rudimentary NWOBHM workouts (the vocals seem a bit strained in places), although the band were fairly energetic in their musical approach, suggesting comparisons with the likes of RENEGADE and HAMMERHEAD. Assuming, therefore, that this bunch didn't subsequently reinvent themselves and go on to release a pair of fairly decent post-NWOBHM albums in the mid-80's (*vide infra*), it looks as though the original version of SATANIC RITES had ceased all operations shortly after their debut single had made its way into the shops (maybe it was merely a one-off get-together in the studio, which might explain the complete lack of information relating to the participants, and the fact that they didn't get out and about much), so I guess they must have become disillusioned within a remarkably short space of time. As usual, any supporting or contradictory evidence should be submitted to the court at a later date…

7" Singles
»Live To Ride« Heavy Metal 1981

Compilation Appearances

"**Hit And Run**" on »NWOBHM Vol.6« Bootleg CD 1992 + »Heavy Metal Records Singles Collection Vol.1« CD British Steel 1996
"**Live To Ride**" on »Heavy Metal Records Singles Collection Vol.1« CD British Steel 1996

SATANIC RITES (II)

Deborah Webster (v)
Stuart Page (g)
David Ingham (b)
Kevin Doyle (k)
David Kershaw (d)

The mid-80's incarnation of SATANIC RITES (a name which would do any Black Metal outfit proud), based in Yorkshire, appear to have come and gone within a relatively short space of time, although the enterprising ensemble still managed the impressive feat of releasing a pair of privately-pressed albums during their brief existence. The quintet first came to prominence with the self-financed »Which Way The Wind Blows« effort (issued in a pretty accomplished sleeve) in 1985, which revealed this bunch to be resident at the heavier end of the female-vocal spectrum. In spite of some promising song titles, however, it doesn't quite reach the intensity of WAR MACHINE, the whole affair being more along the lines of SIEGE or RAMPENT. It was a reasonably varied set (with a few perfectly acceptable keyboard contributions in places), though, boasting a number of strong inclusions such as "Burn In Hell", "Turn Around" and "Slam The Door". There was, at times, also something of a CANIS MAJOR influence, especially on the epic title track, and a couple of instances where the group displayed a somewhat more powerful style, vaguely suggestive of OVERDRIVE or the West Midlands version of SCARAB. The record didn't attract a great deal of attention in the national press at the time, and the release would appear to have experienced a fairly limited distribution, but it doubtless won favour with some of the local rock fans.

The band returned a couple of years later (they were hardly conspicuous in terms of live appearances at any stage, so it's hard to comment on their activities during the preceding months) with another full-length effort, this time titled »No Use Crying« (with a rather less impressive sleeve). They had recruited a new keyboard player (Graham Dyson) in the interim, and their vocalist was now identified as Deborah Ingham, presumably having become spliced to the group's bassist sometime after the first album. Their second long-player was a considerably more restrained and lightweight affair, even bordering on pop/rock on a couple of occasions, which was a genuine surprise after their comparatively substantial debut. It wasn't a total disaster, though, and the likes of "Changling" and "Cast My Spell" were reasonably capable inclusions, but the flimsy, semi-progressive compositions which comprise much of the remainder of this particular album are just so utterly nondescript that they can actually be quite irritating at times. Again, the record failed to set the world on fire, and the members of SATANIC RITES were soon disappearing back into the obscurity from whence they came.

LP's
»**Which Way The Wind Blows**« Chub 1985
»**No Use Crying**« Chub 1987

SAVAGE

Chris Bradley (v, b)
Andy Dawson (g)
Wayne Renshaw (g)
Dave Lindley (d)

Nottinghamshire's much-loved SAVAGE (not to be confused with some Dutch namesakes from the same period) first got the metal bug in around 1978, the band's original members finding themselves being magnetically attracted to the strong ambition and personality of frontman Chris Bradley, who had big plans for the outfit. Joining up in the first instance were Andy Dawson (g), Wayne Renshaw (g) and Dave Lindley (d), and the group soon set about the task of extracting something marketable from their experimental musical fumblings, the lads making good use of such well-worn influences as THIN LIZZY, JUDAS PRIEST and UFO. Realising that *'overnight success'* was something of a mythical concept, the down-to-earth quartet resigned themselves to the inevitable routine of demos, rehearsals and local gigs, hoping that their activities would, nevertheless, raise a major-label eyebrow or two at some point. In spite of many favourable appearances throughout the Midlands at the turn of the decade, however, they still had to wait until 1981 (by which time they already had a demo or two under their belts) for their first crack at the big time, which came with an offer from the local Suspect Records (most familiar for their patronage of SPARTA's early career) for SAVAGE to appear on their forthcoming metal compilation, a modest local-band collection entitled »Scene Of The Crime«.

It was a welcome and timely invitation, and the lads jumped at the chance to see their name gracing a piece of vinyl at last, laying down "Let It Loose" and "Dirty Money" for the project. The pairing showed SAVAGE to have mastered a heavy, blistering style of metal which can only properly be described as *'quintessential NWOBHM'*, something to which a great many

bands aspired, but which pitifully few actually managed to deliver. Assisted by a more-than-adequate production, the group were able to shine with their faithful interpretation of the NWOBHM archetype, their material eliciting comparisons with the likes of CHARIOT, EXCALIBUR, DARK HEART and SAMURAI. Admittedly, they hadn't been pitted against outstandingly talented opposition on this occasion (the other acts featured were PANZA DIVISION, SPARTA, TYRANT and MANITOU), although it was plain for all to see that those charging riffs and heartfelt vocals served to separate SAVAGE from the chasing pack, and this appearance went a long way towards identifying the outfit as worthy of label attention. Still, they were to wait a while longer for fame and fortune to come their way, and 1982 saw the lads indulging in the NWOBHM transfer market for the first (and only) time, with drummer Dave Lindley being released from contract to join up with local rivals DAWN TRADER, while SAVAGE recruited new striker Mark Brown from fellow »Scene Of The Crime« veterans TYRANT. Once they had broken in their new recruit (whose first gig was a prestigious affair, the group supporting DIAMOND HEAD), there would surely be no stopping them...

In the spring of 1982, word of SAVAGE's activities drew the attention of the fledgling Ebony Records, and the lucky outfit were immediately offered the usual compilation appearance to test the water. "Ain't No Fit Place", the powerful number selected to appear on the label's inaugural »Metal Fatigue« sampler, turned out to be another admirably confident effort, and it's fair to say that these young Nottinghamshire hopefuls stood head and shoulders above the rest of the nonentities on display, none of whom managed to progress any further in the music business. The talented SAVAGE, however, were deservedly plucked from relative obscurity to be groomed as one of Ebony's flagship acts of years to come. Still, they had to go through the formal initiation ritual of releasing a 7" single to prove themselves, and so "Ain't No Fit Place" was re-recorded (in abridged form), along with "The China Run", to form the basis of their proper vinyl debut. Although Ebony might not have expected the band to take off straight away, the record was soon shifting an impressive number of units, having garnered some decent reviews (and some word-of-mouth recommendations) within a remarkably short space of time. Realising that they undoubtedly had something of a hot potato on their hands, Ebony were quick to commission a full LP, and, after several months of intensive songwriting and rehearsal sessions, SAVAGE went into the studio facility to create their much-anticipated album.

It seems to have taken quite a while for the recording of SAVAGE's full-length debut to progress to completion, and the group's fairly protracted studio activities appear to have run concurrently with some increasingly-newsworthy jaunts around the country. A particularly notable outing came when the lads were invited to support MERCYFUL FATE at the Hammersmith Clarendon (it was supposed to be a whole tour, but things didn't quite work out as intended), the Danes having come over to lay down a 'Friday Rock Show' session and delight a few unsuspecting audiences at the same time. According to fairly credible reports, Ebony's head honcho (Darryl Johnston) had played King Diamond a selection of tracks (presumably when MERCYFUL FATE were engaged in the task of recording their contribution to the label's »Metallic Storm« sampler) which had previously been recorded at Ebony's own studio facility, and the lowly SAVAGE had impressed the wacky frontman most of all. The one-off gig was a major success, and the outfit were soon able to command a healthy crowd of their own without relying on the help of a more familiar act. After what seemed like an eternity, the group's debut album finally hit the shops, and »Loose 'n' Lethal« was to be the legendary record which well and truly catapulted the talented bunch into the hearts of metal fans worldwide. Having said all that, this 'long-player' was a disappointingly brief affair, and it set an unwelcome precedent for a number of Ebony's future releases, some of which barely scraped over the half-hour mark.

The album featured just eight tracks in total, including all-new versions of four already-familiar numbers, notably "Ain't No Fit Place" and "The China Run" (both from their single), plus "Let It Loose" and "Dirty Money" (from the »Scene Of The Crime« compilation). As strong as these compositions were, it might have been nice to showcase some newer efforts, and a few of SAVAGE's more devoted followers might have felt a bit short-changed by the distinct paucity of exclusive tracks. It was all very enjoyable, nevertheless, and the rough 'n' ready production actually suited the material quite well, giving the whole affair something of a spontaneous, 'live' feel. There was barely a weak number to be found anywhere, and the likes of the excellent "Cry Wolf" (very similar to CHARIOT's "Screams The Night", it has to be said), "Berlin", "On The Rocks" and "White Hot" were all well up to the band's usual high standards. The normally-impassive journalists were universally impressed, and were soon having to invent new superlatives for their reviews of the album. It was all pretty remarkable, and SAVAGE already seemed to have the world at their feet. Sales of the long-player rapidly went through the roof, and tens of thousands of copies proceeded to fly out of Britain as export issues (in particular, they hit exactly the right chord with the American market), and insatiable metal fans around the globe were soon clamouring for more. In due course, the lads were afforded the accolade of appearing at the Aardschok Festival in Holland, alongside the likes of METALLICA (more on them later), VENOM and TOKYO BLADE, and their participation in this memorable, high-profile event surely represented the pinnacle of SAVAGE's career.

Along with the debut albums released by GRIM REAPER and SHY, the phenomenal success of SAVAGE's first long-player undoubtedly served to establish Ebony, and the small-time label (having seen a huge return on its initial investment) was able to expand into a far more ambitious and influential concern by 1984. With money to burn, a brand-new recording facility was commissioned and the power-hungry company began signing semi-talented outfits left, right and centre. Furthermore, American interest in the label's more established acts soon reached fever pitch, with the mighty RCA offering to take some of them under their wing for promotion overseas. While GRIM REAPER and SHY were subsequently given the chance to further their careers with albums for RCA, however, the luckless SAVAGE (to whom precisely the same offer had apparently been extended) were never given the opportunity to progress from their lowly status as Ebony recording artists. This was a pretty baffling state of affairs, and the rationale behind this perverse and mulish decision has never been fully explained, although it's also worth noting that the youngsters themselves were blissfully unaware of all these underhand boardroom shenanigans at the time. Nevertheless, when the reality of the situation finally dawned on the bewildered musicians, they wasted precious little time before terminating their relationship with Ebony, who had already started making preparations for a follow-up release.

In spite of their former label's lack of critical judgement, there seemed little chance that SAVAGE would be left to wallow in self-pity or disappear into obscurity overnight, and there was a suitably happy outcome before the end of the year when Zebra Records stepped in with a well-timed offer to escort some further SAVAGE product into the shops. With the handy patronage of a new label offering them a lifeline, the group's next move was to record a three track EP (featuring "We Got The Edge", "Runnin' Scared" and "She Don't Need You") for imminent release on Zebra. Housed within an excellent and striking cover, the 12" contained a triumvirate of extremely enjoyable compositions, although all seemed marginally less frenetic than the band's early material. In terms of first impressions, therefore, these numbers clearly hinted that SAVAGE might just be preparing to move into slightly more accessible, semi-anthemic territory, although it was evident that these musicians still had some extremely interesting musical ideas up their sleeves. Fortunately, the loyal fans seemed not to develop any particular antagonism towards the group's minor shift in direction, and this latest slice of vinyl was selling by the bucketload within weeks, prompting Zebra to keep the lads under contract for a bit longer. In due course, SAVAGE followed in the footsteps of PERSIAN RISK and built upon the foundations of their Zebra-financed EP by recording a full-length effort for the label, the only difference being that SAVAGE's LP actually appeared as scheduled.

Album number two, »Hyperactive«, hit the shops in 1985, and turned out to be a considerably more melodic effort than many people had anticipated. Even some of the older and more popular numbers from the live set (notably "Keep It On Ice" and "Stevie's Vengeance") appeared to have been reworked to come across less forcefully, but it still represented a capable enough selection of compositions. In particular, the likes of "Hard On Your Heels", "Gonna Tear Ya Heart Out" and "Eye For An Eye" stood out as effortlessly listenable efforts, the overall sound suggesting that elements of ELIXIR, DEF LEPPARD and TYTAN might have been incorporated into SAVAGE's more recent work, so »Hyperactive« definitely wasn't a predictable follow-up to the proto-thrash of »Loose 'n' Lethal« by any means. Sadly, the record failed to win the approval of all that many die-hard fans, which is something of an injustice, since it hardly constituted a full-scale wimp-out, just the sort of logical progression that any forward-looking outfit might have been tempted to investigate sooner or later. In the wake of relatively poor sales (mind you, it would have been difficult to emulate the stellar performance of its predecessor), there seemed little possibility that SAVAGE would be invited to undertake any additional recording sessions for Zebra. In fact, the label concluded that it wasn't even worth releasing a single to promote the album, although an unfeasibly scarce 7" (based around "Cardiac", possibly the weakest cut on the entire set) did eventually sneak out in France, the record appearing on the Black Dragon label, much to the bemusement of the band themselves.

By 1986, things weren't going well at all. The offers of overseas work had long since dried up, the record companies were largely disinterested in SAVAGE's current activities, and the once-proud outfit seemed to have little musical future other than a steadily-declining role on the local club scene. Even then, emerging local favourites such as DEUCE and SABBAT seemed to be stealing their fire somewhat, leaving SAVAGE to consider whether or not they should continue. In the end, the lads made one last stand and recorded a further demo, and they briefly got their hopes up when there was a flicker of interest from one of the more influential labels of the day. Sadly, this came to nothing, and so SAVAGE finally threw in the towel by the end of the year. In the wake of their demise, the outfit split into two factions, with Andy Dawson, Mark Brown and Wayne Renshaw forming REBEL, while Chris Bradley elected to go it alone with XL, an act who were, in all honesty, almost imperceptibly different from SAVAGE themselves. Although both outfits benefitted from the generous patronage of certain sections of the rock press (notably 'Metal Forces'), REBEL soon began showing signs of instability, with Renshaw going back to his day job in 1987 and Brown moving on to pastures new shortly thereafter. Dawson soldiered on alone for a while, but ultimately swallowed his pride and disbanded the outfit, whereupon he teamed up with Bradley in the thriving XL. Joining the duo in the ranks of XL at that time were guitarist Stewart Whawell and drummer Richard Kirk, the group's greatest claim to fame coming with a Friday Rock Show session from late 1988, where the outfit took great pleasure in wheeling out old favourite "Let It Loose" once again.

For some reason, however, XL consistently failed to build upon their considerable early popularity, and had finally called it a day by around the turn of the decade. Bradley subsequently assumed a rather more low-profile level of involvement in the rock scene, although he continued to play the clubs as a member of various traditional rock and blues-based acts, collaborating with former members of LIMELIGHT on occasion. Dawson, meanwhile, formed a succession of small-time rock ventures, notably RED, QUANGO and CLOWNHOUSE, the latter bunch even getting as far as releasing a self-financed CD in the course of their relatively brief existence. In the years since SAVAGE's demise, however, it had become apparent that they still had at least one major fan, that daft Ulrich bloke from America, who would regularly proffer his opinionated views concerning those long-forgotten British hopefuls who originally inspired his own outfit to form and play heavy music in the first instance. It transpired that METALLICA had been avid followers of SAVAGE from the outset, and Ulrich's well-worn copy of »Scene Of The Crime« had served to provide the outfit with two of their earliest cover versions, which they gleefully reworked in the rehearsal studio and at their first batch of live appearances.

Intriguingly, it appears that METALLICA were all set to release their interpretation of "Let It Loose" in an official capacity at one point (possibly on the »Creeping Death« 12", although this eventually paired DIAMOND HEAD's "Am I Evil" with BLITZKRIEG's "Blitzkrieg"), but apparently had second thoughts, so the only way for fans to check out the Yanks' version is by seeking out certain unofficial CD's or the famous bootleg single which couples this track with an equally

523

rough take of SWEET SAVAGE's "Killing Time". In fact, SAVAGE and METALLICA originally crossed paths while both were struggling to climb the ladder of success (at the Aardschok Festival, whereupon they became long-term acquaintances), and the latter were only too keen to express their admiration for SAVAGE in years to come, as Chris Bradley happily revealed: *"We became friends with them in the early days, we got along straight away, as we were both in the same boat at that stage. They told us that they had a copy of the »Scene Of The Crime« album, and liked both songs so much that they learnt to play them. "Let It Loose" and "Dirty Money" were apparently on their first demo, and this helped them to get a deal with Megaforce!"* (Ref: Iron Pages No.35, 1996). Hmmm, I'm not

entirely sure about the validity of that last statement, although there's little doubt that METALLICA were heavily influenced by SAVAGE. Still, it was a bit odd that Ulrich didn't include any of their tracks on his »NWOBHM '79 Revisited« album...

The almost inevitable upshot of all this METALLICA-induced interest in the band was a full-scale SAVAGE reunion (where the ever-dependable Dawson and Bradley were joined by the outfit's original drummer, Dave Lindley), although it's perhaps slightly surprising that it took until 1995 for this to happen. Anyhow, the lads swiftly formed an allegiance with the resurrected Neat Metal, proudly announced that they were bringing out a brand-new CD called »Holy Wars«, and assured everyone that they would soon be taking on the world once again. In fact, their comeback album wasn't really an entirely 'new' set of recordings after all, as it featured an extremely predictable rehashing of the METALLICA-sponsored "Let It Loose" (cunningly retitled "Let It Loose 95"), while the likes of "Anthem", "Fashion By Force" and "Headstrong" were nothing other than remnants from the XL days. Nevertheless, there were a few unfamiliar numbers on display, and the likes of "How?" (as close to THIN LIZZY as you can get without buying a THIN LIZZY album), "Suffer The Children" and "Streets Of Fire" all showed that SAVAGE still had a few surprises in store. Chris Bradley was happy to acknowledge the prominent LIZZY influence in some of their latest material: *"Sure, we all loved the band a lot, they were certainly a huge influence on us, even in the early days. There are two numbers on the new album, 'Fashion By Force' and 'How?', which are very much inspired by them, and that's the direction we intend to follow in future. Even the album title, »Holy Wars«, is slightly LIZZY-ish, so it's sort of a tribute. Even before the SAVAGE reunion, we had got together with a couple of friends and played some sets of LIZZY material in local clubs."* [Ref: ibid.]

After undertaking a few low-key gigs as SAVAGE (the group utilising the services of second guitarist Andy Wilson in the live environment), the lads made the journey to Europe again in mid-1996, in order to play at the Bang Your Head Festival in Germany (organised by 'Heavy Oder Was?' magazine), where they appeared alongside TOKYO BLADE, another act who were enjoying something of a renaissance at the time. That same year, Neat Metal cannily reissued »Loose 'n' Lethal« on CD (after rejecting any notion of a tasteful remix and issuing the whole thing its gloriously-rough original form), and they generously threw in three previously-unheard numbers from SAVAGE's formative years. This was a significant bonus for fans (who previously had to make do with shabby bootleg CD's as an alternative to their crackly vinyl copies), and the pairing of "No Cause To Kill" and "The Devil Take You" (both taken from a 1980 demo tape) represent the outfit's first faltering steps in the world of heavy metal. These weren't classic efforts by any means (still far better than many of their contemporaries, mind you), although these inclusions must surely serve to assist any would-be NWOBHM scholars in their attempts to chronicle SAVAGE's development over the years. Even more remarkably, however, the CD also features their "Back On The Road", a cliché-ridden, hard-rocking track (supposedly their first-ever collective composition) recorded one year previously, which (by the group's own humble admission) clearly exposes their original primary influences, namely the ever-popular duo of UFO and THIN LIZZY.

SAVAGE weren't finished yet, though, and returned in 1997 with an all-new CD (the band now featuring drummer Richard Kirk, one of Bradley and Dawson's former colleagues in XL), this time entitled »Babylon«. In spite of the slightly disturbing fact that the central characters had originally threatened to deliver an entire set of LIZZY-inspired material, however, it was actually an individualistic and immensely interesting effort. This wasn't the NWOBHM-era SAVAGE of old, that's for sure, but these heavy, moody compositions were all extremely listenable, and »Babylon« seemed to represent a shift towards a rather more contemporary writing style. In fact, the album appeared to have considerably more in common with the likes of recent MEGADETH, STONE TEMPLE PILOTS or the unfeasibly excellent (and criminally-overlooked) SKYSCRAPER than anything more directly related to the original NWOBHM ethos, and standout efforts such as "Temple Of Deceit", "Babylon", "TV Nation" and "No Ordinary Day" (the group's gritty lyrics now tending to reflect social issues as opposed to the usual sex 'n' drugs 'n' stamp collecting nonsense) were undeniably outstanding compositions which demonstrated genuinely innovative musicianship. Sadly, the mainstream rock press seems to have given the release short shrift, the journalists probably being reluctant to endorse *'dinosaurs'* such as SAVAGE (no matter how strong their releases are) when they're supposed to be seeking out new *'talent'*. The lads seemed to go to ground after they had delivered this particular set (although they remained involved with the local music scene), but they recently resurfaced with a brand-new effort entitled »Xtreme Machine«, and played a set at Wacken 2000 to get their name back into circulation. Here's hoping their new CD meets with some critical approval and that they decide to stick around for a good few years yet.

LP's
»Loose 'n' Lethal« Ebony 1983
»Hyperactive« Zebra Records 1985

12" EP's
»We Got The Edge« Zebra Records 1984
[Both "Runnin' Scared" and "She Don't Need You" non-LP]

7" Singles
»Ain't No Fit Place« Ebony 1982
[Both tracks different to album versions]
»Cardiac« Black Dragon 1985

CD's
»Loose 'n' Lethal« Reborn Classics 1993
[Bootleg release, also includes SATAN's »Court In The Act« album]
»Holy Wars« Neat Metal 1995
[UK issue]
»Holy Wars« Pony Canyon 1995
[Japanese issue with two bonus tracks]
»Loose 'n' Lethal« Pony Canyon 1996
[Japanese issue with five bonus tracks]
»Babylon« Neat Metal 1997
[UK issue]
»Babylon« Pony Canyon 1997
[Japanese issue with one bonus track]
»Loose 'n' Lethal« Neat Metal 1997
[With three bonus tracks]
»Hyperactive« British Steel 1997
[With three bonus tracks]
»Xtreme Machine« Neat Metal 2000

Compilation Appearances
"Let It Loose" on »Scene Of The Crime« LP Suspect Records 1981 + »NWOBHM Vol.3« Bootleg CD 1992 + »The Metallic-Era« CD Neat Metal 1996
[Different to album version]
"Dirty Money" on »Scene Of The Crime« LP Suspect Records 1981 + »The Metallic-Era Volume II« CD Neat Metal 1999
[Different to album version]
"Ain't No Fit Place" on »Metal Fatigue« LP Ebony 1982
[Different to album and single versions]
"We Got The Edge" on »The Best Of British« LP Zebra 1985 + »Axe Attack« LP M Port 1985/Mausoleum 1986 + »The Best Of Indie Metal« CD Emporio 1998
"Let It Loose 95" on »Neat Metal« CD Neat Metal 1995
"How?" on »Neat Metal« CD Neat Metal 1995
"Space Cowboy" on »Frontiers 6« CD Private 1997
[Free with 'Frontiers' magazine]
"Are You Ready" on »Unbroken Metal« CD Private 1997

SAXON

Peter 'Biff' Byford (v)
Graham Oliver (g)
Paul Quinn (g)
Steve Dawson (b)
Pete Gill (d)

Although many people seem to regard Barnsley's legendary SAXON as pretty much an archetypal example of a NWOBHM outfit, I've always felt that they enjoyed rather more of a happy coexistence with the movement, establishing themselves before it all kicked off, riding along on its early 80's momentum but outlasting it effortlessly, and continuing to ply their trade (with an enviable level of success) even to the present day. It all started back in around 1976, when some youthful Tykes got the music bug (Biff Byford and Paul Quinn had initially jammed together in an act called COAST, where Biff actually played bass, as early as 1974) and formed a knockabout bunch called SON OF A BITCH, who did the rounds in the pubs and clubs of Yorkshire for a couple of years (with Pete Gill joining in the fun in 1977) without ever getting all that much in the way of recognition, before concluding that they either had to call it a day or set their sights considerably higher in the long run. At first, the band's direction of choice had apparently been a fairly haphazard mix of generic rock and boogie, although the lads gradually developed quite a distinctive style of their own, successfully bridging the good-time boogie of VARDIS and the upbeat power of early DEF LEPPARD, something which is quite tricky to pin down in terms of influences, but I reckon they must have been inspired to some extent by a few of the more edgy British acts of the 70's such as GILLAN, NAZARETH and BUDGIE. They adopted the very metal name of SAXON along the way, and their fortunes seemed to be looking up when the French label Carrere took a major risk and offered the lads a contract in the early part of 1979.

SAXON burst forth with an eponymous album several months later, although the general public hardly went crazy for this long-player in the first instance, but it still (especially when you consider how unknown the outfit were and how little pre-publicity there had been) managed to shift a reasonable number of units. Behind the metal-looking logo and heroic sleeve lay a record with a few decent numbers to its name, notably the upbeat "Backs To The Wall" and the unashamedly-titled "Stallions Of The Highway", although it was a patchy affair which also included such mediocre efforts as "Big Teaser" and the two-part "Rainbow Theme/Frozen Rainbow", the latter failing to win the hearts of too many average rock fans at the time. Still, the big NWOBHM explosion was still in its infancy, and SAXON would soon get their chance to shine once they had toughened up their act a bit. In the meantime, »Big Teaser« and »Backs To The Wall« emerged as singles, although they didn't exactly trouble the compilers of the mainstream charts. Carrere remained utterly convinced that they had something worth investing in, though, and encouraged the lads to come up with another full-length effort, on which the outfit commenced work after undertaking some productive touring activities. While the group were already able to draw a sizeable crowd in their locality, gigs further afield only really became viable when they hooked up with bigger attractions, and the likes of NAZARETH, RAINBOW and MOTÖRHEAD were happy to offer SAXON the deserved chance to open the proceedings at various well-attended events around the country. The outfit grabbed the opportunity to redeem themselves in the aftermath of an unremarkable debut long-player, and the punters were soon being won over by a combination of down-to-earth charm and musical ability, setting the stage for album number two.

Early the following year, SAXON recorded their first session for the 'Friday Rock Show', initially transmitted on the 15th of February 1980, where the lads performed a mixture of old and new material. In addition to "Backs To The Wall", "Stallions Of The Highway" and "Still Fit To Boogie" (three of the more capable efforts from the debut LP), they also showcased "Motorcycle Man", a considerably more proficient number which certainly seemed to indicate that they were now getting their act together in time for that second album. The public didn't have to wait very long to find out one way or another, and it duly transpired that SAXON had indeed come up with a bit of a corker. »Wheels Of Steel« emerged in the spring, and represented a marked progression from their unsure debut, with compositions such as "747 (Strangers In The Night)", "Stand Up And Be Counted", the memorable title track and the energetic "Motorcycle Man" all lodging themselves in the public's consciousness almost immediately. Sales of the record took off in an astonishing manner, and the album soon reached a phenomenal 'Top 5' placing in the mainstream charts, after which there was no looking back for SAXON. »Wheels Of Steel« and »747 (Strangers In The Night)« were trundled out as singles, and both hit the 'Top 20', although the more restrained »Suzie Hold On« failed to make much of an impression, so the musicians were soon acknowledging the rather blindingly obvious fact that it was their more upbeat and powerful numbers that were persuading the NWOBHM fans to part with their hard-earned cash. The lads were soon out on tour to promote their latest release, which initially took them around the UK (culminating in a prestigious appearance at the inaugural 'Monsters Of Rock' Festival at Donington, a recording of which was finally made available almost twenty years later), followed by a Stateside jaunt with RUSH, after which they immediately returned to the studio to lay down their second long-player of the year. By now, there was now no stopping SAXON in their inexorable quest for global domination.

It might have seemed a bit too soon for the outfit to be delivering another full album, and there were suggestions that their label might be exerting pressure upon them to come up with another record before they were ready, but they still managed to pull together a pretty respectable selection of material at short notice. »Strong Arm Of The Law« appeared towards the end of 1980, and it contained some very listenable compositions such as "Heavy Metal Thunder", "Dallas 1 p.m." and "20000 Ft.", although sales were rather more modest than those of »Wheels Of Steel«. The fans seemed to be voting with their wallets and refusing to purchase the record in the bulk quantities that their label had originally anticipated, and the album was soon being identified as something of an attempt to cash in on the success of its predecessor. In fact, just one song (the title track) was selected to appear as a single (which failed to sell in significant quantities either) this time, and there was only a brief end-of-year tour to promote the latest release, so it was all a bit of a non-starter. Before much longer, therefore, everyone concerned was putting the whole episode down to experience and thinking about starting off afresh with a properly-conceived set the following year. After a more generous period in the studio, the lads had captured an album's worth of material, and began preparing the world for its imminent release with a handful of European gigs, after which they jetted off to Japan for a couple of shows in front of a brand-new bunch of followers. It was soon back to the UK to oversee the release of »Denim And Leather«, though, and the latest vinyl offering was something of a return to form, the band demonstrating a good ear for melody as well as their usual flair for dynamic, anthemic arrangements. Highlights included "Princess Of The Night", "And The Bands Played On" and "Fire In The Sky", although the stand-out inclusion has to be the anthemic title track, a heartfelt (if slightly tongue-in-cheek) tribute to the whole NWOBHM phenomenon and the sense of community which surrounded the emergence of all the young hopefuls back in 1979. Sniff.

SAXON were back with a vengeance, and the singles were soon hitting the charts once again, with »And The Bands Played On« and »Never Surrender« following each other into the 'Top 20', which more than compensated for the utterly inexplicable failure of »Princess Of The Night« to make much of an impression in terms of sales. Oh well, you can't have everything. The lads were all geared up for some further touring activity, although they lost the services of the long-serving Pete Gill (who later enjoyed a stint with MOTÖRHEAD) towards the end of the year, whereupon they were compelled to enlist the services of stand-in sticksman Nigel Glockler (who had latterly been pounding the skins for wailing harridan TOYAH) to complete their end-of-year jaunt around the UK and Europe. As it turned out, Glockler made such a favourable impression that he was invited to join on a full-time basis, and was officially named as the new SAXON drummer in the early part of 1982. The lads then jetted off to the States again in the spring, where they headlined at some fairly prestigious venues, but returned to the UK in time for a high-profile event or two in the summer. They also performed a memorable live session on BBC Radio, where (on the 25th of April 1982) "20000 Ft.", "747 (Strangers In The Night)", "Dallas 1 p.m." and new number "The Eagle Has Landed" were showcased for the benefit of the station's listeners. There was, however, to be no new studio album from SAXON in 1982, largely due to the difficulty in getting enough recording time in between all their touring commitments (which included bill-topping appearances at both the Mildenhall and Hackney Festivals), but they made it up to the fans by releasing a live set entitled »The Eagle Has Landed«, which turned out to be a highly respectable release in its own right (capturing the power and energy of a SAXON concert remarkably efficiently), even if it failed to sell in equivalent numbers to their recent studio efforts. After some further UK dates in the latter part of 1982, however, it was down to the serious business of beginning work on yet another proper long-player.

»Power And The Glory« hit the shops in the spring of 1983, and successfully carried on the tradition of decent full-length releases, but the band were soon on the receiving end of a post-NWOBHM backlash, the movement having more or less fizzled out by this stage, whereupon the media had a field day with any outfit who stuck to their guns and failed to move with the times. SAXON had little or no intention of hiring a keyboard player, although they soon began wondering if there might be any mileage in a bit of tentative experimentation with some slightly more accessible material. In the meantime, however, sales of the album (and the pair of singles which emerged to promote it) reached respectable levels, so there was no immediate temptation to change a winning formula just to appease the hostile rock press. After a fairly extensive round of touring in the UK, North America and Europe, it was time to write some new material, and another full-length effort was recorded towards the end of the year. »Crusader«, in spite of its unashamedly heroic title and cover, was a record which suggested that the subliminal influence of some cruel reviews might have manifested itself in their latest material after all. Ominous titles such as "Sailing To America" seemed to intimate that a possible DEF LEPPARD-style invasion of the States might be on the cards, although SAXON's transatlantic success never actually came anywhere near eclipsing their performance in the UK. Still, the latest record was, on the face of it, rather more attuned to the MTV mentality, and some radio-friendly titles such as "Rock City", "Just Let Me Rock" and "Bad Boys (Like To Rock 'n' Roll)" (not that 'rock' was becoming their favourite word or anything) suggested a likely move away from the dubious NWOBHM associations of the fondly-remembered past. It was still a well-received set in the UK, however, and the press were soon forced to concede that (even if their singles were no longer charting) SAXON were still relevant after all.

SAXON were now on a roll, and their existence now seemed to revolve around delivering an adequate-but-unremarkable album every year, going out on tour and then repeating the process ad infinitum, as did several of their contemporaries, with varying degrees of success. It was a surprise, therefore, when the band decided to abandon the relative safety of Carrere and make a fresh start with EMI (originally on the Parlophone subsidiary), a label with absolutely no tolerance of amateurs or time-wasters. For SAXON to enjoy the patronage of this affluent concern, they would have to deliver the goods in no uncertain terms, and so the lads were ultimately forced to concentrate on recapturing their mass popularity of the early 80's. Nothing less would do. They swiftly concluded that there was no point in returning to their powerhouse roots, and were soon throwing their hats into the melodic rock ring, laying down an album of extremely polished, radio-friendly compositions which, although competently written and performed, seemed particularly soulless and contrived at times, the musicians apparently going through the motions just to sate their employers and keep themselves in business for the time being. »Innocence Is No Excuse« generally failed to win the hearts of the listening public, however, and sales were way down on their previous efforts (the singles were also largely ignored once again), although a hardcore following were still buying just enough copies for the record to make a marginal impression on the charts. It didn't look good, but EMI were obviously raking in enough money from IRON MAIDEN to be able to subsidise SAXON for the time being, so they charitably gave the lads another chance to deliver something special.

After recording yet another long-player (in between a spate of hectic touring activity, taking in more or less the obligatory series of familiar venues) in a surprisingly short space of time, SAXON returned to the fore with 1986's »Rock The Nations« album, another release which aimed squarely for the raunchy rock market, but which failed to spark any great interest within the UK. All things considered, there was a surfeit of other emergent hopefuls attempting this sort of style, and SAXON weren't even attaining the same sort of musical standard as HEAVY PETTIN or TOBRUK, to be honest, so they had precious little chance of cracking it on either side of the Atlantic. Admittedly, the old stagers still had their capable moments, especially on classy efforts such as "Waiting For The Night", but they seemed to be losing their fan base in major fashion by this juncture. Mind you, their fervent following in Europe remained remarkably faithful, and sales on the continent tended to prop up SAXON's mediocre achievements elsewhere. By this stage, they had already parted company with long-time associate Steve Dawson (who duly moved over to local rivals U.S.I.), whereupon ousted U.S.I. bassist Paul Johnson (a veteran of HERITAGE and STATETROOPER) swiftly assumed his place in SAXON! Surprisingly enough, EMI stuck with the Barnsley lads for the time being, in spite of their dwindling popularity, and proceeded to release several more singles as well as sponsoring the usual round of touring, although their jaunts now seemed to be more, er, 'selective', based around fairly brief excursions which took in more modest venues. An exception was the Reading Festival, where SAXON put in a highly credible performance, but the temptation on such occasions was always to play the nostalgia card and treat the assembled masses to those well-worn classics instead of bombarding them with unfamiliar material. After some North American gigs at the beginning of 1987, it was already time to think about another record. Instead of churning out a brand-new studio long-player almost immediately, however, the musicians took something of a lengthy break for the remainder of the year, during which time they tried out some last-ditch ideas (including the dreaded cover version, which is usually a sign of an act in crisis) in order to reverse their fortunes.

The lads parted company with Nigel Glockler (who moved on to the ill-fated GTR project) during their preparations for the next album, although they were able to draft in another U.S.I. stalwart, Nigel Durham, to bring them back up to strength. The latest incarnation of SAXON (also featuring the keyboard services of a certain Stephen Lawes-Clifford, probably plain old 'Steve Clifford' from CRY/SEVENTH SON) made their debut with »Destiny«, a lacklustre affair which suffered from a very palpable sense of uncertainty. Even the British fans were now largely giving up on their one-time heroes (the album barely scraped the 'Top 50'), leaving just the Europeans (strangely, SAXON never really took off in the Far East) to give the sales figures any semblance of respectability. The singles were also a cop-out, especially the featherweight, keyboard-drenched »I Can't Wait Anymore«, although the Christopher Cross-penned »Ride Like The Wind« was slightly less objectionable. Even so, SAXON were now so far removed from their roots that there seemed to be no way back, and EMI were soon terminating their contract for good, in the wake of both »Rock The Nations« and »Destiny« being utterly pilloried by the reviewers and ignored by the majority of rock fans. There was a brief tour, but Paul Johnson subsequently decided he'd had enough towards the end of 1988, whereupon he made his way back to the ongoing U.S.I. venture. His replacement was Tim 'Nibbs' Carter, who wasn't exactly a household name, but who fitted in perfectly well into the SAXON set-up. The lads were undergoing something of a transitional period once more, and again used the device of a live album as a stop-gap, with »Rock 'n' Roll Gypsies« (it's a pity that SPIDER had used the title already) appearing as a one-off release on Roadrunner during 1989. It was an uneasy mixture of old and new, confusing the fans even more, and even the band themselves seemed to be unsure of their role in rock society at this point in time.

It took the persevering outfit a while to organise a new deal for themselves, but they returned to the fore in 1990 with a handful of low-key dates throughout Europe and the UK, where they tried out some of their newly-penned material, and the overall response appeared to be quite favourable. Before much longer, they were busying themselves in the studio once again, and emerged with a new album for Virgin towards the end of the year. »Solid Ball Of Rock« was a step in the right direction, although it hardly constituted a return to top form, and sales were pretty modest, on the whole. SAXON's brand of rock was now largely being overlooked in favour of considerably more extreme metal or this new-fangled grunge thing, although a few charitable souls found SAXON's dated material quaintly endearing, and gave them a tentative thumbs-up, which was about all they could have hoped for after their late 80's flirtation with the world of melodic rock. More importantly, SAXON's inclusion ("Motorcycle Man") on the Ulrich-sponsored »NWOBHM '79 Revisited« set was something which worked in their favour to some extent, and the European crowds were soon coming out of hiding to cheer the lads on their tour in the spring of 1991. Back in the UK, meanwhile, things weren't quite as straightforward, and poor old SAXON could barely get a sizeable paying audience to turn up at their local venues. There was always the very viable option of shuffling off to Europe and eking out a living by delivering live sets based around material from the good old days, but SAXON were determined to keep plugging away with studio albums, the next of which was 1993's »Forever Free«, which again appeared on Virgin, although a UK pressing also surfaced on the non-illustrious Warhammer label. It was barely differentiable from their previous outing, but served to allow the outfit to vary their live set to some degree, working in some of the newer numbers at the expense of the more poorly-received efforts from the recent long-players, and the lads were soon packing out the concert halls in certain parts of Europe, particularly in Germany, where their once-tarnished reputation was rapidly being salvaged.

By this time, the outfit had more or less given up on the UK, the States and the rest of the world, but were happy to pin all their hopes on Europe, where the metal scene wasn't quite as fickle and prone to backstabbing as it was elsewhere. In due course, they re-signed to the EMI label, who had magnanimously decided to give them another chance, resulting in the release of »Dogs Of War« in 1995. This was much more the sort of thing the fans were wanting to hear, and there appeared to be something of a mini-revival in SAXON's media profile, with their activities in Europe being heralded as major events which were anticipated quite feverishly. Before long, they were picked up by SPV, who were doing their utmost to carry the torch for 'true metal', which resulted in the reissue of their latest album with a more extensive distribution. In the interim, however, long-serving guitarist Graham Oliver had decided to go off to do his own thing, which involved reuniting with erstwhile colleagues Pete Gill and Steve Dawson, one-time SARACEN guitarist Haydn Conway and vocalist Ted Bullet (previously with THUNDERHEAD) to form a new ensemble called (wait for it) SON OF A BITCH! This was all immensely confusing for many fans, especially once the newly-established outfit (whose roots actually lay in an unsuccessful Steve Dawson/Nigel Durham vehicle called WANTED) began gigging with a live repertoire predominantly composed of early SAXON originals, and there was no love lost between the two acts at the time. Eventually, however, SON OF A BITCH began to write their own material and duly released a critically-ignored album called »Victim You«, which only the most dedicated SAXON fans bothered with. Things came to a head a couple of years later, however, when Oliver's group decided to play live (in the UK and in some overseas territories, but not in Europe) under the name of SAXON, whereupon things all got a bit messy, but the lawyers ultimately sorted it all out.

Back in the SAXON camp, though, the lads were soon breaking in new guitarist Doug Scarratt to replace the departed Graham Oliver, and began formulating plans for another album for SPV once all the fuss surrounding the emergence of SON OF A BITCH had died down. Meanwhile, however, a veritable glut of compilations, live albums and retrospectives (some more valid than others) had begun to clutter up the shelves, although the situation appears to have calmed down slightly in more recent times. For a while, though, there seemed to be another SAXON record on display every other week, many of which were only minor variations on the same batch of previously-released material, with some even containing exactly the same tracks in a dif-

Photo: Danillo P.

ferent order and with alternate cover artwork *etc.*, something which has also plagued the likes of GIRLSCHOOL and VENOM in the past few years. SAXON soon had a *'proper'* new album to promote, though, and »Unleash The Beast« (the band gradually regressing to their roots as time goes by) proved to be another winner with the European fans, although it actually got the occasional mention in the British rock press as well, which is nothing short of miraculous. It seemed that, not only had SAXON recaptured the spirit of their youth, but they were even making attempts to innovate once more, and some of their newer numbers were actually quite individualistic in their construction. A further set, »Metalhead« (the group utilising the services of drummer Fritz Randow, a veteran of such outfits as ELOY), appeared in 1999, and (with the lads clearly attempting to cultivate rather more of a tangibly contemporary sound) was afforded some remarkably favourable reviews throughout the world, so it looks as though they're probably back for good this time. I hope these stalwarts stay around a bit longer, but let's face it, they're knocking on a bit now…

LP's

»Saxon« Carrere 1979
»Wheels Of Steel« Carrere 1980
»Strong Arm Of The Law« Carrere 1980
[Gatefold sleeve]
»Denim And Leather« Carrere 1981
[Also issued as limited edition on blue vinyl]
»Highlights« Carrere 1981
[German compilation release, possibly cassette only]
»The Eagle Has Landed« Carrere 1982
[Live album, also issued as limited edition picture disc]
»Power And The Glory« Carrere 1983
[Also issued as limited edition picture disc]
»Crusader« Carrere 1984
[Also issued as limited edition picture disc]
»Strong Arm Metal« Carrere 1985
[Compilation release]
»Innocence Is No Excuse« Parlophone 1985
[Also issued as limited edition picture disc]
»Rock The Nations« EMI 1986
»Destiny« EMI 1988
»Anthology« Raw Power 1988
[Double compilation album]
»Rock 'n' Roll Gypsies« Roadrunner 1989
[Live album]
»Back On The Streets« Connoisseur 1990
[Double compilation album]
»Greatest Hits Live« Castle Communications 1990
[Double live album]

»Solid Ball Of Rock« Virgin 1990
»Best Of Saxon« EMI 1991
[Compilation release]
»Forever Free« Virgin 1993
[European issue]
»Forever Free« Warhammer 1993
[UK issue in different cover]
»Dogs Of War« H.T.D. 1995

12" EP's

»747 (Strangers In The Night)« Carrere 1980
[Includes live version of "Stallions Of The Highway"]
»Power And The Glory« Carrere 1983
[Features live versions of "See The Light Shining" and "Denim And Leather"]
»Nightmare« Carrere 1984
[Features live version of "747 (Strangers In The Night)"]
»Bad Boys« Carrere 1984
[Italian-only release]
»Back On The Streets« Parlophone 1985
['Remix' edition, with two versions of A-side, "Live Fast, Die Young" non-LP]
»Back On The Streets« Parlophone 1985
['Club mix' edition in different sleeve, with two versions of A-side, "Live Fast, Die Young" non-LP]
»Rock 'n' Roll Gypsy« Parlophone 1986
["Krakatoa" non-LP, also features live "Heavy Metal Thunder Medley"]
»Waiting For The Night« EMI 1986
[With two versions of A-side, "Chase The Fade" non-LP]
»Rock The Nations« EMI 1986
[Issued as limited edition on clear vinyl]
»Northern Lady« EMI 1987
[Features live versions of "Everybody Up" and "Dallas 1 p.m."]
»Ride Like The Wind« EMI 1988
[Features live version of "Rock The Nations"]
»I Can't Wait Anymore« EMI 1988
[With remixed A-side, also includes live versions of "Broken Heroes" and "Gonna Shout"]
»Requiem (We Will Remember)« Virgin 1991
[With two versions of A-side, "Reeperbahn Stomp" non-LP]

12" Singles

»Suzie Hold On« Carrere 1980
[B-side live version of "Judgement Day"]
»Strong Arm Of The Law« Carrere 1980
»Sailing To America« Carrere 1984
»Do It All For You« Carrere 1984
»Iron Wheels« Warhammer 1993

7" EP's

»And The Bands Played On« Carrere 1981

7" Singles

»Big Teaser« Carrere 1979
[Original issue without picture sleeve, B-side "Stallions Of The Highway"]
»Backs To The Wall« Carrere 1979
[Original issue]
»Big Teaser« Carrere 1980
[Reissue as part of ten-part 'Heavy Metal' series in special sleeve, B-side "Rainbow Theme/Frozen Rainbow"]
»Backs To The Wall« Carrere 1980
[Reissue as part of ten-part 'Heavy Metal' series in special sleeve]
»Motorcycle Man« Elektra 1980
[Japanese-only release]
»Wheels Of Steel« Carrere 1980
[UK issue]
»Wheels Of Steel« Polystar 1980
[German issue in different sleeve]
»747 (Strangers In The Night)« Carrere 1980
»Suzie Hold On« Carrere 1980
[B-side live version of "Judgement Day"]
»Strong Arm Of The Law« Carrere 1980
»Heavy Metal Thunder« Elektra 1980
[Japanese-only release]
»Never Surrender« Carrere 1981
[B-side "20000 Ft." different to album version]
»Never Surrender« Carrere 1981
[Limited edition in alternate gatefold sleeve, with free single featuring "Street Fighting Gang" and exclusive live track "Bap-shoo-ap!"]
»Princess Of The Night« Carrere 1981
»Power And The Glory« Carrere 1983
[Also issued as limited edition picture disc, B-side live version of "See The Light Shining"]
»Warrior« Carrere 1983
[Spanish-only release]
»Nightmare« Carrere 1983
[Also issued as limited edition picture disc]
»Sailing To America« Carrere 1984
»Do It All For You« Carrere 1984
[UK issue]
»Do It All For You« Carrere 1984
[French issue in different sleeve]
»Rock City« Epic 1984
[Spanish-only release]
»Back On The Streets« Parlophone 1985
[B-side "Live Fast, Die Young" non-LP]
»Rock 'n' Roll Gypsy« Parlophone 1986
[Also issued in poster sleeve and as limited edition picture disc, B-side "Krakatoa" non-LP]
»Waiting For The Night« EMI 1986
[B-side "Chase The Fade" non-LP]
»Rock The Nations« EMI 1986
[A-side different to album version, also issued as limited edition picture disc]
»Northern Lady« EMI 1987
[B-side live version of "Everybody Up"]
»Ride Like The Wind« EMI 1988
»I Can't Wait Anymore« EMI 1988
[With remixed A-side, B-side live version of "Broken Heroes", also released as limited edition 'pouch pack' with free poster and numbered discography]
»Requiem (We Will Remember)« Virgin 1991

Shaped Picture Discs

»Back On The Streets« Parlophone 1985
»Rock The Nations« EMI 1986
»Ride Like The Wind« EMI 1988
»Requiem (We Will Remember)« Virgin 1991

Selected Promotional Releases

»Big Teaser« Carrere 1979
[Promo-only 12" single]
»This Town Rocks« Carrere 1983
[US radio promo 12"]

CD's

»Strong Arm Metal« Carrere 1985
[Compilation release]
»Denim And Leather« EMI 1987
»Anthology« Raw Power 1988
[Compilation release]
»Crusader« EMI 1988
»Innocence Is No Excuse« EMI 1988
»Rock The Nations« EMI 1988
»Destiny« EMI 1988
»The Eagle Has Landed« EMI 1989
[Live release]
»Power And The Glory« EMI 1989
»Rock 'n' Roll Gypsies« Roadrunner 1989
[Live release]
»Greatest Hits Live« Castle Communications 1990
[Live compilation release]
»Solid Ball Of Rock« Virgin 1990
»Back On The Streets« Connoisseur 1990
[Compilation release]
»Best Of Saxon« EMI 1991
[Compilation release]
»Forever Free« Virgin 1993
[European issue]
»Forever Free« Warhammer 1993
[UK issue in different sleeve]
»Saxon« EMI Japan 1994
[Japanese issue]
»Wheels Of Steel« EMI Japan 1994
[Japanese issue]
»Strong Arm Of The Law« EMI Japan 1994
[Japanese issue}
»Dogs Of War« EMI 1995
[Original UK issue]

»**Dogs Of War**« SPV 1996
[German issue]
»**The Collection**« EMI 1996
[Compilation release]
»**A Collection Of Metal**« Disky 1996
[Compilation release, alternate issue of »The Collection«]
»**Champions Of Rock**« Disky 1996
[Compilation release]
»**The Eagle Has Landed II**« Virgin 1996
[Double disc]
»**Donington-The Live Tracks**« CAS Records 1997
[Live release]
»**Wheels Of Steel/Strong Arm Of The Law**« EMI 1997
[Double disc, reissue of early albums with bonus tracks]
»**Unleash The Beast**« SPV 1997
»**The Best Of Saxon**« EMI Japan 1998
[Japanese issue, compilation release]
»**And The Bands Played On**« Neon 1999
[Alternate issue of »Denim And Leather«]
»**Metalhead**« SPV 1999
[Some in limited edition box packaging]
»**Live At Donington 1980**« Angel Air 1999
[Live release]
»**Live-In The Raw**« Zoom Club Records 2000
[Live release]
»**Diamonds And Nuggets**« Angel Air 2000
[Compilation release, includes unreleased live and studio material]

CD Singles
»**Ride Like The Wind**« EMI 1988
[Includes live version of "Back On The Streets"]
»**Requiem (We Will Remember)**« Virgin 1991
»**Iron Wheels**« Virgin 1993
»**Dogs Of War**« EMI 1995

Selected Compilation Appearances
"**Backs To The Wall**" (live) on »Monsters Of Rock« LP Polydor 1980
"**Freeway Mad**" (live) on »Monsters Of Rock« Cassette Polydor 1980
"**Heavy Metal Thunder**" on »Heavy Metal Thunder« LP Carrere 1982
"**Denim & Leather**" on »Heavy Metal Thunder« LP Carrere 1982
"**Motorcycle Man**" on »Heavy Metal Thunder« LP Carrere 1982 + »NWOBHM '79 Revisited« Do-LP/Do-CD Phonogram 1990
"**Rockin' Again**" on »Masters Of Metal« LP Powersaw Records 1986
"**Back On The Streets**" on »Protect The Innocent« Do-LP/Do-CD Telstar 1989
"**Ride Like The Wind**" on »Rock Legends« CD Telstar 1990
"**747 (Strangers In The Night)**" (live) on »Live 'n' Loud« LP/CD EMI 1991
"**747 (Strangers In The Night)**" on »The Metal Box« 3-CD Box Castle Communications 1993
"**Wheels Of Steel**" (live) on »Metal Killers« CD Castle Communications 1993 + »Monsters Of Rock« CD Castle Communications 1995 + »Wild Thing« CD Kaz Records 1995
"**Heavy Metal Thunder**" (live) on »Metal Killers« CD Castle Communications 1993
"**Denim & Leather**" (live) on »Rock Legends« CD Castle Communications 1995

SCARAB (I)

Stevens
Garner
Millard

Just when you thought things couldn't get any more confusing, how about this situation: a pair of British NWOBHM-period outfits who shared an identical name, and who both came from the same geographical area! Roughly speaking, the two versions of SCARAB (which have commonly been regarded as one and the same in the past) were based in the Midlands, but it's thought that the first bunch to assume the identity (about whom precious little else is known) were actually from nearer Birmingham itself. Recording their sole 7" (featuring "Rock Night" and "Wicked Women") single at Diamond Studios in Wednesbury late in 1980 and issuing it on the small (not to mention diverse) Inferno label a few months later, the outfit displayed a style lying somewhere between A II Z, WIKKYD VIKKER and CHINATOWN, not quite as heavy as their later namesakes but with a considerably more talented vocalist. Issued without a picture sleeve, the two-tracker is quite rightly regarded as a collectable rarity these days, and demand is now outstripping supply. The band's subsequent story has yet to be established, although you'd expect that they must have split before the other bunch got together a year or two later. It's unlikely that the name was passed on from one group to another (it happened with DRAGSTER, though), so it's probably just one of those spooky coincidence scenarios. The truth is out there…

7" Singles
»**Rock Night**« Inferno Records 1981

SCARAB (II)

Paul Britton (v, g)
Dave Parrish (g)
Nigel Shaw (b)
Steve Riley (d)

The second version of SCARAB are slightly less of a mystery than their original English namesakes (*vide supra*), the four-piece hailing from the West Midlands and presumably forming in around 1983 or thereabouts. Their early activities no doubt revolved around small-time club appearances and collecting rejection letters from record companies, although they eventually made it to the vinyl stage at some point in 1984. Their one and only single was a heavy slice of NWOBHM which paired the atmospheric "Poltergeist" (later featured on the »NWOBHM Vol.6« bootleg CD) with the somewhat more straight-ahead and pacey "Hell On Wheels", both of which were perfectly listenable. The music itself was a hard and fast variant which elicits comparisons with OVERDRIVE, JAGUAR and early ANGEL WITCH, for example, and duly won SCARAB some honourable mentions in various publications (including the ever-dependable 'High Octane') following its original release. It remains a highly-regarded piece by NWOBHM aficionados of the present day, some of whom insist that it's very much a *'premier league'* effort in terms of status. I wouldn't quite go that far, personally, but »Poltergeist« is an excellent and collectable item, nonetheless, and was issued in an appropriate monochrome cover, supposedly depicting an ancient Egyptian scarab (although it looks more like a wasp to me).

Moving into 1985, the outfit replaced original drummer Steve Riley with the experienced Paul Brookes (who later joined local thrash heroes SACRILEGE before moving on to the considerably heavier BENEDICTION and, more recently, the persevering MARSHALL LAW), and, having allegedly shifted several thousand copies (!) of their debut two-tracker, waited in vain for that fabled major label deal to materialise in front of their eyes. Inevitably, it didn't happen, given that the overwhelming trend at the time was for considerably more commercial material; British groups (even remarkably popular ones) with bullet belts and studded wristbands were invariably being eschewed for those with tasteful keyboards and bouffant hairstyles. With the dejected group disintegrating soon afterwards, little or nothing was heard from the original SCARAB members, although there was speculation that some of them might actually have become involved with the SHADOWLANDS project, given that the latter were apparently the only other ensemble to issue a single on the Pharaoh label. In fact, this later release (from 1986) was in a considerably more accessible style, and it transpires that the original notion of a fundamental connection was completely unfounded.

7" Singles
»Poltergeist« Pharaoh Records 1984

Compilation Appearances
"Poltergeist" on »NWOBHM Vol.6« Bootleg CD 1992

SCORCHED EARTH

Dave Cooper (v, k)
Paul Bodley (g)
Dave Matthews (g)
Tony Badger (b)
Tim Kristic (d)

It looks as though SCORCHED EARTH (not the first act to assume the identity) must have had some influential friends in high places and/or a bit of serious backing in order to explain their high-profile appearances on BBC Radio and their prestigious deal with the mighty Carrere Records (not that they were ever likely to topple the perennial SAXON as the company's highest-grossing act), as they weren't exactly the most exciting musical prospect of the period. First coming to public attention with a 'Friday Rock Show' session (a rather unusual scenario for bands with no previous vinyl releases to their credit), broadcast on the 24th of June 1983, the group showcased three original compositions *viz.* "Where Do We Go From Here", "Tomorrow Never Comes" and "Shangri La", and then waited for the listening public to start worshipping them from afar. As I say, though, it was hardly the most riveting or staggeringly original material ever performed, and their collective intention seems to have been the creation of a bluesy, sophisticated style which would be more likely to appeal to the discerning rock fan of the time rather than the denim 'n' leather brigade.

Following on from this early exposure, the quintet (who were originally from the Midlands, although they presumably relocated to the nation's capital at a fairly early stage) were rewarded with the enviable opportunity to record a four track EP for the aforementioned Carrere label (who hadn't struck gold with RAGE and were now in the process of losing SAXON to Parlophone), who evidently had high hopes for this bunch. First issued in 1984, the »Tomorrow Never Comes« 12" (which, in addition to the title track, also featured "So Long", "Where Do We Go From Here" and "Questions") saw the unit deliver a fairly uninspiring, slightly raunchy combination of ALASKA and SAMSON material from roughly the same period. By this juncture, the outfit featured the well-travelled Andy Beirne (who had served time with DIRTY TRICKS and GRAND PRIX, and who also deputised in LIONHEART at one point) on drums, and the group had apparently roped in the Troy brothers and Bernie Shaw from STRATUS to provide backing vocals (although you'd never know it if

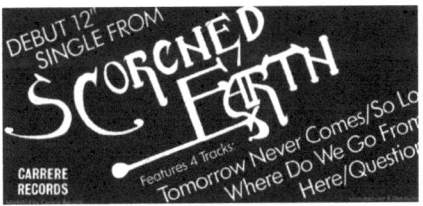

you hadn't been told) and liven things up. The publicity surrounding the guest musicians failed to improve matters, however, and the record flopped miserably, as it would be no exaggeration to say that the vast majority of record-buying punters hadn't the remotest notion who SCORCHED EARTH actually were, not helped by the observation that the lads gigged fairly infrequently.

Surprisingly, though, this wasn't the end of the story, as Carrere took it upon themselves to repromote the EP a year later, this time issuing it in a more eye-catching cover and hoping this would make a world of difference. A *'special UK radio cut'* white-label 7" promo (no sleeve), coupling "Tomorrow Never Comes" and "So Long", was also circulated amongst DJ's in a blatant attempt to glean some much-needed airplay, but I don't recall it being featured on prime-time radio at the time. As if the promotional machine hadn't been used to its fullest capacity, the determined outfit also managed to muscle their way onto the BBC again, this time playing a live, half-hour set (alongside PARTNERS IN CRIME) as part of Radio One's exclusive 'In Concert' series. It was a confident enough performance, the lads taking the opportunity to unveil new numbers such as "Take It Easy", and Carrere must have been optimistic that things would

work out better the second time around. Alas, 'twas all in vain once more. The EP stayed firmly in the racks, forcing the musicians and their management finally (after a few half-hearted support slots in and around the London area, including some appearances at such prestigious venues as the Hammersmith Odeon) to admit defeat. Best filed alongside the likes of GOGMAGOG in the *'well, it seemed like a good idea at the time'* file, I reckon.

12" EP's
»Tomorrow Never Comes« Carrere 1984
[Original issue in black sleeve]
»Tomorrow Never Comes« Carrere 1985
[Second issue in red sleeve]
»Tomorrow Never Comes« Philips 1985
[Greek issue in red sleeve]

Promotional Releases
»Tomorrow Never Comes« Carrere 1985
[White label DJ promo 7" single, B-side "So Long"]

Compilation Appearances
"Where Do We Go From Here" on »NWOBHM Vol.8« Bootleg CD 1996

SCORPIO

Line-up unknown

Another utterly obscure two-tracker with minimal information: no picture sleeve, date, writing credits or studio details, which is always incredibly enlightening. This was, however, the first release on the small Quicksilver (home of PREDATÜR and the odd punk outfit) label, dating it as being from 1981 or thereabouts. A tiny bit of further research suggests that SCORPIO were also a Berkshire band, with their local radio station (who presumably playlisted the record at some point) giving away a few copies of their one-off single (produced by Doug Gleave, who also handled the sole TRACK 4 release in 1982) as competition prizes to lucky listeners at the time. As for the music, it's an energetic, but slightly confusing, hotchpotch of metal and punk tendencies, with noisy keyboards thrown in for good measure. The optimistically-titled A-side, "Taking England By Storm" (which they evidently didn't), is quite a strong effort, evoking either SLEDGEHAMMER's "Fantasia" or METAL MIRROR with a bad attitude, although "Hawks", on the reverse, is in rather more of a garage style, suggesting that degenerates such as the MC5 might have been an additional influence on SCORPIO's musical stance. Hardly a typical NWOBHM release (it seems to have been a one-off, with those responsible retreating to the shadows almost immediately), and one which has surfaced in absolutely tiny quantities thus far, but well worth looking out for...

7" Singles
»Taking England By Storm« Quicksilver Records 1981?

SEDUCER

Chris Hunt (v, g)
Steve Goldsack (b)
Nigel Augur (d)

A band who soon (in the absence of a great deal of competition) became established as Surrey's favourite power trio, SEDUCER (not to be confused with Dutch namesakes) started out in around 1982, rapidly building up their reputation with a never-ending series of local gigs, playing alongside various regional favourites such as STATIC. Their vinyl debut came along fairly quickly, taking the form of the obligatory, small-time 7" single (only a handful of promotional copies were issued with a makeshift picture sleeve showing the band members emerging from the back of a grotty van), the numbers featured being "Call Your Name" and "Survivor". This down-to-earth trio were, in the first instance, clearly perfectly content to churn out a fairly traditional brand of British metal (described as 'quaintly dated' in 'Kerrang'), their anthemic, semi-epic style being reminiscent of similarly non-reconstructed acts such as BATTLEZONE, TYGA MYRA or MILLENNIUM. Nevertheless, it was a competent enough way to start off a musical career, and the tracks in question eventually reached a wider audience after being picked up by Future Earth, who duly allowed their European counterparts at Mausoleum to include the pair on their peculiar »Metal Prisoners« sampler a few months later.

For some reason, however, Future Earth didn't feel compelled to slap a full album contract in front of SEDUCER, and, in the wake of being given their freedom, the group eventually signed instead with Thunderbolt, home of such heavy acts as HERETIC and THUNDERSTICK. The first fruit of the trio's liaison with their new employers turned out to be the relatively disappointing (on the basis of their earlier two-tracker) »Indecent Exposure« EP, an offering which appeared in the summer of 1984 or thereabouts. It was, in all honesty, an entirely unremarkable release, with the combination of banal lyrics and uninspiring music suggesting a shift towards facile, biker-pleasing TANK impersonations. Not only that, the limited vocal talents of Chris Hunt generally fail to come across in a particularly favourable light on this rather listless effort. Nevertheless, the plucky threesome carried on regardless (ignoring the overwhelmingly negative reviews that came their way) and proceeded to recruit new bassist Dave Mandy (supposedly a veteran of the last CHINATOWN line-up) towards the end of the year. Fresh material was swiftly written and recorded for the benefit of their accommodating label, and a full SEDUCER album was in the shops the following year.

By the time their »Caught In The Act« long-player appeared, however, SEDUCER already featured the services of yet another new bassist (Phil Smith), suggesting that the luckless Dave Mandy had ultimately failed to make the grade. Whatever the story, their full-length debut was a major improvement on the lacklustre EP, the album incorporating a reworked version of "Call Your Name" alongside a selection of considerably stronger material. Having said that, these recently-penned songs were a further step away from the outfit's straight-ahead roots (I'd wager that the lads had probably been listening to a fair bit of JUDAS PRIEST's back catalogue in the interim), being mostly intense, upbeat efforts (occasionally reminiscent of FUGITIVE or even a markedly more capable HELLRAZER), some of the more listenable examples being "Do You Believe", "Wednesday" and "Halloween". A rather strange and contrasting inclusion, however, was their cover of "Remember (Walkin' In The Sand)", a track originally recorded by all-girl troupe the SHANGRI-LA'S in the early 60's, but later rocked up by the likes of JACKBOOT and AEROSMITH. I'll never comprehend how three entirely unrelated rock acts could possibly end up playing such an obscure original!

SEDUCER reluctantly parted company with Thunderbolt after the first album's release, suggesting that sales had been modest, although it wasn't long before they found themselves on the books of the short-lived Castle Communications subsidiary known as Stud Records (home of MAD DOG), who invited the musicians to enter the studio and set about recording a follow-up without too much of a delay. The quirkily-titled »Eads Down-See You At The End« set duly materialised in 1986, and was their first vinyl release to feature the talents of recently-acquired sticksman Tim Haywood. To be brutally honest, the second full-length effort basically started where its predecessor had left off, with precious little evidence to suggest that the trio were remotely intent on pushing back the frontiers of metal. There was, however, some marginally more adventurous guitar work on display, and compositions such as "Storm", "Liar" and "Problems" are all quite listenable. Even so, it was barely enough to generate any sustainable interest in the fortunes of the persevering outfit. Furthermore, the lads had failed to win all that many friends in the music press over the years, and the latest SEDUCER album met with the usual lukewarm reception upon its release.

SEDUCER were still a going concern in 1987, incessantly recording new material, attempting to develop a more marketable style and hoping forlornly that their big break might still be lurking around the corner. Another new drummer, Dave Sutherland (formerly with WILD!), was given a trial in a last-ditch attempt to reverse the outfit's dwindling fortunes, but the lads finally admitted defeat (within a year or so) after releasing one last (critically-ignored) four track demo. Second-choice drummer Tim Haywood later cropped up in the ranks of PANIK ATTAK, the outfit formed by JJ Cox after WHITE HEAT, and frontman Chris Hunt (aka Chris Monroe) subsequently played with the knockabout MENTAL HELICOPTERS (who didn't really get much further than an obscure compilation appearance or two), although the whereabouts of the remaining participants remains something of a mystery for now. As far as collectors are concerned, however, the only piece of SEDUCER vinyl worth making much of an effort to find is their debut single, although you'll be very lucky to locate one with a picture sleeve.

LP's
»Caught In The Act« Thunderbolt 1985
»Eads Down – See You At The End« Stud Records 1986

12" EP's
»Indecent Exposure« Thunderbolt 1984
[All four tracks non-LP]

7" Singles
»Call Your Name« Sticky Records 1983
[A-side different to album version, B-side "Survivor" non-LP]

Compilation Appearances
"Call Your Name" on »Metal Prisoners« LP Mausoleum 1983
[Different to album version]
"Survivor" on »Metal Prisoners« LP Mausoleum 1983
"Down Down" on »A Bolt From The Black« LP Thunderbolt 1984

SEVENTH SON

Brian Shaughnessy (v)
Kevin Shaughnessy (g)
Robert White (b)
Jon Shaw (d)

Yorkshire's long-lived SEVENTH SON might have felt slightly unlucky to have been lumbered with the tag of *'poor man's SAXON'* for the majority of their career, but it's fair to say that they sounded remarkably like Biff's bunch on occasion. Growing up in the same town of Barnsley, the members of both bands had plenty in common, and the musicians were to come into contact with one another from an early stage, with SAXON (still known as SON OF A BITCH at the time) playing the local colleges and clubs while the future members of SEVENTH SON were part of the appreciative audience. Clearly, SAXON would be a pretty huge influence when SEVENTH SON finally got going at around the turn of the decade, although it's fair to say that the perennial comparisons acted as something of a double-edged sword in years to come. On one hand, it suggested to many sceptical onlookers that the young group would always remain in the minor NWOBHM league and never achieve great success on their own. On the other hand, however, it meant that SEVENTH SON would always be assured of a healthy reception from small, parochial crowds who still wanted to follow the fortunes of some *'local heroes'* once SAXON had moved onto far bigger things.

After infiltrating the minor club scene themselves, SEVENTH SON rapidly established a good reputation (even managing to get a headlining gig at a local mini-festival in 1981), and finally got to the stage of releasing their first demo in mid-1982. The four-tracker failed to cause much of a commotion among the record company moguls, though, and they were soon forced to travel that well-worn path of issuing a self-financed private single. In due course, the lads set up their own label, Rising Son Records, and would issue several slices of vinyl themselves over the ensuing years. Their first effort was the »Man In The Street« single, their heaviest and most sought-after release nowadays, although it's worth noting that all of their records were issued in the same standard quantity of a thousand copies. The A-side was a fairly short, punchy effort which was, admittedly, very much in the style of prime-era SAXON, with some immensely similar vocal inflections from Brian Shaughnessy. Fortunately, however, the memorable "Immortal Hours" (as featured on the »NWOBHM Vol.4« bootleg) turned out to be a far more individualistic number with an interesting arrangement and some excellent, atmospheric guitar work throughout. The two-tracker sold quite respectably from the outset (the lads score bonus points for sneaking Lurch from 'The Addams Family' into the group photo on the reverse sleeve), and the musicians were soon winning the patronage of various local radio stations, notably Radio Hallam, who gave the record some generous airplay and subsequently offered the lads the chance to contribute some session tracks for future broadcast. During 1983, the lads took the opportunity to showcase such exclusive material as "Alive By Night", "The Rising" and "Out In The Cold", efforts which revealed the outfit to be developing quite healthily and mastering a heavy style with distinct similarities to the likes of HAMMERHEAD, EZY MEAT and LE GRIFFE.

By 1984, the ambitious youngsters had grown in stature and confidence, and were understandably keen to get another slice of vinyl into the shops, whereupon they immortalised a couple of their latest compositions at Fairview Studios in Hull. By this stage, however, a bit of rearrangement had evidently occurred, with the central Shaughnessy brothers (having dispensed with their original rhythm section) now being assisted by drummer John Talbot (Len Parkin from LOTUS CRUISE had also apparently filled in at one point) and bassist Rick Gregory. Their follow-up single (a double A-side) turned out to be a marginally more accessible affair, although neither "Sound And Fury" nor the ludicrously-titled "Metal To The Moon" really helped to deflect the original accusations of blatant SAXON-ism. Nevertheless, both tracks were enthusiastically-performed and competently-played efforts, and sales of the latest record were fairly brisk once again. As with the first single, »Metal To The Moon« was intended to be issued in a picture cover (a rather unusual fold-out effort this time) with a cartoon design, although comparatively few sleeved copies actually made it into circulation as a result of an 'incident' which led to several hundred records being severely water-damaged during storage.

Whoops. As a result, intact copies tend to fetch a relatively high price, but are still, for some reason, valued slightly lower than the first single itself.

The next two or three years passed without any great level of studio activity on the SEVENTH SON front, although the lads continued to tour fairly extensively, still (in spite of the fact that the NWOBHM boom had long since fizzled out) hoping that they might get a proper deal at some stage. One of their compositions from the recent »Sound And Fury« sessions ("Stage Crazy") turned up on one of Torment Records' sporadic and eclectic local-band compilations in 1986, although it wasn't until the following year that the lads finally attracted a bit of attention from outwith their immediate area, when the little-known Music Factory label stepped in with an offer to subsidise their next single. This emerged in the form of »Northern Boots«, the A-side of which was an utterly baffling reworking of NANCY SINATRA's "These Boots Are Made For Walking", with the lyrics 'subtly' altered to celebrate the famous 'North-South divide', an artificial construct of the time which served to associate the North of England with rampant unemployment, strikes, crime and cruelty to ferrets, while the South was its more affluent, smug and highbrow equivalent. It was, and still is, a complete and utter nonsense, although many felt that this was an entirely adequate representation of the country in those days. SEVENTH SON's take on the whole affair was to venerate the North and all its perceived foibles, and it's not particularly clear whether or not it was all meant to be taken with a pinch of salt. In any case, the track drew a fair bit of attention (the more worthy B-side, "Harder You Rock", barely got a look-in) from both fans and the media, with band mainman Brian Shaughnessy being badgered for newspaper, radio and television interviews at every available opportunity.

After this unanticipated piece of publicity had blown over, the musicians set about widening their horizons, and were soon planning a brief jaunt to the South of France to play a few gigs for the benefit of a brand-new audience. By this time, they had picked up a second guitarist, Andy Frost, and the enterprising SEVENTH SON even went as far as to assemble a cassette-album (»Dangerous Kiss«) for exclusive sale at these appearances. The shows appear to have been an overwhelming success, the group playing to far more populous crowds than they were accustomed to at home, and they returned from their sojourn in high spirits, ready to plan their next assault on the unsuspecting public. In fact, they were to suffer something of a blow the following year, when founder member Kevin Shaughnessy announced plans to emigrate to Australia (so much for all that *'Northern pride'*), and his farewell appearance took place at a sold-out local event towards the end of the year. For a while, it looked as though this might place the future of SEVENTH SON in jeopardy, especially when John Talbot and Andy Frost also jacked it all in before the end of the year. Nevertheless, the situation was salvaged when new sticksman Dave Barton and former CRY guitarist Steve Clifford were located in the early months of 1989, bringing the group up to strength once more. It took a relatively short time for the latest line-up to become established, and they demoed a couple of fresh numbers ("Sister Strange" and "Give Me Everything Tonight") in the latter half of the year, mainly to ascertain if anyone was particularly interested in their continued activities.

In fact, there was to be little in the way of response from any record labels of note, although the group received a bit of useful exposure in publications such as 'Metal Forces', and the lads subsequently went ahead with their scheduled programme of releases on their own label. A 12" EP was recorded at the end of the year, utilising their two recent demo selections, plus "What More Do You Want?" and "Bitter Ashes", a quartet of tracks which saw the outfit moving into rather more of a semi-sleaze style, suggesting that new recruit Steve Clifford might have brought a few ideas from his old act into the songwriting side of things. It was a sudden and not-entirely-convincing shift in direction, to be honest, but at least they didn't go the whole hog in terms of the *'big hair and cowboy hats'* image, so maybe it was just a brief period of experimentation. It was also readily detectable (particularly on "Sister Strange") that Brian Shaughnessy now desperately wanted to be THE CULT's Ian Astbury rather than good old Biff, but it's never a good idea to make your influences (whomever they might be) so transparently obvious. In the wake of the public's general dissatisfaction with the release, Steve Clifford was ejected, and new guitarist (the judiciously-named 'Raff') was recruited in an attempt to save the day. The revised version of SEVENTH SON wasted little time before getting another single out, but 1991's »Factory Girls«

(b/w "Last Band In Town") was to be their last vinyl release to date. Significantly, the A-side was one of their older compositions (co-written by Kevin Shaughnessy), and the 7" saw a return to a rather more down-to-earth type of material with a fairly melodic edge.

Although SEVENTH SON have long since abandoned their quest for global fame and fortune, a touring version of the band has continued to play the odd local gig (plus a notable support slot with NAZARETH in 1992) for much of the remainder of the decade, with interest being buoyed slightly by their comparatively recent *'rediscovery'* by a whole new generation of NWOBHM collectors and aficionados. Brian Shaughnessy and Rick Gregory have now been the mainstays of the unit for the best part of fifteen years, the duo's most recent accomplices being guitarist Dave Fox (who has also worked with local rockers BEDLAM CHOIR) and drummer Dave Burge. Interestingly, however, it recently emerged that there were plans afoot to get an enhanced version of the unreleased »Dangerous Kiss« album issued on CD at long last, courtesy of 'IRON PAGES' themselves. Brian Shaughnessy revealed the chain of events leading up to this release: *"The whole idea came from my brother Kevin, who now lives in Australia, when he came back to Barnsley for a visit earlier this year. He had a custom-made CD with him, entitled »Ten Years Gone«. It was the material from the unreleased album, the title making fun of the fact that he'd now been away for ten years and the release had been delayed for that length of time. At first it was only a joke, he had made a CD-R, complete with a makeshift cover featuring Barnsley Town Hall, for each of the members. I liked the idea so much that I considered the possibility of making it commercially available, and then we came into contact with you lot at IRON PAGES..."* (Ref: Iron Pages No.50, September 1999).

The CD has indeed appeared at last, and, in spite of some of the master tapes being of slightly dubious quality, those involved with the project have done a sterling job in mixing the featured material and getting it up to scratch. With a generous fourteen tracks included (the original cassette album has been supplemented with some numbers from later singles and compilation appearances), there's obviously going to be a mixture of good and bad, although there are still some remarkably capable efforts on display, notably "Early Warning", "Dangerous Kiss", "Stage Crazy" and "Never Let You Go". Overall, it's been well worth the effort in getting the album together (I know this wasn't a particularly straightforward project), and it's nice to give the fans a chance to hear some of the band's strongest material at long last. Where (if anywhere) they'll go from here is anyone's guess, though, but I wouldn't be surprised if they decide to stick around for quite a few years to come. I get the distinct impression that, while a modicum of belated recognition and success probably wouldn't go amiss, these guys are perfectly happy to do their thing out of sheer love for the music itself. Bless 'em.

12" EP's
»What More Do You Want?« Rising Son Records 1990

7" Singles
»Man In The Street« Rising Son Records 1982
»Metal To The Moon« Rising Son Records 1984
»Northern Boots« Music Factory 1987
»Factory Girls« Rising Son Records 1991

Promotional Releases
»Up From The Vaults« Rising Son Records 1990
[Very limited box set comprising first three singles, six track cassette and booklet]

CD's
»Dangerous Kiss« Iron Pages 1999
[Compilation of mostly unreleased studio material]

Compilation Appearances
"Stage Crazy" on »Torn In Two« LP Torment Records 1986
"Immortal Hours" on »NWOBHM Vol.4« Bootleg CD 1992
"Metal To The Moon" on »N.W.O.B.H.M. Metal Rarities Vol.3« CD British Steel 1997
"Sound And Fury" on »N.W.O.B.H.M. Metal Rarities Vol.3« CD British Steel 1997

SEVERED HEAD

Danny Morris (v, g)
Cindy Dilling (bv)
Liz Morris (bv)
Mark Squire (g)
Ian Dixon (b)
Lawrence Pledger (d)

Not to be confused with a long-lived and rather noisy electronic outfit from Australia called the SEVERED HEADS, the relatively obscure English rock/metal proposition (the general consensus of opinion being that they were almost certainly based somewhere in the South West, possibly Devon) who operated under the highly similar name of SEVERED HEAD were successful in releasing their own single in a somewhat unconventional manner. Instead of the usual route of recording a privately-pressed 7", sending it off to influential parties such as Tommy Vance and hoping to get a session or radio exposure of some description as a result, this particular bunch did precisely the opposite. In fact, SEVERED HEAD were one of a tiny minority of NWOBHM-era hopefuls who seem to have wangled a coveted slot on the 'Friday Rock Show' via a humble demo tape alone, after which the cunning individuals set about arranging for two of their session recordings (expertly produced by Tony Wilson) to be released on

vinyl. It seemed to be a pretty amicable way of doing things, and the BBC were happy enough to release the tapes, so you have to wonder why so few outfits of the time (with the notable exception of HEAVY PETTIN, who included a couple as B-sides, and EXCALIBUR, who issued a full session as the »Hot For Love« EP, for example) made better use of their own 'Rock Show' recordings.

With the session originally being broadcast on the 18th of March 1983, the tracks "God Of My Father", "Killing The Kidz", "Heavy Metal" (now there's a novel one) and "Two Wheel Mistress" all showed the small-time group to have been a fairly run-of-the-mill, semi-NWOBHM proposition with something of a boogie/biker influence, occasionally reminiscent of SHADER, JOKER or Ireland's COBRA. The upbeat "Two Wheel Mistress" is probably the pick of the bunch, whereas the unusually pedestrian and melancholic "God Of My Father", sounding at times like a miserable extract from a MOONSPELL or TYPE O NEGATIVE album, just never gets anywhere at all. Furthermore, the two female *'backing singers'* (yeah, I'll bet) were entirely superfluous, and the pair (ludicrously, also credited with *'dancing'*) didn't exactly enhance the featured material in any way. From these four compositions, "Heavy Metal" and "Killing The Kidz" (two tracks which, unfortunately, hardly pushed the boundaries of musicianship or lyrical originality in any sense) were selected to be immortalised on vinyl, although the resultant single doesn't appear to have performed all that well upon its release (leading to an inevitably bleak future for the outfit, who presumably called it a day within a year or so), and isn't considered to be a particularly sought-after memento today. You'd be forgiven for expecting something special to lurk behind the sleeve illustration of a decapitated, biomechanoid medusa, but it's hardly an essential purchase by any stretch of the imagination.

7" Singles
»**Heavy Metal**« Plastic Canvas Records 1983

SHADER

George Whitter (v)
Richard Wright (g)
Colin Ramsden (g)
Terry Goillau (b)
Paul Bentley (d)

London's knockabout SHADER certainly had the right idea in terms of their quest for fame and fortune: constantly gigging all over the UK in the late 70's and early 80's, printing their logo upon numerous T-shirts and badges (as evidenced by the group photo on the insert of their one-off single, although I've always felt it to be extraordinarily naff for *any* outfit to wear their own T-shirts) and issuing a private (sleeveless) 7" on the punningly-titled Piston Broke label in 1981 to flog to the adoring masses. Well, that was the cunning plan. In reality, their dull, plodding boogie/blues workouts probably failed to win favour with anyone except a few drunken, STEPPENWOLF-idolising bikers, most of whom would perhaps have preferred the singalong, self-effacing humour of DUMPY'S RUSTY NUTS anyway. Too bad. I'm sure it was fun while it lasted (the lads seem to have called it a day by 1983, having demoed their final batch of material late the previous year), but I suspect that there was never really any real chance of SHADER becoming a household name. Nevertheless, they made the most of their time on Britain's music circuit, and it's worth retelling their story for posterity's sake.

The whole SHADER vision had originally been conceived as long ago as 1976 by the triumvirate of Richard Wright, Terry Goillau and George Whitter, the lads (aided and abetted by some short-term colleagues at first) bravely going against the punk grain and steadily developing an unpretentious, straightforward rock style which, nevertheless, gradually won them many loyal fans throughout their locality. As the hardworking act became more confident over the course of the following three years, the increasingly-ambitious outfit (having acquired permanent drummer Paul Bentley along the way) ultimately began to venture further afield, embarking upon several lengthy treks to make themselves known to the public. Their activities included the charmingly-titled 'Up Yours' tour in the spring of 1980, which saw SHADER taking in various Northern venues (opportunistically recruiting second guitarist Colin Ramsden at one of these shows), followed by the self-explanatory 'Off Our Own Backs' jaunt a year later, which involved beating a path to some even more remote locations (the musicians usually being paid barely enough to cover their travelling expenses) in a bid to win new fans. Such dedication, it brings tears to your eyes.

SHADER's lone single (it was originally intended to be a three-tracker, but a tastefully-titled ditty called "The Pimp" was subsequently dropped, for reasons which weren't explained) appeared later the same year, and finally allowed the general public to hear the group's variation on the biker rock theme. Neither "Bad News Blues" nor the not-remotely-subtle "Banging Like A Shit House Door" are as heavy or energetic as the likes of NO FAITH or CENTURION, for example (possibly more along the lines of a lacklustre A.R.C. ROCK BAND), and both fail to leave a lasting impression for the right reasons. The production is awful, the guitars poorly tuned and the almost unique (on vinyl, at least) concept of spinning out an uneventful number with a lengthy drum solo (!) is utterly risible. Worth picking up (i.e. it's not quite as atrocious as the TOKYO ROSE or WITCHES BREW efforts) if you see it dirt-cheap, but the fact that this item has been sold at three-figure prices is prime evidence that the world has gone completely mad. Predictably, though, it failed to

send SHADER hurtling into the rock charts of the day, so the lads were soon coming to terms with the painful truth that they would never be more than small-time crowd-pleasers.

In fact, the participants kept things going for another year or so, although it looks as though their enthusiasm began to wane before long, especially once a couple of members became involved with certain other projects. After the SHADER empire had finally collapsed for good (they apparently slimmed down to a four-piece towards the end of their existence, utilising a guitarist called Ollie), vocalist George Whitter assembled an entirely novel set of accomplices and resumed activities under the identity of BAD BLOOD. Confusingly, however, a selection of BAD BLOOD and SHADER originals later appeared as the seldom-seen »On My Knees« long-player, a private affair released under the guise of BLOODSHOT EYES (see separate entry) in 1984. It's also worth mentioning, in passing, that the trio of Paul Bentley, Richard Wright and Terry Goillau evidently took time off from SHADER to undertake a spot of moonlighting at some point in 1982, acting as a stand-in backing ensemble for an implausibly untalented female vocalist in the shambolic REAVELL FORMAN AND THE LADS ensemble, who even managed to release a pretty atrocious single (»High Energy Flow«) of their own shortly thereafter. I wouldn't waste too much effort looking for a copy, though.

7" Singles
»Bad News Blues« Piston Broke Records 1981

SHADOWFAX

Martin Harris

It's quite difficult to say why, precisely, but the cover of »The Russians Are Coming«, a fairly obscure two-tracker by SHADOWFAX (an act named after Gandalf's horse from 'Lord of the Rings', in case anyone's remotely interested) certainly looks slightly more punk than metal. Maybe it's the odd style of writing on the front and back, or perhaps the chaotic graphics on the picture sleeve and labels. Mind you, I suppose the only way to find out for sure is to take a chance and play the thing, so does the vinyl inside indeed deliver an extremely objectionable punkathon? Nope, this release (from the heady days of 1980) is pretty much exactly the sort of thing we're always looking for, the group coming across as a snottier version of REINCARNATE or TURBO (particularly with regard to the vocal technique, memorably described as *'babyish'* in a long-forgotten catalogue), the numbers boasting supposedly *'socially conscious'* lyrics, although I don't imagine that they'd hold up to particularly close scrutiny. Both the nominated A-side and the similarly-conceived reverse, "Calling The Shots", reveal SHADOWFAX to have been purveyors of incredibly catchy, memorable compositions, and their brand of tuneful, quirky material should really have secured the outfit a pretty healthy following at the time. Indeed, the ensemble did their utmost to promote themselves further (they were regular fixtures on London's club scene at the turn of the decade), although they don't seem to have gone on to greater things, which is a shame.

It's interesting (well, it is if you're as sad as me) to note that the sleeve credits offer grateful thanks to both Tommy Vance and John Peel (as well as various other radio presenters of the period), suggesting that the group may, in fact, already have enjoyed fairly widespread airplay (either that or they were anticipating a bit of crossover potential amongst the metal/punk communities) before the single hit the shops. It's also notable that, observing the weekly gig guides of the day, SHADOWFAX (not to be confused with an even more obscure Northern bunch called SHADDOWFAX, who had released a pretty unremarkable two-tracker of their own in 1979) were considerably more likely to be found supporting assorted punk/indie weirdos than appearing on rock bills in their locality. It would seem, therefore, that we have here an outfit who were (and still are) genuinely difficult to pigeonhole, which is always a good thing. Keep an eye out for this one, although, as with the likes of RED RAGE, BASELINE and TOO MUCH, you'll be competing against the punk aficionados for any copies which surface from now on.

7" Singles

»The Russians Are Coming« Risky Discs 1980

SHADOWLANDS

Kevin Billington (v)
Dave Martin (g)
Marcus Gardner (g)
Dave Moore (b)
Steve Sprason (d)

Given that there were apparently only ever two singles released on the small-time Pharaoh label, it originally seemed perfectly reasonable for collectors to assume that the two West Midlands ensembles involved (SCARAB and SHADOWLANDS) probably had some sort of fundamental connection, although it transpires that if there is indeed any link, then it's certainly a pretty tenuous one. In any case, as soon as you actually get round to giving the SHADOWLANDS two-tracker a spin, it swiftly becomes evident that there's very little to connect the outfits either musically or lyrically, given that the aforementioned quintet seemed content to adopt a highly melodic rock/AOR stance with remarkably few references to malevolent poltergeists or possessed motorbikes. Their double A-sided 7" (from 1986, two years after the SCARAB single hit the shops), featuring "Cry From The Heart" and "Cold Nights", is distinctly evocative of certain other tuneful bands who were doing the rounds in the mid-80's, particularly CHROME MOLLY or »Burning In The Shade«-era TYGERS OF PAN TANG, but at least we're spared the near-compulsory keyboard backing in this instance.

All things considered, the upbeat "Cry From The Heart" is certainly a far more enjoyable and well-constructed effort than the rather saccharine power ballad on the reverse, although, on the evidence presented here, there's no denying that SHADOWLANDS were a talented and technically-competent outfit with a modicum of major-label potential. They appear to have come and gone in a relatively short space of time, however, without leaving all that much of an impression on the British rock scene, and their one-off single (no picture sleeve known) is a scarcely-sighted item today. Lead guitarist Dave Martin (who had previously been involved with a little-known venture called CHINA WHITE, not to be confused with the similarly-named CHINA-WITE who recorded for Mausoleum and Future

Earth) seems to be the only member to have remained in the business, becoming one of the founder members of MARSHALL LAW in the latter part of 1987, an outfit (who, entirely coincidentally, also featured one of SCARAB's alternate drummers at one stage) who have enjoyed considerably more success over the years with a rather heavier brand of metal.

7" Singles
»Cry From The Heart« Pharaoh Records 1986

SHE

Karen McInulty (v)
Ken Riley (g)
Lee Robertson (g, k)
Billy Germaney (b)
Paul Defty (d)

By the mid-80's, Neat Records was a shadow of its original self, struggling to maintain its former position as the most dependable and credible label of the NWOBHM era. With the initial metal boom having pretty much fizzled out by around 1984, the label decided that the only way to continue was to branch out and sign some of the more lightweight acts who were currently causing a bit of a stir in the unsettled rock climate. One of their most accessible acquisitions were local female-fronted quintet SHE (a name which had been used previously on more than one occasion, notably by Tracey Lamb's post-ROCK GODDESS venture and a transatlantic all-girl group), a recently-formed proposition who had been earning themselves something of a reputation for their entertaining live appearances throughout Tyneside. Within a short space of time, they were on the books of Neat, and a single was hastily recorded (with the assistance of John Verity and Fred Purser) for imminent release. It would appear that Neat were somewhat wary of the fact that there might just be a bit of a backlash on this one, though, and they initially suggested that the record would be coming out on a newly-formed subsidiary which would concern itself with more lightweight or traditional rock acts.

In the event, SHE's »Never Surrender« debut appeared as an entirely conventional Neat release in 1985, the company having presumably decided in the interim that its more lightweight signings of the period (STATETROOPER, MAMMATH, VALHALLA etc.) were somehow strong enough to hold their own in the company

of WARFARE, VENOM and BLITZKRIEG, for example. It was a brave, if foolhardy, move, leaving the metal-loving public to discern for themselves whether or not the SHE offering was actually worth buying. Sadly, the majority decided that it wasn't an essential purchase by any stretch of the imagination, something which is perfectly understandable in view of the chart-friendly, semi-pop/rock material which fills the grooves. "Never Surrender" and "Breaking Away" are fairly interchangeable efforts which elicit a few comparisons with some of the more lightweight selections performed by RUNESTAFF, CANIS MAJOR or ROUGH JUSTICE, although the B-side is actually a slightly stronger number in this case. The 12" version, however, additionally included the listenable "On My Way", a rather raunchier and moodier track in the style of AMAZON or AFTER HOURS, which demonstrates that SHE were (when they put their minds to it) perfectly capable of penning rather more substantial material than their throwaway A-side might have suggested.

The group might not have sparked the public's imagination from the outset, but they had emerged at just the right time in one important respect, given that SHE were one of the lucky acts to be invited onto the 'E.C.T.' television programme to showcase some of their material to a national audience. The outfit duly grasped their chance with considerable enthusiasm, and their high-energy delivery of "Never Surrender" and the previously-unheard "New Start" might just have won them a few additional fans. The hard-working quintet subsequently continued to tour fairly extensively through-

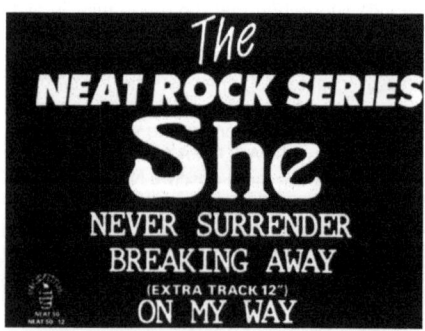

out the North East, and there seemed to be every chance that they would be invited to record further material by one label or another. The following year, however, it became apparent that the unlucky outfit had already parted company with Neat, although the musicians were soon preparing a single for release on their own Elle label. This took the form of the seldom-seen »Captured« 7" (b/w "New Start"), released in the early months of 1986, and again promoted by a tour of the North East. It was another decent enough offering, albeit very much in the style of their vinyl debut, and it looks as though the group were hardly intent on pushing back the boundaries of musical inventiveness or originality.

Sadly, but entirely predictably, SHE's second attempt to deliver a vinyl masterpiece (which, incidentally, doesn't seem to have been issued in a picture sleeve at any stage) appears to have performed fairly dismally in the sales stakes (let's face it, if the band couldn't break through with Neat's patronage and backing, it would surely have been ten times harder to do it on their own), and the world-weary outfit must have begun to wonder whether or not they actually had any long-term future after all. Nevertheless, they were still regular fixtures on the live scene throughout 1987 (even making it down to London for a handful of high-profile appearances), trying out recently-penned material such as "Loving You" and winning the odd semi-favourable mention in the rock press along the way. Eventually, however, the members of SHE appear to have reached a mutual conclusion that they had probably missed their fleeting opportunity to achieve fame and fortune, and it looks as though the curtain finally came down a year or so later.

12" EP's
»Never Surrender« Neat 1985

7" Singles
»Never Surrender« Neat 1985
»Captured« Elle Records 1986

Compilation Appearances
"Breaking Away" on »Powertrax« Cassette Neat 1986
"Never Surrender" on »Heavy Metal Collection 2« CD X-Tra Collection 1993

SHEER KHAN

Phil Brown (v)
Roger Brown (g)
Malcolm Hayes (g)
Nigel Heath (b)
Martin Priddy (d)

The one and only single from Cambridgeshire quintet SHEER KHAN (recorded, for some unfathomable reason, at Pennine Studios in faraway Oldham) suffers from the same basic shortcomings as that of the PURPLE HAZE release *viz.* an unsuitable vocalist who has trouble holding a note and carrying an otherwise reasonable tune. It's not actually all that atrocious, but you get the distinct impression that there must surely have been other hopefuls out there who could have made a far better attempt at the job. Their story goes back as far as 1979, when an amateur-hour bunch called SAMURAI (oh gawd, spare us) started making a bit of a racket in their bedrooms and began to get big ideas about making a name for themselves in the music business. Not much happened for a year or two, though, and the youngsters eventually concluded that they had to reinvent themselves to stand out from the crowd. By 1982, after numerous personnel changes, they had evolved into SHEER KHAN, whereupon their collective ambition seems to have become rather more focused and serious, the outfit making a few inroads into the live scene (although their locality was never the most metal-friendly of regions) and recording a speculative demo tape or two. Still, the record labels expressed little or no interest in the group's activities, and so, after a further period spent gigging and writing new material, they eventually decided to go it alone with a private single.

SHEER KHAN's two-tracker appeared in 1984, and coupled a fairly unremarkable pair of compositions, although I'm sure they were doing their best to come across as semi-melodic contenders with a modicum of individuality. The intro to "Last Generation" kicks off in a similar manner to AFTER DARK's "Evil Woman", but this number soon degenerates into a rather lumpen, JOKER-style effort which tends to drag along pretty uneventfully. The sombre, heavy-handed (and often unintentionally amusing) lyrics, dealing with the plight of Native American tribes at the hands of *'the white man'*, do little to lighten the mood, and the track swiftly becomes tedious. The B-side, "Lady's Dance", is a considerable improvement, with a substantial, DEEP PURPLE/RAINBOW-influenced riff leading into a cheerful and upbeat tune whose construction is markedly more encouraging, slightly comparable to a faster MARZ at times. Again, the lyrics are worthy of mention, having, paradoxically, nothing to do with either *'ladies'* or *'dancing'*. Instead, this appears to be a delightfully tasteless story of public hangings (!) at some unspecified point in history, with the *'lady's dance'* presumably referring to the jerking of the gallows and noose in response to some poor wretch's fight for life. Blimey. I may have to review my opinion that TRACER were the most miserable band in the NWOBHM scene!

The single (with, you guessed it, an anonymous, monochrome picture sleeve) appears not to have succeeded in promoting SHEER KHAN to the masses, and I suspect that extremely few units were actually shifted at the time. As a result, the two-tracker is a genuinely rare record these days, and relatively few collectors possess a copy, but I'll leave it up to you to decide whether or not the usual three-figure asking price is worth the investment. It wasn't quite the end of the story for the members involved, though, as the outfit finally splintered in the summer of 1985, with guitarists Malcolm Hayes (who now also assumed vocal duties) and Roger Brown forming a new venture called NEXT, recruiting a rhythm section consisting of Pete Scrivener (b) and Tim Day (d) to complete a fairly stable line-up. The revamped outfit (whose sound was based around a traditional, THIN LIZZY-style brand of heavy rock) became something of a minor cult in their locality, and even benefitted from one or two lengthy features in various fanzines (notably 'A Dose Of The Heavies'), but they ultimately called it a day within a couple of years in the wake of record company disinterest. A familiar story.

7" Singles
»Last Generation« SRT 1984

SHERWOOD

Fluff (v)
Rick Salter (g)
Phil Johnson (b)
Mark Haddleton (k)
Al Jones (d)

From the outset, it's apparent that Yorkshire's SHERWOOD weren't exactly a *'crash bang wallop'* proposition, but it's hard to pin a label on them. Not AOR, not prog, not mainstream rock...how best to describe the quintet's music? Well, I think the nearest thing is *'classy, polished metal'*, as they were once identified in a surprisingly accurate dealer's catalogue, although *'metal'* might be pushing it a bit. On listening to the title track of their self-financed »Riding The Rainbow« 12" EP from 1986, it's difficult to compare the band to anyone other than MAGNUM,

who clearly (given that one of the protagonists is pictured in one of the latter's T-shirts) influenced the ensemble's sound to a major extent, particularly with respect to the keyboards and distinctive vocal phrasing. On the remaining numbers, "Tonight" (a fairly dull ballad, but some tasteful Knopfler-esque guitar work), "Lost And Lonely" (considerably heavier and closer to traditional NWOBHM territory) and "So Far Away" (slightly more upbeat but still very melodic), the MAGNUM (and, by inference, »Change Of Heart«-era SARACEN) influence is always present, but there are also hints of other semi-prog bands (DAMASCUS, WHITE SPIRIT, CHEMICAL ALICE etc.) to maintain the interest of NWOBHM hardliners. Co-produced by good old Jih Seymour of MENDES PREY, the EP comes in a very nice monochrome sleeve depicting a winged horse, and is regarded as a pretty collectable piece. As I say, it's not a particularly heavy one, but, if you happen to pick up an inexpensive copy, you might (as I did) find yourself enjoying it far more than you thought you would.

12" EP's
»Riding The Rainbow« SRT 1986

SHIVA

John Hall (v, g, k)
Andy Skuse (b, k)
Chris Logan (d)

Avon's immensely talented SHIVA were, it must be said, one of the more atypical and technically-proficient NWOBHM bands, especially when you consider that they ended up on the roster of Heavy Metal Records, a label which was hardly renowned for pushing back the genre's musical boundaries. Initially conceived in mid-1980 by frontman John Hall, the act had successfully established itself as a stable, musically-adept unit (largely without making inroads into the local live scene) by the latter half of 1981, whereupon a speculative demo somehow found its way into the hands of Heavy Metal's Paul Birch, who swiftly offered SHIVA the opportunity to lay down a humble two-tracker. Although the luckless trio would later be lumbered with the unwarranted tag of *'RUSH clones'* at every available opportunity, their debut was actually closer to LED ZEPPELIN, with "Rock Lives On" being a fairly heavy effort with distinctive (but annoying) vocoder effects on Hall's vocals, while "Sympathy" was a perfectly capable power ballad.

Released in the early months of 1982, the 7" was selling in fairly healthy quantities before long, and the A-side duly put in an appearance in the 'Top 30 Kuts' chart in 'Kerrang', a pretty good indicator of its popularity among fans of the time.

In due course, the group demoed some new material, notably "Angel Of Mons", "En Cachent" and "Cut Me To The Quick", tracks which saw the lads attempting more ambitious and technical songs with more than a passing resemblance to (yes, you guessed it) RUSH, although the band's music also contained hints of various other heroes from the 70's, including JUDAS PRIEST, YES and even BLACK SABBATH. A second SHIVA single, featuring "Angel Of Mons" and "Stranger Lands", was lined up for imminent release, although it was postponed for a few months while their label faffed about with distribution problems, and it came to pass that the lads were then given the chance to record a full album while matters were being resolved. In the short term, however, they received further exposure in the 'Armed And Ready' section of 'Kerrang', where their adventurous compositions were praised in a pretty enthusiastic manner. It's fair to say that SHIVA never really pushed the boat out in terms of live appearances, being hindered by a lack of finances and a shortage of suitable acts with whom to play, although the feisty combo were never scared to jump at any opportunity which came their way, even if it meant sharing a stage with non-metal ensembles, as Andy Skuse later recalled: *'We can't be pigeon-holed. Our following is so across-the-board. For example, we did a gig in Bridgwater recently with three punk bands, in front of some two hundred skins and punks-and they went crazy for us!'* (Ref: Kerrang No.40, April 1983).

SHIVA's new album and long-awaited second single finally put in an appearance during the second half of 1982, and their latest material did indeed prove to be rather stronger and more coherent than their original vinyl release. »Firedance«, the long-player, was an undeniably impressive mixture of old and new in terms of musical influences, with the now-familiar LED ZEPPELIN and RUSH comparisons standing alongside similarities to more recently-established acts such as LIMELIGHT (in particular), BLEAK HOUSE, BIG DAISY and WHITE LIGHTNING, the overall effect (both musically and lyrically) suggesting a fairly considerable departure from the traditional NWOBHM ethos. It was, as a whole, an extremely proficient demonstration of melodic, semi-progressive metal, the main accusations of RUSH-ism coming on "Wild Machine" (where the dreaded vocoder puts in an appearance once again), "User" and the richly-textured "En Cachent" (which also turned up on the second »Heavy Metal Heroes« compilation, incidentally), although several other inclusions possess considerably more of an individualistic character, a couple of which (notably "How Can I?" and "Angel Of Mons") even come across as possibly taking their lead from THE POLICE. Admittedly, the album loses its way at times, and runs out of steam slightly towards the end, but it's still a fairly solid effort on the whole.

By this stage, SHIVA were already cult heroes in the West Country, and, judging by the impressive sales of both the album (issued in a distinctive but poorly-executed sleeve) and recent single, they now seemed to be enjoying rather more widespread popularity in the wake of this brace of releases. A few more gigs followed in due course, and the lads were soon experiencing the luxury of the BBC's lavish recording studios, having been invited to lay down a session for the 'Friday Rock Show' towards the end of the year. Eventually broadcast on the 14th of January 1983, the session showcased four tracks from the album, namely "User", "How Can I?", "Borderline" and "Stranger Lands", the recordings exposing the inventive and sophisticated musings of SHIVA to a national audience for the first time. The band then capitalised on their new-found fame with a series of shows supporting MSG, which appear to have gone pretty well in spite of their evident lack of experience in the live environment. Things went rather quiet soon after, however, although the musicians were afforded the honour of a full-page feature in 'Kerrang', where Andy Skuse defended the group against accusations of wholesale plagiarism of a certain Canadian outfit: *'We're certainly not trying to copy RUSH. I guess being a trio with high-pitched vocals does make people link us and them, but there's nothing in it. Not that we object to the comparison. Everyone at our level is compared to someone and, as we all admire RUSH, we're quite happy to be associated with them.'* (Ref: *ibid.*)

In the months that followed, however, it became only too apparent that all was not well between SHIVA and their label, which eventually led to a parting of the ways, forcing the trio to seek out a new home. By the end of the year, though, it had reached the stage whereby drummer Chris Logan was compelled to throw in his hand, after which the new name of Phil Williams was ultimately recruited to the SHIVA ranks.

Together, the revised line-up demoed a batch of novel material such as "Ring Of Fire", "Power Of Persuasion", "Not There", "Window On The West" and "Eden" (none of which was ever circulated particularly widely), and duly announced, with enviable confidence, that their second album would definitely be appearing at some point the following year. Sadly, however, the ensemble appear to have experienced considerably greater difficulty in selling themselves than they had originally anticipated, and it looks as though SHIVA had finally called it a day by the end of 1984, having made little or no real progress in the interim. The members appear to have returned to their day jobs thereafter, no doubt wondering where and when it had all gone awry along the way. Nevertheless, they remain a highly-regarded act from the NWOBHM period, and British Steel's CD reissue of their »Firedance« set appears to have sold in pretty respectable quantities thus far.

LP's
»Firedance« Heavy Metal 1982

7" Singles
»Rock Lives On« Heavy Metal 1982
[Both tracks non-LP, also issued as part of »Munsters Of Rock« singles pack]
»Angel Of Mons« Heavy Metal 1982

CD's
»Firedance« British Steel 1997
[With two bonus tracks]

Compilation Appearances
"En Cachent" on »Heavy Metal Heroes Vol.2« LP Heavy Metal 1982 + »Heavy Metal Heroes Vol.I&II« CD British Steel 1996
"Rock Lives On" on »N.W.O.B.H.M.« LP/CD Heavy Metal 1991 + »N.W.O.B.H.M. Metal Rarities Vol.2« CD British Steel 1996
"Sympathy" on »N.W.O.B.H.M. Metal Rarities Vol.2« CD British Steel 1996

SHOCK TREATMENT

Carr
Evans
Ward
Crowbar Eddie

Further concrete proof, as if any were needed, that there really are always one or two *bona fide*, prime-era NWOBHM rarities just waiting to be discovered by the lucky collector. East Anglia's uncompromising SHOCK TREATMENT (not to be confused with at least one punk band of the same name) would surely now be regarded as having produced one of the genre's most sought-after artefacts, were it not for the simple fact that the single in question is still almost totally unknown, even amongst the major players in the collecting and record dealing worlds. Clearly, the original pressing must have been absolutely minuscule, but it's somewhat surprising to note that the few copies unearthed over the years have failed to send excitable NWOBHM fans into the anticipated frenzy. The excellent monochrome sleeve alone (a masked baddie with a glinting knife) is entirely indicative of the record's provenance, and the five motley individuals shown on the reverse certainly don't look like the type to cross swords with (one of them's called *'Crowbar Eddie'*, for pity's sake) down at their local pub, and I'd suggest that it would be an *extraordinarily* bad idea either to spill their pints or to cast aspersions about their girlfriends.

The A-side of this 1980 offering, the unflinchingly-titled "The Mugger", starts off with an apocalyptic thunderclap and a woman's piercing scream before launching into a seriously heavy tune that brings to mind MOTÖRHEAD or DEMOLITION (the subject matter being not too dissimilar to the latter's "Hooker Hater", incidentally), pretty much the most brutal UK acts of the time. It's a mystery to me why the likes of BLITZKRIEG or JAGUAR are often referred to as *'skull-crushingly heavy'* when bands such as SHOCK TREATMENT have left their musical legacy on vinyl, but I guess we all have our own opinions. On the reverse, meanwhile, "Nuclear Warfare" isn't (surprisingly enough) a cheerful, poppy singalong about lovely little kittens at all. This is a slower, grinding number (the sort of thing that might well have inspired regional heavyweights DEVIATED INSTINCT in years to come) which shamelessly pilfers a few ideas from "Also Sprach Zarathustra" (as featured on '2001: A Space Odyssey') along the way, the track basically being an updated protest song about how the prospect of global nuclear annihilation is actually quite a bad idea. You don't say. Both selections are pretty long, so you'll get quite a lot of music for your money (and let's face it, this one won't come cheap) if you ever have the opportunity to add this gem to your collection. Nevertheless, SHOCK TREATMENT seem to have gone back into hiding almost immediately after their 7" hit the shops, perhaps slightly disgruntled with the lack of media attention and public appreciation. As far as I'm aware, none of them resurfaced in other bands of note, unless they reinvented themselves as the masked lunatics of DEEP SWITCH…

7" Singles
»The Mugger« Skull Records 1980

SHOGUN

Alan Marsh (v)
Danny Gwilym (g)
Toby Martin (g)
Andy Wrighton (b)
Tony Moore (k)
Bob Richards (d)

Having been unceremoniously booted out of TOKYO BLADE following a case of mutual agreement that his vocal performance on the original »Night Of The Blade« LP demos wasn't best-suited to the material, Al Marsh didn't spend too much time licking his wounds before putting together the SHOGUN project towards the end of 1985. There was no shortage of NWOBHM stalwarts queuing up to join him in this new venture, and he was soon roping in ex-TOKYO BLADE colleague Andy Wrighton (also a veteran of the legendary DEEP MACHINE) and Danny Gwilym, who had been at a bit of a loose end since CHINATOWN's demise, and who had latterly been filling in with Gloucestershire's TYRANT. The original incarnation of SHOGUN was completed by second guitarist Toby Martin (who had previously spent time in the last, ill-fated MARSEILLE line-up), keyboard player Tony Moore (who held the distinction of being featured, albeit absurdly briefly, in a very early version of IRON MAIDEN) and unknown drummer Bob Richards (who would later work with Adrian Smith in the UNTOUCHABLES venture). Within a fairly short space of time, the band had secured a deal with an American company, the Attack Music Corporation, and were soon busying themselves in Alaska (presumably the studio as opposed to the state, but you never can tell), where they set about the task of recording their first long-player.

SHOGUN's eponymous debut appeared in 1986, and showed the ensemble to be a rather more lightweight and melodic proposition than TOKYO BLADE had been, with Marsh no longer having to perform vocal gymnastics to reach ridiculously high notes. The majority of the tracks featured are fairly commercial selections sharing common ground with the mid-80's incarnations of outfits such as DEF LEPPARD, WAYSTED and the TYGERS OF PAN TANG, although a few heavier cuts such as "Burning Down The Night" and "Too Late For The Hunter" (all penned by Marsh and Gwilym, incidentally) serve to remind us of the duo's former glories. I'm not entirely sure about the legality (or ethicality, for that matter) of re-using CHINATOWN's "Time Will Tell" and crediting it as a *'Marsh/Gwilym'* composition, though, but nobody seemed to complain. To coincide with the debut set, a single was released, featuring a cover of AMEN CORNER's "High In The Sky", originally a hit from the late 60's; a slightly odd choice, perhaps, but their rocked up version of this poppy effort is, nonetheless, quite listenable. Neither the LP nor two-tracker appears to have sold in great quantities (and are relatively rare pieces today), however, and the outfit remained largely unknown in the UK.

By early 1987, though, things seemed to have flipped around pretty dramatically, and the group, having swung a contract with the Jet label (QUARTZ, GIRL, OZZY OSBOURNE *etc.*), were ensconced in the studio once again, with the result that the second SHOGUN LP, entitled »31 Days« (the period they were allotted to record the set, by all accounts), was soon ready for imminent release. First of all, however, the ensemble (now employing new sticksman Steve Pierce, a long-time compatriot of Marsh's from the KILLER, GENGHIS KHAN and TOKYO BLADE days) issued »Cloak And Dagger« as a single (in both 7" and 12" forms) as a taster for their latest long-player, backing it with numbers from the previous set, but sales were relatively modest. The album itself, which was widely promoted as being SHOGUN's debut LP, turned out to be a fairly blatant exercise in commercialism, with the prominent, AOR-style keyboards lending a distinct flavour of TOBRUK or MAMA'S BOYS to the proceedings. Although there are a couple of reasonably strong moments in the form of "Shock To The Heart" and "Cold Truth", the set as a whole wasn't sufficiently consistent or original to win over too many rock and metal fans of the day, resulting in pretty mediocre sales figures. Reviews in the music press were decidedly mixed, although Tommy Vance featured the album on his radio show to a fair extent, so at least the lads had a few important people in their corner.

A follow-up single, »Voices From The Heart«, was also lifted from the album and issued in 1988, although it seems to have sold very poorly indeed, and it wasn't long before the dejected outfit was in serious trouble in terms of stability. Successive keyboard players Ian Marshall (who, coincidentally, later went on to play with a band from the North West called TOKYO, who had absolutely nothing to do with TOKYO BLADE) and Andy Higgins (a veteran of one of the numerous outfits called ENGLAND) took their turn, as did new bassist Andy Robbins, yet another TOKYO BLADE veteran. However, the latest line-up never really gelled (although they managed to win themselves a coveted support slot with MEATLOAF along the way), and it wasn't too long before both Al Marsh and Danny Gwilym flew the coop, teaming up again in the short-lived MR ICE project before Marsh eventually made his way back to his spiritual home of, you guessed it, TOKYO BLADE. In the SHOGUN camp, meanwhile, things went from bad to worse when Steve Pierce defected to the little-known FROZEN HEART, leaving the remaining members to shift around and gradually metamorphose into something of a new musical venture with Andy Robbins at the helm. However, this all came to a rather abrupt end following the collapse of Myke Gray's original JAGGED EDGE vision, whereupon Robbins was headhunted and duly became a central part of the restructuring act's second (and markedly more successful) attempt at finding commercial success.

LP's
»Shogun« Attack Records 1986
»31 Days« Jet Records 1987

12" EP's
»Cloak And Dagger« Jet Records 1987

[Issued as limited edition on red vinyl]
»Voices From The Heart« Jet Records 1988

7" Singles
»High In The Sky« Attack Records 1986
[A-side non-LP]
»Cloak And Dagger« Jet Records 1987
»Voices From The Heart« Jet Records 1988

CD's
»Shogun« Zoom Club Records 1998

Compilation Appearances
"Time Will Tell" on »NWOBHM Vol.7« Bootleg CD 1996

SHY

Tony Mills (v)
Steve Harris (g)
Mark Badrick (b)
Pat McKenna (k)
Alan Kelly (d)

In contrast to all those NWOBHM-era outfits who have something of a dodgy past, Birmingham's long-lived SHY actually have quite a credible one. In fact, a forerunner of the band had operated since 1980 as TROJAN, a straight-ahead metal proposition who, although well-respected in their locality, soon tired of being merely one of the crowd, whereupon they made a conscious decision to try out a rather different style. By 1982, they had reinvented themselves as SHY, and with the name change came a fairly blatant shift in musical direction, their newer compositions signifying a move towards markedly more commercial material. Along the way, there were a couple of personnel reshuffles, and the lads also brought in a dedicated keyboard player, after which there was no going back to their humble NWOBHM roots. After getting their act together and sending a speculative demo tape to Ebony, the lucky quintet were rewarded with the opportunity to contribute to the lottery of the label's ongoing programme of compilation releases, whereupon "Tonight" was duly selected for inclusion on »Metal Warriors«. Quite evidently, the band were attempting to emulate some of the more commercial acts from across the Atlantic (which, to be fair, relatively few UK outfits were thinking about at the time), and the song in question undoubtedly had more in common with the likes of RAINBOW or DOKKEN than with the majority of their contemporaries on this side of the pond.

Still, the fans must have been relatively appreciative of the compilation offering, and a full SHY album was commissioned without too much delay. Their »Once Bitten Twice Shy« effort was unleashed towards the end of 1983, and represented an undeniably capable selection of original material, even if some of it might have been slightly too commercially-oriented for the metal-loving public of the time. Nevertheless, the likes of "Give Me A Chance" and "Chained By Desire" were enjoyable and well-crafted numbers, and it was clear that SHY, along with the likes of HEAVY PETTIN and TOBRUK, would be more than ready to take on the world if the whole melodic rock thing really took off in the UK in years to come. Mind you, it wasn't a perfect long-player by any stretch of the imagination (it was the kind of remarkably short affair which would soon become par for the course on Ebony), and soppy ballads such as "Reflections" didn't really do them any favours at that point in their career. Mind you, the lads had obviously impressed the powers-that-be at the BBC, and SHY were duly asked to deliver a session for the 'Friday Rock Show'. The group were happy to oblige, and their first exposure to the station's many listeners came on the 25th of May 1984, where they unveiled four freshly-penned numbers, namely "Throwing It All Away", "Behind Closed Doors", "Was I Wrong" and "My Apollo". This appears to have been more or less the last notable contribution of original bassist Mark Badrick, however, and the latter too would make way for erstwhile TROUBLE stalwart Roy Davis, who slotted in to the SHY family quite nicely.

Before long, the lads began growing in stature and were soon picking up a few fairly lucrative support slots with the likes of TWELFTH NIGHT and MAGNUM, all of which was to help establish SHY as an act to watch. Eventually, though, it was back into the studio to capture their second album, which would be their debut release for the giant RCA concern, the latter having now swung a deal with Ebony to take over much of the necessary legwork relating to the promotion of SHY (and labelmates GRIM REAPER) in the global environment. At this point, the ambitious Brummies more or less severed all ties with their original sponsors and allowed themselves to be moulded (the ultimate intention being to crack the American market) by this influential major label. Their first big-budget LP was recorded at the beginning of 1985, and appeared in the spring under the guise of »Brave The Storm«. It didn't exactly constitute a major progression ("Reflections" was even recycled from their debut), but the lads were clearly quite happy to be able to benefit from a more generous studio budget and professional recording conditions, so the long-player seemed to be an adequate beginning for stage two of their career. Nevertheless, the fans were quick to express their disappointment in the latest material, although the group still tried their best to promote themselves at every opportunity (they also saw »Hold On (To Your Love)« and »Reflections« released as singles by RCA in due course, although both were largely ignored by the public), starting with a memorably out-of-tune performance on the famous 'E.C.T.' television show (showcasing "Hold On (To Your Love)" and "Keep The Fires Burning"), where the hapless bunch did themselves no favours whatsoever.

Even so, they still managed to keep things ticking over on the live front, starting off by supporting UFO towards the end of 1985 and subsequently enjoying gigs throughout the following couple of years, taking in extensive tours of UK and Europe (as well as some carefully-selected outings in the States, where Tony Mills took time off to contribute backing vocals to CINDERELLA's debut LP) with GARY MOORE, MEATLOAF and BON JOVI in the process. By the early part of 1987, however, SHY were expected to deliver a further album for RCA, and so the lads were soon ensconced in the recording studio again, desperately trying to come up with something a bit out of the ordinary. The oddly-titled »Excess All Areas« duly emerged in the spring of that year, and, happily, it turned out to be a marked improvement on their previous offering, even if it took a big-budget production and the input of several co-writers to raise the music to the relevant standard. The likes of "Can't Fight The Nights", "Emergency" and "Talk To Me" showed a capable and polished outfit at the height of their powers, even though the soppy "Just Love Me" and "When The Love Is Over" (not to mention the pointless cover of CLIFF RICHARD's "Devil Woman") were rather less inspiring. The whole release was surrounded by a veritable blaze of publicity, and the band were soon giving as many interviews as humanly possible, after which they returned to the BBC to lay down their second 'Friday Rock Show' session, whereupon the lads showcased (on the 5th of June 1987) versions of "Telephone", "Young Hearts", "Break Down The Walls" and "Can't Fight The Nights", all taken from their new opus.

Before long, there were more singles (»Break Down The Walls« and »Young Heart«) which needed to be promoted, and there was no let-up

551

in the group's hectic touring schedule, which memorably took in a bottle-dodging appearance at the 1987 Reading Festival (a veritable trial by ordeal, the musicians being lucky to escape with their lives), although their reception on this occasion was hardly representative of a typical SHY gig. Their latest album actually proceeded to sell in relatively impressive quantities, although it still didn't constitute the kind of stellar success that RCA were evidently anticipating, and so the luckless SHY were unceremoniously dropped without much further ado, leaving them with no deal at the end of 1987. Help was just around the corner, though, as Tony Mills was to make a few contacts at FM Records while assisting on the debut TORINO long-player, which more or less resulted in SHY being offered the chance to release a one-off EP on the label. The four-tracker was assembled in no time at all, and merely featured an alternate version of "Just Love Me" plus some live material, so there wasn't really much of an incentive for the fans to part with their hard-earned cash, but at least it kept the outfit's name in the press while they sought out a new deal. Fortunately, they struck lucky at some point in 1989 when they hooked up with MCA, and so another long-player was soon on the cards. »Misspent Youth« appeared later in the year, but was hardly the release which would reverse SHY's fortunes overnight, although it had its moments. Nevertheless, it seemed to be something of an ill-judged experiment in vaguely sleazy party rock at times, and the fans failed to respond in a particularly favourable manner.

RCA tried their best to salvage the situation with a handful of tie-in singles (»Give It All You've Got«, »Money« and »Broken Heart«), but none of these sparked the public's imagination to any great extent, and the label was soon cutting its losses and leaving SHY to their own devices by the latter half of 1990. In the event, the lads began experiencing serious personnel trouble even by early 1991, when Tony Mills elected to depart and attempt to establish his own project, initially teaming up with certain ex-members of SAD CAFE and 10 CC to form a new ensemble, although this notion soon fizzled out. Before long, however, he had formed SIAM (originally SIAM SLAM), bringing in musicians from a variety of small-time local acts such as BAJJ-ON and RECKLESS DAUGHTER, this all-new venture eventually releasing a couple of critically-ignored albums of their own in the mid-90's. Back in the SHY camp, meanwhile, things had reached crisis point, and it looked as though they would soon be forced to call it a day. In fact,

1992 saw them recruiting a new frontman (erstwhile AFTER HOURS singer John Francis) and renaming themselves BLACKCAT, although this turned out to be an extraordinarily unsuccessful and short-lived piece of experimentation. Within a year or so, they were trying again with another vocalist (another one-time TROUBLE man, John Ward, who had latterly been earning a crust in the States) and yet another new identity (the hopeless CRAZY CRAZY), but this also stiffed in terms of public reaction, after which they bowed to pressure and resurrected the SHY name.

The revitalised SHY were clearly of the opinion that they still had something to offer the rock world, and were fortunate to be given another chance to deliver the goods when the little-known Granite Records eventually stumped up the cash to finance yet another long-player. Sadly, 1994's »Welcome To The Madhouse« (an album which also saw a licensed release in Japan, where they had latterly developed something of a cult following) escaped with virtually zero publicity, and few additional fans could have been tempted to check out the band's latest material. After that, the name of SHY became less and less prominent, and had more or less faded away into disuse within a year or two. However, after Tony Mills had finally decided to call time on his SIAM venture towards the end of the decade, it came as a pretty major surprise when the singer reunited with his former colleagues in SHY (who were now seeing much of their back catalogue being re-released on such labels as BMG and Pony Canyon), with the eventual result being that the lads signed a contract with Neat Metal. The latter concern (after putting out their debut album on CD for the first time) injected a significant amount of cash into the project, and allowed SHY to kickstart their dwindling career, which has thus far seen the prolific bunch issuing two brand-new studio efforts (»Regeneration« and »Let The Hammer Fall«) as well as their self-explanatory »Live In Europe« set. Although this batch of recent offerings have largely failed to make much of an impression in the general rock press, renewed interest in the group's fortunes appears to be remarkably strong at the present time, and I'm sure they'll plough on with their release programme for the benefit of a pretty loyal fan base, no matter the amount of commercial success they achieve in the long run.

LP's
»**Once Bitten Twice Shy**« Ebony 1983
»**Brave The Storm**« RCA 1985
»**Excess All Areas**« RCA 1987

»Misspent Youth« MCA 1989

12" EP's
»Hold On (To Your Love)« RCA 1985
["Strangers In Town" non-LP, also includes live version of "Two Hearts"]
»Reflections« RCA 1985
[Includes 'Once Bitten' mix of "Deep Water"]
»Break Down The Walls« RCA 1987
[Also released as limited edition in gatefold sleeve, "Only You" non-LP]
»Young Heart« RCA 1987
[Both "Run For Cover" and "Don't Wanna Lose Your Love" non-LP]
»Just Love Me« FM Records 1988
["Just Love Me" different to album version, also features live versions of "Deep Water", "Hold On (To Your Love)" and "Break Down The Walls"]
»Give It All You've Got« MCA 1989
[Both "She's Got What It Takes" and "How Does It Feel" non-LP, also issued in limited edition gatefold sleeve with free stencil]
»Money« MCA 1990
["If You Want It" non-LP, also includes live version of "Make My Day", some promo copies in special sleeve]
»Broken Heart« MCA 1990
[Includes live versions of "Emergency" and "Give It All You've Got", some promo copies in special sleeve]

7" Singles
»Hold On (To Your Love)« RCA 1985
[B-side "Strangers In Town" non-LP]
»Reflections« RCA 1985
[Also released as limited edition in gatefold sleeve with free single featuring "Behind Closed Doors" and "Give Me A Chance"]
»Break Down The Walls« RCA 1987
»Young Heart« RCA 1987
[B-side "Run For Cover" non-LP]
»Give It All You've Got« MCA 1989
[B-side "She's Got What It Takes" non-LP]
»Money« MCA 1990
[B-side "If You Want It" non-LP]
»Broken Heart« MCA 1990
[B-side live version of "Emergency"]

Promotional Releases
»Under Fire« RCA 1987
[Three track 7" given free with 'Kerrang' magazine, in picture sleeve, "Break Down The Walls" different to album version]

CD's
»Excess All Areas« RCA 1987
»Misspent Youth« MCA 1989
[UK issue]
»Misspent Youth« MCA Japan 1989
[Japanese issue]
»Emergency« Bootleg 199?
[Unofficial release with live and studio material]
»Welcome To The Madhouse« Granite Records 1994
[UK issue]
»Welcome To The Madhouse« Phonogram 1995
[Japanese issue with alternate tracklisting]
»Excess All Areas« BMG Japan 1996
[Japanese issue with three bonus tracks]
»Brave The Storm« BMG Japan 1996
[Japanese issue with six bonus tracks]
»Once Bitten Twice Shy« Neat Metal 1998
[UK issue with one extra track]
»Once Bitten Twice Shy« Pony Canyon 1998
[Japanese issue with two extra tracks]
»Regeneration« Neat Metal 1999
»Live In Europe« Neat Metal 1999
[Live release]
»Regeneration/Live In Europe« Pony Canyon 1999
[Japanese issue, double disc]
»Let The Hammer Fall« Neat Metal 1999
[UK issue]
»Let The Hammer Fall« Pony Canyon 1999
[Japanese issue with one extra track]

Mini-CD's
»Give It All You've Got« MCA 1989
»It's Only Rock And Roll« Granite Records 1994

Compilation Appearances
"Tonight" on »Metal Warriors« LP Ebony 1983
[Different to album version]
"The Hunter" on »Let Them Eat Rock« LP RCA 1986
"If It Ain't Love" on »Hard Roxx Taster Vol.10« CD Private 1999
[free with 'Hard Roxx' magazine]

SHYWOLF

Phil Toone (v, g)
Steve Littlewood (v, b)
Jay Melbourne (d)

The humble origins of SHYWOLF lie in the popular Midlands outfit SPOONFULL, whose roots extend quite far back into the 70's, and whose main (indeed, only) claim to fame is the fact that two of their easy-going compositions ("On Your Trail" and "Nine 'Til Five") were included on the infrequently-sighted »Brum Beats« compilation in 1980. With the threesome having been recorded in concert (at one of their final shows, by the looks of things) alongside the likes of SPEED LIMIT and MAYDAY, the lads gave the impression that they were content to plod along as ever-present crowd-pleasers, although they appear to have harboured a hidden desire to move into heavier territory. Within a year or so, the dastardly plan was put into action, whereupon the central duo of Phil Toone and Steve Littlewood (who shared vocal duties quite democratically) parted company with tubby sticksman Don Bailey, recruited the youthful Jay Melbourne to the fold and swiftly reinvented themselves as a proper NWOBHM concern called BLITZ, who won themselves a few support slots with the likes of BUDGIE and (improbably) TOM ROBINSON as a result. However, given that several other combos (mostly of the knockabout punk variety) had also adopted the same identity, confusion was rife until the lads finally settled on the rather more innovative and individualistic moniker of SHYWOLF early in 1982.

The ambitious trio soon got ideas about jumping on the vinyl bandwagon, and duly entered Midland Recording Studios in Walsall a couple of months later, laying down the tracks "Lucretia" and "California Jam" for imminent release as a self-financed (given that they hadn't exactly been inundated with offers from major labels in the preceding months), double A-sided 7". Issued in a well-presented picture sleeve showing their logo and a drawing of a wolf (how staggeringly original), the single demonstrated that these experienced characters (particularly on the energetic and catchy "Lucretia") were now evidently going for the full-on metal approach in a big way, with the aforementioned selection being an upbeat effort sounding like a cross between HELLANBACH and GILLAN. Flipside "California Jam", on the other hand, was considerably closer to traditional rock territory (and to the combo's direction of choice in their original incarnation as SPOONFULL), the track bringing contemporaries such as SLENDER THREAD, FACTORY and DAWN TRADER to mind. The production isn't especially competent, admittedly, but the guitar work and vocal performance are pretty respectable throughout, and it looks as though the record was sufficiently convincing to shift a fair number of units to the metal community.

Although the band were fortunate enough to gain valuable exposure in the 'Armed And Ready' section of 'Kerrang' later in the year (for some reason, their two-tracker wasn't reviewed in the magazine until several months after its release), they don't appear to have gone on to greater things, and presumably called time on their quest for fame within a year or two. Their single was largely forgotten for almost an entire decade, although it was rediscovered by fanatical NWOBHM collectors in the 90's, and demand soon sent the asking price into orbit, although its value appears to have stabilised in recent times. It's not a classic, but it's still a decent release which is worth adding to serious collections. To be honest, though, I would imagine that SHYWOLF might have suffered from a slight image problem, especially with the two 70's throwbacks out front (dressed in comfortable shirts and sensible trousers) being backed by a precocious upstart with a penchant for impressively-studded wristbands. Maybe Toone and Littlewood had a rethink and went back to their traditional rock roots in the pubs and clubs of the Midlands…

7" Singles
»Lucretia« Private 1982

SIAN

Line-up unknown

I'll happily admit that this obscurity stumped me (and pretty much everyone else) for quite a while, given that it's another of those infuriatingly uninformative releases, with (apparently) no picture sleeve and precious little to work with on the label itself. In fact, had it not been established that SIAN's lone two-tracker definitely dates from 1981, then it would have been slightly risky mentioning it here. Mind you, the self-financed 7" in question tends to skirt unconvincingly around the NWOBHM periphery, and only just scrapes in musically, so it might be prudent to be as brief as possible. The unrenowned ensemble (if I was forced to hazard a guess at their origins, I'd probably plump for the Home Counties) delivered a largely inoffensive, female-fronted brand of rock/pop (the music being penned by a certain Les Payne, presumably the central character from 70's lightweights MAINLAND, who has been operating as a solo artist in more recent years) with only a very faint resemblance to the rough'n'ready archetype, although the semi-capable A-side (the promisingly-titled "Fight The Dragon") just about qualifies as a worthy contribution to the genre.

The aforementioned effort (as per usual, any song which mentions the word *'dragon'* and isn't on a DIO album is almost invariably about drugs as opposed to mythological creatures) is an undeniably catchy number which benefits from some reasonably heavy guitars and heartfelt vocals (similar to LOST PROPERTY), the overall effect being vaguely reminiscent of a particularly lightweight ROCK GODDESS or a markedly less feisty AMAZON. After this semi-decent start, however, things take a nosedive on the unremarkable reverse ("Look Before You Leap"), which turns out to be an eminently forgettable piece of pop nonsense that brings to mind the nauseatingly bad TOKYO ROSE single on Guardian, so this composition barely warrants any attention whatsoever. All in all, therefore, you can easily live without this scarcely-sighted two-tracker unless you're a female-vocal obsessive (and I have no doubt that such individuals do indeed exist), but any further information concerning SIAN's personnel or exploits would still be greatly appreciated. Incidentally, this bunch shouldn't be confused either with any of the bands who adopted the identity of SIAM or with a second (male vocal) SIAN who recorded a tuneful 'Friday Rock Show' session in 1990, as there doesn't seem to be any obvious connection.

7" Singles
»Fight The Dragon« Big Bet Records 1981

SIDEWINDER

Line-up unknown

Another outfit with a promising name but a relatively lightweight musical outlook were the rather mysterious SIDEWINDER (although an identically-monikered pair of acts from Yorkshire and Sussex, both of whom actually remained on the rock scene until the late 80's, would be the main suspects in this instance), whose sole contribution to the vinyl universe appears to have been a self-financed, double A-sided single from 1983. Featuring "The Game" and the bafflingly-titled "Basil Herd", this little-known release reveals the ensemble to have been operating in a slightly unusual style for the time, their allegiances lying somewhere between the laid-back, 70's-influenced material of URCHIN or TRADER, and the semi-prog histrionics of contemporaries such as ATLANTIS RISING or LIAISON. Evidently, this must have been a one-off attempt for SIDEWINDER to make themselves known outwith their local area, but it looks as though they were probably swamped by the sheer number of like-minded hopefuls doing precisely the same thing, leaving the participants to abandon any notions of global supremacy thereafter. As per flipping usual in such circumstances, there's no picture sleeve and virtually nothing to report on the label (not a solitary writing credit, producer or mention of a studio), so it's another of those 'let us know if you have any further information' scenarios. Comparatively few examples of the single have surfaced to date, but it's not regarded as a highly-coveted item at the present time.

7" Singles
»The Game« SRT 1983

SIEGE

Sharon Thompson (v)
Al Stringer (g)
Dave Glover (b)
Rachel Glover (k)
Ray Lawrence (d)

Not to be confused with the legendary American hardcore outfit of the same era, Hampshire's SIEGE were one of a rare breed of NWOBHM groups, one in which the vocalist *happened* to be female. Don't get me wrong, we've already established that plenty of femme-fronted outfits were active on Britain's music scene back then, it's just that I get the unnerving feeling (I mean, why were female drummers and guitarists so thin on the ground in comparison?) that many might have been cynically fabricated *i.e.* 'we've got a girl on vocals, doesn't that make us stand out from the crowd?' or 'maybe if we put a semi-talented dolly bird out front, people won't notice how uninspiring our music is.' Added to the observation that many female-fronted NWOBHM acts of the period (especially in the very early 80's) tended to churn out an extraordinarily similar brand of semi-bluesy, raunchy rock, it's hardly surprising that the majority had a severely limited shelf-life. As I say, though, I'd classify SIEGE (as with WAR MACHINE, RAMPENT, SATANIC RITES and, to a slightly lesser extent, RUNESTAFF) as a decent, heavy proposition in their own right, rather than merely lumping them in with all the *'female-fronted rock'* clones.

SIEGE, who appear to have started out in around 1984, didn't arrive on the rock scene with much fanfare at all (although the band were a popular act in their region and even appeared in the 'Top Ten' poll of local hopefuls in 'Forearm Smash' fanzine at the time), and it's only in recent years that their privately-issued »Goddess Of Fire« 7" (B-side "Don't Punish Me") from 1985 has attracted any kind of general interest from NWOBHM fanatics. Musically, the A-side, in the style of SOLDIER or FIREBIRD, is far superior, with good guitar work on display; the uninspiring reverse, on the other hand, is a tad simplistic and disappointing in comparison. Still, the two-tracker (issued without a picture sleeve) sold reasonably well throughout their locality, and the group subsequently made a concerted effort to spread their name to the masses. To this end, SIEGE toured extensively (alongside emergent heavyweights such as EXPLORER) around the South Coast (showcasing a lengthy repertoire of original material including "The Bomb", "Mindblower" and "He Said, She Said") on the back of this release in search of that big break. Sadly, however, their potential doesn't seem to have been unleashed fully in the short term, and the musicians were soon struggling to maintain a stable line-up with which to further their careers. As a result, their profile gradually dwindled quite dramatically over the ensuing months, after which there seemed to be little or no mention of SIEGE for quite some time.

In fact, it wasn't until early 1987 that the persevering outfit (who had, by this time, ditched their hapless keyboard player and recruited some new blood, namely guitarist Les Black and heroically-named bassist Mark Conquer) would suddenly re-emerge from the wilderness, gaining a piece of valuable national exposure in the form of a prestigious 'Friday Rock Show' session. The reshuffled group grasped the opportunity to unveil some of their latest compositions, their slot (broadcast on the 6th of February 1987) showcasing "Wait For Me", "Red Light", "How Does It Feel" and "Wasted Time". Sadly, however, these new offerings ultimately failed to win the hearts of the listening public, and SIEGE spent the following six months trying to maintain a stable line-up while gigging locally with the likes of HOLOSADE. In the end, though, they reluctantly conceded defeat, and had already disbanded even before the year was out. Vocalist Sharon Thompson subsequently attempted to form a new outfit, and soon advertised for applicants through the pages of 'Kerrang', but she doesn't seem to have been overwhelmed by the response. The SIEGE single, meanwhile, perhaps due to its comparatively tardy issue, isn't generally regarded as particularly collectable at present, but there aren't all that many copies in circulation.

7" Singles

»Goddess Of Fire« Private 1985

SILVERWING

Dave Roberts (v, b)
Stuart MacFarlane (g)
Rob Ingham (g)
Steve Roberts (d)

The origins of Cheshire's infamous SILVERWING actually date back to the mid-70's, when glam-obsessed teen brothers Dave and Steve Roberts first took up their instruments and proceeded to annoy the neighbours no end with their early 'rehearsals'. By 1979, however, the dynamic duo had become the nucleus of a more genuine band, drafting in talented guitarists Stuart MacFarlane and Rob Ingham to make up the necessary numbers. Over the following few months, a fairly wide range of original compositions were penned, with the likes of "Love Ya", "Teenage Love Affair" and "Shoot To Kill" all eventually making it to the demo stage. With the young outfit's general inclination being in much the same vein as acts such as GIRL, ROX and WRATHCHILD, SILVERWING immediately assumed their place as firm favourites in the mini-'glam revival' scene of the early 80's, the latter movement being swept along quite conveniently by the momentum of the earlier NWOBHM explosion. It wasn't too long before SILVERWING reached the vinyl stage, their first exposure coming with the energetic "Rock And Roll Are Four Letter Words", their contribution to the legendary »New Electric Warriors« compilation in the autumn of 1980. This marked a pretty successful start to their career, and, within a couple of months, the lads had raked together enough money to finance their debut 7", a three track affair (on their own label, Mayhem Records) featuring a different version of their compilation number, plus "High Class Woman" and "Hot City Streets".

The success of the debut EP took everyone by surprise (not least the band themselves), and the initial pressing had already sold out by the end of the year. SILVERWING rapidly developed a phenomenal following, their live appearances becoming a much-anticipated rock'n'roll circus (the lads taking a few cues from their heroes, KISS) which would draw the punters from far and wide. A down-to-earth attitude served them well, as it became apparent that the musicians didn't regard themselves as being all that different from their fans, Steve Roberts being quoted thus: 'I hope that we wouldn't cut ourselves off from the fans if we did get big. We always take a lot of time with people. It's very important to retain personal contact, which we intend to do even if we eventually end up living in America. That's come through because we too are fans. We've been to gigs and tried to meet bands we liked afterwards, and when we haven't met them we've been so disappointed.' (Ref: Phoenix, Issue 1, 1980). Things were looking rosy for SILVERWING when, out of the blue, founder member Rob Ingham decided he wasn't happy with his role in the venture, and duly left (early in 1981) to pursue his own interests. He was swiftly

replaced by new recruit Alistair Terry, an extremely capable guitarist who would also contribute to the vocal side of things in years to come. By the time SILVERWING were confirmed as unlikely special guests on DIAMOND HEAD's extensive summer tour (preceded by an eventful appearance at the legendary metal festival at U.M.I.S.T. in Manchester), the revised line-up was already firmly established, and the musicians regularly took the opportunity to showcase an extensive repertoire of newly-penned material such as "Rock Tonite", "Rock'n'Roll Romance" and "Weary Traveller" alongside a well-received cover of "Rock'n'Roll All Nite" by old favourites KISS.

On the strength of their vinyl debut, the group came to an agreement with City Records (see also GIRLSCHOOL, SPIDER and TERRAPLANE)

that the label would assume the responsibility of releasing their second single, coupling "Rock And Roll Mayhem" and "Love And Leave". Although this was scheduled to appear in the second half of 1981, it never saw the light of day, for some peculiar reason (most likely to have been a lack of finances, as the band actually outlined this perennial problem in a 'Kerrang' interview at the time), which was a cruel blow for the emergent outfit. Whatever the story, it was to prove the end of the road for the unsettled Stuart MacFarlane, who (fancying himself as something of a guitar hero) immediately set about establishing MACAXE, which was essentially a solo vehicle designed to showcase his many talents. Mind you, it wasn't exactly a great success, to be honest, and the chap was subsequently reduced to helping out in sundry projects such as BIG AMONGST SHEEP (guesting on the »Terminal Velocity« album in 1982) and KOZAKADE, the ill-fated quintet assembled by ousted ROX vocalist Kev Kozak a couple of years later. New guitarist Trevor Kirkpatrick was, meanwhile, brought in as MacFarlane's immediate replacement in SILVERWING, and the latest axeman proceeded to establish himself as a worthy successor in the testing live environment.

Moving into 1982, with the outfit having failed to capture any significant label interest in the wake of the abortive deal with City, the lads were to issue their follow-up release (again, on their own label), the »Sittin' Pretty« single, issued in both 7" and 12" forms this time. The 7" version also featured "Teenage Love Affair", while the 12" EP additionally included versions of "Rock And Roll Mayhem" and "Love And Leave". Interestingly, the latter pair had been the compositions scheduled to appear on the cancelled single, but the particular versions committed to vinyl were actually (strange as it may seem) unreleased studio demos from 1980, featuring their original guitarists MacFarlane and Ingham. The latest SILVERWING record didn't quite set the world on fire to the same extent as its vinyl predecessor, although it was still a well-received offering which made its way into the Heavy Metal charts of the day. Before the end of the year, the lads issued yet another single, coupling "That's Entertainment" with "Flashbomb Fever", and housed within a poster sleeve. Again, the sales figures took a bit of a dip, and it appeared that the group were facing something of an uphill struggle to maintain their original fan base in the face of a melodic rock onslaught from across the Atlantic.

By the spring of 1983, SILVERWING (who,

bizarrely enough, had even welcomed Stuart MacFarlane back into the ranks in the interim) appeared to be in serious decline, although they were still wowing audiences with their live activities (which had become rather more toned-down than before), most notably at the Salford Glamfest and the Marquee in London. Within a few months, it came as no surprise to learn that they had pretty much called it a day, although not before Bullet Records had stepped in and issued an album of live and studio material (entitled »Alive And Kicking«) in the second half of the year. It was a fitting way to say goodbye to the first incarnation of SILVERWING, and the inclusion of a handful of previously-unreleased demo recordings was a generous bonus for the fans, while the live material (all taken from the aforementioned Salford date) revealed the sheer energy and conviction of the group, particularly on numbers such as "Rock And Roll Mayhem" and their interesting interpretation of JAPAN's "Adolescent Sex". The following year, the new name of PET HATE (see separate entry) emerged from the ashes of the last SILVERWING line-up, and this venture saw the Roberts brothers, Alistair Terry and Stuart MacFarlane getting back together with new recruit Michael Parris for a couple of moderately-successful albums and singles on the Heavy Metal label before eventually drifting apart in around 1986.

Somewhat unexpectedly, however, the Roberts brothers managed to orchestrate a SILVERWING reformation in the early months of 1988, luring Trevor Kirkpatrick back to the fold and recruiting new guitarist Ivor Griffiths (who would share the vocal duties with Dave Roberts at first) to make up the numbers. A demo tape, featuring a reworked version of "Rock And Roll Are Four Letter Words" in addition to the unfamiliar pairing of "Young And Wild" and "Just One Kiss", was circulated in order to gauge public reaction, much to the surprise of many casual observers, most of whom were completely unaware of this oddly-timed reformation. After meeting with a charitably favourable response, though, the lads duly set about organising a few low-key club outings to get back into the swing of things. Reviews at the time were decidedly mixed, although many of their original fans welcomed their return to the fore with open arms, and the band proceeded to play a fair number of shows over the ensuing months. Kirkpatrick was soon to leave, however, whereupon former CITY HEAT guitarist Paul Roland was brought in as a replacement. Following this change, the lads had a rethink, allowing Griffiths to concentrate solely on vocal duties and abandoning the two-guitar sound, their intention being to begin writing material in a slightly different style to their previous efforts.

By mid-1989, however, that initial enthusiasm had already worn off once again, and the lads eventually came to a mutual decision that they wouldn't be continuing after the end of the year. A couple of farewell shows in December marked the end of SILVERWING (again) and permitted the restless Dave Roberts to pursue some other options. He rapidly established a new musical venture which operated under the identity of the WILD ONES, the latter being an overlooked act who managed to catch a few handy support slots in London, but who eventually fizzled out without making much of a name for themselves. Undeterred, the persistent chap tried yet again in the early 90's, this time in a three-piece outfit (featuring erstwhile PET HATE colleague James Page) called THE UNLOVED, but this bunch appear to have fared equally poorly. Will SILVERWING ever return from the musical wilderness, you ask? Stranger things have happened, you know…

LP's
»Alive And Kicking« Bullet 1983
[Includes both live and unreleased studio material]

12" EP's
»Sittin' Pretty« Mayhem Records 1982
["Love And Leave" non-LP and "Rock And Roll Mayhem" different to album version]

7" EP's
»Rock And Roll Are Four Letter Words«
Mayhem Records 1980
[A-side different to album version, "High Class Woman" and "Hot City Streets" non-LP]

7" Singles
»Sittin' Pretty« Mayhem Records 1982
»That's Entertainment« Mayhem Records 1982

Compilation Appearances
"Rock And Roll Are Four Letter Words" on »New Electric Warriors« LP Logo 1980/CD British Steel 1997
[Different to either album or 7" version]

SINGAPORE

Nigel Potter

I can't fathom what lay behind the fascination with all things oriental in the NWOBHM era, with all the TOKYO and CHINA bands, SHANGHAI, SAIGON, SHOGUN, KOREA, TORA TORA, KAMIKAZE, GENGHIS KHAN, SAMURAI, SIAM etc., but here's yet another addition to the ever-growing list…SINGAPORE. A popular group in the thriving Welsh rock/metal scene at around the turn of the decade, these hopefuls (from Mid-Glamorgan) cultivated a sound with decidedly prominent leanings towards certain 70's acts, particularly THIN LIZZY and BOSTON, something which probably distanced them from the new metal explosion to some extent. Even so, they managed to issue a self-financed single as early as 1979, setting something of a precedent for all the heavier outfits who would follow in their footsteps. The bafflingly-titled "Launching", featuring a fairly strong vocal performance, brings to mind one or two mild-mannered NWOBHM-era combos such as MEANSTREAK and SPEED LIMIT, whereas the B-side ("A Bird With No Wings"), with its harmonised vocals and slightly odd structure, is markedly less enjoyable. No doubt SINGAPORE shifted a reasonable number of units at their small-time, provincial gigs, but I reckon that comparatively few examples made it into wider circulation at the time, rendering it a fairly scarce item these days.

Although the long-forgotten outfit appear to have been on the go for a fair old number of years, undertaking regular live excursions throughout their existence (there's evidence that they even made it up to London on a handful of occasions), their one-off (sleeveless) single seems to have been their only appearance on vinyl, and the members of SINGAPORE appear to have called it a day sometime in the mid-80's, having failed to win favour with any of the influential record companies. To be honest, they were probably flogging a dead horse with such polite material, which was neither raucous enough to please the nation's headbangers nor sufficiently sophisticated to appeal to the AOR brigade. Various one-time members of SINGAPORE (guitarists Del Boy Butler and Huw Jenkins, plus keyboard player Steve Von Haag, who may or may not actually have featured on their single) subsequently teamed up with former TINTAJEL personnel to form the run-of-the-mill, late 80's outfit TEACHER'S PET, veterans of a couple of forgettable compilation appearances (the »Rock Meets Metal« LP on Ebony and the »Battleaxe« 7" on Other Records) but not, as far as I know, responsible for any vinyl product of their own.

7" Singles

»Launching« SRT 1979

SINNER

Ian Gow (v, b)
Graham Cumming (g)
Pierre Jacob (d)

The Home Counties version of SINNER (as opposed to the obscure London bunch who appeared on Ebony's »Metal Warriors« compilation or various overseas namesakes) were, in all honesty, more of a heavy 'pub rock' variant than anything closer to the NWOBHM archetype. Nevertheless, it's entirely possible that bands such as SINNER, who issued their own product towards the end of the 70's, paved the way for the first influx of NWOBHM outfits, even if they didn't exert a direct influence upon the particular style of music to which the later groups tended to gravitate. Released on the small Whitetower label (in a reasonably professional fold-out cover, the front of which appears to feature a melting face), SINNER's debut EP featured "Need Your Love", "Beggar" and "God's In His Heaven", three highly-similar tracks which were extremely primitive in terms of construction and presentation (bringing to mind the likes of SHADER, WENDY HOUSE or NO FAITH), none of which exactly threatened to set the world on fire. The production is, for the most part, quite odd, which seems to have been a direct consequence of Whitetower's patented 'binaural stereo' recording process, a development which was intended to give better spatial clarity within recordings (all those tiresome techno buffs must have been wetting themselves in anticipation), but which actually just tends to make things echo a bit.

Whitetower apparently took it upon themselves to promote this supposedly 'revolutionary' technique at every opportunity (the inside sleeve provides a description of the equipment and processing involved in mind-numbingly-excessive detail), even going so far as to issue a further generous selection of vinyl offerings such as the enthralling 'Seven Comedy Sketches With Music' and (wait for it) 'The Superb Sounds Of Steam Trains'. Good grief. Needless to say, being associated with this complete and utter absurdity did SINNER no good whatsoever in the long run, and they evidently disappeared without making further vinyl appearances. Nowadays, their EP is another one for those among us with more money than sense (personally, I don't have much of either), as it's not a cheap item by any means and the musical contents certainly don't reward the level of investment required to obtain a copy.

7" EP's
»Need Your Love« Whitetower Music 1979

SKITZOFRENIK

Mike Muskett (v, g)
Mick Howard (b)
Steve Cabbage (k)
Ian Fleetham (d)

One of the more obscure bands from the musically-prolific North East to feature on Guardian's legendary »Roxcalibur« compilation in 1982, it transpires that Cleveland's SKITZOFRENIK had actually released their own 7" on the very same label one year previously, although it doesn't seem to have made much of an impact at the time. Contrary to popular opinion, there were a fair old number of relatively unknown singles issued on Guardian over the years (even the company failed to keep track of their myriad releases with any great efficiency), although the vast majority of those which occasionally surface (GINSENG SPARTA, RED ALERT, PIRANHA BROTHERS, PRIME EXAMPLE, SKIN DEEP, CIRKUS, STORMBOYS *etc.*) are of utterly minimal interest to NWOBHM fanatics (even so, they may be prized by devotees of other genres). To be honest, I was only made aware of the SKITZOFRENIK single in the first instance after a one-time acquaintance of the group mentioned it in passing, and it took a surprisingly long time to track down someone who owned a copy, so the »U.S.A.« 7" seems to have been an extraordinarily obscure release, even by Guardian's standards.

Anyway, both of the featured numbers (exhibiting a fairly unusual guitar style and a bit of indie-style keyboard backing) come across as broadly similar to the standard of material the combo would ultimately contribute to »Roxcalibur«, with "U.S.A." (resembling a meeting of JAMESON RAID and MITHRANDIR) being very much in the vein of "Keep Right On" from the compilation under discussion. "Lonely Road", on the other hand, is an epic power ballad (although it takes a while to get going properly) in the manner of SLOWTRAIN's "Ronnie", with the impressive, heartfelt vocals really carrying the tune along nicely. At this point in time, incidentally, the group were operating as a quintet who chose to perform under comedy aliases such as *'Muski'* and *'Fifi'*, although their true identities (you genuinely have to feel pity for someone with the surname *'Cabbage'*) were revealed a year later on the poster given away free with a handful of copies of »Roxcalibur«. By then, the outfit had slimmed down to a quartet, with their guitarist (Mike Muskett) taking over vocal duties. On "Exodus", particularly, the all-new SKITZOFRENIK demonstrated a rather more forceful style which clearly outshone the likes of BRANDS HATCH and the incredibly weak UNTER DEN LINDEN (it's hard to believe that BLITZKRIEG's Brian Ross was once involved with the latter, but it's apparently true) on what turned out to be a pretty patchy album.

Yet again, though, the story seems to be that the luckless outfit eventually disintegrated within a couple of years of their last vinyl appearance, presumably having found it difficult to maintain a great deal of momentum in the face of mounting public apathy and continued label disinterest. Of the various members, only Mike Muskett seems to have retained a musical role of note, assuming the vacant guitar slot in local rivals MILLENNIUM (see separate entry), a position which had been generated by Dave Merrington's post-LP departure towards the end of 1984. Although Muskett subsequently collaborated on a demo tape or two with his new cohorts, however, MILLENNIUM themselves had also split within a couple of years, having experienced internal difficulties and a serious loss of direction. As with most of Guardian's

NWOBHM-era vinyl, the SKITZOFRENIK single is an immensely scarce release (although I strongly suspect that it won't take over from HOLLOW GROUND and SATAN as one of the ultra-collectables of the genre), and was issued in a distinctive, monochrome sleeve featuring a gruesome creature holding an actor's mask.

7" Singles
»U.S.A.« Guardian 1981

Exclusive Compilation Appearances
"Exodus" on »Roxcalibur« LP Guardian 1982/CD British Steel 1998
"Keep Right On" on »Roxcalibur« LP Guardian 1982/CD British Steel 1998

SLEDGEHAMMER

Mike Cooke (v, g)
Terry Pearce (b)
Ken Revell (d)

Berkshire's heavy power trio known by the uncompromising moniker of SLEDGEHAMMER were amongst the first of the emergent NWOBHM contenders to attract the attention of journalists and fans at the end of the 70's, the timing of their first single coinciding impeccably with Geoff Barton's 'new metal' exposé in 'Sounds', which more or less provided the impetus for the whole movement. Their vinyl debut, the inventively-titled »Sledgehammer« single, was initially released as a fairly modest pressing on their own Slammer label in 1979 (no sleeve issued), but was rapidly picked up by the larger Valiant Records and afforded the honour of a far more extensive and widely-distributed release the following year, this time in a (rather unremarkable) picture sleeve. To regress slightly, the outfit had originally formed in 1978, and enjoyed the distinction of supporting none other than MOTÖRHEAD at their very first local gig. After further live outings of their own, including some notable appearances at the Marquee in London, the lads furthered their cause with a well-received series of shows with APRIL WINE in 1979, which brings us neatly back to their debut single. Both "Sledgehammer" and (to a lesser extent) "Feel Good" were no-frills, down-to-earth metal efforts (although not quite capturing the band's live aggression) in the general prime-era manner of OVERKILL, TORA TORA or NIGHTIME FLYER. For some reason, however, the 7" captured the public's imagination from the outset, after which the emergent trio soon found themselves going from strength to strength.

On the back of their debut release, the group were plucked from relative obscurity to feature on EMI's first »Metal For Muthas« compilation, although it was slightly disappointing that they utilised "Sledgehammer" yet again (a different recording, admittedly) for their contribution. Shortly thereafter, however, an unfamiliar number ("Fantasia") was to be heard on MCA's »Brute Force« sampler, and it was well up to the standard of their debut single, suggesting that SLEDGEHAMMER wouldn't merely be one-hit-wonders. Indeed, recording sessions for a full-length album (to be produced by John McCoy) were scheduled to take place a short time later, but these early plans were thrown into turmoil when original bassist Terry Pearce elected to take a sabbatical from the outfit (former FRASER NASH bassist John Jay stepping in to help out at short notice) without having given much of an advance warning. Fortunately, however, Pearce was soon to return, and a big break subsequently came SLEDGEHAMMER's way in August 1980, when the lads were included on the bill of the Reading Festival (as local favourites), where they set the stage for the likes of the TYGERS OF PAN TANG, DEF LEPPARD and WHITESNAKE. Following on from this memorable experience, the three-piece issued their »Living In Dreams« two-tracker (B-side "Fantasia"), once again on their own Slammer label, and decorated the rear sleeve with a photo of their triumphal appearance at Reading.

Strangely, however, the much-anticipated SLEDGEHAMMER album failed to appear at any point in 1981, or 1982 for that matter. The band's activities were low-key (to say the least) during this period, and it looks as though they were actually on the brink of calling it a day after struggling with continual personnel problems. Eventually, however, they were encouraged to get their act together properly, and resurfaced in 1983 with the »Blood On Their Hands« long-player for the little-known Illuminated label (which tended to favour darker, indie-style acts), a set which featured mostly new material. By this time, stand-in bassist John Jay (aka John J. Hennessey) had been re-recruited as a full-time member (although he also found time to collaborate with former ORE vocalist Gordon MacArthur in the ill-fated SPRINGHEEL JACK), and it rapidly became apparent that the outfit's repertoire had now expanded considerably, this selection of varied, adventurous efforts (notably "1984", "Garabandal" and "Over The Top 1914") demonstrating a more confident edge to the all-new SLEDGEHAMMER. The original fans, meanwhile, were possibly more attuned to such well-worn favourites as "Perfumed Garden" and the ludicrously-titled "Food And Sex Mad", so there should, in theory, have been something for everyone. Sadly, though, the long-player wasn't a phenomenal success, not least because the band's loyal devotees soon discovered that it wasn't particularly easy to get hold of a copy. The existence of two separate album covers (one with the logo, one with a pair of hands) has led to speculation that it may even have been withdrawn at some stage, although there's little in the way of supporting evidence. Perhaps the lads just had second thoughts about the original artwork and commissioned a batch of replacement sleeves, or perhaps there were actually two separate (but very limited) pressings.

If the initial failure of the album had been attributable to poor distribution, however, there can have been no similar accusations levelled at its reissue by the Mausoleum label in 1984, where the long-player was repackaged in a gatefold sleeve and issued with a bonus 12" EP (a device the company also used to bolster WITCHFYNDE's »Lords Of Sin«) in an attempt to secure a few additional sales. Bizarrely, however, the 7" version of "Sledgehammer", which was originally intended to appear on the bonus 12", was somehow replaced by the QUARTZ track "Wildfire", an utterly baffling mix-up, given that there's no fundamental connection between the bands. Nevertheless, the repackaged set sold reasonably well throughout mainland Europe, and the outfit (now featuring yet another bassist in Gerry Sherwin, a veteran of MAYA, TROUBLESHOOTER and the ENGLISH ROGUES) proceeded to release a further EP on Illuminated (issued as a 'sledgehammer'-shaped picture disc, just to make it marginally more exciting), featuring "In The Queue", "Oxford City" and "1984". Once again, however, the limited distribution of this release, added to the simple fact that relatively few outlets were prepared to stock shaped discs in the first instance, meant that it constituted another comparatively poor performer in sales terms. One of the outfit's last attempts to promote themselves involved recording a live video at London's Marquee, a sad affair due to the fact that SLEDGEHAMMER were unable to attract anything approaching a sizeable audience by this juncture (a major advertising cock-up didn't help), and the video, when it was eventually released in the second half of the year, suffered from the ignominy of having some completely over-the-top crowd noises dubbed in to save their embarrassment. Cringe.

By the mid-80's, SLEDGEHAMMER had more or less wound down their studio activities (Gerry Sherwin went on to collaborate with Paul Samson, notably in the PAUL SAMSON'S ROGUES project, while his predecessor, John Hennessey, later worked with both ORE and DRIVESHAFT), but a version of the band continued to make the odd local appearance at small clubs in years to come. Eventually, however, mainman Mike Cooke felt compelled to commit a further pair of songs to vinyl, and the seldom-seen »We Don't Like Porno Peat« 7" (b/w "In The Middle Of The Night") was recorded under the SLEDGEHAMMER name as late as 1988. This was very much a case of Cooke's social conscience getting the better of him, however, and these two tales concerning domestic and physical abuse (which was all part of some multi-media project at the time) stood very little chance of persuading the headbangers to part with their hard-earned cash, no matter how worthy the frontman's intentions might have been. Shortly thereafter, another 7" (coupling "In The Middle Of The Night" and the original version of their well-worn "Sledgehammer" anthem) was issued as a sort of '10th Anniversary Celebration' affair, but remarkably few units appear to have been shifted once again. Since then, the various one-time members have elected to keep rather more of a low profile (although Mike Cooke was the brains behind a further single called »A Kind Of Madness« in 1990, credited to ONE VOICE), and most seem to have gone back to their day jobs in recent years (Cooke himself is a full-time teacher), although it's worth noting that the evergreen Gerry Sherwin still takes to the stage with the resurrected ENGLISH ROGUES from time to time.

LP's

»Blood On Their Hands« Illuminated Records 1983
[Issued with two different covers, "sledgehammer" version more common than 'hands' version]
»Sledgehammer« Mausoleum 1984
[Reissue of »Blood On Their Hands« LP in gatefold sleeve with free 12" EP featuring "In The Queue", "Oxford City", "Living In Dreams" and "Sledgehammer", the latter actually being "Wildfire" by QUARTZ]

7" Singles

»Sledgehammer« Slammer Records 1979
[First issue without sleeve, both tracks different to album versions]
»Sledgehammer« Valiant Records 1980
[Second issue in picture sleeve, both tracks different to album versions]

»Living In Dreams« Slammer Records 1980
[Both tracks non-LP]
»We Don't Like Porno Peat« Sambec Music 1988
[Both tracks non-LP]
»In The Middle Of The Night« Slammer Records 1988
[A-side non-LP, B-side original single version of "Sledgehammer"]

Shaped Picture Discs
»In The Queue« Illuminated Records 1984
[Also a few uncut white vinyl test pressings, both "In The Queue" and "Oxford City" non-LP, "1984" different to album version]

Compilation Appearances
"Sledgehammer" on »Metal For Muthas« LP EMI 1980/CD Airraid Records 2000 + »The Bible Of Hard Rock« CD Toshiba 1990 + »NWOBHM '79 Revisited« Do-LP/Do-CD Phonogram 1990
[Different to either album or single version]
"Fantasia" on »Brute Force« LP MCA 1980
"In The Queue" on »Metal Killers« LP Kastle Killers 1984
[Miscredited as "Lepers Queue"]
"Over The Top 1914" on »Heavy Metal Monsters« Do-LP Cambra Records 1985
"Garabandal" on »Heavy Metal Monsters« Do-LP Cambra Records 1985
"Sledgehammer" (live) on »NWOBHM-The Days On Stage« Bootleg CD Taurus Records 1993

SLENDER THREAD

Paddy
Baz
Lex
Dave

SLENDER THREAD's single may now be fairly well-known amongst the NWOBHM fraternity, but the band themselves remain something of a mystery in terms of their county of origin (the consensus of opinion now seems to be somewhere in the West Midlands) and how long they were on the scene. Recorded at Modello Sound Studios in deepest Herefordshire (where DIAMOND HEAD famously laid down their »Diamond Lights« EP) at some point in 1980, the two-tracker wasn't particularly representative of the general NWOBHM ethos, although the featured compositions were still reasonably heavy and competently-written pieces. The A-side ("I See The Light"), for example, is a bluesy, hard-rocking number with raunchy vocals in the style of XERO or ORE, with the overall sound suggesting a faster and heavier combination of STREET LEGAL and TRADER. The energetic flipside ("Where Is The Beat?"), meanwhile, is a much speedier offering with some blistering guitar work in places, all of which tends to imply that SLENDER THREAD's intention may have been to pass themselves off as a seriously souped-up Mississippi blues band rather than the next big thing in the rock world. Not that they were blatantly ripping off JOHN LEE HOOKER/B.B. KING or anything (I'm not a great fan of the traditional blues style by any means), but it's still a fairly valid reference point for the kind of heavy material on display.

With the two-tracker being issued on the unimaginatively-named Rock Records (motto: *'Play Loud!!'*) label (one of at least three record companies to adopt this identity at around the turn of the decade) without a picture sleeve, SLENDER THREAD's one and only release was quite competently distributed at the time, and sold in pretty healthy quantities through outlets such as Bullet Records. Having said that, the outfit (who appear to have been a quartet) don't seem to have made much of an impression on the club circuit and were seldom, if ever, mentioned in the national music weeklies of the day, suggesting that they were probably a relatively short-lived concern. In spite of the observation that a reasonable number of copies of »I See The Light« have surfaced in recent years, a surprisingly consistent level of demand from collectors has allowed it to remain a fairly highly-valued item, although it hardly justifies silly prices on musical merit alone. If you can find it cheaply enough, however, the single certainly deserves a place in any serious NWOBHM collection.

7" Singles
»I See The Light« Rock Records 1980

SLOWTRAIN

Steve Twohill (v)
Dave Ross (g)
Tim Rumble (b)
Ray Fowler (k, d)

Wow, where's this one been hiding? Clearly, this must be a bit of an unknown entity, or it would surely be on many more wants lists than is currently the case! The monochrome cover housing

SLOWTRAIN's unassuming single from 1980 (a guitar-playing genie emerging from a magical flask), which was presumably drawn by a particularly untalented ten-year-old, certainly shouts 'NWOBHM alert!' at considerable volume, and the musical contents aren't a let-down by any means; just imagine splicing together a few genes from the MYTHRA, JAMESON RAID and HAMMERHEAD chromosomes and you're virtually there. The B-side ("Just One Way") actual-

ly turns out to be the stronger effort of the pair, with an upbeat riff carrying an effortlessly catchy tune which seems to last no time at all before a keyboard sweeps in and the track suddenly metamorphoses into an extended guitar freakout. The nominated A-side, meanwhile, the confusingly-titled "Ronnie" (telling the, er, *'moving'* story of a runaway girl), is a more restrained semi-ballad, which is vaguely reminiscent of some of the more laid-back efforts on the VOLTZ album. It wasn't too objectionable, admittedly, but I reckon the lads might have been better-served by showcasing two examples of more energetic material at this point in their career.

Remarkably few examples of this one-off single (issued by the youthful outfit on their own Spirit label, which shouldn't be confused with the identically-named company who subsequently sponsored the careers of no-hopers such as SILHOUETTE) have ever surfaced (despite the fact that it wasn't an excessively limited pressing), and most were sold within an extremely restricted area in the first instance. This was perfectly understandable, given that the cash-strapped group (based in the Southern outskirts of London) weren't phenomenally active on the club circuit at the time, and seldom got out and about to promote themselves to the masses. In fact, it transpires that the whole SLOWTRAIN empire crumbled within a relatively short timescale after their debut release had been recorded, following the decision of a couple of members that it might be better in the long term to go back to college and gain some qualifications rather than aiming for big-time recognition in the dog-eat-dog music business. Disturbingly sensible, if you ask me. All serious NWOBHM collectors should make a point of seeking out a copy of »Ronnie« at the earliest opportunity, but I reckon you might have to part with a hefty bundle of cash. Just one final thought: how on earth did anyone manage to play drums and keyboards simultaneously, particularly in the live environment?

7" Singles
»**Ronnie**« Spirit Records 1980

SMART

Dave Martin (v, g)
John Pilka (g)
Geoff Myles (b)
Roger Travis (d)

Originally performing under the rather unrepresentative name of THE SMART (which, unsurprisingly, caused many people to assume that they were a mod outfit), this four-piece became the more concise SMART (still, it has to be said, not the most metal of identities) in early 1982 or thereabouts, having presumably got together a year or two previously. With experienced guitarist John Pilka being a veteran of Surrey's STORMTROOPER (whose sole »I'm A Mess« single was released by Solent Records in 1977, two full years after the original outfit's demise), you might have expected SMART to share the same pub rock/punk affinity to some extent. In fact, they turned out to be more of a melodic rock concern with a slight glam edge, slotting in somewhere between GIRL, DEF LEPPARD and FORGER, with the merest hint of SHADOWFAX in places. Their one and only slice of vinyl, issued towards the end of 1982, coupled "This Time" (a number originally recorded by CHERIE AND MARIE CURRIE after the former's defection from the RUNAWAYS to team up with her sister) with "Mr. Right", the latter being a more capable effort in terms of songwriting, although the A-side benefitted from a highly memorable chorus. In fact, CHERIE AND MARIE CURRIE had themselves issued the main track as a single two years earlier, so this seemed a rather peculiar way for SMART to introduce themselves.

With 1982 also bringing the members of SMART a reasonably successful and potentially-lucrative support slot on the British tour undertaken by JOAN JETT AND THE BLACKHEARTS (keeping the RUNAWAYS connection going strong, by the looks of things), it originally looked as though this might just signal the start of something pretty big. The lads won a highly favourable review of their two-tracker in 'Kerrang', followed by a praiseworthy live report (with a risqué composition called "See You Next Tuesday" being singled out for an honourable mention) in due course, all of which seemed to bode pretty well for the future. Surprisingly, however, things went inexplicably quiet once the year was out, and there was to be little or no news concerning SMART's studio or live activities thereafter, leading to the almost inevitable conclusion that they had, for some reason, split rather suddenly following their initial success. It was all a bit of a mystery, but it was probably nothing more sinister than disillusionment or personnel problems. As a consequence of the band's relatively short lifespan, comparatively few copies of the single (issued in a picture sleeve with a group photo) appear to have made it into circulation, rendering it a collectable, mid-priced rarity these days.

7" Singles
»This Time« Complex Records 1982

SMOKIN ROADIE

Rue Philips (v, g)
Steve 'Dingo' Bell (v, d)
Aldo Mazzei (b)

SMOKIN ROADIE, an ambitious trio of musicians from the Midlands (although they eventually based themselves in Yorkshire), were one of those outfits who didn't, unfortunately, manage to stand the test of time too well. It's entirely possible that they were working as a low-profile club act prior to 1983, although there was little or no mention of their activities in the music press until the summer of that year, when they were reported as touring the North of the country with their repertoire of JIMI HENDRIX-influenced material. The obligatory private 7" (recorded under the auspices of producer Terry Rowley at the oft-frequented Old Smithy Studios) followed in due course, although it's impossible to detect much of a resemblance to HENDRIX within the grooves of "Midnight", this being an example of lightweight, borderline rock (quite poppy in places) which fails to leave much of a decent impression. As is so often the case, however, the reverse ("Rip Off") is considerably faster and heavier than the nominated A-side, and would probably have been a more prudent choice for the main focus of attention. Overall, it was a bit of a formulaic throwback to days gone by, and it was, in all honesty, probably closer to pub rock than to the NWOBHM archetype. For those few serious collectors who have, nevertheless, been tempted to seek out this fairly unremarkable effort (interest was piqued by the inclusion of "Midnight" on the »NWOBHM Vol.5« bootleg a few years back), the asking price for the single (issued in a colourful sleeve picturing the band in action) has been surprisingly steep in recent years.

By 1985, the nucleus of Rue Phillips and Dingo Bell had recruited new bassist Lee Faulkner (founder member Aldo Mazzei subsequently found his way into the ranks of RADIO MOSCOW) and recorded a further quirky single under the identity of TEMPEST (see separate entry), before the outfit ultimately decided to revert to their original SMOKIN ROADIE moniker. After a somewhat ambitious attempt to crack the American market (which involved jetting over to the States and gigging like maniacs for most of 1986), however, the trio duly returned to the UK and set about recording a complete album's worth of material, again at the Old Smithy. In the event, their full-length debut (»Overnight Stay«) remained unissued until 1989, and only ever materialised in finished form in Japan, by which time the outfit (crediting guest keyboard player Malcolm Bruce and drummer Kofi Baker, who was also involved with the ATOMGOD project) had elected to be known by the feeble identity of THE NOW. With the album (only released on CD format by Teichiku) featuring mostly older SMOKIN ROADIE material (it also included a version of TEMPEST's "Hell Fire" and a cover of MARVIN GAYE's "I Heard It Through The Grapevine"), the rather dated contents failed to elicit a favourable response from the Japanese market, after which the group disappeared into total obscurity within a mercifully short timescale. Rue Phillips later helped out on BILL WARD's »Ward One« album, but the other members played little part in the rock scene thereafter.

7" Singles

»Midnight« Zone To Zone Records 1983

Compilation Appearances
"Midnight" on »NWOBHM Vol.5« Bootleg CD 1992

SNAKEBITE

Grant Hawthorne (v)
Bobby Irvine (g)
John Boag (rg)
Gary Boag (b)
Gordon Duff (d)

One of the more talented acts to have emerged from the Scottish rock scene during the NWOBHM period were the five-piece known as SNAKEBITE, who came together on the outskirts of Edinburgh at some point in 1981. Unashamedly claiming to be heavily influenced by LED ZEPPELIN and THIN LIZZY, the lads started off by playing the inevitable selection of cover versions to appreciative local audiences, gradually introducing some of their own numbers as time went on. Within a few months, they had laid down their first proper demo, featuring "Black Horizons", "Angels", "Once Ain't Enough" and "Fight For Yourselves", with which they hoped to draw a modicum of interest from various influential parties. For some reason, though, the cassette wasn't widely circulated (although a track or two received airplay on local radio stations) and few individuals were privileged enough to hear the fruits of this inaugural visit to the studio. However, a second tape, recorded at the beginning of 1982, appears to have benefitted from a wider distribution, and listenable copies still survive. It transpires that SNAKEBITE's original material was entirely representative of the NWOBHM archetype, the band coming across as a heavy-but-melodic act to rival the likes of DEALER, HERITAGE and KARRIER, particularly on the excellent "Waster" and the reworked "Fight For Yourselves", whereas the epic "The Message" turned out to be a weighty effort resembling the works of the DESOLATION ANGELS or OMEGA. The real jaw-dropper, however, was the astonishing "Burning Sky", a composition quite unlike anything else from the NWOBHM era. To this day, I can scarcely believe that the track wasn't actually penned by Bob Mould, as I reckon this melodic masterpiece could easily have originated either on a HÜSKER DÜ or SUGAR album. Incredible.

In the spring of 1982, the lads received valuable coverage in the 'Armed And Ready' section of 'Kerrang', where they were touted as having *'the biggest rock following in lowland Scotland'* (they didn't elaborate on who the favoured act in the Highlands might have been), which might have impressed one or two people. It was a slightly contentious claim, perhaps, but it was backed up by some convincing tales of sold-out shows at venues such as the Nite Club in Edinburgh (where HOLOCAUST famously recorded their live album) and successful support slots with high-profile touring acts including DIAMOND HEAD. At this point, the outfit made it crystal clear that they were intending to release a three track EP featuring "Burning Sky", "Waster" and "The Message", a self-financed effort (having failed to solicit much response from the majors) in an edition of a thousand copies. Despite the fact that this item appears on numerous wants lists, however, it never actually materialised, so you can safely stop looking for a copy. As with various other cancelled releases, the reasons behind the non-appearance of this record (which would surely have become one of the true classics of the genre) have never been established, although it must have come as something of a disappointment (to say the least) for the unfortunate four hundred souls who had trustingly placed advance orders...

Now, do you want the good news or the bad news? Well, the good news is that a SNAKEBITE single did eventually appear, but not until 1983. The bad news, however, is that it was totally inferior to their early demo material. I've absolutely no idea what might have happened to the group in the months following their exposure in 'Kerrang', but their belated vinyl debut made it perfectly clear that the protagonists were now operating in an entirely dissimilar style, seemingly closer to the likes of AC/DC and LED ZEPPELIN than to their original musical direction of choice. To be honest, it sounds like a completely different ensemble, so I wouldn't be remotely surprised if there had been some serious personnel rearrangement in the interim. Anyway, the main focus of attention (the disappointing "Blow You Away") is basically ZEP's "Rock And Roll" revisited, with a dash of good old AC/DC (Brian Johnson era) chucked in for good measure, but the flipside was the record's saving grace. The raunchy "Thin Ice" turned out to be a markedly more original and adventurous number (featuring a genuinely excellent guitar interlude which belongs in a different song altogether, and comes perilously close to a section of IRON MAIDEN's "To Tame A Land") falling somewhere between OXYM and Hampshire's LONE WOLF. It wasn't an unmitigated disaster, although, on the evidence of their early demos, SNAKEBITE should have been able to conjure up something considerably more inspiring.

The band didn't hang around for too long after their single finally appeared (the participants all appear to have given the music business a wide berth in later years), and, given that they had, for some unfathomable reason, taken it upon themselves to press several thousand copies in readiness for the orders which were bound to flood in from all corners of the globe (presumably having convinced themselves that there would be an unprecedented demand), the central characters were lumbered with something of a vinyl surplus when they finally called it a day. In the 90's, however, various one-time members were relieved of their *'burden'* by some philanthropic dealers, who proceeded to offer the single (which was never issued in a picture sleeve) for sale at grossly inflated prices. Nowadays, the original hefty tag has come down to something approaching a vaguely sane level, so there's no need to shell out quite as much for a copy, should you decide that you can't possibly live without it.

7" Singles
»Blow You Away« Astor Records 1983

SNATCH-BACK

Ste Platt
J. Cowley
Micky
Ian

An early and very obscure NWOBHM release comes courtesy of the enigmatic SNATCH-BACK (peculiar name, that), who appear to have been a Mancunian quartet, although nobody in the relevant area seems to remember them with any great certainty, suggesting that they weren't particularly serious contenders. Their sole vinyl release, the self-financed »Eastern Lady« 7" from 1979 (recorded at Central Sound Studios in Manchester itself), is an eminently respectable stab at NWOBHM (although the nonexistent production leaves a lot to be desired), occasionally reminiscent of a more forceful OMEN SEARCHER or BASHFUL ALLEY. The A-side opens with an unusual, choppy riff which doesn't really seem to fit the song structure too well, but the track is still extremely listenable once it gets going properly. The reverse ("Cryin' To The Night") is better still, however, this being a memorable, catchy number in the WIKKYD VIKKER scheme of things. Overall, it was a pretty decent start, but it seems not to have led to greater things for the oddly-monikered ensemble, which is a shame. Virtually nothing else is known about the outfit at the present time (there have been some tentative suggestions that they might belong somewhere in the hopelessly convoluted BUDGIE family tree, possibly linked to the short-lived FREEZ, but these conjectures are built upon pretty shaky foundations), so any additional information would, as ever, be greatly appreciated. The two-tracker, which seems not to have been issued in a picture sleeve, appears to have been the group's only attempt to get their big break, and extraordinarily few copies have surfaced thus far. Expect to hand over a fair bit of dosh for this one!

7" Singles
»Eastern Lady« CSS Records 1979

SNOWBLIND

Tony Mason (v)
Andy Simmons (g)
Geoff Gillespie (b)
Ross Bingham (k)
Kevin Baker (d)

With bassist Geoff Gillespie having played a major part in the success of Surrey's talented SABRE (see separate entry), it was natural that people's expectations would be pretty high when details of his all-new outfit, SNOWBLIND, were announced in the latter part of 1983. In fact, Gillespie had, following the demise of SABRE, briefly joined forces with Noel Jones in STATIC, the aforementioned vocalist having recruited several former members of another local outfit called SPHINX in a last-gasp attempt to keep his own band alive. When things didn't work out in the long term, Gillespie took three of his latest accomplices with him, recruited new vocalist Tony Mason (from the ranks of the little-known British OMEN), and set about recording new material under the snappy moniker of SNOWBLIND (if this was indeed taken from the BLACK SABBATH song, there was precious little influence in terms of their musical direction). With a stable line-up having been achieved pretty swiftly, it didn't take long for things to happen for the lads (although tentative plans to issue a single at the beginning of 1984 were hastily shelved), and a demo tape from a few months later (featuring such originals as "Look On Up", "On Our Own", "Possession" and "Pride Before A Fall") was soon attracting a fair bit of label interest.

Having finally been offered a deal by Mausoleum Records by the end of 1984 (presumably having been referred to the Belgian company by the bosses of Future Earth in the UK), the quintet proceeded to knock out their eponymous debut long-player in the first few months of 1985. The lads also took a few hours off at the start of the year to record a session for the 'Friday Rock Show', a performance (broadcast on the 22nd of February 1985) showcasing four future LP tracks in the form of "Walk The Line", "Chasing The Dragon", "Losing My Place" and "Hold On". Whether or not this exercise successfully whetted the public's appetite is open to conjecture, however, as the album itself turned out to be something of a major disappointment. Even the long-player's ill-advised cover came in for some serious flak from the outset: although bewilderingly poor sleeves were par for the course on labels like Mausoleum, SNOWBLIND's effort (a frost-bitten eskimo) still stands out as a particularly ludicrous example of not-remotely-metal artwork. Sadly, the musical contents turned out to be just as uninspiring as the packaging, the group delivering little more than some American-oriented wimp-rock in the style of JOURNEY or TOTO, rendering this particular album as one which can hardly be recommended to the average NWOBHM fan (unless they happen to be partial to a bit of STRATUS or mid-80's TYGERS OF PAN TANG) with any great vigour.

With the much-hyped LP dying a death in no uncertain terms, the dejected outfit began falling apart relatively soon after its release, and vocalist Tony Mason had already moved on to pastures new (a minor club act called CAPRICE) by the second half of the year. Nevertheless, SNOWBLIND persevered at first, recruiting new frontman Trevor McGowan from the little-known SLOWHAND, after which they added guitarist Matt Haslett, a former member of ONYX. Rehearsals for a speculative second album (although they had no firm offers to release one at that stage) began towards the end of 1985, although it would appear that their latest selection of material failed to come up to scratch. Key character Gillespie finally disbanded SNOWBLIND in the early months of 1986, having decided that a move into management might prove to be a more lucrative career, and the enterprising chap spent several years handling the affairs of some of Surrey's up-and-coming hopefuls such as PEROUX (an act, featuring erstwhile SNOWBLIND guitarist Matt Haslett, which went on to enjoy marginally greater success after evolving into NAUGHTY NAUGHTY), although none of them ever looked particularly likely to make him a millionaire. In more recent years, the industrious chap has played a major role in the fortunes of Zoom Club Records, a company who have already unleashed some perfectly respectable CD's of archive NWOBHM material. Various other former members of SNOWBLIND supposedly resurfaced in the appallingly-named HUGH AND WHO'S ARMY towards the end of the 80's, but I reckon this venture actually amounted to little more than some frivolous mucking around in rather more of a knockabout pub rock style.

LP's
»Snowblind« Mausoleum 1985

CD's
»Snowblind« Mausoleum Classix 1994
[Unofficial release]

SOLDIER

Garry Phillips (v)
Ian Dick (g)
Steve Barlow (b)
Ian Astrop (d)

One of the better minor NWOBHM outfits who never got the breaks, Northamptonshire's SOLDIER first appeared on vinyl as a four-piece, contributing "Storm Of Steel" to the legendary »Heavy Metal Heroes« compilation which well and truly put Heavy Metal Records on the map. Although this was an excellent effort, it showed the group at their heaviest, and this DESTROYER/CHARIOT hybrid direction was soon eschewed in favour of a slightly more reserved and melodic (but still satisfyingly heavy) style of music. They had clearly impressed those at Heavy Metal, though, and the lads were duly invited to record a single for the label, whereupon their »Sheralee« two-tracker (b/w "Force") was issued in the early months of 1982 (the A-side made it into the 'Top 30 Kuts' chart in 'Kerrang', incidentally), the record revealing a move towards the confident musical inclinations of acts such as TRESPASS or early PRAYING MANTIS. Even by this time, though, the outfit had already begun to reorganise themselves (as with many others, SOLDIER suffered chronically from personnel difficulties throughout their existence), having recently added Nick Bicknell as second axeman and replaced original drummer Ian Astrop with Steve Taylor, an accomplished veteran of Leicestershire hopefuls the DISTRAINERS (see separate entry), a bunch who had recently mutated into ALIEN, having failed to last the distance in their original incarnation.

With SOLDIER's sound now having become rather more rounded and accessible, their popularity soared over the coming months (even to the extent of establishing an official fan club based in Holland), and, having toured extensively throughout much of Britain (including memorable support slots with both BUDGIE and WISHBONE ASH, in addition to numerous headlining appearances of their own), the lads prepared to record their much-anticipated debut album for Heavy Metal Records. Promoted in the 'Armed And Ready' section of 'Kerrang' in October 1982, the ensemble (now featuring a certain Nick Lashley in place of departed guitarist Ian Dick) garnered some richly-deserved praise for their latest efforts, having presented the reviewers with a demo featuring such gems as "Infantrycide" (the long-player's intended title), "Fire In My Heart", "Don't Throw Your Life Away" and "Lost In Time", a selection of impressive, accomplished compositions in the general manner of their earlier single, although "Lost In Time" additionally showed a willingness to experiment with the odd CRYER-style epic. Towards the end of the year, SOLDIER also circulated an official live cassette (mainly for their loyal fan club members) entitled »Live Forces«, recorded at a memorable performance at one of their regular haunts (the Old Five Bells venue in Northampton), which included a generous selection of unreleased material such as "Man From Berlin", "Making A Stand" and "Stay".

As you'll no doubt be aware, however, the projected SOLDIER long-player never actually materialised, and it doesn't, in fact, even exist in finished tape form. Drummer Steve Taylor explains the circumstances: 'I'm afraid that »Infantrycide« was never recorded-we did loads of demos for it and then had a huge bust up with Paul Birch who owned Heavy Metal Records, they wanted us to sign a five year deal with no money and all the options on their side.' (Ref: Private communication, March 1997). Despite receiving a fair bit of interest from other labels, the group suffered serious internal problems thereafter, and were forced to eject founder members Steve Barlow and Garry Phillips in the summer of 1983, replacing the pair with ex-GASKIN (well, he had played about one rehearsal with them) bassist Mark McKenzie (who later had a brief stint with the unsuccessful SHAKETOWN) and ex-GIRL vocalist Phil Lewis (who went on to join the NEW TORPEDOS, before subsequently linking up with TORMÉ and then ultimately having an extremely busy time of it in the prolific L.A. GUNS venture). Once the revised line-up had managed to get their act together, the lads

eventually got around to demoing some fairly commercial material such as "Charlotte Russe" and the excellent "Heartbreak Zone" (bringing to mind the likes of LYADRIVE and ENERGY), and they soon found themselves attracting the attention of Music For Nations, among others.

Although the persevering SOLDIER were apparently considered strong contenders for a possible album deal, the aforementioned label failed to come up with a firm offer, eventually deciding that TANK were actually a markedly better commercial option! Having suffered years of bad luck and cruel rejection, the band began to lose heart, and, understandably, they had ultimately thrown in their hand by 1984. Guitarist Nick Lashley, however, having been involved in various short-lived projects throughout the 80's (he even helped out in the ranks of GIRLSCHOOL at one stage), is now on a nice little earner, given that he was later plucked from obscurity to become a full-time member of million-selling angst-merchant ALANIS MORISSETTE's backing group! The well-travelled Steve Taylor has also maintained a notable role in the business, composing a diverse range of original material (from incidental music to considerably heavier selections) and performing (under such bizarre aliases as GODDWARF) as a solo artist on occasion, even to the present day.

7" Singles
»Sheralee« Heavy Metal 1982
[Also released as part of »Munsters Of Rock«

singles pack]

Exclusive Compilation Appearances
"Storm Of Steel" on »Heavy Metal Heroes« LP Heavy Metal 1981 *[Issued in two different sleeves]* + »Heavy Metal Heroes Vol.I&II« CD British Steel 1996

Compilation Appearances
"Sheralee" on »NWOBHM Vol.1« Bootleg CD 1992 + »N.W.O.B.H.M. Metal Rarities Vol.3« CD British Steel 1997
"Force" on »N.W.O.B.H.M. Metal Rarities Vol.3« CD British Steel 1997

SO WHAT

Tommy Smillie (v, b)
Rod Earl (g)
Des Duffy (g)
Gerry Duffy (d)

An energetic bunch from North of the border, SO WHAT got their first break as early as 1982, when they were one of several heavy hopefuls from the Ayrshire area to be allocated a track or two on the seldom-seen »Kikrock« showcase album, lovingly assembled by small-time label Kik Records (the one-time home of bands such as the PENETRATIONS). After a quick trip to the studio, the lads duly contributed the unremarkable, semi-boogie of "Fool's Love" and the considerably more proficient "Me And You" to the little-known sampler, and, even at that stage, SO WHAT certainly stood out as one of the more capable acts on display. It's worth noting that the outfit clearly featured a slightly different line-up in the early days (I suspect that erstwhile JOE LETHAL mainman Alan Aitken may well have been involved at the outset), but it's fair to say that their general sound had more or less become fixed by this juncture. Following this handy exposure, the lads basically concentrated on live work for a year or two, earning themselves a useful local reputation in the process, although they finally (after a couple of personnel changes became necessary in order to achieve genuine stability) decided to introduce themselves to the rock cognoscenti by touting around an impressive and well-recorded eight track demo.

Encompassing an enviable variety of original compositions, from the *'early TOKYO BLADE meets prime-era UFO'*-style, twin-guitar attacks of "Bad Boys" and "Searching For Love", to the EXCALIBUR-soundalike "Visions", the selection of material was consistently excellent, with a considerable level of musical aptitude on display all round. Elsewhere, such capable efforts as the hard-rocking "Young Girls" and a revamped version of the aforementioned "Me And You" were extremely enjoyable too, so it looked as though SO WHAT had plenty of potential for the future. With their latest batch of material presumably having met with critical approval from Tommy Vance at the BBC, the lucky group (who had signed a management deal and relocated to the capital by mid-1985) were offered the chance to lay down a prestigious session for the 'Friday Rock Show', and the lads wasted little time before grasping the opportunity with both hands. Broadcast on the 13th of December 1985, their slot showcased "I Don't Know Why" (featuring an instrumental segment of "Auld Lang Syne", for no apparent reason), "I've Got To Go", "Promises" and "I'll Be Your Friend", all of which represented strong, gutsy pieces of melodic rock, perhaps marginally more in the vein of later 80's ensembles such as CRYWOLF and FAST KUTZ than before. Apart from "I'll Be Your Friend", which was vaguely reminiscent of TRIUMPH, the selections were again all very British-sounding (something of a novelty, given that so many home-grown hopefuls succumbed to the insidious North American influence at around this time), although it appears that the foursome might have been trying to move with the times and distance themselves from their earlier (more metallic) roots.

The move towards mainstream material, however, had become even more blatant by the time the outfit's debut single (the prophetically-titled »Is It All Over«) put in an appearance in the early months of 1986. The A-side was, sadly, an extremely poor example of utterly formulaic, gutless, mid-80's melodic nonsense, the quartet delivering a pauper's version of STRATUS or STATETROOPER without the omnipresent keyboards. Admittedly, the reverse ("Now I Don't Want You Around") was a tad heavier, suggesting TERRAPLANE on a bad day, but it failed to save the situation. The ensemble seemed to have lost the plot in major fashion, but didn't actually remain a going concern as SO WHAT for very long after the (sleeveless) 7" appeared, as they had evolved into NINJA (one of several acts to adopt the name) by 1987, whereupon they were honoured with a generous, full-page feature in 'Kerrang' and heralded as *'new'* contenders for the melodic rock crown. After some high-profile appearances at the Marquee under this guise, a demo was circulated the following year, although this uninspiring effort, featuring THE SWEET's "Action" (again) and "Visions Of Youth", didn't exactly set the world on fire. Predictably enough, the lads evidently called it a day shortly thereafter, but this inauspicious fall from grace fails to alter the fact that SO WHAT were once a very fine band indeed. It appears that their long-time chums in SPIDER agreed, as the boogie-meisters actually elected to cover the excellent "Bad Boys" (and a remarkably good job they made of it, too) on their swansong »Raise The Banner« LP.

7" Singles
»Is It All Over« Private 1986

Exclusive Compilation Appearances
"Fool's Love" on »Kikrock« LP Kik Records 1982
"Me And You" on »Kikrock« LP Kik Records 1982

SPARTA

Karl Reders (v)
Tony Foster (g)
Snake Reders (g)
Tony Warren (b)
Paul 'Radge' Reders (d)

Nottinghamshire's SPARTA formed in the early part of 1980, their members having been assimilated from a couple of less-successful, late 70's Midlands outfits (Tony Foster and Tony Warren had been in XEROX, while the Reders brothers operated as something of an amateur-hour trio) who had failed to amount to much. Originally working their way up from the elementary, ground-level pub gigs with local hopefuls such as OVERDRIVE, to some more prestigious support slots with (allegedly) the likes of DIAMOND HEAD, URIAH HEEP, PRAYING MANTIS, LIONHEART and BUDGIE (although the actual evidence for such claims would appear to be scant), the group's heavy and energetic brand of metal soon allowed them to establish themselves as firm regional favourites. Releasing their first 7" (in a sleeve featuring a half-inched comic-book illustration of some ancient warriors) within around six months of their initial formation, by which time a fan club and merchandising operation had already been set up in their area, the outfit were rewarded with the accolade of *'Heavy Metal Single Of The Week'* in 'Sounds' magazine. The two-tracker (sponsored by the short-lived Suspect Records concern), pairing "Fast Lane" and "Fighting To Be Free", was a heavy slice of NWOBHM with a very distinctive vocal style, musically reminiscent of the likes of MARZ or early DEF LEPPARD from time to time.

SPARTA built upon the success of their debut with yet more regional gigging, and a follow-up single (another double A-side, this time in a fold-out cover) was in the shops by the following year, this new release coupling "Angel Of Death" (which, in due course, would put in an appearance in the 'Local Chart' section of 'Kerrang') and "Tonight". By now, the quintet had evidently added a slightly more forceful edge to their sound, suggesting possible comparisons with outfits such as RICOCHET and the West Midlands version of SCARAB. In fact, 1981 was to be a busy year for the SPARTA lads, and the group were fortunate enough to be featured on the Suspect Records compilation »Scene Of The Crime« (delivering the exclusive contribution "Lords Of Time") as well as being promoted in the 'Armed And Ready' section of 'Kerrang', so things appeared to be going swimmingly at that stage. By the start of 1982, however, they had parted company with original frontman Karl Reders, and it was to be several months before a capable replacement, an unknown quantity called Trevor Morgan, filled his shoes. Nevertheless, a few newer SPARTA compositions were laid down before much longer, and some (including "Rock For You", "Dogs Of War", "Streetwalkin'", "Shady Lady", "Lady Evil" and "Hot Rock") were even featured in session on Radio Hallam. Now featuring a more traditional vocalist, the outfit appear to have been attempting a more straightforward, rocking style in the vein of BATTLEAXE or FUGITIVE, although the material was hardly outstanding in its originality or execution. Plans for a third single were outlined, but this project never seems to have made it to the vinyl stage, and, following a few gigs towards the end of the year, everything went ominously quiet.

In fact, the lads continued in low-profile mode for a few years (recruiting yet another vocalist, Mark Henshaw), and made tentative plans (after demoing some new numbers such as "Soldier Of Fortune", "Welcome To My Nightmare" and "The Legend Of Doctor Bill") to release another single in the mid-80's, but no further vinyl offerings subsequently materialised. Tony Foster, the main songwriting force, flew the coop in 1985, which destabilised the outfit considerably, although the remaining members struggled on until around 1987 before finally conceding defeat. Nevertheless, a version of SPARTA appears to have come out of the woodwork at around the turn of the decade, when the Reders brothers got back together for one last crack at making it big, and duly undertook a couple of studio sessions as a trio. It's entirely possible, therefore, that the SPARTA who apparently contributed a track to one of Ebony's late 80's compilations (one of the »Full Force« albums which appeared on the Reaction subsidiary) were indeed a direct descendent of the original bunch, but I guess we'd better wait for confirmation. The working partnership of Tony Warren and Tony Foster continues in the clubs to this day, incidentally, as the duo still play together in a more bluesy concern called the SOUND COMPANY.

7" Singles
»Fast Lane« Suspect Records 1980
»Angel Of Death« Suspect Records 1981

Exclusive Compilation Appearances
"Lords Of Time" on »Scene Of The Crime« LP Suspect Records 1981

Compilation Appearances
"Tonight" on »NWOBHM Vol.5« Bootleg CD 1992

SPARTAN WARRIOR

Dave Wilkinson (v)
Neil Wilkinson (g)
Paul Swaddle (g)
Tom Spencer (b)
Gordon Webster (d)

Tyneside's heroically-named SPARTAN WARRIOR were, without any question, one of Guardian's better signings, and they appear to have been in existence for a relatively short time before the company took a vested interest in their activities. Initially, the quintet were afforded the opportunity of contributing two tracks to the »Pure Overkill« compilation in 1983, but swiftly progressed to a full album of their own following the favourable response to these early numbers. The compositions in question were "Comes As No Surprise" and "Steel'n'Chains", the latter of which would be recycled as the title track of their debut long-player. From the outset, the group's upbeat, twin-guitar style identified them as potential heroes to all those who appreciate such powerful, speedy outfits as SALEM, RAVEN, BLACKWYCH and SAMURAI, for example. SPARTAN WARRIOR's recordings for Guardian yielded an extremely capable album, with particular highlights from the »Steel'n'Chains«

set being the energetic "Stormer" and atmospheric "Witchfinder", plus the truly excellent "Breakin' Sweat". It wasn't exactly ground-breaking stuff in any sense, but the truly enviable level of enthusiasm and commitment serves to elevate the LP to a much higher plane of enjoyment. It seems to have been a popular purchase at the time, and the lads were soon to capitalise on their new-found fame by undertaking a couple of reasonably extensive tours of the North before thinking about a follow-up release.

Album number two, 1984's eponymous effort, saw the lads recording at Guardian under the auspices of Terry Gavaghan once again, although the end product was actually issued by the more influential Roadrunner label. The energy and speed had now taken a bit of a dip, although the record was still a very powerful effort (highlights including such heavy offerings as "Sentenced To Die" and "Mercenary") with occasional tinges of DEALER and TYGA MYRA. Mind you, the outfit lose quite a few brownie points for some nauseatingly puerile lyrics on "Hanging On", the kind of thing that comes straight out of MÖTLEY CRÜE's practical guide to amateur misogyny. Sadly, Roadrunner's attempts to break the group in the global metal market appear to have been limited to a solitary compilation appearance around the time of the album's release (maybe they spent their entire promotional budget on the extremely accomplished cover artwork), and the band consequently failed to make much of an impact either in mainland Europe or in their homeland thereafter. The end appears to come fairly shortly afterwards (the lads attempted to start afresh by recruiting a new vocalist, Steve Taylor, in the early months of 1985, although the revised line-up appears to have failed to record), with none of the original members proceeding to team up with any other acts of note. A great pity.

LP's
»Steel'n'Chains« Guardian 1983
»Spartan Warrior« Roadrunner 1984

Compilation Appearances
"Steel'n'Chains" on »Pure Overkill« LP Guardian 1983
"Comes As No Surprise" on »Pure Overkill« LP Guardian 1983
[Retitled as "Easy Prey" on »Steel'n'Chains« album]
"Mercenary" on »The Metal Machine« LP Roadrunner 1984
"Cold Hearted" on »NWOBHM Vol.8« Bootleg CD 1996

SPEED

Bruce Bruce (v)
Steve Adams (g)
Paul White (b)
Gary Edwards (k)
Jeff Moody (d)

Forget URCHIN, the monumentally rare SPEED single pretty much represents the Holy Grail as far as fanatical NWOBHM collectors and IRON MAIDEN completists are concerned, featuring, as it does, the earliest known recording of the *'air raid siren'* himself, Bruce Dickinson (aka Bruce Bruce). With the tracks in question having supposedly been recorded in around 1978, but remaining unissued until 1980, it would appear that XERO weren't the only shameless opportunists who identified the lucrative possibility of cashing in on some of their archive studio material, although the quantity of SPEED singles actually pressed must have been truly minimal in comparison, with only a single-figure quantity known to survive today. With the two-tracker being released with a cheap, double-sided insert as opposed to a proper sleeve, the scoundrels involved in this exploitation affair evidently tried to blur the facts somewhat, insisting that the band had formed in Essex as recently as 1979 (interesting, that) and crediting Dickinson only as a *'guest vocalist'* (hmmm, naughty). It was also implied that the frontman was actually *'on loan'* from SAMSON at the time, and that the single was indeed recorded in 1980, which seems to be quite at odds with Dickinson's own version of events *(vide infra)*. In any case, it seems to have sold in staggeringly modest quantities upon its release, so you have to wonder whether or not it was really worth the effort.

The track "Man In The Street" has, in recent years, been heard by a wider audience, having been featured on the »NWOBHM Vol.7« bootleg, prompting a bit of gentle interrogation from the 'IRON PAGES' crew. Bruce Dickinson reveals: *'That's a studio recording from when I was still at college. The original SPEED had already formally disbanded by that time, but Noddy White asked me whether or not I'd come back and sing on this number, which he intended to record with a couple of his mates. So I agreed to help him out, and we even got as far as laying down a second track, a boogie number, the title of which I've forgotten. SPEED were, even back then, a kind of NWOBHM outfit, we played PRIEST and STRANGLERS songs alongside our own material and toured in and around London in the late 70's. On a couple of occasions we shared a stage with ANGEL WITCH.'* (Ref: Interview, Matthias Mader, March 1997). Clearly, even Dickinson himself was unaware of the single's existence, which tends to suggest that he wasn't consulted before it hit the shops. As to the virtues of the music on display, though, it's not exactly typical NWOBHM fodder after all, more of a *'VARDIS with garage-style keyboards'* approach, but I dare say all the MAIDEN fans would still wet themselves at the extremely slender prospect of finding a copy. The B-side, "Down The Road", is probably the stronger effort of the pair, with those distinctive vocals largely overshadowing the rest of the musicians. Evidently, this was their only (belated) vinyl output as an ensemble, and this version of SPEED shouldn't be confused with the Irish group who issued the »Big City« 7" a year or two previously (or with the unrelated act who appeared on the »Green Metal« compilation several years later). Start saving your money *now* if you ever want to own this one!

7" Singles
»**Man In The Street**« Private 1980

Compilation Appearances
"**Man In The Street**" on »NWOBHM Vol.7« Bootleg CD 1996

SPEED LIMIT

Acker Appleby (v)
David Morris (g)
Brian Smith (g)
Dougie Dennis (b)
Tony Baylis (d)

Generally regarded as founding fathers of the crowd-pleasing, good-time rock'n'roll scene which established itself in the pre-NWOBHM era were the legendary SPEED LIMIT, whose famous exploits in the Midlands from the mid-70's onwards paved the way for later knockabout reprobates such as EAZIE RYDER, SPLIT BEAVER and the STARFIGHTERS to follow in their footsteps. All things considered, their live reputation was truly enviable, with numerous reports of over-the-top appearances with massive crowd participation, all helped along by the outfit's down-to-earth attitude and slacker ethics (evidenced by ditties such as "Watching TV", "Down The Boozer" and "Doing Time"). Sadly, however, their notoriety as debauched hellraisers largely fails to come across on their debut album (the »First Offence« effort), an unremarkable set recorded for the little-known Satril label in 1978. Although there are a handful of numbers, such as "Motorbike Kid", "Down At The Ritz" and "Speed Limit", where the band allowed themselves to rock out a bit more, the majority of the album consists of pretty bland and perfunctory proto-NWOBHM of the kind peddled by ANGEL STREET, TRADER, SINGAPORE and so forth. It wasn't entirely the musicians' fault, though, given that the muted, MOR-style production had removed a great deal of energy from a group whose real forte was in the live environment.

Mind you, matters weren't helped by the fact that Satril subsequently elected to issue the album's weakest cut (the awful "Wino" semi-ballad) as a single to promote the new long-player, especially when the flipside ("Motorbike Kid") was immeasurably stronger. To be honest, I imagine the band's many followers were utterly bewildered by their first batch of vinyl releases, and the lacklustre album probably failed to win over too many new fans at the time. Almost immediately, rumours began circulating that SPEED LIMIT would be calling it a day within a short space of time, apparently being immensely disappointed with the public reaction to their debut long-player. It wasn't to be the case, however, although they were to issue no further recordings of their own at any stage. Eventually, though, after many years of solid gigging, their farewell gigs were announced, culminating in an appearance at Birmingham's Barrel Organ in June 1980. As luck would have it, this actually coincided with the recording of several shows for future release as a live compilation album to celebrate the Midlands rock scene.

In the event, two of the outfit's previously-unrecorded numbers ("Alright On The Night" and ever-popular singalong "CJ") were included on the sampler, the »Brum Beats« double set issued on Big Bear Records a couple of months later. These particular tracks finally saw justice being done, capturing SPEED LIMIT at their most intense and energetic, the capacity crowd savouring every last moment of what they assumed would surely be the final appearance by their heroes. In fact, it appears that they were lured out of retirement on at least two further occasions, first towards the end of 1980 and then in the early months of 1981 (by which time their bassist, Dougie Dennis, was firmly established as a paid-up member of the STARFIGHTERS), although these pretty much seem to have been one-off get-togethers. To sum up, if ever there was a group who should, like A II Z, CHINATOWN, STAMPEDE, SURFACE et al., have introduced themselves to the masses with a live album, it was SPEED LIMIT!

LP's
»First Offence« Satril Records 1978

7" Singles
»Wino« Satril Records 1978

Exclusive Compilation Appearances
"Alright On The Night" (live) on »Brum Beats-Live At The Barrel Organ« Do-LP Big Bear Records 1980
"CJ" (live) on »Brum Beats-Live At The Barrel Organ« Do-LP Big Bear Records 1980

SPIDER

Col Harkness (v,g)
Dave 'Sniffa' Bryce (g)
Brian Burrows (b)
Rob Burrows (d)

Few of SPIDER's many die-hard fans will be aware just how early their Merseyside heroes actually got to the vinyl stage (having formed in the mid-70's), as it's something that the quartet tried (remarkably successfully, it must be stated) to conceal in their NWOBHM-period interviews. Some of you might be sitting there quite smugly, thinking 'I know all about their early releases on the Alien label, thanks very much', but I'm talking about an even earlier effort, of which relatively few collectors and fans have the remotest knowledge. Recorded for the small Pennine label, SPIDER's first vinyl appearance came in the form of a 7" single featuring "Back To The Wall" and "Down And Out", issued in a blackmail-friendly sleeve showing the youngsters (looking not a day over fifteen) posing against a wall in shiny cabaret suits with bell-bottomed trousers. How stylish. Although this offering isn't dated explicitly (furthermore, Pennine's catalogue system isn't the most straightforward to decode), it turns out to have been issued at the tail end of 1977, the first reviews appearing in the music weeklies soon after. Even by the standards of the 'crypto-NWOBHM' genre, however, this is a monumentally scarce record (the vast majority of discographies omit it completely), and examples have been unearthed considerably less frequently (especially with the coveted picture cover) than URCHIN's »Black Leather Fantasy« over the years.

There's absolutely no suggestion that SPIDER (not to be confused with a punky outfit who appeared on an obscure »Battle Of The Bands« EP in 1978 or a lightweight American act who once recorded for the Dreamland label and later changed their name to SHANGHAI) ever played anything other than QUO-influenced boogie the vast majority of the time, and their vinyl debut set the tone for what was to be a prolific career which took them from label to label over the following ten years or so. Having said that, there was, after this early effort, something of a hiatus before additional vinyl started appearing, and their activities in the interim appear to be shrouded in mystery (maybe they went back to

school). Although they gradually developed a reputation as a live act at around the turn of the decade, SPIDER kept something of a low profile whilst looking for a proper deal, although they still enjoyed playing to appreciative crowds whenever possible, getting their performances down to a fine art, as Brian Burrows explained early in 1980: *'We've learnt that the secret is to grab them by the balls and hold them. The danger is that you can get an audience up so far and if you don't watch it you can just lose them. It's a case of building and building until at the end of the night they're ready for anything and don't want to go home.'* (Ref: Teenage Depression, Issue 12, 1980).

Eventually, the lads became affiliated with the little-known Alien label (more of a punk concern), who proceeded to release a couple of SPIDER singles (»Children Of The Street« and »College Luv«) in 1980. These appear to have sold in reasonable quantities for an independent brace of releases, and they certainly served to introduce the outfit to a slightly wider audience than before. Having said that, surprisingly few copies appear to have survived the ensuing years in playable condition, and both are now valued quite highly, especially with picture sleeves. SPIDER's next port of call was the fairly dependable City Records (who also released product from the likes of GIRLSCHOOL and TERRAPLANE), although this proved to be another brief relationship, the lads moving on after just one single, the »All The Time« two-tracker from 1981. At around this point, the outfit found time to record the first of their two sessions for the 'Friday Rock Show', which resulted in "9-5", "A.W.O.L.", "Rock'n'Roll Forever Will Last" and "What You're Doin' To Me" being broadcast on the 19th of June 1981. The following year, the group had yet another new label (the rather less prestigious Creole, future home of VIRGINIA WOLF), for whom they issued another sole single, this time taking the form of the »Talkin' 'Bout Rock'n'Roll« 7". The foursome's sales figures had been improving with every release, and they were starting to get bigger support slots with acts such as SLADE and GILLAN, but the lads felt that their big break was still just around the corner, and they were soon to be proved right.

1982 turned out to be a good year for SPIDER, in that their hectic and relentless touring schedule (in addition to support dates and headlining gigs of their own) took in an appearance at the Reading Festival, where they shared a bill with the likes of TERRAPLANE, CHINATOWN and Y&T. Not only that, they were picked up by the influential RCA concern, who were soon encouraging their new protégés to lay down their debut album. SPIDER realised that this really was their big chance at last, and duly relocated to the capital in order to start work on their first long-player. »Rock'n'Roll Gypsies« appeared later in the year, and it was a decent enough representation of the outfit's no-nonsense style of boogie-influenced NWOBHM, including versions of old stage favourites such as "Did Ya Like It Baby" and "What You're Doin' To Me", although there was still the odd surprise in store, with "'Til I'm Certain" showing that there was more than one dimension to the supposedly formulaic and derivative music of SPIDER. The album sold well, as did two hastily-issued singles (»Rock'n'Roll Forever Will Last« and a re-promoted version of »Talkin' 'Bout Rock'n'Roll«), and things now seemed to be going SPIDER's way in no uncertain terms. Moving into 1983, the lads embarked upon a successful European tour alongside UFO, and their label issued another couple of singles in the shape of »Why D'ya Lie To Me« (featuring entirely exclusive material) and »Part Of The Legend«, although the latter (which tied in with some kind of advertising campaign) only seems to have emerged in Spain.

Nevertheless, in spite of their apparent success with RCA, the restless combo (who were, by this time, widely acknowledged as an act who were more than capable of attracting a fairly large crowd to their own headlining appearances) were soon on the move once again, signing with A&M Records later in the year. Almost immediately, they began work on their second long-player, which appeared in the early months of 1984 as »Rough Justice«. This contained several compositions which were a surprising departure from the straightforward boogie norm (notably the complexity of "The Minstrel" and the utterly bizarre folk-boogie of "Midsummer Morning") alongside more typical SPIDER fare, although there was a tendency towards some slightly heavier riffing on the likes of "Death Row" and the title track, whereas "Martyred (For What I Love)" (a number quite reminiscent of the type of melodic NWOBHM purveyed by PRAYING MANTIS) showed that the lads were more than capable of breaking out of the narrow boogie niche after all. The latest LP may have won the lads a few new fans, but it seems to have alienated a considerably greater number of their original followers (after all, STATUS QUO have peddled heads-down boogie for thirty-odd years, why couldn't SPIDER have followed their example rather than getting any clever ideas?), resulting in an album which was ultimately regarded as something of a commercial failure. After two tie-in singles (»Here We Go Rock'n'Roll« and »Breakaway«, the latter based around an obscure original which had been performed as early as 1977 by the little-remembered DEAD END KIDS) had been issued to overwhelming public disinterest, the band found themselves in the unenviable position of looking for yet another new label.

Strangely, however, SPIDER found that they were still able to pull the crowds whenever they played live (as long as they didn't try out any of that 'fancy' stuff), and they continued to trek around the country at every available opportunity, with one of their most notable appearances of 1984 coming at the Kerrang Festival at the seaside resort of Caister (highlights of which were later broadcast on the 'Friday Rock Show'), where the group took their turn to entertain a receptive and appreciative crowd alongside the likes of DUMPY'S RUSTY NUTS, WAYSTED and MOTÖRHEAD. Moving into 1985, the headlining appearances continued apace, although they also took time off to appear on the much-lambasted 'E.C.T.' television programme, performing old favourite "All The Time" and the unfamiliar effort "Rock Tonite" for the benefit of an easily-entertained bunch of freeloaders (sorry, I meant to say 'sincere and knowledgeable rock fans'). Before much longer, yet another company became interested in the outfit's activities, this time in the slightly unexpected shape of Mausoleum Records (who would, in fact, have been SPIDER's seventh label). Contracts were duly exchanged, and the quartet proceeded to lay down their third album towards the end of 1985, although it rapidly became worryingly apparent that the cash-strapped Mausoleum were now in no position to release any product by the hapless group after all, leaving them with no option but to tout around the master tapes and then sell to the highest bidder.

In the meantime, however, the lads took the opportunity to showcase some of their latest material with another set for their old friends at the 'Friday Rock Show'. Their second session was transmitted on the 31st of January 1986, the featured numbers being "Need To Know About You", "Mind, Heart, Body and Soul", "I'm Not The Only One" and "Gimme Gimme It All", all of which were firmly in the grand old SPIDER tradition, suggesting that they had outgrown their brief period of experimentation. In the event, remarkably little record company interest came SPIDER's way in the wake of the broadcast, and they were eventually forced to go with the small-time PRT label (which, to all intents and purposes, meant that it was a self-produced affair) just to get the third album released at all. When »Raise The Banner« finally appeared later in 1986, the SPIDER empire was already on the brink of collapse after all the trials and tribulations of the previous months, although they remained together long enough to promote the album to some extent. As might have been expected on the basis of their latest radio session, the LP saw a return to their original style on most tracks, although there were a couple of more daring compositions ("Games In The Park" and "So Sorry") towards the end which came across as a more lightweight version of LE GRIFFE, but it was too little, too late. The record appears to have been pressed in quite limited quantities, but it sold in pitifully small numbers, and the writing was on the wall for the unfortunate SPIDER.

Ironically, there was one truly excellent song on »Raise The Banner«, but the credit actually belonged to another little-known NWOBHM band. The superb "Bad Boys" had originally been penned by Scottish hopefuls SO WHAT (see separate entry) a couple of years previously, and SPIDER (who had played with the aforementioned outfit on numerous occasions in the past) picked up on the track while recording their latest opus. To be honest, it sticks out like a sore thumb compared with their own compositions, but it still provides the listener with a unique chance to hear SPIDER attempting (and very successfully, too) some twin-guitar riffing in the best tradition of TOKYO BLADE! The lads made one final effort to win back the fans by issuing »Gimme Gimme It All« as a single, but it flopped once again, leaving them with a fairly dismal future ahead of them. SPIDER played their last gig in the summer of 1986, whereupon Sniffa decided to pack it all in and quit the music business in disgust. Peculiarly, however, the remaining members announced that they would be continuing with a replacement guitarist (former HERETIC axeman Stu Hurwood), although this line-up never actually appears to have made any progress whatsoever, splitting by the end of the year without recording any new material or playing in public. In the wake of SPIDER's demise, the members drifted away from the rock scene and returned to the non-glamorous life of working-class drudgery in order to pay the bills, although the name of Brian Burrows has graced a number of record sleeves in recent years, the talented chap having turned his hand to graphic design with considerable aplomb.

LP's
»**Rock'n'Roll Gypsies**« RCA 1982
»**Rough Justice**« A&M 1984
»**Raise The Banner**« PRT 1986

12" EP's
»**Why D'ya Lie To Me**« RCA 1983
[All three tracks non-LP]
»**Here We Go Rock'n'Roll**« A&M 1984
["I Just Wanna Make Love To You" non-LP]
»**Breakaway**« A&M 1984
[A-side non-LP]
»**Gimme Gimme It All**« PRT 1986
[Includes live version of "Did Ya Like It Baby"]

7" Singles
»**Back To The Wall**« Pennine Records 1977
[Both tracks non-LP]
»**Children Of The Street**« Alien Records 1980
[Both tracks non-LP]
»**College Luv**« Alien Records 1980
[Both tracks non-LP]
»**All The Time**« City Records 1981
[A-side different to album version, B-side "Feel Like A Man" non-LP]
»**Talkin' 'Bout Rock'n'Roll**« Creole Records 1982
[Original issue, B-side "'Til I'm Certain"]
»**Rock'n'Roll Forever Will Last**« RCA 1982
[Initially packaged with free single featuring special track "Amazing Grace Medley" (Parts 1 and 2)]
»**Talkin' 'Bout Rock'n'Roll**« RCA 1982
[Second issue in different sleeve, B-side "Down'n'Out" non-LP]
»**Why D'ya Lie To Me**« RCA 1983
[Both tracks non-LP]
»**Part Of The Legend**« RCA 1983
[Spanish-only release]
»**Here We Go Rock'n'Roll**« A&M 1984
»**Breakaway**« A&M 1984
[A-side non-LP]
»**Gimme Gimme It All**« PRT 1986
[A-side different to album version, some copies packaged in plastic wallet with free single featuring live versions of "Get Down And Get With It" and "Rock'n'Roll Forever Will Last"]

Shaped Picture Discs
»**Here We Go Rock'n'Roll**« A&M 1984

Compilation Appearances
"What You're Doing To Me" on »The Friday Rock Show« LP BBC Records 1981
[Different to album version]
"All The Time" (live) on »Reading Rock Vol.1« Do-LP Mean Records 1982
[Different to album version]
"All The Time" on »Give 'Em Hell« CD Nectar Masters 1995 + »The Best Of Indie Metal« CD Emporio 1998
"Feel Like A Man" on »Rock Out!« Do-CD Emporio 1996 + »The Best Of Indie Metal« CD Emporio 1998

SPITFIRE

Line-up unknown

It's hard to believe that this particular SPITFIRE (not to be confused with about three million other namesakes throughout the world) was a *'proper'* band in any sense, as their single has the distinct feeling of a jokey side-project or a (rapidly thrown together) cash-in (*cf.* the pointless »Status Rock« 7" credited to the HEADBANGERS). I've no idea who might have played a part in this misguided venture, although the ensemble's reworking of the lengthily-titled A-side (a standard originally recorded by the BYRDS as long ago as 1967) is a pretty decent, hard-rocking effort which brings forth a few comparisons with the likes of FIST, MORE or the STARFIGHTERS, with the fairly powerful vocals failing to shine in the presence of such hackneyed lyrics. Mind you, it's worth pointing out that SPITFIRE weren't the first (or the only) bunch to cover this particular number by a long way, as THE MOVE saw fit to issue their own version soon after the original was released. The disposable B-side ("Spitfire Boogie", credited to 'SPITFIRE and the Blackpool Barmies'), on the other hand, is a rather unsubtle SPIDER/STATUS QUO pastiche featuring many a familiar riff and lyric, the 'we're laughing all the way to the bank' refrain at the end providing us with a pretty good idea of how seriously we're supposed to take all this nonsense. This sleeveless 1982 oddity, sponsored (implausibly enough) by the Carrere label (home of SAXON, RAGE and SCORCHED EARTH), has been regarded as something of a collectable rarity for a number of years, although the catalogue value far exceeds its musical merit. Whatever you do, don't get conned into thinking this is a true NWOBHM classic!

7" Singles
»So You Want To Be A Rock'n'Roll Star«
Carrere 1982

SPITZBROOK

Dave Bolton (v)
Ant Baker (g)
Terry Golding (b)
Josh Phillips-Gorse (k)
Andy Dovey (d)

The curiously-monikered SPITZBROOK, a five-piece proposition from the musically-flourishing area of Kent, contrived to deliver one of the NWOBHM genre's most remarkable vinyl offerings, although I suspect that relatively few of you will have been aware of this masterpiece until now. Issued on the small-time Ace label (home of regional heavyweights DENIGH) back in 1981, their »Stranger« 7" stands way above most other independent releases of the time, not only in terms of musicianship, but also with regard to the lyrical content and production.

Mind you, if you expect a heads down, full-on guitar assault, you'd be sorely disappointed, as the band clearly took their lead from more progressive, technical acts, notably RUSH. In particular, the A-side (dealing with the topic of cryogenic suspension) is unmistakably reminiscent of "Spirit Of Radio", with excellent keyboard work and some superb vocals from Dave Bolton, plus a blistering guitar solo in best Brian Tatler tradition; it's slightly spooky, therefore, that keyboard player Josh Phillips-Gorse would actually hook up with DIAMOND HEAD two years later! The flipside ("Looking At You"), meanwhile, is somewhat unusual in its construction, the subject matter being a parable of illicit naughtiness at the English coast (drug smuggling is the obvious implication) and consequent foul play amongst the participants. The chorus seems rather ill-advised and out of place, though:

'Come with me, you can get some too
When I'm looking at you, looking at you
Much better than sniffing glue
When I'm looking at you, looking at you.'

Believe me, regardless of all these unseemly *'sniffing glue'* references, there's absolutely *zero* punk influence here, folks! Despite gigging exhaustively around their native county at the time, the talented bunch evidently didn't hang around for all that long after their single made its way into the shops, which is a real pity, but I suspect that the sophisticated sound the lads were trying to develop just wasn't in favour with the vast majority of metalheads in the early 80's. They might well have enjoyed marginally more success later in the decade, I suppose, but SPITZBROOK were one of countless acts whose only crime was to be different. Seek this one out if you appreciate some of the more adventurous and cerebral NWOBHM outfits such as SHIVA, BIG DAISY or even the more progressively-inclined LIAISON, but you'll undoubtedly discover that copies of »Stranger« (particularly the minority with the generic picture sleeve) are somewhat thin on the ground these days.

7" Singles
»Stranger« Ace Records 1981

SPLIT BEAVER

Darrell Whitehouse (v)
Mike Hoppett (g)
Alan Rees (b)
Keith Allen (d)

Right from day one, Midlands combo SPLIT BEAVER (prudes might be reassured to know that the name actually has literary origins, believe it or not) antagonised people with immense efficiency, which may or may not have been the intention all along. Formed at the tail end of 1979, the band's original line-up featured two guitarists, although one was rapidly ejected, leaving vocalist (and Clint Eastwood wannabe) Darrell Whitehouse, guitarist Mike Hoppett, bassist Alan Rees and drummer Keith Allen, the latter having previously been involved with local modsters the CIRCLES, veterans of a single or two on the diverse Graduate label. SPLIT BEAVER were fortunate enough to receive early exposure in the 'Armed And Ready' section of the very first issue of 'Kerrang', by which time they had already signed to the Heavy Metal label, and their first vinyl forays came with a double A-sided single featuring "Savage" and "Hounds Of Hell", closely followed by an appearance on the »Heavy Metal Heroes« compilation with "Running Wild". The group were revealed to be a fairly enthusiastic, but ultimately unremarkable, proposition owing a considerable debt to the boogie/rock'n'roll foundations laid by local heroes SPEED LIMIT and the STARFIGHTERS, as well as the bludgeoning assault of MOTÖRHEAD and TANK. It was, however, clearly a sufficiently capable start that the lads procured a full album deal within a matter of months, and recording sessions for their debut long-player began in the new year, by which time the outfit featured a new drummer in the form of Mick Dunn, whose past was entirely unbesmirched by dubious musical associations.

SPLIT BEAVER's album, entitled »When Hell Won't Have You«, didn't exactly win the hearts of too many music journalists at the time (although various numbers were regularly featured in the Heavy Metal Charts of the period), being vilified in the likes of 'Kerrang' for its musical mediocrity. Actually, it's not quite as bad as it was originally painted by the press, although the reviewers were probably more influenced by the outfit's unseemly moniker, tracks with such utterly puerile titles as "Gimme Head" and some decidedly SPINAL TAP-worthy artwork (drawn by a woman, you'll be intrigued to discover). Overall, though, the mixture of heavy boogie, blues, full-on rock and the occasional sedate effort didn't constitute a ground-breaking or memorable release by any stretch of the imagination. Unsurprisingly, a second set was never commissioned, although this apparent failure didn't result in the SPLIT BEAVER name being laid to rest indefinitely. In fact, a version of the group continued to gig sporadically around the Midlands for the remainder of the decade (and possibly beyond), taking in small club appearances with other persevering scenesters such as the HANDSOME BEASTS and the STARFIGHTERS in the late 80's. The lads even got as far as issuing a brand-new demo tape in 1988, so perhaps SPLIT BEAVER were considering the possibility of a comeback and subsequently had second thoughts. Since then, however, there have been very few sightings of this elusive beast.

LP's
»When Hell Won't Have You« Heavy Metal 1982
[Initial quantities with textured cover]

7" Singles
»Savage« Heavy Metal 1981
[Relatively few in picture covers, some in company sleeves, most in plain sleeves, issued with either silver or green labels]

Exclusive Compilation Appearances
"Running Wild" on »Heavy Metal Heroes« LP Heavy Metal 1981 *[Issued in two different sleeves]* + »Heavy Metal Heroes Vol.I&II« CD British Steel 1996

Compilation Appearances
"Hounds Of Hell" on »N.W.O.B.H.M.« LP/CD Heavy Metal 1991 + »Heavy Metal Records Singles Collection Vol.1« CD British Steel 1996
"Savage" on »Heavy Metal Records Singles Collection Vol.1« CD British Steel 1996

SPLITCROW

Rob Davidson (v, g)
John Dickinson (g)
Barry Winlow (b)
Nigel Stawart (d)

Although the curiously-named SPLITCROW (yet another of Terry Gavaghan's hopelessly obscure discoveries from the North East) attempted to pass themselves off as something of a bar-room boogie outfit to rival the likes of ZZ TOP, the reality of the situation was that they could actually be a pretty listenable, hard-rocking, bluesy foursome when they felt like it. In fact, their one and only album, the largely-overlooked »Rockstorm« effort from 1984, showed their preferred style to lie closer to the raunchy rock of TERRAPLANE, ANGEL STREET or HOLLAND than to anything more closely affiliated to the world of boogie. True, there are a couple of riffs which could quite easily breach several copyright laws (I suspect that ZZ TOP's lawyers failed to hear the long-player, though), and there's a rather annoying tendency (especially on side two) to experiment with some slide guitar, acoustic interludes, piano etc., but these episodes (the ill-judged "Little Darlin", in particular, is truly atrocious) are, mercifully, few and far between.

There are, admittedly, certainly a few moments that bring forth some facile comparisons with the likes of SPIDER, SHADER, ROKKA and so on, but the most enjoyable material ("Back Door Blues", "Nobody's Gonna Stand In My Way" and "In The Heat Of The Night") sees SPLITCROW admirably holding their own amongst the most accomplished of BAD COMPANY copyists (and let's face it, that was the whole *raison d'être* of certain outfits). You can be assured that this isn't an album for the NWOBHM purist, but you certainly won't be getting *'genuine Southern Boogie'* (seek out the seldom-seen STREET LEGAL single for a closer impersonation) for your money, no matter what the sleeve insists! Nevertheless, the boogie-loving Xavier Russell wrote a gushing review of both the album (comparing it to the likes of MOLLY HATCHET and FOGHAT, so maybe I'm missing something here) and one of the band's local gigs in 'Kerrang' a year or so later, although it appears to have failed to save the dwindling outfit (who were, admittedly, quite a popular attraction in their locality) from going down the tubes within a predictably short space of time.

LP's
»**Rockstorm**« Guardian 1984

SQUASHED PYRANNAH

Kev Carroll (v)
Steve Wadley (g)
Martin Treasure (g)
John Box (b)
Dave Parfitt (d)

Although the NWOBHM explosion eventually affected the British Isles in its entirety, it looks as though the local talent was a bit thin on the ground in certain parts of the country, with the South West of England being particularly severely affected, for some inexplicable reason. It would appear that, while good old heavy metal was clearly just as popular in this region as anywhere else, comparatively few outfits from counties such as Cornwall, Devon, Dorset, Wiltshire and Shropshire seem to have made it to the vinyl stage, which is a bit odd. Mind you, these areas don't seem to have yielded all that many bands full stop, so I guess metal wasn't likely to be any different. In any case, another of those with a fairly minimal NWOBHM presence appears to have been Somerset (my own pet theory implicates the region's unfeasibly strong

cider, repeated imbibition of which probably rendered the local inhabitants unable to stand up properly, let alone play a musical instrument), although the utterly obscure and bizarrely-named SQUASHED PYRANNAH have finally come to the rescue, saving Somerset from an eternity of disgraceful NWOBHM anonymity.

Admittedly, nothing particularly illuminating is known about this long-forgotten bunch of hopefuls, save for the fact that they recorded a seldom-seen single entitled »Heartstop« (b/w "Dr Jekyll") for a local concern (the little-known Rapp Records, who weren't exactly prolific in terms of vinyl releases) in 1982, issued in a cartoon-style sleeve showing a fearsome yokel, er, squashing some unfortunate piranhas, for no apparent reason. See what I mean about the evils of alcohol? The quintet's music itself was in a fairly basic, hard-rocking, 70's-tinged style reminiscent of NWOBHM-era contemporaries such as SLENDER THREAD and DAWN TRADER, but it's all perfectly listenable nonetheless. Their 7" (which seems to have been a one-off) is a comparatively recent discovery, with a minimal number of examples having come out of the woodwork thus far, but I can't imagine it will ever become regarded as one of the more sought-after artefacts of the period. Furthermore, there isn't exactly an abundance of useful information on the sleeve or label, so the story leading up to the release of this vinyl oddity will have to remain a bit of a mystery for the time being. Any additional revelations would be greatly appreciated...

7" Singles
»**Heartstop**« Rapp Records 1982

STAGEFRIGHT

Terry Clarke
Randall
Taylor

Another relatively obscure band first brought to prominence by the laudable (but slightly naughty) Japanese series of bootleg compilation CD's, STAGEFRIGHT issued a fantastic three track EP in the early months of 1985 which has now become one of the most highly sought-after collectables of the era. Featuring, without question, one of the most talented singers of the entire NWOBHM genre, the outfit offer a very melodic, but satisfyingly heavy, style of metal in the vein of BABY TUCKOO, MENDES PREY or IONA, with strategically-placed keyboards serving only to enhance the overall sound. "Stranger In The Night" is undoubtedly the pick of the bunch, an instantly-memorable classic which, musically, more than compensates for the ultra-clichéd (*'there's danger in the darkness, there's danger in the air'*) lyrical nonsense. On the other hand, "Heartless" and "Rock City" (the latter possibly inspired by a certain popular Midlands music venue?) are well-crafted rockers (with a distinct SAPPHIRE influence) which again suffer from *'crap lyric syndrome'* but which are elevated by the excellent musicianship and vocal performance. Very few copies of this sleeveless EP have ever surfaced, and even the group's area of origin in uncertain (although, given that the title track was featured in a 'Local Chart' compiled for 'Kerrang' by a Midlands venue, I'd suggest that Nottinghamshire or Derbyshire would be the best bet), as STAGEFRIGHT was a surprisingly popular choice of name for heavy acts in the 80's. Further information on this bunch would be particularly welcome!

7" EP's
»**Stranger In The Night**« S.T.N. Records 1985

Compilation Appearances
"**Stranger In The Night**" on »NWOBHM Vol.6« Bootleg CD 1992

STAMPEDE (I)

Reuben Archer (v)
Laurence Archer (g)
Colin Bond (b)
Alan Nelson (k)
Frank Noon (d)

The London-based outfit known as STAMPEDE (not to be confused with German namesakes) came into existence towards the end of 1981, when Reuben and Laurence Archer (both formerly with the unsuccessful LAUTREC, the elder of the pair also having had a brief stint in LIONHEART) severed their ties with WILD HORSES (see separate entry) in order to form a brand-new act of their own. Enlisting one of their associates from WILD HORSES (the much-travelled Frank Noon) and another ex-LAUTREC member (Alan Nelson), the original line-up was duly completed by the unknown quantity Colin Bond on bass guitar. Although this venture was initially regarded as something of a revived LAUTREC, however, the musicians involved rapidly made it clear that this was an all-new outfit with a distinct identity of its own. STAMPEDE started off inconspicuously enough, with a couple of minor club appearances, but their energetic brand of rock soon had tongues wagging all over the capital, so it looked as though they had hit the nail squarely on the head from the outset. The lads demoed some original material in the early months of 1982, after which they duly came to the attention of Tommy Vance at the BBC, who was suitably motivated to offer STAMPEDE a 'Friday Rock Show' session before they had even accepted a record deal. Broadcast on the 28th of May 1982, the session allowed listeners to hear four of the outfit's own compositions, namely "Photographs", "Moving On", "The Other Side" and "Shadows Of The Night", and it was apparent that STAMPEDE, featuring a hard-rocking attitude in the UFO, MENDES PREY or STAGEFRIGHT vein, were a considerably more polished and accessible act than the rough'n'ready LAUTREC had ever been.

Further exposure rapidly came their way in the form of a Capital Radio session, an appearance on the BBC's 'In Concert' programme (alongside GIRLSCHOOL) and a slot at the Mildenhall Rock Festival (the restless Frank Noon was replaced by Eddie Parsons along the way, but this failed to hinder their progress in the slightest), and it wasn't long before Polydor Records stepped in with a deal which met with

581

the band's acceptance. A single was prepared with little hesitation, although the initial (promotional) pressings of the 7" used "Photographs" as the A-side and "Days Of Wine And Roses" as the flipside, and the order was reversed by the time the commercial version appeared. There was also a 12" issue, which additionally featured "Moving On" (a marginally longer recording of which had already been included on the »Steel Crazy« compilation, alongside LAUTREC's "Mean Gasoline") and "Missing You", which would prove to be the only time the latter pair would be made available as studio versions. The single was timed to coincide with the group's appearance at the Reading Festival, where they did a splendid job of warming up the crowd for the likes of PRAYING MANTIS, DIAMOND HEAD and BUDGIE. Everything seemed to be going STAMPEDE's way, and there was little doubt that a full album would soon follow as a matter of routine.

Strangely, however, Polydor elected to issue a live debut album, culling tracks from the recordings made at the Reading and Mildenhall Festival appearances. It seemed a peculiar decision for an affluent label to make (they had done the same with A II Z, remember), and this suggested to many observers that they were out to save money at every opportunity, although it's entirely possible that they may have had more obscure or shrewd reasons for promoting live albums. The long-player eventually appeared as »The Official Bootleg« (the original title was the baffling »Way Up In The Air«), with correspondingly minimalist packaging and presentation. In terms of sound quality, it was acceptable enough, although I'm sure the majority of fans would rather have heard what the group were capable of producing in the studio environment. The featured material was mostly familiar to those who had already heard STAMPEDE's radio sessions and their earlier vinyl, although there were a couple of more recent efforts such as "The Runner" and "Hurricane Town" to liven things up slightly. Even so, it was still a rather uninspiring release, and it didn't exactly shatter any sales records.

Within a very short space of time, however, Polydor allowed the lads to enter the studio in order to lay down a proper album, the recording sessions for which took place in the early months of 1983, around the time that STAMPEDE were touring the UK with GARY MOORE. By this stage, however, Alan Nelson had jumped ship (he later resurfaced in STRATUS, JAGGED EDGE and MAMA'S BOYS), and the outfit were forced to draft in MAGNUM's Mark Stanway to contribute the necessary keyboard sections. Sadly, »Hurricane Town« proved to be a rather overproduced, commercialised affair, presumably designed to appeal to the DEF LEPPARD market rather than the original NWOBHM community, but it ultimately failed to convince many observers that STAMPEDE were heading in the right direction. There was little evidence of their live energy or enthusiasm, even on the revamped versions of "The Runner" and "Hurricane Town", and much of the 'newer' material (strangely, "Girl" was given a Street Tunes publishing credit, suggesting that it may actually have dated back to the formative LAUTREC days) seemed pretty disposable. It was hardly an impressive or top-selling effort, and the group's label began to lose interest in their activities almost immediately.

The dejected outfit persevered for a while, but it was all over by 1984, when Laurence Archer and Mark Stanway defected to Phil Lynott's ill-fated GRAND SLAM project, while bassist Colin Bond (aka James C. Bond) joined forces with TORMÉ, initially as a guest, but later as a full member. Stanway eventually made his way back to good old MAGNUM (via ROBIN GEORGE), while Archer Jr. has dabbled in the occasional piece of production work (WRAITH, for instance) as well as helping out in numerous heavy acts ever since (some of the more notable examples including RHODE ISLAND RED, UFO and BRIAN SPENCE), as well as recording a critically-acclaimed solo album (primarily for the Japanese market), which was released under the functional title of »L.A.« and is now extremely difficult to locate. Archer Sr., meanwhile, is still also heavily involved in the music business, albeit in more of a behind-the-scenes capacity, and is currently responsible for some extremely worthy, music-related websites.

LP's
»**The Official Bootleg**« Polydor 1982
»**Hurricane Town**« Polydor 1983

12" EP's
»**Days Of Wine And Roses**« Polydor 1982
["Days Of Wine And Roses", "Moving On" and "Missing You" all different to album versions, "Photographs" non-LP]

7" Singles
»**Days Of Wine And Roses**« Polydor 1982
[A-side different to album version, B-side "Photographs" non-LP]
»**The Other Side**« Polydor 1983
[A-side different to album version]

Promotional Releases

»**Photographs**« Polydor 1982
[7" single, a few copies only, no sleeve issued, B-side "Days Of Wine And Roses", tracks later reversed and issued commercially in picture sleeve]

CD's
»**The Official Bootleg**« Bootleg 199?
[Unofficial release with four extra tracks]

Compilation Appearances
"**Moving On**" on »Steel Crazy« LP Abstract Records 1982
[Different to album version, very slightly different to 12" version]
"**The Runner**" **(live)** on »A Little Bit Of Light Relief« LP Polydor 1982
"**There And Back**" **(live)** on »Reading Rock Vol.1« Do-LP Mean Records 1982

STAMPEDE (II)

Norman Evans (v, g)
Brian Evans (v, d)
Chris Barnes (g)
Dave Anderson (b)

Oddly enough, it transpires that there was another STAMPEDE on the go in the NWOBHM era, and this little-known bunch actually got to the vinyl stage a couple of years before their familiar counterparts, although their one-off 7" is so staggeringly rare that I guess few collectors are aware of its existence. You'll gather that very little is currently known about the quartet's history, although this appears to have been another small-time, family affair centred around some youthful characters (*cf.* the equally-ramshackle MITHRANDIR), as evidenced by the heartwarming *'special thanks to mum and dad'* on the sleeve. Indeed, it seems likely that this was a minuscule pressing organised for friends and relatives as opposed to a record which showcased a genuine group with their sights on the future, and the credits suggest that the musicians had more or less been assembled specifically for this particular release. Anyway, the EP (issued way back in 1980) opens with "Notch On Your Gun", a number which is unlikely to win any points for musicianship or originality, being much in the manner of such glorified pub rock ensembles as GROUND ATTACK, PRESENCE or even the MEAN STREET DEALERS. Still, it drags on far too long, and, having pretty much run out of steam after only a couple of minutes, the participants attempt (and fail) to divert attention from their lack of songwriting experience by utilising a yawn-inducing instrumental mid-section.

Over on side two, meanwhile, "On My Way" is a twangy, semi-acoustic affair which, to be perfectly frank, leaves very little in the way of an impression (either favourable or unfavourable), although things pick up slightly on closing number "The Simple Life", more of a boogie/bluesy effort with occasional glimpses of DESPERATE OATES or PANZA DIVISION (undeniably similar to the latter's "The Day Delta 4 Played Mars"), all of which saves the record from being completely disposable. I suppose it wasn't as atrocious as certain other efforts from the same era, although it looks as though these lads probably needed another couple of years of rehearsals to hone their writing skills. The record was issued in a hand-drawn picture sleeve (typically awful artwork) featuring some characters from the Wild West, and was presumably pressed in microscopic quantities at the time, so I wouldn't hold out many hopes of finding a copy. It was, incidentally, recorded at Foel Studios (also frequented by the likes of REQUIEM), so I guess STAMPEDE were from the same neck of the woods, namely the West Midlands. Predictably, though, the lads seem to have gone to ground after just one EP, so their involvement with the music business may have ended within a matter of months, and perhaps they never even got to the stage of playing any gigs. No doubt mum and dad were really proud, though.

7" EP's
»**Notch On Your Gun**« Punchbowl Music 1980

STARFIGHTERS

Steve Burton (v)
Stevie Young (g)
Pat Hambly (g)
Doug Dennis (b)
Spencer Scrannage (d)

It's fair to say that Birmingham's biker-friendly rock'n'roll legends known as the STARFIGHTERS (affectionately referred to as the *'fightstarters'* for fairly obvious reasons) became something of an overnight sensation after their original formation in the latter part of 1979, although a fair bit of their appeal seemed to hinge on the fact that guitarist Stevie Young was actually a cousin of AC/DC's Malcolm and Angus. Given that the STARFIGHTERS (who also featured erstwhile SPEED LIMIT bassist Doug Dennis and well-travelled vocalist Steve Burton, who, strange as it may seem, had fronted such disparate acts as the knockabout SUBURBAN STUDS and the more grandiose CRYER during the previous couple of years) primarily operated in a broadly similar area to the likes of AC/DC or ROSE TATTOO (bands who were enjoying truly phenomenal levels of success in the UK at the time), the comparisons would be understandably hard to shake off in years to come. Naturally, there were always a few sceptics who would gleefully deride the quintet as guilty of shamelessly hanging onto the coat-tails of AC/DC, accusations which reached a peak when the act (who were yet to be picked up by a major label) were awarded a lucrative support slot with the Aussies themselves in the autumn of 1980. Mind you, it's not as if they were no-hopers, and the lads had already released a single on the small local Motor City Rhythm concern (see also LÉARGO, for example), which showcased "I'm Falling" and the lengthy "Heaven And Hell", two well-performed numbers with sufficient personality of their own to kick the ubiquitous AC/DC comparisons firmly into touch.

In terms of NWOBHM similarities, the likes of MORE and SPLIT BEAVER would probably be their nearest musical neighbours, both being fairly analogous in terms of raunchy metal with a distinct biker-rock influence. It came as no particular surprise when the STARFIGHTERS began attracting a fair bit of major label interest during 1981, although they found the whole process of getting a deal to be a frustratingly protracted and contrived process, and they eventually went with the first company who actually put a firm offer on the table. That label was Jive, who weren't known for very much apart from representing a few minor pop acts, so the lads freely acknowledged that they were taking something of a calculated risk. Their first product for their new sponsors was a full LP (by this stage, Steve Bailey, formerly with HOLLY AND THE ITALIANS, had replaced original drummer Spencer Scrannage, who later resurfaced in the THE ALLIANCE), an eponymous effort whose generous recording budget had allowed the outfit to shine rather more brightly than they had done on their under-produced debut. Nevertheless, there were perilously few tracks ("Help Me" and "Silver Lady" weren't too bad) that stood out as particularly memorable or individualistic, even though the overall standard was reasonably high. It proved to be quite a popular release at the time, however, although their label was apparently less-than-overjoyed with the sales figures.

Steve Burton later reflected on the fact that Jive may have had ulterior motives for signing the outfit: 'It was the golden goose being thrown before us, but now we wish we'd stuck to our guns. We wonder at this point if they were really into us as a band at all or if they were more keen on jumping on the NWOBHM thing by signing a token heavy rock band.' (Ref: Kerrang No.36, February 1983). Certainly, it would appear that their label had started out with good intentions, promoting the STARFIGHTERS with some wide-

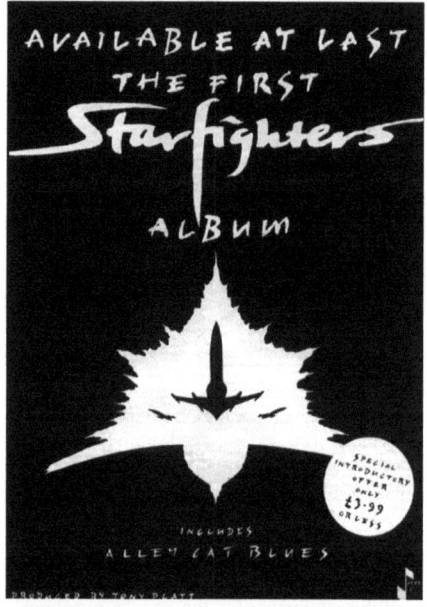

spread advertising and releasing two singles (»Alley Cat Blues« and »Power Crazy«, each in both 7" and 12" forms, with a smattering of non-LP cuts as B-sides) to further their cause, but rapidly withdrew their financial backing when it became apparent that the group weren't going to be selling millions of records after all. Nevertheless, the ensemble were more than capable of handling things themselves, and started off by recording a well-received session for the 'Friday Rock Show' (broadcast on the 4th of September 1981), where the quintet powered their way through energetic versions of "Power Crazy", "Alley Cat Blues", "Killing Time" and "Devil's Driving", all taken from their debut long-player. The lads then set their sights on promoting themselves through productive live work, and were soon touring the UK with MSG, after which their name was recognised slightly more widely than before. In the early months of 1982, they managed to grab a support slot with OZZY OSBOURNE, which saw them travelling to the States for some well-attended shows at capacious arenas, and they also grasped the opportunity to undertake a few headlining appearances of their own at smaller venues. Returning to the UK, the lads seemed to be slightly happier with their circumstances, and were clearly relieved when Jive finally agreed to allow the STARFIGHTERS to lay down a second album.

The follow-up long-player was recorded in due course, only for their label to have second thoughts about releasing it after all. After considerable pressure from the group, it finally made it into the shops on both sides of the Atlantic, although it had been a bit of a struggle, as Stevie Young admitted: *'We had to fight just to get this album released, cos Jive couldn't decide whether to put it out or not. But we like the songs more than the first album, cos they're fresher. The tracks for our debut LP were over a year old when we recorded them and the spark was a little gone. We've progressed a lot with this new one. It shows we're more than just a riff band.'* (Ref: *ibid.*) The record (»In-flight Movie«) finally saw the light of day at the end of 1982, and showed the lads to be flirting with more lightweight material (worryingly reminiscent of ROD STEWART at times), much of which was considerably closer to traditional hard-rocking territory than had been apparent on their first clutch of releases. It was actually quite a listenable effort, though, and tracks such as "Who Cares" and "Working Girl" would probably have gone down reasonably well in the States, particularly among fans of acts such as the CARS. In terms of its appeal to the British market, however, it was probably a backwards step for the STARFIGHTERS. They subsequently parted company with Jive (who had refused to promote the album at all or issue any accompanying singles this time) in 1983, but affirmed their intentions of persevering and doing their own thing regardless of the diminishing amount of media recognition which was coming their way.

They were ultimately fighting a losing battle, though, and were to call it a day in 1984, following one last batch of gigs to try to get things going again. Strangely, however, the duo of Steve Burton and Stevie Young resurrected the STARFIGHTERS name in 1987 (after doing precisely zilch in the intervening years), amid strong rumours that the ensemble fully intended to issue another album of freshly-penned material. Joining the vocalist and guitarist in the revived outfit were axeman Rik Sandford (who, as he was keen to point out, was not to be confused with his near-namesake in LEGS DIAMOND), bassist Steve Redvers and semi-permanent drummer Jamie Hawkins, who was still very much involved with the fortunes of his other outfit, melodic rockers SURFACE. The new STARFIGHTERS gradually began playing the odd local gig (with various minor rock hopefuls and the persevering SPLIT BEAVER, for example) to gauge public reaction, which still seemed to be overwhelmingly favourable. Even so, by 1988, their original plan to release a full-length comeback album had now metamorphosed into a rather more modest four track EP. Sadly, even that failed to materialise in the long term, and, after a few more gigs in the area (including the odd appearance at some well-attended rock/metal all-dayers), things began to go wrong yet again.

Stevie Young was sequestered by none other than AC/DC to assist on the touring front late in the year, and, although the STARFIGHTERS attempted to plough on as a four-piece until he returned, further pressure was placed upon the group when Rik Sandford was recruited by UFO for the same reason. After that, the remaining members also decided that they should be able to help out in other acts, with Steve Redvers proceeding to work with TOTALLY SUSPECT before holding an incredibly brief tenure in BLACK SABBATH. Jamie Hawkins, on the other hand, along with his commitments related to SURFACE, also became involved with UFO's studio sessions in due course, and, with all these side-projects taking up so much time, things never really got going for the STARFIGHTERS again. The project officially disbanded in 1989, with Steve Burton (who very nearly became involved with the FOUR HORSEMEN at one point) going on to enjoy stints with outfits such as the bluesy E NUMBERS in the next couple of years, while Steve Redvers eventually found a slightly more permanent position in THE GRIP. Redvers also reunited with Stevie Young in the early 90's in a group known as LITTLE BIG HORN, who contrived to get a 'Friday Rock Show' session under their belts at an early stage, but who never really managed to hit the big time. If you were to compose a fitting obituary for the STARFIGHTERS, you would almost certainly have to say that they were one of those bands who, like local pioneers SPEED LIMIT, were probably best appreciated in the live environment, and whose vinyl offerings repeatedly failed to capture them at their most powerful and charismatic.

LP's
»Starfighters« Jive 1981
»In-flight Movie« Jive 1982

12" EP's
»Alley Cat Blues« Jive 1981
["Rock 'Em Dead" non-LP]
»Power Crazy« Jive 1981
[Both "Get Out While You Can" and "I Want You" non-LP]

7" Singles
»I'm Falling« Motor City Rhythm 1980
[Both tracks non-LP]
»Alley Cat Blues« Jive 1981
[UK issue, B-side "Don't Touch me"]
»Alley Cat Blues« Teldec 1981
[German issue, B-side "Power Crazy", slightly different sleeve]
»Power Crazy« Jive 1981
[B-side "I Want You" non-LP]

Compilation Appearances
"Alley Cat Blues" on »Steel Crazy« LP Abstract Records 1982

STATETROOPER

Gary Barden (v)
Steve Johnson (g)
Paul 'Fasker' Johnson (b)
Bruce Bisland (d)

The unashamedly lightweight proposition known as STATETROOPER (who based themselves in the nation's capital) initially came into existence towards the end of 1984, after the demise of Michael Schenker's much-loved MSG allowed ambitious vocalist Gary Barden to establish his own project at long last. At first, the frontman was assisted in his activities by the former HERITAGE duo of Steve (g) and Fasker (b), the musical Johnson brothers, plus WILDFIRE (the Mausoleum recording artists) drummer Bruce Bisland, the latter acting as a locum for the time being. Some formative demo compositions were immortalised on tape within a matter of months, and the makeshift ensemble's original material was, even at that stage, soon causing a bit of a stir among some of the influential labels of the day. In due course, a slightly more stable line-up gradually emerged from the chaos, this all-new incarnation of STATETROOPER having been established *via* the recruitment of keyboard player Steve Glover and drummer Eddie Stratton (a relatively unknown pair of musicians), and things appeared to be going swimmingly for a short time.

Even so, things were to fall apart pretty rapidly, resulting in the sudden departure of the Johnsons and Eddie Stratton (the three of them would ultimately resurface in the ill-fated U.S.I. venture, although Fasker additionally enjoyed a fleeting stint with SAXON), leaving the nucleus of Barden and Glover to start afresh in the summer of 1985 with an entirely different set of accomplices. As luck would have it, however, the aforementioned WILDFIRE unit had disintegrated shortly beforehand, leaving the former members free to pursue new options. In the event, Gary Barden proceeded to recruit no fewer than four of the musicians in question (Martin Bushell, Jeff Summers, Jeff Brown and good old Bruce Bisland), a move which determined that many people (being unfamiliar with the band's early history) would consider STATETROOPER to be nothing more than WILDFIRE Mk.II as opposed to a genuine Barden project. It took the revised version of the group a relatively short time to re-establish themselves on the rock scene (hardly surprising, given that four of the musicians had been happily collaborating for the best part of three years in their previous outfit), and they soon set about the task of writing a selection of original material.

From day one, however, the new-look STATETROOPER had *'ill-advised post-NWOBHM piffle'* written all over it, and it wasn't long before the rock community was afforded the chance to make up their own minds, as the band were given a one-off opportunity to record a humble slice of vinyl for Neat (surprising, that, considering the fact that the majors had allegedly been *'falling over themselves'* to sign the outfit in the first instance) in due course. Eschewing the label's own Impulse Studios facility, the outfit simply ensconced themselves in a nearby establishment a short time later, whereupon "She Got The Look", "Set Fire To The Night" and "Veni, Vidi, Vinci" (the best of the three) were captured for posterity. With "She Got The Look" being selected as the main focus of attention, STATETROOPER's debut single was duly issued in both 12" and 7" formats, the latter omitting "Set Fire To The Night". As expected, it transpired that the ensemble were one of those typical mid-80's *'supergroups'* who delivered a highly accessible (verging on pop) style of melodic rock, very much along the lines of other post-

NWOBHM propositions such as LIONHEART, STRATUS or BLUE BLUD. The material was, admittedly, quite proficiently written and performed, as you would expect from musicians of this stature, although the sheer politeness of the numbers took many by surprise.

By early 1986, the stabilised group had writ-

ten an album's worth of material, played various high-profile gigs at venues such as the Marquee in London (as well as the odd support slot with the likes of BLUE ÖYSTER CULT), and recorded a session for the 'Friday Rock Show'. Broadcast on the 14th of February 1986, the session saw the lads running through versions of "Set Fire To The Night", "Too Late", "She Got The Look" and the never-released "Faster Than Light". It exposed the band to a national audience, and this would evidently have been the ideal time to release their first album, something which the musicians had envisaged from an early stage. In the event, however, it proved to be a further year before their eponymous debut long-player finally materialised (for reasons which are not particularly obvious), this time on the FM label. It's hard to comprehend why it took quite so long to generate a usable set of compositions (guitarist Martin Bushell had, in fact, already left by the time it eventually dawdled its way into the shops), given that they recycled all three of their earlier Neat recordings, threw in a couple of live tracks (one of them being a rather cheeky cover of MSG's "Armed And Ready") and included a grand total of just four 'new' studio efforts.

A later interview with Jeff Brown failed to explain either the timing or content of the album, with certain statements being particularly bewildering: 'Our management caught up with us while we were out in Europe and matter-of-factly informed us that we now had a record deal and that our debut album would be released next week. What album? We weren't prepared for this at all, but the record appeared anyway. I think the two live tracks were the best numbers, even Gary Barden himself considered that version of "Armed And Ready" to be better than the Schenker original!' (Ref: Interview, Matthias Mader, March 1996). It certainly looks as though the recordings had been ready for some time, and that the long-player was rapidly bundled together at comparatively short notice, which is a bit odd. Whatever the reason for the delay (perhaps it was nothing more sinister than waiting for a suitable deal to materialise, given that Neat had expressed no interest in sponsoring a full-length release), the initial buzz about the band had died down considerably, with many adhering to the belief that STATETROOPER had actually ceased to exist. Sales of the record were disappointingly poor, and the contents hardly represented the most inspiring selection of compositions ever committed to vinyl, with only "Shape Of Things To Come" standing out as a reasonably strong effort.

It's a widely-held misconception that STATETROOPER actually issued their sole album posthumously, but this wasn't the case at all. In fact, they were still very much a going concern (on paper, at least) throughout 1987, although their once-stable line-up was to alter quite a bit over the ensuing months. With the group still actively seeking a replacement for the departed Martin Bushell, they were extremely fortunate to attract such an experienced guitarist as Brian Robertson (previously employed by such luminaries as THIN LIZZY, WILD HORSES and MOTÖRHEAD) to the project at relatively short notice. His arrival only helped to stabilise the dwindling outfit in the short term, though, and their chronic personnel afflictions were soon mounting up once again. Steve Glover was the next to go (towards the end of the year), closely followed by recent addition Brian Robertson (who had never really settled into his new role with any great level of enthusiasm, and who eventually hooked up with the HELLFIRE CLUB), after which STATETROOPER appear to have been unable to locate permanent replacements at any stage. Nevertheless, the remaining members attempted to start composing new material on their own, but the whole thing was to collapse irretrievably in the spring of 1988.

The long-anticipated fragmentation of STATETROOPER was to lead to the formation of various offshoots and side-projects, the first of these being the short-lived and little-remembered HEAD 2 HEAD, an unsuccessful proposition which roped together Summers, Bisland and

Glover. Brown and Bisland subsequently teamed up with the latter's erstwhile colleague in WEAPON, vocalist Danny Hynes, in the occasional outfit PADDY GOES TO HOLYHEAD, an act (also featuring a couple of one-time members of THE SWEET) who still perform to this very day. Bisland has additionally worked with PRAYING MANTIS in recent years, while he and Jeff Brown also guested in the ranks of THE SWEET themselves (in one of their later incarnations) at some of their shows in the 90's. Gary Barden, on the other hand, after attempting to instigate a solo career at the turn of the decade (enlisting members of BABY TUCKOO as a backing ensemble), as well as enjoying a brief stint with the aforementioned PRAYING MANTIS, was also one of many musicians to have been roped in to contribute to those fairly atrocious ALL STARS/TRUE BRITS projects, which I'm sure everyone would rather forget about. He's now attempting to launch yet another group of his own, apparently, so let's wish him all the best with these musical endeavours.

LP's
»Statetrooper« FM Records 1987

12" EP's
»She Got The Look« Neat 1985

7" Singles
»She Got The Look« Neat 1985

CD's
»Statetrooper« FM Records 1987

Compilation Appearances
"She Got The Look" on »Powertrax« Cassette Neat 1986 + »Heavy Metal Collection 3« CD X-Tra Collection 1993
"Stand Me Up" on »Coast To Coast« LP/CD FM Records 1987

STATIC

Noel Jones (v, g, k)
Tony Dugdale (g)
Peter Buckler (b)
Neil Dowling (d)

Surrey's popular STATIC were originally conceived as far back as 1978, their formation being masterminded by a certain Peter Buckler (brother of Rick Buckler, famous sticksman from THE JAM), the outfit's ever-dependable bassist.

With the act originally employing the services of a vocalist named Gary Frost, it soon became apparent that the aforementioned frontman's aspirations involved pushing the outfit in a semi-AOR direction, creating a style reminiscent of TOTO or FOREIGNER. This suggestion met with serious disapprobation from the other members, however, and the hapless singer was soon on his way, with Noel Jones subsequently stepping in to fill the vacancy. The line-up was, in the first instance, completed by former ACE HIGH guita-

rist Tony Dugdale and drummer Neil Dowling, and this version of the band recorded the first STATIC demo (featuring "Someone Like You", "Too Long Free" and "Lady Money") in December 1979. The group initially resembled a pretty typical, late 70's rock proposition with the standard twin influences of UFO and THIN LIZZY, although they gradually began taking on more of an individualistic personality. A couple of further recording sessions took place the following year, the lads trying out newer material (in more of a CHINATOWN vein than anything else) such as "Gotta Lose Ya", "Last Train", "Believe In Me" and "Silent Angels", although these were to mark the final involvement of Tony Dugdale (who would subsequently play a major role in the quirky FOUR WHEEL DRIVE project), the latter being replaced by Paddy Chambers (formerly with a minor local concern called TANK, who, confusingly, had absolutely no connection with Algy Ward's mob) in the spring of 1980.

With their new, relatively stable line-up, the group played gig after gig in their locality, even venturing up to the capital itself on occasion. Support slots soon began coming their way, notably with TRUST (following on from their trek around Britain with IRON MAIDEN), WEAPON and MARILLION. In the early months of 1981, however, the rhythm section (including founder member Peter Buckler) flew the coop (Neil Dowling initially found his way into the ranks of L.A. HOOKER, although he would later become

Tony Dugdale's business partner in the FOUR WHEEL DRIVE venture), and the remaining duo of Jones and Chambers (who rapidly evolved into STATIC's main songwriting force) were compelled to draft in new boys Kieran McCleary (d) and Andy Rose (b) to make up the numbers once again. There were even a few suggestions that STATIC might be releasing their debut single on Heavy Metal Records before the year was out, but nothing seems to have come from their initial association with the company, which is a shame. Following on from yet more successful regional gigging on the appreciative pub/club circuit, some further demo recordings (the lads now operating in a rather more accessible style, having penned the likes of "Heavy Heart" and "Voice On The Line") and regular exposure on local radio, the group were featured in the 'Armed And Ready' section of 'Kerrang' in the summer of 1982. Although the lads had hoped to attract some level of serious record company interest by this point, they eventually came to terms with the fact that the only way they were likely to get to the vinyl stage was now to release a self-financed product themselves.

STATIC's debut single ended up being issued only a couple of months later, pairing "Voice On The Line" with "Stealin'", two listenable enough efforts in the general style of URCHIN or early SAMSON, not overly heavy (compared with some of the material they had demoed a year or two earlier, anyway) but still reasonably strong on the guitar front. The two-tracker, issued on the band's own Eeyo label (allegedly derived from, er, *'Extremely Excellent Yodelling Organisation'*) wasn't issued in a picture cover at any stage, although some sleeves were simply stamped with the STATIC logo to liven things up slightly. The record shifted a worthwhile number of units, and the lads duly promoted its release with yet more touring and some productive support slots with the likes of DUMPY'S RUSTY NUTS and the JACKIE LYNTON BAND, consolidating the ensemble's rapidly-developing position as well-received crowd-pleasers. Within a relatively short timescale, however, certain members of STATIC began to express dissatisfaction with their apparent lack of progress, all of which culminated in a fairly amicable split towards the end of that year. Undeterred, Noel Jones set about assembling some likely accomplices to assist in his inexorable quest for fame and fortune, and eventually (after soliciting applications through the pages of 'Kerrang') hooked up with Andy Simmons (g), Ross Bingham (g,k), Pete Blanchard (b) and Kev Baker (d), all of whom had actually been members of an unsuccessful local outfit called SPHINX. Blanchard stayed a very short while, though, before a more suitable replacement was found in the form of ex-SABRE bassist Geoff Gillespie.

It looked as though the popular STATIC name would soon be riding high once again (in fact, the catchy "Voice On The Line" even made an appearance in the 'Local Chart' section in 'Kerrang' early in 1983) once the lads got their act together and made a few trips to the recording studio. Sadly, however, it didn't work out for the revised version of the band (who played just one gig, alongside rising local hopefuls SEDUCER), and, inevitably, the outfit splintered for good shortly thereafter. Gillespie and the three ex-SPHINX musicians proceeded to form their own SNOWBLIND (see separate entry) offshoot soon afterwards, while Noel Jones took stock of the situation and eventually (after playing a part in the short-lived ICEMON venture) returned with the considerably more distinctive and successful WHITE LIGHTNING (see separate entry) operation. The STATIC single remains a fairly collectable piece (intriguingly, aficionados of the power pop genre have also picked up on it), although the fact that a considerable quantity of unsold copies have been released by the band members in recent years means that the typical asking price has failed to escalate to ridiculous levels in the interim.

7" Singles
»**Voice On The Line**« Eeyo Records 1982

Compilation Appearances
"**Voice On The Line**" on »N.W.O.B.H.M. Metal Rarities Vol.3« CD British Steel 1997
"**Stealin'**" on »N.W.O.B.H.M. Metal Rarities Vol.3« CD British Steel 1997

STEEL

Paul Tunnecliffe (v)
Dave Brookes (g)
Paul Roe (g)
Stefan Cartwright (b)
Simon Atkins (d)

One of the better outfits who ended up on Neat's never-ending roster of bands at the height of the NWOBHM explosion, the roots of Staffordshire's STEEL lay in the realms of traditional 70's rock, with vocalist Paul Tunnecliffe and drummer Simon Atkins having played, in days of yore, in a variety of long-forgotten groups with fellow scenesters such as Ian 'Truff' Threlfall of BASHFUL ALLEY. The very first incarnation of STEEL came into existence in around 1980, at which point the ensemble featured bassist John Fox (whose brother, Roger, was a member of local rivals BIG DAISY), although the latter was to be replaced by new lad Stefan Cartwright within a matter of months. The musicians swiftly built up a reasonable following throughout their area, playing to appreciative crowds on a regular basis, and were soon attracting the attention of various small record companies. With the enterprising Neat label casting their net far and wide in an attempt to catch up-and-coming metal acts, the emerging STEEL were ensnared and rewarded with the opportunity to record their debut release for the company.

Their »Rock Out« single (B-side "All Systems Go") escaped in 1981, much to the delight of rock fans throughout the nation, and the two-tracker rapidly became a remarkably good seller for their label. With the record representing an excellent attempt at dynamic NWOBHM, the tracks come across as a capable mixture of HOLLOW GROUND's energy and STAGEFRIGHT's melody, although it has to be pointed out that "Rock Out" does, in places, bear an undeniable similarity to "Detroit Rock City" by KISS! It was a more-than-adequate start, and it looked as though the outfit surely had an extremely healthy future ahead of them, but it turned out not to be the case after all, which is still quite difficult to comprehend. Sadly, the criminally-overlooked STEEL never went on to greater things (their major achievement being a support slot with the mighty IRON MAIDEN, something to which a suspiciously high proportion of minor NWOBHM acts lay claim), and, after their "All Systems Go" effort had been recycled (in its original form, unlike most of the other material featured) on Neat's »60 Minutes Plus« promotional cassette in 1982, the group started to drift apart.

Talented frontman Paul Tunnecliffe was the first to do a bunk, and the remaining members subsequently relocated to the rock'n'roll capital of the world (Wolverhampton) in an attempt to get things started again, apparently securing the services of future MAMA'S BOYS/GRAFFITI vocalist Rick Chase to plug the gap. Ultimately, though, things didn't work out for the new line-up and STEEL eventually disintegrated (after demoing fresh numbers such as "End Of The Line" and playing a final gig or two with MAGNUM) in around 1984. Simon Atkins (who was himself replaced by Ian West towards the

very end of STEEL's existence) went on to enjoy a short residency at the DARK STAR drumstool (appearing on their comeback album in 1987), having replaced the unrelated, but similarly-named, Steve Atkins, before moving on to pastures new. In later years, he undertook a great deal of session work as well as playing with a not-remotely-famous indie band called the WHISPERING MESSERSCHMITTS. Apart from that, though, there's little to suggest that the other ex-members of STEEL persevered in the music business.

7" Singles
»Rock Out« Neat 1981

Compilation Appearances
"All Systems Go" on »60 Minutes Plus« Cassette Neat 1982/CD Teichiku 1992 + »All Hell Let Loose« LP Neat 1983

STOLEN THUNDER

G. Scales

Appearing out of nowhere with their »Tough Touch Mama« single at the tail end of 1982, London's STOLEN THUNDER were hardly a band intent on pushing back the boundaries of metal, being pretty much stuck in a previous decade in terms of musical influences. Their one and only record, featuring "Tough Touch Mama" and the rather weak "Dirty Denise", was *'privileged'* enough to be reviewed in 'Kerrang' (the kiss of death for most British groups), where it was described as containing music which *'harks back to a bygone age'*. Nevertheless, the reviewer seemed to enjoy it, comparing them to the legendary CREAM, which is a fair enough observation, particularly with respect to the powerhouse drumming on the A-side. I'd say that there are certainly other influences from the late 60's or early 70's, including some of the heavier material attempted by the likes of HUMBLE PIE and THE WHO at times, with additional similarities to early NIGHTWING also becoming apparent on occasion. Overall, it's a musical area into which few of their NWOBHM contemporaries (with the odd exception such as ZORRO and CLIENTELLE, in their formative days) ventured, and it probably failed to strike the right chord with the rock community, to be honest. As a consequence of relatively poor sales at the time, therefore, the unassuming two-tracker (which seems not to have been issued with a picture sleeve at any stage) is a scarcely-sighted piece today.

By as early as the beginning of 1983, however, it became apparent that all was not well in the STOLEN THUNDER camp, with what looks like a fairly significant personnel defection having taken place remarkably shortly after the single's release, this being followed by an announcement in the pages of 'Kerrang' that the remaining nucleus were intending to recruit a new guitarist, drummer and keyboard player in order to get things going again. Given that the outfit were, by this stage, describing themselves as writing *'in-depth lyrics draped across a rock'n'roll landscape of driving music you can listen to'* (a hopelessly optimistic and pretentious statement bearing no resemblance whatsoever to their earlier knockabout material), it may be the case that attempts were now being made to steer the stricken ensemble in a somewhat more ambitious direction than before. However, it looks as though the revamped version of STOLEN THUNDER, if it ever got past the planning stage at all, didn't make much of an impression on the music scene in the long term, and the participants no doubt went back to their day jobs thereafter.

7" Singles
»Tough Touch Mama« Kenetic Trigger Records 1982

STORMCHILD

Chris Mitchell
Neil McCurley
Geoff Harwood
Ian Bridge
Joe Rodmell

Lancashire's little-known STORMCHILD (not the only band to use the identity by any means) contrived to press up one of the most scarcely-sighted artefacts of the NWOBHM era, with no more than a few hundred copies of their »Rockin' Steady« single (B-side "Last Night") being manufactured way back in 1982. The quintet's music was, in fact, rather more restrained than their JAGUAR-approved moniker might have suggested, and 'Kerrang' were keen to sing the group's praises when the 7" was submitted for review at the time. Musically, it was mid-paced, melodic NWOBHM with similarities to the likes of LYADRIVE, BLACK AXE and CRYS, the lads using strategically-placed keyboard sections to enhance the overall sound with considerable finesse. No doubt they shifted a fair number of copies at local gigs at the time, but most of these seem to have disappeared over the ensuing years (there's undoubtedly a *'Bermuda Triangle'* effect going on with some of these rarities), which is a great pity. Consequently, few lucky NWOBHM aficionados had heard either of these studio recordings until the A-side was conveniently included on the »NWOBHM Vol.6« bootleg a decade later, and only a tiny handful of modern-day collectors actually possess a copy, which originally came in a pretty basic, monochrome picture sleeve featuring the outfit's spiky logo and song titles.

Needless to say, the STORMCHILD single is going to be a big-money item whenever an example comes onto the market, so I guess most of us will never see a copy first hand. Boo. The group seem to have had quite a good reputation as a live act, and were often to be found gigging throughout the North West in the early 80's, appearing alongside similarly-minded rock hopefuls most of the time, but perfectly happy to share a stage with more noisy punk and new wave acts when necessity demanded. Still, STORMCHILD (not to be confused with the East Anglian bunch who contributed to Ebony's »The Metal Collection Vol.II« sampler) seem to have been pretty realistic about their chances of success and the number of singles they would be able to shift, and must have called it a day sometime towards the middle of the decade after finally acknowledging the fact that they were never particularly likely to headline Wembley Stadium.

7" Singles
»Rockin' Steady« Private 1982

Compilation Appearances
"Rockin' Steady" on »NWOBHM Vol.6« Bootleg CD 1992

STORMQUEEN

Chris Glyn-Jones (v)
Dave Morse (g)
Neil Baker (g)
Bryn Merrick (b)
Neil Clements (d)

Proving, yet again, that the Welsh were often more than a match for their high-profile English counterparts in the early 80's, Gwent's little-known STORMQUEEN (more sci-fi fans, as the name suggests) put out a cracker of a single in 1982 which absolutely typifies the NWOBHM sound and attitude. The outstanding "Come Silent The World" bursts forth from the speakers like prime-era BLITZKRIEG, the commanding vocal performance from Paul Burnett even including the occasional Brian Ross-style shriek! Other minor similarities would be to combos such as ENERGY and PHYNE THANQUZ, so you can see for yourselves that this record has a pretty respectable pedigree in terms of NWOBHM comparisons. The appropriately-titled flipside ("Raising The Roof") is, as you might expect, an upbeat, straightforward NWOBHM rocker, more in the vein of prime-era TYGERS OF PAN TANG than anything else, but still hugely listenable throughout. Definitely one for the wants list (no picture sleeve, but a nice logo on the label), although there are literally only a handful of examples currently known amongst collectors. Just to confound the completists, however, I'm compelled to reveal the existence of two minor variations; the original red-label issue quoted the wrong title (many were still sent out as promotional devices, although the remainder were supposedly destroyed), while the error had been corrected on the later black-label version. Only a few hundred copies of each were ever pressed, though, so you'll be extraordinarily lucky if you ever see one.

STORMQUEEN had initially gravitated together at around the turn of the decade, and were something of a cosmopolitan act in terms of personnel, although it transpires that both of their 'imported' guitarists (Dave Morse and Neil Baker) had, in fact, relocated to Britain (from the USA and Canada, respectively) at a comparatively young age. The lads proceeded to record their first demo tape (the »Battle Of Britain« four-tracker, featuring such efforts as "Captives Of The Moon" and "Lady Night") at some point in 1980, which led directly to useful local airplay, after which the lads duly began making a name for themselves on the regional club circuit.

Things went swimmingly for a while, the lads sharing a stage with various other small-time hopefuls and turning in many memorable performances. Eventually, however, the original line-up began to disintegrate, the first to go being bassist Bryn Merrick, who had been offered a dream job in THE DAMNED, and so the lucky individual proceeded to play a part in the latter's fortunes for quite some time. Soon after Merrick's departure, frontman Chris Glyn-Jones also got the boot, as the remaining members had reached the conclusion that they needed a slightly more capable singer. Fortunately, they were able to recruit the pairing of Paul Burnett (v) and Nicky McCormack (b) from the ranks of the recently-demised ASHMATA, whereupon they became a more serious proposition and ultimately got around to issuing their self-financed single, which elevated the lads to an entirely new level of popularity.

The outfit remained on the local scene for a further couple of years, occasionally operating under the assumed identity of the FAMOUS FIVE (for reasons which are too complicated to go into), but they ultimately failed to progress to the mythical status of national heroes. By 1984, part one of the STORMQUEEN story had drawn to a fairly natural conclusion, whereupon they evolved (replacing Neil Baker with former MULTI-STORY guitarist Andy Carney) into an act called VANCOUVER, although this proved to be a disappointingly short-lived concern. Dave Morse later inveigled his way into a variety of bands, including the local heavyweights known as LORD, before retreating to the States for a while and playing a role in the fortunes of little-remembered outfits such as EVE'S TATTOO. He's now back in the UK, however, lining up with erstwhile colleague Neil Clements in a forceful concern called DEFACE. The in-demand Paul Burnett (does anyone else get the impression that there was a distinct paucity of singers in Wales back then?), on the other hand, after fitting in relatively brief stints with TREDEGAR and London's CARRERA, subsequently made valiant attempts to get ASHMATA off the ground again in the latter half of 1986. Now boasting several ex-NWOBHM scenesters (including former members of MAMMATH and TRUFFLE) in their ranks, and (rather optimistically) promoting themselves as a *'supergroup'*, ASHMATA didn't leave the world any vinyl legacy, although they did get around to recording an album's worth of material (never released in any form, sadly) at one stage. The busy chap also found time to help out in TALAN, a capable late 80's unit which additionally featured certain former PREYER and SAMURAI personnel, although he had already been succeeded by a full-time vocalist (Dave Hughes from STALLION) by the time their one-off »Spellbinder« single appeared in 1989.

7" Singles
»Come Silent The Night« Real Fire Records 1982
[Original withdrawn red label pressing with wrong title, most destroyed]
»Come Silent The World« Real Fire Records 1982
[Second pressing with black label and correct title]

STORMTROOPER

Paul Merrell (v)
Bob Starling (g)
Boggy (b, k)
Nick Hancox (d)

Although numerous British acts (and quite a few overseas ones, for that matter) elected to adopt the identity of STORMTROOPER in the NWOBHM era or thereabouts, relatively few actually made it to the vinyl stage in the long term, two notable exceptions being Surrey's pub/punk combo, whose scarce »I'm A Mess« two-tracker was issued (after their demise) as early as 1977, and Yorkshire's more metal-oriented version, whose sole vinyl outing was an appearance on the »New Electric Warriors« album with the oddly-titled "Grind'n'Heat". More significant, however, were the short-lived Avon bunch, formed at the tail end of the 70's, who recorded their one-off single in the early months of 1980. On "Pride Before A Fall", the quartet come across as an enjoyably heavy, riff-inclined proposition in the general mode of SALEM or OVERKILL, with atmospheric keyboards reminiscent of AXIS adding to the overall sound. Flipside "Still Coming Home", meanwhile, is in much the same style, although it's a relatively messy and unmemorable effort in comparison. Issued on the predominantly punk-biased Heartbeat label in a somewhat uninspiring, black and white picture sleeve, the 7" has turned up in fairly noteworthy quantities over the years, but it still commands a reasonably high price among NWOBHM collectors.

It was a decent enough way to kick off a career in the music business, although the whole venture had more or less collapsed before it even got off the ground properly, which was a bit of a shame. With STORMTROOPER having already run into intractable problems and elected to disband within approximately a year of their debut single hitting the shops, the various members were left with no option but to attempt to find employment elsewhere. Of the four protagonists, vocalist Paul Merrell was undoubtedly the most successful, initially hooking up with London's quirky HELLRAZER (see separate entry) for a few months in 1981, before eventually making his way back to the West Country and joining forces with local heroes JAGUAR (who had recently parted company with founder member Rob Reiss) at the beginning of 1982, making his first appearance with the band at a prestigious festival date a matter of days later. It rapidly became apparent that Merrell was obviously well up to the job (in spite of the fact that his vocals had occasionally sounded quite strained on the earlier STORMTROOPER compositions), and he was to remain at the helm for the remainder of JAGUAR's eventful (but relatively successful) career.

7" Singles
»Pride Before A Fall« Heartbeat Heavies 1980

Compilation Appearances
"Pride Before A Fall" on »NWOBHM Vol.2« Bootleg CD 1992 + »N.W.O.B.H.M. Metal Rarities Vol.2« CD British Steel 1996
"Still Comin' Home" on »N.W.O.B.H.M. Metal Rarities Vol.2« CD British Steel 1996

STORYTELLER

Mark Tipping (v)
Kevin 'Ted' Hickey (g)
Steve Andrews (g)
Gary Farmer (b)

Tony Slater (d)

Even if STORYTELLER's obscure »Mystery Girl« single from 1985 hadn't been dated explicitly, you wouldn't really have had much doubt as to the approximate time of its release, given that it constitutes an extremely representative example of the type of mid-paced, melodic rock/metal being churned out by various post-NWOBHM propositions such as IDOL RICH, JOKERS WILD and FORGER by the mid-80's. It's a pretty solid effort, all the same, and at least we're spared the almost obligatory keyboard passages, but it's still not quite up to STRUTZ standard, for example. Not a great deal is known about the musical activities of these young Worcestershire hopefuls on the rock scene at the time, and they don't seem to have constituted one of the bigger attractions in their locality at any stage. Nevertheless, both the commercially-minded A-side and the marginally more substantial "Easy Living" (laid down at the popular Zella Recording facility in Birmingham) are sufficiently competent rockers to put a smile on the face of the average NWOBHM fan. Mind you, I bet a few people have been disinclined towards buying this offering over the years, as the colourful sleeve depicting the 'mystery girl' in question (and a right old slapper she looks, too) would tend to suggest far poppier material than is actually featured.

The group ultimately appear to have faded away into total obscurity in the years following their debut, and nothing else seems to have been committed to vinyl at any stage, so it looks as though they struggled to maintain their momentum after their single hit the shops. The ultimate demise of STORYTELLER wasn't a particularly newsworthy event at the time, although erstwhile frontman Mark Tipping remained in the music business thereafter (his one-time colleagues seem to have forgone their aspirations of rock stardom completely, though), and eventually turned up in a markedly heavier ensemble called SHERE KHAN (not to be confused with a couple of near-namesakes), who released at least one full album (»Killing For Harmony«, a private release from 1996 which was produced by MARSHALL LAW's Andy Faulkner) of capable power metal but failed to elicit a great deal of media interest at the time. It's perfectly possible that this group is still doing the rounds in the Midlands, but I reckon their chances of achieving widespread recognition are pretty slim by now.

7" Singles
»Mystery Girl« Private 1985

STRATEGY

Dave Cook (g, b)
Ron Emms (d)

It has to be said that Ebony seldom went out on a limb to sign acts who deviated significantly from the NWOBHM archetype (in their early days, at least), but Worcestershire's STRATEGY were undoubtedly cast from an entirely different mould to the vast majority of their contemporaries. Comprised of two multi-talented individuals in the form of Dave Cook and Ron Emms, STRATEGY was very much a studio project, exploiting recording technology to great effect and relying on multi-tracking practices to achieve a sufficiently rounded and complex sound. Their one and only single (issued in the latter half of 1982), which featured the instrumental pairing of "Technical Overflow" and "Astral Planes" (recorded, strangely enough, at different studio facilities), soon found a champion in the unlikely shape of 'Kerrang', who included STRATEGY in their 'Armed And Ready' section and praised the duo's originality and virtuosity in no uncertain terms. If you ask me, this level of adulation was a bit excessive, as the tracks (despite their rather progressively-inclined titles) tend to come across more like a cobbled-together collection of Eddie Van Halen's guitar solos than anything more cohesive. It's not a bad effort, considerably heavier than either DAGABAND or MADE IN ENGLAND, but it's not the sort of thing that would have given EMERSON, LAKE AND PALMER (which, oddly, was the main comparison when the two-tracker came to be reviewed in 'Kerrang') too many sleepless nights.

As it turned out, however, the humble STRATEGY two-tracker didn't actually proceed to sell in anything approaching massive quantities, despite the fact that Cook and Emms eventually took it upon themselves to solicit mail-order sales via the music weeklies of the day. All things considered, STRATEGY's brand of experimentation was hardly the sort of thing that was going to appeal directly to the general NWOBHM fan base, and the central characters ultimately decided not to follow up their critically-ignored vinyl debut at any stage. By 1983, however, the duo had already been assimilated into the ranks of local oddballs JEDDAH (see separate entry), another remarkably short-lived concern who conspired to issue a 7" based around an off-the-wall cover of the old BEATLES chestnut "Eleanor Rigby" (which again won praise in 'Kerrang', not that I'm suggesting they might have had relatives working for the magazine or anything) before ultimately ceasing all operations within the blink of an eye.

7" Singles
»Technical Overflow« Ebony 1982

STRATUS

Bernie Shaw (v)
Tino Troy (g)
Chris Troy (b)
Clive Burr (d)

After finally parting company with IRON MAIDEN in the early months of 1983, there was initial speculation that Clive Burr would (or possibly should) be taking an extended break from the music business. In fact, this turned out not to be the case, and he actually ventured over to Europe for several months, helping out French rockers TRUST in the recording studio. On returning to Blighty later in the year, however, Burr formulated plans to get a new band of his own off the drawing board, and soon roped in a likely trio of conspirators in the capable shape of Tino Troy, Chris Troy and Bernie Shaw, all three of whom had suddenly become available for employment following the recent demise of PRAYING MANTIS. The quartet hurriedly demoed some freshly-penned material, although pretty much all of these formative efforts were rapidly shelved, and the musicians (who originally used the occasional services of keyboard player Don Garbett) subsequently began reworking some of the unissued PRAYING MANTIS compositions from the latter part of their career. In due course, the newly-established group (initially lumbered with the rather unwieldy handle of CLIVE BURR'S ESCAPE) would begin to incorporate such familiar numbers as "Raining In Kensington", "Enough Is Enough" and "Romancer" in their ever-expanding repertoire, although they were soon also composing their own efforts, notably "Fantasy", "Top Of The Mountain", "Born Evil" and "Woman Of The Night", all of which were eminently listenable.

Understandably, there was widespread speculation as to the precise musical direction that STRATUS would ultimately adopt, and Tino Troy proffered an honest impression of their choice of material at an early stage: *'It sounds MANTIS-ish to me, but it's also certainly got a new feel to it. We've been trying to do this kind of stuff for two years and, while the name of PRAYING MANTIS started to hinder us in the end, we never gave up on the musical style because it's what we all believe in and it's what we all feel most comfortable playing, Clive included.'* (Ref: Kerrang No.58, December 1983). Their live debut, a packed-out date at London's Marquee in December 1983, saw the ensemble delighting the assembled throng with their blend of old and new, throwing favourites such as "Tell Me The Nightmare's Wrong" and "Turn The Tables" into the set to keep the legions of PRAYING MANTIS fans happy. Within a matter of weeks, CLIVE BURR'S ESCAPE already found themselves recording a session for the 'Friday Rock Show' (by which time their ranks had been swelled by the addition of full-time keyboard player Alan Nelson, formerly with LAUTREC, WILDFIRE and STAMPEDE), whereupon the tracks "Romancer", "Enough Is Enough", "Take No Prisoners" and "Top Of The Mountain" were showcased for the benefit of the station's listeners on the 24th of February 1984. It had been a pretty healthy start, and the rapidly-developing outfit continued to gig whenever possible, picking up occasional support slots (with SPIDER, for example) as well as headlining their own shindigs, and things seemed to be going according to plan in every sense.

Still, there was trouble lurking just around the corner, and the hapless bunch were, in the wake of a potential law suit from another band called ESCAPE, soon forced to change their identity to the rather more original TIGON. This proved to be an unpopular choice, however (more importantly, it had also been registered by other groups), and so the metamorphosis into STRATUS occurred within a remarkably short space of time. By this stage, however, the outfit had already become something of a studio project (one of their few gigs as STRATUS was apparently in support of MÖTLEY CRÜE), their ultimate objective being simply to release a full album. In due course, the recording sessions for this opus were undertaken towards the end of the year (plans to precede it with a single based around "Back Street Lovers" were rapidly shelved), and the resultant LP, entitled »Throwing Shapes«, finally (after initially looking as though it might only see the light of day in Japan) received a European release on Steel Trax, an obscure Belgian label. It was much as expected, particularly for those who had been exposed to the original CLIVE BURR'S ESCAPE material (some of which has recently been included on the PRAYING MANTIS »Demorabilia« retrospective set, incidentally), although it might have seemed just a tad lightweight for fans of the first PRAYING MANTIS long-player. The overall feeling was that the participants had perhaps assumed an overly-commercial stance, the main NWOBHM-period comparisons being with acts such as STATETROOPER, GRAND PRIX, SNOWBLIND and JOKERS WILD, and the individual compositions were, although all competently written and performed, ultimately rather disposable.

The album's initial distribution was, understandably enough, severely limited, and few fans outside mainland Europe and Japan were able to get hold of the long-player at the time, although an exclusive number ("Top Of The Mountain") put in an appearance on Zebra's patchy »The Best Of British« compilation. The upshot, however, was that the quintet rapidly lost faith in themselves, and, being unable to secure any additional live work to promote their activities, proceeded to go their separate ways. Bernie Shaw, for example, soon hooked up with URIAH HEEP, while Clive Burr went back to session work, assisting the likes of (ahem) GOGMAGOG, ELIXIR and DESPERADO. Alan Nelson, on the other hand, donated his keyboard skills to the lesser-known of the two acts who went by the name of JAGGED EDGE (although this was a fairly unfruitful liaison) before teaming up with MAMA'S BOYS towards the end of 1987. The Troy brothers, meanwhile, ultimately found themselves unable to resist the urge to reform PRAYING MANTIS, starting with a one-off reunion show in 1987, and subsequently progressing to a complete renaissance of this legendary outfit, who are still enjoying a staggeringly prolific and successful career, fuelled predominantly by fanatical interest and support from the Far East.

LP's
»Throwing Shapes« Steel Trax 1985
[European issue]
»Throwing Shapes« CBS/Sony 1985
[Japanese issue]

CD's
»Throwing Shapes« Reborn Classics 1993
[Bootleg release, also features IRON MAIDEN's »Soundhouse Tapes« EP]
»Throwing Shapes« CBS Japan 1994
[Japanese issue]

Exclusive Compilation Appearances
"Top Of The Mountain" on »The Best Of British« LP Zebra 1985

STREETFIGHTER

Lee Fenton (v)
John Sykes (g)
Dave Westrop (g)
Merv Goldsworthy (b)
Gary Taylor (d)

In spite of the observation that the »Crazy Dream« EP, released by Lancashire's STREETFIGHTER (not to be confused with their rather obscure namesakes from Germany) in 1982, has often been given the enticing *'featuring John Sykes'* sales pitch, it's not actually true, folks. Although the young lad (who had apparently been working as a labourer in Blackpool prior to his appointment) started off his career with this local outfit at the tail end of the 70's, he had already been shamelessly pilfered by the TYGERS OF PAN TANG by the autumn of 1980. However, the guitar legend *does* feature on STREETFIGHTER's very first vinyl appearance, the capable "She's No Angel" track on Logo's »New Electric Warriors« compilation. Although this contribution was harshly dismissed as merely *'average'* in the hard-to-please 'Phoenix' fanzine upon its release, it's not actually too bad, with hints of DRIVESHAFT or early DEALER, plus a bit of a THIN LIZZY influence coming across in the guitar department. By the time the compilation finally hit the shops (its release was delayed by a typically British strike at the pressing plant), however, Sykes had already been tempted away by the offer to join a more high-profile concern, and so a new recruit (Dave Senczak) was rapidly brought in to serve as his immediate replacement.

To regress slightly, the origins of STREETFIGHTER date back to around 1977, when youthful axemen John Sykes and Dave Westrop first started swapping playing tips, which soon led the pair to formulate some fairly ambitious ideas about forming a heavy act of their own. Within a matter of months, one-time JENKS bassist Merv Goldsworthy had been recruited to the cause, with drummer Gary Taylor and vocalist Lee Fenton becoming permanent fixtures some time later. The next couple of years were no doubt spent gigging throughout their local area and developing a bit more of a fan base, and the outfit's well-timed compilation appearance might easily have led to greater things in the heady days of 1980. In fact, this exposure didn't exactly propel the name of STREETFIGHTER into the realms of stardom, and it took another year or two of hard graft before the rejigged band eventually decided to take the plunge and finance their own vinyl product. The resultant four-tracker certainly wasn't a landmark release, although it's passable enough (something of a let-down after their promising sampler appearance, perhaps), with both "Crazy Dream" and "City Girls" coming across as raunchy, boogie-tinged rockers in the style of a heavier MASAI or VARDIS. On the other hand, "Livin' On The Red Line" has more of a SNAKEBITE feel to it, while "Streetfighter" is undoubtedly the pick of the bunch, a heavy-but-catchy number evocative of ENERGY. Overall, a semi-decent effort, and a 7" (issued without a picture sleeve) which has remained a popular, mid-priced item for NWOBHM collectors over a number of years.

Even so, the EP ultimately failed to send STREETFIGHTER hurtling into the NWOBHM premier league, and the participants presumably went back to the drawing board thereafter, but failed to think of any better way to promote themselves to the masses. The ensemble had presumably disintegrated completely by 1983 at the very latest, having struggled to come up with the kind of original material which would see them outlasting the NWOBHM boom, although most of the ex-members subsequently managed to find gainful employment elsewhere. Departed guitar wizard John Sykes had a remarkably busy time of it, with post-TYGERS OF PAN TANG stints in BADLANDS, THIN LIZZY, WHITESNAKE and BLUE MURDER (not to mention his solo efforts), while in-demand bassist Merv Goldsworthy proceeded to lend his services to such luminaries as DIAMOND HEAD, SAMSON and FM, as well as a very obscure project called BAT. Sticksman Gary Taylor, meanwhile, found work with BUFFALO (as did his fly-by-night predecessor, Paul Milek) and TANK, while Dave Senczak played with slightly less successful outfits such as BLACKFOX, CANNES, MORITZ and FIRST STRIKE, the latter being best-known for their involvement with the godawful ALL STARS project.

7" EP's
»**Crazy Dream**« Private 1982

Exclusive Compilation Appearances
"**She's No Angel**" on »New Electric Warriors« LP Logo 1980/CD British Steel 1997

STREET LEGAL

Lonestar Willy (v)
Matt Foster (g)
Wayne Boon (g)
Neil Darbyshire (g)
Marc Dempsey (b)
Bob Darnell (d)

You would be forgiven for expecting a band called STREET LEGAL to be purveyors of biker rock in its purest form, but you'd be mistaken in this instance. Bizarrely enough, this particular bunch elected to deliver a pretty decent imitation of Southern Boogie in the grand old manner of BLACKFOOT or LYNYRD SKYNYRD, although the absurdity of a group from the Northern wastelands of Cheshire being fronted by a character called 'Lonestar Willy' (who happily extols the virtues of 'mississippi moonshine') is considerable. If you can get over this mental hurdle, however, the outfit's music is really quite passable (considerably more authentic than the faltering attempts of SPLITCROW to create a similar effect), but hardly metal in its purest form, although this ensemble should at least be praised for trying something different from 99% of their peers. To be honest, though, they might well have struggled to get onto rock bills with bands of a similar inclination, given that (with the possible exception of SLENDER THREAD) there really weren't many compatible acts doing the rounds in Britain at the time.

STREET LEGAL's debut two-tracker (a modest, self-financed effort, needless to say) appeared in 1984, and this pretty much served to introduce the little-known group to the rock community. The ZZ TOP-influenced A-side ("Rolling On") was undoubtedly the stronger effort of the pair, a raunchy and memorable affair with a passing similarity to the likes of MORE or the STARFIGHTERS. The reverse (the campfire singalong of "Mississippi Moonshine"), on the other hand, was something of an unmitigated disaster, and certainly wasn't enhanced by the clapping sounds, I'm afraid! Admittedly, this type of material was probably better-suited to the pubs and clubs, but it was still a perfectly valid release, even if it failed to propel the act into the realms of stardom in the long term. Indeed, the six-piece concern (who boasted no fewer than three guitarists, which was at least one more than they actually needed) seem to have come out of nowhere before releasing their single (in the obligatory, anonymous, monochrome sleeve) and disappearing back into complete obscurity, rendering this piece of vinyl a collectable memento of their (presumably) brief existence. Who knows, maybe they all bought cowboy costumes and moved to Texas…

7" Singles

»Rolling On« Weeird Brothers Records 1984

STRUTZ

Karen Sambrook (v)
Graham Wood (g)
Dave Hellon (rg)
Alan Harter (b)
Jeff Stevens (k)
Andy Davis (d)

I reckon we might be able to clear up a bit of a long-standing mystery here. At some point in the dim and distant past, some bright spark decided to include a STRUTZ 7" on their NWOBHM wants list, but the only thing that the dealers could turn up was the »Start/Stop« 7" by an obscure Scottish band on Braw Records. In spite of the fact that this is an abysmal piece of electro-pop, it has indeed been passed off as a *bona fide* NWOBHM release in the past, although not, as far as I know, at outlandish prices. In more recent times, however, the genuine article has finally been located, condemning the rogue STRUTZ to its rightful place in the bargain bins. Captured at Cavalier Studios in Stockport (as with the DRAGONSLAYER EP), the double A-sided single from this particular Mancunian combo (recorded shortly after their formation, in the days when they still had a male vocalist) is a pretty good stab at melodic rock/metal with keyboards, broadly similar to »Blackhearts«-era TOKYO BLADE or early BRIAR. "Mixed Emotions" is the stronger of the two compositions on display, incorporating a cracking, widdly riff that the outfit would do well to patent and sell to the likes of IN FLAMES or any of the multifarious NWOSDM pretenders for widespread use on their next album. "Come Back", on the other hand, doesn't leave quite such a favourable impression, but it's still a decent enough effort all the same. Happily, though, the keyboards (which had become virtually compulsory amongst tuneful British wannabes by 1985) aren't particularly out of place, and seem to complement the music pretty well in this case.

All things considered, the music of STRUTZ was energetic stuff (performed with considerably more conviction than most of their featherweight rivals), and the popular group deservedly became quite a successful act on the club circuit in the second half of the decade. No doubt they took the opportunity to shift a few copies of their vinyl offering at these regular shindigs throughout the North West, although it appears to have been a fairly limited pressing in the first instance. A brand-new demo tape (featuring the tracks "Alright Mama", "Breakaway", "Never Surrender" and "Sweet Dreamer") was issued a year or two later, to the approval of several local radio stations, and the outfit duly mentioned plans (which don't seem to have come to fruition) to shoot a professional video to promote themselves even further. Although the big break never came their way, the band persevered, in various forms, until around 1989, recruiting a female singer (Karen Sambrook, later of BLUE 46) along the way, their overall sound (on newly-penned demo selections such as "Won't Cry" and "I Still Love You") supposedly veering more towards HEART after this point. There's not much else to report about the activities of STRUTZ at this juncture, and we've yet to establish who the original vocalist was, but their (sleeveless) vinyl rarity is well worth seeking out nonetheless.

7" Singles
»Come Back« Sticky Label Records 1985

STRYDER

Joe Wearan (g)

Ireland's little-known STRYDER were one of the first metal bands in their homeland to make it to the vinyl stage, and their one-off (I presume it was a one-off, anyway) single hit the shops as early as 1980. The energetic A-side, "Forcin' Thru'", was an enjoyable, upbeat number, quite heavy on the guitar front (very much in the SWEET SAVAGE or MASTERSTROKE scheme of things) and occasionally reminiscent of the likes of GEDDES AXE, PERSIAN RISK or DEALER. The flipside ("Settle Down"), on the other hand, could almost pass for a THIN LIZZY composition (the ideal to which most Irish rock hopefuls aspired, quite understandably), although it's another capable effort (recorded live, oddly enough) which shows the outfit to have been a highly confident and enthusiastic bunch in their own right. Nevertheless, I don't imagine STRYDER ever made it to the mainland at any stage, and I'm not even convinced that they ever managed to hook up with any of the bigger touring acts who occasionally ventured over to the Emerald Isle. In the face of considerable local popularity but complete disinterest further afield, therefore, it seems as though the project must ultimately have lost momentum within a couple of years, and it all seems to have fallen apart by 1983, whereupon guitarist Joe Wearan made his way to the South of England and teamed up with the long-lived ENGLISH ROGUES, who didn't get much further than an appearance on the »Rockworks« compilation. The STRYDER single (which doesn't appear to have been issued in a picture sleeve), meanwhile, is a very scarcely-sighted item which would no doubt fetch a pretty hefty price on the open market.

7" Singles
»Forcin' Thru« Quartz Records 1980

SURFACE

Gez Finnegan (v)
Mark Davies (g)
Mike Cheshire (g)
Ian Hawkins (b)
John Bennet (k)
Jamie Hawkins (d)

Although Birmingham's long-lived SURFACE originally got together at the very height of the NWOBHM explosion in 1980, they rapidly decided not to impersonate the majority of their contemporaries in terms of musical direction, electing instead to cultivate a rather more polished and accessible sound. It had all started when axeman Mike Cheshire (formerly with the little-known XENON) and sticksman Jamie Hawkins attempted to get a new rock group together, their first recruit being former GOOD GRIEF vocalist Gez Finnegan, who was swiftly followed by bassist Ian Hawkins (Jamie's brother) to establish something of a stable unit. The line-up was duly completed, in the first instance, by a second guitarist (Mike Davies) and keyboard player (John Bennet), after which SURFACE gradually began making an effort to get themselves known to the masses. Mind you, they initially found it reasonably difficult to get onto local bills on account of their lightweight tendencies, although the gradual shift in musical outlook of the general public (leading to the emergence of regional favourites such as TOBRUK, FORCE and SHY, for example) eventually allowed them to develop a significant following. Before long, therefore, SURFACE had become a regular fixture at the likes of the famous Railway Inn, where they were always assured of pulling a loyal and enthusiastic crowd.

Up until the beginning of 1984, however, SURFACE had been content to function as a live attraction, and elected to wait until they had established themselves before circulating any demo tapes of their own. Their first studio recordings materialised in the shape of a four track cassette, featuring numbers such as "Confusion", "Someday" and "Fading Faster", a selection of early material which was to feature in the band's setlist for several years. The tape failed to garner much in the way of a favourable response from the record companies (although they were rapidly heralded as nothing less than the saviours of rock'n'roll by the over-enthusiastic 'High Octane' fanzine, who were soon devoting multi-page features to these relative unknowns), so the lads went back to the continual grind of touring the pubs and clubs, even venturing over to France for an eventful series of shows in due course. Towards the end of the year, SURFACE issued an official live tape, although this effort was more of a souvenir for their fans than something with which to impress the labels. Moving into 1985, the outfit recruited a new keyboard player, Dean Field, who was soon making his mark on their next demo tape, another four track affair. This time, however, the cassette (featuring such compositions as "Paris", "Hideaway", "Don't Try" and "Different Story") seemed to do the trick, and the labels were soon beating a path to their door.

SURFACE, to their credit, didn't rush into the first offer that came their way, and the patient Brummies carried on playing live at every available opportunity, securing a useful support slot with the TYGERS OF PAN TANG along the way. Eventually, however, they elected to sign on the dotted line with Killerwatt (who were handling the affairs of the revived ANGEL WITCH at the time) towards the end of that year (by which juncture they had replaced founder member Mike Cheshire with new boy Loz Rabone), and so a full SURFACE album was finally on the cards. Strangely, however, their new sponsors elected to issue a live set instead of a properly-financed studio affair, the end product being the »Race The Night« long-player (mixed by DEMON's Les Hunt), which hit the shelves in the early months of 1986. In spite of the low-budget limitations of the recording, though, it turned out to be a pretty decent release, the outfit coming across as rather more forceful-sounding than they had previously done on cassette. Compositions such as "Night Creature", "Hideaway" and the title track itself were all undeniably strong efforts, very much in the manner of BLUE BLUD, KOOGA or IDOL RICH. Unfortunately, however, the record failed to sell in particularly noteworthy quantities in the first instance, and so the lads were soon being left to pick up the pieces and attempt to get their career back on track before a follow-up could be issued.

In fact, there would be no further vinyl product from the outfit, and even their once-prolific live appearances had begun to tail off considerably by mid-1987. In view of the observation that SURFACE already seemed to be winding down their activities in major fashion, many casual observers simply assumed that the group would disappear sooner than later. Surprisingly, however, it was duly reported in 1988 that some of Killerwatt's releases from the previous year or two (notably those of ANGEL WITCH and SURFACE) had been picked up by the JCI concern in the States and would soon benefit from reissues for the benefit of the American market. In due course, it transpired that SURFACE's debut was to be repackaged under the alternate title of »Beneath The Surface« (with new cover artwork), and this piece of serendipity appeared to kickstart the ensemble's waning enthusiasm to some extent. In spite of their reduced public profile, the group was apparently still a going concern at this stage, and there was even talk of a series of hastily-organised American shows to promote the 'new' release. Whether or not this actually occurred is open to debate, although their fortunes were hardly to change dramatically in the wake of this re-promotion.

Nevertheless, the dogged band still soldiered on regardless, and, even when drummer Jamie Hawkins hooked up with the reformed STARFIGHTERS a couple of months later, he ostensibly remained fully involved with the activities of SURFACE. Further sporadic touring followed (although they never really got to the stage of headlining particularly capacious venues), and the persevering group eventually appeared to be getting their act together again by the latter half of 1989. Unfortunately, however, it finally all fell apart for the lads the following year, the luckless combo having already given it their best shot for a full decade. Loz Rabone subsequently worked with local hopefuls FELONY (who never received a great deal of media attention) and MERCILESS (ditto, although sharing your name with death metal groups is never a particularly good idea), whereas the other musicians in question have been rather less prominent in their post-SURFACE activities.

LP's

»Race The Night« Killerwatt Records 1986
[Original UK issue, live album]

»Beneath The Surface« JCI Records 1988
[US reissue of »Race The Night« in different cover]

SUSPECT

R. Winfield

The little-known SUSPECT were yet another on the never-ending list of minor hopefuls who put out a very limited private single through the Ellie Jay pressing facility in the NWOBHM era. This fairly anonymous Sussex quintet seem to have started out in 1980 or thereabouts, and they must have reached the vinyl stage pretty quickly, no doubt hoping to boost their appeal to the local fan base by having something to sell at gigs. Issued in 1981, their double A-sided effort (recorded at Wave Studios in Twickenham) coupled two semi-restrained numbers with a vague feeling of the genuine NWOBHM spirit, with "Working It Out" being the better of the pair; a rather sombre, moody composition (fairly similar

to LEGEND in their »Frontline« period) with the odd tinge of TRACER thrown in for good measure. "In The Night", on the other hand, is more of an upbeat, lightweight cut which additionally brings forth comparisons with the likes of H.G.B. or SINGAPORE. Not a bad effort at all, but it's certainly not a prime candidate for classic NWOBHM status, and it clearly didn't sell in staggering quantities at the time. SUSPECT's activities on the live front appear to have petered out somewhat after the single's release, suggesting that the anticipated positive feedback from Britain's rock community just wasn't there, and the participants probably went back to their day jobs soon afterwards. Nevertheless, their two-tracker is now an extremely rare piece (issued in a flimsy sleeve showing a photo of some sunglasses, a knife and a razor blade), and is likely to set you back a fair bit of dosh if you go in search of a copy.

7" Singles
»Working It Out« Ellie Jay 1981

SWEET SAVAGE

Raymond Haller (v, b)
Vivian Campbell (g)
Trevor Fleming (g)
David Bates (d)

I wonder just how many bitter ex-musicians from the NWOBHM era are sitting out there in minimum-wage-land, cursing their luck that METALLICA's benevolent patronage didn't quite extend as far as their own outfit. Admittedly, Ulrich's mob hardly wielded the sort of power which could have saved the likes of DIAMOND HEAD, HOLOCAUST, BLITZKRIEG and SAVAGE from extinction at the time, although it's notable that all of these acts got a second bite at the cherry in the wake of their posthumous adulation. By far the most obscure act to have been afforded the honour of having one of their tracks covered by METALLICA (originally in their formative 'garage' sessions of 1981), however, were the pride of Northern Ireland, SWEET SAVAGE. An embryonic version of the band first came together in early 1979, originally taking the rather uninspiring name TEASER, but soon finding a more individualistic identity for themselves (although the good name of SWEET SAVAGE was later besmirched by an abysmal American pretty-boy outfit), whereupon they could mount their assault on the pubs and clubs of the nation. Based in Belfast, but maintaining fairly strong links with Dublin throughout their career, the lads started out by treating the rock-starved crowds to the obligatory selection of covers from the likes of THIN LIZZY (but of course) and DEEP PURPLE, although they soon progressed to an enviable repertoire of self-penned numbers.

By early 1980, the NWOBHM was in full swing, and Ireland had its own range of emergent rock/metal outfits (it's open to debate whether or not the Irish scene developed independently, but it's hard to conceive that the goings-on in the mainland failed to have any sort of knock-on effect in the Emerald Isle), although the vast majority were consigned to a predictable fate (given the extreme difficulty in making themselves known to fans and labels in the rest of Britain) of local popularity and nothing more. For the talented SWEET SAVAGE, however, things started looking rosy when they were invited to support WISHBONE ASH (one of the few touring acts whose itinerary included Irish dates) on the local leg of their latest jaunt, and this early exposure was to go a long way towards establishing the band as a capable opening act with the potential to go on to greater things. Even better was to come towards the end of that year, however, when the foursome were asked to travel to the mainland and support BUDGIE on their forthcoming UK tour. Hardly surprisingly, SWEET SAVAGE jumped at the chance, and the ambitious young musicians proceeded to enjoy a productive time of it while they were playing away from home, as it were. Apart from the obvious benefits of travelling around the country, performing in unfamiliar cities and experiencing far larger audiences than they were used to, the lads somehow managed to fit in a visit to the BBC's own studios, where they laid down a session for the 'Friday Rock Show'.

To this day, I still haven't the remotest idea how the then-unknown SWEET SAVAGE wangled that early session. It's possible that they had recorded a demo in the past, which could have found its way to Tommy Vance and his cohorts by some circuitous route or other, although I suspect (knowing the quantity of charm, not to mention sheer nerve, possessed by most Irish citizens) that they probably turned up unannounced, plugged in their equipment and recorded four tracks before the bewildered employees of the station actually had the remotest inkling as to what was going on. In any case, their session was initially transmitted on the 19th of December 1980, when the upstarts showcased four original numbers, "Killing Time", "Eye Of The Storm", "Into The Night" and "Queen's Vengeance". It was an extraordinarily confident debut, with some heavy arrangements, strong guitar work and distinctive, throaty vocals, the outfit setting a precedent for the kind of powerful, upbeat metal later purveyed by countrymen such as EZY MEAT, DRIVESHAFT and TROJAN, although there are also similarities to mainland acts such as TRIDENT, DEALER and (to a lesser extent) ELIXIR. The broadcast was received with immense enthusiasm by the programme's listeners, and "Eye Of The Storm" would subsequently be chosen to appear on the BBC's »The Friday Rock Show« showcase compilation, one of two extremely worthy albums to be assembled from session highlights.

Upon their eventual return to Northern Ireland, the jubilant SWEET SAVAGE finally turned their thoughts to the once-distant possibility of getting some vinyl into the shops. With little or no prospect of a major deal, however, they were forced to go it alone, so their debut appeared as a private release on the Park label. Issued in a picture sleeve showing a photo of the group, SWEET SAVAGE's inaugural single (produced by the talented Chris Tsangarides) coupled the semi-raunchy "Take No Prisoners" with the upbeat, proto-thrash of "Killing Time", as previously heard on their BBC appearance. It was a pretty decent way to kick off their career proper, although it's worth pointing out that they already had far better numbers than "Take No Prisoners" in their repertoire by this stage. Nevertheless, the two-tracker received a predictably warm welcome from their many fans at home, and was soon selling in healthy quantities at gigs (their activities took in a few dates with WILD HORSES) and by mail order, with many a copy making its way to the mainland and disappearing into one collection or another (yes, a number of people really did collect NWOBHM pretty seriously in those days). With the first pressing being a typically limited affair, the stocks were soon exhausted, and the band went back to local gigging to keep themselves busy while their management attempted to win them a proper deal. They suffered a blow, however, when Trevor Fleming went back to his day job later in the year, although the outfit managed to teach their repertoire to his replacement, Ian Wilson, without too much effort, and little momentum was lost.

SWEET SAVAGE's continual hard graft in the live environment was ultimately rewarded when the quartet started picking up some rather more prestigious and lucrative gigs, including a modest billing at a popular rock festival held in the grounds of Slane Castle, where the lads set the stage for such luminaries as ROSE TATTOO, U2 and THIN LIZZY, the latter being so impressed with SWEET SAVAGE's performance (it was Fleming's last gig) that they invited the youngsters to support them on their UK tour towards the end of 1981. By all accounts, the band were received with great warmth throughout the jaunt, and treated the audiences to a wide and varied set, featuring original compositions such as "Finders Keepers", "Sweet Surrender", "Bottle Of Wine" and "Lady Marion". Mention was made at the time that the outfit intended to record a second single based around "The Raid" (the most likely B-side being "Prospector Of Greed"), which would see the light of day early the following year, although plans for this release were apparently shelved in favour of further touring

activities, as drummer David Bates later confirmed: 'We actually recorded »The Raid« back then, it should have come out as our second single. Chris Tsangarides, who had already produced our debut single, was involved again, and we recorded it in Morgan Studios in London while we were on tour with THIN LIZZY. As far as I'm aware, though, not even one test pressing of this single exists. We were recording loads of demos at around that time, and eventually hoped to release an album, but it never happened.' (Ref: Interview, Matthias Mader, September 1996).

With the release of their second single initially being delayed for a few months and then cancelled altogether (it makes you wonder why some individuals insist on claiming to have seen such an item, though), SWEET SAVAGE decided that the time had come to progress to slightly more accessible material, and came to a mutual agreement that frontman Ray Haller should revert to bass duties and make way for a dedicated singer. To this end, talented new recruit Robert Casserley (aka Rob Cass) was drafted in towards the end of the year, and the outfit briefly existed as a five-piece concern while a selection of original material was being written. The group evidently hadn't been forgotten, however, as the inclusion of "Take No Prisoners" in the 'Top 30 Kuts' chart in 'Kerrang' during the summer of 1982 showed (not only that, a studio version of "Lady Of The Night" also turned up on an extraordinarily obscure local-band compilation), and a great number of British fans were clearly eager to hear a lot more from SWEET SAVAGE. The lads continued their hectic schedule of touring, recording and promotion as they moved into 1983, and further radio and television exposure was to follow, notably an appearance on a networked Irish rock programme, where the combo ran through versions of "Bottle Of Wine", "Straight Through The Heart" and "Moving On", the latter pair moving into considerably more melodic territory and showcasing the considerable vocal talents of their latest acquisition.

Once they had firmly re-established themselves once again, the group began giving serious thought as to their next move on the vinyl front. It seemed inevitable that another single would definitely be forthcoming this time, although their immediate plans were seriously disrupted when talented guitarist Vivian Campbell was lured away by an unexpected offer to join the newly-formed DIO (bassist Jimmy Bain recalled seeing the youngster in action when SWEET SAVAGE had shared a stage with WILD HORSES in the past), resulting in the band's reduction to a humble quartet once again. It's notable that the enterprising Campbell clearly took some of his own riffs and musical ideas to his new venture, and there were, as a result, some pretty remarkable similarities between the two outfits at times. Even so, I'd still refute the occasionally-made suggestion that at least half of DIO's truly excellent »Holy Diver« album was actually comprised of reworked SWEET SAVAGE compositions. Mind you, "Rainbow In The Dark" was certainly a variation on the theme of "Lady Marion", "Invisible" bore a passing similarity to "Queen's Vengeance" and "Caught In The Middle" unashamedly nicked the intro to "Straight Through The Heart" (confusingly, the DIO long-player had an entirely separate track called "Straight Through The Heart"), but that's about it, as far as I'm concerned.

It took SWEET SAVAGE a few months to recover from the loss of Campbell, but they eventually went ahead with the release of their long-awaited second single, supposedly recorded while the departed guitarist was still in the band. »Straight Through The Heart« (b/w "Teaser") emerged towards the end of 1983 on the small-time Crashed label, and the record more or less completed the metamorphosis of SWEET SAVAGE into a radio-friendly act with mainstream aspirations, a move which failed to win favour with all that many of their original fans. To be honest, their latest material was actually quite strong, although the move into soft rock territory (with occasional similarities to the likes of DEF LEPPARD, ALKATRAZZ or MOTHER'S RUIN) seemed to have come across as a betrayal of their NWOBHM roots. The record (never issued in a picture sleeve) sold in pretty modest quantities, and is currently valued at a pretty extortionate price which is hardly justified by the contents. Its musically-superior predecessor, meanwhile, is also usually regarded as a three-figure item, but has turned up considerably more frequently, although you should be aware that copies were actually manufactured on at least two separate occasions. Examples of the coveted original have red and yellow labels, while the second pressing (organised by Dato Records, whoever they were) features black and yellow labels and a 'Dato Records' credit. I've no idea just how official this alternate pressing was (it seems to be rather more plentiful), or when it came about, although I would suspect that it was an attempt to cash in on Vivian Campbell's new-found fame in the wake of the immense success of the first DIO album.

SWEET SAVAGE were understandably disappointed by the failure of their new direction to win the hearts of the listening public, and proceeded to suffer a slight crisis of confidence thereafter. Nevertheless, they remained active during 1984, and continued to try out new material in the valiant hope that an album deal would still come their way in the long term. Sadly, however, none of the influential labels of the day appear to have been overly-impressed with their brand of melodic metal (a pretty ridiculous situation, especially when you consider that their former label, Crashed Records, somehow considered BLACKWYCH to be deserving of a full album), leaving the outfit high and dry with regard to getting further product into the shops. In the end, it all fell apart in the early months of 1985, with Ray Haller moving over to a non-illustrious position of bassist in the long-forgotten EMERALD, while Rob Cass was headhunted by a variety of melodic rock projects, notably Neal Kay's ill-fated VENTURE, plus ALASKA and MGM. A year or two after their demise, however, Lars Ulrich began singing the praises of various NWOBHM heroes, and singled out SWEET SAVAGE for attention on quite a regular basis. Their fondly-remembered "Killing Time" had been one of the drummer's particular favourites at the time of its release, and had been played numerous times at rehearsals in METALLICA's formative years, along with SAVAGE's "Let It Loose" and half of DIAMOND HEAD's back catalogue, for example.

Within a couple of years, Ulrich had achieved his vision of assembling an official tribute to his original NWOBHM influences, and SWEET SAVAGE's "Eye Of The Storm" was duly included on the »NWOBHM '79 Revisited« retrospective in 1990. More significantly, METALLICA's energetic interpretation of "Killing Time" finally emerged officially (a very rough take had appeared on a bootleg single several years previously) on

Photo: Tobias Thiem

the reverse of 1991's »The Unforgiven« single, and this move heralded a serious revival of interest in the career of the Belfast boys. The first to cotton on were the bootleggers, who soon prepared a lovingly-assembled CD (featuring both singles, their BBC session and a much-traded audience tape of an appearance at Hammersmith Odeon, taken from the THIN LIZZY tour of 1981), and released it as a self-titled set in 1992. Paralleling the TRESPASS situation (the very same bootleggers released a CD of the latter's demos at more or less the same time), the former members of SWEET SAVAGE subsequently found out about the release, noted how well it was selling, and rapidly concluded 'hey, we could do better than that' (or words to that effect). As a result, a reformed SWEET SAVAGE, featuring Haller, Bates, Wilson and Fleming (sadly, Campbell couldn't be tempted to join in the fun, being far too busy with his other musical endeavours, which have included WHITESNA-

KE, RIVER DOGS, SHADOW KING and, most recently, DEF LEPPARD), got together for some low-key gigs late in 1992.

The quartet's activities took in a memorable appearance at the Marquee in London, where they modestly opened the proceedings for LIONSHEART and LILLIAN AXE, but must have been hoping that a few of those present might have had some notion that they were witnessing something a bit out of the ordinary. Sadly, the vast majority failed to recognise any of the material (they played their trump card, "Killing Time", right at the start, but to no avail), and merely formed the collective opinion that this was presumably a new bunch of hopefuls from across the water. It was a great pity, as the all-too-brief SWEET SAVAGE set included many an old favourite (some of which had actually been given a major overhaul), including "The Raid", "Bottle Of Wine" (now retitled "Ground Zero") and "Eye Of The Storm", in addition to a highly respectful cover of THIN LIZZY's "Suicide" (dedicated to 'a band who helped us out a long time ago'). Intriguingly, however, there was even a brand-new selection ("D.U.D.", which bore more than a passing similarity to THE ALMIGHTY) on display, which suggested that the lads might just have been considering a proper comeback at that juncture. In fact, things appeared to cool off pretty quickly after this initial bout of unabashed enthusiasm, and it looked as though SWEET SAVAGE had almost certainly gone back into retirement, this time permanently.

Surprisingly, however, the outfit re-emerged once again in 1996, having been given the opportunity to record an album for the resurrected Neat Metal concern (who had presumably first come into contact with SWEET SAVAGE when seeking permission to include "Killing Time" on their »The Metallic-Era« exploitation release) at their convenience. With the reliable nucleus of Haller, Bates and Fleming now being joined by youthful guitarist Simon McBride (who, rather embarrassingly, was still in nappies when the rest were originally doing the rounds), their »Killing Time« (didn't see that title coming a mile off, oh no) CD finally provided the lads with a chance to capture some old favourites for posterity, the musicians additionally making full use of the opportunity to showcase a selection of newer material. Consequently, well-worn efforts such as "Killing Time" (inevitably), "The Raid", "Eye Of The Storm", "Prospector Of Greed", "Ground Zero" and "Vengeance" (originally "Queen's Vengeance") sat happily alongside a range of more contemporary offerings, namely

"D.U.D.", "Reach Out", "Welcome To The Real World", "Thunder", "Parody Of Wisdom" and the disarmingly-subtle "Why?". With the lads battling valiantly against a very odd production, the album turned out to be an eminently listenable affair, and I'm happy to say that it wasn't a one-off event; after a handful of promotional appearances to let the world know they were back from the dead (including an appearance at the Wacken Festival in 1998, alongside the likes of BLITZKRIEG), the outfit proceeded to record a brand-new CD called »Rune« (now as a slimmed-down trio, Trevor Fleming having moved on), another release which has been on the receiving end of some pretty favourable reviews thus far. I've no idea where they'll go from here, or how long they'll stick around, but I'm glad they're back. I love a happy ending.

7" Singles
»**Take No Prisoners**« Park Records 1981
[Original issue with red/yellow labels, different version of B-side "Killing Time" appears on »Killing Time« CD]
»**Take No Prisoners**« Park Records/Dato Records 198?
[Re-pressing with black/yellow labels]
»**Straight Through The Heart**« Crashed Records 1983

CD's
»**Sweet Savage**« Bootleg 1992
[Unofficial release, includes live recording from 1981 plus single and compilation tracks]
»**Killing Time**« Neat Metal 1996
[UK issue, mixture of new and re-recorded older material]
»**Killing Time**« Pony Canyon 1996
[Japanese issue with one bonus track]
»**Rune**« Neat Metal 1998

Compilation Appearances
"**Eye Of The Storm**" on »The Friday Rock Show« LP BBC Records 1981 + »NWOBHM '79 Revisited« Do-LP/Do-CD Phonogram 1990
[Appears unofficially on »Sweet Savage« bootleg, different version appears on »Killing Time« CD]
"**Lady Of The Night**" on »Now In Session« LP Downtown Radio 1982
[Studio take, live version appears unofficially on »Sweet Savage« bootleg]
"**Killing Time**" on »NWOBHM Vol.1« Bootleg CD 1992 + »The Metallic-Era« CD Neat Metal 1996
[Different version appears on »Killing Time« CD]
"**I Am Nothing**" on »Hard Roxx Taster Vol.5« CD Private 1998
[Free with 'Hard Roxx' magazine]

SYAR

Martin Berkeley (v)
Grant Kirkhope (g)
Buzz Nixon (g)
Roger Gibbons (b)
Nigel Harrison (d)

The peculiarly-named SYAR were a pretty classy metal proposition who took their first faltering steps in Yorkshire's flourishing rock scene in 1982 or thereabouts. Within a comparatively short space of time, they had begun to make a few useful inroads into the club circuit, and proceeded to lay down a speculative demo or two just to see if anyone was particularly impressed. In the event, it took a year or so for anything major to happen for the lads, but they ultimately won favour with those at Future Earth Records, who, after assessing their chances of breaking these hopefuls in Britain, eventually elected to pass the quintet on to their European counterparts at Mausoleum. With a freshly-signed contract clutched in their hands, the young Tykes locked themselves away in Strawberry Studios and eventually resurfaced with a pretty good debut effort. Their »Death Before Dishonour« long-player appeared on Mausoleum in 1984, and was an opus which sounded rather more European in style than most of their British contemporaries. Although the cover image of a warrior valiantly attempting to slay a giant sea serpent (bloody show-off, anything to impress the girls) tended to suggest that the LP might contain some laughably poor, sub-GRIM REAPER heroics, it transpired that SYAR didn't quite fit in with either the power metal scene (most commonly found in the West Midlands) or the riffy, twin-guitar onslaught of the East End bands.

Instead, the group occupied a musical region which few of their NWOBHM contemporaries inhabited, although, in terms of the more memorable compositions (such as "Taking A Gamble", "High Flyer" and "Deep In The Night"), their closest UK allies would, perhaps, be MIDAS, EAZY STREET and (at their very heaviest) even the DESOLATION ANGELS. Aside from the aforementioned inclusions, there are a couple of more epic numbers (the title track itself is particularly lengthy), although they're not overly ambitious or pretentious. All in all, it's an extremely listenable piece, but it's another which (as Future Earth seem to have predicted) might not have performed quite as well in the British market as it did overseas. Even so, the long-player received a fair bit of welcome praise upon its release ('Kerrang' even afforded it the honour of a decent review, although their lazy comparisons with SAXON suggested they hadn't listened too far beyond the opening track), with "Speeder" even attaining a high place in the Heavy Metal Chart in 'Melody Maker'. The outfit continued to tour for the remainder of the year to promote the album, unveiling a few unreleased compositions such as "Get Up, Get Down" and "Alone Again" in the process, and it looked as though they definitely planned to record a follow-up at some stage.

Once again, however, things were to fall apart within a remarkably short space of time, with three of the five members (Grant Kirkhope, Nigel Harrison and Roger Gibbons) defecting to another local act, the more varied and commercially-successful MAINEEAXE (taking some of their original compositions with them), after a fairly brief interval. With most of the original outfit having moved on to pastures new, therefore, it would appear that the luckless SYAR ceased to exist almost immediately, which is a bit of a shame, and we'll never know for sure if they had a cracking second album up their sleeves. Their sole LP, however, has latterly been exhumed by the fly-by-night Mausoleum Classix label and reissued on CD, along with long-deleted albums by the likes of LIMELIGHT, CHASAR, EF BAND etc., although it's worth noting that the absolute legality of this action has actually been called into question. You might not go to jail for buying these releases, but please be aware that they almost certainly weren't approved by any of the bands themselves, and royalties have not been forthcoming thus far.

LP's
»**Death Before Dishonour**« Mausoleum 1984

CD's
»**Death Before Dishonour**« Mausoleum Classix 1994
[Unofficial release]

S.Y.Z.

Roy Henson (v)
Mark Gibson (g)
Mick Atkins (g)
Tony Speakman (b)
Wez (d)

With the gradual disintegration of Nottinghamshire's original NWOBHM scene towards the mid-80's came the formation of S.Y.Z. (allegedly the SCREAMING YELLOW ZONKERS...hey, that's a *really* great name, guys...honestly), a knockabout outfit who were hardly likely to become major-label heroes at any point. Nevertheless, this *'supergroup'* of scenesters (with the notable inclusion of HELL stalwart Tony Speakman and Mark Gibson of PARALEX) laid down the tracks "Rock & Roll Children" and "Heavy Rider" for release as a debut single in around 1986, which more or less coincided with the final demise of both of the aforementioned outfits. With the quintet delivering a good-time, irreverent sound reminiscent of a carefree mixture of METAL MIRROR, FUGITIVE and PROWLER (with a hint of NO FAITH-style biker rock thrown in too), the music is pretty undemanding on the ears but still reasonably satisfying to the NWOBHM palate, and is entirely consistent with much of the material that was doing the rounds five years earlier. While they may have been regarded as something of an anachronism by the mid-80's, I'll bet this bunch were an absolute riot when and if they ever hit the clubs, and they no doubt attracted an unruly rabble of motley individuals who worshipped them from afar. Their self-financed 7", released without a picture sleeve and with minimal details provided on the labels, appears to have been a one-off foray into the vinyl world, however, and is known to exist in truly minuscule quantities today.

7" Singles
»**Rock & Roll Children**« Private 1986?

T34

Steve Williams (v)
Mick Clee (g)
Colin Stuart (b)
John Baker (d)

Lurking behind the undeniably nondescript moniker of T34 (a name with military significance, as I'm sure MARDUK would tell you, given that it refers to a class of tank) lies a rather quirky ensemble from the East End of London, although this bunch didn't conform to the usual stereotype of IRON MAIDEN wannabes by any means. Ironically, however, guitarist Mick Clee was himself a member of the legendary SMILER in the dim and distant past, but he was one of the minority who wasn't actually called up to the MAIDEN ranks at any point. First appearing on the capital's gig guides early in 1981 (with regular appearances at the legendary Ruskin Arms taking place in the following months), T34 proceeded to become a permanent fixture on the live circuit, carving out a niche for themselves by delivering an original brand of metal which (for better or worse) separated them from the rest of the pack. The ambitious foursome were clearly keen to do their own thing in terms of their musical approach, and ultimately ended up veering away from the facile heavy metal style, although, in the early days at least, these guys certainly cranked up those guitars in fairly major fashion.

Having developed a suitably expansive and loyal following with their endless club appearances, the band soon began making a few trips to the recording studio to see what they could come up with as a unit. Their first batch of material appears not to have been particularly widely circulated, however, and it looks as though the musicians simply decided to debut with a self-financed slice of vinyl in order to spread their name further. The first T34 single hit the shops even before the end of the year, and this coupled "Mind Your Own Business" with "Computer Dating", the latter being one of those dreaded 'comedy B-sides' favoured by contemporaries such as CHEEKY and E.S.P., but which are better left to the likes of IAN DURY or the SMALL FACES. In spite of its blatant shortcomings, however, the track features some pretty impressive guitar work, so it's a pity they didn't go for the all-out NWOBHM assault. The reverse was a markedly more enjoyable listening experience, though, this being a semi-heavy and immensely catchy number with elements of such outfits as BLAZER BLAZER, GOGMAGOG, EARTHBOUND and even (wait for it) JAPAN, although it's an extremely distinctive style which fails to elicit many direct comparisons (JEDDAH, perhaps) within the NWOBHM spectrum.

Moving into 1982, things started going the outfit's way in many respects, as they began to enjoy a limited amount of press coverage in the likes of 'Kerrang'. On the live front, meanwhile, they were incredibly fortunate to be added to the bill of the Hackney Festival (organised by the Hells Angels, no less) in July of that year, an event headlined by MOTÖRHEAD and SAXON, and also due to feature SPIDER, ANGEL WITCH, LIGHTNING RAIDERS and SLEEK. In the event, however, it looks as though T34 and ANGEL WITCH stayed away, the latter deciding that the Mildenhall Festival was a better option. Nevertheless, 'Kerrang' subsequently elected to review one of T34's own gigs in the capital, offering generally favourable comments ('*interesting, danceable metal*') about the set, which included numbers such as "A Look From Your Eye", "Fire Down Below" and their rather odd choice of cover version in the form of "Rock On", a track originally performed by another East End hero, DAVID ESSEX. Towards the end of that year, the outfit (who had now recruited full-time keyboard player Wayne Baker to the fold) decided to issue their second single, evidently hoping to build upon their new-found popularity. Strangely, though, they chose to make their offbeat interpretation of "Rock On" the main focus of attention, pairing it with the equally dubious "Looking After Me (Looking After You)", a track, bordering on synth-pop, which owed little to their debut and distanced the lads from the NWOBHM movement in major fashion.

With the single being issued in a rather arty sleeve that would be far better suited to housing a VISAGE effort, I reckon the group had misjudged their audience in a big way. Ultimately, it looks as though »Rock On« went down like the proverbial lead balloon among the bemused rock community of the day, presumably leaving the band to take stock of the situation and think again about what they actually wanted to achieve. Although the lads were already keeping a very low profile by the end of 1983, and had almost certainly split by the middle of the decade, it's quite possible that they reformed for a few appearances in 1989, as their name was advertised for a gig or two at venues such as the Walthamstow Royal Standard at the time, and it seems highly improbable that a second outfit could somehow have adopted the same identity. In all probability, you're unlikely to encounter either of the T34 singles very often (their debut is by far the rarer, and only a tiny minority seem to have been housed within a flimsy, odd-looking picture sleeve), although these shouldn't be regarded as high-priority items by the majority of modern-day collectors.

7" Singles
»**Mind Your Own Business**« Divage Records 1981
»**Rock On**« Galaxy Records 1982

TANK

Alasdair 'Algy' Ward (v, b)
Peter Brabbs (g)
Mark Brabbs (d)

For all its limitations, it's fair to say that the NWOBHM could lay claim to a couple of notable achievements as it began to take shape: for one thing, it inspired hundreds of bands to form and do their own thing in the first instance (admittedly, the vast majority failed to amount to anything), when large sections of the media were trying to brainwash everyone into believing that heavy metal was a thing of the past. Secondly, the music of the genre's pioneers provided a welcome starting point (sadly, many made no attempts to do anything except imitate) for many existing or newly-formed acts who were struggling to establish an identity and who were desperately seeking a relevant style with which they could affiliate themselves. For South London's much-loved TANK, who came together in the spring of 1980, this handy renaissance in heavy music was something which hadn't come a moment too soon, the members having served time in various knockabout punk and rock'n'roll outfits over the preceding few years, none of which were going anywhere in particular. Experienced frontman Algy Ward, for example, had latterly been helping out in the ranks of THE DAMNED, while the Brabbs brothers (Peter and Mark) had been in a small-time act called the HEROES, although they gravitated together with the express intention of creating something which would appeal to both punks and metalheads.

Taking the unambiguous name of TANK to signify their heavy and forceful personality, the trio set about the daunting task of fusing together punk attitude, rock'n'roll guitar and NWOBHM dynamics, and, in all fairness, they made a pretty good fist of it. In fact, they were to experience a remarkably short period of probation before things started happening, and their strong links with the members and management of MOTÖRHEAD (which went back several years) would serve them well in their forthcoming activities. First of all, this amicable relationship resulted in TANK's debut gig (supporting none other than GIRLSCHOOL) taking the form of an enviably high-profile affair, and the lads duly became a sought-after live attraction, blandished by promoters and clubs throughout the capital and beyond. In due course, the threesome came to the attention of Kamaflage Records (whose only other signings of note appear to have been TYTAN and BARON ROJO) at some point in 1981, and, with a contract having been drawn up with immense haste, TANK's first vinyl assault was soon being planned with all the finesse of a top-secret military operation. In a classic pincer movement (a 7" version in the UK, a 12" version in Europe), the »Don't Walk Away« EP was unleashed upon an unsuspecting public, and saw TANK bringing elements of (for example) MOTÖRHEAD, EDDIE COCHRAN and the RUTS to the fray. It was all an ungodly racket, but strangely compelling, and the EP (completed

by "Shellshock" and "Hammer On") was soon endearing itself to an entire generation of rock fans.

TANK might not have been the first (or last) heavy act who attempted to develop a bit of crossover potential (the likes of the LIGHTNING RAIDERS, ROGUE MALE and MAYHEM all offered their variation on the punk/metal theme at one time or another), but they were certainly the most successful exponents of this kind of material, and their much-anticipated gigs were soon attracting a remarkably cosmopolitan selection of music fans. Towards the end of 1981, they were given another big break when their chums in MOTÖRHEAD offered TANK the opportunity to accompany them on their forthcoming European jaunt, and the trio proceeded to enjoy a productive series of gigs throughout the continent. Returning to the UK, they began work on their debut album for Kamaflage, and the »Filth Hounds Of Hades« set duly emerged in the spring of 1982, at around the time that TANK were undertaking the second part of MOTÖRHEAD's tour, this time covering the British dates. The long-player, produced by Fast Eddie Clarke himself, was a typically brusque affair, although the individual tracks were all weighty and memorable enough, and it featured several numbers which would become mainstays of the outfit's live set for years to come, notably "Blood, Guts And Beer", "T.W.D.A.M.O.", "(He Fell In Love With A) Stormtrooper" and "Turn Your Head Around". It also gave the first indications that TANK might just be a tiny bit obsessed with the old war malarkey, with overtly-militaristic titles such as "Heavy Artillery" paving the way for the numerous belligerent compositions of later years.

All things considered, it was a most successful debut, and sales of the record (which initially came with a free single featuring a live version of "Don't Walk Away" and the otherwise-unavailable "The Snake") were soon amounting to quite impressive figures, so it came as no surprise that a brace of tie-in singles were subsequently trotted out to rake in a bit more ready cash for Kamaflage. The lengthily-titled »(He Fell In Love With A) Stormtrooper« appeared in the form of a picture disc (in the UK, at least), backed with a live version of "Blood, Guts And Beer", while the blistering »Turn Your Head Around« (the A-side being the closest to the NWOBHM archetype on the album) also included the exclusive "Steppin' On A Landmine" on the reverse. Both sold in healthy quantities, and the world seemed to be TANK's oyster, their next move being to record that inevitable session for the 'Friday Rock Show'. Broadcast on the 30th of April 1982, the band's debut showcase saw them delivering powerful versions of "Stormtrooper", "Heavy Artillery", "Hammer On" and "Don't Walk Away", and a warm reception from listeners suggested that there was now no looking back for TANK. The trio continued to play live at every opportunity, and began to be added to more prestigious bills, with appearances at the Wrexham Festival and the rather more illustrious Reading Festival following in due course. Before long, though, they were being encouraged to return to the studio and commit another long-player to vinyl.

The group's second album, »Power Of The Hunter«, appeared towards the end of that year, its release coinciding with their extensive UK tour in support of the immensely popular DIAMOND HEAD. Predictably, TANK had seen little or no reason to change a winning formula, and delivered a fairly analogous record the second time around. It wasn't quite as intense or overpowering as their debut had been, though, and some of the material seemed a bit too restrained for its own good (threatening to drift into mediocre hard rock territory at times), although they approached top form on compositions such as "Walking Barefoot Over Glass", "T.A.N.K." and their energetic cover of "Crazy Horses" by THE OSMONDS (the original is actually a fairly powerful number, so it's not quite as obtuse a selection as you might think). Only one ancillary single was to emerge this time, though, coupling the aforementioned "Crazy Horses" with the exclusive "Filth Bitch Boogie", although neither the long-player nor single performed particularly well in terms of sales, and TANK were soon coming to terms with what must have seemed like an overnight loss of popularity. 1983 proved to be a difficult year for the group all round, with the collapse of Kamaflage leaving them without a deal, while personnel problems led to some hasty rearrangement and restructuring. At first, however, the changes were pretty minor, as former AXIS/WHITE SPIRIT guitarist Mick Tucker was brought in to bolster the outfit's sound somewhat, and the newly-expanded TANK had relatively little difficulty in winning a new deal after impressing Music For Nations.

TANK's first album for their new label appeared in mid-1983, and »This Means War« represented a fairly radical departure for a bunch of so-called 'MOTÖRHEAD clones', the long-player seeing a confident move towards longer and more ambitious compositions. It was, at times, quite an accessible (there were even keyboards in places, something which would have been anathema in the band's early days) collection of tracks, and the presence of some rather more flashy guitar work showed that the much-mocked TANK might actually be a more substantial and forward-looking act than many casual observers had originally assumed. Efforts such as "Just Like Something From Hell", "Hot Lead Cold Steel" and "(If We Go) We Go Down Fighting" were all very listenable, while "This Means War" and "Echoes Of A Distant Battle" constituted the obligatory war-related numbers. A single was released (in both 7" and 12" formats) to capitalise on the album's already-impressive sales, with "Echoes Of A Distant Battle" being used as the main track and some exclusive selections included as B-sides. Not only was TANK's latest material indicative of an unquestionable return to form, it had seen the quartet making a significant progression into far more accomplished territory, and Music For Nations were keen to hang onto their new musical investment, commissioning a follow-up release without too much delay.

However, the band hadn't quite finished with their enforced restructuring, and it was a considerable disappointment for the fans that TANK couldn't retain a stable line-up in the wake of the latest LP's release, something which pretty much scuppered any touring plans. During this transitionary period, both of the Brabbs brothers were eventually to depart by the end of 1983 (Pete apparently disappeared off the face of the earth, whereas Mark moved on to DUMPY'S RUSTY NUTS, although he also took time off to help out in a diverse range of musical projects such as THE BLOOD, PAUL SAMSON'S EMPIRE, UK, SAVIOUR, RIGHTEOUS and BAM BALAM, and he's now to be found working with yet another heavy act called the RAZOR BABIES), leaving Algy Ward and Mick Tucker (who was, by this stage, playing a major role on the songwriting front) to rebuild the project around themselves by drafting in drummer Graeme Crallan, one of Tucker's erstwhile colleagues from WHITE SPIRIT. Subsequently, however, the musicians concluded that it would be best to persevere with the four-piece structure which had worked so effectively on »This Means War«, and so experienced session man Cliff Evans (who had latterly been mucking about with nondescript club performers such as CHICKEN SHACK) was handed the vital role of second guitarist.

With things back on schedule at last, TANK were apparently able to make a handful of live appearances once again (although Algy Ward, having been keen to develop his skills as a producer, would become somewhat distracted by his subsequent involvement with the recording of WARFARE's debut album), but the quartet eventually turned their thoughts to their own studio activities. Long-player number four, »Honour And Blood« (their second for Music For Nations), was recorded over a fairly lengthy period during 1984, finally emerging quite late in the year, by which time the members of TANK were already immersed in the task of preparing for a fairly extensive tour of large European venues with none other than METALLICA. It looked, on the face of it, like a marriage made in heavy metal heaven, but I'm sometimes tempted to wonder if this was the case after all. I assume, in the absence of any contradictory evidence, that the two outfits got on perfectly amicably at the time (the Brits were more than happy to credit the Yanks on a record sleeve or two), but TANK were a notable and fairly inexplicable omission on Lars Ulrich's »NWOBHM '79 Revisited« compilation (I suppose they had to draw the line somewhere, or it could easily have ended up as a ten-album set) all those years later...

The newly-released TANK album turned out to be a hit-and-miss affair which largely lacked the impact of its predecessor, although they had kept the extended song structures and dumped any notions of commercial appeal by losing the keyboard backing and rejecting any overly-tuneful interludes. Even so, several of the featured compositions still failed to leave all that much of a positive impression, although the situation was salvaged from potential catastrophe by such inspired inclusions as "Chain Of Fools" (a rocked-up soul/r'n'b number from the 60's which had originally been written for ARETHA FRANKLIN), "W.M.L.A" (a song in a remarkably different style, with an extremely refined vocal performance from Algy Ward) and the title track itself. At times, TANK had begun to resemble certain NWOBHM hopefuls, notably SABRE (a bunch from the same neck of the woods) and CRUCIFIXION (on "Too Tired To Wait For Love" and the tenderly-titled "Kill", for example), although the overall strength of their newest material just wasn't sufficiently high to consolidate their position as national heroes. It was a great pity, but the ruthless Music For Nations had precious little sympathy for TANK's plight, and, in the wake of this perceived commercial failure, no further albums or singles would appear on this particular label. Undeterred, the lads continued to ply their trade during 1985, although they were forced to recruit a replacement drummer early in the year when Graeme Crallan packed his bags (he later had spells with minor acts BRITON and PANAMA), but new member Gary Taylor (a veteran of such outfits as STRE-

ETFIGHTER and BUFFALO) turned out to be an eminently capable substitute.

With no contract and nothing to lose, TANK made their way across the Atlantic for a mid-1985 series of appearances in the States, whereupon they discovered audiences who afforded them a pretty rapturous reception whenever and wherever they played. This was something of a surprise for the lads themselves, and the members rapidly came to the conclusion that they might be better off staying in America and attempting to kickstart their career by means of hard graft in the live environment. Back in Britain, however, the newly-established Raw Power label was in the process of assembling one of their infamous retrospective collections (see also VENOM, TOKYO BLADE, RAVEN etc.),

Photo: Tobias Thiem

which appeared later that year as the suitably-titled »Armour Plated«. It was an entirely representative (indeed, it covered most of their back catalogue) selection of TANK material, and it might well have raked in a few much-needed pennies at the time, but the lack of exclusive (or even hard-to-get) tracks must have been a serious disappointment for most of the die-hard fans. Nevertheless, the persevering TANK continued to write new material and play some increasingly low-key gigs (some of which were in support of the touring RAVEN) in the States in order to gauge public reaction, although it took quite a while to convince any record labels to plough some investment into their future projects. In the end, however, GWR Records (home of, you guessed it, MOTÖRHEAD) were inspired to commission another TANK album, which finally emerged as an eponymous effort (with one of the least interesting covers I've ever seen) towards the end of 1987.

The »Tank« set had actually been recorded in 1986, although the tapes had languished in the studio while the band patiently waited for a deal to come their way. In the interim, guitarist Mick Tucker had decided to return to the UK and go back to his day job, leaving TANK to struggle on as a three-piece concern. The album itself consisted of a pretty typical bunch of TANK originals, although it was beginning to sound rather tired and uninspired, as though they were simply going through the motions by this stage. Side one was particularly weak, with a selection of lengthy, laboured compositions which went absolutely nowhere, although things picked up a bit on side two, where "The Enemy Below" and "It Fell From The Sky" were a tad more lively and memorable. It didn't prevent the long-player receiving an utter drubbing from the vast majority of journalists, though, and even the faithful patronage of Tommy Vance at the 'Friday Rock Show' failed to reverse too many opinions. Predictably, the group made light of all the criticism, insisting that they had a fanatical following in the States who would always welcome them with open arms, as Algy Ward explained: 'Throughout the world there are a lot of people who want us, but not necessarily in England. We gave up with England years ago. Out there [America] rock'n'roll isn't just fashion, it simply happens.' (Ref: Kerrang No.184, April 1988).

In fact, the truth of the matter was that the latest TANK album hadn't even been released in the States at that time, and it wasn't until 1989 that Restless Records finally picked up on the LP and gave it a welcome American release. Nevertheless, the outfit (who now featured former FASTWAY drummer Steve Clarke in place of the recently-departed Gary Taylor) hastily arranged a series of promotional dates to boost sales in America. For some reason, however, even their supposedly-loyal fans across the pond were equally unimpressed by TANK's latest studio offerings, and this entire tour appears to have been a dismally-attended and disastrous affair. Since it seemed that the dejected members of TANK apparently hadn't a friend in the world by the end of 1989, the lads reluctantly called it a day rather than letting things drag on much longer. Algy Ward was still an in-demand musician, however, and his eventual return to the UK allowed him to play an important role in the activities of post-NWOBHM ventures such as ATOMGOD (with the likes of Bill Liesegang from XERO), WARHEAD (with Evo from WARFARE) and the considerably-heavier NECROPOLIS (basically a revamped version of ATOMGOD). He was, incidentally, joined in both the ATOMGOD and NECROPOLIS projects by erstwhile colleague Steve Clarke, so the TANK connection was pretty strong in each case.

By 1997, however, NECROPOLIS were taking something of a break while the members attended to unrelated projects (their last offering was the »End Of The Line« album in 1996), which allowed Algy Ward to turn his attention to various compositions which had been co-written with Mick Tucker since TANK's demise. Having decided that the world deserved a chance to hear some of these unreleased tracks, the frontman reassembled a version of the outfit with the assistance of Cliff Evans (who had latterly been employed by Paul Dianno's KILLERS) and Mick Tucker, while the much-travelled Steve Hopgood (another recent alumnus of the KILLERS school) took his place at the drumkit. The quartet then proceeded to undertake a modest tour of Germany (a land with a near-fanatical following, with national institution SODOM having committed no less than three TANK originals to vinyl over the years), where the reception was so favourable (particularly at their triumphal Wacken Festival appearance) that a full-scale reformation was instigated, the first fruits of which came in the form of their »The Return Of The Filth Hounds-Live« CD, issued by Rising Sun in 1998. The album featured recordings from their recent German tour, plus a couple of exclusive new studio tracks, and the release was welcomed by many of TANK's long-standing fans around the world. With the outfit having now established itself as a going concern once more, their activities have recently included a handful of UK gigs (appearing alongside GIRLSCHOOL at some of them) and further European touring. They also played an important role in the '20th Anniversary' NWOBHM festival held in Japan in the latter part of 1999, and appear on the live CD set released to commemorate the event.

It's worth noting that one of the reasons lying behind Algy Ward's decision to reform TANK was an apparent endorsement which came from an unexpected (to say the very least) source. His long-time associate, Cliff Evans, was happy to provide an explanation of the band's collective motivation at the time: *'Obviously, the interest in TANK was always still there. Looking back, I remember reading an article in an Italian rock magazine, in which Kurt Cobain was interviewed a few weeks before his suicide. He was asked what his major influences were, and he actually said that one of the biggest influences was TANK. When NIRVANA started out, they often experimented by messing around with TANK songs.'* (Ref: That's It, Issue 11, 1997). No, don't laugh, it's wicked to mock the afflicted. Come to think of it, though, it actually makes a fair bit of sense, and I suppose that certain acts (particularly MUDHONEY and GREEN RIVER, and possibly even NIRVANA themselves) who came to prominence later in the decade *could* have taken on board a few influences from the early punk/metal crossover of TANK and their ilk. So there you have it, it turns out that Algy Ward's mob were officially the forefathers of grunge. Who'd have thought it?

LP's
»Filth Hounds Of Hades« Kamaflage 1982
[Some copies with free single featuring "The Snake" and live version of "Don't Walk Away"]
»Filth Hounds Of Hades« Kamaflage/DJM Records 1982
[French issue with different cover]
»Los Perros Inmundos Del Infierno« Kamaflage 1982
[Spanish issue of »Filth Hounds Of Hades« with titles in Spanish]
»Power Of The Hunter« Kamaflage 1982
»This Means War« Music For Nations 1983
[UK issue, also released as limited edition picture disc]
»This Means War« Roadrunner 1983
[Dutch issue]
»Honour And Blood« Music For Nations 1984/Roadrunner 1984
[UK/Dutch issue]
»Armour Plated« Raw Power 1985
[Double compilation album]
»Tank« GWR Records 1987
[Original UK issue]
»Tank« Restless Records 1989
[Later US issue]

12" EP's
»Don't Walk Away« Kamaflage 1981
[German-only issue, A-side and "Hammer On" non-LP, "Shellscock" different to album version]
»Echoes Of A Distant Battle« Music For Nations 1983

[Both "The Man Who Never Was" and "Which-catchewedmycuckoo" non-LP]

7" EP's
»Don't Walk Away« Kamaflage 1981
[A-side and "Hammer On" non-LP, "Shellshock" different to album version]
»Don't Walk Away« Kamaflage/DJM Records 1981
[Spanish issue in different sleeve]

7" Singles
»Don't Walk Away« (live) Kamaflage 1982
[Free with some copies of »Filth Hounds Of Hades« LP, A-side different to EP version, B-side "The Snake" non-LP]
»(He Fell In Love With A) Stormtrooper« Kamaflage 1982
[UK issue, limited edition picture disc, B-side "Blood Guts And Beer" (live), both tracks different to album versions]
»(He Fell In Love With A) Stormtrooper« Kamaflage 1982
[Spanish issue with different sleeve image and titles in Spanish, B-side studio version of "Blood Guts And Beer"]
»Turn Your Head Around« Kamaflage 1982
[B-side "Steppin' On A Landmine" non-LP]
»Crazy Horses« Kamaflage 1982
[A-side different to album version, B-side "Filth Bitch Boogie" non-LP]
»Crazy Horses« Kamaflage 1982
[Spanish issue with different reverse sleeve]
»Echoes Of A Distant Battle« Music For Nations 1983
[B-side "The Man Who Never Was" non-LP]

CD's
»Tank« GWR Records 1987
[Japanese-only issue]
»This Means War« Roadrunner 198?
[Japanese issue]
»Honour And Blood« Roadrunner 198?
[Japanese issue]
»Filth Hounds Of Hades« Repertoire 1992
»Power Of The Hunter« Repertoire 1992
»This Means War« Apollon 1993
[Japanese issue with one bonus track]
»Honour And Blood« Apollon 1993
[Japanese issue with one bonus track]
»This Means War« High Vaultage 1997
[With one bonus track]
»Honour And Blood« High Vaultage 1997
[With one bonus track]
»The Return Of The Filth Hounds-Live« Rising Sun 1998
[Live release with bonus studio tracks]
»Metal Crusade 99« Pony Canyon 1999

[Japanese-only live double CD set, shared with SAMSON, PRAYING MANTIS and TRESPASS]

Compilation Appearances
"Don't Walk Away" on »Pop Rocky« LP Metronome 1981
"Hammer On" on »Pop Rocky« LP Metronome 1981
"Laughing In The Face Of Death" on »Metal Battle« LP Neat 1983/Roadrunner 1983
"Just Like Something From Hell" on »Hell On Earth« LP Music For Nations 1983
"The War Drags Ever On" on »Welcome To The Metal Zone« Do-LP Music For Nations 1985
"Run Like Hell" on »Metal Killers Kollection I« Do-LP Castle Communications 1985 + »Metal Killers« LP Raw Power 1986 + »Rock Out!« Do-CD Emporio 1996
"Echoes Of A Distant Battle" on »Music For Nations-The Singles Album« Do-LP Music For Nations 1986
"Blood Guts And Beer" on »Metal Killers« LP Raw Power 1986 + »Metal Masters« 4-CD Box Castle Communications 1993 + »Rock Out!« Do-CD Emporio 1996
"Reign Of Thunder" on »Metal Masters« 4-CD Box Castle Communications 1993
"Run Like Hell" on »NWOBHM Vol.7« Bootleg CD 1996
[Alternate version]
"Echoes Of A Distant Battle" (live) on »NWOBHM Live« CD Emporio 1997
"This Means War" (live) on »NWOBHM Live« CD Emporio 1997
"That's What Dreams Are Made Of" (live) on »NWOBHM Live« CD Emporio 1997

TARGET UK

Pete Stacy (v, b)
Andy Hart (g)
Dave Hackett (d)

As with the VOYAGER situation, I would imagine that TARGET UK merely added the suffix to avoid potential confusion with another outfit (in this case, presumably the lightweight Canadian TARGET from the mid-70's, since the powerful Belgians didn't trundle along until later), rather than displaying an excessive amount of national pride. In any case, this heavy Worcestershire trio appear to have released just the one single back in 1985, which is a shame, as they were one of the more talented and energetic of the British outfits to have emerged towards the middle of the decade. Their vinyl offering, expertly produced by John Thomas of BUDGIE, displayed a highly competent style of catchy, hard-rocking material, with the snappy "Alive And Kickin'" (a very lighthearted ditty with a 'Frankenstein' theme) borrowing from DIAMOND HEAD's "Trick Or Treat", whereas the lengthier "F.B.I." was a more commercial number falling somewhere between ACE LANE, CHARIOT and STORYTELLER. All things considered, both tracks were laudably well-written and capably performed, and the standard of musicianship and enthusiasm was remarkably high for such a young act. Deservedly, the two-tracker got the thumbs-up from those at 'Kerrang', although it doesn't appear to have won the group many new fans in the long term.

Judging by the title of the B-side, it would appear that these lads may have had a bit of an unhealthy fascination with all things American, although it remains something of a mystery why a small-time musician from the West Midlands would be all that concerned about the possibility of a transatlantic criminal investigations organisation pursuing him for alleged firearms offences. Mind you, I suppose it's slightly more romantic than singing 'the local village policeman wants to question me about some missing apples', which would, quite possibly, have been the more realistic eventuality. Housed within a generic, monochrome picture sleeve, the single is, in spite of its relatively recent date of issue, a rarely-seen (and fairly highly-valued) NWOBHM collectable whose main (indeed, only) claim to fame was hitting the 'Local Chart' section in 'Kerrang' a year after its release. The individual band members appear not to have gone on to other projects (maybe they're all doing fifteen to twenty in the state penitentiary) and there don't seem to be any additional TARGET UK recordings in circulation, so we're left to wonder, yet again, if the situation might have been different if they'd been around at the start of the decade.

7" Singles
»Alive And Kickin'« Flying V Records 1985

TEMPEST

Rue Phillips (v, g)
Lee Faulkner (b)
Steve 'Dingo' Bell (d)

It transpires that the self-styled 'power trio' known as TEMPEST (not to be confused with later outfits from the USA and Germany, or with some identically-named British heavyweights who recorded for Bronze in the 70's) were actually a side-project (or possibly an extremely ill-conceived alter ego) of Midlands rockers SMOKIN ROADIE (see separate entry), and this particular incarnation of the band seems to have been in existence barely long enough to oversee the release of their curious »Hell Fire« two-tracker in 1985. The A-side (produced by the eccentric Roy Wood of WIZZARD) is a pretty feeble and unpalatable offering, a chart-friendly piece of disco-metal (yes, really) which appears to feature the profoundly distasteful use of a drum machine. Ugh. On the other hand, flipside "Waistin' Time" is an infinitely more enjoyable listening experience, this being a slice of infectious, upbeat NWOBHM in the general style of early TOKYO BLADE. All immensely confusing, on the whole, and I'm sure the rock community failed to make all that much sense of the 7" upon its release, leading to predictably modest sales figures.

Your guess is as good as mine as to why TEMPEST elected to showcase two numbers in such markedly dissimilar modes, but I suppose it's reasonable to speculate that the musicians involved might just have taking full advantage of their assumed identity to try something a bit different. It didn't really work to their advantage in the short term, though, and the whole episode was brushed under the proverbial carpet before long. Nevertheless, the 7" (issued in a distinctive red sleeve with a live-action shot) is well worth picking up (if only for the B-side) if you see it cheaply enough. Following on from this poorly-received piece of experimentation, the members of TEMPEST simply reverted to the dependable SMOKIN ROADIE moniker and touted their wares around for a further couple of years (which, surprisingly enough, included a fairly productive residency in the States), although their plans to release an album in 1987 had to be abandoned in the wake of overwhelming label disinterest. Eventually, however, the central characters resurfaced under the unfamiliar guise of THE NOW (not a unique name by any stretch of the imagination), who belatedly got around to issuing a Japanese-only CD (entitled »Overnight Stay«) in 1989, the latter featuring a reworked (and considerably heavier) version of "Hell Fire".

7" Singles
»Hell Fire« Mak Rekords 1985
[Alternate version of A-side later appeared on »Overnight Stay« album by THE NOW]

TERRAPLANE

Danny Bowes (v)
Luke Morley (g)
Nick Linden (b)
Gary James (d)

The South London legends known as TERRAPLANE evolved from the rather less successful NUTHIN FANCY (see separate entry) in the second half of 1981 (confusingly, an identically-named GROUNDHOGS offshoot had been operational a year or two previously), when Luke Morley and Danny Bowes recruited the rhythm section of Nick Linden and Gary 'Harry' James (aka Gary Aitken) from little-known local hopefuls MOONTIER and WHITE NOIZ, respectively. The initial line-up additionally featured the services of second guitarist Tony Myers (who later resurfaced in the unrenowned SING SING), although the lads must have concluded pretty rapidly that they could manage just as well without him. After spending the best part of a year in the shadows, writing an all-new repertoire and playing a few low-key gigs, the quartet were fortunate enough to be allocated a slot on the 'Friday Rock Show'. Broadcast on the 20th of August 1982, their session showcased "Gimme The Money", "If You Could See Yourself", "The Beginning Of The End" and "Let The Wheels Go Round", four numbers which would all resurface as single B-sides in due course. A mere week later, the lads were playing a *slightly* larger gig than they had been used to, as they nervously took to the stage at the Reading Festival (friends in high places, obviously), unsure of how the paying public would respond to their raunchy rock efforts. Fortunately, it all went swimmingly, and two excerpts from the set ("Turn Me Loose" and "I Want Your Body") subsequently appeared on the commemorative double album issued by Mean Records as a souvenir of the event. It was apparent from the outset that TERRAPLANE were operating in a highly similar style to the original NUTHIN FANCY prototype, their semi-bluesy, mid-paced compositions bringing forth fairly straightforward comparisons with the likes of TRUX, NATIONAL GOLD and HOLLAND, owing as much of a debt to BAD COMPANY as the NWOBHM movement itself.

By the end of the year, the group had already supported acts such as BUDGIE and GRAND PRIX, and it wasn't too long before they were picked up for a one-off single by the diverse City label (see also SPIDER and GIRLSCHOOL), culminating in the release of »I Survive« (in both 7" and 12" formats) in 1983. It was a strong debut with an undeniably commercial edge, and it became something of an instant hit among devotees of the more traditional, hard-rocking outfits of the day. Within a matter of months, a contract was being waved under their collective noses by the influential Epic label, and the lads didn't waste much time before agreeing to the terms. They were soon hard at work in the studio, and had recorded at least an album's worth of material before the end of the year, but, for some reason, Epic chose to delay the release of a long-playing effort until they had tested the water with a single or two. In the event, no less than four (»I Can't Live Without Your Love«, a reissue of »I Survive«, »When You're Hot« and »Talking To Myself«) were trotted out before the company finally had the conviction to release a full album at the start of 1986, by which time the outfit (who had been featured on the BBC's 'In Concert' programme alongside TOBRUK (in the interim) were becoming more than a little frustrated at not getting their songs heard by the public. Nevertheless, »Black And White« (the working title had been the bizarre »Talking To You On The Great White Telephone«, a colourful euphemism which was presumably vetoed on grounds of taste) sold in healthy quantities, the band having fleshed out their sound somewhat by employing additional guitarists (the much-travelled Dave Colwell, formerly with the likes of HOTLINE, ANGEL STREET and 720, plus the gifted Rudi Riviere, erstwhile DRAGONFLY and SAPPHIRE axeman) to help out during the recording process. In due course, Riviere (who had, up until that point, still been lending a hand in various minor acts such as BLACK MAIL and the NEW TORPEDOS) was assimilated into TERRAPLANE as a full-time fifth member, and he was soon contributing to their studio activities.

The lads promoted the album with a series of well-received gigs, but wasted little time before starting work on a follow-up, having written a great deal of material while waiting for »Black And White« to dawdle its way into the shops. Their second set, entitled »Moving Target«, turned out to be a considerably more lightweight pop/rock affair (accompanied by an ill-advised image change involving smart clothes and worryingly short hair), which, predictably, didn't go down too well with the majority of their original fan base. Luke Morley subsequently provi-

ded a rationale of what appeared to be an overnight shift in musical direction: *'Some people might think it sounds drastically different, but that's because »Black And White« was actually recorded in 1984 and in the three years since then we've naturally progressed in our writing quite a bit. This new album's a much better record than the last one; we were very green the first time around, but now we're much more technically aware of things, and consequently the album sounds more modern and mature, I think.'* (Ref: Kerrang No.148, June 1987). The new long-play-er had been preceded by yet another single, »If That's What It Takes«, and was soon followed by even more attempts to storm the mainstream charts (»Good Thing Going«, the A-side of which was an unashamedly commercial effort which had the reviewers spitting bile in no uncertain terms, and »Moving Target«), neither of which struck the right note with the fans, who avoided the record in droves. There's little doubt that TERRAPLANE's latest album was a rather poor seller in comparison with the debut release, although the lads tried to save the day with an energetic performance at the 1987 Reading Festival, where their recently-penned material was rocked up a bit. Nevertheless, things were going downhill fast, and the end of the year saw new lad Riviere departing in acrimonious circumstances, the guitarist later forming an unsuccessful semi-glam outfit with the atrocious name of BAM BALAM.

It came as little surprise when TERRAPLANE were eventually dropped (after one last pointless reissue of »If That's What It Takes«) by their unsympathetic label in the aftermath of their second album's failure, leaving them without a deal in the early months of 1988. After an aborted attempt to start afresh with more down-to-earth material, the lads eventually called time on their latest venture, and the name of TERRAPLANE was laid to rest at the beginning of 1989. For Morley, Bowes and James, however, there was to be a happy ending after all. The trio (Nick Linden did his own thing with BAD BREED, but didn't achieve a great deal of recognition) resurfaced a mere year later, recruiting two new compatriots in the form of Ben Matthews (g) and Mark Luckhurst (b) before reinventing themselves as THUNDER. With the revamped outfit now reverting to their original brand of raunchy rock (and somehow managing to induce a more contemporary edge), which was soon to enjoy something of a major renaissance in the popularity stakes, the mammoth EMI concern were only too keen to pick up on this hot musical proposition. As a result, the band have enjoyed a lengthy and fruitful career (experiencing a considerable amount of mainstream chart success along the way) ever since. Seldom has the phrase *'third time lucky'* seemed so appropriate.

LP's

»**Black And White**« Epic 1986
[Cassette version includes three extra tracks]
»**Moving Target**« Epic 1987

12" EP's

»**I Survive**« City Records 1983

[Original issue, "Gimme The Money" non-LP, also includes live versions of "Turn Me Loose" and "I Want Your Body"]
»**I Can't Live Without Your Love**« Epic 1984
[Two alternate sleeve designs, "Let The Wheels Go Round" non-LP, "Beginning Of The End" only on cassette version of album]
»**I Survive**« Epic 1985
[Second issue, "Money" non-LP, "All Night And Day" only on cassette version of album]
»**When You're Hot**« Epic 1985
["If You Could See Yourself" non-LP, "Tough Kind Of Love" only on cassette version of album]
»**Talking To Myself**« Epic 1985
["Gimme The Money" non-LP]
»**If That's What It Takes**« Epic 1986
[Original issue with remixed A-side, both "Living After Dark" and "Drugs" non-LP]
»**Good Thing Going**« Epic 1987
[Both "A Night Of Madness" and "The Good Life" non-LP, cassette version includes extra remix of A-side]
»**Moving Target**« Epic 1987
["When I Sleep Alone" only on CD version of album, also includes live versions of "I Survive" and "I Can't Live Without Your Love"]
»**If That's What It Takes**« Epic 1988
[Reissue as limited edition with poster sleeve, both "Living After Dark" and "Drugs" non-LP]

7" Singles
»**I Survive**« City Records 1983
[Original issue, B-side "Gimme The Money" non-LP]
»**I Can't Live Without Your Love**« Epic 1984
[B-side "Beginning Of The End" only on cassette version of album, also issued in gatefold sleeve with free single featuring live versions of "All Night And Day" and "I'm The One"]
»**I Survive**« Epic 1985
[Second issue, B-side "All Night And Day" only on cassette version of album]
»**When You're Hot**« Epic 1985
[B-side "Tough Kind Of Love" only on cassette version of album]
»**Talking To Myself**« Epic 1985
»**If That's What It Takes**« Epic 1986
[Original issue, B-side "Living After Dark" non-LP, also issued as limited edition double single]
»**Good Thing Going**« Epic 1987
[B-side "A Night Of Madness" non-LP]
»**Moving Target**« Epic 1987
[B-side "When I Sleep Alone" only on CD version of album, also issued with free single featuring live versions of "I Survive" and "I Can't Live Without Your Love"]
»**If That's What It Takes**« Epic 1988
[Reissue, B-side "Living After Dark" non-LP]

Shaped Picture Discs
»**If That's What It Takes**« Epic 1986

Promotional Releases
»**I'm The One**« Epic 1986
[Promo-only live 7" flexi disc in picture cover]

CD's
»**Moving Target**« Epic 1987
[With four bonus tracks]
»**Black And White**« Sony 198?
[Japanese issue]
»**Back To Innocence**« Jailbait 199?
[Live bootleg, material taken from 1985 and 1986 shows]
»**Black And White**« Columbia 2000
[With three bonus tracks]

Compilation Appearances
"I Want Your Body" (live) on »Reading Rock Vol.1« Do-LP Mean Records 1982
"Turn Me Loose" (live) on »Reading Rock Vol.1« Do-LP Mean Records 1982
"Living After Dark" on »Sounds EP« 7" EP Epic 1986
[Free with 'Sounds' magazine]
"I Survive" on »Give 'Em Hell« CD Nectar Masters 1995 + »The Best Of Indie Metal« CD Emporio 1998
"Gimme The Money" on »Rock Out!« Do-CD Emporio 1996 + »The Best Of Indie Metal« CD Emporio 1998

THIN END OF THE WEDGE

Babs Norris (v, k)
Steve Norris (g)
Terry Steers (g)
Phil Arthur (b)
Bill Campion (d)

I'm not quite sure why Merseyside's THIN END OF THE WEDGE (what a truly awful name) seem to have been lumbered with the dreaded 'prog rock' tag, but it certainly implies that some individuals haven't listened to their one-off single too closely (or perhaps they were just prejudiced against female vocalists?) in the past. Sure, there are disconcerting sleeve credits for both keyboards and flute (which indicates they weren't of the MOTÖRHEAD school of thought), and the B-side does indeed have a couple of mildly folky interludes, but, in the main, their music was basically an accessible brand of rock/metal which more than merits inclusion here. The nominated A-side ("Lights Are On Green") was a strong effort in the vein of CANIS MAJOR or AFTER HOURS, with a raunchy vocal performance from Babs Norris and some highly impressive guitar work on display all round, while "I'm Not Dead Yet", on the reverse, incorporated some unusual ideas and changes of pace along the way but still conformed to an underlying, semi-NWOBHM ethos. It was a pretty respectable debut, all things considered, and it seems to have attracted a fair amount of attention in the local rock community (relatively few copies actually made it out of the North West) upon its release in 1981. In fact, it raised their profile to such an extent that the talented Terry Steers was subsequently poached by fellow Scousers RAGE, appearing as second axeman on their »Nice'n'Dirty« album (although credited, rather bizarrely, as *Tony* Steers) a year later.

Refusing to allow this piece of minor misfortune to affect their chances, THIN END OF THE WEDGE bravely soldiered on with a revised line-up (a chap called Dave Bridge assumed the vacant guitar position), and ambitiously entered the second national *'Battle Of The Bands'* contest, winning their local leg and even appearing on the compilation album released by RCA as a souvenir of the televised grand final. Their featured composition ("The Letter") was, however, in a considerably more commercial style, a power ballad featuring both piano and saxophone (an accessory which deserves to be made illegal at the earliest opportunity), something which no doubt came as a major disappointment to those who had enjoyed the strong debut single. In spite of the band's increasingly-mainstream aspirations, though, they don't appear to have capitalised on their new-found *'celebrity status'* (or to have benefitted from the studio time they had won as a prize in the first instance), and the quintet had presumably disbanded within a year or two. The pairing of Dave Bridge (who nowadays teaches classical guitar) and Bill Campion, however, proceeded to form part of the original line-up of DAMASCUS (see separate entry), an act with considerably greater appeal to the average metalhead. The THIN END OF THE WEDGE single, which comes in a monochrome sleeve with images of the musicians' faces, isn't a major-league rarity at present, but it's a pretty good effort, all the same.

7" Singles
»Lights Are On Green« Jungle Records 1981

Exclusive Compilation Appearances
"The Letter" on »Battle Of The Bands Vol.2« LP RCA 1982

THUNDERSTICK

Vinni Munro (v)
Colin Heart (g)
Neal Hay (g)
Ben Reeve (b)
Barry 'Thunderstick' Purkis (d)

It seems probable that the masked individual known simply as Thunderstick (aka Barry Purkis, Barry Graham) will forever be remembered as the unacceptable face (in more ways than one) of the NWOBHM, his ill-advised stage persona frequently offending those of fragile sensibilities (his photo originally took pride of place on the proof sleeve for the »NWOBHM '79 Revisited« LP in 1990, but the image was eventually obscured, mainly at the behest of SLEDGEHAMMER's Mike Cooke), although the accusations of some hysterical parties that his very existence actually condoned rape was certainly a bit excessive. Anyway, the much-travelled drummer (who had been in the business since the early 70's) had played a major role in the early years of SAMSON, appearing on three full albums before finally giving way to Mel Gaynor, and he also enjoyed brief stints with the likes of IRON MAIDEN, COLIN TOWNS, GILLAN and the ELECTRIC GYPSIES at one point or another. Having now been given his freedom from SAMSON (quite literally, as he had actually performed in a makeshift *'cage'* on a few occasions), however, the ambitious chap began considering the possibility of assembling his own musical venture, announcing at a relatively early stage that THUNDERSTICK'S LIGHTNING (as the project was originally conceived) would become major contenders in the rock field before long.

It took a while to get going, however, and it wasn't until the early part of 1982 that momentum had built up sufficiently to attract public interest in the ensemble, now simply called THUNDERSTICK. The first stable line-up saw the drummer teaming up with vocalist Vinni Munro and unknown (although they had all been players on the minor club scene) accomplices Ben Reeve (b), Colin Heart (g) and Neal Hay (g), and, after circulating the obligatory demo, the outfit's thoughts soon turned to releasing some product of their own. Plans for a THUNDERSTICK single were originally outlined during mid-1982, at a time when the quintet had still to play a solitary gig, although they rapidly shelved the idea of debuting with a vinyl release. Instead, they started making the occasional high-profile appearance in and around the capital, where the ensemble were revealed to be an unashamedly theatrical proposition who relied just as much (if not more) on visual impact as on the strength of their songs themselves. The viewing and listening public were largely unconvinced on both counts, however, and it looked as though the whole project might die a remarkably swift death if the situation wasn't rectified at the earliest opportunity. In due course, original chantress Vinni Munro was given the push, as was

THUNDERSTICK

her immediate replacement, former CHEVRONS singer Ana Marie Borg (not before the latter had recorded a batch of studio material, though), both of whom had failed to make the grade.

By the second half of 1983, however, a suitable candidate had materialised in the form of American import Jodee Valentine, and so the necessary reorganisation was soon being undertaken. Colin Heart had also flown the coop by this time, however (new guitarist Cris Martin was quickly broken in), while their other axeman, Neal Hay, had now reinvented himself as the wacky 'Wango Wiggins', for reasons best known to his psychiatrist. With a more stable and appropriate line-up having been achieved at last, the group were finally ready to make a real attempt at cracking the market, and THUNDERSTICK's first release would be the »Feel Like Rock'n'Roll« 12", the outfit having been conveniently picked up by the Thunderbolt label (who now owned the rights to certain early SAMSON material) in the previous month or two. The debut four-tracker (which, in spite of the credit for Jodee Valentine, actually featured her fly-by-night predecessor) was a slightly odd affair, the bland music seeming ill-at-ease with their over-the-top theatrical posturing and occult lyrical proclivities. In fact, the likes of "Alecia", "Runaround" and the title track were fairly innocuous, tuneful pieces with occasional similarities to PET HATE, SIAN or LOST PROPERTY, for example, so it wasn't too enthralling, on the whole. There was, admittedly, some reasonably competent guitar work on display at times, but barely enough to hold the attention, although the weightier "Buried Alive" was a somewhat stronger effort.

In spite of this relatively inauspicious opening gambit, however, the group remained supremely confident of their ability to deliver a world-beating album. Furthermore, the drummer was keen to defend his venture against allegations that they were a manufactured concern: *'Other bands, I won't mention any names, do certain things for publicity. They don't really believe in it, it's just a game, and once they get success it all goes out of the window. This is me, not a game. Bank managers dress for their job and I dress for mine.'* (Ref: Kerrang No.55, November 1983). Before long, a full THUNDERSTICK LP was in the shops, and the rock fans of the day were able to make up their own minds as to whether or not »Beauty And The Beasts« was worthy of accolade. In fact, the album was a mediocre offering (their inexplicable fondness for spoken overdubs was acutely annoying), neither as intense as GIRLSCHOOL (if you're going for the facile female-vocal comparisons) nor as inventive as CANIS MAJOR (a few more tracks like "Heartbeat (In The Night)" might have helped), and the public reaction was one of utter indifference. If the group were to prosper, it looked as though it would be *'back to the drawing board'* once again. In fact, the original version of the outfit elected instead to call it a day within a fairly short timescale (they had, towards the end, tried out new guitarist Bengt Sorensen, formerly with SPRING-HEEL JACK, in place of Cris Martin), although the drummer eventually got things going again in 1986, roping in Jodee Valentine (whom he had married in the interim!) and (in the long term) working alongside the all-new guitar pairing of Dave Kilford and Paul Lewis.

In fact, it transpires that a second THUNDERSTICK album, entitled »Don't Touch, I'll Scream«, had apparently been recorded on the sly (oddly enough, by the previous line-up) at some point beforehand, but was eventually pulled from release due to various problems with the minor label who were due to issue their later output. There was, however, little or no evidence that these recordings still existed until comparatively recently, when the long-lost "Dark Night Black Light" and "Shining" were exhumed for inclusion on a budget compilation entitled »The Best Of British Metal«. Mind you, there had been little musical progression, so it's not as if we had been cheated out of a classic release by any means, although it now seems quite possible that the set may yet see a belated release after all. The band had finally thrown in the towel (again) by 1987, with their masked figurehead going back to session work and touring activities with various minor club acts (plus an ill-fated reunion of the original SAMSON line-up around the turn of the decade), while his erstwhile colleague Cris Martin subsequently tried his hand in a number of projects such as MARINO, MASTER (no, not Paul Speckmann's bunch), BLACKFOX and FIRED UP, none of whom were spectacularly successful in the long term. Thunderstick himself, meanwhile, having attempted to establish another venture called (appropriately enough) MASK in the early 90's, is now happily back in the SAMSON fold for the umpteenth time (having recently played at the '20th Anniversary' NWOBHM mini-festival held in Japan in the latter part of 1999), and looks as though he'll remain a part of their set-up for the foreseeable future.

LP's
»Beauty And The Beasts« Thunderbolt 1984

12" EP's
»Feel Like Rock'n'Roll?« Thunderbolt 1983
[All four tracks non-LP]

Exclusive Compilation Appearances
"Dark Night Black Light" on »The Best Of British Metal« CD Delta Music 1999
"Shining" on »The Best Of British Metal« CD Delta Music 1999

Compilation Appearances
"Runaround" on »A Bolt From The Black« LP Thunderbolt 1984

TITAN (I)

Rocky Shades (v)
Martin Schell (g)
John Floyd (g)
Chris Johnson (b)
Pete Travis (d)

The original British TITAN (who were almost certainly the first recording band of WRATHCHILD's future frontman, Rocky Shades) established themselves in the West Midlands at the very height of the NWOBHM, but turned out to be an extremely short-lived concern, which is a shame, as they were actually rather good. Nevertheless, the quintet managed to get a privately-financed single pressed in 1980, coupling "East Wind, West Wind" with "Losing The Fight". TITAN's debut two-tracker, issued on the little-remembered Wild Dog label, featured a pair of original compositions of the highest NWOBHM pedigree (the former being a catchy, upbeat effort, while the latter was a slightly moodier affair), both of which bring forth comparisons with SLOWTRAIN, CYNIC, METAL MIRROR and BOLLWEEVIL, for example. There was also a subtle hint of MARC BOLAN in the vocal department (Shades was evidently trying to outdo METAL MIRROR's Cameron Vagges), with the talented frontman unveiling a considerably more varied and impressive range than ever became apparent in his later efforts with WRATHCHILD. This certainly wasn't mediocre, anthemic glam, that's for sure! The hyper-rare 7" was issued without a picture sleeve, and has turned up in truly minimal quantities in recent years, suggesting that incredibly few copies were shifted at the time, which is perfectly understandable, given that the group fragmented so soon after its release.

In fact, the talented TITAN appear to have fallen apart at some point in the second half of 1980 (a great pity, really), with Rocky Shades going on to join the ranks of the developing WRATHCHILD almost immediately. Nevertheless, TITAN had composed quite an extensive repertoire of original material, and some of these (including "Slow Motion Suicide", "Writhing In Ecstasy", "Lady Desire" and the epic "Invasion") were even immortalised on tape in embryonic form. It's unfortunate that the lads didn't persevere, as they had the potential to become one of the more popular outfits of the period, and they captured the mood of the time to perfection. Martin Schell and Pete Travis soon formed an all-new venture of their own, however (Chris Johnson, meanwhile, may well have resurfaced in HIGHWAY, but it's such a common name that I can't be sure), the punningly-monikered SCHELL SHOCK, who reworked some of TITAN's original material (*e.g.* "East Wind, West Wind" and "Slow Motion Suicide") in their live routine, although they were soon writing strong numbers of their own. Again, this was yet another group who were more than deserving of a modicum of success, but their sole vinyl exposure was to be the "Steel Breeze" track on Ebony's »Metal Fatigue« compilation. A SCHELL SHOCK single was apparently in the pipeline at one stage, but appears to have been cancelled on financial grounds (there are some tantalising rumours that it got to the test pressing stage, though), and the promising outfit eventually gave up the ghost in the mid-80's, following on from the usual cycle of personnel instability and public disinterest.

7" Singles
»East Wind, West Wind« Wild Dog Records
1980

TITAN (II)

Colin Whittaker
Malcolm McCarthy
Damian Gibson
Linda

I'd heard the rumours but didn't believe them. Furtive glances, barely-suppressed sniggering and whispered references to JAMES GALWAY and *'flute solos'* had sparked my curiosity but seemed even less credible once I actually held a copy of this legendary item (TITAN's »Imaginary Lady« single, that is) in my own hands. The monochrome picture cover, showing a diaphanous female apparition and some decidedly hairy individuals lurking in the background, could hardly have looked more promising. The amateurish, hand-written reverse sleeve was equally impeccable, so it was without trepidation that the vinyl hit the turntable. Bloody hell, it's all *true*! The A-side is indeed a bass-backed instrumental affair, although I reckon the aforementioned *'flute'* description is open to debate. To my ears, it sounds more like pan pipes (as in the original INCANTATION and their famous "Cacharpaya" effort), or, more realistically, a Fairlight on a *'pan pipe'* setting. Either way, it tootles along for a jaw-dropping two and a half minutes without going anywhere at all and then stopping rather abruptly. Er, not exactly my idea of metal, matey.

The not-remotely-ironically-titled B-side ("Guaranteed You Won't Like It") kicks off in much the same manner, unfortunately, although the tootling ceases mercifully quickly in this instance, whereupon a fairly decent (and rather more conventional) NWOBHM rocker takes over. With occasional hints of CAMARGUE, SLOWTRAIN and HAZZARD, but retaining its own sense of identity throughout, this effort additionally features folky, female backing vocals from time to time, proving once and for all that bands such as DARK TRANQUILLITY didn't invent the concept. Clearly, Yorkshire's TITAN (not to be confused with their later French namesakes, the mystery metal outfit who contributed to »The Whinging Album« or Rocky Shades' genuinely excellent pre-WRATHCHILD combo, who were actually doing the rounds a year or two earlier) were an act with originality

in mind, although I'd say that they certainly overdid it with the ill-judged »Imaginary Lady« (surely all the possible permutations on the *'lady'* theme must have been well and truly exhausted by now), which originally hit the shops at some point in 1982. Peculiarly, however, there seems to have been more than one pressing (I can hardly believe that the general public were falling over themselves to buy a copy, though), and an alternate issue in a different sleeve (a shadowy female figure and little else) also crops up every now and again.

As it turns out, TITAN appears to have represented more or less a one-man-operation, a studio-based venture conceived by a certain Colin Whittaker, who composed and performed much (if not all) of the original material himself. Mind you, he clearly had three hapless individuals helping out on the first release, but I reckon they probably weren't a permanent part of the picture. As such, there wasn't all that much chance of TITAN getting out and about in the regional pubs and clubs (unless Whittaker did indeed have a backing ensemble on standby for these occasions), which is probably just as well, really, as I can't imagine the biker community giving him/them a particularly easy ride (as it were). Understandably enough, it seems that an utterly pitiful quantity of singles were actually shifted at the time, so you wouldn't really have expected Whittaker to have kept plugging away for several years thereafter. It comes as a major surprise (to say the least), therefore, to discover that a second TITAN single (bafflingly, credited to THE ORANGE WORLD OF TITAN on the cover) was recorded as late as 1990, on which the mainman seems to have been the sole participant.

The seldom-seen 'follow-up' 7" consists of two versions of a track called "Big Baby", with the instrumental take (complete with tootles) being entirely disposable, although the vocal one is a semi-listenable (weakened by a hopeless song construction and the multi-layered effects) piece of pop/rock, none of which bears any relation whatsoever to the original NWOBHM sound, so you shouldn't really be too upset if you can't locate a copy. The mainman is, incidentally, pictured on the front cover, posing against a wall with examples of the original TITAN single in the background, while the shot on the reverse shows him complete with flute-style object, so I guess this really was his own gimmick all along. Even so, it looks as though this belated offering was another dead loss in terms of sales, leaving Whittaker to call time on TITAN before much longer. The first single, however, is a hopelessly rare piece (notwithstanding the existence of two different issues), and, with the dealers having hyped it to a ludicrous extent in recent years, your chances of ever owning a copy (assuming you'd want to) are now directly proportional to the size of your wallet.

7" Singles
»Imaginary Lady« CDLM Records 1982
[Issued in two different picture sleeves]
»Big Baby« Private 1990
[Includes two versions of "Big Baby"]

TNT

Nick Williams
Nobby Brett
Mark Smith
Gary Stevenson
Colin French

Kent's unrenowned TNT were somewhat unfortunate to choose a name which would become seriously over-subscribed in years to come (clearly, the most successful version were to be the hairspray-heavy Norwegians), and they might, in retrospect, have been better-served by a more distinctive moniker. Having started out (at around the turn of the decade) as a strictly amateur-hour covers concern playing numerous small-time gigs purely for the benefit of local rock fans, the outfit nevertheless progressed to the stage whereby they felt sufficiently confident to demo a handful of their own numbers for various record companies of the day. Although major-label deals had become few and far between by that time, the TNT lads were still to attract a modest amount of interest from the smaller companies, and were duly invited to contribute their perfunctorily-titled "Sorry" effort to Ebony's »Metal Warriors« compilation in 1983. With the latter featuring an impressive twin-guitar attack and powerful vocals, the group already exhibited some of the considerable talent of outfits such as HAMMERHEAD, MYTHRA and early DEF LEPPARD, a framework which was to serve them well in the future.

Following on from this early vinyl appearance, the outfit proceeded to take the slightly unconventional step of signing for one of Ebony's arch-rivals, namely Neat, and subsequently issued the »Back On The Road« single a year later. The A-side turned out to be a fairly strong and catchy number in the general manner of their compilation offering, although the rather more commercial and uninspiring flipside ("Rockin' The Night") was possibly a slight disappointment in comparison. Mind you, it was still a far more accomplished release than many NWOBHM hopefuls managed to achieve in their entire careers, so give credit where it's due. TNT really deserved to get further, but they didn't get all that much assistance from Neat, who were failing to promote emergent prospects to the same extent by this juncture (concentrating on proven acts such as RAVEN and VENOM, although they still found it in their hearts to sponsor the unremarkable PHASSLAYNE), and it looks as though the luckless band faded away into nothingness without any of the more affluent labels of the day offering to take them under their wing. None of the original participants can be confirmed as having resurfaced in other acts of note, though, so I guess TNT just represented a brief flirtation with the fickle world of rock'n'roll after all.

7" Singles
»Back On The Road« Neat 1984

Exclusive Compilation Appearances

"Sorry" on »Metal Warriors« LP Ebony 1983

TOAD THE WET SPROCKET

Mick Mustofa (v)
Mark 'Curly' Rideaut (g)
Pete Austin (b)
Martin 'Witik' Wightwick (d)

Just in case there's still *someone* on the face of the planet who's having a hard time coming to terms with the apparently mind-blowing fact that two disparate sets of musicians, a full decade apart and on either side of the Atlantic, could possibly both come up with the utterly ludicrous TOAD THE WET SPROCKET as the name of their band, let's just run through the oft-recalled story one last time. The original *'T.T.W.S.'* was, in fact, an entirely fictitious group created for the purposes of a one-off 'Monty Python' sketch back in the 70's, although this completely hilarious (or not) moniker apparently tickled the fancy of both of the later outfits so much that they subsequently decided that they just *had* to use it for their own ensemble. So there you go, it was nothing more fantastical than that. The equally-silly name ETHEL THE FROG, incidentally, was pinched from a highly similar source, this being the title of one of the numerous album tracks recorded by the aforementioned comedy team.

Having gravitated together in Bedfordshire in the mid-70's, the lads initially struggled to find their identity amongst the hippy hangers-on and punk upstarts of the day, and later claimed that they had been given a rough time for wanting to play heavy music. In fact, there's reliable evidence to suggest that the lads weren't actually playing *'out and out metal'* right from the start, and that they originally settled on a style that borrowed equally from metal, punk and pub rock, and it was only in later years that their own material began to drift towards the newly-created NWOBHM ideal. In any case, the lads ultimately got in on the *'do it yourself'* ethos, and their self-financed »Pete's Punk Song« (the title of which might just have contained a subtle hint that the outfit didn't consider themselves to be a full-on metal concern at that stage) single appeared (as did its successor, in a monochrome, gatefold sleeve) in 1979 to overwhelming public disinterest. Perhaps the title discouraged members of the metal community from buying a copy, but I don't recall it doing brisk business among the punkers either. In any case, this description wasn't particularly accurate; the A-side turned out to be a truly bizarre and confusing concoction, combining a fairly traditional rocker (with a reasonable vocal effort) and a knockabout, piano-based backing from the implausibly-named *'Pip Domino'* (actually Nick Rideaut, Mark's brother), all of which was very odd indeed. Mind you, the disposable reverse ("Feel It") is even more tacky, a 70's-styled bit of lounge-bar *'easy listening'* which was surely intended as a joke…wasn't it?

After this, er, *quirky* start (which might all have been a great laugh but resulted in very poor record sales), the lads decided to stop arsing about (their earlier vinyl outing was later conveniently denounced as *'unrepresentative'*), and they finally got around to releasing a proper metal record a year later. Their »Reaching For The Sky« single (b/w "One Glass Of Whiskey") is a heavy slice of mid-paced rock/metal which brings to mind early 80's outfits such as SLEDGEHAMMER, NIGHTIME FLYER or Coventry's CHAINSAW, and which has long been held

up as an exemplary demonstration of the original NWOBHM archetype. The A-side, in particular, is a pretty decent example of a prime-era contribution to the genre, and this offering has latterly been appreciated by numerous modern-day fans on the »NWOBHM Vol.3« bootleg CD. Earlier in the year, meanwhile, the quartet (by this time having supported the likes of NUTZ, BUDGIE, VARDIS, SAMSON, GIRL, ANGEL WITCH and IRON MAIDEN) had been featured on the Neal Kay-assembled »Metal For Muthas« compilation with the pointless, laid-back, raunchy rock of "Blues In A", a throwaway track which hardly did their reputation any favours, and this whole exercise seems to have been a completely wasted opportunity to promote the band to a vastly enhanced audience.

Interviewed in a fanzine (after taking part in

the *'Herts And Beds Rock Contest')* at around the time of the second single's release, the protagonists were asked about their progress thus far. Mick Mustofa replied: *'We feel we are doing well but we want to do better. We know that playing commercial music would help us but we feel people should like our music, not the stuff that other people play just to get into the charts. Many HM bands are cashing in on the rise of HM but they play commercial crap, they are only interested in making money.'* (Ref: Teenage Depression, Issue 13, 1980). How true. After the obligatory interrogation about the origin of their name, the outfit also commented on their much-criticised (lack of) image. Pete Austin revealed: *'I feel many HM bands use gimmicks to get their name around but we feel that the music is all that counts. We are lively on stage and feel clothes and other gimmicks are not necessary. We wear mainly jeans and T-shirts and if we become famous we wouldn't want to change. We believe our music is good and that's all that counts.'* (Ref: ibid.) Fair enough.

The group were also fortunate enough to be invited onto the 'Friday Rock Show' that same year, performing specially-recorded versions of "Just Another Game", "Rock And Roll Runner", "One Glass Of Whiskey" and "Big Deal". Broadcast on the 27th of June 1980, the session served as a pretty reliable indicator of the outfit's talent, with the energetic "Big Deal" (evocative of A II Z) being particularly impressive. Elsewhere, "Just Another Game" and old favourite "One Glass Of Whiskey" represented fairly interchangeable (but perfectly capable), slower numbers, whereas "Rock And Roll Runner" was a reasonable enough mid-paced rocker, although not quite showing the ensemble at their very heaviest. The session may not have made TOAD THE WET SPROCKET a household name (which is understandable enough) in the first instance, but it certainly didn't harm their reputation in any way, and it no doubt inspired a few additional fans to seek out a copy of their most recent single. The following months saw the quartet touring fairly extensively, their activities including several regional headlining shows in addition to gigs with other local favourites such as BLEAK HOUSE, CLIENTELLE and HIGH TREASON, with the lads developing a healthy fan base in the process.

For some strange reason, though, it would appear that the band failed to make much of an impact in the music press at the time ('Kerrang', for instance, didn't seem to cotton on to the outfit's existence until the early part of 1982), although the foursome were, admittedly, keeping a rather low profile by this point. With the lads having undertaken only the occasional live outing in recent months to confirm that they were still an active unit after all, 'Kerrang' even proceeded to include them in their 'Armed And Ready' section for *'unsigned, upcoming bands'*. Hmmm. By this stage, however, the outfit's *'latest'* vinyl offering was now the best part of two years old, and so this ill-timed feature can hardly have served to promote them particularly effectively. Indeed, the disillusioned group appear to have disappeared from the scene with great haste (an utterly disposable effort called "Charlie" subsequently appeared on a somewhat obscure local-band compilation, although, given that it was much along the lines of their first two-tracker, this could easily have been one of their older numbers) without making any further recordings. Too bad. Drummer Martin 'Witik' Wightwick, incidentally, became a part of RIO's touring ensemble in the latter half of 1985, although the remaining ex-members of TOAD THE WET SPROCKET all appear to have vanished completely in later years.

7" Singles
»Pete's Punk Song« Sprockets Records 1979
»Reaching For The Sky« Sprockets Records 1980

Exclusive Compilation Appearances
"Blues In A" on »Metal For Muthas« LP EMI 1980/CD Airraid Records 2000 + »The Bible Of Hard Rock« CD Toshiba 1990
"Charlie" on »Lend An Ear 1992?« LP Vroom Records 1982

Compilation Appearances
"Reaching For The Sky" on »NWOBHM Vol.3« Bootleg CD 1992

TOBRUK

Stuart 'Snake' Neill (v)
Nigel Evans (g)
Mike Newman (g)
Steve Woodward (b)
Jem Davis (k)
Alan Vallance (d)

In view of the observation that melodic rockers TOBRUK were eventually to develop something of a reputation as the pride of the Midlands, it's therefore slightly surprising to note that the embryonic version of the group actually formed in Bedfordshire in around 1980. The original

TOBRUK (the brainchild of guitarist Mike Newman) was very much an amateur-hour concern, however, and it wasn't until Nigel Evans, Snake and Jem Davis were recruited (all from the ranks of the defunct STRANGER) in the latter half of 1981 that the band evolved into something vaguely resembling a serious proposition. Early the following year, the lads made that vital decision to relocate to the thriving musical centre of Birmingham, and the members were soon properly established in their new habitat. After a few minor reshuffles, the line-up was completed by drummer Allan Vallance and bassist Steve Woodward, whereupon the all-new TOBRUK set about gigging and laying down some demo material for public consumption. Their early visits to the recording studio yielded versions of tracks such as "Running From The Night" and "Midnight Rider", and it wasn't long before their activities came to the attention of those responsible for commissioning material for the 'Friday Rock Show'. The outfit installed themselves in the BBC's enviable studio facility late in the year, laying down "Motel Love", "Wild On The Run", "The Show Must Go On" and "Rage Of Angels", all of which would become firm favourites among fans in due course.

The session, broadcast on the 22nd of October 1982, placed TOBRUK on the first rung of the ladder to success, and the lads were soon building on this early exposure, cultivating a fair bit of label interest, and their greatest hope was that a worthwhile deal would come sooner rather than later. Indeed, they only had to wait a matter of months before Neat stepped in with an offer to promote the band with a 7" single, and the members concluded that this would be a perfectly acceptable way to get their first product into the shops. By this time, they had broken in a new drummer, Eddie Fincher, and the outfit duly reworked "Wild On The Run" and "The Show Must Go On" from their radio session for the purposes of the debut release. This two-tracker was a radical departure from the expected Neat offering, and TOBRUK's brand of accessible, raunchy, melodic rock/metal (they were, at their heaviest, comparable to the likes of MAINEEAXE, BLADE RUNNER or EXCALIBUR, but were just as happy in more mainstream mode) was soon capturing the public's imagination, the group enjoying a great deal of radio exposure (particularly in the Midlands) in due course. Nevertheless, the majors remained unconvinced, and it took another two years of hard graft in the live environment (including support tours with DIAMOND HEAD, MANOWAR and UFO) before the lads finally got some further product on the market. In the spring of 1984 (by which time the lads had parted company with original bassist Steve Woodward, bringing in Mike Brown to fill the gap), some deserved label recognition had come TOBRUK's way, and the band subsequently became involved with the giant EMI corporation, for whom they demoed some strong material, including "Under The Gun", "Like Lightning" and "Shine A Light".

On the basis of their latest selection of studio recordings (and in view of the fact that TOBRUK were now an established act with a healthy following of their own), the lads were passed on to EMI's Parlophone subsidiary, after which they were invited to lay down a full album for the label. The first fruit of TOBRUK's liaison with the company arrived in the form of their »Wild On The Run« set, a long-player (issued in the early months of 1985) which adeptly combined old and new, with an extremely charismatic performance from their ophidian frontman raising the standard of the material quite considerably. There was, on occasion, a slight tendency to slip into anthemic, semi-AOR territory in the HEAVY PETTIN or GLASGOW vein, but the inaugural LP was, as a whole, a strong melodic rock effort, with stand-out tracks including the excellent "Falling", "Running From The Night" and "Poor Girl". The combo gigged quite extensively to promote the release, and were also lucky enough to be featured on the BBC's 'In Concert' programme (alongside TERRAPLANE), following up this useful piece of exposure with a fairly prestigious outing at the Heavy Sound Festival in Europe, where they shared a stage with the likes of TOKYO BLADE. The busy musicians also found time to put in an appearance on the 'E.C.T.' television programme, performing "Breakdown" and "Falling" in front of a rabid crowd of strangely-attired rock fans. Parlophone, meanwhile, seemed committed to the group's cause, and released both »Falling« and »On The Rebound« as singles in their own right, each proceeding to perform in sufficiently impressive terms that the label swiftly decided to commission a follow-up album.

TOBRUK returned to the studio in 1986, and duly captured an album's worth of brand-new material on tape without making too much of a fuss about it. Their »In Motion« set was scheduled to be released by Parlophone a short time later, but the label were apparently entirely dissatisfied with many of the compositions which were now being offered to them, whereupon they insisted on a never-ending cycle of remixes and re-recordings in an attempt to come up with an acceptable finished product. By 1987, the lads had assembled a selection of apparently-suitable material, and the delayed album (now retitled »Rock & Roll Casualty«) was once again readied for imminent release. During the final build-up to the record's issue, however, the musicians started to lose faith in the project, and constant bickering and in-fighting ultimately led to an acrimonious fragmentation of TOBRUK in mid-1987, after which the inseparable duo of Snake and Eddie Fincher proceeded to inveigle their way into IDOL RICH. In the event, Parlophone decided that there wasn't much point in issuing an album by an act who no longer existed, and, despite pleas from the remaining members that they would find replacements for the departed duo, the release was shelved. However, just when it seemed as though the world would forever be deprived of that second TOBRUK album, FM Records stepped in with an offer to release the record after all (they also got hold of HEAVY PETTIN's »Big Bang«, which was cancelled by Polydor in similar circumstances), and it finally appeared as »Pleasure And Pain« in 1988.

After this considerable delay, the album turned out to be a slightly disappointing effort, and it saw the band delivering a selection of inadvisably lightweight material with an emphasis on accessible, keyboard-dominated compositions in something of a mainstream style, much more along the lines of SHOGUN, JOKERS WILD or BRIAR. Nevertheless, there were a few reminders of their undoubted talent, notably "Girl Crazy", "No Paradise In Heaven" and "Cry Out In The Night", although the long-player as a whole was generally unremarkable. Again, advance publicity for the release dropped a few hints that a revised version of TOBRUK was covertly being assembled, and that they would soon be active in the live environment once again. However, even if these promises were actually sincere (and I have my doubts), there never seems to have been any genuine attempts to resurrect TOBRUK, and their name was finally laid to rest after sales of the much-delayed record began to tail off. Jem Davis later teamed up with former colleague Eddie Fincher (following the demise of IDOL RICH) in MIDNIGHT BLUE, a melodic rock proposition who had a modicum of success in the late 80's, before Davis moved on to pastures new, lending a hand in the recording and touring activities of acts such as PRAYING MANTIS, FM and UFO. Certain other ex-TOBRUK personnel (presumably including Nigel Evans himself) supposedly resurfaced in a reformed version of the long-forgotten STRANGER at around the turn of the decade, although details are sketchy at present, while former frontman Snake's last notable activity in the music business appears to have been a very brief stint as vocalist in the WILDHEARTS.

LP's
»Wild On The Run« Parlophone 1985
»Pleasure And Pain« FM Records 1988

12" EP's
»Falling« Parlophone 1985
[A-side different to album version, both "Like Lightning" and "Under The Gun" non-LP]
»On The Rebound« Parlophone 1985
["Falling" different to album version]

7" Singles
»Wild On The Run« Neat 1983
[A-side different to album version, B-side "The Show Must Go On" non-LP]
»Falling« Parlophone 1985
[B-side "Like Lightning" non-LP]
»On The Rebound« Parlophone 1985

Promotional Releases
»Hotline« Parlophone 1985
[One-sided promo 12" with excerpts from »Wild On The Run« LP]

CD's
»Wild On The Run« Reborn Classics 1993
[Bootleg release with two extra tracks, also features BLACK KNIGHT's »Master Of Disaster« album]
»Pleasure And Pain« FM Records 1988
[With two extra tracks]

Compilation Appearances
"Wild On The Run" on »Kerrang Kompilation« Do-LP EMI 1985

TOK-IO ROSE

Chris Moore (v)
Rob Skrines (g)
Martin Slade (g)
Tony Godwin (b)
Les Foster (d)

Some bands wear their influences like a badge, naming themselves after the song titles of their mentors (INTERNATIONAL HEROES, NO QUARTER, PALI GAP etc.), while others are directly influenced by their local peers. Barnsley's

SEVENTH SON, for instance, owed a considerable debt to SAXON, while Nottingham's SABBAT frequently acknowledged the legacy of HELL. Similarly, it's hard to believe that Cardiff's TOK-IO ROSE would have come into existence without the pioneering PERSIAN RISK having preceded them. Formed in the early 80's, these lads wisely chose to dissociate themselves from all the other 'Tokyo' clones by adopting the distinctive spelling at the outset, and swiftly began promoting themselves as genuine contenders. TOK-IO ROSE got off to a healthy start by issuing a well-received demo tape (featuring "Whispered Anticipation" and "Bad Girls") in around 1983, and, by the time their privately-pressed single appeared (in an unusually professional sleeve) a year or so later, they had clearly become a very polished outfit indeed. Both the re-recorded "Bad Girls" and the newer "Desperate Situation" were eminently listenable, melodic-but-heavy offerings which could quite feasibly have passed for PERSIAN RISK material from the same period, the vocals of Chris Moore, in particular, being uncannily similar to Carl Sentance's dulcet tones. Along with the talented TRAITORS GATE, this bunch were clearly capable of becoming firm regional favourites in the long term, and might even have pinched some of PERSIAN RISK's fan base as the latter started to lose their way.

Sadly, however, things didn't work out too well for the original line-up, with a split occurring in 1986 (the earlier defection of sticksman Les Foster to the ailing JAGUAR hadn't helped matters), the dejected outfit citing *'mismanagement'* and the expense of travelling up to London for gigs as the crucial factors. However, the central cadre of Moore, Skrines and Godwin subsequently decided to have a second bite at the cherry, and eventually regrouped in 1988, recruiting guitarist Will Smith (no, not the Fresh Prince) and drummer Tony Brussalis (ex-JINX) to the fold. Featured in a fairly extensive 'Welsh Metal Special' in the pages of 'Kerrang' shortly thereafter, the revitalised group were clearly in a better frame of mind by this stage, as Rob Skrines explained: *'There are no drawbacks to being based in Wales if you've got the backing.'* (Ref: Kerrang No.174, February 1988). The all-new TOK-IO ROSE soon announced their intention to bolster their sound with a keyboard player (ex-KOOGA stalwart Neil Garland had been identified as a likely target), and made tentative plans to issue a new single ("Julie-Anne" and "Doesn't Matter" were both mooted as possible A-sides) during the course of the ensuing months, although these particular records seem to be extraordinarily hard to come by, and I suspect that they were never actually pressed at all.

In fact, the most interesting TOK-IO ROSE development of 1988 was the surprise replacement of Chris Moore by none other than Mr Rent-a-voice himself, Carl Sentance! With the latter having additionally served time in the previous couple of years with such acts as TOKYO BLADE, TREDEGAR, the GEEZER BUTLER BAND and MONRO, this was evidently quite a coup for the TOK-IO ROSE lads, who immediately took the opportunity to incorporate the odd GEEZER BUTLER BAND and PERSIAN RISK composition into their live repertoire. Things looked pretty rosy for the ensemble at that stage, and the rock community duly prepared to receive further vinyl offerings from TOK-IO ROSE. Alas, something must have gone badly wrong along the way, and no official product hit the shops thereafter. Although the group (now featuring Stefan Chelmis in place of Will Smith, plus new keyboard player Tim Ransome) were still active in 1989 (making occasional live appearances with the likes of EXCALIBUR), the split must have come relatively shortly afterwards, possibly with Carl Sentance's decision to emigrate to the States to try his luck there. Still, keep an eye out for that debut single, and any other later releases that may or may not be out there somewhere!

7" Singles
»**Bad Girls**« Private 1984

TOKYO BLADE

Alan Marsh (v)
John Wiggins (g)
Andy Boulton (g)
Andy Robbins (b)
Steve Pierce (d)

After a couple of ill-fated attempts to start off their quest for world domination under the identities of KILLER and GENGHIS KHAN (see separate entry), Wiltshire's favourite NWOBHM outfit finally got lucky the third time around, after reinventing themselves as TOKYO BLADE. The quintet's first move under their new name was to recruit former DEEP MACHINE guitarist John Wiggins (also a veteran of such acts as BLACK FRIDAY and Paul Dianno's LONEWOLF) to take the place of the ousted Ray Dismore, and repackage the two records from the withdrawn GENGHIS KHAN double pack as *bona fide*

TOKYO BLADE singles, printing up proper sleeves and hastily plastering new labels over the original records to facilitate a somewhat slipshod transformation. The first pair of TOKYO BLADE offerings (»If Heaven Is Hell« and »Midnight Rendezvous«) were released/reissued simultaneously, and these were soon proving a popular purchase among devotees of the type of twin-guitar power metal pioneered by the likes of IRON MAIDEN and JUDAS PRIEST. All things

considered, TOKYO BLADE were one of the earliest and most accomplished exponents of the style to emerge in the NWOBHM era, although they would find musical allies such as ELIXIR, PROWLER and VIRTUE in years to come.

Even before the final metamorphosis into TOKYO BLADE had taken place, the lads had developed a healthy following thanks to many well-attended shows in the South of England, with regular pilgrimages to various rock-friendly haunts in London having been part of the outfit's itinerary since the very beginning. As a result, TOKYO BLADE seemed to come out of nowhere and take the rock scene completely by storm, although the truth of the matter was swiftly established. The minor revelation that TOKYO BLADE were actually old hands in the rock business failed to detract from their appeal as an emergent metal act, however, and the group's material was strong enough to see them becoming more and more popular with every release which followed. First up was a single for Powerstation, which coupled "Powergame" and "Death On Mainstreet", a record which sold sufficiently well to compel their sponsors to demand a full album before the end of the year. The eponymous long-player was recorded in a matter of days, but still served to showcase the outfit's skills pretty efficiently, and TOKYO BLADE were soon benefitting from some overwhelmingly favourable reviews from around the globe. In fact, the quintet seemed to have the best of both worlds: the power to appeal to the IRON MAIDEN followers and the melody to keep the DEF LEPPARD fans happy, so the potential market was huge. To capitalise on their new-found success, the four tracks from the GENGHIS KHAN release were re-recorded and trundled out yet again, this time in the form of the »Midnight Rendezvous« 12" EP. They certainly got their money's worth from those titles...

With the outfit having become something of an *'overnight success'* in Europe, they were soon being invited to play at some remarkably high-profile events, with two notable examples being the Aardschok and Earthquake Festivals, held in the early months of 1984. The band (who parted company with original bassist Andy Robbins at around this time, bringing in another graduate of the recently-expired DEEP MACHINE, Andy Wrighton) were exposed to a sizeable audience on each occasion, and the members still look back on these appearances (especially Aardschok) with particular fondness. Next up was a hastily-organised tour of France, where the outfit hitched a ride with MAMA'S BOYS, the dates coinciding with a couple of licensed issues (the album, retitled »Midnight Rendezvous«, and a French-only single based around the new title track) on the Bernett label. In due course, the long-player would benefit from a variety of issues, including a rejigged American pressing on Combat, giving TOKYO BLADE a very realistic chance of cracking the global rock market in the long term. Even by the summer of 1984, the outfit were prepared to record their second album for Powerstation, and all seemed to be going according to plan until it came to the post-production stage, whereupon some ungallant soul expressed serious concern about Alan Marsh's vocal performance. After a bit of enforced soul-searching, the lads eventually formed the collective opinion that the set couldn't be released in its original form, and so these recordings were subsequently scrapped (although, interestingly enough, they were ultimately exhumed and released by High Vaultage in the 90's), whereupon everyone came to a fairly amicable agreement that Marsh should leave the group and go off to do his own thing. It wasn't that he had a terrible voice or anything, just that the material was a bit too demanding at times.

Having tactfully broken the news to Powerstation that the album would now be slightly delayed, TOKYO BLADE went off in search of a capable singer, and they swiftly brought in a little-known lad called Vicki James Wright (previously with various unrenowned hopefuls such as TOPAZ and the laughably-named BOBO), to re-record the whole thing. Fortunately, the newcomer was a quick learner, so it didn't take too long to complete the studio work, and, happily, the long-player was soon in the can (again). The public were introduced to the new vocalist (although they were initially a bit cagey about their change of personnel) by means of the enjoyable »Lightning Strikes« three-tracker, which showed the talented frontman to be the possessor of a powerful voice and an impressive range, albeit marred by a slightly whiney intonation that suggested he might have been more at home in a sleaze outfit. After that, the album appeared as intended, and »Night Of The Blade« suggested that TOKYO BLADE might be testing the water with respect to moving in a more commercial direction. They were still hedging their bets at this stage, presumably wary of any adverse reaction to such a move, and the record included something of a mixture of the traditional ("Night Of The Blade", "Unleash The Beast") and accessible ("Someone To Love", "Rock Me To The Limit"), although it was all carried off with a fair bit of finesse. It was also quite reassuring that they now seemed to be concentrating on using their own compositions at the expense of covers, as the Russ Ballard-penned "Tonight" had undoubtedly been one of the debut album's low-points.

The group were still in understandably high demand for live events on the continent, and would make a number of appearances before the year was out, including a slot at the Breaking Sound Festival in France, a pilgrimage to the legendary Dynamo in Eindhoven and a short European jaunt in the winter. They also found time to record a session for the 'Friday Rock Show' (Tommy Vance had already been playing their records on a regular basis), where (on the 19th of October 1984) the listening public were treated to energetic versions of "Night Of The Blade", "Someone To Love" and "Lovestruck", as well as the unfamiliar "Breakout". Moving into 1985, there was no let-up in the group's activities, and they were soon off to Europe once again, this time taking in a more extensive range of venues throughout some of the more rock-friendly territories such as France and Germany. By this juncture, TOKYO BLADE had become *bona fide* headliners, playing unusually lengthy sets which incorporated much of the material from their first two LP's. Almost everywhere the lads ventured, they were on the receiving end of rapturous praise, suggesting that the group would presumably go from strength to strength in years to come. For some strange reason, however, the unsettled outfit parted company with Powerstation later that same year (after the release of the disappointing »Madame Guillotine« 12" EP) and elected to go it alone for a while, a bold move (which may even have been inspired by Powerstation's decision to sell the rights to their early material to Raw Power, who proceeded to manufacture the shabby »Warriors Of The Rising Sun« cash-in compilation) which, nonetheless, seems to have set TOKYO BLADE on a bit of a downward spiral.

Still, the line-up remained relatively stable for the time being, and the lads were soon returning to the studio to capture yet more freshly-penned material for future use, resulting in a spate of further TOKYO BLADE releases before the year was out. First up was a self-styled *'official bootleg'*, a (deliberately) poorly-presented EP entitled »The Cave Sessions«, which featured four previously-unheard efforts from (presumably) a one-off trip to Cave Studios in Bristol. Given that there's no information whatsoever apart from the song titles (it's certainly the Vic Wright version of the band as opposed to Alan Marsh), though, it's difficult to ascertain when these efforts might have been immortalised on tape. Maybe it was even a post-Powerstation demo (it certainly sounds rough enough) pressed up on vinyl. These numbers were something of a departure once again, and suggested a shift towards a heavy, sleazy variant, which was undeniably powerful ("Monkeys Blood" almost bordered on thrash) and original in its conception, although this kind of experimentation was still guaranteed to alienate the vast majority of their original fans. One way or another, TOKYO BLADE would soon have to make up their minds whether to follow the heavy or sleazy path. In the meantime, however, the lads continued plugging away in the live arena, consolidating their enviable reputation as crowd-pleasers by turning in a capable performance at the Heavy Sound Festival (alongside the likes of TOBRUK) in Europe, after which they even recorded an official live video at a specially-organised London show a few months later.

By the tail end of 1985, the lads had recorded their third full album, which they proceeded to release on their own label (T.B. Records), having either shunned the advances of various unsuitable record companies or (more probably) failed to solicit all that much label interest in their future activities. Either way, »Blackhearts And Jaded Spades« appeared (in a well-presented gatefold sleeve) shortly thereafter, and the latest TOKYO

BLADE long-player revealed that the outfit (who, thanks to liberal use of make-up and hairspray, were now looking a lot *'prettier'* than before) had indeed made an overwhelming move towards the dreaded sleaze style, with recently-penned compositions such as "Dirty Faced Angels", "Tough Guys Tumble", "Undercover Honeymoon" and "Make It Through The Night" all conforming to the utter musical and lyrical mediocrity of the genre's pioneers. In spite of a dominance of clichéd *'big hair'* rock, dire ballads and the odd semi-acoustic affair, it wasn't quite an unmitigated disaster (the catchy title track and the reworked "Monkeys Blood" were listenable enough efforts, and "Dancing In Blue Moonlight" was a surprisingly classy number), but the largely-uninspiring album saw the *'true metal'* aficionados crying *'sell out'* and deserting TOKYO BLADE in huge numbers, leaving the ensemble's immediate future hanging in the balance.

Still, the plucky individuals carried on, releasing the unremarkable »Undercover Honeymoon« 12" EP in a futile attempt to boost sales, but it made little or no difference. It seemed to be a case of *'back to the drawing board'* once again, although the workmanlike TOKYO BLADE had yet another European tour coming up at the beginning of 1986, so the outfit would soon be able to see for themselves just how many loyal fans they actually had left. Unfortunately, vocalist Vic *'I didn't get where I am today without knowing a sinking ship when I see one'* Wright duly handed in his notice, whereupon he jetted off to the States and formed the imaginatively-named and short-lived VICKI JAMES WRIGHT BAND, before trying again and enjoying considerably more success with his JOHNNY CRASH venture. By this stage, the lads barely knew which way to turn, and there was a very real chance that they would soon cease to exist, especially when the reaction to their latest album had been so poor. Andy Boulton freely admitted that »Blackhearts« had been something of a disaster in a subsequent interview: *'The third album was a mistake, there's no doubt about that! Alan and I had written the first two albums ourselves, then Vic Wright came in as an additional songwriter, which changed our sound quite a bit. There were several tracks on »Blackhearts And Jaded Spades« which sounded nothing like typical TOKYO BLADE. The album flopped completely, and the band basically came to an end there and then.'* (Ref: Iron Pages No.35, 1996).

TOKYO BLADE had apparently played in numerous parts of the world in the preceding couple of years (they even made it to the States at one point, but it wasn't a particularly well-publicised jaunt), so they were certainly experienced campaigners by this juncture. The lack of a vocalist, however, was a serious problem, and the musicians had precious little time to find a replacement in the short term, so they were compelled to bring in the ever-obliging Carl Sentance (who was still a paid-up member of PERSIAN RISK) to fill in at their European dates, where they supported rock veterans BLUE

ÖYSTER CULT. The tour was a bit of a struggle to get through, and it was painfully apparent that TOKYO BLADE were now enjoying a far more *'selective'* following than before. The cracks were already beginning to show, and things began falling apart almost immediately upon their return to the UK. John Wiggins was first to pack his bags, lured away by a better offer to join BATTLEZONE, and things got much worse within a matter of weeks when the duo of Steve Pierce and Andy Wrighton followed suit, swiftly teaming up with former colleague Alan Marsh in the rather more melodic SHOGUN venture (a group which would also feature original TOKYO BLADE bassist Andy Robbins towards the end of their existence). This left only the hapless Andy Boulton to soldier on alone, but he subsequently made some valiant attempts to keep the name of TOKYO BLADE alive. In the first instance, he recruited an entirely new set of assistants, namely Brian George (v), Sean Cooper (g), Alex Lee (d) and former JESS COX/TYGERS OF PAN TANG stand-in Dave Donaldson (b), to make up the numbers, but this particular incarnation appears to have been staggeringly unsuccessful, and had fallen apart completely within a matter of months.

Undeterred, Boulton bounced back the following year with yet another group of backing musicians, retaining Alex Lee and trying out unknown bassist Chris Stover (who later worked with erstwhile TIGERTAILZ vocalist Steevi Jaimz in his unsuccessful WAR PARTY venture) and former SHARK vocalist Peter Zito. By some underhand method, the mainman somehow wangled a deal with an unsuspecting German company (Scratch Records), whereupon the outfit released the »Ain't Misbehavin'« set (prominently credited, on the cover at least, to *'Andy Boulton's Tokyo Blade'*) without making much of a song and dance about it. The latest long-player signified a further departure from TOKYO BLADE's power metal roots, and represented a move into semi-AOR territory of the type purveyed by MAMA'S BOYS, ALKATRAZZ or GRAND PRIX. It was melodic-rock-by-numbers (with suitably-hackneyed song titles such as "Hot For Love", "Don't Walk Away" and the obligatory "Heartbreaker"), although it was quite listenable on the whole. It hardly pushed the musical boundaries in any sense, however, and TOKYO BLADE were soon coming to terms with the fact that they would have to come up with something a tad more imaginative if they were going to survive in an oversaturated melodic rock market. Three tracks from the album subsequently showed up on their »Movie Star« 12", the latter being issued by the outfit's own (short-lived) Areba Records (who also sponsored FAIR WARNING's »Rocking At The Speed Of Light« EP at around the same time), although this British-only release doesn't really appear to have helped TOKYO BLADE's cause at home. The lads (who, confusingly, had credited Andy Catlin as bassist on their recent EP as opposed to Chris Stover) persevered with their relentless touring schedule, and proceeded to venture quite far afield, playing in some previously-uncharted parts of Europe towards the end of 1987.

In the wake of considerable public apathy, however, Andy Boulton swiftly concluded that the latest version of his beloved TOKYO BLADE had failed to capture the imagination of all that many rock fans, and the mainman must have been sorely tempted to give up the ghost completely at that point. Indeed, he appears to have dissolved the group once more in the early months of 1988 (Peter Zito moved over to the little-remembered INSIDE OUT), and there seemed to be little chance of a glorious comeback at any point thereafter. Nevertheless, Boulton confounded the sceptics yet again, and returned in 1989 with the umpteenth incarnation of TOKYO BLADE, although it was basically a solo vehicle by this stage. His latest conspirators were a trio of aspiring German musicians, two of whom (vocalist Michael Pozz and drummer Astor Mannheim) came from the little-known DEAD BALLERINAS, while the third (unknown bassist Martin Machwitz) was presumably a hastily-recruited session man. After spending some months over in Europe with his new cohorts, Boulton had written and recorded an album's worth of originals, and a deal was struck with a German company, Hot Blood Records (licensed in the US by Apocalypse), to release the fifth TOKYO BLADE LP. Sadly, »No Remorse« turned out to be a truly horrendous affair, completely marred by a disastrous production (particularly the hopelessly over-processed vocals), tenth-rate musical ideas (half of which were blatantly pinched from the likes of AEROSMITH and EUROPE, while others were just so utterly nondescript that they truly defied belief) and some excruciatingly embarrassing lyrics (although I suspect that most of the blame for the latter could be laid squarely upon the shoulders of Boulton's co-writers rather than the man himself). It was an immensely difficult album to listen to in one sitting, with all the featured tracks seeming to drag on for an eternity, and it would be virtually impossible to identify any highlights, although "Fever" (nothing to do with the outfit's identically-titled track from the »Lightning Strikes« 12") was probably the best of a *very* bad bunch. Remarkably, a tie-in 7" even escaped in Germany itself, coupling "Dark Night Over Paradise" with the reprehensible "Five Inch Catwalk", although this seems to have sold about half a dozen copies in total.

The album was the last straw for the critics, who had been reluctant to write off TOKYO BLADE completely until now, and »No Remorse« was to earn itself some of the most damning reviews ever committed to paper. Boulton soon conceded that it had all been a terrible mistake, and swiftly called it a day, laying the band to rest for the foreseeable future. The guitarist found it hard to stay away from the music business for long, however, and he soon began formulating dastardly plans to have another crack at achieving commercial success. In 1990, Boulton formed a friendly alliance with one of his former cohorts, original TOKYO BLADE vocalist Alan Marsh, whose SHOGUN venture had now run its course, and he soon persuaded the singer (plus erstwhile SHOGUN guitarist Danny Gwilym) to join him in a new venture. The trio subsequently brought the unit up to strength by recruiting bassist Colin Riggs (ex-BEG TO DIFFER), drummer Mark Angel (ex-STERLING/HARD GRAFT) and session keyboard player William 'Attila' Jackson, best-known for his work with MAINEE-AXE. Appreciating the fact that the media would, quite naturally, be wary of any further attempts to revive the now-reviled name of TOKYO BLADE, the outfit was given a false identity in the first instance, and so the press were soon being informed about the emergence of an all-new concern called MR ICE. Before long, the lads had recorded a four track demo, showcasing compositions such as "1000 Nites", "Hard Getting Over You" and "No Resistance To Love", and the general response to the cassette seemed to be pretty favourable.

In due course, MR ICE brought out a mini-LP (Danny Gwilym didn't hang around long enough to be credited, though), entitled »Have An Ice Day« (in an unrepresentative cover which would have been far better suited to a rap release), and this relatively obscure release (on the little-known Hama label, which almost certainly masked a self-financed effort) showed something of a semi-convincing return to form, the latest material generally tending to fall somewhere between the original TOKYO BLADE (in their »Blackhearts And Jaded Spades« period) and Alan Marsh's ill-fated SHOGUN themselves, with various additional influences coming across within the individual tracks. Opener "Hot Breath", for example, is a fairly blatant take on ZEPPELIN's "Kashmir", whereas "Poor Little Rich Kid" is more of an EXTREME-style funk-o-metal experience, although the entire six-tracker (with the possible exception of the irritating "Young, Bad And No Good") was pretty enjoyable, particularly so "Women And Love" and "Boyz Will Be Boyz". Over the following year or so, the band alternated between the MR ICE and TOKYO BLADE identities, although they kept a pretty low profile most of the time, concentrating on making the occasional live appearance in the South of England. They did, however, participate in a brief round of European touring (with URIAH HEEP) in the spring of 1991, although, given that the new mini-album had been such a limited pressing, I suspect that few overseas fans were even aware of its existence.

By 1992, things had gone ominously quiet once again, and it looked as though TOKYO BLADE had finally been consigned to the 'where are they now?' file. Surprisingly, however, the nucleus of the MR ICE version of the group (Marsh, Boulton, Riggs and Angel) reassembled once again in 1995, roping in old mate John Wiggins (who had been at a loose end since BATTLEZONE's demise) to make up the numbers. The outfit swiftly wrote and recorded a grand total of fifteen numbers, three of which ("Burning Down Paradise", "Flashpoint Serenade" and a reworked "Women And Love") were circulated as a promotional cassette in an attempt to draw some label attention. Fortunately, their luck was in, and the German company SPV expressed an interest in releasing the band's (latest) comeback album. With the tracks having been recorded and mastered in advance, it took little time for the long-player to be pressed up, and »Burning Down Paradise« was hitting the shops even before the end of the year. It was a very competent release, and it almost saw a return to »Night Of The Blade«-era material, with compositions such as "Burning Down Paradise", "Get Out Of My Face", "Flashpoint Serenade" and "Only The Strong" all being immensely listenable efforts. The selection of original material featured ("Women And Love" and "Hot Breath" were additionally recycled from the MR ICE record) wasn't flawless by any means, though, and some inclusions seemed a bit lengthy and lacking in personality. Still, it was the strongest TOKYO BLADE release for a decade, so let's give credit where it's due.

Immediately after the album appeared, there seemed to be a pretty major resurgence in TOKYO BLADE-related interest, and the lads were invited to play at 1996's Bang Your Head Festival in Europe, where they shared the bill with the revived SAVAGE. The warm reception afforded to the ensemble by the local crowd must have come as a considerable relief, and it looked as though there would certainly be further mileage in the TOKYO BLADE name for the time being. In fact, things went quiet soon afterwards, and there have, as yet, been no reliable indications that additional releases will be recorded in the immediate future. Andy Boulton is still reported to be writing new material himself, and may even bring out a solo album at some stage, but there's serious doubt as to whether the TOKYO BLADE name will ever be resurrected properly. With John Wiggins, Mark

Angel and Colin Riggs having all been lending their services to the revived BATTLEZONE in recent times, their future involvement with any of Andy Boulton's musical activities must remain uncertain, so we'll just have to wait and see what happens. In the meantime, fans have recently been treated to a fairly generous programme of CD reissues from labels such as High Vaultage and Zoom Club, one of the latest to appear being an album called »Pumphouse«,

culled from unreleased studio material recorded in the 90's. In fact, PUMPHOUSE was the name of Al Marsh's low-key project from 1993 or thereabouts (the line-up was practically identical to that of MR ICE, though), so I reckon it probably wasn't conceived as a genuine TOKYO BLADE release in the first instance.

LP's

»**Tokyo Blade**« Powerstation 1983
[Original UK issue]
»**Midnight Rendezvous**« Bernett 1984/Banzai 1984
[French/Canadian issue of »Tokyo Blade« album]
»**Tokyo Blade**« Roadrunner 1984
[Dutch issue]
»**Night Of The Blade**« Powerstation 1984/Bernett/Roadrunner 1984
[UK/French/Dutch issue]
»**Midnight Rendezvous**« Combat 1985
[US issue of »Tokyo Blade« album with three alternate tracks]
»**Night Of The Blade**« Combat 1985
[US issue]
»**Warrior Of The Rising Sun**« Raw Power 1985
[Double compilation album]
»**Blackhearts And Jaded Spades**« T.B. Records 1985/Steamhammer 1985
[UK/German issue, gatefold sleeve]
»**Ain't Misbehavin'**« Scratch Records 1987
»**No Remorse**« Apocalypse 1989
[US issue]

»**No Remorse**« Hot Blood 1989
[German issue in different sleeve]
»**One Night In Ludwigsburg**« Bootleg 198?
[Live bootleg from 1985]

Mini-LP's
»**Madame Guillotine**« Banzai 1985
[Canadian issue with six tracks]
»**Have An Ice Day**« Hama Records 1990
[Under the name of MR ICE]

12" EP's
»**Midnight Rendezvous**« Powerstation 1984
["Midnight Rendezvous", "Meanstreak" and "Highway Passion" all non-LP]
»**Lightning Strikes**« Powerstation 1984
["Attack Attack" and "Fever" non-LP]
»**Madame Guillotine**« Powerstation 1985
[Three track UK version, "Madame Guillotine" and "Breakout" non-LP]
»**Madame Guillotine**« Roadrunner 1985
[Four track Dutch version]
»**The Cave Sessions**« Private 1985
["School House Is Burnin'" and "Jezzabell" non-LP, "Shadows Of Insanity" different to album version]
»**Undercover Honeymoon**« T.B. Records 1985
["Stealing The Thief" and "Bottom End" non-LP, "Undercover Honeymoon" and "Playroom Of Poison Dreams" different to album versions]
»**Movie Star**« Areba Records 1987

7" Singles
»**If Heaven Is Hell**« Blade Records 1983
[Reissue of GENGHIS KHAN single with new labels and sleeve, B-side "Highway Passion", different versions of both tracks later featured on »Midnight Rendezvous« 12"]
»**Midnight Rendezvous**« Blade Records 1983
[Reissue of GENGHIS KHAN single with new labels and sleeve, B-side "Meanstreak", different versions of both tracks later featured on »Midnight Rendezvous« 12"]
»**Powergame**« Powerstation 1983
[A-side different to album version, B-side "Death On Mainstreet" non-LP]
»**Midnight Rendez-vous**« Bernett 1984
[French issue in different sleeve, B-side "If Heaven Is Hell"]
»**If Heaven Is Hell**« Victoria 1984
[Spanish issue in different sleeve, B-side "Liar"]
»**Dark Night Over Paradise**« Hot Blood 1989
[German-only release, A-side non-LP]

Promotional Releases
»**Monkeys Blood**« Private 1985
[Promo 7" flexi disc, given free with 'Enfer' magazine]

CD's

»Blackhearts And Jaded Spades« Steamhammer 1985
»Ain't Misbehavin'« Hard'n'Heavy 1987
[German release]
»No Remorse« Apocalypse 1989
[US issue with two bonus tracks]
»No Remorse« Hot Blood 1989
[German issue with different cover]
»Tokyo Blade« Roadrunner 1989
»Night Of The Blade« Roadrunner 1989
»Ain't Misbehavin'« Brainstorm 1990
[Swiss release]
»Burning Down Paradise« SPV 1995
»Tokyo Blade« High Vaultage 1996
[With five bonus tracks]
»Night Of The Blade« High Vaultage 1997
[With eight bonus tracks]
»Night Of The Blade-The Night Before« High Vaultage 1997
[Unreleased demo version of second album with original vocalist, with six extra tracks]
»Blackhearts And Jaded Spades« Zoom Club Records 1998
[Reissue]
»Pumphouse« Zoom Club Records 1998
[Compilation of unreleased studio material from early 90's]
»Have An Ice Day« Zoom Club Records 1999
[Under the name of MR ICE, reissue of original mini-album with four bonus studio and live tracks]

Mini-CD's

»Have An Ice Day« Hama Records 1990
[Under the name of MR ICE]

Compilation Appearances

"Attack Attack" on »Wango Tango Vol.1« LP Bernett 1984
"Fever" on »Wango Tango Vol.1« LP Bernett 1984 + »12 Commandments In Metal« LP Roadrunner 1985 + »Megalomania« LP Powerstation 1986
"If Heaven Is Hell" on »Metal Hammer« LP Roadrunner 1984 + »Megalomania« LP Powerstation 1986
"Night Of The Blade" on »Metal Killers Kollection I« Do-LP Castle Communications 1985 + »Metal Killers Kollection« CD Castle Communications 1991
"Lightning Strikes" on »Axe« LP Banzai 1985
"Rock Me To The Limit" on »Megalomania« LP Powerstation 1986
"Sting In The Tail" on »Unbroken Metal« CD Private 1997

TOKYO ROSE

Val Ophield (v)
Peter Barclay (g)
Derek Buckham (b)
Steve Blenkinsop (k)
Graeme Wright (d)
Derek Smith (sx)

As with the RED ALERT/WILDFIRE affair, this one unquestionably needs a bit of urgent clarification. Contrary to some previous reports, the particular version of TOKYO ROSE who recorded a one-off single for Guardian in 1983 weren't actually related to the identically-named outfit who appeared on the same label's »Pure Overkill« compilation within a matter of months (and who later contributed personnel to HOLOSADE and DARK HEART). It seems a inexplicably bizarre coincidence, but, when you contemplate just how many groups (at least half a dozen, both within the UK and elsewhere) adopted the TOKYO ROSE identity from the early 80's onwards (suggesting that RIOT probably have a lot to answer for), and, when you further consider that (incredibly enough) there were even at least two British versions of TOKYO BLADE on the go at roughly the same time, the reality of the situation becomes a bit easier to comprehend. Clearly, rock musicians have never been the most original characters when it comes to thinking up names for their own outfits.

In any case, the little-remembered bunch who issued the Guardian single (entitled »Dry Your Eyes«) certainly *looked* the part (as evidenced by their photos on the reverse of the picture sleeve, the front of which shows a tearful woman in military regalia), although the musical contents are, if truth be known, utterly abysmal. This disaster is really only on the very verge of the rock style, and sounds more like a slushy pop/rock effort than anything remotely resembling NWOBHM. In fact, it's far less listenable than ROUGH JUSTICE's »Million To One« EP, a record which (having been offered for sale at ridiculously high prices over the years) now seems to be almost universally despised by collectors, for some strange reason. If anything, the utterly nonsensical flipside ("This Is Tokyo Rose") is even worse than the dreary ballad on the A-side, and, in both cases, the feeble lyrics, amateurish arrangements, embarrassingly coy vocals and inclusion of saxophones are all monstrously dire. Surprisingly, therefore, I wouldn't recommend that you look for a copy, unless you intend to throw darts at it.

Nothing much is known about this particular band or their musical history (and I don't imagine anyone really cares, to be honest), but it looks as though they only chose to inflict one vinyl debacle upon us, so we should probably be grateful for small mercies. Although this shocker of a single has even been touted around at obscene three-figure prices (yes, I'm afraid so) over the years, I can assure everyone that there's absolutely no justification for spending more than a fiver on it, should any of you decide that you just can't bear to have unsightly gaps in your Guardian collection. I've absolutely no idea what possessed the normally-sensible Terry Gavaghan to get involved with utter tripe like this, and it's hardly surprising that the Guardian label found itself in critical financial trouble within a year or so of this dreadful record's release.

7" Singles
»Dry Your Eyes« Guardian 1983

TOO MUCH

Colin John Bates (v)
Russ Sollof (g)
Dick Conolly (b)
Dave Mew (d)

More borderline punk/metal material comes courtesy of TOO MUCH, whose two 7" releases on the eclectic Lightning label (both of which predated the original metal explosion by at least a year) appear to have been adopted as genuine NWOBHM by many (as with outfits such as MAYHEM and RED RAGE, however, their records tend to fetch higher prices among punk fans), although I'm sure the band themselves would have denied being remotely 'metal' at the time. The quartet's musical progression pretty much mirrors that of the LIGHTNING RAIDERS, with their first single, the »Who You Wanna Be« (B-side "Another Time Another Place") effort from early 1978, containing a couple of fairly disposable, knockabout punk selections with very little to offer the majority of metalheads. Certainly, the *'moody types posing on a hill'* image on the cover pretty much typified the band's early sound, and this particular release was an altogether unremarkable affair. Like many of the singles issued by Lightning in the late 70's, the TOO MUCH debut wasn't pressed in huge quantities, and has remained a scarcely-sighted item ever since, although NWOBHM collectors can safely give this one a wide berth.

In spite of the relatively modest performance of their first release, however, the band were fortunate enough to be retained by Lightning, who invited them to deliver another slice of vinyl before the year was out. The second TOO MUCH 7", however, turned out to be considerably more rocking, with both "Kick Me One More Time" and "It's Only For Me" coming across as passable crossover material in the general style of GROUND ATTACK, RED RAGE or LEFT HAND DRIVE. The remaining track, "Be Mine", is nothing to write home about, though, so it's very much a *'take it or leave it'* release for the average metal fan. With the record being issued in a rather misleading gatefold sleeve (depicting a reasonably well-illustrated, fantasy battle scene) which certainly *looks* like a typical NWOBHM release, the group's intention was surely somewhat ironic, rather than suggesting they had indeed *'gone metal'* since their first vinyl outing. Both TOO MUCH releases currently fetch a disproportionately high price for what they actually are, to be honest, and they should really only be of interest to the fanatical NWOBHM collector.

7" EP's
»Kick Me One More Time« Lightning 1978
7" Singles
»Who You Wanna Be« Lightning 1978

TORA TORA

Brenn (v)
Paul Wheeldon (g)
Peter North (g)
Ian Dalglish (b)
Simon Wright (d)

Although a couple of American outfits subsequently adopted the name, the original TORA TORA were an extremely youthful bunch of Mancunians who first got together in around 1979. With remarkable haste (although the ensemble had presumably paid their dues in the live environment beforehand), their debut »Red Sun Setting« single (which came in a fairly unremarkable picture sleeve) was recorded (at the famous Cargo Studios in Rochdale) and issued as a self-financed effort in mid-1980, at which point the average age of the musicians was still a mere seventeen. Even so, TORA TORA acquitted themselves pretty respectably on this introductory vinyl outing, where both the energetic A-side and the musically-analogous "Highway (Shooting Like A Bullet)" come across as mid-paced, straightforward, heavy fare in the manner of CHAINSAW, SLEDGEHAMMER or TORTURE, fairly typical of the early days of the NWOBHM, but hardly pushing the musical boundaries in any sense. Considering the youngsters' lack of experience on the recording front, however, it wasn't a bad way to introduce themselves to the masses, although it's certainly not the most sophisticated material you're ever likely to hear.

Following the debut single's release, the group were soon to part company with their enigmatic frontman *'Brenn'* (contrary to speculation, this apparently wasn't the well-travelled Bren Spencer, later of GASKIN *et al.*) and bassist Ian Dalglish, the latter being replaced by Nigel Blythe (who, worryingly enough, also dabbled with keyboards on occasion), while guitarist Peter North won a promotion and subsequently took over vocal duties. With this short-lived line-up, the lads circulated a new demo featuring "Rod Of Iron", "Burn Down Ya Stack" (whatever the hell that means) and a cover of UFO's "Shoot Shoot", hoping to build upon their ever-developing local popularity, which had allowed the band to tour successfully throughout the North West in the preceding months. The revised version of TORA TORA seems not to have been a massive success, however, and a few more personnel reshuffles were in order before a more satisfactory line-up was finally established. The chaps kept a low profile during this period of instability (which was understandable enough), but it must have come as a relief when they managed to assemble a more suitable collection of musicians, whereupon they began working on some brand-new material.

The latest version of the group centred around the long-serving Paul Wheeldon and Peter North, who found themselves being assisted by newcomers Mick Leach (v), John Murney (b) and Kevin Whitehead (d). With a stronger line-up having emerged from the chaos of the preceding months, the revitalised TORA TORA swiftly recorded a cassette featuring "Night Of The Demons", "Island Of Gods" and "Rockin' In The UK", which duly received high praise in Howard Johnson's 'Phoenix' fanzine. A short time later, the lads had several of their demo selections aired in a session for their local Piccadilly Radio station, this useful exposure being followed by a prestigious appearance at the legendary U.M.I.S.T. Metal Festival, held in Manchester in May 1981, where they shared a stage with local rivals SACRED ALIEN, VENOM (before they became ROX), SILVERWING and headliners DIAMOND HEAD. The lads were also privileged enough to be featured in the 'Armed And Ready' section of the inaugural issue of 'Kerrang', which spread their name to a national audience. A number of gigs further afield followed as a matter of routine, including the occasional trip to the rock-friendly capital, and the outfit (whose business affairs were largely handled by family members as opposed to a professional management team) allowed themselves to look to the future with considerable optimism.

The band's follow-up single, another self-financed effort entitled »Don't Want To Let You Go« (b/w "Sorry I Broke Your Heart"), is, however, something of a baffling mystery. There's no picture sleeve, no date of release, and it appears to have escaped with virtually zero publicity, such that relatively few NWOBHM collectors are actually even aware of its existence these days. Apart from the ever-present nucleus of Paul Wheeldon and Pete North, however, I'm not even sure who was involved by this stage, although it appears to feature yet another new vocalist (to be honest, I'd have to admit that Mick Leach had quite an annoying style), and I couldn't say for sure when it might have been released. Mind you, since TORA TORA's overall direction had now moved towards a considerably more polished and melodic style reminiscent of SHERWOOD or GRAND PRIX, I'd suggest that it's most likely to have been from around 1984 or thereabouts, as opposed to the irritatingly vague *'early 80's'* tag which the majority of dealers tend to ascribe to it. Given that this ill-advised and poorly-promoted release was almost certainly a complete and utter commercial disaster, though, you might well have expected it to signal the end of the outfit for good.

After a hiatus of a further few years, however, yet another revised version of the band (now simply calling themselves TORA) came out of the woodwork, the Wheeldon/North backbone now being complemented by the returning Nigel Blythe on bass, plus relative unknowns Pete Jackson (v), Paul Quinn (d) and Kevin Brannie (k). Before long, a capable demo cassette and some well-received live appearances began drawing the attention of 'Kerrang' and one or two of the smaller fanzines, although the word on the street was that the ensemble's musical inclinations had apparently shifted once more during the wilderness years. Indeed, when their »Deja Vu« single (b/w "She's History") was unleashed upon the listening public (with no picture sleeve and featuring an extraordinarily amateurish label design) shortly thereafter, it rapidly became evident that TORA had now adopted a considerably more commercial stance (falling somewhere between RADIO MOSCOW and VOYAGER UK) which bore precious little resemblance to their original gutsy NWOBHM sound, although I suppose it was still a fairly logical progression after their melodic »Don't Want To Let You Go« two-tracker. Still, this comeback release seems to have made little or no impression on the rock community at the time, and sales of »Deja Vu« were extremely modest, so you can't help but wonder if slightly more forethought in terms of presentation or promotion might have helped their cause.

Towards the end of their existence, the persevering TORA's personnel problems seem to have become particularly exaggerated, although the lads had already become accustomed to drafting in a variety of local scenesters to plug the gaps which arose on a depressingly regular basis, and one of their final acquisitions was frontman Pete McGuckian, an individual who had contributed backing vocals to ALISTAIR TERRY's solo »Yonge At Heart« album way back in 1985. Although the revamped outfit remained on the scene for the rest of the decade (their activities including a few gigs with FM and support slot on a DOGS D'AMOUR tour in 1988), gaining the odd live review and honourable mention in the rock press along the way, they don't seem to have survived the transition to the 90's. It looks as though TORA eventually ran out of both accomplices and enthusiasm, whereupon the central characters ultimately pulled the plug in the wake of continued media disinterest, after which they finally took their leave of the music scene. Although the long-serving veterans failed to resurface in acts of note, it's worth mentioning that a couple of TORA TORA members moved over to other metal-related projects after leaving the fold in the early 80's. Bassist John Murney, for example, held a fairly brief tenure with fellow Mancunians SACRED ALIEN, while their original drummer, Simon Wright, after initially pottering around with various NWOBHM hopefuls such as A II Z, TYTAN and AURORA, eventually made his mark with some considerably more high-profile acts, including AC/DC, DIO and, latterly, UFO.

7" Singles
»Red Sun Setting« Mancunian Metal Records 1980
»Don't Want To Let You Go« Tora Records 198?
»Deja Vu« Laminate Records 1987
[Under the name of TORA]

TORTURE

Ray Askew (v,g)
Clive Robinson (g)
Mark Kenyon (g)
Pete Ditchfield (b)
Mic Young (d)

The individual members of Kent's TORTURE (not to be confused with heavier American namesakes from later in the decade) were all to be found playing in various small-time local bands immediately prior to the main NWOBHM explosion, the original five musicians coming together to form the all-new TORTURE entity in 1979. The threesome of Clive Robinson, Mic Young and Mark Kenyon were all veterans of the recently-demised LOCO, while vocalist Ray Askew had latterly been busy with an act called MORDOR. Completing the line-up in the first instance was bassist Pete Ditchfield, whose previous credits included a stint with the hopelessly-named LIVE ANTEATER. With an earth-shattering triple-guitar attack at their disposal, this powerful new outfit were soon being described by casual observers (those who managed to retain their hearing, that is) as an extraordinarily loud mixture of AC/DC, MOTÖRHEAD, KISS and the SEX PISTOLS, whereupon TORTURE began developing a strong local following *via* their numerous outings in the pubs and clubs of the region. Towards the end of 1980, the band finally managed to install themselves in Red Studios in Rochester, where they laid down a speculative demo, a three track affair featuring "On The Run", "Galactic Warriors" and "Motorvating Thing". Mind you, just when things were starting to take off, original drummer Mic Young flew the coop at short notice, although Dean Swift was, er, *swiftly* brought in to save the day.

The TORTURE lads had another bit of rearrangement in store in February 1981, however, when bassist Pete Ditchfield decided to pack in the music business in favour of pursuing his Geology studies at college, which is possibly the least rock'n'roll thing I've ever heard in my entire life. Even so, Clive Robinson duly took over on bass without making much of a fuss about it, and the outfit soldiered on with their slimmed-down line-up, proceeding (almost immediately) to record the tracks which would constitute their self-financed vinyl debut (predictably, the group hadn't benefitted from any major-label patronage in the interim) at the nearby Oakwood Studios facility. Pressed in a relatively modest quantity of around seven hundred copies (strange amount, that), TORTURE's 7" EP featured three unusually varied selections, the memorable opener "Last Post" (an incredibly raw and energetic, upbeat composition in the mould of early TYGERS OF PAN TANG or DRAGSTER) being easily the pick of the bunch, while the punk-tinged "Lucky" is, perhaps, more along the lines of VIRGIN STAR or the LIGHTNING RAIDERS. "Finding My Way Home", on the other hand, is a knockabout, singalong, good-time rock'n'roll number (with the 'Captain Pugwash' theme thrown in for good measure) in the best tradition of VARDIS or SPIDER. Weird.

The record proved to be a major success for the band, with regional sales exceeding their wildest dreams and landing the lads a number one position in the 'Sounds' Heavy Metal Chart of the day. Clive Robinson more or less became their spokesman at around this time, and was even invited to provide some ready quotes for the hacks at a local newspaper, one representative example being: 'We hope to get a few more gigs as a result of the single, although it would be nice enough if we could just spread our name around in this way.' How utterly fascinating. At this point, the group entered their most successful phase, recruiting a full-time bassist in the shape of Pete Sollis (Clive Robinson moving back to guitar duties) and stepping up their activities in the live environment. The aforementioned Robinson was clearly something of an eccentric character, as he was apparently in the habit of taking to the stage in a brown fur costume complete with horns (and you thought MANOWAR were ridiculous enough), the band members obviously having a particular fondness for certain mighty creatures (the observation that they named their label Wildebeest Records was a bit of a giveaway) of this ilk (or possibly *elk*). Bizarrely, they even went so far as to *'sacrifice'* an effigy of the aforementioned animal at one of their many appearances...er, keep taking the pills, lads.

Unfortunately, TORTURE consistently failed to procure a suitable management team at any point (maybe Clive's wildebeest costume frightened them all off), such people being a necessary evil for any acts who wished to attract a significant amount of major (or, more realistically, independent) label attention. As a result, the band were never offered that lucrative deal which would bring in some serious wonga. Eventually, the lads began to lose heart, and, after a seemingly mismatched support tour with NINE BELOW ZERO, the disenchanted outfit rapidly started to grow apart, and had splintered within a matter of months. Ray Askew, Dean Swift and Pete Sollis proceeded to hook up with a talented guitarist called Mick Bennett, forming a capable, but ultimately unsuccessful, proposition known as MEANSTREAK (one of countless groups to adopt the identity), who failed to make all that much of an impression at the time. Bonkers guitarist Clive Robinson, on the other hand, after taking some time off to reassess the situation, unexpectedly reformed TORTURE a year or so later, enticing former cohorts Mark Kenyon and Mic Young back into the ranks, the line-up being completed by new bassist Andy Stilwell and frontman Mick Hoare. It proved to be a remarkably fleeting second attempt, however, and this particular incarnation gave up the ghost for good (after a mere two gigs) within a couple of months.

Interest in the scarce TORTURE 7" (which was never issued in a picture sleeve) was stirred up by the high prices which were suddenly being charged for the item in the early 90's, whereupon the musicians were kind enough to release a significant quantity of unsold copies onto the market, ensuring that the asking price would never reach particularly insane levels. Once the erstwhile members had been contacted, it emerged that Clive Robinson had been spreading himself pretty widely over the intervening years (presumably having abandoned any notions of becoming a full-time gnu impersonator by this stage), the latter having lent a hand in such hopelessly obscure post-TORTURE projects as ART ZONE, JANUS STARK (no, not the ENGLISH DOGS offshoot), DRESDEN STYLE, the EARTHMOVERS and CARNIVAL OF SOULS. What a busy chap. His erstwhile colleague Mick Hoare, on the other hand, has spent a considerable amount of his time in recent years at the helm of a covers band called FREE SPIRIT (I can't possibly imagine what sort of material features in their set) and running an excellent record shop named Rock Bottom.

7" EP's
»**Last Post**« Wildebeest Records 1981

Compilation Appearances
"**Last Post**" on »NWOBHM Vol.7« Bootleg CD 1996

TOSH

Howard 'Tosh' Midlane (v, g)
Tony Cousins (v, k)
Dave Palmer (v, d)
Steve Turner (g, b)
Steve Jackson (d)

Phil Boucherat (sx)

In spite of the observation that they had comparatively little competition in the rock sphere (with the notable exception of CHAIN REACTION, FLIGHT 77 and the GOLANT PISTONS), Cornwall's unpromisingly-monikered TOSH (the central character's nickname) appear not to have made much of a name for themselves anywhere in the South West, suggesting that they probably didn't get out and about too often. Indeed, inspecting the credits on their one-off slice of vinyl, it looks very much like a studio endeavour, especially with the multiple vocalists, drummers and so forth. Still, the privately-issued »One More For The Road« set (which surfaced in 1982) was a semi-interesting collection of original material, with one side being very much inclined towards more progressive musings, while the reverse is practically pub rock. Very strange, if you ask me. Their long-player opens with two extremely lengthy efforts ("Julius" and "Queen Of Tiger Bay"), these being the more ambitious numbers by far, showcasing some reasonably innovative examples of musicianship and eliciting a few tentative comparisons with the likes of SARACEN, BACKLASH, MOVIE STARS or even SHAFTSBURY. It was rather self-indulgent, admittedly, and I reckon twelve-minute songs should probably be banned outright by the Geneva Convention, but these particular efforts weren't too obnoxious at all.

On side two, however, TOSH reveal another aspect of their personality, one which they would have been well-advised to keep hidden, but never mind. The lightweight, crowd-pleasing tracks ("Millionaire", "Little Runaway Sister", "Life's High Trapeze" and "One More For The Road") trundled out for inspection are all pretty throwaway and unsubstantial, suggesting some comparisons with the likes of WENDY HOUSE, DEDRINGER and SMOKIN ROADIE. Even the dreaded saxophone puts in an unwarranted appearance on a few occasions, and this batch of numbers seems to possess virtually no redeeming features whatsoever. It was all very disappointing, although I suppose a carbon copy of side one might have rendered the album a pretty heavy-going experience, so at least we were spared another pair of epics in this instance. The long-player appears to have been pressed in fairly minuscule quantities, and most NWOBHM aficionados remained unaware of its existence until the mid-90's, when a few copies were unearthed and offered for sale at hugely-inflated prices. Predictably, though, once word got around that this wasn't exactly a true classic of the genre after all, its value dropped quite dramatically, but I reckon it's still an item that most modern-day collectors can leave off their wants lists in the long term.

LP's
»One More For The Road« Bicycle Records 1982

TOUCHED

Ronnie Wolstenholme (v)
John Hull (g)
Mark Caffrey (b)
Martin Schofield (d)

The entity known as TOUCHED came into being in the second half of 1983, following the demise of two popular bands from the North West viz. ARAGORN (from whence came guitarist John Hull) and DRAGSTER (who had 'acquired' their identity from the earlier act who had recorded for Heavy Metal and were now 'resting'). The new outfit (who based themselves in Lancashire) swiftly assembled a repertoire of usable compositions, some of which were demoed for the attention of the ever-accommodating Ebony, who graciously stumped up some cash and encouraged the lads to come up with a full album. The debut TOUCHED set (the tastefully-titled »Back Alley Vices«) was eventually unleashed towards the end of 1984, having been preceded by a single coupling "Dream Girl" with the non-LP effort "We'll Fight Back". Significantly, the combo were still using a few old DRAGSTER compositions such as "Warrior" and "Heartbreaker" at this juncture, so they had probably been given little opportunity to develop a significantly novel repertoire of their own during the earlier part of the year. The material on display was pretty substantial in general, but occasionally quite melodic and accessible, the main comparisons being with the likes of METAL MIRROR, A II Z, TNT or MIDAS. It was an energetic collection (marred by the usual bog-standard production), with highlights including the catchy "Nothing To Lose" and "Running", although the overall standard was pretty variable.

TOUCHED subsequently endured a 'review' in 'Kerrang' which basically amounted to little more than a premeditated character assassination (somebody surely got out of the wrong side of bed that day), before stepping up their touring activities to promote the release. It soon became apparent that their live appearances were limited by the amount of time the lads could take off work, as they were all still holding down day jobs at that stage. Even so, their gigs tended to be lively, enthusiastically-received (if not exactly well-attended) affairs, the group treating crowds to a selection of original material as well as carefully selected covers from the likes of MONTROSE and VAN HALEN. Notwithstanding the lack of support from the big players in the publishing field, the band enjoyed loyal patronage from various fanzines and radio stations, developing a reasonably substantial following over the ensuing months. Mark Caffrey, in particular, was later keen to give thanks to the part-time writers who served to promote the music of small-time hopefuls: *'They give a genuine opinion of the music, whereas you get the impression with bigger magazines that a lot of money might go west in order to say the 'right' thing about the 'wrong' band. Definitely more honest and it's more in touch with the roots as well.'* (Ref: A Dose Of The Heavies, Issue 4, September 1986).

By the summer of 1986, a second TOUCHED album was finally on the cards, and so the lads were soon doing their thing in the recording studio once more. The finished product came in the shape of the starkly-presented »Death Row«, a long-player which saw the group attempting a less frenzied and more varied set of compositions. The production was certainly a slight improvement on the hatchet-job of their debut, and allowed the individual tracks (two of the better efforts being "When I Call Your Name" and "Through The Night") to take on something of an identity of their own, rather than just merging into one overwhelming blur as had been the case on the »Back Alley Vices« set. Overall, it was a fairly major step in the right direction, and it seems that the musicians themselves were considerably more satisfied with the end result. Sadly, however, the outfit still appear to have lost a bit of confidence after this release hit the shops, and subsequently struggled to find a direction which would suit the musical needs of each member. Things looked fairly ominous, but there was still a real chance that TOUCHED would resolve their various problems and return to the fray.

In the end, though, it was to prove an intolerable situation for vocalist Ronnie Wolstenholme, and, following his inevitable departure, the remaining members were obliged to draft in new recruit Rob Bowker to make up the numbers. This revised version of TOUCHED re-emerged in 1988 (having already parted company with Ebony by this juncture), brandishing a two track demo (featuring "Angel Face" and "Trial By Combat") with which to tempt various labels into furnishing them with lucrative contracts. In the event, however, no particularly viable offers came their way, and the group began to fragment within a matter of months. Three of the four members (Martin Schofield, Mark Caffrey and John Hull) from the last line-up, incidentally, later resurfaced in a boogie rock outfit known as the OUTSIDERS, who released a private album entitled »Skin« in 1991, following this with the »Ripped Shirt« set a couple of years later, by which time Mark Caffrey was the only one of the three still involved. It's entirely possible that the OUTSIDERS might actually still be a going concern in one form or another (erstwhile COBRA stalwart Paul Edmondson was lending a hand as drummer at one point), although their plans to issue a third album called »The Proud Ones« (originally due towards the end of 1997) seem to have fallen through for the time being. Mark Caffrey also hooked up with the *original* DRAGSTER after they got going again in the 90's, just to confuse matters even further, and he features on several tracks (produced by erstwhile TOUCHED colleague John Hull) which have recently been included on British Steel's »The Very Best Of Dragster« retrospective.

LP's
»Back Alley Vices« Ebony 1984
»Death Row« Ebony 1986

7" Singles
»Dream Girl« Ebony 1984
[B-side "We'll Fight Back" non-LP]

TRACER

Ron Laity (v)
Aubrey Williams (g)
Mark Daghorn (b)
Nigel Amy (d)

Compared with the semi-success achieved by LEGEND, the other NWOBHM-period bands from the Channel Islands ultimately failed to make themselves known further afield, one of Jersey's minor contenders being the little-remembered TRACER, whose »Chanelled Agression« EP (well done chaps, you thought of a great pun but contrived to spell both words incorrectly) represents a major-league rarity. Clearly, this particular bunch were taking their lead from the aforementioned LEGEND in terms of going it alone and releasing their own vinyl rather than waiting for the labels to come calling, and it's fair to suggest

that they shared an equivalently-gloomy outlook. Is life on Jersey really that bad? The four miserably-titled compositions on show are pedestrian, melancholic pieces in the vein of a particularly woeful REQUIEM, ARC or RENEGADE (Kent version), with "Don't Bless The Warrior" being the most familiar, this number having been included on the »NWOBHM Vol.8« bootleg. Elsewhere, "Memories Always Kill", "Pain, Pain" and "Neon Town" are much the same, and some of the lyrics would almost certainly be a bit pejorative to the mental state of anyone who already felt slightly 'down in the dumps'. In fact, it's difficult to recommend this release to anyone except those of you who genuinely enjoy morose material, as the musicianship and songwriting is average and the production is basic, to say the least. It's reasonably heavy, though, and, as a proto-doom offering, it's probably of historical interest in terms of the genre's development over the years.

Other studio material recorded by the quartet, however, a year or so after their debut EP was originally released, tended to suggest that the lads had actually adopted a slightly more upbeat style with less mournful vocals. The lyrics, meanwhile, still evoke a rather nihilistic view of life, especially on the non-cheerful "Blinded By A Lie" and "Nightstalker" (musically reminiscent of Avon's BOULEVARD and the American group DRUID, respectively). Otherwise, "In The Heat Of The Night", "Shoot Out The Lights" (hey, those titles look a bit familiar) and "City Lights" (shouldn't that be *Diamond* Lights"?) were more of the same, although the riffs are marginally better and the shouted backing vocals tend to lift the mood slightly. Nevertheless, the outfit (who probably gigged locally throughout their existence but didn't necessarily make it to the mainland at any point) didn't manage to follow up their debut vinyl release in later years, suggesting that they fragmented towards the second half of the decade. Things appear to have gone wrong in the wake of Nigel Amy's departure in 1985 (although a temporary stand-in was found in the shape of Dean Shepherd, borrowed from local part-timers JONAH), and it's entirely possible that the lads failed to get a revised version of the group off the ground after this period of instability.

The TRACER 7" comes in a generic picture sleeve featuring the band logo (their identity having been taken from a type of luminous bullet, no doubt a subject close to their hearts) and the EP title itself. On the reverse, the four manic depressives pictured look as though they've just been told that there's been a Prozac embargo on the very day that all their families have been wiped out in a series of bizarre gardening accidents. As if this wasn't enough, the following cheery aphorism is given at the base of the sleeve: 'There is no end in sight, no winners in this fight'. How uplifting. I wonder if any of them are actually still alive? The last TRACER member to be heard from was Mark Daghorn, who, in later years, appeared in more melodic outfits such as THE AVENUE (who even got to the stage of issuing an EP) and VARIOUS AREAS, although the fact that the latter trio were mercilessly ridiculed in the cruel 'Ugliest Men In Rock' feature in 'Kerrang' might finally have tipped him over the edge.

7" EP's
»Chanelled Agression« Mousehole Records 1983

Compilation Appearances
"Don't Bless The Warrior" on »NWOBHM Vol.8« Bootleg CD 1996

TRACK 4

Cliff Robertson (v, g)
Mark Bickerstaffe (v, g)
Rob Sheppard (b)
Steve Kirby (d)

Not quite as hopelessly esoteric as some of the monumentally scarce records documented in this volume, this privately-issued three-tracker is included on a considerable percentage of wants lists, although there has still been a fair amount of confusion over the band's name in recent years. To put everyone straight, the quartet in question (from Berkshire) were definitely called TRACK 4 (still an utterly feeble choice, though) and their sole vinyl offering (issued at the tail end of 1982) was titled »Mr Charisma«, not the other way round! It's a fairly schizophrenic release, to be honest, with only "Chalk And Cheese" setting our NWOBHM pulses racing to any extent, this being a pretty weighty number in the vein of RENEGADE (the Kent version, that is). The title track and "Freetime", on the other hand, were rather more lightweight and throwaway rockers in the easy-going manner of ANGEL STREET, STATIC or NO SWEAT, with the merest hint of old masters THIN LIZZY shining through every now and again. It was slightly disappointing, all things considered, and it's a shame this bunch didn't simply go for the full-on approach with more conviction. I can't imagine that the record was a particularly extensive pressing, though, and it seems likely that few units were shifted upon its release.

TRACK 4 seem to have been the epitome of the local, small-time outfit with big ambitions but a critical lack of musical innovation with which to attract the attention of the major (or, for that matter, independent) labels. Surprisingly, however, it looks as though they persevered, in one form or another, until at least 1984, laying down further demos along the way, although their various recordings consistently failed to win favour with any record companies of note. Only a few hundred copies of the band's EP are likely to have been manufactured (rendering it a fairly highly-priced item for the modern-day NWOBHM collector), and they certainly don't come out of the woodwork too often. If you fancy one, though, keep an eye out for (you guessed it) a generic, monochrome cover which, if you're very lucky, may also contain a one-sided insert which gives an entertaining insight into the ensemble's rather off-the-wall lyrical concepts. It's entirely possible, by the way, that certain TRACK 4 personnel (notably guitarist Mark Bickerstaffe) also contributed to the fortunes of another local outfit, PREDATÜR, although we still await confirmation of this.

7" EP's
»Mr Charisma« Private 1982

TRADER

Wrann
Hayter
Blake
Appleton

Hampshire's little-remembered TRADER certainly won't be troubling the likes of DEMOLITION or SHOCK TREATMENT for the coveted title of 'most brutal NWOBHM band', but their laid-back direction just about warrants inclusion in this book. The selections showcased on their seldom-seen single viz. "Back Street Trader" and "Love On The Run", are extremely lightweight, 70's-influenced efforts in the general style of BLAZER BLAZER or URCHIN (let's face it, would either of these outfits *ever* have been considered genuine NWOBHM contenders were it not for certain future members of IRON MAIDEN being involved?), with a detectable undercurrent of more mainstream acts such as THE EAGLES or STEELY DAN. In other words, if you happen to appreciate the undemanding material delivered by some of the more borderline NWOBHM-era groups (ANGEL STREET, CAGEY BEE, H.G.B. or ISENGARD, for example), then you might well enjoy this one as well. If not, steer well clear! TRADER failed to achieve anything other than moderate club success during their time on the South Coast rock scene, and their lone two-tracker (dating from 1979, so they were there at the very inception of the movement) was unquestionably the high-point of their career. Their single came in a yellow sleeve picturing the band members, and remarkably few copies have ever surfaced (even in their home county), suggesting that most were shifted at local gigs and are only occasionally liberated from dusty collections and offered for sale these days. If you manage to find one, therefore, then you've done pretty well.

7" Singles
»Back Street Trader« Bos Records 1979

TRAITORS GATE

Robby Jones (v)
Andy Turner (g)
Steve Colley (b)
Paul House (d)

The excellent TRAITORS GATE (confusingly, there appears to have been at least two additional identically-named acts on the go in the UK at around the same time, although neither seems to have made it to the vinyl stage) were yet another group who emerged from the thriving rock scene of South Wales in the NWOBHM era. These talented natives of Gwent initially started out in around 1982 and soon got into the swing of things by playing the usual circuit of club gigs before sending their lovingly-crafted demo tapes to all the influential companies of the day, but the lads weren't exactly inundated with major-label offers in the short term. In fact, it wasn't until the latter half of 1984 that a five track cassette finally won them a deal with the ambitious Bullet concern. The outfit laid down their debut EP a short time later (I suspect that some of them might also have helped out on the obscure NIGHT GAMES record beforehand), although its release appears to have been delayed by the financial and distribution problems which blighted the hapless company at around this time, and it's entirely possible that the majority of finished copies didn't actually make it into general circulation until the early months of 1985.

The TRAITORS GATE three-tracker was undoubtedly the most impressive of all the releases which came from the Bullet stable, the band's style of powerful, pacey metal being very much in the manner of their fellow countrymen PERSIAN RISK and TOK-IO ROSE. The title track, "Devil Takes The High Road", is certainly the pick of the bunch, its heavy-but-melodic arrangement and superb vocal performance elevating it to the highest standards of the genre, and suggests that this bunch would certainly have given PERSIAN RISK a good run for their money if the two acts had ever had a showdown on stage. The accessible "Love After Midnight", on the other hand, was slightly too commercial for its own good (is that a keyboard I hear?), although Robby Jones acquitted himself as an extremely charismatic frontman once again, saving this number from sinking into the mire of semi-AOR mediocrity. Rounding things off was the energetic "Shoot To Kill", another cracking effort with a rather more rudimentary structure, but still showing the ensemble to have been a highly confident and competent set of musicians with some truly outstanding material at their disposal. Quite rightly, the quartet's seldom-seen EP is generally regarded as the most collectable and musically-important release on Bullet, and it truly deserves to be a part of every serious NWOBHM collection.

As you will be aware, however, TRAITORS GATE somehow managed to defy the odds and fail to become household names in the long term. It's hard to say why, exactly, although the old *'personnel problems'* chestnut certainly affected them pretty severely from a fairly early stage. In fact, talented guitarist/songwriter Andy Turner had already left by the time the debut EP was eventually released (his successor being Andy D'Urso), and it's entirely possible that the resultant incarnation failed to come up with comparably strong material thereafter. As if that wasn't enough, further ill-fortune was to strike when gifted vocalist Robby Jones (the other half of their original songwriting partnership) also decided to throw in his proverbial hand by the spring of 1985, although the lads persevered with new recruit Chris Ellis in the wake of his departure. However, after a few more shows in their locality (including a prestigious support slot with none other than ANGEL WITCH), they appear to have finally called it a day, which is a great shame. Bassist Steve Colley subsequently lent his services to the little-known IN PURSUIT and the rather more illustrious KOOGA, while Andy D'Urso had a stint with the little-remembered VIGILANTE, and it's also possible that original guitarist Andy Turner resurfaced in local melodic rock hopefuls MONRO, but it's such a common name that I can't be totally sure at this stage.

12" EP's
»Devil Takes The High Road« Bullet 1984

TRANS AM

Reardon
Lock
Dominy
Smith

The extraordinarily obscure TRANS AM (not to be confused with the talented-but-overlooked TRANZZAM from Oxfordshire) are a bit of an enigma at present, although there are at least two pieces of information on their only known single (dating from 1983) which initially suggested that there might be a Yorkshire connection. First, MAINEEAXE are known to have evolved from an amateur-hour concern called TRANS-AM, and secondly, the combined presence of a female vocalist and the reference to *'Chub Records'* tends to start a few alarm bells ringing on the SATANIC RITES front. Mind you, since none of the writing credits quoted on the TRANS AM two-tracker (there's no picture sleeve known for this particular record, by the way) actually match up with any of the musicians from either of the aforementioned acts, it merely seems to be a particularly weird coincidence after all. In fact, there's some fairly solid evidence to suggest that the group under discussion may well have originated from the fertile region of South Wales (Glamorgan, in all likelihood), so that's where my money is going at the moment.

Anyway, the self-financed single features "Crazy World" and "Flash In The Pan", two inoffensive enough numbers (to be honest, the singer doesn't really sound anything like Deborah Webster of SATANIC RITES, so this idea was surely a non-starter), although the over-emphasised, semi-operatic vocal delivery seems slightly excessive, given that the musical backing is pretty rudimentary, on the whole. The designated A-side ("Crazy World") is, perhaps, marginally weaker than the reverse, the latter revolving around a cracking (but immensely derivative) riff which leads into an enjoyable and energetic effort. Indeed, some of the guitar work on display is remarkably effective (primitive in its conception, admittedly, but still extremely convincing), the music eliciting a few convenient comparisons with OVERDRIVE or Kent's RENEGADE, although the main reference point in the vocal sense would tend to lie somewhere between the heavyweight WAR MACHINE and the more accessible RUNESTAFF. Again, this record is a scarcely-sighted item, and would probably fetch a fairly respectable price on the open market. Any further details on the story behind this release would be appreciated...

7" Singles
»Crazy World« Chub Records 1983

TRAXX

Geoff Greenwood (v)
Geoff Hollows (g)
Michael Robinson (rg)
Bob Hollows (b)
Darren Wilcock (d)

Although the fabled »Subway Walker« 7" by VOLTAGE crops up on a number of wants lists (thanks largely to a somewhat premature announcement of its imminent release in 'Kerrang'), the record wasn't actually issued under that name. This Manchester-based outfit did indeed start out with the VOLTAGE handle in around 1983, before becoming the extremely ill-advised KLAN (oh dear) and eventually (after a couple of demos and several personnel changes, including the loss of original bassist Marc Webb to DRAGONSLAYER, plus the defection of drummer Clive Southgate to JAILBAIT) settling on the borderline-glam moniker of TRAXX. Of the three compositions featured on their sole EP from 1986 (a record which received a fairly praiseworthy review in 'Kerrang' shortly after its release), "Subway Walker", "C Red" and "Rock 4 Ever" (hmmm, something of a PRINCE fixation in the song title department, methinks), two were ostensibly 'recorded live in Europe Spring 86', although they sure as hell don't sound like genuine concert recordings to me. Well, I suppose the musicians were indeed 'live' when they laid down the EP, and Manchester is certainly still a part of Europe, so I don't suppose there are any legal grounds for taking them to task over these extremely silly claims...

It's interesting to note that the three-tracker (for which no picture sleeve seems to have been manufactured) was issued on the small-time Heighway Robbery label (responsible for a pretty meagre total of just three or four releases during a period of five years) owned by SACRED ALIEN's manager Warren Heighway, since the musical similarities are quite discernible at times. Indeed, drummer Darren Wilcock was actually a paid-up member of SACRED ALIEN for several months in the latter part of 1982 (he didn't contribute to either of their vinyl releases, however), although TRAXX didn't quite succeed in emulating the former's lyrical ingenuity or technical expertise. Further comparisons would be with ARAGORN or those infamous Londoners DEEP MACHINE, although I guess the latter is one for the demo collectors only! It looks as though they must have jacked it all in after a year or two trying to promote themselves further (sales of their EP appear not to have amounted to much), but I can't imagine that TRAXX ever cultivated a particularly massive local following at any stage. All things considered, though, enjoying the company of this 7" (not an especially highly-valued piece at the time of writing, probably due to the fact that relatively few collectors know about it) is a fairly decent way to spend fifteen minutes of your life.

7" EP's
»Subway Walker« Heighway Robbery Wreckords 1986

TREDEGAR

Ian Hornsby (v)
Tony Bourge (g)
Alan Fish (b)
Ray Phillips (d)

Having been founder members of the Welsh rock colossus known as BUDGIE, Ray Phillips and Tony Bourge were privileged enough to enjoy the glory years of the outfit, although both had departed by the late 70's. After initially tinkering around with an ill-fated project called FREEZ (which also featured future FIRECLOWN stalwart Pete Dutton), the duo formed a new rock proposition in 1982, taking the slightly unimaginative identity TREDEGAR (simply the name of their local area). Joining them in the early days were youthful vocalist Ian Hornsby (their first serious frontman) and seasoned veteran bassist Alan Fish (previously employed by numerous rock outfits, and later of the GROUNDHOGS, DUMPY'S RUSTY NUTS, EGYPT etc.), and things were soon working out pretty well for the ambitious bunch. Original material was demoed early on, and numerous live appearances duly followed (the industrious outfit travelling the length and breadth of the country from a very early stage), although it was an uphill struggle to satisfy the many requests for old BUDGIE classics while attempting to showcase TREDEGAR's own compositions, a sticky situation which mainman Tony Bourge later reflected upon: *'If you're in a no-name band it is much harder to get recognised. When we formed we were looking for a direction, so we took our direction from what we had done before.'* (Ref: A Dose Of The Heavies, Issue 4, September 1986). The unsettled Alan Fish was to take his leave after a couple of years (during which time they added a second guitarist, Andy Wood), however, his immediate replacement being a character called Tom Prince, and the band also took the opportunity to try out a selection of frontmen, including Paul Parry, Paul Burnett (who, after starting out with local heavyweights STORMQUEEN, also worked with CARRERA and ASHMATA) and Carl Sentance (on loan from PERSIAN RISK), before finally settling on ex-MONZA vocalist Russ North.

By 1985, the outfit still had no firm offers from any of the record companies, as Ray Phillips later explained: *'The major ones weren't at all interested in hard rock and the smaller ones didn't wanna know 'cos we weren't a thrash metal band.'* (Ref: Mega Metal Kerrang No.3, 1986). In an act of complete desperation (not to mention utter madness), Phillips re-mortgaged his house in order to raise the necessary capital to release their first vinyl product, which the band envisaged as taking the form of a full-length effort. In the event, however, the ambitious troupe went so far as to produce an album (in an attractive gatefold sleeve), single (the latter featuring "Duma" and "The Jester") and even a video (excerpts from which would receive a modicum of television exposure in due course), all lovingly assembled and admirably presented. The mainman later explained the reasoning behind the manufacture of these unusually lavish affairs: *'We wanted to go beyond just putting out another independent LP, so I designed a gatefold sleeve*

with our logo embossed in gold on the cover, and we've also put out a single, »Duma«, again with an expensive sleeve. To be honest, We've had so many problems along the way that at one time I did wonder what was gonna come out of this but I think the records are ones we can all feel proud of.' (Ref: *ibid.*) The album was a substantial, semi-epic collection of tracks (the lyrics dealing mainly with historical and fantasy themes) lying somewhere between CLOVEN HOOF, SARACEN and TRAITORS GATE. It was an accomplished debut, the musicians acquitting themselves impeccably throughout, and, thanks to some competently-arranged distribution, the eponymous long-player was soon enjoying healthy worldwide sales.

It subsequently became apparent, however, that all was not as it initially appeared, as it transpires that most of the vocal duties on »Tredegar« had actually been handled by the inimitable Carl Sentance himself, the latter (who was still a paid-up member of PERSIAN RISK at the time) recording the majority of the tracks during his brief stint (he also had equally short spells with the likes of TOKYO BLADE and the GEEZER BUTLER BAND) in TREDEGAR. In fact, Russ North, although credited as sole vocalist on the debut set, had actually been recruited fairly shortly before the album was released, and had made little contribution to the recording process. A trifle unfair on Mr Sentance, perhaps? Nevertheless, the lads capitalised on the success of the long-player with yet more gigs, recruiting new bassist Mike Taylor along the way as a replacement for Tom Prince (who later resurfaced in PHANTASM), the latest line-up remaining stable for quite some time. Taylor himself was to leave the following year, however, as was Andy Wood, lured away by an offer to join the persevering CLOVEN HOOF. In the wake of their departure, TREDEGAR tried out a few hopeful musicians, before ultimately selecting one-time TREASON bassist Fabrice Francese and former HAMMERFIST axeman Lee Jones, although the latter (who was to spend a relatively short time with the outfit before also joining CLOVEN HOOF) gave way to former LYIN RAMPANT bloke Kevin 'KJ' Street towards the end of the decade.

TREDEGAR's attempts to get further vinyl product of their own into the shops were repeatedly thwarted by various logistical and financial factors (a second single was originally planned as early as 1987), and things remained in limbo for a while (they kept plugging away in the clubs), although the band's fortunes seemed to be picking up once again by 1990. Their debut set was duly remixed and reissued by an obliging German company called Nibelung Records, the long-player being augmented by a bonus track entitled "Sabre Dance", a classical piece which BUDGIE had tinkered around with in the good old days, but which they had never recorded. Furthermore, the lads were soon whisked off on a memorable European jaunt where they opened for none other than DEMON (although, given that mouthpiece Russ North had latterly become the third member to defect to CLOVEN HOOF, I suspect that Ray Phillips was handling the vocals himself at that particular juncture), a productive series of gigs which Phillips recalls with great fondness: *'It was a great tour, the organisation was just so professional! There was no stress at all, we didn't have to concern ourselves with the equipment or transport, so we were able to concentrate solely on each individual show. We played twelve dates and even included a few old BUDGIE songs in the set, I had a great time! I hadn't been over to Europe for years, and it was evident that rock music has a significantly higher status in Germany than it does back home in England.'* (Ref: Iron Pages No.34, 1995).

Eventually, however, it was make or break time for TREDEGAR, and the final incarnation of the oft-reshuffled group took shape in 1992, where yet another revised line-up was assembled (Bourge and Phillips had now drafted in former STALLION bassist Jason Marsh, guitarist Sam Lees and session singer Trixie Thorne) in order to record that much-postponed second LP. An album's worth of material was duly captured for posterity, although the labels who had originally expressed an interest in releasing the long-player backed out at the eleventh hour, leaving the master tapes to gather dust for a year or two. Eventually, however, those in charge of the BUDGIE Appreciation Society exhumed the recordings and issued the material (along with their debut set) in the form of 1994's »Re-Mix And Re-Birth« package. By this time, though, TREDEGAR had ceased to exist as such, with Phillips and Bourge having brought the first chapter to a logical conclusion around a year previously. The persevering trio of Phillips, Marsh and Lees subsequently started afresh under the name of SIX TON BUDGIE (confusingly, the original BUDGIE moniker, although it had been dropped long before they recorded their first album for MCA), gradually evolving into a line-up which featured Justin Phillips (Ray's son) and one-time TREDEGAR man Tom Prince, after which a couple of representative selections of brand-new SIX TON BUDGIE material (»Unplucked« and »Ornithology«) were made available on CD in the second half of the 90's.

LP's
»Tredegar« Aries Records 1986
[Original UK issue in gatefold sleeve]
»Tredegar« Nibelung Records 1990
[German remixed version with extra track "Sabre Dance"]

7" Singles
»Duma« Aries Records 1986

CD's
»Tredegar« Nibelung Records 1990
[German remixed version with extra track "Sabre Dance"]
»Re-Mix And Re-Birth« Axel Records 1994
[Features second album and includes »Tredegar« set]
»Budgie And Beyond« Vicious Sloth Records 1994
[Compilation release featuring eight TREDEGAR tracks, also includes material from BOMBSHELL, FREEZ, TITUS OATS and SIX TON BUDGIE]

TRESPASS

Mark Sutcliffe (v, g)
Dave Crawte (g)
Richard Penny (b)
Paul Sutcliffe (d)

For a band who only managed to issue a handful of self-financed records during their original time together, it's remarkable just how many people have become acquainted with the music of TRESPASS over the years, so I guess they must have struck the right chord with many fans of the NWOBHM genre. Formed as long ago as 1976, the Suffolk hopefuls were the brainchild of the musical Sutcliffe brothers, Mark and Paul, who assembled a group around themselves and slowly-but-surely became something of a serious proposition as opposed to merely indulging in the bedroom-based fancifulness of the past. By 1979, they were being assisted by bassist Richard Penny and second guitarist Dave Crawte, and the ambitious quartet proceeded to finance their first release, a single featuring "One Of These Days" and "Bloody Moon". From the very outset, TRESPASS displayed an uncanny knack of writing heavy, catchy material with one foot firmly in the 70's (there being an undeniable THIN LIZZY tinge in the guitar department) and the other in the more upbeat and forceful NWOBHM movement, their closest musical allies among the major players of the day being PRAYING MANTIS (in particular) and DEMON (on occasion). Their debut two-tracker (especially the memorable A-side) rapidly became an instant favourite among the nation's rock fans, and TRESPASS already seemed to have a healthy career awaiting them.

In the early months of 1980, a stroke of good fortune was to come the group's way when EMI came a-hunting for new talent, and TRESPASS were rewarded with the opportunity to contribute to the label's second »Metal For Muthas« album. In the event, the outfit (who now featured an altered line-up, with Chris Linscott occupying the bass slot and the slightly more refined tones of Steve Mills succeeding the gruff vocals of Mark Sutcliffe, who reverted back to guitar duties) were privileged enough to be afforded the honour of supplying two songs to the compilation. As requested, the lads came up with a reworked version of "One Of These Days", plus the lengthy and powerful "Stormchild", and saw both numbers included as promised. With the quintet having now received generous exposure *via* widespread airplay of their single and healthy sales of the compilation, they soon came to the attention of the BBC's 'Friday Rock Show', and TRESPASS soon found themselves recording material for imminent transmission. First broadcast on the 2nd of May 1980, their session featured versions of the popular "One Of These Days" (inevitably) and "Stormchild" (again), plus the previously-unheard "Live It Up" and a well-crafted, semi-epic composition entitled "Visionary". The listeners readily voiced their approval of the session, and "Visionary" was duly included on the BBC's »Metal Explosion« sampler later in the year. The group were gaining momentum with every passing week, and their live outings were now anticipated with considerable fervour.

Strangely, however, Steve Mills was to be ousted after only a few months (he later auditioned unsuccessfully for GASKIN, and was last heard of mucking about with various small-time Midlands hopefuls), his replacement being a certain Robert Eckland, and it was this particular incarnation of TRESPASS who recorded their second single towards the end of the year. "Jealousy" and "Live It Up" were more lively and metallic efforts which suggested that the lads were now wholeheartedly embracing the NWOBHM ethos, the pair of energetic originals coming across as broadly similar to some of WHITE SPIRIT's heavier compositions. The musicianship was highly impressive throughout, and

647

you'd also have to concede that Eckland was undoubtedly their most gifted frontman to date, so things certainly appeared to be heading in the right direction. Peculiarly, however, none of the influential labels picked up on TRESPASS, something which baffled many observers at the time, and which makes equally little sense nowadays, especially considering some of the amateur-hour dross which ended up on the books of excitable companies from time to time. Nevertheless, the outfit were unperturbed by their apparent lack of recognition by the majors, and they were more than happy to delight the crowds and sell their self-produced vinyl (several thousand copies of their first two singles were eventually shifted) to dedicated metal aficionados, for whom the lack of big-label endorsement was no indicator of an absence of talent.

It's worth clearing up something of a myth at this juncture. TRESPASS recorded a considerable amount of material during their time together, including a ten track cassette (quite a variable set of compositions, if truth be told) entitled »Through The Ages«, which featured their second vocalist, Steve Mills. At no stage, however, did they press an extremely limited white-label album to tout around as a promotional device. I've no idea how this rumour came to be so firmly established, but you can stop looking now, the confirmation of the record's non-existence comes straight from the horse's mouth. By 1981, the lads were still actively searching for their breakthrough (at their own leisurely pace, mind you) and ventured into the studio to work on a batch of fresh material with their latest acquisition, bassist Bob Irving. Another demo (comprising "Bounty Hunter", "Vendetta" and "Point Of No Return") was recorded in due course, although the tape (featuring a more accessible, but ultimately uninspiring, selection of newer material) was never officially circulated, for some reason. It proved to be the last major contribution from Robert Eckland, however, after which the lads swiftly reverted to a four-piece formation (although the musicians never actually made this particularly clear), with Mark Sutcliffe reclaiming the mike stand once again.

After a short time together, this back-to-basics version of TRESPASS elected to deliver yet another slice of vinyl, which appeared as the obligatory self-financed 7", this time featuring "Bright Lights", "The Duel" and "Man And Machine", the latter pair being well-established numbers from their live set. These were all slightly stronger than much of their recently-demoed material, particularly the interesting guitar work on "Bright Lights" (a composition more reminiscent of SOLDIER than anything else), although the other two were also extremely listenable efforts. The EP was, incidentally, pressed in considerably more limited quantities than the first two releases, suggesting that their savings might have been running a bit low by this stage. In any case, the »Bright Lights« 7" is currently valued somewhat higher (especially the tiny handful which apparently came with a poster) than the earlier efforts, all of which featured fairly unremarkable sleeve designs. Following on from their last vinyl offering, it looks as though the TRESPASS lads suffered a bit of a personality crisis, and couldn't make up their minds whether to retain their heavy identity or to try again with more melodic material. In the end, they opted for the latter, whereupon an even more stripped-down version of the outfit (Bob Irving flew the coop and Dave Crawte switched over to bass) demoed various lightweight compositions such as "After Dark", "Turnin' The Tables" and "I'm On The Outside". Sadly, however, the public had been steadily losing interest over the preceding months, and few took any notice of the group's latest activities. After a further period of ever-dwindling popularity, the dejected TRESPASS lads finally called it a day in the summer of 1983.

The Sutcliffe brothers continued to work together in terms of songwriting, although they kept a rather low profile until the tail end of 1986, when the duo announced that they had begun to work with Dave Crawte once again, forming an all-new proposition called BLUE BLUD (see separate entry). Operating in the melodic rock vein that the original outfit had tried so hard to master, this thinly-disguised (although it fooled many people at first) version of TRESPASS enjoyed considerably more success, delivering a private mini-LP and two full-length efforts for Music For Nations along the way. By early 1992, however, the outfit (who had evolved into a more sleazy variant and changed their identity to BLUE BLOOD in the interim) had lost their way somewhat, and called it a day sooner rather than later. Conveniently, however, an enterprising bootlegger had chosen this precise moment to assemble a CD's worth of unreleased (or, at least, hard-to-get) TRESPASS material, and the finished product surprised many by racking up significant sales in a very short time. The main body of the CD was the aforementioned ten track »Through The Ages« cassette, although the compilers managed to screw up the song order, introduce two efforts ("Life Beat" and "It's All Over") from a completely different source and lose one of the numbers in the process. Nevertheless, there were some reliable indications that the band possessed some pretty decent material, notably "Eight Til Five" and "Assassin (Parts 1&2)", although a couple of the inclusions, notably "Lightsmith" and "Money", just didn't work at all, so it's a good thing that these had remained hidden at the time. If nothing else, the boot demonstrated that TRESPASS might actually have struggled to deliver a particularly competent album at that stage.

Surprisingly, news of the »Live It Up« bootleg came to the attention of the outfit's former members, who rapidly concluded that they could go one better by assembling their own CD of rare material. Within a remarkably short timescale, the lads had set up their own company, Alien Egg Records, and swiftly assembled a CD called »The Works«, which featured most of the tracks from their original singles (with the inexplicable exception of "Man And Machine"), plus assorted demo takes which had been captured over the years. Much of the material would probably have been familiar to their more ardent followers, although "Running Out Of Love" and "Make It Metal" (more anthemic, rock-influenced numbers from the latter days of their original existence) would presumably have been new to virtually everyone. The officially-sanctioned TRESPASS retrospective went on to sell in respectable quantities; so much so that it even warranted a special Japanese release (with an extra track thrown in) to meet demand. It might have come a decade too late, but it was nice to see the lads getting some recognition and critical acclaim at last. As with many NWOBHM bands who were enjoying something of a renaissance at the time, however, TRESPASS soon concluded that it might be worth having another go...

Before long, the name of TRESPASS was back in fashion in certain circles (although their resurrection was greeted with complete and utter apathy in their homeland, which wasn't at all predictable), whereupon the rejuvenated outfit decided to set about recording their first proper album at last. It emerged, in 1993, under the rather quirky title of »Head«, and revealed that the lads had certainly been taking a few additional influences on board since the demise of the commercially-motivated BLUE BLOOD. In fact, the featured tracks were all decidedly weighty, semi-thrash efforts with occasional similarities to the likes of METALLICA (naturally), CORROSION OF CONFORMITY or even PANTERA, something which came as a bit of a surprise to many listeners. Nevertheless, it didn't actually come across as a particularly disingenuous or contrived move to conform to the ideals of the 90's metal world, and their selection of effective and capable numbers (such as "Watch The Skies", "Hole" and "Not Of This World") was sufficient to convince many reviewers that TRESPASS were now back in business with a new musical outlook. Mainman Mark Sutcliffe was keen to give an explanation of their apparent shift in direction: *'It's still typical TRESPASS, but obviously more modern, compact and, above all, heavier! In fact, that was our intention all along, and we knew we could pull it off.'* (Ref: Iron Pages No.24, 1993).

In due course, TRESPASS would appear (alongside HOLOCAUST, another persevering act who had already undergone a considerable musical evolution of their own) at that year's Wacken Open Air Festival, unveiling a set containing a mixture of old ("One Of These Days", "Eight Til Five") and new, although quite heavily biased in favour of the latter. A few more gigs were pencilled in during the course of the next year or so, but there were to be perilously few confirmed sightings thereafter, all of which tended to suggest that the various protagonists might have had second thoughts and gone back into retirement after the initial enthusiasm waned. In fact, this wasn't the case at all, and the chaps resurfaced (having temporarily reverted to their original line-up) at the well-received *'20th NWOBHM Anniversary'* bash in Japan (alongside TANK, PRAYING MANTIS and SAMSON), showing the world that they were still an operational unit after all. More recently, Hellion Records have released »The Works II« (a set assembled using yet more recordings from the early 80's, plus a batch of later selections featuring short-stay vocalist Adrian Lynden, who subsequently joined the SUMO GIANTS), so their name should (hopefully) remain in circulation until they get around to recording something new. Happily, though, it seems that the collective activities of TRESPASS (possibly consisting of both live *and* studio work) is likely to continue for the foreseeable future. Welcome back, chaps.

7" EP's
»Bright Lights« Trial Records 1981
[Very limited quantities with poster]

7" Singles
»One Of These Days« Trial Records 1979
»Jealousy« Trial Records 1980

CD's
»Live It Up« Bootleg 1992

[Unofficial issue with unreleased studio demos and compilation tracks]
»**The Works**« Alien Egg Records 1992
[UK issue, official compilation of early and unreleased studio recordings]
»**The Works**« Pony Canyon 1992
[Japanese issue with extra track "Look Alive"]
»**Head**« Alien Egg Records 1993
»**Metal Crusade 99**« Pony Canyon 1999
[Japanese-only live double CD set, shared with TANK, PRAYING MANTIS and SAMSON]
»**The Works II**« Hellion Records 2000
[Compilation of early and unreleased studio recordings]

Compilation Appearances
"**Visionary**" on »Metal Explosion« LP BBC Records 1980
[Appears unofficially on »Live It Up« bootleg, different version appears on »The Works II«]
"**One Of These Days**" on »Metal For Muthas Vol.2« LP EMI 1980/CD Airraid Records 2000 + »The Bible Of Hard Rock« CD Toshiba 1990 + »NWOBHM '79 Revisited« Do-LP/Do-CD Phonogram 1990
[Different to single version]
"**Stormchild**" on »Metal For Muthas Vol.2« LP EMI 1980/CD Airraid Records 2000
"**Live It Up**" on »NWOBHM Vol.1« Bootleg CD 1992
"**One Of These Days**" on »Give 'Em Hell« CD Nectar Masters 1995

TRIARCHY

Mike Wheeler (v, b, k)
Graham Legg (g)
Mark Newbold (d)

Kent's excellently-named TRIARCHY were one of the region's more innovative and progressively-inclined acts (see also SPITZBROOK and, to a lesser extent, LEGEND), and the talented trio (see, there's some kind of logic here) first got the music bug in the late 70's, grafting some novel synthesizer sections (later adopted by the likes of MARQUIS DE SADE and DAWNWATCHER) onto their elaborate rock constructions in the style of BLEAK HOUSE, LEGEND (the Jersey version this time) or SHIVA. They were, all things considered, one of the very first metal acts to utilise synthesizers quite so effectively, and frontman Mike Wheeler was happy to reflect on the variety of influences which ultimately led to this pioneering stylistic juxtaposition: *'That all came about because, back then, the various members of the band were also listening to certain keyboard-dominated new wave outfits such as JAPAN or ULTRAVOX, for example. We combined this sound with HM music, although our use of keyboards differed from that of traditional heavy rock bands like DEEP PURPLE. I'm pretty sure that no other bands sounded remotely like TRIARCHY at the time.'* (Ref: Iron Pages No.34, 1996).

In 1979, the outfit released their first 7", a privately-issued affair with a bulky, hand-drawn sleeve of a warrior on horseback. It was a very limited pressing (which tends to fetch a hefty price nowadays), demand for which took the unsuspecting musicians entirely by surprise, and it was to be reissued (in a significantly greater quantity) the following year on Direct Records, the second batch serving to placate all of the metal fans who desperately wanted a copy to call their own. This time, the two-tracker

wasn't officially issued with a proper picture sleeve, although there appear to have been a handful of covers left over from the original pressing, and so a few examples of the Direct issue were (confusingly enough) sold with picture sleeves after all. The record itself was an atmospheric release which coupled the excellent "Save The Khan" with "Juliet's Tomb", two highly original and interesting compositions which weren't oversaturated by the keyboards, their sparing and strategic use being far more effective in the long run. Musically speaking, it was certainly a highly capable effort, it's just a pity that a rather unconvincing vocal performance tended to detract from the overall sound somewhat.

Moving into the second half of 1980, TRIARCHY had replaced original guitarist Graham Legg with new recruit Brian Galibardy, and the revamped outfit were soon back in the studio to lay down their second vinyl release for Direct. This time, it emerged as a three track EP (it has been claimed that a tiny number came with a flimsy, fold-round sleeve, although even those associated with the group seem to doubt the existence of such a makeshift cover) which featured "Metal Messiah", "Sweet Alcohol" and "Hell Hound On My Trail", the latter (a ROBERT JOHNSON blues classic from the 1930's) being something of an obscure and unexpected inclusion. The whole affair was, perhaps, slightly closer to traditional metal territory (LIMELIGHT or GASKIN, for example) than their stunning debut had been, but it was still a powerful release which remains a mid-priced and sought-after collectable to this day. The lads gigged around the South East for most of the next two years, playing small-time shows with other local hopefuls (and taking the chance to shift a few more copies of their »Metal Messiah« EP at every opportunity), and occasionally getting together with touring acts from further afield, notably VARDIS. Although the labels continued to keep their distance, it seemed likely that the popular band would remain a going concern purely to satisfy the demands of their followers.

By around 1983, however, the original version of TRIARCHY had dissolved, and band mainman Mike Wheeler was now penning a few more commercially-oriented compositions with cohorts Mark Dawson (formerly of local hopefuls LEGEND) and Paul Gunn. In fact, this amounted to little more than some friendly tinkering around in the studio to see if the musicians could come up with anything that might just be worth capturing on tape, and, in the event, very little in the way of fresh material was kept for posterity. Moreover, the chances of the general public actually getting to hear any of these compositions appeared to vanish completely once the name of TRIARCHY had finally been laid to rest in the mid-80's. However, the group were one of several to be contacted by the ever-dependable dealers (in the early 90's) regarding the possibility of obtaining unsold vinyl, and, as with the likes of LEGEND, NO QUARTER, RHABSTALLION *etc.*, the former members of TRIARCHY were sufficiently motivated by the recent resurgence in their popularity (and that of the NWOBHM genre in general) that they assembled a CD under the auspices of the Vinyl Tap label. However, given that they had disappointingly little in the way of surviving material at their disposal, the tracks from the outfit's two vinyl releases were trotted out once again and augmented by a handful of numbers from Wheeler's later period of experimentation.

»Before Your Very Ears« (strange title, that) eventually emerged in CD form in 1995, and, as something of a bonus, the original TRIARCHY recordings were supplemented by a new version of old stage favourite "Hiroshima", as Mike Wheeler explained: *'Unfortunately, our original version of "Hiroshima" never made it to vinyl at the time. Because we didn't have forty minutes of material for the CD, we had a bit of a get-together and played a new version of this song in the studio. "Hiroshima" is actually my favourite track on the CD, we recorded it at Goldust Studios with Mark Dawson.'* (Ref: *ibid.*) Finally, fans of the band were able to hear previously-unreleased tracks such as "Marionette" and "Ghost Of An Emotion", more melodic (but still undeniably quirky and distinctive) efforts which were more than worthy of a belated piece of exhumation. There was never any serious talk of a full-scale TRIARCHY reformation, though, so I'm afraid that you'll just have to content yourself with the material contained on this (frustratingly short) one-off CD.

7" Singles
»**Save The Khan**« SRT 1979
[Original issue in picture sleeve]
»**Save The Khan**« Direct Records 1980
[Second issue, no sleeve manufactured]

7" EP's
»**Metal Messiah**« Direct Records 1980

CD's
»**Before Your Very Ears**« Vinyl Tap Records 1995
[Compilation of studio material, mostly taken from earlier vinyl releases]

Compilation Appearances
"**Metal Messiah**" on »NWOBHM Vol.1« Bootleg CD 1992
"**Marionette**" on »Noise Level Critical« CD Hallmark 1997

TRIDENT

John Owen (v, g)
Spink
Marshall

Forming in North Wales in around 1982, TRIDENT immediately became an extremely popular live act in their local area (which was, in terms of the sheer quantity of active rock bands, considerably more sparse than the Southern half of the country), their first release being the »Broken Dream« cassette album, issued a year or so after formation. Unfortunately, although this apparently sold well in their own neck of the woods, a minimal quantity of copies seem to have survived, so I've no idea if it was a classic or not. Somebody really should seek out those master recordings and give it the CD release it undoubtedly deserves! Nevertheless, the cassette ultimately drew the attention of Sane Records (also based in North Wales), who were then in the process of compiling a sampler album featuring talented, unsigned rock/metal concerns, and were keen to showcase a few home-grown outfits. As a result, their weighty "Power Of The Trident" was featured on the label's seldom-seen »It's Unheard Of!« compilation, a release which hit the local shops at some point in 1984. TRIDENT's contribution, a substantial, mid-paced number in the general vein of DEALER, DRIVESHAFT or SWEET SAVAGE, was undoubtedly one of the record's highlights (not that the LP sold in staggering quantities at the time, mind you), and it wasn't long before the group were in a position to issue a single of their own.

Recorded at Pink Studios in Liverpool, TRIDENT's capable »Destiny« 7" (which recycled the aforementioned "Power Of The Trident" as its flipside) soon became a popular purchase among the nation's headbangers, no doubt assisted by generous airplay on the 'Friday Rock Show' and a favourable review in 'Kerrang'. Indeed, the record has, in more recent years, become revered as one of the true classics of the genre, especially after the A-side was included on the »NWOBHM Vol.4« bootleg CD in the early 90's. As well as ringing up numerous sales in their local area (and throughout the rest of Britain), however, the two-tracker apparently sold well in countries as diverse as Italy, America and Poland (!), so it looked as though the outfit stood every chance of acquiring a proper deal in due course. Buoyed by the considerable success of their vinyl debut, TRIDENT subsequently played to many large, appreciative crowds throughout both Wales and England, so their future should have been secure. Sadly, the outfit defied the odds and lost their way, eventually drifting apart after four eventful years together, with band leader John Owen citing *'lack of dedication by other band members'* as the fundamental problem.

The dauntless Owen subsequently tried to kick-start a solo career, recording several speculative demos off his own back, touting himself around shamelessly and occasionally utilising the services of a backing band in order to maintain his high-profile presence in the live environment. In the end, however, it was all in vain, and this projected *'solo'* venture ultimately failed to spark much interest, although Owen wasn't quite finished yet. In fact, his original musical vision gradually metamorphosed into the three-piece concern FILTHY RICH (see separate entry), an act who even issued a surprisingly mediocre private single entitled »She's 17« in 1987. The latter's direction was considerably more melodic and basic, however, and shouldn't be allowed to tarnish the good name of TRIDENT, whose sleeveless single is (despite a number of copies being prised from the band in the early 90's) still a fairly major rarity these days.

7" Singles
»Destiny« SRT 1984

Compilation Appearances
"Power Of The Trident" on »It's Unheard Of!« LP Sane Records 1984
"Destiny" on »NWOBHM Vol.4« Bootleg CD 1992

TROBWLL

Richard Morris (v, g)
Steve Lewis (b)
Mark Jones (k)
Mel Turner (d)

Getting in on the *'Welsh-language rock single'* act a year or two before fellow countrymen CRYS, TRYDAN, DIAWLED, CEFFYL PREN and DORCAS (none of whom, predictably enough, made all that much of a name for themselves outside their homeland) were an extremely obscure outfit named TROBWLL, purveyors of a semi-interesting, but not astoundingly heavy, variety of progressive/folky metal. Their only known release was a 7" from 1979 on the microscopic Buwch Hapus (*'Happy Cow'*) label, featuring an epic composition called "Taith" (spread over both sides), the title translating as "Journey". The first part is the slightly heavier side with occasional vocal accompaniment, whereas the sequel/continuation turns out to be a lengthy instrumental which amounts to little more than an extended guitar solo with a bit of backing from the rhythm section. In terms of facile comparisons, you'd probably be looking at the MOVIE STARS or the aforementioned DORCAS, with minor similarities to the likes of CHEMICAL ALICE or LOST FAMOUS at times, but

TROBWLL (which translates literally as 'Whirlpool', although there's a mention of 'Vortex' secreted amongst all the Welsh sleeve notes) were evidently operating on the periphery of the NWOBHM genre.

Practically nothing is known about the exploits or history of this particular ensemble, although they were certainly good chums with the aforementioned CRYS, and TROBWLL's busy mainman (Richard Morris) seems to have been quite keen on moonlighting, given that he subsequently produced the latter's debut single, among others, as well as lending a helping hand to the various music-related activities of several disparate projects. What an obliging chap. It's also worth noting that the pair frequented the same studio facilities, and both acts probably utilised the same godawful graphic artists, by the look of things, with the dingy TROBWLL sleeve (I think it's supposed to be some sort of geometric perspective drawing, but I could be missing the point completely) being even more monumentally dull than the feeble CRYS effort, which is an achievement in itself. One for fans of the more progressive offerings of the period, I would imagine, and not an item that you're particularly likely to come across unless you're on a hill-walking holiday in Wales.

7" Singles
»Taith« Buwch Hapus Records 1979

TROJAN (I)

Dave Kenyon (v)
Pete Wadeson (g)
Andy Halliwell (g)
Brian Bentham (b)
Mick Taylor (d)

Of the numerous groups who assumed the TROJAN name in the NWOBHM era, possibly the most successful were the outfit formed at the very height of the movement in the Manchester area. Led by guitar virtuoso Pete Wadeson (and featuring former ARAGORN stalwart Andy Halliwell in their ranks), the original incarnation of the band recorded a speculative demo tape in 1982 (including such early efforts as "Dealer" and "Renegades"), a release which eventually sold (primarily through the pages of 'Kerrang') several thousand copies worldwide, a hugely impressive feat for such a recently-established act. In due course, TROJAN were invited to contribute to Ebony's »Metal Maniaxe« compilation, the lads delivering a rather unremarkable, upbeat demo offering entitled "Premonition". It seemed like an ideal start, but things weren't going according to Wadeson's master plan, and he soon began thinking about making some changes. After taking stock of the situation, the mainman concluded that he needed to start afresh, whereupon he dissolved the original line-up at some point in 1983 (abandoning plans to release a self-financed EP which had already been recorded) and recruited a trio of new accomplices in the form of Graeme Wyatt (v), Eddy Martin (b) and Sam Hall (d). Freshly-penned material was laid down within a remarkably short timescale, and a cassette from the early months of 1984 (featuring such efforts as "Bring On The Night", "Aggressor", "Tonight We've Got It Made" and "Only The Strong Survive") was soon winning the approval of none other than Roadrunner Records.

Roadrunner were, at that time, still struggling to find a new batch of talented British acts to promote in Europe, as the particular brand of fast'n'furious mayhem that went down a storm at clubs such as the Dynamo in Eindhoven was pretty thin on the ground in the UK. Nevertheless, they had previously picked up on JAGUAR and SPARTAN WARRIOR, both of whom had delivered suitably frenetic vinyl debuts, and who seemed to fit the bill perfectly. Unfortunately, however, this pair of acts had somehow contrived to record considerably more accessible (stupefyingly so, in the case of JAGUAR) follow-ups than the label had anticipated, and both proved to be a bit of a disappointment in the sales stakes. Understandably, therefore, fingers were being firmly crossed that TROJAN would be able to replicate the same level of energy and power on vinyl that they had already demonstrated on their demos. Roadrunner were taking a considerable chance, as it would appear that the outfit were something of a non-touring concern at this stage, meaning that the label had been unable to check out their latest act in the live environment. When the recording sessions were completed, you could almost hear the enormous sigh of relief emanating from Roadrunner's executives.

TROJAN's »Chasing The Storm« long-player was a powerful, pacey concoction with more than a passing similarity to JAGUAR's debut (other facile comparisons being with the likes of SAMURAI and CHATEAUX), and would surely soon be bringing in the money at an impressive rate. In fact, had it not been for a somewhat odd production and a slight lack of variety on the songwriting front, it could easily have become one of Roadrunner's best-selling releases of the period.

653

Nevertheless, the selection of material (much of which had already been circulated in demo form) was rapturously received (the title track and "Icehouse" were amongst the pick of the bunch) by many European power metal fans, and it wasn't long before the musicians were being invited over to the mainland to promote themselves with some high-profile club gigs and a couple of prestigious festival appearances. It looked as though TROJAN had a secure future as crowd-pleasers in certain countries, and they were duly given the opportunity to record a second album. For some reason, though, Pete Wadeson had second (third?) thoughts once again, and, after they had mysteriously parted company with Roadrunner in 1987, the members eventually ceased working together under the name of TROJAN. Wadeson, after one last abortive attempt to get the group off the ground again in 1988, briefly linked up with former colleague Andy Halliwell in the SWEET SIN project (although he didn't feature on their album), before eventually (after recording an instrumental LP which never actually saw the light of day) deciding to try his luck yet again with a new(ish) outfit.

In 1989, Wadeson teamed up once more with vocalist Graeme Wyatt and drummer Johnny Lee Jackson (both of whom had featured in the last, ill-fated version of TROJAN), bringing in bassist Phil Gavin (previously with local heavyweights WOLFPACK and a less-successful bunch named SALEM) to make up the numbers. With the lads having regrouped, the musicians duly set about finding a novel identity for the project, originally taking the name of LETHAL, but (after running into copyright problems) settling on TALION, self-styled purveyors of 'melodic thrash' (now there's an oxymoron for you). A demo was circulated, featuring "Screamin' For Mercy", "Sanctuary", "Premonition" (a reworked version of the old TROJAN effort), "Killing The World" and "Living On The Edge", and the tape was soon drawing the attention of publications such as 'Metal Forces' as well as one or two of the smaller labels. Within a remarkably short space of time, the lads were recording their debut album for Major Records (a subsidiary of Peaceville), and »Killing The World« was to appear in the shops a few months later. TALION was, admittedly, a rather heavier proposition than TROJAN had been, although it was still a bit of a risky signing for Peaceville. Inevitably, the extreme music aficionados (in the UK, at least) failed to take much notice of the record, favouring the latest releases by DEATH and MORBID ANGEL instead, and so the project was thrown into limbo for a while.

Nevertheless, the musicians persevered gamely for a while (touring pretty extensively throughout various far-flung corners of Europe), although Gavin and Jackson finally handed in their notice in 1991, effectively signalling the end of the line for TALION. As a result of these relatively unfulfilling experiences, Pete Wadeson ultimately went back to basics and started doing the old 'guitar hero' thing, recording a couple of instrumental demos (e.g. »Play With Fire« and »Burnout«) with cohorts such as Tony Schofield (b) and Dave Edwards (d), the ensemble performing as the imaginatively-titled PETE WADESON BAND. Aside from a sole inclusion on the »Metal For Muthas '92« CD, however, the poor chap appears to have received little in the way of a meaningful or encouraging response to these recordings, and has subsequently moved into a slightly different line of work. I gather that he's now trying his hand at rock journalism, although I wouldn't be remotely surprised if he feels compelled to strap on his guitar and have yet another attempt at finding fame and fortune at some unspecified point in the future.

LP's
»Chasing The Storm« Roadrunner 1985

Exclusive Compilation Appearances
"Premonition" on »Metal Maniaxe« LP Ebony 1982

TROJAN (II)

Ed Kenny (v)
Tom Harte (g)
Derek 'Dee' Barton (g)
Maurice Cassidy (b)
Fergus Kelly (d)

The Irish version of TROJAN, despite achieving slightly more limited recognition than their English namesakes (vide supra), were, nevertheless, far from an inferior proposition. Initially forming in 1982, their early activities consisted predominantly of live appearances throughout the Emerald Isle, their collective ambition being to develop a sufficiently healthy reputation that they might ultimately be able to venture over to the mainland at some point. While influenced by such heavyweights as THIN LIZZY (but of course), IRON MAIDEN, KISS and JUDAS PRIEST, however, the band rapidly concluded that their cause would certainly be aided if they could perform a mainly original set, without recourse to the well-worn selection of cover versions. This was a pretty good idea, and it served to identify TROJAN as a rather more forward-looking and ambitious act than so many of their crowd-pleasing contemporaries, most of whom never made it out of the pubs. It wasn't until 1985, though, that the fans finally got a taste of the ensemble on vinyl, when the lads contributed "Soldiers Song" and "Charge Of The Night Brigade" to the

decidedly patchy »Green Metal« showcase of Irish talent. This energetic pair of numbers showed TROJAN to be following in the nation's grand tradition of powerful, heavy innovators such as SWEET SAVAGE, DRIVESHAFT and EZY MEAT (although it has to be said that the vocal performance wasn't totally convincing), all of which suggested that, with the continued support of their ever-dependable fan base, a productive future was almost certainly just around the corner.

The following year, TROJAN elected to release a humble two-tracker on their own Wooden Horse label, the numbers in question being "Bombs Away" and "Back To Me". To be honest, these were considerably more accomplished (and more flattering) than their previous compilation efforts, and it was no surprise that the record sold in impressive quantities, not only in Ireland, but also throughout Europe and even as far away as Australia! After their debut single had been recorded, incidentally, vocalist Ed Kenny took time off to lay down some backing vocals for FASTWAY's »Trick Or Treat« album, but was soon back at the helm of the good ship TROJAN. Valuable radio exposure (including American airplay) followed throughout 1987, and the tracks were also picked up by Metalother Records in the UK, who proceeded to include a TROJAN original on each of their »Metal Warriör« and »The Last Warrior« compilations. A further composition, the exclusive "Relentless Pursuit", was duly featured on Ebony's »Rock Masters« debacle, and this was easily the album's stand-out number. In due course, the ambitious outfit recruited a new drummer, Robbie Cahill, and recorded a brand-new cassette (featuring "Chasing The Dragon", "Never Cry Again" and "Danger Zone") to shop around the various record companies of the day. Before long, however, their efforts were rewarded with the chance to record a full LP for Metalother Records themselves.

TROJAN's full-length debut was recorded at the tail end of 1987 (apparently featuring yet another different drummer, Ray Ellis), and eventually surfaced in the early months of 1988. »The March Is On« (which actually appeared on the recently-established G.I. Records concern as opposed to Metalother) turned out to be a fairly inventive and substantial effort, including their three most recent demo compositions plus assorted material (such as the excellent "Troubleshooter" and "War Cry") harvested from their extensive repertoire, and the record was soon garnering healthy reviews and further airplay on both sides of the Atlantic. The long-player was, incidentally, dedicated to the late Phil Lynott, and TROJAN were even invited to play at the latter's memorial convention, where the lads were joined on stage by the original THIN LIZZY drummer, Brian Downey. The group then attempted to capitalise on the album's initial success by going out on tour once again (with, you guessed it, yet another sticksman, a chap called Ernie Tiedt), although their collective activities seem to have dwindled away fairly dramatically thereafter, so we can only assume that the group had called it a day by the end of the decade (perhaps having already exhausted Ireland's limited supply of drummers), crestfallen by their failure to become superstars in the interim. Sadly, the untimely demise of TROJAN meant that live favourites such as "Eastern Eyes" and "The Runner" (both of which were tentatively scheduled for inclusion on their follow-up release) would forever remain unrecorded, something which must have disappointed their devoted fans.

LP's

»The March Is On« G.I. Records 1988

7" Singles

»Bombs Away« Wooden Horse Records 1986
[Both tracks non-LP]

Exclusive Compilation Appearances

"Soldiers Song" on »Green Metal« LP Metal Masters 1985
"Charge Of The Night Brigade" on »Green Metal« LP Metal Masters 1985
"Relentless Pursuit" on »Rock Masters« LP Reaction 1987

Compilation Appearances

"Back To Me" on »Metal Warriör« Mini-LP Metalother Records 1987
"Bombs Away" on »The Last Warrior« Mini-LP Metalother Records 1987

TRUFFLE

Russ Horton (v,b)
John Dunning (g)
Ritchie Stopforth (g)
Peter Patterson (d)

Formed at the height of the NWOBHM influx, Hampshire's TRUFFLE were yet another of those hapless outfits who were plagued by numerous personnel changes during their time together, but were, nevertheless, a popular enough bunch with a genuine chance of making an impression outwith their locality in the long term. Mind you, in spite of an uncanny ability to please the crowds in the live environment, the lads tended to let themselves down a bit (in their formative years, at least) when it came to laying something down in the studio. For concrete evidence, you don't really have to look very much further than their double A-sided single (recorded at the local Chestnut Studio facility) from 1981, coupling the mid-tempo "If You Really Want" with the more restrained semi-ballad "Round Tower", the featured tracks having apparently been selected by their fans themselves. This 7" comes across as a pretty mediocre offering (with elements of outfits such as DORCAS, WHITEFIRE or RAGE), passable enough for a small-time club proposition, perhaps, but hardly pushing the musical and lyrical boundaries in any tangible sense. Nevertheless, the two-tracker (issued in a picture sleeve featuring a motorbike, although it wasn't specifically aimed at the biker community) is still regarded as a highly-rated NWOBHM artefact today. In due course, the band were lucky to be given further useful exposure in the 'Armed And Ready' section of 'Kerrang', which no doubt helped their cause significantly.

TRUFFLE developed a comparatively healthy reputation as a live attraction in the South of England, supporting touring acts such as TANK and DIAMOND HEAD, and even making it up to London on occasion. One of their gigs at the Marquee in the summer of 1982 (the group having recently completed a support slot with SPIDER) was even reviewed in 'Kerrang', who praised the outfit for turning in an enthusiastic and competent performance which featured self-penned numbers such as "Denim And Dandruff" and "City Girl", alongside the near-obligatory cover of "Ace Of Spades". Another memorable show came at the Reading Festival in 1983, although the lads weren't on the official bill, electing instead to delight a rather more *'selective'* audience in the nearby car park! By 1984, TRUFFLE had expanded to a five-piece *via* the recruitment of Mark Mulholland (a one-time member of an obscure outfit called SAHARA), who dabbled in both keyboard and rhythm guitar work, which eventually saw the outfit recording a more accessible five track demo. It wasn't a great success, to be honest, and the latest addition was soon on his way (finding employment in the ASHMATA *'supergroup'* a year or two later), as was John Dunning (who had a brief stint with local nonentities HARD GRAFT before being tempted away by an offer to join the up-and-coming WHITE HEAT), leaving the bewildered TRUFFLE to return to basics. Another single, entitled »Starlight«, was recorded in 1985 and was scheduled to be released on vinyl, but this would appear to have been shelved at the last minute, presumably as a consequence of financial shortcomings.

A year or so later, however, the lads proceeded to issue a lengthy cassette (largely for the benefit of their regional fan base) entitled »The Bacon Slicer Strikes Again« (featuring such stage favourites as the excellent "God Of War", "Street Fighter" and "Thunderbird"), and this seemed to be a huge improvement on their early efforts, with several of the tracks coming across as fairly similar to the sort of material that BITCHES SIN were now performing. Even so, TRUFFLE's dreams of a major record deal had long since evaporated, while their ill-conceived plans to issue a self-financed vinyl album had fallen through some time earlier. The outfit struggled on for the remainder of the decade with various guitarists coming and going (John Bowyer, Greg Watkins, Gary Jeffrey and Paul Jupe were among those who took their turn), winning the occasional mention and live review (with tracks such as "Running Out Of Time" and "Million Miles Away" being singled out for a modicum of acclamation) in the local and national music press, but it had all fallen apart by around 1989, whereupon most of those involved decided to throw in the towel completely. Peter Patterson, however, couldn't stay away from the music business and later (having also played alongside Russ Horton in an obscure side-project called NO FIXED ABODE in the mid-80's) joined forces with a rock covers act called the MAFIA, who may or may not still be a going concern down South.

7" Singles
»Round Tower« Chestnut Records 1981

Compilation Appearances
"If You Really Want" on »NWOBHM Vol.8« Bootleg CD 1996

TRUX

Eddie Allen (v,g)
Marc Noel-Johnson (g)
Roger Newell (b)
Ant Ellerton (d)

It would appear that »Bad Luck«, the title of the one and only single by Cambridgeshire-based TRUX, serves pretty admirably as the band's theme song! Originally conceived in around 1981, the hapless outfit endured countless line-up alterations and shifts in direction over the ensuing years (all in a desperate attempt to secure a loyal following), largely without enormous success. With the only continuity being provided by mainman Eddie Allen, numerous other members (mostly called Mark, by a bizarre quirk of fate) came and went without really having a genuine chance to establish themselves properly, causing confusion amongst their modest fan base and sowing seeds of doubt in the minds of one or two participants, who became rather disgruntled with their lack of musical progression. Eddie Allen explained the situation in a local fanzine interrogation some years later: *'The problem we seemed to come up against with material is that it was so well put together that we couldn't branch out from it and the songs were becoming just a mechanical thing. Whilst the band got better and better, it seemed to lose that sparkle between us and the audiences. The audiences that were turning up at the gigs were expecting something they weren't getting. So we decided maybe it was time to go back and pick up where we left off two years ago.'* (Ref: A Dose of the Heavies, Issue 2, May 1986).

With no major-label interest on the horizon, a self-financed single was practically inevitable, and the item in question duly appeared in 1982, the latter coupling "Bad Luck" and "Moving On", two compositions which represented quintessentially British stabs at bluesy rock in the traditional manner of FREE or BAD COMPANY. It was undeniably similar to NUTHIN FANCY at times, so I'd say that either BABY TUCKOO or early TERRAPLANE would be reasonably appropriate reference points for NWOBHM aficionados. Admittedly, the music of TRUX certainly didn't embody anything staggeringly original or revolutionary, but it was still carried off with enviable sincerity and enthusiasm, even if it ultimately failed to win the lads many friends outwith their locality. While this variety of raunchy material no doubt went down an absolute storm in the regional rock clubs and pubs of the day (or, for example, at the charmingly-titled *'Pegasus Motorcycle Club Horseshit Rally'* in 1983, where TRUX apparently played one of their more memorable gigs for the benefit of the biker community), it was hardly the sort of thing that screamed *'world domination'* at the influential record companies. Even so, their 7" (never issued in a picture sleeve, by the looks of things, but a collectable item these days) did actually receive a fairly praiseworthy review in 'Kerrang', which was an achievement in itself. Mind you, with the chart success enjoyed by SKIN, THUNDER and REEF in comparatively recent times, maybe TRUX should consider re-inventing themselves and having another go!

After innumerable personnel reshuffles (original vocalist Steve Breeze, for example, departed in late 1983 or thereabouts and subsequently hooked up with an obscure melodic outfit called SING SING, while former colleagues such as Mark Stoakes seemingly disappeared off the face of the earth), the persevering ensemble eventually got back on track in the mid-80's with a revised line-up consisting of the ever-dependable Eddie Allen (now assuming vocal duties in addition to guitar), plus Marc Noel-Johnson (g), Ant Ellerton (d) and Roger Newell (b). However, their original enthusiasm seemed to have waned by this point, and, after having spent many years trying forlornly to get their big break in the business, the luckless outfit (who additionally tried alternate axeman Mark Lankshire-Boon, borrowed from local crowd-pleasers the FRIGIDAIRES, towards the end) finally disintegrated at the tail end of 1986 (although there seem to have been some low-key reformation gigs since then), leaving only the following epitaph, as revealed in the aforementioned fanzine: *'Banned from Haverhill pub venue for obscene stage act'*. The mind boggles.

7" Singles
»Bad Luck« Private 1982

TRYDAN

Meic Jones (v,g)
Linda Williams (v)
Sharon Jones (v)
Carol Jones (rg)
Dafydd Elis (b)
Garym Jones (d)

Yet another signing to the popular Welsh label Sain Records were the relatively obscure TRYDAN (*'Electricity'*), a sextet who (in addition to TROBWLL, CRYS, DIAWLED, CEFFYL PREN and DORCAS) also elected to sing in their native tongue. The band appear to have been a fairly democratic mix of male and female members (not too sure about the absolute necessity for three vocalists, though), and their only known vinyl release is a scarce EP (issued in a rather functional sleeve) from 1980, featuring "Mods A Rocers" (a number with a fairly obvious translation, perhaps inspired by the classic 'Quadrophenia', a film released shortly beforehand), "Di-waith, Di-'fynedd" and the quirky, throwaway nonsense of "Mr. Urdd". Their "Mods A Rocers" effort is undoubtedly the pick of the bunch, this being a fairly unremarkable example of metal-by-numbers with a vague feel of SLEDGEHAMMER or VARDIS, whereas the comparatively disposable "Di-waith, Di-'fynedd" (sorry, but the translation technology blew a fuse on this one) is a considerably more lightweight offering, not a million miles away from fellow countrymen DORCAS. Not an essential purchase for NWOBHM devotees by any stretch of the imagination (there could quite feasibly be various other TRYDAN releases out there, as their history hasn't been reported in great detail), but another interesting artefact which serves to remind us of a severely under-documented musical area.

7" EP's
»Mods A Rocers« Sain Records 1980

TURBO

Des Horsfall (v)
Ian Blackburn (g)
Pete Mayhew (g)
Rick Payne (b)
Chris Day (d)

Initially formed, as with so many of their NWOBHM contemporaries, at the tail end of the 70's, TURBO (you wouldn't be daft enough to confuse them with either of their East-European namesakes, would you?) were primarily based in Lancashire, although, just to confuse matters, they additionally appear to have utilised the services of various natives of Yorkshire over the years. Perhaps it was a constant struggle to attract and retain participants of a suitably high calibre, and, judging by the number of writing credits on their two vinyl releases, it looks as though a fair few characters passed through their ranks during the course of the outfit's relatively brief existence. TURBO's early exploits on the music scene aren't well-documented by any means, although it seems pretty safe to assume that they revolved around the usual processes of local gigging, developing their own material (hoping that the public wouldn't confuse them with at least three other small-time ensembles who laid claim to the identity at the time) and attempting to establish something vaguely resembling a stable line-up. There seems to have been little in the way of genuine label interest, though, leaving the lads with no option but to go it alone.

Their first release was a 7" EP, recorded early in 1980 at Cargo Studios in Rochdale (coincidentally, the day after OXYM recorded their own two-tracker at the same facility!), featuring the numbers "Stallion", "Running" and "Take My Life". Issued in a monochrome sleeve depicting an imposing Rolls Royce turbine, the record (which soon received valuable airplay on the 'Friday Rock Show' courtesy of stand-in DJ Ian Gillan) is an excellent example of archetypal NWOBHM, and its scarcity is reflected by a very steep asking price these days. "Stallion" and "Running" (the latter also being included on the seminal »New Electric Warriors« album, and described as 'a fine track' in 'Phoenix' fanzine's review of the same) are mid-paced numbers in the style of MARZ or DESTROYER, whereas "Take My Life" (featuring keyboard work from associate member Chris Riley) is a heavy, atmospheric effort more reminiscent of CRYER or DAWNWATCHER. Their appearance on the aforementioned compilation, meanwhile, also tied in with a kind of 'Battle Of The Bands' contest, and TURBO's popularity duly allowed them to reach the 'grand final' (along with RACE AGAINST TIME and BASTILLE), played at the Marquee in London in January 1981. At some point thereafter, the ambitious bunch even decided to produce a video of themselves in action, presumably for promotional purposes, which, in all probability, very few people are likely ever to have seen.

The band continued to change personnel at an incredible rate (Des Horsfall went on to join RAW DEAL, the outfit who released a single on Neat, before doing some ropy solo work, while Ian Blackburn was last heard of producing WOLF's »See Them Running« 7"), and, by the time their »Charged For Glory« (I think "*Charge For Glory*", which they seem to be singing, makes more sense) single (b/w "Race For The Dawn") was released in the summer of 1982, only Pete Mayhew remained from their earlier line-up. He was now joined by Steve McCann (v), Paul Hartley (g,k), Chris Bartlett (b) and Peter Emmonds (d), although the overall sound had shifted very little in the interim. The vocals were slightly different, perhaps more in the vein of REINCARNATE or SHADOWFAX, but the guitar work was virtually identical. "Charged For Glory" is by far the better song, the latter being a well-constructed, catchy number (in the style of HOLLOW GROUND's "Flying High") with inspiring (if slightly naive) lyrics about doing something constructive with your life and '*not letting the bastards grind you down*', as it were. Cracking stuff, and well worth its place on the »NWOBHM Vol.5« bootleg CD. Many thousands of copies of this two-tracker appear to have been pressed (and sold!) at the time, with a considerable number having remained in circulation ever since. As a consequence, the asking price tends to be a mere fraction of the first EP, and, believe me, it will be one of the most astute NWOBHM purchases (alongside MYTHRA's EP on Guardian, for example) you'll ever make.

In spite of the relative success of TURBO's vinyl releases (not to mention the group's fairly widespread popularity), the project began to fall apart not long after »Charged For Glory« (no picture sleeve issued this time) hit the shops (they finally gave up the ghost in around 1984), which is a real pity, as the musicians involved certainly had enough talent and variety in their songwriting ability to be able to pull off a cracker of an album. The persevering Pete Mayhew eventually resurfaced in the extremely lightweight SILHOUETTE, an act who recorded a couple of disposable singles for the Spirit label, but the fate of the remaining ex-members remains a mystery. Also, while books such as the 'Heavy Metal-The Vinyl Years' by John Allinson refer to yet another TURBO release entitled »Burning«, this record is, if it exists at all, credited to an entirely different outfit, namely the Scottish bunch who featured one-time PRAYING MANTIS vocalist Tommy Jackson in his pre-BERNIE MARSDEN'S S.O.S. days. Even so, I'm still not convinced that this act (who contributed a couple of tracks to the obscure »Kikrock« compilation) actually got as far as releasing their own single.

7" EP's
»**Stallion**« Cargo Records 1980

7" Singles
»**Charged For Glory**« SRT 1982

Compilation Appearances
"**Running**" on »New Electric Warriors« LP Logo 1980/CD British Steel 1997
"**Charged For Glory**" on »NWOBHM Vol.5« Bootleg CD 1992

TUTCH

Truin
Cole
Coote

You can invariably rely on the quirky Gargoyle Records to come up with something a bit out of the ordinary, although it's not necessarily always the most enjoyable piece of listening. One of their early releases, a three track EP by TUTCH, is an unusual mixture of prog, rock and more commercial material, although the overall effect is quite listenable if you're in the right frame of mind. Of the various compositions presented, "The Battle" is certainly the most accomplished, featuring a rather complicated structure reminiscent of ORION and AVALON, for example, although the vocal technique is undeniably impressive in places. The track also has a distinctly baroque feel, bringing to mind CLIENTELLE's "Skyflier" or some of the more adventurous material attempted by heavy groups such as SKYCLAD or SEVENCHURCH a decade later. "You Don't Care", on the other hand, turns out to be a featherweight, forgettable ballad which could easily pass for a STYX out-take, so that's not quite as appealing to the NWOBHM palate. Closing the proceedings, meanwhile, is "Round And Round", a more upbeat, catchy effort (very brief, though) in the general disposition of contemporaries such as H.G.B. or TRACK 4, so it looks as though TUTCH were pretty keen to adopt a few different stances on their vinyl debut. The one-off EP (released in 1980) doesn't appear to have been issued with a picture sleeve, and nothing is currently known about the band themselves, although the fact that they were associated with Gargoyle would tend to suggest a Home Counties connection. I wonder how many other undiscovered curios are still lurking around on the label?

7" EP's
»The Battle« Gargoyle Records 1980

TUXEDO

Stef Erdos (v)
Brian Lumb (g)
Mick Noonan (b, k)
Graham Clarke (d)

TUXEDO? On the Rushmore label? Surely this two-tracker has to be American, right? Actually, no. This is, in fact, a post-NWOBHM curio (recorded in the early months of 1985) from a relatively obscure Yorkshire quartet, although you'd certainly be forgiven for assuming otherwise, especially after hearing the brand of non-aggressive, inoffensive tunefulness on offer. The title of the nominated A-side, "Take It Easy", is apposite enough, this being an undemanding, keyboard-laden melodic workout in the style of "Waiting For A Miracle" by MAMA'S BOYS or (particularly) VAN HALEN's "Jump", the latter having been released only a short time previously (not that I'm suggesting anything). The flipside ("Set Me Free") is also an unashamedly lightweight effort, but without the invasive keyboards, this particular number being reasonably similar in construction to much of the material purveyed by such home-grown acts as VOYAGER UK. Overall, this was a musical style mastered by relatively few (although attempted by many) British hopefuls of the period, and you can rest assured that you're not missing out on a heavy classic if the TUXEDO single is currently absent from your collection. As a consequence of the lightweight contents, the associated price tag for this item (despite being a fairly scarce piece nowadays) remains at fairly modest levels. Incidentally, the monochrome sleeve is rather atypical, with a small group picture and a somewhat arty background of blocks and swirly paint patterns. How odd…

Interestingly (well, maybe not), it transpires that TUXEDO was actually the outfit's second musical identity, since they originally operated under the deceptively-heavy name of EPITAPH, who had earlier managed to issue an official cassette entitled »New Dimensions«, featuring the self-penned compositions "(Do You) No Harm", "Nobodies Fool" and "Heading For My Dreams". Comprising two extremely competent, harder-rocking numbers and one POLICE-influenced effort, this tape suggests that the young lads hadn't quite pledged their allegiances to the gods of AOR at that stage, and were still making up their minds as to what kind of material they wanted to play. Following the unheralded disintegration of TUXEDO, Stef Erdos ended up fronting regional AOR nonentities FKM (who eventually evolved into the extremely capable HARDLAND), while the pairing of Brian Lumb and Graham Clarke subsequently teamed up with bassist Pete Betts and one-time LIZARD frontman Nick Wood to form yet another MEANSTREAK (yawn) in around 1987, a band whose own demo material (such as "United" and "Are You Ready") was in a markedly heavier vein, generally coming across as a worthy combination of CHARIOT and TRIDENT. Unfortunately, it would appear that this outfit turned out to be a very short-lived affair, whereupon the central duo ultimately tried again in an equally unsuccessful, more melodic foursome who went by the moniker of BEDLAM. Since then, however, it looks as though their presence on the national rock scene has diminished completely.

7" Singles
»Take It Easy« Rushmore Records 1985

20/20 VISION

Denvyl Lewis (v, g)
Gerwyn Howley (g)
David Lewis (b)
Steve Preston (k)
Andrew Shortman (d)

Oh dear. Reviewing Christian rock/metal releases is a difficult enough challenge when the music is actually worthy of attention in the first place (BELIEVER, TROUBLE, BARREN CROSS etc.), but this self-financed album is in a completely different league, unfortunately. Still, I suppose it has to be included just for reasons of completeness, and to warn off anyone who's thinking of buying a copy. Recorded at I.C.C. Studios in the sunny South Coast resort of Eastbourne (although the main protagonists in this ill-judged venture seem to have been Welsh) at some point in the early 80's, the peculiarly-titled »In The Town/In The City« set by 20/20 VISION (pronounced 'twenty twenty vision', meaning 'perfect sight') is real 'in your face' stuff, telling us how truly awful the world is, how the good Lord is our only hope of salvation and how the vast majority of the population will end up in the 'Lake Of Fire' for all eternity. Oh well, at least it should be nice and warm.

Of the nine numbers featured on this shocking long-player, only two qualify as anything vaguely resembling bona fide NWOBHM, namely the title track and "The Dealer", both of which are heavy-ish (good guitar in places) pieces in the general style of CHEVY. The remaining selections, however, are unutterably dire ballads (although "Jehovah" and "I Thank You Lord" are marginally more powerful than the others) extolling the virtues of an unblemished lifestyle, all of which are extraordinarily difficult to stomach. Fortunately, though, a lyric sheet hasn't been provided in this case, or I think I would probably have lost my lunch somewhere along the way. The singalong "He's Alive" is an unintentionally mirthsome inclusion, with numerous references to the great 'J.C.' and also a strangely, er, 'familiar' song construction. Hey guys, it's just as well there isn't a commandment which states 'Thou shalt not nick the chorus from DON MACLEAN's "American Pie" note for bloody note and insert it into your own songs', otherwise the unfortunate members of 20/20 VISION would surely be joining the rest of us in the unholy 'Lake Of Fire'. All in all, complete and utter bilge.

I would imagine that the long-forgotten 20/20 VISION, along with similarly-minded hopefuls such as 100% PROOF, the unrenowned MARK 2 and the inordinately mild-mannered 20TH CENTURY (I wonder what their fascination with numbers was all about?), went down an absolute storm at Christian music festivals and progressive church services, but I wouldn't have given them much chance of emerging unscathed from an appearance at a biker rally. In view of its extreme scarcity, you'll almost certainly never encounter this particular long-player (even the record's off-putting cover tries to deliver a typically heavy-handed social message), but, believe me, you really wouldn't want to. Axeman Gerwyn Howley, incidentally, later sold his soul to the devil and joined the goat-worshipping blasphemers of KOOGA in around 1987, although it wasn't long before they too were on the slippery slope to disintegration.

LP's
»In The Town/In The City« Private 198?

TWISTED ACE

Jeff Lever (v)
Phil Haywood (g)
Steve Topping (b)
Jeff Berry (d)

Merseyside's short-lived TWISTED ACE were a reasonable enough semi-NWOBHM proposition, their music coming across as a slightly harder-edged version of more traditional rock from the preceding decade, although they were yet another outfit who didn't get the breaks in the long term. First coming to the general public's notice on the original »Heavy Metal Heroes« compilation back in 1981 (with "I Won't Surrender"), the band were duly offered the opportunity to record their own single for the label towards the end of that year, and so the aforementioned sampler contribution was hastily recycled (in re-recorded form) and paired with the similarly-conceived "Firebird", the outfit's enthusiastic tribute to unnecessarily powerful penis extensions (sorry, I mean racing cars). These particular recordings (the first to credit bassist Steve James) are heavy enough slices of energetic rock/metal with occasional similarities to such diverse NWOBHM-era acts as RAVEN and FLASH HARRY, but both numbers are let down by extremely weak and vapid choruses, unfortunately. Nevertheless, "Firebird" made its way into the 'Top 30 Kuts' chart in 'Kerrang' in due course, suggesting that the lads must have won over a fair few fans in the wider rock community.

A year later, TWISTED ACE were offered another chance to shine, this time on the disappointing sequel to the original »Heavy Metal Heroes« compilation. With "This Fire Inside", the quartet seemed to have made a conscious decision to reinvent themselves, and were clearly now going for a considerably more melodic, keyboard-augmented approach, possibly reflecting the incredible popularity generated by the Joe Lynn Turner version of RAINBOW in the previous year or so. Their label seemed to approve of this new direction, however, and "This Fire Inside" was even lined up to be issued as the main focus of the band's second single a few months later. However, for some strange reason, this release was cancelled without any explanation, so if you've ever wondered why there's an extremely annoying gap (Heavy14) ruining the continuity of your Heavy Metal Records singles collection, you now know. Nothing was heard from the luckless outfit after this mysterious non-event, though, so I guess it's entirely possible that they had even already called it a day by then. The members all failed to resurface in later years, suggesting that they had probably become disillusioned with the music business and returned to conventional employment. Although TWISTED ACE left a modest legacy of just three tracks, these numbers have subsequently been issued on several NWOBHM compilations, so I hope the lads have been suitably reimbursed for their use over the years...

7" Singles
»Firebird« Heavy Metal 1981

Exclusive Compilation Appearances
"This Fire Inside" on »Heavy Metal Heroes Vol.II« LP Heavy Metal 1982 + »Heavy Metal Heroes Vol.I&II« CD British Steel 1996

Compilation Appearances
"I Won't Surrender" on »Heavy Metal Heroes« LP Heavy Metal 1981 *[Issued in two different sleeves]* + »Heavy Metal Heroes Vol.I&II« CD British Steel 1996 *[Different to single version]*
"I Won't Surrender" on »N.W.O.B.H.M. Metal Rarities Vol.3« CD British Steel 1997
"Firebird" on »N.W.O.B.H.M.« LP/CD Heavy Metal 1991 + »N.W.O.B.H.M. Metal Rarities Vol.3« CD British Steel 1997

TYGA MYRA

Mike Jurgens (v, g)
Teggi (g)
Randy Lingham (b)
Steve Dean (d)

Although the bafflingly-named TYGA MYRA allegedly started out as something of a CYNIC (see separate entry) offshoot, such was their rapid turnover of members in their early days (forming in around 1984) that half the population of Gloucestershire and/or Worcestershire seem to have passed through their ranks before a stable line-up was eventually achieved. Still, implausibly-named bassist Randy Lingham (known as plain old Ray Pedlingham in his CYNIC days) appears to have been a pretty permanent fixture, so at least there was some sort of continuity. Along the way, a demo cassette (featuring efforts such as "Rodeo", "Lady Danger" and "Rock'n'Roll Nightmare") was circulated to various influential parties of the day, and there wasn't a huge delay before the act began to attract some genuine interest with their competent and energetic brand of metal. It seems quite likely that the quartet eventually used the influence of friends in high places (notably Nick Bowcott of local heroes GRIM REAPER, who helped out on the recording side of things) to wangle a deal with Ebony, and it wasn't long before the musicians were hard at work in the studio, busily writing and laying down material for their first LP. The finished item eventually materialised in 1986, one of a batch of variable debut releases issued by some of Ebony's recent signings such as DEALER and RANKELSON.

TYGA MYRA's debut long-player, entitled »Deliverance«, was an undeniably heavy variation on the NWOBHM philosophy, building on the framework of local pioneers TYRANT, DEALER and GRIM REAPER to create a power metal proposition to challenge some of the more aggressive invaders from overseas. A couple of compositions, such as the substantial opener "Deliverance" and the atmospheric "Dead Zone", come across as particularly worthy efforts (a significant improvement on the demo recordings, with a far more accomplished vocal performance on display), albeit highly derivative, but TYGA MYRA's first vinyl offering could still quite easily have won the hearts of a fair percentage of British rock fans. Sadly, however, it failed miserably to make any impression whatsoever in the UK (a lukewarm review in 'Kerrang' didn't further their cause in any sense), although the ensemble would probably have fared slightly better in the American and European markets if Ebony had bothered to expend a fraction of the promotion and backing they afforded to their money-spinning flagship acts such as the aforementioned GRIM REAPER. Still, the plucky TYGA MYRA struggled on for around a year after the album's release, although they continued to be cursed by insurmountable personnel problems, and the lads never fully recovered from the departure of drummer Steve Dean in the early months of 1987.

With the act splintering shortly afterwards (abandoning the notion of recording a follow-up LP called »Terminator«, a title which had, in any case, already been used by labelmates PREYER), frontman Mike Jurgens swiftly inveigled his way into the ranks of the recently-established WRECKAGE, an outfit which employed countless scenesters from various West Country/West Midlands groups (including several other one-time members of TYGA MYRA themselves) over the years, but which would also suffer acutely from incurable line-up instability. They did, however, manage to record a semi-decent session for the 'Friday Rock Show' towards the end of 1988, and also contributed to the thrash-dominated »A Taste Of Armageddon« compilation, these representative efforts demonstrating that WRECKAGE were very much in the TYGA MYRA scheme of things, if not a tad heavier. It would appear, though, that the newer outfit never really went on to achieve anything particularly significant after this inauspicious opening gambit, although they kept going a lot longer than most observers would reasonably have anticipated (the group evolving into more of a crowd-pleasing, knockabout act in the process), before calling it a day in the mid-90's or thereabouts, having repeatedly failed either to attract genuine label interest or to release any self-financed product.

LP's

»Deliverance« Ebony 1986

TYGERS OF PAN TANG

Jess Cox (v)
Robb Weir (g)
Rocky Laws (b)
Brian Dick (d)

The origins of Tyneside's legendary (let's face it, the majority of metal fans with only a passing knowledge of the genre would still be able to identify them as one of the archetypal NWOBHM outfits) and extraordinarily prolific TYGERS OF PAN TANG lie in a knockabout act called TRICK, who were doing the rounds in the North East from around 1976 onwards. Apparently more strongly affiliated with the punk camp, TRICK were a notoriously unstable act (the only stalwart being guitarist Robb Weir), and were very much a small-time operation at the outset. As time went by, and as members came and went, however, the band veered more towards a heavier style, and eventually achieved a stable line-up and a fixed musical direction towards the end of 1977. At this point in time, Weir was being ably assisted by Rocky Laws (b), Brian Dick (d) and Mark Butcher (v), although they soon decided that they needed a more metal moniker to get themselves noticed. As luck (well, maybe not) would have it, one of the youngsters was reading Michael Moorcock's 'Stormbringer' novel at the time, and jokingly suggested 'the tygers of pan tang' at one of their early rehearsals. Incredibly, the unwieldy handle won favour with the remaining members, and the group soon unveiled their new identity at some local pub gigs. Original vocalist Mark Butcher failed to last the distance, however, and was out on his ear after around a dozen shows in the early months of 1978, whereupon the TYGERS acquired the services of Jess Cox, who had latterly been fronting a minor outfit called (wait for it) WILLY AND THE WEREWOLVES. By gum, those were some *seriously* bad names, guys...

By mid-1979, the rapidly-improving TYGERS had well and truly established themselves as a popular act in their locality, and were now in the habit of attracting sizeable crowds to their live appearances. Furthermore, they had managed to pocket a few quid in the process, and were soon laying down a demo or two at nearby

Impulse Studios, a facility run by a small company called Neat Records, who had released a couple of unsuccessful mainstream singles in the preceding months, but who weren't exactly renowned for their patronage of rock music at the time. Nevertheless, the label's boss (Dave Wood) took an instant liking to the TYGERS, and offered them the chance to record a one-off 7" towards the end of the year. The youngsters jumped at the opportunity, and duly laid down "Don't Touch Me There", "Bad Times" and "Burning Up" for imminent release. Neither the band nor their label were at all prepared for the response the record was about to elicit. Sales of the debut release from this oddly-named combo rapidly escalated to truly phenomenal levels, and Neat could hardly press enough copies to meet demand. Unwittingly, the TYGERS had tapped into the public's consciousness by delivering precisely the kind of 'new metal' the music press were currently enthusing about, having emerged at just the right time to land themselves a prime seat on the NWOBHM bandwagon. Certainly, they had more in common with the likes of IRON MAIDEN, whose rough'n'ready appeal stemmed from their unpretentious attitude (which, unlike their music, was shared with the punk scene), as opposed to bands such as DIAMOND HEAD and PRAYING MANTIS, who were very much trying to update the traditional heavy rock/metal sound which had been pioneered by musical behemoths such as THIN LIZZY and LED ZEPPELIN in the early 70's. Both schools of thought would exert a considerable hold over the nation's metal aficionados as the movement took shape, although it's fair to suggest that the likes of MAIDEN and the TYGERS were rather more likely to be identified as the very epitome of the NWOBHM spirit.

The colossal impact of the TYGERS debut was single-handedly instrumental in persuading Neat to 'go metal', and the label swiftly turned its attention to seeking out other young hopefuls to see if the phenomenon could be repeated. However, they were soon persuaded to sign over the rights to future TYGERS releases, with a generous offer coming from the mighty MCA, who wished to sponsor the outfit's career from this point onwards (they later repeated the process, with considerably more modest success, for WHITE SPIRIT and FIST). Neat, to their credit, realised that the TYGERS would stand a far better chance of becoming stars if they had the backing of a major company, and subsequently allowed the youngsters to benefit from the financial clout wielded by MCA. Still, I'm not entirely sure if the profits were actually shared, as in the case of FIST and WHITE SPIRIT, whose MCA albums were joint releases with Neat. Within a matter of weeks, the TYGERS were preparing their inaugural release for their new employers, although their initial product on MCA was a straight reissue of their first EP, housed in an identical picture sleeve. Again, this sold in pretty healthy quantities (although not quite as spectacularly as the Neat version, in spite of MCA's assertions to the contrary), and it allowed MCA to trouser a bit of handy cash while the lads were busying themselves on their debut long-player. Next up was the »Rock'n'Roll Man« 7", which (for reasons best known to those responsible for the release) appeared as both a conventional two track single (most without a picture sleeve) and a more common three track EP (the additional numbers being "Alright On The Night" and "Wild Catz"). Sales were brisk, although the puzzling existence of two separate versions (the seldom-seen sleeve for the two-tracker merely blocks out the extra title) must have caused a bit of consternation among the fans of the time.

The TYGERS were allowed to showcase four numbers from their repertoire on the 'Friday Rock Show' prior to the release of the first album, and this valuable piece of exposure must have given their chances a significant boost. Transmitted on the 11th of April 1980, the session included versions of "Don't Touch Me There", "Wild Catz" and "Euthanasia", plus the exclusive "Don't Take Nothin'", which later turned up on MCA's »Precious Metal« compilation. The band's »Wild Cat« long-player appeared in due course (the lads having been out on tour with both MAGNUM and SAXON in the interim), and, surprisingly, it turned out to be a record with massive crossover potential, appealing just as much to the traditional rock/metal fans (hefty MOTÖRHEAD and THIN LIZZY influences coming across in places) as to the followers of the emergent NWOBHM outfits such as ANGEL WITCH and IRON MAIDEN. It was a capable enough debut, if slightly lacking in variety, and the rough vocals of Jess Cox were to come in for some serious criticism, although the overall energy and enthusiasm carried the group through admirably, as well as some impressive musicianship on tracks such as "Killers", "Fireclown", "Badger Badger" and the lengthy "Insanity". The LP proceeded to sell in utterly enormous quantities, impinging upon the mainstream charts and eventually achieving a hugely impressive 'Top 20' position in the long run, propelling the TYGERS OF PAN TANG well and truly into the IRON MAIDEN bracket in terms of units shifted. Truly, the lads were already at the very forefront of the NWOBHM explosion, and were soon capitalising on their popularity with a ceaseless series of tours, hitching a ride with the well-liked SCORPIONS (as well as occasional appearances with DIAMOND HEAD and ANGEL WITCH) before the year was out.

MCA also made good use of the album with regard to getting singles into the shops, starting off with »Suzie Smiled« (backed with a cover of ZZ TOP's "Tush", a live favourite), and the band were soon a sufficiently high-profile act to be able to headline their own tour for the first time. To this end, a lengthy series of dates was scheduled for the second half of the year, kicking off with an appearance at the Reading Festival, where the lads set the stage for the likes of DEF LEPPARD and WHITESNAKE. By this time, though, the TYGERS had come to a mutual agreement that they would benefit from the presence of a second guitarist, and so some auditions were swiftly arranged. After a few no-hopers had courteously been shown the door, in stepped STREETFIGHTER's John Sykes, who impressed the outfit with both his playing and his looks (!), and the lucky lad was soon being invited to join in the fun. Although his first *'official'* appearance was at the festival, the TYGERS weren't quite cruel enough to make Sykes endure such a hellish baptism of fire, and actually allowed him to make his debut at a modest club gig a few days prior to the main event. The whole Reading experience passed without any major hitches, and the jubilant ensemble were soon riding the crest of a wave as they went back out on the road to promote their latest two-tracker, the contentious and ill-advised (but no doubt it was tongue-in-cheek) »Euthanasia« 7" (which appeared in a minimalist black sleeve which didn't even credit the outfit), backed with the non-album cut "Straight As A Die". The single didn't exactly break any sales records (I'm sure many people failed to realise what it was), and its release was largely overlooked at the time, which is just as well, really, as the excitable media would have had a field day with the lyrical contents.

In spite of the tour being a well-attended and critically-hailed success, the group (and, more importantly, their ambitious management) were now of the general opinion that Jess Cox was holding them back with his rudimentary style. Since the TYGERS would almost certainly be attempting to move into more commercial waters with their next release (in order to make an impression on the overseas market), they decided to part company with the frontman (who hastily hooked up with LIONHEART) and seek out an individual with a more powerful set of lungs. After a couple of hectic months (during which time they auditioned over a *hundred* likely candidates), their quest for a new singer was finally accomplished when Jon Deverill, the original voice of PERSIAN RISK, was inducted into the TYGERS hall of fame. The talented frontman was unveiled at a well-attended show at the Marquee at the end of 1980, and he made his vinyl debut on the group's next single, »Hellbound« (b/w "Don't Give A Damn"), a release which (thanks to the freebie »The Audition Tapes« two-tracker being thrown in for good measure) also allowed the fans to hear two tracks taken from Deverill's try-outs. The replacement vocalist acquitted himself admirably on his first vinyl effort, and it looked as though the TYGERS would go from strength to strength from that point onwards. Fresh material was swiftly demoed for the follow-up album, which happily got the thumbs-up from MCA, so work on »Spellbound« began almost immediately. The lads took some time off to play a special show for the BBC's exclusive 'In Concert' programme, where (appearing alongside CHEVY) the TYGERS proceeded to deliver an energetic half-hour performance. Next up was yet another 7", this time a three-tracker to showcase some numbers from the forthcoming long-player. The EP introduced the fans to "The Story So Far" and "Silver And Gold" (two efforts which already showed a considerable shift towards more accessible material), although the highlight was the group's interpretation of the SMALL FACES classic "All Or Nothing".

The much-anticipated »Spellbound« turned out to be quite a varied affair, which embraced the melodic ("Don't Stop By", plus the now-familiar pairing of "Silver And Gold" and "The Story So Far"), the powerful ("Tyger Bay", "Blackjack" and "Gangland", the latter subsequently covered by none other than KREATOR) and even an attempt at the odd power ballad (the surprisingly listenable "Mirror"). Peculiarly, though, the album wasn't to achieve quite the same level of success as its predecessor (it still made a healthy impact on the charts once again), and a considerable number of the outfit's fans seemed to be quite loath to accept the diversification of their much-loved heroes. Still, MCA went ahead with its programme of single releases, although only »Don't Stop By« emerged this time (in both 7" and 12" forms, using live material from their BBC broadcast to act as B-sides), suggesting a slight lack of confidence in the latest TYGERS compositions. Nevertheless, the hard-working lads were soon out on the road once again, headlining a relatively successful and productive series of dates throughout the UK and mainland Europe. MCA's response to the comparatively poor performance of »Spellbound«, however, was to get another LP in the shops as soon as possible, so they duly hit the TYGERS with an ultimatum that they either deliver a full album of new material within a couple of months or risk losing their deal. The pressure was well and truly on, although the lads (who could have done with a few months off to recover from their hectic touring schedule) somehow contrived to assemble the »Crazy Nights« long-player within the required time limit (they also managed to fit in a television appearance on the networked 'Something Else' show), and the *'difficult third album'* hit the shops towards the end of the year, much to the surprise of the fans and rock press.

All things considered, the world wasn't ready for another TYGERS album this soon, and questions were raised as to whether the lads were sacrificing their artistic integrity in order to get more product into the shops as quickly as possible. Unaware of the pressures being applied by the outfit's label, the fans began to view the TYGERS as an avaricious proposition with little or no regard for their followers, and something

of a backlash had been initiated even before the long-player appeared in the shops. The situation might have been salvaged if the record had turned out to be a cracker, but »Crazy Nights« was their worst-selling and most poorly-received offering to date (despite being launched in a blaze of publicity with a packed-out show at the Marquee), and most of the compositions featured were of a particularly low standard. There were, admittedly, a couple of decent numbers, notably "Running Out Of Time" and "Lonely Man", but tracks such as "Never Satisfied", "Down And Out" and "Make A Stand" were all such half-baked, throwaway efforts (I'm sure none of them would have survived if the TYGERS had been given a more generous time to deliver the album) that the overall impression tended to be one of disappointment. The band seemed to be paving the way for a move into more ambitious territory (similarities to DIAMOND HEAD at times), although, on the evidence presented here, they simply didn't possess the requisite songwriting skills to be able to deliver the goods in the short term. Further criticism could also be levelled at frontman Jon Deverill, who, despite being an eminently talented vocalist, was trying *far* too hard to liven up some dismally uninspiring songs with a completely over-the-top display of vocal histrionics, which not only failed to enhance the material, but was just downright annoying.

MCA attempted to boost sales by repackaging the album with a free 12" single (featuring "The Stormlands" and "Slip Away", two compositions of a considerably higher standard, originally included only as bonus tracks on the cassette version and the Japanese release), which presumably helped matters slightly, although their subsequent attempts to rake in a bit of cash from singles seems to have failed pretty miserably. The »Love Don't Stay« 7" (B-side "Paradise Drive") was based around the most lightweight number on the whole set, and failed to shift enough units to make the release worthwhile, but the follow-up (»Do It Good«) was an unmitigated disaster, with hardly any copies even getting into the shops (it was a totally half-hearted affair, by the looks of things, and it seems MCA couldn't even be bothered to fabricate a picture sleeve), so sales were laughably poor as a consequence. The participants were understandably disappointed with the general reaction to their latest long-player, although they seemed to be aware that it was a substandard release even before it hit the shelves, as John Sykes later revealed: '»*Crazy Nights*« *was a mixture of everyone's material, we were all getting sussed to the situation of three versus two and we weren't working as a band.* »*Crazy Nights*« *was a disaster, the worst piece of work I've ever been associated with. The album was thrown together. I could tell it wouldn't be much cop, nobody had their heart in it.* »*Spellbound*« *had a lot more fire and excitement. I was really ashamed of* »*Crazy Nights*«…*I haven't even got a copy of it.*' (Ref: Kerrang No.27, October 1982).

Still, there was always work to be done on the promotional side of things, and the dejected TYGERS were soon putting on a brave face and venturing off to mainland Europe once again, where they hooked up with GILLAN for a reasonably successful series of dates, proving that they still had plenty of devoted fans after all. After returning to the UK to attempt to get things back on track (starting off with a high-profile appearance on the 'Old Grey Whistle Test'), however, the cracks were beginning to show, and it became apparent that John Sykes wasn't happy with his role in the group. The tensions of the previous months had been slowly needling their talented lead guitarist, who was very much at the end of his tether, having formed the opinion that the original TYGERS members (Rocky, Brian and Robb) had now closed ranks, and were reluctant to let the *'newcomers'* (Sykes and Deverill) exert much influence on the songwriting or creative side of things (see the *'three versus two'* reference in the preceding quote). It was surely only a matter of time before the axeman finally left, and he eventually jumped ship after an offer to tour the States with OZZY OSBOURNE, although things didn't work out quite as expected, with the arrangement falling through at short notice, leaving him to team up with John Sloman's ill-fated BADLANDS project for an incredibly brief spell before moving on (*via* an ostensibly *'solo'* single) to THIN LIZZY. After hurriedly auditioning for a suitable replacement, the TYGERS made the surprise announcement that their latest recruit was a chap called Fred Purser, who had previously earned a wage playing with new wave heavyweights PENETRATION, a group who were, on the face of it, the utter antithesis of the NWOBHM archetype. Nevertheless, the guitarist was soon putting everyone's fears at rest, assuring the press that PENETRATION and the TYGERS had considerably more in common than you might think. Hmmm. Still, the new boy settled in quite nicely, and was soon making his live debut on a brief tour of France, which seems to have gone without any major hassles.

By mid-1982, the lads were being ushered back in the studio once more, where they desperately tried to assemble an album's worth of usable material within the usual short timescale. The long-player was preceded by a single (recorded while John Sykes was still in the outfit) featuring "Love Potion No.9", a cover of a popular r'n'b standard (originally a hit for the CLOVERS as far back as 1959), an immensely catchy number which took the TYGERS into the singles charts for the first time, and which led to the lads filming a reasonably mirthsome promo video set in a courthouse. The TYGERS were back with a vengeance, and it looked as though the public might be willing to forgive them for the »Crazy Nights« debacle after all. This time,

however, they really were struggling to come up with novel material, given that the departed John Sykes had co-written many of their compositions of recent months, and these were now unavailable for the TYGERS to use themselves. New recruit Fred Purser valiantly came up with a few efforts ("Tides", "The Actor" and "You Always See What You Want To See", an interesting trio of capable numbers which were undeniably similar to TYTAN in places, plus a brief instrumental called "The Cage", the album's intended title) within a fairly short space of time, but the remaining members had something of a creative block and failed to come up with anything (apart from the entirely mundane "Making Tracks") of a remotely comparable standard. The outfit's label and management ended up having a bit of a discussion about this worrying situation, and ultimately decided to pad out the LP with a selection of cover versions and specially co-written efforts. The band's long-time acquaintance, the prolific Steve Thompson, was brought in to pen a few catchy ditties ("Paris By Air", "Lonely At The Top" and "Letter From L.A."), and things were duly rounded off with "Love Potion No.9" (again), "Danger In Paradise" and "Rendezvous".

In the end, things actually worked out quite well, and this selection of predominantly chart-friendly material (with Fred Purser also now contributing keyboards) effectively represented almost an entire album's worth of singles, something which MCA could use to their considerable advantage in their attempts to break the TYGERS in the States at long last. In fact, »The Cage« was to sell incredibly well on both sides of the Atlantic (it proved to be their most successful album of all time in the UK), and confirmed unequivocally that the band were still a lucrative and highly-regarded act after all. Three singles (two of which dented the mainstream charts once again) were unleashed over the ensuing months, and it was actually the more accessible efforts ("Rendezvous" and "Paris By Air") which ultimately turned out to be the more popular A-sides, with the subsequent »Making Tracks« single (released as both 7" and 12", the latter incorporating a pointless and overly-long remix) failing to achieve a comparable level of sales. A major headlining tour was organised to coincide with the album's release, and the lads kicked things off with a triumphal return to the Reading Festival (where they appeared second on the bill to IRON MAIDEN) before taking to the road for a UK tour with (oddly enough) TYTAN in tow. The gigs were pretty successful, and the general public were now accepting the TYGERS with open arms once again, their tuneful new direction winning the hearts of many followers. With the outfit's popularity now seemingly at an all-time high, the lads were also duly shipped over to Japan for a brief (but immensely well-received) series of club appearances. A couple of these shows were even recorded professionally, and some of this material later surfaced on a Japanese-only vinyl release entitled »Live In Japan« (although it's listed as an eponymous affair in some reference sources). The TYGERS rounded off 1982 with another attention-grabbing television appearance, this time on 'The Tube', a notoriously anarchic and chaotic networked show of the time.

Perversely, just when things seemed to be going the group's way once again, things soon started to go pear-shaped in major fashion, although the quintet still remained under contract to MCA for another long-player, on which the lads began working in the early months of 1983. In fact, they actually got as far as demoing an entire album's worth of material, none of which ever saw the light of day officially (the tracks were "With You", "Square One", "Travel The World", "Darkest Cloud", "Time Flies", "Real Life", "Samurai", "Fake Diamonds" and "Answers"), although the public wasn't really being deprived of anything spectacular, the compositions all being very much in the melodic, lightweight, unremarkable style which had been pioneered on some of the lesser numbers from »The Cage«. After recording this mediocre material, long-serving members Robb Weir and Brian Dick (who were becoming increasingly frustrated at their lack of creative input) jumped ship to form the ill-fated SEARGENT (or SERGEANT, depending on whom you choose to believe) in the wake of various management problems and contractual wrangling. Following their departure, the remainder of the band swiftly disintegrated, leaving MCA with no usable material for a fifth album. Undeterred, the grasping label concluded that they were still entitled to another TYGERS long-player after all, and hastily threw together a 'greatest hits' compilation (the contents mostly being plundered from singles) with the predictable title »The Best Of The Tygers Of Pan Tang«. Bizarrely, MCA even pressed up a 7" (»Lonely At The Top«) to coincide with this release, although it seems to have been another inept attempt to rake in a bit of additional cash, and hardly any copies made it into circulation (again, there wasn't even a picture sleeve) at the time.

With Weir and Dick immersed in their new project, little was heard from the members of the TYGERS OF PAN TANG for a couple of years, although the failure of SEARGENT eventually led to media speculation that the TYGERS might get back together for another crack at recapturing their fan base. Towards the end of 1984, Jon Deverill and Brian Dick 'reformed' the group (pointing out that there had never actually been an official split), although Robb Weir couldn't be enticed back into the ranks (he later formed the TYGER TYGER offshoot with original vocalist Jess Cox) for love nor money. In the first instance, Deverill and Dick attempted to kick-start the TYGERS by recruiting guitarists Mick Procter and Neil Shepherd (both formerly associated with the defunct JESS COX venture), plus bassist Paul Irwin (previously with local rivals WARRIOR), although Procter (who, as well as playing on the NATO single, subsequently guested on BLITZKRIEG's »A Time Of Changes« album) was soon ousted in favour of former SEARGENT axeman Steve Lamb. Irwin, on the other hand, lasted slightly longer, although he was still superseded by Dave Donaldson (yet another JESS COX veteran) after a couple of months. Within a fairly short space of time, the revamped TYGERS had wangled a deal with Music For Nations, and (having already knocked out their fifth long-player well in advance) saw the comeback album hitting the shops without too much of a delay.

With Steve Thompson having been brought in to collaborate with Jon Deverill once again, the TYGERS seemed to be involved in a fairly blatant conspiracy to recapture the glory days of »The Cage«, and the public were given the chance to offer their opinion of the latest material when the LP (lumbered with the confusing and clumsy title of »The Wreck-Age«) appeared in the spring of 1985. It was a very patchy affair, to be honest, and featured a keyboard-dominated style of chart-friendly melodic rock which veered from the listenable ("Waiting", "The Wreck-Age", "All Change Faces") to the far-too-close-to-LIONHEART-for-my-liking ("Innocent Eyes" and "Women In Cages", both penned by someone outside the band), and I'm sure the lads could easily have come up with something stronger if they had been a tad more patient and hadn't rushed headfirst into things in their (now-customary) haphazard fashion. Still, the outfit were back in the limelight and determined to make the most of it, and (in spite of some decidedly lukewarm reviews for their comeback opus) were soon doing their utmost to promote themselves, starting off with an appearance on the 'E.C.T.' television programme, where they ran through energetic versions of "The Wreck-Age" and "Desert Of No Love", the tracks sounding far stronger live than they did on vinyl. Next up was a session for the ever-obliging 'Friday Rock Show', where they were temporarily joined by keyboard player Pete Whalan (Steve Thompson had done the honours on the latest album) for their four track showcase (broadcast on the 6th of September 1985). The lads ran through versions of "The Wreck-Age", "Desert Of No Love", "Waiting" and "Women In Cages" for the benefit of the station's listeners, and were soon jetting of to the States for the first time, playing a handful of select dates before returning to the UK and repeating the process.

In spite of reasonable album sales and a fairly successful presence on the British club circuit for much of 1986, however, the hapless group (now featuring new keyboard bod Gordon Hall) soon found themselves without a deal once again. Around this time, though, Neat Records stepped in with a generous offer to release some of the outfit's early demos, and the »First Kill« set appeared after the briefest of negotiations. It was, without doubt, a great opportunity for the dedicated TYGERS fans to hear the original versions of some of their old favourites, as well as unfamiliar material such as "Angel", "The Final Answer" and "Shakespear Road". It would appear that Neat had something of a hidden agenda for getting the album into the shops, however, as they cunningly used the opportunity to sneak on a TYGER TYGER number ("Small Town Flirt", entirely comparable to the formative TYGERS themselves, albeit rather more anthemic) as a 'bonus', hoping to generate some interest in the latest Cox/Weir project, who were now on Neat's books and who were expected to deliver an album of their own before the year was out. In fact, the TYGER TYGER venture (the other members being one-time EMERSON bassist Brian Emerson and mysterious drummer Mr. Roland) failed to spark the public's imagination to any great extent, and finally drifted apart within a couple of years without ever getting to the vinyl stage after all. Still, at least the TYGERS had managed to get an album out of Neat at last, keeping their career afloat for the time being, although the label would decline the opportunity of signing up the lads for a brand-new LP in the wake of relatively modest sales of »First Kill«.

Undeterred, the main members of the TYGERS OF PAN TANG (Jon Deverill, Brian Dick and Steve Lamb) ploughed on regardless (Dave Donaldson having defected to TOKYO BLADE and Neil Shepherd going back to occasional session work) and sought out a new deal with Zebra Records. Brian Emerson briefly stepped in to help on bass, but old faithful (Steve Thompson) subsequently took over both keyboard and bass duties for the recording of the forthcoming long-player for their new label, the band concluding that they could manage perfectly well without a second guitarist. Sadly, »Burning In The Shade« turned out to be the last TYGERS album, and it was a very poor way for them to bow out, given that the record consisted almost entirely of feather-light melodic rock and unsubstantial ballads (not even genuine power ballads now), with barely a solitary 'highlight' of note, although closer "The Memory Fades" was a semi-decent (but immensely soppy) effort. The lads went out on a lengthy spring tour of the UK (although they were no longer able to fill the major venues) with the rapidly-improving BLUE BLUD in tow, although the latter act appear to have shown the more experienced headliners exactly how to please the melodic rock contingent at every opportunity. Still, the TYGERS refused to quit, and returned to the clubs (increasingly minor ones, that is) towards the end of the year, although this series of gigs appears to have been a total disaster, with few fans bothering to turn out on the cold nights to cheer on these fallen heroes. By the early weeks of 1988, the TYGERS had fallen apart for good.

Surprisingly, few of the outfit's one-time members made any further impression on the rock scene, although Steve Thompson soon went back to his songwriting activities, and continues to pen many a cheery tune for various acts even today. Jon Deverill, on the other hand, joined forces with Pete Way to record some new demos for the ailing WAYSTED project in the early months of 1988, although this relationship proved to be a short-lived affair. The charismatic vocalist subsequently had talks with German rockers VICTORY about the possibility of fronting them throughout their forthcoming touring schedule (Deverill even undertook a couple of studio rehearsals with the outfit), but nothing much came of that notion either, and the dejected chap soon disappeared into obscurity. By the early 90's, however, it became apparent that there was still a hardcore interest in the TYGERS in some parts of the globe, and the dedicated Japanese market was apparently ripe for exploitation. To this end, MCA Japan swiftly issued an exclusive compilation of the outfit's more popular 7" offerings (imaginatively titled »Singles«), although the bootleggers soon jumped on the bandwagon and pressed up a couple of live CD's, which was much more the sort of thing the

669

obsessive fans really wanted to hear. A few years later, the revived Neat Metal concern (run by Jess Cox himself) acquired the rights to the group's MCA back catalogue and reissued all four albums on CD (on their Edgy imprint), complete with numerous bonus tracks and comprehensive sleeve notes.

There was a further treat in store for TYGERS fans at the 1998 Wacken Festival in Europe, when Jess Cox got up on stage with BLITZKRIEG and belted out versions of "Money" and "Suzie Smiled", much to the delight of the assembled masses. They went one better at Wacken in 1999, however, when Jess Cox reunited with Robb Weir and (assisted by BLITZKRIEG's rhythm section) delivered a curtailed set (drat those pesky curfews) under the TYGERS OF PAN TANG name once again. The reception was extremely favourable, although there have been no specific moves (yet) to get a bona fide version of the TYGERS off the ground once again, but the fans will always remain hopeful. Nevertheless, there are still plenty of potential releases in the pipeline, including an official live album (recorded during their glory days of 1981) and possibly yet another retrospective (if there's enough genuine demand) or a new compilation of unreleased material. If you're a TYGERS aficionado, it certainly looks as though there could be some interesting CD's on the way in the next couple of years, but, given the difficult relationships which exist between some of the original members, that full-scale reformation is another matter entirely…

LP's

»Wild Cat« MCA 1980/Beograddisk 1980
[UK/Yugoslavian issue]
»Spellbound« MCA 1981/Jugodisk 1981
[UK/Yugoslavian issue]
»Crazy Nights« MCA 1981
[Some copies with free 12" featuring "The Stormlands" and "Slip Away", cassette version includes both tracks]
»Crazy Nights« MCA Japan 1981
[Japanese issue with two extra tracks]
»The Cage« MCA 1982
[UK issue with eleven tracks]
»The Cage« MCA 1982
[US issue with different running order, also omits "Lonely At The Top"]
»Live In Japan« MCA Japan 1982
[Japanese-only compilation release of live and studio material]
»The Best Of The Tygers Of Pan Tang« MCA 1983
[Compilation release]
»Wild Cat« Fame 1983
[Reissue]
»The Wreck-Age« Music For Nations 1985
»First Kill« Neat 1986
[Compilation of early demos]
»Burning In The Shade« Zebra Records 1987
»Hellbound« Repertoire 1989
[German-only double album featuring »Wild Cat« and »Spellbound«]

12" EP's

»Don't Stop By« MCA 1981
[Features exclusive live versions of "Slave To Freedom" and "Raised On Rock"]

12" Singles

»The Stormlands« MCA 1981
[Free with some copies of »Crazy Nights« LP, both tracks non-LP]
»Making Tracks« MCA 1982
[With extended remix of A-side, different to album version, B-side "What You Saying" non-LP]

7" EP's

»Don't Touch Me There« Neat 1979
[Original issue, "Burning Up" non-LP, A-side different to album version, "Bad Times" different to version on »First Kill« set]
»Don't Touch Me There« MCA 1980
[Second issue]
»Rock'n'Roll Man« MCA 1980
[Three track version in picture sleeve, A-side non-LP, "Alright On The Night" different to version on »First Kill« set]
»The Story So Far« MCA 1981
[A-side different to album version, "All Or Nothing" non-LP]

7" Singles

»Rock'n'Roll Man« MCA 1980
[Two track version, most in company sleeves, A-side non-LP, B-side "Alright On The Night" different to version on »First Kill« set]
»Suzie Smiled« MCA 1980
[A-side different to album version, B-side "Tush" non-LP]
»Suzie Smiled« Beograddisk 1980
[Yugoslavian issue in different sleeve]
»Euthanasia« MCA 1980
[B-side "Straight As A Die" different to version on »First Kill« set]
»Hellbound« MCA 1981
[B-side "Don't Give A Damn" non-LP, limited edition with free »Audition Tapes« single featuring exclusive demo versions of "Don't Take Nothin'" and "Bad Times"]
»Hellbound« MCA 1981
[German issue without free single]

»Don't Stop By« MCA 1981
[B-side exclusive live version of "Slave To Freedom"]
»Love Don't Stay« MCA 1981
[A-side different to album version, B-side "Paradise Drive" non-LP]
»Do It Good« MCA 1981
[B-side "Slip Away" non-LP]
»Love Potion No.9« MCA 1982
[B-side "The Stormlands" non-LP, also released as limited edition picture disc with different image]
»Love Potion No.9« MCA 1982
[German issue with different sleeve]
»Love Potion No.9« MCA Japan 1982
[Japanese issue with different sleeve]
»Rendezvous« MCA 1982
[Limited edition in poster sleeve, also issued on red, white and blue vinyl, A-side different to album version, B-side "Life Of Crime" non-LP]
»Rendezvous« MCA 1982
[German issue in different sleeve]
»Paris By Air« MCA 1982
[Initially with free earring, also issued as limited edition picture disc, B-side "Love's A Lie" non-LP]
»Making Tracks« MCA 1982
[A-side different to album version, B-side "What You Saying" non-LP]
»Lonely At The Top« MCA 1983

CD's
»Wild Cat« Repertoire 1990
»Spellbound« Repertoire 1990
»First Kill« Castle Communications 1991
[Compilation of early demos]
»Wild Cat« MCA/Victor 1992
[Japanese issue]
»Spellbound« MCA/Victor 1992
[Japanese issue]
»Crazy Nights« MCA/Victor 1992
[Japanese issue]
»The Cage« MCA/Victor 1992
[Japanese issue]
»Singles« MCA Japan 1992
[Japanese-only compilation]
»Money« Real Life 1996
[Live bootleg from 1980]
»First Tyger« Nightlife 1996
[Live bootleg from 1980]
»Wild Cat« Edgy 1997
[With seven bonus tracks]
»Spellbound« Edgy 1997
[With five bonus tracks]
»Crazy Nights« Edgy 1997
[With three bonus tracks]
»The Cage« Edgy 1997
[With four bonus tracks]
»On The Prowl (The Best Of)« Half Moon 1999

[Compilation release]
»The Wreck-Age« Edgy 2000

Compilation Appearances
"Don't Take Nothin'" on »Precious Metal« LP MCA 1980 + »The Metal Box« 3-CD Box Castle Communications 1993 + »Give 'Em Hell« CD Nectar Masters 1995
"The Story So Far" on »Hammer« LP Ariola 1981
"Love Potion No.9" on »Heavy« LP K-Tel 1983 + »Metal Treasures And Vinyl Heavies« LP Action Replay Records 1984
"Rendezvous" on »Metal Killers« LP Kastle Killers 1984
"Waiting" on »Beyond Metal Zone« Do-LP Music For Nations 1986
"Killers" on »NWOBHM '79 Revisited« Do-LP/Do-CD Phonogram 1990
"Angel" on »Heavy Metal Collection 1« CD X-Tra Collection 1993
"Wild Catz" (live) on »NWOBHM-The Days On Stage« Bootleg CD Taurus Records 1993
"Straight As A Die" on »Metal Killers« CD Castle Communications 1993
"Euthanasia" on »Metal Killers« CD Castle Communications 1993
"Bad Times" on »Wild Thing« CD Kaz Records 1995 + »The Metal Box« 3-CD Box Kaz Records 1995
"Sweet Lies" on »Rock Out!« Do-CD Emporio 1996
"Hit It" on »Rock Out!« Do-CD Emporio 1996 + »The Best Of Indie Metal« CD Emporio 1998
"Are You There" on »The Best Of Indie Metal« CD Emporio 1998

TYRANT

Mark Kelser (v)
Jim Merritt (g)
Gary Atkins (g)
Pete Antonious (b)
Mark Walker (d)

For some peculiar reason, epic power metal just never took off in the UK during the 80's, in spite of the fact that many fans around the world regarded this to be the natural successor to the original NWOBHM sound. Nevertheless, overblown, bombastic vocal performances and heroic, sword-wielding lyrics never went down as well with cynical British audiences as those in the States or Europe, and, consequently, few resident bands attempted the style at any point in time. However, Gloucestershire's TYRANT (not to be confused with their better-known American or German namesakes) were another atypically heavy NWOBHM proposition whose colossal »Hold Back The Lightning« two-tracker sits comfortably alongside early 80's vinyl releases such as ARC's »War Of The Ring«, AFTER DARK's »Deathbringer« and DRAGONSLAYER's »I Want Your Life« in the *'unusually heroic'* file. Indeed, it's quite difficult to come to terms with the fact that this particular quintet were actually British citizens at all, sounding at times more like MANOWAR than the *'kings of metal'* themselves!

After forming in 1982 and touring extensively throughout England and Wales before issuing a well-received six track demo tape featuring such gems as "Shadows Of The Night" (an alternate version of their single's A-side), "Take It To The Dragon" and "Clash Of The Titans", the lads swiftly decided that they wanted a piece of the action as far as vinyl product was concerned. To this end, TYRANT duly laid down "Hold Back The Lightning" and "Eyes Of A Stranger" at Millstream Studios in Cheltenham, two numbers which would comprise their debut single (a self-financed affair) the following year. Deservedly, this release (very much in the mould of powerful outfits such as ELIXIR, the DESOLATION ANGELS or Leicestershire's PROWLER) received its fair share of airplay on various regional radio stations, and was soon selling in pretty respectable quantities to some of the country's more accommodating metalheads. On the face of it, things seemed to be going quite well at this stage (mind you, the record was on the receiving end of the usual disadvantageous review in 'Kerrang'), although the hapless members of TYRANT appear to have lacked the crucial ability to build upon the initially-favourable reception and establish themselves as genuine contenders.

As with so many others, the group seem to have struggled to maintain a stable line-up, losing both guitarists in the early months of 1984 and bringing in scenesters such as Danny Gwilym (better-known for his involvement with CHINATOWN and SHOGUN) and Phil Vokins (aka Phil Wrathchild, who also collaborated with the likes of WRATHCHILD, CRASH KO, PERSIAN RISK and BILL WARD over the years) to make up the numbers. Additional demo tracks such as "Mirror Image" and "Haunted Dreams" apparently drew a limited amount of record company interest, but no deal ever materialised. Sadly, the inevitable split occurred soon afterwards (bassist Pete Antonious jumped ship, ostensibly to try his luck with a pop outfit, and the shellshocked group never fully recovered), with talented vocalist Mark Kelser (who had allegedly turned down the opportunity to join ACCEPT at one point) subsequently joining the ranks of the ever-changing CARRERA. Naturally, the TYRANT single (for which no picture sleeve was manufactured) is, to say the least, a bit of a rarity, and modern-day collectors are unlikely to get hold of a copy without handing over a fair amount of cash. Mind you, if the multitudinous IRON MAIDEN fans became aware of its existence, the asking price would surely go through the roof, so let's be grateful that they're generally more preoccupied with tracking down URCHIN releases. Incidentally, there's absolutely no connection with the other British TYRANT, who earlier appeared on Suspect's »Scene Of The Crime« compilation, although there's more than a passing similarity in terms of lyrics and songwriting styles.

7" Singles
»**Hold Back The Lightning**« SRT 1983

TYSONDOG

Clutch Carruthers (v)
Alan Hunter (g)
Paul Burdis (g)
Kevin Wynn (b)
Peter Reeve (d)

Tyneside heavyweights TYSONDOG (supposedly named after a dog called Tyson, absurdly enough) became a serious proposition in around the summer of 1982, and were soon making waves with a well-received three track demo, which they circulated to all the usual labels to see if anyone would take the bait. It wasn't too much of a shock when Neat stepped in with an offer, given that the outfit's brand of powerful metal (with some top-notch vocals from Clutch Carruthers) was entirely representative of the fabled *'Neat sound'*, their music containing elements of contemporaries such as BLITZKRIEG, TRIDENT and CLOVEN HOOF. TYSONDOG's debut for Neat was a modest two-tracker featuring "Eat The Rich" and "Dead Meat", a pair of highly capable efforts which immediately allowed the quintet to become firm favourites among the metalheads of the day, after which they were encouraged to follow up this promising start with a full-length release. By the early months of 1984, the lads had already drafted in a new drummer, Ged Wolf, and had also permitted axeman Alan Hunter to deputise as SATAN vocalist (he had actually served as TYSONDOG's own frontman at the very outset) for a few vital gigs, after the departure of Brian Ross had left the aforementioned outfit in severe danger of losing out on some important appearances in Europe. Once things had settled down again, the lads got around to recording their »Beware Of The Dog« opus, an album which contained its fair share of substantial numbers such as "Hammerhead", "The Inquisitor" and "Day Of The Butcher". It was a heavy and varied long-player, and it certainly consolidated TYSONDOG's position as firm favourites, particularly in the North East.

Neat were keen to hold on to the popular band, and the lads remained loyal to their label from that point onwards, building upon their initial popularity with a wide-ranging series of gigs throughout the country. Ged Wolf was to prove a fairly short-term member of the group (he went on to join ATOMKRAFT), however, and the sticksman soon gave way to new recruit Rob Walker after the debut album had been recorded. In 1985, the public were able to hear the first recordings made by the revised TYSONDOG line-up, when the group issued an EP featuring the freshly-penned "Shoot To Kill", "Changeling" and "Back To The Bullet", as well as a reworked version of the excellent "Hammerhead". It was another strong and well-received effort (a fifth track from these studio sessions, "T.W.A.T.", turned up exclusively on Roadrunner's »12 Commandments In Metal« sampler), and the public looked forward to the outfit's second full album with a considerable degree of anticipation. Sadly, however, vocalist Clutch Carruthers was to experience a fairly severe health scare shortly thereafter, and was forced (amid genuine fears that he would have to give up the music business completely) to take an extended break from all TYSONDOG-related activities with immediate effect. Fortunately, he was to recuperate reasonably quickly, although his condition had undoubtedly caused the hapless outfit to lose momentum in the interim. Nevertheless, they tried to get back on track with their sophomore effort, the »Crimes Of Insanity« (the original title of »Taste The Hate« having been rejected in the long run) long-player, which emerged in 1986.

By this time, Alan Hunter was no longer acting as a full-time member of TYSONDOG (he later resurfaced as vocalist in the 90's version of PARIAH), although he contributed a few guitar parts to the new album all the same. The latest TYSONDOG long-player wasn't a bad effort at all (the likes of "Blood Money" and "Street Thunder" were listenable enough numbers), but it failed to catch the public's imagination in the same way as the earlier releases had done. There was a fairly prominent move towards semi-anthemic power metal in places, and it was a heavy set of compositions, admittedly, but the individual tracks failed to leave much of a lasting impression. The faltering TYSONDOG's last vinyl outing took the form of a single (released in both 7" and 12" forms) featuring an unremarkable rehashing of ALICE COOPER's "School's Out", which had previously been featured on »Crimes Of Insanity«. Sadly, it hit completely the wrong note with both fans and reviewers ('Kerrang' concluded that the whole exercise was *'utterly pointless'*, which was harsh but fair), and the record failed to sell in worthwhile quantities. It came as no particular surprise, therefore, when TYSONDOG announced that they would be going their separate ways in the early months of 1987, citing *'various internal problems'* as the main contributory factor. Most of the members seem to have abandoned the music scene completely, although Kevin Wynn worked with Jess Cox in his ill-fated TYGER TYGER project for a while before this initially-promising venture finally fell apart a couple of years later.

LP's
»Beware Of The Dog« Neat 1984
»Crimes Of Insanity« Neat 1986

12" EP's
»Shoot To Kill« Neat 1985
[Labels credit tracks in wrong order, "Shoot To Kill", "Back To The Bullet" and "Changeling" all non-LP, "Hammerhead" different to album version]
»School's Out« Neat 1986
["Back To The Bullet" non-LP]

7" Singles
»Eat The Rich« Neat 1983
[Both tracks different to album versions]
»School's Out« Neat 1986

CD's

»Beware Of The Dog/Crimes Of Insanity«
Neat Metal 2000
[Double disc, includes both albums and three bonus tracks from the »Shoot To Kill« EP]

Exclusive Compilation Appearances
"T.W.A.T." on »12 Commandments In Metal« LP Roadrunner 1985

Compilation Appearances
"Eat The Rich" on »British Steel« LP M Port Records 1984/Steel Trax 1986 + »Metal Killers Kollection II« Do-LP Castle Communications 1986
"Taste The Hate" on »Powertrax« Cassette Neat 1986 + »Heavy Metal Collection 2« CD X-Tra Collection 1993
"School's Out" on »Heavy Metal Collection 3« CD X-Tra Collection 1993
"Hotter Than Hell" on »Metal Masters« 4-CD Box Castle Communications 1993 + »Heavy Metal Collection 4« CD X-Tra Collection 1993 + »Metal Mania« CD Castle Communications 1994

TYTAN

Kal Swan (v)
Stuart Adams (g)
Stevie Gibbs (g)
Kevin Riddles (b)
Dave Dufort (d)

The passing of the original incarnation of ANGEL WITCH in the second half of 1981 came as a genuine shock and a disappointment for many metal fans, although the period of mourning had barely begun when bassist Kevin Riddles announced that he would, in fact, be keeping the spirit alive in a new venture called TYTAN. For those who expected more or less a carbon copy of Heybourne's musical vision, however, there was something of a surprise in store, as Riddles (and his main partner in crime, vocalist Kal Swan) had something pretty remarkable in mind. Within a matter of weeks, the media buzz surrounding this project (completed, in the first instance, by guitarists Stevie Gibbs and Stuart Adams, plus another old stager from the ANGEL WITCH ranks, Dave Dufort) had reached fever pitch, and yet they had still to play a major gig or release a proper demo. A feature in the 'Armed And Ready' section of 'Kerrang' introduced the public to the quintet, and even provided a couple of song titles, but the protagonists soon adopted a *'less is more'* philosophy and gave little away, letting everyone's imagination run wild for a while. Eventually, however, they made a headlining appearance at London's packed Marquee Club in January 1982, an epoch-making event which served to reveal an immensely confident and inventive outfit who had already crafted some extraordinary tracks which managed the near-impossible feat of combining power and melody to create songs which were both original and memorable.

There seemed little doubt in anyone's mind that TYTAN would be the next big-money signing to take the world by storm, but the combo didn't hurry themselves at all. Confident that the labels would soon get to hear of their undisputed talent, they refused to circulate a demo, relying on word of mouth to spread the news that there was a hot new proposition in town. Amazingly, their confrontational attitude worked out in the long term, as many of the more influential record companies made it their mission to get TYTAN to sign on the dotted line as soon as humanly possible. Nevertheless, the lads weren't going to commit themselves until the time was exactly right, and, after a bit of reorganisation (former A II Z guitarist Gary Owens was drafted in to replace the ousted Stuart Adams, who later found his way into the ranks of Scottish also-rans LYIN RAMPANT, an act who eventually recorded an extremely mediocre album in 1987), the group finally deigned to proffer the general public a few examples of their genius *via* a session for the 'Friday Rock Show'. Broadcast on the 26th of March 1982, the session saw the talented outfit showcasing a varied and accomplished set of original compositions, veering dextrously from the heavy and aggressive "Cold Bitch" to the subtle and unpredictable arrangements of "Far Side Of Destiny" and "The Watcher", with the impressive and thought-provoking "Blind Men And Fools" being the ace in the pack without doubt. The imposing vocals of Kal Swan, coupled with an array of truly majestic riffs, all served to suggest that TYTAN were, in terms of both status and musical style, the missing link between ANGEL WITCH and DIAMOND HEAD, creating a standard of material which saw them rising head and shoulders above the vast majority of their NWOBHM contemporaries.

Eventually, TYTAN did indeed sign a contract (with TANK's early label, Kamaflage), and they even demoed some new material such as the haunting "Sadman" and bonkers-as-you-like "Ballad Of Edward Case", as well as continuing to play live with the likes of DIAMOND HEAD and appearing at more prestigious events such as the Monmore Festival. In due course, the first single was readied for imminent release, and the excellent "Blind Men And Fools" was chosen as the main track, with the quirky "Ballad Of Edward Case" on the reverse and "Sadman" included as a bonus selection on the 12" format. It was, all things considered, a truly cracking way to start off a career, and the record sold in serious quantities, making its way into most of the charts of the day, and it looked as though things were going swimmingly for TYTAN. Tragically, however, things went inexorably downhill from that point onwards, starting with the departure of Dave Dufort (who, after a series of ill-fated musical projects such as KAMIKAZE, NEVADA FOXX, TROY and PHANTASM, has been keeping a much lower profile in recent years) and Gary Owens (who, for some reason, failed to hook up with his former A II Z colleagues in their new AURORA venture). All these reshuffles destabilised the act considerably and led to a procession of drummers (former JUDAS PRIEST man Les Binks, whom TYTAN subsequently 'lent' to LIONHEART, MONEY's Tony Boden and TORA TORA's Simon Wright) and guitarists (Steve Mann, on loan from LIONHEART, and the unknown Dave Harrison) coming and going without making their mark in any great sense.

Nevertheless, the lads managed to continue in one form or another, and won a valuable support slot on tour with the TYGERS OF PAN TANG towards the end of the year. Gigs in Europe followed in the early months of 1983, and the persevering outfit finally began work on their long-awaited debut album shortly thereafter. Around this time, Kamaflage also came to an amicable agreement with CBS in the States, meaning that any future product from the group would almost certainly be licensed for worldwide release. In fact, there was a suggestion that »Women On The Frontline« would even be issued as a single to introduce the outfit to the American market, but this idea appears to have fallen through at a fairly early stage. TYTAN's efforts in the studio eventually yielded a set of recordings from which ten tracks were selected to feature on their long-player, these numbers being "Far Cry", "Nothing Ever Lasts", "Forever Gone", "Far Side Of Destiny", "Blind Men And Fools", "Money For Love", "Don't Play Their Way", "Women On The Frontline", "Rude Awakening" and "Hold On". Advance tapes were circulated (to almost universal approval) to various interested parties, but the record repeatedly failed either to be issued or even to be given a firm release date. Disastrously, Kamaflage were experiencing serious financial problems, which eventually culminated in the label going bankrupt, leaving TYTAN without a leg to stand on.

At first, the band members assured everyone that it would all work out in the end and that they would soon permit the set to be issued on one label or another, but the blow had hit them harder than they admitted. Inevitably, the outfit began to drift apart while trying to sort out their affairs, and they eventually called it a day (with great reluctance and considerable sadness) towards the end of 1983. It genuinely was a great injustice, and there seemed to be a minimal chance of reconciliation, especially once Kal Swan had jetted off to the States in order to initiate a new venture (he wasted little time before founding LION, an act who enjoyed considerable commercial success in America and Japan, although the frontman eventually started afresh in the early 90's with the rather less well-received BAD MOON RISING), since there was approximately zero chance of locating an equivalently-gifted singer. Before long, the other central characters also moved on to new musical ventures, with Stevie Gibbs enjoying a brief stint in the ailing CHINATOWN towards the end of their existence, while Kevin Riddles hooked up with the laughable MAX AND THE BROADWAY METAL CHOIR before earning a crust with the rather more credible PAUL SAMSON'S EMPIRE. With the one-time members of TYTAN having all now dispersed, there seemed to be precious little likelihood of their LP ever seeing the light of day.

Happily, though, it wasn't quite the end of the TYTAN story, and the shelved album finally appeared courtesy of Metal Masters, who picked up the rights to various recordings (also including PERSIAN RISK's abortive demos for Zebra) in the mid-80's and who facilitated the release of a posthumous TYTAN long-player (with the ever-so-apt title of »Rough Justice«) in 1985. It wasn't, in fact, the album which the band had originally envisaged; out had gone "Nothing Ever Lasts" (which bore an uncanny resemblance to LIONHEART's "Give Me The Light", which is especially suspicious in view of the fact that these two acts 'shared' personnel) and "Hold On", but a few additional numbers ("Cold Bitch", "Ballad Of Edward Case", "Sadman" and "The Watcher") were brought in to provide value for money. With many of the tracks being familiar to those who had heard TYTAN's radio session and introductory single, there was little doubt that this would be anything less than a genuinely worthy long-player, and inclusions such as the bombastic "Rude Awakening" (based around a towering riff that DIAMOND HEAD would surely have been proud to call their own), the catchy "Forever Gone" and the upbeat "Don't Play Their Way" were all of an equivalently high standard.

All things considered, it was an extremely strong selection of material, and the overwhelmingly enthusiastic response of the rock community confirmed that Metal Masters had been entirely justified in going to all the effort of exhuming the master tapes and finally giving the set a belated release. The »Rough Justice« album (dedicated to *'everyone who hears us, saw us, liked us and mourned our passing'*) won widespread approval from critics, and copies were soon being snapped up by numerous metal fans of the day, but there was no possibility whatsoever of a reformation by this stage. It was, nevertheless, a fitting and dignified tribute to an extraordinarily talented act who had been dealt a very poor hand indeed, and who should have been hailed as heroes while they were still a going concern. I reckon someone would do well to get that album out on CD (it was bootlegged a few years back) one of these days, and give the current generation of NWOBHM aficionados the chance to appreciate TYTAN's music.

LP's
»Rough Justice« Metal Masters 1985

12" EP's
»Blind Men And Fools« Kamaflage 1982

7" Singles
»Blind Men And Fools« Kamaflage 1982

CD's
»Rough Justice« Bootleg 1992
[Unofficial release]
»On The Frontline« Bootleg 1996
[Unofficial release featuring live material from 1982]

URCHIN

David Hall (v)
Adrian Smith (g)
Maurice Coyne (g)
Alan Levett (b)
Barry Tyler (d)

The legendary URCHIN were one of the many lightweight acts who established themselves

through hard graft in London's rock clubs and pubs (particularly in some of the more insalubrious haunts of the East End) from the mid-70's onwards, although they would almost certainly have disappeared into utter obscurity (as with similarly-minded non-luminaries HOTLINE, ANGEL STREET, GYPSY'S KISS, REMUS DOWN BOULEVARD, UNITED, SMILER *etc.*) by now were it not for the earth-shattering observation that a couple of future IRON MAIDEN stalwarts played a part in their fortunes at one time or another. First, their youthful lead guitarist was a certain Adrian Smith (whose musical career had started at the tender age of fifteen, his first faltering steps having been taken with acts such as the long-forgotten EVIL WAYS), a hard-working individual who also contributed to the activities of various short-lived hopefuls such as BLAZER BLAZER (see separate entry) over the years. Furthermore, Smith's erstwhile schoolfriend Dave Murray also featured in the URCHIN line-up for the best part of six months (while on an extended sabbatical from the emerging IRON MAIDEN themselves), although the latter failed to contribute to either of the band's vinyl releases. Aside from this pair, quite a few musicians passed through the ranks of URCHIN after their initial formation in the mid-70's, and many of these names are now lost in the mists of time.

With the individual founder members having been strongly influenced by such acts as THIN LIZZY and UFO, it came as little surprise that URCHIN gradually (and quite purposefully, I'm sure) developed an accessible, melodic rock style with which to storm the charts. Well, their rise to stardom might not have been quite as meteoric as the musicians originally anticipated (this being at a time when 'NWOBHM' was but a twinkle in Geoff Barton's eye), but signing a deal with the influential DJM label (the famous home of ELTON JOHN) seemed a pretty good way to start. The first of two URCHIN singles would appear before the end of 1977, their debut 7" being constructed around the raunchy biker anthem "Black Leather Fantasy" (b/w "Rock'n'Roll Woman"), the lengthy A-side being a reasonably heavy and memorable piece, even if the boogie-tinged flipside was a bit of a throwaway effort. Most examples of the single (and DJM wisely didn't manufacture all that many in the first place) were issued without picture sleeves, although a handful of promotional copies featured the generic yellow DJM design with a few band details (and the spookily-prophetic quote *'URCHIN could prove to be the forerunners of a new revival of heavy British rock music'*). As you can imagine, a truly minimal quantity remain in circulation after all this time, with fierce competition between IRON MAIDEN completists and fanatical NWOBHM collectors over the years having driven the asking price of this item to the most extreme end of the market.

A second single followed in 1978, a slice of vinyl which sold in considerably more impressive quantities at the time and which resides in a far higher percentage of collections than the debut. Mind you, the asking price for this item has also gone through the roof in recent years, and the constant demand from enthusiasts shows no signs of slowing down. Coupling "She's A Roller" and "Long Time No Woman", the two-tracker was a highly melodic and commercial effort (with little or no evidence to support the assertion that the outfit might actually have been quite a heavy proposition in the live environment) in the style of MARSEILLE, TRADER, BROOKLYN, MAYDAY and so forth, although it captured the hearts of many fans at the time. Adrian Smith later provided the background to their affiliation with DJM: *'We were still very young when we signed with DJM. I knew nothing about them at the time, and I'm not even sure if they still exist. Our management got some money out of the record label, and we ended up having to knock out these awful pop songs on vinyl. At least we were paid for it and were able to buy ourselves some new equipment. The company then saw us playing live for the first time and were surprised how heavy we were. These were very difficult times for heavy rock, it was all punk back in 1978!'* (Ref: Interview, Matthias Mader, March 1996).

Fascinatingly, however, there's even a brief video clip of URCHIN in existence, which shows the youthful group performing the A-side of their second single at a small-time gig in the capital, and this excerpt famously appears on IRON MAIDEN's »12 Wasted Years« video. The story behind this one-off piece of filming was bizarre, to say the least, as Smith later revealed: *'Every Friday night for two years, we played in a pub called The Squire in South London, which was in a pretty dangerous part of town. It was a big place, where the National Front held meetings-that's something we kept well away from. Nevertheless, we had our own fans who came to see us every week, and they were tolerated for a while, even though the National Front supporters were well-known for their aggressive tendencies. On a couple of occasions, however, they decided there were too many 'longhairs' in their pub, kicked our equipment to pieces and started a few punch-ups. One week prior to one of these bust-ups, a film crew from the political television programme 'Panorama' had been present, in order to compile a report about these individuals and their connection to football hooliganism. While they were there, they also filmed us playing "She's A Roller", which is incredible but true!'* (Ref: *ibid.*)

It's fair to say that URCHIN developed a loyal fan base in the pubs and clubs of the capital, but it's equally fair to say that they had little chance of competing with the more aggressive and speedy upstarts who were rapidly emerging as the NWOBHM boom took hold. Having given it their best shot for a number of years, the URCHIN story finally drew to a close towards the end of 1980, the remaining members finding it impossible to carry on in the same form after founder member Adrian Smith had elected to move on to pastures new. As we all know, the axeman was lured away by a tempting offer to join forces with his former colleague Dave Murray in IRON MAIDEN, a group who had themselves often shared a stage with most of Smith's earlier outfits. Needless to say, this was an opportunity the ambitious guitarist couldn't afford to miss, and so his fond memories of those small-time beginnings were soon being filed away for good. Nevertheless, various URCHIN numbers have still been belted out in the live environment from time to time, notably whenever Smith's knockabout club act, THE ENTIRE POPULATION OF HACKNEY, takes to the stage for one of their increasingly-infrequent outings.

7" Singles
»Black Leather Fantasy« DJM Records 1977
[A few promo copies issued with semi-generic picture sleeve]
»She's A Roller« DJM Records 1978

Compilation Appearances

"Black Leather Fantasy" on »NWOBHM Vol.8« Bootleg CD 1998

US

T. John (v, b)
John James (g)
Bob Lane (g, k)
Bob 'B.J.' Harding (d)

With three of the founder members of the little-known US (an act formed at the beginning of 1985) having previously been involved with the heavy Essex version of SAMURAI (who evolved out of the excellent »Brute Force« PROWLER, an act which allegedly employed future US front-man T. John and axeman John James in the dim and distant past), you might just have expected their newer quartet to share a broadly similar musical viewpoint. Mind you, SAMURAI had already been moving into markedly more commercial territory by the mid-80's (remarkably, the latter kept things going after the defection of three members to US, and even issued a single after reverting to the PROWLER identity), so there was certainly an equal (if not greater) probability that the splinter outfit would maintain their original desire to crack the melodic rock market. The all-new US (difficult to ascertain whether this was supposed to be 'U.S.' or 'Us', but either way it's a hopeless choice) was completed by former FIRST ATTACK guitarist Bob Lane and drummer Bob Harding, who (as well as being the third SAMURAI veteran) additionally featured in one of the numerous concerns going under the name of ROUGH JUSTICE, so they weren't exactly inexperienced youngsters. Indeed, it took the ensemble little time to become established as a genuine proposition, and they soon revealed themselves to be one of the innumerable melodic rock acts who seemed intent on cluttering up Britain's mid-80's music scene.

The musical activities of US were decidedly low-key in the first instance, but no doubt they were toiling away in the live environment while they developed a marketable style, planning their future assault on the rock scene with military precision. By 1986, the tuneful foursome finally concluded that they were ready to strike, and, having saved some pennies in the interim, issued that self-financed 7" of their dreams. Their two-tracker was released in a pretty unremarkable picture sleeve showing the band members looking extremely self-conscious, and featured the pairing of "Where Are You Now" (originally recorded in 1985) and "Losing Touch" (a number dating from as far back as 1984, which, given that it was ostensibly laid down before US had officially formed, might even be an old SAMURAI composition). As expected, the all-out metal assault of their earlier NWOBHM-era combos had now metamorphosed into a rather more radio-friendly, accessible rock stance akin to a decelerated STRATUS with less prominent keyboards (the sort of thing FILTHY RICH and FIREBRAND churned out with equivalently little success) and the single presumably flopped like the proverbial lead balloon, with very few copies having come up for sale in recent times. Nothing much was heard from the characters involved in this melodic endeavour in later years, suggesting that their quest for fame was probably fairly short-lived and unrewarding.

7" Singles

»Where Are You Now« Private 1986

V8

Nigel Duval (v, k)
Stuart Lee (g)
Paul James-Evans (g, k)
Paul (b)
Nick Hayes (d)

Yet another contribution to the New Wave Of South Wales Heavy Metal (now there's a term that just trips off the tongue with ease), Glamorgan's succinctly-named V8 recorded an unashamedly melodic 7" at Cardiff's Music Factory Studio towards the end of 1983, coupling the extremely listenable "Lonely Days" with "Only My Love". With their two-tracker boasting an unusually capable production for an independent release of the time, the featured material borders on AOR, but is still sufficiently substantial to justify inclusion here. The catchy "Lonely Days", with its TOTO-style keyboards and Paul Stanley-influenced vocals from the talented Nigel Duval, brings contemporaries such as GRAND PRIX, MOSELLE and TUXEDO to mind, while the reverse is rather more of an upbeat, bluesy number in the vein of WHITESNAKE or the first AFTER DARK 7". It was a perfectly decent way for these emergent hopefuls to open their account, and it seemed to have paved the way for a healthy future. Strangely, though, V8 were relatively minor personalities on the regional music scene, and appear not to have achieved a great deal of recognition during their spell together, suggesting that they might have been slightly ahead of their time. Their one-off single is undeniably likeable, though, and you would do well to seek it out, even if it resides at the more lightweight end of the NWOBHM spectrum. Inevitably, it has a monochrome sleeve (a tad more professional-looking than most self-financed Welsh releases of the day, if we're being totally truthful), this time featuring the outfit's attractive logo and a (reassuringly tasteful) photo of a female torso.

7" Singles
»Lonely Days« Music Factory Records 1983

VAGABOND

Line-up unknown

Another mystery outfit, VAGABOND issued a sleeveless, double A-sided 7" single in 1985 which doesn't give much away as to who was actually in the band or where it might have been recorded. It does, however, have quite a nice drawing of a tramp (that's 'vagrant' to our American readers, OK?) on the label itself, so at least it gives you something to look for. The featured tracks are reasonably heavy on the guitar front, and the frontman ably displays a powerful vocal style with an equally impressive range, although it's certainly more refined than many of the raucous offerings from earlier in the decade. First up is "Deep Water" (an epic tale of legendary, seafaring races), which comes across as a meeting of minds between RADIO MOSCOW and the TYGERS OF PAN TANG circa 1987, with a hint of ELIXIR's "Pandora's Box" thrown in for good measure. The reverse, the bizarrely-titled "Yanoyo" (although this would appear to be an acronym derived from 'You Are Never On Your Own'), is somewhat pacier, and is more akin to "Giving The Game Away" by the DICK SMITH BAND than anything else. Not a bad effort at all, so keep your eyes peeled and you might get lucky. Still, this self-financed affair appears to have been a one-off, and I suspect that the outfit were a pretty fleeting concern. Most known copies of this 7" (and there aren't many at all) have turned up in the South, so it's a distinct possibility that VAGABOND were yet another of those who tried valiantly (but unsuccessfully, by the looks of things) to get their big break via London's thriving club circuit.

7" Singles
»Deep Water« SRT 1985

VALHALLA (I)

Nigel 'Leg' Hopkins (v)
Mark Evans (g)
Joe (rg)
Chris Stretton (b)
Steve 'Waz' Bee (d)

Although the name was subsequently adopted by one of Neat's later (and poorer) signings, the original version of VALHALLA were, to be completely honest, an infinitely better proposition, so it's a real tragedy that they disappeared into obscurity without ever being heard by the masses at the time. Formed in Leicestershire during the summer of 1980, the workmanlike quintet proceeded to lay the foundations for a successful future with numerous local gigs, rapidly establishing the usual healthy regional following, thanks mainly to their 'very exciting stage show', to quote the protagonists themselves. It wasn't long before the lads became familiar with studio technology, laying down their own material (employing the services of a lyricist in the shape of Martin Minard, who was very much the outfit's unsung sixth member) and, on occasion, even helping out by acting as session musicians for solo artists. Inevitably, they soon began thinking about issuing their own product, and, from one of their regular trips to the studio (the Sounds Good facility in Windsor, to be precise), two tracks emerged which seemed particularly suitable for future use. In due course, therefore, these formed the basis of VALHALLA's double A-sided debut, which the youngsters released on their own Asgard label a short time later.

Unleashed in the early months of 1981, VALHALLA's one-off single is truly an undiscovered classic of the genre, with the superb "Lightning In The Sky" coming across as a heavy mixture of OVERDRIVE, SNATCH-BACK and PROWLER, with an excellent vocal performance (and some quite interesting drumming, which isn't something I'm in the habit of noticing) throughout. Wonderful stuff. On the reverse, "These Sunday Nights" is a rather less intense number, but still constitutes an impressively-written piece of metal lying somewhere between TRESPASS and DRAGONFLY. I'd get this one on the wants list at the earliest opportunity, folks! Very few copies are known to have surfaced, however, and it doesn't seem to have been issued with a picture sleeve at any stage. Although guitarist Mark Evans jumped ship to hook up with local rivals WIKKYD VIKKER a year or so after VALHALLA's 7" hit the shops, it's entirely possible that the band carried on for a while in slightly different form. Nevertheless, further vinyl offerings don't seem to have been forthcoming, which is a great shame. Another sad loss to the NWOBHM scene, but their one and only single remains an item which seems set to attain legendary status in years to come.

7" Singles
»Lightning In The Sky« Asgard Records 1981

VALHALLA (II)

Dave Howard (v)
Kevin Hunter (g)
Ian Glenister (g)
Kevin Kershaw (b)
Ian Parsons (k)
Mick Simkins (d)

Tarnishing the good name of the outstanding Leicestershire bunch who had originally adopted the identity (*vide supra*), the later version of VALHALLA (who were based in the Home Counties) somehow made it onto Neat's books with their overly-poppy interpretation of the NWOBHM style. Their debut single from late 1982, featuring "Coming Home" and "Through With You", wouldn't have been nearly as bad (the flipside's actually quite listenable in places) if it hadn't featured the kind of oppressive keyboard tootlings that ruined the MAYDAY single, as the group weren't actually a million miles away from the WHITE SPIRIT prototype. Dave Howard's capable and powerful vocals (which were, in all honesty, truly wasted on this type of average material) could surely have been put to far better use by a more adventurous outfit, though. The small-time band (who really had no use for twin guitarists, but never mind) also contributed an unremarkable and excessively soppy ballad entitled "Maybe Someday" to Neat's »60 Minutes Plus« cassette at around the same time, although, following this initial exposure (given that sales of the first two-tracker were evidently very poor), I suspect that few people expected to hear anything from VALHALLA ever again. Amazingly, however, not only were the outfit still a going concern by 1984 (having played a

fair number of local gigs with the likes of CLIENTELLE in the interim), but Neat somehow felt compelled to offer VALHALLA another crack at achieving success, which wasn't a common scenario for groups who weren't actually based in the North East itself. As a result, their follow-up 7" appeared in the shape of a double A-sided effort featuring "Still In Love With You" and "Jack", a pretty dire pairing which saw the outfit deserting the rock style even further (having ditched Ian Glenister after the first release, before recruiting new bassist David Warminger in place of Kevin Kershaw) and attempting some extremely mainstream, lightweight material. Modest sales followed once again, and the group went into hiding once more. This time, however, it really was the end, and we should be grateful that this particular bunch were never offered the chance to record a full album. VALHALLA remain one of Neat's more ill-advised and anonymous signings, and I reckon the outfit had already packed it in by 1985, with bassist David Warminger going on to hook up with the ill-fated SCHUTT (what an atrocious name), a motley act who boasted ex-members of local nonentities such as JOKER, TIGON and BLACK TIGER, but who never delivered any vinyl of their own. He later turned up in an extraordinarily capable melodic bunch called VAGRANT towards the end of the decade, who truly deserved to get further, but who gave up the ghost after being critically ignored once too often.

7" Singles
»Coming Home« Neat 1982
»Still In Love With You« Neat 1984

Exclusive Compilation Appearances
"Maybe Someday" on »60 Minutes Plus« Cassette Neat 1982/CD Teichiku 1992

VARDIS

Steve Zodiac (v,g)
Alan Selway (b)
Phil Medley (d)

Yorkshire's much loved boogie merchants VARDIS first set the ball rolling as far back as 1977, when eccentric frontman Steve Zodiac (not a traditional English surname, that) decided to form a band whose compositions would encompass a variety of influences from the glam, rock and pop worlds, notably (in his own words) T. REX, JEFF BECK and the ROLLING STONES, plus (in my own humble opinion) THE SWEET, MUD and STATUS QUO. His musical vision originally took the rather grandiose and grammatically-incorrect identity of QUO VARDIS (that's *'quo vadis'*, young Zodiac, take a hundred lines), although the early moniker was abbreviated to the more familiar VARDIS (presumably to dissociate themselves from any unwanted QUO connotations) after only a few weeks. The vocalist/guitarist (who had been tinkering around with his axe since 1974 or thereabouts) was originally assisted in his pursuits by bassist Tony Boulton, although the latter was soon to find more lucrative employment elsewhere (most significantly, playing a key role in the fortunes of MENDES PREY), whereupon the first *'proper'* VARDIS line-up was established, the picture being completed by bassist Alan Selway and drummer Phil Medley. After finding their feet on the local live circuit, the threesome made the first of many visits to the studio, and eventually emerged with a tape which would ultimately form the basis of their debut vinyl release, a four track 7" on the small-time Redball label.

The »100 M.P.H.« EP (issued in a very dull sleeve featuring a low-grade photo of the band) hit the shops in 1979, although it failed to cause all that much of a commotion at the time, the four featured tracks ("100 M.P.H.", "Blue Rock", "Destiny" and "The World's Insane") coming across as fairly average rockers and failing to pack much of a punch. With the pressing being pretty limited (a couple of thousand at most, few of which seem to have escaped from the clutches of local fans), relatively few copies remain in circulation, which goes some way towards justifying the record's absurdly high asking price (in fact, it was one of the first *bona fide* NWOBHM collectables, even by 1980!) in today's collecting scene. In spite of this inauspicious start, however, the lads remained a popular live attraction, and things began to work out slightly better for VARDIS as they moved into 1980. By the time their second slice of vinyl was being recorded (for the Castle label this time), the trio had recruited new drummer Gary Pearson, and the latest 7" (coupling "If I Were King" and "Out Of The Way") made a significantly better impression than their modest debut, selling in far healthier quantities in the process. Shortly thereafter, VARDIS were to become firmly associated with the NWOBHM movement (something which Zodiac always felt to be utterly absurd) when they were invited to contribute a track of their choice to Logo's »New Electric Warriors« compilation, and so the lads duly supplied a considerably more upbeat version of "If I Were King" to the set. It was getting better all the time, but it still appeared that VARDIS were struggling to come across as effectively on vinyl as they did in the live environment. Mind you, such problems could be rectified quite easily...

VARDIS had clearly impressed the bosses of Logo with their compilation appearance, and the label were soon waving a genuine contract under the band's noses. At that time, Logo were largely unfamiliar with the rock scene (although they had such borderline acts as STRAIGHT EIGHT and BLAZER BLAZER on their books in the late 70's), so it looks as though their patronage of VARDIS (and, to a lesser extent, QUARTZ), represented their entire involvement with the NWOBHM genre. Even before the end of 1980, VARDIS had their first album in the shops, although »100 M.P.H.« (they seem to have been quite fond of that title) had been hastily cobbled together from various recordings of the lads in action during the previous year's touring. Nevertheless, releasing a live album was an inspired move, this being the most beneficial way to introduce the music of VARDIS to a considerably wider audience, and tracks such as "Destiny", "Situation Negative", "Let's Go" and "Living Out Of Touch" gave a pretty favourable indication of the kind of high-energy performance to which the trio were now treating their audiences on a regular basis. With regard to their contemporaries in the NWOBHM scene, it was something of a peculiar mixture, not exactly the out and out boogie of SPIDER, ROKKA or 100% PROOF, but, on the other hand, not conforming to the lyrical triteness or ludicrous image of SILVERWING and their glam-obsessed cohorts. Perhaps their closest allies would be the comparatively obscure MASAI, although the latter can hardly claim to have experienced anything like the same level of success.

With VARDIS finally having managed to release a flattering piece of vinyl at last, they set about establishing something of a monopoly on good-time, 70's-influenced, glam-tinged boogie. Hardly surprisingly, there wasn't a great deal of competition at the time, and the musicians were soon finding themselves in great demand for support slots and festival appearances. Mind you, they hadn't finished with their programme of vinyl releases just yet, and proceeded to issue two studio singles (»Let's Go« and »Too Many People«, both released as *'limited edition'* double packs) before the year was out. Both went on to sell in quite staggering quantities, and the name of VARDIS was now well and truly lodged in the public's consciousness. The lads wasted little time before delivering a follow-up in the spring of 1981, but there was no easy way to avoid the studio this time (only DUMPY'S RUSTY NUTS could get away with multiple live albums), and long-player number two, »The World's Insane«, would almost certainly be the make-or-break album for VARDIS. Predictably, however, it failed to live up to the standard of its predecessor, with unremarkable efforts such as "Power Under Foot", "Money Grabber", "Police Patrol" (with its ludicrous *bagpipe* intro) and "Steamin' Along" (none of which made the remotest attempt to progress in a musical sense) failing to leave a particularly good impression, although "Curse The Gods" and "Love Is Dead" were passable, I suppose. Attempting to capitalise on the release, the lads then delivered a session for the 'Friday Rock Show' (broadcast on the 29th of May 1981), where they ran through typically upbeat versions of "Let's Go", "Love Is Dead", "Steamin' Along" and "Power Under Foot", possibly winning over a few listeners in the process.

The band's rocked-up version of HAWKWIND's "Silver Machine" had been a strange inclusion on their latest album, and sounded more like "Let's Do The Timewarp Again" from 'The Rocky Horror Picture Show' than anything else. Nevertheless, it was trotted out as a single in due course (rather pathetically, the B-side, "Come On", had some extremely unconvincing *'crowd noises'* dubbed in to make it sound like a live recording), and it proceeded to achieve fairly high placings in several rock charts of the day, so I guess there's no accounting for taste. The next offering took the shape of »All You'll Ever Need«, a three track EP whose most interesting feature was a competent cover of "Jumpin' Jack Flash" by the ROLLING STONES, and which failed to make much of an impact in terms of sales. After this flurry of vinyl activity, the group took some time off to play a few gigs (including a bit of valuable exposure at the *'Heavy Metal Holocaust'* all-dayer in Stoke and an appearance at the Reading Festival, having been a last-minute addition to the bill) and to record an official live video, a slightly misguided venture, given that so few of their followers could actually make use of such an item. In spite of the fact that their second album had been slightly disappointing for both VARDIS fans and Logo Records, however, a third LP soon became a viable commodity, and the lads embarked on yet another productive spell in the recording studio.

The fruit of their labours, the »Quo Vardis« long-player, emerged in the early part of 1982, and saw the group attempting to bring a few novel ideas (some better than others) into their writing style. All in all, it was a more moody and varied affair than any of their previous vinyl outings, with efforts such as "Please Do", "Dream With Me" and "Together Tonight" standing out as the most capable numbers on display. Having said that, there were still a few traditional VARDIS rockers to keep their more easily-pleased fans happy. The lads certainly hadn't severed all ties with live recordings, though, as evidenced by the fact that initial quantities of the new album contained a bonus live EP, featuring some of their more popular material and an energetic cover of the T. REX classic "Jeepster", a mainstay of their live set. Zodiac was keen to convey his admiration for the late Marc Bolan in an interview at the time: *'When I first heard "Get It On" and "Jeepster" I had no option but to rush out and get the album (»Electric Warrior«) that they both appeared on. One play and I knew what I was gonna do for a living. It was the desire to get up on stage and do what Bolan was doing, rather than wanting to play similar material'*. (Ref: Kerrang No.12, March 1982). Just one single slipped out this time, a double A-sided effort which coupled "To Be With You" and "Gary Glitter Part One", a track which hasn't featured on too many playlists of late. Inevitably, it was business as usual on the hectic live circuit (including a few shows with SLADE), and VARDIS also managed to fit in a show at the Monmore Festival alongside the likes of TYTAN and LIMELIGHT.

Sadly, it was all downhill for VARDIS after the end of 1982, when they became embroiled in sundry hassles related to their management and business affairs, which tended to preclude any further activity on the recording front until matters had been completely resolved. It was, in addition to being a considerable inconvenience for the outfit themselves, a major blow for their loyal label, who intended to churn out at least one new album a year, and Logo eventually succumbed to temptation by throwing together an extremely pointless long-player (as something of a 'greatest hits' retrospective) entitled »The Lion's Share« (it also appeared on the Razor label) to bring in a few bucks while the band were in a state of semi-disarray. It wasn't a worthwhile release in any respect, given that there was a total absence of exclusive material, and even the inclusion of 'alternate takes' and 'unreleased versions' failed to tempt all that many people to part with their hard-earned cash. Things got worse for VARDIS when long-standing bassist Alan Selway threw in his hand towards the end of 1983, although the surviving duo rapidly managed to locate a suitable stand-in, former DIRTY TRICKS stalwart Terry Horbury. It took a while for the revised version of the band to get going again properly, although they were soon back in action on the gig front, touring throughout 1984, and they even managed to wangle a one-off deal with Big Beat Records to get some long-awaited new product onto the market.

The trio's 'comeback' release came in the shape of a single based around yet another old favourite, "Standing In The Road", a composition originally recorded by Midlands heroes BLACKFOOT SUE. By all accounts, however, the record (backed with "Freezing History", the 12" also adding "Who Loves Ya Baby") was met with unanimous disinterest from the rock community, in spite of the fact that it was a reasonable enough stab at something rather more commercially-oriented. Nevertheless, VARDIS soldiered on regardless, demoing new material in 1985 and hoping that someone would still be prepared to take a chance on their music, which was now beginning to look a bit insubstantial and dated in the context of the new generation of power metal and melodic rock hopefuls. Surprisingly, however, the NWOBHM-friendly Raw Power concern saw enough money-making potential to commission a full album, and »Vigilante« finally hit the shops the following year. It transpired that VARDIS had felt the need to rope in former DEEP MACHINE/ROGUE MALE sticksman Steve Kingsley to assist in some capacity or another (the sleeve provides precious few clues as to what this might have been), although his presence hardly seems to have made any discernable impact in the outfit's overall sound. Yep, this was a pretty standard VARDIS offering, although there were some slightly more bluesy (and, on occasion, Southern Boogie) influences thrown in this time, but it failed to save the combo from almost inevitable critical apathy.

To be honest, it wasn't a particularly atrocious album (the likes of "I Must Be Mad" and "Running" weren't bad at all), but the inconsequential sales which followed must finally have rammed home the rather unpleasant (albeit unavoidable) message that the ensemble's glory days had long since passed. Thankfully, VARDIS knocked it on the head within a mercifully short space of time, whereupon the participants simply dispersed without making much of an impression on the rock scene thereafter. Still, the once-revered name of VARDIS has been kept alive by a select clique of NWOBHM/boogie aficionados since their demise (the well-worn "If I Were King" effort even showed up on the »NWOBHM '79 Revisited« set in 1990), although only their first EP is now regarded as a particularly sought-after piece (mind you, there are also a fair number of obscure and intriguing foreign releases which are yet to be documented comprehensively) by the majority of collectors. A couple of years ago, however, there was an unexpected bonus for VARDIS fans when British Steel assembled a retrospective CD with the typically unimaginative title of »The Best Of Vardis«. As you might reasonably anticipate, there was no sign of any previously-unheard material whatsoever (I suspect that the vaults had been well and truly plundered by this juncture), but it's fair to say that this well-intentioned release served its purpose and would surely have made a few people happy.

LP's

»100 M.P.H.« Logo 1980
[Live album, some with free poster]
»The World's Insane« Logo 1981
»Metal Power« Logo 1981
[Belgian issue of first two albums in gatefold sleeve]
»Quo Vardis« Logo 1982
[Some with free four track »Guaranteed No Overdubs« live EP]
»The Lion's Share« Logo 1983/Razor 1983
[Compilation release]
»Vigilante« Raw Power 1986

12" EP's

»Standing In The Road« Big Beat Records 1984
[With extended version of A-side, all three tracks non-LP]

7" EP's

»100 M.P.H.« Redball Records 1979
[All four tracks different to album versions]
»All You'll Ever Need« Logo 1981

["All You'll Ever Need" different to album version, "Jumpin' Jack Flash" non-LP, "If I Were King" different to album and original single version]
»Guaranteed No Overdubs« Logo 1982
[Four track live EP given free with some copies of »Quo Vardis« album. "Jeepster" non-LP, "Situation Negative" and "Steamin' Along" different to album versions, "Too Many People" different to single version]
»Guaranteed Live« Logo 1982
[Belgian-only live release]

7" Singles
»If I Were King« Castle Records 1980
[Both tracks different to album versions]
»Let's Go« Logo 1980
[Limited edition with free single featuring live versions of "100 M.P.H." and "Out Of The Way", all four tracks different to album versions]
»Let's Go« Logo 1980
[German issue in different sleeve]
»Let's Go« Logo 1980
[Spanish issue in different sleeve]
»Too Many People« Logo 1980
[Limited edition with free single featuring "Blue Rock" and "Dirty Money". "Too Many People" non-LP, other three tracks different to album versions]
»Power Under Foot« Logo 1981
[Spanish-only release]
»Silver Machine« Logo 1981
[B-side "Come On" non-LP]
»To Be With You« Logo 1982
»Standing In The Road« Big Beat Records 1984
[Both tracks non-LP]

Promotional Releases
»Promo E.P.« Logo 1981
[Four track 12" sampler for »The World's Insane« LP, issued in plain stamped sleeve, some with photo insert]

CD's
»The Best Of Vardis« British Steel 1998
[Compilation release]
»The World's Insane« Essential 2000
[Compilation release, double disc]

Compilation Appearances
"If I Were King" on »New Electric Warriors« LP Logo 1980/CD British Steel 1997 + »NWOBHM '79 Revisited« Do-LP/Do-CD Phonogram 1990
[Exclusive take, different to 7", EP or LP version]
"Silver Machine" on »Pop Rocky« LP Metronome 1981
"Steaming Along" on »Pop Rocky« LP Metronome 1981

VENOM

Conrad 'Cronos' Lant (v, b)
Jeff 'Mantas' Dunn (g)
Tony 'Abaddon' Bray (d)

When it comes to telling the story of Tyneside's legendary VENOM, it's remarkably easy to fall into the trap of swallowing all of the ludicrous hyperbole, fanciful embellishments and downright untruths which have surrounded their activities from day one. Many writers have dutifully reported on the sheer spectacle of the hell-raising outfit's early gigs during their pre-vinyl days (there weren't any, you know) and recounted such lurid tales as the original guitarist having his contract terminated by finding a dead cat nailed to his front door (beats a boring old P45, I suppose). It all makes for a good yarn, but it still tends to get a bit tedious when a consider-

able number of objectionable and humourless oiks regularly adopt a poker face and attempt to tell the world that VENOM really *were* unholy blasphemers, actually, and that they really *did* spend every weekend ravishing virgins and sacrificing goats (or possibly *vice versa*), and that they would wholeheartedly approve of the present generation of pasty-faced Scandinavians doing unmentionable things in forests, disposing of their best friends (or themselves, if they haven't got any chums) for a laugh and helpfully cutting down on heating bills at their local church. Some people really should get out more, if you ask me. Fair enough, you can take Satanism as seriously as you like, but it's hardly fair to implicate VENOM when it comes to all this modern-day tomfoolery, they were just three mad Geordies having a laugh...

Although the roots of VENOM date back to around 1979, it hardly constituted a real band at first, just a bit of fun for Conrad 'Cronos' Lant (an employee of Impulse Studios) and one or two of his close friends. Lant played the bass in his spare time, and he had garnered a fair bit of studio expertise after helping various new wave and punk nonentities to record their demos and singles during the previous year or two. After a while, he and his cohorts (Jeff 'Mantas' Dunn and Tony 'Abaddon' Bray) finally ventured into the studio themselves and laid down an abominable cacophony which served to make up VENOM's first demo tape. Proud of the results, Cronos allowed his boss (Dave Wood, who had now established Neat Records) to hear his musical creation, although the latter was utterly bewildered by the unholy racket which had been captured for posterity. Although Wood's initial reaction was (a) to tell Cronos not to give up his day job and (b) to make a mental note of the phone number of the local loony bin, he ended up subscribing to the heretical theory that VENOM might actually have some sort of genuine potential after all. The frontman had already sent out a copy or two of the demo to selected parties, however, and there was even a tentative thumbs-up to the material from some enlightened individuals, so Wood eventually agreed to sponsor a one-off single on Neat if the lads kept up their end of the bargain and put in a bit of practice.

In the spring of 1981, the unsuspecting public finally got a taste of VENOM's musical vision when the group's »In League With Satan« (some famously crediting "In League With *Satin*" on the label) single (B-side "Live Like An Angel, Die Like A Devil") was unleashed. It was a horrendously-produced affair, but there were a few fairly innovative ideas on display nonetheless. It was all extremely intense, like MOTÖRHEAD jamming with BLACK SABBATH on a particularly rowdy building site, but the heavy, grinding "In League With Satan", with its fearsome vocals and tribal drums, was a highly distinctive effort, while the flipside had rather more in common with the NWOBHM archetype, an upbeat number which even boasted some twin-guitar sections. All in all, it was an uncompromising start, and the two-tracker was soon selling in surprisingly healthy quantities, whereupon Neat concluded that there might just be some mileage in VENOM after all. Next up was an appearance on Neat's »Lead Weight« sampler with the chaotic "Angel Dust", after which the trio went into the studio to lay down their first full album. »Welcome To Hell« appeared a couple of months later, and basically continued where their single had left off, with numbers such as "Schizo", "Poison" and "Witching Hour" all being very intense, heavy inclusions which bludgeoned the listener into submission. It wasn't exactly a flawless opus, though, since "Red Light Fever" was a complete mess and the funky interlude during "1000 Days In Sodom" was very odd indeed, but, overall, it was a decent enough debut. The reviewers and radio presenters mostly seemed to think it was all a bit over-the-top, however, but the fans still shelled out for a staggering number of copies, whereupon Neat soon hatched big plans to market VENOM as their flagship act, especially now that money-spinning groups such as the TYGERS OF PAN TANG, FIST and WHITE SPIRIT had all defected to MCA.

Moving into 1982, VENOM were already showing signs that they most certainly weren't a novelty act after all, and that they would outlast most of the British hopefuls (DEMON PACT, SHOCK TREATMENT, DEMOLITION *etc.*) who had also attempted to break through with a similarly forceful brand of metal in the previous year or two. In fact, only SATAN seemed to be keeping up with them, although the latter would soon be branching out into more of a power metal style, leaving VENOM to stand alone as the UK's most feared bunch of evil blasphemers. The trio were soon hard at work on their follow-up to »Welcome To Hell«, but the next product to emerge was another single, unleashed in the summer of 1982. The latest two-tracker coupled "Blood Lust" and "In Nomine Satanas" a pair of unfamiliar numbers which, in addition to a few quirky rhythm changes and unusual ideas, actually contained some pretty capable musicianship, especially in the guitar department. If some people had originally viewed VENOM as a musical joke, it was no longer a laughing matter. The lads even became ambitious enough to play their first ever gig, at the Heavy Sound Festival in Belgium, where they did their thing in front of a pretty hefty audience, although it rapidly became evident that this would be strictly a one-off appearance for the time being. Their initial reasons for not playing live had centred around their inability to find a suitable range of venues which could cope with all the special effects and pyrotechnics (hardly the most convincing explanation of all time), although their rationale soon shifted towards their reluctance (well, point blank refusal) to play as a support act, no matter who the headliners might be. It was all a bit silly, to be honest. Anyway, the new album followed later in the year, and it duly became apparent that VENOM had spawned a monster with »Black Metal«, a record whose title alone was enough to inspire a brand-new sub-genre.

»Black Metal« wasn't, to be honest, all that different from its predecessor in the musical sense, and it seemed, at times, to merge into a bit of a monotonous blur, but strong selections such as "Countess Bathory" and the title track compensated for the interchangeability of the rest of the material on display. Mind you, "Teacher's Pet" was something of an oddity, and stood out like a sore thumb with its juvenile lyrics and bluesy middle section. Still, the new long-player seemed to spark the public's imagination to an even greater extent than the band's debut, and an entire generation of fans around the world were soon coming to terms with the fact that VENOM were setting the stage for a whole new breed of metal outfits. The latest LP might not have been a ground-breaking release in terms of its musical contents, but the whole Satanic image and demonic lyrical stance, coupled with the intense and weighty music, represented a sufficiently novel variation on the heavy metal theme that a vast number of impersonators (or, at least, groups who had taken a considerable VENOM influence on board) were soon cropping up on both sides of the Atlantic. In North America, for example, we had the likes of DEATH, POSSESSED, SLAYER and RAZOR, while the European community had their own representatives with HELLHAMMER, SODOM, BATHORY and BULLDOZER. Abaddon was later happy to acknowledge his outfit's influence on the metal scene: *'In around 1982, it was pretty dangerous for anyone to attempt to distance themselves from the term 'Heavy Metal', although the press seemed happy to identify our style as Black Metal, taken from the album title itself. I remember we did an interview, I think it was with 'Aardschok', when we just said 'Yes, we're Heavy Metal, Black Metal, Power Metal, Thrash Metal'. The journalist immediately began writing it all down, and within a couple of years there were all these sub-genres, so we really must have been ahead of our time.'* (Ref: Interview, Matthias Mader, February 1997). Before the year was out, the fans were treated to another new track, when "Bursting Out" put in an appearance on Neat's »60 Minutes Plus« cassette, although I'm sure they would have preferred a gig or two instead. Indeed, the possibility of some end-of-year shows in the UK was mooted, but this notion was scrapped before too long.

In spite of the band's extreme inability to get themselves out and about in the live environment, they were still going from strength to strength on reputation alone, and each release was now selling more extensively than the preceding offering. In due course, the *'Venom's Legions'* fan club was established, and many followers from all around the world were soon benefitting from regular newsletters which detailed their heroes' every activity. In the spring of 1983, however, VENOM found a couple of venues who were prepared to host their live extravaganza, although the outfit had to trek all the way to the States to do so. After a handful of well-received shows on the East Coast (where they were supported by a young bunch called METALLICA), the lads returned home in good spirits, and soon concluded that this touring lark wasn't quite as big a deal as they had been making out. The dates had coincided with the release of their »Die Hard« single (B-side "Acid Queen"), the US edition of which (on Megaforce) came as an exclusive (and strictly limited) picture disc, which now fetches a hefty price on the open market. The European fans, on the other hand, got a 12" version (on Roadrunner) with an extra track (an all-new recording of "Bursting Out"), so there was something for everyone. Mind you, things didn't go completely the group's way, and a headlining appearance at the Aardschok Festival had to be pulled after their gear failed to make its way back from the States in mysterious circumstances. A new VENOM long-player was widely expected to appear before the year was out, but, in the long run, the legions had to make do with the »Warhead« single (which appeared in both 12" and 7" forms, the latter with three sleeve variations) as the only other release from 1983. At least the featured selections (the others were "Lady Luck" and "Seven Gates Of Hell") were all exclusive this time, and the release led to a monumental episode in the history of Radio One, when Tommy Vance conspired (by offering to pay a sum of money to charity) to get the not-very-radio-friendly A-side played during daytime programming, to the distress and bewilderment of many sensitive souls. Chortle.

In the early months of 1984, VENOM decided to go out on a limb and play a modest handful of gigs in Europe (with METALLICA in tow once again), taking them to the likes of France, Italy and Germany before ending up with a legendary headlining (naturally) appearance at the Aardschok Festival in Holland (they actually got to play this time), where the trio proceeded to go down an absolute storm with the rabid crowd of metal merchants. Before long, they were back home and working on their next long-player, although they finally bowed to considerable pressure and played their first UK gig, a much-heralded show at the Hammersmith Odeon which was attended by a significant number of personalities from the music scene of the time, as well as some fanatical followers who had waited several years for this opportunity. The lads made good use of the event, capturing the show on both audio and video tape, the latter being used to form the basis of their »Seventh Date Of Hell« release in due course. Before much longer, though, VENOM emerged from the studio with their new LP, which took the form of »At War With Satan« (the outro on the previous album had served as a taster for the record to follow), an offering which represented something of a (semi) concept piece. In fact, one whole side of the latest set was occupied by the epic title track itself, although it was, to be frank, a somewhat self-indulgent piece of experimentation which failed to impress the majority of metalheads. The other side, though, comprised the usual batch of chaotic compositions, and the likes of "Genocide" and "Rip Ride" were up to their usual standard, but it's fair to say that VENOM weren't exactly pushing the musical boundaries from one album to the next. For some reason, though, the new record began shifting an incredible number of units almost immediately, and sales were sufficiently plentiful that it even managed to achieve a placing in the mainstream charts (not a high placing, but, even so, it's pretty astonishing) at one stage.

The workshy band didn't bother playing any more gigs for the remainder of 1984, but carried on tinkering around in the studio every now and then, helping out their mates in WARFARE (who were recording their debut long-player) before laying down an end-of-year single based around new number "Manitou". Neat really went to town with this release, issuing it on virtually every format known to mankind (7", 7" picture disc, 12", shaped picture disc and cassette single), and it was only too clear that VENOM's huge popularity was already breeding seriously unhealthy levels of avarice in certain quarters. Worse was to come, though. Still, this release (another pair of unfamiliar numbers, "Dead Of The Night" and "Woman", were used as B-sides) was another extremely popular purchase for the adoring masses, and at least the quirky A-side was something a bit different. Moving into 1985, VENOM soon decided to push the boat out and record a brand-new album without any further ado. Within a matter of months, »Possessed« was hitting the shelves and earning itself a critical panning in many quarters, the first VENOM offering to have elicited such a widespread reaction of disapproval. It's hard to say why, as it's pretty much the sort of thing they had been doing all along, but perhaps that was the very problem. VENOM had not only failed to make much of a progression, they now seemed to be going backwards with slapdash, formulaic numbers which must have taken at least five minutes to write in each case. In contrast to the indulgence of »At War With Satan«, the latest compositions seemed to reach the other extreme, and the majority whizzed past without running the risk of overstaying their welcome. Still, the hardcore fans were happy to part with their hard-earned cash.

The outfit then proceeded to play another handful of well-attended dates in North America during the spring (with stand-in guitarists Les Cheetham from AVENGER and Dave Irwin from FIST, who deputised for the not-very-well Mantas), before coming back to the UK to formulate their plan of campaign for the rest of the year. Their activities in the coming months took in an appearance on the 'E.C.T.' television show, where they performed versions of "Too Loud For The Crowd", "Nightmare" and "Die Hard", which famously ended with Cronos diving headfirst into the crowd, bass still attached! Next up was a session for the 'Friday Rock Show', where (on the 16th of August 1985) the lads ran through versions of "Blood Lust", "Nightmare", "Black Metal" and "Too Loud For The Crowd", the recordings later being made available on the »Radio Hell« CD alongside the WARFARE and RAVEN sessions. After that, the VENOM lads put in an appearance at the Metal Hammer Festival in Germany, an event which was filmed and later broadcast (in the form of selected highlights) on television. There was no stopping the lads now that they had finally managed to motivate themselves to get out and about, and their next task was to organise an end-of-year tour to promote their new release, a single based around "Nightmare", a number the outfit had been showcasing a great deal in recent times. Once again, the latest record was to appear in multifarious formats, including a picture disc which barely made it into the shops, a picture sleeve for the 12" version (showing a horny creature getting up to some real naughtiness on a four-poster bed) which was withdrawn after a bit of a fuss was kicked up by someone-or-other, plus the usual motley array of shaped discs, cassettes and the like. Still, the odd bit of controversy never did sales any harm, and the release itself was actually of a rather higher standard than their most recent album might have suggested, so there were signs that VENOM might just salvage the situation after all.

Their winter schedule took in a tour of the UK (yes, several whole appearances this time, not just a one-off in the capital, although they still managed to cancel half of the dates), where

CHARIOT and EXODUS came along for the ride, and then it was off to Europe, where ATOMKRAFT took CHARIOT's place and opened the proceedings quite satisfactorily. Once again, their Hammersmith Odeon appearance had been captured for posterity, and this set of recordings were subsequently utilised to assemble a couple of official live releases, the first of which appeared very shortly afterwards as the »Hell At Hammersmith« EP, a limited edition which, nevertheless, failed to tempt all that many fans to shell out for a copy. Even so, VENOM were perfectly happy to sanction quite a few slices of ropy vinyl over the next couple of years, notably the infamous series of »Assaults« (has anyone actually seen that alleged Italian one?), which were supposedly conceived as a strictly-limited souvenir of each of their overseas jaunts (correct me if I'm wrong, but they never actually made it to Scandinavia), but which eventually started to be churned out on a regular basis in order to fleece their loyal fans around the world. Boo. In the spring of 1986, it was back across the pond for some North American dates, and a couple of hectic nights at the Ritz in New York were additionally taped for future use. In due course, the Hammersmith and New York recordings formed the basis of the band's »Eine Kleine Nachtmusik« live set, which, in addition to a generous helping of original favourites, introduced the fans to a couple of newies, notably "Love Amongst The Dead" and "The Chanting Of The Priests". As the first official VENOM live album (the bootleggers were already doing a roaring trade), the set soon won favour with the public, and a healthy number of units were shifted in no time at all. Before long, however, Neat got slightly carried away and duly started re-pressing much of the group's back catalogue, varying things a bit by using such gimmicks as picture discs and coloured vinyl releases to create a few instant collectables which would hopefully encourage even more fans to part with their money. Double boo.

By the second half of the year, the lads were hard at work on their next album, which had already been given the tentative title of »Deadline«, when things started to go quite horrendously wrong, resulting in a great deal of infighting which ultimately culminated in Mantas going off to do his own thing. Although the axeman initially restricted himself to a bit of instrumentalist tinkering around in the studio, he had formed his own MANTAS solo venture within a couple of years, an act who got to the stage of releasing an album (»Winds Of Change«) of polished melodic metal before calling it a day within a remarkably short space of time thereafter. Back in the VENOM camp, however, things were in a state of complete disarray, and the lads failed to deliver the anticipated album for Neat, who soon terminated their contract. They still managed to undertake a tour of Brazil at the end of 1986 (by which time another couple of cash-in releases had now appeared on different labels) using a pair of stand-in axemen (Mike Hickey and Jim Clare), who worked out so well that they swiftly became permanent fixtures in the VENOM line-up. After getting their act together over the ensuing months, the newly-expanded quartet finally came up with an effort called »Calm Before The Storm« (on the Filmtrax label) in 1987, which took quite a few observers by surprise, and the reviewers were soon announcing that VENOM had at last *'discovered melody'*, although I wouldn't quite go that far, personally.

Nevertheless, the latest long-player was still a break with tradition as far as VENOM were concerned, and the majority of the tracks featured were indeed considerably more accessible than on previous vinyl outings. It wasn't bad in places (notably "Under A Spell", "The Chanting Of The Priests" and "Gypsy"), but the general standard was pretty variable, and the fans were largely nonplussed by the whole affair, leading to fairly disappointing sales around the world. The outfit didn't even bother to promote it particularly heavily, and their only touring activity at the time was a very brief jaunt to Japan (where they were never all that popular) towards the end of 1987. It appeared that VENOM had undoubtedly lost the plot to some extent, and were now finding it extremely difficult to appeal to a significant proportion of the metal fans in the face of a glam/thrash tidal wave. In fact, an emergent *'second generation'* of VENOM-inspired hopefuls were now beginning to break through, many of whom were somewhat more extreme and forward-looking than the original clutch of unashamed copyists had been. On both sides of the Atlantic, it seemed that countless youthful ensembles were dusting off their old copies of »Welcome To Hell« and taking things one step further in order to lay the foundations of the death and black metal scenes which would ultimately reach unprecedented levels of popularity during the 90's. In North America, for example, we now had the likes of MORBID ANGEL, NECROPHAGIA, SLAUGHTER and AMON (later DEICIDE), while the phenomenon was repeated further afield by the likes of Norway's MAYHEM, Australia's ANGEL OF DEATH, Brazil's SARCOFAGO and Japan's SABBAT, to name but a few.

Meanwhile, however, VENOM themselves were rapidly fading into disregard while these young pretenders came to the fore.

There was very little to report on the VENOM front during 1988, although they started thinking about a new album (for the Under One Flag label) the following year. Things began to fall apart at a pretty early stage, though, and Cronos soon decided to pack his bags and leave (taking Mike Hickey and Jim Clare with him) to form his own eponymous venture, which almost didn't get off the ground at all (an abortive US tour was dismally promoted and ended in a complete shambles), but which eventually spawned three critically-ignored albums in the 90's. Back in the VENOM camp, sole survivor Abaddon soon reunited with original guitarist Mantas, whose solo project had died a bit of a death, and the axeman brought in one of his erstwhile colleagues (Al Barnes, another guitarist) to bolster the sound. All that they needed was a new frontman (preferably one who could double up as a bassist), and they swiftly identified the ideal candidate in the shape of ATOMKRAFT's Tony Dolan (or 'The Demolition Man', as he soon became

known), who was happy to lay his previous outfit to rest and start all over again with VENOM. Within a remarkably short space of time, the revamped act had another record on the market, although »Prime Evil« was hardly the return to form that they had originally promised the world.

While the latest album wasn't nearly as accessible as its predecessor, the fans failed to detect any redeeming features whatsoever in the new material, and the overwhelming opinion was that VENOM should call it a day before they became something of an embarrassment. In the face of hefty criticism, however, the thick-skinned musicians ploughed on regardless, and they even played a couple of low-key shows in Europe during the early months of 1990 to introduce their new frontman to the fans. Later in the year, the group brought out a mini-album called »Tear Your Soul Apart«, although it relied rather heavily on reworkings of older material, and hardly won them any new friends in the long run.

In 1991, VENOM tried again with »Temples Of Ice«, another set of newly-penned compositions which met with the usual level of utter indifference from both fans and reviewers, and modest sales saw the outfit continuing on their inexorable downward slide. It was all very ironic, especially with all these newer outfits paying tribute to VENOM's original ground-breaking style, and I reckon that relatively few of them actually realised that the old stagers were still on the go, such was the lacklustre performance of their most recent studio albums. It was all too much for guitarist Al Barnes, who soon defected to emergent local hopefuls XLR8R, whereupon he was replaced by Steve White (another ATOMKRAFT veteran, latterly with WAR MACHINE), who fitted in to the VENOM line-up without any great difficulty. The lads had more or less given up on the live appearances by now, but were still determined to show the public that they could indeed return from the cold and deliver a world-beating album after all these years. Sadly, 1992's inauspicious »The Waste Lands« wasn't the record which would reverse their fortunes overnight, and it seemed as though the hapless participants barely had a friend left in the world by this stage, even though there was still a roaring trade in all the reissues, compilations, bootlegs and retrospectives which covered the early part of their career. The situation with these exploitation releases soon escalated to absurd levels, and some 'new' VENOM product seemed to be hitting the shops virtually every other week during the mid-90's. Admittedly, some of them (notably »In Memorium« and »Skeletons In The Closet«) were, by virtue of their unreleased material, worthy additions to the VENOM catalogue, while some of the others (including those which were only differentiable by their cover artwork or title) were cynically designed to part the fans from their money without any regard to the validity of the release.

By 1993, VENOM had pretty much fallen apart in the wake of adverse publicity following their latest batch of releases, and so the musicians went their separate ways for a while. Abaddon became involved in the day-to-day running of the Bleeding Hearts concern, while Mantas got all spiritual and immersed himself in various martial arts activities. Meanwhile, Cronos was still toiling on his eponymous musical project (as well as working as a fitness instructor to pay the bills), but his third solo album (issued in 1995 on the revived Neat Metal concern) was something of a surprise, as »Venom« (clever title, that) featured a bunch of 'covers' (if you can call them covers) of VENOM classics such as "In League With Satan" and "7 Gates Of Hell". It now seemed as though Cronos was willing to put all the disagreements of the past behind him, and it wasn't long before a widely-anticipated reunion of the three original forces of evil was being confirmed as a reality. The reaction in the metal world was astonishing, demonstrating that people didn't hate VENOM after all, just the pale imitation of the band that had been doing the rounds since 1986. As ever, though, the chaps didn't exactly take the world by storm with an extensive world tour, and the first signs of renewed activity came with an anonymous-looking mini-CD called »Venom '96«, which introduced the fans to a couple of freshly-penned compositions. After that, there was just one gig to show that the boys were back in town, a triumphal return to form at the Dynamo Festival in 1996, where the original trio blew away most of the hapless impersonators in attendance. The whole event was professionally filmed and taped, after which it appeared as a CD/video package called »The Second Coming«, a limited edition which sold out in no time at all.

VENOM were back with a vengeance, and the world was soon getting a taste of the threesome's new writing style when their »Cast In Stone« set emerged during 1997. The lengthy release (a double CD or triple album, which appeared on both the little-known CBH and the more influential SPV labels) was generally well-received by both the rabid fans and the rock press as a whole, the consensus of opinion being that the

trio had defied considerable odds and delivered a release which was relevant to the modern-day music scene without merely resorting to rehashing some of their half-formed ideas from the early 80's. Sales of this particular set were extremely respectable, and the outfit capitalised on their return to form with another brace of gigs, namely a memorable show-stealer at the Milwaukee Metalfest and a long-promised destruction of Greece. After that, however, they were gone, returning to the shadows to plan their next assault (as it were) on an unsuspecting public. Every now and again, however, there were fairly reliable indicators that VENOM would be coming out of hiding to play a one-off festival date or even a club tour (several trips to the States have fallen through in pretty mysterious circumstances), but nothing ever came of the initial speculation.

Eventually, however, the lads finally managed to complete work on their (long-anticipated) studio follow-up to the highly successful »Cast In Stone« set (although their drummer elected not to take part in this case, and went off to do a solo album instead), and an all-new effort called »Resurrection« (featuring stand-in sticksman Anton) has appeared (the industrial-flavoured ABADDON offering, »I Am Legion«, actually hit the shops first, which means that all three original members now have eponymous releases under their belts) comparatively recently. All that remains is to wait and see how the general public will react to the latest selection of VENOM originals, which will no doubt be followed by further wild speculation as to if and when they'll finally return to the live arena, although their addition to the bill of Wacken 2000 was a promising start. Given that virtually every death and black metal outfit currently on the music scene seems to regard the unholy threesome as being the very epitome of extreme music (as evidenced by the recent spate of tribute albums, as well as extraordinarily healthy sales of VENOM T-shirts and numerous honourable mentions in magazine interviews), there's no fundamental reason (unless they screw everything up by falling out again or refusing to play live to promote their latest studio offering) why these musicians shouldn't be able to recapture some of the utterly phenomenal popularity they once enjoyed in their early 80's heyday.

LP's

»Welcome To Hell« Neat 1981
[Also issued as limited edition picture disc and on purple vinyl, a few examples on other coloured vinyl]
»Black Metal« Neat 1982
[Also issued as limited edition picture disc and on grey marbled vinyl, a few examples on other coloured vinyl]
»Welcome To Hell« Bernett 1983
[French issue]
»Black Metal« Bernett 1983
[French issue]
»At War With Satan« Neat 1984
[UK issue, initially with gatefold sleeve and booklet, also issued as limited edition picture disc and very few examples on coloured vinyl]
»At War With Satan« Roadrunner 1984/Bernett 1984
[Dutch/French issue]
»Welcome To Hell« Combat 1985
[US issue with two extra tracks]
»Black Metal« Combat 1985
[US issue with three extra tracks]
»At War With Satan« Combat 1985
[US issue with extra tracks]
»Possessed« Neat 1985
[UK issue, also released as limited edition picture disc and on blue vinyl]
»Possessed« Bernett 1985/Combat 1985/Tonpress 1985/Banzai 1985
[French/US/Polish/Canadian issue]
»From Hell To The Unknown« Raw Power 1985
[Double compilation album, includes »Welcome To Hell« album plus previously-released material, most are either on black/black or black/red vinyl, very few on black/white vinyl]
»Eine Kleine Nachtmusik« Neat 1986/Tonpress 1986
[UK/Polish issue, double live album]
»Live-Official Bootleg« American Phonograph 1986
[Live release, also issued as limited edition picture disc]
»The Singles 80-86« Raw Power 1986
[Compilation release]
»Calm Before The Storm« Filmtrax 1987
[Original UK issue]
»Calm Before The Storm« K-Tel 1987
[US issue with slightly different cover]
»Live In Concert« Qwil Records 1987
[US live release with material taken from »Eine Kleine Nachtmusik« album]
»Welcome To Hell« Roadrunner 1989
[European reissue]
»Black Metal« Roadrunner 1989
[European reissue]
»At War With Satan« Roadrunner 1989
[European reissue]
»Possessed« Roadrunner 1989
[European reissue]
»Eine Kleine Nachtmusik« Roadrunner 1989

[Double live album, European reissue]
»Japanese Assault« VAP 1989
[Compilation release for Japanese market]
»Prime Evil« Under One Flag 1989
[Also issued as limited edition picture disc]
»In Memorium« Music Collection 1991
[Double compilation album with booklet, includes previously released material]
»Temples Of Ice« Under One Flag 1991
»The Waste Lands« Under One Flag 1992
»Cast In Stone« SPV 1997
[Triple album]
»Resurrection« SPV 2000
[Double album, issued as limited edition picture disc set]

Mini-LP's
»Canadian Assault« Banzai 1985
[Compilation release]
»French Assault« New Records 1985
[Compilation release]
»American Assault« Combat 1985
[Compilation release]
»Scandinavian Assault« Neat 1986
[Compilation release]
»German Assault« Roadrunner 1987
[Compilation release]
»Tear Your Soul Apart« Under One Flag 1990

12" EP's
»Die Hard« Neat/Roadrunner 1983
[All three tracks non-LP]
»Warhead« Neat 1983
[With extended A-side, all three tracks non-LP, also issued as very limited edition on blue vinyl]
»Warhead« Roadrunner 1983
[Dutch issue]
»Manitou« Neat 1984/Roadrunner 1984
[UK/Dutch issue, all three tracks non-LP, cassette version with Dutch radio interview added]
»Nightmare« Neat 1985
[Both "Nightmare" and "F.O.A.D." non-LP, first issue in withdrawn 'devil' sleeve, also released as limited edition picture disc and cassette, both with live version of "Warhead" as extra track]
»Nightmare« Roadrunner 1985
[Dutch issue in 'devil' sleeve with extra track]
»Nightmare« Neat 1985
[Second issue in 'faces' sleeve]
»Hell At Hammersmith« Neat 1985
[Live release]

7" Singles
»In League With Satan« Neat 1981
[Both tracks different to album versions, various minor label and sleeve differences, some credit A-side as "In League With Satin"]
»Blood Lust« Neat 1982
[Both tracks non-LP, some with poster, also issued as very limited edition on purple vinyl]
»Die Hard« Neat 1983/Bernett 1983
[UK/French issue in picture sleeve, both tracks non-LP]
»Acid Queen« Megaforce 1983
[US issue picture disc, very limited quantities, later counterfeited, tracks same as UK »Die Hard« single]
»Warhead« Neat 1983
[With edited A-side, both tracks non-LP, issued with three picture sleeves featuring individual band members, also very few copies on coloured vinyl]
»Manitou« Neat 1984
[Both tracks non-LP, also issued as limited edition picture disc]
»Nightmare« Neat 1985
[A-side non-LP]
»In League With Satan« Bootleg 1997
[Unofficial picture disc reissue of first single, very limited quantities]

Shaped Picture Discs
»Manitou« Neat 1984
[B-side "Woman" different to version on other formats]
»Nightmare« Neat 1985

Promotional Releases
»Here Lies Venom« Combat 1985
[Very limited box set with US pressings of first three albums, plus exclusive »American Assault« picture disc]
»Bursting Out« New Records 1985
[Split 7" flexi given free with 'Enfer' magazine, other track "Pull The Trigger" by BLITZKRIEG]
»Interview with Venom« Baktabak 1985
[Interview 12" picture disc]
»Fire« K-Tel 1988
[US promo-only 12"]

CD's
»Black Metal« Neat 1986
»At War With Satan« Neat 1986
»The Singles 80-86« Raw Power 1986
[Compilation release]
»Live-Official Bootleg« Magnum 1987
[Live release]
»Calm Before The Storm« Filmtrax 1987
»Metalpunk« Soundwings 1987
[Alternate European issue of »Calm Before The Storm«]
»Eine Kleine Nachtmusik« Neat 1987
[Live release]
»Live In Concert« Qwil Records 1987

[US live release with material taken from »Eine Kleine Nachtmusik« album]
»At War With Satan« Neat/Roadrunner 1989
[European reissue]
»Japanese Assault« VAP 1989
[Japanese compilation release]
»Prime Evil« Under One Flag 1989
[With one extra track]
»At War With Satan« Roadrunner 199?
[Japanese issue with five bonus tracks]
»Acid Queen« Marble Arch 1991
[Compilation release]
»In Memorium« Music Collection 1991
[Compilation release]
»Temples Of Ice« Under One Flag 1991
»Black Metal« Castle Communications 1992
[Reissue]
»Welcome To Hell« Castle Communications 1992
[Reissue]
»At War With Satan« Castle Communications 1992
[Reissue]
»The Singles 80-86« Castle Communications 1992
[Reissue]
»The Waste Lands« Under One Flag 1992
»Book Of Armageddon« Relativity 1992
[Compilation release]
»Kissing The Beast« Disky 1993
[Compilation release]
»Leave Me In Hell« Success 1993
[Compilation release]
»Old, New, Borrowed And Blue« Bleeding Hearts 1993
[Compilation release]
»Skeletons In The Closet« Castle Communications 1993
[Compilation of rare and unreleased material]
»The Official Bootleg« Magnum 1996
[Reissue]
»Black Reign« Receiver 1996
[Compilation release]
»The Second Coming« CMA 1996
[Issued as part of video/CD package]
»From Heaven To The Unknown« Snapper 1997
[Double disc, compilation release]
»New, Live And Rare« Bleeding Hearts 1997
[Double disc, compilation release]
»Cast In Stone« CBH 1997/SPV 1997
[UK/German issue, double disc]
»Eine Kleine Nachtmusik« Neat Metal 1998
[Reissue, live release]
»Calm Before The Storm« Neat Metal 1998
[Reissue in same sleeve but different colour scheme]
»Buried Alive« Receiver 1999
[Compilation of live and studio material]
»Greatest Hits And More« Deadline 1999
[Triple disc, limited edition box set featuring »New,

Live And Rare« and »In Memorium« releases]
»Resurrection« SPV 2000
»The Court Of Death« Receiver 2000
[Compilation release]
»The Collection« Connoisseur Collection 2000
[Compilation release]
»Beauty And The Beast« Dressed To Kill 2000
[Another alternate version of »Calm Before The Storm«]

Mini-CD's
»Tear Your Soul Apart« Music For Nations 1990
»Venom '96« Private 1996

Compilation Appearances
"Angel Dust" on »Lead Weight« LP Neat 1981/CD Teichiku 1992
[Different to album version]
"Bursting Out" on »60 Minutes Plus« Cassette Neat 1982/CD Teichiku 1992 + »All Hell Let Loose« LP Neat 1983
[Different to version on »Die Hard« 12"]
"Leave Me In Hell" on »Metal Battle« LP Neat 1983/Roadrunner 1983 + »War On The Planet« LP CP Records 1986?
"Poison" on »Metal Hammer« LP Roadrunner 1984 + »Heavy Metal Collection 2« CD X-Tra Collection 1993
"Woman" on »Wango Tango Vol.1« LP Bernett 1984 + »Metal Inferno« LP Castle Communications 1985
"Warhead" on »Wango Tango Vol.1« LP Bernett 1984 + »British Steel« LP M Port Records 1984/Steel Trax 1986
"Witching Hour" on »British Steel« LP M Port Records 1984/Steel Trax 1986
"Black Metal" on »Metal Inferno« LP Castle Communications 1985 + »Metal Killers Kollection I« Do-LP Castle Communications 1985 + »Metal Concussion« LP Bandit 1986 + »Metal Killers Kollection« CD Castle Communications 1991 + »Heavy Metal Collection 3« CD X-Tra Collection 1993 + »Wild Thing« CD Kaz Records 1995 + »The Metal Box« 3-CD Box Kaz Records 1995
"Black Metal" on »Speed Kills« LP Music For Nations 1985
[Different to album version]
"Voyeur" on »12 Commandments In Metal« LP Roadrunner 1985
"Manitou" on »Axe Attack« LP M Port 1985/Mausoleum 1986 + »Metal Mania« Do-CD Duet 1995 + »The Metal Box« 3-CD Box Kaz Records 1995
"Witching Hour" (live) on »Powertrax« Cassette Neat 1986
"Countess Bathory" on »War On The Planet«

LP CP Records 1986? + »Metal Mania« Do-CD Duet 1995 + »Metal Mania« 3-CD Box Kaz Records 1995
"Angel Dust" (live) on »Heavy Metal Holocaust« Bootleg 3-LP Box Metallic Death 198?
"Angel Dust" on »NWOBHM '79 Revisited« Do-LP/Do-CD Phonogram 1990
"Welcome To Hell" on »Giants Of Rock-The Metal Decade Vol.1« Do-CD Teldec 1990 + »Metal Killers« CD Castle Communications 1993 + »Metal Mania« Do-CD Duet 1995 + »The Metal Box« 3-CD Box Kaz Records 1995
"Acid Queen" on »Deeper Into The Vault« CD Music For Nations 1991
"Black Metal" on »Radio Hell« CD Raw Fruit 1992 *[Different to album version]*
"Nightmare" on »Radio Hell« CD Raw Fruit 1992 *[Different to single version]*
"Too Loud For The Crowd" on »Radio Hell« CD Raw Fruit 1992 *[Different to album version]*
"Blood Lust" on »Radio Hell« CD Raw Fruit 1992 *[Different to single version]*
"Die Hard" on »The Metal Box« 3-CD Box Castle Communications 1993
"Rip Ride" on »Metal Masters« 4-CD Box Castle Communications 1993 + »Metal Mania« CD Castle Communications 1994
"In League With Satan" on »Heavy Metal Collection 1« CD X-Tra Collection 1993 + »Metal Mania« Do-CD Duet 1995 + »The Metal Box« 3-CD Box Kaz Records 1995
"Sons Of Satan" on »Heavy Metal Collection 4« CD X-Tra Collection 1993
"To Hell And Back" on »Give 'Em Hell« CD Nectar Masters 1995

VERMILION

Vermilion Sands (v)
Kenny Alton (g)
Fritz (b)
Pete Davies (d)

Lying squarely on the shaky boundary of punk and metal at the inception of the NWOBHM phenomenon (if not even a bit earlier) were VERMILION, a pretty impassioned quartet named after their confrontational frontwoman, the American-born Vermilion Sands. Based in London, the no-nonsense ensemble formed in the late 70's and soon made their intentions known by gigging around the pubs and clubs of the capital, delivering a rowdy brand of music which borrowed equally from VICE SQUAD (Beki Bondage's pre-BOMBSHELLS venture) and BOW WOW WOW (with the merest hint of ROCK GODDESS thrown in for good measure), winning a few fans from both metal and punk communities in the process. Although the combo styled themselves as a hard-rocking, biker/punk proposition with lyrics highly biased towards the hedonistic sex, bikes and rock'n'roll ethic, their general disposition deviated quite considerably from the norm as far as crossover material was concerned, although they still managed to deliver some semi-listenable compositions from time to time. Before long, they were courted by a couple of the minor record labels, and ultimately chose to go with one of the more established companies rather than trusting their future to some fly-by-night operation.

Signing to the punk-dominated Illegal concern (the original home of THE POLICE) in mid-1978 or thereabouts, VERMILION's first vinyl offering emerged in the shape of a humble 7" EP, the latter including "Angry Young Women" (featuring some extraordinarily annoying vocals), the uncompromising "Nymphomania" (so much for lying back and thinking of England) and the biker-friendly "Wild Boys (Ride Their Bikes)". The record, issued in a fairly metal-looking and distinctive picture sleeve, rammed home the slightly unconvincing message that those who followed the biker/non-stop-rampant-nookie lifestyle had a considerably better time of it than the rest of us (er, I mean them), and the sheer spectacle of the frontwoman attempting to pose seductively (chortle) with a Triumph Bonneville on the back cover could hardly have been a more blatant move to pander to the group's intended audience. Musically speaking, it might have been a reasonably successful release at the time, but their debut now seems a rather uneasy and contrived affair which will appeal only to a limited number of NWOBHM enthusiasts. Some time after the release of »Angry Young Women«, though, Ms. Sands decided to recruit an entirely novel set of accomplices, and eventually teamed up with Steve Tannett (g), Charlie Casey (b) and Noel Martin (d), all formerly of recently-demised, legendary punk outfit (and fellow Illegal recording act) MENACE, whose exploits are fully documented in 'Oi! The Book Vol.1' by Mader *et al.*

Adopting the revised identity VERMILION AND THE ACES, the revamped outfit proceeded to lay down another slice of vinyl (a two-tracker produced by Mick Farren of the infamous DEVIANTS) for Illegal in 1979, this time pairing "The Letter" with the entirely self-explanatory "I Like Motorcycles". Surprisingly, however, this potentially explosive mixture of musicians actually yielded something remarkably coherent and accessible (compared with the shambolic VERMILION 7", anyway), suggesting a crossover style lying somewhere between THIN END OF THE WEDGE and the LIGHTNING RAIDERS. The outfit's material had become far more attuned to the NWOBHM ethos by this stage, and it looked as though the musicians might be able to inveigle their way into the metal scene if they played their cards right. VERMILION AND THE ACES played quite a few live gigs to promote themselves to the masses, where freshly-penned efforts such as "Gladiator Rock" were unleashed upon the hapless audiences of the day, and most of these tended to attract comparatively favourable reviews in the music press. However, it looks as though VERMILION and her ACES had parted company by the early 80's, with the ACES going on to pursue a brief career of their own, culminating in the release of a scarce single entitled »One Way Street« in 1982. I've no idea what happened to Ms. Sands herself, but I prefer to think she's now something like a bonkers performance artist rather than a dull housewife...

7" EP's
»Angry Young Women« Illegal Records 1978

7" Singles
»The Letter« Illegal Records 1979
[Under the name of VERMILION AND THE ACES]

VHF

Harrod
Trimby

Much as it pains me to say so, but VHF's »Heart Of Stone« 7" from 1980 is a remarkably irritating record. It's not that the music itself was unreservedly abysmal, just that a reasonable NWOBHM band somehow managed to corrupt two otherwise decent tracks with appalling vocals, clumsy arrangements and ill-conceived ideas. Exhibit A: "Heart Of Stone". Excellent start, a good heavy riff and mid-range vocals in the TORTURE or TYGERS OF PAN TANG vein. Then the second *'singer'* comes in, delivering a tuneless, high-pitched screech that's about as easy on the ears as nails on a blackboard. Throw in some incredibly awkward time changes and an initially-decent composition is rendered virtually unlistenable.

Exhibit B: "Cheatin' Stealin'". A heavier, slower number which is occasionally reminiscent of ARC's "Ice Cream Theme" or some of the weightier tracks from the first QUARTZ long-player. All fine and dandy until approximately halfway through, when the participants decide that a tuneless, acoustic, folky interlude is in order before returning to the original theme. Sorry lads, leave that kind of nonsense to BOB DYLAN. Again, another utter shambles.

In my humble opinion, this sleeveless effort should almost certainly be filed with the likes of ORION in the *'what the hell were they thinking?'* department, although it's still not quite the most atrocious release from the period. Mind you, the two-tracker hardly goes any way towards justifying the hefty price tag which tends to be slapped upon it with monotonous regularity these days, so don't be hoodwinked into thinking that it might actually be a decent offering after all. Incidentally, VHF was a pretty common identity in the UK during the 80's, and I don't believe that this particular bunch (I think they came from the Essex area or thereabouts) released anything else (thankfully), so they shouldn't be confused either with the obscure ensemble (possibly from the Midlands) who issued the lightweight »First Impressions« 7" in 1981 or with the London-based group (who had evolved out of Scottish act SATAN'S EMPIRE after the latter's relocation to the capital) responsible for the scarce »Insanity« EP six years later.

7" Singles
»Heart Of Stone« Lion Records 1980

VIRGINIA WOLF

Steve Lawrence (v)
Dale Williams (g)
Dave Sheridan (g, k)
Pete Morgan (b)
Brian Taylor (d)

Not to be confused (although, thanks to some irritatingly lazy journalism over the years, they frequently have been) with the mid-80's AOR group (who, at one time, featured Jason Bonham and recorded for the Atlantic label), the original Welsh version of VIRGINIA WOLF first appeared on the nation's thriving rock scene in the early 80's, and, having established themselves by paying their dues in the live environment (mainly in their locality and the North West of England, by the looks of things), introduced themselves to the masses in 1982 with an unheralded two-tracker based around their energetic reworking of THE SWEET's "Action". Issued on the Creole label (the group perhaps having been picked up as the company's token rock act following SPIDER's defection to RCA), the 7" (the B-side was the largely-unremarkable "Where Do We Go From Here?", incidentally) was a faithful, but heavy, interpretation of the original (already covered by RAVEN, along with "Hellraiser", the previous year), the band coming across as a listenable combination of MARSEILLE, JESS COX and SILVERWING, with some fairly prominent keyboards.

The ambitious outfit subsequently attempted to capitalise on their debut single's release (the two-tracker even managed to dent the 'Top 30 Kuts' chart in 'Kerrang' at one point, so they must have had a few loyal fans locally, if nowhere else) with some rather more illustrious club appearances, including an ill-fated trip to the Marquee in London, which was reviewed in the aforementioned publication by an unforgiving Dave Ling. With the unfortunate VIRGINIA WOLF showcasing a repertoire of relatively mediocre original material (which included such humble offerings as "The War", "Surrender Your Love" and "Entertaining You", none of which were ever destined to be immortalised on vinyl), the journo's verdict on the set as a whole (observed by a pitifully modest paying audience, apparently) was spectacularly damning: *This was the first time I'd seen VIRGINIA WOLF and it will probably be the last. Although the band showed initial promise this was definitely not one of the year's better gigs.*' (Ref: Kerrang No.15, May 1982). It looks as though they'd unwittingly made an enemy for life there...

Undeterred, the lads merely kept plugging away regardless and proceeded to record a follow-up release for their slightly erratic label, this time pairing "Walkie Talkie Boy" with "One Night Stand", although comparatively few examples made it into general circulation, for some reason. In spite of Dave Reynolds' assurance (in the commemorative NWOBHM supplement compiled by 'Kerrang' in 1989) that this two-tracker was *'never commercially issued'*, finished copies *do* exist, although I suppose these may conceivably have been manufactured for promotional purposes only ('Kerrang' certainly received a copy for review, although they didn't exactly shower it with praise), after which the general release was cancelled. Anyway, the mundane tracks showed little or no progression from the quintet's first vinyl offering, and, with the public showing virtually no interest in VIRGINIA WOLF's future activities, the dejected group presumably went into self-destruct mode soon after. Contrary to reports elsewhere, however, they certainly didn't evolve into V8, so I've absolutely no idea how that conjecture came about. Should you decide to go in search of the singles, meanwhile, they both came in colourful, AOR-style picture sleeves as opposed to the usual monochrome efforts of the period, but they're still pretty thin on the ground.

7" Singles
»**Action**« Creole Records 1982
»**Walkie Talkie Boy**« Creole Records 1982

VIRGIN STAR

Paul Taylor (v)
Russell Simon (g)
Guy Tittley (b)
Mark Simon (d)

Although the Worcestershire-based ensemble known as VIRGIN STAR made it perfectly clear that they saw themselves as a rebellious bunch of punk/glam terrorists, it actually took quite a while for them to live up to this promise. Having originally formed in 1980 or thereabouts, the outfit endured the usual round of personnel changes and hapless fumblings in the live environment, but began to get their act together properly by around 1982, whereupon the lads ventured into the studio to lay down formative efforts such as "Day Dreamer" and "Hit And Run". To be honest, it was nothing spectacularly original or impressive at that stage, and the group seemed content to churn out a rather unremarkable brand of music, occasionally resembling something of a pop/glam cross (entirely befitting of their dodgy moniker) along the lines of PET HATE or FORGER. Before long, though, they received some useful exposure in the 'Armed And Ready' section of 'Kerrang', which divulged that the quartet had recorded a demo called »**Four More For The Road**«, featuring such new selections as "Giving It Up", "Rocket Ship", "Toulouse Ya" and "Tigers Eye". Admittedly, their latest batch of compositions certainly showed the occasional glimpse of creativity (a few similarities to METAL MIRROR), although there was still a long way to go if VIRGIN STAR were ever to rise above the rest of Britain's emergent hopefuls.

Over the following couple of years, it looks as though the group made a conscious decision to toughen up their act pretty dramatically, and endured another reshuffle or two (new bassist Benjie Brittain joining in the fun along the way) before making an attempt to gain a record deal. In due course, they attracted the attention of the tiny Welsh-based Official Records, and were soon offered the chance to release their debut single. With the VIRGIN STAR lads now styling themselves as a genuine glam/punk hybrid (their intended direction being more along the lines of MARIONETTE or WRATHCHILD than anything else), the public would soon be able to see for themselves whether or not the musicians had completed the transformation successfully. Indeed, the two-tracker turned out to be a pretty scathing slice of vinyl, with the A-side ("When The Reds") speculating at length on what might happen *'when the reds come over the hill'*, suggesting a possible reference to either football or war (not much difference, when you think about it), but the largely indecipherable lyrics (you can just about make out the odd *'revenge'*, *'retribution'* and *'no solution'*) tend to mask the intended message, and matters aren't exactly helped by a rather cack-handed production. Cheery stuff this isn't, although the mixture of metal and punk sensibilities doesn't clash (no pun intended) quite as catastrophically as on some other efforts of the period.

All things considered, you can (and probably should) quite happily ignore the questionable lyrical sentiments and enjoy the music, which charges along furiously with a decidedly punky guitar influence in places, although this fails to detract from the overall metal sound in the vein of DENIGH or BOLLWEEVIL. The B-side, "Shake The Towers", is pretty decent too, with its SEX PISTOLS-style guitar breaks, although this effort is even more lyrically ambiguous than the reverse. Given that the members of VIRGIN STAR had been outlining their musical influences from a pretty early stage, often claiming to be heavily influenced by the ROLLING STONES, the NEW YORK DOLLS and HANOI ROCKS, they finally managed to come up with the goods on their debut single, and they had certainly developed more of an authentically-punky edge than many of their glam-affiliated contemporaries. Even the notoriously hard-to-please 'Kerrang' seemed to approve of the two-tracker, and were keen to praise »When The Reds« upon its release, although there was to be no meteoric rise to stardom for VIRGIN STAR thereafter. Even so, the record is well worth adding to your collection (a handful of promo copies boasted a picture sleeve) if you like things slightly raucous. I just hope no nasty *'accidents'* subsequently befell the musicians, as it's possible that their lyrics might just have upset the wrong kind of people...

Although their first release had served to pave the way for a fairly successful and productive career in the music business, it transpires that VIRGIN STAR actually ceased to exist within a surprisingly short space of time after their vinyl debut made its way into the shops, with drummer Mark Simon being poached by local heroes GRIM REAPER in the early part of 1985, following the sudden departure of Lee Harris. Interestingly, he was eventually joined (in 1988) by one of his erstwhile VIRGIN STAR colleagues, bassist Benjie Brittain, although this particular incarnation of GRIM REAPER (their numbers being completed by Steve Grimmett and Nick Bowcott) never reached the vinyl stage. The nucleus of the last VIRGIN STAR line-up (centred around Paul Taylor and Russell Simon), meanwhile, evolved into an act who went under the quirky identity of the IPANEMA KATZ (see separate entry), who had become established within a matter of months. This all-new proposition represented more of an overtly-sleazy concern (they even issued a single or two of their own in the second half of the decade), although the full album which was also scheduled for subsequent release appears not to have seen the light of day.

7" Singles
»When The Reds« Official Records 1984

VIRTUE

Tudor Sheldon (v)
Matt Sheldon (g)
Adrian Metcalfe (g)
Brian Reader (b)
Ian Lewington (d)

Oxfordshire's VIRTUE, despite their relatively late arrival on the metal scene, still managed to create one of the most highly-regarded NWOBHM singles of all. Appearing (so it would seem) out of nowhere in 1985 with their double A-sided offering on the local Other label (a recently-established venture with links to Endangered Musik, a company predominantly concerned with punk upstarts), the unfeasibly young band (typically in their mid-to-late teens at the time) drew considerable praise from various publications ('High Octane' fanzine, in particular) at the time, and it's not too difficult to see why. The two-tracker, housed in an admirably-presented yellow picture sleeve showing a whip-wielding, shadowy figure, comes across as a highly energetic mixture of PROWLER and IRON MAIDEN, the ensemble's twin-guitar riffing on both "We Stand To Fight" and "High Treason", coupled with excellent and distinctive vocals, raising the material to the highest standards. Understandably, the record has become one of the more sought-after artefacts from the period, and demand from NWOBHM/power metal aficionados has been pretty consistent in recent years.

In fact, VIRTUE's intriguing story can actually be traced back as far as 1981, the whole operation being yet another of those small-time, good-natured, family affairs at the outset. Initially, it was merely a case of musical brothers Matt and Tudor Sheldon messing about after school, valiantly trying to emulate their heroes in established, powerful bands such as IRON MAIDEN and JUDAS PRIEST, although the duo gradually roped in some similarly-youthful cohorts to make up the numbers as time went on. By early 1984, the ensemble (who assumed the heroic identity of VIRTUE to represent their musical intentions and pay tribute to their influences) was, unmistakably, a genuine proposition, the Sheldons being joined by second guitarist Adrian Metcalfe, bassist Brian Reader and Ian Lewington on drums. A speculative cassette (entitled »Virtue-Defenders«) was eventually recorded, a low-budget effort which didn't exactly show the band's skills off to greatest effect, and their collective disappointment in the end product (the participants swiftly concluded that the public had to be *'protected'* from the musical contents, so it never made it into wider circulation) almost resulted in the outfit throwing in the towel before they had even got off the blocks properly.

Fortunately, however, the lads persevered, although the two central characters ultimately decided that a new set of musical accomplices would certainly be required if VIRTUE were ever to progress beyond small-time aspirations. In the end, a revised backing ensemble was successfully recruited, with Boz Beast (g), Darren Prothero (b) and Simon Walters (d) signing up for action, whereupon the revamped band (after getting their act together) rapidly set about the task of winning themselves a few gigs in the rock-friendly pubs and clubs of Oxfordshire. Still, it was something of a constant struggle at first, and the precocious combo initially found it frustratingly difficult to infiltrate the venues in question, although they eventually developed an audacious tactic to inveigle their way onto rock bills, as Matt Sheldon explains: *'We didn't have enough money to record a proper demo tape so we'd turn up at venues wearing our stage clothes (as you did in those days) and then demanded to see the manager. Because we looked like a band, the manager would sometimes let us support some of the bigger bands without having heard what we sounded like.'* (Ref: Private communication, September 1999). By all accounts, this sly technique seems to have worked remarkably efficiently, although it wasn't long before VIRTUE were being invited to appear rather more legitimately.

At some point in 1985, the lads concluded that they could just about manage to scrape together enough cash to finance a (very) limited vinyl release. Tracks were laid down at Matinee Music in Reading and the band started to spread the word that a VIRTUE single was imminent. In fact, luck was on their side, as they played the tapes to a benevolent individual (who had only been approached to publicise the group's intentions in the first instance) who was so taken with the material that he decided to establish Other Records merely to be able to issue the record himself. The 7" duly appeared, was received rapturously by local fans, and soon gained airplay on a significant number of radio stations. A considerable quantity were sent out as promotional devices, and various companies indicated that they would be interested in hearing more from the youngsters. In particular, it's notable that none other than EMI took note of the group's activities, although it's hard to believe that they would have been groomed to become one of the label's major acts; they did, after all, already have IRON MAIDEN on their books! In the event, however, the material demoed for EMI failed to yield a deal, so it was back to earth with a bump for VIRTUE.

With the band's debut vinyl release shifting an impressive number of units from the outset, it's hardly surprising that the original issue of around five hundred copies (not all of which came with the picture sleeve, incidentally) was insufficient to meet public demand, and so a re-pressing was hastily organised by Other (later Metalother) a year later. With hindsight, it's quite fortunate that this occurred, otherwise collectors would probably be paying an extortionate price for this cracking item today! Towards the end of 1986, the outfit prepared the ground for their second release, the three track »Fool's Gold« EP, the latter scheduled to be issued by another local concern, Hatchet Records. Moving into 1987, however, it soon became apparent that things weren't going to plan on the »Fool's Gold« front. Delays, pressing problems, financial shortcomings and general cock-ups meant that the EP never actually received a proper release on vinyl. However, official cassette versions were circulated, with "Fool's Gold", "Hideaway" and "Seek And Destroy" (no, not that one) showing that the »We Stand To Fight« 7" wasn't a one-off, and that the talented musicians had plenty of similar material in their repertoire. In all honesty, "Fool's Gold" is perhaps a bit *too* close to "High Treason" for comfort, but the other two compositions are a tad more varied in their structures. It's a genuine tragedy that this release fell through, as I'm sure it would have consolidated the group's position as top-notch metal contenders to take over from once-popular outfits such as the faltering SAVAGE and CHARIOT.

VIRTUE were occasionally mentioned in the pages of 'Kerrang' over the years, with details being given concerning their vinyl intentions and proposed live appearances (most of which were local, although they made it down to London for the occasional performance at venues such as The Wellington), but I get the distinct impression that the musicians could possibly have done slightly more to promote themselves in order to glean the media attention they surely deserved. Mind you, it's not as if VIRTUE had a powerful or influential management company on their side, so it's all perfectly understandable. Following on from the disappointment of the »Fool's Gold« debacle, the band began to endure line-up changes (new bassist Bob Duffy was drafted in for a brief stint towards the end, before joining Lou Taylor's TOUR DE FORCE project, and subsequently moving on to minor acts such as KID WICKED), with the resultant instability causing a split in around 1988. The protagonists all soon went their separate ways, leaving little or no chance of reconciliation, which was a great pity, but never mind. Matt Sheldon gallantly shoulders much of the blame for VIRTUE's failure himself: *'It was all my fault, I didn't realise the band's potential at such a young age, I should have kept it going. I decided that Tudor wasn't a very good singer and managed to convince him to give up.'* (Ref: *ibid.*) If only you'd been ready in 1981, lads, you'd have been absolutely huge...

It wasn't the end of the story for the musicians involved, however, with guitarist Matt Sheldon going on to spend time in relatively minor groups such as TRANSMIT THIS and ROUNDHOUSE, before eventually reuniting with former VIRTUE colleague Boz Beast (aka Boz Bozlee) in the early 90's, whereupon the pair formed a brand-new, five-piece melodic rock proposition (with the assistance of vocalist Mazz Barclay, bassist Dan Cunningham and ex-ROUNDHOUSE drummer Pete Newdeck) called THE SHOCK. After early support slots with the likes of LILLIAN AXE and a couple of well-received demos, the outfit finally started to get some attention *via* their involvement with the Now And Then label, and a couple of CD releases (»Against The

World« and »Pinultimate«) have now been made available to the fans. With one-time VIRTUE bassist Bob Duffy (who, like drummer Pete Newdeck, additionally worked with none other than Paul Dianno in the 90's) also joining the ranks of THE SHOCK at one stage, we were getting tantalisingly close to a full-scale reunion of their original outfit, but things now seem to have cooled off somewhat, leaving the whole project in limbo for the time being. You just never know what might happen in the future, though, so keep your fingers crossed and VIRTUE might even get back together one of these days. Until a genuine reformation actually comes about, however, you could certainly do a lot worse than to check out THE SHOCK...

7" Singles
»We Stand To Fight« Other Records 1985

VOLTZ

Glen Leinster (v, g)
Mark Fisher (g)

Paul Hancock (b)
Gary Leinster (d)

Having emerged towards the end of 1979 from the ashes of a small-time act called AIRLINE, the embryonic incarnation of Hampshire's VOLTZ (featuring, in their very early days, second guitarist Rick Over, formerly of the imaginatively-named RICK OVER BAND) wasted little time before setting about the unenviable task of promoting themselves as dependable crowd-pleasers, initially as a glorified covers outfit. As time progressed, though, the slimmed-down unit started to write their own songs (which were, apparently, fairly typical of the primitive, hard'n'heavy NWOBHM style) and finally made a few attempts to get their name known to those who really mattered. The quartet's activities garnered regular mentions in the local press, and their first proper demo tape even received a limited amount of airplay on regional radio, so things looked quite promising for VOLTZ at that point. However, the musicians involved (for reasons best known to themselves) somehow reached the conclusion that things weren't working out too well, and so they elected to go their separate ways at the beginning of 1981. Although there was no additional activity on the VOLTZ front for much of the year, the nucleus of the Leinster brothers continued to work on the rudiments of the existing compositions and, after a while, eventually began penning newer, guitar-heavy material. Towards the end of the year, a version of VOLTZ was resurrected with an altered line-up, although it wasn't long before original members Mark Fisher and Paul Hancock returned to the fold to try their luck again. Feeling much happier as an ensemble with the fresh material, the outfit recorded a second demo in more of a sophisticated hard rock style than before, which was soon drawing the attention of various influential parties such as the local Airship Records concern.

After impressing Airship (also responsible for the likes of CHINATOWN, HIGH RISK and PARADYNE) with the depth and maturity of their recently-composed material, VOLTZ set about recording their debut album for the eclectic label by booking sessions at the nearby Chestnut facility (also frequented by bands such as TRUFFLE) and at Toucan Studios (with erstwhile member Rick Over helping out on the production side of things). The end result of this period of frenzied activity was the epic »Knight's Fall« album, released in the summer of 1982, and now regarded by many as one of the classic LP releases of the genre. Hard-hitting, heavy compositions with a respectful nod towards BLACK SABBATH and LED ZEPPELIN, particularly opener "After Armageddon" and the memorable "Badon Hill" (bringing forth comparisons with the likes of CRACKED MIRROR and QUARTZ), alternated with more reflective numbers such as "In A Dream", although both stylistic extremes were carried off with equal aplomb. In spite of a rather tepid review in 'Kerrang' (which tended to suggest that VOLTZ were a bit of a 70's-style anachronism with nothing to offer the modern fan), the album sold extremely well in local shops, and, thanks to several selections being given exposure on BBC Radio's rock programmes, the group soon developed a solid following. Indeed, their reputation swiftly grew to an extent whereby a handful of gigs in London became a possibility for the first time (the band supporting the likes of GRAND PRIX on such occasions), including productive trips to such well-attended venues as the Marquee and Hammersmith Clarendon.

Surprisingly, in addition to making quite an impact in the UK itself, a considerable quantity of VOLTZ albums had somehow made their way overseas within a matter of months, resulting in a significant level of interest being generated in mainland Europe, which culminated in a little-known French label called Amidisque taking the talented bunch under their wing. Following some rather protracted negotiations during 1983, both parties finally agreed on a recording contract which suited each other adequately, and it was soon all systems go for a second VOLTZ long-player. Things went swimmingly at first, and the quartet's supportive label stumped up the necessary cash for the lads to undertake recording sessions at several well-appointed studio facilities in the coming months. A handful of demos were laid down in due course, and VOLTZ soon had more than enough usable material to fill another LP. However, notwithstanding the fact that numerous studio visits had already been completed at quite considerable expense, and, despite the relevant observation that VOLTZ had recently played an incredibly well-received series of sold-out gigs at the City Rock club in Paris, Amidisque got cold feet for no particular reason and eventually backed out of the deal at short notice. The dejected outfit had little option but to pack their bags and return home, wondering exactly what had happened to their record deal.

Upon their subsequent return to England, it wasn't long before VOLTZ lost the services of disenchanted guitarist Mark Fisher, although the latter was rapidly replaced by new recruit

Graham Bushell, and the revised quartet were soon appearing in front of several hundred appreciative fans at the South Parade Pier in Portsmouth, having successfully reached the semi-finals of one of the countless 'Battle Of The Bands' competitions being organised throughout the country at the time. Within a matter of days, however, the ailing Glen Leinster was admitted to hospital, whereupon the singer underwent a much-postponed operation on his damaged vocal cords, something which forced the entire project to be placed on ice once more. This time, however, temporarily suspending their activities effectively signalled the end of the road for the luckless outfit, as the participants never really managed to get things going again properly after this enforced break. It was a great pity, and I've no doubt that the second VOLTZ LP would have been a worthy offering, so hopefully it'll be exhumed at some point in the future. Nowadays, Glen Leinster continues to pursue his musical interests at his own facility (Track Studio), and the frontman also collaborates with drummer Mike Payne and bassist Johnny Hatch in an occasional project entitled ZED, an act who even include a selection of unreleased VOLTZ originals in their live repertoire.

LP's
»Knight's Fall« Airship 1982

VOYAGER UK

Ivan Markovic (v)
Dave Thompson (g)
Paul Harkin (g)
Steve Holton (b)
Andy Wells (k)
Dave Wood (d)

I'm not entirely convinced that VOYAGER UK (the rather irksome 'UK' suffix presumably added to distance themselves from their namesakes in the MOR field) wasn't actually a government-funded initiative to remove unemployed ex-NWOBHM musicians from the streets of Yorkshire. Mind you, taking into account all of their previous credits, the collective talents of Andy Wells (VERITY), Dave Thompson (RHABSTALLION, VENTURE), Ivan Markovic (ARENA), Steve Holton (CYRKA), Dave 'DD' Wood (guest musician, a member of HARLEQUYN) and Paul Harkin (another guest, with no previous convictions, letting the side down a bit here) should certainly have been perfectly able to produce something special on vinyl. Originally formed as a small-time studio project by Wells and Thompson in 1986, the rapidly-developing ensemble subsequently expanded into a bona fide touring outfit (they didn't exactly break any records in terms of live appearances, though), and their lightweight brand of keyboard-soaked rock gradually began to win favour with a significant percentage of Yorkshire's rock community. Before long, the lads were turning their collective thoughts towards vinyl product (mainly as a promotional device) as opposed to demos, and raked together the cash (intriguingly, a local chain of pubs helped to sponsor the release) for a self-financed single.

VOYAGER UK's debut (issued in a generic, monochrome sleeve), to which many dealers tend to ascribe the incorrect date '1985', was more likely to have been from early 1987 (the group having recorded a four track demo tape shortly beforehand), although I suppose late 1986 is a remote possibility too. In any case, both "Run Away Heart" and "Don't Hold Back" were tuneful slices of rock/AOR crossover in the general vein of TUXEDO, MAMA'S BOYS or V8, with a pretty good vocal effort throughout. With increasing levels of popularity developing over the ensuing months, fuelled by local press and radio coverage, 1987 turned out to be a busy year for the lads, although personnel instability necessitated the eventual recruitment of a full-time drummer (Rick Smith) and successive stand-in bassists (Martin Barber and Paul Smith, the latter having recently parted company with BABY TUCKOO) in due course. Two compositions ("Don't Hold Back" and the otherwise-unreleased "Without Your Love") credited to the altered line-up were subsequently included on the not-quite-as-good-as-it-might-have-been »The Vinyl Frontier« sampler (compiled by the infamous Bailey Brothers), which also featured the likes of KOOGA and THE ALLIANCE. It probably gave the lads a minor boost at the time, but I reckon the album sold in such utterly pitiful quantities that few rock fans actually got to hear the material, which is a shame.

On the 28th of August 1987, VOYAGER UK were featured in session on the 'Friday Rock Show', showcasing "Razor's Edge", "Line Of Fire", "Rock This Town" and the ubiquitous "Don't Hold Back". These efforts were well up to their usual standard, and the session was warmly received by the show's listeners, so it looked good at that stage. Nevertheless, the project went down the tubes a year or so later, which is a familiar story for such melodic outfits of the day, their seniority having been usurped by markedly heavier and sleazier groups in the late 80's. Taking this into account, Ivan Markovic and Rick Smith eventually went on to establish the more forceful HARDLAND (from the ashes of an earlier outfit called FKM, which featured the original vocalist from local strugglers TUXEDO) in early 1990. The new group were another to be featured on the »Metal For Muthas '92« CD, with the track "Hammerfall" (!), the latter displaying a markedly heavier direction than had been the case in VOYAGER UK. As the CD-booklet helpfully explains, *'All members have been very much influenced by the late 70's/early 80's sound of twin-guitar bands and want to return to those sounds in the 90's, far away from the AOR and American bands that are dominating the music scene.'* Slightly ironic, perhaps, coming from the very same people who were only too keen to embrace the *'AOR/American sound'* only a few years previously, especially when Rick Smith permanently abandoned the notion of heavy music and hooked up with erstwhile colleague Dave Thompson in the unashamedly-melodic LOST WEEKEND concern a short time later…

7" Singles
»Run Away Heart« The Fighting Cock Records 1986?

Exclusive Compilation Appearances
"Without Your Love" on »The Vinyl Frontier« LP BB Records 1987

Compilation Appearances
"Don't Hold Back" on »The Vinyl Frontier« LP BB Records 1987

WARFARE

Evo (v, d)
Gunner (g)
Falken (b)

I suspect that few of you will be aware just how phenomenally popular Tyneside's uncompromising WARFARE actually were in their late 80's heyday, although it took them a few years to reach such incredible levels of adulation. To put the band's popularity into perspective, it's worth considering the fact that »A Conflict Of Hatred« is fairly well-established as Neat's best-selling album of all time in the global market, something which will doubtless shock a few VENOM and RAVEN fanatics. WARFARE itself represented the brainchild of Paul Evo, former drummer with THE BLOOD (and, in his youth, MAJOR ACCIDENT and the ANGELIC UPSTARTS), and the conspirators were officially first brought together in mid-1984, although embryonic versions of some of their original material had actually been laid down by the mainman even earlier. Within a remarkably short timescale after their *'official'* inception, the trio were offered a deal with Neat, and were soon assembling their introductory aural assault on a bewildered public, which came in the shape of the suitably-titled »Noise, Filth And Fury« EP, featuring such tender ditties as "Burn The Kings Road" and "The New Age Of Total Warfare". The rapid emergence of WARFARE very much mirrored the VENOM situation (obtaining a deal without going through the usual route of a properly-circulated demo tape and numerous small-time gigs), and their music bore more than a passing similarity, too, although there were also strong elements of TANK, MOTÖRHEAD and assorted punk heavyweights thrown into the melting pot. It certainly wasn't a typical NWOBHM sound, although WARFARE (and some of their musically-similar contemporaries such as ATOMKRAFT, DEEP SWITCH and ROGUE MALE) were clearly intent on pushing the boundaries of metal into considerably more brutal and lyrically-contentious territory.

The next release came in the form of a 12" EP based around a complete demolition of chart hit "Two Tribes", the original having been laid down by one of several acts (FRANKIE GOES TO HOLLYWOOD, in this case) for whom WARFARE developed an extremely healthy disrespect during the course of their career. Still, the record puzzled the reviewers and fans, who didn't know for sure if it was merely a joke (if so, it was vaguely funny for about a nanosecond) or a bona fide cover version. I'd say it was a lot closer to the former than the latter, to be honest. In fact, the release appeared to serve little purpose other than to pave the way for the outfit's full-length debut, which finally appeared towards the end of 1984 under another appropriate title of »Pure Filth«. With TANK's Algy Ward lending a hand at the production helm, the unsuspecting public were treated to a relentless aural barrage of almost unprecedented ferocity, with uncompromising, intense efforts such as "Let The Show Go On", "Limit Crescendo" and "Break Out" all setting out WARFARE's stall in no uncertain terms. It was, for the average rock aficionado, just too over-the-top to cope with, although many fans of VENOM and their ilk were soon drooling over this obdurate blur of noise and hatred. To be honest, it was basically the same basic formula repeated *ad infinitum*, although it's fair to say that WARFARE were hardly the only NWOBHM-era outfit to build an entire career upon just one or two novel ideas. It's worth noting that VENOM themselves even got in on the act on this occasion, lending their services to an unholy shambles called "Rose Petals Fall From Her Face", one of numerous WARFARE numbers (along with the likes of "Rape") which was to tackle the kind of subject matter which (rightly or wrongly) the vast majority of metal acts wouldn't have touched with a ten foot barge-pole.

The lads had a few tracks left over from these recording sessions, and soon saw a handful being released as the »Total Death« EP, whereupon they finally bowed to pressure and decided to give a few selected performances of their repertoire to some lucky audiences. It would be a gross understatement to say that WARFARE weren't exactly prolific in terms of live appearances, their much-anticipated gigs coming in ones or twos rather than in the form of lengthy treks around the country, although they played a handful of shows (in both the UK and Europe) to promote their first LP, with ATOMKRAFT's Ged Wolf helping out on drums in some instances, allowing frontman Evo to concentrate on his vocal delivery. The gigs were fairly well-received affairs in general, the band attracting an eclectic mixture of followers from the metal, punk and indie camps, although any reviews of such outings tended to refer to an impenetrable *'wall of noise'* rather than commenting objectively on the merits of individual numbers. Nevertheless, sales of the debut long-player had been sufficiently bounteous to warrant a follow-up, and so work duly began on the »Metal Anarchy« set later in the year. This time, none other than Sir Lemmy himself was to be found helping out in a production capacity, so it looks as though those WARFARE lads were particularly adept at winning over some fairly influential chums in the business. The LP emerged towards the end of 1985, and was practically a carbon copy of their debut album (the trio incorporating some slightly more varied and substantial riffs at times), with unyielding selections such as "Warfare", "Electric Mayhem" and the title track itself all maintaining the original level of intensity.

The outfit didn't exactly wear themselves out touring to promote the latest offering, deciding that they were more or less going to be a studio project from this point onwards. It hardly mattered, as their fans now seemed happy to buy everything that WARFARE could throw at them, and there appeared to be little chance of significantly expanding their following through live appearances. Surprisingly, they began work on their third album within a matter of months, although only half of the necessary studio work had been undertaken when disenchanted bassist Falken decided to part company with the outfit (he then quit the music business completely), leaving the remaining duo in a bit of a sticky situation with regard to the completion of their recording activities. In the event, they utilised VENOM stalwart Cronos as session bassist for a short while to get the album finished, but eventually took the bull by the horns and recruited new permanent member Zlaughter. With things back on track, it was time to make another pilgrimage to Europe, although it transpires that they only managed to play one solitary gig in Germany (which saw a short-tempered WARFARE baiting an inexplicably restive audience) before thinking better of it and returning to the relative safety of the UK. It was clear that the group were heading for imminent armageddon if they didn't buck up their ideas, and Neat seemed to be getting increasingly jittery about the behaviour of their most obstreperous act. WARFARE's next publicity stunt, meanwhile, was to play an impromptu *'open air'* gig on the back of a truck, which they confrontationally parked outside the Hammersmith Odeon during a METALLICA (another outfit whom they appear to have held in particular contempt) concert, before being cordially invited to accompany a couple of members of Her Majesty's constabulary to their nearby nick.

At this point, their sensible label appears to have made attempts to defuse a rapidly-escalating situation, and more or less put a stop to WARFARE's relentless programme of hellraising, delaying the release of their next album until at least the end of the year. After allowing things to cool off, Neat must have been praying that the lads had finally composed themselves and that the long-player would be an entirely trouble-free release. Oh dear. True to form, WARFARE elected to call their third LP »Mayhem F**kin Mayhem«, a pointlessly offensive and obnoxious title which, predictably, ran into serious trouble immediately. There were suggestions that the sleeves would have to be housed within outer covers or censored by hand, but the band ultimately capitulated to pressure from the industry (in view of assurances that many retailers would refuse to handle it) to redesign the sleeve layout and pretty much censor the title themselves. With the record finally hitting the shops at the beginning of 1987, the fans and reviewers were soon being given the opportunity to see if WARFARE had managed to progress in any sense whatsoever. Unsurprisingly, it was still much the same as before, with such titles as "Projectile Vomit" and "Atomic Slut" (muscling in on MENTORS territory, perhaps) giving ample advance indication that there probably weren't any soppy ballads included on the latest offering. Still, the likes of "Ebony Dreams" clearly hinted at a slightly more ambitious level of songwriting, and the album also contained another knockabout *'cover version'*, a typically-raucous interpretation of "You Really Got Me" by the KINKS. It seemed to be a *'love it or hate it'* release for the journalists of the day, most of whom adhered to the latter philosophy, with one notable exception being a glowing review from 'Metal Forces'. Predictably, the fans all bought the record anyway.

In the wake of the new album's release (and the inevitable hectic touring schedule of no gigs whatsoever), the group were once again left to their own devices, and few clues as to their future intentions were gleaned for the best part of six months, whereupon WARFARE eventually resurfaced with a cunning plan to gain a further bit of notoriety. Their grand idea was to record a brand-new single, their latest target of vilification being ROBERT PALMER's "Addicted To Love", which they would ruthlessly destroy by reworking the song's chorus as *'addicted to drugs'* (my, how witty) and waiting for some manner of public outcry. Clearly, they hadn't yet given up their aspirations of getting up as many noses as possible. In the event, however, they didn't get much of a chance to offend any sensibilities, as the lawyers descended almost immediately, citing defamation and copyright infringement as very good reasons why the release shouldn't go ahead. The band then attempted to get the single out by offering to retitle the offending number "Addicted (Mayhem Mix)", but it didn't wash. Eventually, the release was cancelled for good, the only legacy being (supposedly) ten test pressings, none of which have ever come up for sale, as far as I'm aware, although 'Metal Forces' gave one away as a competition prize sometime afterwards. In any case, it would appear that the tracks from this aborted release (the B-side was a live version of "Hungry Dogs") later appeared officially, originally on an extremely limited cassette-only release entitled »Annihilation Anaesthetized« (which the outfit compiled in 1989 to commemorate their fifth anniversary), and were then scheduled to appear (although I can't confirm that they actually did) as bonus selections on the CD version of their »A Conflict Of Hatred« album.

In the immediate aftermath of the »Addicted« debacle, the lads kept even more of a low profile than usual, but eventually returned to the studio later in the year, since they already had a few ideas for yet another album. This time, WARFARE appeared to be brimming with confidence (after all, sales of their last long-player had been extremely healthy), and were now of the opinion that they could branch out into a more ambitious style without a catastrophic loss of popularity. They brought in a session player, Lazer, to contribute a few strategically-placed keyboard passages, and this period of experimentation turned out to be so successful that the lucky individual was retained as a permanent fixture thereafter. Further major surprises were in store when various members from more mainstream acts (including regional lightweights LINDISFARNE) were invited to appear as honoured guests, leading to some intriguing contributions from folky female backing singers, acoustic sections and even the odd appearance from the dreaded saxophone. The album (»A Conflict Of Hatred«) materialised in the early months of 1988, and came as a surprise to those who had originally painted WARFARE as nothing more than talentless throwbacks to the punk scene. Their newer material was considerably more accomplished than before, and both the general musicianship and songwriting ability had come on in leaps and bounds, although there were still frenzied numbers such as "Deathcharge" and "Fatal Vision" to keep the thrashers happy. As stated at the outset, this album was a staggering success, no doubt related to the fact that WARFARE seemed to be fitting in perfectly with the late 80's thrash/hardcore scene (some of their musical allies now including BOMB DISNEYLAND, ENERGETIC KRUSHER and DEVIATED INSTINCT), the increasingly-accepted band no longer being the despised janissaries who were originally hellbent on shaking up the world of heavy music.

The lads promoted their latest LP with their first session for the 'Friday Rock Show', where (assisted temporarily by Algy Ward on keyboards) they ran through versions of "Burn Down The King's Road", "Ebony Dreams", "Revolution" and "Deathcharge" for the delectation of the station's listeners. Happily, the session (transmitted on the 8th of April 1988) turned out to be a fairly warmly-received broadcast, and the whole thing can now be found on the »Radio Hell« CD, issued in 1992. Next up was a gig or two (literally), one of which was in support of TESTAMENT, although this marked the end of WARFARE's activities for quite some time (the fans were treated to a video, »A Concept Of Hatred«, to go along with the album), as they then conceived an extremely grand notion which was ultimately to spell disaster for the hapless outfit. WARFARE parted company with Neat in 1989, and were soon talking to Hammer Film Music (Evo being a huge fan of classic horror movies) about the prospect of collaborating on a musical celebration of the studio's first forty years in the film-making business. This took a while to come about, but contracts were eventually signed, and the group began committing their musical interpretation of a variety of film titles to tape. Promotional examples of the new WARFARE album (»Hammer Horror«) were being handed out at the end of the year as originally planned, although most commercial copies didn't actually make it into circulation until the early part of 1990, something which seemed to defeat the whole object of the exercise, but never mind.

In spite of this minor drawback, the musicians seemed to be extraordinarily happy with the results, and were just as content with the fact that they had been afforded the opportunity to contribute to an ambitious project which also featured the voices of some of their screen idols (most notably, Christopher Lee and Peter Cushing) from time to time. It certainly showed another side to the ensemble (not necessarily one that their fans wanted to see, though), but it was hardly a *bona fide* WARFARE release at all. This was basically a soundtrack album, incidental music for an atmospheric horror film which would never see the light of day. It was a labour of love for the members of the outfit, but people were less-than-impressed with the end result. Sales of »Hammer Horror« (which had surfaced on the FM label) turned out to be understandably poor, and there was no denying the fact that the fans were now turning their backs on WARFARE, given that they seemed to be moving wholesale into the world of film scores. Nevertheless, the group had already played a grand one-off London show (at the Hippodrome) to promote the release, which turned out to be quite a well-attended affair, although the public were soon expressing the general opinion that the lads should now call it a day. Long-standing guitarist Gunner seemed to feel that these criticisms were entirely justified, and quit the project soon after, leaving the remaining members with little option to bring in a temporary replacement once more.

This time, it was a certain JJ Dunn (aka Mantas from VENOM) who stepped in to help out in the live environment, although things were rapidly sliding downhill by this stage. An extensive nationwide tour with CRONOS was scheduled for the early months of 1991, which must have come as a shock for many followers of this notoriously-reluctant touring concern, although few of the scheduled gigs appear to have gone ahead as planned. Still, one of the band's recently-recorded shows was subsequently released in the form of the »Deathcharge« album for the small RKT label, but sales were modest, and there seemed to be little sustainable interest by this stage. Tentative plans were then outlined to deliver a second long-player for Hammer Film Music at some point in 1992, although the members of WARFARE must have come to terms with the futility of releasing another record that no-one would buy, leading to the venture being shelved and the group as a whole being laid to rest shortly thereafter. Evo took a couple of years away from the music scene before forming his WARHEAD offshoot, where he collaborated with a couple of very familiar characters (Algy Ward from TANK and Würzel from MOTÖRHEAD) on some pretty hefty material, eventually recording some finished product for the Communiqué label. Since then, things have been all quiet on the Evo front, but I somehow doubt that there will be a WARFARE reunion in the foreseeable future.

LP's

»Pure Filth« Neat 1984
[UK issue in black sleeve, some with free single featuring "This Machine Kills" and "Burn The King's Road"]
»Pure Filth« Roadrunner 1984
[Dutch issue in red sleeve with two extra tracks]
»Pure Filth« Banzai 1984
[Canadian issue with free »Two Tribes« 12"]
»Metal Anarchy« Neat 1985
»Mayhem F••kin Mayhem« Neat 1987

[Cassette version contains exclusive extra track "F.A.I.T.S."]
»A Conflict Of Hatred« Neat 1988
»Hammer Horror« FM Records 1989
»Deathcharge« RKT Records 1991
[Live album]

12" EP's
»Two Tribes« Neat 1984
[All three tracks non-LP]
»Total Death« Neat 1985
["Burning Up", "Rape" and "Destroy" all non-LP]

7" EP's
»Noise, Filth And Fury« Neat 1984
[Both "Burn The King's Road" and "The New Age Of Total Warfare" non-LP]

7" Singles
»This Machine Kills« Neat 1984
[Given away free with some copies of »Pure Filth« album, both tracks non-LP]

Promotional Releases
»Addicted To Drugs« Neat 1987
[7" single, B-side live version of "Hungry Dogs", white label promo copies only, general release cancelled]

CD's
»A Conflict Of Hatred« Neat 1988
[With two extra tracks]
»Hammer Horror« FM Records 1989
[Original issue]
»Deathcharge« RKT Records 1991
[Live release]
»Crescendo Of Reflexions« Kraze 1992
[Compilation release]
»Decade Of Decibels« Bleeding Hearts 1993
[Compilation release]
»Hammer Horror« Silva Screen 1993
[Re-recorded version with one extra track]

Compilation Appearances
"Burn The King's Road" on »The Best Of British« LP Zebra 1985 + »Metal Killers Kollection II« Do-LP Castle Communications 1986
"Metal Anarchy" on »Powertrax« Cassette Neat 1986 + »A Rather Nasty Dream« LP RKT Records 1989 + »Heavy Metal Collection 4« CD X-Tra Collection 1993
"Deathcharge" on »Radio Hell« CD Raw Fruit 1992
[Different to album version]
"Burn The King's Road" on »Radio Hell« CD Raw Fruit 1992
[Different to single version]
"Ebony Dreams" on »Radio Hell« CD Raw Fruit 1992
[Different to album version]
"Revolution" on »Radio Hell« CD Raw Fruit 1992
[Different to album version]
"Hammer Horror" on »The Metal Box« 3-CD Box Castle Communications 1993
"Fatal Vision" on »Metal Masters« 4-CD Box Castle Communications 1993 + »Metal Mania« CD Castle Communications 1994

WAR MACHINE

Bernadette Mooney (v)
Steve White (g)
Lez Fry (b)
Brian Waugh (d)

Tyneside's WAR MACHINE were one of the later additions to Neat's roster, although it transpires that the original version of the outfit was initially conceived by ex-ATOMKRAFT guitarist Steve White as far back as 1983. Talented frontwoman Bern Mooney and bassist Lez Fry (neither of whom were particularly well-known, admittedly) were recruited at a fairly early stage, although the ever-evolving outfit were to try out numerous long-forgotten drummers in their formative days before the youthful Brian Waugh (who shouldn't be confused with his namesake from HEAVY PETTIN) was eventually drafted in to complete a stable line-up at some point in 1985. Their lucrative deal with the local Neat concern seems to have followed as a matter of course, at a time when the label was branching out into signing a range of more mainstream acts (SHE, STATETROOPER etc.) as well as promoting the likes of ATOMKRAFT, WARFARE and their semi-thrashy cohorts. Mind you, WAR MACHINE were undoubtedly more closely affiliated with the latter division, offering a substantial brand of metal which was, in all honesty, significantly more powerful than that delivered by most of the UK's other female-fronted bands of the era.

Their debut album, the »Unknown Soldier« effort from 1986 (featuring several compositions which dated right back to the quartet's inception), was, undeniably, an individualistic and capable affair, although there were, in terms of Bern Mooney's vocal characteristics, minor similarities to the likes of SIEGE and SATANIC RITES. The band impress with their heavy, technical riffing (even vaguely reminiscent of the mighty WATCHTOWER on occasion), and a couple of tracks feature some pretty flashy guitar work in places, so it would appear that the group were supremely confident of their collective abilities. Having said all that, WAR MACHINE elected to play their trump card right at the outset viz. the excellent "Sacred Hold", a memorable number which outshines everything else on the LP by quite a long way. Nevertheless, strong inclusions such as "On The Edge" and "The Power" (a demo version of which had earlier featured on Neat's »Powertrax« cassette sampler) are highly listenable selections, bringing to mind the likes of PROWLER and DEALER, although not quite as intense as either of these acts. Sadly, the musicians appear to run out of innovative ideas pretty quickly, and side two, which often sees the unit operating in similar territory to WARLOCK or ZED YAGO, is fairly repetitive.

WAR MACHINE appear to have been a relatively unsuccessful act in terms of sales (it's yet another of those releases which probably failed to capture the hearts of the British public), and their label seems to have been reluctant to commission a follow-up. The outfit lay low for a year or two, but returned with a three track demo in 1988, featuring "Storm Warning", "Gun Metal Sky" and "The Chain", although it wasn't long before vocalist Bern Mooney and stand-in drummer Chris Buggy were to depart for pastures new. A decent replacement for the latter was swiftly located in the shape of Mark Savage, although their efforts to recruit a suitable new vocalist met with repeated failure. The final straw seems to have come with Savage's increasing level of active involvement with the MANTAS project (he later moved on to local rockers XLR8R), which limited the amount of time he could devote to WAR MACHINE. By the end of the decade, it was all over, although band mainman Steve White still managed one last piece of glory with a brief stint in the ranks of the declining VENOM in the early 90's.

LP's
»Unknown Soldier« Neat 1986/Roadrunner 1986
[UK/Dutch issue]

Compilation Appearances
"The Power" on »Powertrax« Cassette Neat 1986 + »Heavy Metal Collection 1« CD X-Tra Collection 1993
[Different to album version]
"No Place To Hide" on »Heavy Metal Collection 3« CD X-Tra Collection 1993
"Dangerous" on »Heavy Metal Collection 4« CD X-Tra Collection 1993
"On The Edge" on »Metal Masters« 4-CD Box Castle Communications 1993

WARRIOR (I)

Clive Murray (v)
Dave Cooper (g)
Steve Birley (rg)
Gary Pinning (b)
Sev Lewkowicz (k)
Paul Humfrays (d)

There seems, during the early 80's, to have been a little-known English by-law which stated that every town with a population of over fifty thousand inhabitants was legally required to play host to metal outfits called WARRIOR, LEGEND, RAW DEAL, ROUGH JUSTICE and, if at all possible, PROWLER. Fortunately for the sanity of modern-day collectors, relatively few of these no-hopers ever made it out of their local pub, but serious NWOBHM aficionados will already be familiar with three or four British versions of WARRIOR (*vide infra*) who either contrived to get their own vinyl product into the shops or appeared on compilation albums (there was one on »New Electric Warriors«, for example) at around the turn of the decade. Just to confuse matters even further, though, along comes yet another variant (probably not the last, either), this time from the general Hampshire/West Sussex area. Unlike their contemporaries from elsewhere in the land, however, this particular WARRIOR managed to release a full-length effort (on the tiny Goodwood label), which was quite an achievement in the heady days of 1980. Mind you, we're certainly not talking prime-era NWOBHM here, in spite of the observation that many dealers attempt to pass it off as such.

In fact, the majority of tracks comprising the outfit's »Troublemaker« LP are fairly unremarkable, boogie-type workouts and occasional SLEDGEHAMMER/VARDIS hybrids, although there's also a rather embarrassing tendency to drift into a sub-EAGLES brand of MOR at times, notably on the depressing (in more ways than one) "Isn't Life Lonely", "Can't Stop Crying" and "Through For You" (hey, get over it man, she probably wasn't worth it). The highlights, such as they are, come in the shape of "Stay Away", "Give Me Your Love" and the title track itself, where the guys rock out a bit more, although the sky-high asking price for this (admittedly very scarce) piece of vinyl is extremely difficult to justify on the basis of musical merit alone. It would appear that the record sold in fairly limited quantities (it wasn't a particularly extensive pressing in the first instance) upon its release, and the WARRIOR quest for global domination

707

seems to have come to a grinding halt shortly thereafter. Their album's cover is certainly worthy of mention, however, where five of the participants (their occasional keyboard player, Sev Lewkowicz, who also contributed to the first ANGEL WITCH long-player, isn't pictured) are portrayed as 'rough boys from the wrong side of town', posing in an insalubrious doorway clutching a variety of makeshift 'weapons' including a pitifully small pen-knife and a broken bottle. Laughable.

LP's
»Troublemaker« Goodwood Music 1980

WARRIOR (II)

Dave Hewitt (v)
Steve Allsopp (g)
Mick Bannister (rg)
Kev Barsby (b)
Barry Bingham (d)

As far as the heavyweight acts mentioned in this particular book are concerned, I reckon the outfit who landed themselves with the heroic WARRIOR identity in the first instance were the Derbyshire band, a musical force which had initially gravitated together as long ago as 1977. As was the case with many of their downtrodden, hard-rocking contemporaries of the period, their own music had practically nothing in common with the snotty punk upstarts who were attracting so much media attention at the time, the members electing instead to build upon the basis of an unassuming brand of 70's-influenced material with elements of blues and prog rock. In fact, WARRIOR's overall direction was considerably closer to guitar-heavy outfits such as STRAY, WISHBONE ASH or DIRTY TRICKS than anything more typical of the NWOBHM era. Nevertheless, they were still able to work their way up from humble pub roots to headlining appearances in front of several hundred fans in their early 80's heyday, cultivating an enviable reputation as crowd-pleasers in the process. Even so, the lads failed to be picked up by any of the major (or minor) labels in the immediate wake of the NWOBHM explosion, and there seemed to be little chance of getting any vinyl into the shops at this stage.

By the spring of 1980, however, it had finally dawned on the group that they would be perfectly capable of issuing their own private record, as so many other outfits were doing at the time.

In WARRIOR's case, however, their collective finances actually stretched to a full album rather than the obligatory 7" single. Still, it turned out to be an extremely modest pressing of just five hundred copies, a quantity which turned out to be more or less sufficient to meet local demand. Recorded at Rainbow Studios in Nottingham, their eight track effort (»Let Battle Commence«) featured a selection of lengthy compositions with a great deal of emphasis on guitar technique (the comparatively sparse sound being only marginally affiliated with the brusque archetype of the NWOBHM movement), although there are, nevertheless, distinct similarities to the vinyl offerings of CRACKED MIRROR, VOLTZ and PHOENIX RISING, for example. The debut long-player was very much a self-produced (in more ways than one) affair, as Dave Hewitt later explained: 'I actually designed the cover myself while I was at work. I was employed as a bookkeeper at the time, and if the bosses had found out about it, I would have been kicked out straight away. We financed the whole thing ourselves, using the savings from our gigs and with money borrowed from our families. We had no idea how to go about getting a deal, we were totally naive!' (Ref: Interview, Matthias Mader, July 1996). Inevitably, the sheer scarcity of the WARRIOR record would, in later years, lead to many completists seeking to add it to their collection, merely on the basis of it being a rare rock LP. In due course, the price shot up dramatically as a few NWOBHM aficionados were ensnared by stories of this lost 'classic' of the genre. In all honesty, it's quite an average effort (perfectly adequate as a traditional rock album, but not a NWOBHM monster), and hardly justifies its three-figure price tag.

Aside from the fact that they had issued a private record, there was little to connect WARRIOR with the youthful energy of many of their NWOBHM counterparts, although there was a general tendency to spout the usual lyrical twaddle about battles and so forth. In the midst of this quagmire of clichés, however, came a notable exception in "Ulster, Bloody Ulster", an impassioned inclusion which concerned the political unrest and paramilitary activities taking place throughout Northern Ireland, a theme more commonly associated with punk outfits of the time. Hewitt was later allowed to elaborate on this number: 'That was a political song. My cousin had been shot at and wounded in Belfast, several years before we'd recorded our album. I got the impression that both the press and the man in the street had become disinterested in the bloody civil war that was ongoing in Northern Ireland. I firmly believed at the time, and still do, that the opinions of songwriters were being suppressed, and so I didn't think it was out of place for me to vent my anger in this way. Perhaps I was writing in a semi-punk style, since I was listening to a lot of punk music at the time.' (Ref: ibid.) Conclusive evidence that certain rock musicians actually have a bit more grey matter than they're usually given credit for, I'd say.

The album failed to turn WARRIOR into superstars overnight, and the group persevered only until 1981 (at which point both Steve Allsopp and Mick Bannister had to move away from the area due to professional commitments), having sold a limited number of records at gigs around the Midlands. After the band finally splintered, Kev Barsby and Dave Hewitt hooked up with guitarist Chris Cuttriss and drummer Mark Newman, whereupon they formed a short-lived outfit called AXIS (not to be confused with various namesakes who made it to the vinyl stage). Sadly, however, this promising venture came to an abrupt end in 1982, when poor old Dave Hewitt suffered a nervous breakdown at a regional show, an experience which proved to be so distressing that the frontman later swore that he would never again have anything to do with the music business. In fact, Hewitt kept his word for an entire decade, although he was finally coaxed back into the rock world, taking his place (this time as bassist) at the helm of a local outfit called STORMWATCH. In 1996, the act signed to Vinyl Tap Records (the label having already reissued WARRIOR's long-lost album on CD a couple of years previously) and delivered a very decent selection of traditional power metal entitled »Patriot« soon afterwards. As far as I'm aware, STORMWATCH remain a going concern (although Dave Hewitt and guitarist Ron Reynolds are apparently deputising in the LUTHER BELTZ WITCHFYNDE project at the time of writing), delighting a brand-new generation of fans who have absolutely no inkling of the bassist's long-forgotten musical past.

LP's
»Let Battle Commence« Rainbow Sound 1980

CD's
»Let Battle Commence« Vinyl Tap Records 1994

Compilation Appearances
"Yesterday's Hero" on »NWOBHM Vol.4« Bootleg CD 1992
"Invaders" on »Noise Level Critical« CD Hallmark 1997

WARRIOR (III)

Roy Metté (v, g)
Martin Jones (b)
Steve Halford (d)

Blissfully unaware of the fact that numerous heavy namesakes were doing their own thing throughout Britain at the time, the Essex version of WARRIOR were yet another of those late 70's concerns who, rather fortuitously, got to the vinyl stage at more or less the height of the NWOBHM explosion. In fact, the threesome were very much in the right place at the right time, and benefitted indirectly from a government grant which had been issued by the Department Of Education And Science (!) shortly beforehand. This facilitated projects such as the founding of the local Rambert Records concern, and WARRIOR became one of the very first acts (and pretty much the only heavy bunch, given that Rambert tended to sponsor mainstream hopefuls in years to come) to be offered the chance to record for this newly-established label via the so-called 'Make it Yourself' initiative (see also the obscure MADE IN ENGLAND single on Gargoyle, for example). The lads took full advantage of this piece of serendipity, and duly laid down the tracks "Don't Let It Show", "Silver Lady" and "The Lord's Prayer" for release as an EP. Unusually, however, they chose to issue it on the uncommon 10" format, something which appears to have been shared only by FIRECLOWN in the NWOBHM genre.

This particular WARRIOR were, quite clearly, only operating on the periphery of the NWOBHM style, having more in common with raunchy, guitar-based rockers such as SLENDER THREAD, FULL MOON and STREET LEGAL, all of whom were considerably closer to heavy 70's acts than anything that was coming out of the woodwork at the height of the new metal explosion. Nevertheless, their three-tracker was a very competent release which showcased some heavy, catchy riffing, and this would certainly appeal to fans of the aforementioned outfits, although the asking price is currently staggeringly high. It's a rare record, admittedly, especially with the coveted (but generic) picture sleeve, but, with several unsold copies having been extracted from the band members over the past few years, I think it's about time the price started coming down to more realistic levels. It's quite fortunate that most of the groups who adopted the WARRIOR moniker were fairly unambitious, amateur-hour outfits, or things

709

might have become a bit messy when they all started vying for national acclaim. As with their relatively unsuccessful South Coast and Derbyshire namesakes, however, I reckon the Essex version had abandoned all hope of world domination after just one vinyl release, and none of the musicians involved seem to have maintained any role of note in the business thereafter.

10" EP's
»Don't Let It Show« Rambert Records 1980

Compilation Appearances
"Don't Let It Show" on »NWOBHM Vol.8« Bootleg CD 1996

WARRIOR (IV)

Eddy Smith (v)
Dave Hall (g)
Tony Watson (rg)
Barry 'Baz' Smith (b)
Rob Mills (d)

Possibly the best-known of the four bands called WARRIOR to be featured in this book (none of whom should be confused with the minor Lancashire outfit who were featured on the »New Electric Warriors« compilation), the Tyneside version were probably the last to establish themselves on the scene, as there's little or no evidence to suggest that they were active prior to 1980. The quintet first came to prominence the following year, when their "Flying High" was included on Neat's »Lead Weight« compilation, although this unspectacular offering (lying somewhere between BLACKWYCH and the TYGERS OF PAN TANG at their most formulaic) failed to shine particularly brightly. Nevertheless, Neat still identified some sort of potential in WARRIOR, and encouraged the lads to release a three track 7" (a great fuss was made of the fact that the featured material was recorded live in the studio) in 1982, by which time their original guitarist Dave Hall had been replaced by new recruit Dave Dawson. The EP, titled »Dead When It Comes To Love«, saw a marked improvement in the group's songwriting ability, with the energetic title track having more of a HIGH TREASON feel to it, while "Stab You In The Back" and "Kansas City" were more along the lines of SABRE. This line-up, incidentally, also contributed an alternate version of "Kansas City" to Neat's »60 Minutes Plus« compilation, and recorded an official live tape entitled »Live In A Dive«, which featured a selection of stage favourites such as "Addiction", "Troops" and the laughably-titled "Rock'n'Roll Rockstar".

In the wake of this early patronage from Neat, however, the outfit soon severed all ties with the label and elected to go it alone, recording new material sporadically and releasing their own vinyl as and when they managed to accumulate the finances required. The first of these offerings didn't surface until mid-1983, though, by which time the unstable ensemble had undergone something of a radical reconstruction, with only Tony Watson and Dave Dawson now remaining from the previous line-up. Joining them were new bassist Steve Telford, gravel-throated vocalist Eddie Halliday and erstwhile RAVEN/SATAN drummer Sean Taylor, who was merely acting in a guest capacity. The revised WARRIOR issued a five track mini-LP (in an extremely heroic-looking sleeve with an image of a warrior's helmet) entitled »For Europe Only« (strange, as it was available pretty much everywhere else thanks to a Bullet/Neon distribution), featuring reworked versions of "Flying High" and "Kansas City", plus a trio of live favourites in the form of "Prisoner", "Suicide" and "Warrior", the latter being a very lengthy effort with a SHADER-style drum solo (and a rather long one, at that) for no particular reason. It didn't, however, constitute a staggeringly successful release (for one thing, it was marred by an amateurish production), and WARRIOR's continued lack of press attention proved to be something of a setback in their quest for global domination. Nevertheless, the musicians continued to tour extensively, offering a wide range of merchandise to their fans, and they were considerate enough to keep the public informed of their future intentions (via a series of official newsletters) along the way.

It's apparent that WARRIOR attracted a fair bit of record company interest in their time, but it looks as though the offers repeatedly failed to match up to their expectations, and so the band elected to proceed with their plan of campaign as originally scheduled. They fully intended to issue a four track EP before the end of 1983 (by which time they had brought in yet another singer, Martin Clerkin, plus new bassist Paul Irwin), supposedly in a pressing of several thousand copies (anticipating a huge demand, obviously), but this never emerged in its intended form. Instead, a three-tracker was prepared for release in the early months of 1984, featuring guest drums courtesy of Malcolm (or could it have been TYGERS OF PAN TANG stalwart Brian?) Dick. In the event, it looks as though they might have run out of money, as the pressing was severely limited (only a few hundred copies), with hardly any examples actually making it as far as the shops. Anyway, the record (issued in the kind of cheaply-printed, cut-out sleeve which had housed their Neat 7") featured "Breakout", "Dragon Slayer" and "Take Your Chance", tracks which saw WARRIOR moving into a slightly more epic style of metal, their high-range vocalist bringing forth a few comparisons with JUDAS PRIEST, GRIM REAPER, MITHRANDIR and Kent's LEGEND. The three-tracker suffered from another immensely unflattering production, however, and the musicians evidently decided to withdraw it from sale at a pretty early stage, regarding it as doing them a disservice, given that it was supposedly a sampler for their forthcoming album, which had already been given the working title of »Invasion Imminent«. With so few copies making it into circulation, therefore, it's hardly surprising that the »Breakout« EP constitutes WARRIOR's most scarce and highly-valued release.

The full-length WARRIOR album was scheduled to surface in the second half of 1984, with all of the relevant material having already been written well in advance. It would appear that the set was indeed recorded as planned, and rough tapes were touted around various labels in an attempt to get a last-minute deal. With little or no interest being shown, however, the musicians investigated the possibility of financing the release themselves. Unfortunately, they soon discovered that albums cost a lot more to produce than singles, and it would appear that this enterprise proved way beyond their means. Before long, the valiant members of WARRIOR decided that they were fighting a losing battle (I'm sure I haven't included quite as many belligerent phrases as I could have, so be thankful for that), and eventually laid down their swords for good (oh dear, another one sneaked in at the end), probably even before the year was out. Martin Clerkin went on to have a fleeting involvement with FAST KUTZ, incidentally, but he was soon out on his ear once his new employers discovered the full extent of his vocal limitations. Similarly, bassist Paul Irwin's stint with the restructuring TYGERS OF PAN TANG towards the end of 1984 appears to have been an equivalently short-lived arrangement.

Mini-LP's
»For Europe Only« Warrior 1983

7" EP's
»Dead When It Comes To Love« Neat 1982
["Kansas City" different to mini-LP version]

»Breakout« Warrior 1984

Compilation Appearances
"Flying High" on »Lead Weight« LP Neat 1981/CD Teichiku 1992
[Different to mini-LP version]
"Kansas City" on »60 Minutes Plus« Cassette Neat 1982/CD Teichiku 1992 + »All Hell Let Loose« LP Neat 1983
[Different to mini-LP or 7" version]
"Dragon Slayer" on »NWOBHM Vol.5« Bootleg CD 1992

WEAPON

Danny Hynes (v)
Jeff Summers (g)
Barry Downes (b)
Bruce Bisland (d)

For an outfit who were only around for a couple of years in the first instance, and who didn't exactly go overboard in terms of vinyl releases, it's remarkable how much of a legacy the London-based quartet known as WEAPON seem to have bequeathed to the metal world. Their name is instantly recognised by an extremely high percentage of NWOBHM enthusiasts, and they were honoured by their notable inclusion on Lars Ulrich's commemorative album in 1990, so they somehow appear to have made a significant impact on a great many individuals! The venture first came together at around the turn of the decade (originally operating under the shockingly-bad moniker of FAST RELIEF), the group consisting of certain characters who had featured in various 70's acts of, er, *varying* credibility (bassist Barry Downes, for instance, came from the not-remotely-interesting HAWKWIND offshoot INNER CITY UNIT) in their ranks. Vocalist Danny Hynes, meanwhile, was an Irish import who had settled in the English capital some time previously, whereas talented guitarist Jeff Summers was a wily individual (with no major skeletons in his closet) who used his handy contacts in the music business (notably his brother Steve, a one-time member of the long-forgotten pop/rock ensemble LIP SERVICE) to locate a suitable drummer (Bruce Bisland), who had played alongside Steve Summers in the aforementioned no-hopers. It was all systems go...

A prudent name change to WEAPON occurred at a mercifully early stage, after which the newly-christened group enjoyed an enviably rapid rise to prominence following a relatively modest series of club appearances in the capital. In due course, the ensemble became affiliated with Virgin Publishing (although they didn't actually sign to the Virgin label itself), and the lads were fortunate to be selected to open for MOTÖRHEAD on their UK tour towards the end of the year. Most of these shows were, by all accounts, wildly successful affairs, and the release of the outfit's vinyl debut was timed to coincide with this series of appearances, as Bruce Bisland explained: *'It was released just in time for the tour. Virgin were merely the publishers, so we brought the single and 12" out on our own label. After the tour, we were hoping to sign with a major, well that was the plan.'* (Ref: Interview, Matthias Mader, March 1996). WEAPON's privately-issued single (with a fairly widespread distribution, admittedly) coupled "It's A Mad Mad World" and "Set The Stage Alight" (the latter being the selection featured on »NWOBHM '79 Revisited« a decade later), two eminently listenable, mid-tempo rockers ("Set The Stage Alight", the designated B-side, was actually the more energetic and enjoyable effort) in the general style of SAPPHIRE, BLACK AXE or LE GRIFFE, and it was a debut which should have set the stage (as it were) for a long and healthy career in the wacky world of rock.

It remains something of a mystery as to why WEAPON chose to release their single in both 12" and 7" forms, though, as both formats (issued in identical and unremarkable picture sleeves) feature exactly the same versions of both songs, and it's also particularly ludicrous that the 12" edition is now regarded as considerably more valuable and collectable than its diminutive counterpart! In spite of their auspicious start, however, WEAPON contrived to burn themselves out almost as rapidly as they had exploded onto the scene, and no further tracks ever made it to vinyl. It's a pity, as they demoed some highly capable material (such as "Liar", "Midnight Satisfaction", "One Night Stand" and "Take That Bottle Away"), and also tried out a different line-up in the second half of 1981 after recruiting second guitarist Rob Angelo (from PRAYING MANTIS) and new drummer Jon Phillips. Their efforts to salvage the situation were ultimately unsuccessful, though, and the receivers were called in before the year was out. In the aftermath of WEAPON's collapse (which occurred at truly breakneck speed), the participants redistributed themselves, with Bisland and Summers ending up in the newly-formed WILDFIRE (see separate entry), while Angelo retreated to the clubs with various small-time, bluesy outfits, before recording a couple of albums as a solo artist many years later. There seemed to be no chance whatsoever that WEAPON would return.

It came as something of a surprise, therefore, when rumours of a possible WEAPON reunion began circulating out of the blue in the spring of 1984. Nevertheless, it was all true enough, and much was duly made in the press of this unforeseen reformation, spearheaded by Hynes and Bisland (who was now acting in a guest capacity), their partners in crime being guitarists Mal McNulty (of THE SWEET) and Ian Simmons, plus much-travelled bassist Billy Kulke (later of JAGGED EDGE, FIRST STRIKE, SOLE ASYLUM *et al.*), all of whom were eminently capable musicians. Almost inevitably, however, the hype exceeded the reality of the situation, and this much-heralded return fizzled out pretty quickly, with very little (if any) studio activity actually taking place at any point. Mal McNulty proceeded to lend his services to the German version of HAZZARD, while Bisland and Summers continued to work together in their WILDFIRE venture, before the inseparable duo moved on to STATETROOPER in the second half of the decade. The jovial Bisland later found occasional work with the likes of PRAYING MANTIS, THE SWEET and the knockabout PADDY GOES TO HOLYHEAD, in which he was (and still is, from time to time) joined by erstwhile colleagues Danny Hynes and Mal McNulty.

12" Singles
»It's A Mad Mad World« Private 1980

7" Singles
»It's A Mad Mad World« Private 1980

Compilation Appearances
"Set The Stage Alight" on »12 Commandments In Metal« LP Roadrunner 1985 + »NWOBHM '79 Revisited« Do-LP/Do-CD Phonogram 1990
"It's A Mad Mad World" on »NWOBHM Vol.3« Bootleg CD 1992

WENDY HOUSE

Roy Hamilton (v, b)
Keith Hyde (g)
Kelvin Purcell (d)

Be honest, given the choice of seeing either a band called WENDY HOUSE or an outfit called something like REINCARNATE or TORTURE, which would you go for? Me too. I suspect, however, that Surrey's aforementioned WENDY HOUSE weren't really all that interested in world domination or being part of the original NWOBHM explosion. For one thing, they didn't release their seldom-seen »Storeys« EP until 1985, by which time the earlier kerfuffle had died down considerably. Secondly, the gimmicky fold-out cover, depicting three beer-swilling inebriates (including a frontman who would have been a surefire bet in any Dumpy Dunnell lookalike contests) residing within a garish cartoon house, suggests that the trio were probably little more than a regular fixture in the corner of a rustic pub in their home county. However, it appears that, 'due to public demand', a vinyl souvenir of their knockabout gigs ultimately became a viable commodity, so a self-financed release was duly organised. Of the selections on the EP, "Charmaine" and "Today" (ballads which border on Country and Western material) are both unreservedly awful, while "Belle Of The Ball" and "See No Reason" are fairly unremarkable rockers in a vaguely VARDIS style, although I'd imagine the three-piece probably spent more time listening to acts such as the ROLLING STONES and the KINKS than anything more contemporary.

In fact, it transpires that WENDY HOUSE actually evolved from the ashes of a prolific biker/pub rock concern named JEEP, who released around half a dozen singles (worth picking up if they're dirt-cheap, but not particularly edifying) on the small Airport label between 1979 and 1983, and who shared a broadly similar musical philosophy. Both JEEP (who featured Roy Hamilton and Kelvin Purcell in their ranks) and WENDY HOUSE are the sort of comedy/covers outfit that could, quite feasibly, still be in existence today, probably going down a storm with locals who, after eight pints of gut-rotting traditional English ale, don't honestly care who's on stage, as long as they make a fair bit of noise and everyone has a nice, jolly singsong along the way. As for the group's »Storeys« EP, well, you can easily live without it unless you're a completist, and it's not really worth paying over the odds for.

7" EP's
»Storeys« Wendy House Records 1985

WHITEFIRE

Tim Wright (v)
Simon Jhons (g)
Jim Beswick (b)
Stuart Sheffield (k)
Eddie Byron Taylor III (d)

I've no doubt that whichever NWOBHM lunatic first unearthed a copy of WHITEFIRE's sole EP (issued in the pre-explosion days of 1978) must have taken one look at the monochrome sleeve depicting a flame-haired temptress and curving logo, before concluding that they had discovered a monster. Sadly, the three-tracker, recorded at the famous Cargo Studios facility in Rochdale, doesn't quite live up to such high expectations, being fairly firmly rooted in the early 70's in terms of convenient musical reference points. However, the record illustrates that this Lancashire outfit were perfectly happy to attempt a reasonably wide variety of styles, with "Suzanne" being a semi-heavy rock ballad falling somewhere between the likes of BILL THE MURDERER and a considerably more restrained DAWNWATCHER. The throwaway "Teresa Green", meanwhile, is pretty awful (the sort of thing that Dave Edmunds was churning out on a regular basis in his ROCKPILE days, so it's not really genuine NWOBHM fodder at all), but at least it doesn't last long. The ambitious "Parades Of Glory", on the other hand, is an epic composition which, despite beginning and ending rather feebly with mellowed-out, HAWKWIND-influenced segments, really explodes into life in the mid-section. With a heartfelt vocal performance and excellent guitar work, the band had clearly been studying at the LED ZEPPELIN academy in their spare time, and successfully found a niche somewhere between DIAMOND HEAD and NO QUARTER on this occasion.

As you'll no doubt be aware by now, the mid-to-late 70's were slightly difficult times for emergent rock/metal bands (in the transitional period prior to the genre's mass acceptance), and outfits such as WHITEFIRE were probably a bit of an anomaly in those days (in the sense that non-punksters weren't supposed to be issuing private singles and EP's). While they might have had slightly more success if they had formed two or three years later (a gigging version of the group was, incidentally, still fairly active as late as 1981, although it transpires that an identically-named Mancunian outfit from the latter part of the decade were an entirely unrelated concern), they don't seem to have established themselves as regional favourites at any point in time. Their rare 7", however, is now approaching the three-figure mark in terms of its usual asking price, but this seems rather steep when you consider that collectors could probably land a TORTURE or DESTROYER single for less. As VARDIS sagely stated, 'The World's Insane'...

7" EP's
»Suzanne« Private 1978

WHITE HEAT

John Dunning (v)
Jon 'JJ' Cox (g)
John Tucker (b)
Kevin Cassidy (d)

With the JJ'S POWERHOUSE project (see separate entry), having basically represented a one-off vinyl showcase for the guitar talents of band mainman Jon 'JJ' Cox, the axeman subsequently found himself living in London and touting his wares around the capital's rock clubs. Within a fairly short timescale, he had already teamed up with bassist John Tucker and drummer Kevin Cassidy in a small-time outfit with a notoriously unstable line-up, although this still provided him with the opportunity to get his foot in the door and make an impact on the local music scene. With frontmen initially coming and going at an

alarming rate, the arrival of a chap called Ian Aidey finally brought a brief period of stability, whereupon the group decided to reinvent themselves as WHITE HEAT, the moniker being taken from a James Cagney film. With the newly-christened outfit (not to be confused with various foreign namesakes or the strange British bunch

who recorded for the Valium label in the early 80's) getting their act together at some point towards the end of 1983, the ambitious group set about developing a heavy, powerful style with which to win the hearts of the nation's headbangers.

Before much longer, however, their latest frontman flew the coop, whereupon former TRUFFLE/HARD GRAFT stalwart John Dunning (who had previously manned the microphone in the both outfits from time to time, but didn't actually sing on TRUFFLE's »Round Tower« two-tracker) was drafted in to strut his funky stuff at the mike stand. With the ensemble now featuring no less than three members called Jon/John (disappointingly, it appears that no drummers with that forename were available at the time), the comic possibilities were endless, and I'm sure their rehearsals must have been quite eventful. Given that the quartet had now become a rather more serious and capable proposition in the wake of Dunning's arrival, WHITE HEAT swiftly began writing the sort of material that would go down a storm with fans of no-nonsense heavy metal. Even by mid-1984, the lads had formed an alliance with Rick Le Page's small-time Rock Shop label (who, for some inexplicable reason, were now calling themselves RSR), having presumably been introduced to the Hampshire-based concern by local boy John Dunning. A concerted charm offensive led to them swinging a deal for a one-off 7", and all that remained was to stump up the readies for the recording session, which wasn't a major problem, given that the lads had raked in some ready cash via encouragingly healthy sales of the original JJ'S POWERHOUSE single at their early gigs.

WHITE HEAT's debut two-tracker, engineered by good old Ray Dorset (MUNGO JERRY's mainman), began hitting the shops within a matter of weeks, so the fans and journalists were soon getting an earful of "Soldier Of Fortune" and "Lovemaker". The weighty A-side, in particular, turned out to be an extremely substantial and memorable offering (later taking its place on the »NWOBHM Vol.7« bootleg CD), reminiscent of equivalently high-powered outfits such as SALEM, CHARIOT and (naturally) JJ'S POWERHOUSE themselves, whereas the reverse was a rather more commercial and raunchy number which, to be perfectly honest, seemed completely at odds with the forceful "Soldier Of Fortune". I guess they were just trying to show their diversity, but I know for a fact that most of the outfit's own material (which included the likes of "Out Of My Life" and "Breaking Free") tended to be in the more powerful style, and had rather more in common with the likes of LAAZ ROCKIT than with any of their British counterparts. The WHITE HEAT single was, incidentally, issued in a very colourful and eye-catching picture sleeve showing an image of a gun-toting desperado against a flaming background, all of which must surely have helped to shift numerous copies to metal fans at the time. This release is a scarcely-sighted rarity these days, though, and currently fetches an impressively high price, although examples have been known to surface occasionally in the areas where the foursome played most of their gigs (notably Hampshire itself), so keep looking!

Regular club outings followed as a matter of course, the lads becoming a popular live attraction, and they were honoured with a high placing in the 'Best Local Band' poll in 'Forearm Smash' fanzine at the time. Not only that, WHITE HEAT developed something of a cult following in parts of mainland Europe, and they subsequently proceeded to play some rapturously-received shows in metal-friendly countries such as Belgium and Holland (even being filmed at one of their gigs in Amsterdam) over the ensuing months. Still, John Dunning eventually tired of his role within the group, and was to be replaced (after a few no-hopers had failed to impress) by new boy Tim Bromfield after a couple of years at the helm. Sadly, it all went seriously awry within a remarkably short space of time thereafter, with mainman JJ Cox finding it increasingly difficult either to maintain a stable line-up or to attract suitably high-calibre musicians to back up his considerable talents, so the outfit eventually called it a day. After the demise of WHITE HEAT in the second half of 1986, bassist John Tucker remained in the musical wilderness for only a few months, whereupon he inveigled his way into the ranks of Kent's foundering DEUCE, although the observation that this particular outfit had ceased all operations before the end of 1987 suggests that he was able to make only a relatively minor contribution to their activities.

JJ Cox, on the other hand, was undaunted by the ultimate collapse of WHITE HEAT, and soon set about forming yet another group of his own, the little-known PANIK ATTAK. This venture actually took shape following the guitarist's relocation (again!) to Cornwall, a remote region (where WHITE HEAT had played with great success on numerous occasions) with a strong fan base for heavy music, but which boasted very few home-grown rock outfits, for some peculiar reason. Recruiting vocalist Derek John Hodd (who once fronted Cornwall's self-proclaimed 'heaviest band', CHAIN REACTION, and who had also spent time with CLOVEN HOOF), drummer Tim Haywood (ex-SEDUCER) and unknown bassist Ivan Wellington, the quartet rapidly became a popular live attraction throughout the region, and eventually got around to releasing their »Shout« 12" EP in 1990. With the highly impressive three-tracker displaying a slightly more contemporary direction (quite similar, in places, to some of BUFFALO's more recent output), with flamboyant guitar work from Cox himself, there was certainly enough of a NWOBHM influence to keep fans of his previous outfits more than happy. Although the restless chap has now called time on PANIK ATTAK and moved on to pastures new (recently collaborating with erstwhile colleagues John Tucker from WHITE HEAT and Ozzy Davies from QUAD/JJ'S POWERHOUSE on a selection of freshly-penned material), he remains extremely active in the rock field, and is currently putting together a studio facility to allow his various musical ideas to be captured for posterity. We await future developments with bated breath!

7" Singles
»Soldier Of Fortune« RSR 1984

Compilation Appearances
"Soldier Of Fortune" on »NWOBHM Vol.7« Bootleg CD 1996

WHITE LIGHTNING

Noel Jones (v)
Simon Pengilly (g)
Gerald Goff (b)
Jeff Ward (d)

After the eventual demise of Surrey's popular STATIC in the early months of 1983, mainman Noel Jones decided that he wasn't quite finished in the music business. While his erstwhile colleagues from the last STATIC line-up proceeded to form the AOR-friendly SNOWBLIND (see separate entry), however, Jones envisaged a rather more ambitious project. Within a year or so (after an ill-fated venture called ICEMON, where he worked alongside guitarist Greg Hart), he had teamed up with a brand-new set of accomplices (who were initially brought together through advertisements in the music papers of the day) to form WHITE LIGHTNING, an outfit with a slightly more progressive edge to their music. After finding their feet and recording a couple of early demos, the quartet decided to release their own single to get their name into the public's consciousness. Issued on their own Wild Party label in 1985, the record featured "This Poison Fountain" and "Hypocrite", two enjoyable selections (illustrating the considerable vocal talents of the frontman, something which had been less apparent in STATIC) which revealed the ensemble to be following the path of earlier acts such as SHIVA, CANIS MAJOR or BIG DAISY, carving a technical, semi-progressive niche for themselves, this being at a time when RUSH-influenced music was finding little favour amongst those in the music industry.

The single was a fairly remarkable debut, with confident arrangements and original lyrics (the heartfelt "This Poison Fountain" addressing the issue of pollution, while the scathing "Hypocrite" was inspired by those whose blind faith in organised religion serves to isolate them from the outside world), and the outfit were delighted with the favourable reaction from the rock fraternity. Nevertheless, the patient musicians were to lurk in the shadows for a further year or two while they plotted their ultimate strategy for global domination. Along the way, bassist Richard Max Goddard was brought in as a replacement for Gerald Goff, the new recruit being a talented individual who had played a minor role in the fortunes of regional oddballs MOURNBLADE in recent times. Indeed, the bands enjoyed a friendly rivalry, with WHITE LIGHTNING drummer Jeff Ward having also lent a hand to the former's recording activities at one point. Compared with the prolific STATIC, it must be stated that WHITE LIGHTNING played considerably fewer gigs, although a notable live appearance was at a 'Battle Of The Bands'-style showcase event in London, where the quartet took to the stage alongside various minor hopefuls such as ATTILA, FAHRENHEIT, UGLY, TOKYO and EXCALIBUR (the whole shebang being headlined by VOW WOW) in order to impress as many fans and industry types as possible. They also completed an all-new demo at around this time, which featured "Love Really Hurts Without You", "Danger Man" and "Lesson One", which soon set the media tongues wagging in no uncertain terms.

In 1988, WHITE LIGHTNING finally entered the studio (the grandly-named Sound Theatre facility in Middlesex, which, in reality, turns out to have been nothing more illustrious than Jeff Ward's old bedroom at his family home, an arrangement which necessitated the drumkit being squeezed into the nearby garage during the recording process) in order to lay down their (long-overdue) debut full-length release. By the end of the year, the whole album was safely in the can, and it only remained for the musicians to attract a bit of label interest to get the finished product into the shops. In an ideal world, this shouldn't really have posed too much of a problem, but a suitable record deal was to prove frustratingly elusive in the first instance, and so the long-player (»…As Midnight Approaches«) initially appeared (in fairly limited quantities, admittedly) on the group's own Wild Party label once again. It was, overall, an extremely impressive and individualistic effort, and it was interesting to note the inclusion of revamped versions of "Hypocrite" and "This Poison Fountain" in addition to a number of less-familiar tracks. There was, admittedly, something of a shift towards marginally more accessible territory in places, when the band attempted a style more in keeping with RADIO MOSCOW or THE STORM, but numbers such as "Right Between The Eyes" were very much in the vein of their first single.

The ambitious outfit were understandably keen to get their latest product into the hands of as many rock fans as possible, although their limited finances dictated that a more extensive pressing of the album would be virtually impossible unless they were picked up by a more affluent company. Things appeared to be looking up the following year, however, especially after WHITE LIGHTNING became affiliated with the recently-established G.I. Records, who issued two tracks, "Dealer" (a non-LP effort) and "As Midnight Approaches" (actually an outro taken from a longer album track entitled "Frightened Children"), on their seldom-seen »Shooting From The Hip« compilation. Sadly, though, the company didn't feel compelled to release any additional WHITE LIGHTNING product (either the original album or a brand-new follow-up), and things looked fairly ominous in terms of getting further vinyl releases onto the shelves until the little-known Workshop Records (nothing to do with LEGEND's own label) stepped in at the last minute to obtain the rights to the ensemble's debut set. Much to the musicians' collective relief, »…As Midnight Approaches« was finally reissued (this time in more generous quantities) in 1990, and the long-player was soon attracting a significant amount of attention in the music press of the day.

The re-promoted album benefitted from a fairly respectable review in 'Kerrang' (who, oddly enough, suggested influences as diverse as MARILLION and U2), and the benevolent Tommy Vance also saw fit to playlist various selections on the 'Friday Rock Show'. Furthermore, their new label somehow managed to garner the lads a one-off show (on the Isle Of Man) supporting none other than MEATLOAF, where the lucky WHITE LIGHTNING performed in front of several thousand appreciative fans, which can't have done their reputation any harm whatsoever. The outfit also developed quite an enviable following of their own, headlining capacious venues such as the Marquee in London and playing to packed houses on an increasingly regular basis. By this juncture, however, the band had now parted company with long-time guitarist Simon Pengilly, drafting in an unknown character (John Storey) to make up the numbers, but it failed to hamper their progress in any sense. Indeed, in the wake of the overwhel-

mingly favourable response to »...As Midnight Approaches«, a second album was commissioned by Workshop almost immediately, and so the outfit were soon happily ensconced in a 'proper' recording facility (Woodcray Studios in Berkshire, where BLACK SABBATH had just completed work on their »Tyr« opus), whereupon the lads proceeded to lay down the tracks for their »Paradise...At A Price« set.

With the album recordings all ready for imminent release, WHITE LIGHTNING should have experienced little or no difficulty in getting their sophomore LP into the shops, but things didn't quite go according to plan. Cruelly, Workshop began to express serious concern as to the long-term potential of the group, and eventually reneged on the deal (feebly claiming that the lads had assured them that their second effort would be a chart-friendly album of mainstream material), whereby the company refused to release the much-anticipated LP, Rotters. At this point, mainman Noel Jones actually offered to buy back the master tapes (so he could try to arrange a new deal elsewhere), a request which fell upon deaf ears. In fact, the fate of these recordings remains a mystery, as they were nowhere to be found when the receivers were finally called in to liquidate the failed company's assets a few years later. Sadly, this whole sorry episode ultimately led to the demise of WHITE LIGHTNING, a talented outfit who could, with a bit of luck on their side, have gone considerably further than they managed during the course of their existence.

LP's
»...As Midnight Approaches« Wild Party Records 1988
[Original issue]
»...As Midnight Approaches« Workshop Records 1990
[Reissue]

7" Singles
»This Poison Fountain« Wild Party Records 1985
[Both tracks different to LP versions]

CD's
»...As Midnight Approaches« Workshop Records 1990

Exclusive Compilation Appearances
"**Dealer**" on »Shooting From The Hip« LP G.I. Records 1989

Compilation Appearances
"**As Midnight Approaches**" on »Shooting From The Hip« LP G.I. Records 1989
[Different version appeared as outro to "Frightened Children" on »...As Midnight Approaches« album]
"**This Poison Fountain**" on »N.W.O.B.H.M. Metal Rarities Vol.3« CD British Steel 1997
[Different to LP version]
"**Hypocrite**" on »N.W.O.B.H.M. Metal Rarities Vol.3« CD British Steel 1997
[Different to LP version]

WHITE SPIRIT

Bruce Ruff (v)
Janick Gers (g)
Phil Brady (b)
Malcolm Pearson (k)
Graeme Crallan (d)

Cleveland's WHITE SPIRIT had been active on their local music scene, in one form or another, from as early as 1975, although they struggled to maintain a stable line-up and a consistent musical direction until around 1979, when the familiar quintet came together and started making a serious name for themselves with well-attended shows throughout the North East. The outfit were fairly heavily into the basic DEEP PURPLE sound, delivering hard-rocking compositions with keyboard backing, although many of their more adventurous tracks began to incorporate rather more intricate and progressively-inclined keyboard work, bringing to mind some of their NWOBHM contemporaries such as CHEMICAL ALICE, SHERWOOD or Yorkshire's WILDFIRE. By early 1980, their activities (including support slots with the likes of GIRL, BUDGIE and IRON MAIDEN) had attracted the attention of Neat Records, and so the band were encouraged to follow in the footsteps of the TYGERS OF PAN TANG and FIST by recording a single for the label. The lads duly obliged by supplying "Back To The Grind" and "Cheetah", the keyboard-heavy former being chosen as A-side at the expense of the more traditional heavy rock of "Cheetah". The 7" proved to be another top seller for Neat, and WHITE SPIRIT were (as with the TYGERS and FIST) swiftly licensed to MCA in order to record their debut album with a decent studio budget.

The recording sessions for the eponymous long-player took place in the summer of 1980 (by which time WHITE SPIRIT had also contributed a couple of tracks to EMI's »Metal For Muthas Vol.II« and »Muthas Pride« compilations), and the finished product would appear at around the same time as the group were being added (at pretty much the last minute) to the bill of the Reading Festival. The response of the festival crowd turned out to be surprisingly favourable, and the outfit were soon out on tour with GILLAN to promote their new LP (which had, incidentally, been produced by the latter's John McCoy) even more effectively. WHITE SPIRIT's debut album was an effective and well-balanced mixture of their more progressively-inclined approach (the superb "Red Skies" and "High Upon High", for example) and DEEP PURPLE-influenced rockers (such as "Midnight Chaser", "Don't Be Fooled" and "No Reprieve"), with just seven fairly lengthy (particularly the epic "Fool For The Gods") selections comprising the set as a whole. Sales were extremely respectable from the outset, and so a couple of tie-in releases were hurriedly trotted out to further the group's cause. The first of these was the »Midnight Chaser« 7", which backed an edited take of the A-side with the complex "Suffragettes", a non-LP number which, with its semi-acoustic intro and heartfelt (if rather heavy-handed) lyrical sentiments (bonus points awarded for inclusion of the word 'emancipation'), could almost have been the prototype for METALLICA's "Nothing Else Matters". Happily, this particular single sold in fairly healthy quantities, and is now regarded as a collectable slice of NWOBHM vinyl, especially with the coveted picture sleeve.

The second 7" to be lifted from the debut album utilised an edited version of "High Upon High" (a more rocking effort than its predecessor had been, although it wasn't the strongest track in their repertoire) as its main focus of attention. The flipside actually contained two numbers, "No Reprieve" and "Conversations With Arthur Guitar", although the latter is basi-

THE PORTERHOUSE
20 Carolgate, Retford, Notts
Friday 16th January   Adm £2.0

WHITE SPIRIT + Support

cally nothing more than some pointless and rather annoying lo-fi arsing about in the studio. I've no idea who the ubiquitous 'Arthur Guitar' actually was (Bernie Tormé?), but it's worth noting that this pseudonymous individual was additionally credited as playing on the COLIN TOWNS track featured on the »Brute Force« sampler, so there's no doubt some sort of GILLAN connection once again. The lads presumably had high hopes for this offering (which wasn't issued in a picture sleeve, incidentally), but it seems to have performed relatively poorly in terms of sales (it would appear that comparatively few copies actually made it into the shops, for some reason, as with FIST's »Collision Course« 7"), failing to capture the public's imagination to any great extent. As a result of this disappointing response at the time, few copies of »High Upon High« have ever been in circulation, and this is now regarded as the most sought-after and highly-valued WHITE SPIRIT collectable. Predictably, its lack of chart impact didn't exactly fill MCA with confidence, although the lads would remain on the company's books for the time being.

Moving into 1981, however, it was all change on the WHITE SPIRIT front, and the outfit seemed to be renewing their links with their original home, especially when their "Cheetah" number was recycled on Neat's »Lead Weight« compilation. This piece of exposure seemed to raise their public profile slightly, however, and so the lads toured fairly widely in the spring to keep the momentum going. All the while, they were composing new material and making regular trips to the recording studio, so, even when the inevitable split with MCA was confirmed, there didn't seem to be any particular cause for concern at that point. Mind you, the group's plans to seek out a new deal were thrown into total confusion later in the year when star guitarist Janick Gers was headhunted by GILLAN to replace the newly-departed Bernie Tormé. Understandably, the axeman jumped at the chance (he went on to play a major part in the fortunes of IRON MAIDEN, having also been roped into the GOGMAGOG disaster), leaving WHITE SPIRIT at something of a loose end. Notwithstanding the fact that they eventually (after a protracted auditioning process) got around to naming a replacement (one-time AXIS stalwart Mick Tucker), things had cooled off by that stage, and the band's collective activities rapidly tailed off considerably. Following the loss of Janick Gers, incidentally, it was announced that two tracks ("Nowhere To Run" and "Can't Take It") had been recorded shortly beforehand, and there were even a few tentative plans to issue these as a one-off single on Neat, although this notion appears to have fallen through at an early stage.

In fact, WHITE SPIRIT kept a remarkably low profile until the second half of 1982, whereupon they began gigging once again (having relocated to the capital in the interim) with something of a drastically-altered line-up. The disgruntled Bruce Ruff and Phil Brady had flown the coop (the latter subsequently hooked up with local rivals AXIS, although the capable frontman seemed to vanish off the surface of the planet), and the lads had drafted in a couple of new faces. After briefly utilising the services of a certain Ian Shuttleworth, the band recruited much-travelled bassist Toby Sadler (who, over the years, spent time with acts such as AIRRACE, SAMSON, LISA DOMINIQUE and IF ONLY, more often as a keyboard player than bassist) and talented vocalist Brian Howe, previously with a little-known Hampshire bunch called SHY, who had no connection with the more familiar ensemble from the Midlands. The revised version of WHITE SPIRIT played a mixture of old and new material at their shows, although the only track from this period to make it to the vinyl stage was "Watch Out", which (after initially turning up on Neat's »60 Minutes Plus« cassette) appeared on the »All Hell Let Loose« compilation. It was a decent enough effort, although far closer to raunchy AOR territory than their original direction, and it proved to be a move which failed to secure all that much interest in the group. With the members suffering a total breakdown in self-confidence, they finally went their separate ways in 1983, with the various characters from the last line-up all proceeding to find further employment in the music business.

Mick Tucker, for example, was soon finding a stable position as second guitarist in TANK (he's still playing an important role in the revitalised version of the Filth Hounds), who had finally taken the decision to expand to a quartet. At one point, he was joined by erstwhile colleague Graeme Crallan, although the latter subsequently moved over to the unsuccessful BRITON and PANAMA. Malcolm Pearson later worked with Toby Sadler in the ranks of the LISA DOMINIQUE band towards the end of the decade, while talented vocalist Brian Howe was to get his big break when he was (after a brief stint with TED NUGENT) called up to join the ranks of the revived BAD COMPANY in the early part of 1986. WHITE SPIRIT are fondly remembered by many, however, including original guitarist Janick Gers, who reflected on his experiences with the outfit many years later: *'You know, I actually listened to the CD once again when I was in Japan, and I felt that the music still seemed pretty fresh. Of course, we weren't totally happy with the sound at the time, the recording process took just ten days including mixing, but the songs are still fresh. Naturally, I would change a few things nowadays, for example the drum sound, but I'm not suggesting it would benefit from a remix, things should be left just as they are! I was very proud of the album back then, and that's still the case.'* (Ref: Interview, Matthias Mader, December 1995). I happen to know that at least another album's worth of unreleased WHITE SPIRIT material exists on tape, and it would be a great bonus for their devoted fans if some of these selections could be exhumed for future release, but I've no idea whether or not this is a genuine possibility.

LP's
»White Spirit« MCA 1980

7" EP's
»High Upon High« MCA 1980
["High Upon High" different to album version, "Conversations With Arthur Guitar" non-LP]

7" Singles
»Back To The Grind« Neat 1980
[Both tracks non-LP]
»Midnight Chaser« MCA 1980
[A-side different to album version, B-side "Suffragettes" non-LP]

CD's

»White Spirit« Black Ghost 1991
[Bootleg release]
»White Spirit« MCA Japan 1992
[Japanese issue with three bonus tracks]

Exclusive Compilation Appearances
"Watch Out" on »60 Minutes Plus« Cassette Neat 1982/CD Teichiku 1992 + »All Hell Let Loose« LP Neat 1983 + »NWOBHM Vol.3« Bootleg CD 1992

Compilation Appearances
"High Upon High" on »Metal For Muthas Vol.2« LP EMI 1980/CD Airraid Records 2000 + »The Bible Of Hard Rock« CD Toshiba 1990
[Different to album or single version]
"Red Skies" on »Muthas Pride« 12" EP EMI 1980
[Different to album version]
"Back To The Grind" on »Brute Force« LP MCA 1980 + »Give 'Em Hell« CD Nectar Masters 1995
"Midnight Chaser" on »Double Hard« LP Ariola 1981
"Cheetah" on »Lead Weight« LP Neat 1981/CD Teichiku 1992 + »NWOBHM '79 Revisited« Do-LP/Do-CD Phonogram 1990 + »Metal Masters« 4-CD Box Castle Communications 1993
"Suffragettes" on »NWOBHM Vol.1« Bootleg CD 1992
"Fool For The Gods" (live) on »NWOBHM-The Days On Stage« Bootleg CD Taurus Records 1993

WIDOW

Re Beth (v, g)
Phillip Damien Hyde (b)
Rex Duval (d)

The eponymous long-player released by a mysterious bunch called WIDOW back in 1983 has always (well, ever since it was reviewed in the pages of Kerrang) been a source of intrigue among the NWOBHM fraternity and fans of heavy music in general, although the item itself is such a rare piece that few individuals have been privileged to encounter a copy in recent times. Entirely predictably, therefore, it has been the subject of rumour and counter-rumour over the years, the legendary musical contents varying between such extremes as '*a classic of the black metal genre*' and, well, rather less charitable views. In fact, there was even doubt that a homegrown act was responsible after all, given that so many overseas namesakes seemed to exist, whereas nobody could really remember anyone (apart from the part-timers from Merseyside who evolved into KAMARG) using the identity in this country. As it turns out, though, the unrenowned threesome (masked by some remarkably silly pseudonyms) were indeed based in the UK, their LP being recorded at Wickham Studios in Surrey and the sleeve notes crediting various other facilities in and around London, so I suspect that they probably originated from this general area. In any case, WIDOW's debut LP emerged on the trio's own Legend label at the beginning of 1983, although this unheralded offering well and truly failed to take the nation by storm, a situation exacerbated by the (presumably) microscopic pressing, the observation that it was practically impossible to get hold of (I don't even remember 'Shades' advertising it) and the peculiar fact that nobody in the entire country appeared to possess the remotest knowledge of the band.

Still, the 'Kerrang review' had been fairly interesting, if not exactly gushing with praise, and this seemed to paint WIDOW as demonic wannabes from the WITCHFYNDE academy, something which should have garnered them a few fans in due course. Indeed, the cover artwork (a colourful drawing of a nubile wench behind the obligatory gothic logo) and a couple of those song titles ("Come To The Ritual" and "Never For Evil") seemed indicative of an act with quasi-satanic pretensions, although the music itself turns out to be rather unremarkable, semi-doomy, miserablist metal in the manner of VOLTZ, PHOENIX RISING, OMEGA and Jersey's LEGEND, for example. There are also, admittedly, some effective, upbeat efforts, although the likes of the epic title track and "Morning Star" appear to be more representative of the outfit's direction of choice. Mind you, the musicianship is undeniably rudimentary, and the unflattering production does the protagonists no favours whatsoever, but it's mostly listenable, notwithstanding the fact that there are perilously few original musical ideas (which are regularly stretched to breaking point) on display. In particular, "Rebecca", "Journey" and "Burning" tend to come and go without making much of an impact, and a couple of numbers threaten to fall apart completely, giving the impression that they weren't properly finished. All in all, therefore, it suggests that WIDOW didn't have enough decent material at their disposal to justify a full-length release (they even utilise around five minutes of rather pointless '*thunderstorm*' sound effects to pad things out), although, given that their compositions were hardly suited to a conventional 7" single, I suppose an album was a logical enough option if the lads desperately wanted to get some self-financed vinyl into the shops.

Clearly, WIDOW were never a high-profile name on the music scene at any time, and I suspect that they were merely a fly-by-night concern who failed to escape from the recording studio or progress to the stage of playing any gigs of note. Predictably, therefore, they were never destined to become local heroes, and most of the regional metalheads probably remained oblivious to their existence. With the participants having used soubriquets to conceal their identities, I guess there's only a slim chance of finding out who was actually responsible, which is a bit of a shame, especially if one of them still has a box of unplayed copies nestling under his bed. It's a struggle to make sense of this peculiar album, to be perfectly honest, and it's plausible that this was either a youthful bunch who were trying to make a breakthrough (and who were sincere about the whole metal lark), or a gaggle of old stagers who had grown weary of pub rock and decided to try their hand (with limited success) at the devil's music. As with the likes of INCUBUS, though, a satanic-looking sleeve and some promising song titles doesn't qualify them as genuine black metal contenders, so I'd strike this release off the wants list if you were hoping WIDOW might be VENOM clones. As I say, the album seems to have sold in pitiful quantities at the time, and virtually none remain in circulation, so most of us should accept the fact that we're probably not going to find one in our local charity shop.

LP's
»Widow« Legend Records 1983

WIKKYD VIKKER

Dick Boorman (v)
Gary Butler (g)
Andy Harrison (b)
Adrian Bates (d)

Formed in mid-1981, the original version of Leicestershire's questionably-named WIKKYD VIKKER was conceived as a four-piece proposition, and it came as a pleasant surprise to many when it transpired that they weren't a particularly glam-influenced act at all. In fact, the quartet initially favoured a slightly more restrained and down-to-earth approach, something which seemed to be rather at odds with their SILVERWING-approved moniker. Even so, their early fumblings on the rock scene failed to turn many heads, but things soon began to pick up as they grew in stature and confidence. By early 1982, a sizeable quantity of original material had already been written and immortalised on tape, and it wasn't long before the youngsters were invited to contribute a representative track to one of those infamous Ebony samplers. With "Phoenix" and "Super Rocker" being demoed for this purpose, the label put their faith in the latter (a pretty mundane effort, it must be said), which duly appeared on »Metallic Storm« a few months later. Predictably, the Ebony experience failed to propel WIKKYD VIKKER into the realms of stardom in the short term (let's face it, "Super Rocker" had been a mediocre cut on an overlooked compilation), and little or no outside interest was stirred up as a result, leaving the lads with no option but to go it alone. Soon afterwards, however, the musicians were fortunate enough to be featured in the 'Armed And Ready' section of 'Kerrang', where the virtues of this hopeful troupe were extolled for the benefit of the nation.

In due course, the ambitious WIKKYD VIKKER took the bull by the horns and expanded to a quintet *via* the addition of former VALHALLA guitarist Mark Evans, who more or less took over the songwriting side of things completely. The ensemble entered the studio some time later, whereupon they laid down two freshly-penned compositions ("Black Of The Night" and "Release") for an introductory 7" single. Issued on the tiny Boogie label in the first half of 1983, the two-tracker turned out to be a major improvement on their unspectacular "Super Rocker" effort, with "Black Of The Night", in particular, being an excellent, heavy number with a memorable and interesting structure, the overall effect bringing forth comparisons with the likes of GEDDES AXE, SNATCH-BACK and DEALER. The flipside, on the other hand, was a rather less inspiring piece, a slower, more mainstream-sounding track (vaguely reminiscent of certain early ENERGY compositions) with an unusually lacklustre vocal performance. Surprisingly, perhaps, the record won an uncharacteristically ebullient review from 'Kerrang' (by this time, however, the lads had decided that their name wasn't doing them any favours, and had now reinvented themselves as PRETTY WIKKYD, although it's hard to see how this was any sort of improvement), and the group's fortunes seemed to be looking up at this juncture.

Sadly, the assorted activities of the freshly-christened PRETTY WIKKYD (who, according to a promotional photo which was circulated at the time, were starting to look more like an out and out glam act by the minute) failed to raise too many major-label eyebrows during the following year or so, although they still received the occasional mention in the rock press, with 'Kerrang' even reviewing one of their shows alongside LYADRIVE and some long-forgotten minor hopefuls. In the end, however, it had all started to fall apart by the mid-80's, with the various musicians finally deciding to call it a day and return to their day jobs without making too much of a song and dance about it. Nevertheless, the group's original name has been kept alive by enthusiasts and collectors in recent times, and their excellent "Black Of The Night" even took pride of place on the »NWOBHM Vol.4« bootleg CD a few years back. The one-off WIKKYD VIKKER single (which was never issued in a picture sleeve) is, needless to say, an incredibly scarce and highly-valued piece nowadays, and this prized slice of vinyl currently resides in relatively few NWOBHM collections.

7" Singles
»Black Of The Night« Boogie Records 1983

Exclusive Compilation Appearances
"Super Rocker" on »Metallic Storm« LP Ebony 1982

Compilation Appearances
"Black Of The Night" on »NWOBHM Vol.4« Bootleg CD 1992

WILDFIRE (I)

Doug Edwards (v)
John Lockton (g)
Rocky Newton (b)
Alan Nelson (k)
Frank Noon (d)

As fans will be only too aware, the WILDFIRE/RED ALERT situation is hugely confusing due to the sheer number of bands using each name virtually simultaneously, and most well-intentioned attempts to clarify matters haven't really helped that much, to be blunt, so let's try to sort out this story once and for all. Once upon a time in Yorkshire (now there's a potential movie title that Sergio Leone appears to have overlooked) there was a threesome called the NEXT BAND, who issued an EP of proto-NWOBHM entitled »Four By Three« way back in 1978. Having been overtaken by some of the county's emergent musical hopefuls, however, the central characters in this venture (Rocky Newton, Frank Noon and John Lockton) ultimately decided to reinvent themselves as a rather more metal-oriented concern known as RED ALERT, inspired by one of their original song titles. Evidently, the protagonists were keen to adopt a powerful stance which was more in keeping with the general NWOBHM ethos, and so they duly roped in a couple of likely candidates (one-time LAUTREC keyboard player Alan Nelson and unknown singer Doug Edwards) to assist them in their future activities.

This particular RED ALERT (who have, in their time, been confused with both a legendary punk band and the bluesy outfit who appeared on the »Metal For Muthas Vol.II« compilation with "Open Heart") wasted little time before penning a few brand-new selections and getting some vinyl product of their own onto the market. In the second half of 1980, the combo recorded a self-financed, double A-sided single pairing the energetic "Run To Ground" with "Wild Dog", these capable efforts featuring high-range vocals and widdly keyboard sections in the general manner of WHITE SPIRIT or CHEMICAL ALICE. Before the debut two-tracker had even been officially released, however, the musicians were selected for inclusion on the forthcoming »Muthas Pride« 12", a sampler EP conceived as something of a follow-up to the »Metal For Muthas« albums. With EMI presumably pointing out that an act possessing an identical handle had been featured on one of the label's aforementioned compilations only a few months previously, the outfit decided that a name change was in order, and (rather unfortunately, although it transpires that this was apparently their management's choice) plumped for WILDFIRE. Under this new moniker, "Wild Dog" was duly featured on the mini-sampler, but left the lads with the small matter of several boxfuls of singles still credited to RED ALERT. Oops.

In the event, however, a rather pragmatic solution was found (later adopted by DRAGONSLAYER after their name had been expanded out of necessity), and the band adorned their records (luckily, no sleeves had been printed, or these would presumably have had to go in the bin) with hand-written stickers to reveal their new identity prior to shipping them out to the shops. Whether or not the newly-christened WILDFIRE were actually around long enough to promote the release to any extent is open to debate, though, as the apparently inseparable duo of Newton and Noon had hooked up with LIONHEART by around November of that year, whereas John Lockton defected to WILD HORSES virtually simultaneously. Alan Nelson, meanwhile, resurfaced in STAMPEDE, although Doug Edwards vanished off the face of the earth. It's entirely possible, by the way, that the poorly-distributed »Run To Ground« 7" didn't get into general circulation until the early months of 1981 (by which time the participants were all settled with their latest projects), although it wasn't released as a posthumous affair. It was, all things considered, an extraordinarily unusual set of circumstances (there are also some unstickered copies, perhaps sent out as advance promos), and even the one-time members have little recollection of what really happened. In some respects, therefore, it's quite fortunate that this group had ceased all operations by the time the next WILDFIRE (Paul Mario Day and Co.) arrived on the scene to cause even more bewilderment amongst fans and collectors of the genre. Phew!

7" Singles
»Run To Ground« Steel City Records 1980

Compilation Appearances
"Wild Dog" on »Muthas Pride« 12" EP EMI 1980

WILDFIRE (II)

Paul Mario Day (v)
Jeff Summers (g)
Martin Bushell (g)
Jeff Brown (b)
Bruce Bisland (d)

Although they were neither the first nor the last band (either in Britain or overseas) to adopt the very metal WILDFIRE moniker, the London-based act who recorded for Mausoleum Records can quite safely lay claim to being the most successful of all. Depending on whose version of events you choose to believe, however, the story of how it all started can vary quite considerably, although the most plausible background seems to centre around vocalist Paul Mario Day, who had left his previous act, MORE (see separate entry), halfway through the recording sessions for the latter's second album. In the wake of his departure, he collaborated with long-time associate Martin Bushell on what was essentially 'solo' material, and some speculative demos (laid down towards the end of 1982) were apparently of sufficiently high quality to arouse the interest of Mausoleum, who hurriedly snapped up the emergent 'band' (who still had no name and no fixed line-up at that stage) before anyone else could get in on the act. Before long, however, the central nucleus of Day and Bushell had conspired to rope in Jeff Summers and Bruce Bisland (both from the recently-deceased WEAPON), and duly began working with guest bassist Brian Day, who was still very much a part of the MORE set-up.

By early 1983, however, the project had acquired both an identity (the lads having rejected their label's own suggestions for a suitable name, notably VOODOO) and a permanent bassist in the form of Jeff Brown, a much-travelled scenester who had been enticed away from his cushy position in DUMPY'S RUSTY NUTS for something a bit more ambitious. With an album's worth of material having been captured on tape within a matter of weeks, the first WILDFIRE long-player was soon being assembled (it was actually recorded in Belgium), and »Brute Force And Ignorance« (inspired by a RORY GALLAGHER song title, I reckon) appeared a short time later, encased in a pretty minimalist cover. The record revealed WILDFIRE to be continuing in the raunchy, heavy rock tradition of DEEP PURPLE and RAINBOW, although, as with similarly-minded NWOBHM acts such as WHITE SPIRIT, AFTER DARK and TWISTED ACE, they successfully managed to infuse something of a contemporary twist into the material, their extremely capable singer helping matters considerably. It was also a bold move for the outfit to unveil a selection of songs which oscillated between the extremes of accessible rock and heavy(ish) metal; the powerful "Violator" and "Redline" (boasting some highly accomplished twin-guitar work at times) contrasting with the melody of "Victim Of Love" and "If I Tried" (overlooking the utterly bizarre snippet of "Scarborough Fair" at the start, that is), for example. All in all, WILDFIRE's debut was certainly a confident and impressive affair (it wasn't a flawless slice of vinyl, though) which suggested that a pretty healthy future awaited the talented quintet.

The lads kept something of a low profile for the next year or so, electing to spend a great deal of time in Europe, where they busied themselves by writing and recording new material for a follow-up album (Bruce Bisland also took time out to assist in an ill-fated WEAPON reformation). It would have been the ideal opportunity for WILDFIRE to try out some of their newer numbers in the live environment, although it seems that their label was to plead poverty at every available opportunity, scuppering any prospective tours before they could even get past the planning stage. A few gigs did take place at home, however, including a memorable occasion when they shared a stage (sort of) with none other than METALLICA, as Bruce Bisland later recalled: *'It was at the opening of a new club belonging to a friend of ours, and he was handing out free booze to all the guests. We were doing our thing on stage, and then in came METALLICA! They asked us if they could get up and play a couple of songs, but I wasn't all that happy about them using my drumkit! That must have been in 1984, METALLICA were in England but their tour had been cancelled because too few tickets had been sold. They were really terrible that evening, they started arguing amongst themselves and we just said to ourselves: they'll never make it! Well, anyone can make a mistake…'* (Ref: Interview, Matthias Mader, March 1996). Just be grateful that nobody bootlegged that show…

In due course, the second WILDFIRE album was recorded (again in Belgium, this time utilising the occasional keyboard section from guest member Austin England), the set being released towards the end of 1984 as »Summer Lightning«. In truth, it was something of a disappointment after their comparatively strong debut, and the lacklustre compositions (supposedly a collective effort, with all of the members being credited as co-writers this time) barely managed to capture the listener's attention at any point. In all likelihood, the fact that the musicians had been unable to gauge public reaction to the latest material in advance may have been their undoing. There were, nevertheless, a handful of reasonable inclusions, notably the fairly powerful "Gun Runner", "Screaming In The Night" and "Natural Selection", although it was a release which ultimately failed to exude the sheer confidence of its predecessor, and it often seemed that Paul Mario Day was trying just a bit too hard with his vocal performance, going slightly over-the-top on occasion. With the majority of numbers sinking into sub-BRONZ mediocrity, it came as little surprise when the latest WILDFIRE long-player failed to perform particularly well in terms of sales, although the musicians and their management attempted to salvage the situation by lining up »Nothing Lasts Forever« as a tie-in single and arranging to record a slot for the 'Friday Rock Show'. Broadcast on the 9th of November 1984, the session showcased three tracks from the latest LP ("Summer Lightning", "Nothing Lasts Forever" and "The Key"), as well as a traditional poem-set-to-music called "Jerusalem", a truly dreadful dirge which surely qualifies as one of the more ill-advised *'cover versions'* of the period.

The struggling outfit persevered into 1985, having failed to reverse their fortunes in the previous few months, at which point they took the monumentally laughable decision to utilise their overblown interpretation of "Jerusalem" as the main focus of attention on their next 7", a futile move which ultimately yielded one of Mausoleum's worst-selling singles of all time (no mean feat, I can assure you). WILDFIRE's last noteworthy piece of musical activity was an appearance on the 'E.C.T.' television programme in the spring of 1985, a truly painful experience which saw the hapless bunch performing their "Natural Selection" and a worse-than-ever rendition of "Jerusalem" in front of a bemused audience. Even the musicians themselves must have realised that they had contrived to lose the plot completely by this stage, and the curtain came down mercifully swiftly, with four of the full-time members (Brown, Summers, Bisland and Bushell) defecting *en masse* to Gary Barden's shamelessly melodic STATETROOPER venture (see separate entry) a short time later. Paul Mario Day, on the other hand, worked sporadically with acts such as THE SWEET (as did the likes of Jeff Brown and Bruce Bisland) in later years, although he appears to be keeping himself to himself these days, having emigrated to Australia some time back.

LP's
»**Brute Force And Ignorance**« Mausoleum 1983
»**Summer Lightning**« Mausoleum 1984

7" Singles
»**Nothing Lasts Forever**« Mausoleum 1984
»**Jerusalem**« Mausoleum 1985

[A-side non-LP]

CD's
»Brute Force And Ignorance« Mausoleum Classix 1994
[Unofficial release]
»Summer Lightning« Mausoleum Classix 1994
[Unofficial release]

WILD HORSES

Jimmy Bain (v, b)
Neil Carter (g)
Brian Robertson (g, k)
Clive Edwards (d)

The original incarnation of WILD HORSES (not to be confused with the KINGDOM COME-related bunch who issued the »Bare Back« album in the early 90's) first came together in 1978, following the departure of Jimmy Bain and Brian Robertson from RAINBOW and THIN LIZZY, respectively. Although cynics suggested that this would be little more than a cash-in to make a bit of money from fans of the aforementioned outfits, it was certainly a genuine project (their assurance that it would sound nothing like their previous groups was to prove slightly misleading, however), as evidenced by the fact that the outfit were more than happy to start again from scratch and work their way up from modest early gigs in a variety of small club venues. In the first instance, the central duo recruited experienced guitarist Neil Carter (who had latterly been pottering around in a minor club act with future GRAND PRIX stalwart Phil Lanzon) and drafted in drummer Kevin Johns to make up the numbers. In the event, however, the first-choice sticksman failed to measure up to their stringent requirements, whereupon erstwhile LONE STAR skin-pounder Dixie Lee was targeted as his successor. The latter was soon also shown the door, though, as Brian Robertson frankly explained: *'We had to sack him because he was a nutcase.'* (Ref: Acne'n'Dandruff, Issue 1, May 1980). Former FILTHY McNASTY/ELECTRIC SUN/PAT TRAVERS man Clive Edwards was swiftly identified as a suitable replacement, and, happily, things ran slightly more smoothly for a while. Surprisingly, Bain had decided that a dedicated frontman would not be a fundamental requirement of WILD HORSES, and assumed most of the vocal duties in this new venture himself, although he happily handed over the mike stand to Robertson on occasion.

The outfit's progression was a swift one (helped along by a support slot with RUSH), and they became one of EMI's first proper rock/metal signings (along with the ill-fated KICK) at some point in 1979, shortly before the label's involvement with the NWOBHM really took off. The lads were fortunate enough to be included on the bill of that year's Reading Festival before they even had a solitary 7" release to their name, and they proceeded to play a fairly comprehensive set which appeared to go down very well with the assembled masses. Before the end of the year, their first single hit the shops, coupling "Criminal Tendencies" with the inadvisably-titled "The Rapist", which is best glossed-over. The two-tracker was indicative of a fairly unremarkable, heavy rock style with a slight American inclination (and more than a hint of THIN LIZZY), reasonably close to the type of material found on the MEANSTREAK and AURORA releases. An eponymous longplayer followed in the new year, although it was a limp affair which enjoyed only a marginal relationship with the NWOBHM (it completely failed to capture any of the group's live charisma), the limitations of Bain's vocals being displayed with painful efficiency. Inevitably, however, the loyal THIN LIZZY fans were soon gleefully handing over their hard-earned cash for a copy, eventually sending the record into the album charts of the day. Two singles (»Face Down« and »Flyaway«) were churned out over the ensuing months, and a further support slot with TED NUGENT came their way in the summer. Towards the end of the year, the group jetted off to Japan, where they had contrived to develop a cult following before the album had even been released, and played a successful series of shows to near-hysterical audiences. To say that anything LIZZY-related was a guaranteed success in the Far East would be something of an understatement…

By 1981, the outfit had drafted in ex-NEXT BAND/WILDFIRE guitarist John Lockton in the aftermath of Neil Carter's sudden defection to UFO (he later worked alongside Gary Moore), and they were soon back in the studio to lay down a second album for EMI. Fortunately, however, the musicians had toughened up the sound somewhat by the time »Stand Your Ground« appeared in the spring, and the set was rather more attuned to the brand of heavy music that was in vogue at the time. It still wasn't full-blown NWOBHM by any means (reasonably similar to STAMPEDE and GRAND PRIX in places), but it was a hell of a lot closer than their backward-looking debut. Perversely, though, it actually failed to rival its full-length predecessor in terms of sales, so their sponsors were soon having second thoughts about keeping the WILD HORSES on their books. A (supposedly) limited-edition double single was issued to promote the LP, featuring "I'll Give You Love" and the otherwise-unavailable "The Kid", plus two live tracks from their Japanese tour (an interminable version of the JOE WALSH dirge "Rocky Mountain Way" and "On A Saturday Night", another obscure cover, this time of a BLUES BROTHERS BAND original), although this package doesn't appear to have sold in particularly stellar quantities either. A final two-tracker was scheduled to appear shortly thereafter, coupling the outfit's interpretation of the old LOVE AFFAIR chestnut "Everlasting Love" with "The Axe", although remarkably few copies appear to have made it into the shops, for some reason, and this particular record is a seldom-sighted item nowadays.

The outfit were featured on the BBC's 'In Concert' radio programme in June 1981 (alongside the thriving EXPORT), where they showcased some of their newer compositions, but it was all starting to go wrong by this time. Robertson and Edwards flew the coop in the autumn (the former going on to work with MOTÖRHEAD and STATETROOPER, the latter enjoying stints with LIONHEART, S.O.S., INFIDEL, GRAND PRIX and UFO), and it wasn't long before the ousted LIONHEART drummer, Frank Noon, offered his services to WILD HORSES, bringing vocalist Reuben Archer with him. In due course, Reuben's stepson Laurence (the pair had earlier played together in LAUTREC) was roped in to replace Robertson, and the all-new five-piece version of WILD HORSES (with Reuben Archer taking over on vocals) soon began to establish itself in terms of rehearsals. Not only that, they proceeded to book a generous chunk of studio time later in the year, their intention being to work on a new selection of material for a possible third album. Ultimately, however, it all fell apart with great speed when the three new members announced that they couldn't work productively with Bain in the studio environment, and so the WILD HORSES were soon being consigned to the knacker's yard for good. Soon after, the Archers/Noon triumvirate departed in order to start up their ambitious STAMPEDE project, while John Lockton went on to have a stint with German rockers VICTORY. Jimmy Bain failed to get a new outfit of his own off the ground in the short term, and was eventually to accept an offer to join DIO, where he subsequently spent many happy years as bassist.

LP's
»**Wild Horses**« EMI 1980
»**Stand Your Ground**« EMI 1981

7" Singles
»**Criminal Tendencies**« EMI 1979
[B-side "The Rapist" non-LP]
»**Face Down**« EMI 1980
[UK issue]
»**Face Down**« EMI Japan 1980
[Japanese issue in different sleeve]
»**Flyaway**« EMI 1980
[Most issued on white vinyl, some demo copies on black]
»**I'll Give You Love**« EMI 1981
[B-side "Rocky Mountain Way" (live) non-LP, also issued as limited edition in gatefold sleeve with free single featuring "The Kid" and "On A Saturday Night" (live), both non-LP]
»**Everlasting Love**« EMI 1981
[A-side non-LP, very few copies in circulation, possibly promos only]

CD's
»**Wild Horses**« EMI Japan 199?
[Japanese issue]
»**Stand Your Ground**« EMI Japan 199?
[Japanese issue]
»**Mad Axe Attack**« Nightlife 1996
[Live bootleg from 1979]
»**Wild Horses**« Zoom Club Records 1999
[With two bonus tracks]
»**Stand Your Ground**« Zoom Club Records 1999
[With two bonus tracks]

Compilation Appearances
"**Criminal Tendencies**" on »Metal Mania« LP EMI 1980 + »Heavy Duty« LP Harvest 1980
"**Face Down**" on »The Bible Of Hard Rock« CD Toshiba 1990 + »The Rainbow Family Album« CD Connoisseur 1994

WILDSMITH ST.

Line-up unknown

More mystery men from South Wales, whose only claim to notoriety appears to have been issuing a single *via* their local Note Pad label (a small-time operation who put together the odd parochial compilation in their time) sometime in the early/middle part of the NWOBHM era. The mid-paced "Oh No Not Again" turns out to be a fairly substantial slice of rock/metal with some pretty gruff vocals, occasionally bringing to mind the A.R.C. ROCK BAND or a slightly more cheerful and less war-obsessed TANK (let's face it, folks, it's hard to imagine a *more* war-obsessed TANK). In stark contrast, however, the B-side ("Please Don't Phone") is a much more lightweight effort (complete with some immensely irritating *'telephone'* effects), coming across as quite similar in style to bands such as H.G.B., ANGEL STREET or BILL THE MURDERER. Not bad, all the same, and this scarcely-sighted single (like everything else on Notepad) remains a pretty rare piece of vinyl today. No picture sleeve appears to have been issued, unfortunately, and there's virtually no information on the anonymous-looking record itself, so any further details would be appreciated. Another good name for a heavy outfit, it certainly sounds as though WILDSMITH ST. would have been an interesting place to live...

7" Singles
»Oh No Not Again« Note Pad Records 198?

WINTER'S REIGN

Billy 'Bo' Larkin (v)
Leo Larkin (g)
Paul Dixon (b)
Brian Lynch (k)
Stuart MacMillan (d)

While Ireland's prolific WINTER'S REIGN are undoubtedly most familiar to rock enthusiasts through their late 80's releases, they actually formed right at the start of the decade, although a stable line-up wasn't realised until the latter part of 1982. Their first known vinyl releases (although there may still be some even earlier examples) are a couple of scarcely-sighted singles, issued (in customised company sleeves) on the Irish Scoff label (one-time home of MAMA'S BOYS) in around 1984. The first of these features "Save It" and "I Keep Trying", while the second couples "Karen" with "I'm Getting Out", and both efforts represent a pretty decent attempt at keyboard-infused, melodic rock/metal in the manner of JOKERS WILD, VOYAGER UK or GENERAL WOLF. A year or two later, having recruited new keyboard player Mick Cavanagh and supported the likes of GARY MOORE in their homeland, the group issued their confusingly-titled »The Mini Album«, which is actually a full LP but which has a picture of two mini-skirted posteriors on the cover (highly comical, I'm sure). With the exception of "I Keep Trying", the tracks from their earlier singles are all recycled (including two extremely similar versions of "Karen", for no good reason), alongside a selection of newer numbers such as "Is This The End", "Can You Keep A Secret" and a couple of soppy ballads, all of which are in the same general mode.

By the time the outfit's second set was recorded in 1987, however, only bassist Paul Dixon and Mick Cavanagh (the latter now assuming guitar duties) remained from the previous line-up, with new boy Robbie 'Animal' Hurley joining them on vocals and keyboards. No permanent drummer is credited this time (although SAXON's Nigel Glockler is a prominent inclusion on the thanks list), so it looks as though they probably used guest musicians and/or a drum machine during the recording process. With the LP being given the title of »The Beginning...«, it might well have been regarded as signifying a new start for the experienced act (it was even widely advertised as their *'superb debut album'*), although no fundamental alteration of their musical stance was particularly apparent. Mind you, it certainly seemed to be the case that the lads had been affected by the phenomenal success of EUROPE and BON JOVI during the previous year or so, and "White Fury" (which, despite its contentious title, is actually about boxing) is a reasonably strong opener in this style (it may also have been issued as a single at some point, but I'm not entirely sure). Elsewhere, "Take It Away" is listenable enough, although the rest of the album (including a tribute to Phil Lynott and a cover of a HORSLIPS number, suggesting a great deal of national pride) is, unfortunately, far too lightweight and slushy for all but the most easily-assuaged melodic rocker. Incidentally, some copies of the LP were issued with a free single (featuring two exclusive tracks) as a bonus. Whoopee.

On the back of this full-length release, the lads secured a couple of prestigious appearances on Irish television as well as the odd vinyl/live review in the likes of 'Kerrang' and 'Metal Hammer', although these weren't always particularly favourable. Nonetheless, the ensemble continued to do their thing, becoming a proper five-piece concern with the addition of drummer Wataru Noguchi (now there's an Irish name if ever I saw one) and Robbie Block on keyboards. Showing their caring side, they recorded a single (coupling the BEATLES number "Ticket To Ride" with their own throwaway effort "What Do You Call It") in order to raise funds to cover the medical bills incurred by a young relative of their manager. Bass duties on this release were handled by new recruit Rodney Pepper, and Robbie Block had apparently flown the coop (Robbie Hurley taking over on keyboards once again) by the time WINTER'S REIGN had been picked up by the influential GWR label (home of MOTÖRHEAD, GIRLSCHOOL, FASTWAY et al.) a year or so later. The fruit of this liaison seems to have been a lone, eponymous album (although, for some reason, few copies appear to be in circulation) and a 7" coupling "Go For Gold" with "Mayday" (the latter also featuring on an obscure Legacy/GWR compilation). Although slightly over-produced, this new material was stronger than before, but it seems not to have reversed their collective fortunes, leaving the band to fade into obscurity soon after; in recent years, things have been remarkably quiet on the WINTER'S REIGN front.

LP's
»The Mini Album« Q Records 1985
»The Beginning...« Loop Records 1987
[Some copies issued with free single featuring "Rock Me" and "A Quickie"]
»Winter's Reign« GWR Records 1990

7" Singles
»Save It« Scoff Records 1984
[B-side "I Keep Trying" non-LP]
»Karen« Scoff Records 1984
»Rock Me« Loop Records 1988
[Free with some copies of »The Beginning...« album, both tracks non-LP]
»Ticket To Ride« War Records 1989?
[Both tracks non-LP]
»Go For Gold« GWR Records 1990

CD's
»The Beginning...« Loop Records 1987
[Includes two bonus tracks]
»Winter's Reign« GWR Records 1990

Compilation Appearances
"Mayday" on »Iron Brew« LP/CD Legacy Records 1990

WITCHES BREW

Ron Göbl (v, g)
Barry McCabe (b)
Sean Maguire (d)

In the immortal words of SPINAL TAP's Nigel Tufnel, *'Is this a joke?'* Fair enough, we've all encountered the odd NWOBHM-period single which includes one reasonable side and one *'not so good'* effort (TEMPEST's »Hell Fire«, RADAR's »Leave Her Alone«, TOAD THE WET SPROCKET's »Pete's Punk Song« etc.), but this absolute shocker (by the long-forgotten WITCHES BREW) elevates the sub-genre to an entirely new level. The cover, featuring the group's logo and a cauldron, seems inoffensive enough, and the musicians look like fairly typical metallers with their bullet belts and regulation facial hair, so what could be the problem? Well, if you can honestly listen to »Angeline« without thinking of "Last Christmas" by WHAM! (come on, we've all heard it), then I reckon you deserve a special prize for services to metal. Honestly, this grotesque song, with its saxophones (was somebody selling them wholesale?) and harmonised vocals, would be rejected by most pop hopefuls for being obnoxiously saccharine, and it's virtually impossible to rationalise the philosophy behind the pairing of this odious monstrosity with "Reach For The Night", which is, in truth, a vaguely acceptable attempt at straight ahead metal with attitude, although the vocal performance is pretty dire. Clearly, this hapless Irish threesome had some serious identity problems, and even roping in Pat McManus from MAMA'S BOYS to help with the recording session evidently failed to postpone their inevitable demise at the hands of a baying mob of headbangers. Avoid like the plague.

7" Singles
»Angeline« Pussy Records 1981?

WITCHFINDER GENERAL

Zeeb Parkes (v)
Phil Cope (g)
Toss McCready (b)
Steve Kinsell (d)

It's hard to comprehend why some NWOBHM bands have been elevated to quasi-mythical status in the years since their demise (or, at least, since their glory days): VENOM, once considered a poor musical joke, are now widely regarded as the godfathers of black metal, while the likes of ANGEL WITCH and DIAMOND HEAD (immensely popular acts in their heyday, admittedly) have, in recent years, been lionised by the NWOBHM community to such an extent that their original vinyl offerings can barely do justice to the self-perpetuating legend. On the other hand, WITCHFINDER GENERAL seem to be the definitive example of an outfit who were *'discovered'* by means of retrospection, as they hardly amounted to a hill of beans at the time. Their story goes back to the late 70's, when Zeeb Parkes and Phil Cope (both experienced players from the West Midlands music scene) gravitated together to form a songwriting partnership which would ultimately yield some unashamedly heavy music. With the pair taking their inspiration from some of the region's legendary musical forefathers, notably an obscure bunch of heavyweights called EARTH (who apparently later changed their name to something-or-other), a shared appreciation of classic horror films (particularly those produced by the legendary 'Hammer' studio), plus a predilection for gothic imagery and macabre lyrics, the entity known as WITCHFINDER GENERAL gradually took shape in their twisted minds.

By the tail end of 1978, a considerable amount of original material had already been written, whereupon the central duo roped in a variety of fly-by-night drummers (including Cope's cousin) and bassists (most of whom had very silly names indeed) to help out with their projected live appearances. The initial series of WITCHFINDER GENERAL gigs finally took place in the early months of 1979, after which the lads took the opportunity to play the local clubs whenever possible. Over the following year or so, however, the outfit's activities generally failed to raise too many eyebrows, with most spectators regarding the oft-reshuffled quartet as little more than a curiosity which would soon be disappearing back into obscurity. Nevertheless, a plateau of stability appeared to have been reached by the second half of 1980, with bassist Toss (I bet nobody ever made fun of his name at all) McCready and drummer Steve Kinsell being recruited to the fold, whereupon the band managed to undertake a considerably more successful (if not particularly widespread) jaunt towards the end of the year. Moving into 1981, the lads somehow (I'm not actually convinced they even recorded a demo) attracted the attention of their local label, Heavy Metal Records, and were one of the first batch of hopefuls to be encouraged to lay down a single for the newly-formed company.

WITCHFINDER GENERAL's first visit to the recording studio was a fairly memorable (but not particularly satisfying) affair, as Zeeb Parkes later recalled: *'It was diabolical. We must take much of the blame for it, cos our inexperience in the studio came through. What made it even worse, though, was that something went wrong during the cutting of the record and the bass lines were all distorted. And the studio itself (Ginger) were also partly at fault, a fact they conceded by allowing us some free time as a way of making up for it.'* (Ref: Kerrang No.29, November 1982). So there you have it. Conclusive evidence that the heaviness and fuzziness of the outfit's early numbers may have been partially due to studio limitations and mastering ineptitude! Whatever the story, there's little argument that their earliest material was their heaviest, and it's these particular releases which have largely drawn the attention of doom fans in recent times. The result of their initial studio activities was a batch of four or five tracks, including "Burning A Sinner" and "Satan's Children", two excellent efforts which bore little resemblance to what was going on in most of Britain at that time (aside from that odd pocket of atypically heavy outfits such as ARC and REQUIEM, most of whom were actually also based in the West Midlands), and had far more common with the considerably more doomy acts who were doing the utmost to create their own scene across the Atlantic, notably PENTAGRAM (in particular) and ST. VITUS. Nevertheless, the lads found a few new fans in the UK, and undertook a handful of local gigs (they were never the most prolific of touring acts) to promote their new single.

As previously mentioned, WITCHFINDER GENERAL still had some additional studio material from that initial recording session at their disposal, and they soon began to make pretty good use of it. First, "Rabies" was trotted out for their label's original »Heavy Metal Heroes« compilation, and the lads were subsequently given the go-ahead to assemble a 12" EP, which featured the heavy "Soviet Invasion" (which, significantly, saw a move away from the usual horror-style lyricism) as its title track, plus "Rabies" (again) and a not-terribly-convincing *'live'* version of "R.I.P." (*i.e.* some Wembley Arena-style crowd hysterics dubbed on before and after the track itself). In fact, the chronology of events becomes a tad strange and convoluted here, as this EP wasn't actually released until the second half of 1982, several months after WITCHFINDER GENERAL's debut album had itself been recorded. However, the long-player was also kept back for some considerable time (for reasons which will become apparent shortly), and so the EP would still hit the shops first. By this stage, however, the outfit had undergone a couple of personnel changes, necessitated by the fact that their latest rhythm section had steadfastly refused to commit themselves to the project on a full-time basis. As a result, they were both *'permitted'* to go back to their day jobs, whereupon new bassist Woolfy

729

(yes, that's *Woolfy*) Trope was drafted in fairly swiftly. Recruiting a permanent drummer proved to be rather more problematic, however, and an unnamed session sticksman (possibly the bizarrely-nicknamed 'Derm The Germ', who is known to have lent a hand in the studio from time to time) was employed for the album recordings. In due course, though, a more suitable candidate emerged in the form of Graham Ditchfield, who was to remain something of a permanent fixture from that point onwards.

Now, WITCHFINDER GENERAL's masterplan for world domination basically involved the release of an album which would, one way or another, attract a fair old bit of attention from the media as a whole, and so the publicity machine undoubtedly went into overdrive in the months prior to its release. Tales were spun concerning the utterly grotesque lyrics (no printer was prepared to process the intended lyric sheets, apparently) and lurid cover (which would be banned instantaneously, apparently), although it looks as though relatively few of the jaded journalists in the rock world actually took the bait. The tabloid press, however, jumped at the chance to denounce these unholy blasphemers who were about to shake the very foundations of society with their moral turpitude and devil's cacophony. Inevitably, it all blew over pretty quickly after the initial hysteria; the record (when Heavy Metal eventually got around to releasing it) wasn't banned and comparatively few eyebrows were raised at the cover image, depicting the mock-sacrifice of a nubile wench who had somehow mislaid most of her garments. In fact, the general (as it were) opinion was one of derision rather than utter repulsion, and many onlookers regarded WITCHFINDER GENERAL as a rather pitiful bunch of overgrown adolescents who had stooped pretty low to make their name known to the masses.

In fact, the album (»Death Penalty«) wasn't as musically atrocious as the packaging might have suggested, and it contained a few decent enough efforts, most notably the lengthy and complex "Invisible Hate" and "Death Penalty" itself. Having said that, however, most of the other inclusions were (while heavy enough, admittedly) just too darn *cheerful* (especially the proto-stoner philosophy of "Free Country") to qualify as *bona fide* doom metal in its purest sense of agonised despondency. Nevertheless, virtually every self-styled doom concern formed after 1982 have somehow felt compelled to quote WITCHFINDER GENERAL as a prime influence (I wonder how many of them could name more than three of their tracks?), although they surely have far more in common with such *'groovy'* outfits as ORANGE GOBLIN, ACRIMONY or (later) CATHEDRAL than with the utter bleakness of DREAM DEATH, WINTER or GRIEF, for example. In fact, WITCHFINDER GENERAL were really (on their albums, anyway) only a doom band in the same sense as DESOLATION ANGELS, PAGAN ALTAR, DEMON or ANGEL WITCH, their music employing some unusually heavy guitar work at times, but tending to favour the NWOBHM dynamism rather than sludgy, tortuous riffs. If all you doomsters were actually to abandon your preconceptions and listen to »Death Penalty« with an open mind, I'm sure you'd be forced to concede that it's nowhere near as heavy as people seem to have been brainwashed into thinking…

The album sold in reasonable quantities, although the lads appear to have been increasingly reticent to get out on the road to promote themselves, and they were to make no further vinyl appearances for the best part of a year, with the exception of "Free Country", which was recycled on the second »Heavy Metal Heroes« compilation. In fact, they had been suffering continued personnel problems, with Woolfy (and I haven't even made any *'freedom for Tooting'* references until now) having gone back to the woods after the long-player had been recorded, leaving the group to recruit a new bassist with the disappointingly sensible name of Rod 'Corks' Hawks. It would appear that Graham Ditchfield was also unsettled in his new post, although the outfit managed to retain the sticksman in a *'guest'* capacity for their future recording sessions. In due course, WITCHFINDER GENERAL were back in the studio one again, and another long-player was scheduled for release in the second half of 1983, leading to conjecture that they might have smartened up their act a bit and abandoned the tacky covers and silly lyrics. Had they bollocks. »Friends Of Hell« was more of the same, and this time the sleeve featured a veritable bevy of young ladies (who, predictably, had made a few glaring errors when getting dressed that morning), once again being ravished in a graveyard by the leering band members (who, by the looks of it, had a good thing going with the local fancy dress shop). Oh dear, some people never learn.

In fact, the music was pretty decent once again, possibly even more varied and accomplished than on their debut LP, with some slightly more original musicianship on display. The likes of "Friends Of Hell" and "Requiem For Youth" certainly had one or two interesting ideas, for example, and the surprisingly sensitive "I Lost You" was something of an unexpected inclusion. Elsewhere, the lyrics now occasionally deviated from the occult path, and there also seemed to a tangible move towards rather more traditional NWOBHM territory, with occasional similarities to the likes of SATAN, KRAKEN and BLITZKRIEG. Nevertheless, the heavy riffs were still present, but this was, overall, even less of a *'doom'* album than its predecessor. Even so, the novelty of the act appeared to have worn off by now, and the sales figures turned out to be disappointingly modest. A single, »Music«, was trundled out to promote the latest full-length release, but it failed to make much of an impression, and the outfit seemed to be in decline as they moved into 1984. In fact, things appear to have ground to a halt over the ensuing months, with few (if any) sightings of WITCHFINDER GENERAL in the live environment, and no subsequent reports of further studio activity filtering through at any stage. It looked bad, and, in the absence of any official announcement, the public were left to assume that the members had finally gone their separate ways.

It's ironic that WITCHFINDER GENERAL ultimately fell apart in such inauspicious circumstances, given that their popularity later rocketed to levels which had been utterly unknown while the group were still a going concern, and, to be honest, I reckon their musical legacy has been blown out of proportion in recent years. They were a decent enough band, but they didn't change the world or do anything that hadn't been tried a decade earlier. The main members of the combo, Zeeb Parkes and Phil Cope, have long since joined *'respectable'* society, and the only one-time member of WITCHFINDER GENERAL to have maintained any sort of role in the music business is a certain bassist known as Zak Bajjon (another award-winning name), who has shamelessly advertised himself as an *'ex-WITCHFINDER GENERAL'* bod at every conceivable opportunity since he first formed his own outfit called BAJJON way back in 1986. In fact, it would appear that this guy was only involved with WITCHFINDER GENERAL for about half an hour (well, maybe a bit longer) in the early part of 1979, but I suppose a modicum of blatant name-dropping (especially when it helps to further a flagging career) is excusable every now and then. In spite of the cheeky chap's slightly misleading credentials, though, it's worth mentioning that he later cropped up in LIONSHEART, and has been working more recently with emerging metal acts such as CROWFOOT and RAINMAKER.

LP's
»**Death Penalty**« Heavy Metal 1982
[Also released as limited edition picture disc and on both red and clear vinyl]
»**Friends Of Hell**« Heavy Metal 1983
[Also released as limited edition picture disc and on both blue and silver vinyl]

12" EP's
»**Soviet Invasion**« Heavy Metal 1982
[Both "Soviet Invasion" and "Rabies" non-LP, also includes 'live' version of "R.I.P."]

7" Singles
»**Burning A Sinner**« Heavy Metal 1981
[A-side different to album version, B-side "Satan's Children" non-LP]
»**Music**« Heavy Metal 1983
[A-side different to album version, also released as limited edition silver vinyl 'picture disc']
»**Burning A Sinner**« Old World Records 1998
[Limited edition numbered reissue, issued in original picture sleeve with inverse colour scheme]

CD's
»**Death Penalty**« Teichiku 1990
[Japanese issue in gold cover]
»**Death Penalty**« Heavy Metal 1996
»**Friends Of Hell**« Heavy Metal 1998

Compilation Appearances
"Rabies" on »Heavy Metal Heroes« LP Heavy Metal 1981 *[Issued in two different sleeves]* + »Heavy Metal Heroes Vol.I&II« CD British Steel 1996
"Free Country" on »Heavy Metal Heroes Vol.2« LP Heavy Metal 1982 + »Heavy Metal Heroes Vol.I&II« CD British Steel 1996
"Friends Of Hell" on »Metal Inferno« LP Castle Communications 1985 + »Metal Killers Kollection II« Do-LP Castle Communications 1986
"Witchfinder General" on »NWOBHM '79 Revisited« Do-CD Phonogram 1990
"Music" on »N.W.O.B.H.M.« LP/CD Heavy Metal 1991 + »Give 'Em Hell« CD Nectar Masters 1995
"Soviet Invasion" on »NWOBHM Vol.3« Bootleg CD 1992

WITCHFYNDE

Steve Bridges (v)
Montalo (g)
Andro Coulton (b)

Gra Scoresby (d)

Initially conceived as long ago as 1975, Nottinghamshire's oddly-named WITCHFYNDE (something that caused a fair bit of confusion when the similarly-monikered WITCHFINDER GENERAL came along a few years later) appear to have considered themselves to be the very epitome of occult rock/metal, although they were, in all honesty, yet another of the many bands who merely flirted with the pseudo-satanic imagery as and when it suited them. Their early attempts to convince the masses of their talents were largely ignored, and it took the lads several years to attain the status of a remotely credible proposition. Eventually, however, they became the first rock act to be picked up by the

rather inconsistent Rondelet (or 'Round Records', as they styled themselves at the outset) label, the first fruit of this relationship being their »Give 'Em Hell« two-tracker, released towards the end of 1979. The A-side was, admittedly, quite a weighty effort, building on the foundations laid by the familiar occult/theatrical pairing of BLACK SABBATH and BLACK WIDOW (see also HELL, PAGAN ALTAR etc.) to produce a slightly more contemporary and substantial contribution to the burgeoning NWOBHM scene. Having said that, the flipside ("Gettin' Heavy") was an extremely unremarkable composition all round, and showed a slightly disconcerting tendency to slip into rather more of a primitive style, almost bordering on pub rock.

Nevertheless, the single became an extraordinarily popular purchase (the original limited pressing on Round Records would be exhausted pretty swiftly) for many NWOBHM fans of the day, and a full WITCHFYNDE album was soon being worked upon. Released in the early months of 1980, »Give 'Em Hell« (the album, that is) was, to be honest, a rather inauspicious and pedestrian effort, although there were a couple of reasonably listenable inclusions, notably the more pacey and hard-rocking "Ready To Roll" and "Pay Now-Love Later", both of which bore fairly strong similarities to the likes of MARZ, RENEGADE and Cheshire's WOLF. As you might expect, the outfit's high-concept pieces turned out to be rather more heavy-going (although not necessarily particularly *heavy* in a musical sense), the best of the bunch being a capable effort called "The Divine Victim", a historical retelling of Joan Of Arc's sticky end. "Unto The Ages Of The Ages" (a mystical tale of something-or-other), on the other hand, had a few good ideas, but lasted an eternity (maybe that was the whole idea), while the impenetrable nonsense of "Leaving Nadir" (which would actually put in an appearance on the »NWOBHM '79 Revisited« set in 1990) was completely disposable. In spite of its shortcomings, however, the record still proceeded to shift a highly impressive number of units, and the public were soon treated to a reissue of »Give 'Em Hell« (the single, that is).

The lads went out on the road to promote their recently-unveiled album, initially undertaking a few headlining shows of their own and then hooking up with unlikely tour associates DEF LEPPARD for a successful series of dates. Reports of the time generally painted WITCHFYNDE as a talented and energetic live act, although there was little or no mention of the quartet's supposed fascination with theatrical imagery and occult lyrical concepts, so I reckon they weren't actually branded as 'wannabe satanists' until later on. In fact, the group's more straight-ahead material was often stronger than their 'darker' efforts, so it might actually have been a better idea to concentrate on the more accessible compositions and distance themselves from all that diabolical (in more ways than one) piffle. Just to be really awkward, WITCHFYNDE did precisely the opposite, becoming more and more dependent on the occult themes as time went on. To their credit, however, they didn't go the whole hog and try to pass themselves off as direct competition to VENOM, and their next album, recorded towards the end of 1980, was a considerably more upbeat and listenable effort than their debut. That being said, »Stagefright« (the first release to feature new bassist Pete Surgey) was an inconsistent mishmash of material, and the heavier numbers (such as "Wake Up Screaming" and the title track itself) sat uneasily alongside the likes of "Moon Magic", "In The Stars" and "Trick Or Treat", which now saw the band moving into PRAYING MANTIS territory. Furthermore, several other inclusions were even more lightweight, such as the 70's rock of "Would Not Be Seen Dead In Heaven", the dismal ballad "Madeleine" and the abysmal semi-pop of "Big Deal", which could easily have passed for a SMOKIN ROADIE or DEDRINGER composition.

Having apparently ditched the dreary and lengthy dirges for the time being, it looked as though WITCHFYNDE would win a few new fans with their more punchy, accessible material, although »Stagefright« appears to have sold rather more poorly than its predecessor, suggesting that many remained unconvinced that the outfit really meant business. Nevertheless, »In The Stars« (b/w "Wake Up Screaming") was trotted out as a single, which appears to have been a slightly more worthwhile release. In due course, however, the group were to lose their original vocalist, Steve Bridges, and the comically-named Chalky White had been drafted in as a replacement by the early part of 1981. Within a fairly short space of time, the revised version of WITCHFYNDE were recording their first session for the 'Friday Rock Show', and they took the opportunity to showcase "Gettin' Heavy", "Give 'Em Hell", "Moon Magic" and "Belfast", the session being broadcast on the 13th of February 1981. "Belfast" was something of a major departure for WITCHFYNDE, a power ballad (written by their new frontman) with a strong political message (their associates in WARRIOR had already penned something of an analogous effort in their "Ulster, Bloody Ulster"), although it seems to have been a one-off, and they appear not to have pursued this particular direction with any great sense of conviction. Still, the track was considered worthy of inclusion on the BBC's »The Friday Rock Show« tie-in album from later in the year.

By this time, however, WITCHFYNDE were encountering serious problems with their label, who refused to finance further live outings, as Gra Scoresby later explained: *'After »Stagefright«, the record company's promotional activities left a lot to be desired. Touring is extremely expensive, and since we had to finance everything personally, we had to organise the shows ourselves. That sort of thing doesn't go down particularly well with the promoters. Our management was also our record label at the time, and they just didn't didn't want to know. So we had to do everything ourselves and in the end the stress was just too much.'* (Ref: Metal Forces No.7, 1984). Whether or not there was ever a possibility of another album being financed by Rondelet is open to debate, although it all became purely academic the following year, when the cash-strapped company finally went to the wall, leaving WITCHFYNDE with no option but to seek out a brand-new home. At first, there was speculation that the group might even have called it a day, as there seemed to be little or no evidence to suggest that they were still making trips to the studio. Given that the lads no longer had any kind of benefactors to subsidise such activities, though, it was understandable. In time, however, the protagonists began making valiant attempts to distract attention from their apparent inactivity by circulating a few cock-and-bull stories (I distinctly recall one laughable episode when they tried to convince everyone that Trevor, sorry, *Montalo* had apparently gone missing in mysterious circumstances) and insisting that they were still hard at work, *'researching'* a few lyrical concepts by immersing themselves in every grimoire and necronomicon they could get their hands on. I bet they were really down the pub all along.

However, WITCHFYNDE confounded the sceptics by resurfacing in 1983 (ostensibly with yet another new vocalist, although it transpires that Chalky White had merely reinvented himself as the King Diamond-soundalike *'Luther Beltz'*), and the lads soon had another full album to offer the world, having been snapped up by Expulsion Records in the interim. Their debut set for the label, »Cloak And Dagger« (a release which also appeared on Roadrunner), turned out to be a more substantial effort than their previous offerings, and the semi-operatic vocals lent more of a MERCYFUL FATE feeling to the proceedings. The heavier compositions, such as "The Devil's Playground", "Crystal Gazing" and "Cry Wolf" (complete with "Hall Of The Mountain King" intro) were the pick of the bunch, although even the more lightweight and tuneful numbers ("Somewhere To Hide", "Living For Memories") were played with considerably more panache than before. It wasn't a flawless album by any means, though, and it ran out of steam towards the end, with a couple of throwaway efforts ("Rock'n'Roll" and "Stay Away") serving little purpose other than merely filling up space. Nevertheless, the record (housed in a suitably cabalistic sleeve) went on to sell enough copies (as did »I'd Rather Go Wild«, which appeared as a tie-in single) to persuade the lads that it might be worth hanging around a bit longer. It was the end of the line as far as their record company (the cash-strapped Expulsion) and bassist (Pete Surgey) were concerned, though...

The early months of 1984 saw the persevering WITCHFYNDE signing to Mausoleum for their fourth long-player, and erstwhile PANZA DIVI-

SION bassist Alan Edwards was brought in to help out on the recording front, although a character called 'Edd Wolfe' (I strongly suspect that this was an assumed identity for their latest recruit) was eventually confirmed as Surgey's permanent replacement. Presented in another demonic-looking cover, »Lords Of Sin« appeared some time later, the first pressing (I'm not even sure if there was ever a second run, though) being housed within a gatefold sleeve with a bonus four track EP thrown in. The album itself was a fairly blatant attempt to deliver some slightly more classy hard rock/metal material, with lengthier songs and a far more restrained vocal performance from Luther Beltz being the order of the day. Sadly, however, the majority of the featured selections were so utterly nondescript and unmemorable that the reviewers slaughtered the record, which, understandably, proceeded to die a bit of a death in terms of sales. In fact, the likes of "Stab In The Back" and "Wall Of Death" weren't all that bad, and the long-player had one genuine ace in the form of "Scarlet Lady", an excellent, upbeat NWOBHM effort which, despite losing its way in the middle, could almost pass for MYTHRA. Incidentally, the freebie record which came with the album featured recent 'live' (strange, I don't remember them playing any gigs whatsoever after 1981, although it successfully gives the impression of a proper soundboard recording) versions of some of their early favourites (viz. "Cloak And Dagger", "I'd Rather Go Wild", "Moon Magic" and "Give 'Em Hell"), although it seems unlikely that many additional sales were solicited by its inclusion in the long run.

WITCHFYNDE were in serious decline after the initial failure of »Lords Of Sin« to sell in significant quantities, and their financially-struggling label could do little to bail them out. A single (»Conspiracy«) eventually appeared (in a very limited pressing, admittedly) the following year, although it's hard to see what purpose this could possibly have served after such a long interval. In any case, the lads had more or less decided to call it a day by this point, and nothing further was heard from the group in the second half of the decade. They still remained a pretty highly-regarded act by many NWOBHM fans, however, and interest in the band's career was briefly rekindled a few years ago when British Steel acquired the rights to Rondelet's back catalogue and assembled a CD with the slightly optimistic title of »The Best Of Witchfynde«. Apart from that, however, there was little else to report concerning the future activities of these ill-fated necromancers, and there didn't really seem to be much chance of a reformation, especially as the musicians apparently hadn't been maintaining any significant level of involvement with the local rock scene in the intervening years. By the late 90's, however, there were a few tantalising suggestions that WITCHFYNDE might be preparing for a long-awaited comeback after all. In the event, Luther Beltz finally came out of the wilderness to supply a solo track to a well-received DEMON tribute album (»The Day Of The Demon«), after which he reunited with his former colleagues Gra Scoresby, Montalo and Pete Surgey, and so it suddenly looked as though a fully-operational version of WITCHFYNDE could well be on the cards once again.

Peculiarly, however, Beltz soon decided to go off and do his own thing, although the remaining members were unperturbed by his departure, and simply recruited new frontman Harry Harrison, an experienced veteran of local acts such as NIGHTVISION and REBEL. In a bizarre twist, though, it transpires that Luther Beltz has now proceeded to assemble an entirely new backing ensemble (who, just to confuse matters, are operating under the not-very-catchy identity of LUTHER BELTZ WITCHFYNDE) consisting of Dave Hewitt (b), Ron Reynolds (g), Rick Gilliat (g) and Tez Brown (d). Even with two of these members (Hewitt and Reynolds) being borrowed from regional favourites STORMWATCH, this seems to be a pretty genuine attempt to get things going once again (they've demoed some impressive new material, and have even undertaken a high-profile appearance or two, although a proposed trip to Wacken never actually happened), but I'm positive we haven't heard the last of this rivalry between the two separate versions of the band. The 'original' WITCHFYNDE have recently gone as far as to create an official website to promote themselves, but I'm not sure if any new material has actually been written as yet. Mind you, I suppose the existence of these doppelgängers (confusing though it may be) doubles the chances of a sustained comeback, so it's entirely possible that further WITCHFYNDE releases may be forthcoming at some point...

LP's
»Give 'Em Hell« Rondelet 1980
»Stagefright« Rondelet 1980
»Cloak & Dagger« Expulsion 1983
[UK issue, also released as limited edition picture disc]
»Cloak & Dagger« Roadrunner 1983
[Dutch issue]

»**Lords Of Sin**« Mausoleum 1984
[Initially issued in gatefold sleeve with bonus »*Anthems*« *four track live 12" EP]*

7" Singles

»**Give 'Em Hell**« Round Records 1979
[Original issue]
»**Give 'Em Hell**« Rondelet 1980
[Second issue in identical sleeve]
»**In The Stars**« Rondelet 1980
»**I'd Rather Go Wild**« Expulsion 1983
[A-side different to album version]
»**Conspiracy**« Mausoleum 1985
[A-side different to album version]

CD's

»**Give 'Em Hell**« Pony Canyon 1992
[Japanese issue]
»**Stagefright**« Pony Canyon 1992
[Japanese issue]
»**Lords Of Sin**« Mausoleum Classix 1994
[Unofficial release]
»**The Best Of Witchfynde**« British Steel 1996
[Compilation release]
»**Cloak & Dagger**« Private 2000
[Official remastered release]

Exclusive Compilation Appearances

"**Belfast**" on »The Friday Rock Show« LP BBC Records 1981

Compilation Appearances

"**I'd Rather Go Wild**" on »Metal Battle« LP Neat 1983/Roadrunner 1983
"**Leaving Nadir**" on »NWOBHM '79 Revisited« Do-LP/Do-CD Phonogram 1990
"**Give 'Em Hell**" on »Give 'Em Hell« CD Nectar Masters 1995 + »Rock Out!« Do-CD Emporio 1996
"**Pay Now Love Later**" on »Rock Out!« Do-CD Emporio 1996

WOLF (I)

Wally Rumsey (g)
Clowes
Mason
Tunstall

Beating their Cumbrian counterparts (formerly BLACK AXE) to the name by at least a year (although both lose out, in terms of seniority, to Darryl Way's original outfit from the early 70's), the other North West version of WOLF (from Cheshire, in this instance) recorded their one and only slice of vinyl at Cargo Studios in Rochdale in 1981. Co-engineered by Colin Richardson and TURBO's Ian Blackburn, the sleeveless, double A-sided 7" (coupling "Creatures Of The Night" with "See Them Running") demonstrates a heavy, fairly technical style, quite similar to some of WITCHFYNDE's early material at times. It was one of the more distinctive private releases of the period, and both tracks were well-performed and competently-produced efforts, so it's a bit surprising that the band weren't picked up by the likes of Ebony or Heavy Metal and given the chance to release another single (or, at least, appear on a compilation). For some reason, however, WOLF never drew much attention from any labels of note, and they were (like so many of their anonymous contemporaries) left to wither and die without ever making a name for themselves outside their locality. It's a pity, as it might have been nice to hear additional releases from this bunch, even if their only option had been to persevere with those self-financed records. In any case, WOLF's one-off 7" is now regarded as a sought-after item by many collectors (although a quantity of unsold copies came out of the woodwork some years back), and the three-figure asking price certainly reflects this fact.

Although WOLF presumably disintegrated within a couple of years of releasing their single (assuming they were a genuine touring act in the first place, and not just a short-lived studio project), guitarist Wally Rumsey had, by the mid-80's, established a new quartet called KRUIZER. After offering the world their five track »Suicide« (my, what a cheerful title) demo, the emergent outfit won praise in 'High Octane' (to be brutally honest, few British hopefuls failed to win the approval of these staunch patriots) for compositions such as "Borderline" and "Take The Strain", supposedly heavy numbers in a slightly more commercial vein. KRUIZER struggled on valiantly for quite some time, and apparently even persevered into the 90's in one form or another, although they don't seem to have achieved further recognition or released any vinyl of their own at any stage. The rest of WOLF's personnel remain somewhat anonymous at present, but, if I had to hazard a guess at the identity of the mystery participants, I wouldn't be remotely surprised if the *'Clowes'* credited on the label is actually Dave Clowes, one-time bassist in SACRED ALIEN. On the other hand, *'Tunstall'* could be Phil Tunstall, a musical associate of DEMON's, but I couldn't say for sure who *'Mason'* might have been. Anyone know for certain who else was a member of this particular WOLF?

7" Singles

»See Them Running« Gremlin Records 1981

Compilation Appearances
"Creatures Of The Night" on »NWOBHM Vol.7« Bootleg CD 1996

WOLF (II)

Chris English (v)
Simon Sparkes (g)
Bill Keir (g, k)
Stewart Richardson (b)
Mike Thorburn (d)

At first, signing to Chrysalis must surely have seemed like a dream career move for BLACK AXE: bigger recording budgets, better promotion, more lucrative support slots and powerful financial backing. It rapidly turned into a complete and utter nightmare, however, beginning with their label's bizarre decision to lumber their new acquisition with the hopelessly generic name of WOLF (probably inspired by TREVOR RABIN's latest album for Chrysalis) and attempting to turn them into mainstream rock stars. Almost immediately, the lads were encouraged to relocate to the capital and install themselves in the studio, whereby they would lay down a selection of material which was supposedly going to make their new label very rich indeed. The first fruits of these endeavours were to be unveiled in the early months of 1982, with the release of WOLF's »Head Contact« single (B-side "Soul For The Devil") in both 7" and (somewhat pointlessly) 12" forms. For all those fans who had grown accustomed to the endearingly rough'n'ready sound of BLACK AXE, this release must have come as a complete surprise, and, to be honest, the lavish production values and the tasteful keyboard overlays didn't really do the musicians any favours at all, diminishing their original energy and enthusiasm to a major extent, and rendering WOLF as merely another anonymous melodic rock/metal band.

Nevertheless, the single proceeded to sell in reasonably healthy quantities, and "Head Contact" itself eventually found its way into the 'Top 30 Kuts' chart in 'Kerrang'. In order to showcase their latest protégés, Chrysalis conspired to install WOLF as support act on the lengthy SCORPIONS tour in April 1982, a series of gigs which provided the group with a valuable piece of exposure in front of some seriously large audiences. By all accounts, WOLF acquitted themselves extremely well (one of their appearances being reviewed remarkably favourably in 'Kerrang'), and certainly weren't treated as an endurance test prior to the main attraction, as was undoubtedly the case with various minor hopefuls who somehow ended up with such support slots. In the wake of their debut single as WOLF, however, it became apparent that drummer Mike Thorburn no longer wished to be identified as a full-time member, and it was therefore necessary to recruit a stand-in (John Shearer, a highly experienced session player who had served time with STEVE HACKETT and also Noel McCalla's MOON during the late 70's)

for their forthcoming studio sessions. The chaps then proceeded to record a plentiful assortment of tracks for inclusion on their debut long-player, scheduled for release towards the end of the year, but this batch of recordings failed to win the approval of Chrysalis, for some unfathomable reason. With little in the way of formality, WOLF were unceremoniously dumped by the wayside, resulting in the release of their much-anticipated album being cancelled forthwith.

Having now had the proverbial rug pulled from beneath their feet, WOLF were now at a loss as to how (indeed, *whether*) they should proceed. Eventually, the lads concluded that, without the backing of a suitably influential company, they were extremely unlikely to achieve any notable success, and ultimately decided to call it a day for good. However, the musicians retained the master tapes and the rights to the music (Chrysalis effectively washed their hands of the whole affair), which finally allowed them to organise a posthumous release through Mausoleum in 1984. WOLF's long-overdue album, entitled »Edge Of The World«, turned out to be a collection of competently-written and well-played numbers (at least half of which dated back to their BLACK AXE glory days, these actually being the strongest efforts on the set), although the general feeling (on the newer compositions) was perhaps more along the lines of KARRIER or even mid-period ANGEL WITCH as opposed to the youthful exuberance displayed in the outfit's formative years. It's also extremely obvious that the featured selections were recorded under a variety of studio conditions (the musicians appear to have elected to use their original BLACK AXE recordings in most cases), and there's very little in the way of equalisation to ensure anything resembling a consistent sound profile.

In spite of its limitations, the record was, nevertheless, given a charitably warm reception at 'Kerrang', who offered the following opinion: 'WOLF had a distinct advantage over most of the NWOBHM competition in that they actually concentrated on writing songs, letting the innate rock'n'roll power speak for itself.' (Ref: Kerrang No.72, July 1984). Whether or not such sincere plaudits actually led to increased record sales is open to debate, but it hardly mattered by that time, given that there was no serious talk of getting the outfit off the ground again. In fact, the participants all seem to have taken their leave of the rock scene thereafter, having presumably become both bitter and completely disillusioned with the fickle music business. As a slightly vindictive parting shot, the back cover of their LP (which remains a highly-regarded and collectable release in some quarters) prominently identifies the band as 'WOLF a.k.a. BLACK AXE', suggesting that the lads weren't entirely enamoured of the utterly nondescript moniker which Chrysalis had foisted upon them with little or no consultation. It was all a bit of a shambles, really, as the group (whatever they preferred to call themselves) deserved so much better...

LP's
»Edge Of The World« Mausoleum 1984
[Includes material from BLACK AXE period]

12" Singles
»Head Contact« Chrysalis 1982
[With extended version of B-side "Soul For The Devil", different to album version]

7" Singles
»Head Contact« Chrysalis 1982

[Issued on both black and clear vinyl, clear copies more common]

WRATHCHILD

Rocky Shades (v)
Phil Wrathchild (g)
Marc Angel (b)
Brian Thunderburst (d)

You might suspect that Worcestershire's self-styled 'glam gods', WRATHCHILD, would have stuck out like a sore thumb in a local scene which was practically dominated by proto-doom and power metal hopefuls, although these pretty boys actually started out as a markedly heavier proposition, with early reports of their theatrical live appearances even identifying the group as (wait for it) 'black metal wannabes'! Well, I'm not entirely convinced by such contentious claims, but it would appear that the outfit's formative material certainly wasn't particularly representative of the unremarkable style they eventually chose to inflict upon the world. Whatever the story, the WRATHCHILD lads got together towards the end of 1980, following the virtually simultaneous disintegration of the excellent TITAN (from whence came vocalist Rocky Shades) and the little-known SINNER (not to be confused with various recording acts of that name), the founder members having also previously been employed by numerous obscure West Midlands ensembles such as SWEET ACID, NIGHT CREATURES and the DUMMIES. In the first instance, Shades (aka Robert Berkley) was joined by guitarist Phil Wrathchild (aka Phil Vokins), bassist Marc Angel (aka Stan Wood) and drummer Brian Thunderburst (aka Brian Parry, a chap who also had a brief tenure in GRIM REAPER), whereupon they set about creating a rock'n'roll entity to take the world by storm.

Well, it would appear that the world just wasn't ready for the musical delights of WRATHCHILD in 1980, and it took the lads a couple of years to make any impression whatsoever, gradually winning over the initially-hostile crowds with their flamboyant and self-assured live appearances, and their once-derided demos were soon being taken rather more seriously. The outfit's first big break came towards the end of 1982, when their increasingly-glammy style of music came to the attention of the newly-formed Bullet label. The quartet had undergone something of a radical reconstruction in the interim, and their »Mascara Massacre« demo (featuring original compositions such as "Rock The City Down" and "Rockin' To The Top") had been recorded with the help of drummer Eddy Starr (aka Eddy Smith) and guitarist Lance Rocket (aka Lance Perkins), both of whom had been recruited from the ranks of local hopefuls MEDUSA. With the fresh line-up (erstwhile drummer Brian Parry later resurfaced in ORIGINAL SIN, while the much-travelled Phil Vokins had stints with CRASH KO, TYRANT, PERSIAN RISK, BILL WARD, FIREWORX and ROGUE ISLAND) came a new sense of conviction, and, having already signed their lives away to Bullet Records by this juncture, the lads were rewarded with the chance to record a 12" EP for their benevolent label.

The »Stackheel Strutt« EP featured four passable enough glam anthems ("Rock The City Down", "Lipstick Killers", "Trash Queen" and "Teenage Revolution"), although many rock fans were slightly alienated by the record's semi-punk attitude, which served to distance WRATHCHILD from more traditional glam revivalists such as ROX, GIRL, SILVERWING or FORGER. In due course, they would eventually find a handful of musical allies such as MARIONETTE and VIRGIN STAR, but establishing a solid fan base was far from straightforward at the outset. Nevertheless, Bullet stuck to their guns (as it were) and commissioned a follow-up before the end of that year, a single (issued in both 7" and 12" formats) which coupled "Do You Want My Love" and "Twist Of The Knife". It sold in slightly more impressive quantities, although apparently not well enough to compel Bullet to stump up the cash for a full album, and WRATHCHILD were already looking for a new home as they entered 1984. Fortunately, however, the Heavy Metal label was on the lookout for some new acts to take over the mantle of national rock heroes, the company's early signings (the likes of BITCHES SIN, SPLIT BEAVER, WITCHFINDER GENERAL *et al.*) having all failed miserably to make piles of money. However, it appeared that they had formulated a brand-new vision of the future of heavy music, and, funnily enough, WRATHCHILD seemed to fit the bill perfectly, so they were soon signing on the dotted line.

The ludicrously-titled »Stakk Attakk« long-player turned out to be a surprisingly capable (if underproduced) effort, and the featured tracks were sufficiently varied to dispel any possible accusations that the quartet were happy to churn out *'mindless anthemic glam twaddle'*. In fact, the hapless outfit were still singled out for precisely this kind of attack by the rock press,

suggesting that the reviewers in question might have made up their minds about WRATHCHILD long before they had turned their attention to the album. The fans, on the other hand, voted with their wallets, and the long-player was soon to become a firm favourite among some of the more open-minded metalheads of the day. Admittedly, it wasn't a perfect release by any stretch of the imagination, and some of the numbers undoubtedly harked back to the glory days of SLADE and THE SWEET, although the likes of "Too Wild To Tame", "Wreckless" and "Kick Down The Walls" were all eminently listenable. A tie-in single was trotted out in due course, based around a pretty uninspiring interpretation of GARY GLITTER's "Doing Alright With The Boys", a chart hit from 1975, and (despite the fact that this really *was* mindless anthemic glam twaddle) it can't have done their chances any harm at that stage (still, I'd be surprised if emergent hopefuls are queuing up to cover any of the jailbird's tracks nowadays). With the variable reviews having failed to diminish sales of the LP to any great extent, and, with the group's popularity having reached something of a peak, they even took the relatively unusual step (for such a minor act) of issuing a live video, recorded at a high-profile London gig towards the end of 1984.

With one reasonably successful LP under their belts already, it came as no surprise when the lads soon announced plans for a follow-up, and »Wrath Of The Gods« was subsequently scheduled for release at some point during 1985. Sadly, however, things didn't quite pan out as anticipated, and the project was put *'on hold'* until the situation rectified itself (the band continued to tour fairly extensively in the meantime, and even managed to fit in an appearance on 'The Tube', a popular television programme). By the end of the year, however, it became apparent that matters had now reached something of an impasse, and the fans had to make do with a hastily-assembled compilation of early recordings (»Trash Queens«, released by Castle) for the time being. WRATHCHILD's activities came to a fairly abrupt halt in the early months of 1986 (after they had announced a batch of new track titles for the second album, including "Blood On The Blade", "Howitzer" and "Rebel Run Wild"), when mounting problems with labels, abortive record deals and management hassles came to a rather nasty head, whereupon the stressed-out musicians concluded that it might now be best to take a break for a while, assuming that things would somehow sort themselves out in the interim. Given that this type of painfully-familiar scenario tends to result in bands drifting apart and never getting back together, however, there was genuine concern (or, in some cases, optimism) at the time that we might well have seen the last of WRATHCHILD.

With the band playing approximately zero gigs for the best part of the next two years, it began to look as though there was no way back, especially when it was reported that Rocky Shades had teamed up with DISCHARGE (!) in the early part of 1987. In fact, the frontman stayed with the punksters just long enough to pose for a couple of photos (the whole sorry episode smacked of a pretty desperate publicity stunt all round), and he was soon back in the WRATH-

CHILD camp once more. By the end of that year, the lads had begun making a few low-key appearances in the live environment, although they remained tight-lipped when questioned about the possibility of a comeback album. After a few more gigs in the early months of 1988, the elusive characters seemed to disappear once again, and nobody seemed to know what was going on with any great certainty, so it was something of a surprise when they suddenly re-emerged in the second half of the year, having recorded a new album with virtually zero pre-publicity. Asked why they had decided to have another bite of the cherry after all this time, Rocky Shades offered some logical reasoning: 'We started a whole lot of things that are coming back in now. All these glam/sleaze bands are coming out with LP's that sound worse than our demos, and they're getting credit for it when we started the whole thing off.' (Ref: Metal Forces No.33, November 1988).

The brand-new album, the wisecrackingly-titled »The Biz Suxx (But We Don't Care)«, had been recorded for the FM concern (with Heavy Metal having branched out and formed various subsidiaries in the interim) several months previously, and the set appeared in a blaze of advertising and media hype towards the end of 1988. It was, fortunately, quite a decent comeback, and saw the lads moving in more of a punk/sleaze direction, combining a variety of influences from the 70's (RAMONES, SEX PISTOLS) and 80's (THE CULT, ZODIAC MINDWARP) to yield a reasonably forceful and heavy product. The likes of "Wild Wild Honey", "Hooligunz" and "She'z No Angel", in particular, stood out as the most enjoyable numbers on display, although it was the anthemic "Nukklear Rokket" which formed the basis of the next single, issued in both 7" (featuring a live version of "Trash Queen" on the reverse) and 12" formats, the latter adding a raucous live take of SEX PISTOLS favourite "Pretty Vacant". The lads were back with a bang, although there was one stumbling-block which still needed to be resolved, the outfit having been involved in a minor altercation with their recently-formed transatlantic namesakes over the rights to the WRATHCHILD moniker. Happily, the original owners were to emerge victorious in the early months of 1989 (the Yanks were legally compelled to rename themselves WRATHCHILD AMERICA thereafter) on the grounds that they had been an established act for the best part of a decade.

With all these sundry distractions now being consigned to the past, WRATHCHILD were able to concentrate on delivering a further album, and they were hard at work once more within a matter of months. Their next long-player for FM emerged at the tail end of 1989, although »Delirium« failed to come across as favourably as its predecessor, and this selection of ill-advised ballads and unremarkable rockers with some suspiciously PRINCE-influenced titles (notably "Long Way 2 Go", "Only 4 The Fun" and "That's What U Get") had little to offer the average rock fan. In the aftermath of poor sales, their label decided to cut its losses and cancel any proposed singles which might have been on the cards initially, and WRATHCHILD were left high and dry in terms of promotion and support. Unsurprisingly, this proved too much for the hapless quartet to cope with, and they duly elected to call it a day before the end of 1990. The charismatic Rocky Shades tried his luck again a couple of years later in a fairly obscure bunch of post-glam also-rans named ONE TRACK AND DIRTY, although their brief activities on the UK rock scene failed to raise too many eyebrows. The unmasked Stan Wood, on the other hand, appears to have turned his back on metal altogether, and the treacherous bassist (usually calling himself 'Stan Lee' by this juncture) subsequently earned a crust playing in indie no-hopers BANG BANG

MACHINE in the early 90's.

LP's

»**Stakk Attakk**« Heavy Metal 1984
[Also released as limited edition picture disc and on green vinyl]
»**Trash Queens**« Castle Communications 1985
[Compilation release of early material]
»**The Biz Suxx (But We Don't Care)**« FM Records 1988
[Also released as limited edition picture disc and on pink vinyl]
»**Delirium**« FM Records 1989
[Also issued as limited edition in gatefold sleeve with free poster]
»**Cock Shock Rock**« Bootleg 198?
[Live bootleg from 1984]

12" EP's

»**Stackheel Strutt**« Bullet 1983
[Also issued as limited edition on red vinyl]
»**Nukklear Rokket**« FM Records 1989
[Also issued as limited edition on purple vinyl, A-side remixed, "Pretty Vacant" (live) non-LP, also includes live version of "Trash Queen"]

12" Singles

»**Do You Want My Love**« Bullet 1983

7" Singles

»**Do You Want My Love**« Bullet 1983
[Also issued as limited edition picture disc]
»**Alrite With The Boys**« FM Records 1984
»**Nukklear Rokket**« FM Records 1989
[B-side live version of "Trash Queen"]

CD's

»**The Biz Suxx (But We Don't Care)**« FM Records 1988
»**Stakk Attakk**« Heavy Metal 1989
»**Delirium**« FM Records 1989

Compilation Appearances

"**Trash Queen**" on »Heavy Metal Records« LP Heavy Metal 1984
"**Teenage Revolution**" on »Metallergy« LP Bandit Records 1985
"**Twist Of The Knife**" on »Metal Killers Kollection I« Do-LP Castle Communications 1985 + »Metal Killers Kollection« CD Castle Communications 1991
"**Nukklear Rokket**" on »Metal Hammer's Best Of British Steel« Do-LP/Do-CD FM Records 1989 + »Protect The Innocent« Do-LP/Do-CD Telstar 1989
"**Stakk Attakk**" on »The Metal Box« 3-CD Box Castle Communications 1993

XERO

Moon Williams (v)
Bill Liesegang (g)
Boon Gould (b)
Barry Fitzgerald (d)

It's a real pity that the good name of London's XERO eventually became firmly associated with rock'n'roll infamy (as a result of the major kerfuffle surrounding by their first vinyl release), as they were actually a pretty talented proposition in their own right. Initially formed at the tail end of 1979 by former solo artist Moon Williams and self-styled guitar hero Bill Liesegang, the outfit's early activities on the live front swiftly captured the attention of many observers, and it wasn't long before the lads were afforded the considerable honour of appearing on MCA's »Brute Force« compilation, assembled in the summer of 1980. Their contribution, "Hold On", was an excellent slice of melodic metal, with an impressive, bluesy vocal delivery from Williams bringing forth a few handy comparisons with ORE, AFTER DARK and LAUTREC. It was an extremely confident way for an emergent bunch to open their account, and further good fortune was to come XERO's way before long, when the lads somehow came to the attention of EMI, who promptly included the band's "Cutting Loose" on their second »Metal For Muthas« compilation. It was another enviably capable effort, and, with the album ultimately finding its way into the hands of Tommy Vance, it swiftly led to a session appearance on the 'Friday Rock Show'.

A slightly rearranged version of XERO (now featuring new bassist Peter Solinsky and second guitarist Tony Murphy) took full advantage of the BBC's well-appointed studio facilities and laid down "Cutting Loose", "Lone Wolf", "Don't You Think It's Time" and "Can You See Me" early the following year. Broadcast on the 10th of April 1981, the session showed the group to have a powerful and varied range of material at their disposal, and the response to this slot was overwhelmingly positive. In due course, this particular take of "Cutting Loose" was included on the BBC's »The Friday Rock Show« sampler of session favourites, and XERO were now firmly established as a bunch to watch. Mind you, it rapidly became apparent that the lads wouldn't be able to survive on compilation appearances alone, so they finally got around to laying down a few representative compositions for the benefit of various record companies. Over the coming months, a significant number of XERO originals were captured for posterity (peculiarly, the lads alternated between Moon and an understudy called Billy Little, although the experienced man was ultimately favoured), including strong selections such as "Hi Living", "No More Crying", "As Far As The Eye Can See" and "Easy Does It". In fact, it appears that one or two new members (second guitarists, in the main) were tried out along the way, although the central nucleus of Williams, Liesegang and Fitzgerald seems to have been relatively stable.

In 1983, XERO finally signed a fateful deal with the small-time Brickyard Records, who decided to issue their first slice of vinyl in both 7" and 12" formats. The unremarkable "Oh Baby" was soon chosen as the lead track, with the rather more engaging "Hold On" bringing up the rear. Then, in a moment of temporary insanity, Bill Liesegang turned up at the studio with a dusty old tape of "Lone Wolf" (a track which had been in XERO's repertoire since their inception, and which the group had utilised on their 'Friday Rock Show' session two years earlier), which the outfit's management decided to add to the forthcoming pressing at the last minute, turning the proposed two-tracker into a more substantial EP. Nothing particularly odd about that, you might think, only the truth of the matter was rather more nefarious. In fact, it transpired that this particular version of "Lone Wolf" wasn't a bona fide XERO recording after all; this take had actually been laid down by one of Liesegang's previous outfits, SHOTS. Having said that, there probably wasn't anything to prevent the XERO lads from presenting the track as their own. I mean, who could possibly object to its commercial use? Well, the original SHOTS vocalist, for one, a young chap called Bruce Dickinson who was now doing rather well for himself. Oh dear, do I detect a swarm of voracious lawyers starting to circle overhead?

Blissfully unaware of the legal implications of their naive actions, the band oversaw the release of the EP's as scheduled, the advertising shamelessly proclaiming that there was a 'bonus' track on each featuring the current IRON MAIDEN vocalist. Since neither XERO nor their label appear to have been familiar with the concept of The Copyright Act, both parties heroically failed to anticipate that Dickinson or his employers might actually kick up a bit of a fuss about all this. They couldn't have been more spectacularly wrong. MAIDEN's influential management came down on XERO like a ton of bricks, forcing the record to be withdrawn, but not before a considerable percentage of the original pressing had made it into circulation. Dickinson himself later explained the bizarre chain of events surrounding the illegal release of "Lone Wolf": 'That was a demo of a band called SHOTS, which I was in before SAMSON. Their guitarist was Bill Liesegang, who later played for a while with NINA HAGEN. After that, he hooked up with XERO, but he still had copies of these tapes. XERO's manager came up with the idea that they could use this track, which had been recorded on an eight-track machine, as a B-side in order to sell a few more copies of their single. I never even received a copy of it.' (Ref: Iron Pages No.36, 1995). At least that explains why the quality is so rough, and it just goes to prove that Bruce was never actually a member of XERO after all!

Well, the audacious ploy had ultimately backfired for the hapless XERO (it didn't work for SPEED, either, but at least the latter apparently owned the rights to the material featured on their cash-in single), and they were left with no option but to bring out new versions of »Oh Baby«. The second pressing of the 12" replaced "Lone Wolf" with the throwaway instrumental "Killer Frog", while the revised 7" simply omitted the contentious track altogether. Paradoxically, the second issues have always been far more scarce than the originals, although each of the variations remain pretty collectable. The whole affair was all monumentally embarrassing, but the thick-skinned XERO continued unabashed, and their sponsors eventually announced plans to issue another single (»Don't You Think It's Time«), again in 7" and 12" formats, with "Nightmare" and "All In Vain" being the planned B-sides. Not only that, a full album (entitled »First Mission«) was even scheduled for release in the spring of 1984, the intended tracks including the aforementioned trio, plus "Don't Say Don't Say It", "Can You Ever See Me", "Kamikaze", "Cutting Loose", "Hold On" and "Killer Frog". In the event, however, these projects were both cancelled (not before some rough artwork for the album had been prepared), possibly as a result of Brickyard's financial instability (they later reinvented themselves as Loose Records and made a pig's ear of getting a LYADRIVE record into the shops). In any case, it was to signal the end of the road for XERO, who had called it a day by the middle of the decade.

Bill Liesegang swiftly returned to session work, as did original bassist Boon Gould (who later cropped up in the not-remotely-metal LEVEL 42), while Moon Williams began composing material for a wide range of projects (often using pseudonyms), some of which would be used as incidental music for television programmes. By the late 80's, however, two XERO veterans (Bill Liesegang and Barry Fitzgerald) reunited in an outfit called DIRTY DOGS (later KILLER DOGS), who also featured such stalwarts as vocalist Tony Lawrence (ex-PANAMA) and bassist Harris Joannou (ex-GEORGE HATCHER BAND). This short-lived venture proceeded to record a powerful 'Friday Rock Show' session in 1989, but failed to last the distance, with Liesegang subsequently joining the ATOMGOD project, appearing on the »History Re-written« album in 1991. Since then, he has recorded a solo album (with the help of several well-kent faces) entitled »No Strings Attached«, lent a hand to the much heavier NECROPOLIS concern (an act who are now recording for Neat Metal), and has occasionally been spotted on stage with the likes of JOHN WETTON in recent years, so he seems to be keeping busy.

12" EP's
»Oh Baby« Brickyard Records 1983
[Original withdrawn version in stickered sleeve, includes "Lone Wolf"]
»Oh Baby« Brickyard Records 1983
[Second issue, includes "Killer Frog"]

7" EP's
»Oh Baby« Brickyard Records 1983
[Three track withdrawn version with "Lone Wolf" included]

7" Singles
»Oh Baby« Brickyard Records 1983
[Two track version omitting "Lone Wolf", slightly different sleeve]

Exclusive Compilation Appearances
"Cutting Loose" on »Metal For Muthas Vol.2« LP EMI 1980/CD Airraid Records 2000 + »The Bible Of Hard Rock« CD Toshiba 1990
"Cutting Loose" on »The Friday Rock Show« LP BBC Records 1981
[Different to »Metal For Muthas« version]

Compilation Appearances
"Hold On" on »Brute Force« LP MCA 1980 + »NWOBHM Vol.2« Bootleg CD 1992 + »N.W.O.B.H.M. Metal Rarities Vol.2« CD British Steel 1996
"Oh Baby" on »N.W.O.B.H.M. Metal Rarities Vol.2« CD British Steel 1996
"Killer Frog" on »N.W.O.B.H.M. Metal Rarities Vol.2« CD British Steel 1996

YOUNG BLOOD

Stewart Goodchild (v, g)
Dave Cadman (v,b)
Andy Webb (d)

The humble origins of YOUNG BLOOD, a talented trio from County Durham, can be traced back to a variety of small-time pop/rock outfits who were doing the rounds at the turn of the decade but who all failed to make much of an impression in the long term. Nevertheless, the experience was to serve the participants well, and the gradual demise of these bands eventually paved the way for Stewart Goodchild, Dave Cadman and Andy Webb to get together (initially under the name of CIVILIAN) and develop into a rather heavier proposition. The name of YOUNG BLOOD (not to be confused with one of Cozy Powell's innumerable recording acts from much earlier) duly appeared, seemingly out of nowhere, in the latter part of 1983 (they had, in reality, been active as a unit since 1981, but were apparently playing considerably more lightweight material in their formative years), the trio making themselves known with a few modest club appearances. After that, the lads proceeded to circulate some strong demo material which aroused a fair bit of interest, and ultimately led to them being snapped up by the erratic Landslide label (home to DUMPY'S

RUSTY NUTS at one point) the following year. With the unannounced release of the group's debut EP (the »First Blood« 12") coming a relatively short time later, the record provoked something of an astonished reaction from reviewers at 'Kerrang', who heaped plentiful praise upon this new and exciting prospect.

Recorded at Woodlands Studio in West Yorkshire (the outfit using the services of an additional session bassist, John Wood), the EP featured four excellently-produced melodic rock tracks in the shape of "Hold On To Love", "Your Money Or Your Life", "Good Time Tonight" and "Dangerous Games". These all turned out to be competently-performed, catchy efforts in the general manner of NWOBHM-era propositions such as ETHEL THE FROG, TERRAPLANE and ALKATRAZZ, albeit quite varied in terms of content (moving from AOR to raunchy rock via boogie). It was a mature, commercially-motivated release, and the glowing write-up in 'Kerrang' ('this young band have produced a truly magnificent debut that should worry all their contemporaries') can't have done these young pretenders' chances any harm whatsoever. In fact, YOUNG BLOOD ended up being a fairly short-lived concern (notwithstanding a full-page 'exposé' appearing in 'Kerrang' after the EP had been issued), with no further releases materialising on vinyl at any stage. Their greatest success was, perhaps, a support slot with none other than MOTÖRHEAD (although the lads also shared a stage with the likes of MAMA'S BOYS and GRAND SLAM) at the legendary Hammersmith Odeon, as Stewart Goodchild later recalled: 'Really, I prefer playing the smaller gigs because I can see the whites of the audience's eyes and it's easier to relate to a small crowd, but I'm itching to play the bigger halls all the same, so the MOTÖRHEAD gig was a great experience.' (Ref: Kerrang No.70, June 1984).

Despite making an impressive start, the lads were keeping a comparatively low profile even within a year of their record hitting the shops, so things clearly weren't going swimmingly. By early 1986, musical differences had finally driven the trio apart (drummer Andy Webb later resurfaced in the ranks of SMASH ALLEY), leaving mainman Stewart Goodchild to start again on his own, his intention being to relocate to the capital after finding some talented accomplices with whom to collaborate in an all-new project. In due course, he teamed up with bassist Ian Rigby and drummer Paul Stirk in a new venture called RUBICON (confusingly, at least two unrelated rock outfits of that name issued their own vinyl product in 1987 or thereabouts), who were

all set to storm the charts with their supposedly irresistible brand of original rock, but who eventually fizzled out before they were afforded a chance to prove themselves properly. Goodchild subsequently tried again under the identity of SAVIOUR, roping in erstwhile PAULINE GILLAN BAND bassist Chris Wing and much-travelled drummer Mark Brabbs to form another melodic trio, although this new bunch also failed to achieve a great deal during their brief existence. The YOUNG BLOOD record, meanwhile, has never really achieved cult status among the majority of NWOBHM collectors, mainly due to its comparatively lightweight musical content, and examples can still be picked up at a fairly reasonable price nowadays.

12" EP's
»First Blood« Landslide Records 1984

Compilation Appearances
"Dangerous Games" on »Metal Killers II« LP Kastle Killers 1984 + »Metal Masters« 4-CD Box Castle Communications 1993
"Hold On To Love" on »Metal Masters« 4-CD Box Castle Communications 1993 + »Rock Out!« Do-CD Emporio 1996

ZENITH

Andy Sayers (v, g)
Cliff Evans (g)
Hayden Palmer (b)
Mark Helmore (d)

Time to get up on my soapbox for a moment, I reckon. The all-embracing and increasingly-common phrase *'second wave NWOBHM'*, as exemplified by the freebie four track EP given away by 'Metal Hammer' magazine in 1987, can be a bit of a misnomer, really. To lump together any old metal acts from the late 80's and attach such an arbitrary label is both unconstructive and misleading, so I think it's time it was discontinued. Whereas *'second wave'* might *almost* be an appropriate term for outfits such as ELIXIR, DEUCE or FAIR WARNING (who were clearly influenced by the NWOBHM movement itself, but who didn't properly establish themselves or come into their element until the mid-to-late 80's, by which time the earlier Metal boom had long since fizzled out), the same does not really apply to old stagers such as SAMSON, CLOVEN HOOF or HEAVY PETTIN, who unquestionably *were* successful players on the scene back in 1982, and who steadfastly carried on after most of their contemporaries had gone back to their day jobs. Neither is it remotely helpful to attach this lazy and meaningless label to virtually *all* the British groups who issued private rock/metal releases during the second half of the decade in the vain hope of hiking up the asking prices by implying that there's some sort of NWOBHM connection. A considerable number of outfits from this period have been excluded from this volume on the basis of their lack of relevance to collectors of the genre, although they may still be advertised as such by some of the less knowledgeable or more unscrupulous dealers.

There's no such problem, however, with ZENITH (not to be confused with German namesakes), natives of the county of Avon, who originally seem to have come to prominence with a ten track demo of fairly traditional British metal, which was circulated amongst various industry types in the first half of 1985. Sadly, but predictably, the album-length cassette completely failed to attract the attention of any of the more influential labels of the day (Ebony must have been cutting back on their roster by that stage), leaving the group with little option but to go it alone and release their own vinyl product. ZENITH's impressive three-tracker was recorded locally at the beginning of 1986 (by which time they had already broken in new bassist Andy Jamieson and drummer Keith Townsend) and unleashed upon an unsuspecting public a few months later. Generally speaking, the material on display falls somewhere between EXOCET, BLACKWYCH and a rather more cheerful DESOLATION ANGELS, although the group's lyrics themselves were pretty grim, particularly on "Not Guilty" and "Death By Misadventure". Still, the memorable "Heavy Heart" is, perhaps, the most accomplished of the featured selections, this being a slightly more melodic effort in the manner of TRAXX or EAZY STREET. All in all, it was a highly respectable debut EP which genuinely deserved to be heard by a wider audience than their local fan base.

No doubt this particular ZENITH (one of several outfits to adopt the name in the UK) went down well with the loyal metal crowds at Bristol's Granary or Bierkeller, but the band don't seem to have made all that much of an impression outwith their locality. It looks as though the lads were unable to get out and about as much as they would have liked, something which no doubt contributed to their downfall in the long term. The members from the last line-up all appear to have drifted away from the music scene shortly after their record was released, and (for those of you who might be wondering) it transpires that guitarist Cliff Evans *wasn't* actually the same chap who was involved with TANK and Paul Dianno's KILLERS. The group's original bassist (Hayden Palmer), incidentally, after a comparatively brief residency in London's VHF, subsequently guested as one of TILT's stand-in guitarists at a handful of live appearances at around the turn of the decade, so at least one of them kept busy. A few copies of ZENITH's 7", with a rather flimsy picture sleeve showing a live-action shot, surfaced in their home area about five years ago, but the supply seems to have dried up for the moment. Keep your eyes peeled and you might be lucky...

7" EP's
»Heavy Heart« Zen Records 1986

ZORRO

Mark Newman (v)
Terry Bunting (g)
Kevin Longman (b)
Galen Littlewood (k)
Fritz Wright (d)

Originally formed in the second half of the 70's as a knockabout bunch of snotty rock upstarts, the popular East Anglian ensemble who went by the wacky name of ZORRO hardly epitomised the NWOBHM archetype at all, choosing instead to take their lead from such raucous acts as the HEAVY METAL KIDS. As time went by, however, the band gradually became less ramshackle and more focused, and things began to take shape properly as the outfit restructured itself around ever-present keyboard player Galen Littlewood. In due course, a new vocalist and bassist (Dave Smith and Alan Fish, respectively) were brought in, the pair having previously played together in the recently-demised POACHER. With their repertoire expanding at an impressive rate, the lads soon began attracting a healthy following to their local shows, as original sticksman Fritz Wright confirmed: 'We had a hell of a following around Norwich, Great Yarmouth and Ipswich. Dave Smith was a great singer and frontman who really drew the crowds. We could pack places like Whites in Norwich or the Royal William in Ipswich.' (Ref: Private communication, June 2000). Eventually, however, ZORRO started making inroads into the capital's bustling rock scene, although there were yet more personnel changes in store before long. In fact, they proceeded to lose the services of two long-serving members (Terry Bunting and Fritz Wright) in quick succession, whereupon the remaining characters drafted in Ronnie Newson (g) and Ricci Titcombe (d), recruited from the ranks of local punk strugglers THE CRABS.

With a stable line-up having been established at last, the quintet finally began thinking about the possibility of getting some vinyl product into the shops, and their affiliation with the Bridge House label ultimately led to the release of a somewhat quirky three track EP in 1979. Although ZORRO's music has been unfairly dismissed as merely 'pub rock' elsewhere, however, this debut offering was, in truth, really nothing of the sort. Both "Arrods Don't Sell'em" (bizarrely, a peculiar bunch called THE UNION issued an identically-titled single in the late 80's, but there's absolutely no connection) and "Soldier Boy" are slightly odd concoctions lying somewhere between the SMALL FACES and TOAD THE WET SPROCKET's "Pete's Punk Song", with some similar snotty vocals and moog keyboards (see also LYNX, for example) thrown in for good measure. The enjoyable "Starfight" (one of their older compositions), on the other hand, is a considerably more metal effort (those distracting keyboards are still present, though) in the vein of a more laid-back REINCARNATE or SHADO-WFAX, so it's a pity that the whole EP wasn't in this style. Incidentally, the aforementioned "Soldier Boy" is apparently a cover version (I've no idea who might have performed the original), but it's clearly an unusually obscure one.

Overall, ZORRO's EP doesn't quite stand up as a definitive NWOBHM release, although it should still be of interest to a fair percentage of collectors, particularly those who enjoy some of the more 'borderline' outfits of the period. Of the band members identified on the scarce, flimsy cover (which, for some reason, pictures just one of the five individuals involved), only the familiar name of bassist Alan Fish stands out, this presumably being the same busy character who featured in numerous rock (and several non-rock) outfits throughout the 70's and who later lent his services to the likes of the GROUNDHOGS, TREDEGAR and DUMPY'S RUSTY NUTS before subsequently deciding to settle down and form the bizarrely-named AUTOLAND COMMAND (who soon evolved into the persevering EGYPT). Original drummer Fritz Wright also continues to pound the skins for such small-time acts as BLUE WAVE and the ENTIRE BAND, although his cohorts seem to have drifted away from the scene altogether, the group having fragmented in the early 80's as the metal world returned to relative normality. ZORRO's lone 7", meanwhile, remains a collectable artefact, particularly with that coveted picture sleeve, and it's just about the only thing on the (predominantly punk/mod-biased) Bridge House label that's actually worth paying good money for.

7" EP's
»**Arrods Don't Sell'em**« Bridge House Records 1979

COMPILATIONS

You might imagine that it's a fairly trivial matter to document all the NWOBHM compilations that have come onto the market since the early days of the movement, but you'd be surprised just how many have actually appeared. There were a fair old number issued at the time, and considerably more started to appear during the 90's, fuelled by the mini-revival which was underway back then. Even so, many of the collections churned out by labels such as Castle (and all its offshoots) tend to feature pretty standard selections, and are frequently guilty of duplication (certain well-worn tracks by ANGEL WITCH, GIRLSCHOOL and VENOM have now been round the block *far* too many times), so these are only of marginal interest to serious NWOBHM fans. Similarly, a range of budget-price releases have cropped up in mainland Europe, the States *etc.* (predominantly to introduce acts to a novel market), and these also tend to recycle relatively familiar material, so there's often precious little incentive to track down such sets. There are, in addition, a great many samplers which incorporate a significant quota of NWOBHM, even if they didn't set out to be dedicated compilations, so the best idea is probably to take an arbitrary figure of 50%, and include in this section any records which approximate or surpass this level of NWOBHM content. There may, admittedly, be certain albums with just one or two worthy tracks, but the majority of the more interesting ones are likely to be documented separately in the discussion of local-band and themed compilations.

Samplers continue to be remarkably popular items among most types of NWOBHM collector, given that they offer a fairly cost-effective means of checking out a variety of acts before taking the plunge and purchasing expensive singles or EP's. Indeed, a handful of modern-day labels (such concerns as Emporio, Hallmark and Delta Music) are still assembling brand-new sets of archive material, and others (notably British Steel and Neat Metal) have additionally been responsible for CD reissues of highly-regarded classics such as »Roxcalibur« and »New Electric Warriors«. Also, the »Metal Rarities« series has shown these labels to be heading in the right direction at last, and have proved that the obscure stuff sells just as healthily (if not more so) as material from the big-name acts. I hope someday we'll see something (legal) on a par with the Japanese bootleg series, either featuring ultra-rare singles (preferably taken from master tapes and not crackly vinyl copies) or even compilations of totally unreleased studio material from decent bands who didn't make it to the vinyl stage originally. Although notoriously difficult in terms of licensing, those blessed with sufficient energy and finances should be able to pull it off, so keep your fingers crossed...

»Axe Attack« LP M Port Records 1985/Steel Trax 1986
Side 1:
    AVENGER "Too Wild To Tame"
    DEMON "Wonderland"
    PERSIAN RISK "Too Different"
    HAWKWIND "Psy Power"
    WAYSTED "Hurts So Good"
    STORMBRINGER "Searchin"
Side 2:
    VENOM "Manitou"
    LIMELIGHT "White Fire"
    SAVAGE "We Got The Edge"
    BERNIE TORMÉ
    "My Baby Loves A Vampire"
    NIGHTWING "Back On The Streets"
    DEDRINGER "Comin' Out Fighting"

Nothing to do with the original »Axe Attack« compilation which was assembled by K-Tel way back in 1980, this particular sampler appears to have been thrown together for the American market in the first instance, but was ultimately picked up for a European release. Some of the featured numbers (those by PERSIAN RISK, SAVAGE and LIMELIGHT) also appeared on a Zebra sampler entitled »The Best Of British« at around the same time, so there may well have been some underlying connection. Anyway, this set showcases a few NWOBHM hopefuls who were apparently ripe for promotion in the States, plus some rather more borderline candidates such as BERNIE TORMÉ, WAYSTED and HAWKWIND (how they qualify for these compilations is beyond me), so it's a bit of a mixed bag. It's also quite misleading, especially when the sleeve proclaims the contents to represent *'the cutting edge of England's newest heavy metal'* (I'm sure PERSIAN RISK were just *delighted* by that one), as it's certainly not all metal and I'm pretty sure STORMBRINGER weren't even British, let alone English. Furthermore, DEDRINGER (both the song title and band name are actually miscredited, as is the NIGHTWING track) and LIMELIGHT had pretty much called it a day by this stage, so it's not easy to fathom the logic behind their inclusion. There's nothing fundamentally wrong with any of the selections, but the whole album just seems a bit pointless and rather haphazard in its construction. It's worth picking up if you desperately want to hear the LIMELIGHT number (taken from a soundtrack), but hardly an essential item otherwise. In spite of the best intentions of the compilers, I suspect that the LP failed to assist too many of those featured, with only VENOM and WAYSTED going on to achieve any level of recognition on the other side of the pond.

»Battleaxe« 7" EP Other Records 1987
Side 1:
  HOLOSADE "Love It To Death"
  BLACK RIDERS "Chosen Few"
Side 2:
  TEACHER'S PET "Joanne"
  KES "Saturday Night"

An enjoyable *'mini-compilation'* (slightly too late to be classed as prime-era NWOBHM, but never mind) from the Other label which, aside from the utterly derivative heavy rock of the forgettable TEACHER'S PET, tends to favour outfits with a markedly heavier style, almost bordering on power metal rather than NWOBHM. Pick of the bunch is undoubtedly "Chosen Few" by the BLACK RIDERS, a truly excellent contribution which would appear a year later, in slightly inferior form, as the title track to their album on G.I. Records. (Note to unscrupulous record dealers: please stop trying to pass off undated G.I. releases as being prime-era NWOBHM from 1984, as we're well aware that the label didn't even exist then). HOLOSADE, as we now know, evolved from DARK HEART and later went on to record an LP for Powerstation, although the fate of minor North-East hopefuls KES remains a mystery. I guess Other Records (aka Metalother, before they became G.I.) were simply using the sampler as a device to gauge who might be worth retaining, so they were perhaps taking their lead from the likes of Ebony and Neat. Nevertheless, this modest four-tracker apparently shifted a couple of thousand units at the time, which can't have been a bad result.

»Belfast Rocks« LP Rip Off Records 1979
Side 1:
  PRETTY BOY FLOYD AND THE GEMS "Spread The Word Around"
  BLUE STEAM "Cortina Cowboys"
  COBRA "Looking For A Lady"
  THE JUMPERS "Jimmy Jump"
  NO SWEAT "You Should Be So Lucky"
  THE DETONATORS "Cruisin'"
Side 2:
  BLUE STEAM "Lizard King"
  NO SWEAT "Start All Over Again"
  COBRA "Graveyard Boogie"
  PRETTY BOY FLOYD AND THE GEMS "Rough, Tough, Pretty Too"
  THE JUMPERS "Baby C'mon"
  THE DETONATORS "Light At Your Window"

Ireland's Rip Off label made good use of its initial batch of single releases (which started appearing in 1978), and several of these two-trackers were cobbled together early the following year (more or less coinciding with the beginnings of the NWOBHM explosion) as the »Belfast Rocks« album. This sampler of local talent was a real mixed bag, with only the boogie of COBRA and the catchy punk/metal of NO SWEAT resembling anything that might constitute genuine early NWOBHM. Elsewhere, unremarkable acts such as BLUE STEAM, THE JUMPERS and THE DETONATORS are of little or no interest to the majority of metalheads, and are really only situated on the periphery of the rock scene. Similarly, PRETTY BOY FLOYD AND THE GEMS are more punk than metal, but are a rather more interesting proposition (they actually released quite a few singles in their time) due to the presence of future ROGUE MALE frontman Jim Lyttle. In fact, one of the numbers on show ("Rough, Tough, Pretty Too") was reworked by his later ensemble and even turned up as a B-side on (appropriately enough) their »Belfast« 12". All in all, »Belfast Rocks« was an unspectacular release, but affords modern-day collectors the opportunity to hear some of Ireland's minor contenders without having to pay extortionate prices for the original singles.

»British Steel« LP M Port Records 1984/Steel Trax 1986
Side 1:
  BRONZ "Loneliness Is Mine"
  ROX "Love Ya Like A Diamond"
  ALASKA "The Sorcerer"
  JESS COX "One In A Million"
  HAWKWIND "Kings Of Speed"
  VENOM "Witching Hour"
Side 2:
  MOTÖRHEAD "Ace Of Spades"
  VENOM "Warhead"
  TYSONDOG "Eat The Rich"
  TWELFTH NIGHT "The Ceiling Speaks"
  ALASKA "Suzie Blue"
  ROX "Daylight Robbery"

Contentiously subtitled 'England's Latest Heavy Metal Invasion', which is pushing it a bit with regard to the participation of HAWKWIND, ALASKA and TWELFTH NIGHT, this is yet another of the many 'half and half' NWOBHM compilations which emerged in the mid-80's, largely for the benefit of the overseas market. The »British Steel« set appeared initially on M Port Records in the States in 1984, and was later picked up by Steel Trax, whereupon it was reissued for the European community in 1986. Predictably, there's nothing unreleased or remotely out of the ordinary here, with VENOM, ROX and ALASKA being afforded two tracks each, the remainder of the LP being filled up with an assortment of NWOBHM and mainstream outfits. Not exactly an essential purchase, and I can't imagine that this unrepresentative selection of British talent sold in any great quantities at the time.

»Brute Force« LP MCA 1980
Side 1:
  DIAMOND HEAD "It's Electric"
  FIST "Brain Damage"
  RAVEN "Let It Rip"
  PROWLER "Gotta Get Back To You"
  SLEDGEHAMMER "Fantasia"
  COLIN TOWNS "Breakdown"
Side 2:
  MICK UNDERWOOD "Earthquake At The Savoy"
  WHITE SPIRIT "Back To The Grind"
  QUARTZ "Can't Say No To You"
  XERO "Hold On"
  CRYER "Day To Day"
  MAY WEST "Black Queen"

Although they didn't manage to pick up on the NWOBHM explosion as quickly as EMI, the giant MCA concern soon made up the lost ground, and duly issued their own compilation of emergent talent a few months later. »Brute Force« was a generous sampler, giving exposure to a number of young(ish) metal hopefuls, although I'm not too sure why two GILLAN members (Mick Underwood and Colin Towns) were allowed to contribute solo tracks. Still, several of the acts (e.g. FIST, RAVEN, SLEDGEHAMMER, QUARTZ, DIAMOND HEAD and WHITE SPIRIT) were, while not exactly fresh-faced newcomers, only just reaching their full potential, so it was a timely LP in terms of propelling some of these talented ensembles onto the next rung of the ladder. The aforementioned acts all come up with listenable enough numbers (none of them are exclusive, sadly, but at least the RAVEN and QUARTZ tracks appear in different form to their album counterparts), although I reckon the most interesting feature of the »Brute Force« set (for the modern-day aficionado, at least) probably comes with the humble contributions from the rather more modest outfits, namely PROWLER (the Essex version as opposed to the later Leicestershire version), XERO, MAY WEST and CRYER. Of these, XERO's cracking "Hold On" was later recycled on their debut 7", as was CRYER's august "Day To Day" effort, which subsequently appeared on the album recorded after the latter's reinvention as FORCE. Meanwhile, PROWLER's excellent "Gotta Get Back To You" was one of the highlights of the LP, and this upbeat number should have set the stage for a healthy career. Sadly, it wasn't to be, and the luckless group were beset with sundry name changes, personnel problems and shifts in direction in years to come, although they eventually released an overly-melodic single in the mid-80's. That just leaves the unrenowned MAY WEST, whose "Black Queen" is another highly listenable offering in the style of OMEN SEARCHER, and which showed plenty of potential, although it looks as though this bunch just never got the breaks and fell apart soon after. It was an extremely worthy release back then, but doesn't have quite the same kudos nowadays, given that so many of the tracks later appeared elsewhere. Still, it's worth a few quid of anyone's cash.

»Give 'Em Hell« CD Nectar Masters 1995
  DIAMOND HEAD "Am I Evil"
  WHITE SPIRIT "Back To The Grind"
  GIRLSCHOOL "Take It All Away"
  TYGERS OF PAN TANG "Don't Take Nothin'"
  FIST "Name, Rank And Serial Number"
  RAVEN "Don't Need Your Money"
  WITCHFINDER GENERAL "Music"
  BERNIE TORMÉ "All Around The World"
  QUARTZ "Buried Alive"
  VENOM "To Hell And Back"
  TERRAPLANE "I Survive"
  JAGUAR "Back Street Woman"
  TRESPASS "One Of These Days"
  ANGEL WITCH "Straight From Hell"
  SPIDER "All The Time"
  WITCHFYNDE "Give 'Em Hell"

This budget-price compilation sneaked out in 1995 on the Nectar Masters (who?) label with minimal publicity, and, although it's apparently still available today, it's not often to be found in the CD racks of the larger music emporia. At least it looks as though somebody reasonably knowledgeable was behind the project, although a few of these inclusions have been recycled so many times that they're beginning to wear a bit thin by this stage. It should now be blindingly obvious to record companies that, while NWOBHM is certainly an eminently collectable genre, you can't merely throw together a random selection of tracks that virtually all self-respecting aficionados will have in their collection already and just wait for the money to pour in. It's notable that Geoff Barton (the very individual who first coined the phrase 'New Wave Of British Heavy Metal' during his time at 'Sounds') was roped in to pen the accompanying booklet, although it's surprising that someone so erudite should resort to a lazy rehashing of all the old clichés (punk was entirely responsible for the NWOBHM explosion, 80's bands were all rebelling against the progressive 70's, the Bay Area thrash scene would never have existed without the NWOBHM influence *etc.*) and fail to offer a more personal opinion. Yawn. What about the late 70's political upheavals, the effects of social disillusionment, the fact that privately-pressed records only became a financial viability at this time? Couldn't some of these, along with the fact that music has a natural tendency to evolve in cycles, have had *something* to do with the inception of the NWOBHM movement?

»Green Metal« LP Metal Masters 1985
Side 1:
 ASSASSIN "Don't Run For Cover"
 ASSASSIN "U.X.B."
 BLACKWYCH "Metal Mania"
 BLACKWYCH "Out Of Control"
 APRIL SOUTH "Oro Se Do Bheatha Bhaile"
 APRIL SOUTH "Rock'n'Roll Rodeo"
Side 2:
 KRUGER "Firefight"
 KRUGER "Thunder On The Plains"
 STONESNIPE "A Change From Yesterday"
 SPEED "A Real Live Wire"
 TROJAN "Soldiers Song"
 TROJAN "Charge Of The Night Brigade"

Following on from the pioneering »Belfast Rocks« set, the »Green Metal« sampler of emergent Irish talent (assembled jointly by Crashed Records and Metal Masters) turned out to represent a far more accomplished selection of regional hopefuls, with a couple of them (BLACKWYCH and TROJAN) going on to issue full albums in later years. Admittedly, TROJAN were a highly capable bunch, but BLACKWYCH were (in my humble opinion) entirely average, and I'd much rather have seen the youthful ASSASSIN being given the nod, as their energetic, BLACK ROSE-style approach was considerably more listenable. Still, ASSASSIN managed to organise a handful of seldom-seen singles and win themselves a 'Friday Rock Show' session later on in the decade, so they didn't just disappear completely. Elsewhere, APRIL SOUTH's mundane Gaelic offering (which I can't even be bothered to translate) is pretty dismal, as is its English-language counterpart (although this act also managed to issue a single or two of their own), while KRUGER (a fairly decent set of musicians) shouldn't have been allowed to appear until they had replaced their truly awful vocalist. The strangely-named STONESNIPE and SPEED, meanwhile, are allocated a single track each, the former being a reflective number with a modicum of promise, the latter weakened by another tuneless vocalist and a rudimentary arrangement. Overall, though, it's a passable collection of original material (comparatively little of which is available elsewhere), and an LP (issued in a truly pitiful sleeve) which is always worth picking up.

»Hammer« LP Ariola 1981
Side 1:
 MOTÖRHEAD "Ace Of Spades"
 MICHAEL SCHENKER GROUP "Armed And Dangerous"
 GIRLSCHOOL "Hit And Run"
 UFO "Chains, Chains"
 POINT BLANK "Nicole"
 DEDRINGER "Direct Line"
Side 2:
 ANGEL WITCH "Angel Witch"
 KROKUS "Smelly Nelly"
 TYGERS OF PAN TANG "The Story So Far"
 TOKYO "Tokyo"
 GILLAN "Future Shock"
 PRAYING MANTIS "Children Of The Earth"

A slightly peculiar compilation from Germany, which seems to have served little purpose other than to showcase some of the global acts licensed to Ariola at the time. It's a real mixed bag, with a few of our NWOBHM favourites (and DEDRINGER), some established Brits who were already major names on the rock scene (MOTÖRHEAD, UFO and GILLAN, as if you didn't know), plus a handful of heavy invaders from overseas (SCHENKER, KROKUS, the unremarkable POINT BLANK and the little-remembered TOKYO, few of whom were in dire need of this kind of exposure), none of which is particularly enthralling. Nothing exclusive or hard-to-get, inevitably, and not really a sampler that you should be losing sleep over if it doesn't currently reside in your collection.

»Heavy Metal Collection 1« CD X-Tra
Collection 1993
  VENOM "In League With Satan"
  TYGERS OF PAN TANG "Angel"
  BLITZKRIEG "A Time Of Changes"
  GEORDIE "Bless My Soul"
  CRONOS "Dancing In The Fire"
  JAGUAR "Cold Heart"
  RAVEN "Hellraiser"
  AVENGER "Yesterday's Heroes"
  DEDRINGER "Rock Night"
  WAR MACHINE "The Power"
  MANTAS "Nowhere To Run"
  FIST "Turn The Hell On"

The obscure »Heavy Metal Collection« series of CD's appears to have been conceived as a long-running set of releases. Although only four volumes seem to have emerged thus far. Certainly, the discs in question have been spotted for sale in some far-flung parts of the globe (both individually and as a weighty box set), and this repackaging of material (all of which was originally recorded for the Neat label) appears to have been an officially-sanctioned undertaking. It may be completely irrelevant for all the collectors who possess most of Neat's releases, although I suspect that those responsible were intending to capitalise on the perceived NWOBHM revival, and assumed that these acts were sufficiently credible to justify a few compilations. In any case, each of these CD's showcases a pretty representative selection of Neat's major players, and tends to skirt around all of those hopefuls who delivered a single or two before disappearing back into obscurity. The first volume is unremarkable, in the main, and the inclusion of outfits such as GEORDIE, CRONOS and MANTAS indicates a broad range of acts in terms of style and timescale. There's nothing particularly hard-to-get, but no doubt a few fans were happy to pick this up, purely for the convenience of having some of these titles on CD for the first time.

»Heavy Metal Collection 2« CD X-Tra
Collection 1993
  GEORDIE "No Sweat"
  BLACK ROSE "California USA"
  ATOMKRAFT "Your Mentor"
  RAVEN "Hell Patrol"
  PERSIAN RISK "Ridin' High"
  VENOM "Poison"
  SARACEN "We Have Arrived"
  SHE "Never Surrender"
  TYSONDOG "Taste The Hate"
  MANTAS "Let It Rock"
  CRONOS "Speedball"
  ARTILLERY "Time Has Come"

I suppose the second release in this series is marginally more interesting than its unremarkable predecessor, if only because of the inclusion of PERSIAN RISK and ATOMKRAFT, the latter's "Your Mentor" offering (a number which was scheduled to feature on an EP which never saw the light of day) having appeared only on the relatively obscure »Powertrax« promo cassette, suggesting that those responsible for these CD's might actually have made genuine attempts to locate hard-to-get material. It's possibly a semi-important compilation for the avid ATOMKRAFT collector, therefore, but it hardly represents an essential purchase for the rest of us. As before, GEORDIE, CRONOS and MANTAS all put in an appearance, as do Danish thrashers ARTILLERY, which pretty much scuppers any notion of these being dedicated NWOBHM collections. Perhaps the compilers failed to appreciate that Neat diversified as time went on. Bit of a mystery, really.

»Heavy Metal Collection 3« CD X-Tra
Collection 1993
  RAVEN "Take Control"
  STATETROOPER "She Got The Look"
  VENOM "Black Metal"
  MANTAS "Desperado"
  BLACK ROSE "Don't Fall In Love"
  AVENGER "Steel On Steel"
  GEORDIE "We Make It Rock"
  TYSONDOG "School's Out"
  CRONOS "Bad Reputation"
  DEDRINGER "The Eagle Never Falls"
  WAR MACHINE "No Place To Hide"
  JAGUAR "Raw Deal"

There's nothing much to write home about on the third instalment, to be frank, and things were already looking a bit formulaic by this time, with the obligatory selections coming from the ever-present VENOM (plus the related CRONOS and MANTAS) and RAVEN (perfectly understandable, given that they were Neat's big-name acts), although I can't really fathom why GEORDIE also turned up on every volume. Elsewhere, the additional presence of DEDRINGER and STATE-TROOPER hardly threatens to tempt all that many NWOBHM aficionados to part with their hard-earned cash, so it was quite variable in terms of quality control. I sincerely hope that these CD's were relatively inexpensive releases, as none of the volumes were to include a generous or particularly interesting assortment of tracks.

»Heavy Metal Collection 4« CD X-Tra
Collection 1993
AVENGER "(Fight For The) Right To Rock"
BLACK ROSE "Walk It How You Talk It"
VENOM "Sons Of Satan"
TYSONDOG "Hotter Than Hell"
WAR MACHINE "Dangerous"
WARFARE "Metal Anarchy"
RAVEN "Faster Than The Speed Of Light"
GEORDIE "Time To Run"
CRONOS "Painkiller"
MANTAS "Deceiver"
JESS COX "Piece Of The Action"
BLITZKRIEG "Vikings"

No surprises whatsoever on the fourth and final volume (so far) in this peculiar series, which pretty much replicates the manner of the initial three releases. Again, there's little to cause a great deal of excitement among all but the most easily-placated collectors, although at least the likes of JESS COX, BLITZKRIEG and WARFARE provide a bit of welcome variety. I shouldn't imagine that there will be a significant demand for further instalments of the »Heavy Metal Collection« series (although I could easily be proved wrong), and I suspect that those responsible for the assembly of this batch might ultimately have been disappointed with the eventual sales figures.

»Heavy Metal Heroes« LP Heavy Metal 1981
Side 1:
TWISTED ACE "I Won't Surrender"
GRIM REAPER "The Reaper"
JAGUAR "Stormchild"
SOLDIER "Storm Of Steel"
BITCHES SIN "Strangers On The Shore"
METAL MIRROR "Hard Life"
Side 2:
HANDSOME BEASTS "Local Heroes"
BUFFALO "Cold As Night"

EXPOZER "Rock Japan"
SPLIT BEAVER "Running Wild"
DRAGSTER "Do It!"
WITCHFINDER GENERAL "Rabies"

After issuing a handful of singles in the early months of 1981, the Heavy Metal label decided to branch out and begin releasing full albums, but started off by throwing together a compilation to see which of their acts might qualify as stars of the future. The original »Heavy Metal Heroes« volume showcased a fairly wide range of acts, some of whom (BUFFALO, DRAGSTER, SOLDIER, TWISTED ACE, JAGUAR) didn't get past the stage of releasing singles for the label, although others (notably WITCHFINDER GENERAL, BITCHES SIN, SPLIT BEAVER and HANDSOME BEASTS) were evidently better-received by the listening public, and were ultimately afforded the chance to record full-length offerings. Even so, much of the material on display is exclusive to this compilation (it's also a rare opportunity to hear GRIM REAPER as fronted by Paul de Mercado), so it still represents a worthy purchase for fans of the genre. In fact, the only contentious inclusions are perhaps those from METAL MIRROR and EXPOZER, both of whom had earlier released private singles, but who were never all that likely to make it out of the minor league. As most of you will be aware, this LP was issued in two different sleeves (for reasons which were never particularly obvious), with the red version (a pretty functional affair with little more than the band names and song titles) being markedly less common than the one with the proper 'guitar' cover. Still, both of the »Heavy Metal Heroes« albums are becoming quite hard to locate in their original form, so the fact that the pair have now been made available on a single CD by British Steel should make a number of fans happy.

»Heavy Metal Heroes Vol.2« LP Heavy Metal 1982
Side 1:
LIONHEART "Lionheart"
SHIVA "En Cachent"
PALLAS "Arrive Alive"
MENDES PREY "What The Hell's Hoing On?"
MANTLE-SWALLOW-PALMER "Ice Cold Diamond"
OVERKILL "Out Of My Head"
Side 2:
JESS COX "Devil's Triangle"
TWISTED ACE "This Fire Inside"
WITCHFINDER GENERAL "Free Country"
NO FAITH "Oh Well"

PERSIAN RISK "Calling For You"
NO QUARTER "Power And The Key"

The Heavy Metal concern was well and truly established as a force to be reckoned with by the tail end of 1982, but they were still on the lookout for new talent, and so the second instalment of their »Heavy Metal Heroes« series sought to introduce the public to a few of the nation's young wannabes as well as a couple of the company's major prospects viz. SHIVA and WITCHFINDER GENERAL. Even so, it was surprising just how many of the other outfits featured had already released their own vinyl product (PALLAS, MENDES PREY, OVERKILL, NO FAITH and PERSIAN RISK), so it wasn't really giving exposure to all that many emergent hopefuls at all. Mind you, OVERKILL, MENDES PREY and the superb PERSIAN RISK all delivered some eminently listenable contributions, and there were early glimpses of the music of LIONHEART and JESS COX. Elsewhere, NO QUARTER and MANTLE-SWALLOW-PALMER (whoever the hell they were) proceed to tough it out for the title of 'most desperate ZEPPELIN wannabes', although Scottish proggies PALLAS were an odd choice for inclusion, even if "Arrive Alive" represented one of their more substantial efforts. Again, there was a fair old quota of exclusive material, so the album is another useful purchase for NWOBHM fans. Still, none of the acts promoted on this particular set (apart from SHIVA and WITCHFINDER GENERAL) went on to enjoy a productive career with Heavy Metal (although a couple found more accommodating labels elsewhere), so it seems to have been a fairly futile attempt to unearth a few possible additions to their roster. A third volume in the »Heavy Metal Heroes« series actually emerged as late as 1990 (mainly to showcase the still-functioning HANDSOME BEASTS, I reckon), although the other acts on display had little or no connection with the original NWOBHM movement.

»Heavy Metal Records Singles Collection Vol.1« CD British Steel 1996
    HANDSOME BEASTS "All Riot Now"
    HANDSOME BEASTS "The Mark Of The Beast"
    HANDSOME BEASTS "Breaker"
    HANDSOME BEASTS "Crazy"
    HANDSOME BEASTS "One In A Crowd"
    BUFFALO "Battle Torn Heroes"
    BUFFALO "Women Of The Night"
    DRAGSTER "Ambitions"
    DRAGSTER "Won't Bring You Back"
    LAST FLIGHT "Dance To The Music"
    LAST FLIGHT "I'm Ready"
    SPLIT BEAVER "Savage"
    SPLIT BEAVER "Hound Of Hell"
    SATANIC RITES "Live To Ride"
    SATANIC RITES "Hit And Run"

Hmmm, the 'HANDSOME BEASTS singles collection', more like. Well, I suppose some people might have been sufficiently tempted by the other featured tracks to spend a few quid on this one, but this early British Steel compilation is a bit of an oddity, and seems to have been a case of simply raking together some vaguely-scarce singles (although they evidently couldn't get the rights to the sought-after WITCHFINDER GENERAL one) and chucking them on a CD (officially, that is) for the first time. There's really nothing too inspiring here, to be perfectly frank, and little that hasn't been featured on other compilations, bootlegs or album reissues, although I suppose the well-intentioned booklet notes might have helped things along. A second volume has failed to materialise thus far, and I suspect that British Steel now have rather more of an idea about what makes NWOBHM collectors tick.

»It's Unheard Of!« LP Sane Records 1984
Side 1:
    INCUBUS "Lost Soul"
    RUNESTAFF "The Games You Play"
    PYRAMID "Time Forgets A Hero"
    AVALANCHE "Night Creeper"
    DED ENGINE "Renegade"
    RESEARCH DEPT "Mrs. Poe"
    HAMMERHEAD "Lochinvar"
Side 2:
    CRY WOLF "Seventh Sister"
    SHYLOCK "Egypt"
    TRIDENT "The Power Of The Trident"
    NU-TRICX "Cry"
    SAPPHIRE "Encounter"
    KRAKEN "Rat Race"
    INCUBUS "Way Of The World"

This extremely rare LP, compiled by the Welsh label Sane Records (presumably something of a play on the name of the much larger Sain Records), has, in recent years, become a fruitful source of material for the Japanese series of NWOBHM bootleg CD's, as the majority of tracks included are otherwise unreleased. Familiar groups such as HAMMERHEAD, RUNESTAFF (in their original, male-vocal incarnation) and TRIDENT feature alongside an assortment of obscurities such as PYRAMID, AVALANCHE, SHYLOCK and NU-TRICX, while DED ENGINE

(USA) and RESEARCH DEPT (Italy) constitute the (slightly superfluous) overseas contingent. The remaining bands, namely INCUBUS (honoured with two tracks, for some reason), CRY WOLF, SAPPHIRE and KRAKEN, *aren't* to be confused with their more familiar British namesakes, with this being the only known vinyl appearance of these particular outfits. There are few *bona fide* classics on display, but it's a pretty good selection, all the same. Furthermore, considering the fact that the featured cuts were apparently all lifted directly from demo tapes, the sound quality is remarkably listenable throughout, and the combination of musical styles isn't bad at all. Sane Records apparently did their best to promote hopefuls from a variety of genres, issuing further (equally-scarce) album samplers such as »Subtle Hints« (Electro-pop) and »On The Street« (Punk), but they don't seem to have been in a position to issue any singles of their own (being a *'non-profit making, one-man operation'*), which is a real pity, as whoever was responsible did a particularly good job with this compilation. Even so, only RUNESTAFF managed to get any further, after recruiting a female vocalist and signing to Heavy Metal the following year, although the Merseyside-based KRAKEN ultimately evolved into a melodic proposition called PLATINUM-HI, who (after relocating to London) ended up working under the feeble identity of LO GIRLS, an act who contributed to the »Metal For Muthas '92« compilation.

»Kent Rocks« LP White Witch Records 1981
Side 1:
 RENEGADE "Last Warrior"
 STIF CREMONA "People Like You"
 MICROGRAMMA "Bus To Amsterdam"
 DERVISH "Cyclone"
 LEGEND "Heaven Sent"
Side 2:
 DEMON PACT "Escape"
 K.C.B. "Tomorrow"
 JERRY SCALES BAND "The Man"
 SHANE "My Song"
 REPLACEABLE HEADZ "Primeval Ooze"
 RAW DEAL "Cut Above The Rest"

Although the legendary »Kent Rocks« album has long been viewed as a genuine NWOBHM ultra-collectable, the record is really just one of those local-band samplers, albeit one with a fair number of metal hopefuls on display. Issued by the White Witch label at the height of its powers, the compilation gave valuable exposure to eleven of Kent's wannabes, although several of those featured are utterly unworthy of a place on vinyl. For example, the indie twaddle of STIF CREMONA and the abysmal mess vomited up by the JERRY SCALES BAND (whose shocker of a track sounds as though it was originally recorded on a wax cylinder) are nothing short of a complete disgrace, while both MICROGRAMMA and the REPLACEABLE HEADZ manage to extricate themselves from their 'Freak Brothers' comics just long enough to deliver some totally pointless, sub-HAWKWIND sonic burblings with no musical merit whatsoever. At least the K.C.B. offering is mercifully brief, although their punk/mod concoction is a reasonably jolly effort. The good stuff comes from RENEGADE and RAW DEAL (both of whom would record their own singles for the label and contribute exclusive numbers here), plus LEGEND and DEMON PACT, whose self-financed singles were also sold through White Witch. Again, the DEMON PACT offering is one which didn't appear on their subsequent two-tracker, but LEGEND let the side down slightly by recycling "Heaven Sent" on theirs. That only leaves the mysterious DERVISH, whose weighty selection showcases some impressive musicianship and an extremely capable vocalist, the overall effect being very much in the HOLLOW GROUND scheme of things, so it's a great pity this bunch didn't get any further. The album was a spartan affair in terms of presentation, with just a double-sided insert serving as a makeshift *'cover'*, and the quantity pressed was pretty minimal (I don't trust the figure quoted by the label), so you'll be slightly lucky to pick one up dirt-cheap. To be honest, though, it doesn't justify the massive price tag at all, even taking into account the exclusive material from certain outfits. As some wise men once said, don't believe the hype.

»Kikrock« LP Kik Records 1982
Side 1:
 SO WHAT "Fool's Love"
 TURBO "Soddom And Gommorrah"
 ELECTRIQUE HOBAUX "Silly Games"
 SMOKEY BEARS
  "Another Notch In The Headboard"
 STRAW DOGS "Ralston Wall"
 BLOODY MARY "Hard To Get"
 SMOKEY BEARS "Something On My Mind"
 THE FEDS "Things That Go Bump In The Night"
Side 2:
 PLAY DIRTY "Seems That You Can't With Me"
 BLOODY MARY "Rock Suicide"
 SO WHAT "Me And You"

TURBO "Take Me High"
ELECTRIQUE HOBAUX "Plane To Tokyo"
THE FEDS "Good Times"
STRAW DOGS "Scotland"

This one's so obscure that even the majority of die-hard NWOBHM collectors are unaware of its existence, and the »Kikrock« album, assembled by Kik Records (responsible for issuing singles by acts such as the PENETRATIONS) in 1982, was presumably pressed in such tiny quantities that few examples have ever come onto the market. This particular sampler is a collection of rock/metal talent from the West of Scotland (mostly Ayrshire), and most of the outfits on display are utterly unknown, although SO WHAT and TURBO (not to be confused with their English counterparts) may be familiar to a few NWOBHM aficionados. This was pretty early in SO WHAT's career, though, and the outfit seemed quite content to churn out some largely unremarkable semi-boogie on "Fool's Love" (although "Me And You" is a huge improvement), whereas TURBO were clearly operating in a melodic rock style with a vaguely celtic feel, fairly similar to early MAMA'S BOYS in the main. Elsewhere, the feebly-named ELECTRIQUE HOBAUX are rather poppy and disposable, and it's back to comparatively mundane boogie territory for the VARDIS-style rock of the SMOKEY BEARS. The STRAW DOGS (one of several heavy acts to adopt the name over the years), meanwhile, seem to have been a pretty knockabout crossover proposition, and basically stick out like a sore thumb (the supposedly 'anthemic' "Scotland" effort is truly diabolical), but never mind. BLOODY MARY, on the other hand, come across as a substantial, female-fronted bunch operating in a broadly similar style to RAMPENT or SIEGE, while THE FEDS deliver a catchy brand of quirky material with occasional similarities to T34 and JEDDAH. Ironically, the only band to be afforded a single track turn out to be the pick of the bunch, and PLAY DIRTY's "Seems That You Can't With Me" is a superb, energetic offering which brings forth some extremely strong comparisons with the excellent SABRE. Shame that a couple of those no-hopers couldn't have been left off in order that this ensemble could have contributed another number, but there you go. As I say, a very scarce album indeed, and one that few of us are ever likely to encounter.

»Lead Weight« LP Neat 1981/CD Teichiku 1992
Side 1:
RAVEN "Inquisitor"
WHITE SPIRIT "Cheetah"
VENOM "Angel Dust"
AXE "SS Giro"
BLITZKRIEG "Inferno"
ARAGORN "Noonday"
Side 2:
FIST "Throwing In The Towel"
AXIS "Messiah"
BITCHES SIN "Down The Road"
WARRIOR "Flying High"
SATAN'S EMPIRE "Soldiers Of War"

Although Neat's »Lead Weight« sampler started off life as a humble promotional cassette, it subsequently emerged (in Italy, at least) as a proper vinyl pressing, and it was certainly a valid enough release in terms of showcasing some of the label's talent of the day. In fact, only three of the featured tracks were recycled from earlier releases (the ARAGORN, WHITE SPIRIT and AXIS numbers were all lifted from singles), the remainder either being exclusive or different to the versions which would show up elsewhere. In particular, BLITZKRIEG's "Inferno" was taken from their first demo, while the selections from RAVEN, VENOM and WARRIOR all differ to their album/EP counterparts, so there's a fair amount of interest generated by these inclusions alone. Even better, though, the excellent BITCHES SIN and FIST compositions are completely exclusive to this compilation, and there's also a unique opportunity to hear AXE (a defunct combo who had already evolved into FIST, so their presence is slightly difficult to comprehend) and SATAN'S EMPIRE, a talented Scottish bunch of hopefuls who subsequently relocated to London and plied their trade for several years before metamorphosing into one of many acts going by the name of VHF. Understandably, the AXE cut ("SS Giro") wasn't exactly a million miles away from the version which later appeared on the second FIST album, but never mind. The SATAN'S EMPIRE number was another highlight of the set, this epic composition coming across as broadly similar to GEDDES AXE or DEALER, so it's a great pity they didn't achieve any further recognition in their original form. All things considered, »Lead Weight« is an excellent compilation, but it's a shame that it's so difficult to track down (even the tape version is extremely scarce), so it would be nice if it was made available again. The album has only ever appeared on CD in Japan, although there are suggestions that Neat Metal might be thinking about a CD reissue in the near future, which would doubtless be welcomed by a great many fans.

»Megalomania« LP Powerstation 1986
Side 1:
   CHROME MOLLY "Take Me I'm Yours"
   BATTLEZONE "Voice On The Radio"
   MAX AND THE BROADWAY METAL CHOIR "Placebo Effect"
   TOKYO BLADE "Rock Me To The Limit"
   MAINEEAXE "The Game"
   ALEX HARVEY "Billy Bolero"
   SERGEANT "Movin'"
Side 2:
   PAULINE GILLAN BAND "Damage Is Done"
   CHROME MOLLY "Lonely"
   MAX AND THE BROADWAY METAL CHOIR "Almighty Dollar"
   TOKYO BLADE "If Heaven Is Hell"
   ALEX HARVEY "Shoeshoes Thompson"
   BATTLEZONE "Rising Star"
   CHROME MOLLY "Set Me Free"
   TOKYO BLADE "Fever"

Featuring, in the main, an unremarkable selection of later bands who were (at best) loosely affiliated with the original NWOBHM movement, this compilation additionally serves to illustrate just how much second-rate poo-plop Powerstation had on their books at the time. I mean, how many of us are remotely interested in ALEX HARVEY (who had kicked the bucket a good few years earlier) or the 'hilarious' antics of the hopelessly contrived MAX AND THE BROADWAY METAL CHOIR? Furthermore, while a sticker on the front cover proudly announces the inclusion of 'previously unreleased tracks', pretty much all of them did, in fact, appear on either earlier or subsequent releases (some in slightly different form, admittedly), so you're not getting too many exclusives after all. Clearly, with three whole selections included here, TOKYO BLADE were rightly regarded as the company's flagship act when the LP was being assembled (although they had pretty much gone off on their own by the time it hit the shops), and, to be honest, the remainder of Powerstation's signings simply can't be regarded as residing in the same league.

»Metal Battle« LP Neat 1983/Roadrunner 1983
Side 1:
   RAVEN "Mind Over Metal"
   ANVIL "Motormount"
   BATTLEAXE "Ready To Deliver"
   MERCYFUL FATE "Black Funeral"
   TANK "Laughing In The Face Of Death"
Side 2:
   VENOM "Leave Me In Hell"
   JAGUAR "Run For Your Life"
   WITCHFYNDE "I'd Rather Go Wild"
   HELLANBACH "Dancin'"
   SATAN "Hunt You Down"
   SANTERS "Racing Time"

The »Metal Battle« compilation, released both on Neat and on the fledgling Roadrunner label (the latter issue featuring a rather more elaborate gatefold sleeve with condensed band biographies), was basically a showcase for the predominantly British roster of acts signed to (or licensed by) the labels at the time. It might have been nice to make an effort to include one or two unreleased tracks, as there was certainly a lot of unused material in Neat's vaults, although I suppose the logistics of promoting a variety of acts on a relatively novel label (Roadrunner) in this manner might have been a bit problematic. A reasonable compilation, all the same, but not nearly as interesting as Neat's »Lead Weight« or »All Hell Let Loose« sets.

»Metal Explosion« LP BBC Records 1980
Side 1:
   SAMSON "Take It Like A Man"
   PRAYING MANTIS "Johnny Cool"
   TRESPASS "Visionary"
   TAURUS "Paper Chaser"
Side 2:
   MORE "Soldier"
   MONEY "Leo The Jester"
   GILLAN "If You Believe Me"
   ANGEL WITCH "Extermination Day"

One of the BBC's better ideas in days gone by was to make some of their session material available to the general public, but it's a pity that metal fans were only given an allowance of two compilation albums, while indie types were appeased with dozens of »Peel Sessions« EP's and mini-albums over the years. Maybe we'll actually see a belated series of »Vance Sessions« EP's at some future date (wouldn't that be dandy?), but I wouldn't hold your breath. Getting back to those compilations, the first one was »Metal Explosion«, which showcased some of the more popular session favourites from 1979 and 1980, supposedly from the 'new breed of metal bands', so heaven knows what GILLAN were doing on there. Much of the material was exclusive to the compilation at the time, although the vast majority of tracks later turned up (in different form, admittedly) on regular releases, so it's not such a big deal nowadays. Still, it's nice to hear the original session versions of familiar numbers, as these were often works-in-progress at that stage, and changed quite perceptibly before they were made available officially. The *bona fide* coup for this particular set, though, was the inclusion of a TAURUS original, an immensely capable ensemble who never enjoyed the best of luck and who, despite offers from major labels, contrived to defy the odds by failing to release any product of their own thereafter. By virtue of this track alone, »Metal Explosion« represents an important album for NWOBHM completists, and it surely deserves a place in every serious collection.

»Metal Fatigue« LP Ebony 1982
Side 1:
    HEADHUNTER "Headhunter"
    SAVAGE "Ain't No Fit Place"
    HOT WIRE "Ain't Gonna Beg"
    SCHELL SHOCK "Steel Breeze"
    STRONTIUM DOG
    "Getting In From The Outside"
Side 2:
    J.D. BAND "Too Late"
    ASSASIN "Lonely Southern Road"
    INNER VISION "Stage Play"
    MODUS OPERANDI "Something Inside"

The Ebony label first introduced itself to the rock public with a series of compilation albums, the earliest example of which (»Metal Fatigue«) hit the shops in 1982. With the exception of the excellent SAVAGE (following up their triumphal appearance on the »Scene Of The Crime« set), the young hopefuls featured are horrendously obscure (I'm assuming, in the absence of any other information, that each of them were based in Britain), and, to be honest, I can't really provide additional details about any of these acts with the exception of Birmingham's SCHELL SHOCK, who emerged from the ashes of the capable TITAN and who proceed to deliver one of the more listenable numbers on display, this effort resembling BASHFUL ALLEY at times. Elsewhere, however, many of those under scrutiny just weren't ready to appear on vinyl, and didn't do themselves any favours by revealing their musical inadequacies to the fans and labels. STRONTIUM DOG and the J.D. BAND are particularly atrocious, although ASSASIN (who may or may not have been a HAZZARD offshoot) and INNER VISION aren't far behind in terms of non-talent. Poor MODUS OPERANDI were lumbered with a very unflattering production, but showed a modicum of promise, while HEADHUNTER (energetic but ramshackle) and HOT WIRE (raunchy but derivative) were passable, at least. It wasn't exactly the best way to start off a record label, and the selection of acts was pretty awful, but Ebony's compilations got better as time went on, fortunately.

»Metal For Muthas« LP EMI 1980/CD Airraid Records 2000
Side 1:
    IRON MAIDEN "Sanctuary"
    SLEDGEHAMMER "Sledgehammer"
    EF BAND "Fighting For Rock And Roll"
    TOAD THE WET SPROCKET "Blues In A"
    PRAYING MANTIS "Captured City"
Side 2:
    ETHEL THE FROG "Fight Back"
    ANGEL WITCH "Baphomet"
    IRON MAIDEN "Wrathchild"
    SAMSON "Tomorrow Or Yesterday"
    NUTZ "Bootliggers"

As far as the major labels are concerned, EMI were undoubtedly the trailblazers in the NWOBHM era, and the company initially picked up on the new metal explosion at the tail end of 1979, whereupon they identified (under the aegis of Neal Kay) some of the emergent hopefuls (mostly from London and its environs) who might benefit from exposure on a compilation album. That LP was the legendary »Metal For Muthas«, and it was soon selling in pretty impressive quantities upon its release at the beginning of 1980. A couple of the acts already had vinyl product on the market by that juncture, but it still represented an incredibly beneficial showcase for the majority of the featured contenders, particularly IRON MAIDEN, ANGEL WITCH, ETHEL THE FROG and SAMSON, all of whom were retained for further releases. Of these, it was MAIDEN who lasted the distance, although the likes of NUTZ (aka RAGE), ANGEL WITCH, SAMSON, the EF BAND and PRAYING MANTIS all went on to enjoy success with a variety of other labels, so this sampler pretty much constitutes the most efficient showcase for unsigned NWOBHM talent. For the modern-day collector, it's also an important release, given that each of the cuts are (with the exception of ETHEL THE FROG's contribution) either exclusive or different to the versions which appeared elsewhere, and interest in the MAIDEN tracks alone (demo versions recorded specifically for this set) has been sufficient to elevate it to the status of an evergreen collectable. Recently, though, the material has been made available on disc (much of the two »Metal For

Muthas« sets appeared in Japan as »The Bible Of Hard Rock«) courtesy of Bruce Dickinson's Airraid label, so fans can finally upgrade from their crackly old vinyl.

»Metal For Muthas Vol.2« LP EMI 1980/CD Airraid Records 2000
Side 1:
 TRESPASS "One Of These Days"
 EAZY MONEY "Telephone Man"
 XERO "Cutting Loose"
 WHITE SPIRIT "High Upon High"
 DARK STAR "Lady Of Mars"
Side 2:
 HORSEPOWER "She Gives Me Candy"
 RED ALERT "Open Heart"
 CHEVY "Chevy"
 THE RAID "Hard Lines"
 TRESPASS "Stormchild"

With the first »Metal For Muthas« album becoming such a massive success for EMI almost immediately, it came as little surprise when the label began sniffing around for talent to feature on a sequel, which hit the shops a matter of months later. The second set showcased another strong selection of hopefuls, some of whom (DARK STAR, CHEVY, WHITE SPIRIT) were soon snapped up by other labels, but it's curious that EMI didn't feel compelled to offer contracts to any of the acts on show this time. Predictably, the three aforementioned bands all deliver capable numbers, as do the excellent TRESPASS (honoured with two tracks), XERO and THE RAID (aka JAMESON RAID), although there were also some unspectacular offerings from HORSEPOWER (who later issued a mediocre single), EAZY MONEY (fly-by-night Londoners who allegedly featured guest vocalist Marc Storace of KROKUS) and RED ALERT (a complete and utter enigma, seemingly unrelated to any of the other recording acts of that identity), all of which lower the standard quite considerably. Still, it was a passable enough selection, even if it failed to make quite the same impact as its predecessor, and the presence of some exclusive tracks and alternate versions has been enough to keep collectors interested for two decades since its release. As with the first set, »Metal For Muthas Vol.2« is also now available on CD, but this volume proved to be a turning point for EMI, who concluded (after chucking together the half-hearted »Muthas Pride« 12" EP) that compilations weren't the way forward after all, whereupon they merely threw all their weight behind the immensely popular IRON MAIDEN.

»Metal Hammer« LP Roadrunner 1984
Side 1:
 MERCYFUL FATE "Evil"
 RAVEN "Mind Over Metal"
 VENOM "Poison"
 SATAN "No Turning Back"
 THUNDERFIRE "Danger"
 CLOVEN HOOF "Crack The Whip"
Side 2:
 METALLICA "Motorbreath"
 TOKYO BLADE "If Heaven Is Hell"
 RODS "Born To Rock"
 BATTLEAXE "Running Out Of Time"
 EXCITER "Saxons Of The Fire"
 ANTHRAX "Metal Thrashing Mad"

Following on from the success of their »Metal Battle« sampler of recent signings, Roadrunner's next compilation album, released as a collaboration with 'Metal Hammer' magazine, again featured a cross-section of bands from the label's impressive roster, of which approximately half are NWOBHM in this case. There's nothing out of the ordinary here, although the choice of tracks is pretty respectable, and the company subsequently continued the formula with their »12 Commandments In Metal« long-player before taking a break from compilations for a while. Incidentally, one of the most energetic cuts on the »Metal Hammer« sampler comes from an obscure bunch of youthful REINCARNATE copyists called METALLICA; I wonder whatever happened to them?

»Metal Inferno« LP Castle Communications 1985
Side 1:
 VENOM "Black Metal"
 WITCHFINDER GENERAL "Friends Of Hell"
 CRUCIFIXION "Green Eyes"
 CLOVEN HOOF "Laying Down The Law"
 DEMON "Don't Break The Circle"
Side 2:
 DEMON "Beyond The Gates"
 THE BLOOD "Incubus"
 VENOM "Woman"
 ANGEL WITCH "Dr Phibes"
 CLOVEN HOOF "Gates Of Gehenna"
 WIDOW "Come To The Sabbat"

An early compilation from Castle, which saw the label plundering the back catalogues of acts such as CLOVEN HOOF, DEMON and VENOM, having presumably come to an arrangement with the likes of Heavy Metal and Neat to license selected material. Things are padded out with some peculiar choices, namely THE BLOOD and WIDOW, the latter act (whoever the hell they were) delivering a version of BLACK WIDOW's "Come To The Sabbat" (originally recorded as long ago as 1970), and there are a handful of NWOBHM standards from ANGEL WITCH, WITCHFINDER GENERAL and CRUCIFIXION, all of which appear to be pretty much connected in terms of some underlying occult theme. Scary. It's not a bad compilation at all, although it sold incredibly poorly at the time, and relatively few copies are currently in circulation. Even so, it's worth picking up if it's a cheapie, and would be a good introduction to a couple of non-premier-league outfits.

»Metallic Storm« LP Ebony 1982
Side 1:
MERCYFUL FATE "Black Funeral"
TANTRUM "You Won't Live Forever"
SCIMITAR "That's The Way I Want It"
TAROT SUTRA "The Fool"
MEAN MACHINE "Gods And Devils"
CONFESSOR "Secrets"
JURY "Don't Go"
Side 2:
WELLS FARGO "Hellride"
MERCINARY "Not The Time"
WIKKYD VIKKER "Super Rocker"
PENTAPUS "Breakout"
DETROIT "USA Lights"
MOBY DICK "Can't Have My Body Tonight"

Ebony's second collection turned out to be a dramatic improvement on the disposable »Metal Fatigue«, and »Metallic Storm« contained a far more generous and varied selection of talent, including a couple of visitors from overseas (WELLS FARGO and MERCYFUL FATE), and at least the sleeve actually revealed the origins of the acts this time. Even so, only a couple of the British hopefuls (MOBY DICK and WIKKYD VIKKER) went on to release vinyl product, so it looks as though this sort of sampler tended to be of relatively little use when it came to promoting new groups. Still, there was plenty of listenable material from the unknowns, with most of the selections falling conveniently into either the straight-ahead metal (SCIMITAR, MERCINARY, PENTAPUS) or the more raunchy rock (TANTRUM, JURY, DETROIT) camps, while there's a bit more in the way of originality from TAROT SUTRA, MEAN MACHINE and CONFESSOR, whose offerings are reminiscent of CRYER, MARQUIS DE SADE and HELL, respectively. There aren't any turkeys on display at all this time, so all credit to Ebony for getting their act together and seeking out some genuinely deserving bands. Mind you, few of them were ever heard from again, although CONFESSOR and DETROIT subsequently contributed vocalists to CHATEAUX and MARSHALL LAW, respectively. By this stage, Ebony were beginning to release a handful of singles to promote some of the more worthy acts who were now coming to their attention, but there were still several more samplers to come.

»Metal Mania« CD Castle Communications 1994
VENOM "Rip Ride"
HAWKWIND "Ghost Dance"
GIRLSCHOOL "Kick It Down"
RAVEN "Break The Chain"
LISA DOMINIQUE "Back To Back"
JUICY LUCY "Who Do You Love?"
WARFARE "Fatal Vision"
BLITZKRIEG "Buried Alive"
GROUNDHOGS "Razor's Edge"
MOTÖRHEAD "Limb From Limb"
TYSONDOG "Hotter Than Hell"
CRONOS "Fantasia"

Another of those 'semi-NWOBHM' samplers that seems to be filled out with a random selection of tracks with no logical connection. There's nothing remotely out of the ordinary here, but at least the RAVEN, MOTÖRHEAD and GIRLSCHOOL contributions aren't the best-known selections from their respective back catalogues, so it makes a change not to have to endure "Ace Of Spades" for the umpteenth time. Elsewhere, it's nice to see BLITZKRIEG, WARFARE and TYSONDOG being featured alongside the bigger names, although the inclusion of HAWKWIND (isn't it utterly amazing how often they crop up on supposedly 'metal' compilations?), JUICY LUCY and the GROUNDHOGS (really contemporary acts, those) tends to spoil things a bit. I assume (and sincerely hope) that this was merely a budget-price sampler designed to introduce people to names they might not be familiar with, as the modest running time of forty-odd minutes scarcely warrants a full-price release. Looking at the CD insert detailing Castle's back catalogue, meanwhile, it's absolutely incredible to see just how many cheapo compilations they've seen fit to bung out over the years, a great percentage of which (e.g. »The Mighty Wurlitzer«) sound as though they'd be utterly atrocious. Anything for a quick buck, eh?

»Metal Maniaxe« LP Ebony 1982
Side 1:
UNCLE SIRUS "Midnight Rendezvous"

MAD AVENUE "Bad Girl"
CHATEAUX "Young Blood"
MADAME GUILLOTINE "Machine Run"
OMUN "Chosen One"
MENACE "Hard Way"
Side 2:
TROJAN "Premonition"
FALLEN ANGEL "The Man"
MIRAJ "Trapped"
ANGEL UNDERGROUND "New Life"
CRY WOLF "Behind The Smile"
STRANGER "Call Of The Wild"
EMERALD "Deb"

After assembling their solid »Metallic Storm« collection, Ebony contrived to take two steps backwards with their follow-up, as »Metal Maniaxe« contained a largely-unremarkable selection of obscurities (annoyingly, there were no details of origin this time), few of which shone out as particularly capable, although both CHATEAUX and TROJAN (English version) went on to greater things in years to come. Elsewhere, though, much of the material on display is staggeringly mediocre (MADAME GUILLOTINE and OMUN offer a pair of fairly substantial numbers, while both STRANGER and MAD AVENUE conspire to demonstrate a keen ear for melody on their individual tracks), although there's nothing remotely out-of-the-ordinary here. There aren't any real stinkers, mind you, just an overwhelming lack of originality and dedication, so it's hardly a great surprise that so few of these acts achieved any further recognition or success in the business. Perhaps Ebony were guilty of trying to squeeze out one too many sampler (this being their third of the year) at a time when there was something of a dearth of new talent, or maybe they just had a bad hair day when this one was being thrown together.

»**Metal Plated**« LP Ebony 1983
Side 1:
DEMON EYES "Les Deux Maudites"
BADGER "The Traveller"
COMA "All In The Name Of Rock And Roll"
BLASPHEME "Jehova"
Side 2:
VULCAIN "Vulcain"
DOUBLE AGENT "Madman"
STEEL WINGS "Live Your Life"
STALLION "Don't Wait Too Long"

»Metal Plated«, the fifth and last of the original cluster of Ebony compilations, was something of a half-hearted affair, and featured four European propositions (mostly quite a bit heavier than their British contemporaries at the time) and an equivalent number of NWOBHM acts, the best of which would undoubtedly be the twin-guitar assault of BADGER (who may or may not have proceeded to release a couple of slices of vinyl thereafter) and STALLION (members of whom subsequently took up residence in BLADE RUNNER and MAMMATH), the latter unit coming across as a passable mixture of JAMESON RAID and TOBRUK. On the other hand, COMA (sounding like a mundane cross between SNAKEBITE and WRATHCHILD) and DOUBLE AGENT (staggeringly average rock with a tuneless vocalist) fail to leave a good impression. Excuse me for not writing about the foreigners, but you'll have gathered by now that this is a volume about Brits and Brits alone. Still, this particular LP is quite enjoyable (despite the relatively modest number of selections), and it's certainly all good old heavy metal, although you'll have to be an ardent fan of both NWOBHM and Eurometal to get the most enjoyment out of it.

»**Metal Prisoners**« LP Mausoleum 1983
Side 1:
CHINAWITE "Blood On The Streets"
SEDUCER "Call Your Name"
ACID "Demon"
FACTORY "You Are The Music"
ACE LANE "Never The Same"
Side 2:
CHINAWITE "Ready To Satisfy"
SEDUCER "Survivor"
ACID "Heaven's Devils"
FACTORY "The History Of The Turkey"
ACE LANE "Emotion"

A peculiar and slightly pointless compilation from the fledgling Mausoleum label, the »Metal Prisoners« effort (issued in a fairly uninspiring sleeve) cobbled together a few heavy acts signed to (or at least affiliated with) the Future Earth concern in the UK, a couple of whom (CHINAWITE and FACTORY) had already seen their own singles issued by the latter company. Strangely, however, the very same compositions were happily trundled out for inspection once again, which was disappointing, and there was also nothing exclusive from either ACE LANE (two numbers taken from their LP on Expulsion) or SEDUCER (the brace of tracks comprising their single on Sticky), so it was a dead loss in terms of giving the fans something special for their money. Still, I suppose it saves a few modern-day aficionados shelling out their hard-earned cash for a handful of reasonably scare singles. Why the compilers felt the need to pad out the set with two numbers from Belgian metal merchants ACID is a complete mystery, however, especially when WITCHFYNDE or LIMELIGHT would probably have been happy to allow some of their own material to be used. A pretty ropy compilation, but one that shouldn't cost an arm and a leg if you're desperate to add it to the collection.

»Metal Warriör« Mini-LP Metalother 1987
Side 1:
　DEUCE "Power Of The Realm"
　CRISIS "Keep Fighting"
　FIRST OFFENCE "Into The Night"
Side 2:
　TROJAN "Back To Me"
　NOT FRAGILE "Cheltenham"
　EZY MEAT "Massacre"

The small-time Other/Metalother label was a relative latecomer to the post-NWOBHM scene, although they soon progressed to the stage of issuing their own compilations, the first of which was the »Metal Warriör« six-tracker from 1987. As well as four acts from the UK, the label were keen to showcase a couple of foreign hopefuls, namely CRISIS (from the States) and NOT FRAGILE (from Germany), so it was all quite egalitarian. To be honest, it's not a staggeringly-impressive selection of tracks, but there are a few glimpses of talent from time to time. The contribution from DEUCE (Kent version), for example, was far stronger than might have been anticipated on the basis of their earlier single, but the band were already beginning to struggle by this stage. FIRST OFFENCE, meanwhile, acquit themselves reasonably well with their powerful effort, but fail to

push too many musical boundaries. Ireland's TROJAN deliver a passable slice of metal, but this is hardly the strongest number they ever committed to vinyl, while EZY MEAT's "Massacre", a track which had originally appeared on the outfit's second album, rounds things off in fine, THIN LIZZY-influenced style, although it's a pity it didn't help the group to get any further. This sampler may have been a pretty decent way to introduce a few unfamiliar acts to the public back then, but it's a release that doesn't really stand up too well after all this time. Still, Metalother assembled a follow-up, »The Last Warrior«, shortly afterwards, and also commissioned full albums from FIRST OFFENCE, NOT FRAGILE and TROJAN (although the latter ultimately appeared on G.I. Records, as did a set by the DEUCE offshoot ST. HELLIER), so I guess there must have been a bit of positive feedback from fans.

»Metal Warriors« LP Ebony 1983
Side 1:
　SHY "Tonight"
　HIGH LEVEL "Devil's Gate"
　FLYTE "Oh For The Brains Of A Ludwig"
　MITCHELL TROY "Playing Soldiers"
　WISH "Night Life"
　OMEGA "Blood Sacrifice"
Side 2:
　SORTILEGE "Cyclope De L'etang"
　LYADRIVE "We've Got The Rock"
　TNT "Sorry"
　VORTEX "The Devil's Voice"
　SINNER "Destiny"
　RANDOM BLACK "Ophelia"
　BREEZE "Do You Want To Love Me"

Ebony seemed to be getting back on the right track when their fourth compilation hit the shops, and »Metal Warriors« not only featured a more capable selection of hopefuls, but also gave useful exposure to several acts (SHY, OMEGA, LYADRIVE, TNT) who would subsequently get their own vinyl product onto the market. Of the remainder, we have another couple of European imports (HIGH LEVEL and SORTILEGE) to make up the numbers, although the home-grown talent is actually pretty decent this time. FLYTE's offering, for example, is far more enjoyable than its ludicrous title would tend to suggest, while MITCHELL TROY's contribution is another well-crafted slice of metal. WISH are a rather less inspiring outfit, though, whereas VORTEX and RANDOM BLACK, while heavy enough propositions, are both lacking in the songwriting department. SINNER (not to be confused with the trio responsible for the »Need Your Love« 7") would have been more effective if they had recruited a decent frontman, and the cheery singalong of BREEZE would probably have gone down far better with the mod fraternity, to be honest, so it's a somewhat baffling inclusion here. Still, with four of the UK acts going on to achieve some level of fame in later years, you have to regard this sampler as a success. Mind you, Ebony were already beginning to wind down their programme of compilations, and were concentrating mainly on albums by individual artists.

»Muthas Pride« 12" EP EMI 1980
Side 1:
 WILDFIRE "Wild Dog"
 QUARTZ "Back In The Band"
Side 2:
 WHITE SPIRIT "Red Skies"
 BABY JANE "Baby Jane"

After two successful volumes of »Metal For Muthas«, it came as something of a surprise when EMI elected to abandon the idea of a third instalment, and contented themselves with the »Muthas Pride« EP, featuring a mere four acts. Still, it was a fairly interesting selection, and WILDFIRE's contribution was a capable opener (even though it also appeared on their one-off single), while WHITE SPIRIT's "Red Skies" appears here in different form to the album version, making it a worthwhile purchase for fans. Even better, the QUARTZ track was exclusive to this particular EP, and represents one of their better numbers of the period, so it looks as though EMI weren't just trotting out some familiar material to rake in more cash. Mind you, I've absolutely no idea how they contrived to dredge up the totally unknown BABY JANE, whose self-titled offering was a peculiar combination of raunchy rock with vaguely reggae-influenced guitar work. Not particularly impressive, to be honest, and I reckon this was probably the only time this mystery ensemble ever reached the vinyl stage. Overall, though, a perfectly respectable release which is worth a few quid of anyone's money.

»New Electric Warriors« LP Logo 1980/CD British Steel 1997
Side 1:
 TURBO "Running"
 BUFFALO "Battle Torn Heroes"
 STREETFIGHTER "She's No Angel"
 STORMTROOPER "Grind'n'Heat"
 TAROT "Feel The Power"
 BASTILLE "Hard Man"
 OXYM "Hot Rain"
 DAWNWATCHER "Firing On All Eight"
Side 2:
 VARDIS "If I Were King"
 SILVERWING "Rock & Roll Are Four Letter Words"
 RHABSTALLION "Chain Reaction"
 COLOSSUS "Holding Back Your Love"
 JEDEDIAH STRUT "Workin' Nights"
 WARRIOR "Still On The Outside"
 KOSH "The Hit"
 RACE AGAINST TIME "Bedtime"

As the somewhat pompous and pretentious (well, it's easy to get a bit carried away when you feel particularly passionate about something) sleeve notes reveal, the »New Electric Warriors« LP was conceived at the very height of the NWOBHM explosion as one of the earliest showcases for grass-roots talent. It came about when journalist Nigel Burnham got together with Logo Records and began the task of assembling a selection of young hopefuls who hadn't yet had the merest sniff of major-label interest, and who were, in the opinion of the compilers, worthy of an appearance on vinyl. In the event, a mammoth sixteen outfits were somehow shoehorned onto a single album, and these were (at that stage) a motley assortment of both the semi-familiar and the complete unknowns. Of the familiar outfits, there was a subdivision into those whose tracks can be found elsewhere (BUFFALO, SILVERWING, VARDIS, TURBO) and those whose contributions are all exclusive to this long-player (STREETFIGHTER, RHABSTALLION, DAWNWATCHER, OXYM), while the remainder seem to have been unable to make any further impression in the business. In some cases, it's fairly easy to see why, as the likes of STORMTROOPER (a Yorkshire act, not to be confused with their Bristol namesakes), WARRIOR (yet another one, from Lancashire this time) and RACE AGAINST TIME (featuring future HELL frontman Dave Halliday) were nothing to write home about, while the atrocious KOSH effort is a complete and utter travesty which shouldn't have crept onto the finished article. Mind you, the fact that the superb TAROT (like a more rough'n'ready MIDAS) were never snapped up is a total disgrace, and I'm sure that BASTILLE (powerful), COLOSSUS (tuneful) and JEDEDIAH STRUT (who actually recorded their own two-tracker, but it never saw the light of day) could all have been coaxed into producing something special if they had been given a modicum of encouragement. Even so, this generous sampler is, on the whole, an extremely respectable and varied affair, which (as I've said elsewhere) just about represents the best introduction to the genre for the total NWOBHM novice.

»N.W.O.B.H.M.« LP/CD Heavy Metal 1991
Side 1:
 HANDSOME BEASTS "All Riot Now"
 TWISTED ACE "Firebird"
 PERSIAN RISK "Calling For You"
 SHIVA "Rock Lives On"
 GRIM REAPER "The Reaper"
Side 2:
 BUFFALO "Battle Torn Heroes"
 QUARTZ "Buried Alive"
 WITCHFINDER GENERAL "Music"
 PRAYING MANTIS "Captured City"
 [Credited as "Ambitions" by DRAGSTER]
 JAGUAR "Back Street Woman"
 SPLIT BEAVER "Hounds Of Hell"

And the award for 'least imaginative album title' goes to Heavy Metal for their »N.W.O.B.H.M.« collection. This was something of a shameless cash-in, rushed out in the wake of Lars Ulrich's celebratory compilation (which, in itself, hardly threatened to break any sales records), although it represents a pretty good cross-section of some of the label's more talented acts of yore. The featured tracks are taken from a variety of sources, namely singles, albums and compilations, and it's all listenable enough, although the reviewers tended to focus on the now-legendary *faux pas* which resulted in "Captured City" by PRAYING MANTIS appearing instead of the intended DRAGSTER contribution. It was an utterly laughable mistake, and one which suggested that the company might have been slightly careless whilst assembling their, er, *'source material'*. Even so, it's not exactly a distasteful record to have in your collection, and is still relatively easy to find, given that dozens of unsold copies have been cluttering up the bargain bins ever since its release.

»NWOBHM Demo Tapes« CD Bootleg 1992
 SATAN "Into The Firerial By Fire"
 SATAN "Blades Of Steel"
 SATAN "No Turning Back"
 SATAN "Break Free"
 SATAN "Pull The Trigger"
 SATAN "The Ritual"
 GRIM REAPER "Entrance/All Hell Let Loose"
 GRIM REAPER "Loser In Love"
 GRIM REAPER "Liar"
 GRIM REAPER "See You In Hell"
 GRIM REAPER "Suck It And See"
 GRIM REAPER "Now Or Never"
 KRAKEN "Kill The King"
 KRAKEN "Executioner"
 KRAKEN "The Kraken"

This unofficial Japanese CD collection, assembled around SATAN's »Into The Fire« demo (which featured short-stay vocalist Ian Davison Swift) and a couple of GRIM REAPER studio tapes, could have been a pretty decent release, were it not for the slapdash presentation (a JAGUAR demo is shown on the cover, for no good reason) and ludicrous spelling mistakes (apparently, an outfit called *'Grim Peaper'* are featured extensively), not to mention the staggeringly-obvious fact that this particular KRAKEN, by virtue of the fact that they were actually Canadian (this being the ensemble whose unreleased album was bootlegged on vinyl at around the same time, as opposed to either of the UK recording acts of that name), don't exactly qualify as NWOBHM in the first place. Throw in some extremely ropy mixing and editing (tracks being lumped together three or four at a time, making it an unnecessarily tedious process to access individual numbers), and we're left with a pretty dodgy release, but I suppose it's still interesting enough, in its own way. GRIM REAPER's surprisingly melodic "Loser In Love" composition never put in an appearance on vinyl, for example, and the other selections are sufficiently dissimilar to their album counterparts to warrant a modicum of attention. Meanwhile, this batch of SATAN offerings, which all later appeared officially, constitute the only available studio recordings with Swift on vocals, before he moved over to AVENGER and was replaced by Brian Ross. Furthermore, "Pull The Trigger" never appeared on any SATAN releases at all, although it showed up in different form on BLITZKRIEG's »A Time Of Changes« album. All in all, the CD is worth picking up if you're a die-hard fan of GRIM REAPER or the SATAN family, but it's not a particularly easy item to locate these days.

»N.W.O.B.H.M. Metal Rarities Vol.1« CD
British Steel 1996
 LEGEND "Hideaway"
 LEGEND "Heaven Sent"
 PRAYING MANTIS "Praying Mantis"

PRAYING MANTIS "High Roller"
MYTHRA "Death And Destiny"
MYTHRA "Killer"
MYTHRA "Overlord"
MYTHRA "U.F.O."
HOLLOW GROUND "Flying High"
HOLLOW GROUND "Warlord"
HOLLOW GROUND "Rock On"
HOLLOW GROUND "Don't Chase The Dragon"
ANGEL WITCH "Loser"
ANGEL WITCH "Suffer"
ANGEL WITCH "Dr Phibes"
GASKIN "Mony Mony"
GASKIN "Queen Of Flames"
HERITAGE "Strange Place To Be"
HERITAGE "Misunderstood"

XERO "Hold On"
XERO "Killer Frog"
PARALEX "White Lightning"
PARALEX "Travelling Man"
PARALEX "Black Widow"
SAMSON "Mr Rock'n'Roll"
SAMSON "Drivin' Music"
SHIVA "Rock Lives On"
SHIVA "Sympathy"
EF BAND "Another Day Gone"
EF BAND "Night Angel"

As well as acquiring the rights to various archive material from the Heavy Metal concern (which yielded the »Heavy Metal Records Singles Collection Vol.1« CD), British Steel's early activities also saw them garnering long-lost recordings from the likes of Guardian and Rondelet, companies which had either gone into liquidation or ceased to exist many years earlier. Before long, British Steel had assembled the first in a series of NWOBHM compilations, and their original »Metal Rarities« set saw them putting acts such as HOLLOW GROUND, MYTHRA, HERITAGE and GASKIN onto disc, and padding things out with tracks from ANGEL WITCH, LEGEND (Kent version) and PRAYING MANTIS, all of which seems to have been legal and above board, even if a couple of the groups themselves may not have been informed of these undertakings at the time. It's extraordinarily easy to criticise labels for such behaviour, but it's also perfectly understandable, especially if they come into possession of tapes quite legally, and they can hardly be expected to track down every single ex-band member to see if they have any objections to their music being reissued. Still, I'd expect them to behave in an appropriate manner as and when these people come out of the woodwork and demand a few free copies or some modest royalty payments.

»N.W.O.B.H.M. Metal Rarities Vol.2« CD
British Steel 1996
SAMSON "Telephone"
SAMSON "Leavin' You"
STORMTROOPER "Pride Before A Fall"
STORMTROOPER "Still Comin' Home"
JANINE "Crazy On You"
JANINE "Candy"
XERO "Oh Baby"

The initial instalment of the »Metal Rarities« series represented a decent enough purchase for NWOBHM fans, and was pretty much the first time that the likes of MYTHRA and HOLLOW GROUND (apart from the odd compilation) had officially appeared on CD. The follow-up was a fairly mixed bag, and saw a few more small label/privately-pressed releases being included (PARALEX, JANINE, STORMTROOPER, XERO), as well as some commonly-encountered singles from SHIVA, SAMSON and the EF BAND. To be honest, relatively few die-hard collectors would be particularly bothered about possessing the latter trio of acts on CD, and would be far more interested in the obscure stuff. In that respect, the other acts featured are well worth a place on disc, although the only really noteworthy inclusion is XERO's "Killer Frog" instrumental, a track which appeared on comparatively few copies of the outfit's »Oh Baby« 12", having replaced the offending number ("Lone Wolf") which appeared illegally on the original pressing. Even so, this CD represents a considerable saving for those devotees whose main priority is to be able to get hold of the music, and who aren't overly-concerned about owning the (often incredibly expensive) vinyl items.

»N.W.O.B.H.M. Metal Rarities Vol.3« CD
British Steel 1997
GIRLSCHOOL "Take It All Away"
GIRLSCHOOL "It Could Be Better"
TWISTED ACE "I Won't Surrender"
TWISTED ACE "Firebird"
SOLDIER "Sheralee"
SOLDIER "Force"
JAGUAR "Back Street Woman"
JAGUAR "Chasing The Dragon"
DENIGH "No Way"
DENIGH "Running"
STATIC "Voice On The Line"
STATIC "Stealin'"
SEVENTH SON "Metal To The Moon"

SEVENTH SON "Sound And Fury"
WHITE LIGHTNING "This Poison Fountain"
WHITE LIGHTNING "Hypocrite"
DRAGONSLAYER "I Want Your Life"
DRAGONSLAYER "Satan Is Free"
DRAGONSLAYER "Broken Hearts"

British Steel continue with their heroic attempts to plunder the vaults of various small record labels and secure the rights to a number of privately-issued singles. In the third volume of the »Metal Rarities« series we encounter old favourites from JAGUAR, SOLDIER and TWISTED ACE, all originally issued by the Heavy Metal label, plus relatively (compared with GIRLSCHOOL, that is) minor bands such as STATIC and SEVENTH SON. I would imagine that the main interest in this particular compilation will again be from those who wish to check out some of the more obscure and powerful outfits, making the excellent DENIGH and DRAGONSLAYER the prime selling points of this collection. There's a chance that one or two further volumes may still appear as and when the labels and musicians are contacted (a genuinely tortuous process, but the 'Iron Pages' lads have made a sterling effort in this respect), as British Steel appear to be an honourable label (no, they're not paying me to say this, and I'm not on their 'freebie' list either), and aren't in the habit of issuing tracks that they're not legally entitled to use. This might ultimately limit their choice of material somewhat, but they've still managed to ensure that their compilations don't come across as hurriedly-assembled, haphazard cash-ins. Other companies take note!

»NWOBHM-The Days On Stage« CD
Taurus Records 1993
SAMSON "Hard Times" (live)
GIRLSCHOOL "Watch Your Step" (live)
SLEDGEHAMMER "Sledgehammer" (live)
WHITE SPIRIT "Fool For The Gods" (live)
DEF LEPPARD "Wasted" (live)
DIAMOND HEAD "Am I Evil?" (live)
TYGERS OF PAN TANG "Wild Catz" (live)
IRON MAIDEN "The Ides Of March" (live)
IRON MAIDEN "Sanctuary" (live)

To be honest, I've never actually seen an original copy of this scarce Italian bootleg (Taurus Records also put out live sets by the likes of EXODUS and RIOT, incidentally), but the quirkily-titled CD (which incorporates a fairly modest batch of tracks) has evidently been assembled from various recordings made at the Reading Festival in the early 80's, at a time when a fair number of popular NWOBHM acts were invited to appear. As a result, the sound quality is variable, the best source material (from radio broadcasts) eclipsing the audience tapes by quite some way, but it's all supposedly listenable enough for the average NWOBHM aficionado. Clearly, one or two of these outfits didn't make any of their live recordings available officially, so this is a rare opportunity to hear such selections on disc (which isn't to say that the material is necessarily CD quality), and it's possibly a worthwhile release for die-hard devotees of SLEDGEHAMMER or WHITE SPIRIT, although the official live albums issued by IRON MAIDEN, SAMSON etc. tend to represent considerably better value for money. It actually seems quite a peculiar idea for anyone to assemble a bootleg compilation of live material, to be honest, and I wonder if individual CD's of the featured acts might have been a better concept. Not that I'd actually condone the naughty practice of bootlegging, officer.

»NWOBHM Live« CD Emporio 1997
SAMSON "Red Skies" (live)
SAMSON "Drivin' With ZZ" (live)
SAMSON "Riding With The Angels" (live)
GIRLSCHOOL "C'mon Let's Go" (live)
GIRLSCHOOL "Emergency" (live)
GIRLSCHOOL "Take It All Away" (live)
ANGEL WITCH "White Witch" (live)
ANGEL WITCH "Angel Of Death" (live)
ANGEL WITCH "Angel Witch" (live)
TANK "Echoes Of A Distant Battle" (live)
TANK "This Means War" (live)
TANK "That's What Dreams Are Made Of" (live)

In contrast to the Taurus Records bootleg (*vide supra*), Emporio's »NWOBHM Live« CD was a perfectly legal sampler, the selections (from SAMSON, GIRLSCHOOL, ANGEL WITCH and TANK) all being lifted (I presume) from already-released live albums (not entirely sure about the source of the TANK material, though, given that their »Return Of The Filth Hounds« set didn't emerge until a full year later), so I guess you're not getting anything too enthralling for your money, assuming you can actually track down a copy in the first place. To be honest, it's hard to judge who the label were targeting with this one, as die-hard fans of the outfits in question would no doubt have multiple versions of these numbers anyway, and newcomers to the genre would surely go for samplers of studio recordings rather than live material. I suppose those concerned should be praised for getting NWOBHM compilations onto the market at regular intervals, although it would be nice to see a few exclusive selections if at all possible.

»NWOBHM '79 Revisited« Do-LP/Do-CD
Phonogram 1990
Side 1:
DIAMOND HEAD "It's Electric"
SWEET SAVAGE "Eye Of The Storm"
SAXON "Motorcycle Man"
WHITE SPIRIT "Cheetah"
RAVEN "Don't Need Your Money"
PARALEX "White Lightning"
Side 2:
DEF LEPPARD "Getcha Rocks Off"
WEAPON "Set The Stage Alight"
SAMSON "Vice Versa"
HOLLOW GROUND "Fight With The Devil"
GIRLSCHOOL "Demolition Boys"
WITCHFYNDE "Leaving Nadir"
Side 3:
IRON MAIDEN "Sanctuary"
JAGUAR "Back Street Woman"
TYGERS OF PAN TANG "Killers"
GASKIN "I'm No Fool"
SLEDGEHAMMER "Sledgehammer"
VENOM "Angel Dust"
Side 4:
ANGEL WITCH "Extermination Day"
TRESPASS "One Of These Days"
HOLOCAUST "Death Or Glory"
VARDIS "If I Were King"
BLITZKRIEG "Blitzkrieg"
DIAMOND HEAD "Helpless"
CD Bonus Tracks:
DRAGSTER "Ambitions"
A II Z "Treason"
WITCHFINDER GENERAL "Witchfinder General"
BLACK AXE "Red Lights"
FIST "SS Giro"
PRAYING MANTIS "Captured City"

Whether you care to admit it or not, this compilation is the one that really kicked off the collecting boom in the early 90's. As you'll all be aware, it came about (as the sleeve notes explicate in rather sensationalistic detail) when Messrs Ulrich and Barton (Lars and Geoff to their mates) put their heads together and came to the conclusion that the New Wave Of British Heavy Metal should finally be brought out of the closet and venerated as a genre in its own right. Admittedly, quite a number of individuals (mostly outwith the UK) were already doing just that: writing about the subject with immense fondness, collecting the vinyl passionately and generally campaigning for DEEP MACHINE to reform. Well, it takes all sorts. Having said that, the NWOBHM aficionados were a reclusive and isolated bunch, and there were no high-profile figures championing the movement at that stage, so the patronage of this pair really was a major boost to a musical phenomenon that was beginning to give new meaning to the word 'underground'. The plan to celebrate the NWOBHM era centred around the assembly of a commemorative retrospective, with many of the bigger names from the period (take your pick, they're almost all there) being featured alongside several of those who had achieved rather more limited success, such as PARALEX, SWEET SAVAGE, WEAPON and HOLLOW GROUND.

The set didn't just hit the shops unannounced; Ulrich took every opportunity to promote the release in the months leading up to its (delayed) release, with the end result being that a great many metal aficionados (a considerable proportion of whom were METALLICA fans, and who were already aware of the legacy of these long-forgotten acts) forked out for the double album when it finally materialised in 1990 (a year late, given that it was supposed to be a '10th Anniversary' deal). Many of the hardcore NWOBHM devotees snubbed the set completely, complaining that it was a 'rip-off' which contained nothing to interest them, which was missing the point entirely, but a lot of the curious fans who invested in the compilation soon began checking out some of the more obscure NWOBHM vinyl. In due course, the dealers were doing a roaring trade, and the demand for NWOBHM peaked a few years later. The collecting boom may not have been exclusively due to this release, but it undoubtedly had a hell of a lot to do with it. Anyway, the compilation features a representative selection of NWOBHM talent, the tracks on display mostly being lifted from standard albums and singles, although a handful came from other sources, and the 'Friday Rock Show' session take of IRON MAIDEN's "Sanctuary" was something of a coup. Understandably, this set wasn't pressed in massive quantities (ironically, it has itself become a fairly collectable piece), although enough units were apparently shifted to make this 'labour of love' a worthwhile endeavour.

»NWOBHM Vol.1« CD Bootleg 1992
PRAYING MANTIS "Praying Mantis"
QUARTZ "Satan's Serenade"
BITCHES SIN "Ice Angels"
SOLDIER "Sheralee"

TRESPASS "Live It Up"
GASKIN "Sweet Dream Maker"
DIAMOND HEAD "Diamond Lights"
BLEAK HOUSE "Rainbow Warrior"
BASHFUL ALLEY "Running Blind"
WHITE SPIRIT "Suffragettes"
BUFFALO "Mean Machine"
TRIARCHY "Metal Messiah"
SWEET SAVAGE "Killing Time"
BLACK ROSE "Sucker For Your Love"
BLACK AXE "Highway Rider"
ANGEL WITCH "Hades Paradise"

As something of a knee-jerk response to the glut of officially-sanctioned compilations which were suddenly surfacing at around the turn of the decade, but which were offering the die-hard NWOBHM fans comparatively little in the way of exclusive or hard-to-get material, certain enterprising individuals in Japan began to assemble a series of do-it-yourself bootlegs, all lovingly-prepared (the featured cuts being mastered off vinyl of varying quality), and with covers showing some of the more sought-after artefacts of the period. Admittedly, the compilers started off fairly inauspiciously, with the first volume of the functionally-titled series containing a selection of numbers which, in the main, were actually quite easy to locate. Still, the likes of TRIARCHY, BLEAK HOUSE, SWEET SAVAGE and BASHFUL ALLEY were a bit more interesting, and enough collectors shelled out for a copy (it wasn't actually pressed in huge quantities) to make further volumes a worthwhile proposition. Over the years, several more instalments would appear, as would bootlegs devoted to the likes of PRAYING MANTIS, HOLOCAUST, TRESPASS and SWEET SAVAGE (using source material which varied from live/demo tapes to recordings from vinyl rarities), and these pretty much showed the official labels the sort of thing the true aficionados actually wanted to hear.

»NWOBHM Vol.2« CD Bootleg 1992
HOLOCAUST "Heavy Metal Mania"
QUARTZ "Back In The Band"
CRUCIFIXION "On The Run"
BADGE "Silver Woman"
AXIS "Messiah"
MOTHER'S RUIN "Turn Another Corner"
MYTHRA "Killer"
EF BAND "Night Angel"
JAMESON RAID "It's A Crime"
OXYM "Music Power"
LIMELIGHT "Metal Man"
DARK STAR "Rock'n'Romancin'"

XERO "Hold On"
STORMTROOPER "Pride Before A Fall"
HIGH TREASON "Saturday Night Special"
HERITAGE "Misunderstood"
DAMASCUS "Open Your Eyes"
DIAMOND HEAD "I Don't Got"

By the second volume, the compilers had already cottoned on to the fact that there would be a fair bit of mileage in obscure B-sides and compilation appearances, and they duly began scouring their collections for interesting inclusions. In this case, many of the tracks were considerably less familiar to the majority of collectors, and things were once again livened up by some little-known gems from the likes of DAMASCUS, HIGH TREASON and MOTHER'S RUIN. They were certainly heading in the right direction, and the fans applauded their efforts to bring them something slightly out of the ordinary.

»NWOBHM Vol.3« CD Bootleg 1992
SATAN "Oppression"
SAVAGE "Let It Loose"
JAGUAR "Stormchild"
AURORA "I'll Be Your Fantasy"
CHEVY "Skybird"
FIST "Forever Amber"
PERSIAN RISK "50000 Stallions"
WHITE SPIRIT "Watch Out"
BLITZKRIEG "Inferno"
WITCHFINDER GENERAL "Soviet Invasion"
TOAD THE WET SPROCKET
"Reaching For The Sky"
WEAPON "It's A Mad Mad World"
HOLLOW GROUND "Flying High"
LEGEND "Hideaway"
CRYER "Day To Day"
AXIS "Flame Burns On"
BLEAK HOUSE "Inquisition"
[Miscredited as "Isandhlwana"]
A II Z "Danger UXB"

The last of the original batch of compilations was another strong selection, and there were virtually no *'common'* inclusions this time, the CD featuring some sought-after tracks from hard-to-find samplers such as »Lead Weight« and »60 Minutes Plus«, as well as the usual hoard of B-sides and sundry rarities, the latter coming in the shape of BLEAK HOUSE (again), CRYER, AURORA and TOAD THE WET SPROCKET. As far as the fans were concerned, the bootleggers could churn out as many collections of this general standard as they could manage, but the compilers were already preparing some considerably more interesting selections for their next batch of CD's...

»NWOBHM Vol.4« CD Bootleg 1992
  TRIDENT "Destiny"
  PARALEX "Travelling Man"
  SATAN "Kiss Of Death"
  AFTER DARK "Evil Woman"
  MARQUIS DE SADE "Black Angel"
  A II Z "No Fun After Midnight"
  SCRATCH "Metal Breaker"
  DRAGONFLY "Silent Nights"
  MENDES PREY "On To The Borderline"
  DAWNWATCHER "Hall Of Mirrors"
  DEALER "Better Things To Do"
  LIMELIGHT "White Fire"
  HAMMERHEAD "Time Will Tell"
  WIKKYD VIKKER "Black Of The Night"
  SEVENTH SON "Immortal Hours"
  WARRIOR "Yesterday's Hero"

The second batch of CD's (apparently issued later the same year) began with the fourth volume, which saw the bootleggers raising the stakes in terms of the sheer unavailability of the tracks on display. Almost without exception, the numbers were all plundered from very scarce singles, EP's, LP's and compilations, and this was the first time that the likes of MARQUIS DE SADE, DRAGONFLY, WARRIOR and WIKKYD VIKKER had been heard by a wider fan base, as only a handful of collectors had managed to acquire the original vinyl at that time. It really was an extremely impressive sampler (possibly the best one of them all), in terms of both exclusivity and musical standard, although the inclusion of the Swedish group SCRATCH was a bit of a cock-up, even though their "Metal Breaker" track (very much along the lines of BLACK SABBATH's "Die Young") is a genuine classic of the period.

»NWOBHM Vol.5« CD Bootleg 1992
  ENERGY "Fight For Your Freedom"
  REINCARNATE "Take It Or Leave It"
  SMOKIN ROADIE "Midnight"
  LE GRIFFE "Where Are You Now"
  SPARTA "Tonight"
  SAPPHIRE "Jealousy"
  OVERDRIVE "On The Run"
  TURBO "Charged For Glory"
  WARRIOR "Dragon Slayer"
  DICK SMITH BAND "Way Of The World"
  BLEAK HOUSE "Down To Zero"
  MIDAS "Can't Stop Loving You Now"
  DEMOLITION "Hooker Hater"
  RUNESTAFF "The Games You Play"
  BIG DAISY "Footprints On The Water"
  LIONHEART "Lionheart"
  PROWLER "Forgotten Angel"
  NO QUARTER "Racing For Home"

There seemed to be no prospect of topping the impressive fourth volume, but the compilers almost managed it with its successor, which was now featuring such horrendously obscure material (BIG DAISY, DEMOLITION, MIDAS, ENERGY) that many NWOBHM aficionados were now able to hear outfits that they hadn't even been aware of in the first instance. Added to the excellent cover image, picturing a generous percentage of the rare-as-you-like records included, and it's fair to say that the collectors really were getting something truly out of the ordinary for their hard-earned cash. Again, the selection of material is eminently respectable, with superb inclusions from the likes of ENERGY, REINCARNATE and OVERDRIVE, although I reckon the compilers could possibly have used alternate tracks from MIDAS, PROWLER and WARRIOR. Still, copies of the disc were soon making their way around the world (and they weren't always particularly easy to obtain, either), although the bootleggers, to their credit, didn't start getting ideas above their station, and basically restricted themselves to producing affordable, functionally-presented releases, all of which were pressed in modest quantities.

»NWOBHM Vol.6« CD Bootleg 1992
  ELIXIR "Treachery"
  DUCHESS "Your Love"
  GEDDES AXE "Six-Six-Six"
  SAPPHIRE "Let It Burn"
  STORMCHILD "Rockin' Steady"
  SATAN "Heads Will Roll"
  MEANSTREAK "Played It Right"
  RICOCHET "Midas Light"
  SCARAB "Poltergeist"
  SATANIC RITES "Hit And Run"
  STAGEFRIGHT "Stranger In The Night"
  SALEM "Reach To Eternity"
  LYADRIVE "Anytime"
  HAMMERHEAD "Lochinvar"
  LIAISON "Only Heaven Knows"
  ANGEL WITCH "Flight 19"

If anything, the sixth volume was a slight step backward, with numbers from ANGEL WITCH, SATANIC RITES and GEDDES AXE being a bit too common for some people's liking, although the rarities were well up to scratch once more, with the excruciatingly rare STORMCHILD, RICOCHET and STAGEFRIGHT all showing that some of the most obscure outfits actually managed to produce some of the most enjoyable music of the period. Elsewhere, the likes of LYADRIVE, MEANSTREAK, DUCHESS and SALEM were all extremely deserving of a piece of exposure, and a significant number of NWOBHM fans were now becoming inspired to expand their once-modest wants lists quite considerably, whereupon many individuals began looking for some of these utterly obscure singles themselves, all of which led to the collecting scene taking off in a big way and sending some of the asking prices into orbit.

»NWOBHM Vol.7« CD Bootleg 1996
RADIUM "Angel Of Fear"
WOLF "Creatures Of The Night"
FUGITIVE "Need My Freedom"
DRIVESHAFT "Take A Chance On Me"
FRENZY "This Is The Last Time"
LOTUS CRUISE "Tonight"
TORTURE "Last Post"
RENEGADE "Lonely Road"
SPEED "Man In The Street"
TEMPEST RIDE "Another Time, Another Place"
TANK "Run Like Hell"
HAZZARD "Snake In The Grass"
WHITE HEAT "Soldier Of Fortune"
PYRAMID "Time Forgets A Hero"
SHOGUN "Time Will Tell"

After a necessary break of around four years, the compilers had evidently expanded their vinyl collections somewhat, and began to assemble a couple of new compilations. The seventh instalment in the series (with a slightly different presentation, although the covers still pictured the inevitable cache of typically-rare sleeves) featured the usual generous selection of obscurities, and relatively few aficionados would have heard ensembles such as RADIUM, LOTUS CRUISE, HAZZARD and DRIVESHAFT prior to this CD being circulated. Mind you, much of the material wasn't quite as listenable as on some of the previous volumes, and the likes of FRENZY, WOLF and FUGITIVE aren't really too special, to be quite honest. Certain other (space-filling?) inclusions were slightly questionable, notably SHOGUN's lengthy "Time Will Tell", although the TANK number on display is actually an alternate version taken from a European single, so that's quite a nice one for fans of the Filth Hounds. Rare compilations (»It's Unheard Of!« and »The Bridge Album«) were now being plundered for tracks by PYRAMID and TEMPEST RIDE (later LYADRIVE), although the real coup this time was surely SPEED's "Man In The Street", a track (gleaned from an unfeasibly scarce single) featuring Bruce Dickinson during his college days. Worth the price of the disc alone for MAIDEN fans, I reckon.

»NWOBHM Vol.8« CD Bootleg 1996
JJ'S POWERHOUSE "Running For The Line"
MARZ "Lady Of The Night"
SPARTAN WARRIOR "Cold Hearted"
TRACTOR "Average Man's Hero"
APOCALYPSE "Stormchild"
DEMON PACT "Escape"
WARRIOR "Don't Let It Show"
LAUTREC "Shoot Out The Lights"
TRUFFLE "If You Really Want"
URCHIN "Black Leather Fantasy"
BOULEVARD "Dawn Raid"
TRACER "Don't Bless The Warrior"
LONE WOLF "Nobody's Move"
SCORCHED EARTH "Where Do We Go From Here"
ANTHEM "England"

The last (so far) instalment in the bootleg series was a real mixed bag, ranging from the excellent and rare (JJ'S POWERHOUSE, MARZ, APOCALYPSE, LAUTREC, ANTHEM), to the fairly unremarkable and comparatively easy to obtain (SPARTAN WARRIOR, LONE WOLF, SCORCHED EARTH), and the inclusion of 70's no-hopers TRACTOR (with their unpleasant bandwagon-jumping effort from 1981) is a complete waste of time. There seems to have been a bit of a cock-up on the sleeve front, too, given that the last three numbers are omitted completely, leaving one of two fans scratching their heads as to what they might be. Still, it's another pretty good selection for curious aficionados of obscure NWOBHM, even if a few of the numbers are a bit lacking in listenability. I've no idea whether or not the series will ever be resurrected (people seem to think it's run its course), but there's certainly plenty of material that eager collectors would be absolutely delighted to hear at some point in future. The bootlegs undoubtedly served their purpose, so their importance to the resurgence of general NWOBHM appreciation and the development of the collecting scene shouldn't be understated. Even so, some of the official samplers (from the likes of British Steel) are now beginning to resemble the sort of things that the fans want to hear, so maybe there's not enough room in the market for the bootleggers these days. Now there's a challenge...

»Noise Level Critical« CD Hallmark 1997
ROCK GODDESS "Turn Me Loose"
TIGERTAILZ "Noise Level Critical (Live)"
SAMSON "Losing My Grip (Live)"
SIX TON BUDGIE "She Gives It All"
LYADRIVE "Sign Of The Hunted"
EGYPT "King Of Hearts"
TRIARCHY "Marionette"
STORMWATCH "Lest We Forget"
LEGEND "My Heart Is There"
WARRIOR "Invaders"
NO QUARTER "No Stopping It Now"
CHINATOWN "No Time To Kill"
RHABSTALLION "Shock'n'Roll"
SIX TON BUDGIE "Southern"
LYADRIVE "Steal Away The Night"
ROCK GODDESS "Streets Of The City"
SAMSON "Vice Versa (Live)"
TIGERTAILZ "Love Bomb Baby (Live)"

A cheap and cheerful CD compilation (brandishing the utterly unashamed slogan *'Classic British Heavy Metal'*) which, judging by the inclusion of such acts as TIGERTAILZ, SIX TON BUDGIE, EGYPT and STORMWATCH, obviously takes a fairly liberal view of what actually constitutes *bona fide* NWOBHM material. Even so, this sampler, featuring a significant quantity of tracks which had originally appeared on Vinyl Tap's (now dormant) series of NWOBHM reissues, is still quite interesting in spite of its lack of exclusive material. The selections are all very listenable, and it makes a change to hear a NWOBHM compilation which doesn't feature all the old chestnuts (DIAMOND HEAD, ANGEL WITCH, TYGERS OF PAN TANG *etc.*), as good as they may be. Perhaps Hallmark will try again (assuming anyone actually bought this one) and deliver the goods on their next disc...

»One Take No Dubs« 12" EP Neat 1982
Side 1:
ALIEN "Could Have Done Better"
AVENGER "Hot'n'Heavy Express"
Side 2:
BLACK ROSE "Knocked Out"
HELLANBACH "All Systems Go"

It's a pity that Neat never really went the whole hog in terms of compilations (unlike Ebony, who churned them out on a weekly basis), as they certainly had enough talent on their books to make such releases worthwhile. One of their few vinyl samplers was the »One Take No Dubs« (all tracks recorded live in the studio) effort from 1982, which introduced the general public to new signings such as AVENGER, HELLANBACH and BLACK ROSE (all of whom went on to become relatively popular acts), plus the criminally-overlooked ALIEN, who surely deserved to be offered the chance to release their own product. Still, it was a decent enough sampler, given that the AVENGER contribution (which had featured on their first demo) never actually appeared elsewhere (officially, at least), while the rough-but-energetic BLACK ROSE and HELLANBACH takes were different to the versions which later showed up on their respective albums. It's just a pity that the luckless ALIEN never got the opportunity to shine, as their own brand of CRUCIFIXION-style metal (also shown to great effect on their equally-superb "Absolute Zero" contribution to the label's »60 Minutes Plus« cassette) outclassed a great number of Neat's more mediocre signings. I reckon somebody messed up big time by not waving an album contract under their noses at the earliest opportunity...

»Overtone 3 – The Rock Album« LP Overtone Records 1984
Side 1:
NEAT SPEED "Long After Dark"
THE REVZ "Killing Time"
SHADY DEAL "Instant Communication"
MENACE "Eyes Of The Dark"
OUTPUT ZONE "Live For Rock"
NATHAN "Shout It Out"
A SKELETON FAMILY "Cowboys"
AVALANCHE "New York City"
Side 2:
MENACE "Lucifer Never Cries"
NATHAN "Candidate For Love"
AVALANCHE "No Way"
OUTPUT ZONE "In The Rain"
SHADY DEAL "Don't Look"
THE REVZ "Turn As They Fall"
NEAT SPEED "Eyes Of The Law"
A SKELETON FAMILY "Zion"

As with the Sane label from Wales, who issued a series of vinyl compilations with the purely altruistic intention of promoting worthy bands regardless of musical style, Scotland's Overtone Records evidently had much the same idea, issuing at least three full-length samplers of its own. After »The Modern Album« and »The Progressive Album« came »The Rock Album«, featuring two numbers each from a handful of Scotland's unsigned hopefuls of the time. Interestingly, AVALANCHE were also featured on »It's Unheard Of!« (both were issued in 1984), while SHADY DEAL had seen a track included on the obscure »G-Force« 7" EP the year before. MENACE, however, aren't the same outfit who appeared on Ebony's »Metal Maniaxe« in 1982 (nor are they the famous punk act), but are undoubtedly the pick of the bunch, with "Eyes Of The Dark" and "Lucifer Never Cries" (good titles, those) each coming across as a top-notch mixture of MYTHRA and IRON MAIDEN. Otherwise, the SNAKEBITE-style rock/metal of AVALANCHE and the FRENZY-tinged rock of THE REVZ are the best tracks on offer here. Elsewhere, NATHAN, NEAT SPEED and SHADY DEAL all emanate from the more lightweight end of the spectrum (vaguely similar to LORELEI, BRUNEL and ANGEL STREET, respectively), whereas the disposable OUTPUT ZONE and A SKELETON FAMILY (who later became known as THE EAST, incidentally), with their quirky material, hardly qualify as rock at all. Quite a respectable album for its day, but a pity there weren't a couple more really heavy groups on it, as there were plenty to choose from in Scotland. Mind you, if an obscure MENACE single ever turns up (a metal one, that is), I'll be the first in line for it!

»Parkside Steelworks« LP LiL Records 1985
Side 1:
MENDES PREY "Red Alert"
CYRKA "Price Of Love"
GYPSY "Street Fighter"
EAST TO WEST "You Mean Everything"
VIRGIN "Glittering Diamonds"
Side 2:
EAST TO WEST "I Want You Back"
CYRKA "New Direction"
VIRGIN "So Bad"
GYPSY "Ride From Hell"
LYZARD "The Loving Kind"
MENDES PREY "Cry For The World"

This scarce compilation of Yorkshire's post-NWOBHM rock and metal talent (issued by the tiny LiL label) has recently become one of the genre's top collectables, although there was a time when it could be picked up relatively inexpensively, so it's hard to say why it's now inspiring such feverish competition among the NWOBHM community. Those featured vary from the familiar (MENDES PREY, who had already released a 7" of their own, and VIRGIN, who had shared a two-tracker with SACRED ALIEN) to the unrenowned (EAST TO WEST, GYPSY and CYRKA), while the utterly obscure LYZARD are a mystery even to me. Anyway, the material is all exclusive to this sampler, and the excellent pair of MENDES PREY selections would surely be enough to spark a fair bit of interest on their own. Elsewhere, tuneful trio CYRKA create a keyboard-flavoured pop/rock amalgam which lies somewhere between BOMBAY and BLAZER BLAZER, while EAST TO WEST also offer up a lightweight brand of melodic rock, which largely fails to make a strong impression. The glam-obsessed VIRGIN, meanwhile, manage to acquit themselves slightly better than on their earlier vinyl appearance, having moved into more of a mid-80's TYGERS OF PAN TANG vibe by this time, while GYPSY appear to have been major SCORPIONS fans, even down to the immensely irritating vocalist. The enigmatic LYZARD (who were only allowed to contribute one track), on the other hand, were a fairly heavy proposition, but their sole effort is a complete mess with no sense of identity whatsoever. Hardly an exemplary selection of prime-era NWOBHM, therefore, and a record which wins no prizes in terms of production values (no doubt the budget was microscopic) or presentation, so it's not really one that deserves a hefty price tag. Incidentally, none of the acts featured got much further in their original form: MENDES PREY were already beginning to lose their way, and called it quits after the lukewarm reception given to their »Wonderland« single, whereas VIRGIN and LYZARD were never heard from again. Jan Cyrka, meanwhile, proceeded to disband his eponymous project and carve out a successful career as a guitar hero (as well as reinventing himself as *'Flash Bastard'* when serving time in ZODIAC MINDWARP), while EAST TO WEST and GYPSY ultimately evolved into ANTIGUA and LADY LUCK, respectively, each failing to make their breakthrough in their new guises.

»Pop Rocky« LP Metronome 1981
Side 1:
MOTÖRHEAD "Motorhead"
MOTÖRHEAD "Beer Drinkers & Hell Raisers"
VARDIS "Silver Machine"
VARDIS "Steamin Along"
ACCEPT "Burning"
ACCEPT "I'm A Rebel"
Side 2:
TANK "Don't Walk Away"
TANK "Hammer On"
QUARTZ "Satan's Serenade"
QUARTZ "Bloody Fool"
STEVE WHITNEY BAND "Judy In Disguise"
STEVE WHITNEY BAND "She's A Lady"

This ludicrously-titled German compilation is a bit of an oddity, with four British outfits sharing the grooves with a couple of European-based acts, so I've really no idea what the connection was supposed to be in the first instance. Even so, it's still a vaguely interesting piece for the NWOBHM completist by virtue of the VARDIS, TANK and QUARTZ material, although there's nothing either exclusive or hard-to-get here.

»Powertrax« Cassette Neat 1986
Side 1:
 STATETROOPER "She Got The Look"
 WARFARE "Metal Anarchy"
 TYSONDOG "Taste The Hate"
 SARACEN "We Have Arrived"
 ARTILLERY "Time Has Come"
Side 2:
 VENOM "Witching Hour (Live In 85)"
 ATOMKRAFT "Your Mentor"
 WAR MACHINE "The Power"
 SHE "Breaking Away"
 MANTAS "Lothlorien"

One of Neat's more obscure releases, this ten track cassette sampler was put together primarily for promotional purposes, although it does feature the odd exclusive selection or two. First, the ATOMKRAFT contribution ("Your Mentor") was intended to form the basis of a 12" EP, although this notion obviously fell through in the aftermath of personnel problems, whereupon the »Queen Of Death« Mini-LP was released instead. Curiously, however, "Your Mentor" (as with most of the other numbers on display here) subsequently turned up on the cheapo »Heavy Metal Collection« series of compilations in the 90's. Another notable inclusion was the MANTAS instrumental "Lothlorien", originally envisaged as the theme to an unreleased Neat video, tastefully entitled »Metal Bitch«. This composition is, to my knowledge, unavailable elsewhere, and predates the guitarist's solo LP by a couple of years, so it's probably of interest to all the diehard (as it were) VENOM followers. The remaining inclusions all feature on other standard Neat releases, although WAR MACHINE's contribution is a 'studio demo' for their LP, and SARACEN's "We Have Arrived" is supposedly lifted from the »Metal City« video (not that anyone would notice, I'm sure) as opposed to their 7". As I say, this tape was probably never sold commercially, but Neat had (and may still have) a stockpile of copies left in the late 80's, and were in the habit of giving them away to people who bought a few items from their back catalogue.

Maybe if you asked them nicely…

»Pure Overkill« LP Guardian 1983
Side 1:
 RISK "Comin' For You Baby"
 MILLENNIUM "Steal Your Heart"
 TOKYO ROSE "Lost In The Heat"
 SPARTAN WARRIOR "Steel'n'Chains"
 TOKYO ROSE "Give Me Back My Heart"
 INCUBUS "Ain't Runnin' For You"
Side 2:
 SPARTAN WARRIOR "Comes As No Surprise"
 MILLENNIUM "Rock Was Meant For Me"
 TOKYO ROSE "When The Lights Go Down"
 INCUBUS "Caught Red Handed"
 MILLENNIUM "Magic Mirror"
 TOKYO ROSE "Victim Of Love"

After their »Roksnax« and »Roxcalibur« samplers, Guardian got back into the swing of compilation albums with their »Pure Overkill« set, showcasing a number of local hopefuls who might be worthy of a full contract at some stage. It features a very odd distribution of tracks, though, varying from one (provided by the little-remembered RISK) to a mighty four (from the lucky TOKYO ROSE), so it wasn't a remotely democratic arrangement. Still, it provided the fans with their first taste of INCUBUS, SPARTAN WARRIOR and MILLENNIUM, all of whom went on to record full albums for the label (the latter pair happily recycling their compilation numbers, while INCUBUS started afresh), these being outfits who could easily write a decent metal track when they put their minds to it. On the other hand, TOKYO ROSE (not to be confused with the shockingly-atrocious bunch of no-hopers who vomited up a single for the same label) were a semi-decent proposition, although they seem to have called it a day fairly soon afterwards, with members making their way into the ranks of DARK HEART and HOLOSADE, both of whom managed to get an album into the shops. That just leaves RISK, who were as unremarkable as their name suggests, and who surely can't have been serious contenders for a deal at any stage. There aren't any real gems on this LP, if we're being totally frank, and the mis-spellings and miscredits on the sleeve are irritating, but it's still a worthy purchase which tends to command a relatively modest value in comparison to its predecessors.

»Radio Hell« CD Raw Fruit 1992
 RAVEN "Lambs To The Slaughter"
 RAVEN "Hold Back The Fire"

RAVEN "Hard Ride"
RAVEN "Chainsaw"
VENOM "Black Metal"
VENOM "Nightmare"
VENOM "Too Loud For The Crowd"
VENOM "Bloodlust"
WARFARE "Death Charge"
WARFARE "Burn Down The King's Road"
WARFARE "Ebony Dreams"
WARFARE "Revolution"

Although the Raw Fruit concern (which now seems to have died a natural death) preferentially plundered BBC Radio's archives for live material, this innovative release, comprising three hugely popular sessions from the 'Friday Rock Show', should have been a major seller amongst the many fans of the ensembles featured. Somehow, however, these characters managed to cock it up along the way, and the disc just never got advertised or distributed effectively, so pitifully few copies made it to the shops. Nice one, guys. Added to the fact that the shoddy packaging makes it look like a bootleg issue, and you've got a veritable disaster on your hands. Nevertheless, those who actually managed to lay their mitts on a copy were rewarded with a respectable release in terms of sound quality, allowing them to relegate all those knackered tapes to the back of the cupboard. A worthy release, in a sense, but the compilers clearly hadn't a clue what they were doing. I'm not sure how many intact sessions still survive in the BBC vaults, but here's a thought: given that we die-hard NWOBHM fans are perverse creatures who like to seek out utterly obscure music, how about assembling a CD with the sessions laid down by such also-rans as DAMACLES, ROUGH JUSTICE and ANACONDA? You'd probably sell ten times as many copies...

»Reading Rock Vol.1« Do-LP Mean Records 1982
Side 1:
 WHITESNAKE
 "Walking In The Shadow Of The Blues"
 TERRAPLANE "I Want Your Body"
 MARILLION "He Knows You Know"
 JACKIE LYNTON BAND "Slow Rider"
 BUDGIE "Superstar"
Side 2:
 BERNIE MARSDEN'S S.O.S. "S.O.S."
 CHINATOWN "I Wanna See You Tonight"
 RANDY CALIFORNIA "Come On Woman"
 STAMPEDE "There And Back"
 TWISTED SISTER "Shoot 'Em Down"

Side 3:
 MICHAEL SCHENKER GROUP
 "Attack Of The Mad Axeman"
 MARILLION
 "Three Boats Down From The Candy"
 TERRAPLANE "Turn Me Loose"
 JUST GOOD FRIENDS "You Really Got Me"
 UFO "Hot And Ready"
Side 4:
 BUDGIE "Panzer Division Destroyed"
 GRAND PRIX "Keep On Believing"
 SPIDER "All The Time"
 CHINATOWN "Caught On The Wrong Side"
 JACKIE LYNTON BAND "Hedgehog Song"

The Reading Festivals of the early 80's were usually captured for posterity by a mobile recording unit or two (including one from the BBC, who were in the habit of broadcasting excerpts from the three-dayer on the 'Friday Rock Show'), and 1982 turned out to be a bumper year for the professional bootleggers. Within a few months, the little-known Mean Records had managed to secure the rights to some of these recordings, and the company duly threw together a double live album to commemorate the event. It was a strange affair, padded out (for no tangible reason) with tracks from WHITESNAKE and BUDGIE, which had actually been recorded at earlier festivals, but there was still a fairly high proportion of material to interest the NWOBHM fans. For example, it was an early taster of TERRAPLANE's music, given that they were yet to sign a contract, and a rare opportunity to hear the short-lived BERNIE MARSDEN'S S.O.S. venture (the forerunner of ALASKA), who called it a day soon afterwards. Elsewhere, there were capable contributions from CHINATOWN and STAMPEDE, although, given that both acts issued live albums of their own, this was rather less of a novelty than hearing concert recordings from GRAND PRIX and SPIDER, for instance. BUDGIE and MARILLION are listenable enough, if that sort of thing tickles your fancy, but RANDY CALIFORNIA, JUST GOOD FRIENDS and the JACKIE LYNTON BAND are slightly out of place, so it's a pity there wasn't any material from the other NWOBHM acts (DIAMOND HEAD, ORE, TYGERS OF PAN TANG, IRON MAIDEN, OVERKILL, TANK, PRAYING MANTIS, ROCK GODDESS) who took to the stage that weekend. Still, the set seems to have sold in fairly respectable quantities (there were two separate issues, one with a single cover and one with a gatefold), but probably not enough to warrant a sequel.

»Rock Masters« LP Reaction 1987
Side 1:
    TROJAN "Relentless Pursuit"
    FAR CRY "Julie's Home"
    RACER "Poor Little Rich Girl"
    RENDEZVOUS "Lock Me Away"
    CALIBRE "Just A Little Bit"
    DEL RIO "Love Strippers"
Side 2:
    TERRA NOVA "Under Fire"
    M-16 "(Standing) On Top Of The World"
    ZELA "Leaving"
    SYLENT KNIGHT "The Beast Within"
    STORM "High Class Girl"
    PREY DON'T PRAY "Somebody Stole My Soul"
    M.B.M. "By My Side"

The absolute nadir of Ebony's history undoubtedly came with the release of the ill-judged »Rock Masters« set on its newly-created (and short-lived) Reaction Records subsidiary. It's apparent that the wayward label had obviously lost the plot completely by this juncture, and this compilation must surely have sounded the death knell. Apart from the saving grace of TROJAN (Irish version, that is), there's absolutely zero indication of any talent whatsoever on this shameful waste of vinyl. A few compositions are actually embarrassingly bad, others just poorly written and performed, and none of the acts got any further, as far as I'm aware. It's a sad indictment of the state of Britain's metal scene in the late 80's (those memories had been temporarily relegated to the back of my mind), and it's no wonder that so many of us got into the thrash and death genres at that point! In conclusion, therefore, I would strongly advise you to blow your money on something slightly more listenable than this disaster.

»Rock Meets Metal Vol.1« LP Ebony 1987
Side 1:
    STRANGER "Tokyo Road"
    CIRCUS "Down And Out"
    E.S.T. "S.O.S."
    TEACHER'S PET
    "Could Have Been Love (Tonight)"
    APRIL 16TH "Thursdays Child"
    ST. VALENTINE "Always Together"
    TOMB "Dungeon Gates"
    MASQUE "Going Home"
Side 2:
    SPELLBINDER "Babylon By Night"
    CHARLIE MOUSE "Get Up And Party"
    CRASH DIET "Stagestruck"
    ROULETTE "Who's Crying"
    DARK CRUSADE "Lady In Black"
    PARADISE LOST "Watch The Spider"
    RAM "Eternal Grave"
    SWEET CYANIDE "Natural Born Loser"

Another mammoth sixteen-tracker from the rapidly-ailing Ebony concern, this set again features a couple of hopefuls who went on to marginally greater things (APRIL 16TH, MASQUE) alongside the usual motley selection of hapless nonentities. Again, half of this is utterly unworthy of a place on vinyl, although the weightier bands featured (TOMB, RAM, DARK CRUSADE) aren't too bad, I suppose, and the melodic rock of STRANGER, ROULETTE and PARADISE LOST (the Bristol version, that is) is enjoyable too, each of these tuneful acts boasting frontmen who have actually mastered the difficult task of learning to sing, as opposed to simply talking or growling into the microphone. As I say, poor old Ebony was far removed from its NWOBHM roots by this stage, and was desperately seeking the *'next big thing'* with which to resurrect their fortunes. Sadly, none of the acts featured on this sampler were anywhere near talented enough, and, a short time after creating the ill-fated Reaction Records subsidiary, Ebony was no more.

»Rock Meets Metal Vol.2« LP Ebony 1987
Side 1:
    CZAKAN "Tears In My Eyes"
    ANNEXE "Shadows Of Insanity"
    ALLEGIANCE "Waiting For The Bomb"
    WILD PUSSY "Feel Fire"
    7TH ERA "Is Anybody Out There?"
    STEEL "I Still Want You"
    EZY MEAT "Warrior"
Side 2:
    ETERNITY "Children Of The Sun"
    TARYN "Self Destruct"
    JEALOUS "Tell Me Lies"
    MAXIMUS THRAXX "Vault Of The Disciple"
    TRANSMISSION "No Reason, No Rhyme"
    BLACK RIDERS "Addiction"
    UNREAL TERROR "Pullin' The Switch"
    CREAM SODA "Just Sixteen"

In a move of quite astonishing ineptitude, Ebony contrived to follow up »Rock Meets Metal Vol.1« with, er, »Rock Meets Metal« (presumably having forgotten they'd already released the first instalment in the series), featuring an identical sleeve design (blue instead of grey) to confuse the situation even further. To simplify matters somewhat, therefore, I think we'd better refer to

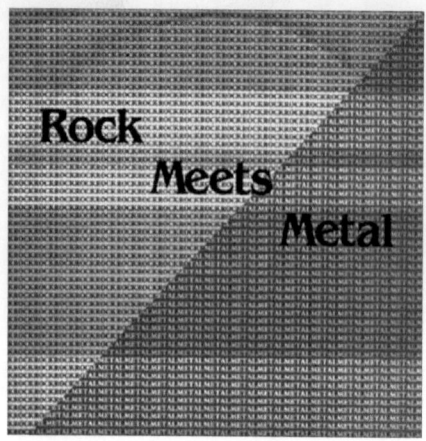

this one as »Rock Meets Metal Vol.2«, don't you? Anyway, this volume features the same general standard of obscure acts as its predecessor, including several visitors from mainland Europe in the shape of the equally-unrenowned CZAKAN, STEEL, ETERNITY and UNREAL TERROR. Of the home-grown talent, the only *'big'* names on display are EZY MEAT and the BLACK RIDERS, reliable outfits who stand out from the rest of the amateur-hour hopefuls, although it's worth pointing out that WILD PUSSY managed to issue a long-player of their own a year or two later, whereas the laughably-named MAXIMUS THRAXX were subsequently afforded a generous piece of exposure on the ridiculed »Diminished Responsibility« thrash sampler. Elsewhere, there's very little to write home about, and this feeble exercise must go down as yet another dark chapter in the chequered history of Ebony Records.

»Rock Out!« Do-CD Emporio 1996
Disc 1:
MOTÖRHEAD "White Line Fever"
TANK "Blood, Guts & Beer"
URIAH HEEP "Holy Roller"
QUIREBOYS "Devil Of A Woman"
SAMSON "Too Late"
TORMÉ "T.V.O.D."
WITCHFYNDE "Pay Now Love Later"
TYGERS OF PAN TANG "Sweet Lies"
HAWKWIND "Night Of The Hawks"
THOR "Let The Blood Run Red"
GIRLSCHOOL "Take It All Away"
GASKIN "Burning Alive"
PERSIAN RISK "Jane"
NEW ENGLAND "Money"

HERITAGE "Attack Attack"
YOUNG BLOOD "Hold On To Love"
SPIDER "Feel Like A Man"
EXCALIBUR "Come On And Rock"
DIRTY STRANGERS "The Biggest Mouth"
MAN "Kerosine (live)"
DISC 2:
WITCHFYNDE "Give 'Em Hell"
HAWKWIND "Motorhead"
RUNAWAYS "Black Leather"
GIRLSCHOOL "Nothing To Lose"
TERRAPLANE "Gimme The Money"
TYGERS OF PAN TANG "Hit It"
SAMSON "The Silver Screen"
THOR "Thunder In The Tundra"
URIAH HEEP "Still Calls His Name"
HAWKLORDS "Who's Gonna Win The War"
RED DOGS "Wrong Side Of Town"
EXCALIBUR "Devil In Disguise"
GASKIN "End Of The World"
TATTOOED LOVE BOYS
"Why Waltz When You Can Rock'n'Roll"
MICK RALPHS "All It Takes"
TANK "Run Like Hell"
HERITAGE "Remorse Code"
WOLFPACK "Maniac"
GIRLSCHOOL "Not For Sale"
QUIREBOYS "Whippin' Boy"

The Emporio label seems to have been instigated by Cherry Red to run concurrently with its more familiar British Steel imprint, and this introductory effort was itself compiled by the latter's Mark Brennan. It's not a NWOBHM compilation as such, but around half of the acts certainly come under that general banner, even if most of the tracks on display seem to emanate from the latter part of their careers. Of the remaining bands featured, most are mainstays of the 80's British metal scene, although the inclusion of the RUNAWAYS, THOR, MICK RALPHS, HAWKWIND (yet again) and MAN (good grief) tends to obfuscate whatever grand concept originally lay behind the project. Overall, though, this seems to have been a *'let's see what we can secure the rights to and bung together a tenuously-linked rock compilation'* release than anything more coherent. There's a generous quantity of tracks squeezed onto the two discs, however, and it's nice to see outfits such as PERSIAN RISK and YOUNG BLOOD featured. No previously-unreleased material, but I suspect that their budget didn't stretch to such measures. Oh, and Mark, you lose a *lot* of NWOBHM credibility by referring to one of the groups featured (in more than one instance) as the *'Tygers Of Pang Tang'*...

»Roksnax« LP Guardian 1980
Side 1:
 SAMURAI "Die Or Deliver"
 HOLLOW GROUND "Rock On"
 SARACEN "Speed Of Sound"
 HOLLOW GROUND "Fight With The Devil"
 SAMURAI "Temptress"
 SARACEN "Fast Living"
Side 2:
 HOLLOW GROUND "Flying High"
 SARACEN "Feel Just The Same"
 SAMURAI "Knights In Painted Castles"
 HOLLOW GROUND "The Holy One"
 SAMURAI "Spirits Of The Lost"
 SARACEN "Setting The World Ablaze"

Guardian Records had been in business for a year or two before the NWOBHM explosion really took off, but the wily company soon cottoned on to the popularity of metal, and began releasing the odd single and compilation to test the water. Their first metal sampler was recorded towards the end of 1980, and the strangely-titled »Roksnax« LP showcased just three of the local hopefuls, namely HOLLOW GROUND, SAMURAI (not to be confused with the Welsh act who later signed to Ebony) and SARACEN (nothing to do with the bunch who recorded for Nucleus and Neat), each of whom were permitted to contribute a generous four tracks. Unsurprisingly, the gifted HOLLOW GROUND acquitted themselves best of all, their classy batch of compositions paving the way for an excellent EP the following year (admittedly, they didn't achieve much after that), although SAMURAI weren't too bad in places, their upbeat, semi-heroic metal evoking the likes of TRIDENT and BLACKWYCH at times. Mind you, SARACEN (fronted by future BLIND FURY stalwart Lou Taylor) were a rather unremarkable proposition, their style of choice being pretty similar to PARALEX, but the material was unconvincing on the whole. This record evidently shifted a fair old number of units at the time (plentiful sales through outlets such as Bullet Records helped things along nicely), although it ultimately failed to propel any of the featured groups into the superstar bracket.

In fact, I reckon all three acts had pretty much called it a day within a couple of years, and most of the musicians appear to have drifted away from the scene completely. Some members of HOLLOW GROUND are still doing their thing in the clubs, however, and two SAMURAI bods cropped up in a melodic bunch called DIRTY SECRETS towards the end of the decade. Lou Taylor, on the other hand, eventually left his memories of SARACEN behind and teamed up with Kevin Heybourne in the ill-fated BLIND FURY venture (the latter would rework SARACEN's "Feel Just The Same" as a ballad in their live set, incidentally) before joining forces with the reconstructing SATAN in the, er, ill-fated BLIND FURY venture (bit of *deja vu* there). Mind you, the fact that the newer group also elected to use "Feel Just The Same" (on their sole 'Friday Rock Show' session) suggests that the vocalist was rather proud of this composition! The »Roksnax« set has always been a sought-after item (mainly due to a couple of HOLLOW GROUND exclusives, although "Fight With The Devil" later took pride of place on the »NWOBHM '79 Revisited« compilation), and is still a worthwhile (but expensive) purchase nowadays. Given that the CD release of »Roxcalibur« performed reasonably, however, maybe it'll also be reissued on disc one of these days.

»Roxcalibur« LP Guardian 1982/CD British Steel 1998
Side 1:
 BLACK ROSE "No Point Runnin'"
 BRANDS HATCH "Brands Hatch"
 BATTLEAXE "Burn This Town"
 SATAN "Oppression"
 MARAUDER "Battlefield"
 UNTER DEN LINDEN "Wings Of Night"
 SKITZOFRENIK "Exodus"
Side 2:
 BATTLEAXE "Battleaxe"
 MARAUDER "Woman Of The Night"
 BLACK ROSE "Ridin' Higher"
 UNTER DEN LINDEN "Man At The Bottom"
 SKITZOFRENIK "Keep Right On"
 SATAN "The Executioner"
 BRANDS HATCH "No Return"

After assembling its »Roksnax« compilation at the tail end of 1980, Guardian waited until the beginning of 1982 to deliver another metal sampler, but »Roxcalibur« was a more democratic arrangement, with seven hopefuls each getting the chance to lay down a pair of representative numbers. The set gave some early exposure to SATAN, BLACK ROSE, BATTLEAXE and SKITZOFRENIK (all of whom were getting to the stage of releasing their own vinyl product), whereas MARAUDER, UNTER DEN LINDEN and BRANDS HATCH represented the unknown quantities on this occasion. Of these, I'd say that BRANDS HATCH were the most capable musicians, and they also had a pretty decent singer, whereas MARAUDER were an entirely disposable bunch with a gravel-throated frontman. The confusingly-named UNTER DEN LINDEN, though, just weren't ready for a vinyl appearance, and "Wings Of Night" is a forgettable effort all round, while the utterly dismal "Man At The Bottom" is just plain embarrassing. Clearly, BATTLEAXE, BLACK ROSE and SATAN were the success stories this time, whereas the luckless SKITZOFRENIK and BRANDS HATCH struggled to retain any momentum after the LP's release, and seem to have called it quits before long. Predictably, MARAUDER and UNTER DEN LINDEN (both of whom actually exchanged personnel with BLITZKRIEG during their time) failed to last the distance, and few of the musicians involved proceeded to hook up with other outfits in the North East. The album is still a popular purchase for collectors (examples with the rare poster are particularly sought-after), although the recent CD reissue by British Steel has probably tempered demand for the original vinyl.

»Scene Of The Crime« LP Suspect Records 1981
Side 1:
PANZA DIVISION "Blitz"
MANITOU "Manitou"
SAVAGE "Let It Loose"
SPARTA "Lords Of Time"
Side 2:
TYRANT "Day Of The Knight"
PANZA DIVISION
"The Day Delta 4 Played Mars"
SAVAGE "Dirty Money"
TYRANT "Sanctuary"
MANITOU "Overlord"

The tiny Suspect label wasn't around for all that long, but they still managed to make a pretty decent job of furthering SPARTA's career, issuing two popular singles before branching out into the world of compilation albums with the famous »Scene Of The Crime« effort. The sampler showcased a selection of emergent talent from England's central belt, including an exclusive track from SPARTA themselves, although there were some other gems from SAVAGE (with two excellent, energetic takes which were later reworked on their debut album for Ebony), while PANZA DIVISION deliver a couple of typical, boogie-flavoured compositions, these being exclusive to this compilation. The names of TYRANT (not to be confused with the bunch responsible for the »Hold Back The Lightning« single) and MANITOU (who, contrary to popular opinion, didn't release a single themselves) are less familiar, the latter coming across as a reasonable enough proposition with certain similarities to NO QUARTER, although TYRANT's heroic brand of metal (with the occasional nod to SKITZOFRENIK and MITHRANDIR) doesn't really work particularly well. Even so, it was a perfectly respectable release for a small label, but I suspect (oops) that the costs incurred by the project were crippling, and this may even have led directly to the company's collapse shortly thereafter. Only SAVAGE went on to greater things, although PANZA DIVISION (later the LONELY HEARTS) also managed to keep things going for a good few years, so at least »Scene Of The Crime« served its purpose. The album remains a sought-after item, and has been a popular, mid-priced collectable for many years.

»60 Minutes Plus« Cassette Neat 1982/CD Teichiku 1992
Side 1:
RAVEN "Live At The Inferno"
STEEL "All Systems Go"
CRUCIFIXION "The Fox"
GOLDSMITH "Give Me Your Love"
VALHALLA "Maybe Someday"
JAGUAR "Dirty Tricks"
AXIS "Flame Burns On"
PERSIAN RISK "50000 Stallions"
Side 2:
DEDRINGER "Lucy"
VENOM "Bursting Out"
SABRE "Cry To The Wind"
WHITE SPIRIT "Watch Out"
WARRIOR "Kansas City"
ALIEN "Absolute Zero"
HELLANBACH "All The Way"
FIST "Lost And Found"

Neat's first foray into the world of compilations (»Lead Weight«) was an extremely enjoyable release, but it's immensely peculiar that it only escaped on vinyl as something of an afterthought. Clearly, the company were quite wary of issuing vinyl samplers (I can't imagine why), and their »60 Minutes Plus« promotional showcase from late 1982 received the same treatment, appearing in truncated form the following year (again, in mainland Europe alone) as a seldom-seen vinyl set called »All Hell Let Loose«, with four tracks (from GOLDSMITH, VALHALLA, DEDRINGER and FIST) being omitted for reasons of length. Nevertheless, the cassette version of the sampler was another excellent release, with much of the material being exclusive or different to the versions on later product, although the RAVEN, FIST and STEEL tracks can be found in identical form elsewhere. Still, there were some decent versions of favourites by CRUCIFIXION (whose energetic take is even more enjoyable than the one on their debut single), VENOM, WARRIOR and HELLANBACH, although I suspect that most fans will be more interested in the genuine exclusives. Of these, the real crackers come from PERSIAN RISK, WHITE SPIRIT (exhibiting their more melodic later direction), SABRE and JAGUAR, although it's nice to see some of the less-familiar acts (DEDRINGER, VALHALLA, AXIS, GOLDSMITH) getting a fair crack of the whip. Mind you, my main problem with the set is that the stand-out track comes from the criminally-ignored ALIEN, whose "Absolute Zero" effort is of the same standard of genius as their contribution ("Could Have Done Better") to the »One Take No Dubs« EP, so it's a complete mystery how this mob failed to land a deal, either with Neat or anyone else. Needless to say, the original vinyl and cassette formats are extraordinarily hard to find (several of the tracks have been plundered for various bootlegs, though), but it looks as though there might be a CD reissue (inevitably, the Japanese collectors have already seen an official release) coming along to save the day.

»Southern Comfort« LP Spectrum Records 1983
Side 1:
    PRAVDA "Minds Eye"
    STRAIGHT SIX "Heavy Rain"
    FLOORS "Freeman"
    RAISING CAIN "Murder In Paradise"
    DEUCE "Mystery Lady"
Side 2:
    DEUCE "Sail Me Away"
    STRAIGHT SIX "Belt It Out"
    FLOORS "Wasted Years"
    RAISING CAIN "September Rain"
    STRAIGHT SIX "Rock & Roll"
    AMADEUS "Grey Skies"

Brazenly subtitled 'A rock compilation album from the South', the »Southern Comfort« sampler was one of those local-band affairs which showcased hopefuls from a specific area, in this case Kent and its environs, so I guess Spectrum Records probably took their lead from the seminal »Kent Rocks« album of 1981. Of the acts on display, only DEUCE are remotely familiar, this being the bunch who managed to issue their inexplicably-poor »Radar Love« single as late as 1986, and who clearly reveal that they were actually considerably better in their early days.

Still, they're not the best group on the compilation, and the mysterious STRAIGHT SIX outclass them with three capable contributions, showcasing some highly flamboyant guitar work, classy arrangements and decent vocals, occasionally reminiscent of »Loser«-period ANGEL WITCH. PRAVDA, meanwhile, represent a rather more progressive outlook, their widdly keyboards and restrained musicianship evoking a few handy comparisons with the likes of CHEMICAL ALICE and the MOVIE STARS, although they seem to have been a semi-decent prospect for a modicum of success. Elsewhere, however, the 'rock' definition gets stretched to its limit with both FLOORS (a feeble bunch of indie no-hopers) and RAISING CAIN (extremely lightweight, poppy material with synthesizers and weak vocals, neither of whom are particularly suited to this album. That just leaves AMADEUS, who only get to deliver one composition, this basically being a solo vehicle for busy keyboard player Ian Penman-Dick, who actually contributed to all of the PRAVDA and RAISING CAIN material on the album. Even so, it's a completely disposable piece of background music that serves no useful purpose. All in all, the »Southern Comfort« set is a semi-interesting release (few copies of which have come out of the woodwork in recent years) which appears to have had comparatively little impact in terms of furthering the careers of most of those included, but it remains a collectable piece nowadays, no doubt helped by the obscurity of the groups and the exclusivity of the material.

»Southern Comfort III« LP Spectrum Records 1984?
Side 1:
    DEUCE "Madhouse Parts 1/2"
    DAKKA DAKKA DAKKA "Sweet Dreams"
    DAKKA DAKKA DAKKA "Goodbye"
    EXERCISE 1 "Time To Choose"
Side 2:
    QUEST "In My Back Garden"
    QUEST "Want Your Loving Tonight"
    EXILES "Virgo Girls"
    EXILES "The Bigger They Are"
    WARDOG "Wheels On The Road"
    WARDOG "I've Been Running"
    DOOMWATCH "Devils Dream"

As it turns out, Spectrum's original »Southern Comfort« release wasn't actually a one-off; this series is now believed to have yielded a grand total of four volumes (the second instalment is proving remarkably elusive, however), each featuring a variety of Kent's more obscure rock/indie acts. DEUCE's epic "Madhouse" gets the third long-player off to a suitably substantial start, but the dull DAKKA DAKKA DAKKA (what a bloody awful name) are more indie than rock, and the JOY DIVISION-influenced racket of EXERCISE 1 is hopelessly out of place too. Over on side two, an obscure bunch of rockers named QUEST offer poppy, female-vocal material, while the EXILES return the listener to upbeat indie territory. The excellently-named (but not uniquely-named) WARDOG, however, are a major improvement, their numbers suggesting a few easy comparisons with SLENDER THREAD, VARDIS and DAWN TRADER in terms of musical direction. The most capable inclusion, perhaps, is kept until last, with DOOMWATCH (another non-unique identity) coming across as genuine NWOBHM contenders with an accomplished track reminiscent of OVERDRIVE or PROWLER. With the exception of DEUCE, none of those featured appear to have had any longevity whatsoever, but I suppose the set is another fairly interesting snapshot of a few fly-by-night hopefuls. Mind you, it's a pity that the compilers didn't have a stricter definition of 'rock', I mean, there's no reason to include indie jokers just because they feature the odd bit of guitar work, is there?

»Southern Comfort 4« LP Spectrum Records 1984?
Side 1:
PAUL BELTON/DEUCE "Intro"
T. BONE "Going To A Party"
T. BONE "Too Young To Realise"
CHAOTIC CHILDREN "Writing On The Wall"
CHAOTIC CHILDREN "Chaotic Children"
X DIRECTORY "Public Schoolboy"
Side 2:
ROUGH DIAMOND "She's So Aware"
ROUGH DIAMOND "Fine Night"
DESIGN "The Girl Of My Dreams"
DESIGN "Deborah"
ROB THE PACK "Lady"

Probably the last contender in the series of self-styled 'rock compilations from the South', the fourth volume is a bit short on genuine 'rock', to be honest. Really scraping the bottom of the barrel by this stage, there's hardly any out and out metal here at all. After a completely pointless (but very brief) intro piece by PAUL BELTON, the poorly-named T. BONE offer us their "Going To A Party" effort, which, despite being vaguely heavy, is extraordinarily annoying due to the poor vocals and hoedown (!) arrangement. It's virtually impossible, therefore, to come to terms with the fact that "Too Young To Realise" is actually by the same bunch of musicians, this one (the album's stand-out cut by a long way) coming across as very much in the fashion of SAPPHIRE or PERSIAN RISK. Elsewhere, CHAOTIC CHILDREN and X DIRECTORY are also quite heavy, but the arrangements and vocals suggest that these acts would be better-suited to new romantic and punk collections, respectively. Opening side two, meanwhile, ROUGH DIAMOND are a fairly unmemorable traditional rock outfit who are hindered by some rather weak vocals, while DESIGN yield two lightweight ballads, although "Deborah" has a decent guitar freakout at the end. Finishing off the album is ROB THE PACK's "Lady", an unnecessarily long, slower rock track with virtually no redeeming features. After this, it looks as though there were few Kent hopefuls left to inflict upon the unsuspecting public, and the series drew to a natural close. Needless to say, these LP's are remarkably thin on the ground nowadays, but do let us know if you have the missing one...

»Steel Crazy« LP Abstract Records 1982
Side 1:
THE RODS "Get Ready To Rock'n'Roll"
TWISTED SISTER "I'll Never Grow Up"
STAMPEDE "Moving On"
STARFIGHTERS "Alley Cat Blues"
ANVIL "Bedroom Games"
Side 2:
GEORDIE "Keep On Rocking"
PRAYING MANTIS "Running For Tomorrow"
KROKUS "Bedside Radio"
LAUTREC "Mean Gasoline"
GIRLSCHOOL "Take It All Away"

To be honest, Abstract Records weren't exactly a particularly credible proposition, and never really seemed to get to grips with the state of the music market, their attempts to push a selection of indie nonentities into the public eye meeting with repeated disinterest from punters and media alike. One of their few forays (they promised that others would follow, but these never materialised) into the rock world, however, was the »Steel Crazy« sampler from 1982, which again demonstrates a real lack of forethought, from the bizarre cover image (on a par with the »Parkside Steelworks« effort) to the haphazard selection of acts on display, and there seems to have been no logical reason to go to all the effort of licensing this unremarkable collection of tracks from a variety of record labels. Anyway, it's a fairly egalitarian mixture of Brits and overseas imports, and I suppose the inclusion of PRAYING MANTIS, STAMPEDE and the STARFIGHTERS make it semi-interesting for NWOBHM fans. The real saving grace, however, is the presence of LAUTREC's "Mean Gasoline", which was scheduled to appear on the latter's cancelled single, so I guess that makes »Steel Crazy« a pretty respectable purchase for many serious collectors of the genre. If it wasn't for that, though, most copies of this LP would probably be gathering dust in junk shops, covered in countless marks resulting from the repeated impact of ten foot barge-poles.

»The Best Of British« LP Zebra 1985
Side 1:
  PERSIAN RISK "Too Different"
  MARSEILLE "Walking On A High Wire"
  STRATUS "Top Of The Mountain"
  WARFARE "Burn The King's Road"
  JAGUAR "(Nights Of) Long Shadows"
Side 2:
  EMERSON "Maybe Someday"
  DIANNO "Antigua"
  LIMELIGHT "White Fire"
  SAVAGE "We Got The Edge"
  BABY TUCKOO "Broken Heart"

Sharing quite a few tracks with the »Axe Attack« album released by M Port Records in the same year, this collection features a couple of Zebra's own acts (namely PERSIAN RISK and SAVAGE) of the time, plus various bands signed to several other labels, so I'm not quite sure what the ultimate objective was (apart from making money, that is, which is not something that compilations of this type were particularly efficient at doing) in this case. The only *'unreleased'* tracks are those by EMERSON (and how many of us were even aware that they were still doing the rounds in 1985?) and LIMELIGHT, whose "White Fire" (which also cropped up on »Axe Attack« and subsequently on the »NWOBHM Vol.4« bootleg) was originally commissioned as part of a soundtrack for a film of the same name, although the version included here appears to be slightly different. Not an essential purchase, it's fair to say, but yet another item that you might occasionally encounter quite cheaply.

»The Best Of British Metal« CD Delta Music 1999
  GIRLSCHOOL "Screaming Blue Murder (live)"
  SAMSON "Turn Out The Lights (live)"
  ANGEL WITCH "They Wouldn't Dare"
  ROCK GODDESS "The Party Never Ends"
  LYADRIVE "Another Time, Another Place"
  THUNDERSTICK "Dark Night Black Light"
  ROCK GODDESS "So Much Love"
  TIGERTAILZ "Call Of The Wild (live)"
  ANGEL WITCH "Sorceress (live)"
  THUNDERSTICK "Shining"
  GIRLSCHOOL "Wild At Heart"
  LYADRIVE "White Dress"
  TIGERTAILZ "Love Overload (live)"
  SAMSON "Voodoo Chile (live)"

From the team that brought us »Noise Level Critical«, we have another cheap and cheerful disc featuring two tracks each from some of the key protagonists of the mid-80's metal scene, most of whom had been operational since the inception of the NWOBHM. For a budget compilation of this type, it's surprising to note that there's even some previously-unreleased material on offer, this coming in the form of the THUNDERSTICK compositions (which might not be a huge selling point, admittedly) and the pair of SAMSON live takes (the label fail to disclose the source of the latter, though), so all credit to these chaps for seeking out a few exclusive selections. Elsewhere, there's a generous helping of live material and tracks which aren't immediately familiar to the majority of aficionados, so hats off to Delta Music for not inflicting the same old tosh on us for the umpteenth time. Oh, by the way, please don't blame me for the brevity of the sleeve notes, they were *heavily* edited...

»The Best Of Indie Metal« CD Emporio 1998
  TERRAPLANE "I Survive"
  GIRLSCHOOL "Take It All Away"
  SPIDER "All The Time"
  HAWKWIND "Motorhead"
  BERNIE TORMÉ "All Around The World"
  TYGERS OF PAN TANG "Hit It"
  SCORPIONS "Wind Of Change"
  SAVAGE "We Got The Edge"
  TERRAPLANE "Gimme The Money"
  PERSIAN RISK "Too Different"
  SCRUBS "Time For You"
  GIRLSCHOOL "It Could Be Better"
  HAWKWIND "Hurry On Sundown"
  SPIDER "Feel Like A Man"
  TORMÉ "Star"
  TYGERS OF PAN TANG "Are You There"

After Emporio's »Rock Out!« and »NWOBHM Live« efforts, they came up with a confusingly-titled (not to mention inaccurate) sampler called »The Best Of Indie Metal«, rounding up the usual suspects from the NWOBHM (GIRLSCHOOL,

TERRAPLANE, TYGERS, SPIDER) and non-NWOBHM (the ubiquitous HAWKWIND and TORMÉ) scenes to create yet another instant compilation. How some of these major-label acts qualify as 'indie' either in design or status is a complete and utter mystery, however, and gawd alone knows what the SCORPIONS are doing on this set. Still, I suppose it has a few redeeming features, with a couple of smaller outfits (SAVAGE and PERSIAN RISK) being given equal billing, although the chosen selections aren't particularly inspiring. The real shocker, though, is the effort by the SCRUBS, a worthless combo formed by lags serving life sentences at one of Her Majesty's hotels. Not only was it a pretty tasteless project, the group's music (they managed to get two singles pressed, believe it or not) was as atrocious as you would expect, and it seems utterly bizarre that someone sat down and listened to "Time For You" a decade after its release and decided to devote valuable disc space to it. Anyway, it's fair to say that this release failed to arouse much interest at the time, and it's really only for the fanatical NWOBHM maniac. The British Steel releases tend, on the whole, to be *far* more worthy offerings...

»The Bridge Album« LP Bridge Records 1982
Side 1:
   ROUGH CUT "Gunship"
   STELLA REBELLA "School Life"
   HERETIC "In Time"
   SWITCHBACK "How You Made Me Cry"
   NORTH STAR "It's Only Money"
Side 2:
   MINT "Underworld"
   TEMPEST RIDE "Another Time, Another Place"
   THE JON BAND "Dressed In Cream"
   CHERRY ARMADILLO "Cocaine Cocktail"
   TAKEAWAY "Reflections"

One of the plethora of local band samplers/themed compilations of the early 80's (which, as with »Kent Rocks« or »The Rockworks Album«, just happens to feature a fair percentage of noteworthy cuts), »The Bridge Album« is now threatening to become the next source of obscure tracks for the bootleggers. The record's stand-out piece, "Another Time, Another Place" by TEMPEST RIDE (an act who had metamorphosed into LYADRIVE even before the sampler hit the shops), has already been plundered for use on the »NWOBHM Vol.7« CD, and it may not be much longer before HERETIC (with a markedly heavier and more atmospheric style than was apparent on their dismal »Burnt At The Stake« EP) or the mid-paced rock of NORTH STAR follow suit. Elsewhere, the upbeat rock/metal of the little-recalled ROUGH CUT (nothing to do with Paul Shortino) is eminently listenable, as is the epic semi-ballad contributed by TAKEAWAY, whose incorporation of progressive and folk influences adds to the track's strength. Otherwise, things are pretty dire, with the new wave of STELLA REBELLA, the pop/rock of SWITCHBACK and THE JON BAND, the reggae of MINT and the downright awfulness of the eccentric CHERRY ARMADILLO. The premise of this album was to showcase outfits who used the Bridge rehearsal rooms/studio in Uxbridge, and both LYADRIVE and NORTH STAR went on to record singles for the Bridge label itself, so, in that respect, it was a moderate success. Few copies have survived, though, so snap it up if you ever see one at a reasonable price.

»The Friday Rock Show« LP BBC Records 1981
Side 1:
   SPIDER "What You're Doing To Me"
   DIAMOND HEAD "Don't You Ever Leave Me"
   SWEET SAVAGE "Eye Of The Storm"
   LAST FLIGHT "Dance To The Music"
Side 2:
   DEMON "One Helluva Night"
   BLACK AXE "Edge Of The World"
   WITCHFYNDE "Belfast"
   XERO "Cutting Loose"

The »Metal Explosion« set was evidently enough of a success to inspire the BBC to assemble another album of session highlights from the 'Friday Rock Show', which emerged (a year later) under a rather more functional title. It was nice to see some of the less-established acts winning the chance to be appreciated on vinyl, with XERO, SWEET SAVAGE, BLACK AXE and LAST FLIGHT all unveiling songs which easily hold their own alongside DIAMOND HEAD, WITCHFYNDE and DEMON. In fact, this was a consistently-enjoyable set, and it's just a pity that most of the material (with the exception of WITCHFYNDE's atypical "Belfast") would eventually turn up elsewhere. XERO's offering had already made an appearance on the second »Metal For Muthas« set, while LAST FLIGHT's contribution also took pride of place on their single, so I wonder if the bands were even consulted to see which songs they wanted to use. Mind you, there's no way that anyone could have predicted that the BLACK AXE (after they had become WOLF) and SWEET SAVAGE numbers would be recycled several years later, so I guess it was just bad luck in that sense. Elsewhere, the DIAMOND HEAD (quite different to the version which eventually cropped up on the »Living On Borrowed Time« album), DEMON and SPIDER numbers are all worthy of scrutiny from their die-hard followers, but I'd say that this is a worthwhile purchase for virtually all NWOBHM lunatics.

»The Last Warrior« Mini-LP Metalother 1987
Side 1:
  ARMOURED HEART "Far Beyond The Sun"
  BLACK RIDERS "Coma"
  DIAMOND LADY "Lady Of The Night"
Side 2:
  TROJAN "Bombs Away"
  JEALOUS "Resistance"
  SPECIAL GUESTS "Attack"

Metalother followed up their initial »Metal Warriör« set with a similarly-conceived mini-album, which hit the shelves within a matter of months, so you have to wonder why they didn't simply assemble a proper full-length offering in the first instance. Still, the second instalment was a listenable enough collection of post-NWOBHM, with a couple of the featured acts being fairly obscure. Ireland's TROJAN had already participated on the label's introductory set, and this was a second outing (following their original appearance on the »Battleaxe« EP) for the capable BLACK RIDERS, whose HOLOGRAM-style effort is one of the more powerful numbers on display. Elsewhere, ARMOURED HEART's contribution is a capably-performed affair with occasional similarities to BLEAK HOUSE, whereas DIAMOND LADY epitomised the type of unremarkable, female-fronted act who tended to win favour with comparatively few metal fans. The utterly obscure JEALOUS and SPECIAL GUESTS, meanwhile, came up with similar-sounding, semi-quirky efforts in the general manner of METAL MIRROR, although neither is overly-exciting. Although this set was mainly intended to give exposure to some aspirational young outfits (with full contact addresses on the sleeve), it was only a partial success; TROJAN and the BLACK RIDERS both ended up recording an album for G.I. Records, but the others appear to have drifted back into obscurity with great haste.

»The Metal Collection Vol.I« LP Ebony 1986
Side 1:
  BLOOD MONEY "Metalyzed"
  HIGH VOLTAGE "End Of Time"
  CHARGER "Rock"
  MOTHER'S RUIN "Mother's Ruin"
  HELLRAZER "Made Of Metal"
  RANSOM "Nightmare"
  BAD REPUTATION "How Long"
Side 2:
  TORQUE SHOW "The Hour Of The Slowest Clock"
  STATE OF MIND "The Dream"
  RICHTER "Leather'n'Lace"
  DARK HEART "Stone Cold Hearted"
  HOLOSADE "Cries In The Night"
  S.E.X. "Overlord Of Rampant Rock"
  ACCRYL "Victims In Chains"

After a gap of several years, Ebony unwisely decided to get back into the world of compilation LP's with their »Metal Collection« series, each volume utilising the same cover image (anything to save a bit of cash), but in different colours. With the first instalment showcasing European imports (HIGH VOLTAGE and ACCRYL) alongside the Brits, monikers such as HOLOSADE, CHARGER (both of whom engaged a very busy Colin Bell at that point in time), BLOOD MONEY, DARK HEART and HELLRAZER are relatively familiar to many of us, although the obscure West Country version of MOTHER'S RUIN (who were ultimately forced to change their identity to THE RUIN) featured here aren't the band who recorded for the Spectra label. The other *'unknown'* acts are mostly fairly forgettable, although the likes of RANSOM and RICHTER aren't too bad, I suppose, so it wasn't a complete disaster. A reasonable compilation, on balance, but still hardly achieving the heights of those original releases of the early 80's.

»The Metal Collection Vol.II« LP Ebony 1987
Side 1:
  FALSE WITNESS "Ride The Tiger"
  CENTURION "Lord Of The Rock"
  WAYWARD ANGEL "Rise Up And Fight"
  PHOENIX "Let Me Know"
  DEALER "Bring The Walls Down"
Side 2:
  FAST KUTZ "Midnight Love"
  STRAND DER VARD "I Don't Know"
  STORMCHILD "Holocaust City"
  CRIER "Fantasy World"
  DRAGONSLAYER "Rock The Radio"

Following on, around a year later, from the original entry in this three-volume series, this compilation features a mere ten tracks (financial cutbacks?) and fewer recognisable names. FAST KUTZ, DEALER and DRAGONSLAYER are surely familiar to most, but neither CENTURION nor STORMCHILD are related to the groups who released private singles back in the heady days of 1982, which is a bit of a shame. Nevertheless, the standard of this set is quite high throughout, with the capable contributions of FALSE WITNESS, CENTURION and PHOENIX standing out as being especially enjoyable. A salutary lesson, perhaps, that quality is generally preferable to quantity (well, it's always a reassuring thought when you step out of the shower on a cold day), and this one's easily the most worthwhile LP in this series.

»**The Metal Collection Vol.III**« LP Ebony 1987
Side 1:
FROZEN EYES "Intruder (World Of Madness)"
PURSUIT "Wastelands"
NITELYNE "Winners Or Losers"
COVENANT "Breaker"
MOBIUS STRIP "Shout To The Top"
OUT OF ORDER "Illusion Of Fear"
PASSIONTIDE "Can't Live Without Your Love"
CRY "Party After Dark"
Side 2:
SIOUX "Too Late"
CERBERUS "Alpha Centauri"
KAMIKAZI "Meet Your Maker"
MK II "Twilight Zone"
STRANDED "Love Lost Forever"
ALIBI "Breakout"
PAINT IT BLACK "The Next Show"
SUDDEN COMFORT "Compulsory Purchase"

By this stage, although long-players by individual bands such as BLOOD MONEY, RANKELSON and FAST KUTZ were still being churned out by the label, Ebony were now featuring such obscure acts on their compilations that few of us will recognise more than a couple of the outfits involved (it's a sad day when CRY are the best-known ensemble on a collection of this nature). Added to the fact that some of them might even have been European in origin, we're left wondering, yet again, why the company was often so infuriatingly vague about band details. Squeezing a mammoth *sixteen* tracks onto vinyl this time (even exceeding the overly-generous fourteen on the original volume), most of the groups featured are remarkably untalented WOLFSBANE clones or semi-thrash wannabes, although the likes of PASSIONTIDE and STRANDED are somewhat less objectionable than most. Still pretty awful, on the whole, and, although Ebony (towards the end of its existence) was now veering away from its NWOBHM roots, it still managed to inflict additional compilations on us, such as the dire »Rock Meets Metal«.

»**The Metallic-Era**« CD Neat Metal 1996
SAVAGE "Let It Loose"
DIAMOND HEAD "Sucking My Love"
SWEET SAVAGE "Killing Time"
DIAMOND HEAD "Am I Evil?"
BLITZKRIEG "Blitzkrieg"
DIAMOND HEAD "The Prince"
HOLOCAUST "The Small Hours"
DIAMOND HEAD "Helpless"
BUDGIE "Crash Course In Brain Surgery"
KILLING JOKE "The Wait"
BUDGIE "Breadfan"
ANTI NOWHERE LEAGUE "So What"

I suppose the only surprising thing about this compilation is that it took so long to come about, but it seems to have been a reasonably efficient means of parting METALLICA fans from their hard-earned cash. The simple premise, clearly, was that people had heard the latter's cover versions over the years (although it's worth pointing out that their knockabout interpretation of "Sucking My Love", one of four DIAMOND HEAD tracks on display, can only be found on one or two scarce bootlegs), and could now compare them with the originals, if they particularly wanted to. As it turned out, quite a number of devotees were sufficiently intrigued to purchase the set, and so Neat were soon gleefully raking in the cash; so much so that these shrewd businessmen couldn't resist the temptation to throw together a sequel of sorts a couple of years later. It wasn't a bad collection, all things considered, just one that seems rather superfluous for NWOBHM enthusiasts rather than METALLICA fans.

»**The Metallic-Era Volume II**« CD Neat Metal 1999
MOTÖRHEAD "Overkill"
DIAMOND HEAD "It's Electric"
SAVAGE "Dirty Money"
JAGUAR "Stormchild"
NICK CAVE AND THE BAD SEEDS "Loverman"
MERCYFUL FATE "Evil"
LYNYRD SKYNYRD "Tuesday's Gone"
HOLOCAUST "Master Of Puppets"
HOLOCAUST "The Small Hours" (live)
MOTÖRHEAD "Too Late Too Late"
MERCYFUL FATE "Curse Of The Pharaohs"
BLUE ÖYSTER CULT "Astronomy"

Given that the original version of »The Metallic-

Era« turned out to be such an unanticipated money-spinner for Neat Metal, you can hardly blame the company for a bit of serious barrel-scraping in order to bring out a sequel. Fortunately for them, METALLICA were obliging enough to release their »Garage Inc.« effort, featuring another generous batch of covers, although the NWOBHM content was extremely low in this instance. Nevertheless, yet another DIAMOND HEAD original ("It's Electric") was trundled out for inspection (why don't METALLICA just issue their own version of »Lightning To The Nations« and be done with it?), and various other tracks from the aforementioned release are presented in their original form (it looks as though Neat couldn't secure the rights to THIN LIZZY's "Whiskey In The Jar", though). In order to flesh out this follow-up with a tad more NWOBHM content, however, we're treated to a live recording of HOLOCAUST's "The Small Hours" (an utterly pointless exercise, given that the studio take had appeared on »The Metallic-Era« itself), plus HOLOCAUST's own interpretation of "Master Of Puppets", an abstruse inclusion which, to be blunt, defeats the purpose of the whole album. We're also rewarded with seemingly-random tracks from SAVAGE and JAGUAR, although there's no concrete evidence to suggest that METALLICA ever played these particular numbers either live or in rehearsals. Decent enough selections, perhaps, but it's stretching the gullibility of the fans somewhat. No doubt we'll soon be treated to further releases such as »Lars Really Likes These Songs, Honest«, and »METALLICA Would Probably Cover These Ones Too If They Had Time«. Ooh, such cynicism.

»The Rockworks Album« LP SRT 1982
Side 1:
  L'ART BLANC "Why? (Song For Piers)"
  NO ANGRY MAN "What Goes Up"
  SLICE "Sabda Brahma"
  EPIDEMIC "Let's Make War"
  PHAETON "Phaeton (Lost In Space)"
  CALIBRE "Nowhere To Hide"
Side 2:
  ENGLISH ROGUES "Radio Song"
  SHOCKING CONDITION "Hot On Your Heels"
  EXCHANGE "Someone"
  SLICE "Never Never"
  PHYSICAL DIGNITY "Can You Hear Me"
  RUSTIC NERVE "Change Your Mind"
  BMA "Change Or Die"

It would appear that 'Rockworks' was the name of an early 80's organisation which promoted local bands by helpfully arranging regular live music events in Surrey, with most of the hopefuls included on this tie-in album hailing from that particular neck of the woods. The outfits on display tend to be either rock or reggae/two tone, with approximately half of those featured being of interest to us. The album's outstanding track is undoubtedly CALIBRE's "Nowhere To Hide", an out and out metal effort with a vocal performance uncannily similar to Trev Robinson, SATAN's original frontman. Elsewhere, RUSTIC NERVE provide an energetic piece of metal/punk crossover, whereas the long-lived ENGLISH ROGUES offer a very melodic chunk of rock in the manner of V8. The strangely-monikered SLICE, on the other hand, are allocated a generous two tracks, with their "Sabda Brahma" effort being a truly awful, semi-acoustic instrumental which surely belongs in the 'easy listening' category, although "Never Never" is a much stronger selection in the general SCORCHED EARTH vein. SHOCKING CONDITION's contribution would be OK if it didn't veer off into reggae territory at times, and EXCHANGE are just too similar to THE KINKS for comfort. Otherwise, the bands are a bit samey and dull, and hardly appeal to our NWOBHM sensibilities to any great extent. The bootleggers don't seem to have cottoned on to this record yet, but when and if they do, I reckon that CALIBRE (not to be confused with the outfit who later cropped up on Ebony's »Rock Masters« compilation) will undoubtedly be the first bunch to see their contribution plundered.

»The 2nd Wave Of New British Metal« 7" EP
Private 1987
Side 1:
  PAUL SAMSON'S EMPIRE "One Day Heroes"
  CHARIOT "Life On The Line"
Side 2:
  HEAVY PETTIN "Heaven Sent"
  STRANGEWAYS "Never Gonna Lose It"

This four track EP, given away with 'Metal Hammer' magazine in April 1987, is an interesting piece of history in terms of the outfits featured. The PAUL SAMSON'S EMPIRE number, their only officially-released track until the »Live At The Marquee« disc finally emerged as late as 1994, is a rare opportunity to hear the band fronted by Mick White as opposed to Sam Blewitt, while CHARIOT's offering was their last vinyl appearance before Pete Franklin decided to try again under various different identities. HEAVY

PETTIN, on the other hand, were still signed to Polydor at this point, with their »Big Bang« LP expected to be released at any time, although it wasn't until two years later that the set finally appeared on the FM label after contractual difficulties. STRANGEWAYS, however, seem very out of place here; their facile, lightweight brand of AOR may have been relatively successful in commercial terms back then, but this hardly qualifies them for inclusion on a 'new metal' sampler. Mind you, it's interesting (and not a little perplexing) that so many rock publications of the day, from biggies such as 'Kerrang' and 'Metal Hammer', to several of the ground-level fanzines, adhered to the notion that there was a tangible 'second NWOBHM' in full swing, at a time when 'true metal' was actually in serious decline in the UK and the main contenders were, by that stage, either glam or thrash outfits. Wishful thinking, perhaps?

»12 Commandments In Metal« LP Roadrunner 1985
Side 1:
    BITCHES SIN "Ain't Life A Bitch"
    HELLION "Run For Your Life"
    WARHEAD "Whore"
    TOKYO BLADE "Fever"
    TYSONDOG "T.W.A.T."
    EARTHSHAKER "More" (live)
Side 2:
    SLAYER "The Antichrist" (live)
    WEAPON "Set The Stage Alight"
    ANTHRAX "Soldiers Of Metal"
    VENOM "Voyeur"
    SATAN "Oppression"
    OMEN "Torture Me"

After »Metal Battle« and »Metal Hammer«, Roadrunner delivered another selection of global talent with their »12 Commandments In Metal« set, showcasing acts signed to a fairly wide variety of labels. Once again, only half of those featured are genuine NWOBHM contenders, but at least some sort of effort appears to have gone into the selection process, and it's fair to say that the VENOM and TOKYO BLADE contributions aren't as familiar as some of their oft-recycled favourites. Elsewhere, the WEAPON and SATAN tracks were useful inclusions, given that both originally appeared on long-deleted pieces of vinyl, whereas the BITCHES SIN and TYSONDOG numbers were actually exclusive to this collection at the time, which was certainly something of a coup. Mind you, the BITCHES SIN composition subsequently put in an appearance on their »Invaders« long-player, although it looks as though this is the only place you'll find TYSONDOG's tastefully-titled ditty, so I guess that's something which might inspire a few collectors to seek out a copy.

Local-band Compilations

For those jaded souls among us for whom the novelty of private rock/metal singles, albums and compilations eventually wears a bit thin (or for those individuals who, quite reasonably, object to shelling out truly obscene amounts of moolah for supposedly rare pieces), the only recognised route for getting our grubby mitts on incredibly obscure NWOBHM is to join the clandestine tape-trading world and thereby expose ourselves to demo and live recordings from bands who never achieved anything greater at the time. Mind you, it's not particularly straightforward getting hold of such material these days, and you're often rewarded for your efforts with a virtually unlistenable, twentieth generation copy of a tape that wasn't too hot in the first instance. Well, there *is* an alternative to this route after all. Quite by chance, the NWOBHM era happened to coincide with a second phenomenon, the proliferation of local-band compilations released by tiny labels throughout the 80's. Admittedly, records of a similar description were assembled in most parts of the world at one time or another, but it's fair to say that the sheer volume issued in Britain in and around the time of the original NWOBHM explosion was truly extraordinary.

There are literally dozens, if not hundreds, of such small-time samplers, either showcasing

bands from a fairly restricted geographical area or collating aspiring acts with some sort of connection or general theme. The most familiar of these to the NWOBHM collector would be the likes of »Kent Rocks«, »Southern Comfort«, »Belfast Rocks«, »The Bridge Album« etc., these being fairly well-established releases which just happened to include a relatively high proportion of rock/metal talent. The majority of local/themed compilations, however, are much more likely to feature only one or two outfits of interest, and are therefore valued considerably lower, the upshot being that most of them tend to be overlooked by dealers. On the occasions that you come across such records as a collector, they will, more often than not, be extremely inexpensive, so it's worth taking a gamble with your money (it always helps if the groups are actually pictured on the sleeve or insert, and one or two of them happen to look a bit hairy) and you might even, from time to time, find a jewel amongst the dross.

The following section is intended to serve as a rudimentary introduction to this often-neglected field of vinyl collecting, not a comprehensive attempt to document the phenomenon of local-band compilations (this would be a futile and pointlessly time-consuming task) and offers the merest glimpse of a fraction of the multifarious compilations issued in the NWOBHM era. Please be aware of the fact that, if any of you go forth and purchase obscure albums of this type, you will be forced to suffer some astoundingly bad punk, reggae, synth-pop, new romantic and two-tone drivel (even on samplers which style themselves as *'rock compilations'*) in order to find even one decent metal track (if you're particularly unlucky, you might even get a compilation with absolutely no heavies whatsoever), so kindly proceed with extreme caution. At the time of writing, this is an area into which relatively few NWOBHM collectors venture (the punks are a bit more on-the-ball), and nobody really knows what's out there, so you could easily make a great discovery!

There's no particularly logical place to start, so let's just venture as far South as possible and work our way up from there, shall we? Issued on the C-Side label in 1983, »Feet On The Street« is ostensibly a collection of bands based on the Isle Of Wight (an island off the South Coast of England, best-known for its early 70's festivals), although I find it incredibly hard to believe that such a sparsely-populated isle could have boasted a thriving music scene (it certainly doesn't nowadays, from what I can gather), and I'm pretty sure that several of the acts on display were actually from the mainland. In any case, there's a fair smattering of rock and metal here, such as MECHANIX (that would make a decent album title, you know), who sound vaguely like LYADRIVE or a keyboard-augmented OMEN SEARCHER on "Can't Quit You", RENDEZVOUS (not related to the Cambridgeshire outfit who recorded the »For Crying Out Loud« album) and their brand of RAINBOW/TOTO-style melody on "Decisions In Love", and ENFORCE, whose "Eagle's Edge" (lying somewhere between early SATAN and SKITZOFRENIK) is easily the heaviest track on the whole album. Elsewhere, there are a couple of borderline candidates in the shape of the very peculiar ABANDON CITY (an oddball outfit who somehow wangled a 'Friday Rock Show' session in their time), whose "Swinging Date" sounds like early (quirky) TOAD THE WET SPROCKET, the female-fronted but pop/rock of CASSIE (one of them's wearing a GIRL T-shirt in the photo, though), the HALL & OATES-wannabes GARAGEBAND and finally MUMBO JUMBO, whose melodic rock is seriously overpowered by some LEVEL 42-style, thwacky bass work. Not a bad return for your money, though, assuming you'd only paid a couple of quid for it.

Moving a bit further North to the mainland, we come across the tastefully-titled »Spit 'n' Finish« LP, pressed (on fetching red vinyl, no less, but with a pretty unassuming sleeve) by the tiny Toucan concern at some point in 1983. Issued as a means of promoting obscure outfits from Hampshire and its environs, this particular compilation boasts the otherwise-unreleased "Pyramid Blue" from the LED ZEPPELIN-influenced FRIENDS (a number which preceded the ensemble's own single on Rock Shop), the enjoyable "All Systems Go" from the excellently-named DARK HARVEST, who would appear to have been unashamed BLUE ÖYSTER CULT copyists, plus the more commercial rock of RELATIVE EASE, who deliver a listenable effort entitled "Run From My Mind". Of the remaining groups on display, most seem to be peculiarly lightweight indie acts, none being grossly objectionable (which is unusual) but none of which are worthy of anything but the briefest attention from the majority of NWOBHM enthusiasts. Again, however, two or three reasonably heavy tracks signifies a pretty good result in this case.

Remaining on the South Coast, but travelling East towards Sussex and its environs, we encounter the famous Airship Records and their *'wittily'*-titled »Seaside Rock« (the confectionery on the cover ramming home the obvious pun as on the earlier »Belfast Rocks« effort from 1981. A well-packaged double LP set (most of the artists featured being afforded two tracks) which actually includes a booklet containing line-up details and photos, this would be a lot better were it not for the sickening fact that it incorporates a grand total of one metal act. Moan. As with many others, however, the use of the word 'rock' in the album title is either deliberately misleading or just downright lazy. Anyway, the composition of interest here is VALKYRIE's "Cradle To The Grave", and it's actually quite a corker. This is an epic, heavy offering which begins with an ambitious, symphonic section (eat your hearts out, all you black metal copyists) before launching into a track reminiscent of a slightly less accomplished CYNIC. Cracking stuff, and it's a great pity that this long-lived combo (they persevered until at least the mid-80's) weren't rewarded with the opportunity to record their own single/EP for Airship. Elsewhere, the only other acts remotely deserving of the 'rock' tag are BLUE ORION, X-IT and ORANGE, although their respective contributions were all pretty abysmal, if truth be told. Some incredibly talentless ensembles feature on the rest of the set, and it suggests that the Sussex scene wasn't the healthiest in terms of originality or variety at the time.

Nevertheless, Airship organised another local-band sampler a year later, an offering entitled »Listen To Me« (issued in a far-too-arty-for-its-own-good cover), although it's fair to say that this monumentally shabby collection didn't do anyone any favours. Admittedly, this one didn't actually set out to be a 'rock' compilation per se, but the musical contents are fairly atrocious on the whole, with only the progressively-inclined LEGAL SIN and MIRAGE (and you'll hear about an infinitely more worthy band of that name later) coming anywhere near real rock territory with their allotted tracks. Tellingly, however, the sleeve notes reveal that the label played an entirely marginal role in this particular LP's assembly, with the responsibility for deciding which numbers to use lying wholly in the hands of the groups themselves. On the evidence presented here, I'd say that a modicum of quality control wouldn't have gone amiss, and you can rest assured that you're certainly not being deprived of any undiscovered talent here.

Moving towards London, we discover a few compilations which are generally linked in terms of recording studios, with groups who frequented certain facilities being rewarded with appearances on hastily thrown-together albums (by all accounts, they often had to pay for the privilege) in order to expose them to a wider audience. Without exception, the diverse acts featured are all extraordinarily obscure, and none of them, as far as I'm aware, went on to achieve greater success in the music business, so it looks as though this sort of thing was the only vinyl legacy of numerous long-forgotten wannabes. First up is »Baby Don't Jump«, a sampler issued by V.U. Records of Tottenham in 1982. The only remotely worthwhile contribution as far as most NWOBHM devotees are concerned, however, is "I'm A Fool For You" by the feebly-named READY RUBBED, an offering which comes across as a kind of lightweight LOTUS CRUISE, but it's hardly a world-beater. Apart from that, though, it's all unreservedly atrocious, but there's a dubious 'highlight' and potential blackmail opportunity in the form of a number by RAY WINSTONE, who's now a relatively well-known 'hard man' type of actor who has appeared in quite a few critically-acclaimed films of late. Chortle.

Next up is the rather functionally-titled »Compilation 1« LP from Starforce Studios, again issued at some point in 1982, which more or less seems to have represented the peak of local-sampler activity. This one is, however, an immensely peculiar compilation (with a monumentally off-putting sleeve), and the bias is towards hopelessly pretentious electro-pop/new romantic piffle (including an outfit called the HELLFIRE CLUB, although, disappointingly, it turns out not to be the metal version from the West Midlands who recorded a seldom-seen single on the tiny Romac label), with the notable exception of THE INVISIBLE BAND (a bunch who were, remarkably enough, actually operational for the best part of the 80's, whose "Doin' The Ton", a relatively upbeat exercise in CENTURION-style biker rock with brain-dead lyrics to match, rounds off the set in semi-listenable fashion. Aside from that, however, it's all irritatingly poor, and this sort of release really was a complete and utter waste of vinyl. Not one that should have the NWOBHM collectors fighting among themselves, to be honest.

Also from London is the early Bridgehouse showcase called »A Week At The Bridge E16«, featuring live recordings of various outfits who played at the aforementioned venue in the spring of 1978. Although this predates the NWOBHM explosion by at least a year, it's still a semi-interesting document of the rock music underground at the time, and captures a few bands who were pretty much doing their own thing and not getting sucked into all that punk nonsense. Even so, it's not exactly genuine metal that's on display, and suggests that traditional hard-rockers and bluesy acts could still attract a significant following at the time. In fact, the most interesting aspect of the ensembles featured is actually that they featured a few personalities who were better-known for their work elsewhere. For example, FILTHY McNASTY (a vaguely funky bunch of raunchy rockers) featured much-travelled sticksman Clive Edwards and future solo star Stevie Lange, while the ROLL-UPS (unremarkable snotty types) nurtured the talents of FASTWAY's Lea Hart. There's also the GERRY McAVOY JAM, which is basically a few of RORY GALLAGHER's cronies enjoying a bit of extra-curricular activity, the perennial JACKIE LYNTON'S HAPPY DAYS and the utterly disposable SALT, none of which really sets the pulse racing. The remaining band, REMUS DOWN BOULEVARD, are the most interesting of the lot, being the outfit which featured future IRON MAIDEN stalwart Dennis Stratton and one-time ANGEL WITCH bassist Gerry Cunningham, and their pair of contributions ("Only For You" and "Gunrunner") are the closest thing to proto-NWOBHM on the entire set. One for MAIDEN fans, certainly, but it's an item (released as a single album with a bonus 12" EP) which doesn't come up for sale too often.

Staying in the same general cartographic area, we have »The Best Of The Rest Vol.1«, an LP issued by Catman Boogie Records (these company names get worse by the second) of Essex, whose apparent intention was to promote some of the bands who recorded at Indigo Blue Studio. Although undated (the label were issuing compilations as late as 1987), it certainly looks as though it could represent an early effort, and, with a mammoth eighteen hopefuls featured, there's a strong statistical likelihood of unearthing some rock or metal. Indeed, there's a fair quota in the shape of "Heart User" by HARD TIMES, "Struck By Lightning" by FEMME FATALE (no, not that lot), POSITIVE I.D.'s "Victim Of Your Heart" and "Sleepless Nights" by an act with the promising name of THE PREY, all of which were reasonably heavy and strong on guitars. Even so, you wouldn't say that any of these combos were committed to playing full-on metal, as there are distinct influences from various other genres in each case (and take it from me, metal with SPANDAU BALLET-style vocals isn't a winning combination), which confuses matters slightly. Very odd, overall, and it seems to suggest that most of the weighty contenders from the region weren't in the habit of frequenting Indigo Blue, for some strange reason. It's still a compilation worth picking up if you see it cheaply, though.

Working our way North to the posh suburbs of Hertfordshire, we meet up with some old friends at Lost Moment Records, who saw fit to issue their bafflingly-titled »Colours Of The Bastard Art« sampler (a self-proclaimed *'alternative compilation'*), containing a snapshot of the label's *'talent'* (and, believe me, I use the expression guardedly), in 1985 or thereabouts. No contribution from JOKER, unfortunately, but the rather weird ORION are here, with an entirely different arrangement of "Storm" to the version which had appeared on their earlier single for the label. Apart from a reasonably acceptable (but rather quirky) number (entitled "Jericho") from the SUGAR GLYDERS (who also released a single or two of their own through Lost Moment at more or less the same time), however, this particular compilation reaches Zen heights of awfulness (in case you were wondering, it comes in a colourful sleeve with the band names boldly emblazoned thereon) and it can't really be recommended to anyone other than die-hard ORION fans, if there are any.

Another fairly obscure compilation from the Hertfordshire area, which presumably showcases yet another cross-section of the local hopefuls, is the private-as-you-like (a plain cover with paste-on artwork and credits) »Rupert Preaching At A Picnic« (there's definitely something a bit flipping weird about some of these titles) effort, assembled by a minor concern called Naive Records in 1981. In the main, it's all pretty atrocious indie piffle, but there's a semi-decent number entitled "Sword" from an act known as OBLIVION II, whose music is occasionally similar to MITHRANDIR, although their slightly irritating, indie-style vocalist lets them down. Apart from that one, however, there's very little to write home about, although it's just about worth mentioning the noisy punk mayhem which emanates from the INNOCENT VICARS and DERANGED. I've no doubt that this one was pressed in utterly minuscule quantities, so it's not a compilation you're going to see very often, and one that shouldn't tempt all that many NWOBHM fans.

Staying in the Home Counties, however, we find »The Quest Tapes«, an album (issued in 1982) showcasing several outfits who used the facilities at Luton's Quest Studios. Sadly, many of the more respected NWOBHM acts who are known to have frequented the place (CLIENTELLE, TOAD THE WET SPROCKET, BLEAK HOUSE and so on) are notable by their absence, although the LP pulls off something of a major coup with its two exclusive tracks from the excellent HIGH TREASON, whose "Cake" and "The Siren Song" are undoubtedly the record's highlights. Elsewhere, however, there's a pretty patchy selection of compositions (most bands being afforded two numbers each), although ZTORM, with their CHEMICAL ALICE-style widdly prog on their sole "Evensong" effort, seem to have been a vaguely capable bunch. The ODD ENDS and THE DRIVERS show the occasional glimpse of musical ability, but not enough to allow them to be recommended with any great enthusiasm. If you should ever see this particular album cheaply, though, it's well worth buying (mind you, an unremarkable cover means you could easily overlook it) just for the HIGH TREASON content.

Strangely, however, while many of the region's bands were clearly beavering away happily at Quest Studios, an equal number appear to have been ensconced in the nearby Wopalong facility more or less simultaneously, the end result being the oddly-titled »Lend An Ear 1992?« sampler, which also appeared (on the unrenowned Vroom label) in 1982. Again showcasing a variety of Home Counties hopefuls, the most notable inclusion is TOAD THE WET SPROCKET, who deliver the otherwise-unavailable "Charlie", although this complete shambles (with saxophones and all sorts) is more along the lines of their first single than their second, so it's hardly a major selling-point for this album. Elsewhere, the mysterious GIANT HOAX are the best of a relatively bad lot, their pair of upbeat rockers ("Floating Above It All" and "Micky And The Cowboys") occasionally eliciting comparisons with FRAMED or VARDIS, whereas SLICE and FADED SECRET are passable, although both are only on the periphery of the NWOBHM style. Once again, it's an acceptable purchase if it's cheap enough, although yet another unspectacular, irrelevant cover increases the chances of this LP failing to grab your attention.

In nearby Cambridgeshire, meanwhile, there's a sampler LP entitled »No Cause For Alarm«, although it's virtually impossible to discern the criteria which resulted in these particular acts being selected for inclusion, as there's absolutely no connection either in terms of locality (the outfits come from as far away as Wales and Scotland) or the music on display (it's the usual mixed bag), so it's all a bit of a mystery at present. In fact, this collection (lovingly assembled by Plectrum Records in 1980 and presented in the usual minimalist sleeve) is pretty ropy in general, with no genuine NWOBHM on display at all, but the DEAD SOULS (with "Pouring Rain") and the PRIZE GUYS (with "Don't U Mess Around") come closest, with some fairly cheerful metal/punk crossover material. Elsewhere, though, it's all pitifully awful, and the sampler even includes two equally-untalented acts called NO EXIT just to confuse matters further. A pretty dismal effort in the main, and one that really shouldn't be giving too many NWOBHM collectors any sleepless nights.

The bizarre »The Whinging Album« (subtitled 'Clutching At Straws'), meanwhile, takes in an unusually wide catchment area, including bands from as far afield as North London and the Home Counties, to Northamptonshire, Oxfordshire and so on. Issued on Whinging Records itself at some point in the early 80's, this set takes the 'do it yourself' ethos to the letter, and the record is housed within an extraordinarily low-budget, fold-round cover which appears to have been thrown together at short notice and which actually looks half-finished. Still, there are a handful of extremely deserving acts on display (along with the motley no-hopers) this time, the pick of the bunch being TELLURIAN, whose disarmingly-heavy music (very much in the manner of WITCHFINDER GENERAL and OVERDRIVE) should have taken them a lot further in the business. Sadly, though, this seems to be the only place to hear their collective talents, and I reckon the truly excellent "Reborn" and the marginally-less-intense "Trojan Journey" would have made a cracking 7" under different circumstances. Another top-notch bunch of contenders were TITAN (yes, another one), who threaten to deliver a capable piece of ANGEL WITCH impersonation on "Destiny", although the keyboard-tinged mid-section might have been a slightly poor idea. I reckon this bunch had nothing to do with the pre-WRATHCHILD act (it sounds vaguely similar, although the keyboards are a bit of a giveaway, and it doesn't really fit in geographically either), and they certainly weren't connected with the Yorkshire oddballs. Elsewhere, THOR (the little-known London version) contribute "War Of The Roses", a somewhat odd effort which sounds like a glammed-up ELIXIR, whereas ACANTHUS offer "Valley Of The Unknown", a tasteful slice of synth-based rock in the general TRIARCHY manner. Apart from that, it's all mostly listenable, although it's disappointing that the REQUIEM featured are indie wannabes and not the Midlands heavyweights. As I say, it's not dated explicitly, although the unremarkable SPRING OFFENSIVE released a single in 1981, and THOR circulated a demo around a year later, so I'd be very surprised if this LP wasn't from more or less the same period. With five perfectly respectable slices of NWOBHM on display, though, this one can be recommended pretty highly.

Further West, Wiltshire's TW Records (a company who issued a fair old number of singles from punk and indie acts over the years) were responsible for assembling the little-known »Tracks West-Platform 1« collection from 1983, which is a real mixed bag in terms of musical styles. MORROKKO's "Titanic", for example, is a semi-listenable melodic rocker with some anomalously heavy riffing in places, while MAXWELL STREET's plaintive "Sleep With Me Tonight" (been a long time, eh?) is an overly-lengthy, soppy ballad which rapidly outstays its welcome. On the reverse, THE OPPOSITE MAN's "The Extremist Song" is a moderately acceptable example of crossover material, while HI-FI contribute an upbeat pop/rock tune with female vocals (sounding, at times, remarkably similar to RAMPENT, which is a listenable enough effort. I've no idea what the sleeve's supposed to look like, as I'm working with a copy that seems to have lost its cover, but I'd imagine that this one was probably decorated with the kind of atrocious artwork which most of these samplers had in common.

In the NWOBHM wasteland of Somerset, the small-time concern known as Rapp Records (responsible for the seldom-seen SQUASHED PYRANNAH single) assembled their »Forgotten Futures« compilation at some point in 1983, the album (pressed on white vinyl, as if this makes it more interesting) featuring a motley assortment of regional nonentities. Side one is especially awful, showcasing the non-existent musical ability of various no-hopers with an annoying lack of talent and some equally irritating band names. On the reverse, however, things improve marginally with the semi-listenable, female-fronted INDIA, whose uplifting "Now Susan's Dead" barely makes it out of the pop category, while the likes of WOUNDED KNEE, STRIKNENE and QUAZOR (some decent guitar work on the latter's "Another Wasted Soul", although it takes quite a while for the track to get going) are vaguely acceptable (not archetypal NWOBHM by a long stretch, though) if you're in the right frame of mind. Otherwise, the best of a *very* bad lot would probably be the relatively energetic crossover of THE UNIT, whose "Broken Dream" is about as close as we're going to get to genuine metal territory in this instance. Another entirely unremarkable compilation with another anonymous sleeve, but worth picking up if it comes cheaply enough.

Over in Wales, meanwhile, the independent labels were doing their own thing, with an unusually early compilation coming in the shape of »Is The War Over?«, a collection of bands from the Cardiff area which was issued by a concern called Z Block Records way back in 1979. Remarkably, this sampler actually features an extremely youthful MAD DOG, in their original incarnation as a quintet, with "Killer" and "Someone Here Must Like Me". Given that these numbers are entirely consistent with their mid-80's output, though, it's somewhat baffling as to why it took them so long to get their own product out after this early introduction to the masses. The next-best outfit under scrutiny are probably the punk-tinged ADDICTION, who offer three suitably heavy tracks of crossover material in the form of "Violence", "Stampede" and "Seek & Search". Elsewhere, there's some reasonable, SPEED LIMIT-style rock from the inadvisably-named BEAVER on "Mac The Knife" and "Kleptomania", while the only remaining outfit of note are REPTILE RANCH, whose "Waterhole" isn't exactly out and out metal (neither is it the most enthralling of tracks), but their bassist was Philip John, possibly the same chap who went on to pound the skins for NIGHTIME FLYER and PREYER. Apart from that, there's nothing else to write home about, although it's worth mentioning that the YOUNG MARBLE GIANTS, who close the album with two rather insipid offerings, went on to make quite a name for themselves in the indie field.

A further notable entry from the land of song comes from Notepad Records and their undated (although I'd say *ca.* 1984 judging by some of the fashion victims pictured on the sleeve) »Notepad Productions Volume 1« collection, featuring a number of utterly unknown outfits from South Wales. Among these are the likes of HALCYON DAZE, whose "Hang On" contribution is vaguely reminiscent of early BLEAK HOUSE, and the lightweight, borderline rock of GENEVA WALK and SWITCHY AND THE CIRCUIT BREAKERS (what an utterly pathetic name), all of which are reasonably decent. The real corker, however, comes in the form of the unfeasibly capable MIRAGE (not to be confused with the forgettable bunch who cropped up on Airship's »Listen To Me« LP), whose extraordinary "Blind Fury" is truly one of the classic tracks of the entire NWOBHM genre! Lying somewhere between early SAVAGE, DEF LEPPARD and HIGH TREASON, this is a superb, catchy, mid-paced number with an excellent vocal performance from a talented chap called, er, 'Wretch'. Sterling stuff, and it would be a tragedy if this were the only number they ever committed to vinyl. Mind you, Notepad are also known to have issued the odd 7" (e.g. WILDSMITH ST.), so if there's any justice at all, there deserves to be a MIRAGE single out there too. Fingers crossed!

Staying in roughly the same geographical area, we encounter a Sain Records compilation from 1984 entitled »Barod Am Roc 1«, featuring recordings of various Welsh outfits (all singing in their native tongue) which cover a remarkably broad range of years, dating back to the early 70's in a couple of cases. I'm not sure exactly what the underlying concept originally was (no doubt the sleeve notes would offer some sort of explanation if I could be bothered to trawl through them to get a translation), but I suspect it was nothing more than to celebrate the Welsh 'rock' scene in general, utilising contributions from as wide a variety of sources as possible, which is fair enough. Anyway, the highlight of the album would have to be "Barod Am Roc" ("Ready To Rock"), the title track, supplied by the dependable CRYS. This mid-paced number (dating from 1982) originally appeared on their second LP, although the scarcity of their albums means that this compilation still represents a pretty good find for collectors. Among the other obscure acts on display are RHIANNON TOMOS A'R BAND (showcasing a talented female vocalist who later ended up fronting the weighty DIAWLED towards the end of their career), whose "Cwm Hiraeth" ("Yearning For The Valley"), from 1980, is another hard-rocking effort with a powerful vocal performance. Elsewhere, "Majic", by SHWN, is a reasonably catchy boogie tune from 1978, and the lightweight HERGEST (whose similar-sounding track dates from as far back as 1976) featured a certain Derec Brown, who later fronted his own outfit called DEREC BROWN A'R RACARACWYR, an ensemble who released at least one single and a full album in the early 80's. Apart from that, however, it's all pretty disposable, run-of-the-mill rock with various influences, although it's well worth picking up for CRYS and RHIANNON TOMOS A'R BAND, at least. I'm not entirely sure if further volumes of »Barod Am Roc« materialised at any stage, although I wouldn't be remotely surprised if there were others.

Before leaving Wales, it's well worth drawing some attention to an extremely scarce four track, Welsh-language compilation 7" entitled »Gyda Chymorth C.A.C.« (the translation appears to be something along the lines of 'help together', so this might even have been some sort of fund-raising project for whatever 'C.A.C.'

stood for), a mini-sampler of local hopefuls issued by the small Fflach ('flash') label in 1982. Without doubt, the highlight is "Shwt Mae Siapus?" (don't ask, I haven't a clue) by one of the region's heavier acts, DIAWLED, who would issue a single or two of their own in years to come (mind you, this appears to be an exclusive number), although the "Efo Mi" contribution from ERYR WEN is vaguely listenable too, even if the completely bizarre 'trumpet' sections (sounds more like a synthesizer to me) tend to spoil things a bit. The other two acts (filling up space and serving no purpose whatsoever) are totally forgettable, however, but this sampler as a whole (it was, incidentally, relatively uncommon to find compilation EP's at this time) is a reasonably worthwhile investment.

Back over to Staffordshire, there's a healthy percentage of rock and metal talent on display on »To Boldly Go...« (subtitled 'The Potteries Compilation Album'), issued by Rats Kart Records (a cunning alter ego for Star Trak Studios) in 1986. There's one familiar name straight away, although HARRIER proceed to deliver an entirely disposable ballad entitled "Leave Me Now", which is very much in the manner of their not-particularly-impressive EP. Elsewhere, though, there are some promising candidates, notably CHEATER, whose lengthy "Kill Two Birds" is a substantial slice of raunchy rock in the fashion of BABY TUCKOO or MASTERSTROKE, while the unashamedly-named EXECUTIONER come up with a complex, semi-progressive effort ("Fly To The Rainbow") with shades of DAWNWATCHER and SARACEN. The tuneful "Don't Go Away" by WILLIE'S WIFE, meanwhile, is let down by a very messy arrangement and the fact that the band have chosen one of the worst monikers in the history of the universe, while STORIES (with an offering called "Buckshot") come across as a poppy, keyboard-tinged proposition in the style of MAYDAY. STRAFE's "Everybody" is a heavy enough effort, but suffers from an extreme identity crisis, and ends up as neither one thing nor the other, whereas "Our Time" by SOME WEIRD SIN is another weighty offering, but it's nearer to FIELDS OF THE NEPHILIM than traditional NWOBHM territory. All in all, however, a pretty decent sampler with a generous smattering of rock and metal, and it's just a pity that there's absolutely no information given about any of the acts on show.

Staying in the Midlands, a fairly interesting release crops up in the unlikely form of »Brum Beats-Live At The Barrel Organ«, a scarcely-sighted double LP (issued on Big Bear Records) which commemorates a series of gigs held at the famous Birmingham venue to promote local bands in June 1980. With the acts being recorded live specifically for this purpose, all of the material is unique to this compilation, the most interesting to NWOBHM fans clearly being the contributions (two tracks each) of MAYDAY, SPEED LIMIT and SPOONFULL (the latter representing an early incarnation of SHYWOLF), all of which are perfectly listenable. Of these, I'd say that the most enjoyable pair of numbers probably come from local favourites SPEED LIMIT, who deliver "Alright On The Night" and "CJ" (this was, incidentally, supposed to be their farewell gig, but it turned out not to be the case), although MAYDAY (with "Moving In Time" and "Standing On The Edge Of The World") come across as a markedly stronger proposition than on their mediocre »Day After Day« single. Elsewhere, there's quite a lot of fairly traditional rock and blues, although a couple of semi-interesting inclusions are the legendary punk outfit DANSETTE DAMAGE and THE LAZERS, fronted by a very young Carol Decker in her pre-T'PAU days. All in all, it's an energetic and enjoyable compilation, and well worth a couple of quid of anyone's money.

A bit further on, we're presented with the »Castle Rock Compilation«, a private pressing from 1984 which was evidently organised by Radio Trent to promote some of the local hopefuls who had previously recorded sessions for the station. Chiefly of interest to the NWOBHM community is the exclusive "Homebreaker" by DAWN TRADER, an excellent track which displays a considerably more metal attitude than had been apparent on their 70's-style EP. Elsewhere, however, it appears that the Nottinghamshire area was an area of total musical mediocrity, judging by some of the utterly hopeless acts featured here. With the possible exception of the rather lightweight ENGLISH ELECTRIC, it's all completely disposable, and there's absolutely nothing to suggest that this one should ever be up there with »Kent Rocks« in terms of value. In fact, I reckon those involved with the project must have had their doubts about the LP at the time, since compiler/presenter Graham Neale's sleeve notes includes the ominous statement 'I'm not saying they're good, I'll leave that to you'. Er, do you mind if I don't?

Travelling up the motorway to Yorkshire, we come across a compilation of local groups entitled »New Belief In Old Cities«, issued by the New Belief Record Company in 1983. Alongside the usual collection of hapless nonentities there are a couple of extremely worthy contenders (I knew

Yorkshire wouldn't let us down) in the shape of SCREAMING TREE (nothing to do with Mark Lanegan), whose "The Runner" is slightly reminiscent of Kent's TNT, while CURFEW's "Get A Grip On Myself" is a catchy, upbeat affair in the general style of SHADOWFAX. The rest of the acts featured, while not nearly as contrived or pretentious as some of those doing the rounds in London at the time, were still an unpalatable selection, and it's no wonder that the area's indie wannabes often struggled to get themselves known locally, given that Yorkshire has always been a bastion of rock/metal talent. I'd say that this album (issued in a fairly distinctive sleeve) would certainly be well worth picking up, though.

Also in Yorkshire, an even earlier compilation shows up in »The Art Of Solving Problems« from 1980, a record (issued by the small-time Ram Records) which showcased six acts from Leeds and allowed each of them to contribute two tracks to the sampler. Of the six, five are truly atrocious, although SIDE EFFECT save the day, even if their style bordered on quirky punk at times. Still, their "Chain Reaction" composition was a fairly listenable effort with vague similarities to the likes of ZORRO or LYNX, especially when the unusual guitar work and keyboards come into play most strongly. Mind you, their other offering ("Pin Stripe Suit") is a pretty feeble number, a third-rate MEAN STREET DEALERS reject in a pub/punk style which barely holds the attention. Elsewhere, THE CAT and THE FORST (yes, THE FORST) were reasonably heavy at times, but both were just far too off-the-wall to appeal to most NWOBHM fans. Hardly an album to put on the wants list (another silly cartoon cover, too), and probably one that's better suited to the punk fans, on balance.

In the North East, the long-lived Teesbeat label (who put out the first BLACK ROSE single back in 1982) were still doing their best to promote local talent as late as the mid-80's, and were responsible for a couple of compilation albums to show what was going on in their region at the time. First up is »On A Wing And A Prayer« (released in 1985), which gives exposure to six totally unknown acts, each of whom were allowed to contribute two original compositions. In general, the musical standard is head and shoulders above most of the similarly-conceived compilations from elsewhere in the UK, although only one or two acts border on NWOBHM in this case. The pick of the bunch would undoubtedly be TRIXTER (no, not them), who deliver a pair of slightly quirky, mid-paced, semi-NWOBHM numbers, with their "Burn So Bright" and "Fraulien" (somebody get those guys a German dictionary) efforts coming across as vaguely in the SCORPIO or BEG TO DIFFER scheme of things. The next-best act on display would be SECRET GARDEN, although their "Tsantsa" (no, me neither) and "Summer Of Hate" are both in more of a power pop style, with vaguely psychedelic undertones at times, so this isn't really genuine NWOBHM fodder at all. As I say, it's a listenable collection as a whole, and worth a couple of quid of anyone's dosh.

A year later, Teesbeat came up with another compilation, this time called »Rumour Sets The Woods Alight« (yet another title which totally defies logic), a record (issued in a pretty atrocious sleeve) which saw a slight dip in the overall quality of acts, although things are ultimately saved by the unusually-spelled LANSLIDE, a melodic bunch of metallers whose extremely listenable pair ("Following Your Heart" and "All Through The Night") are very much in the manner of early BRIAR, so it's a shame this bunch didn't (as far as we know) get any further. On the rest of the set, the promisingly-monikered WHITE ROSE fail to pose much of a threat to their unwashed cousins, and merely provide some rather insipid, semi-acoustic nonsense. Mind you, the rather more feebly-named STEVE INNOCENT manage to deliver a passable rocker called "I Don't Want Your Freedom", which has a bit of metal-sounding guitar work (the overall effect is still in rather more of a crossover style, though), but their other number ("You Gave Me Life") is completely disposable. A semi-decent purchase for the two LANSLIDE offerings, therefore, but that's about all.

Over in Ireland, meanwhile, the emergent Scoff label was evidently doing its utmost to promote some new talent on their »Vinyl Verdict« set ('A compilation of new Irish rock music'), a long-player which hit the shops in 1981. It was a somewhat disappointing LP in terms of bona fide NWOBHM acts, though (no sign of MAMA'S BOYS or WINTER'S REIGN, for instance), and the only passable bunch on display were THE POSERS (shocking name, mind you), whose catchy "Liar" turns out to be a pretty capable rocker in the manner of TEMPEST or MEANSTREAK. Elsewhere, there are some real musical atrocities from various untalented indie wannabes (who were equally awful across the water), although the respective contributions from NIGEL HAMILTON (quite possibly the ex-COBRA stalwart), DEKE O'BRIEN, CONTACT and TEEN COMMANDMENTS (groan) are fairly

Iron Pages
Books & Distribution

Iron Pages Records

Address:
I.P. Verlag Jeske/Mader GbR, Haydnstr. 2, 12203 Berlin, Germany
Tel. 0049/30/86 20 09 81 Fax 0049/30/86 20 09 82
E-Mail: pages@ip-verlag.de Homepage: www.ip-verlag.de

inoffensive slices of tunefulness, albeit on the very periphery of the melodic rock/pop style. It's not an album you're likely to encounter very often, to be honest, and I'd only recommend parting with a nominal amount of cash if you happen to see a copy for sale.

As previously stated, it's less common to find compilation 7" or 12" EP's from the NWOBHM era, although another exception to add to the list is the fairly obscure »G-Force« 7" sampler of Scottish bands, issued by the unrenowned Mouth concern in 1983. The outfits featured are BLYTHE BROCKETT (female-fronted rock/pop in the style of SHE or ROUGH JUSTICE), DEAD LOSS (dated, bluesy rock in the DR FEELGOOD vein), SHADY DEAL (who also showed up on the »Overtone 3« rock compilation a year later) and EGYPT (indie no-hopers, not to be confused with the identically-named group formed by Alan Fish in the late 80's), with the heaviest of the bunch coming in the shape of SHADY DEAL's "Boys In The Media", although the track is worrying funky in places. It's interesting (well, almost) to note that BLYTHE BROCKETT and SHADY DEAL shared virtually identical writing credits, so maybe they were actually different projects from essentially the same group of musicians. Not a particularly fascinating piece of vinyl, really, but just about worth keeping half an eye out for.

A further 7" EP comes in the form of a rather mysterious four-tracker which was issued by D.T.A. Records (whoever they were) in 1983. There's no title for the EP, and no information on the label as to what might have been the connection between the bands, which tends to suggest that a picture sleeve might have been issued originally, this having possibly gone missing in the interim. Unfortunately, when such records are known to exist in terms of only one or two examples, you can't be sure about these things. In any case, the various ensembles featured are, again, hopelessly obscure, with the lightweight, utterly nondescript contributions of the APPLICATORS and FREETIME being instantly forgettable, whereas "Hidin'n'Runnin", by the MIDNIGHT RAMBLERS, is an energetic punk/metal collision quite similar to the STRANGLERS. The saving grace, however, the superb "Goddess Of The Night" by the impossibly enigmatic DREQUON, is a classic number falling perfectly between the styles of BLEAK HOUSE and Jersey's LEGEND. Outstanding. A great pity that this bunch got no further, and I'd like to find out more. As I say, I haven't the remotest idea where these outfits were based, so if anyone actually remembers them, get in touch!

Rounding off the section on NWOBHM-era releases are the two LP's issued by RCA Records to celebrate their annual 'Battle Of The Bands' contest of the early 80's, a nationwide competition which saw the winners from a variety of regional heats competing against each other in a televised grand final (which tended to be of a similar standard to the Eurovision Song Contest). The first volume, based around the 1981 event, is considerably more worthy than the sequel, and includes the otherwise-unavailable "Bad Boy" from Manchester's 100% PROOF, plus "Stop Crying" from COBRA (the little-known Suffolk version who were once featured in the 'Armed And Ready' section of 'Kerrang'), who come across as a less-accomplished BASHFUL ALLEY, and Merseyside's long-lived ASYLUM, whose "Nowhere To Run" shows them to be followers of the JAMESON RAID school of NWOBHM. In the event, the hopeless twaddle of CARL GREEN AND THE SCENE somehow got the nod, and so they were duly rewarded with studio time and their own vinyl release on the label, as were the two runners-up. Inevitably, the highest-placed rock outfit (COBRA) came in fourth, and just missed out on having a single pressed, which is a shame.

The second (and final) instalment of the brief »Battle Of The Bands« series of compilations followed a year later, and was marked by a serious decline in musical talent. In fact, the only remotely NWOBHM-linked ensembles featured were the mysterious 3X (there wasn't any information concerning the contenders' origins this time), whose "Echo Of Guilt" sounds a bit like LORELEI, and Merseyside's familiar THIN END OF THE WEDGE, with the otherwise-unreleased "The Letter". However, by this time, the latter outfit had sunk into commercial pop/rock territory, choosing to deliver a very soppy ballad featuring saxophones (good grief), which was immensely dull and disappointing. Furthermore, with the rest of the material on display being extremely lightweight and overly-commercial, this particular compilation can only be of marginal interest to NWOBHM collectors. I vaguely remember watching the final on telly at the time, and seem to recall that PRIVATE I.D. won this one, although it's hard to understand why, listening to their utterly average contribution.

Although the sheer number of such minor-band compilations had seemingly fallen away exponentially by the mid-80's, you may, very occasionally, find one from slightly later in the decade. Clearly, however, there's usually little or no relevance to the original NWOBHM scene, although there are always exceptions. Two such examples worth picking up cheaply are those albums issued by Academy Records in 1987, showcasing hopefuls from areas such as Surrey and the Southern outskirts of London. First up, »The Academy Record Collection Vol.1« (featuring the all-too-honest phrase *'Just what the world needs-another bloody record'* on the cover, so full marks for coming to terms with the sheer futility of releasing this kind of album) incorporated a fair amount of semi-listenable rock/metal from the long-lived BUZZARD (with a particularly unremarkable reworking of GOLDEN EARRING's "Radar Love"), OHMADON ("Stealer"), SHELTERED LIFE ("Round The World") and BRONX ("Knocking On The Door Of Love"), although it's fairly lightweight stuff (as with most of Ebony's later samplers, for example) on the whole. Still, possibly worth a couple of quid if you're feeling slightly generous.

The second Academy compilation (seemingly issued within a matter of months of the first instalment) also featured the lucky BUZZARD lads (mind you, they had actually issued a single or two of their own in the earlier part of the decade, so they weren't exactly the most deserving of *'unknown'* acts), this time with an original composition, the otherwise-unavailable "Deep Lust" (not the most captivating track ever penned, though). Also showcased were STRIPTEASE, whose "Midnight Fix" is very much in the FLASH HARRY scheme of things, and AUNT LUCY, whose "Right Or Wrong" is an entirely average rocker with unnecessarily-long instrumental sections. The other hopefuls on display, however, all prove to be talent-free areas, so it's somewhat disappointing in general. Not anywhere near as good as the first volume, in short, and I imagine that there probably wasn't sufficient interest to justify a third instalment in the series. Even so, it's another one worth picking up if you happen to see it at a giveaway price, which I suppose is always a possibility.

So there you have it, a very brief introduction to the weird and wonderful world of local-band compilations. There are always more to be discovered, so keep your eyes peeled for those give-away, poorly-drawn, horrible covers when

Liste mit über 2.500 7", LP's, 12", Pictures, sortiert nach US Metal NWoBHM • Scandinavian Metal • European Metal • World Metal Superbands • Punk/HC gegen 2,20 DM Rückporto anfordern.

Full list for 2 I.R.C.'s! Wants lists welcome.

H.M. Mailorder
Lichtenbergweg 13, D-30974 Wennigsen,
Tel./Fax 05103/3137

flicking through boxes of cheap records, and take a chance with your hard-earned money every now and again. If you find further examples of interesting samplers, featuring outstandingly obscure NWOBHM bands who never made it, be sure to let us know!

Epilogue

With three increasingly-hefty 'IRON PAGES' volumes having been published thus far, covering the general NWOBHM phenomenon and the bands of the period, you may well ask where this might all be heading. Will revised editions continue to emerge every few years, or do we need to take things in a new direction? There certainly seems to be sufficient interest in the subject as a whole to justify undertaking further comprehensive projects of a similar nature, given that people around the world genuinely desire information on both the better-known names and also the amateur-hour hopefuls. Given that obscure pieces of vinyl will continue to be discovered (at an ever-decreasing rate), there will always be more groups to document, although I now suspect that the final toll of British acts who got to the vinyl stage during the era will tend to peak at around the 600 mark. As a result, the possibility of a supplementary volume to this tome seems highly improbable (it would be a pretty slim addition to the series), but we should, over an extended period of time, be able to gather together enough new information, interviews *etc.* to convince everyone that at least one revised/expanded edition of 'The NWOBHM Encyclopaedia' would be a worthwhile endeavour. Mind you, it's worth giving some perusal to the limitations of text, and the logical (albeit vastly time-consuming and hugely expensive) next step might be to consider slapping all of this info onto CD-ROM, together with more pictures, archive material and interviews, plus (copyright hassles permitting) sound files and video clips. It's just an idea…

It's important to accept that there are always going to be gaps in our collective knowledge of any subject, and we'll only get progressively closer to the whole truth if people involved with the NWOBHM scene start to share information freely. Let's face it, we'll never uncover absolutely every act who released a private slice of vinyl back then, no matter what. Mysterious curios will invariably come out of the woodwork to surprise us all, which is a good thing, and it means that no-one will ever be able to claim (as do some hopelessly deluded individuals at the moment) that they own *'everything'* from the NWOBHM period. Another area which will never be documented authoritatively is the realm of compilation albums (especially those bewildering local-band samplers), such is the sheer number and incredible variety of such releases. Again, it's a case of waiting to see what turns up, doing some detective work and adding the extra information when possible. This applies to some of the records themselves: it's inevitable that a few singles which have been described as *'never issued in picture cover'* will, in reality, exist with promo-only/handmade efforts which were produced in extremely limited runs, so this is a matter to be resolved by fans swapping information as time goes by. I trust that those with access to additional details or corrections (missing line-ups/origins, incomplete histories/discographies and so forth) will have the decency to spill the beans rather than (as some selfish halfwits are prone to do) playing dumb. Needless to say, revelations concerning the smaller outfits would be appreciated most of all, given that the luminaries (LEPPARD, MAIDEN, SAXON and their ilk) occupy more than enough space already. The 'IRON PAGES' series of NWOBHM volumes (which would, in an ideal and egalitarian world, seek to provide approximately equal coverage to all) may not be error-free or totally all-encompassing, but they're a pretty good starting point, and you can help to make them even better…

It's open to debate whether or not the books being written on this subject should be extended to document some of the acts who, for various reasons, didn't get to the vinyl stage at all. No doubt, certain aficionados of the genre would happily devour every available piece of information on even the most minor and short-lived of hopefuls. In many cases, however, giving exposure to such ephemeral outfits would be hopelessly out of context. I mean, I could regale everyone with tales of a youthful ensemble called NIGHTHAWK who played (to a largely-bewildered audience) at our school disco in 1979, but who probably never recorded a demo tape, or some of the ramshackle, fly-by-night *'bands'* who rehearsed locally, the majority of whom probably never even had a name, but why? If you ask me, to link such utter nonentities with the more accomplished outfits of the day serves merely to cheapen and demean the genre as a whole; you have to draw the line somewhere. However, it might be worth documenting some of those part-timers who, for the sake of argument, were allocated a slot on the 'Friday

Rock Show' and whose sessions still exist on tape. Many of us will be familiar with TAURUS, for instance, but what about some of the others, namely GARRISON, EUPHORIA or ROUGH JUSTICE (the Yorkshire version), who may or may not have appeared on vinyl at any stage? Some of the more deserving demo groups may also be worth mentioning at some point in the future, not least the legendary DEEP MACHINE (whose convoluted history, offshoot bands and ever-evolving personnel could be reported in considerably greater detail than some of the 'mystery' acts who somehow issued a single during their fleeting existence), BURN, CHAIN REACTION, NO MERCY, DESTROYA or TREASON. Also, what about the multifarious combos whose sole claim to fame was a track on one of Ebony's many samplers, for example?

Basically, we're open to suggestions from now on. A bit of feedback on what might be worth including in future volumes or revised editions would be much appreciated. Also, if you think the format could be improved (assuming we stick to humble books and don't eventually branch out into multimedia projects), want to see more/fewer pictures or sleeve reproductions, a bit more in the way of constructive input from the ex-musicians, writers and scenesters themselves (they were a remarkably reclusive and reticent lot at the outset, but increasing numbers are finally coming out of the woodwork these days) or whatever, it's always worth chipping in with a few suggestions. Don't feel that this is the end of the road by any means. As far as I'm concerned, it's only the beginning...

HEAVY ROCK RECORDS
Specialists in NWOBHM and Classic Rock

The Damien Story
(Damien)

Previously unreleased studio live & bunker recordings of the late great Anglo-German rock band. Together with a commentary of their anthology.

Reincarnation Vol.1
(various artists)

The first in a series of NWOBHM compilations Featuring: *Ricochet, Quartz, Razorback, Demolition, The Handsome Beasts* and *Damien*.

buy these and more on-line at:
WWW.HEAVYROCK.CO.UK

Acknowledgements

It's conventional, in these circumstances, to give thanks to as many people as possible (including long-forgotten schoolfriends, distant relations and complete strangers who once bought you a pint ten years ago) in order to show what an utterly fantastic person you are and how many great mates you've got. At the risk of being regarded as somewhat inferior, I'd prefer to limit my gratitude to those who helped in a meaningful way. I'm indebted to the following people (pity about the dearth of female names, as this flies in the face of evidence that some women actually have good taste in music) for making this book a reality. Many of them assisted in an extremely fundamental way, by furnishing me with records, tapes, memorabilia, information or access to their collections. Others have been rather more peripheral in terms of their contribution, such as involvement with the tape-trading scene (going back a long way, in some cases) or simply being enthusiastic, supportive or encouraging with regard to the project or to the promotion of NWOBHM in general. In all cases, however, they've been instrumental in getting a certain someone to the stage whereby they're regarded as sufficiently clued-up to write a volume about a subject that means a lot to them. The ever-accommodating 'IRON PAGES' crew (Matthias Mader and Otger Jeske) clearly deserve the biggest cheer, however, since there wouldn't be a book at all if they hadn't been charitable enough to approach me in the first instance. Cheers, folks.

Mats Ahlstedt, Lyndon Allen, Marc Alton-Cooper, Tsutomu Ando, Reuben Archer, Chris Aylmer, Keith Bage, Shane Ballard, Pete Barnes, Geoff Bate, Chris Baumgartner, Greg Belton, Jeff Berry, Neville Billings, Pascal Boland, Horst-Gunter Borgardts, Tony Boulton, Ricky Bruce, Bron Buick, Lee Burrows, Oliver Butz, Phil Caine, Steve Cattle, David Clarke, Pete Cowie, Jess Cox, Jon Cox, Pete Davis, Paul Dianno, Bernard Doe, William Dunsmore, Malc Finlay, Neil Finnegan, Paola Fowler, Paul Gaskin, Steve Goldby, Andrew Goodwin, Andy Goodwin, Steve Goodwin, Scott Gorman, Chris Goulstone, Rob Grain, Tim Gray, Andy Gregory, Steve Gregory, Danny Gwilym, Dave Harman, Patrick Harman, Sean Harris, Peter Haworth, Liam Hayes, Jurgen Hegewald, Scott Heller, Mark Henshaw, Dave Hewitt, Scott Higham, Jon Hinchliffe, Perry Hodder, Ralph Hood, Bob Hooker, James Hooker, Craig Hughes, Henrik Johansson, Nick John, Ade Jones, Noel Jones, Terry Jones, Thilo Kelling, Hans Kern, Martin King, Nigel King, Oliver Klemm, Laura Koritz, Hartmut Kreckel, Ivan Lavery, Steve Lee, Phil Lentz, Richard Leskens, Ron Levine, Gabriel Lilliehook, Eddy Mackay, Jim Mallard, Roger Marsden, Cole McKinney, John Merikoski, Thierry Mias, Tatsu Mikami, Greg Moffitt, Oleg Moiseev, Pierre Moix, Brian Moore, Wayne Morgan, David Morse, Yuichi Nagano, Greg Nelson, Kenny Nicholson, Frank Noon, Phil Noon, Dave O'Brien, Roland Oei, Mario Panciera, Steve Peck, Simon Pepper, Edilson Pichiliani, David Poole, Mick Priestley, Laurent Ramadier, Vinnie Reed, Jim Rillings, John Roach, Jay Robohn, Bill Robson, Paul Rote, Brian Russ, Paul Samson, Dave Shakespeare, Jonathan Sharp, Matt Sheldon, Georgios Sidiropoulos, Russ Smith, Michael Smyth, Paul Solynskij, Al Spremo, Tony Stokes, Al Strachan, Guy Strachan, Tina Sullivan, Mark Sutcliffe, Robert Sweeten, Brian Tatler, Steve Taylor, Kostas Theos, Alun Thomas, Russ Tippins, Bernie Tormé, Panos Tsioubris, Paul v.d. Burght, Luc van Parys, Jason Visick, Alexis Vlastos, Phil Wang, Chalky White, Chris Wood, Fritz Wright, Matthias Wulf, Bryan Yorke, Keith Young, Charlie (GDM Records), Chris (Lost Horizons), Silvio (Ocean Records), Mil (Record Mill), Chris (Rock Of Ages), Gerry (Roxcalibur), Tony (Vinyl Tap).

BUYSELL**TRADE**

MATTHIAS AEBY
P.O. BOX 118
9542 MUENCHWILEN
SWITZERLAND

Tel/Fax: +71/966'52'84
matsaeby@gmx.net

coming soon:
www.sikkie.ch

BUYSELL**TRADE**

N.W.O.B.H.M. Survey

For Iron Pages, this book is just the beginning of numerous other projects related to Heavy Metal in general and the New Wave Of British Heavy Metal specifically! If you could spare five minutes of your precious time, please fill in this form and send, fax or e-mail your answers to the following address:

I.P. Verlag Jeske/Mader GbR, Iron Pages, Haydnstr. 2, 12203 Berlin, Germany
Fax 0049/30/86 20 09 82
e-mail: pages@ip-verlag.de

If you wish to be informed about any N.W.O.B.H.M. news or future Iron Pages books, please include your postal address and/or e-mail!

1. Where did you obtain this book?
    a) Mailorder
    b) Record Shop
    c) Book Shop
    d) Internet
    e) Elsewhere:

2. Have you been aware of any other Iron Pages books?
    a) No
    b) Yes, namely:

3. Which other encyclopedias would be worth your money regarding an English edition?
    a) U.S. Metal
    b) Death Metal
    c) Black Metal
    d) German Metal
    e) Scandinavian Metal
    f) Others:

4. What's more important for you...
    a) the number of pages
    b) to have as many photos as possible

5. How did you like the presentation of "The N.W.O.B.H.M. Encyclopedia"?
    a) I would have liked more photos, flyers, single sleeves
    b) It's more important to get the facts right!

6. Would you be interested in a CD-Rom edition of "The N.W.O.B.H.M. Encyclopedia"?
    a) Yes
    b) No, cause...

7. Did you know that Iron Pages also releases rare N.W.O.B.H.M. albums on CD?
    a) Yes
    b) No

8. Are there any (obscure) bands you would like to see released on CD via Iron Pages?
    a) Yes, I would fancy:
    b) No, can't be bothered!

9. If you had the choice, would you prefer new Iron Pages Records titles to come out on...
    a) on CD
    b) on vinyl

10. Completing your N.W.O.B.H.M. collection, what format do you prefer?
    a) I only buy vinyl originals, even if they gonna cost me a fortune
    b) If a CD is cheaper (and has extra tracks), I am going for the CD instead of the vinyl

Thanks for your time!